CIVIL WAR

Album

COMPLETE PHOTOGRAPHIC HISTORY
OF THE CIVIL WAR

CIVIL WAR

Album

COMPLETE PHOTOGRAPHIC HISTORY
OF THE CIVIL WAR

FORT SUMTER TO APPOMATTOX

Edited by
WILLIAM C. DAVIS AND BELL L. WILEY
Under the direction of
THE NATIONAL HISTORIC SOCIETY

Tess
Press

NEW YORK

Originally published in six separate volumes as:

The Image of War 1861-1865, volume One: Shadows of the Storm
The Image of War 1861-1865, volume Two: The Guns of '62
The Image of War 1861-1865, volume Three: the Embattled Confederacy
The Image of War 1861-1865, volume Four: Fighting for Time
The Image of War 1861-1865, volume Five: The South Besieged
The Image of War 1861-1865, volume Six: The End of an Era

Published by Tess Press an imprint of Black Dog & Leventhal Publishers,Inc.
151 West 19th Street
New York, NY 10011
Jacket design by Filip Zawodnik

Manufactured in Hong Kong
h g f e

ISBN-10: 1-57912-409-7
ISBN-13: 978-1-57912-409-0

THE EDITORS

Editor
William C. Davis

Senior Consulting Editor
Bell I. Wiley

Photographic Consultants
William A. Frassanito
Manuel kean
Lloyd Ostendorf
Frederick ray

Editorial Assistants
Deborah A. Berrier
Karen K. Kennedy
Denise Mummert
James Rietmulder

Contents

Introduction

WILLIAM C. DAVIS

The origins of the *Civil War Times Illustrated History of the Civil War* are just about as obscure and unlikely as they could be. At their remotest distance, they date from 1960 in a cramped two-bedroom bungalow in Sebatopol, California, in the heart of redwood and wine country. Not exactly a place one associates with the Civil War.

But there I was, aged almost fourteen, having read perhaps two books on the "late unpleasantness," and vaguely aware that I found the general subject interesting. Then I saw and advertisement in the now long-defunct "True Magazine". It was for a book titled *Campfire and Battlefield of the Civil War*, and emphasized that the volume included almost 1,000 photographs from the conflict. In fact, though the ad did not bother to say so, it was a reprint of one of the very first Civil War photographic books, put together by Rossiter Johnson and first published at the turn of the century when the development of the halftone process made it practical to reproduce photographs in books and magazines.

To a typical fourteen-year-old—meaning one with no job and no money— the terms were alluring. The book cost $15.00 plus postage and handling, could be ordered on approval with no money down, and paid for in four installments of $3.95 each. Remember, this is 1960, and begging even $3.95 a month from financially hard-pressed parents was no easy feat. As I recall, I ordered the book unilaterally, trusting that I would find the money somewhere later on.

When the book arrived I experienced something like unto an epiphany. Day after day I poured over the book. I never read the text then or later. To this day I have not read it, nor would I advise anyone else to do so, for intervening years of experience have taught me how unreliable was most of the material being written at the time.

But the photographs transfixed me. The reproduction was awful. Even the originals were not too clear, for halftone printing was still fairly primitive when Campfire and Battlefield first appeared. The reprint I bought was merely photographed from an original copy, and with little given to quality. Nevertheless, it was what was in the photos, and not their quality, that seized me. Here were the actual faces and figures of the men and women of the Civil War, their weapons, their homes, their forts and railroads. These were not just stilted paintings or crude woodcuts at the time, but the faces of the Civil War exactly as they appeared to each other.

I treasured that book, and have it still. It was the very first Civil War book I ever bought (eventually someone made those $3.95 payments, though I cannot remember who). More to the point, it inaugurated a fascination with the photographic record of the conflict that has lasted to this day, and that along the way has produced some of the most exhilarating moments of my life, and with them this new volume of the *Civil War Times' The Civil War Album*.

No one is interested in the life stories of historians, and wisely, I might add, so I will skip the next eighteen years and pick up the story in 1978. Through a series of accidents, fortuitous circumstances, and only occasional design, by then I was editor of "Civil War Times Illustrated", the nation's largest and leading magazine devoted to the conflict, and living in central Pennsylvania where it is published. One of the happiest aspects of editing that magazine was that almost every week, thanks to its wide circulation and reputation, the magazine's editorial offices received letters out of the blue regarding new discoveries in Civil War photography. Collectors sent in copies of the treasures they uncovered in flea markets and antique stores. Dusty attics disgorged long hidden images of the great and small. And in the course of researching illustrations for articles, our editors and art director constantly found overlooked rarities in public archives.

With no particular object in mind, I filed all of this in the back of my mind along with all the rest of the clutter that a historian carries around. Then in 1978 the thunderbolt struck. At nearby Carlisle sat the United States Military History Institute, the Army's chief repository of books and documents. In that year the Institute received an incredible bequest. A defunct Civil War veterans organization, the Massachusetts commandery of the Military Order of the Loyal Legion of the United States, seeking a secure home for its fabulous collections of documents and artifacts before they were vandalized into oblivion, turned most of the material over to the Army. Among the donation were some photographs.

About 40,000 to be exact! The Massachusetts MOLLUS commandery—the acronym by which the group was known—had accumulated in the last two decades of the nineteenth century the greatest collection of Civil War photographs in existence, yet for years it had been virtually unknown outside the MOLLUS membership. Even the people at "Civil War Times Illustrated", which by then had been publishing for almost two decades, had never heard of the collection. I'll never forget the day the 100 and more leather-bound volumes arrived at the institute. Colonel George Pappas, then director of the Institute, piled them on a metal trolley and wheeled load after load into the archives room, where I and a couple of other expectant Institute staff attacked them greedily. Almost every page yielded something new, something never-before-published. Here were portraits of generals we had never known to exist, regiment after regiment standing at attention for the camera, nurses at work in the hospitals, even photos of the photographers themselves at work. The magnitude of the collection was staggering, dwarfing by several multiples of the largest known holdings of the time.

As near as I can recall, that same evening, stunned by what I had seen, I lay awake most of the night turning over in my mind just what could be done with that collection. It was out of that sleepless night, whose own roots went all the way back to a fire lit in 1960, that the *Civil War Times Illustrated Photographic History of the Civil War* eventually emerged.

SHADOWS OF THE STORM

The Coming of the War

T. HARRY WILLIAMS

America goes mad, and to war with itself

"Let Freedom Ring." Symbols of American independence—Congress Hall, the Pennsylvania State House, and Philadelphia's old City Hall, in 1855. Here began the epic of American nationhood. Here, too, the Founding Fathers planted unknowingly the seeds of dissolution. (FREE LIBRARY OF PHILADELPHIA)

THE MOST SENSATIONAL NEWS in the big city newspapers of the United States in 1855 and 1856 concerned events in far-off Kansas Territory. There, according to reports of correspondents, settlers were committing widespread acts of violence on other settlers, burning and destroying property and engaging in wholesale murder. A certain amount of violence occurred in every frontier area undergoing settlement, and although this was duly recorded in the press, it did not attract special attention. What set the disorders in Kansas apart was that they resulted from, or seemed to result from, a difference in ideology between contesting individuals and groups. Kansans were not killing each other in a spirit of passion or lawlessness but in a mood of crusading zeal. They were fighting to make Kansas a free state—or a slave state. As the turmoil mounted and the deaths increased, the term "Bleeding Kansas" became a national by word.

The question of whether slavery should be permitted to enter the territories was an old one in American politics. It had first arisen in 1819 when Missouri applied for admission as a state with a constitution establishing slavery, and northern opponents of slavery and southern influence in the federal government had attempted to block admission. Although Missouri won entrance in the following year, the bulk of the then existing national domain was declared closed to slavery in the Missouri Compromise. The issue slumbered for years thereafter, but criticism of slavery continued; in deed, beginning in the 1830s more and more persons in the North began to say that slavery must be eradicated, be either abolished immediately or phased out gradually. The territorial issue reappeared in 1848 at the close of the Mexican War. As a result of that conflict, the United States had acquired a huge region to the southwest of the existing boundary, and hardly was the ink dry on the peace treaty when men in the North and the South began to argue about the status of slavery in the new possession.

As the dispute deepened, three proposals to solve the situation were advanced. Most Southerners contended that slaveholders had a constitutional right to take their human property into the recently acquired territory, or for that matter, into any part of the national domain, and to be protected in holding their property by the federal government. The most confirmed antislavery Northerners held that Congress had a constitutional power and a moral duty to exclude the institution from the new territory, or from any other territory; they believed that if slavery was prevented from expanding, it would ultimately die a forced death. In between these diametrically opposed views was a third formula that drew its strongest support from Democrats in the northwestern states. Known as popular sovereignty, it recommended that Congress should make no pronouncement on the status of slavery in the Mexican cession territory nor, by implication, in any other territory. Slave holders should be permitted to enter, and the position of the institution would be determined by the territorial legislature, or, as advocates of the doctrine liked to say, by the people themselves. Although popular sovereignty did not formally exclude slavery, it was actually a subtle exclusion prescription—the majority of settlers in a territory would undoubtedly come from the more populous North.

Popular sovereignty found enough support to be enacted into law as a part of the Compromise of 1850, which attempted to settle the territorial dispute and other issues which had arisen between the sections. Comparative calm prevailed for several years after passage of the compromise act. But in 1854 Senator Stephen A. Douglas of Illinois offered a measure that stirred fresh and even more bitter controversy. The leader of the northwestern Democrats, Douglas was a believer in popular sovereignty and in the future of the West. Both principles influenced the provisions that he put into his bill. To speed settlement of the western region, he proposed to organize two new territories, Kansas and Nebraska, which lay north of the line proscribing slavery in the Missouri Compromise. But to get southern support for the bill, he had to insert a section that repealed the exclusion clause of the old and revered Missouri law, leaving the determination of the condition of slavery in the proposed territories to their legislatures. The whole North seemed to blaze with fury at passage of the Kansas Nebraska Act. Antislavery leaders cried that the South had used its malign influence to extend its immoral institution and that this latest threat to freedom must be checked—Kansas, the southernmost of the two territories, must be settled by people from the North who would vote to make it a free state. Southern leaders responded to the challenge by urging their people to immigrate to the territory to vote for slavery. Kansas was about to become a prize to be contended for by the sections.

Many of the settlers who went to Kansas did so for the reasons that usually impelled families to move to a new area—they were looking only for a better life. But others entered to support a cause— dedicated enemies of slavery from the northeastern states and dedicated adherents of the institution from the neighboring state of Missouri who were willing to become transitory and illegal voters. Some men on both sides were not content to rely on voting to decide the issue, and soon the intimidation and the shooting started. Violence was superseding the normal democratic process.

The Kansas question stirred men to passion everywhere, including on the floors of Congress. In May 1856 antislavery senator Charles Sumner of Massachusetts delivered a bitter speech attacking various southern colleagues for supporting what he called "The Crime Against Kansas." Representative Preston Brooks of South Carolina, a younger kinsman of one of the senators attacked, was so enraged at the speech that he armed himself with a cane and went over to the other chamber and beat Sumner into bloody unconsciousness. The episode was but one of many examples of actual or threatened violence in Congress. Some members came to sessions wearing thinly concealed pistols, several fist-swinging brawls occurred between individual Northerners and Southerners or between groups, and challenges to duels were freely passed. The violence in halls dedicated to debate, like the violence in Kansas, was a symbol dark with portent for the future. Americans were becoming so aroused about the question of slavery in any of its manifestations that they were not satisfied to discuss it or to vote on it. They could relieve their feelings only by committing physical harm on those who disagreed

Left: It is a thriving, bustling nation, full of itself and its ever-stretching power and prosperity. Already in 1860, Broadway in New York City is one of the busiest streets in the world. (U.S. ARMY MILITARY HISTORY INSTITUTE, CARLISLE BARRACKS, PA.)

Below: To St. Joseph, Missouri, where immigrant trains jumped off into the Great Plains for the trek to Oregon and California. Albert Bierstadt took this 1859 view of the "Pike's Peak Passenger & Freight Express Co." (KANSAS STATE HISTORICAL SOCIETY, TOPEKA)

Above: On Saturday, October 13, 1860, J. W. Black of the firm of Black & Batchelder loaded his camera into a balloon operated by Professor Samuel A. King, and up they went, several hundred feet above Boston. There below them they captured the image of one of the principal trading cities of the world. Washington Street runs diagonally from lower right, Old South Meeting House at its other end. (U.S. AIR FORCE)

Right: It is a nation moving west, leaving in train thousands of rural still lifes such as this unidentified scene. (JOE M. BAUMAN)

Above: West to Nebraska spread the tentacles of a voracious America, taking root in the rich farmlands that produced abundant grain for sale in the East. Steamboats like the Colorado here at Omaha brought the produce to the railhead for the Hannibal & St. Joe and other new railroads to move speedily to market.
(NEBRASKA STATE HISTORICAL SOCIETY, LINCOLN)

Below: To the mining camps and burgeoning cities of the mountains like Central City, Colorado. (DENVER Pu,BLIC LIBRARY, WESTERN HISTORY DEPARTMENT)

Left: To Illinois expansion spread, to Galena, and a leather store run by Grant Perkins. Ulysses S. Grant. (CHICAGO HISTORICAL SOCIETY)

with them. Their anger flowed in part from the contradictions in American society, a society that was homogeneous but also diverse, that was experiencing an expansion of wealth and power but was being torn apart by ideological division.

The United States in 1860 was a land of imposing physical dimensions. The writ of American authority ran from the Atlantic Ocean to the Pacific Ocean, from the Canadian border to the Mexican border. A large part of the expanse west of the Mississippi River was as yet unpeopled except by Indian tribes. A tier of states just beyond the river marked the farthest line of settlement, and beyond them was wilderness stretching to California and Oregon on the Pacific coast. But already emigrants were pushing into the distant areas—the movement to Kansas was one example—and a constant increase in the population of the older regions gave promise that the eruptions would continue and that more states would soon be added to what popular orators liked to call "the galaxy of the Union."

The population of the thirty-three states then in the Union was approximately 31,000,000 persons, almost double the number of inhabitants in 1840. Nearly half of these lived west of the Appalachian mountain chain, a distribution that revealed the newer states were growing in influence at the expense of the older ones. Another demographic development, and at the moment a more ominous one, was the disparity in population between the free states and the slave states. The former numbered about 22,000,000 persons and the latter 9,000,000 persons of whom one third were black slaves. The South was becoming a minority, losing strength in the House of Representatives and the Electoral College every decade.

Most Americans lived, as their fathers and grandfathers had lived, in rural surroundings, on farms or in small towns. But beginning in the 1840s a significant shift of population toward cities occurred. New York City, the largest urban center, counted over 800,000 persons in 1860; Philadelphia, 565,000 persons; and Boston, 165,000. The most sensational growth was experienced by Chicago, which in little more than twenty years grew from 250 to over 100,000 inhabitants. Not participating in the trend toward urbanism was the South. If Baltimore, with its 200,000 people, is excepted as a border town, the region could boast of but one large city, New Orleans, whose 165,000 population was small in comparison with the teeming northern centers. Richmond and Charleston, next greatest in numbers, had only 40,000 each.

An increasing population was but one manifestation of national growth. Also expanding was the economy, the most dramatic and significant inflation occurring in industry. Textile, iron, and other plants dotted the Northeast, and manufacturies were beginning to spread into the Northwest and, although to a lesser extent, into the South. Accompanying the revolution in production was a revolution in transportation and communication. Railroads, superseding other means of conveyance, laced the eastern half of the country, the greatest concentration of lines being in the Northeast and the Northwest. The effect of the coming of the railroads on American life was like that of the great technological innovations of the twentieth century—a conquest of time and space had occurred. In the 1830s a traveler required three weeks to go from New York to Chicago or St. Louis; by 1860 he could complete the trip in two to three days. The transportation revolution bound the various parts of the country into a greater if uncomfortable unity.

The section least affected by the transforming changes of the time was the South. The region below the Potomac and the Ohio stood apart, or wanted to stand apart, from the mainstream of progress. The South was still distinctive—rural, agricultural, conservative, maintaining an ordered and orderly social structure, and boasting in its plantation lords the closest approach to an American aristocracy. Above all other differences, the South was the only part of the country that contained in large numbers a race of another color than white, a race held in slavery. Southerners of all classes stood determined to uphold slavery and the system of race relations based on it against all outside attacks. Their peculiar culture, they proclaimed, was superior to that of the North. One spokesman, denouncing free society as a "monstrous abortion," described his own society as a "healthy, beautiful and natural being." The refusal of Southerners to consider any modification of their system was a key to the conflicts that rent the nation during the last half of the 1850s.

The presidential election of 1856 took place against this backdrop of continuing violence in Kansas and continuing debate over the status of slavery in the territories. The Democrats nominated James Buchanan of Pennsylvania as their candidate and offered popular sovereignty as a formula to settle the territorial question. Their opposition was a new party, the Republicans, just two years of age. The Republican organization had been formed in the anger that swept the North after the enactment of the Kansas-Nebraska Act and had absorbed most northern members of the former Whig party and some antislavery northern Democrats. The Republicans nominated as their candidate John C. Fremont of California, famous as an explorer of the Far West, and submitted as their platform congressional exclusion of slavery from all national territories. A one-idea party, they were also a sectional party, having their main strength in the North with only a smattering of support in the border slave states.

The Democrats, although troubled by sectional division, were still a national party, and they elected Buchanan and a majority to Congress. However, the young Republican party had made a surprising showing. Fremont carried eleven of the sixteen northern states and rolled up a large popular vote. A slight shift of votes in a few states would have made the sectional party the majority party.

James Buchanan was a dignified "elder statesman," almost sixty-six years of age at the time of his inauguration, and an amiable and well-meaning public servant. But he lacked resolution of character and flinched from taking strong action in a crisis. Enjoying the company of Southerners, he was inclined to let himself be guided by southern leaders. Cast into office in a period of storm, he could not have controlled all events; he rarely tried to control any of them.

Most of the crises of his administration were concerned with the issues in controversy

Right: To Minnesota's Castle Rock it spread. (MINNESOTA HISTORICAL SOCIETY)

Below: And with "California or Bust," they completed the conquest of a continent, drawn by land, adventure, and gold. This early daguerreotype by Shaw & Johnson shows a gold claim in the early 1850s. (CALIFORNIA HISTORICAL SOCIETY LIBRARY)

Below: To the once barren wastes of Utah, where Salt Lake City sprang from the desert and Brigham Young's dream. (UTAH STATE HISTORICAL SOCIETY)

Right: Northwest to Oregon went America, to Table Rock City, on stirring stories of the Oregon Trail. (SOUTHERN OREGON HISTORICAL SOCIETY)

Left: It was a nation thriving on commerce, whose fast clipper ships traded with the world and turned the docks at the end of New York's Wall Street into a forest of masts. (NEW-YORK HISTORICAL SOCIETY)

Below: Yet there were two Americas. While the northern states and their people pushed and built and traded and manufactured, another America took a slower pace. The South, too, had its major trading cities like Charleston, South Carolina, and to be sure, its skyline evidences a few factory smokestacks.

between the sections and every outcome exacerbated sectional bitterness and moved the nation closer to dissolution. In Kansas the turmoil between the contesting factions continued unabated, with efforts now concentrated on electing a convention to write a state constitution. Buchanan used his influence to aid the proslavery side, which was clearly a minority. His action enraged Republicans and disgusted popular sovereignty members of his own party, and Congress refused to accept the constitution presented by the slavery adherents. Kansas remained a territory, and an issue of discord.

At the height of the Kansas dispute the Supreme Court handed down a pronouncement on the question of whether slavery could enter a territory in Dred Scott v. Sanford. The case had a complicated background, but in the broadest meaning it involved the exclusion clause in the Missouri Compromise. The majority opinion (seven of the nine justices were Democrats) held that this clause was in violation of the constitutional provision that forbade Congress to take property without "due process of law." The Congress of 1820 had acted illegally in barring slavery, and no Congress could exclude the institution. Translated into the language of current politics, the decision declared the platform of the Republican party to he unconstitutional. By implication it also disallowed popular sovereignty,

Above: And the factory came to America, the sweatshop, the women and child labor, the endless days at machines producing textiles. There was great prosperity, but it cost great toil. (USAMHI)

Right: Trade between the states flourished, borne on iron rails and man-made waterways like the Chesapeake & Ohio Canal. (NATIONAL ARCHIVES, WASHINGTON, D.C.)

for if Congress could not prohibit slavery in the territories neither could a territorial legislature that was created by Congress. The voice of the highest tribunal did not calm but rather excited sectional passions. A typical Republican effusion denounced the Court as the "last resort behind which despotism is sheltered," and Republican leaders proclaimed that when their party gained control of the government they would reconstitute the Court and retry the case.

Northern anger at the Dred Scott decision was more than matched by southern rage at an event occurring in 1859. John Brown, a fierce foe of slavery who had migrated to Kansas and participated in the killings there, reappeared in the East full of a plan to strike at slavery in the South itself. With encouragement and monetary support from certain abolitionists, who realized his general purpose, he proposed to seize the Federal arsenal at Harpers Ferry in western Virginia, and from this base to incite an armed slave insurrection. In October he and eighteen followers descended on the town and captured the arsenal. No slaves came in to join him, and he was pinned down in his position by attacking citizens and local militia. News of the raid alarmed official Washington, and President Buchanan, reacting with unusual vigor, dispatched a contingent of marines under Robert E. Lee of the Regular Army to Harpers Ferry to

Right: The barons of industrial expansion discovered the riches beneath the earth, and profits came to be measured in barrels. Oil Creek Valley, near Rouseville, Pennsylvania already the scars of industry blotted the landscape. (DRAKE WELL MUSE-UM, TITUSVILLE, PA.)

Below:. . . of their river cities like Vicksburg on the mighty Mississippi. H. J. Herrick took this view from the Louisiana side of the river, Vicksburg's courthouse towering over all. (OLD COU,RT HOUSE MUSE-UM, VICKSBURG, MISS.)

Above: But Southerners preferred to think of themselves in a different way, as the last outpost of a more graceful, pastoral mode of life that existed more in myth than in actual memory. They thought of the beauty of Wade Hampton's garden at his plantation in Columbia, South Carolina. (USAMHI)

Right: Their pride lay not in capitalism, but in cotton, piled in bales on Charleston's wharves awaiting shipment to northern and European textile mills. WRHS)

Below: Despite differences in their economies and ways of life, North and South still managed to accommodate each other peaceably enough in the first half of the century. Both rejoiced in the young nation's expanding horizons, and celebrated their common heroes on days like the July 4, 1859, celebration at New York Harbor. (USAMHI)

Above and right: Slaves were bought and sold, and between transactions were often kept in pens like this one at Alexandria, Virginia, almost within sight of the Capitol in Washington City. (USAMHI)

deal with the crisis. Brown resisted the onslaught of Lee's force, but with ten of his men killed he finally had to surrender. The national government handed him over to Virginia to be tried for treason against the state.

Brown's raid aroused fury in the South, and also horror. The whites lived in constant fear of a slave uprising, and now it seemed that outside agitators, abolitionists or Republicans, had attempted to incite an insurrection. Southern suspicions were heightened by the praise heaped upon Brown by abolitionist leaders who hailed him as a saint, an "angel of light" in the words of New England writer Henry David Thoreau. Thoreau and others hoped that Brown would not escape hanging and would become a martyr to the cause of freedom. They need not have feared. Brown was duly tried and executed. In his last message to the world he wrote that he was certain the crimes of "this, guilty land" would never be purged away "but with Blood." The stage was set for the fateful presidential election of 1860.

All the boiling tensions in the country came to a head in 1860. The election in that year marked the apogee of sectionalism. Parties represented largely sectional interests, and the result prompted the South to withdraw from the Union. It is the only contest in American history in which the losing side felt that it could not live with the consequence of defeat.

The Democrats were the first to meet in convention. Gathering in historic Charleston in April, they plunged into angry debate on the issue of slavery in the territories. Southern delegates demanded that the platform affirm the right of slaveholders to take their chattels into any part of the national domain, and northern delegates held out for a popular sovereignty plank. When the latter triumphed, a number of southern delegations walked out of the hall. The managers thereupon adjourned the convention to meet again in Baltimore in June, hoping that time would cool the passions of the opposing factions. However, at Baltimore anger was even more intense, and another southern exodus occurred. The remaining delegates nominated Stephen A. Douglas to run on a popular sovereignty platform. The bolters nominated John C. Breckinridge of Kentucky to stand for the rights of slavery in the territories. There were now two Democratic parties in the field, and although each had adherents in the other section, one was a northern party and one was a southern party. The only national political organization in the country had at last split on

Above: Whitney made only part of the work easy. The rest, the picking, must be done by hand, by slaves, the captive labor force of the South, the legacy of a problem the Founding Fathers chose not to solve. Timothy O'Sullivan photographed this slave family on a South Carolina cotton plantation in 1862. (LIBRARY OF CONGRESS, WASHINGTON, D.C.)

Above: They grudgingly gave credit to Yankee Eli Whitney's invention of the cotton gin for making possible the large-scale production and harvest of the fiber. Gin houses like this one on Edisto Island in South Carolina hummed with activity throughout the 1850s. (WRHS)

Above: They planted the fields on Pope's Plantation at Hilton Head, South Carolina.

Below: Over the nation loomed the haunting specter of sectionalism, of slavery, of southern pretensions for a nationhood of its own. South Carolina's John C. Calhoun, ardent champion of states' rights and secession, might lie dead in his tomb in Charleston, but what he stood for still lived. (USAMHI)

Left: Slaves became not only a work force, but a measure of wealth as well. These blacks of all ages and sex are gathered in Baton Rouge, Louisiana. (OCHM)

Below: And they brought their day's pickings in every evening to put it through Mr. Whitney's machine. George N. Barnard's post-war photograph was taken near Charleston, South Carolina. (NYHS)

the rock of sectionalism.

The Republicans met in bustling Chicago in May in a huge building, the Wigwam, built by the Republicans of the city to house the convention.

Elated at the promise of victory held out by Democratic division, the party managers were determined to present a platform and a candidate that would appeal to the broadest spectrum of northern opinion. They were especially concerned that the party should not appear to be a collection of wild eyed crusaders who had no other objective but to attack slavery. Now the Republicans were to stand before the voters as men of moderation whose vision embraced many issues. The platform embodied the new strategy. Although reaffirming their opposition to slavery's expansion into the territories, the Republicans declared that they had no intention of interfering with the institution in the states where it already existed. Other planks emphasized economic

Below: Sectional schism was seemingly averted in 1856 when the contest for the presidency First saw a young Republican party, northern for the most part and antislavery in character, defeated at the polls. Democrats in the South paraded horse-drawn "ships of state" in their streets. They elected their candidate, routed Republicanism, and, so they thought, ensured peace. (JMB)

Above: Of all the men ever to hold presidential office, the people chose the one least suited. James Buchanan lacked almost everything, necessary in a President, most of all a firm will and resolution. The collapse of the Union began almost at once. (NA)

Above: They picked the cotton under the eye of their white overseers, as in this postwar image. (NA, WOMEN S BUREAU)

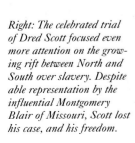

Right: The celebrated trial of Dred Scott focused even more attention on the growing rift between North and South over slavery. Despite able representation by the influential Montgomery Blair of Missouri, Scott lost his case, and his freedom.

Right: Violent men like James Lane led bands of marauders who proved little better than ruffians in the quest to wrest control of Kansas from their opposition . (u SAM Hi)

issues. The party endorsed a high protective tariff, internal improvements (national financial support to transportation projects), and a homestead bill (free land to settlers in the West). In a shrewd bid for victory the Republicans had combined the idealism of the antislavery impulse and the aspirations of the principal economic groups in the North.

The party showed the same sense of practicality in choosing a candidate. Passing over the best known leaders who had records that might alienate some voters, the convention nominated Abraham Lincoln of Illinois. Lincoln was, in the language of politics, an "available" candidate. He had a national reputation, but he had not been on the national scene long enough to accumulate a list of enemies. He had spoken out against the Kansas Nebraska Act, but he was not thought to be a "radical" antislavery man. His views on slavery squared with those of the mass of Republicans. He believed that the institution was wrong and that it should persistently be labeled as wrong. He would not interfere with the institution where it existed, but he would uncompromisingly oppose its expansion with the purpose of bringing about its demise. The opponents of slavery, he said, must "place it where the public mind shall rest in the belief that it is in the course of ultimate extinction."

The appearance of three major parties indicated an unusual splintering of popular opinion. And this was not the end of it. Still a fourth party entered the lists, the new and hastily formed Constitutional Union party. Composed of former Whigs, it nominated John Bell of Tennessee as its candidate and presented as a platform only support of the Constitution and the Union. The apparent softness in its position was a deliberate strategy. The leaders thought that with so many candidates dividing the vote no one of them would gain a majority of the electoral vote and that the election would be thrown into the House of Representatives. There their conservative nominee might emerge as the victor.

The result of the election in November reflected the division of parties and populace. Although Lincoln had a minority of the popular vote, about 40 percent of the total, he rolled up a clear electoral majority, 180 votes. His margin was the consequence of success in the northern states with large electoral votes; he carried every free state except New Jersey, which he divided with Douglas. (The Republican sweep did not, however, bring in a majority in Congress.) Breckinridge carried the Lower South and three border slave states and stood second in the electoral vote. Bell took three border states and came in third. Douglas won only one state, Missouri, and divided New Jersey with Lincoln. However, his popular vote was second to Lincoln's, about 30 percent of the total. If it is assumed that his popular sovereignty followers were voting against the expansion of slavery, 70 percent of the voters had registered a verdict to pen up slavery where it was.

During the campaign, extremist leaders in the Lower South had tried to impress upon their people that if the Republicans won the contest, the interests of the South would not be safe in the Union. The "Black Republicans" would sooner or later be driven to attack slavery, that is, to interfere with the prevailing racial patterns, and to prevent this dire eventuality southern states should secede from the Union. One of the loudest sounders of the cry to get out was Robert Toombs of Georgia, and he became even more strident after the election. Addressing the Georgia legislature in November, he urged secession before the Republicans, "your enemies," took office on March 4, 1861. "Then strike," he thundered, "strike while it is yet time." Leaders in other states reechoed his demand.

The threats of secession were heard in the North with mixed feelings. Many persons refused to believe that the danger was serious,

Left: Then violence erupted at Harpers Ferry, Virginia, and the North and South were so polarized that there seemed no cementing them back together. John Brown of Ossawatomie, a free-state fighter from Kansas, led a band of men across this bridge on the Potomac, turned right, and . . . (USAMHI)

Right: The conflict reached the floor of the United States Senate when Charles Sumner of Massachusetts, decrying the "Crime Against Kansas" in a violent antislave speech, was attacked and caned senseless by Preston Brooks of South Carolina. For three years Sumner's chair remained empty, itself a powerful symbol for the abolitionist forces.

Below: Kansas came to be "Bloody Kansas" as it sought statehood. Antislave men flocked to the territory while proslave interests, fearing that the slave states would soon become a minority in Congress, did likewise. Each hoped to provide a majority to bring Kansas into statehood. The conflict between them led to open warfare on the plains, fought by units like this Free-State Battery at Topeka in 1856. (KANSAS STATE HISTORICAL SOCIETY, TOPEKA)

Right: In 1858 the battle continued in Illinois, where Stephen A. Douglas and Abraham Lincoln vied for a Senate seat. Douglas won the election, but Lincoln won nationwide prominence thanks to their celebrated series of debates. Photograph by Calvin Jackson of Pittsfield, October 1, 1858. (USAMHI)

Left: . . . swarmed down this street to the United States Arsenal. Here they hoped to capture arms to lead a slave uprising in the South that would end slavery forever. Instead, the townspeople quickly organized against them, and Brown and his men found themselves cornered across the street . . . (CHESAPEAKE & OHIO RAILROAD CO.)

Left, right and below: In Richmond, Virginia's governor issued the call for troops to suppress this outrage, and many stepped forward. The 1st Virginia Militia, the "Richmond Grays," answered the call. They did not take part in the final capture of brown, but they did arrive in Charles Town, Virginia, in time to form a hollow square around a gallows where old John Brown was hanged after his trial. One of their number present was john Wilkes Booth, an actor, who rather pitied Brown, 'na brave old man," he said. These four views, two of them not previously published, show the Richmond Grays at the time of Brown's trial and hanging.

Right: . . . in an engine house. (CHESAPEAKE & OHIO RAILROAD CO.)

thinking that the South was only bluffing to wring concessions from the national government. Other men were acutely alarmed, realizing that the Union was threatened with dissolution. One who was especially concerned was lame-duck President Buchanan.

In his message to Congress in early December, Buchanan took note of the gathering sentiment behind secession in the Lower South. He denied that a state could constitutionally leave the Union, but he also denied that the federal government could force a state that had left to return, or, as he put it, could "make war against a state." To avert secession, he urged Congress to frame an amendment to the Constitution that would guarantee the existence of slavery, ensure the right of slaveholders to enter the territories, and guarantee the privilege of owners to recover fugitive slaves. In pleading for compromise Buchanan thought that he was acting the part of a patriot. He did not seem to realize that his idea of compromise was weighted heavily in favor of the South.

Both houses of Congress took Buchanan's advice, appointing separate committees to frame an amendment. The House committee was never able to come up with a complete plan; it agreed on an amendment guaranteeing the existence of slavery, but arrived at no accord on the question of slavery in the territories. The Senate committee gave earnest consideration to a proposal submitted by Senator John J. Crittenden of Kentucky and known therefore as the Crittenden Compromise. This measure also ensured the existence of slavery and contained a provision to satisfy southern demands as to fugitive slaves. Most important, Crittenden attempted to deal with the troublesome territorial problem. His solution was to establish the demarcation line of the Missouri Compromise, the thirty sixth parallel, in all of the territory of the United States then held or thereafter acquired—slavery would be prohibited north of the line and permitted south of it. Southern members of the committee

Above: Here the old man, who had grown a beard since this 1856 photograph was made, fought desperately, even while his sons were being killed beside him. (KANSAS STATE HISTORICAL. SOCIETY, TOPEKA)

indicated that they would accept this division if the Republicans as a party would support it. Before returning an answer, Republican leaders sought the reaction of President-elect Lincoln, waiting in Springfield to come to Washington. Lincoln returned a negative answer. There could be "no compromise" on the question of extending slavery, he said. "The tug has to come & better now than later," he wrote in one letter. The Senate committee had to abandon its labors.

The attempts at compromise failed for various reasons. Many men on both sides felt that they could not yield their beliefs, either out of devotion to principle or to party. Some men on both sides would have been willing to give way if they had thought war would follow, but they convinced themselves that they could have their desires without war. And there were some in each section who did not care if war came, who, in fact, welcomed it, if for no other reason than to relieve tensions that were becoming unbearable.

While the efforts to compromise were drag-

Right: L.eadership from the Executive Mansion, the "White House," was nonexistent. Here Montgomery C. Meigs, the engineer supervising the expansion of the Capitol building, used his stereo camera to provide a deceptively peaceful image.

Left: The man who led the capture of brown, Colonel Robert E. Lee—a photo taken in l 85 1 . (CH S)

Below: Many in the North refused to abide by the Fugitive Slave Law, part of the Compromise of 1850. When this slave, "Old Peter," nearly one hundred years old, escaped to the home of Slater Brown in Lancaster, Pennsylvania, the Quaker refused to return him to his former master.

Below: Never was there greater pressure on the leaders in Washington to compromise, to lead. Yet, just as they could not agree to finish the monument to the nation's first President, so could they not agree on a course to save the country from disunion. (NA)

Left: The situation was worse at the opposite end of Pennsylvania avenue. The Congress, like the building in which it met, seemed to be in pieces. Montgomery Meigs's photog;raph shows the old Capitol dome, which he would soon replace, and the partially completed new Senate wing. (LC)

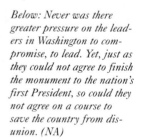

Above: Buchanan and his Cabinet proved hopelessly ineb'ectual. The two members seated at left, Jacob Thompson and John B. Floyd, were suspected of financial malfeasance. Both would become secessionists. Secretary of State Lewis Cass, behind them, had long since ceased to be a poten: force in public affairs. Ilowell Cobb of Georgia, standing just right of Buchanan, would support secession as well. Only Jo.seph Holt, standing at far right, and Jeremiah Black, seated far right, were men of real force and strong, Union sentiment. Isaac Toucey, seated to the left of Black, remained an unknown quantity. A divided administration could hardly unite a country. (LC)

ging to a sad conclusion in Washington, in the deep South states the adventure in secession got off in a mood of gaiety and exultation. South Carolina, long the leader of southern separatism, acted first. A convention elected to consider the course the state should take proved unanimously secessionist. Meeting in Charleston, the convention voted on December 20 to take the state out of the Union. The news of its action was greeted in the city with wild rejoicing. An English newspaper correspondent visiting in Charleston a short time later caught the spirit of the citizens. "Secession is the fashion here," he wrote. "Young ladies sing for it; old ladies pray for it; young men are dying to fight for it; old men are ready to demonstrate it."

Six other states soon followed the example of South Carolina. They were, in the order of their leaving, Mississippi, Florida, Alabama, Georgia, Louisiana, and Texas. Not all of them went out rejoicing as South Carolina had done. In some conventions there were men who opposed secession, not the right but the need to secede; they counseled delay and cooperative sectional action rather than individual state action. And there were other men who accepted secession reluctantly, and with heavy hearts voted to sever relations with the Union. But the seceders were in

Below: Here compromise failed. The old House of Representatives chamber about 1861. (LC)

Above: The Capitol from Pennsylvania Avenue in 1860. There is still much work to be done—on the building and the Union. (LC)

Below: There the once powerful voice of Henry Clay had managed compromise from discord. But Clay's voice was stilled, and none stepped forward to take his place. (I\'YH S)

Above: Instead the hotbloods took the floor, the "fire-eaters" like Senator William L. Yancey of Alabama. Dazzled by the idea of a southern nation, and perhaps their own political ambitions within it, they spurned compromise. (NYHS)

Above: Meigs's camera captures Secretary of State Cass standing at a table, and his own image in the mirror in the background. (LC)

Above: Buchanan's Secretary of the Treasury Howell Cobb gaze the secessionists tacit support. (LC)

Below: The fiery W. G. "Parson" Brownlow of Tennessee made strident exclamations for the Union, and published his newspaper called the Rebel Ventilator. (USAMHI)

Above: Alexander H. Stephens, cong,ressman from Georgia, one-time friend of Lincoln, spoke for those who interpreted the Constitution so strictly that secession seemed justified, if not actually legal.

Above: Not all Southerners were fire-eaters, though. The old hero of the Texas Revolution, Sam Houston, spoke out against secession and for the Union, even at personal risk. (NA)

Right: Virginia's governor Henry A. Wise, from his experience with John Brown's raid in his own state, felt more keenly than most the fear of slave uprising and northeln aggressions against slavery. (JACK MCGUIRE)

control in every convention and carried their will. The process was completed by February 1.

The secession leaders realized that their states could not exist separately. Their intention from the first had been to create a new and a southern Union. Accordingly, representatives of the seven states met in February at the little city of Montgomery, Alabama (population, 8,800), to write a provisional constitution and form a provisional government. They called their nation the Confederate States of America and chose as its president Jefferson Davis of Mississippi. Davis came to Montgomery to be inaugurated on February 18. In his address he affirmed unrelenting devotion to the cause of southern independence.

Less than a month later Abraham Lincoln was inaugurated President of what had been the United States in a Washington tense with rumors of impending civil conflict. Although in his address he pled with the seceded states to return, he made it clear that he would not offer any concessions to induce them to come back. He denied that any state could lawfully leave the Union, repudiating secession as the "essense of anarchy." The portion of his remarks that most angered Southerners was the announcement that he would "hold, occupy, and possess" Federal properties within the confines of the Confederacy. He did not have to identify the places that he was referring to, offshore forts that the seceding states and the Confederate government had not been able to seize. Two of these forts particularly occupied public attention, Sumter in Charleston harbor and Pickens near the coast at Pensacola, Florida. The Davis government was mounting military preparations to assault them if this was necessary to secure them, and Lincoln was letting Davis know that they would be defended.

Lincoln's policy, although stated subtly, was nevertheless plain—he hoped that the Union could be restored peaceably but if this was not

Left and above: A bitter reminder to the southern cadets were the cannon captured during the war with Mexico a decade before. Southern soldiers contributed considerably to that war, and they had hoped to bring much of the conquered territory into the Union as slave states.

Left: In the midst of the sectional agitation, and largely stimulated by it, a martial spirit grew rapidly North and South. Cadets at the United States Military Academy at West Point, New York, found themselves divided, often in heated argument. From their practice batteries overlooking the Hudson . . .

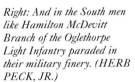

Right: . . . to their field exercises at Camp Walker, they argued and took their sides.

possible, he was willing to employ force, to resort to war. Davis's policy was also clear—the seceded states would not voluntarily return to the Union and the Confederacy would maintain its independence by force if it had to. The policies of both men and both governments accorded with the feelings of the northern and the southern people. Most Northerners valued the Union and would fight to keep it inviolate. Most Southerners valued the political and social system represented by the Confederacy and would fight to defend that. A martial spirit was rising in both sections. It could be seen in the bellicose declarations of leaders, in the cry for action from ordinary people, and, in a picturesque but dangerous manifestation, in the many volunteer and militia groups of young men that were springing into being throughout the once united land and that were loudly eager to demonstrate their manhood.

Only an incident was needed to touch off war.

Below: Now young men, like these members of the class of 1864, pondered just what their budding military careers held for them, and who their first battles would bring against them. Standing at left is Ranald MacKenzie, soon to be a general, and in years to come a noted Indian fighter in the West. (USAMHI)

Right: And in the South men like Hamilton McDevitt Branch of the Oglethorpe Light Infantry paraded in their military finery. (HERB PECK, JR.)

Right: Even less experienced were the volunteer and militia units springing up everywhere. What they lacked in field knowledge, they made up for in natty attire and precision at drill. Here officers of the 6th New York State Militia and, standing second from the left, E. Elmer Ellsworth, in July 1860. A favorite of Abraham Lincoln, Ellsworth led one of the North's finest drilled units, his "Fire zouaves." (CHS)

Above: The old Regular Army was undermanned, ill equipped, and officered largely by men with no real combat experience, and those that did know battle were acquainted with a kind of war that would never be fought again. Colonel Joseph Plympton and his black orderly. (PEARL KORN)

Left and below: And in Louisville, Kentucky, in August 1860, the State Guard held a much publicized encampment. The holiday atmosphere of it all, with a refreshment stand and ice cream, barely concealed the rattling sabers. (KENTUCKY HISTORICAL SOCIETY,]CENTUCKY MILITARY HISTORY MUSEUM, FRANKFORT, KY.)

Below: By 1860, the last remaining hope of maintaining the Union was the Democratic party. Friendly to southern interest.s, it could keep the South in the nation if it stayed united and defeated the Republicans in November. Instead, the party fragmented. The chiefly northern wing nominated Stephen A. Douglas, the "Little Giant" of Illinois. Immensely popular, he still came in last in the electoral ballot. (USAMHI)

Above: Cincinnati, Ohio's "Guthrie Grays," ready for the foe, whoever it might be. (CINCINNATI HISTORICAL SOCIETY)

Left: The Mobile Cadets from Alabama refined their marksmanship. (HP)

Left: Shortly after his nomination for the Presidency, a still beardless Lincoln unbends his lanky frame for a full-length portrait in his home town of Springfield, Illinois. (LC)

Above: Their election brought jubilation in much of the North, as in Mohawk, New York, where the "Mohawk Wide Awakes" and their band paraded in honor of the victory. (LLOYD OSTENDORF COLLECTION)

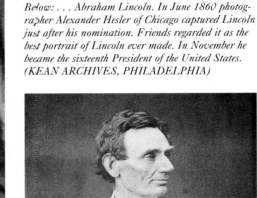

Left: Animated by years of heated rhetoric, exaggerated fears and hatreds, irresponsible politicians, and an impulse for southern nationalism, South Carolina called a convention here in Secession Hall. The outcome was never in doubt. In December 1860 they adopted here an ordinance of secession. The broadsides on the streets the next day read "The Union Is Dissolved. (USAMHI)

Below: . . . Abraham Lincoln. In June 1860 photographer Alexander Hesler of Chicago captured Lincoln just after his nomination. Friends regarded it as the best portrait of Lincoln ever made. In November he became the sixteenth President of the United States. (KEAN ARCHIVES, PHILADELPHIA)

Above: Elected with him, as Vice-President, was Hannibal Hamlin of Maine. (USAMHI)

Above: The more conservative Northerners and the southern rights men nominated Buchanan's Vice-President, John C. Breckinridge of Kentucky. The only candidate with nationwide appeal, his popular vote was evenly divided between North and South, but he placed second in the Electoral College. (LC)

Left: Six other states did the same in the weeks to follow, and on February 18, 1861, in Montgomery, Alabama, new capital of the Confederate States of America, they inaugurated their first President, Jefferson Davis of Mississippi. A. C. McIntyre of Montgomery sensed something historic taking place, and set his camera to capture the scene. The Alabama statehouse clock says 1 P.M. Davis and Howell Cobb stand at the doorway between the center columns. The Confederacy is begun. (NA)

Above: But there was no rejoicing in Charleston, South Carolina. Despite Lincoln's earnest promises not to interfere with slavery where it already existed, Southerners saw in his election a dagger poised at their labor system, their way of life, and their honor. (NYHS)

Left: In the North, four days after Davis's inauguration, President-elect Lincoln arrived in Philadelphia. Here, on Washington's birthday, he symbolically raised the flag at Independence Hall. The Union, he promised, would be preserved. Frederick D. Richards caught the scene with his camera while the dignitaries stood at prayer. Lincoln is visible directly above the star on the left of the lqag, while men view the scene from trees. (LO)

Above: And on March 4, 1861, a crozud gathered before the stands on the Capitol steps in Washington. Meigs set his camera to record the scene. (LC)

Below: Then Lincoln took the oath of office and told the nation that the Union must be preserved. "We are not enemies, but friends," he told the South. "We must not be enemies." "In your hands, my dissatisfied fellow-countrymen, and not in mine, is the momentous issue of civil war." Meigs certainly could not have heard the President, but his camera caught the moment forever. (LC)

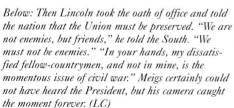

Above: Jefferson Davis, photographed in 1859 by Montgomery Meigs. An unpublished portrait which shows him with a hint of a smile. After 1860 he would rarely smile again. (LC)

Above: The Republicans, in the face of a Democratic split, were ensured of success. New York's William H. Seward, standing at left, had hoped for the nomination, but he lost it to Douglas's old foe from Illinois . . . (NYHS)

Below: The word spread across the nation, to a host of men then little known and not likely to be remembered. In Cairo, Illinois, to a man standing just left of the post office pillar, Ulysses S. Grant . . . (CHS)

Right: . . . to three friends from West Point days, Philip H. Sheridan in the center, and George Crook at left. (u. s. MILITARY ACADEMY ARCHIVES)

Below: . . . to an adjutant general in the Army, Lieutenant Colonel Don Carlos Buell. (USAMHI)

Left: . . . to a firebrand Unionist in Missouri, Nathaniel Lyon. (USAMHI)

Above: . . to a captain in the United States Topographical Engineers, George G. Meade. (USAMHI)

Below: . . . to a professor at the Virginia Military Institute, seen here in Mexican War uniform, Thomas Jonathan Jackson. (USAMHI)

Below: . . to a dashing Virginian who had helped Lee corner John Brown, James Ewell Brown Stuart.

Above: . . . to a young southern officer, Ambrose Powell Hill.   (MUSEUM OF THE CONFEDERACY)

Right: And to Chnlleston went the word. It was in their hands, said Lincoln. (LC)

Above: . . . to men like Captain A. W. Reynolds.

Left: In the hands of Brigadier General Pierre G. T. Beauregard, commanding the Confederates gathered in Charleston. (OCHM)

Above: . . . to a sour, humorless, Mexican War veteran, Braxton Bragg. (SOUTHERN HISTORICAL COLLECTION, UNIVERSITY OF NORTH CAROLINA, CHAPEL HILL)

The Guns at Fort Sumter

W.A. SWANBERG

A Charlston April shatters America's innocence

Above: The ghostly face of Fort Sumter in Charleston Harbor, almost lost in this scratched and faded ambrotype. It is the only known photo of the fortress before its bombardment. (VM)

Left: Brigadier General Pierre G. T. Beauregard, commanding Confederate forces in and around Charleston. He appears in his uniform as colonel of engineers in the Provisional Army of Louisiana, shortly after the time he served briefly as superintendent of the Military Academy at West Point. Filled with grand ideas of warfare—and his potential part in it—this Creole officer looked forward to firing on Fort Sumter as soon as the authorities gave him the word. (USAMHI)

"I HAVE THE HONOR TO REPORT," Major Robert Anderson wrote on December 26, 1860, after his night-shrouded move across a mile of water to Fort Sumter, "that I have just completed, by the blessing of God, the removal to this fort of all my garrison." The anger which this clandestine shift of a mere seventy-odd men caused in the South, and the joy it aroused in the North, bespoke the sectional strife of which the major and the Charleston forts had become a symbol.

President Buchanan saw in it none of God's work. "Are calamities never to come singly!" he lamented. Yearning to finish his nine remaining weeks in office and to leave the secession crisis in the lap of the man who had caused it, Lincoln, he had said that there would be no "hostile act" in the harbor. Three South Carolina commissioners, just arrived in Washington to parley about the forts, said Anderson's move was a hostile act. Mississippi Senator Jefferson Davis, soon to be Confederate President, told the President, ". . . you are surrounded with blood and dishonor on all sides." Exultant headlines in the North and outraged ones in the South told the real significance of the major's action. Secretary of War John B. Floyd telegraphed Anderson in anger:

> Intelligence has reached here this morning that you have abandoned Fort Moultrie, spiked your guns, burned the carriages, and gone to Fort Sumter.... Explain the meaning of this report.

But Floyd was a Virginian who had been implicated first in a financial scandal and then in an effort to ship cannon from Pittsburgh to southern points, where they would be useful to the new Confederacy if it came to war. Buchanan had asked him to resign. Floyd had not yet got around to it. His continued presence in the Cabinet was one of the errors of a lame-duck President whose power to govern had virtually become paralyzed. Floyd had sent Anderson to Charleston in the first place because of the major's background as a Kentuckian who had married a Georgia girl, had until recently owned a few slaves, and expressed a sympathy for the South equaled only by his reverence for the Union. At Moultrie he had been deserted by the secretary—left in an untenable fort without reinforcements, his requests for instructions usually ignored. Moultrie, in the midst of extensive repairs, had gaps in its walls entered by neighborhood dogs, children, or secessionist leaders who watched, took notes and photographs, and called the Union presence there "coercion." From secessionist homes overlooking the fort it would be possible for snipers to pick off cannoneers. A well-armed force could overpower the garrison. Anderson's father, Major Richard Clough Anderson, had defended Moultrie against the British in 1779 and been captured—one particular footstep the son preferred not to follow in. He was aroused by Charlestonian threats and insistence that the forts be handed over, noting, "They are making every preparation (drilling nightly, &c) for the fight which they say must take place and insist on our not doing anything."

Indeed, few outsiders could gauge the Carolinian intensity. Francis W. Pickens had learned this when he returned from a recent tour as minister to Russia, talked with his good Democratic friend Buchanan in the White House, agreed that the Palmetto people were being hasty, and said he would quiet them when he got home. But Pickens, immediately running for governor of the state, found his moderating speeches so disdained that he quickly became a hotspur and was elected. Now, with Anderson in Sumter, the governor seized Moultrie, the United States arsenal (with 22,000 muskets), the customs house, and post office.

That was an error, for the chances were good that if Pickens had only protested, Buchanan would have ordered Anderson back to Moultrie. Now, if the President did such a thing, he would be hanged in effigy in a hundred northern cities and probably impeached. And now he was confronted by Secretary Floyd, whom he considered already fired, coming to him and resigning because of the President's "dishonorable" acceptance of the move to Sumter—a wily exit indeed. And when the South Carolina commissioners left after calling Buchanan lying and deceitful, he seemed more affected by this insult to his person than by the various discourtesies to the Union. Anderson, he said heavily, would have to be reinforced.

At Sumter, Chaplain Mathias Harris led a prayer of thanksgiving. Major Anderson raised Old Glory with slow dignity. The band played "Hail, Columbia" as the battery presented arms, then the men broke into spontaneous cheers, both in enthusiasm for their leader and in relief at escaping Moultrie. Yet, while it was true that Sumter was entirely surrounded by water, four times as big as Moultrie, and planned for three tiers of 146 guns served by 650 men, it was anything but impregnable in its present condition. Work on the fort had been impeded by the current quarrels. The barracks were unfinished, only fifteen guns had been mounted, many embrasures were wide open, the parade was choked with building materials as well as 5,600 shot and shell and sixty-six unmounted guns. The place could have been taken by a few hundred men with scaling ladders. Luckily, this was not known in town. "Twenty-five well-drilled men could hold it against all Charleston," said the Charleston Courier in dismay.

The garrison began mounting more guns. Abolitionist officers such as Captain Abner Doubleday and Captain John G. Foster, who had suspected Anderson of excessive southern sympathies, praised the skillful move to Sumter, and morale was high until the Star of the West arrived from New York on January 9 with two hundred men and supplies for the garrison. It was typical of the confusion and irresolution in government that the men were sent in a rented, unarmed merchantman rather than a Navy warship, and that Major Anderson had not been informed of its dispatch whereas the Charlestonians had. Buchanan's secessionist Secretary of the Interior, Jacob Thompson of Mississippi, had telegraphed the news to Governor Pickens and then resigned his post. Anderson was utterly perplexed when the vessel hove into view and was fired on by one of the Carolina batteries— arguably the first shot of the War Between the States, fired by a young cadet named George E. Haynsworth. Other batteries let fly, with aim mostly poor. Anderson, whose orders had been to act "strictly on the defensive," had his gunners ready but so longed for an

Right: His antagonist, Major Robert Anderson, commanding in Fort Sumter. A native of Kentucky, Anderson's sympathies were severely torn by the sectional crisis, but he saw his duty to the Union as paramount. (USAMHI)

Below: Castle Pinckney in Charleston. Here and at other works like this, the Confederate volunteers gathered during the early months of 1861, to train and await the time of their taking the Yankee fort that taunted them in their own harbor. (VM)

Left: Probably Confederates lounging inside Castle Pinckney, ready to fill its cannon with the shot stacked all about them and send the missiles on their way to Sumter. (SOUTH CAROLINA HISTORICAL SOCIETY)

The Charleston Zouave Cadets in Castle Pinckney, smart, well equipped, and anxious. (USAMHI)

Lieutenant R. C. Gilchrist, standing second from the left, carries a sword more like a scimitar than a saber, but the cadets in their pipe-clayed crossbelts dare not smile. Neither do their black orderlies at the rear. A year before most southern states had statutes on their books preventing slaves from reading or gathering together. Now they were uniformed and sometimes even trusted with arms as they came to the front to see to life's amenities while their masters met the enemy. (VM)

Right: Simon Cameron, Lincoln's Secretary of War, was slow in appreciating Anderson's helpless situation at Sumter, and slower still in doing anything about it. (USAMHI)

Below: Some military organizations that existed before the war, as much fraternal groups as real armed units, readied for the coming fight. Prominent were the men of Charleston's own Washington Light Infantry. They bivouacked in Camp Truesdale on the east end of Sullivan's Island. This faded old print shows their officers before their tent, equipped in a manner that two years hence would be only a fond memory. (WASHINGTON LIGHT INFANTRY)

amicable settlement between the states that he was loath to give the order to fire. As he pondered, the Star took two minor hits and fled. Doubleday and others were incensed at this failure to defend the flag, whereas soldiers with southern sympathies, such as Lieutenant R. K. Meade, thought Anderson's restraint wise. As for the fire-eating Robert Barnwell Rhett's Charleston Mercury, it hailed the striking of the first blow, saying, "It has wiped out a half century of scorn and outrage."

Governor Pickens was in the odd position of heading a self-styled South Carolina republic that still used United States stamps. Its congressmen were using their franking privileges to propagandize for the new Confederacy, and Pickens himself was asking for a $3,000 balance due him as minister to Russia, although he had forbidden the U.S. Subtreasury in Charleston to cash any more drafts from Washington. That cost him dearly when Washington, with intentional irony, sent him a $3,000 draft on the Subtreasury whose payments he had stopped. Pickens sent out his secretaries of state and war, Judge A.G. Magrath and General D.F. Jamison, under a flag of truce to urge Anderson to look to his own safety and evacuate Sumter peacefully since, they said, the United States government itself was crumbling. The major declined, urged diplomacy with Washington, and kept his men at the task of mounting more guns. Meanwhile, Colonel Samuel Colt of Hartford was shipping thousands of firearms south and building himself a mansion, and a Connecticut munitions firm sold 300,000 pounds of powder to Governor Pickens. Treason? Not at all. Did not the President himself declare that the seceded states were still part of the Union?

"The people of the South are mad," old Lewis Cass said; "the people of the North are asleep. The President is pale with fear.... God only knows what is to be the fate of my country!"

With South Carolina spending $20,000 daily for defense, and shipping now avoiding its greatest harbor, bankruptcy became a threat. Yet other southern leaders urged Pickens to go slowly, arguing that northern Democrats would sustain Buchanan whereas if a confrontation could be delayed until Lincoln took office, the Democrats would oppose him and the North would be divided. A new voice in Washington was that of William Henry Seward, Secretary of State-designate for Lincoln, who let it be known that he had plans (as yet unspecified) to resolve the whole quarrel and save the Union too. Other voices rumored that secessionists plotted to seize the capital on February 13, when the electoral votes would be officially counted and Lincoln formally declared the winner. They inspired the aged, Virginia-born General Winfield Scott, head of the Army, to colorful utterance:

> I have said that any [such person] should be lashed to the muzzle of a 12-pounder and fired out of a window of the Capitol. I would manure the hills of Arlington with fragments of his body.... It is my duty to suppress insurrection—my duty!

The day passed without incident. Buchanan's severity had given way once more to caution. He had swallowed the Star of the West affront. He wavered about reinforcing Anderson at all. He hoped that the new Confederate government would be less demanding than Pickens, that the crisis could be put off for his remaining days in the White House. On the complaint of Southerners that it was "warlike," he was ready to cancel a Washington's Birthday parade of six hundred soldiers until the spirited New York Congressman Daniel Sickles exploded that Washington was a Virginian, a national hero. The President was, critics said, ready to "give up part or even the whole of the Constitution to save the remainder."

Lincoln arrived quietly next day, having taken an earlier train to foil a rumored plot to assassinate him. The delegates from the seceded states had already met in Montgomery, elected Jefferson Davis president, and taken pains to remove the question of the forts from the excitable Pickens, who was now only a governor again. The men at Sumter froze in a heatless fort and ran low on tobacco while the aristocratic Carolinians enjoyed madeira, champagne, Spanish cigars and spoiled for a fight. Major Pierre Beauregard, U.S.A., recently deprived of his post as commander at West Point because of his southern allegiance, arrived in Charleston to take charge as Brigadier General Beauregard, C.S.A. He had been Anderson's pupil when the latter taught gunnery at West Point. He respected his one-time teacher but soon realized that he could overpower or starve out the meager Sumter garrison if he could prevent its reinforcement. Anderson, the man of honor, was wrestling also with the problem of what he should do in case his own state of Kentucky seceded, in which event it seemed to him that no matter what course he took there would be dishonor involved. A popular ditty in the North ran:

James is in his Cabinet
  Doubting and debating;
Anderson's in Sumter,
  Very tired of waiting.

Pickens is in Charleston,
  Blustering of blows;
Thank goodness March the Fourth is near,
  To nip Secession's nose.

On the fourth, Lincoln gave his inaugural in a city bristling with police and soldiers against a threatened secessionist coup, saying among other things, "...no state, upon its own mere notion, can lawfully get out of the Union," and "The power confided in me will be used to hold, occupy and possess the property and places belonging to the government." He had earlier said more colorfully that the Union was not a "free love arrangement" which any state could repudiate at will. The new Confederate commissioners arrived in Washington to parley with Lincoln through an intermediary, since the President would not recognize the C.S.A. Secretary Seward launched into an irresponsible and unauthorized course, letting the commissioners know that Lincoln was untutored in national affairs but that he, Seward, would soon bring him around and that Sumter would be peacefully evacuated. Seward's policy was based on his certainty that there was great innate love for the Union in the South and that if the states were permitted to secede, this love

Above Left:Another group of Confederates in Charleston, fully equipped for the field, their knapsacks on their backs, their Harpers Ferry rifles on their shoulders. (VM)

Above Right:Secretary of State William Seward played several ends against the middle in attempting to avoid the outbreak of hostilities in Charleston. In so doing he lied, overstepped his authority, and severely tried the patience of Lincoln. (USAMHI)

Right: Reminder of an earlier brave, now buried at Fort Moultrie. Osceola, the Seminole leader, effectively defeated the U. S. Army's attempt to subdue his people until the government admitted that it had lost the contest. His example was hardly lost on the high-spirited Southrons gathered at Charleston. (VM)

Above Left:Hurt most by Seward's interference was septuagenarian Lieutenant General Winfield Scott. Once the foremost soldier of the young republic, he was now an obese old man, a picture of ruined magnificence. Yet his mind was as active as ever, and he appreciated at once the hopelessness of reinforcing Anderson in Sumter without precipitating war. He advised that the fort be evacuated. Lincoln would not have it. (KA)

And that left Major Robert Anderson caught squarely in a trap. Charleston photographer George Cook took his camera out to Sumter in February 1861 and persuaded Anderson and his officers to sit for him. A tongue-in-cheek broadside soon appeared describing how "Col. George S. Cook, of the Charleston Photographic Light Artillery," stormed Sumter, "heroically penetrated to the presence of Maj. Anderson, and levelling a double barrelled Camera, demanded his unconditional surrender." The broadside appeared under the headline, MAJOR ANDERSON TAKEN! It looked like war was going to be fun. (VM)

Above: Anderson and his officers "captured" by Cook. Most of them would be heard from in the war to come. Seated from the left are Captain Abner Doubleday, Anderson, Surgeon Samuel W. Crawford, and Captain John G. Foster. Standing from the left are Captain Truman Seymour, Lieutenant G. W. Snyder, Lieutenant Jefferson C. Davis, Lieutenant R. K. Meade, and Captain T. Talbot. All but Snyder, Meade, and Talbot will become generals. (USAMHI)

Right: Talbot, Crawford, and Seymour posed separately, enjoying the distinction of being "captured" twice. (USAMHI)

Above: There were those who would help Anderson, and finally a relief expedition was sent, led by Gustavus V. Fox, Assistant Secretary of the Navy. But it could not dare Charleston's guns, and so it sat on the horizon, within sight but not reach of Anderson's exhausted command. (NAVAL PHOTOGRAPHIC CENTER)

Below: The Confederates, from their lookout tower at Fort Washington, expected Fox's coming. Several of them are here waving their caps in celebration, perhaps at the Union fleet's failure to test their batteries. (WASHINGTON LIGHT INFANTRY)

would combine with loss of trade and internal bickering to make them clamor to rejoin the Union within a year or so.

A message from Major Anderson staggered the new administration, for it told of the steady buildup of Confederate forces, the fact that Sumter had supplies for less than forty days, and gave an estimate (in which Anderson's officers substantially agreed) that it would take reinforcements of 20,000 men to hold the fort.

Twenty thousand men! No such force was available, nor were there enough Navy men-of-war to carry them if there had been. General Scott, much under Seward's influence, agreed with Anderson's estimate and told Lincoln, "Evacuation seems almost inevitable."

The idea was repugnant to the President. It would violate his "hold, occupy and possess" promise in his inaugural. It would begin his administration with a surrender which not even the irresolute Buchanan had contemplated. It would outrage the North and subject him to the contempt of the South—indeed, the whole watching world. Seward pressed him with the evacuation idea and the theory of an affectionate South which, if given its way, would spring back into the Union as if on a rubber band—a theory Lincoln deeply suspected. Determined to get the facts, he sent Gustavus Vasa Fox, a former Navy captain who yearned to lead an expedition to reinforce Anderson, to Charleston to confer with the major and find the actual condition of the fort and garrison. He dispatched Ward Lamon and Stephen Hurlbut separately to Charleston to sound officials and private citizens and see if they were, as Seward supposed, affectionate Unionists in a temporary fit of bad temper.

There were signs of spring in Charleston, ladies and gentlemen were promenading on the Battery, and the rumor that Sumter would soon be evacuated—which had appeared in the local papers— added spice to the air. The Army in South Carolina now numbered ten regiments of 8,835 men. Local photographers did a large business perpetuating the likenesses of these young men in their new uniforms. One photographer, George Cook, went to Sumter and persuaded the officers to sit for a group portrait despite Doubleday's conviction that he was a spy. In the city there was a magnificent St. Patrick's Day parade, and the feeling toward Anderson and his tobaccoless and short-rationed men softened enough so that cigars and several cases of claret were sent out for the officers. Captain Fox was permitted to visit Anderson and to observe, without mentioning it to the major, that reinforcement of the fort appeared feasible if done skillfully in darkness. Ward Lamon, Lincoln's close friend, apparently believed that there was now no choice but to quit Sumter, for he clearly gave Governor Pickens that impression and, on visiting Anderson at the fort, left him with the conviction that he would be withdrawn. Hurlbut, a native of Charleston who was now an Illinois lawyer, devoted himself to a survey of relatives and friends he had in the city. He decided that Seward's theory was absurd, that "there is a unanimity of sentiment" against the Union that was deep and unrelenting.

It is doubtful that there was ever so important an issue on which there was so much disagreement, so many misinterpretations and errors, so many men at cross purposes, often utterly mistaken and snarled in confusion.

Anderson was relieved that the issue, as he now believed, was to be settled by his withdrawal and that war would be averted. But as the days passed in Charleston (where there were rumors that the major had resigned his commission and that Captain Doubleday had gone insane and was in irons), impatience grew at the failure of the garrison to decamp. General Beauregard, hearing talk that demolition charges might be left in Sumter, wrote Anderson to suggest discreetly that the fort be left undamaged when he departed. The Confederacy in Montgomery was angry at the delay. In Sumter, the garrison was ready to pack and go north where pork chops, apple pie, and beautiful women were realities instead of dreams. Sumter was down to its last barrel of flour, as Anderson reported on April 3 to the new Secretary of War, Simon Cameron, urgently asking instructions. No instructions came.

The Confederate commissioners in Washington now found through an intermediary that Seward was no longer certain that Sumter would be evacuated. The secretary had done his best to impose his policy on the new President and, in failing, had caused misunderstanding and provoked accusations of bad faith. On April 8, a messenger from Lincoln handed Governor Pickens a paper whose single sentence exuded blunt honesty:

I am directed by the President of the United States to notify you to expect an attempt will be made to supply Fort Sumter with provisions only, and that if such attempt be not resisted, no effort to throw in men, arms or ammunition, will be made, without further notice, or in case of an attack upon the Fort.

At the same time, Anderson received his first instructions from the new administration: an expedition would attempt to supply him "and, in case the effort is resisted, will endeavor also to reinforce you." He had reconciled himself to his mortifying failure to defend the Star of the West on the ground that he had saved the peace. Now he had mortification and war too. As for Sumter's men, to whom their fort had become a prison, they reacted with a kind of glorious cussedness and cheered lustily at the news that they would have a chance to throw iron at the Carolinians who had made their lives so difficult.

Anderson declined a last offer by Beauregard permitting him to salute his flag if he would leave peacefully. With food left for perhaps sixty hours, he put his men on stern rations. The Carolinians now had at least thirty guns and eighteen mortars bearing on Sumter from six widely separated emplacements, some of which Sumter could not touch. To save his men, the major ordered them to serve only the guns in the more protected casemate tier, which limited them to twenty-one guns, most of them only 32-pounders, and not a single mortar.

The first shot on Fort Sumter was fired from Fort Johnson on James Island at 4:30 A.M. April 12, 1861. It woke up Doubleday, who commented, "[It] seemed to bury itself in the masonry about a foot from my head." He stayed in bed as the firing became an intermittent roar. Sumter did not answer until after 6 o'clock reveille and a

Left: And finally came war. At 4:30 A.M., or shortly after, April 12, 1861, a signal gun was fired from Fort Johnson. Seconds later Edmund Ruffin, fire-eating secessionist from South Carolina, jerked a lanyard . . . (NA, BRADY COLLECTION)

Below: . . . on one of these eight-inch columbiads in the Iron Clad Battery moored off Morris Island, and launched one of the first hostile shots of the war against Sumter's parapet.

A rare, previously unpublished photograph by Osborn & Durbec of Charleston showing the interior of the Iron Clad Battery, taken April 17, 186 just five days after the firing. One of these guns, or a third not shown, fired Ruffin's hostile shot. (CHS)

Left: The first answering Federal shot of the war was fired by Captain Doubleday, who gladly sent a ball toward the Iron Clad Battery, though it bounced harmlessly off its roof. (USAMHI)

Left: The Surgeon Crawford began firing his gun, sending his shells toward an unusual and ungainly apparition. . . (USAMHI)

Above: The iron-sheathed Floating Battery at Sullivan's Island mounted two 42-pounder cannon and two 32-pounders, and proudly flew the flag of the new Confederacy overhead. A photograph taken on April 16, 1861, by an unidentified photographer, shows the Floating Battery in position off the island. This print has not been published in nearly seventy years. (VM)

Left: After thirty-three hours of bombardment, former Senator Louis T. Wigfall of Texas, aide to Beauregard and an ardent secessionist, carried a truce flag to Sumter and asked Anderson to surrender. Seeing the hopelessness of further resistance, the major gave up. (CIVIL WAR TIMES ILLUSTRATED)

Below: On April 14, Anderson and his command left the fort to its conquerors. The flag of the Confederate States of America went up a makeshift staff, and the next day photographer F. K. Houston of 307 King Street in Charleston became the first to bring a camera into Fort Sumter. Elated soldiers feigned action poses while he made his slow exposure, but the proud new flag would not stay still. (USAMHI)

Below: That day and in those following, several cameramen came to the fort. The names of some are now lost, but thankfully not their photographs. One of them, probably Osborn & Durbec, made a panorama from three separate images of Sumter that shows vividly the damage done by Beauregard's batteries. They claimed to have made these shots the very day of the surrender. (USAMHI)

breakfast consisting of fat pork and water. "Be careful of your lives," Anderson cautioned, ordering his men to stay in the casemates as much as possible. Doubleday, his second in command, was given the honor of firing the first shot against the rebellion—one he accepted with zest, reflecting, "To me it was simply a contest, politically speaking, as to whether virtue or vice should rule." Private John Carmody, knowing that the bigger barbette guns above were loaded and aimed at Moultrie, disobeyed orders, stole up there, and fired them one by one, making a great noise but with little effect on the well-protected Confederate batteries. It was an unequal battle, what with Sumter's lack of mortars and inability to fire shell (there were no fuses), not to mention the poor provender. Enemy fire, gaining in accuracy, cleared the parapet and started fires in the wooden barracks inside, which took smart work to extinguish. Sumter's most visible achievement was a ball that crashed into the large frame Moultrie House hotel, which sent dozens of battle-watchers scurrying.

Early in the afternoon a Sumter watchman saw a United States man-of-war far out beyond the bar. Reinforcements and food! A shout of joy went up from the exhausted gunners—all in vain. The expedition led by Captain Fox had been broken up by confusion in New York and by a storm that drove two of its fighting ships and its tugs off course. The tugs were the heart of Fox's careful plan for reaching the fort, and the guns were essential to protect the tugs. Fox was waiting for help that never came.

The Sumtermen loosed curses the next morning when they saw the "rescue" vessels still waiting in the distance. Cartridges got so low that they restricted their firing to one gun every ten minutes. The barracks took fire again so that there was no putting it out. Flames crept slowly toward the magazine where 275 barrels of powder were stored. The magazine was banked with earth for protection, but flying embers touched off stockpiles of shells and grenades that had been placed at strategic spots along the gorge wall, sending down showers of sparks and broken masonry. The main gates were now ablaze. Smoke poured into the casemates, choking the men serving the guns. From the shore the smoke and flame made it seem impossible that Sumter could continue the battle, and there was Carolinian admiration when its guns kept firing. Texas Senator Louis Wigfall, now a Confederate colonel, who had damned the Union and cheered the attack, marveled at this display of courage but thought it had gone far enough. He got a boat and was rowed to the fort, unseen by the smoke-blinded defenders. He entered an open embrasure, carrying a white flag on his sword, and came upon a sooty-faced Major

Anderson, whose coolness astonished him.

"You have defended your flag nobly, sir," Wigfall shouted. "It's madness to persevere.... General Beauregard wishes to stop this, and to ask upon what terms you will evacuate this work."

Anderson at length agreed to parley. Only three cartridges remained. His men were spent. The larder was all but empty. There was danger of explosions in the fort. The effort to reinforce him had somehow collapsed. It would indeed be madness to persevere.

After thirty-three hours of bombardment, the Sumter flag went down at 1:30 P.M. April 13. A few men on each side had been injured by flying debris, but the only fatality of battle was a horse killed on Morris Island by a Sumter ball. Charleston was in transports over the victory. Headlines in the North used the word "WAR." Young men, North and South, began flocking to the banners. It was, as Horace Greeley said later, a comparatively bloodless beginning for the bloodiest conflict America ever knew.

Sumter's eastern terreplein and parapet, April 15, 1861. Just over the wall can be seen a steam sidewheeler that transported more and more Confederates into the captured fort, and sightseers from Charleston as well. One such is the top-hatted man standing at right. The man at left is Major Nathan G. Evans, who will shortly be a brigadier general at Bull Run. The man in the middle is Lieutenant Robert Pringle. (CHARLESTON LIBRARY SOCIETY)

Top Right: But Anderson's men did some damage, too, and the camera artists were not loath to show it. Here on April 16 the soldiers' barracks at Fort Moultrie showed the effect of Sumter's fire. (CHARLESTON POST-COURIER)

Below Right: So, too, did Moultrie's northwest angle. (CHARLESTON MUSEUM)

Bottom Left: April 15, the interior of Sumter, showing the destroyed western barracks and, in the right foreground, columbiads that Anderson had mounted in the ground to use as mortars. (VM)

Bottom Right: April 15, another view of the southwest angle showing officers' quarters and soldiers' barracks. Elated Confederates stand in groups retelling their experiences while watching the bombardment. (VM)

April 15, the southwest angle of the fort, a panorama formed of two separate images. Dressed smartly on parade, the conquering Confederates line up for the camera, while their flag floats gently overhead. Anderson built the earth bank at left to protect the lower tier of soldiers' quarters. The fort's beacon lantern, removed from its place on the parapet, rests in the parade ground. These two images have never before been juxtaposed to give this wide view of the interior of the fort. (VM)

Right: The only known photograph of the interior of Sumter's casemate, and the guns that Doubleday, Crawford, and others manned in defense. (TU)

Below Left: Another view, April 17 or later, showing the effects of the fire from Charleston upon the mortar and masonry of the fort. (USAMHI)

Below Right: The main sally-port into Sumter, showing the confusion of rubble and the damage done by Beauregard's cannon. (NYHS)

On April 17, 1861, and probably for two or three days thereafter, two special photographers visited not only Fort Sumter, but also all of the Confederate installations that fired against it. They were James M. Osborn and F. E. Durbec of "Osborn & Durbec's Photographic Mart" at 223 King Street in Charleston. They operated a rather extensive establishment, advertising their "Cheap Photographs! Cheap Ambrotypes! Cheap Daguerreotypes! Cheap Ivorytypes! Cheap Melainotypes!" and advised that strangers visiting Charleston "would do well to give us a call before going elsewhere." They sold views of Egypt, photo cases in some five thousand different patterns, and even carried cameras for sale. They are today forgotten, but on those days in April 1861 they took a place beside Brady and Gardner and Edwards and the rest of the war's immortal chroniclers.

Their stereo camera captured over forty scenes in Sumter and the Charleston batteries, the most complete record ever made of the site of a Civil War engagement. Apparently they later attempted to market their stereo views, but the war and the Federal blockade probably prevented their ever getting sufficient chemicals and supplies to manufacture the prints. As a result, very few of their images survive in more than one copy, and all but a few have been entirely lost to view until now.

What follows—in addition to the Osborn & Durbec views already presented in this and the previous chapter—is a nearly complete collection of their work. Two thirds of these images have never before been published and are newly discovered.

As for Osborn & Durbec, their partnership did not survive the war. By 1866 they had gone their separate ways. They left behind a priceless record of the first sad evidence of war between the states.

Left: A group of Confederate dignitaries in front of the shot furnace on Sumter's parade ground. Beside them is one of the columbiads that Anderson mounted to use as mortars against Charleston. They were never fired. The tall figure in the center has long been believed to be Wade Hampton. Others probably include Governor Francis Pickens. (TU)

Below: The sally-port at Fort Sumter seen from the wharf. Already the conquering Confederates are at work cleaning out the rubble and rebuilding. (TU)

Below Left: The southwest face of the fort, showing the damage done by Edmund Ruffin and members of his Palmetto Guard as they fired the columbiads in the Iron Clad Battery. (CHS)

Below Right: The southwest corner, and the effects of shots fired from Morris Island and the Floating Battery. The opening at left is an embrasure for one of Sumter's guns. (CHS)

Above Left: Damage done by Confederate guns firing from Cumming's Point. (TU)

Above Right: The southeast side of the parade, the hot-shot furnace, and the soldiers' east barracks. (CHS)

Above Left: The ruins of the sally-port at right, and to its left the officers' quarters. (CHS)

Above Right: Cleaning up the parade ground in front of the sally-port. (MHS)

The ruined officers' quarters on the southwest side, and a row of cannon Anderson did not emplace. (CHS)

The stair tower at an angle in the perimeter, and jaunty Confederates atop their captured guns. (TU)

Above Left: Damage done by the Iron Clad Battery on the interior of Sumter. (CHS)

Above Right: In the left rear, the powder magazine, protected by an earth traverse. It is on the side facing Charleston, since Sumter was built to withstand an attack from the sea, not the land face. (TU)

Left: Behind the makeshift flagstaff can be seen the effects of Fort Moultrie's fire on the officers quarters and sally-port. (NA,BRADY COLLECTION)

Above: The rear of the same parapet, another dismounted gun, and a traverse built of sand bags to protect men from the fire from Sullivan's Island. (CWTI)

Above: More of the cleanup, with two men working while the others watch. (TU)

Left: The shot furnace and, to the right, Anderson's flagstaff, which was shot off during the bombardment. The new flag of the victors flutters overhead. (CHS)

Right: Sumter's parapet. Fort Moultrie is in the distance, while the guns shown are trained on the Iron Clad Battery. The gun in the foreground has been dismounted by Confederate fire. (CHS)

Far Right: Confederates on Morris Island, very probably men of Colonel J. H. Trapier's Mortar Battery. (SOUTH CAROLINA HISTORICAL SOCIETY)

Below: The Trapier Mortar Battery on Morris Island and, in the right background, Osborn & Durbec's pyramidal portable darkroom. (TU)

Above: Another view of the Trapier Battery, this time manned for action. At the very right of the image, behind the dimly seen man at the edge, is a corner of the portable darkroom. (CHS)

Below: A view of the Iron Clad Battery at Morris Island from the rear. The railroad "T" iron cladding has been removed from its wooden beamed roof. One of the columbiads with which Ruffin sent the first shots against Sumter can be seen within. (SOUTH CAROLINA HISTORICAL SOCIETY)

Left: The harbor face of Fort Moultrie, its shot furnace in the foreground. Since it was assumed that any attacker would come from the sea in wooden ships, the U. S. Army, when building these coastal forts, provided for sending red-hot shot like fireballs into attacking vessels. Just above the gun at the right can be seen a long dark object. It is Fort Sumter. These guns no longer bear upon it. (TU)

Left: Another view of Moultrie's shot furnace, with the officers' quarters behind it. Heated shot from here set ablaze the wooden roofs in Sumter and caused fires that threatened the powder magazine. (TU)

Top Left: The eastern angle of Moultrie, on Sullivan's Island. Damage done by Sumter's return fire can be seen in the roof of the right wing of the large house. (TU)

Top Right: Moultrie's northwestern angle. (TU)

Left: Moultrie's western barracks overlooking the parade ground, and the damage done by Captain Doubleday. (TU)

Right: A house on Sullivan's Island riddled by Surgeon Crawford's shot as he fired on the Floating Battery (TU)

Bottom Left: More of Doubleday's handiwork on the western barracks. It was small recompense. (TU)

Bottom Right: Empty gun emplacements on Sullivan's Island and, in the harbor beyond, Fort Sumter. The bloodless beginning to a bloody war. (TU)

The Boys of '61

BELL I. WILEY

Euphoric thousands enlist before they miss "the fun"

Above: As Lincoln and Davis issued their calls for the boys of '61, the first to be ready were those already enrolled in the scores of active militia units in North and South. New York photographer Charles D. Fredericks turned his camera out his own studio window on July 4, 1860, to catch this resplendent unit at parade. The bearskins would soon disappear. (USAMHI)

THE TREMENDOUS WAVE of patriotism that swept over North and South in the wake of Fort Sumter produced an epidemic of volunteering. Very few of the recruits had any prior military experience. Conversion of the hordes of civilians into effective soldiers presented an enormous challenge, but authorities on both sides rose to the occasion and the results proved better than might have been expected.

Since governors usually took the lead in mobilization, most recruits had a brief stint of state service before they were sworn in as Federal or Confederate troops. First came a physical examination, usually a perfunctory test consisting largely of responses to questions put by the doctors concerning the recruits' medical history. Then came formal muster into national service—inspection by the muster officer, pledging allegiance to the United States or the Confederacy, promising to obey orders, swearing to abide by the 101 articles of war to which recruits listened while standing in company formation, and signing the company muster roll.

On both sides recruits chose their officers. As a rule the rank and file elected only their company officers (lieutenants and captains), who in turn chose the field grade officers (majors, lieutenant colonels, and colonels), but in some units soldiers elected all officers, from corporals to colonels. Those who took the lead in raising units were generally chosen to command them, but when, as was sometimes the case, more than one candidate vied for a position, lively campaigns ensued. Victors in these contests sometimes celebrated their success by hosting drinking parties.

During the first weeks in camp, recruits within the various companies organized themselves into informal groups known as messes. These varied in size from six to a dozen men, drawn together by similarity of inclination and interest. Members took turns in drawing rations, gathering wood, and cooking. Ties became very close with continuing association. An Illinois soldier wrote early in 1862: "Cap wanted to take some more men in our mess but we told him we would rather not, we wanted mess No. one to remain as it was....Ours...is the most intelligent mess in this Reg[iment], the best fellows, the bravest boys, can kill more Secesh & Eat more hard Crackers & stand more hard marching, waid deeper mud & do less grumbling than any other mess in the Northern army."

As the time approached for departure from home for "the seat of war," volunteers took part in a series of farewell activities. One of these was the presentation of a flag by one of the feminine patriots who had helped to make it. As the pretty donor made the presentation, she delivered a flowery speech, extolling cause and country and calling on the recipients to protect the emblem from the vile creatures who sought to defile it. The officer receiving the colors, usually a colonel, responded in words glowing with patriotism and pledging himself and his associates to defend the banner with their lives.

On the day of departure friends and neighbors gathered at the railway station or steamboat wharf or some other place of rendezvous to bid the soldiers farewell. After a prayer by a local minister, the recruits took their leave amid a chorus of good-byes and best wishes. The volunteers joked and laughed to mask their sadness, and loved ones left behind did their best to fight back the tears that filled their eyes.

The trip to the fighting zone, made sometimes by train and sometimes by boat, was a boisterous experience. Troops traveling by rail sometimes obtained better ventilation and visibility by knocking holes in the sides of boxcars; many rode on top of the cars, despite the admonitions of the officers. Escape from home restraints and the prospect of new and exciting experiences brought a holiday attitude. So did the hearty cheering of pretty girls who greeted them along the way. Many volunteers added to their joviality by taking generous swigs from liquor bottles which they had slipped into their baggage before taking leave of their loved ones. The first casualties experienced by some units came not from hostile bullets but from tipsy soldiers falling from trains. The congestion and filth of some of the trains and boats that transported soldiers were enough to provoke excessive drinking. In March 1862 an Illinois Yank wrote home from West Tennessee: "We was aboard the steamer Memphis 8 or 9 days. We was in dirt, lice, shit, grease & Hard crackers."

Arrival at the front, whether in Tennessee, Kentucky, Missouri, Maryland, or Virginia, brought a change in the character of soldiering. During the initial period of service when the men were near their homes, discipline was lax and duties relatively light. Recruits frequently called their superiors by their first names or addressed them as "sarge" or "cap." Leaves were easy to obtain, and officers and men spent much of their time in nearby towns or cities. But the proximity of the enemy and the certainty of combat gave serious and urgent purpose to training. Recruits and their officers came under the control of hard-bitten professionals like Joseph E. Johnston, Braxton Bragg, U.S. Grant, and George B. McClellan. These commanders knew that the novices flowing in from farms, shops, and factories had to undergo a swift and drastic transformation before they could win battles. And they set themselves to effecting the change with determination and vigor. Men who previously treated soldiering as a lark now complained of the hardness of their lot. "I don't believe God ever intended for one man to pen up another and keep him in this manner," wrote a Reb to his homefolks; he added, "Dam Old Abe and Old Jeff Davis. Dam the day I 'listed." Another Reb wrote from a camp near Richmond in May 1861, "A man may come here with as much devil in him as they please, but they will soon tame him." A Georgian, after his transfer to Virginia in the fall of 1861, wrote his father: "I love my country as well as any one but I don't believe in the plan of making myself a slave.... A private soldier is nothing more than a slave and is often treated worse. I have during the past six months gone through more hardships than anyone of ours or Grandma's negroes; their life is a luxury to what mine is sometimes." But this soldier came to realize the value of discipline, and while he never completely gave up the cherished practice of grumbling, he eventually accepted and approved the new order. The same was true of most of his comrades and of the men they fought.

In the fighting zones, platoons, companies, and regiments had to be fitted into larger organizations. Two platoons, each commanded by a

Above: The Kentucky State Guard encampment at Louisville in August 1860 proved a training ground for several future Confederate companies. Commander of the Guard was Brigadier General Simon Bolivar Buckner, soon to be a trusted commander of the Confederacy. This group, the Lexington Rifles, was raised and captained by John Hunt Morgan. In the fall of 1861 he would lead them into the rebellion, to become a part of his famed cavalry. For now they are content to pose and drink and feast on watermelon. (KHS)

Above: Buckner's own unit, the Citizen Guard, and more bearskins. (KHS)

Left: But militia were not enough. New volunteer armies must be raised. Though defeated by Lincoln in 1860, Stephen A. Douglas stood firmly behind his antagonist's administration, and now took to the stump in speaking to raise support and volunteers. He wore himself out in the process, and died that summer. The last words of his final public address declared his stand for the Union: "United, firm, determined, never to permit the Government to be destroyed. (USAMHI)

Right: Lincoln's old friend Senator Edward Baker of Oregon helped raise a regiment. He would lead it to destruction, and his own death, at Ball's Bluff in October. (RICHARD C. OSTERHOUT)

Right: Colonel E. Elmer Ellsworth, once a denizen of Lincoln's Illinois law office, brought his New York Fire Zouaves, composed chiefly of New York City firemen, to Washington soon after the crisis came to shots at Sumter. (NYHS)

Below: To the War Department in Washington fell the task of organizing, equipping, training, and assigning the largest army ever raised in the hemisphere. No one had any experience in dealing with such numbers. (CHS)

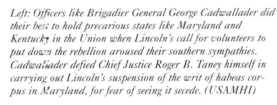

Left: Officers like Brigadier General George Cadwallader did their best to hold precarious states like Maryland and Kentucky in the Union when Lincoln's call for volunteers to put down the rebellion aroused their southern sympathies. Cadwallader defied Chief Justice Roger B. Taney himself in carrying out Lincoln's suspension of the writ of habeas corpus in Maryland, for fear of seeing it secede. (USAMHI)

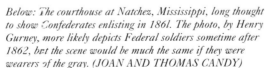

Below: The courthouse at Natchez, Mississippi, long thought to show Confederates enlisting in 1861. The photo, by Henry Gurney, more likely depicts Federal soldiers sometime after 1862, but the scene would be much the same if they were wearers of the gray. (JOAN AND THOMAS CANDY)

lieutenant, comprised a company, led by a captain; ten companies formed a regiment, commanded by a colonel; two or more regiments comprised a brigade, led by a brigadier general; two or more brigades combined to make a division, commanded by a major general; two or more divisions comprised a corps, commanded by a lieutenant general on the Confederate side and a major general on the Union side; and two or more corps made an army, commanded by a full general on the Confederate side and a major general on the Union side. In the artillery, the battalion, consisting of four batteries, each containing four to six guns, was a standard organization. The squadron (known also as the troop and the equivalent roughly of the infantry company) consisting of two or more platoons was a distinctive feature of the cavalry organization. Combination of arms normally began with the attachment of artillery (usually a battery) and cavalry to an infantry brigade. Engineer, signal, and other supporting elements were added on the corps or army level.

The basic unit on both sides was the infantry company, which at full strength numbered something over one hundred officers and men. But, after the first few months of service, companies commonly dwindled to about half their authorized strength and subsequently some experienced even greater attrition. Long and intimate association and the sharing of perils and hardships of soldiering promoted a relationship among company officers and their men very much like that of a family. The captain was the father who supervised daily routine, saw that his men were equipped, fed, clothed, and sheltered, heard their complaints, administered punishment for minor offenses, looked after their health, and led them in combat. He knew every man by name and had some acquaintance with the soldier's home circumstances. He sometimes mediated domestic squabbles, wrote letters for illiterates, supervised religious worship, buried the dead, and wrote letters of sympathy to bereaved wives and mothers. The lieutenants and noncommissioned officers were the captain's helpers and their role was very much like that of the elder children in a large family. A key member of the group was the company's first or orderly sergeant, who called the roll, kept the records, and translated the captain's wishes into orders.

On the Confederate side, and to an increasing extent among the Federals, blacks were obtained to help clean quarters, launder clothing, clean boots and shoes, cook, and perform other menial chores. Early in the war some enlisted men even had one or more Negroes, usually body servants, to lighten the burdens of camp life, even to the extent of standing guard under the supervision of their masters. But after a few months most of these servants went home; those who remained were usually the personal aides of officers, or blacks assigned to companies and regiments as hostlers or teamsters. The blacks encountered in northern camps were ex-slaves hired for a pittance to relieve officers and men of some of the more burdensome aspects of army service. Home letters of many Yanks in 1861 and later told of the writer's good fortune in having obtained the service of black menials. Private Andrew Rose of an Ohio regiment stationed in middle Tennessee wrote his parents in

1863: "The captain got two nigers for our company; every company has got them; all we do when we want nigers is to send a company after them." In 1862 a Maine captain wrote from Louisiana: "Officers & men are having an easy time. We have Negroes to do all fatigue work, cooking and washing clothes." In both armies black servants were often called on to dance and provide music for the entertainment of officers and soldiers. The Negroes sometimes sought diversion for them selves by gambling and drinking. During the last two years of the war, about 200,000 blacks were recruited by the Federals for service as soldiers. Inspection reports show that colored troops were often required to do more than their share of labor and that sometimes their white commander treated them more like menials than as fighters.

The training received by Johnny Reb and Billy Yank was very much alike. Hardee's Tactics—written by William J. Hardee, a Confederate general—was the most widely used infantry manual on both sides. In accordance with rules prescribed by Hardee for "the school of the soldier" recruits mastered such fundamentals as saluting or standing erect; facing left and right; marching forward, to the rear, by the flank, and obliquely; shifting arms to the various positions; parrying and thrusting with the bayonet; and loading and firing their guns standing, kneeling, and lying down. Most Yanks and Rebs were armed either with the Springfield or the Enfield rifled musket. Since both were muzzle loaders, much time and patience were required for their effective use. For loading the gun Hardee specified nine movements, each initiated by the instructor's command. At the order "Load!" the soldier dropped the butt of his gun to the ground, grasped the barrel with his left hand and with his right hand reached for the cartridge box hanging from his belt. In response to subsequent commands he bit the end from the paper cartridge; poured the powder into the barrel; inserted the bullet, with hollow base down, into the muzzle and with a ramrod pushed it to the other end of the barrel; returned the ramrod to its place beneath the barrel; took a percussion cap from a leather pouch on his belt and placed it on the nipple of the tube extending from beneath the hammer into the barrel; and shifted the gun to his right shoulder. Firing was then accomplished by movements executed at the commands "Ready," "Aim," "Fire." Despite the complexity of the procedure, a well-trained infantryman could load and fire his gun twice a minute.

After obtaining proficiency in the use of their rifles, soldiers were taught progressively to march and maneuver in squads, companies, regiments, brigades, and divisions. However, drills by units larger than brigades were infrequent and "sham battles," with infantry, artillery, and cavalry functioning together, were almost unknown until after the first year of the war, and even then they were rare.

Other branches followed a training routine com parable to that of the infantry. In the artillery much practice was required for each member of the gun crew to become proficient in his duties; the most widely used field piece on both sides was the 12-pounder smoothbore called the Napoleon. Functioning by numbers, from 1 to 10, each crew man not only had to

Right: A recruiting scene in an unidentified town. These men, perhaps, are Confederates. Certainly they have the rugged look of those rough-edged, tough men of the trans-Appalachian west who, North and South, proved to be the fiercest fighters—and worst disciplined—of the war. (JMB)

Left: They came in whole families, like these four brothers in blue with their target rifles. (LO)

Below: They spoke in strange tongues, like men of this all-German artillery unit. Tens of thousands of Germans marched behind the Federal banners, often induced to volunteer by high rank being given—sometimes unwisely—to prominent Germans. (AMERICANA IMAGE GALLERY)

Left: They came in baggy pants, the uniform of the French Chasseur. (USAMHI)

Right: They came magnificently equipped, like Sergeant Dore of the 7th New York State Militia. (USAMHI)

Right: They came, like Lieutenant A. Kintzing Post of the 45th Massachusetts, enlisting for and expecting a nine-month war. (USAMHI)

Below: They came like these two brothers of Company I, 2d New Hampshire Volunteers, with their deceptively light colored blouses and rather distinctive headgear. (HP)

Right: And they came young. This unknown boy wears the fatigue blouse and cap, common dress for most Federal infantry. (ROBERT MCDONALD)

Below: And younger still they came. A photograph taken in 1861 by Lieutenant Henry Digby of Ohio, of drummer boys William Ambrose and Jimmy Carvill. (AMERICANA IMAGE GALLERY)

make the specific movement associated with his number, such as removing the shell from the ammunition chest, passing it on to another, placing it in the muzzle, and ramming it down, but he also had to learn the movements as signed to all the other numbers so that when casualties were experienced shifts could be made without loss of efficiency.

While learning to drill and to use their weapons, recruits had to adjust to the regimented routine of army life. The soldier's day was ordered by drum or bugle calls, which ordinarily ran to about a dozen. First came reveille, sounded about dawn, to wake the soldiers and summon them to roll call. After lining up and responding to their names, they were dismissed until a second call a half-hour later ordered them to breakfast. The third call sent the ailing to the regimental surgeon and the well to such duties as cleaning quarters, tidying company grounds, and cutting wood. About eight o'clock, the musicians sounded the call for guard mounting, at which the first sergeant of each company turned out his guard detail for the next twenty-four hours' duty, inspected them, and marched them to the regimental parade ground. There the guards were formed into line, inspected by the adjutant, and sent to their respective posts. Details were so arranged that each member stood guard only two hours out of every six.

Next came the call for drill, which ordinarily lasted until drummer or bugler signaled "roast beef," which was the call for lunch. Following a brief post-luncheon period of relaxation, soldiers were summoned to another drill which normally lasted from one to two hours. Then the men returned to their quarters, brushed their uniforms, blacked their leather, polished buckles and buttons, and cleaned their weapons in preparation for retreat, which consisted of roll call, inspection, and dress parade. Both officers and men took pride in the dress parade, held sometimes by regiment and sometimes by brigade, and always to the accompaniment of music. Dress parades were the occasion for reading orders and making official announcements.

Supper call came shortly after retreat, followed not long after dark by tattoo, which brought an other roll call, after which the men returned to their quarters. The final call of the day required the cessation of noise and the extinguishing of lights. In the course of the war this call became "taps."

This was the typical routine of an infantry regiment in camp during a season of quiet. Practices varied to some extent in different camps and with changing situations. Sunday routine differed from that of other days. The major event on the Sabbath was a general inspection of quarters, grounds, personnel, and equipment. After a preliminary check by the units' own officers, the regiment or battalion formed by companies. The inspector, usually the brigade commander or one of his staff, proceeded up and down the open ranks, carefully observing clothing, weapons, and other equipment. The soldiers were then required to stack arms, unsling and open their knapsacks, and lay them on the ground for examination. The inspector checked the contents of the knapsacks, and if he found a dirty garment he rebuked the offender. Further reproof for this and any other faults discovered by the inspector was given by the unit commander after the men returned to their quarters. The inspecting officer made the rounds of guardhouse, hospital, sutler's shop, kitchen, and such other facilities as he chose to examine. He concluded the inspection shortly before noon by going through the company quarters and checking floors, bunks, and walls. Soldiers usually spent Sunday afternoons writing letters, playing games, reading, or gambling. Those of religious inclination might attend prayer meetings or listen to sermons delivered by the regimental chaplain or by one of their comrades.

Every other month soldiers were mustered for pay. Standing in company formation, each soldier certified his presence by responding "here" when his name was called. After the mustering officer had accounted for every man listed on the roster, he forwarded a copy of the muster roll to the adjutant general in Washington, or Richmond. At the beginning of the war the monthly pay on both sides was $11 for infantry and artillery privates and $12 for cavalry. Early in the conflict the Union government increased the pay of privates in all three branches to $13 a month and in May 1864 to $16. Confederates received only one raise and that was on June 9, 1864, when the monthly stipend of infantry and artillery privates was increased to $20 and that of cavalry privates to $21; by that time the gold value of the Confederate dollar had shrunk to about five cents. Pay was often in arrears, sometimes as much as four months on the Union side and six to twelve months among Confederates.

An essential part of the transition from civilian to soldier was getting accustomed to military clothing. On both sides the first uniforms worn by some soldiers were those in which they had paraded as militiamen. These varied considerably in color and design. Concerning troops whom he observed in Washington in the early summer of 1861, General William T. Sherman stated: "Their uniforms were as various as the cities and states from which they came." When Northerners wore gray militia uniforms into battle and Southerners wore blue, as was the case in some of the early engagements, they had the unhappy experience of being fired on by their comrades. In 1861 and later, both sides had some Zouave units that wore fezzes, red bloomers, gaily colored vests and sashes, and white gaiters. Considerable variation in dress persisted throughout the war, but a fair degree of standardization was achieved in both armies before the end of 1861.

The usual outfit of a Federal infantryman was a long woolen dress coat of dark blue with a high stiff collar; a dark blue jacket or blouse which for field service was much preferred to the dress coat; light blue trousers; black brogan shoes; a flannel shirt; long flannel drawers; socks; blue cap with black visor; and a long blue overcoat with cape. Artillery and cavalry dress was the same as for the infantry except the coats were shorter and boots were normally worn instead of shoes. In both armies each branch had distinctive trimmings (red for artillery, blue for infantry, and yellow for cavalry). Branch was also indicated by insignia worn on the front of the headgear; Union officers below the grade of generals wore crossed cannons for artillery, a bugle for infantry, crossed sabers for cavalry, turreted

Left: And still younger. David Wood, aged ten. The children came to be drummers, but many, the larger ones, often passed for beyond their years and took their place in the battle. The veterans sometimes sang nursery songs in camp when they spied these boys of '61. But it was a young man's war. Some "boys" would be generals before they were old enough to vote. (RICHARD E. WOOD)

Below: C. C. Taylor, J. D. Jackson, and a man named Porter, all from Georgia, enlisted in the 3d Georgia Infantry, but did not leave for war before posing for this ambrotype. The numbers were against them. In this war, nearly one of every three Confederates would die. (MC)

Right: The Southrons flocked to their country's call, too. At Fredericksburg, Virginia, in June 1861, these confident young Virginians posed in a mixture of military and civilian dress. For many it was the best they would ever get. (JOHN A. HESS)

Right: They came to photographers who supplied them with props like Roman short swords and sometimes ungrammatical patriotic expressions. (PRIVATE COLLECTION)

Below: They came with boyish bravado and clowning. (C.D.W. NELSON)

Above: They came with double-barreled shotguns, huge bowie knives, and a look of wild determination. (HP)

Left: Some looked rather bemused by it all. (WILLIAM A. ALBAUGH)

castle for engineers, and flaming shell for ordnance, along with a brass numeral designating regiment and, when applicable, a brass letter specifying company. Union privates wore brass letters and numerals on their caps to indicate company and regiment; on the Confederate side, branch was designated by the color of the cap crown.

Confederate Army regulations specified a double-breasted coat for both officers and enlisted men, but among enlisted men this garment was rarely seen after the first few months of the conflict. In its stead a short, gray single-breasted jacket was worn, thus giving to Johnny Rebs the nickname "gray jackets." Confederate Army regulations also specified trousers of dark blue, but from the beginning, until the use of homemade dyes produced a yellowish brown or "butternut" hue, trousers, like coats, were of gray. Confederate shoes and socks at first were very much like those worn by Yanks, but after the northern blockade became effective, inferior shoes made of home-tanned leather had to be used, though many Rebs equipped themselves with sturdier footwear by appropriating the shoes of Yankee battle casualties. Some Confederates, especially those of rural background, regarded drawers as superfluous. Regulations of both armies listed leather stocks or ties as standard items of issue, but these were rarely worn. Many soldiers in both armies wore soft hats instead of caps. Well-meaning relatives North and South frequently loaded the soldiers down with "extras" such as havelocks to protect necks from sun and rain, sleeping caps, scarfs, and mittens, but these were usually discarded soon after the recruits arrived in camp, if not before.

The soldier's prescribed equipment included a haversack for his food, a canteen, a knapsack for extra items of clothing, stationery, toilet articles, and other personal items, a leather cartridge box, and a small leather pouch for percussion caps. But comfort, convenience, and other considerations led to a shedding of some of this equipment. Knapsacks were frequently discarded and the contents rolled in a blanket which the soldier threw over his left shoulder and tied at the ends above his right hip. Many Rebs and Yanks regarded tin cups and small skillets as essential items of equipment. These they suspended from their belts. The cups some times were used for boiling coffee over the coals of the campfire.

During their period of breaking in as soldiers, Yanks and Rebs frequently had to sleep on the ground under the open skies. Those fortunate enough to have shelter usually were occupants of either Sibley or "A" tents. The Sibley tent, shaped like a bell or wigwam and supported by a vertical center pole, was eighteen feet in diameter and twelve feet high. Its twelve or more occupants slept with their feet to the center and heads near the outer edge, like spokes in a wheel. Guns were stacked around the center pole and other equipment arranged according to comfort and convenience. "A" tents, known also as wedge tents, consisted of a large sheet of canvas draped over a long horizontal bar supported by upright poles, placed at each end. Front and rear were covered by two other pieces of canvas which, when tied together, had the shape of an "A." Each tent housed from four to six men;

occupants could stand up right only when directly beneath the center ridge pole, and in sleeping they found maximum comfort when arranged in spoon fashion; but this meant that when one turned over, all had to do likewise. Officers normally were housed in wall tents, which, in effect, were "A" tents elevated two to four feet from the ground and walled with canvas. They were much more commodious and comfortable for their one or two occupants than were the Sibley and wedge tents.

After 1861 Sibley and "A" tents generally were replaced by lighter and less expensive dwellings known as shelter tents, or dog tents. These were two-man habitations made by buttoning together the rectangular pieces of canvas known as half shelters which each soldier carried as a part of his equipment. These halves, when combined, were made into a miniature wedge, with both ends open. Sometimes four soldiers would combine their half shelters to make a larger covering. Lacking a partner, a soldier could stretch his half shelter horizontally over a framework of four horizontal sticks, one placed at each corner. Ingenious Rebs and Yanks arranged their shelters in various other ways to satisfy their tastes and comforts.

In seasons of cold, when the military situation was quiescent, soldiers winterized their tents or built log cabins. A winterized tent was a rectangular log pen, about four feet high, roofed with sloping canvas and with the interior dug out perhaps to a depth of two feet to provide more standing room and warmth. Log cabins were one-room huts, chinked and daubed like frontier dwellings. Roofs were of boards, grass, or canvas. Spaciousness of the huts was sometimes increased by digging out the interiors. Both huts and winterized tents were heated by fireplaces with chimneys built of logs and chinked and lined with clay. Often chimneys were topped with barrels or kegs to in crease the draft, provide better combustion, and keep the dwellings free of smoke. Sometimes chimneys would catch fire and cause a great commotion in the soldier community.

Many soldiers laid wooden floors to increase the comfort of their winter residences. They drove nails or pegs around the walls for the hanging of hats, haversacks, and cartridge boxes. They made stoves and tables of boxes or barrels obtained from the commissary or of boards taken from nearby barns or residences. Some built double or triple-deck bunks along the walls to conserve space. Bayonets were stuck into floors or walls and candles inserted in the sockets to provide illumination. Photographs, books, and writing materials were conveniently arranged on shelves and tables. Some soldiers added a humorous touch by placarding the entrance of their huts with designations such as "Buzzard Roost," "Astor House," "Howlers," and "Growlers." Many Yanks and Rebs boasted to their womenfolk about the comfort and attractiveness of their winter quarters. A Texan stationed in Virginia wrote his mother on January 14, 1862: "Our house is about 12 feet square... Our guns are in racks on the walls; our utensils consist of one skillet, a stew kettle, a bread pan, a frying pan, & a large kettle. Our china ware is a half dozen plates and the same number of forks & spoons (silver of course), our cups are of tin, 4 quart cups and two pint cups.

Above Right: They came looking ready and alert, like Henry Kelley of the 1st Virginia, with his Colt revolving rifle. (RONN PALM)

Above Left: And they came without spit or polish or posture. (LES JENSEN)

Left: They came with poise and dignity, obviously the sons of the first families. (WENDELL W. LANG, JR.)

Right: And they, too, came young. Brother privates, William E. Spach and Bennett Spach, of the 1st Battalion of North Carolina Sharpshooters. (JOHN T. SPACH)

Above: North and South, the departure of the volunteers for the front was a major occasion. With great ceremony the town fathers or state officials presented the regiments with their colors. Here the 1st Michigan Infantry receive their flags in Detroit on May 1, 1861. (BURTON HISTORICAL COLLECTION, DETROIT PUBLIC LIBRARY)

Below: Then it was off to the war. In April 1861, the 1st Rhode Island Infantry marched to the railroad depot in Providence to ride to the South, their governor, William Sprague, at their head. (RHODE ISLAND HISTORICAL SOCIETY)

Just above the fireplace you will see something which we call a mantle piece.... There are only four of us in this house." A member of the 16th Maine Regiment wrote from near Fredericksburg, Virginia, in January 1863: "Max and I built generously, and inside our finished house, in the warmth of a roaring blaze, we set up bedsteads and overlaid them with pine boughs for mattresses, and covered the boughs with blankets for counterpanes. How proudly we gazed upon those beds!"

Members of some regiments, after completing their huts, built ornate entrances to their camping area. A New Englander stationed near Falls Church, Virginia, wrote his homefolks in January 1862: "The 2nd Maine have erected arches and other fancy works over the entrance to each avenue. These are made of cedar boughs and trees set in and around their camps. Nor has the 17th N.Y. been behind in beautifying their grounds. Over the entrance is placed the name of 'McClellan'—below and on the right is 'Porter' (commanding division), on the left Butterfield (commanding brigade) ." Because of the comfort of their winter dwellings, and the respite from marching and fighting that came with cold weather, most soldiers came to regard winter as the most tolerable of their wartime seasons.

For many recruits the most undesirable feature of breaking in to army life was being "put through the measles." Troops from rural areas, largely be cause they had not been exposed to this malady in childhood, were more susceptible to it than were those from towns and cities. Measles usually struck during the first few months of military service and with devastating consequences. In the summer of 1861, one out of every seven Confederates of the Army of Northern Virginia had measles, and in one camp of 10,000 recruits, 4,000 men were stricken with the disease. Early in 1863 a soldier of Grant's army wrote from near Vicksburg: "Mesles... is what kilde the most of our boys—thay would take the measels and haf to lay out in the rain and storm and thay wod only laste abot 2 days." Comparatively few men died from measles alone, but the tendency to get up too soon often led to complications which proved fatal. A soldier of the Army of Northern Virginia wrote in August 1861: "We have some 5 or 6 that is very sick ones in our company.... They all had the measles, & were getting well & they turn out to drill too soon after it and they all have relapsed." Recruits of 1861 also had dysentery, malaria, typhoid, pneumonia, and other diseases that plagued Civil War armies, but the incidence of measles was much greater among new soldiers than among veterans.

Yet sickness, discomfort, drill, and discipline paled in comparison to the real business of soldiering, and all too soon these boys of '61 would mature in fire and blood to become the men of Bull Run.

Left: Camps of instruction like Camp Chase outside Columbus, Ohio, appeared all over the divided nation, as volunteers poured in to be made into soldiers. (OHIO HISTORICAL SOCIETY)

Left: Hasty makeshift bivouacs sprang forth in most major cities, crowding even major public buildings and filling the square in front of Philadelphia's Independence Hall. (LO)

Above: The 7th New York State Militia on review in 1861 at Camp Cameron. The drill and review were all too new to the recruits of 1861. It would become all too familiar in the years to come. (MHS)

Left: "I have seen Him in the watch-fires of a hundred circling camps," wrote Julia Ward Howe. The camp of the 1st Connecticut Artillery, near Washington. (CHS)

Above: The 9th Mississippi on parade near Pensacola, caught by J. D. Edwards in April 1861. They, too, however rustic in appearance, learned the intricacies of the drill manual, though it often baffled them. They fought back by giving to the evolutions their own peculiar appellations. A right wheel soon became a "stauchendicilar to the right." (MC)

Above: Exposed for the first time to large numbers of their fellow countrymen in close quarters, the boys of '61 were as well exposed to their germs. Hospitals and camps went in tandem all across the land. Here a tent hospital at Kendal Green, near Washington. (LC)

Right: The best respite from the drill and fatigue duty attendant to training came at meal times. Everyone took a hand, though early in the war tasting the soup could be as dangerous as an enemy bullet. At least there were women in camp to do the laundry. And others followed the camps, tending the men's needs of the flesh. (USAMHI)

Left: The officers dined together and fought in imagination the battles and triumphs they would visit upon the enemy. Here the officers of Company F, 8th Massachusetts Infantry, at Camp Brightwood in the District of Columbia. (USAMHI)

Right: The men in the ranks looked forward to their boxes from home, the letters and liquor and delicacies sent by mothers and sweethearts. Men of the 8th Massachusetts. (USAMHI)

Right: Men of the 5th Company, Washington Artillery of New Orleans, at Camp Lewis, near Carrolton, Louisiana. This new camp life was for them, as for their Yankee counterparts, a lark in the days when the war was young and bound only to last a few months. A photograph by J. W. Petty of New Orleans. (CM)

Left: The soldiers read, relaxed, played cards, tickled each other in the ear with feathers, and even stacked the deck for the camera. The gambler to the left holds a "full house," kings and twos. Even a passing bird stops to perch on the cannon's sponge for the photographer. The 1st Massachusetts Light Artillery. (USAMHI)

Above Left: Swords and pistols must be polished bright. The man seated burnishes and cleans his Starr revolver, while his mates of the 1st Massachusetts Light Artillery squint at the camera. (USAMHI)

Above Right: For some in these first days of the war, campaigning was no reason to dispense with the luxuries of home life. The Washington Light Infantry of Charleston, South Carolina, lounge contentedly before their tent, awaiting baskets of food and wine served in glass goblets by their black servants (WASHINGTON LIGHT INFANTRY)

Left: Many Confederates, even private soldiers, appeared for muster with their bodyservants in tow. Andrew Chandler brought his slave Silas Chandler with him, and both armed for a fight. Men who once feared arms in the hands of slaves now thought little of handing them knives and shotguns. (STERLING CHANDLER AND RICHARD S. YOUNG)

Right: Yankees, too, enjoyed the services of blacks when they could get them. Here is the little servant of Captain Aspenwall of the 22d New York. (USAMHI)

Above: Most of all the men North and South did as American soldiers have done in all wars, make the best of it. Confederates of the Washington Artillery relaxed, indifferent to what lay ahead. When they left New Orleans they were told, "May the Lord of Hosts be round about you as a wall of fire, and shield your heads in the day of battle! (JAN P. REIFENBERG)

Above Right: They and their foes to the north, like the 7th New York, will be ready, or think they will. None of them, in their bright uniforms. . . (USAMHI)

Right: . . . their gaily festooned quarters for Phunny Fellows . . . (USAMHI)

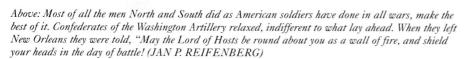

Above: . . . their striped trousers, their blouses decorated with flannel badges and galloping horses . . . (USAMHI)

Right: . . . none of them, for all their pretended preparedness, really know what is coming. (USAMHI)

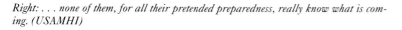

Above Left:Instead, they smile and pose. The 23d New York Infantry. (USAMHI)

Above Right: They pose in little groups. The 33d New York Infantry, the man at right armed with a "Volcanic" repeating pistol in his belt. (USAMHI)

Above: They pose by companies, their lady friends often with them. The 22d New York State Militia. (USAMHI)

Above: They gather around the colors they expect to lead to glory, and defend with their lives if need be. The colors of the 7th New York State Militia, at right and left the general guides, at left center the regimental banner, and right center the national colors. (NA)

Left: The officers and men join together for the camera. Colonel William Wilson, center, and men of his 6th New York Infantry, "Wilson's Zouaves." (USAMHI)

Left: They clowned indoors at mock battle. (LO)

Left: With bread and cider and camaraderie, they passed the summer days of soldiering. But it would not last. These militiamen are guarding the Chain Bridge over the Potomac at Washington in 1861. (RINHART GALLERIES INC.)

Right: Washington was a threatened capital. With Virginia across the Potomac hostile, and Maryland filled with southern sympathizers who attempted to block Federal communications and reinforcement from the North, Lincoln and his city were almost blockaded. Then Benjamin F. Butler, a Massachusetts Democrat and now an ardent supporter of the war, acted under his major general's commission and led an expedition to secure . . . (MICHAEL J. MCAFEE)

. . . the Baltimore & Ohio Railroad junction at Relay House, Maryland, thereby holding open a rail route for troops to reach Washington. From May 6, 1861, onward, troops like these flowed through Relay House and on to the capital. (MHS)

The First Bull Run

JOSEPH P. CULLEN

Reality at last in the heat and dust and blood of Manassas

Above: In the wake of Fort Sumter, the pressure on Lieutenant General Winfield Scottóshown here with his staffóbecame intense. The Union must strike back, put down the Rebellion. ⁄NA)

Left: First Washington must be made secure and troops brought in from the North Benjamin F. Butler's occupation of Relay House on the vital Baltimore & Ohio ensured that. (USAMHI)

IT WAS ALREADY HOT that morning of July 16, 1861, when they marched out of the camps around Washington to fight the first major battle in what has been called the last of the old wars and the first of the new. And the camera would be there, or not far behind, to record for posterity the men of the armies and the scenes of battle—a hill, a stream, a field, a copse of woods; a bridge, a church, a house, a barn. Ordinary everyday things in ordinary, everyday life, but these simple things assumed importance beyond their functional purposes. They became landmarks to show where men fought and died; landmarks to be photographed and recorded for future generations.

Since April, when the guns of Fort Sumter roared out their message that North and South were at war, troops had poured into the Washington area until the surrounding heights blossomed white with tents in a care-free, carnival atmosphere. And the untrained, undisciplined citizen-soldiers, with their gaudy, multicolored uniforms—the flamboyant 11th New York Zouaves in their blue and scarlet shirts and jackets and white turbans; the checked flannels of Michigan lumberjacks; the colorful Garibaldi Guards—added a picturesque touch. A few were army regulars, some state militia, but most were three-month volunteers with romantic ideas about wars in general and battles in particular, who fully expected to end the war with one battle and be home at the end of their brief enlistment.

Many tried to bring the comforts of home with them into the field. One volunteer admitted that his knapsack held "a pair of trousers, two pairs of drawers, a pair of thick boots, four pairs of stockings, four flannel shirts, a blouse, a looking glass, a can of peaches, a bottle of cough-mixture, a button-stick, chalk, razor and strop, a Bible, a small volume of Shakespeare, and writing utensils," in addition to a "tailor's shop," usually made of leather or cloth and "containing needles, pins, thread, buttons, and scissors." He also carried a rubber blanket and a woolen blanket and "a belt bout the body, which held a cartridge-box and bayonet, a cross belt, also a haversack and tin drinking cup, a canteen." The cartridge-box held forty rounds of ammunition and the haversack three days' rations of "salt junk, hardtack, sugar and coffee." Altogether a load to challenge a mule.

There was an air of excitement, a feeling akin to a sudden unexpected holiday, a welcome break in the humdrum monotony of everyday living. And that feeling was very much in evidence that morning as 35,000 men in their colorful uniforms, carrying the stiff new flags clinging to their shiny staffs, marched off to battle with bands blaring and drums rolling. They knew nothing of wars or battles or any of the realities of actual combat. They expected to march for a few days and then line up somewhere in formation and shoot at the enemy from afar. Then when the Southerners ran back to Richmond it would be over and they could all go home as heroes. So they went to war as if to a picnic.

After a few days of marching in the brutal heat and choking dust, however, many of these civilian soldiers began to have second thoughts about the glorious adventure ahead of them. "My canteen banged against my bayonet," one recruit noted, "both tin cup and bayonet badly interfered with the butt of my musket, while my cartridge-box and haversack were constantly flopping up and down." Blistered feet and aching muscles soon dictated that loads had to be lightened, so various pieces of equipment were surreptitiously dropped along the way. Thus would they learn the hard way—by experience.

In command of this ragged mass of men marching out of Washington was Irvin McDowell, a native of Ohio recently promoted to brigadier general of volunteers. A graduate of the U. S. Military Academy, McDowell was forty-three years old, a robust, heavy-set man with dark cropped hair and an iron-gray beard. He had served creditably in the Mexican War in staff positions, but had never commanded a large body of troops in the field. A quiet, introverted person who neither smoked nor drank, he was too reserved to be popular with his fellow officers, and definitely not the type to inspire men. Still he was a professional and as such recognized the weaknesses of his raw recruits. He did not want to fight until the men had been trained sufficiently to at least act like soldiers rather than civilians. "This is not an army," he told his superiors. "It will take a long time to make an army." But the times were against McDowell. The enlistments of most of the three-month volunteers was about up and the people of the North became impatient. "Forward to Richmond" screamed the newspaper headlines. And the government listened to the voice of the people. McDowell was ordered to move against a lesser Confederate force at Manassas, Virginia, about twenty-five miles southwest of Washington. To be sure, there was another Confederate force to the west in the Shenandoah Valley, but it was to be pinned down by other Federal troops and thus prevented from reinforcing the Confederates at Manassas. "You are green, it is true," President Lincoln told the reluctant McDowell, "but they are green also."

And green they were. A few days after the firing at Fort Sumter, Virginia seceded from the Union. In Richmond there was dancing in the streets and bonfires burned to celebrate the historic event. Cannon were dragged by hand from the state arsenal to Capitol Square to fire a salute. The new Confederate flag fluttered proudly atop the capitol building. Virginians by the thousands flocked to the newly opened recruiting stations, fearful the fighting would end before they could play a part in it. Then in May the Confederate Congress, in session at Montgomery, Alabama, voted to move the Confederate capital to Richmond. Now the city underwent a dramatic change. When hundreds of regiments from farther south streamed in, Richmond took on the appearance of a vast military camp. At night the glow from thousands of campfires lit the sky. One observer noted, "One of the remarkable features of the times is that men of all classes and conditions, of all occupations and professions, are of one mind."

Although a Richmond newspaper could bluster, "There is one wild shout of fierce resolve to capture Washington City, at all and every human hazard," that was not the immediate objective of the new government. If the South could not secede from the Union peacefully, then it was determined to defend every acre of territory and maintain its independence to the last. As Confederate President Davis proclaimed: "All

Below: With men of the 7th New York and other regiments garrisoning the camps around Washington, the capital was safe. That done, it was time to press the war and end the Rebellion. Within weeks these boys of '61 would become men in battle. (WRHS)

Above: The first move was to occupy Alexandria, Virginia, just across the Potomac from Washington. Confederate flags flying over the city taunted Lincoln, and on May 24 Colonel Elmer Ellsworth led his Fire Zouaves, now the 11th New York, across the Potomac. (USAMHI)

Left: There Ellsworth saw a Rebel banner flying above the Marshall House. He personally went to the roof and removed it from the staff still visible. On his way to the ground floor, he was met by the house's proprietor, who murdered him on the spot. Ellsworth became the nation's first great martyr, and Lincoln grieved sorely for his dead young friend. (USAMHI)

Left: With Winfield Scott too old to take active field command, a member of his staff, Irvin McDowell, was elevated to brigadier general and given the unenviable task of molding an army and advancing to meet the enemy in Virginia. (USAMHI)

Above: Men of the 1st Rhode Island at Camp Sprague, outside Washington, well trained and ready (LC)

Above: The engineer company of the 8th New York in Arlington, Virginia, in June 1861. Photograph by Brady or an assistant. (LC)

Above: Colonel Ambrose Burnside and officers of the 1st Rhode Island Infantry formed a part of McDowell's developing army. (USAMHI)

we ask is to be left alone." With this philosophy there was nothing to be gained by invading the North. Rather, the South wanted to exploit the advantages of a defensive posture, which would require fewer men and allow it to use its interior, or shorter, lines of communications and supply to best advantage. In addition, all the various government departments, as well as an army, had to be created, organized, and staffed to carry on a war, while at the same time a government had to be set up to pass laws governing what was hoped would be a new nation.

So thousands of young men streamed into Richmond to prepare to defend their independence, and like their counterparts in Washington, their uniforms exhibited an amazing variety. The various state militia colors mixed with fancy home made uniforms, while some regiments had nothing but civilian clothes. Some of the higher ranking officers still wore the dress of the United States Army. And like the Northerners, the new recruits posed stiffly for portraits, followed the bands down the springtime streets, waved to the cheering girls, and set about, they thought, getting the war over with in a hurry. As one lady recorded in her diary, "There was much music and mustering and marching, much cheering and flying of flags, much firing of guns and all that sort of thing."

With Richmond now the Confederate capital, the area of Manassas, about seventy-five miles to the north, became strategically important to the defense of the city. The central point was Manassas Junction, a small railroad settlement consisting of a handful of decrepit buildings scattered carelessly about the railroad crossing. Here two railroads joined. The Orange & Alexandria, running north and south, connected with both Washington and Richmond; and the Manassas Gap Railroad, which extended westward through the Blue Ridge mountains to the rich, fertile valley of the Shenandoah. There were many good roads also, east and west, north and south, the main one being the Warrenton Turnpike, which led through the town of Centreville to Alexandria and Washington. The surrounding area was a gently rolling country of soft ridges, small farms, rail fences, crooked creeks, and quiet woods. About midway between Manassas and Centreville, Bull Run Creek meandered peacefully through the plains, the trees along its banks forming a leafy tunnel with the sun sifting through to form lacy gold patterns on the water, while picturesque arched bridges spanned it.

In June the South moved to protect this vital point. In command was Brigadier General P. G. T. Beauregard, hero of the firing on Fort Sumter. A classmate of McDowell's, his last United States Army assignment had been as Superintendent of the Military Academy at West Point, New York. A small, graceful man in his early forties, Beauregard was a proud Creole from Louisiana who had distinguished himself in the Mexican War as a staff officer but, like McDowell, had never commanded a large body of troops in the field. Outspoken and critical of others, yet sensitive to criticism himself, he generally found it easier to make enemies than friends. But he too was a professional, and now with about 22,000 raw civilian-soldiers he set his line of defense along Bull Run. Although the creek itself was a formidable obstacle to any attacking force with its steep wooded banks,

Left: The 2d Michigan came a long way to be in on the one battle that would surely end the war. (THE BURTON HISTORICAL COLLECTION, DETROIT PUBLIC LIBRARY)

there were many fords and two bridges to be defended. On his right flank he destroyed the railroad bridge at Union Mills; built fortifications at McLean's, Blackburn's, and Mitchell's fords; and stationed other forces at Ball's Ford, Lewis Ford, and the Stone Bridge on the Warrenton Turnpike, his extreme left flank. At Manassas Junction itself massive fortifications were erected running out in different directions from the little station. And across Bull Run he established advance guard posts at Centreville and Fairfax Court House and several strategic crossroads to warn of the approach of the enemy. Sixty miles away to the west across the mountains sat another force under Brigadier General Joseph E. Johnston. If Beauregard was outnumbered and attacked, he hoped to be reinforced by Johnston's troops. They would come on the cars of the Manassas Gap Railroad.

Left: The camp of the 1st Minnesota, near Edwards Ferry, Maryland. They were eager to march south and put down the Rebellion. (MHS)

While these preparations were being made, the recruits were constantly marshaled and drilled in a desperate attempt to give them some training before the battle they knew must come. Yet the camps, like the ones in the North, had a gay, festive atmosphere about them, with constant visitors at all hours of the day and night. In them could be found well-prepared meals, "caddies of tea, barrels of sugar, and many articles better suited for a picnic or a party in a summer house than to soldiers in the field." A young lady visitor wrote that they "were able during those rallying days of June to drive frequently to visit 'the boys' in camp, timing the expeditions to include battalion drill and dress parade, and taking tea afterward in the different tents. Then were the gala days of war, and our proud hosts hastened to produce home dainties dispatched from far-away plantations."

Left: McDowell marched his arriving regiments across the Long Bridge and others leading from Washington to the Virginia side, and trained and organized his army in and around Arlington. (USAMHI)

Such was life in the Confederate camps when McDowell left Washington that July 16. Beauregard received word at once that he was coming from a female spy in Washington. Not that it was any secret anyway—everyone in Washington and in the Army knew where they were going. Beauregard immediately requested that Johnston's troops in the valley be sent to him. Two days later the Union Army concentrated on the heights of Centreville overlooking the plains of Manassas as the Confederate outposts fell back to their main line behind Bull Run. McDowell spent the next two days probing for a weak spot in the Confederate line. A reconnaissance in force was repulsed in the center at

Left: He made his headquarters in the stately mansion, Arlington House, that, until a few weeks before, had been the home of Robert E. Lee. Mrs. Lee was still there when he moved in, and he took great care not to discomfort her. Here he planned his campaign. (USAMHI)

Above: Old General Robert Patterson was to keep the Confederate Army of Joseph E. Johnston occupied in the Shenandoah Valley so that it could not reinforce Confederates around Manassas when McDowell attacked them. If Patterson failed, McDowell could be in grave danger. (USAMHI)

Above: On July 16, 1861, McDowell's army moved out of its camps on the road toward Manassas and the Rebel Army. This image of the 8th New York was taken that same day as they prepared for the march. (MJM)

Above: Charles P. Stone, inspector general of the District of Columbia militia, would command one of Patterson's brigades. (USAMHI)

Above: As they marched they passed historic Falls Church, where George Washington had worshipped. (USAMHI)

Mitchell's and Blackburn's fords, and no suitable terrain for attack appeared on the right. On the Confederate left, however, two unguarded fords, Popular and Sudley, were discovered. A crossing here would put the troops on the Sudley road, which led to the Warrenton Turnpike near the Stone House, and behind the Confederate left.

So on the afternoon of July 20, McDowell issued his battle order for the attack the next morning. His plan was simple but sound. Realizing the center of the Confederate line was too strong for a frontal attack by inexperienced troops, he ordered just a feint there, and then a long flanking march to the right to Sudley and Popular fords to circle and crumple the enemy left. Although McDowell could not know it, the two-day delay in preparing his plan was to prove fatal. Even as he issued his orders the first of Johnston's troops from the valley arrived on the railroad cars at the Junction. When they all got there the Confederates would have about 32,000 men.

Word that the battle would be fought the next day, a Sunday, quickly reached Washington and hundreds of people made frantic preparations to get there to see it. "Every carriage, gig, wagon, and hack has been engaged by people going out to see the fight," wrote an English newspaper reporter. "The French cooks and hotelkeepers, by some occult process of reasoning, have arrived at the conclusion that they must treble the prices of their wines and of the hampers of provisions" the people were ordering to take with them. "Before the battle," wrote a congressman from Ohio, "the hopes of the people and of their representatives are very elated and almost jocosely festive."

The next morning the road to Centreville jammed with nervous horses and handsome carriages, pretty ladies in bright crinoline dresses carrying picnic baskets filled with cool wines and tasty snacks. Senators and congressmen, foreign dignitaries, bureaucrats, and reporters, dressed in their light summer clothing and carrying spyglasses and revolvers and flasks of Bourbon,

Above: They passed by Taylor's Tavern, outside Falls Church, Virginia. (WRHS)

Above: On July 17 the Federals skirmished with the enemy around Fairfax Court House. (NA)

Above: And the next day McDowell occupied Centreville, until that morning a fortified Confederate camp. (USAMHI)

Right: From Centreville, McDowell sent Colonel Daniel Tyler forward with his division to reconnoiter the enemy positions along Bull Run. He was ordered not to bring on an engagement. (USAMHI)

Above: Instead Tyler and his chief lieutenant, Colonel Israel B. Richardson, became engaged in a hot fight at Blackburn's Ford, and were repulsed. (PENNSYLVANIA—MOLLUS COLLECTION, WAR LIBRARY AND MUSEUM, PHILADEL-PHIA)

Above: Three days later, McDowell launched his battle plan, sending his marching columns toward Bull Run, shown here in a July 1862 image by Timothy O'Sullivan. (LC)

Above: McDowell's coming was detected well in advance by men in signal towers built and super-vised by Beauregard's signal officer, Captain Edward Porter Alexander, a Georgian who graduat-ed from West Point four years before. He appears here in his cadet uniform, probably in 1857. (LSU)

Above: By contrast, McDowell's signal officer, Captain A. J. Myer, spent most of the day unsuccess-fully attempting to launch an observation balloon from which to spy enemy movements. (LC)

Above: July 21, 1861, was Brigadier General David Hunter's fifty-ninth birthday. As he led McDowell's flanking column that was to assail the Confederate left via Sudley Ford, he received a birth-day present in the form of a serious wound that put him out of the battle. (USAMHI)

rushed to Virginia to watch the great event, greeting friends, laughing and joking.

To the men in the Union ranks the occasion was not so festive, however. Since two-thirty that morning the flanking march had been taking place under bright moonlight. Across the Turnpike, over Cub Run Creek, through the woods and fields, heading for the Sudley fords. About three hours later, as the first gray streaks of dawn turned the landscape from brown to green, they heard the roar of a Union cannon near the Stone Bridge shatter the early quiet. The first major battle of the Civil War had begun. By seven o'clock they should have been crossing Bull Run at the fords, but these civilians in uniform could not march that fast. They were still more than two hours away, and already the heat was oppressive. Now they were hot and tired, the fancy uniforms covered with choking dust. Even though the maneuver was already several hours behind schedule, the recruits still straggled after ripe blackberries, stopped for a refreshing drink, or just rested in the shade of the trees. It was about nine-thirty before they reached the fords, and then a Confederate officer high atop a signal tower spotted the glint of the sun on a brass cannon. The surprise was lost.

Quickly the Confederates swung their left flank back to Chinn Ridge behind the Stone House and rushed up reinforcements to counter the threat. Shortly after ten o'clock the Union troops came charging out of the woods into the fields on either side of the Sudley road and drove the Confederates back across the Turnpike to a new position on the plateau around the Henry and Robinson houses. The battle had opened

Above: Hunter's men passed the Thornton House, shown here in a March 1862 image by George N. Barnard. (LC)

Above: Then they passed the Sudley Springs Ford and crossed over Bull Run to move toward Beauregard. Photograph by Barnard, March 1862. (USAMHI)

Above: Sudley Church, above Bull Run. The Federals swarmed past it on their way to the first major engagement of the war. (WRHS)

Above: Burnside led his brigade in the initial assaults against Confederate defenders on Mathews' Hill. (USAMHI)

Right: Colonel Andrew Porter was next into the fray with his brigade. He felt that Burnside had attacked with "perhaps, too hasty vigor," but he immediately moved to Burnside's support and took command of the division after Hunter's wound. Porter stands at center in this image taken prior to the battle. (P-M)

Above: One of Burnside's regiments, the 2d Rhode Island Infantry, was the first of Hunter's column to engage the enemy. They fought bravely, even after their colonel was killed and many of their officers put out of the fight. They are shown at drill here in a photograph taken several months following the battle. (USAMHI)

Above: The 8th New York, perhaps the most resplendent of regiments in McDowell's army, went into battle with Porter. (TERENCE P. O'LEARY)

Above: They were fighting an army led by the hero of Fort Sumter, P. G. T. Beauregard, now a brigadier general in the Confederate Army. (LC)

Above: William Weir's house Liberia was not far from the home of Wilmer McLean, where Beauregard made his headquarters. McLean himself was so disturbed by the war's coming to his very doorstep that he moved where he thought it would never find him again. Appomattox. (WRHS)

Right: Major Samuel Jones was Beauregard's chief of artillery, but, in fact, Confederate cannon would play a minor role in the battle unfolding. (LC)

Above: George Barnard's March 1862 photograph of the battlefield at Bull Run, looking over the Warrenton Turnpike. (USAMHI)

Right: The man who stopped the initial assault by Hunter's column, and several succeeding attacks, thus buying time for Beauregard to rush troops to the threatened left, was another veteran of Fort Sumter. Brigadier General Nathan G. Evans, called "Shanks" by friends, was a rough, uncouth braggart whose orderly always stood behind him with a "barrelita" of whiskey. He would later claim that he alone, with the aid of the Almighty "and a few private gentlemen, won the battle. (SOUTH CAROLINIANA LIBRARY)

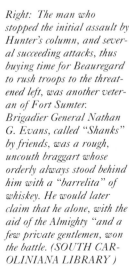

with frightening reality. Yellow sheets of flame flashed along both lines as regiment after regiment exploded into action with a metallic roar. Gigantic crashes of artillery split the air. Shells screamed overhead, exploding in clouds of earth, horses, and men. The noise roared to a crescendo that left men dazed and confused, as the fighting surged back and forth, the issue in doubt, into the afternoon.

On a hill just below Centreville overlooking the plains of Manassas, the carriages from Washington were drawn up as if at a country horse race. Surprisingly, their presence did not seem to bother the troops who saw them. "Near Cub Run we saw carriages and barouches which contained civilians who had driven out from Washington to witness the operation," one soldier remembered. "We thought it wasn't bad idea to have the great men from Washington come out to see us thrash the Rebs." The visitors had a panoramic view of the lovely wooded

Above: A few of those "private gentlemen" who held the line with Evans. Major Roberdeau Wheat's battalion of Louisiana Zouaves, commonly called Wheat's Tigers. They are photographed here in New Orleans in 1861. (LC)

Above: As the battle between Hunter's and Evans's troops developed, Brigadier General Samuel P. Heintzelman's division came into the fight. He, too, would be wounded, but acted heroically in attempting to hold his command together in the confusion of its first fight. (USAMHI)

Above: Soldiers like this rugged-looking woodsman from the 4th Michigan went into the action in Orlando Willcox's brigade of Heintzelman's division. The Michiganders fought like demons, the first Westerners to do battle in the East. (HP)

Above: While the battle raged on the Confederate left, Colonel William T. Sherman led his brigade across a ford near the Stone Bridge in the center of the line and assailed Evans's depleted command. Sherman is shown here as a major general in an 1865 photo. (NYHS)

Above: Colonel Michael Corcoran, center, and officers of the 69th New York crossed with Sherman. (MJM)

Above: So did Colonel James Cameron of the 79th New York. The son of Secretary of War Simon Cameron, he would not recross Bull Run. He died in battle. (USAMHI)

Below: Battery E, 3d United States Artillery, commanded by Captain Romeyn B. Ayres. Called Sherman's Battery because it was formerly led by Thomas W. Sherman, this unit was greatly feared by the Confederates because of its mighty Parrot rifles. This image shows the battery on July 24, 1861, in Washington, three days after the battle. (BRUCE GIMELSON)

Above: Erasmus D. Keyes, like Sherman, a colonel of a brigade in Tyler's division, also crossed Bull Run, but played a lesser role in the fighting along the Warrenton Road. (USAMHI)

Above: The 3d Connecticut of Keyes's brigade. Their gallantry, he believed, "was never surpassed." (LC)

Above: The fighting raged first around the Matthews' House on Matthews' Hill, where the advancing Federals slowly forced Evans and his outnumbered command back to the Warrenton Turnpike. (USAMHI)

Above: Evans's command retreated past the Stone House on the Warrenton Road, shown in this March 1862 photo by Barnard and James F. Gibson, and up the slopes of Henry Hill. (USAMHI)

Above: And on Henry Hill the fighting raged for most of the rest of the day. Soon after Evans's arrival, sharp fighting took place on the right of the hill near the Robinson House, where Sherman attacked the line held by yet another veteran of Fort Sumter… (USAMHI)

country, dotted with green fields and cleared lands. According to one observer, "undulating lines of forest marked the course of the streams which intersected it and gave by their variety of color and shading an additional charm to the landscape which, enclosed in a framework of blue and purple hills, softened into violet in the extreme distance, presented one of the most agreeable displays of simple pastoral woodland scenery that could be conceived." Somehow it was difficult to believe that men would actually shoot at and kill each other across this beautiful scene. But then the woods echoed to the roar of cannon, thin lines of dirty gray haze marked the angry muttering of musketry, white puffs of smoke burst high above the treetops, bayonets flashed in the glaring sun, and clouds of dust shifted constantly back and forth across the landscape. One lady spectator with an opera glass "was quite beside herself when an unusually heavy discharge roused the current of her blood—"That is splendid. Oh, my! Is not that first-rate? I guess we will be in Richmond this time tomorrow."

All afternoon the battle lines surged back and forth across the plateau, around the Henry House and the Robinson House, on Chinn Ridge, and along the Turnpike as men died by the hundreds in the woods, in the fields, on the banks of Bull Run, in a nightmare battle of mistakes fought by untrained volunteers led by inexperienced officers. Then when the last of Johnston's fresh Confederate troops reached the field late in the afternoon, because the Federal force had failed to hold them in the Shenandoah Valley as planned, McDowell realized any chance of victory was gone and ordered a withdrawal. The exhausted troops started an orderly retreat from the field. The battle was over. "There was no confusion or panic then," one soldier remembered, but the men cursed their generals because they did not have fresh reinforcements as the enemy did. The orderly retreat quickly turned to confusion and then panic when the Confederates pursued, while the civilian spectators and their carriages and buggies created a frenzied jam among the army wagons, caissons, guns, and ambulances. "Infantry soldiers on mules and draft horses with the harness clinging to their heels, as much frightened as their riders," wrote a reporter. "Negro servants on their masters' chargers; ambulances crowded with unwounded soldiers; wagons swarming with men who threw out the contents in the road to make room, grinding through a shouting, screaming mass of men on foot who were literally yelling with rage at every halt." No longer under any effective control, many of the soldiers headed for Washington, a confused mob with little semblance of order or discipline. By sundown it was a question of whether or not they should try to make a stand at Centreville. McDowell decided against it. "The condition of our artillery and its ammunition," he reported, "the want of food for the men, and the utter disorganization and demoralization of the mass of the army seemed to admit of no alternative but to fall back."

For miles the roads leading into Washington became strewn with the paraphernalia of war—caps, coats, blankets, rifles, canteens, haversacks. "I saw the beaten, foot-sore, spongy-looking soldiers," a reporter wrote, "officers and all the

Above: … Colonel Wade Hampton, commanding Hampton's Legion. Hampton himself was wounded, but he held his line. (VM)

Above: Lieutenant Thomas M. Logan of Hampton's Legion played a conspicuous part in the fighting around the Robinson House. In February 1865 he would become a brigadier general.

Above: Colonel Francis S. Bartow of Georgia exposed himself recklessly on the battlefield in leading his brigade against the Federals. It cost him his life. (VM)

Above: The fighting became even more fierce in the center of the Confederate line on Henry Hill. There Brigadier General Barnard E. Bee of South Carolina fought desperately against several enemy assaults. His very presence on the field was a harbinger of victory, for he and his brigade had been sent to Beauregard from the Shenandoah. Johnston had eluded Patterson, and even as the battle raged, more of his regiments were on their way. Bee would fall with a mortal wound but not before bestowing on another of Johnston's brigade commanders an immortal sobriquet. Attempting to rally his men after a charge, he pointed to a brigade of Virginians behind them and said… (VM)

Above, right: … "There stands Jackson like a stone wall." It was the brigade of General Thomas J. Jackson, shown here in a 1855 daguerreotype. A man of inordinate peculiarities, he would become the greatest legend of the war. (NATIONAL PORTRAIT GALLERY, SMITHSONIAN INSTITUTION, WASHINGTON, D.C.)

Right: Officers of the Washington Artillery of New Orleans, who helped Jackson stand like a wall. They are brothers, Miles Taylor Squires, Samuel Smith Squires, and Charles W. Squires. (W. H. T. SQUIRES, JR.)

Right: The battle raged for hours on Henry Hill, often around the Henry House itself, where poor old widow Henry, who refused to leave, was blown out of her bed by a shell that severed her foot and mortally wounded her. An 1862 view by Barnard. (USAMHI)

debris of the army filing through mud and rain, forming in crowds in front of the spirit stores." Muddy, hungry, and scared, they staggered through the streets begging food and buying liquor, dropping in exhaustion on porches, lawns, and sidewalks. Many of the younger officers, completely demoralized, filled the hotel barrooms and cheap saloons. One of the civilian casualties who walked forlornly back to Washington was a photographer, already noted for his portraits, who would later become famous, Mathew Brady. He and his assistants had lost the wagon with his camera and all his equipment in the panic, or so he claimed.

And on the plains of Manassas the soul-searing moans of the wounded and dying echoed through the still night air. Motionless forms covered the ground in grotesque positions, as if someone had carelessly heaved them from a wagon. The Federals suffered almost 3,000 casualties in killed, wounded, and missing; the Confederates almost 2,000. All through the night the stretcher-bearers, doctors, friends, and even relatives worked tirelessly among the dead and wounded, the flickering flames from the candles and lanterns casting weird shadows among the dark, silent trees.

"The capture of Washington seems now to be inevitable," a frightened government official declared. "The rout, overthrow, and utter demoralization of the whole army is complete." This, of course, was an exaggeration. A more sober, realistic view of the situation was made by another close observer of the events. "We have undertaken to make war without in the least knowing how," he wrote. "We have made a false start and we have discovered it. It only remains to start afresh." A lesson had been learned—a hard lesson. It was not going to be a short, easy war. The politicians now realized that all the powerful resources of the North would have to be organized and directed in preparation for a long, bitter struggle. And the war was not going to be won by the theatrical heroics of untrained three-

Left: Nearly as badly used up as Ricketts's battery was Battery D, 5th United States Artillery. Captain Charles Griffin obeyed orders to take it nearly to the brow of the left of Henry Hill. Once there, Griffin mistook an enemy regiment dressed in blue for his own troops, and discovered the mistake too late. All of his cannoneers were shot down and only three of his six guns escaped, and two of them had to be abandoned later. (P-M)

Above: In desperate fighting on the forward slope of Henry Hill, Captain James B. Ricketts of Battery I, 1st United States Artillery, was wounded four times and captured along with all six of his cannon and forty-nine horses. He would recover to become a brigadier general in less than a year. (USAMHI)

Above: Former Governor of Virginia William "Extra Billy" Smith, now colonel of the 49th Virginia, took a place in the Confederate line just in time to assist in the destruction of Ricketts's and Griffin's batteries. He is shown here in the uniform of a brigadier general, probably in 1863. (USAMHI)

Above: Patterson's failure in the Shenandoah allowed Brigadier General Joseph E. Johnston to bring almost his entire army to assist Beauregard. Johnston arrived on the field and took overall command of operations the day before the battle. This rare photo of Johnston has never before been published. (VM)

Above: The unexpected arrival of Johnston's last brigade to reach the field, led by Colonel Arnold Elzey, threw McDowell's right flank into a panic. (VM)

Above: Colonel Oliver O. Howard, commanding a brigade of Heintzelman's division, was at the right flank when Elzey arrived. Heroic efforts by him brought few results, and before he received orders to retire, his men were doing it on their own. He stands at left here, shortly after his promotion to brigadier general. (WRHS)

Left: While his right crumbled into a disorganized retreat, McDowell found his left threatened when Confederates like Colonel Micah Jenkins led the 5th South Carolina across Bull Run. There was little left for McDowell but a general retreat. For Jenkins there would be a brigadier's promotion a year and a day later. (LC)

Left: Colonel Joseph B. Kershaw spearheaded the pursuit with his 2d South Carolina and, along with old Edmund Ruffin, helped turn retreat into rout when they managed to disable the main bridge over Cub Run that led to safety for the Federals. (SHC)

Below: McDowell's chief of staff, Colonel James B. Fry, made extraordinary efforts to control the retreat, but to no avail. Most of the army did not stop until it reached Centreville, and many soldiers fled all the way to Washington. (P-M)

Above: With the enemy on the run, Brigadier General Milledge L. Bonham's South Carolina brigade took over the pursuit. He would leave the Army in a few months to go to the Confederate Congress, then serve as governor of his state, then don his uniform again in the war's last days. (VM)

Right: McDowell had a reserve division commanded by Colonel Dixon S. Miles stationed at Centreville, but Miles took no part in the battle. In fact, he got drunk and could not give coherent orders to his officers. (USAMHI)

Left: … and Stahel will get his first star in November. These German and Hungarian officers were enormously popular, and the Lincoln Administration hoped that giving them high command would encourage the thousands of their nationality in the North to enlist. It also put great responsibility in the hands of men with little ability. (USAMHI)

Above: Miles's soldiers, like flamboyant Colonel Louis Blenker, shown here with men of the 8th New York, chafed at being left out of the battle. Standing just left of Blenker is Lieutenant Colonel Julius Stahel. In two weeks Blenker will be a brigadier… (NA)

Above: Another popular foreigner, Colonel Frederick G. D'Utassy (third from the right) and the staff of his 39th New York, the "Garibaldi Guard." They, too, sat out the battle at Centreville. (MJM)

Above: And for some who missed the fight, the war was already over. The 4th New Jersey and its officers shown here mustered out of service ten days after the battle . (USAMHI)

month volunteers and comic opera officers. Large armies would have to be raised, trained, and equipped, with the enlistments for three years or the duration, not three months. Washington would have to be adequately protected against the slightest chance of capture, for if the capital fell there would be no United States as such.

While the North thus learned a vital lesson from this first major defeat, the South seemingly was lulled into a false sense of security by the victory. "We are resting on our oars after the victory at Manassas," a clerk in the War Department in Richmond recorded in his diary. The articulate and observant wife of an aide to President Davis put it more succinctly. "That victory did nothing but send us off into a fool's paradise of conceit, and it roused the manhood of the Northern people." Indeed, there was much indignant criticism of the generals because they did not immediately follow up the victory by marching into Washington right then and there to end the war. But the fact was, as General Johnston tried patiently to explain, that "the Confederate army was more disorganized by victory than that of the United States by defeat." In addition, the men were near exhaustion, they were short on rations and ammunition, the raw troops lacked proper discipline and training, stragglers were numerous, the Federals had erected powerful fortifications around Washington, and the broad Potomac River would have had to be crossed. Also, many of the soldiers now believed the war was just about over anyway. "Exaggerated ideas of the victory among our troops cost us more men than the Federal army lost by defeat," Johnston reported. "Many left the army—not to return." Despite this premature complacency, the South was determined to resist to the bitter end, thus assuring the nation of a long, bloody struggle.

A young lady from Virginia wrote after Manassas:

A few days later we rode over the field. The trampled grass had begun to spring again, and wild flowers were blooming around carelessly made graves. From one of these imperfect mounds of clay I saw a hand extended.…Fences were everywhere thrown down; the undergrowth of the woods was riddled with shot; here and there we came upon spiked guns, disabled gun-carriages, cannon balls, blood-stained blankets, and dead horses. We were glad enough to turn away and gallop homeward.

For the men in the armies, however, that home ward turn lay distant years ahead in the uncertain future.

Above: Still, there were many heroes of the battle. One was the son of amateur photographer—and now quartermaster general of the Union Army—Montgomery C. Meigs. John R. Meigs served as a volunteer aide to Colonel Israel Richardson. "A braver and more gallant young man was never in any service," said Richardson. Here his father photographed him and his sister on his return from the battle, perhaps looking at the elder Meigs's own stereo photographs. Three years later, in the Shenandoah, Confederate guerrillas would kill him. (LC)

Above: The famous "Sherman Battery" came through the battle with all of its guns, and was the object of much curiosity afterward. Here, again, it was photographed in Washington. (MHS)

Left: For many of the men of Bull Run, however, there was no welcome home. Hundreds were captured and sent south to makeshift prisons. Many, like these men of Corcoran's 69th New York, were placed in Castle Pinckney at Charleston. They kept their spirits high, lightheartedly decorating their quarters with a sign reading "Music Hall 444 Broadway." (USAMHI)

Above: For many of the Bull Run regiments, defeat or not, there was a triumphal welcome when they returned home to muster out of service. Many of these were three- and nine-month regiments. They will be replaced by regiments enlisted for three years or the war. The North now knew that it would not be over quickly. The return of the 1st Michigan for mustering out in Detroit, August 7, 1861. (BURTON HISTORICAL COLLECTION, DETROIT PUBLIC LIBRARY)

Left: Men of Cameron's 79th New York suffer the same fate. (VM)

Below: But many still never pose again. Barnard's 1862 photograph of the rude graves of Federal soldiers buried by the Confederates at Bull Run. (XA)

Above: And Irvin McDowell will not go unscathed. Not entirely to blame for his loss, still he must be replaced. A new general from the west comes to take over, a man with Napoleonic pretensions and the nickname "Little Mac," Major General George B. McClellan. For the next year the war in the East will be his war. He stands at center here, hand in blouse, with the principal generals of the Army in August 1861. From the left they are Brigadier General William F. Smith, Brigadier General William B. Franklin, Heintzelman, Porter, McDowell, McClellan, Major General George McCall, Brigadier General Don Carlos Buell, Blenker, Brigadier General Silas Casey, and Brigadier General Fitz John Porter. They pose with hats on… (LC)

Below: … and with hats off. (AMERICANA IMAGE GALLERY)

Above: Barnard's 1862 image of a "hecatomb" where 100 Union soldiers sleep below the Sudley Church. For them the war was over. (KA)

The Navies Begin

VIRGIL CARRINGTON JONES

Improvisation and innovative technology clash on the water

Above: The U.S.S. Constitution, *symbol of past naval glory, and of an out-of-date United States fleet in 1861. (LC)*

EVEN BEFORE the Confederate triumph at Bull Run, the Civil War enhanced the stature of Stephen Russell Mallory, Confederate Secretary of the Navy. He took office and accepted the seemingly impossible task of sending against the enemy a fleet that did not exist. At the end of 1861, however, he had things so well organized that he was posing a threat which caused the Union to try to find effective ways to stop him.

Little about Mallory as an individual explained why the President of the new-born Confederate States of America, Jefferson Davis, so quickly singled him out for the job he held. He was rather naive and had dabbled at various occupations—town marshal, real estate dealer, admiralty lawyer, county judge, customs collector, newspaper correspondent, political leader. At age twenty-four he had had a touch of soldiery in the Seminole War. And then, in 1851, he was elected to the United States Senate from Florida, serving in that capacity for ten years, and rising in time to the chairmanship of the important Naval Affairs Committee, a responsibility that unquestionably drew Davis's attention to him.

As his record shows, he was in no sense a quitter. This was demonstrated in his wooing of a Spanish beauty who was bored by his manners at first, but later accepted his proposal of marriage. It was a trait that stood him in good stead when the burden of creating a navy was placed upon his shoulders. While participating in a losing cause, he strove so diligently to succeed that he helped revolutionize the field of naval science. Under his guidance, the Confederacy took part in history's first battle between ironclads, produced the first submarine to sink a ship, and developed the underwater mine or torpedo as an effective weapon of defense.

The war still was nearly two months away when Mallory took office, but the threat was strong. Ominously, the widely scattered ships of the Union began sailing homeward, some of them steering for southern ports. At the mouth of the Mississippi River, vessels passing up or downstream were searched. Floridians surprised and captured the United States Coast Survey schooner Dana.

Some of the seceded states demanded that Union ships within their ports be turned over to them. Among the commanders who refused to do so and fled with their vessels were John Newland Maffitt, later an outstanding Confederate naval officer, and David D. Porter, equally as staunch a Unionist.

Leaders who formed the nucleus of the Confederacy gathered in early February at Montgomery, Alabama. Even before the government was organized, a committee was named to summon "all such persons versed in naval affairs as they may deem advisable to consult with." Only a few United States Navy officers of high rank—five captains and four commanders—had "gone South" at this time, their action hinging on the secession of their respective states. Nevertheless, telegrams were immediately sent to all officers thought to be southern in their sympathy. The response was favorable. By June, a fifth of the officers so contacted had resigned, among them sixteen captains, thirty-four commanders, and seventy-six lieutenants.

One of these officers was Commander Raphael Semmes, a member of the Lighthouse

Board at Washington and only a short period away from one of the most outstanding privateering careers in history. Another was John M. Brooke, already recognized for the banded guns of his own design he was having manufactured at the Tredegar Iron Works in Richmond. Still another was John Taylor Wood, Naval Academy instructor and grandson of President Zachary Taylor.

When the Confederate Navy was created by formal act, it was soon announced that it was to be headed by chubby-faced, side-whiskered Mallory. He took office immediately, heading a fleet that existed only on paper. He had little to draw from. The South possessed virtually no merchant bottoms, no large force of skilled mechanics, and only a few seamen, for seafaring pursuits were not a favorite among its people. It had only two navy yards, one at Pensacola, Florida, and one at Norfolk, Virginia; only three rolling mills, two in Tennessee and one in Georgia, the latter unfitted for heavy work; and no machine shops of superior workmanship. Its sole foundry capable of casting heavy guns was at Richmond, soon to replace Montgomery as the capital of the Confederacy. The only raw material available was standing timber. All else, including iron, would have to be acquired. Only seven steam war vessels had ever been built in the South, and the engines of only two of these had been contracted for in the states involved.

Confronting Mallory as Union Secretary of the Navy was Gideon Welles, described as a small town politician. His task would be one of organization, for the fleet at his disposal was recognized as third in world power. It consisted of eighty-nine vessels, forty-two in commission, twenty-six available but not in commission, and twenty-one rated unserviceable. Although considered very slow, Welles took immediate action for the purchase of 136 vessels, to be altered and commissioned, and the construction of fifty-two others.

Abraham Lincoln's inauguration on March 4 added to the burden Mallory faced, for the new President announced a policy of reoccupying and holding the forts in the South. As the approach to the most important of these was by water, it meant the Confederacy must do something promptly about its deficiency in naval armament. Water mines were settled upon as the answer.

Along with the South's plans for a navy also came the original move for the training of personnel. At Montgomery on March 16, the Congress passed an act providing for a Confederate States Naval Academy, but it would be 1863 before steps actually were taken to bring such a facility into service. At this later period, an academy was actually set up in Richmond and the steamer Patrick Henry, formerly of the James River squadron, was used as a schoolship. The Union in the meantime took action to protect its important Naval Academy at Annapolis, Maryland. Because of its proximity to southern soil, it was transferred, along with its training ship, to Newport, Rhode Island.

On April 1, Commander Semmes, who had been sent North on a buying tour, detrained at Montgomery. He had had little success, finding no ships available which were suitable for service on the high seas. The only purchase he had made was a large amount of ordnance stores.

Above: The Navy Department in Washington, faced with the herculean task of building quickly a new navy to blockade the southern coast and conquer its rivers. To organize and run this mammoth undertaking, Lincoln selected… (LC)

Right: … a Connecticut newspaperman, Gideon Welles. He wore an ill-fitting wig, lacked humor, and proved to be one of the most capable and loyal members of Lincoln's Cabinet. (NA)

Above and below: War of 1812 frigates like the Santee and Constitution were still in service and totally unsuited for the war to come. They are shown here at Annapolis, Maryland, at the United States Naval Academy. (USAMHI)

Left: Many of the personnel were even older and more out of date. Captain William B. Shubrick had been in the Navy since 1806 and served aboard the Constitution *in the War of 1812. (USAMHI)*

Below: Flag Officer Charles Stewart, senior officer in the Navy, had been born in 1778, and commanded the Constitution *when Shubrick served aboard her. He was eighty-three years old when war broke out and still on the active list. (NYHS)*

Left: And promising younger officers like David D. Porter, son of an earlier naval hero and brother of "Dirty Bill" Porter, who would serve on the Mississippi. *(USAMHI)*

Meanwhile, James D. Bullock, captain of the United States mail steamer *Bienville*, and another who had resigned to side with the South were dispatched to England to make arrangements for the construction of ships.

The fall of Fort Sumter was simultaneous with one of Lincoln's most important decisions, for on this same date, April 14, 1861, the sailing frigate *Sabine*, equipped with forty-four guns, began a blockade at Pensacola. Soon it would be extended along the entire southern coast—more than 3,500 miles, the longest ever attempted by any nation—and eventually would rank as one of the North's most effective steps of offense.

Two days later, Lincoln issued a call for 75,000 troops. A counter proclamation came from President Davis on April 17, an offer of letters of marque under the seal of the Confederate States against ships and property of the United States. This was a direct strike against the Union's extensive merchant fleet.

The seventeenth brought other important action. Virginia seceded, affording an answer as to what was to be done with the Gosport Navy Yard at Norfolk, one of the largest in the nation. For weeks, the North had been undecided, withholding action in the hope that Virginia would remain in the Union. When the state seceded, officials at Washington decided to abandon the yard. This was one of the greatest strokes of luck that Mallory would have in his efforts to build a navy.

While ships and buildings at the yard were set afire before they were abandoned, Southerners moved in time to salvage much of what was at hand. Six ships, among them the *Merrimack*, the drydock, large supplies of ammunition and food, and more than a thousand guns were recovered. Without these guns, the Confederacy would have had to wait for months to arm some of its posts. And on April 18, the *Sumter*, a passenger ship converted into a raider, slipped out of the port of New Orleans. At its helm was Raphael Semmes, commencing the career that would afford him his place in history.

Right: But there was new blood, and wood, in the Navy as well. The U.S.S. Hartford *was a powerful 24-gun sloop launched in 1858, shown here after her commissioning at the Boston Navy Yard in 1859. (LC)*

Before the end of the war, he would capture 305 ships, bond ten of them and burn fifty-five, making a contribution in money and destruction valued at more than $5,000,000.

By May, the South had the nucleus of a navy—ten vessels carrying fifteen guns. Some had been seized, some purchased, and some were captured slavers. The Confederacy was not alone in its quest for additional craft. The United States was just as persistent and soon acquired every available steamer in Canada.

Mallory became more and more convinced that ironclad ships would help substantially in offsetting the South's fleet discrepancy. On May 8, he wrote: "I regard the possession of an iron-armored ship as a matter of the first necessity. Such a vessel at this time could traverse the entire coast of the United States, prevent all blockades, and encounter, with a fair prospect of success, their entire navy."

His reference to the blockade was at the moment no exaggeration. All along the Atlantic coast it was mostly a matter of bluff. Lincoln realized this and appointed an overall commander to strengthen it. The assignment went to Commodore Silas H. Stringham, a born seaman and experienced officer. Almost at the same time, the North took steps to block the Mississippi River. They were encouraged by James B. Eads, a veteran shipbuilder thoroughly familiar with the western rivers, who came to Washington to propose blocking the Mississippi to commerce, thereby shutting off a main artery by which the Confederacy could get food, as well as an important route by which it could move cotton to sea. Commander John Rodgers, capable and efficient, was assigned the task of developing a naval force along that major stream.

By July, Mallory was able to report:

The frigate *Merrimack* has been raised and docked at an expense of $6,000, and the necessary repairs to hull and machinery to place her in her former condition is estimated by experts at $450,000. The vessel would then be in the river, and by the blockade of the enemy's fleets and batteries rendered comparatively useless. It has, therefore, been determined to shield her completely with three inch iron, placed at such angles as to render her ball-proof, to complete her at the earliest moment, to arm her with the heaviest ordnance, and to send her at once against the enemy's fleet. It is believed that thus prepared she will be able to contend successfully against the heaviest of the enemy's ships, and to drive them from Hampton Roads and the ports of Virginia.

The *Merrimack* was only one phase of the Confederacy's program to provide its navy with iron clad ships. As it was considered impracticable to purchase these in Europe, plans were pursued to build them in the waters of the South. Contracts were let for a supply of all classes of iron. In this connection, it was learned that the Union was preparing an ironclad fleet of gunboats at St. Louis, Missouri. The Navy Department at Richmond sent reliable mechanics to that city to obtain employment on the vessels and to report on their strength and fighting character, as well as the progress made on them. In time, this information was made available to Mallory, influencing him to concentrate on the

Above: As in all navies in all times, Welles would find more than enough eager young officers hoping to see action after he retired the men now too old to command. (NAVAL HISTORICAL CENTER)

Below: Sailors must be enlisted to crew the growing fleet. A naval recruiting station at the Battery in New York City. They advertised a bounty of $400 to those who would enlist. (WENDELL W. LANG, JR.)

Left: Time did not allow the building of a complete fleet. To have a Union naval presence in the South's waters as soon as possible, Welles bought merchant steamers and even New York ferry boats like the Commodore Perry *and converted them quickly into river gunboats. (USAMHI)*

Right: There was also the safety of the Naval Academy to consider. At Annapolis it was too exposed and vulnerable to Confederate sympathizers in Maryland. (USAMHI)

Above: Welles moved it temporarily to Newport, Rhode Island, where it continued to produce officers for the Union, as this class in 1863. (RP)

Right: And this group of stern-faced young Nelsons. (RP)

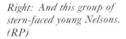

Left: The midshipman of 1861 could affect a jaunty air, but many felt grave fears that there would not be enough action for them in this war. (USAMHi)

defense of New Orleans against an attack from above rather than from the Gulf of Mexico.

The first attack would come elsewhere, however. By August, the North was ready to launch a naval blow against the South. So far as the blockade was concerned, the seat of troubles was at Hatteras on the North Carolina coast. Since May, it had developed into a haven for both runners and privateers, creating such a threat to northern commerce that newspapers referred to it as "a nest for pirates." Hampered by a succession of gales, a fleet for an expedition against Hatteras slowly assembled in Hampton Roads under the direction of Major General John E. Wool, commanding at Fort Monroe. Foremost among the vessels it consisted of were the flagship *Minnesota*, the *Wabash, Cumberland, Monticello, Pawnee*, and *Harriet Lane*, as well as three troop carriers, the steamers *Adelaide* and *George Peabody*, and the tug *Fanny*. The frigate *Susquehanna* would join it at its destination. On August 26, the ships started moving southward. At four o'clock the next afternoon, they were sighted off Hatteras.

Early on the morning of the twenty-eighth, the signal for a landing was given. The South had nothing on hand with which to combat such a fleet, and Forts Clark and Hatteras, defending the point, lowered their flags within a matter of hours. The surrender gave the North a foothold along the southern coast and put it in possession of the main passage to the North Carolina sounds. It was the first sizable victory for the Union since its troops had suffered defeat in the Battle of Bull Run. Prisoners included 670 officers and men. Guns found in the forts had been a part of the armament made available to the Confederates on the abandonment of the Gosport Navy Yard.

The moral effect of the victory was most important, for there were indications that the South was moving ahead in its efforts to build a navy, as well as to arm its troops. The United States consul at London reported the Rebel agents, with more funds at their control than previously, were buying at random. He revealed that the ship *Bermuda* had sailed from England with a million-dollar cargo made up of cannon, rifles, powder, cartridges, and other munitions of war. Her destination was Savannah, Georgia.

Also, the South's shipbuilding program had been stepped up considerably. Construction of two war ships, the *Arkansas* and the *Tennessee*, had been started at Memphis, while two others, the *Mississippi* and the *Louisiana*, were under way at New Orleans. Lieutenant Bullock, meanwhile, was meeting with success in England. He had arranged for the building of two vessels, the *Florida* and the *Alabama*, that would eventually become grave threats to the North's ocean-going commerce. In addition, individual states were forming their own navies, later to be turned over to the Confederacy. South Carolina in March had prepared for sea the first ship she had launched since the Revolution.

As Mallory hurriedly pressed forward, October found the North ready for its second naval expedition. This time the destination was Port Royal Sound, a body of water on the coast of South Carolina. Early in the war, the Union Navy Department listed it as one of three points that would serve as bases from which to combat blockade running. So easily could it be defended that the Federals feared the Confederates would make it impregnable before it could be taken over.

Again the starting point was Hampton Roads. There, under the command of Commodore Samuel Francis du Pont, head of Lincoln's Naval Advisory Board, a fleet of fifty ships assembled. The expedition sailed on October 29 amid much secrecy. But within a matter of hours after the fleet started moving, the Confederacy's Acting Secretary of War, Judah P. Benjamin, was able to wire military authorities at Savannah that the destination was Port Royal. This warning did little good. The Confederates again had nothing to stop a powerful fleet. The forts at Port Royal quickly fell.

While the North now had two naval victories to its credit, it still aimed no decisive blow at the South. By November, the blockade runners were nearing the peak of their activity. Eight out of every nine were getting into port, picking their destinations at random and using every trick to avoid the blockaders. It was not long before lanterns went out of style among the Union vessels standing guard off the southern coast, for it was found these lights at night were like buoys to the ships trying to make shore. Meanwhile Mallory, by December, had a fleet he no longer could count on his fingers. Thirty-five ships and sailing craft of various classes and armaments had been equipped by the Confederacy. Twenty-one of these were steam vessels, most of them small and built for speed rather than power. A majority had fewer than five guns. Some were protected by bales of cotton. He had entered into thirty-two contracts for the construction of forty gunboats, floating batteries, and vessels of war. In addition, the Navy Department had vessels under construction at its own direction. Progress was made in other quarters. A powder mill, engine mill, boiler mill, machine shops, and ordnance workshops were erected. Also completed was a ropewalk capable of making all kinds of cordage, from a rope yard to a nine-inch cable, with a capacity of 8,000 yards a month.

At Washington, Navy Secretary Welles also had been busy. By December, the Union fleet consisted of 264 vessels, carrying 2,557 guns and manned by 22,000 seamen. But the imbalance between the two navies was not the point of interest at this stage of the war. Rather, attention focused on the blockade runners. They brought the guns and ammunition, the vital items needed to make the Confederacy's armies more formidable, more able to repeat their early victories. The runners would have to continue to bear this responsibility until the South could further expand its facilities. Mallory had started office with appropriations of only $17,300. In the first eighteen months of operations, he would have available $14,605,777.

In the offing, he gained a reputation of doing much with nothing. But time would bring a kaleidoscopic pattern as the Union armies marched southward and the Union fleets gave them much needed support in times of desperation. And after the initial Union successes at Hatteras and Port Royal, the focus of attention, land and water, turned to the West.

Left: They learned the art of naval gunnery... (NA)

Below: And practiced aboard the old Constitution, *which moved to Newport as well. (USAMHI)*

Above: One hundred miles to the south of Washington, another naval secretary grappled with the problems of creating a navy. Stephen R. Mallory of Florida displayed a talent for innovation which left his personal stamp on the whole course of Confederate naval operations. It was he who would implement the building of the first ironclad. (SHC)

Below: A stroke of good fortune was the seizure of the Gosport Navy Yard at Norfolk, shown here in Timothy O'Sullivan's image taken in the spring of 1862 after its recapture. Battlefield artist Alfred R. Waud sits in the foreground. (USAMHI)

Below: Lieutenant John Mercer Brooke, shown here in United States uniform around 1852, went to work for Mallory developing the strong and powerful naval guns that would be a major addition to the new navy. He, too, was responsible for much of the concept for the new ironclad Virginia, *converted from the* Merrimack *found at Norfolk. (GEORGE M. BROOKE)*

Above: Commander George N. Hollins, in prewar uniform, made the Confederate Navy's first capture, the St. Nicholas, *on the Potomac in June 1861. The next month Mallory sent him to oversee naval defenses at New Orleans. (OCHM)*

Above: Raphael Semmes, another former officer in the United States Navy, went to the North before Sumter and actually purchased naval supplies for Mallory. Soon he would outfit and command the C.S.S. Sumter, *first of the South's great commerce raiders. This photograph was probably taken in England in 1864. Semmes rests his arm on an early Confederate flag. (NAVAL PHOTOGRAPHIC CENTER)*

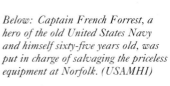

Below: Captain French Forrest, a hero of the old United States Navy and himself sixty-five years old, was put in charge of salvaging the priceless equipment at Norfolk. (USAMHI)

Below: Mallory depended on what was captured at United States installations at the war's outset. The Warrington Navy Yard at Pensacola yielded much, as well. This superb J. D. Edwards photograph, taken in April 1861, hints at what the Confederates seized. Row upon endless row of solid shot, ship's parts; and being refitted, the sidewheeler Fulton. *A previously unpublished image recently discovered. (SHC)*

Below: The Confederacy, too, needed a naval academy for training new officers. Hubbard T. Minor was one of its cadets, shown here in an 1864 photo by Howell & Brown of Savannah, Georgia. (KENNETH HATHAWAY)

Below: The sons of the South's notables attended the new academy, located aboard the C.S.S. Patrick Henry. *General John C. Breckinridge's son attended, and here, at left, is Daniel M. Lee, nephew of Robert E. Lee. (TU)*

Left: Welles quickly put as many ships as possible at sea to implement Lincoln's declared blockade. The U.S.S. Pensacola *had to pass Confederate batteries on the lower Potomac to reach Alexandria in early 1861, but she helped open the river. (USAMHI)*

Above: Soon the wharves at Alexandria saw all manner of vessels coming and going, on all kinds of missions. The mail steamer State of Maine. *(USAMHI)*

Above: The U.S.S. Sabine, *a frigate that took thirty-three years in the building, was one of the first to go on station in the Atlantic blockade. She also carried relief to the garrison at Fort Pickens at Pensacola in April 1861. (NA, U. S. BUREAU OF SHIPS)*

Above: The deck of the Hudson, *the first blockade runner captured in what would be a four-year game of cat and mouse. (NA)*

Above: One of Welles's first captures, the Confederate steamer Thomas Collyer, *taken at Alexandria on May 25, 1861, by the U.S.S.* Pawnee. *(USAMHI)*

Above: And here at the Washington Navy Yard. An 1864 image. (NYES)

Above: The tiny Marine Corps was also the Navy's responsibility, and Welles augmented that arm somewhat. Here a battalion of Marines drill at the Philadelphia Navy Yard. (USAMHI)

Right: They will play a minor role in this conflict, and chafe at their inactivity. (USAMHI)

Below: The Naval Observatory in Washington. Every branch of the Navy's operations was enhanced during Welles's tenure. (USAMHI)

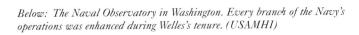

Above: The sail loft at the Boston Navy Yard. Though this was the era of steam, many of the Union's lesser ships still relied on the wind, and even steam vessels were equipped with sails to augment their speed. (USAMHI)

Left: The Washington Navy Yard, launching and refitting site for much of the burgeoning Union fleet. (LC)

Above: Captain Joseph Smith, chief of the Bureau of
Navy Yards and Docks, ran the commission which
made the commitment to go ahead with ironclad
design and building. (USAMHI)

Left: Captain Samuel Barron, the unsuccessful
Confederate defender at Hatteras, spent eleven
months in prison after his capture. (CHS)

Left: September 17, 1864, the launch of the frigate
U.S.S. Franklin at the Portsmouth, New Hampshire,
Navy Yard—a common scene in the years after Welles
took command. This screw frigate itself never saw
action. (NA)

Above: Then came the time
for offensive action.
Commodore Silas A.
Stringham, one of Welles's
most trusted confidants,
commanded the Atlantic
blockading squadron and
planned and led the successful attack on Fort Hatteras.
(USAMHI)

Left: The steam frigate
Minnesota, Stringham's
flagship in the attack on
Forts Clark and Hatteras.
(NA)

Above: Captain Charles H. Davis, fleet captain of Du Pont's seventeen ships as they attacked Forts Walker and Beauregard. (USAMHI)

Above: The U.S.S. Wabash, *flagship of Captain Samuel F. I. du Pont, standing in the center of the group of three officers. In it he led the attack on Port Royal. (USAMHI)*

Above: Port Royal, South Carolina, the next scene of Union naval victory. A Timothy O'Sullivan photograph, probably taken in early 1862. (USAMHI)

Above: O'Sullivan's photograph of the Coosaw Ferry to Port Royal Island. (USAMHI)

Right: The deck of the U.S.S. Pawnee, *an early veteran of the attempt to relieve Sumter, and the attacks on Hatteras Inlet and Port Royal. The screw sloop will be part of the backbone of the blockade in the years to come. (CHS)*

Above: A Federal pontoon wharf at Coosaw Ferry after the capture of Port Royal. (NYHS)

Right: Confederate Fort Walker on Hilton Head, seen from the rear, by O'Sullivan. (USAMHI)

Below: Fort Beauregard, showing ten heavy guns within its earthworks. From its commanding position on Bay Point, it still could not deter Du Pont's fleet. (USAMHI)

Left: The interior of Fort Beauregard, the Union's first strong foothold in South Carolina. (USAMHI)

Left: O'Sullivan's 1862 photograph of one of the Confederate guns inside Fort Beauregard. (USAMHI)

Right: Members of the 79th New York, veterans of Bull Run, could be happy about a victory for a change. After the battle they built this mock battery at Seabrooke Point on Port Royal Island. (USAMHI)

Left: The Mills Plantation on Port Royal Island, where life went on much as usual. (USAMHI)

Right: Quickly the Union took advantage of its capture, and enhanced it. The wharf at Hilton Head that fed a constant stream of supplies to the South Carolina Federals. (USAMHI)

Right: The boat landing at Beaufort began to bustle with Federal craft. (USAMHI)

Above: A man torn by conflicting loyalties. Commander Percival Drayton was a native of South Carolina, yet he stayed with the Union. He commanded the U.S.S. Pocahontas in the attack on Hilton Head. The commander of the Confederates defending Hilton Head was… (USAMHI)

Above: … his brother, Brigadier General Thomas F. Drayton. (USAMHI)

Above: Private homes like the Fuller House became officers' headquarters. (USAMHI)

Right: The generals, like Isaac I. Stevens seated here for O'Sullivan, were a commonplace sight. (SOUTH CAROLINA HISTORICAL SOCIETY)

Above: Workshops and bar-racks sprang up on the sand. (USAMHI)

Left: Hilton Head would soon become an area of great importance for repair of the Navy's blockade fleet. The chief engineer's quarters at Bay Point. (USAMHI)

Above: Guns came aboard ships, ready to renew the offensive against the enemy. (USAMHI)

Below: And the photographer could once again look for scenic beauty rather than the scars of war. (USAMHI)

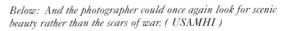

Right: And the price of any great gain in this war, the graves of the dead. Eight men were killed aboard Du Pont's ships. They are buried here on Hilton Head. Photograph by O'Sullivan. (USAMHI)

Right: By November 16, 1861, with two significant successes to its credit, the Union Navy could justifiably preen for its President. The men of the U.S.S. Pensacola man the yards in honor of a visit in Alexandria by Abraham Lincoln. (WRHS)

The War Moves West

ALBERT CASTEL

Names like Grant and Sherman and Shiloh emerge in battle

Above: The broad Tennessee River cut through the South like a crooked knife, from Paducah, Kentucky, to Knoxville. (WRHS)

IN THE PREDOMINANTLY RURAL WEST the camera, like the war itself, was still a novelty in 1861. Moreover, just as more words were printed about military operations in the East, so were more photos taken. The majority of western photographers remained in their studios. Only a few ventured forth to the battlefields.

Perhaps this was because of the different character of the war in the West. In the East combat took place in a small area and it was comparatively easy for Brady and Gardner and others to haul their cumbersome paraphernalia to the scene. Out West, on the other hand, the fighting sprawled from the Appalachians to the Mississippi, from the banks of the Ohio to the Gulf of Mexico. Furthermore, it was hard to predict where or when a battle would occur. In fact, for a long time after the bombardment of Fort Sumter there were no battles of consequence at all.

The western soldiers, Union and Confederate alike, were eager enough. Brandishing flintlocks, butcher knives, and a hodge-podge of other impractical weapons, they looked most bellicose. However, they had to wait awhile to hear the bullets buzz and the cannons roar. First of all both North and South at the outset concentrated most of their forces near Washington in expectation that one big battle there would decide the war. Then, when the western armies did begin building up after Bull Run, they could not get at each other because of Kentucky.

As with other slave-holding border states, public opinion in Kentucky was fragmented. Many Kentuckians favored the Confederacy. Many more adhered to the Union—more or less. But in 1861 the majority preferred neutrality. Realizing this, both Lincoln and Davis refrained from sending troops into their native state for fear of pushing it into the enemy's camp. As Lincoln commented, for the Union to lose Kentucky would be to "lose the whole game." On the other hand, should the North secure control of the state, it would be in a position to penetrate the southern heartland.

Hence during the summer of 1861, increasingly strong Federal and Confederate forces stood poised on Kentucky's borders, neither daring to be the first to cross them. Meanwhile Kentucky Unionists and Secessionists formed military units which sometimes drilled simultaneously in different parts of the same town! Also at Camp Andrew Johnson, Lieutenant Samuel P. Carter of the United States Navy, acting on Lincoln's orders, organized regiments of Unionist refugees from East Tennessee. Lincoln was anxious to liberate that region from Confederate rule.

Sooner or later the Bluegrass impasse had to end. It did so on September 3 when Confederate General Leonidas Polk seized Columbus on the Mississippi River. He claimed that the Yankees had planned to do the same thing, but his real purpose was to obtain a stronger position from which to resist a Union thrust down the Mississippi.

In any event he made the first and greatest of his numerous contributions to southern defeat. His incursion outraged most Kentuckians and transformed hosts of neutralists into Unionists. At the same time it provided the Federals with a legitimate excuse to invade Kentucky also. On September 6, Brigadier General Ulysses S. Grant

Above: For over two years the course of the war in the West would follow its meanderings, its water stained red with the blood of America. (USAMHI)

Left: Simple places with names like Shiloh and Chickamauga would, in years to come, assume a symbolic importance, as would rude churches, and humble dwellings marked by the war. Here in Washington, Kentucky, is the birthplace of Albert Sidney Johnston, a romantic figure who became a general in the Texas revolution of 1836, fought in the Mexican War, and on the plains as colonel of the 2d United States Cavalry. (WRHS)

Right: With war coming to the West, troops must be raised. Existing units, like the Kentucky State Guard, provided many companies already trained and equipped for the Confederacy. Standing at center, in the top hat, is Kentucky's governor, Beriah Magoffin, in this August 1860 photograph. When called on to furnish volunteers to suppress the Rebellion, he refused to aid "the wicked purpose" with Kentucky soldiers. (KHS)

countered Polk's move by occupying Paducah. Other Union forces soon took control of the northern two thirds of the state. General Albert Sidney Johnston, top Confederate commander in the West, sent troops up from Tennessee to block their further advance.

Still, no serious fighting occurred. Each side grossly overestimated the other's strength and so held back from a confrontation. Brigadier General William Tecumseh Sherman, commanding the center of the Union line south of Louisville, was so sure that the Rebel army at Bowling Green would overwhelm him that he nearly suffered a nervous breakdown.

It was Grant who struck the first blow. Earlier in the war, while chasing guerrillas in Missouri, he learned that the enemy was just as scared as he was, and that the secret of military success was to make his foe more scared. Applying that lesson, on November 7 he loaded 3,000 troops onto transports at Cairo, Illinois, steamed down the Mississippi, and attacked an outpost Polk had established at Belmont, Missouri, across the river from Columbus. Superior Confederate numbers finally drove him away, but he gave the Southerners a jolt and strengthened their belief that the main Union offensive would be down the Mississippi.

On the night of the day after the fight at Belmont, bands of Unionists burned five railroad bridges in East Tennessee. This strike had been approved by Lincoln, who hoped thereby to cut a vital southern supply line and at the same time set the stage for the liberation of East Tennessee. The Confederate authorities rushed troops into the area, declared martial law, jailed scores of "Tories," and hanged suspected bridge burners. Hundreds of Unionists fled northward to escape persecution; others remained to wage a ruthless guerrilla war against their persecutors.

The movement of a Federal army commanded by Brigadier General George H. Thomas toward East Tennessee led to the next important battle in the West a little over two

Above: Officers of the Kentucky State Guard at Louisville in August 1860. Almost all of them will become Confederates. The officer at right shaking hands with a civilian is Colonel Thomas H. Hunt, who would later command the 9th Kentucky Infantry in the celebrated Orphan Brigade. (KHS)

Above: The Federals flocked to the banners in even greater numbers; here a group of Iowa volunteers pose in their training camp. (MISSOURI HISTORICAL SOCIETY)

Right: The status of Kentucky, key to Union and Confederate war plans, was precarious. Declared neutral, she had to depend on both sides to honor that stance. Neither did. Major General George B. McClellan, commanding Ohio state forces in April and May, refused to recognize that neutrality, and thereby helped hold Kentucky in the Union. An 1861 photograph by the Brady studio. (USAMHI)

Right: "We are coming, Father Abraham," they sang. The 28th Wisconsin, bound for Kentucky. (NA)

Below: Officers of the 1st Minnesota gather at the home of the commandant at Fort Snelling in May 1861, ready to go to war. (MHS)

months later. This time the scene was eastern Kentucky and the Confederates were the aggressors. Early on the morning of January 19, 1862, at Logan's Crossroads near Mill Springs, some 5,000 of them under Major General George B. Crittenden made a surprise attack on Thomas's somewhat smaller force. At first driven back, Thomas's troops rallied, then routed the ill armed Southerners who were demoralized by the death of their popular second-in-command, Brigadier General Felix Zollicoffer. The ragged, famished remnants of Crittenden's army retreated into East Tennessee, which now lay open to northern occupation. However, much to Lincoln's frustration, supply problems prevented the Federals from pushing further southward.

Thomas's victory wrecked the right wing of Johnston's long line across Kentucky. The following month Grant and the United States Navy smashed the left wing. First, on February 6, Commodore Andrew H. Foote's gunboats captured Fort Henry on the Tennessee River. Five days later Grant marched his army to the Cumberland River, where on February 13 he invested the large Confederate garrison at Fort Donelson. An attack by Foote, who had steamed back down the Tennessee to the Ohio and then up the Cumberland, failed on February 14. The following day the Confederates almost broke out to the south—indeed, probably would have had not their commander, Brigadier General John Floyd, lost his nerve. On the other hand, Grant, again applying the lesson he had learned in Missouri, promptly counterattacked and drove the Rebels back into their fortifications.

On February 16 Brigadier General Simon Bolivar Buckner, who had succeeded Floyd as commander, asked Grant for terms. Grant replied: "No terms except unconditional and immediate surrender.... I propose to move immediately upon your works." Buckner had no choice except to comply. Close to 12,000 Confederates became prisoners of war.

It was the biggest Union victory so far in the war. Along with the fall of Fort Henry it opened middle Tennessee to Federal invasion via the Cumberland and Tennessee rivers, made Polk's position at Columbus untenable, and forced Johnston to retreat hastily from Kentucky all the way to Corinth, Mississippi.

There he began concentrating his hitherto scattered forces. By April he had 40,000 troops organized into four divisions commanded by generals Polk, Braxton Bragg, William J. Hardee, and John C. Breckinridge. On April 3 he set out to attack Grant at Pittsburg Landing on the Tennessee. His plan, which had been devised by General P. G. T. Beauregard, who had been posted from Virginia to serve as second-in-command in the West, was to surprise and destroy Grant's 42,000-man army before it was joined by another large Union force under Major General Don Carlos Buell heading down from Nashville. If successful, central Tennessee would be redeemed and the tide of the war in the West reversed.

It was only twenty miles from Corinth to Pittsburg Landing. But the roads were bad and the march discipline of the raw Rebel troops worse. Hence, instead of striking Grant on the morning of April 5 as planned, the Confederates found them selves on the evening of that day still several miles from their objective. Beauregard, despairing of achieving surprise, advised returning to Corinth. However, Johnston, believing that a retreat would be more demoralizing than a defeat, ordered the attack to be made at dawn on April 6.

And so it was—and with great success. Despite the fact that some of their patrols had heard, seen, and even clashed with advance units of Johnston's army, most of the Federals were taken by surprise. Grant, who had been promoted to major general for Fort Donelson, simply had not expected Johnston to bring the battle to him. Furthermore, he had posted his troops with a view to drilling rather than defense—nor, as usual during the early period of the war, had they bothered to entrench. Consequently the Confederates, charging with a ferocity that henceforth would be their trademark, drove back Grant's men, thousands of whom fled in wild eyed panic. It seemed that Johnston's prediction to his staff as the battle got under way, "Tonight we will water our horses in the Tennessee River," would come true.

However, most of the Northerners fought with a stubbornness equal to the Southerners' dash. In particular several thousand of them under Brigadier General Benjamin Prentiss, stationed in a sunken road which soon and ever after was called The Hornets' Nest, repulsed assault after assault. Nearby, scores of wounded from both sides mingled as they sought to quench their thirst in "The Bloody Pond." At 2:30 P.M., Johnston, while urging his men on against the Yankee strongpoint, bled to death when a bullet severed an artery in his right leg. Not until late in the afternoon, after surrounding him, did the Confederates force Prentiss to surrender. By then Grant had been able to form a compact defense line around Pittsburg Landing with his 7,000 remaining effectives, who were bolstered by massed artillery, gunboats, and several regiments from the vanguard of Buell's army. When at twilight a few thousand exhausted Rebels—the most Beauregard, who had replaced Johnston, could muster—made a last desperate effort to drive the Federals into the river, withering fire flung them back.

It was a hideous night of torrential rain falling on thousands of untended, moaning, screaming wounded. During the night 5,000 Union troops under Brigadier General Lew Wallace, who had been encamped to the north of Pittsburg Landing, belatedly joined Grant's army. More importantly, 20,000 of Buell's men also arrived. In the morning Grant counterattacked. Beauregard, who had no more than 20,000 muskets in his firing line, slowly gave way. Finally, late in the afternoon, seeing that victory was impossible and defeat inevitable, he ordered a retreat back to Corinth. The Federals, happy to see the Confederates leave, did not pursue.

Pittsburg Landing, as the North called it, or Shiloh, as the South named it after a log church around which much of the fighting centered, was the biggest and bloodiest battle of the war to that time. Nearly 11,000 Confederates and over 13,000 Federals were killed, wounded, captured, or missing—a loss for each army of 25 percent of the troops actually engaged. Strategically it clinched the Union gains resulting from Forts Henry and Donelson. Psychologically it was a tremendous blow to Confederate morale and

Above: By the fall, Federal recruiting and training camps appeared in the Bluegrass, at places like Camp Nelson, complete with bakeries... (NA, U.S. WAR DEPT. GENERAL STAFF)

Above: ... well-supplied workshops... (NA, U. S. SIGNAL CORPS)

Right: ... and even reservoirs with picket fences. (NA, U. S. SIGNAL CORPS)

Left: Even larger camps of instruction like Camp Butler, near Cairo, Illinois, began to produce the regiments that would fight the western war. (ILLINOIS STATE HISTORICAL LIBRARY)

Left: And in came the volunteers. The 52d Illinois paraded through Elgin, Illinois, on its way to put down rebellion. (ILLINOIS STATE HISTORICAL LIBRARY)

Above: Members of the 9th Missouri try to look their best on the street in St. Joseph, but these western soldiers will ever appear unkempt… and rugged as hell itself . (STATE HISTORICAL SOCIETY OF MISSOURI)

Left: Friends and families saw them off to war in front of their courthouses, as here at Paris, Illinois, in April 1862. While the speeches were made and the colors presented, the wagons loaded with their gear awaited the march to Dixie. (EDWARD STEERS)

Right: From farther west they came by river steamer, like these Nebraska soldiers aboard the Henderson at Bellview, Iowa, in 1861. (NEBRASKA STATE HISTORICAL SOCIETY)

gave the northern soldiers of the West something of the same sense of superiority that the Southerners in Virginia derived from Bull Run. Yet if Johnston had been able to attack on the day planned, probably he would have destroyed Grant, although it is unlikely that his army would have been in condition to follow up the victory.

As it was, the Federals failed to exploit fully their success. After the battle Major General Henry W. Halleck, overall Union commander in the West, took personal charge of operations. He soon revealed himself to be more at home at a desk than in the saddle. Although he accumulated over 120,000 men, he moved with excessive slowness and caution on Corinth, where Beauregard, despite reinforcements from the Trans-Mississippi under Major Generals Earl Van Dorn and Sterling Price, mustered barely 50,000. Then, when he finally forced Beauregard to evacuate Corinth on June 7, he neither pursued nor struck for Vicksburg, which as a result of the Union captures of Island No. 10, Fort Pillow, and Memphis during the spring was the last remaining major Confederate stronghold on the Mississippi north of Baton Rouge. Instead he broke up his host into a number of separate armies spread between Memphis and the approaches to Chattanooga. By so doing he gave the Confederates, now commanded by Bragg, a breathing spell which they put to good use.

Kentucky and Tennessee were not the only western states to witness a Confederate rollback during the early months of 1862. The same occurred from the opposite direction in Louisiana and Mississippi. On the night of April 24, in a daring surprise move, Flag Officer David Farragut, United States Navy, ran his wooden warships past Forts St. Philip and Jackson guarding the mouth of the Mississippi. A Confederate attempt to stop him with gunboats, rams, and fire rafts failed, and on the afternoon of April 25 he seized New Orleans, the South's largest city and main port. He then proceeded up the river to capture Baton Rouge on May 12 and Natchez six days later.

However, strong fortifications and the powerful ironclad *Arkansas* foiled him at Vicksburg during June and July.

Meanwhile, Union troops commanded by Ben Butler, a political general from Massachusetts, garrisoned New Orleans. There some of the women expressed their resentment of the Yankee presence by spitting on blue-clad soldiers. In retaliation Butler on May 15 issued an order declaring that "hereafter when any female shall by word, gesture, or movement insult… any officer or soldier of the United States she shall be regarded and held liable to be treated as woman of the town plying her vocation." This order enraged Southerners, who denounced Butler as a "beast." But it stopped the spitting.

Numerous male Louisianans expressed their opposition to northern rule by forming guerrilla bands which harassed Federal outposts and shipping. On May 28 forty of these bushwhackers fired on a boat from Farragut's flagship *Hartford*, which was putting ashore at Baton Rouge. Outraged, Farragut promptly opened up with his heavy cannons, wrecking the state capitol along with many other buildings.

Not all Louisianans resisted Yankee domination. Hundreds of free blacks—many of whom were in fact white-skinned—joined the 1st Louisiana Native Guards, the formation of which had been authorized by Butler on August 22, a full month before Lincoln issued the Preliminary Emancipation Proclamation. Mustered in at New Orleans on September 27, it was one of the first Negro regiments to serve in the Union Army.

Baton Rouge suffered further devastation on August 5 when 2,600 Confederates under Breckinridge tried to retake it. At first they drove the 2,500-man Union garrison toward the river. But then they came under heavy fire from gunboats and eventually retreated. Plans had called for the ironclad *Arkansas* to assist Breckinridge's assault, but owing to engine trouble she failed to arrive in time and on the following day her crew blew her up in order to prevent her capture by Federal warships. Both sides lost heavily at Baton Rouge, with the northern commander, Brigadier General Thomas Williams, being among the slain.

Six days after the battle the Federals evacuated the town, which was given over to pillaging and burning by Negroes and convicts released from the state prison. As for Breckinridge, he withdrew to Port Hudson, where he fortified the bluff overlooking the Mississippi. The approximately 150-mile stretch between that point and Vicksburg constituted the last link between the eastern and western halves of the Confederacy.

In northern Mississippi Bragg spent the early part of the summer reorganizing and training the army he had taken over from Beauregard. His men hated his harsh discipline and him for it, but they became better soldiers and, perhaps, even better fighters. By late July he was ready to launch an offensive which had as its object nothing less than the liberation of Tennessee and the occupation of Kentucky. Leaving behind 15,000 men under Sterling Price to keep an eye on Grant in West Tennessee and another small army under Van Dorn to guard Vicksburg, he transferred his remaining 35,000 troops by rail from Tupelo through Mobile and Atlanta to Chattanooga. By this maneuver, the most brilliant of its kind during the war, he outflanked the entire Federal front in the West. In addition, raids by the hard-riding gray troopers of Frank Armstrong, Nathan Bedford Forrest, and John Hunt Morgan caused Buell's army, which had been slowly advancing on Chattanooga, to fall back to Nashville, thus opening a path into Kentucky.

On August 28 Bragg began marching north. "Fighting Joe" Wheeler's cavalry led the way; the infantry jubilantly sang "Dixie." Two days later another Confederate army, 7,000 men under Major General Edmund Kirby Smith, who had moved up from Knoxville, routed 6,500 Federals at Richmond, Kentucky, then occupied Lexington. Expecting to be attacked next, the people of Cincinnati frantically constructed fortifications as thousands of Ohio and Kentucky militia hastened to their aid. But Kirby Smith neither advanced northward against Cincinnati nor moved westward to reinforce Bragg: He was too cautious to do the former and too reluctant to give up his quasi-independent command to do the latter.

Above: A troop transport loaded with soldiers lands at Cairo, Illinois, where the men will train for the war. These men come aboard the Aleck Scott, *unaware that before the war she was piloted briefly by a writer who will take his pen name from the cry of a steamboat leadsman, "Mark Twain." At the moment, he is still Samuel L. Clemens, and now a young and very scared Confederate soldier. (LO)*

Above: But these Confederates are not at all frightened. Officers all, their cigars and miniature flags proclaiming their bravado, they look forward to the coming fray. (LSU)

Above: Southerners who remained loyal to the Union enjoyed wide popularity in the North, and often obtained high rank. Samuel P. Carter of East Tennessee outdid them all. A graduate of the United States Naval Academy, he was commissioned a brigadier general in the Army in 1862, simultaneously holding that rank and a commander's commission in the Navy. He was invaluable in stirring Union sentiment in Tennessee, and in 1862 was leading loyal Tennesseans in raids against their enemies. (NA)

Right: The first scene of conflict was Missouri, soon to be one of the most hotly contested areas of the war. The Federal commander there was a man of international stature, native of Georgia, California's first senator, unsuccessful Republican presidential candidate in 1856, and a man of almost no military capabilities—Major General John C. Fremont, the celebrated "Pathfinder" of the West. He proved to be a martinet and constant thorn in Lincoln's side. (NYHS)

Above: The first action came bloodlessly on May 10 when a body of secessionist Missouri militia training at Camp Jackson near St. Louis was seized by the man who almost single-handedly saved Missouri for the Union. (MISSOURI HISTORICAL SOCIETY)

Above: Captain Nathaniel Lyon. A Unionist fire-brand who brooked no obstacle to his single purpose of keeping Missouri out of the hands of the secession-ists. When meetings with Missouri Confederates look-ing toward compromise produced nothing, he stated to them laconically, "This means war." A previously unpublished portrait probably taken after his promo-tion to brigadier. (NA)

Above: Missouri Confederates did not give in peace-fully. The flamboyant Colonel M. Jefferson Thompson, in 1860 mayor of St. Joseph, marched on Cape Girardeau with nearly 5,000 men when Fremont took command in the state. Later, after the general issued an ill-advised and unauthorized proclamation of emancipation, Thompson promul-gated his own proclamation countermanding Fremont's. He would remain throughout the war one of the most colorful figures of the western Confederates. (JM)

Above: Lyon's foe was a Tennessean commanding Arkansas troops, Brigadier General Ben McCulloch, a man who disdained a uniform and went into battle attired, as here, in a black velvet suit. In 1835 he went to Texas with Davy Crockett. In March 1862 he would die in battle at Pea Ridge, Arkansas. (VM)

Below: Lyon was right when he said there must be war. In attempting to rid the state of Confederates, he led his little army against that of General Benjamin McCulloch at Wilson's Creek, near Springfield, on August 10, 1861. It was war, and here, where the numeral "2" rests on the horizon, Lyon fell in battle. Probably an early postwar photo. (WRHS)

Above: Mosby Monroe Parsons, former Missouri attorney general and a commander of Confederate Missouri state guardsmen at Wilson's Creek. (LSU)

Above: Men of Missouri's Union State Guard. No other state, even Kentucky, would suffer as much from divided loyalties and families. (MISSOURI HIS-TORICAL SOCIETY)

Above: The next month Confederates led by Sterling Price besieged and captured Lexington, Missouri, defended by Colonel James A. Mulligan and his 23d Illinois Irish Brigade." (USAMHI)

Above: By early 1862, Missouri still had not been firmly taken by either side. On March 7-8, the largest battle west of the Mississippi took place at Pea Ridge, Arkansas, its outcome deciding the fate of Missouri. Ben McCulloch would die in the battle. Brigadier General Alexander S. Asboth, leading a Union division, would be wounded. (USAMHI)

Left: Confederate Brigadier General Albert Pike was a native of Boston, Massachusetts, but raised Indian troops for the South in Arkansas and led them ingloriously at Pea Ridge. A fellow general said he was "either insane or untrue to the South." He resigned soon thereafter, and spent much of the rest of his life writing the ritual and dogma for Masonry. (NYHS)

Below: Brigadier General Daniel M. Frost, a native of New York who sided with the South, was offered command of a brigade at Pea Ridge, but refused to accept such a small command and instead watched the battle "from a convenient height." (LSU)

All the while Buell, believing that Bragg was aiming for Nashville, remained at the Tennessee capital with his 50,000 troops. Not until September 7 did he realize that the Confederate objective was Kentucky and so set out in pursuit.

Given his long lead, Bragg by rapid marching might have taken Louisville—a stroke which would have panicked the Northwest. However, Davis had instructed him not to take unnecessary risks, and he feared being caught between the forces protecting that city and Buell's army moving up from Tennessee. Therefore, after capturing a 4,000-man Federal garrison at Munfordville, Kentucky, on September 17, 1862 (the same day as the Battle of Antietam), he swerved eastward to link up with Kirby Smith. Ten days later Buell reached Louisville, where he began readying a counteroffensive. His preparations were somewhat disrupted when on September 29 Brigadier General Jefferson C. Davis murdered Brigadier General William "Bull" Nelson after the three-hundred-pound Nelson slapped him during an altercation at a hotel.

Back to the south: Price, having been instructed by Bragg to enter middle Tennessee, advanced to Iuka, in northeastern Mississippi, on September 14. Grant countered by sending a column under Major General William S. Rosecrans to strike Price from the south while Major General E. O. C. Ord's army hit him from the north. However, owing to an atmospheric freak condition, neither Ord nor Grant (who accompanied him) heard the sound of battle when Rosecrans assaulted Price on September 19. Consequently they did not attack, and Price, after beating off Rosecrans, slipped out of the trap that night.

Late in September Van Dorn came up from Vicksburg to join Price at Ripley, Mississippi. Taking command of their combined force of 22,000, he marched for Corinth, which was held by 23,000 Federals under Rosecrans. On October 3 he drove Rosecrans from his outer for-

Above: Brigadier General William Y. Slack was mortally wounded on the first day at Pea Ridge and died two weeks later. It was nearly a month later that the Confederate Senate promoted him to brigadier, the news of his death not having reached them. The uniform in this photograph has been painted on. (VM)

Right: A Confederate commander whose capabilities were as grand as his name, John Sappington Marmaduke. Educated at Yale and Harvard, he graduated from West Point in 1857, when this photograph was taken. Colonel of Missouri and Arkansas troops, he fought gallantly at Prairie Grove, Arkansas, in December 1862, and rose steadily in ability. He was the last Confederate to win promotion to major general, on March 18, 1865, and was later governor of Missouri. (LSU)

Above: Native of Kentucky, Brigadier General James F. Fagan also distinguished himself in the Confederate defeat at Prairie Grove. (JM)

Left: While the war west of the Mississippi dragged on in its bloody and tragic course, one of the Union's first victories came in January 1862 at Mill Springs, Kentucky. Brigadier General George H. Thomas, a native of Virginia, led part of his division against the Confederate command in southeast Kentucky. (USAMHI)

Above: The Confederates Thomas faced were led by Major General George B. Crittenden. His father was Senator John J. Crittenden, who unsuccessfully attempted a last-minute compromise between North and South in 1861. His brother was a major general in the Union Army; so were Kentucky families divided. This previously unpublished photograph shows him probably in 1862. He was forced to give battle to Thomas at Mill Springs, thanks in part to disobedience to his orders from a subordinate... (LSU)

Above: ... Brigadier General Felix Zollicoffer of Tennessee, who was killed when he accidentally rode into Union troops during the battle. (JM)

Above: Assisted by Federal gunboats under the command of Flag Officer Andrew H. Foote, Grant moved against Confederate bastions on the Tennessee and Cumberland rivers. (LC)

tifications but the next day suffered hideous losses in an attempt to storm the town. A column sent by Grant blocked his retreat, but thanks to Armstrong's cavalry he managed to escape. Shortly after the battle a photographer took pictures of Texans killed assaulting a Union redoubt known as Battery Robinette. They are among the most grim photos of the war. Any civilian viewing them would immediately realize that real-life—or rather real-death—battlefields bore little resemblance to the scenes depicted in Currier and Ives prints.

Bragg and Kirby Smith had expected swarms of recruits in Kentucky—indeed without them they could not hope to hold the state. Instead only about 2,500 joined their ragged legions. Disgusted, Bragg decided to resort to conscription. To that end he arranged for the installation of Richard C. Hawes as Confederate Governor of Kentucky. But the inauguration ceremonies, held at Frankfort, the state capital, on October 4, were abruptly terminated by Union shellfire. Buell had launched his counteroffensive—and sooner than Bragg had anticipated, with the result that he caught the Confederates badly scattered.

Bragg fell back, planning as he did so to regroup his units for a stand west of Lexington. However, on October 8, being pressed by advancing Federals near Perryville, he lashed back at them. Charging through sheets of cannon and rifle fire, 15,000 of Polk's and Hardee's veterans hurled back the Union line, which was held by 14,000 troops, many of them raw. Then, after being reinforced, the Northerners rallied,

Right: Mill Springs destroyed the right of the Confederate defensive line in Kentucky. Now a new general, Ulysses S. Grant, went to work on the left of the line. (USAMHI)

Above: Foote had four new river ironclads, among them the U.S.S. Cincinnati, *one of the powerful "city class" gunboats. (NHC)*

Above: Another was the U.S.S. Carondelet, *heavily armed and armored, and here tied at the bank on one of the western rivers. (NHC)*

counterattacked, and regained much ground. Ferocious but indecisive fighting continued until nightfall. The Confederates lost 3,400 and the Federals 4,200 of the 22,000 men they had engaged.

Bragg thought that he faced at Perryville only a portion of Buell's army, most of which he believed heading for Lexington by way of Frankfort. In actuality Buell had threatened Frankfort with a small column of 7,000 while his main force, 54,000 strong, had advanced on Perryville. Furthermore, Bragg's assault fell on Buell's left wing alone. Fortunately for the Confederates, Buell was so far to the rear that he did not even know a battle was taking place until two hours after it started! And then, again through ignorance plus poor staff work, he failed to exploit a splendid opportunity to crush Polk's and Hardee's divisions by striking them in the flank and rear with his virtually unopposed center and right. In brief, both Bragg and Buell were lost in the fog of war.

That night Bragg, belatedly but in time, realized that he faced Buell's concentrated power at Perryville, whereas his and Kirby Smith's forces still were dispersed. He also learned of Van Dorn's debacle at Corinth, which meant that he could not expect any help from him but that Grant was free to aid Buell—or else sweep southward. Consequently he at once retreated, first to Harrodsburg, then to Bryantsville. There on October 12 he and Kirby Smith decided to return to Tennessee before the Federals cut them off from Cumberland Gap.

Twelve days later the last of the foot-sore Confederates trudged through Cumberland Gap on the way to Knoxville. Their invasion of Kentucky, like Lee's of Maryland the month before, had ended in failure after a brilliant beginning. Many Southerners then and afterward denounced Bragg for abandoning Kentucky without an all-out battle. Bragg, however, saw no point in risking his army fighting for the Confederate cause in the Bluegrass State when so few of the Kentuckians themselves were willing to fight for it.

Lincoln urged, indeed expected, Buell to follow the Confederates to Knoxville, defeat them, and liberate East Tennessee. Instead Buell headed for Nashville. Lincoln thereupon

Above: A markedly different ironclad was the U.S.S. Essex, *a converted centerwheel steamboat whose arming was personally overseen by her commander... (USAMHI)*

Above: One of Foote's three wooden gunboats, the U.S.S. Tyler. *It would do workhorse duty on the western waters, though even great warships still had to dry their laundry now and then. (USAMHI)*

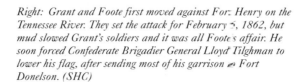

Right: Grant and Foote first moved against Fort Henry on the Tennessee River. They set the attack for February 5, 1862, but mud slowed Grant's soldiers and it was all Foote's affair. He soon forced Confederate Brigadier General Lloyd Tilghman to lower his flag, after sending most of his garrison to Fort Donelson. (SHC)

Above: ... William David Porter. Called "Dirty Bill" because of his unlikable manner and sometimes less-than-honest methods, he was the son of Commodore David Porter of the original Essex. *His brother was Admiral David D. Porter, his half-brother Admiral David Farragut. He would be badly scalded by steam when a shot from Confederate Fort Henry penetrated the* Essex's *boiler. (USAMHI)*

Right: Donelson would be a different matter entirely. Commanding there was General John B. Floyd, who a year before was Buchanan's Secretary of War. On February 13, Grant launched his land attack with the division of Brigadier General Charles F. Smith, his one-time teacher at West Point. (NA)

Right: Two days later, facing a hopeless situation, Floyd decided to escape, abandoning his command to General Gideon J. Pillow. A man of reprehensible character, Pillow, too, chose to flee rather than share the fate of his soldiers. In January 1863, at the Battle of Stones River, he would be seen hiding behind a tree while his brigade went into battle. Thereafter he gave perjured testimony against fellow generals in the political infighting that would always plague the Confederate Army of Tennessee. (VM)

Above: Unidentified western Confederates, probably from Louisiana, men of the stamp of those who gallantly defended Donelson until it was hopeless. (CM)

Below: Men of the 2d Kentucky Infantry almost cut a way out of Grant's trap, but they were called back before they could take advantage of it. Some of these members of the National Blues, Kentucky State Guard, made up the 2d Kentucky. (KHS)

Below: Refusing to abandon his men as did Floyd and Pillow, the dashing Brigadier General Simon B. Buckner, formerly commander of the Kentucky State Guard, stayed with them and finally asked his old friend Grant for terms. (SHC)

replaced him with Rosecrans—who completed the move to Nashville, then remained there through November and most of December despite repeated orders and even pleas from Washington to advance. Like Buell he believed that a winter invasion of mountainous, thinly populated East Tennessee would be logistically impractical and strategically barren. He preferred instead to accumulate a large stockpile of supplies before doing battle with Bragg, who in the meantime had shifted his forces—now and thereafter known as The Army of Tennessee—to Murfreesboro, thirty miles southeast of Nashville.

Both Buell and Rosecrans were not without justification in their concern about supplies. Late in December cavalry raids by Van Dorn and Forrest caused Grant to abandon an attempt to capture Vicksburg by marching south through Mississippi. Similarly Morgan and Wheeler snipped away at Rosecrans's communication lines in Tennessee and Kentucky, delaying thereby his preparations.

Finally, on the day after Christmas, Rosecrans moved out from Nashville with 45,000 troops and an immense wagon train containing twenty days' rations. Bragg waited for him west of Murfreesboro, his 40,000 men straddling easily fordable Stones River. The Federals arrived in front of the Confederate position on December 29, having been slowed by Wheeler's cavalry. Each commander made preparations to attack with his left. The only difference was that Bragg struck first. On the morning of December 31 the redoubtable southern infantry, spearheaded by Irish-born Patrick Cleburne's division, rolled back Rosecrans's right wing until it was at a 90-degree angle to his left. However, the Federals, whose defense was anchored by Irish-descended Phil Sheridan's division, managed to hold just short of the Nashville Pike, their lifeline to the north. A gallant but foolish Confederate attempt to break the Union center at the "Round Forest" failed and the mutual slaughter—for such it was—ceased with the coming of darkness.

That night Rosecrans asked his generals if he should order a retreat. Bearlike George H. Thomas, awakened from a doze, said, "This army doesn't retreat," then went back to sleep. The army stood.

Both sides spent the first day of 1863 (the date the Emancipation Proclamation went into effect) recuperating and redeploying. Then on January 2 Bragg threw Breckinridge's division at Rosecrans's left. The blue infantry broke, but massed Federal artillery tore Breckinridge's ranks to pieces. During the night of January 3 Bragg, who had lost 10,000 men, retreated. Rosecrans did not pursue beyond Murfreesboro. He had suffered 13,000 casualties and Wheeler had destroyed many of his precious wagons. Although actually a draw, the battle was hailed as a victory in the North, where it revived morale that was flagging badly after Burnside's bloody fiasco at Fredericksburg.

Thus ended the first year of fighting in the West. Clearly the North had gained much, the South lost much. Indeed, it would scarcely be an exaggeration to say that while the South had been winning *battles* in the East, in the West the North had been winning the *war*.

But the western Confederates remained undaunted and dangerous. Union Colonel Abel

Above: Gallant defenders of Donelson like Colonel Adolphus Heiman and his 10th Tennessee were downcast at the prospect of going to a northern prison. Heiman would die as a result of his confinement. (HP)

Above: Bushrod R. Johnson of Ohio was one general who would not stay captured. After the surrender he escaped. (VM)

Above: Then came Albert Sidney Johnston and his surprising attack on Grant's army at Pittsburg Landing on April 6. It was Johnston's first and last battle of the war. Shot in the leg, he bled to death, dying in the arms of his brother-in-law…(USAMHI)

Left: Major George B. Cosby of Kentucky carried Buckner's request for surrender terms to Grant. He would later become a brigadier. A previously unpublished portrait. (SHC)

Left: And there was another Confederate who would not accept surrender. A lieutenant colonel of the 7th Tennessee Cavalry, a rich man before the war, Nathan Bedford Forrest would be heard from in this conflict. (LC)

Above: … Colonel William Preston, former Kentucky congressman and Buchanan's minister to Spain. He would become a general in another week. (VM)

Above: Upon Johnston's death, command of the Confederates at Shiloh passed to the seemingly ubiquitous hero of Sumter and Bull Run, General P. G. T. Beauregard. He consolidated the gains of the first day's fighting, aided largely by his confidant and adjutant... (NA, U. S. SIGNAL CORPS, BRADY COLLECTION)

Below: ... Thomas Jordan, who will be made brigadier for his gallantry in this battle. (LC)

Above: Colonel James B. Walton ably commanded his... (THE HISTORIC NEW ORLEANS COLLECTION)

Below: ... Washington Artillery of New Orleans in the fight, the first for this branch of the famed organization that also sent several companies to the Virginia front. (CM)

D. Streight found this out the hard way. On April 11, 1863, he invaded Alabama with 1,500 mounted infantrymen, intending to destroy factories and railroads in North Georgia. Forrest, with 1,000 cavalry, pursued. Guided part of the way by sixteen-year-old Emma Sanson, who rode with him on his horse, he overtook Streight, harried him relentlessly, and finally captured his entire command on May 3.

Meanwhile Rosecrans's Army of the Cumberland, as it was now called, and Bragg's Army of Tennessee, lay motionless throughout the winter and spring, recuperating, skirmishing with cavalry, and steeling themselves for the fighting to come. That there would be more fighting—a great deal more—was obvious to all. It was just that no one knew when it would be, or where—although probably some general, gazing at the map, had already noted a stream, not far away in Georgia, with a strange name: Chickamauga, an Indian word meaning "River of Death."

Above: Private John Rulle of the 2d Tennessee Infantry came to Shiloh ready for a fight, from the look of him. His unit were mostly Irishmen from Memphis. (HP)

Left: Others, too, won laurels. Benjamin Franklin Cheatham a brigadier from Tennessee, will be promoted to major general in recognition of his service at Shiloh. (MC)

Left: A magnificent photograph, taken May 10, 1861, of the "Clinch Rifles," men of the 5th Georgia. The variety of clothing and pose, with their black servant in the background, are among the most interesting to be found in Confederate images. They were to be far less relaxed at Shiloh. (JOSEPH CANOLE, JR.)

Above: The officers and noncommissioned officers of Captain A. M. Rutledge's Tennessee Battery, photographed on July 4, 1861. Their guns at Shiloh would severely discomfit the Federals. (TENNESSEE HISTORICAL SOCIETY)

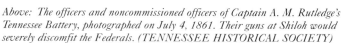

Left: The peach orchard at Shiloh. Through here swarmed the Confederate corps of Brigadier General… (CHS)

Right: … John C. Breckinridge, formerly Vice President and a presidential contender. No believer in secession, and almost certain that the Confederacy could not win, he was forced out of the Union and nevertheless took a command from President Davis. (NA)

Left: Breckinridge's corps and others were bottling up the Federal division of Brigadier General Benjamin M. Prentiss in a place called… (USAMHI)

Right: … the Hornets' Nest. It was in one of their attacks that A. S. Johnston fell mortally wounded . (CHS)

Above: It was a bitter fight. Westerners like these used their Colt revolving rifles to deliver heavy fire power against the Confederates. (RP)

Above: Brigadier General Daniel Ruggles, a native of Massachusetts, retaliated by massing some sixty-two cannon against the Hornets' Nest. (USAMHI)

Above: In the final encirclement of Prentiss, Kentuckians of the Orphan Brigade closed the final trap. Colonel Thomas Hunt, standing eighth from the left here, commanded one of the Kentucky regiments that sealed the Federals' fate. (KHS)

Below: More of the Kentuckians, photographed in August 1860, who would eventually man the Orphan Brigade. (KHS)

Above: Finally Prentiss could not hold out longer, and beneath this tree he surrendered. An early postwar photo. (CHS)

Left: Meanwhile dour Major General Braxton Bragg continually pushed the Federals back toward the Tennessee River.

Above: Finally, as evening approached, a last line was established by Grant and Sherman. These 24-pounder siege guns were a part of it, and here the Federals stood . (USAMHI)

Right: They held on stubbornly, men like Colonel Madison Miller of the 18th Missouri. (LC)

Above: On the Federal right, Brigadier General William T. Sherman, like Beauregard a veteran of Bull Run, fell back under heavy Confederate attacks. (USAMHI)

Below: Men of the 7th Illinois Infantry, armed with their Henry repeating rifles. (ILLINOIS STATE HISTORICAL LIBRARY)

Left: And boys like Johnny Clem, the "drummer boy of Shiloh," acted like men. (LC)

Left: Even bandsmen, usually noncombatants, took arms in holding the last line. (CHICAGO PUBLIC LIBRARY, SPECIAL COLLECTIONS)

Above: The arrival of a relief column under Brigadier General Don Carlos Buell late that evening finally ensured that Grant would not be pushed into the Tennessee. (USAMHI)

Above: The next day, April 7, thanks to Buell's troops arriving here at Pittsburg Landing, and the exhaustion of the Confederates, Grant forced Beauregard to retire from the field. This photograph was taken a few days after the battle. The steamer at right is the Tycoon, *sent by the Cincinnati Sanitary Commission with stores and medical supplies for the wounded. Next to it is Grant's headquarters boat, the* Tigress. *(USAMHI)*

Above: At right, the Universe unloads more supplies for Grant's command. The Tigress *is at the center, and across the stream stands the woooden gunboat* Tyler. *The guns from Foote's fleet played a large part in halting the Confederate drive on April 6. Shiloh was not exactly a victory for Grant, but not a defeat either, and in the aftermath of several Union disasters, that was more important. (USAMHI)*

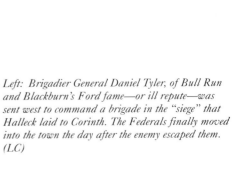

Above: Four days after Shiloh, Major General Henry W. Halleck took command from Grant. Called variously "Old Brains" and "Old Wooden Head," he was an able administrator, and a miserable general. Outnumbering Beauregard two to one, he still could not catch the Confederates at Corinth. (MJM)

Left: Brigadier General Daniel Tyler, of Bull Run and Blackburn's Ford fame—or ill repute—was sent west to command a brigade in the "siege" that Halleck laid to Corinth. The Federals finally moved into the town the day after the enemy escaped them. (LC)

Above: Later in the year, with a Federal command under Major General William S. Rosecrans stationed in and around Corinth, the Confederates were not so slow. Major General Sterling Price led his little army to Iuka on the way to Corinth, and was there attacked by Rosecrans on September 19. A previously unpublished portrait of Price in 1862. (TU)

Above: Two weeks after Iuka, the armies collided again at Corinth, on October 3-4, 1862. (CHS)

Left: It was an important railroad depot and supply center for Rosecrans and his growing army of 21,000 men. A Howard & Hall photograph taken before the battle. Their tent studio appears just left of the Tishomingo Hotel. (USAMHI)

Left: Rosecrans's army were western men, men of the 47th Illinois... (WILLIAM M. ANDERSON)

Below: ... and the 2d Minnesota, which bore much of the brunt of the fighting. (MHS)

Above: Price's most trusted subordinate, Brigadier General Lewis Henry Little, was killed at Iuka while talking with Price by a bullet that first passed under Price's arm. (CHS)

Left: His opponent was the colorful Major General Earl Van Dorn of Mississippi, the loser at Pea Ridge. (MISSISSIPPI DEPARTMENT OF ARCHIVES & HISTORY)

Right: Their commander, Major General William S. Rosecrans, was himself a western man, born in Ohio. He is seen here, with a hint of a smile, taken by Corinth photographer George Armistead of Armistead & White, sometime prior to the battle. (LC)

Right: For two days they fought. The 8th Indiana Artillery was heavily engaged for the Union. (RP)

Left: Fifty-two-year-old Brigadier General Thomas J. McKean led one of Rosecrans's divisions, even though he was considered too old for active command. He is seated here with members of his staff. (NYHS)

Right: Samuel Jones, like many of these men in Mississippi in 1862, was another veteran of Bull Run. He commanded a division under Van Dorn, and was also in the process of making himself the second most photographed general of the Confederacy. (VM)

Above: Major General Mansfield Lovell, a native of Washington, D.C., joined Van Dorn after he lost New Orleans to Farragut, and skillfully commanded the Confederate retreat from Corinth. (CHS)

Above: It was a costly battle. Here in front of Federal Battery Robinette, the Confederate dead and their horses were piled deep. This photograph, taken the day after the battle, shows the horse of Colonel William P. Rogers in the center, and to the left of it, the body of Rogers himself. (WRHS)

Above: Several of the Confederate dead in front of Robinette. Colonel William P. Rogers of the 2d Texas lies at left, and to his right, leaning on his shoulder, is the body of Colonel W. H. Moore, who led a brigade of Missouri and Mississippi troops in futile assaults against Robinette. (ALABAMA STATE DEPARTMENT OF ARCHIVES AND HISTORY)

Left: The Confederate threat gone, Corinth became undisputedly a Union town, and the men of Rosecrans's army enjoyed it as they could. Supplies came in regularly, and Howard & Hall expanded their gallery next to the Tishomingo. (CHS)

Above: Officers like Brigadier General Grenville Dodge established their headquarters in the better homes of the city. (CHS)

Left: Life returned to normal for the inhabitants. (CHS)

Left: The soldiers patronized the local business establishments. (CHS)

Above: They built their winter quarters like Camp Davis, home for the 66th Illinois, south of the city. (ROBERT YOUNGER)

Above: But it would not be a peaceful winter in Mississippi and Tennessee, nor in Kentucky. Brigadier General Jefferson C. Davis, once an officer in Fort Sumter, in late September shot and killed his superior, William Nelson, after an altercation. It could not have come at a worse time, for after a year of seeming security, Kentucky was being invaded by the Confederate Army of Tennessee, commanded now by Beauregard's successor... (LC)

Above: Their bands tuned for the season's demands for entertainments. Here the 97th Indiana musicians. (CHS)

Above: And their earthworks and tents dotted the landscape for the winter ahead, while the firms of Armistead & White and Howard & Hall kept busy with their captive clientele. Winter quarters could mean a small fortune to a photographer. (CHS)

Above: ... General Braxton Bragg. This previously unpublished image of Bragg was made by McIntyre of Montgomery, Alabama, just a few weeks prior to his launching of the Kentucky campaign. (CM)

Above: Commanding the Federals who would resist Bragg was Major General Don Carlos Buell, of Shiloh. (USAMHI)

Below: Bragg and Buell finally met at Perryville, Kentucky, along Doctor's Creek. Probably an early postwar view. (USAMHI)

Above: Bragg's offensive was spearheaded by a Floridian, Major General Kirby Smith, who had been wounded leading a brigade at Bull Run. At Richmond, Kentucky, he defeated Nelson in the only real Confederate battle victory of the campaign,

Above: Leading Bragg's cavalry was a young brigadier who turned twenty-six during the campain, Joseph Wheeler. He would become one of the war's premier cavalrymen. (LC)

Above: Rousseau aligned his command beside a 100-year-old tree that, miraculously, survived the battle.

Below: Federal artillery placed on this high ground, plus numerical superiority, finally gave the battle to Buell. (USAMHI)

Above: The H. P. Bottoms House near the position of Brigadier General Lovell Rousseau, who gallantly led a division against repeated enemy attacks. (USAMHI)

Above: Brigadier General J. Patton Anderson of Tennessee led one of Bragg's divisions to no avail . (USAMHI)

Above: Losses were heavy. General S. A. M. Wood took a serious wound from Federal fire . (VM)

Above: Union Brigadier General William R. Terrill of Virginia was struck in the side by a piece of shell and died that night. His brother was a general in the Confederate Army, and would die in the war as well. (USAMHI)

Right: Heavy fighting along this lane cost Buell even more casualties, but the battle was his. (USAMHI)

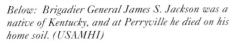

Below: Brigadier General James S. Jackson was a native of Kentucky, and at Perryville he died on his home soil. (USAMHI)

Right: Bragg watered his army at this spring, and retreated into Tennessee, his dream of conquering Kentucky gone in smoke. (USAMHI)

Left: In December the armies meet again, this time at Murfreesboro, Tennessee, and the Federals are once again commanded by Major General William S. Rosecrans. He is seated fourth from the left in this pose with his staff. The man sitting next to him on the right is Brigadier General James A. Garfield, who will become his chief of staff after the battle and, years later, President of the United States. To the far right sits Philip H. Sheridan who, as a brigadier, commands a division at Murfreesboro, and wins promotion. (USAMHI)

Above: The courthouse in Murfreesboro. The town remained in Confederate hands during the battle. (USAMHI)

Above: Rosecrans fought a largely defensive battle, letting Bragg hurl his divisions against tough fighters like the 38th Indiana, shown here in Murfreesboro in April 1863. (JMB)

Left: Those attacks were overseen by Bragg's corps commanders. Lieutenant General William J. Hardee of Georgia was known widely in both armies, thanks to his authorship of Hardee's Tactics, a standard manual North and South. (LC)

Above: The telegraph office from which Bragg boastfully—and prematurely—wired President Davis that he had won a great victory. (USAMHI)

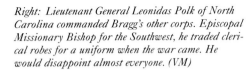

Right: Lieutenant General Leonidas Polk of North Carolina commanded Bragg's other corps. Episcopal Missionary Bishop for the Southwest, he traded clerical robes for a uniform when the war came. He would disappoint almost everyone. (VM)

Above: Some of the greatest infantry assaults of the war took place at Murfreesboro, and they were terribly bloody. Brigadier General Roger Hanson of Kentucky, commander of the Orphan Brigade, fell mortally wounded when the fuse from an exploding shell struck his leg. While being carried from the field he cheered his men, telling them that it was a glorious cause to die for. (JM)

Right: Brigadier General James E. Rains was killed leading his division of Hardee's corps into a charge. His last word was "Forward!" (USAMHI)

Below: Determined resistance by Sheridan and others finally forced Bragg to abandon the field and retreat into the interior, leaving the Federals the field and the victory. (USAMHI)

Above: The Federals occupied Murfreesboro for most of the rest of the war. Here the headquarters from which Rosecrans sent Lincoln the good news of a victory for the New Year, 1863. (USAMHI)

Photographer of the Confederacy: J.D. Edwards

LESLIE D. JENSEN

Prolific yet unknown chronicler of rustics in rebellion

Above: The ever-frowning brow of General Braxton Bragg. He commanded the regiments of rustics forming at Pensacola when Edwards made his historic visit in April 1861. (CHS)

With only four exceptions, all of the J. D. Edwards photographs reproduced here are published for the first time. Several others were published in 1911, but the originals from which they were reproduced have since disappeared. The images that follow are all taken from surviving original prints newly unearthed.

BEFORE the war guns really roared, East or West, on May 14, 1861, the citizens of New Orleans, reading the military columns of their newspapers, came across the following advertisement:

THE WAR !

Views of Pensacola, Forts Barancas, McRae and Pickens; of the Companies there—"Orleans Cadets" "Crescent Rifles" "Chausseurs a Pied," Mississippi and Alabama Regiments and of the U.S. Fleet—39 different Photographic Views, taken by an accomplished artist on the spot, will be on sale tomorrow at the Book Stores, Picture and Looking Glass Stores. They are very large and taken superbly. Price $1 per copy.

The "accomplished artist" was J. D. Edwards, a shadowy figure who remains obscure to this day, yet a man who had accomplished a feat that would not be repeated in the Confederacy. Edwards had produced a comprehensive photographic panorama of the forts, guns, barracks, shipyards, and most importantly, the men who comprised the Confederate Army. Were it not for Edwards, photographic coverage of Confederate military events would be limited to a mere handful of isolated pictures, many of them taken in northern prison camps.

Little is known about Edwards personally or of his life before his Pensacola views went on sale, and practically nothing is known of him afterward. In 1860, he was working in New Orleans. Edwards was twenty-nine years old at the time, had been born in New Hampshire, and gave his occupation as "Ambrotype Portrait." His wife, Mary, a Missourian by birth, was twenty. The Edwardses could not have been in New Orleans long, for their son Edouard had been born in Massachusetts only eight months before. The remainder of the household consisted of Eliza Zeigler, a nineteen-year-old German servant, and Edwards's two assistants, B. Barker, a twenty-nine-year-old native of Massachusetts, and a twenty-four-year old Canadian named Johnson. Edwards valued his personal estate at $3,000.

Yet, though a newcomer to New Orleans, Edwards must have made an impression of being innovative and willing to take on unusual business assignments. When the U. S. Treasury Department and Custom House and the Marine Hospital were under construction in June 1860, Edwards took twenty-three views of the former and twelve views of the latter for the U. S. Army Engineer in charge of the work, a native Louisianan named P. G. T. Beauregard. This assignment may well have started a tradition for both men, outdoor photography for Edwards, and the inclusion of photographs with reports for Beauregard, a practice he continued during the 1861 and 1863 Charleston operations.

By 1861, Edwards operated a studio at 23 Royal Street, yet, though he was listed in the alphabetical section of a city directory, he was still not established enough to be included in the separate section devoted to photographers. Later in the year he moved to 19 Royal Street, occupied when the directory was put out by a photographer named E. J. Newton, Jr. It is not known whether Edwards bought out Newton's operation or went into business with him.

After the firing on Fort Sumter, only one

Right: Fort Pickens photographed from Fort Barrancas, across Pensacola Harbor. The ship is probably the Federal flag-of-truce boat U.S.S. Wyandotte. (SHC)

Above: First Lieutenant Adam J. Slemmer of the 1st United States Artillery, the thorn in Bragg's side who refused to give up Fort Pickens, thus ensuring the mighty bastion for the Union as a base deep in Confederate territory. Edwards never captured Slemmer as Cook did Major Anderson and his men at Fort Sumter, but more than once he turned his camera toward the low, brooding profile of Pickens, a constant reminder of Federal power and determination. (USAMHI)

Left: Guns in the old Spanish part of Fort Barrancas, trained on Fort Pickens in the distance. "I was rather interested with Fort Barrancas," wrote William H. Russell, "built by the Spaniards long ago— an old work on the old plan, weakly armed, but possessing a tolerable command from the face of fire." (SHC)

major U.S. bastion remained in the Confederacy: Fort Pickens, guarding the harbor of Pensacola Bay, Florida. The importance of Fort Pickens has often been overshadowed by other events, and particularly because no major battles were fought to control it. Yet, in April 1861, it was one of the most important areas of potential trouble. As the last Union stronghold on Confederate soil, it was not only irritating to southern pride, but it blocked the bay to southern shipping and restricted the use of the splendid former U. S. Navy Yard at Warrington, just across the bay from the fort. Moreover, it could, and in time did, become a base for operations against the Confederacy. Whoever controlled Fort Pickens controlled the use of one of the best anchorages on the Gulf Coast.

Theoretically, the Confederates, vastly outnumbering the Union troops in the area, should have had little trouble taking control of the bay, but the unexpected stubbornness of Lieutenant Adam Slemmer's tiny Union command, supported by an ever growing Union fleet, kept the Confederates at bay until Union reinforcements arrived. By late April, Confederate volunteers poured into the area, preparing for what every-

Above: The rear of Fort Barrancas and a Confederate regiment camped beyond, probably the 1st Alabama. The variety of tents, the makeshift nature of the camp, and lack of uniformity in the dress of the Confederates drawn up in line, all attest to the informal and inexperienced nature of the Southrons who flocked to Pensacola in 1861. (GULF ISLANDS NATIONAL SEASHORE)

Left: A side view of part of Fort Barrancas as Bragg's men move yet another cannon into place. (SHC)

Above: The sand battery at Fort Barrancas, and a stand of the ill-formed shot. Despite the seemingly strong positions of these guns, Russell believed that if Bragg opened fire on Slemmer, Fort Pickens "ought certainly to knock his works about his ears." (SHC)

Above: Edwards captioned this a "View of two Sand Batteries, showing subterranean passages connecting them together, with Fort Pickens in the distance." Pickens has now disappeared from this faded print, but the crude board shoring of the tunnels is visible in the foreground. Much work remains to be done, but Russell did not find the summer soldiers anxious about it. "The working parties, as they were called—volunteers from Mississippi and Alabama, great long-bearded fellows in flannel shirts and slouched hats, uniformless in all save brightly burnished arms and resolute purpose—were lying about among the works, or contributing languidly to their completion." (TU)

Below: A water battery at Warrington. In the distance to the right is the lighthouse. Bragg did not wish to open fire on Pickens, and the Englishman Russell believed him right. "The magazines of the batteries I visited did not contain ammunition for more than one day's ordinary firing," he wrote. "The shots were badly cast, with projecting flanges from the mould, which would be very injurious to soft metal guns in firing." One of these rustics, standing at the wheel of the front gun, holds a shot in his hand, while his mates sham preparing to fire. The poor man at the second gun, seeing his chance for immortality about to be blocked by a cold iron cannon, had to stoop to present his face to the camera. In the right center is a hot-shot furnace for heating incendiary projectiles. (NA, OFFICE OF THE CHIEF OF ENGINEERS)

one thought would be the next big showdown of the war. Many of the Confederates headed for Pensacola were from New Orleans, and J. D. Edwards apparently saw in this an opportunity to create a pictorial record of the war, make a reputation for himself, and turn a profit by selling his products to the soldiers and the folks back home. Accordingly, sometime in late April, he too headed for the scene of the war's next big battle.

Happily, because Edwards numbered at least some of his negatives in the order he took them, it is possible to follow his work pattern in the Pensacola area with a fair degree of certainty. He seems to have started at the Navy Yard itself, where General Braxton Bragg had his head quarters and where Edwards probably had to go to get permission to take his photographs. He took pictures looking across the bay toward Fort Pickens and photographed the steamer Fulton in dry dock, surrounded by the vast quantities of shells the Confederates had both captured and were making in the yard's foundry. From there, he moved west, photographing Coppens's Louisiana Zouave Battalion at drill on the grounds of the Marine Barracks. He spent a great deal of time at Fort Barrancas, photographing it inside and out, including its old Spanish half-moon battery. From there, Edwards photographed some of the sand batteries and then found himself drawn to the lighthouse. Its 165-foot height provided a perfect view of the coast, and Edwards took his camera to the top, photographing the forts and camps below. He spent considerable time in the camps themselves, mostly in those of the 1st Alabama and 9th Mississippi regiments, before moving on to the Confederate bastion on the right flank, Fort McRee. On the way back, Edwards may have

Above: The lighthouse west of Fort Barrancas. Built in 1859, it quickly attracted Edwards's eye, and he and his camera were soon at its top taking the first aerial photos of the war. (PENSACOLA HISTORICAL SOCIETY, PENSACOLA, FLORIDA)

Below: Looking east from the lighthouse. Barely visible on the shore in the right center is a two-gun sand battery. Just above the right-hand row of tents is another. And just above the tents at left, distinguishable by the straight horizontal line of its parapet, is Fort Barrancas. The buildings to its left are the Barrancas Barracks, while the tall building with cupola in the distance to the right of the barracks is the Marine Hospital. This is, arguably, the first "aerial" photograph in military history. (SHC)

Right: Confederate camps and a four-gun sand battery immediately below the lighthouse. The "subterranean passages" connecting the guns are clearly visible, as are several Confederates lounging in the vicinity. These are Alabama troops. In the distance on the low spit of sand dune is Fort McRee, "weak and badly built," thought Russell, and "quite under the command of Pickens." (GULF ISLANDS NATIONAL SEASHORE)

taken additional camp scenes, and at some point, probably toward the end of his stay, he went to Bayou Grand, just north of Warrington, where he photographed the camp of the Orleans Cadets. Exactly how long Edwards stayed in the Pensacola area is unknown, but given the volume of work that he did and the probable work and travel time, he may have been there a week or more.

The photographs went on sale in New Orleans on May 15, but curiously, Edwards only ran his notice for three days. The various newspapers made some editorial comment on the photographs, but beyond confirming that the advertisement indeed refers to the work of J. D. Edwards, they tell us little. The New Orleans Bee, however, suggested that the photographs would "make an interesting souvenir for the parlor, particularly in the event, considered now so near at hand, of the capture of Fort Pickens."

Some of the photographs made their way north with surprising speed. On June 15, a woodcut appeared in Harper's Weekly entitled "INTERIOR OF A SAND-BAG BATTERY BEARING ON FORT PICKENS.

Harper's claimed that it was the work of their special artist, Theodore Davis, but close comparison with Edwards's photograph No. 33, "Perote Sand Batteries 10 inch Columbiads," reveals the wood cut to have been pirated from Edwards. It is entirely possible that Davis, who had been in Pensacola with William Howard Russell at about the time Edwards was photographing, knew Edwards's work and either made a sketch from the photograph or simply sent the photograph on to Harper's, who incorrectly captioned it. A week later, Harper's ran another woodcut with the caption BIVOUAC OF REBEL TROOPS AT GENERAL BRAGGíS CAMP AT WARRINGTON, FLORIDA, and this time admitted that it was from a photograph, although they did not identify the photographer. The scene was the well-known one of men cooking around a campfire in the 9th Mississippi's camp, but Harper's, not content with the original photograph, rearranged the figures.

Edwards's photographs seem to have been rather widely distributed at the time. Some ended up in the hands of S. H. Lockett, an officer in the 1st Alabama, and somehow Charles Allgower, a member of the 6th New York and an occasional artist for Harper's, also acquired some,

Above: A Confederate encampment just south of Bayou Grande, near Pensacola, probably the Orleans Cadets. This may be the finest Confederate camp scene to survive, excellent not only for its clarity, but for what it shows as well. Almost every aspect of camp life is depicted. A bugler with his instrument to his lips, a soldier with fishing pole in hand, men reading letters and newspapers, others cleaning their rifles, a fatigue detail with shovel on shoulder, two Johnnies feigning a spar, and at right, pipe in mouth, a company officer handing orders to a saluting corporal. To the left are piled boxes of fresh rations. In this image Edwards outdid himself. (STATE PHOTOGRAPHIC ARCHIVES, STROZIER LIBRARY, FLORIDA STATE UNIVERSITY)

Above: The encampment of the Louisville Blues, the 1st Alabama, near the lighthouse. There is a definite lack of order in this camp, blankets and clothing and equipment hanging wherever convenient. These men would learn a lot about soldiering in the years ahead, and about sanitation, too. A trench, perhaps a latrine, is just a few feet to the left of their tents and mess area. Disease, in this war, will kill far more men than bullets. (RP)

Left: Camps of Mississippi regiments behind the lighthouse. (TU)

Left: Edwards did not move his camera after capturing the Mississippi camps. Instead, he moved the Mississippians. Here they parade in all their sartorial chaos. Top hats, stovepipes, slouch and military caps, hunting shirts, bow ties, flannel checks, and their captain in front in a decidedly unmilitary vest. Yet they all have rifles, and an unshakable determination. Nowhere in the world was there another soldiery like them. (PHS)

The 9th Mississippi in camp, and for an Edwards photo, an unusually clear surviving print. Rarely can one see such a brilliant representation of the Confederate soldier of 1861. Especially eye-catching is the soldier crouching to the left of the stand of rifles at left. The significance of the numeral "4" on his shirt is unknown, but his resplendence is unarguable. They all have the lean, hardened look of the American backwoods. Such men could be unbeatable. (RP)

One of Bragg's five big siege guns, a 10-inch columbiad, and, to its right, a tunnel passage to the next gun. There are more uniforms here, more of a military look, but the same posturing for the camera of all these Southrons of 1861. The war was still a lark to them. Most had never been this far from home in their lives. They expected to be home again before the fall. (TU)

The second 10-inch columbiad in this Perote sand battery. It is manned by more Mississippians, the Quitman Rifles. (PHS)

A quiet moment in camp for men of Company B, 9th Mississippi, the Quitman Rifles. These are men from Holly Springs, Mississippi, and at least one of them is probably writing home. His tent mate reads a book, while their friend in the shadows behind their rifles appears to be peeling potatoes. Three years from now the Confederate soldier will regard this simple tent and its furnishings as unimaginable luxury. (PHS)

Company B of the 9th Mississippi again. The man stooping over the frying pan is Kinlock Falconer. One day he will serve on Bragg's staff. For the moment, he is about to serve some fried pork. The closest thing to a uniform for this company would appear to be checkered pants. (LC)

probably while his regiment was stationed in the Pensacola area. Despite Edwards's claim that he produced thirty-nine views, it is now clear that the actual total was much higher. Known views, many of them published in 1911 but since lost, total forty-four. However, Edwards's negative numbers run as high as sixty-eight, and there is at least one photograph numbered "2B." Thus, despite the large number of Edwards photographs which are presented here for the first time, there may be as many as twenty or more yet unaccounted for, including at least two, those of the Crescent Rifles and the Chausseurs a Pied, referred to in the ad.

One wonders whether the appearance of the woodcuts in Harper's Weekly may have been a spur to another photographer, the nation's finest, Mathew B. Brady. The Confederates had already scooped him in the early coverage of the war, and the fact that their photographs were appearing in northern papers, competing with his own portrait work, may well have helped to inspire Brady to take his camera teams into the field.

The fact that the Pensacola front never produced any major battles and was eventually abandoned by the Confederates may have hurt the long-term sales of Edwards's work, but in any case, after the appearance of the photographs, he slipped once more into obscurity. Two of his negatives were seized by U.S. authorities after the fall of New Orleans, and prints from them were turned over to the U. S. Engineers office in Washington in 1863. Unfortunately, we do not know the circumstances of the seizure, and while the prints survive, the negatives have disappeared. Francis Trevelyan Miller claimed that Edwards later worked for the Confederate secret service, but no hard evidence to support the claim has come to light. Yet, there is one tantalizing clue which may indicate that Edwards was an even more important photographer than his Pensacola series indicates. Roy M. Mason, one of the searchers sent by Miller to locate Confederate photographs for the 1911 Photographic History of the Civil War, recalled his experiences in the armory of the Washington Artillery in New Orleans. He noted that the one-armed armorer, Sergeant Dan Kelly, "said that there were no photographs, but consented to look in the long rows of dusty shelves which line the sides of the huge, dark armory. From almost the last he drew forth a pile of soggy, limp cardboard, covered with the grime of years. He passed his sleeve carelessly over the first, and there spread into view a picture of his father sitting reading among his comrades in Camp Louisiana forty-nine years before. The photographs were those of J. D. Edwards, who had also worked at Pensacola and Mobile. Here were Confederate volunteers of '61 and the boys of the Washington Artillery which became so famous in the service of the Army of Northern Virginia." Some Washington Artillery photos were by J. W. Petty of New Orleans, but if

Mason's implication is correct, Edwards may have continued to photograph Confederate troops at least as late as early 1862, when the 5th Company, Washington Artillery was photographed just before Shiloh. If so, Edwards may be responsible for a larger body of Confederate photographs than he has been given credit for.

Yet, if early 1862 was the last time that Edwards may have been at work, it is also the end of any documentation on his Civil War work. The man simply disappears for the next two decades. In the late 1880s he reemerges, working his trade in Atlanta, and there he dies in 1900. How much more wartime work he did, if any, and how much more of it survives, is a mystery.

Miller called Edwards a "pioneer camera man," but apparently even Miller was not aware of just how much of a pioneer Edwards was. In this country there was virtually no tradition of war photography, and while the Crimean War photographs of Roger Fenton and others were known, there was no one who could set the pace in this new art. While enterprising Confederates in Charleston were the first on the scene of America's bloodiest war, their job was made easier by the fact that they were photographing local events. The established photographers remained in their studios, content to take the portraits of the generals and soldiers who would fight the war. Into this scene stepped J. D. Edwards, packing his equipment over miles of swamps and bayous and into a war zone, taking pictures at least as good as Brady's and then marketing them with little apparent financial backing other than his own. At the time Edwards's work was of a far wider scope than anything any other photographer was producing, and while he was eclipsed by the superior resources of Brady, Gardner, and hundreds of others, it was J. D. Edwards, whether known by name to these other photographers or not, who showed the way a war could be photographed. In the Confederacy, no one else would match his work for innovation and sheer importance. If there was anyone who could claim the title Photographer of the Confederacy, it was the obscure Yankee from New Orleans, J. D. Edwards.

Above: A mortar in the water battery just west of the lighthouse, which can be seen above the trees at left. Some of the projecting flanges William H. Russell mentioned can be seen on the shot stacked at right. There is much evidence of work, but apparently it was not necessarily done with perfect harmony. "Considerable improvements were in the course of execution," found Russell, "but the officers were not always agreed as to the work to be done. Captain A., at the wheelbarrows: 'Now then, you men, wheel up these sandbags, and range them just at this corner.' Major B.: 'My good Captain A., what do you want the bags there for? Did I not tell you, these merlons were not to be finished till we had completed the parapet on the front?' Captain A.: 'Well, Major, so you did, and your order made me think you know darned little about your business; so I am going to do a little engineering of my own.'" Such was American democracy in action. (NA, OFFICE OF THE CHIEF OF ENGINEERS)

Above: The Orleans Cadets and their leader, Captain Dreux, a well-uniformed unit for a change. New Orleans was particularly anxious to know the doings of her native sons at Pensacola, and Edwards was aware of the commercial possibilities of selling photographs of them at home. "Any of them will form an interesting souvenir for the parlor," read his advertisement for the prints in New Orleans, "particularly in the event, considered now so near at hand, of the capture of Fort Pickens." (TU)

Above: But the only Confederate who would capture Fort Pickens would be Edwards himself, and here he takes not only the fort, but a Federal ship as well, the U.S.S. Macedonian. His epic task done, J. D. Edwards, truly the "Photographer of the Confederacy," would take back with him to New Orleans a priceless record of Southerners in the early days of their bid for nationhood. Yet his images would be all but lost, and Edwards a forgotten man. He and they deserved better. He was truly a man with vision. (USAMHI)

The North at War

MAURY KLEIN

Life in a country in conflict, yet still growing

The North at war was a bustling place. The great cities grew greater, frontiers moved farther west, business and industry expanded. An early postwar view of New York and, in the foreground, its city hall. (USAMHI)

UNLIKE THE SOUTHERNERS captured by J. D. Edwards and others, for most Northerners the Civil War was a distant event. They did not witness its carnage firsthand, and their cities and farms escaped the devastation that blighted large areas of the South. Seldom did the din of combat reach their ears or the menace of invading troops disturb their daily routines. Life went on, if not as usual, at least with a minimum of disruption.

But distance from the battlefield could not protect Northerners from the effects of a long and bloody war. The ordeal of sustaining so massive a struggle intruded upon people's lives in countless ways. The most obvious of these was, of course, the absence of friends and kinfolk in the service. Every town and hamlet watched its young men depart for the front, some to die and others to return home with bodies maimed or spirits broken. Concern for the safety of loved ones permeated house holds throughout the North, aggravated by the slowness with which accurate details or casualty lists reached home after a major battle. Thus did distance from the seat of war breed anxiety as well as security.

The presence of men in uniform, whether home on leave or forming into newly organized units, also served as constant reminders to civilians. Soldiers could be found on the streets of cities and villages everywhere. Returning wounded brought home stark evidence of their ordeal in combat. Rare was the town that did not welcome home a veteran minus an arm or leg or worse. Army camps and prisoner-of-war compounds were opened in many towns, and by 1862 conscription officers had begun to replace recruitment drives and became objects of loathing wherever they appeared. Through all these agents the war came home to every northern community. Those who did not join the army found their lives affected in other ways. The northern war effort depended not only upon its advantage in men and guns but also upon its superior industrial and agricultural might. In terms of productivity the war was fought as much at home as on the battlefield, and the fight enlisted men, women, and children alike. The drain of manpower for military service, coupled with increased demand for goods, meant simply that there were fewer people to do more work. Farm and factory alike responded to this need in two ways: by increasing their use of machinery to replace human labor and by putting more women and children to work.

The North relied upon its staple crops both to feed its people and army and to produce surpluses which could be sold abroad for sorely needed gold. As thousands of men left the farms to fight the war, women, children, and older men took up the heavy field work. At the same time the use of agricultural machinery spread rapidly, a fact which delighted manufacturers who sniffed bonanza profits. As Cyrus McCormick reminded one of his salesmen in Illinois, "Don't be so blue over the prospects. Remember 20,000 militia have to leave this state… and these men will have to come, many or a large share of them, from the farms."

Mowers and reapers were still relatively new machines in 1860; by 1864 production of them exceeded 70,000, or twice the output of 1862. These wondrous devices saved human labor and could be operated even by women and children. Other machines, including the horse-rake, culti-

vators, new harrows, corn planters, steam thresh-
ers, and grain drills were also devised and marketed. The use of machinery increased the scale
of agriculture and enabled farmers to bring more
land under cultivation, especially in the West.

The results of this effort were impressive.
Northern farmers produced large enough corn,
oat, and wheat crops during the war years—
including record crops in 1862—to fill domestic
needs and still sell large quantities to England,
which experienced three straight years of crop
failures. Hog and cattle output also increased
dramatically, and wool production jumped from
60 million pounds in 1860 to 140 million pounds
in 1865. During that same period the number of
sheep in the North doubled, an important gain
since wool offered the most common substitute
for the cotton supply diminished by the South's
secession.

Apparently photographers, like other
Northerners, took great pride in this record of
productivity; at least they delighted in capturing
scenes showing the new machines at work. But
when they turned their attention to the factories,
something more than productivity caught the
eye. Pictures of giant machines sweeping across
fields, or of fishing boats plying the waters of
Nantucket, conveyed a sense of majesty, even
charm. However, scenes of women and small
children toiling in a factory, although they might
suggest the sacrifice and productivity so vital to
the war effort, were utterly lacking in beauty or
nobility. Unlike the sight of a man or woman
astride a reaper, no charm attached to the spectacle of people young and old harnessed to
machines inside dingy mills.

But the mills and factories played a major role
in carrying the North to victory. From their
bustling, clanging interiors came a swelling
stream of muskets, cannon, equipment, locomotives, rails, wagons, tools, uniforms, shoes, and
thousands of other items. Wartime needs spurred
the development of other industries besides
agricultural implements and armaments. The
demand for uniforms and shoes prompted
increased use of sewing machines. One by-product of this work was the discovery that uniforms
and shoes manufactured in a few basic sizes
would fit most men. This standardization simplified the production of uniforms and shoes in
quantity and after the war stimulated the rise of
the ready-made clothing industry. Military needs
also lent a strong impetus to the canned food
industry, including Gail Borden's canned milk.
The desire to produce canned food quickly and
in quantity led to improvements in canning techniques and machinery.

As its farms and factories responded to the
war effort, an aura of prosperity settled across the
North. Newspapers and politicians alike waxed
eloquent over the nation's material well-being.
The New York Times noted in 1864 that
Northerners were better housed, clothed, and
fed than ever before "in the midst of the most
gigantic civil war… yet seen." Wholesale farm
prices doubled during the war years while nona-
gricultural wages rose 43 percent. Farm land values soared, as did real estate values in general.

For most Northerners, however, this prosperity proved more apparent than real. As always,
war time brought a sharp inflationary trend
which in many cases erased gains in wages or
income. Wholesale prices more than doubled

Left: Fifth Avenue, looking north from the southeast corner of Twenty-eighth Street, New York, 1865. (NYHS)

Left: Away from the eastern coast, the market towns and county seats continued to thrive as before the conflict. Indeed, the presence of large-scale armies boosted business in many communities. The market square in Carlisle, Pennsylvania, in 1862. (LC)

Left: Chestnut Street in Philadelphia just before the war. Hotels, booksellers, typesetters, engravers—the North bustled with the work of tradesmen and artisans. (FREE LIBRARY OF PHILADELPHIA)

Right: Hanover Junction, Pennsylvania, around November 1863. Like hundreds of minor railroad towns, its townspeople saw little of the war and felt its effects even less, except when the trains came through loaded with soldiers going to the front. (USAMHI)

Right: St. Paul, Minnesota, a city that grew largely from the speculations in the 1850s of Washington politicians and bankers, several of them now Confederates. (MHS)

Above: An apple seller in Cincinnati, Ohio, typical of the street vendors that every large city spawned. (LO)

while the consumer price index increased from 102 to 177. According to one recent calculation, the real wage index actually declined from 102 in January 1861 to 67 in January 1865.

Wage earners suffered most from the ravages of inflation, but attempts to improve their lot through organization made little headway during the war. Most wartime trade unions began at the local level, primarily in New York, Pennsylvania, and Massachusetts, and boasted some 300 locals with an estimated 200,000 members by 1865. City federations, begun in Rochester in March 1863, soon sprang up in most major industrial centers. Intended only as advisory bodies, the federations assumed such tasks as organizing trades and boycotts, generating publicity during strikes, and opposing the importation of strike-breakers. They also founded labor newspapers and in thirty-six cities and towns helped establish cooperative stores.

Attempts to revive national trade associations made some gains, but the national organizations were loose bodies with little effective power over their locals. In general the labor movement remained weak during the war. Unskilled workers, especially women, children, and blacks, endured starvation wages and sweatshop conditions with little hope of improving their lot.

Wartime conditions imposed unusual hardships upon workers. According to a Senate report, industrial workers provided the Union Army with about one third of its troops. The Conscription Act of 1863, with its provision that service might be evaded by hiring a substitute or paying a three hundred-dollar commutation fee, especially rankled laborers. On several occasions resentment against the draft boiled into bloody riots. The most spectacular of these occurred in New York City in July 1863 when a mob wrecked the recruiting station, demolished rail and street-car lines and ship yards, closed factories, attacked the homes of leading Republicans, and killed several blacks. Similar riots engulfed other cities in turmoil but brought no relief to workers.

Strikes proved equally futile in wartime. The public regarded them as disloyal and the government sometimes responded with troops. On several occasions President Lincoln felt obliged to intervene in an attempt to salve the feelings of workers and preserve their loyalty to the war effort. At the same time the government took

Right: Travel and sightseeing increased, even among the notables, and especially among the soldiers and foreign observers and dignitaries. Here Secretary of State William Seward entertains a host of diplomats in a pastoral setting. Those seated are, from the left, Molena, Nicaraguan minister; Seward; Baron de Stoeckel, Russian minister; and Mr. Sheffield, the British legation attaché. Standing from the left are Donaldson of Seward's State Department, a man unidentified, Secretary Bodesco of the Russian legation, Swedish minister Count Piper, Italian minister Bertenattie, Hanseatic minister Schleider, French minister Henri Mercier, and Lord Lyons, minister from Britain. (NA)

Above: Main Street in Salt Lake City, Utah, October 24, 1861. Western Union, impelled largely by the war, completes the first transcontinental telegraph. Beneath the backdrop of the mighty mountains, a simple ceremony marks the occasion. With great good fortune, Western Union's "Telegraph Office" is right next to a combination liquor store and "Ambrotype Gallery." The result was this ambrotype of an historic moment. (LO)

steps to increase the labor supply diminished by military service and a decline in immigration. In both 1861 and 1862 immigration, which had averaged 281,455 people a year during the 1850s, fell off to slightly less than 92,000. The figure rose to 176,282 in 1863, but the following year Congress, prodded by Lincoln and concerned industrialists, passed a law which permitted the importation of contract laborers. What ever the effect of this act, immigration rose to 193,418 in 1864 and 248,120 in 1865.

But if workers found prosperity elusive, many businessmen reaped fat profits from wartime opportunities. Alert contractors were quick to take advantage of the government's needs. Some were content to earn legitimate fortunes while others resorted to dishonest means to make their killings. Never had the nation created so large an army or required armaments and equipment on so vast a scale. The scale of operations, as well as the urgency of purchasing so much so quickly, invited corruption of unprecedented dimensions. Revelation after revelation rocked the public, prompting the New York Herald in June 1864 to denounce the "gross corruption prevailing in nearly every department of the government." Large commissions went to men whose only service was to procure lucrative government contracts for firms.

On the stock and gold exchanges, speculators thrived on the uncertainties of wartime. Good news from the front boosted the prices of gold and stocks; bad news sent them crashing downward. Hordes of speculators, including some women braving ridicule in a traditionally male arena, plunged into the treacherous currents of Wall Street seeking a quick fortune. One crafty manipulator, Daniel Drew, recalled that "Along with ordinary happenings, we fellows in Wall Street had the fortunes of war to speculate about.... It's good fishing in troubled waters."

Above: Russian sailors like these were a new sight in New York and San Francisco, where the czar's fleet made showings of support for the Union. (WRHS)

Right: The mode of transporting a Rodman by rail, suspended from a bridge truss. (LC)

Below: Federal commanders did rule over certain threatened parts of the country. Major General John A. Dix exercised considerable authority over largely secessionist Maryland. (USAMHI)

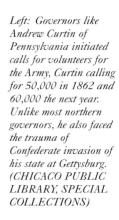

Left: Governors like Andrew Curtin of Pennsylvania initiated calls for volunteers for the Army, Curtin calling for 50,000 in 1862 and 60,000 the next year. Unlike most northern governors, he also faced the trauma of Confederate invasion of his state at Gettysburg. (CHICACO PUBLIC LIBRARY, SPECIAL COLLECTIONS)

Right: Even on Broadway in New York the recruiters worked, and at right, behind the flag, stands the evidence of their success, an army barracks in the heart of the city. No wonder an enterprising vendor selected this spot to sell his sarsaparilla and beer at 3 cents per glass. (USAMHI)

Above: Recruiting offices appeared in every city of any size, as here on New York's State Street. The three main buildings house the United States Quartermaster's office, but the partially obscured house on the far right has a flag in front, and a broadside offering a three-hundred-dollar bounty to men who enlist. (USAMHI)

Right: Photographer Fuller of Madison, Wisconsin, visited his local recruiter, not to enlist, but to shoot. "Enlist—Veteran Regiment" reads the broadside. Perhaps more than a few boys were induced to join after sampling the bottles and jugs, but the significance of the fencing match is, alas, lost. (USAMHI)

Above: All through the war the United States Military Academy at West Point continued to produce officers for the armies. (NA, U. S. SIGNAL CORPS)

Young Jay Gould went one step further: he devised an ingenious system whereby he obtained by telegraph advance information on Union victories or defeats and shifted his speculations accordingly.

Not all northern businessmen were corrupt or dishonest, and not all made fortunes. But the war created a free-wheeling, opportunistic atmosphere that proved irresistible to many people. It is important to remember that not all Northerners bothered to fight the war or even tender it active support. Some people lacked strong interest in the conflict and either ignored it as best they could or resented it as an intrusion into their private affairs.

Among this group were men who found the wartime situation a golden opportunity for self-advancement. Their activities escaped the camera's eye, as did those of the plungers on Wall Street and the hustlers of government contracts, but their ultimate importance rivaled anything that took place on the battlefield. These ambitious young entrepreneurs used the war years to establish themselves in business while their peers were caught up in the clash of arms. Some made their fortunes even before the war ended, while others planted the roots of what were to be long and prosperous careers.

Within this group could be found a surprising number of the business titans who were to dominate the economy, and therefore much of American life, during the half century between the Civil War and World War I: Andrew Carnegie, J. P. Morgan, John D. Rockefeller, George F. Baker, James J. Hill, Gustavus Swift, Charles A. Pillsbury, George M. Pullman, Mark Hanna, Marshall Field, Jay Gould, John Wanamaker, and Peter Widener, to name but a few. Each of these men, and others like them, ignored the call to arms and concentrated instead upon the windfall business opportunities bred by wartime conditions. Few of them even tried to enlist, fewer still stayed home because of disability, and several (Carnegie, Gould, Morgan, Rockefeller, and Philip D. Armour among them) hired substitutes.

In later years some of these men grew defensive about their failure to enter the service. "I was represented in the army," Rockefeller insisted. "I sent more than twenty men, yes, nearly thirty. That is, I made such arrangements for them that they were able to go." The majority, however, seemed content to concentrate on the business at hand. One son of banker Thomas Mellon begged his father for money to speculate in wheat. Writing from Wisconsin, he observed that people "continue growing richer and don't care when the war closes." Mindful of the educational value afforded by prevailing conditions, the elder Mellon flatly forbade another son from enlisting:

I had hoped my boy was going to make a smart intelligent businessman and was not such a goose as to be seduced from duty by the declamations of buncombe speeches. It is only greenhorns who enlist. You can learn nothing in the army.... In time you will come to understand and believe that a man may be a patriot without risking his own life or sacrificing his health. There are plenty of other lives less valuable or ready to serve for the love of serving.

To most of these men, wartime opportunities

brought financial nest eggs from which huge fortunes later hatched. For them, and for many others who advanced their prospects during those turbulent years, prosperity was anything but illusory.

Social activities reflected this mood of rising affluence, especially in the cities. As the war dragged on through month after weary month of bloody battles that produced defeat or indecision, Northerners sought diversions to dispel the gloom of uncertainty that clouded the future. So frenetic did the quest for amusement and gaiety become that stern observers periodically denounced the populace for their indifference to the suffering and hardships endured by soldiers at the front.

In rural areas, where the workday was always long and sources of amusement few, life went on much as it had before the war. There were church socials, husking bees, country fairs, and occasional barn dances. Young men played baseball or competed in foot races, wrestling, and shooting matches. A religious revival or camp meeting, accompanied by picnics and other festivities, might enliven a farm community for a week or more. Many a small town possessed an "opry house" that never saw an opera but welcomed touring lectures, dramatic companies, or minstrel shows. Occasionally too a traveling circus might wend its way through the countryside, thrilling farm folk with its menagerie of strange animals and exotic freaks. No event rivaled the celebration of national holidays like the Fourth of July, for which families gathered from miles around to enjoy barbeques, games, fireworks, oratory, and dancing, usually accompanied by liberal swigs from jugs of whiskey or hard cider.

City life offered far more varied and sophisticated amusements. As always the upper class set the standards and indulged themselves most freely. Dinners, receptions, and elegant parties occupied the fashionable in every city, especially Washington and New York. Roller-skating made its appearance in 1863 and New York's social denizens seized upon it as a pleasure which they hoped to confine to "the educated and refined classes." Ice-skating parties lightened the tedium of winter while periodic visits to fashionable resorts in Newport, Narragansett Pier, or upstate New York helped pass the summer months. Every major city had its lyceums and lecture halls, and in New York the Academy of Music offered the cultured elite a sampling of grand opera imported from Europe.

Crowds flocked to the theaters of every city in unprecedented numbers. Comedies were the staple fare, both in the high-tone playhouses and in lower-class theaters like those in New York's Bowery, where huge crowds gathered to yell and whistle, cheer and hiss, chew peanuts and spit tobacco juice. Although the emphasis upon comedy reflected a desire to escape the war, at least for a few hours, dramas based upon recent battles also proved popular. One energetic producer opened a play about Bull Run within a month of the battle, and later engagements were put on the boards by adapting a standard script to each occasion.

Besides theater, northern urbanites patronized minstrel shows, burlesque, dance halls, winter gardens, prizefights, cockfights, and the saloons. In New York, P. T. Barnum's American Museum drew enormous crowds, as did imitation counter parts in other cities. To the rest of

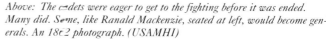

Below: Two cadets of the class of 1864. They will have their chance for glory. (USAMHI)

Above: The cadets were eager to get to the fighting before it was ended. Many did. Some, like Ranald Mackenzie, seated at left, would become generals. An 1862 photograph. (USAMHI)

Left: They, like many of the generals North and South now battling all across the country, learned their military science from Professor Dennis Hart Mahan. His alumni formed a register of nearly all the high command of both armies. (USAMHI)

Left: The Army's military posts in the North continued their functions as before, only now incredibly more busily. The second oldest post in the nation was Carlisle Barracks, Pennsylvania. Here we see guard mounting at the cavalry school of practice in 1861. Portions of the barracks behind them will be sacked by Jeb Stuart's cavalry in 1863. (T. SCOTT SANDERS)

Left: The evidences of a nation at war were not hard to find. Fort Ellsworth in Alexandria, Virginia, named for the Union's first martyr. (USAMHI)

Right: Forrest Hall Military Prison in Georgetown, D.C. Next door a candy store, with jars of peppermint sticks in the window. (USAMHI)

Above: Industry for the war. A Du Pont powder mill near Wilmington, Delaware.(E.I. DU PONT DE NEMOURS & CO.)

Right: The Schuylkill Arsenal in Philadelphia. (KA)

Right: The blacksmith and wagon repair shop at Camp Holt, near Jeffersonville, Indiana. (INDIANA HISTORICAL SOCIETY LIBRARY)

Left: While fighting all along its southern "borders," the Union also had to cast a careful eye to its northern boundaries, should Great Britain decide to aid the Confederacy. Then Canada would be a natural launching place for invasion. Major General John 1-Peck commanded the troops along the North's Canadian frontier in 1864-65. (P-M)

the North Barnum sent his traveling circus, the Grand Colossal Museum and Menagerie, with curiosities borrowed from the American Museum and animals gathered from every corner of the world.

As always in wartime, amusements offered a counterpoint to anxiety and uncertainty. To outward appearance, at least as the photographer captured it, life in the North hewed as closely to its normal patterns as was possible in an era of great duress. The camera recorded with an unblinking eye scenes of a wartime society clinging to its familiar habits while adjusting to changes imposed by the conflict. In so doing it portrayed the landscape of northern society unembellished and often unadorned. This fidelity freed later generations from the illustrator's imagination. Unlike the artist's drawing, the photograph offered viewers not an interpretation of a scene but some raw materials of a scene which one might interpret for himself.

More than this the camera could not do. For one thing the technology of photography was still in its infancy. Photographers still relied upon the wet-plate collodion process, a cumbersome and complicated business which required a wagonload of equipment, including a traveling dark tent for immediate developing, for all work done outside the studio. In effect the photographer could not operate abroad without carrying his laboratory with him. Even then he could not take action pictures with the equipment at his disposal.

In a real sense, then, the camera could capture little more than the bare surface of northern life during the war. On one hand, most of what was important took place beyond the photographer's—or anyone else's—eye; on the other, the technology of photography was unprepared to record the dynamism that was the essence of life in the North during these years.

War is not a still life, either on the battlefield or on the home front. The camera could preserve the residue of battle but not battle itself, the portraits of heroes but not their heroic deeds. Similarly, it might depict the stage, scenery, and characters of northern life, but not the dramatic action or inner moods and conflicts of the play itself. That realm still belonged to the writers, the painters, and the illustrators.

It is not possible to reconstruct the North at

war through photographs or any other artifacts. Through the camera's eye we may look down Broadway in New York or inspect a prison in Chicago or pause at a corner in Hanover Junction. We can feel the heat and drabness of a textile mill or watch track layers at work or fishing boats casting their nets off Narragansett Bay. Each of these pictures represents neither an action nor a scene but a single-frame, a fleeting moment of time frozen and preserved for our imaginations to mull over.

Nothing before the camera had the power to do even that. To those who possess an insatiable appetite for knowledge of the past and of our ancestors, these frozen fragments remain a towering achievement and a precious legacy. Previously it was scarcely possible to preserve intact even the faces, structures, and artifacts of history. In that sense the advent of the camera divides the historical record into two distinct epochs: that about which we have read or heard or viewed the remains of, and that which we have glimpsed with our own eyes, if only fleetingly and in part.

It is fortunate indeed that the Civil War lies, if only barely, upon the latter side of that division. Without these photographs our sense of what life was like in those terrible years would be much the poorer.

Above and Left: In all the major cities and ports, the barracks. Fort Richmond on Staten Island, New York. June 29, 1864. (USAMHI)

Below: Gunboats like the U.S.S. Michigan, *the Navy's first iron-hulled warship, built in 1844, cruised the Great Lakes during the war. (NAVAL PHOTOGRAPHIC CENTER)*

Left and below left: In the larger cities the churches and civic groups operated entertainment centers for the soldiers home on leave or recovering from their wounds. Here the "Union Volunteer Refreshment Saloon" in Philadelphia catered to the soldiers' tastes for food and beverage, if not ladies. (LO)

Below: But for most Northerners, the most common war experience was seeing the ever-present soldiers, either going or coming, in city and country. Hanover Junction, Pennsylvania, in November 1863, saw several, some obviously recuperating from wounds and walking with canes. (USAMHI)

Above: In the larger cities the churches and civic groups operated entertainment centers for the soldiers home on leave or recovering from their wounds. Here the "Union Volunteer Refreshment Saloon" in Philadelphia catered to the soldiers' tastes for food and beverage, if not ladies. (LO)

Above: The guard of honor for the funeral of Lieutenant Colonel George E. Marshall of the 40th Massachusetts, killed at Cold Harbor, Virginia, in June 1864. Here at home in Fitchburg, even the eagle above him is draped in mourning. (USAMHI)

Above: Happy were the men of the regiment whose enlistment expired. The 45th Massachusetts, at Readville, July 7, 1863, the day before they muster out. (MICHAEL J. HAMMERSON)

Below: The Ottawa, Illinois, home of Brigadier General W. H. L. Wallace, mortally wounded at Shiloh. His portrait, his riderless horse, the flag for which he died tell the whole story. (CHS)

Left: Homecoming for all too many, however, meant crepe and tears and the cold ground. It was a sight the North would become used to. (NA)

Above: Finally they will come in such numbers that the government must set aside special sanctuaries for its honored dead. A. J. Russell's photograph of the military cemetery at Alexandria. (NEIKRUG PHOTOGRAPHICA, LTD.)

Above: Only on a few occasions will the North actually feel the sting of the enemy's sword, and nowhere more than in Chambersburg, Pennsylvania. In July 1864, Confederates set the torch to the town when it could not raise a ransom. The fire devastated much of the town. This view by the Zacharias brothers looks down Queen Street. (MAURICE MAROTTE, JR.)

Below: There, in rank upon rank, they will sleep through the ages. (NEIKRUG PHOTOGRAPHICA, LTD.)

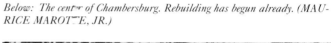

Below: The center of Chambersburg. Rebuilding has begun already. (MAURICE MAROTTE, JR.)

Left: Greater crises faced the nation than enemy raids. The men of the Supreme Court had to deal constantly with the limits of authority in an emergency, with habeas corpus, and the safety of the nation versus the rights of the individual. (NA)

Right: In December 1864, this military commission tried and convicted Indiana dissenter Lambden P. Milligan of treason and sentenced him to death. Two years later, in ex parte Milligan, the Supreme Court would reverse that conviction. (INDIANA STATE LIBRARY)

Above: Riots against the military draft in 1863 turned New York City into a bedlam, and left over 100 people dead. Lieutenant Commander Richard W. Meade, Jr., nephew of General George G. Meade, subdued the rioters. (USAMHI)

Above: "Copperhead" newspapers, those seemingly disloyal or opposed to the war on whatever grounds, were often mobbed and destroyed. In Portsmouth, New Hampshire, a mob gathers in front of the States & Union office angrily denouncing its editorial stance. The sudden appearance of rain dampened their ardor, and the newspaper was not molested. (USAMHI)

Right: In the North, war news came chiefly from the press, and the industry capitalized whenever possible on the salability of the most recent news. Here on June 9, 1862, the Pittsburgh Dispatch office advertises LATER FROM RICHMOND & MEMPHIS, Genl McClellan's Report of the Battle, Our loss in killed wounded & missing 5,134." Three days before, thirteen Union and Confederate ships met in the last fleet battle of the war at Memphis. On June 1 the Battle of Fair Oaks in McClellan's Peninsula Campaign concluded. The Dispatch was reporting both, and its billboard sign probably lists Pittsburghers injured in the battles. The editor, Joseph Singerly Lare, appears in top hat seated at the right on the second-floor ledge. (MRS. ALBERT MCBRIDE)

Far right: The Dispatch took offices above J. M. Fulton's Drug Store on Fifth Avenue. Interested citizens gathered outside on the sidewalk for the early edition with the latest news from the fronts. (MRS. ALBERT MCBRIDE)

Right: The most notorious copperhead of all was Ohio's Clement L. Vallandigham, pictured here in the center. Expelled from the Union, he went south, but Jefferson Davis did not want him either. He spent some time in Canada, then returned to Ohio in 1864, hoping vainly to cause an uprising of antiwar feeling that would defeat Lincoln at the polls. (LC)

Above: Running against Lincoln was his one-time general, George B. McClellan. Virtually shelved after Antietam in the fall of 1862, "Little Mac" accepted the Democratic nomination in 1864. There was no beating Lincoln. (USAMHI)

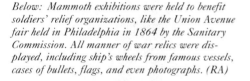

Left: Meanwhile, the people of the North watched and waited. The ladies sewed mammoth flags for the soldiers. These are the ladies of the Pennsylvania Academy of Fine Arts. (LO)

Below: Mammoth exhibitions were held to benefit soldiers' relief organizations, like the Union Avenue fair held in Philadelphia in 1864 by the Sanitary Commission. All manner of war relics were displayed, including ship's wheels from famous vessels, cases of bullets, flags, and even photographs. (RA)

Below: Art exhibited at the Sanitary Fair, including Emanuel Leutze's heroic depiction of Washington crossing the Delaware. (NA)

Right: New York's great Metropolitan Fair, the largest of its kind, attracted thousands. (NA)

Above: They saw a wondrous array of relics, displayed in that cluttered fashion so beloved of the Victorians. Here the uniform of the martyr Elmer Ellsworth, stained with his holy blood. (NA)

Below: Captured enemy flags and relics of the battlefields. (NA)

Above: Suppliers of military hardware displayed their stock. Here a complete exhibit of the pistols and accessories made by the Colt firearms company of Connecticut. The war made Samuel Colt a millionaire, and he sold to both sides. (NA)

Right: Giant projectiles, swords, rifles, axes, even items totally unrelated to the war, and much of it for sale to a souvenir-hungry public. "Relics from Vicksburg Sold Here." (NA)

Above: All manner of weapons, and even soldier art works, like miniature churches fashioned during the long hours in winter quarters. (NA)

Above: And for those not interested in the current war, a little something from an earlier era. (NA)

Right: Young girls shammed at soldiering for the camera, often to send to boyfriends in the Army. (WENDELL W. LANG, JR.)

Left and below left: For those who could not see the great fairs, the photographers provided ample souvenir cartes de visite of soldiers celebrating victories. Fetter of Logansport, Indiana, captured these two sailors, one of them a double amputee, carrying a box marked "Remember Fort Fisher." For such men, pity would be their only livelihood. (DAVID FINNEY)

Above: And a few women who actually passed for men or otherwise served the Army, made capital of it at home. Actress Pauline Cushman (not a very good actress) publicized widely her activities as a spy (not a very good one) in Bragg's army. (LO)

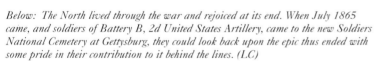

Below: And they looked back on one who told them this time would come, and that they should look ahead "with malice toward none." Abraham Lincoln's second inauguration, March 4, 1865. Lincoln is seated, hands in his lap, just to the left of the small white lectern. On his right is Vice-President Andrew Johnson. (WRHS)

Left: Another popular image, the old bugler and his dog. A Brady gallery photo taken at West Point in 1864. (LO)

Below: The North lived through the war and rejoiced at its end. When July 1865 came, and soldiers of Battery B, 2d United States Artillery, came to the new Soldiers National Cemetery at Gettysburg, they could look back upon the epic thus ended with some pride in their contribution to it behind the lines. (LC)

The Photographers of the War

FREDERIC E. RAY

Historians with cameras
and their journey for posterity

America, even more than Europe, fell in love with the camera. All across the land the photographers and their apparatus set to work. By 1860 there were over three thousand plying the trade, like this dour fellow, lens cap in hand, recording America and Americans. It is noted Oregon artist Peter Britt. (SOUTHERN OREGON HISTORICAL SOCIETY),

WHEN AMERICA WENT TO WAR, the camera went with it, and by 1861 neither was a stranger to the other. Photography, as an art and an industry, had already marked its first quarter century before the guns sounded. It had come a long way.

A Frenchman, Joseph-Nicephore Niepce, experimented with the camera obscura in the 1820S and in 1826 produced probably the first successful photograph on a polished pewter plate. The exposure took eight hours. Nine years later an Englishman, Henry Fox Talbot, developed the first practical imaging process. He called it the calotype and produced it by using paper sensitized with silver salts.

But it remained for another Frenchman, one time partner of Niepce, to make the photograph truly attainable. Louis-Jacques-Mande Daguerre announced his "Daguerreotype" in 1839. He used a sensitized, silver-coated copper plate to capture light images in less than one half hour. Unlike Talbot, Daguerre made his methods public and the daguerreotype quickly found enthusiastic acceptance in Europe.

Thanks to two remarkable men of genius, it also found its way to America almost from the moment of creation. Samuel F. B. Morse, inventor of the telegraph, visited Daguerre in Paris in 1839 and brought back with him the process. The next year he and John W. Draper, a noted New York physicist, began experiments which led shortly to a reduction in exposure time from half an hour to half a minute. At once a lucrative portrait business mushroomed in the country, and one of the principal proponents of this new process was upstate New Yorker Mathew B. Brady, whose fashionable New York and Washington studios would soon attract the notables of the day. Before long a "Brady" became the commonplace term for a portrait.

In 1851, seven years after Brady went into business, another Englishman, Frederick Scott Archer, developed the collodion or wet-plate process. By recording his image on a glass plate, thus producing a negative, he and his revolutionary invention enabled the multiple duplication of photographs printed on salt-or albumen-treated paper, whereas the daguerreotypist could make one image, and one only. Archer's soon became the accepted process for portrait photographers, and their profession spread throughout America. By 1860 there were 3,154 photographers, ambrotypists, daguerreotypists, calotypists, melainotypists, and practitioners of other varieties of the art, spread from New York to San Francisco, from Chicago to New Orleans. The image took America by storm.

By the early 1860s almost every middle-class family owned an album, filled not only with portraits of their own, but also with copies of mass produced images of their presidents, public figures, even actors and actresses. The carte de visite, a calling card-sized photograph ideally suited for albums—and for calling cards—became a rage. And for those wanting more realism, there was the stereoscopic view. The camera made two images simultaneously from two different lenses. They were mounted side by side on a card which, when viewed through a hand-held stereoscope, produced a three-dimensional picture. Thousands were sold to the parlors of America in the late 1850s.

With this market burgeoning just as the

Left: A burgeoning industry begins. In the years immediately prior to the Civil War, the homes of Europe and America discovered the photograph. Here, in an English shop, workers cut and mount stereoscopic views for home consumption, and the public's appetite was voracious. The raw prints hang in the background. The man in the white vest seated at the center is cutting them. Ladies at the table prepare the mounting boards and glue the prints to them, while the two boys standing at the left run the finished pieces through a press. And even here the camera captures not just a scene, but history. Times are starting to change. Men and women are working together in the same shop. Yet some things have not changed, for children are working with them, too, and the clock in the background shows it is nearly 6 P.M., with the day's work not yet done. (NYHS)

Right: Alexander Gardner's own 1863 image of his gallery on 7th and D streets, N.W., in Washington, D.C. Here one of the foremost photographers of the war made his headquarters when not in the field with the armies. Here he thumbed his nose at his one-time employer, Mathew B. Brady, whose own gallery stood nearby. While proclaiming his magnificent "Views of the War" being available on one side of his building, Gardner was a good enough businessman to devote even more advertising to the real bread and butter for all cameramen of the era, the portrait work in cartes de visite, ambrotypes, and a variety of other techniques. (LC)

nation went to war in 1861, the economic potential of supplying war scenes to the public became self evident. And others had already led the way in previous conflicts. Fifteen years before, an anonymous daguerreotypist went to Saltillo during the war with Mexico and made at least four outdoor military images that have survived. One shows Major General John E. Wool and his staff astride their horses in the streets of the city and is remarkable for its clarity. Several years later, during the Crimean War, a British artist turned photographer, Roger Fenton, employed the collodion process to capture over 350 images of the war in the Crimea.

And then the Civil War. In fact, the first artists to recognize and attempt to exploit its possibilities were southern photographers, and it is a happy thing for posterity that they did. Just a few months later the blockade so restricted the necessary imported chemicals and supplies that Confederate artists could no longer afford the highly speculative business of taking outdoor war views. After 1861 they almost exclusively used their carefully husbanded materials for the indoor portrait work that made their livelihood.

Simultaneously they descended on Charleston and Pensacola. Within days after the surrender of Fort Sumter, F. K. Houston of 307

Above: Brady and Gardner had the big studios, but hundreds of others like Bowdoin, Taylor & Company's gallery at 204 King Street in Alexandria, Virginia, operated the studios that most Americans saw. Always there was the large opening in the roof to let in the sunlight essential for the camera and always the case of samples displayed outside the front door. (T. SCOTT SANDERS)

Right: And once the war came, the photographers proved nearly as fascinated by themselves at their work as they were with the conflict itself. Just as the Confederates fired the first shots of the war, so, too, did Confederate photographers take the first shots, both of the war and themselves. Even before the pioneering J. D. Edwards went to Pensacola, the remarkable Osborn & Durbec of King Street in Charleston captured Fort Sumter as surely and completely as did Beauregard.

Among their host of images stands this faded stereo print. It is unique, from a photographic viewpoint perhaps the most important Confederate picture from the entire war. The chief focus of attention are the men and two guns of the Trapier Mortar Battery on Morris Island, guns that bombarded Sumter. But what makes this photo so important is what lies hidden in the background. Lost for over a century and here published for the first time, this is the only known view of Confederate photographic apparatus in the field. Behind the mortar on the right stands a large pyramidal object, and just faintly visible on it are the words "Osborn & Durbec 223 King St." This is their portable darkroom, required for the speedy development of the emulsions of the era.

One of the great misfortunes of a tragic war is that the scarcity of chemicals and materials prevented artists of the caliber of Edwards and Osborn & Durbec from doing for their side of the conflict what Brady and others did for his. (TU)

Right: Mathew B. Brady, the entrepreneurial genius who so identified himself with Civil War photography that for over a century afterward almost every Civil War image was just naturally assumed to be a "Brady." This somewhat retouched image purports to show him in field costume on July 22, 1861, the day he returned to Washington from the battlefield at Bull Run. Brady's whole story of his trip to the battle with McDowell's army is highly suspect, but the evidences of his showmanship in this photo are undeniable. Already he had begun to make Americans believe that he was the war photographer. (USAMHI)

Below: Thanks to his failing eyesight, Brady probably spent little if any time behind the camera during the war. But he certainly spent a lot of time in front of it. In top hat he poses next to General Samuel P. Heintzelman and with members of the general's staff on the steps of Arlington House, the former home of Robert E. Lee, in Arlington, Virginia. It is the late summer of 1861, following the debacle at Bull Run. (LC)

Right: At Blackburn's Ford, by the waters of Bull Run, two photographers pause for a glass in March 1862. (LC)

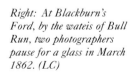

King Street in Charleston set his camera within the parade ground of the fortress and captured it himself on his wet plates. On April 17 arrived James Osborn and F. E. Durbec of Osborn & Durbec's Southern Stereoscopic & Photographic Depot on 223 King Street, at the "sign of the Big Camera." Their epic coverage of the fort and its environs would not be surpassed during the rest of the war. And at the same time, far away in Pensacola, Florida, J. D. Edwards of New Orleans began his own epic. Others, George S. Cook of Charleston and J. W. Petty of New Orleans, for instance, made less ambitious forays from their studios, but after the first spring of the war, they rarely did so again. Only Cook took one brief sortie in 1863, again to Sumter. For the rest of the war they would not be heard from again.

Then came Brady. "I can only describe the destiny that overruled me by saying that, like Euphorion, I felt that I had to go." So he said, and so he did. Perhaps he was urged by the example of Edwards and the others—for he and the North knew of their work—but more likely he and they had the same idea at the same time. In July 1861, excited by the prospect of capturing scenes of the then three-month-old war, he claimed to have accompanied McDowell's army on the road to Bull Run.

"I went to the first Battle of Bull Run with two wagons," he said. His innovative portable dark room, a wagon hooded in black, was dubbed the "what-is-it" wagon. Clad in linen duster and straw hat, Brady says he "got as far as Blackburne's Ford." "We made pictures and expected to be in Richmond next day, but it was not so, and our apparatus was a good deal damaged on the way back to Washington." So Brady claimed thirty years later. In fact, no verifiable images from the first expedition have survived. Some that Brady later said were taken then, actually date months later, calling into question his entire account of his first trip to the front. Brady was first and foremost a businessman, a promoter, and his stories of many of his war exploits are highly colored by exaggeration.

Brady's eyesight was failing and he relegated the actual camera work to his assistants. He appears frequently in front of the camera in a number of his war views, but it is probable that he did not expose any images in the field himself. Throughout the war years, he only occasionally ventured to the armies, and instead spent his time in New York and Washington, supervising his flourishing portrait business and amassing the collection of views taken by his assistants and others that he would produce as "Brady's Album Gallery" and other series. In addition, his views were widely published by the illustrated weeklies of the day, *Harper's* and *Frank Leslie's*, whose artists rendered the images into woodcuts.

The men actually following the armies for Brady were a remarkable array of artists: Alexander and James Gardner, Timothy O'Sullivan, William Pywell, George N. Barnard, David Woodbury, E. Guy Foux, James F. Gibson, Stanley Morrow, James Reekie, and several others. Some were out standing. O'Sullivan would produce many of the best-known war scenes. Alexander Gardner and O'Sullivan together were unequaled in their coverage of the Army of the Potomac and both captured many scenes which transcended photography to be come genuine art. Gibson would become Brady's partner late in the war. Woodbury and others would journey to Gettysburg in November 1863 to preserve for the future the historic gathering at the dedication of the National Cemetery. Lincoln can be discerned on the speakers' platform from which he would deliver his now famous address. Gardner, too, would capture Lincoln in the field, during his visit to General McClellan at Antietam in 1862. Several, most notably Gardner and O'Sullivan, eventually leave Brady when he refuses them credit for their work.

In fact, there were several varieties of photographers with and around the armies during the Civil War. Very few enjoyed a truly official position. Indeed, probably only one, Captain A. J. Russell, can be called a genuine Army photographer. Working for the U. S. Military Railroad, he operated the War Department's only photographic laboratory. His images are among the best that survive from the war.

Far more common were the artists who occasionally took contracts from the War Department for special assignments. George N. Barnard is the most notable for his series of views of the fortifications around Atlanta following its capture. Samuel A. Cooley was paid to photograph government warehouses and other installations at Hilton Head, South Carolina, in 1864. And several, among them Alexander Gardner, worked at enlarging and photographically copying maps for distribution in the armies.

Yet most of the war photographers, like Brady and his assistants, enjoyed no connection at all with the authorities. Rather, they were businessmen looking for profits. If they could obtain a pass from the generals commanding, they might travel freely among the troops, capturing scenes for their stereo and carte de visite series to sell in the North, and doing a lucrative trade in selling portraits to the soldiers. And many of them simply happened to be in the right place at the right time. The war came to them. When the armies reached Corinth, Mississippi, Howard & Hall and Armistead & White were there ready to take their trade. When the Federals occupied Baton Rouge, McPherson & Oliver and the prolific

Above: At Sudley Springs on the Manassas battlefield, the cameramen left their equipment wagon across the stream, then waded over to capture the scene, and with it their footprints in the mud. (LC)

Left: One of the war's finest young photographers was Timothy O'Sullivan, among the first northern cameramen to return to South Carolina with the invading Federals. At Beaufort, in April 1862, he recorded an outstanding series of images, and this one probably includes himself, seated second from the right, at his 'mess.' (USAMHI)

Left: Photographers went with the army of McClellan to Yorktown in May 1862. (LC)

Left: Their portable darkroom intrigued a boatload of soldiers at White House on the Pamunkey River. (WRHS)

Right: Timothy O'Sullivan, "Our Artist at Manassas," the brilliant and energetic cameraman who covered most of the Civil War in the East, and later took his lenses to the West and to Central America. (LARRY J. WEST)

Above: When the armies returned to Manassas in July 1862, so did O'Sullivan, who pauses here for a drink beside his "what's it" wagon on the Fourth of July. (LC)

Above: The equipment box in the front of the wagon says "Brady's Washington." The men are two of his numerous assistants, the one seated at left probably being David B Woodbury, arguably the best of the artists who stayed with Brady throughout the war. (LC)

Right: Timothy O'Sullivan's wagon stands at the end of a bridge built by McDowell's engineers across Bull Run in August 1862, just before he met defeat for the second time on the same ground. (LC)

Andrew D. Lytle happily accommodated them, doing a brisk business not only in studio portraits, but also in outdoor views. At New Bern, North Carolina, J. L. Dowling gladly obliged the Massachusetts troops occupying the town by accepting their custom. Of those who took their operations where the soldiers were, Samuel Cooley proved the most ambitious. He operated four separate galleries, three in South Carolina and one in Jacksonville, Florida. And surely no one surpassed the flair for scenic back drop of R. M. Linn. Perched atop Lookout Mountain, his "Gallery Point Lookout" offered the grandeur of the valley of Chattanooga as background for the portraits he made. A few northern artists made special trips to the field just to capture the doings of home state boys for civilian consumption. G. H. Houghton of Brattleboro, Vermont, made scores of outstanding images with the Vermont regiments in McClellan's army on the Peninsula, then took them home to sell to friends and loved ones.

By contrast, as already noted, Confederate field photography almost ceased to exist after 1861. Thus, the photographic record of the Confederacy is limited largely to formal studio portraits of its statesmen and military figures. Charles Rees of Richmond did venture outdoors in 1863 or 1864 to capture two images of the infamous Libby Prison, and another of Belle Isle in the James River. A. J. Riddle of Georgia took his camera to Andersonville in 1864 and there made a handful of poignant scenes of the thousands of Union prisoners in captivity. And at Brownsville, Texas, A. G. Wedge of Matamoros, Mexico, took his camera across the Rio Grande to photograph the Confederate evacuation. But these were the exceptions.

As the war stretched on, photographers followed the armies through most major campaigns, capturing nearly everything in sight. The most trivial things seemed to fascinate them, and they dearly loved to catch themselves at their work as well. A time exposure of several seconds was necessary for the successful transmission of light on the collodion plate, and the pictures thus nec-

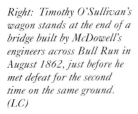

essarily resulted in somewhat frozen "still life" images. There are no real "action" pictures from the war. Artists deceptively posed many of their views to appear to be action scenes—cannoneers positioned at their guns, troops on parade and drill field. And at times the camera came close to battle, as at Antietam and in front of Petersburg. George Cook actually recorded accidentally the explosion of a Federal shell inside Fort Sumter in 1863. Yet for most practical purposes, the darkroom wagon could only be deployed behind the lines because of the time-consuming procedures required for taking such pictures.

These operations were tedious and exacting. The usual medium for the images was a supply of clear glass plates varying in size, but usually eight by ten inches or about four by ten inches for stereo views, carried in dust-proof boxes. When ready to expose, the artist carefully coated a plate with collodion made of a solution of gun cotton in equal parts of sulphuric ether and 95 proof alcohol. Bromide and iodine of potassium or ammonia were then added, sensitizing the surface of the plate. After letting the ether and alcohol evaporate to the right texture, the plate was immersed for three to five minutes in a bath holder solution of silver nitrate. This must be done in absolute darkness, or at best a dull amber light. The sensitized plate then went into a holder for insertion in the camera, which had already been aimed and focused. Uncapping the lens permitted an exposure of from five to thirty seconds, depending on available sunlight. Then the operator had just a few minutes to remove the plate from the camera, return it to the darkroom wagon, and develop it in a solution of sulfate of iron and acetic acid. Then it was washed to remove surplus silver with a solution of cyanide of potassium, and finally washed again, dried, and varnished.

Considering the conditions under which the war photographers worked, and the attendant chances of spoiling their plates during any one of the thirteen separate steps, the degree of quality and clarity achieved in their images is truly remarkable. A century later the best techniques could hardly do better.

The darkroom wagons in which they worked, and which so often appear in the background of their images, were well described by photographer George Rockwood some years after the war as "an ordinary delivery wagon of the period."

[It] had a strong step attached at the rear and below the level of the wagon floor. A door was put on at the back, carefully hung so as to be light-proof. The door... came down over the step which was boxed in at the sides, making it a sort of well within the body of the wagon rather than a true step. The work of coating or sensitizing the plates and that of developing them was done from this well, in which there was just room enough to work. As the operator stood there the collodion was within reach of his right hand, in a special receptacle. On his left also was the holder of one of the baths. The chief developing bath was in front, with the tanks of various liquids stored in front of it again, and the space between it and the floor filled with plates.

On exceptional occasions in very cold weather the life of a wet plate might be extended to nearly an hour on either side of the exposure, the coating or the development side, but

Left: The men who made the pictures. The first publication of a remarkable image taken at Berlin, Maryland, October 28, 1862. Standing at right is Mathew Brady. David B. Woodbury crouches to the right of him. The other assistants are, left to right, Silas Holmes, a cook named Stephen, E. T. Whitney, Hodges, and a teamster named Jim. No other surviving image from the war shows Brady and his assistants in such detail, and their equipment as well. These are some of the men who did the real work for which Brady took credit. (KA)

Right: Brady surveys the ruins of the United States Arsenal at Harpers Ferry in October 1862. He stands at right in this image by his assistant David B. Woodbury. (USAMHI)

Below: Brady, standing at right, again by Woodbury. He looks across the Potomac River, with the Arsenal ruins in the background. (LC)

Right: Major General Ambrose Burnside had no idea this shot of him was being taken. He just finished posing for Brady's camera operator and had sat down on a sack of oats to read a newspaper. Brady, in the straw hat, instructed his assistant to take another shot and then sat in the chair facing the general. He loved to pose with the generals. (USAMHI)

Left: When the armies came to Gettysburg, so did the cameras. William H. Tipton sits aboard the Tyson Brothers' darkroom wagon in front of the house that served Union General George G. Meade as head-quarters during the battle. (DONALD TYSON)

Above: O'Sullivan's photograph of his winter quarters with telegraphers at Brandy Station, Virginia, in 1863. (LC)

Right: The tent of an army photographer in camp along the Rappahannock in 1863. (DON W. MINDEMANN)

Left: At Chattanooga, Tennessee. Morse from Huntsville, Alabama, and his "Gallery of the Cumberland.') (USAMHI)

ordinarily the work had to be done within a very few minutes, and every minute of delay resulted in loss of brilliancy and depth in the negative.

To be sure, other processes were used as well. Most of the portraits of private soldiers that were made in the camps were ambrotypes, or tintypes, cheap processes within reach of the lowly private's pocketbook. The image on a tin-type was caught on a small iron sheet plated with tin and coated with black lacquer. The ambrotype was a glass negative mounted against a dark background to produce a positive image. Unlike the true print derived from the collodion negatives, daguerreotypes, ambrotypes, and tin-types, were almost always mirrored copies of the subject. This reverse image called for some simple ingenuity on the part of the photographer in posing his subjects. Accoutrements were often reversed on the person of the sitter to present them correctly in the finished picture. Even belt plates bearing the letters "US" were turned upside down, presenting a perfect "S" to be sure, but a somewhat peculiar "U."

With these hundreds of photographers traveling the country, there was little that they missed, and most of what they caught has survived. Yet, there are still the "might have been's." A Chambersburg, Pennsylvania, photographer named Bishop is supposed to have arranged his camera in a window in anticipation of the arrival of General Lee during 1863's Gettysburg Campaign. The camera attracted the attention of Confederate soldiers and teamsters along the curbstones who arose to get into the image, thereby blocking Bishop's view of their general and robbing posterity of a memorable moment in time. Off Cherbourg, France, in 1864, the photographer Francois Rondin set up his camera and made an exposure of the battle raging at sea between the U.S.S. *Kearsarge* and the dreaded Confederate commerce raider C.S.S. *Alabama.* Seen widely at the time in the window of Rondin's Cherbourg shop, the priceless print has disappeared. A dozen or more wartime images of Abraham Lincoln are known to have been taken, but are now lost. A much rumored photograph taken from aloft in a Federal observation balloon has yet to surface, if indeed it was ever really taken.

Yet what does survive is truly staggering. An enormous debt is owed for the legacy left by those enterprising men with their little wagons, rolling over rutted roads with their fragile contents, hauling their clumsy cameras in camp and battlefield, occasionally risking their lives, and recording history as it had never been done before.

Mathew Brady, as usual, speaks for all of them, and largely it was through his energy and initiative that they all preserved for generations to come the image of the war and its people. "I felt that I had to go," he would say. "A spirit in my feet said 'Go' and I went."

Left: The tent of an army photographer in camp along the Rappahannock in 1863. (DON W. MIN-DEMANN)

Above: Jefferson Rock at Harpers Ferry, overlooking the Shenandoah River, and the "Jefferson's Rocks Photographs" establishment. A soldier poses on the rock while the artist aims the camera out the window of the "gallery." (RP)

Above: At Chattanooga again. (USAMHI)

Above: And at Lookout Mountain, near Chattanooga, in 1864. Royan M. Linn was the "Brady" of itinerant portrait photographers. He sold himself almost as well as he sold his carte de visite portraits taken at his "Gallery Point Lookout." Establishing himself on the summit of this scenic promontory, Linn sold thousands of images of generals and soldiers posing on the point. Here "Linn of Lookout" himself sits, cane in hand, beside a stereo camera. Over his shoulder is spread the majesty of the Tennessee River. Here was a man with an eye for grandeur. (NA)

Above: Linn once again at Pulpit Rock, another favorite posing place for his subjects. (KA)

Left: Disdaining Brady's taste for notables, when Linn posed with others he selected commonplace people. Brady would never have been seen in a stovepipe hat aboard an ox-drawn wagon.
(TERENCE P. O'LEARY)

Left: Linn fascinated himself. Here he or an assistant photographs Brigadier General Thomas Sweeny, standing above the group of soldiers at left. (USAMHI)

Above: Western photographers, though less numerous than those in the East, still made their mark, and put themselves in the picture.

A landmark of the western campaigns was Corinth, Mississippi's Tishomingo Hotel. Usually unnoticed in the war images of the hotel is the rather considerable establishment to its left, "Howard & Hall Photographers." They could boast no less than three sunlights in their roof. (CHS)

Above: Vicksburg's "Washington Photograph Gallery," headquarters of Joslyn & Smith. (JOHN A. HESS)

Above: Competition among these western artists was sometimes stiff When Brigadier General Grenville Dodge and his staff posed beside their campaign maps for Howard and Hall... (MICHAEL J. HAMMERSON)

Below: ... photographers Armistead & White of Corinth took almost exactly the same image, probably Howard & Hall's also, and published it under their own imprint. (LC)

Above: Little Rock, Arkansas, in 1863 went onto emulsion for posterity in a splendid series of views taken by "White's Photograph Gallery." The studio appears at the lower right, its awninged sunlight extended toward the Arkansas River. Unusual for their striking clarity and quality, White's photographs have never been published before. (NA)

Right: A. D. Lytle of Baton Rouge, Louisiana, one of the most prolific of the western artists. Besides extensive portrait work, he took his camera outdoors and captured a remarkably complete record of a southern city under Union occupation. It was erroneously believed after the war that he used his camera to furnish information via photographs to the Confederates. (LSU)

Above: In 1864, with the main focus of the war in the East, so was the chief focus of the cameras. Stanley J. Morrow, a soldier stationed at the Point Lookout, Maryland, prison camp, learned the trade—from Brady himself he would claim—and opened his own studio. If his sunlight cover looks rather makeshift, how much more so is his business sign. Hopefully Morrow planned his darkroom operations better than he did the lettering for his "Picture Ga…" (STANLEY J . MORROW COLLECTION, W. H. OVER MUSEUM)

Above: James Gardner, brother of Alexander, one of the many unsung true photographic artists of the war. (LJW)

Above: Timothy O'Sullivan caught on June 13, 1864, this almost ghostly scene of a photographer and his camera, just beneath the tree at left, about to shoot a private soldier at Charles City Court House, Virginia. (LC)

Above: Timothy O'Sullivan again, like his profession, a little older and experienced in war. (LJW)

Above: "Bergstressers' Photographic Studio." Attaching themselves to the V Corps of the Army of the Potomac, three brothers, A. J., S. L., and J. Bergstresser, took their tintype or "melainotype" establishment to the front and flourished. The Pennsylvanian artists stayed with the Army for two years or more and took, said an observer, "the Lord only knows how many thousand portraits." Operating more than one gallery, and charging one dollar for a portrait, they sometimes took 160 in a day. "If anybody knows an easier and better way of making money than that," said a New York newspaper, "the public should know of it."

The Bergstressers were not only enterprising, but also innovative. Rather than building a permanent sunlight into this rude log studio, they put in a sliding roof. (USAMHI)

Above: The interior of a photographer's winter quarters. On the wall behind him to the right hang several of the brass or copper frames used for cased ambrotypes. (RP)

Above: One of Brady's wagons at Cold Harbor in June 1864 The photographer could develop his negatives at the back of the wagon, under the black hood. (LC)

Above: June 1864, Bermuda Hundred, Virginia. The signal tower built by General Benjamin F. Butler, a flag-holding signalman atop it, seems almost an extension of the Brady wagon and operator. (LC)

Above: Soldiers posing for the camera are joined by a one-eyed visitor, the camera on the ground at lower left. (NA)

Right: Sherman's great photographer during the Atlanta Campaign, George N. Barnard, posing for Brady's camera. One of the very few artists to be paid by the United States Army, Barnard was commissioned to record photographically Atlanta and its defenses. (KA)

Above: A photographer's printing room at Bermuda Hundred. (JOHN A. HESS)

Right: Barnard's portable darkroom, chemicals, and other equipment attract the attention of several of Sherman's "bummers" in abandoned Confederate trenches southeast of Atlanta. (LC)

Above: Henry P. Moore opened his "DAGTYPS" gallery on Hilton Head, South Carolina, in 1862, and concentrated his efforts chiefly on the men of the 3d New Hampshire. Outdoor views like this one, however, were not daguerreotypes but wet-plate photographs. (LC)

Above: "Sam A. Cooley. U.S. Photographer. Department of the South." That is how he billed himself, never hesitant to make capital on his quasi-official position as a contract artist for the Army in South Carolina. Hucksterism aside, he proved to be one of the most talented camera artists of the war. (WRHS)

Above: "Robbers' Row" in Hilton Head. Here the sutlers and camp followers set up their wares to lure the soldiers' money. Moore was one of them, and his gallery stands second building from the left, the simple sign "PHOTOGRAPHS" stating his business. (USAMHI)

Above: "Cooley's," headquarters in Beaufort, South Carolina, for the enterprising Samuel Cooley. (WRHS)

Above: Cooley, Center, with his associates and his own improved version of the "what's it" wagon. It paid to advertise. (USAMHI)

Right: Paid by the War Department to photograph government supply buildings, Cooley occasionally got himself into the picture. Here is Commissary Store House No. 3 on Hilton Head Island, South Carolina, September 16, 1864. And in the foreground stands the shadow of Cooley and camera. (USAMHI)

Left: For many of the war's photographers, their images of themselves at work are all by which we can remember their names. Take J. L. Dowling of New Bern, North Carolina. He made a remarkable series of prints of the Federal troops occupying his town in 1862 and 1863; yet, while they survive, he is totally forgotten. His recognition depends entirely on this one photograph of his "Ambrotype & Daguerreotype Gallery" situated on a second floor above a drug store. The focus may seem to be the men of the 25th Massachusetts lounging below. But the real attraction is in the window above Dowling's sign. There, standing beside his camera, is the artist himself. This was a man with style. (USAMHI)

Above: George S. Cook, the Confederate photographer who, in 1863, braved Federal fire to take his camera out onto Fort Sumter to record the ruin caused by the enemy's bombardment. Two years before, he made the same trip to capture the images of Major Robert Anderson and his officers as they were about to become the targets of the first shots of the war. (VM)

Above: Alexander Gardner established a great reputation in the Civil War, then enhanced it by going to the Far West immediately afterward to record the opening of the new country. (LJW)

Above: One of Brady's photographic wagons at City Point, Virginia, during the Siege of Petersburg. A familiar sight by now, the "what's it" wagons no longer attracted the attention they once enjoyed. (NA, U. S. SIGNAL CORPS PHOTO, BRADY COLLECTION)

Right: Three photographers lie asleep in the shade of their tent near Petersburg, their wagon in the background, while a fourth writes a letter and a Zouave private apparently wanders into the picture. (LC)

Left: Some artists' chief official services for the War Department came in copying maps for the Topographical Engineers Corps. Here in March 1865, in front of Petersburg, a camera is ready to shoot a map for reproduction. (USAMHI)

Above: "Photographic Wagon, Engineer Department." Perhaps part of Gardner's equipment, shown amid the bomb proofs at Petersburg in the fall of 1864. (LC)

Above: The goal of four years at last attained. Richmond, taken from the south side of the James River, in April 1865. In the foreground stands a portable darkroom and operator at work, which explains the blur of the cameraman who is developing his image. Across the river, the large brick building, painted white on its lower stories, is the infamous Libby Prison. An Egbert G. Foux image, an associate of A. J. Russell. (WRHS)

Left: Richmond in Federal hands, and a stereo camera ready to complete the conquest. (THE MESERVE COLLECTION)

Above: A heavily retouched photo of Messrs. Levy & Cohen of 9th and Filbert streets, Philadelphia. Their series of photographs taken in Richmond immediately after its fall are among the best produced by anyone. Levy's untimely death six months later from a heart attack prevented the firm from publishing and distributing their prints. Instead, their negatives were sold, and never presented to the public until now. (KA)

Left: April 8, 1865, while Grant is cornering Lee at Appomattox, Brady is already in Richmond posing for his own cameras. Here at Pratt's Castle on Gambler's Hill, he stands in top hat, the war that made him great almost done. (USAMHI)

Right: Federal artists were quick to make use of captured Confederate photographs, and one of their favorites was southern photographer Charles Rees's print of Libby Prison in Richmond, taken probably in 1863. It was found after Richmond's fall, and several northern operators published it over their own copyright. This print was part of "Levy & Cohen's Views of the Rebel Capital and Its Environs." It is one of the very few photographs showing Confederate men and officers outdoors. Libby's commandant, Richard Turner, stands third from the left in the foreground. (KA)

Below: At the end of the long road, the war and the camera have come full circle. Here at Fort Sumter they meet again in April 1865, four years after the beginning. Samuel Cooley prepares to photograph the remnant of a once mighty parapet. The guns are now stilled. The war's final shots belong to the camera. (LC)

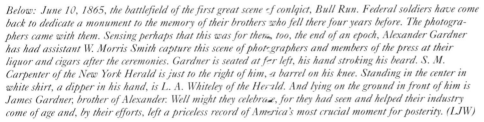

Below: June 10, 1865, the battlefield of the first great scene of conflict, Bull Run. Federal soldiers have come back to dedicate a monument to the memory of their brothers who fell there four years before. The photographers came with them. Sensing perhaps that this was for them, too, the end of an epoch, Alexander Gardner has had assistant W. Morris Smith capture this scene of photographers and members of the press at their liquor and cigars after the ceremonies. Gardner is seated at far left, his hand stroking his beard. S. M. Carpenter of the New York Herald is just to the right of him, a barrel on his knee. Standing in the center in white shirt, a dipper in his hand, is L. A. Whiteley of the Herald. And lying on the ground in front of him is James Gardner, brother of Alexander. Well might they celebrate, for they had seen and helped their industry come of age and, by their efforts, left a priceless record of America's most crucial moment for posterity. (LJW)

Above: Samuel Cooley photographs a soldier in the ruins of Fort Sumter in April 1865. (LC)

THE GUNS
OF '62

Part of the rui_ of 1862. Rolling stock of the Orange & Alexandria Railroad, once used to su_ply a Union Army marching to Manassas, and now destroyed by it to deny it ~o the victorious Confederates. It, like so many other scenes this year, is indica__ve of the almost constant defeat suffered by the North. (U.S. ARMY MILI_ARY HISTORY INSTITUTE, CARLISLE BARRACKS, PENNSYLVA_IA)

Yorktown: The First Siege

WARREN W. HASSLER, JR.

A "Napoleon," a "Prince John," and other dignitaries do battle for Richmond

Above: Major General John E. Wool, a hero of the Mexican War, turned seventy-seven just before the outbreak of war. Yet he showed no lack of energy in immediately ensuring the safety of Fort Monroe at Hampton Roads, Virginia, a vital base in Confederate territory, and in the course of the war a staging area for more than one major campaign. In the coming campaign for Yorktown... (U.S. ARMY MILITARY HISTORY INSTITUTE)

YORKTOWN ! Mere mention of the Virginia river port could conjure heroic images of great historical moment to both Northerners and Southerners at the start of the Civil War.

Both sides knew that it was at this quaint town on the south bank of the York River that Lord Cornwallis had surrendered his British Army to General George Washington's Continentals and their French allies, thereby virtually terminating the Revolutionary War with America triumphant. To Abraham Lincoln's Federals, it was well remembered that Washington had been a staunch nationalist, one who had gainsaid the particularism preached by the states' rights doctrinaires. To Jefferson Davis's Confederates—who naturally hoped to be able to retain control of the grass covered redoubts still remaining at Yorktown—there was still fierce pride in the fact that Washington was a native son of the Old Dominion, a stalwart who had been the one indispensable man of the patriots' struggle to establish an independent nation.

And Virginia was destined to be a central battle arena of the Civil War. Even though they had occupied the great National naval base at Norfolk and had emerged victorious over the Union Army at the First Battle of Bull Run on July 21, 1861, the Southerners were well aware of Federal pressure on their seaward littoral. From the start of hostilities, blue-clad soldiers had maintained control of the most powerful Gibraltar in North America—Fort Monroe, located at Old Point Comfort at the tip of the historic Peninsula between the York and James rivers—a stronghold their forces would hold throughout the war.

Yorktown was a charming, staid village of tree lined streets and neat, impressive houses. It was a prize the North coveted. Even though Confederate forces under John Bankhead "Prince John" Magruder and Daniel Harvey Hill had easily repulsed the inept and feeble attacks on June 10, 1861, of Benjamin Franklin Butler's troops at Big Bethel, a few miles from Old Point Comfort, by early 1862 the Union garrison at Fort Monroe under John E. Wool would be enlarged to some 12,500 soldiers. And the strategic offensive would remain with the Federals, now near Washington, D.C., being molded by the "Young Napoleon," George B. McClellan, into the truly superb Army of the Potomac.

"Little Mac," as the latter was called—a West Point graduate, a twice-brevetted hero of the War with Mexico, an official observer in the Crimean War, and a railroad president—argued long and hard with Lincoln and Secretary of War Edwin M. Stanton over what route the Army of the Potomac should take to move against the Confederate capital of Richmond. The administration favored the overland route through Manassas, but McClellan strongly recommended taking advantage of superior National sea power by moving his force down the Chesapeake Bay and landing it at Urbana on the lower Rappahannock River, or, as less desirable but nonetheless viable alternatives, disembarking it at Mobjack Bay or Fort Monroe. A quick move to West Point on the Pamunkey River —a tributary of the York—would bring the Federals to the point where they expected to employ the Richmond & York River Railroad to supply their short land march upon Richmond. After much disputation, McClellan was authorized to move with approximately 150,000 men on his amphibious operation. However, when the immense movement—one of the largest amphibious ones in warfare up to that time—actually unfolded in late March 1862, the Union commander's force was reduced—against his strenuous objections—to some 100,000 men.

The Confederate victor of Bull Run, Joseph E. Johnston, had gotten warning of the Federal plans and pulled his army back from Manassas to Fredericksburg on the Rappanhannock River. This rendered inoperative McClellan's scheme to debark at Urbana, so he determined to go ahead with the plan to land at Fort Monroe and advance up the Peninsula via Yorktown and Williamsburg toward Richmond. Further, and, McClellan would claim later, crippling to his strategy, was Lincoln's sudden insistence at the beginning of the operation on withholding Irvin McDowell's I Corps of some 38,000 men near Washington to assure the safety of the National Capital (although McClellan believed he had left Washington perfectly secure). The Union commander had earmarked McDowell's force as a flying column to move swiftly by water up the York to land on the Peninsula across from West Point so as to outflank and take in the rear the Confederate forces under Magruder on the lower Peninsula near Yorktown, where the Southern general had established his headquarters. Additionally, 10,000 of John E. Wool's troops which had been pledged to McClellan were now withdrawn from his use.

Also hampering the Union commander initially was the presence near Hampton Roads of the Confederate ironclad warship CSS *Virginia* (formerly the *Merrimack)*, which was neutralized by the USS *Monitor* in the classic battle of March 9, 1862. The Federal naval authorities assured McClellan that he could now proceed with his Peninsular campaign, and they even promised naval assistance in reducing and running past the enemy artillery batteries and fortifications being constructed by "Prince John" at Yorktown and across the river, which at that point narrows to less than a mile in width, at Gloucester Point. But Lincoln so lacked faith in McClellan that he not only withheld McDowell's corps but also demoted "Little Mac" from General-in-Chief of all the Union armies, a vote of no-confidence which left him in command of just the Army of the Potomac and not even of his base of supplies and communication. The President did not agree with McClellan's contention that the best defense of Washington was the heavy pressure McClellan was about to apply against Richmond. Lincoln was concerned about Rebel forces under "Stonewall" Jackson lurking in the Shenandoah.

Delays in assembling the vast shipping slowed the movement of the Union amphibious force to Fort Monroe, and once the troops began landing there—in the heaviest rains known to the region in twenty years—a shortage of supply wagons further impeded the advance. Only 42,000 men could be initially landed; several more weeks would be required for the rest of the army of about 100,000 to arrive and disembark. And McClellan was a most circumspect general, seldom one to take chances—especially since he was convinced time and preponderant resources were on the side of the North.

So colossal was the Federal undertaking that a foreign observer hailed it as "the stride of a

Right: ... Fort Monroe would play a significant part. The exterior of the officers' quarters. (USAMHI)

Below: The house at Fairfax Court House where McClellan made his headquarters. Here he planned his campaign for the Virginia Peninsula. A Timothy O'Sullivan image taken in June 1863. (USAMHI)

Above: Secretary of War Simon Cameron, his administration tainted by charges of corruption, resigned his portfolio on January 11, 1862. This left McClellan working with a new war secretary,... (NATIONAL ARCHIVES)

Below: ... Edwin M. Stanton, a Democrat who opposed Lincoln's election, but who now became the President's strong right arm. (NA)

Below: Major General George B. McClellan and his staff in the Yorktown operations. "Little Mac" was well named, standing a full head shorter than the rest. Immediately to his left is his chief of staff, Brigadier General Randolph B. Marcy, who also happened to be McClellan's father-in-law. To the left of Marcy stands Brigadier General Stewart Van Vliet, quartermaster. (CHICAGO HISTORICAL SOCIETY)

Left: Like McDowell before him, McClellan built his army in and around Washington and northern Virginia while he formulated his plan of campaign. Several familiar faces from the Bull Run debacle are with him. General Samuel P. Heintzelman stands bearded in front of the pillar on the right, with his staff. Robert E. Lee's Arlington House was a favorite posing place. (USAMHI)

Right: McDowell, too, was to cooperate with McClellan, but when a threat appeared in the Shenandoah Valley, Lincoln held him back to protect Washington. McDowell and staff at Arlington House. (MINNESOTA HISTORICAL SOCIETY)

Below: The always ready-to-pose Brigadier General Louis Blenker, with hand in coat, at his brigade headquarters near Washington. After being left out of the fight at Bull Run, he, too, would be withheld from McClellan. On his left stands Brigadier General Julius Stahel; on his right Prussian nobleman Prince Felix Salm-Salm. (WESTERN RESERVE HISTORICAL SOCIETY)

giant." But Fort Monroe lacked sufficient wharf facilities for so gigantic a movement; therefore, a secondary landing place was brought into use at Ship Point, nearer Yorktown. Without the flying column of the I Corps sweeping up the York to West Point, McClellan—now informed by the navy that it would not be able to join in attacking the Confederate batteries at Gloucester Point and Yorktown, or to run past them—was obliged to slog through the seas of mud and lay siege to the latter strong hold.

Meantime, the Confederates had not been idle. The local commander, John Magruder—a native Virginian—was a tall, erect, dark-haired general of fifty-one who had won brevets in the Mexican War and who, as a master of bluff and legerdemain, could make his 15,000 defenders look much more numerous than they were. There were few more colorful Civil War figures than "Prince John." A dandy dresser, he was an artillerist who had gained a wide reputation in the old army as a bon vivant and bountiful host at a myriad of social functions. Magruder never wearied of penning entreaties to his superiors for more reinforcements of men and artillery. He would in due time be joined by Johnston's main army which would, with Magruder's own force, total some 56,000 troops. The limited wharf facilities in the old river port of Yorktown made it difficult to enlarge his force rapidly, as there was no railroad down the Peninsula from Richmond or Williamsburg, and the few roads, upon which the Southern troops had to march, were infamous in this unusually heavy rainy season.

For many months, Magruder had been working steadily on the fortifications to defend Yorktown and the lower Peninsula. The earthworks immediately around the town were fairly strong, and Magruder incorporated with his own new ones some of the old Revolutionary War British redoubts. The water batteries, down low near the York River, as well as the field entrenchments, were buttressed by cotton bales, used also as breast works. Similarly, Gloucester Point, across from Yorktown, was fortified, though less strongly so.

Noting that the Warwick River ran across the Peninsula at right angles to McClellan's line of advance from Fort Monroe, Magruder determined to erect defenses behind this stream. To make the Federal advance and expected attacks more difficult, the Confederate commander built five dams which backed up water from the Warwick to such an extent that it inundated the countryside. This flooding allowed for only a few dry crossings at such points as Lee's Mill on the Confederate right and Wynn's Mill toward Yorktown, and where these roads passed, the Southerners erected batteries and rifle-pits.

Even to the experienced McClellan and other Union Army engineers, these enemy fortifications looked stronger than they actually were. Moreover, the Federal maps of the area were inaccurate, showing erroneously that the Warwick ran parallel to the York and James and therefore comprised no military obstacle. A probing attack on April 16 at Lee's Mill on the Federal left was repelled by the grayclads. So the Union commander set up his headquarters a little less than a mile west of the Farnholt House, on the Federal right, and began the slow process of a siege of the Yorktown-Warwick River

Right: More of the wealth of ordnance and ammuition shipped to the Peninsula to help subdue Johnson and Magruder. A Brady & Company image taken after the fall of Yorktown. (USAMHI)

defenses by regular approaches. This meant miners and sappers would dig parallels encompassing earthworks and wooden platforms for the cannon, with bombproofs for soldiers and ammunition.

The Federals were assisted by a large captive observation balloon, in the basket of which such high ranking officers as Fitz John Porter ascended to examine the Confederate lines through their field glasses. Aloft almost daily, the Union air force suffered a near-catastrophe on one occasion when it slipped loose from its moorings "and sailed majestically over the enemy's works; but fortunately for its occupants it soon met a counter-current of air which returned it safely" to friendly lines.

Owing to the dearth of experienced engineering officers, McClellan, who in the mid 1850s, had personally witnessed the siege of Sevastopol in the Crimean War, felt obliged to make many personal reconnaissances himself at the front lines of his besieging forces. He was often accompanied by his large and glittering staff, which included several volunteer aides from the French nobility, namely, the Orleans princes, including the Prince de Joinville and the Comte de Paris. On one of these occasions, while observing from a redoubt at the front, McClellan and his aides were spotted by Confederate gunners who opened fire upon them. As an eyewitness described it, when several enemy artillery projectiles struck close by, the startled prince "jumped and glanced nervously around, while McClellan quietly knocked the ashes from his cigar."

The strained relations between the Union commander and the administration in Washington continued during the one-month siege of Yorktown in April 1862. As a petulant McClellan related one such incident in a letter to his wife, "The President very coolly telegraphed me yesterday that he thought I had better break the enemy's lines at once! I was much tempted to reply that he had better come and do it himself." On the Confederate side, when Johnston arrived, his rapport with Davis was not at all good, but the Southern commander was at least blessed in having a general—the masterful

Left: Flattered by the attention from European commanders, the Federal officers delighted in posing with them. Brigadier General William F. Barry with British officers and two French noblemen. (NATIONAL LIBRARY OF MEDICINE)

Right: Several pose here on May 1, 1862, at headquarters in Camp Winfield Scott. Seated in the front row, left to right, are Captain L'Amy of the Royal Army and the Duc de Chartres. In the center row, seated, are Colonel Fletcher of the Royal Army, the Prince de Joinville, and Stewart Van Vliet. Standing from the left are Colonels Beaumont and Neville of the Royal Army, an unidentified man, the Comte de Paris, and another unidentified civilian. (USAMHI)

Above: Louis Philippe Albert d'Orleans, Comte de Paris on the left, and Robert Philippe Louis d'Orleans, Duc de Chartres, on the right. Both wear the Union uniform in their capacity as aides to McClellan. (CHS)

Above: James F. Gibson's May 3, 1862, image of, from the left, the Duc de Chartres, the Prince de Joinville, and the Comte de Paris on the day of Yorktown's fall. (WAR LIBRARY AND MUSEUM, MOLLUS-PENNSYLVANIA)

Above: The Prince de Joinville, a familiar sight in McClellan's army. (USAMHI)

Above: Colonel V. DeChanal, French military observer. (USAMHI)

Robert E. Lee—positioned in Richmond as a buffer between himself and the Confederate President. Lee could and did get along amicably with both Davis and Johnston, and he was responsible in a large degree for amassing the force on the Peninsula that Johnston and Magruder had deployed at the Yorktown-Warwick River line.

As April waned, both sides worked feverishly to strengthen their positions. McClellan—who excelled at this sort of thing—laboriously wheeled into position some 114 big guns, howitzers, and mortars. Some of these were impressive pieces of siege weaponry. For example, close to the Farnholt House near the York River, a Federal battery was established which comprised five 100-pounder Parrotts and one monster 200-pounder Parrott. Others included 10-inch and 13-inch siege mortars. The Confederates, on the other hand, while possessing some large, modern, rifled pieces, also had to make do with older and less effective 32-pounder naval smoothbores and columbiads. After completing a 4,000-yard-long first parallel, McClellan's troops then began a second parallel much closer to the main Confederate defenses. All these activities were slowed by continuing torrential rains, execrable roads, and shortages of supply wagons.

But Joe Johnston saw the writing on the wall. He knew his troops and defenses could not stand up to the greatly superior weight of metal that the mushrooming Union batteries would be able to throw when they were ready to open fire. "We are engaged in a species of warfare," Johnston acknowledged in a message to Davis and Lee on April 30, "at which we can never win. It is plain that General McClellan will adhere to the system adopted by him last summer, and depend for success upon artillery and engineering. We can compete with him in neither." Lee and the Confederate President concurred.

Finally, on May 4, just as the massed Federal artillery was about to open a mammoth bombardment of Yorktown, Johnston wisely withdrew his troops and as many of his guns as he could, blew up some of his powder magazines, and retreated precipitately toward Williamsburg

Above: Gibson's photo of several of the British observers. (LIBRARY OF CON-GRESS)

Above: Lieutenant George T. Munroe, Royal Canadian Rifles. (USAMHI)

Above: The commander of Royal Army forces in Canada, Lieutenant General Sir John Michel, K.C.B. (USAMHI)

Above: H. M. Hippisley of the Royal Navy. (USAMHI)

Above: And best known of all, Colonel Arthur Fremantle of the Royal Army, who wrote of and published his experiences with both Union and Confederate armies. (THE NEW-YORK HISTORI-CAL SOCIETY)

Right: But this campaign was for the Americans. McClellan's topographical engineers, photographed by Gibson on May 2, 1862. The use of the pistols to hold the corners of the map was a bit melodramatic of the engineers, but their services were invaluable in an area for which reliable maps were not available. (LC)

Below: A special feature of McClellan's army was Colonel Hiram Berdan and his United States Sharpshooters, men selected and trained for their marksmanship and equipped with special rifles. (USAMHI)

Above: McClellan's antagonist looked every inch a great general. The resplendent Major General John Barkhead Magruder—"Prince John." He managed to completely mislead McClellan about his strength in the works at Yorktown, thereby delaying the Federals for precious days while Richmond forwarded more Confederates to the front. (LOUISIANA STATE UNIVERSITY, DEPARTMENT OF ARCHIVES AND MANUSCRIPTS)

Left: Isaac M. St. John was Magruder's chief engineer at Yorktown, responsible largely for the defenses that so intimidated McClellan. (USAMHI)

Above: Brigadier General Samuel R. Anderson was nea sixty but still exercised active command of one of Magru brigades. Ill health forced him to resign just one week aft evacuation of Yorktown. (USAMHI)

and Richmond. "Yorktown is in our possession," McClellan telegraphed Washington triumphantly. So was Gloucester Point. Only then could the Union commander speed troops up the York River to Eltham's Landing, near Brick House Point, opposite West Point, to speed the Confederate retreat—a retreat that was made possible by a partially successful rearguard stand made by the graycoats on May 5 at Williamsburg. As McClellan's Army of the Potomac moved into the evacuated Warwick River and Yorktown fortifications, they captured some seventy-seven heavy guns that Johnston had been unable to remove in his hasty retrograde movement—a loss the Confederates could ill afford. But the Federals also discovered, at the cost of some fatalities, a new engine of destruction in the form of primitive but effective land mines, then called "torpedoes." These were apparently innovated and ordered to be placed in positions around wells, springs, and elsewhere by Gabriel J. Rains. These land mines were regular 8-inch and 10-inch columbiad shells buried a few inches in the ground, and rigged with the ordinary cannon friction primer, or fulminate of mercury, so that they detonated when moved or stepped upon. So angered was McClellan at these devices that he ordered Confederate prisoners to discover the torpedoes and remove them. Some Southerners also considered the use of the "torpedoes" unethical, and James Longstreet directed Rains to halt the practice. But later in the war both sides employed land mines efficaciously.

Following the capture of Yorktown, McClellan moved up the Peninsula via Yorktown to close in on Richmond. Yorktown was held by the Federals throughout the remainder of the war, its dockage facilities being used, along with those at Fort Monroe and later of City Point, in the final campaigns of the war against Richmond and Petersburg. Yorktown was the first major operation of the initial massive campaign of the Civil War in the eastern theater of operations, and it drew to the scene a number of photographers who were attracted there not only by the large military movements then unfolding, but also because of the historical associations of the place during the final and pivotal campaign of the revolution which had paved the way for the birth of the republic.

The skillful defense of the Yorktown-Warwick River line by first Magruder and then Johnston, combined with McClellan's caution, enabled Lee to take steps to better defend Richmond with fortifications and additional troops so as to hold the capital of the Confederacy through three more years of grim warfare before the final ennobling scene took

Right: At Lee's Mill, soon after McClellan began his investment of Yorktown, Magruder stood off an engagement on April 16. Here is McClellan's uncharacteristically unpretentious headquarters during the battle. Brattleboro, Vermont, photographer G. W. Houghton, who accompanied Vermont troops to the Peninsula, made this image as part of his excellent series of unpublished photographs. (VERMONT HISTORICAL SOCIETY)

Left: Houghton's portrait of Brigadier General William F. Smith, commanding a division that included the Vermonters. It was taken in April 1862, at the Gaines House. Seated at left is Captain Romeyn B. Ayers, later a noted general. (VHS)

Above: Magruder made his headquarters in the large house on the left in this photo of Yorktown made by Brady's company within days of the evacuation. (USAMHI)

Below: The sally port into the defenses around Yorktown, just after McClellan occupied the quiet town. (USAMHI)

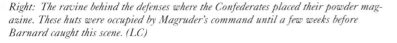

Above: George N. Bernard's photograph of Magruder's headquarters in June 1862. "Prince John" not only dressed in style but lived that way as well. (USAMHI)

Right: The ravine behind the defenses where the Confederates placed their powder magazine. These huts were occupied by Magruder's command until a few weeks before Barnard caught this scene. (LC)

Above: Both North and South drew inspiration from the American successes in the Revolution, and Yorktown was a storied place indeed Here on the right the building that served as headquarters for Charles Lord Cornwallis during Washington's siege of Yorktown. Magruder used it as a hospital, as would Dorothea Dix shortly afterward. Brady & Company's May 1862 image. (KEAN ARCHIVES)

Above: The front line of the works Magruder and St. John built to hold back McClellan. (USAMHI)

Above: Making the best use of the materials at hand, St. John sometimes employed bales of cotton along with sandbags in building his earthworks. When hit, the bales really showed what they were made of. (USAMHI)

Above: Barnard's June photo of a Confederate battery, with McClellan's Battery No. 1 in the distance. The Confederates liked to name their cannons for their generals. As seen by the remnant of an ammunition box in the foreground, this gun—now gone—was named after Major General D. H. Hill. (USAMHI)

Above: A naval battery near the Nelson church in Yorktown, shown on George N. Barnard's July 1862 image. At left are arranged loads of canister—tin cans filled with lead or iron balls—and stands of grapeshot, clusters of a dozen or more larger iron projectiles fired like a scatter-load from the cannon. (LC)

Above: Magruder also erected defenses at Gloucester Point, including this large Dahlgren smoothbore. (USAMHI)

Below: The much-touted Water Battery, strongest of the Confederate works preventing McClellan's easy conquest of Yorktown that he expected. (USAMHI)

Above: The Water Battery became a favorite place for the Federals to pose after Magruder evacuated. Barnard was happy to catch them as they lounged in the works... (USAMHI)

Below: ... and walked the parapet overlooking the York. (USAMHI)

Left: Part of Magruder's defenses, with the York River in the background. (USAMHI)

Below: Gloucester Point, with Yorktown in the distance, and more Dahlgren naval guns. (NLM)

Below: These Rodman guns in the Water Battery bear Magruder's name on their carriages, probably put there when they were being shipped to him from elsewhere in the Confederacy. (LC)

Right: Magruder took as many of his cannons with him as possible when he evacuated. Others had to be abandoned to the enemy, and this one, at least, he did not mind leaving. An exploded gun at one of the inland batteries. By Barnard. (USAMHI)

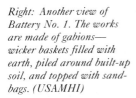

Above: Gibson's photo of Battery No. 4, whose eight mortars lobbed shells into Yorktown constantly. The barge holds their powder and shells. Built into the earth itself are the gunners' quarters, a "bombproof" protecting them from enemy fire. (LC)

Left: McClellan's Battery No. 1 below Yorktown, taken by Gibson in May 1862. McClellan's earthworks are masterpieces. (LC)

Right: Another view of Battery No. 1. The works are made of gabions—wicker baskets filled with earth, piled around built-up soil, and topped with sand-bags. (USAMHI)

Below: The Farnholt House behind Battery No. 1, seen at left. Gunners used the roof to observe the effect of their shells. (USAMHI)

Right: McClellan's headquarters, Camp Winfield Scott, taken by Gibson on the day Magruder evacuated. (USAMHI)

Right: Always the tourists, Federal soldiers visit "Cornwallis' Cave," the small cavern where the British general reputedly took refuge from Washington's artillery in 1781. (NLM)

Left: "Little Mac's" tent in the center, the day of his "victory" over Magruder. (LC)

Left: And officers of the 1st Connecticut Artillery pulled enemy shells from within the cave for jaunty poses like this one, published by Brady & Company. (LC, FITZ JOHN PORTER PAPERS)

Right: Magruder's evacuation was not a simple affair, even given the superb deception he had worked on McClellan. Brigadier General Lafayette McLaws was largely responsible for capably covering the retreat. It won him a promotion. (MUSEUM OF THE CONFEDERACY, RICHMOND)

Above: Magruder used the cave as a powder magazine. Brady's assistants used it as a backdrop for images like this. (USAMHI)

Above: Major General Gustavus W. Smith attacked McClellan's pursuing Federals at Eltham's Landing on May 7 while he covered the withdrawal of Magruder's army. It was effectively the end of the Yorktown campaign. (TULANE UNIVERSITY)

Above: Brigadier General Gabriel J. Rains also contributed his part. One of D. H. Hill's brigade commanders, he laced the roads out of Yorktown with hidden shells triggered to explode when stepped upon. "Infernal machines" they were called, or "torpedoes." He had just pioneered the antipersonnel mine. Even many Confederates thought it a barbarous concept. (USAMHI)

The New Ironclads

WILLIAM N. STILL

Invention went wild in the race for newer and more powerful iron behemoths

Above: The Union Navy granted contracts for three radically different ironclad vessels at first. Here the USS New Ironsides, *powerful and effective, though largely conventional in design. (SMITHSONIAN INSTITUTION)*

ON MARCH 9, 1862, occurred what has rightly been called one of the most important naval engagements in American history. Two iron-armored warships, the USS *Monitor* and the CSS *Virginia*, met in mortal combat, the first such battle in history. Although not the first ironclad warships completed and battle-tested, they were the first completed in North America and the first that fought against each other. They were responsible for the decision by both Abraham Lincoln's and Jefferson Davis's governments to create a powerful naval force of armored vessels.

The Confederates took the first step. Perhaps this was inevitable considering the fact that the South lacked both a navy and the potential to keep pace with their opponents in building warships. On May 9, 1861, Confederate Secretary of the Navy Stephen R. Mallory wrote in an oft-quoted report, "I regard the possession of an iron-armored ship as a matter of the first necessity.... If we... follow their [the United States Navy's]... example and build wooden ships, we shall have to construct several at one time; for one or two ships would fall easy prey to her comparatively numerous steam frigates. But inequality of numbers may be compensated by invulnerability; and thus not only does economy but naval success dictate the wisdom and expediency of fighting with iron against wood." That same day the Confederate Congress appropriated $2,000,000 for the purchase or construction of ironclads in Europe. Although the Confederacy would contract for several powerful armored vessels in England and France, initial efforts were unsuccessful. Secretary Mallory then determined to construct ironclads within the Confederacy. In the middle of July the decision was made to convert the *Merrimack* into the *Virginia*, and six weeks later contracts were awarded for the construction of two ironclads later named the *Arkansas* and *Tennessee* to be built in Memphis; a fourth one, the *Mississippi*, was to be built in New Orleans. In September the *Louisiana* was also laid down in New Orleans. These five initial armor clads were designed to operate on the open sea as well as on inland waters. They were designed not only to break the blockade, but as Secretary Mallory wrote, to "traverse the entire coast of the United States... and encounter, with a fair prospect of success, their entire Navy." In other words, Mallory's initial ironclad strategy was offensive in nature.

The strategy was a failure. Only three of the vessels, the *Arkansas*, *Louisiana*, and *Virginia*, became operational; the other two were destroyed while still under construction. Of the three that were commissioned only the *Arkansas* was used for offensive purposes. During its brief career, it achieved some dramatic success, despite poor design and construction. It was 165 feet in length and carried a battery of ten guns. Its armor was made up of railroad T-rails, and it was powered by inadequate riverboat machinery. The casemate, unlike those found on the other Confederate ironclads, was perpendicular rather than slanted. On July 15, 1862, this awkward-looking warship ran through a large fleet of Union vessels anchored above Vicksburg and successfully resisted several planned attempts to destroy it. In August the *Arkansas* was to participate in a combined operation on Baton Rouge, Louisiana, but because of a breakdown in the machinery, the ironclad was blown up by its crew.

Above: To his credit, Secretary of the Navy Gideon Welles, ridiculous wig and all, supported the ironclad idea from the first. Despite his lack of naval experience he saw what many could not, that wooden ships were things of the past. (NA)

Above: But very effective, and very revolutionary, was the design for the USS Monitor. *Much of the vessel was constructed here on Long Island. (U.S. NAVAL HISTORICAL CENTER)*

The *Louisiana*'s career was briefer and less successful. As envisioned by its builder, E. C. Murray, the armor-clad was to be 264 feet in length, 64 in beam, with a battery of twenty-two guns and propelled by two paddle wheels and two 4-foot propellers. The most unorthodox feature in his design was twin wheels along the centerline, one abaft the other in a well. The ship was still being fitted out when Admiral Farragut's squadron began its ascent of the Mississippi River. The large Confederate ironclad was towed down the river and moored near Fort Jackson. Here as a floating battery it engaged the Union vessels and was destroyed by its crew when the fort surrendered.

The *Virginia* achieved the most notable success of the initial ironclads. It was converted from the captured and partially destroyed sloop-of-war *Merrimack* at the Gosport Navy Yard in Norfolk. Frequently considered to be the prototype of all the Confederate ironclads, it was in fact an experimental vessel constructed only because the Confederacy needed to get a power-

Above: The USS Galena *was not a success, its thin iron sheathing proving easily vulnerable to Confederate shore batteries at Drewry's Bluff in May 1862. James Gibson's photo taken in July. (USAMHI)*

Above: And here it rests in Gibson's July 9, 1862, photograph, taken on the James River. The turret shows the indentations made by the Virginia's *solid shot during their epic battle at Hampton Roads. (USAMHI)*

Above: While monitors would become a mania in the East, in the western waters a different sort of ironclad came about. The first river ironclads were converted snag boats, like the Benton. *With sixteen guns mounted on its deck, it was the most powerful vessel on the Mississippi and flagship of Foote's fleet at Island No. 10 and Davis's fleet in the battle at Memphis. (KA)*

Above: Soon new ships were under construction, however, at places like the Carondelet Marine Railway at Carondelet, Missouri. Here two "city class" ironclads are being built. Their builder, James B. Eads, could construct one in forty-five days, start to finish. (NA, U. S. WAR DEPARTMENT GENERAL STAFF)

Above: Here the finished products rest at anchor at Cairo, Illinois. These "Pook turtles" were the backbone of the Mississippi fleet. At left the USS Baron De Kalb, *in the center the USS* Cincinnati, *and on the right the USS* Mound City. *The De Kalb was formerly the USS* St. Louis, *the first of Eads's boats to launch. (NYHS)*

Above: Another converted snag boat became the USS Essex, *an unfortunate vessel that would be much damaged and beset with difficulty throughout the war. A photograph by Dr. J. T. Field taken while the ship lay moored off Memphis in 1864. Mortar boats lie to its left bow. (CIVIL WAR TIMES ILLUSTRATED COLLECTION)*

ful ironclad operational as quickly as possible in that part of the South. The 262-foot vessel had a casemate 170 feet long, inclined on the sides with the ends horizontally rounded. The rounded ends along with the bow and stern of the hull being submerged were unique; no other Confederate ironclad incorporated these features. The armor, rolled at Tredegar Iron Works in Richmond from railroad iron into plates, was 4 inches thick attached in two layers. The ironclad carried a battery of ten guns, four to a side and a pivot rifle at each end. On March 8, 1862, it attacked units of the North Atlantic Blockading Squadron in Hampton Roads and destroyed the frigate *Congress* and the sloop-of-war *Cumberland.* The following day it fought the *Monitor* and for over a month successfully defended the entrance to the James River. Early in May, Norfolk was captured. With no base to return to and a draft too deep to allow it to ascend the James, the ship was destroyed by its crew to prevent its capture.

With the destruction of the *Arkansas, Louisiana,* and *Virginia,* the first Confederate ironclad program ended. Mallory's vision of a few powerful armored vessels to sweep Union warships from the seas was a failure. Unlike the Confederates', the Union Navy's initial ironclad program was tentative; professional opinion differed over the type of armored vessel to build. Early in August 1861, Congress appropriated $1,500,000 for the "construction or completion of iron or steelclad steamers or steam batteries," and authorized the creation of a board of naval officers to examine proposals and make recommendations. Then in September the board recommended that contracts be awarded for three vessels; a seagoing broadside type of vessel commissioned *New Ironsides,* a lightly armored wooden vessel, the *Galena,* and a revolving turret vessel, the *Monitor.* While the board of naval officers deliberated, the army had already contracted for seven ironclads for service on the Mississippi River and its tributaries.

These seven ironclads have been called "Pook turtles" after their designer, Samuel M.

Above: William "Dirty Bill" Porter designed the conversion of the Essex and commanded her, while also taking a hand in the fashioning of the ungainly Lafayette *and* Choctaw. *(LC)*

Left: Then came the behemoth ironclads, designed by "Dirty Bill" Porter and built by Eads. The USS Lafayette *carried eight heavy guns and a shield of iron laid over rubber, intended to make shot bounce off the casemate. In practice, it did not. (USAMHI)*

Below: Equally formidable in appearance was the USS Choctaw, *it, too, carrying eight heavy cannons. Both ships were ready to ply the rivers by late 1862. (KA)*

Pook, or the "city class," because they were named after western river ports. They were commissioned the *Cairo, Carondelet, Cincinnati, Louisville, Mound City, Pittsburg,* and *St. Louis* (later *Baron De Kalb*). Pook designed wooden, flat-bottomed light draft and low freeboard center-wheelers measuring 175 feet in length. Each gunboat was to be armed with ten 8-inch shell guns. With slanted casemates covered with 2 1/2-inch armor, they were similar in appearance to Confederate ironclads. These ironclads had defects found on nearly all of the armored vessels of this type built by both sides during the war—they were underpowered, too heavy, and vulnerable to high, arched "plunging fire" directed at their roofs. Nevertheless, they saw more service than any other class of river ironclads, fighting in various engagements from Fort Henry to Vicksburg and beyond. Three of them (*Cairo, Cincinnati,* and the *Baron De Kalb*) would be sunk.

The army was also responsible for the conversion of four large river vessels into ironclads. A snag boat was converted into the casemated ironclad *Benton* while the *Essex,* also casemated, was a rebuilt center-wheel ferryboat. The *Benton* carried sixteen heavy guns while the *Essex* carried six. Two side-wheelers named the *Lafayette* and the *Choctaw* were purchased in St. Louis and converted under the supervision of navy Commander William "Dirty Bill" Porter. Although the *Lafayette* would have a sloping casemate, the *Choctaw* would have a stationary turret with inclined sides and a curved top—"a war dome, like the dome on the Court House in St. Louis"—and be pierced to hold four guns. Just forward and aft of the wheels were two small casemates. On top of the forward casemate, which housed two howitzers to sweep the decks

Above: The USS Ozark *was unusual on the Mississippi. It carried a turret of Ericsson's design forward, and mounted four other cannon on the main deck. (USAMHI)*

Above: A variety of less formidable ironclads and "tinclads" plied the Western rivers, boats like the USS General Grant, shown here at Kingston, Georgia. (NA)

Above: David D. Porter had little good to say about any of the Mississippi ironclads. He was a devotee of the conventional Ericsson monitor design. (USAMHI)

Above: And so, obviously, was John Ericsson himself. Arrogant, egotistical, and painfully difficult to work with, he was still a genius of sorts, and the Union turned to him through most of the war for its monitor designs. (NHC)

Above: Admiral Hiram Paulding backed Ericsson's original Monitor design and worked hard to expedite its building and adoption by the navy. He succeeded. (NYHS)

if the enemy should board, was located a conical pilothouse, covered with 2 inches of iron. Commander Porter designed the armor himself. The *Choctaw* had two l-inch layers of iron and a l-inch layer of vulcanized India rubber cushions, while the *Lafayette's* sloping casemate was covered with 1-inch iron over 1-inch India rubber. The navy took over the eleven ironclads after they were completed, and they operated as units of the Mississippi Squadron throughout the war.

The navy also contracted for ironclads on the western rivers. Three of them, the *Chillicothe, Tuscumbia,* and *Indianola,* were built by Joseph Brown in Cincinnati. Each had a small casemate forward containing two 11-inch rifled guns and a casemate astern between two paddle wheels. All three were regarded as inefficient. The *Chillicothe's* first commanding officer pronounced it a "cumbersome scow," and after the battle of Grand Gulf in April 1863, the *Tuscumbia's* captain referred to his vessel as "a Disgrace."

These river ironclads were all laid down or converted during 1861 and early 1862, months before the engagement between the *Monitor* and the *Virginia.* The *Galena* was also under construction at Mystic, Connecticut, during these months.

The *Galena* was, according to Commodore Joseph Smith, senior officer of the Ironclad Board, "a Lighter boat... intended to have more speed than other ironclads to work in part under canvas." It resembled the wooden steam warships of that day except that the upper part of its sides was rounded inward or "tumbled home" at an angle of about 45 degrees to deflect projectiles. A battery of six guns was mounted on a gun deck protected by armor not quite 4 inches in thickness. It had two l-inch plates of armor on its sides separated by an air space in which there were iron bars. Although it was rigged as a schooner, all the masts, except the fore lower mast kept for a lookout position, were removed. It was built by C. S. Bushnell and Company and commissioned in April 1862. In May, the *Galena* was one of the vessels of the North Atlantic

Blockading Squadron that ascended the James River and engaged the Confederate batteries at Drewry's Bluff. It was badly damaged; its thin armor penetrated thirteen times. Later the armor was removed, and the *Galena* completed the war as a wooden-hulled ship.

The *New Ironsides* was a traditional broadside type warship, but 170 feet of its 230-foot hull were covered with iron armor 4½ inches in thickness. The armor belt covered the sides and deck, generally amidship, with bow and stern unarmored. This citadel protected the main battery of sixteen 11-inch Dahlgren guns. Classified a frigate, this large (more than 4,000 tons displacement) and powerful ironclad was built by Merrick & Sons in Philadelphia. *New Ironsides* spent its entire Civil War career with either the South Atlantic or the North Atlantic blockading squadrons. In April 1863 the armored warship participated in Admiral Samuel F. Du Pont's attack on Confederate positions in Charleston harbor, and in this and subsequent attacks it was hit repeatedly by enemy fire without suffering any damage. In October it was slightly damaged by the Confederate torpedo boat *David*, but after repairs it participated in Admiral David D. Porter's attacks on Fort Fisher. *New Ironsides* was the most powerful ironclad completed by the Union during the war and undoubtedly the most effective in the combined operations along the Southern coastline. It was the only seagoing armored cruiser to be completed during the war. An improved armored cruiser, the *Dunderberg*, was laid down but not completed until after Appomattox. The board of naval officers who had recommended the three original armored vessels wrote that "ocean going [armored] cruisers are for the time being impracticable." This report may have had some effect on Union policy concerning armored vessels, but the major factors were the influence of Assistant Secretary of the Navy Gustavus Fox and the *Monitor's*

Above: Above: Captain Francis H. Gregory, a hero of the era of iron men in wooden ships, superintended the construction of ironclads for Welles. (NYHS)

Below: The first turreted ironclads to follow the Monitor *were those of the* Passaic *class, and they were the workhorse ironclads of the Atlantic coast. Here the launch of the* Camanche *of that class. This launch took place in San Francisco, California, where the vessel was shipped in parts and reconstructed. An 1864 photograph by C. E. Watkins. (CHARLES S. SCHWARTZ)*

Above: Chief Engineer Alban Stimers managed most of the construction of the original Monitor, *fought aboard her at Hampton Roads, and later lost his reputation with the unsuccessful Casco class of light-draft monitors. (NHC)*

Above: Officers working under Gregory, like Chief Engineer James W. King, oversaw individual ironclads to completion. King supervised the Manayunk, Catawba, *and* Tippecanoe. *Later he built the* Ozark, Chickasaw, *and* Winnebago, *out west. (LC)*

Above: The anchor well of the Catskill. Note how the anchor could be raised and lowered from within, without exposing men to fire. (NHC)

Above: The USS Catskill, *photographed in Charleston harbor in 1863, one of the most powerful—and most damaged—Passaics. (USAMHI)*

Above: An officer's cabin aboard the Catskill. *A beam of light enters through the skylight scuttle overhead. A watertight bulkhead door is closed behind the desk and above it on the bulkhead is a print of the original* Monitor *at sea. (NHC)*

Above: The Catskill's turret machinery, the enormously heavy turret resting on and being turned by the massive vertical shaft at left. (NHC)

designer, John Ericsson, and the impact of the battle between the *Monitor* and the *Virginia* on Northern public opinion.

As early as December 1861 the Navy Department had requested $12,000,000 to construct twenty additional turreted vessels. As designed, they were to mount a type of turret developed by Captain Cowper Coles of the British Royal Navy. Ericsson, however, persuaded the navy to substitute a turret designed by him for the Coles turret. The *Monitor's* success was primarily responsible for this decision.

The *Monitor* was a unique warship. Designed as a harbor defense vessel, instead of a standard ship hull it had a large armored "raft" 172 feet by 41 feet, 6 inches supported by a lower section of wood 122 feet long and 34 feet wide. The "raft" was designed to increase stability in a seaway and protect the hull from ramming. The vessel's power plant consisted of two boilers and two engines that were of Ericsson's design, as was the revolving turret, which was the armor-clad's most novel feature. The *Monitor* incorporated numerous technical advances for that time including forced ventilation of living spaces, a protected anchor which could be raised and lowered without it or the crew members being exposed to enemy fire, and a protected pilothouse. The turret carried two 11-inch Dahlgren smoothbores. The *Monitor* was completed in early February 1862, and a month later it left under tow to join the North Atlantic Blockading Squadron. Its fortuitous arrival at Hampton Roads in time to challenge the *Virginia* is well known. The *Monitor* won a tactical victory in preventing the destruction of Union vessels in the Roads, and in doing so it produced such an intense enthusiasm in the North that a "monitor fever" swept the Union. From then until the end of the war the Union would concentrate on building monitor-type vessels. It is ironic that the Union Navy which obviously had to assume an offensive strategy in order to win the war, adopted as its principal

Below: A similar, unpublished view of the engine room of the Camanche *while it was being reassembled in San Francisco. (CHARLES S. SCHWARTZ)*

Above: The engine room of the Catskill, *showing part of the steam engine that powered not only the screw, but also the turret machinery. (NHC)*

The USS Nahant *undergoing repairs at Hilton Head, South Carolina, after being heavily damaged in the April 7, 1863, attack on Charleston, carried out largely by* Passaic-*class monitors like the* Nahant. *(USAMHI)*

Left: Rear Admiral Samuel F.I. Du Pont commanded the fleet that attacked Charleston. Seeing the relatively low firepower of the monitors and seeing the heavy damage inflicted on them by Confederate batteries, he formed a poor opinion of monitors as offensive vessels. His entire monitor fleet fired 139 shots in the same time that it received at least 346 hits. (USAMHI)

ironclad a type of vessel that was basically defensive in nature.

On March 21, three weeks after the battle, Ericsson received contracts for six enlarged and improved versions of the *Monitor* while four additional ships of the same class were ordered from other builders. These were the ten *Passaics*—the *Passaic, Montauk, Catskill, Patapsco, Lehigh, Sangamon,* (later renamed *Jason), Camanche, Nahant, Nantucket,* and *Weehawken.* Like the original *Monitor,* each had a single turret, increased thickness of armor, a permanent stack, and a more powerful battery. These vessels as a class were to see more service than any others of the monitor fleet. They were the major ironclad units of both the South Atlantic and North Atlantic blockading squadrons. Monitors of this class participated in the combined operations against Charleston and Savannah, and in the James River.

In 1862 the Navy Department also initiated the construction of double-turreted monitors. The *Onondaga* was built at Continental Iron Works, Greenpoint, New York, under contract with George W. Quintard. Commissioned early in 1864, it was 226 feet long and carried a battery of two 15-inch Dahlgren smoothbores and two 150 pounder Parrott rifles. This vessel spent its entire war career in the James River and was decommissioned after the war. Four additional double turreted monitors were built in navy yards—*Miantonomoh, Monadnock, Agamenticus* (later renamed *Terror),* and *Tonawanda* (later

Left: The next step in improving monitor firepower was two turrets. The Onondaga *was commissioned in March 1864 and proved thoroughly reliable, though it saw very little action. Here it is in the James River, scene of most of its war service. (USAMHI)*

Right: Next came the Miantonomoh *class, ships like the* Tonawanda, *shown here. Only one of them was finished in time to serve in the war, but they were far more seaworthy than their predecessors. (P-M)*

Left: The Miantonomoh *itself actually steamed to Europe, proving the deep-sea capabilities of the monitor type. It appears here at the Washington Navy Yard in 1865. On the left is the USS* Montauk *of the* Passaic *class. In the distance is the light-draft monitor* Chimo *and, just visible behind it, the tall masts of the Confederate ironclad ram* Stonewall. *(NHC)*

Left: Ericsson, meanwhile, turned his mind to much larger seagoing monitors, his Dictator *class. Only two were built, and neither was very successful. Here the* Puritan *peeks out of the shiphouse at the Continental Iron Works at Green Point, New York. (NHC)*

Above: The launch of the USS Dictator, *December 26, 1863, at the Delamater Iron Works. (THE MARINERS MUSEUM, NEWPORT NEWS, VIRGINIA)*

Above: Ready to slide down the ways, the Dictator *looms above the speakers' platform, flag-draped for the dedication ceremonies. (NYHS)*

Above: Stimers's light-draft monitor Casco *on the James River. The* Casco-*type monitors were found to be ill-designed and barely awash, so their turrets were left off and they were turned into torpedo boats instead. (USAMHI)*

Left: The launch of the light-draft USS Modoc, *photographed by the New York artist J. H. Beal in 1864. (NHC)*

Left: James Eads designed powerful light-draft river "monitors" Osage *and* Neosho *to operate in barely four feet of water. Ungainly, they still proved effective against most enemy fire. Here the* Osage, *probably in the Red River in 1864. (LC)*

renamed *Amphitrite*). These vessels were twin-screw, wooden-hulled ironclads over 258 feet in length. Of these four, only the *Monadnock* was completed prior to the end of the war, but it saw no combat. This class, however, was considered the most efficient of the monitor type built during the war and these vessels remained in service for many years afterward.

In September 1862, orders were given to various builders for nine more Ericsson monitors. *Canonicus, Catawba, Oneonta, Mahopac, Manhattan, Tecumseh, Saugus, Manayunk* (later *Ajax*), and *Tippecanoe* (later *Wyandotte*) were similar to the *Passaics*, but with certain significant improvements—a defensive slope around the base of the turret to prevent jamming, a stronger hull, and a heavier battery of 15-inch guns. Five of this class were commissioned in time to see Civil War service, and the *Tecumseh* was sunk during the Battle of Mobile Bay.

The last of the coastal monitors contracted for in 1862 were the two giant single-turret monitors, *Puritan* and Dictator. Displacing more than 3,000 tons each and with large fuel capacities, these vessels were intended as oceangoing vessels. They were built in New York under contract with John Ericsson. Their 312-foot hulls were to be protected by 6-inch side armor. The single turrets would carry two 15-inch Dahlgren smoothbores each. The *Dictator*, after being commissioned in December 1864, joined the North Atlantic Blockading Squadron but saw no action. The *Puritan* was never completed.

The largest single class of monitor-type vessels was the *Casco* class. In the spring of 1863, contracts were signed for the construction of twenty of this type. However, during the war only eight were completed, and they were considered unseaworthy. Five of them were converted to torpedo boats, but none saw action.

Monitors were also constructed for operations on the western rivers. Shortly after the Hampton Roads engagement, James B. Eads received a contract to build three single-turreted monitors of his own design, although the Navy Department insisted that Ericsson's turret be used instead of one designed by Eads. The three river monitors, named *Osage, Neosho*, and *Ozark*, were unlike other monitors in that they were propelled by stern wheels. Unfortunately, the wheels (protected by armored casings) made it impossible for the turrets to turn a full 360 degrees. The *Ozark* was larger and carried additional armament of questionable value—four pivot guns located upon the open deck. They were unusual-looking vessels with virtually nothing showing above the waterline but the turret, the iron-plated house for the stern paddle wheel, and the tall, thin stacks.

Eads received a second contract for monitors. The four vessels built under this contract—*Chickasaw, Kickapoo, Milwaukee*, and *Winnebago*—were double-turreted ironclads, with one turret by Ericsson's design and one by Eads's design. The Eads turret was more sophisticated than Ericsson's. The guns in the turret were mounted on a steam operated elevator which dropped them to a lower deck where they were loaded and then hoisted and run out through ports opened by automatic steam operated shutters. These vessels carried four guns each—two per turret—and were the only monitors ever built with triple screws and rudders. They were prin-

cipally employed with the West Gulf Blockading Squadron operating in Mobile Bay and its vicinity and were generally considered the most serviceable of the river monitors.

The monitor-type had the great advantage of achieving a maximum of impenetrability through two radical factors—low freeboard and the concentration of guns in the armored turret. The guns could be aimed without moving the ship. In confined and sheltered waters the monitors were excellent defensive ships, but they had serious defects that affected Union naval operations. A majority of them were essentially floating batteries that had to be towed from port to port; even in the rivers they could rarely stem the current. They were unseaworthy and had so little reserve buoyancy that a leak could be fatal. For these reasons they were unsuitable for blockade service, the primary mission of the Union Navy. In anything but a flat calm a monitor's deck was awash. The crew had to remain below with hatches battened down. As Admiral Du Pont wrote: "How can such vesels lay off ports… and protect the wooden vessels."

The western rivers were generally more suitable for the monitor type, but even here there were problems. The gunboats' maneuverability was poor, and they had little protection from plunging shot, a serious defect considering the many miles of bluffs along the waterways.

Even more important was their unsuitability for offensive operations. Loading their guns usually required from six to eight minutes. "This delay," as one authority has written, "violated the cardinal principal of naval gunnery, volume of fire." In the attack by the *New Ironsides, Keokuk,* and seven monitors on Fort Sumter in April 1863, only 139 rounds were fired by the combined batteries of the ironclads' guns. At the same time 76 guns in the Confederate forts rained some 2,206 shots on the Union vessels. As Admiral Du Pont wrote Secretary Welles, "I… remind the Department that ability to endure is not sufficient element where with to gain victories, that endurance must be accompanied with a corresponding power to inflict injury upon the enemy… that the weakness of the monitor class of vessels… is fatal to their attempts against fortifications."

The most unusual turreted vessel commissioned during the Civil War was the converted wooden sloop-of-war *Roanoke.* Like her sister ship, the *Merrimack,* converted by the Confederates into the *Virginia,* she was cut down, and three center-line turrets were installed. With a high freeboard, she was not a monitor-type vessel. Because of instability and a deep draft, she was considered unsuitable for active service and spent the war defending New York harbor from possible attack by Confederate cruisers.

While the Union ironclad building program after 1861 emphasized the monitor type of vessel, the Confederate program on the other hand would change from one which stressed offensive vessels in 1861 to one emphasizing defensive vessels. The apparent unseaworthiness of the *Virginia* and the ironclads built in New Orleans and Memphis, the lack of adequate facilities, and qualified technical expertise, the belief that powerful armor-clads could be obtained in Europe, and most important, the growing threat to the Confederacy from invasion and amphibious assault all contributed to this change in poli-

Above: Soon after the Osage *and* Neosho *were begun, Eads started work on another class of light-draft river monitor, the* Winnebagos. *These included turrets designed by Eads, which were far superior to Ericsson's. They did good service on the Mississippi and at Mobile Bay and proved to be the spiritual progenitor of warships for a century to come. Here the USS* Milwaukee, *commissioned at Mound City in August 1864. It struck a "torpedo" on March 28, 1865, and sank. (USAMHI)*

Above: The only three-turreted monitor built during the war, the USS Roanoke. *Originally a steam frigate, sister ship of the* Merrimack, *which the Confederates converted to the CSS* Virginia, *the* Roanoke *also was a conversion. Nearly destroyed by the Confederate ironclad in the battle at Hampton Roads, it was taken to the Brooklyn Navy Yard and the work of making it an ironclad commenced barely two weeks after the battle. The result was not spectacular. The* Roanoke *served two years with the North Atlantic Blockading Squadron, but proved rather ineffective. This previously unpublished photograph shows it at Brooklyn in mid 1865, the old ship-of-the-line USS* Vermont *in the left background . (NHC)*

Above: By the end of the war, sights like these two monitors lying off the Washington Navy Yard were commonplace. The war gave rise to a whole new generation of naval machines in the Union. An unpublished image by Kilburn Brothers of New Hampshire. (USAMHI)

Above: The Confederates looked to a different sort of ironclad, one more compatible with their limited technology and industrial facilities. No photographs of the Virginia *seem to have survived, but all subsequent Confederate ironclads followed the same general pattern originated by John Porter and John Brooke. Here the CSS* Chicora *in Charleston Harbor. On January 31, 1863,* Chicora *and its sister ship* Palmetto State *became the only Confederate ironclads to put to open sea when they steamed out and engaged elements of the blockading fleet successfully, then returned to port. (OLD COURT HOUSE MUSEUM, VICKSBURG)*

Right: Nearly as famous as the Virginia, *the CSS* Albemarle *was equally as unwieldy and slow, yet managed to threaten Albemarle Sound most effectively, sink one enemy warship, and aid materially in the capture of Plymouth, North Carolina. To counter this threat, Lieutenant William B. Cushing attacked it on the night of October 27, 1864, with a torpedo mounted on the end of a spar projecting from a steam launch. The* Albemarle *sank almost immediately and is here shown at the Norfolk Navy Yard in 1865 after being raised by the Federals. (NHC)*

Right: In Georgia's waters, Confederates constructed this casemated ironclad, the CSS Jackson, *only to find themselves so short of iron that it was never completed. The builders destroyed the ship before the Federals could capture it. This image may be by A. J. Riddle, who photographed the Andersonville prison camp in 1864. (TU, LOUISIANA HISTORICAL ASSOCIATION COLLECTION)*

Below: The CSS Atlanta, *now the USS* Atlanta, *patrolling the James. (USAMHI)*

Right: A remarkable unpublished view of the CSS Atlanta, *and perhaps the best illustration extant of the improvised nature of most Confederate ironclads. Taken after the war, this image probably shows the ship laid up at League Island, Pennsylvania, prior to its sale for salvage. It had been converted from the blockade runner* Fingal *in 1862, and the old* Fingal *hull shows clearly below the more streamlined additions that turned it into the* Atlanta. *This deep draft proved its undoing, for in its first engagement it ran aground and surrendered. The Federals later used it to patrol the James River. (THE MARINERS MUSEUM)*

cy. From 1862 until the end of the war, the Confederate naval construction program would concentrate on small, shallow-draft harbor defense armored vessels. Approximately forty of these vessels were laid down, and half of them were completed.

These small defense ironclads were designed by naval constructor John Porter. He developed a standard design which was sent to builders and contractors throughout the Confederacy. The original plan was for a 150-foot flat-bottomed vessel with hull to be partially armored and casemate to be completely covered with iron armor. The iron clad would carry a battery of six guns and be screw propelled. Although this design was utilized by the shipbuilders, it is, nevertheless, almost impossible to generalize about the Confederate armor-clads. There were noticeable differences because of modifications in size, machinery, armor, and battery. In size they ranged from the *Albemarle* and the *Neuse* (139 feet) up to several under construction during the latter months of the war that were over 250 feet in length. The 310-foot *Nashville* was the largest of this class.

The thickness of armor measured from 2 to 8 inches, but all of it was 2-inch laminated iron plate. On several vessels such as the *Arkansas* and *Louisiana* railroad iron—T-rails—was substituted because rolled plates were not available. The marine engines and boilers varied from ship to ship. Some of them were manufactured in the South; more of them were salvaged from other vessels. The method of propulsion consisted of either wheel or screw or a combination of both, as in the *Louisiana*, which had two wheels and two screws. A majority of them were screw steamers with either one or two propellers, but several such as the *Nashville* and *Missouri* were paddle-wheelers because of the accessibility of that kind of machinery. The machinery and propulsion units were notoriously inadequate and inefficient.

The Confederacy had more success in arming its ironclads than in providing motive power for them. There was really never a shortage of heavy guns although some of the ships' initial batteries consisted of a variety of guns. Smoothbores were carried at one time or another by nearly all of the armorclads, but in contrast to the Union Navy, which advocated smoothbores during and after the war, the Confederate Navy concentrated on rifled guns. The standard rifled gun used on the Confederate ironclads was the Brooke gun, a cast-iron banded cannon developed by John Brooke, who headed the Confederate Navy's Bureau of Ordnance and Hydrography. The principal types used on the ironclads were 7-inch and 6.4-inch guns. The Confederate Navy also equipped its ironclads in 1863 with spar torpedoes, egg-shaped copper vessels containing from fifty to seventy pounds of powder, fitted to a long pole attached to the bow of the vessel. Although Union naval officers universally referred to the Confederate ironclads as "rams," only a few of them actually had rams built on.

The 150-foot *Richmond*, laid down at the navy yard in Norfolk and completed in Richmond, was the first of Porter's harbor defense vessels completed. Other 150-foot ironclads commenced included the *Chicora, Raleigh, Palmetto State, North Carolina, Huntsville, Tuscaloosa,* and *Savannah.* Larger vessels included the *Jackson* (renamed *Muscogee), Fredericksburg,* and *Milledgeville* (175 feet); the *Virginia II* and *Charleston* (180 feet); *Missouri* (183 feet); the *Columbia, Texas,* and *Tennessee* (216 feet); and the *Nashville* (310 feet). Porter also designed a smaller vessel of this class to be used in the North Carolina sounds. Only two of these 139-foot ironclads, the *Albemarle* and the *Neuse,* were completed.

Although the casemated ironclad remained the standard "home water" vessel constructed within the Confederacy, two double-ender ironclads with two octagonal casemates were laid down in Richmond and Wilmington. They were similar in appearance to the Union double-turreted monitors, but since the casemates were not moveable turrets, pivot guns were to be utilized. Neither vessel was completed because of the lack of iron armor. No monitor types were constructed in the Confederacy, although one to be built at Columbus, Georgia, was approved. The proposed vessel was apparently never laid down. Secretary of the Navy Mallory preferred the standard casemated ironclad. Less than two months before General Lee surrendered at Appomattox Court House, the secretary was writing, "for river, harbor, and coast defense, the sloping shield and general plan of armored vessels adopted by us... are the best that could be adopted in our situation. In ventilation, light, fighting space, and quarters it is believed that the sloping shield presents greater advantages than the *Monitor* turret."

The ironclads did contribute significantly to the Confederate war effort. They did not break or seriously challenge the Union blockade, but after the spring of 1862, this was not their primary objective. From then until the end of the war their real function was to defend the rivers, inlets, and ports. In this they had some success. Of the five seaports—Savannah, Charleston, Wilmington, Mobile, and Galveston—taken in the last six months of the war, two were taken by land forces from the rear, and two indirectly as a result of pressure from the rear. In all of the cities but one, Galveston, the Confederate Navy had ironclads as part of the harbor defense. Nevertheless, they suffered from serious defects in design and construction. The fundamental problems of weight, speed, seaworthiness, and mechanical inadequacies were never solved.

To a lesser degree the same was true of the Union armored vessels. Yet, they were superior in design and construction—not surprising, considering the available facilities and technological expertise in the North. This was particularly true of the monitors, which would remain the standard armored vessels in the United States Navy until the 1880s.

Like the Confederate ironclads the Union armored vessels played an important role in the Civil War. They were unsuitable for blockade duty, but in the amphibious operations along the coast and in the rivers and confined waters they proved their worth. Truly the Civil War was the ironclad era.

Left: The CSS Tennessee *in Mobile Bay, after its surrender to Farragut. It was commanded in battle by Franklin Buchanan, who commanded the first Confederate ironclad, the* Virginia. *(THE MARINERS MUSEUM)*

Above: The CSS Indianola, *formerly the USS* Indianola. *Captured from the Federals and towed to Vicksburg, the* Indianola *was undergoing refurbishment into a Confederate ironclad when its captors were forced to destroy it before the fall of Vicksburg. (USAMHI)*

Below: A David *class Confederate torpedo boat. These light-draft, semisubmerged "ironclads" were well suited for harbor defense, stealing out in the night to attack blockade ships. They enjoyed little real success, but created considerable consternation among the Federals. (NHC)*

Mr. Cooley of Beaufort and Mr. Moore of Concord

A PORTFOLIO

Two of hundreds of unsung artists, these photographers captured South Carolina long before the Federals

Two of hundreds of unsung artists, these photographers captured South Carolina long before the Federals

THE WORK of two photographers, Samuel A. Cooley and Henry P. Moore, offers a remarkable view of South Carolina during this period.

Samuel A. Cooley represented that special class of quasi-official photographer, like George Barnard and Alexander Gardner, who sometimes did contract work for the government. Whenever possible, this group made private capital of their army contract work, implying that all of their work bore official sanction. Gardner called himself "Photographer to the Army of the Potomac." Cooley would use two titles—"Photographer Tenth Army Corps" and "U. S. Photographer, Department of the South." Perhaps it helped sales of their commercial views. Certainly Cooley could offer an unusual range of images, for he operated permanent establishments in three South Carolina locations, Folly Island, Hilton Head, and Beaufort, and in Jacksonville, Florida. Houses, hospitals, camps, vessels, forts, landscapes, and everything else came before his lenses, and he sold stereo views of all of them.

By contrast, little is known of Henry P. Moore, of Concord, New Hampshire. He operated at Hilton Head in 1862-63, and probably came chiefly to take marketable views of the 3rd New Hampshire for the folks at home. His remarkable images speak for themselves.

The entrepreneur photographer. (USAMHI)

Above: "Cooley's" reads the sign in his Beaufort headquarters, and an unusual "gallery" it is. Clothing, flour, hams, books, butter, stationery, oranges, baskets, watches, and, of course, photographs, all could be bought over Cooley's counter. He stands in the white jacket leaning against his wagon. (USAMHI)

Below: The Fuller House, one of Beaufort's showplaces, and now the headquarters of General Rufus Saxton. A sentry box stands outside the gates to the house. (SOUTH CAROLINA HISTORICAL SOCIETY, CHARLESTON)

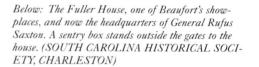

Below: Another view of Cooley's Beaufort gallery, with a little less advertising visible. (USAMHI)

Below: Cooley and assistants with his photographic wagon. Cooley himself stands second from the right, his hand resting on one of his cameras. (WRHS)

Right: Cooley's favorite subject, Beaufort, South Carolina, seen from the river. The artist had a wonderful eye for the still-life possibilities of the camera. (USAMHI)

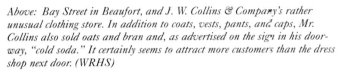

Above: Bay Street in Beaufort, and J. W. Collins & Company's rather unusual clothing store. In addition to coats, vests, pants, and caps, Mr. Collins also sold oats and bran and, as advertised on the sign in his doorway, "cold soda." It certainly seems to attract more customers than the dress shop next door. (WRHS)

Right: A commissary storehouse, shot in October 1864, one of the contract images of government buildings made by Cooley. Right next door stands a fishing tackle and general provisions store. (SOUTH CAROLINA HISTORICAL SOCIETY)

Right: John S. Fyler's store and, next to it, the post office, one example of Cooley's sometimes extraordinary talent for still scenes that have life and seeming movement. (USAMHI)

Above: The Beaufort Hotel and, on its right, the office of the Adams Express Company, one of the early private mail and package carriers in the country. (SOUTH CAROLINA HISTORICAL SOCIETY)

Below: Bay Street in 1862, another view of a typical Southern town. (SOUTH CAROLINA HISTORICAL SOCIETY)

Above: Another Beaufort post office, right next to the Adams Express. Since large sums of money often traveled in the post to and from the soldiers, the ground floor windows are barred with iron mesh to prevent burglary. (USAMHI)

Above: The west side of Bay Street. (USAMHI)

Left: The Beaufort Hotel again and, to its left, the commissary storehouse and fishing tackle shop. The dandies in front of the hotel may be Southern gentlemen who demurred on soldiering, or they may be Yankee traders who followed the army to sell to the soldiers. (USAMHI)

Left: A quiet street scene in Beaufort. (USAMHI)

Above: The one-time home of Dr. John A. Johnson, and now a hospital, with linen and blankets airing on the balcony. (USAMHI)

Left: A house used as a hospital for "contrabands," the slaves who gathered around the Union armies wherever they went, seeking freedom and protection. (SOUTH CAROLINA HISTORICAL SOCIETY)

Below: The Beaufort Arsenal on Craven Street. (SOUTH CAROLINA HISTORICAL SOCIETY)

Left: The United States Marine headquarters on Bay Point, rather a small headquarters, but then it was rather a small Marine Corps. (USAMHI)

Right: A parade, the generals on their white chargers, the men and boys watching from the sideline. Cooley missed no opportunity to shoot a scene with a mass of men. The more subjects in an image, the more who might want to buy a print . . . and perhaps an orange or two from his gallery. (CWTI)

Above: The machine shops at Bay Point and, in the foreground, bits and pieces of the machinery they worked on here, mostly for maintenance on the ships of the South Atlantic Blockading Squadron. (USAMHI)

Above: Hundreds of heavy guns passed through Hilton Head on their way to fight rebellion. They and their accoutrements lie here in some disarray. In the lower left corner, against the sand, can be seen the shadow of Cooley's camera. (USAMHI)

Left. At right the saltwater condenser for purifying water, and in the background several vessels docked awaiting coal. (USAMHI)

Above: The headquarters of Major General David Hunter, now recovered from his Bull Run wound. Cooley did a much more brisk business at Hilton Head than at Beaufort. (USAMHI)

Above: Henry P. Moore, too, went to Hilton Head, where there was more bustle and activity than in sleepy Beaufort. The wharf looked over a bay jammed with warships, transports, tugs, and lighter craft. (USAMHI)

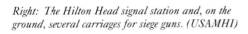

Above: Here immense qualities of supplies for the army besieging Charleston were received. (USAMHI)

Right: The Hilton Head signal station and, on the ground, several carriages for siege guns. (USAMHI)

Left: Moore took his camera atop the signal station to photograph the hospital in the far distance and an ordnance storeyard in the forground. Cannons and carriages lay awaiting shipment to the front. (USAMHI)

Above: Another, larger, signal station was needed in 1863 on St. Helena Island. The engineers who built it based their tower on four existing trees still growing. (USAMHI)

Above: And on Otter Island they built another, which Moore captures in the act of signaling to a ship out on the horizon. (USAMHI)

Left: But at Hilton Head, Moore's best work was his portraits of the men in their camps, and particularly those of the 3rd New Hampshire. Here Lieutenant Colonel J. H. Jackson stands at left, his son Captain T. M. Jackson second from the right, and his servant Cyrus at his right. (USAMHI)

Left: Signal corpsmen, March 1, 1862.

Right: The 3rd New Hampshire's surgeon, A. A. Moulton, and his somewhat gothic-looking wife. (USAMHI)

Above: Cook's galley of Company H. In the hut in back stand tin plates and cups for the mess. In the center foreground stands the cook, G. N. Wheeler, at his camp stove. The man seated on the small barrel is W. Blake, about to grind coffee beans in the grinder at his feet. In the right background an unknown New Hampshire officer peers from his tent to see what Moore is doing. (USAMHI)

Below: The meal prepared, another cook looks on as the bandsmen of the 3rd New Hampshire dine, their drums and fifes set casually about the area. (USAMHI)

Left: A nonchalant group of the New Hampshire boys pose for the artist, their table reflecting their leisure doings. It lies cluttered with books, a cigar, letters from home, cased ambrotypes of female loved one, dominoes, and an ink bottle from which one man is writing his letter. The man seated on the other side of the table reads a page of crude cartoons from an issue of from an issue of Harper's weekly. (USAMHI)

Below: These New Hampshiremen added considerable decoration to their Hilton Head quarters. Seashells, palmettos, cactus, driftwood, all contributed to a scene quite out of the ordinary for Civil War camps. These musicians can enjoy their meal in the most pleasant surroundings. (USAMHI)

Above: The bandmaster's tent with bandmaster G. W. Ingalls at left studying his music while his servant polishes his boots. Sam Brown reads a New Hampshire newspaper at the center of the table, while musician D.A. Brown on the right does the same. Their horns lie on the table. (USAMHI)

Above: And the officers loved their dominoes. (USAMHI)

Left: The splendid plantation residence of John E. Seabrook on Edisto Island, in 1862. At far left is his library—at right, his wine cellar. Lying like a white carpet on the lawn in front of the house is cotton captured aboard the blockade runner Empire and spread out to dry in the sun. (USAMHI)

Left: A closer view of the Seabrook mansion, now headquarters of Colonel E. Q. Fellows and staff. The post adjutant, Martin James, stands under the square marked on the image his office his office by the √, and his sleeping quarters by the #. Made by Moore on April 7, 1862. (KA)

Below: H. P. Moore's images of the Seabrook plantation touched upon art. Here Seabrook's extensive garden as seen from the mansion house. One of Seabrook's slaves, a little boy, stands atop the sundial at right center. Standing with folded arms in the foregrounds in Colonel E. Q. Fellows, commanding the 3rd New Hampshire. It is early spring, April 7, 1862, and already the garden is verdant. Half a continent away, the second day's fighting at Shiloh is raging. (KA)

Above: Seabrook's fishpond, with his house in the distance at left. Bandmaster Ingalls steers the boat. (USAMHI)

Right: More cotton is drying on Seabrook's grounds, being tended by freedmen who were once his slaves. In the distance at center stands the USS Pocahontas. (USAMHI)

Left: Seabrook's library. (USAMHI)

Left: Men who died before Moore could catch them in life pose silent and still in death. Almost all are of the 3rd New Hampshire—almost all died of disease. Hilton Head could kill despite its tropical beauty. (USAMHI)

Left: And however easy it might have been to forget the war, they could not, and neither did Moore. Deceptive in its peacefulness, this scene could turn warlike at any time, and the soldiers reading his letter beside the gun carriage in Fort Wells is certainly not far from his weapon. The sights atop the Rodman gun could fill with enemy vessels or blockade runners, and the tranquility of this image could vanish. Moore, for all his commercial instincts, knew as well that he was capturing a special part of the war for posterity. Thanks to him, these scenes will remain captive for all of time. (USAMHI)

The Peninsular Campaign

EMORY M. THOMAS

The first campaign going "on to Richmond," and the emergence of a general called "Granny" Lee

Above: After Johnston and Magruder abandoned Yorktown, the Confederates found Norfolk untenable and evacuated on May 9. Before leaving they did their best to destroy the navy yard. Timothy O'Sullivan's December 1864 photograph shows how thoroughly they did their task. (P-M)

THE ARMY OF THE POTOMAC was awesome. In the spring of 1862 it was the largest, best equipped armed force ever assembled in the Western Hemisphere. From the masses of volunteers who had descended upon Washington, George B. McClellan had fashioned a mammoth war machine—150,000 men, plus the material to support and sustain this host. With such force McClellan confidently intended to deliver the *coup de grace* to the would-be Confederacy.

McClellan had taken command in the aftermath of the Union debacle at Bull Run in July 1861. He began at once to mold his army and endured pleas and pressure to commit to battle prematurely. Termed "Young Napoleon" by the press, McClellan believed he understood the complexity of "modern war." He first had to spar with ranking United States General Winfield Scott until the aged Scott finally retired from the service in November 1861; then McClellan suffered the "help" of his Commander-in-Chief Abraham Lincoln and other martial amateurs in the administration and Congress.

Having built so splendid an army and waited so long to employ it, McClellan could not afford to err; when he marched, he would have to win. As the campaigning season of 1862 loomed imminent, Lincoln felt the need to rebuild his faith in "Young Napoleon." In frustration, the President issued his own General War Order Number One, which prescribed a "general forward movement" to begin on all fronts on February 22. Beyond this action, he and others in Washington could only chafe at McClellan's caution. Lincoln realized his administration had invested too much in McClellan to cut its losses now. Whatever "Young Napoleon" did or did not do would have to be Union strategy and policy.

Beyond the Potomac waited Confederate armies, the chief of which, commanded by Joseph E. Johnston, occupied the ground around Manassas near the battlefield of Bull Run. Johnston, who ironically held much the same low opinion of his President, Jefferson Davis, as McClellan did of Lincoln, had only some 40,000 troops. But he had 10,000 reinforcements nearby, and he had had all fall and winter to improve a position which had proven impenetrable the previous summer.

For the Army of the Potomac to emulate the tactics of First Bull Run and smash headlong into these waiting defenders seemed to McClellan art less and wasteful. Accordingly he determined to strike the Southerners elsewhere. He wanted to transport his army by water to the tiny port town of Urbana on the Rappahannock and interpose the Army of the Potomac between Johnston's Confederates and Richmond. Johnston, however, foiled the Urbana approach by evacuating Manassas and moving to Culpeper Court House where he might counter attacks from the east and north with equal facility. However sound was Johnston's movement, he acted in haste without fully apprising his President of his intentions. And he had had to destroy at Manassas enormous quantities of supplies his government had labored so diligently to collect. Davis, then, had doubts about Johnston nearly equal to Lincoln's about McClellan.

His Urbana landing scrapped, McClellan shifted to a strategic plan which was even more ambitious. He proposed to transport the Army of

Left: Now McClellan could pursue his original intention of campaigning up the Virginia Peninsula toward Richmond. Here he poses for a Brady camera with members of his staff including, standing at right, Van Vliet. (KA)

Right: Lieutenant General Winfield Scott on June 10, 1862, by Charles D. Fredericks. Taken at West Point after his retirement, it shows a man now bitter at his treatment by the younger McClellan. Two weeks from now, however, "Little Mac" will begin to feel his comeuppance on the Peninsula (USAMHI)

the Potomac by water to Fort Monroe on the tip of the Virginia Peninsula between the York and James rivers. Union troops had maintained possession of the fort throughout the war, and McClellan planned to use this friendly perimeter as a staging area for an assault upon Richmond from the east. The combined army-navy operation and the eastern invasion route may have seemed complicated logistically, but it offered several advantages over a more direct assault. The Peninsular approach would not compel the Federals to cross the many streams and rivers which crossed the direct route to Richmond. The advance would take place on the relatively flat, tidewater coastal plain. The James, York, and Pamunkey rivers would permit the Union Navy to support McClellan's army with both supplies and gunfire during the advance to Richmond. If Johnston or any other commander dared confront the Army of the Potomac on the Peninsula, he would risk the prospect of having a portion of the blue army landed behind him and thus encirclement and destruction. On the other hand, if the Confederates chose to give battle nearer Richmond, McClellan had the siege artillery with which to blast his way into the city and destroy the opposing army at the same time. Withholding McDowell's corps, Lincoln assented to the plan, and McClellan promptly moved his army to the Peninsula and began his month-long siege of Yorktown.

On April 14 in Richmond the Confederate high command met for fourteen hours to plan some response to McClellan's Peninsular approach. Johnston favored a concentration near Richmond because he thought the Federals too strong on the Peninsula. Robert E. Lee, the President's chief military advisor, and Secretary of War George W. Randolph contended that the Southern army would have to confront the threat somewhere and that the Peninsula was as good a place as any. President Davis feared losing his army and capital if the campaign produced siege operations in front of Richmond. Accordingly Davis instructed Johnston to move his entire

Above: One of McClellan's commanders, Brigadier General Edwin V. Sumner, the oldest corps leader of the war. Born in 1797, he was called "bull head" because a musket ball supposedly bounced from his head in Mexico. During the coming campaign, however, he was wounded twice. (USAMHI)

Left: Some of McClellan's generals, on May 14, 1862. Seated from the right they are Brigadier General John Newton, Brigadier General William F. Barry, VI Corps commander Brigadier General William B. Franklin, and Brigadier General Henry W. Slocum. (NLM)

Above: Stewart Van Vliet, McClellan's chief quarter-master in the Peninsular campaign. (KA)

Right: The Army of the Potomac at Cumberland Landing in May 1862, preparing for the push that will take it "on to Richmond." A Wood & Gibson photograph for Alexander Gardner. (LC)

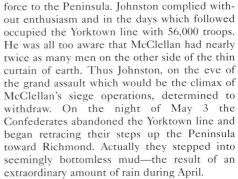

Above: One of Brady's assistants captures a scene at Cumberland Landing. Over 100,000 men await the order to advance against an enemy barely half their numbers. (LC)

Below: A panorama showing the army at camp near Cumberland Landing. (CHS)

force to the Peninsula. Johnston complied without enthusiasm and in the days which followed occupied the Yorktown line with 56,000 troops. He was all too aware that McClellan had nearly twice as many men on the other side of the thin curtain of earth. Thus Johnston, on the eve of the grand assault which would be the climax of McClellan's siege operations, determined to withdraw. On the night of May 3 the Confederates abandoned the Yorktown line and began retracing their steps up the Peninsula toward Richmond. Actually they stepped into seemingly bottomless mud—the result of an extraordinary amount of rain during April.

As Southern columns clogged the spongy roads westward, McClellan's Federals on May 4 rushed empty earthworks. To Washington McClellan announced a great victory at small cost. Then he set about directing the pursuit of his elusive enemy. Five Union divisions plunged into the Peninsular mud, by now well-churned by the retreating Confederates; four more divisions stood ready to move by water up the York to cut off the Southern withdrawal.

Johnston's rear guard (James Longstreet's division) first felt the pressure of the Federal pursuit near Williamsburg. Just east of the old

Left: Two images by James F. Gibson almost form a panoramic view of troops at Cumberland Landing on the Pamunkey River. The landing appears at right. (left, LC; right, USAMHI)

Above: Another Gibson panorama of the camps on the Pamunkey. (USAMHI)

Below: Probably Gibson's finest panorama. The enormity of an army on campaign is evident and overwhelming. (USAMHI)

Right: In mid-May McClellan moved his base to White House on the Pamunkey, formerly the home of one of Robert E. Lee's sons. James Gibson photographed the house on May 17, 1862. (USAMHI)

Below: And G. W. Houghton, the Brattleboro, Vermont photographer, caught this scene of the camps of the army at White House Landing. (VERMONT HISTORICAL SOCIETY)

Left: Gibson's May 17 image of the destroyed bridge of the Richmond & York River Railroad over the Pamunkey. McClellan's people started the work of repair at once and… (NLM)

Below: … soon it was rebuilt, though the steam engine here is on a barge. Tracks have not yet been laid on the bridge. And within a month, McClellan himself will have to destroy it once again when he retreats. (USAMHI)

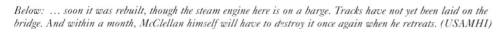

colonial capital on May 5 a sharp fight ensued. The Southerners first stopped the Union advance, then counterattacked, and finally withdrew into the darkness. The Battle of Williamsburg was bloody, but inconclusive. Johnston gained the time he needed to make good his escape, but the Confederate counterattack was a costly failure.

McClellan, meanwhile, was trying to hasten Johnston's envelopment by water. William B. Franklin's division made a landing on the Peninsula opposite West Point, but encountered Gustavus W. Smith's Confederates soon after. The wily Johnston anticipated McClellan's move, and the engagement between Smith's and Franklin's troops on May 7 at Barhamsville (Eltham's Landing) convinced McClellan that his trap had failed. Thereafter he contented himself with a methodical pursuit of his quarry up the Peninsula.

The rival commanders each expressed satisfaction at the developments thus far. Johnston was pleased to have made good his escape, and McClellan took pride in his conquest of the Yorktown line and his pursuit of a fleeing foe. Both generals consumed themselves in cautious movement: Johnston to the vicinity of Richmond and McClellan to the vicinity of Johnston.

In the process both ignored their navies and a succession of military "dominoes" involved in the movement up the Peninsula. When Johnston evacuated the Yorktown line, he left the port city of Norfolk exposed and untenable. When Norfolk fell—the Confederates evacuated the city on May 9—the *Virginia* became a ship without a port. When the *Virginia's* crew failed in their attempt to lighten the heavy-draft vessel sufficiently to steam up the James, they had to destroy the ironclad. This in turn opened the James all the way to Richmond to Union gunboats and troop transports.

Curiously, neither field commander appreciated this circumstance. Lee was the first Confederate to react; he hastened the work on gun emplacements, river obstructions, and "torpedoes" at Drewry's Bluff. McClellan was seemingly too preoccupied even to comprehend the city's vulnerability. Indeed, it was President Lincoln himself, while visiting Fort Monroe, who gave the instructions which led to Norfolk's capture. The Federal Navy then pressed the issue, and on May 15 two ironclads, the *Monitor* and *Galena*, led three wooden gun boats up the James toward Richmond. The small fleet encountered little difficulty until it reached Drewry's Bluff, which was only about seven miles from the Confederate capital. There Southern batteries and channel obstructions halted the Union advance. Had McClellan provided the expedition with a supporting army column of any size, the fight at Drewry's Bluff might have turned out quite differently. As it happened though, this repulse ended the Federal threat to Richmond by water.

Indeed water, in the form of rain, seemed to plague instead of assist McClellan's campaign as the Army of the Potomac advanced nearer Richmond. The Federal route lay up the northern half of the Peninsula to take advantage of supply lines from the York and Pamunkey rivers. At Cumberland Landing and White House the navy deposited massive amounts of supplies for transport overland via road and the Richmond &

York River rail line to the troops. Throughout May unseasonal amounts of rain hampered the movements of men and supplies. Yet even though the Army of the Potomac seemed to ooze instead of march, it moved nonetheless ever closer to Richmond.

As he neared the city McClellan recognized the necessity to broaden his front and position his army on the south as well as the north side of the Chickahominy River, which bisects the Peninsula near Richmond. Two Federal corps had crossed the Chickahominy on May 30 when one of the most violent rainstorms in memory descended upon the area. The fresh rain turned the normally sluggish Chickahominy into a torrent which washed away bridges and left Erasmus Keyes's Union corps isolated from the rest of the army. Joe Johnston recognized his opportunity and determined to strike the exposed Federals with four Confederate divisions.

The Confederate attack appeared simple as long as it consisted only of lines drawn on a map. The lines, representing Southern troops moving along roads, converged at the village of Seven Pines, and there Johnston planned to attack a fraction of the blue army with masses of his own men. On the morning of May 31, however, Johnston's plan came unraveled. James Longstreet seemed most at fault; he took the wrong road and in so doing clogged the Confederate advance. As a result the supposedly coordinated attack degenerated into a series of single blows and an aborted Confederate opportunity. In the aftermath of the day's fighting Johnston fell wounded from his horse, leaving the Southerners not only confused, but also leaderless.

On June 1, after an unsuccessful attempt to salvage victory from the Battle of Seven Pines (or Fair Oaks), Robert E. Lee arrived to assume command and lead the march back toward Richmond. To this juncture, Lee had disappointed himself and others in the Southern cause. Possessed of splendid credentials at the outset of the war, he had directed a doomed campaign in the Kanawha Valley of western Virginia, presided over a retreat from the coast in South Carolina and Georgia, and served in the President's shadow as Davis's military advisor. In this last capacity, Lee had ameliorated somewhat the relations between Davis and Johnston; but of this, no one but Lee was aware. Thus, he took command of Johnston's army in the wake of a bungled battle in the midst of a desperate campaign with little reputation beyond those who knew him. And the first direction he gave to his troops was to dig holes in the ground—to shore up the defensive works in front of Richmond.

Those who crowned Lee with the sobriquet "Granny Lee" or "King of Spades," however, missed his intention. Lee threw up breastworks so that he might defend Richmond with as few troops as possible; with the bulk of his army he determined to attack.

If the new Confederate commander needed time to make Johnston's army his own following the battle, McClellan seemed to be in a cooperative mood. He moved, slowly and cautiously, to consolidate his position before Richmond. Completing his shift of troop units south of the Chickahominy, McClellan stationed four corps (Franklin's, E. V. Sumner's, Samuel P.

Left: George Washington was married in St. Peter's Church near White House. Now it is favored by touring Federals, including white-bearded General Sumner and his staff. (USAMHI)

Left: Another view of St. Peter's, taken by a Brady assistant. (LC)

Below: Contraband blacks flocked to the army's camps to become laborers and servants at White House Landing. (USAMHI)

Right: And another sort of man gathered around the army, the romantic secret service men, the operatives and spies whose "intelligence" McClellan believed unquestioningly. The trouble was, their information proved consistently erroneous. Seated in the background, pipe in mouth, is the most unreliable of them all, Allan Pinkerton. Yet McClellan preferred to believe him since his reports of overwhelming enemy numbers confirmed "Little Mac's" own exaggerated fears. (NLM)

Left: On the march again. David Woodbury caught men of the 5th New Hampshire and 64th New York at work on this military bridge over the Chickahominy in the last days of May, as the Federals are on their way to Seven Pines. (USAMHI)

Above: On the battle line at Seven Pines, or Fair Oaks. Gibson's early June photo of Fort Richardson, near the Quarles House. (NLM)

Right: Gibson's photo taken on the field at Fair Oaks, showing a fresh Union grave at left. (USAMHI)

Heintzelman's and Keyes's) directly east of Seven Pines about six miles from its limits and about one mile from the Confederate works. North of the Chickahominy were the 30,000 troops of Fitz John Porter's corps. McClellan was careful for good reason; his intelligence operatives and spies informed him that the Confederate Army numbered 200,000 men. The estimate, largely the product of Allan Pinkerton's civilian agents, was much exaggerated; Lee had perhaps 65,000 to 70,000 troops with which to confront McClellan's 90,000 to 100,000 at this point. Nevertheless McClellan believed the Army of the Potomac was outnumbered, and he renewed his pleas for reinforcements.

While waiting for his government to appreciate his situation and support him as he believed necessary, McClellan brought up his big guns, 101 pieces of siege artillery. These weapons, he believed, would compensate for his numerical inferiority and enable the Federals to blast their way into Richmond. To his wife, McClellan explained that he planned to "make the first battle mainly an artillery combat." The artillery would "push them in upon Richmond and behind their works." Then he would "bring up my heavy guns, shell the city, and carry it by assault."

With uncanny insight into the mind of his foe, Lee wrote to Davis on June 5, "McClellan will make this a battle of posts. He will take position from position, under cover of his heavy guns, and we cannot get at him without storming his works, which… is extremely hazardous." To counter the Union tactics, Lee proposed "to bring McClellan out," to make the Federals fight in the open, away from prepared fortifications and big guns. First he assured himself that his defensive works before Richmond were as strong as he could make them. Then he dispatched almost four brigades to the Shenandoah Valley to provide "Stonewall" Jackson with the strength to conclude his brilliant campaign there. Lee had need of the hard-hitting Valley Army at Richmond. Finally, he sent J.E.B. Stuart and 1,200 cavalry troopers to scout the Federal right flank.

Stuart left Richmond on the morning of June 12 and rode north twenty-two miles before making camp for the night. Next day the column turned east. The Confederates encountered slight resistance as they moved, and Stuart realized that the Union right flank was unsecured. Nevertheless, he pressed on—completely around McClellan's army and back into Richmond from the south on June 15. Stuart's "ride around McClellan" made him a hero and did wonders for Confederate morale; it also seemed to confirm McClellan's fears about Confederate strength. But most importantly the venture provided Lee with valuable information regarding the Federal flank.

During the latter half of June McClellan hesitated. He considered opening an additional supply route from Harrison's Landing on the James to supplement or supplant his bases on the Pamunkey. He contemplated an all-out assault on Richmond. Eventually he decided upon a limited advance to test Confederate defenses east of the city.

Meanwhile Lee was dreaming larger dreams. On June 23 he convened a meeting attended by Longstreet, D. H. Hill, A. P. Hill, and Jackson, and announced his plans. He would station

Above: Battery C of the 1st Pennsylvania Light Artillery, the extreme front line at Fair Oaks. (NLM)

Above: Two old frame houses, an orchard, and a well, near Fair Oaks, where over 400 dead Federals were buried after the battle. (NLM)

Above: Another view of the twin frame houses beside the orchard. A central main house was meant to connect the two wings, but it was never built. (USAMHI)

Above: Major General Gustavus W. Smith, center, and his staff. After the wounding of Johnston at Fair Oaks, Smith temporarily commanded the Army of Northern Virginia. (CHS)

Left: Union Fort Sumner near Fair Oaks, looking toward the Confederate lines, taken by Gibson a few days after the battle. (USAMHI)

Below: Battery A, 2nd United States Artillery, by Gibson, men who fought at Fair Oaks. (LC)

Left: Lowe replenishing the gas in his balloon Intrepid *from the* Constitution. *Brady's assistant made a series of images of Lowe and his apparatus. (USAMHI)*

Right: While the armies fought at Fair Oaks, Professor T. S. Lowe gained a true bird's-eye view of the fight from his balloon Intrepid. *Here it is being inflated on Gaines's Hill, June 1, 1862. Lowe stands at right with his hand resting against the balloon. (KA)*

Above: "Your message received announcing the success of Balloon and Telegraph combined—the most wonderful feat of the age." So said Thomas T. Eckert of the Union's Military Telegraph. On June 1, 1862, during the Battle of Fair Oaks, a photographer working for Brady captured the scene that made Eckert so ecstatic. Professor Thaddeus Lowe's observation balloon, probably the Intrepid, *is grounded after an ascent. From his observations, telegrapher Parker Spring is sending a dispatch over the portable field key attached to the roll of wire. Lowe may be the man in the white hat seated below him. A third man sits with his back to the camera, sketching the scene on a pad. It was a blending of two new means of rapid communications, a historic moment. "Give my compliments to Prof Lowe and Spring," said Eckert after receiving the first telegram; "if they feel as proud over the enterprise as I do, they have been well repaid and will long be remembered." (KA)*

Right: On his way to the heavens, an officer ascends in Lowe's craft to observe the fighting at Fair Oaks. His climb is controlled by the soldiers anchoring the balloon. (LC)

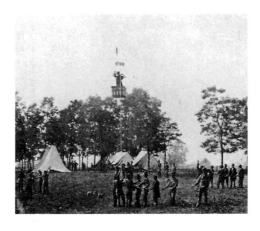

25,000 men commanded by Magruder and Benjamin Huger in the works to the east of Richmond; these troops would have to fend off the entire Union Army if Lee's plan miscarried. The divisions of Longstreet and the two Hills would mass on the Confederate left and strike the Union right at the village of Mechanicsville. And Jackson's Valley Army by rapid and secret marches would join Lee's force and strike the Federals in the rear of their right flank. If all went well, approximately 66,000 Confederates would assault Porter's 30,000 Federals from the flank and the rear. This would "bring McClellan out" of his works and, perhaps, destroy him. If, on the other hand, McClellan realized in time the weakness of the Confederate force covering Richmond, he was capable of blasting his way into the city. The stakes of Lee's gamble were high—victory or disaster.

Lee's campaign, known as the Seven Days Battles, began on June 25 when McClellan launched his limited attack upon the Confederate lines east of Richmond. Two Federal divisions advanced upon the Southern works, tested their strength, and then threw up field fortifications of their own. McClellan believed what Lee wanted him to believe—that the 25,000 Confederates were 50,000. The same day McClellan also learned that Jackson's army was on the way down from the Valley. Immediately he sent a message to Washington announcing Jackson's presence and emphasizing his peril. "I am in no way responsible..." McClellan insisted, "I have not failed to represent repeatedly the necessity for reinforcements... if the result... is a disaster, the responsibility can not be thrown on my shoulders; it must rest where it belongs." Then having prepared his government for the worst and exonerated himself, McClellan hastened to Porter's headquarters.

On June 26 Lee's three divisions formed for the attack on Mechanicsville. The commands of A. P. Hill, D. H. Hill, and Longstreet formed land waited. Nothing was supposed to occur until Jackson arrived, and Jackson was uncharacteristically late. Finally, at three in the afternoon, A. P. Hill could restrain himself no longer. Acting upon the assumption that Jackson must be nearby and poised for attack, Hill began the battle. The Confederates swept across the Chickahominy and through Mechanicsville. Then they crashed head long into Porter's lines behind Beaver Dam Creek.

Left: Brigadier General David B. Birney, son of the abolitionist leader James G. Birney, commanded a brigade at Fair Oaks. He was charged with disobeying an order from his superior,... (USAMHI)

Below: ... Samuel P. Heintzelman, during the battle. Birney was acquitted. (CWTI)

Above: Brady's assistant captures Lowe's balloon during an ascent at Fair Oaks. (BRUCE GIMELSON)

Neither frontal assault nor flank attack could dislodge the Federals. The Confederates sustained 1,484 casualties against 361 Union losses and did precisely what Lee had not wanted to do—attacked the Unionists in their prepared works.

Darkness ended the day's fighting in the Battle of Mechanicsville, and still Jackson's troops had not arrived. Actually the Valley Army reached the vicinity at five o'clock in the afternoon; then Jackson, after being unaccountably late, became incredibly cautious. He made camp within the sound of the battle. The most rational explanation of Jackson's behavior focuses upon an irrational response to stress and exhaustion. He had ridden, fought, and marched too long with too little rest. And now a "fog of war" settled over him and clouded his otherwise clear mind. On the morning of June 27, Jackson finally found the battle. But the fact that the first shells fired by the artillery of the Valley Army landed among some of A. P. Hill's troops portended more confusion on Jackson's part. Lee resolved to continue his attack on June 27; he had little choice. During the previous night McClellan had removed Porter's troops to a new position near Gaines's Mill on Boatswain's Swamp. The Southerners attacked in the early afternoon, and again Porter's men withstood the assault. Jackson was supposed to send his troops crashing down upon the Federal flank, but once more he was late. At last, at seven o'clock in the evening, Lee was able to assemble his army for a concerted drive. In the face of this new attack, Porter's troops, who had been repelling piecemeal assaults for five hours, broke. Confederate infantry tore through the center of the Federal lines. In desperation Union General Phillip St. George Cooke, J.E.B. Stuart's father-in-law, ordered his cavalry to charge the oncoming Southerners. The charge only added to the general confusion, however, when it degenerated into a stampede to the rear in the face of Confederate rifle fire. At Gaines's Mill, at a cost of 8,750 Confederate casualties to 6,837 Union losses, Lee won his first clear victory. Yet during the night Porter was able to cross the Chickahominy and unite his battered men with

Left: And General Oliver O. Howard, who fought at Bull Run, commanded a brigade at Fair Oaks. A bullet there cost him his right arm. He still had both arms in this Brady studio portrait. (USAMHI)

Below: Brigadier General Willis A. Gorman, former territorial governor of Minnesota, shown here with his wife, commanded a brigade in Sumner's corps and won acclaim from several superiors. (NA)

Right: And Brigadier General John J. Abercrombie, born in 1798, was still active enough to lead a brigade at Fair Oaks at the age of sixty-four. Here he was wounded, and he left active service for the duration of the war. (USAMHI)

Below: Another view of the hospital, used by wounded from General Joseph Hooker's division. Even it did not escape the battle, as evidenced in the collapsed chimney and damaged wall. (LC)

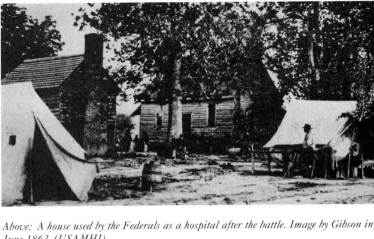

Above: A house used by the Federals as a hospital after the battle. Image by Gibson in June 1862. (USAMHI)

Below: Gibson's photo of the house used as a hospital by General Philip Kearny's brigade. The nondescript looking lot of men here may well be walking wounded. (NLM)

Above: The Quarles House near Fair Oaks. Many Federal dead were interred here after the fight. (USAMHI)

the rest of the Army of the Potomac. McClellan's army was much alive and still a potent force.

McClellan himself was unnerved, however. Fearing for his supply lines to the Pamunkey and for the safety of his army, he determined to retreat to the James and open a new base of supply at Harrison's Landing. Some of his subordinates, notably Joseph Hooker and Phil Kearny, perceived that the Confederate forces directly before Richmond were as weak as they actually were. But McClellan rejected their counsel. He gave the order for his retreat and then vented his frustration upon his superiors in Washington. He dispatched a lengthy telegram in which he explained the situation as he understood it. In conclusion he placed the blame for this circumstance where he thought blame belonged. "If I save this army now, I tell you plainly that I owe no thanks to you or to any other persons in Washington. You have done your best to sacrifice this army." Fortunately for McClellan, the telegraph supervisor in Washington did not transmit these two final sentences to the President.

Satisfied that he had absolved himself of the responsibility for his "change of base," on June 28 McClellan set about saving his army. Confederates could see the smoke from burning

Above: For most of the men in McClellan's army, Fair Oaks was their first real fight. One of these was McClellan's chief of cavalry, Brigadier General George Stoneman, shown here in camp after the battle. He and his cavalry took little part, in fact. (USAMHI)

Above: Stoneman, seated at right, and Brigadier General Henry M. Naglee. The dog is nearly as photogenic as the generals. (USAMHI)

supplies and wagons moving to the southeast. Nevertheless Lee had to act on less than confirmed intelligence when he committed his army to an all-out pursuit. Elements of the opposing armies fought on June 28, but the major effort to cut off and destroy the Army of the Potomac began the following day.

On June 29 Magruder was finally to have the chance for offensive, instead of defensive, action. Moving east, near the old battlefield at Fair Oaks, Magruder was in a good position to strike the retreating Federals. Jackson, too, had the opportunity to fall upon the Union rear. As it happened, though, both Confederate generals failed to move fast enough or decisively enough. Jackson never really got his command into action, and Magruder advanced timidly until his troops encountered the Federals near Savage Station. There, late in the day, the Confederates attacked to no significant effect. Understandably Lee was concerned that he would lose the chance to reap the benefits of his hard-won victories thus far. Accordingly on June 30 he again exhorted his subordinates to press the pursuit. He planned to bring the troops of Longstreet, A. P. Hill, Magruder, Huger, and Jackson together for a climactic battle. Once more, however, Magruder and Jackson were slow, and Huger, too, was late. As a result, Hill's and Longstreet's divisions struck the center of the Federal Army in a battle variously named White Oak Swamp, Frayser's Farm, or Glendale. The combat raged in all three of these places, and more, and the Union line held firm amid fierce fighting.

On the morning of July 1 McClellan seemed to have made good his escape. Porter's corps and the huge wagon train of army supplies were safely at Harrison's Landing. The remaining four

Above: On March 18, 1862, with the threat of McClellan coming up the Peninsula, President Jefferson Davis appointed a new Secretary of War, George Wythe Randolph of Virginia. He appears here in an unpublished portrait. One of the few war secretaries to attempt to exercise real control of the War Department, he only lasted in office until November. But he worked well with the man that he and Davis chose to replace the wounded Johnston at the head of the Army of Northern Virginia,... (UNIVERSITY OF VIRGINIA, EDGEHILL RANDOLPH PAPERS)

Above: ... General Robert Edward Lee. Until now, Lee's war service had been less than glorious. Some called him "Granny Lee," and some, like South Carolina Governor Francis Pickens, doubted that his heart was in the cause. The next month on the Peninsula would answer their fears. (SOUTHERN HISTORICAL COLLECTION, THE UNIVERSITY OF NORTH CAROLINA AT CHAPEL HILL)

Above: Ironically, Lee's opposite number in the Confederate Navy on the Peninsula was his own brother Captain Sidney Smith Lee. "There will be no interference with the naval forces under your command by the land forces serving in conjunction with you," the general wrote to the captain, expressing the hope that "the two services will harmonize perfectly." Even among brothers the age-old rivalry between army and navy had to be resisted . (WILLIAM A. ALBAUGH)

Above: One of the cavalrymen with Stuart, the scout who led him on his ride around McClellan, Lieutenant John Singleton Mosby. Previously unknown, he established his reputation in this war. He appears in this unpublished portrait in the uniform of a colonel. (USAMHI)

Above: The pace of the campaign quickened when, on June 12, Lee sent Brigadier General James Ewell Brown "Jeb" Stuart on a four-day reconnaissance around McClellan's army. Lee gained valuable information, but at the price of alerting McClellan that something was in the wind. (VALENTINE MUSEUM, COOK COLLECTION)

Above: Major General Fitz John Porter and his corps were dangerously isolated north of the Chickahominy River, and late in June Lee determined to attack. (USAMHI)

corps of the Army of the Potomac were drawn up on the slopes of Malvern Hill, the last position they would have to occupy before they reached Harrison's Landing and sanctuary. The Federal position seemed impregnable. Still, Lee hoped for total victory, and so he sent Longstreet to investigate "the feasibility of aggressive battle."

Longstreet believed he had discovered locations from which Confederate artillery might catch the Federals in a devastating cross fire. Lee gave the order to mass the guns where Longstreet indicated and instructed the infantry to charge in the wake of the artillery barrage. However, the Southern artillery never got completely into place or action. Hence Confederate infantry remained in place, and it seemed that there would be no battle.

Then in the middle of the afternoon the Federals began to move; they seemed to be withdrawing. Lee ordered an immediate attack. Southern troops charged up Malvern Hill to find the Army of the Potomac very much in place. The assault was slaughter. Union artillery raked the advancing ranks, and Federal infantry blazed away at the survivors. Yet the series of charges continued until dark. And in the night 8,000 casualties littered the field, 5,000 Confederate, 3,000 Union.

Lee had seized a last chance to destroy his foe and lost. Perhaps he sensed a moment of truth which might not come again. Regardless of the reason the result was disaster.

Although no one knew it for sure at the time, the Battle of Malvern Hill was the last of the Seven Days Battles and the conclusion of the Peninsular campaign. The Army of the Potomac withdrew to Harrison's Landing to recuperate. The Confederates remained nearby for a time; then Lee left a token force and took the bulk of his army to Richmond. The campaign established Lee as savior of the Confederacy. When he took command, the Army of the Potomac was in the suburbs of Richmond; a month later the same army cowered inert under the protection of naval guns twenty-three miles away. Lee was lavish in his praise of his own army, the Army of Northern Virginia. Later in his official report, however, he admitted, "Under ordinary circumstances the Federal Army should have been destroyed."

Although out-generaled, the Army of the Potomac had fought well. The men who had stood firm against the furious Confederate assaults at Gaines's Mill, Malvern Hill, and elsewhere would be back. But McClellan, the "Young Napoleon" who molded this splendid army, had proven himself unable to command it.

Above: Confederate casualties at Mechanicsville ran high. Colonel Mumford S. Stokes of the 1st North Carolina Infantry took a mortal wound. (WRHS)

Left: A group of staff officers on the eve of the fighting on the Virginia Peninsula. The man lying at right with the dog is a twenty-two year old captain, George Armstrong Custer. He too, like Mosby, made a name for himself in this war. (LC)

Left: Mechanicsville, Virginia, photographed in April 1865 by Gardner's assistant James Reekie. Here on June 26, 1862, was fought the second of the Seven Days Battles, when Lee attempted to strike Porter's exposed position north of the Chickahominy. (USAMHI)

Left: Reekie's 1865 image of Ellison's Mill on the battlefield at Mechanicsville. The hottest of the fighting raged around and past this little structure as Porter successfully defended himself before withdrawing. (JA)

Above: Colonel Edward L. Thomas of the 35th Georgia took a bad wound at Mechanicsville. He recovered to become a fine brigade commander and, as pictured here, a brigadier general. (VM)

Right: Faced with heavy numbers against him, Porter withdrew across the Chickahominy on bridges like this one on the Mechanicsville road. (LC)

Right: Porter took a new position near Gaines's Mill, and here on June 27, 1862, Lee attacked again. Reekie's photo shows the destroyed mill in April 1865. (USAMHI)

Below: Brigadier General George Morell was instrumental in defending Porter's corps from Lee's attempted encirclement. (USAMHI)

Right: The Gaines House. Less than two months before, Federal generals were posing for Houghton and others on this porch. Now it is Lee's headquarters. (MUSEUM OF THE CONFEDERACY, RICHMOND)

Above: Brigadier General Andrew A. Humphreys served as McClellan's chief topographical engineer. Poor and inadequate maps plagued both sides on the Peninsula, where local traditions twist names and pronunciations. One road pronounced "Darby" was in fact spelled "Enroughty." (USAMHI)

Above: Brigadier General Arnold Elzey—whose real name was Jones—was a hero at Bull Run. At Gaines's Mill he received a terrible wound which left him unfit for field command for most of the rest of the war. (DUKE UNIVERSITY, BRADLEY T. JOHNSON PAPERS)

Above: Colonel James S. Connor, a veteran of Bull Run and the Hampton Legion, took command of the 22nd North Carolina shortly before Gaines's Mill. In this battle a rifle ball broke his leg. (LC)

Above: Major General Ambrose Powell Hill performed the greatest share of the fighting for Lee at Mechanicsville and Gaines's Mill. He became one of Lee's premier commanders. (FRANK DEMENT)

Right: James J. Archer, appointed a brigadier just before the fighting on the Peninsula began, commanded the Texas brigade at Gaines's Mill with distinction. (P-M)

Above: William Dorsey Pender won promotion to brigadier for his service at Fair Oaks, and now led a brigade for A. P. Hill. One of the army's most brilliant young commanders, he died as a result of a wound at Gettysburg a year later. (USAMHI)

Vermont photographer G. W. Houghton found this tent wrecked after a Confederate shell fired during the Gaines's Mill fighting struck it. (VHS)

Left: Part of the cost of Gaines's Mill. Federal soldiers buried hurriedly in shallow graves by their retreating comrades were exposed by later rains. Reekie found them like this in April 1865. (WRHS)

Right: On June 29 the fighting moved to Savage Station on the Richmond & York River Railroad. It is shown here the day before the battle, photographed by James Gibson. (VM)

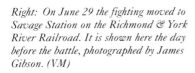

Above: "Prince John" Magruder had been fighting holding actions south of the Chickahominy while Lee attacked Porter. Now Lee ordered him to attack McClellan's rear. He pushed the Federal advance back to Savage Station. (USAMHI)

Above: In the subsequent fighting, over 1,500 Federals became casualties. Here some wounded from Gaines's Mill and earlier fights await transportation to the rear at Savage Station. (USAMHI)

Left: Vermont soldiers particularly distinguished themselves at Savage Station. Here the Green Mountain Boys of the 6th Vermont's Company I at drill. (LC)

Above: McClellan retreated to White Oak Swamp where the forces joined battle again on June 30. There in furious fighting Brigadier General George G. Meade was wounded twice in almost the same moment. (USAMHI)

Left: Sick and wounded of the 16th New York being tended at Savage Station photographed by Gibson on June 28. (MHS)

Above: John Sedgwick, now a brigadier, was once major of the 1st United States Cavalry, whose colonel was Robert E. Lee. Now he led a division in Sumner's corps, but a bullet at White Oak Swamp put him out of the war for several weeks. (NA)

Above: Major General Erasmus D. Keyes, veteran of Bull Run, commanded McClellan's IV Corps without particular distinction at White Oak Swamp. One of his brigade commanders,... (USAMHI)

Right: ... Colonel Philippe Regis Denis de Keredern de Trobriand, was the son of a French nobleman. He became one of the Union's finest brigadiers. (USAMHI)

Above: Brigadier General James L. Kemper, once speaker of the house in the Virginia capital, now led a brigade in the nightmarish morass of White Oak Swamp. (USAMHI)

Above: George M. Sauerbier's image of the "Westchester Chasseurs," the 17th New York on parade. They are among many regiments mauled in the Seven Days fighting and at White Oak Swamp. (NA, BRADY COLLECTION)

Above: The final battle came at Malvern Hill, where the retreating Federals made their stand. On July 1, 1862, Lee attacked repeatedly and with heavy losses. Regiments like the 4th Georgia, shown here in April 1861, could not move the enemy. (GEORGIA DEPARTMENT OF ARCHIVES AND HISTORY)

Above: Despite heavy support from his artillery, commanded by Brigadier General William N. Pendleton, Lee could not break McClellan's line. Pendleton, an Episcopal clergyman, was often mistaken for Lee. When not fighting, he preached in the camps. This photo was probably taken in 1864 after the death of his son, thus the mourning band on his arm. (TONY MARION)

Below: The 19th Georgia took part in repeated attacks. It was largely a family regiment. Standing at right is Lieutenant Colonel Thomas C. Johnson, and seated at right is Lieutenant William H. Johnson. The sergeant standing at back is R. A. Johnson, and the father of all three is seated second from the left. (EMORY UNIVERSITY, PHOTOGRAPHIC SERVICES, ATLANTA)

Above: A remarkable J. D. Edwards image of Gaston Coppens's Louisiana Zouaves on parade in front of the general staff quarters at the navy yard at Pensacola, April 1861. Here was a real trouble regiment. "They are generally small," said a Richmond newspaper, "but wiry, muscular, active as cats, and brown as a side of sole leather." Mutinous, thieving, they never gave their superiors peace. One day's morning report a year from now would show only one man present for duty, the others being absent without leave or under arrest. But they fought like devils at Malvern Hill. The campaign almost destroyed the unit. (SOUTHERN HISTORICAL COLLECTION, THE UNIVERSITY OF NORTH CAROLINA AT CHAPEL HILL)

Above: What stopped Lee at Malvern Hill was the massed guns of McClellan's artillery chief, Colonel Henry J. Hunt. He gathered a hundred cannons to repel enemy assaults. (P-M)

Above: There were no birds perched on the rammers of the 1st Massachusetts Artillery when it took part in Hunt's massive barrage at Malvern Hill. (USAMHI)

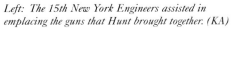

Left: The 15th New York Engineers assisted in emplacing the guns that Hunt brought together. (KA)

Right: Captain August V. Kautz led a company of the 5th United States Cavalry at Malvern Hill, but there was little for the mounted arm to do in this largely infantry campaign. He later became a feared Federal cavalry raider. (AMERICANA IMAGE GALLERY, CUSTODIAN OF THE RINHART COLLECTION)

Above: Lieutenant Colonel Louis Thourot had command of the 55th New York at Malvern Hill when his colonel,… (WRHS)

Above: … Regis de Trobriand, took over a brigade. He stands at right holding a rammer, while members of the 55th New York look on. (AMERICANA IMAGE GALLERY)

Above: Defeated in his purpose to take Richmond and unable to withstand Lee's attacks, McClellan finally withdrew to Harrison's Landing on the James River, thus ending the campaign. His troops occupied "Westover," once the plantation estate of William Byrd, a remarkable Virginia gentleman of a century before. For now the war must move elsewhere. (USAMHI)

Above: Brigadier General John H. Martindale, seated here in 1864 with his staff, reportedly declared that he would sooner surrender than leave behind his wounded at Malvern Hill. A court of inquiry acquitted him of the charge. (LC)

In Camp with the Commom Soldiers

BELL I. WILEY

The real story of the life of the Civil War Soldier; for every day in battle, fifty in camp

Above: Of all the places remembered in afteryears, it is the camp tent with all its associations that soldiers will most clearly call to mind. Lieutenant J. B. Neill of the 153rd New York sits peacefully in his tent, pictures of his wife on the table with his books, his camp cot in the shadows. Arrayed on the shelf above him are the few simple items that he carries from one field to another in this war. (USAMHI)

WHAT MOST YANKS AND REBS had in mind when they enlisted was to meet their foes in battle, and the sooner the better. Instead they learned after a while that fighting was to occupy only a small part of their army service. The long lulls between battles saw them occupied instead with drills, parades, inspections, and routine activities. However good or bad in the fight they might be, all Yanks and Rebs came to excell in "camp life."

Both in camp and on the march the first concern was food. At the beginning of the war the ration officially prescribed for both sides provided a daily allowance for each soldier of twelve ounces of pork or bacon, or twenty ounces of beef, fresh or salted; twenty-two ounces of soft bread or flour, or sixteen ounces of hard bread, or twenty ounces of corn meal; and to every one hundred rations: fifteen pounds of peas or beans and ten pounds of rice or hominy; ten pounds of green coffee, or eight pounds of roasted coffee, or twenty-four ounces of tea; fifteen pounds of sugar; four quarts of vinegar; three pounds and twelve ounces of salt; four ounces of pepper; thirty pounds of potatoes, when practicable; and one quart of molasses. This allowance exceeded that authorized in any European army. Even so, the Union government increased the allowance in August 1861 and the augmentation remained in effect until June 1864, when it was reduced to that provided at the beginning of the war. Experience had shown that the enlarged issue exceeded the needs of the soldiers and promoted wastefulness.

On the Confederate side authorities ordered a general reduction of the ration in April 1862, and later particular items were curtailed. In the autumn of 1863 Commissary-General Lucius B. Northrop reduced the bacon issue to one third of a pound, and the next year the flour or meal ration was cut to sixteen ounces. More often than not, owing to hoarding, bad management, and the breakdown of transportation facilities in the South, Johnny Rebs got considerably less food than that authorized by Northrop and his associates in Richmond.

In both armies the rations specified in regulations and the fare actually served in camp differed considerably. As a rule, Northerners enjoyed greater abundance and variety of food than did Southerners. Billy Yanks were never reduced to the low level of subsistence experienced by Rebs at Port Hudson and Vicksburg in the summer of 1863, but some of them experienced times of great hunger. Those who marched from Chattanooga to Knoxville and back late in 1863 had to subsist for several days on corn gathered from the places where the horses fed and parched over the coals of their campfires. They experienced similar deprivation in Chattanooga before U. S. Grant and William "Baldy" Smith opened up the "cracker line" in October 1863. A Hoosier soldier wrote from Chattanooga on October 22, 1863, that for the past month he and his comrades had lived on "two meals per day and one cracker for each meal."

Mainstays of rations issued to both Rebs and Yanks were meat, bread (or the flour or meal with which to make it), and coffee. Meat was pork or beef, sometimes fresh from recently slaughtered animals, but more often salt-cured or pickled. Salt pork, widely known as sowbelly or sow bosom by the soldiers, was fried in skillets, boiled in pots, or broiled on the ends of sticks held above hot coals. It was also used as seasoning for vegetables cooked in containers suspended above campfires. Fresh beef was usually boiled. Pickled beef, commonly called "salt horse," was sometimes putrid and so briny as to make it unpalatable. An Ohio soldier wrote from camp in Maryland in 1862 that "we drew meat last night that was so damd full of skippers that it could move alone; some of them is stout enuf to cary a musket." A Mississippi Reb stated that the beef issued to his company was so rotten that "the buzzards would not eat it." An Illinois Yank wrote, "Sometimes we draw sow belly and sometimes old bull. The old bull is very good... but the sow belly, phew!"

The bread most often served to Johnny Rebs was cornbread, though sometimes they drew loaves of flour bread and occasionally they had hardtack. When left to their own resources they often converted the flour into hoecakes or biscuits, which they baked on slanting boards placed near their campfires. Some Rebs preferred to wrap bits of dough around a stick or ramrod and convert them into rolls by rotating them above hot coals. Many Southerners were surfeited on cornbread. A Louisianian wrote near the end of the conflict, "If any person offers me cornbread after this war comes to a close I shall probably tell him to—go to hell."

Yanks rarely ate cornbread. They much preferred flour loaves baked in field ovens or prepared by comrades or black servants who cooked for companies or messes. During seasons of active campaigning and sometimes during periods of inactivity the only bread issued to them was hardtack.

Hardtack were crackers 2½ inches wide, 2⅞ inches high, and ⅜ inch thick. They weighed about 1½ ounces and were so hard that soldiers referred to them as "teeth dullers," and said they were more suitable for the building of breastworks than for human consumption. They came packed in boxes or barrels stamped "B.C.," probably for Brigade Commissary, but some soldiers insisted that the abbreviation represented the crackers' date of manufacture. Consumers often increased the edibility of hardtack by pulverizing them with rocks or musket butts, or soaking them in water. Hardtack crumbs were sometimes fried in bacon grease or mixed with soup or coffee.

Coffee, boiled in large kettles for quantity distribution or prepared individually in small cans or tin cups which most soldiers slung to their belts while on the march, was one of the most highly cherished items of camp fare. Soldiers of both armies consumed it in vast quantities. When the genuine "Rio" became scarce in the South owing to the blockade, Rebs resorted to "Confederate coffee" brewed from parched particles of corn, sweet potatoes, peanuts, or rye. Lacking sugar, they added molasses for "long sweetening." Some Rebs professed a fondness for their coffee improvisations, but their tributes reflect more of patriotism than actuality.

White "army beans" and brown Boston beans were often issued to Billy Yanks. Southern counter parts were field peas, sometimes of the black-eyed variety but more often the speckled whippoorwills.

Peas and white beans were usually mixed

Above: Where most of Civil War soldiering took place, the camp. Here the winter tents of the 40th Massachusetts Infantry at Miner's Hill, Virginia, in 1863. (USAMHI)

Above: An unpublished photograph showing the camp of the New Orleans Confederate Guards, probably in 1861, a scene that would be unusual for its neatness and well-equipped appearance by 1863. (TU, LOUISIANA HISTORICAL ASSOCIATION COLLECTION)

Below: The 5th Vermont in camp in 1861, a G. W. Houghton photograph. (LC)

Above: Colonel Henry HoDaman of the 230th New York at his camp table, cigar in hand, clay pipe on the table. And... (NA)

Above: ... his tentmate Major W. M. Gregg at the same table. The occupant of the bed is too tired—or shy—to sit for the camera. (WRHS)

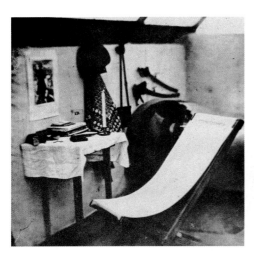

Above: A typical officer's tent interior. Sabers, binoculars, a home-knitted shawl, a kepi, and a print adorn the canvas wall. On the table, a closed cased ambrotype, comb, candlestick, a few books, scissors, and a small sewing kit (NA)

Above: Some officers enjoyed a bit more space and luxury. The same personal and military items hang on the wall. A plumed hat rests on the bed, and the table is set for a meal. There is almost a look of permanence here. (NA)

Right: When winter came, permanence was necessary. The 1st Connecticut Heavy Artillery builds its winter quarters in 1864. (USAMHI)

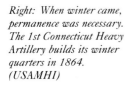

with chunks of pork and boiled in iron pots. New Englanders liked to bake their brown beans in submerged pans surrounded by smoldering coals.

Sweet potatoes, Irish potatoes, and dried fruit were consumed in large quantities in both Union and Confederate camps. Potatoes were often baked in their skins and dried fruit was sometimes stewed and used as filler for fried pies.

Soldier life was conducive to the development of hearty appetites. Private Daniel Peck of New York wrote his sister in December 1862, "I am well and tough and as hearty as ever. I can finish twelve tack a day, three quarts of coffee, one half pound pork or beef, some dried apples & beans. But the beans punish me so I don't eat them. The foretaste is better than the aftertaste."

Yanks and Rebs supplemented commissary issues with boxes of edibles of all sorts sent to them by solicitous relatives and friends at home. Delays in transit often caused spoilage of perishables, and poor packing or rough handling frequently resulted in breakage. But enough of the foodstuff reached its destination in usable condition to keep recipients asking for more.

Foraging, an army euphemism for stealing, was another frequently used source of enrichment of soldier rations. Yanks, partly because they spent most of their time in "enemy" country, were the greater offenders, but Rebs when subjected to hunger, as they frequently were, foraged freely on fellow Southerners. Pigpens, poultry houses, or chards, watermelon patches, cornfields, vegetable gardens, smokehouses, and turkey roosts were rarely immune to soldier incursions in any locality occupied by either Yanks or Rebs.

Another source of ration supplementation was the sutler who set up shop in army camps. Yanks saw more of sutlers than did Rebs because of the dearth of money among Southerners. Sutlers stocked candy, pies, cakes, pickles, canned oysters, sardines, and other edibles, along with stationery, writing pens, books, beverages, and other articles sought by their clientele. Soldiers usually regarded the sutler's prices as

Above: And moves in when they are completed.

Above: Built mostly from scavenged parts and ingenuity, these Confederate huts were good enough that Federals later used them. Manassas, 1862. (WRHS)

exorbitant, and one of their favorite diversions was to raid the merchant's tent and clean out his stock. Civilians too, black and white, residing in areas near army camps often peddled provisions to military personnel. Favorite articles of sale were pies and cakes, which purchasers sometimes referred to as "pizen cakes."

Early in the war soldiers on both sides complained frequently about the quality of their fare. But as the struggle continued and provisions became scarcer, protests centered more on quantity. This was especially true of Confederates. During the Chattanooga campaign a famished Texan of Bragg's army declared that if he ever got home he was going "to take a hundred biscuit and two large hams, call it three days rations, then go down on Goat Island and eat it all at one meal."

The culinary abilities of Yanks and Rebs improved as they adjusted to soldiering and many of them boasted to civilian friends and kin that the food they prepared in camp compared favorably with that served at home. They also bragged about the proficiency acquired in laundering their clothes. On the march they had to wash their garments in streams, lakes, and ponds, as opportunity afforded, and hang them on tree limbs while they lounged naked on the banks waiting for the apparel to dry. But when settled in camp for considerable periods of time, as they usually were in winter, Rebs and Yanks often observed weekly washdays. These resembled the same occasions known at home, except that the washing was done by males with whatever facilities were at hand. Water was usually heated in pots, and clothes were soaped and scrubbed in tubs fashioned from barrels. Sometimes the scrubbing was done on corrugated metal boards, such as those used by the homefolk, but in most instances the dirt was removed by repeated dousing and twisting. Ironing was dispensed with, owing to lack of equipment and the view that wrinkles were an acceptable part of camp life.

Still, practices known at home were considered ideal and in their housing arrangements soldiers were inclined to approximate them to the fullest possible extent. The shelter tents, or pup

Above: Whole cities of log huts dot the Southern landscape every war winter. (USAMHI)

Above: They are Confederate as well as Union. Here Confederate winter quarters of J. E. Johnston's army at Manassas in 1862. (USAMHI)

Left: Union soldiers occupying once-Confederate winter houses at Centreville, Virginia. Winter, rain, and mud erased any care about who built them. "Corduroy" roads and walkways made of logs cross the mud. (LC)

tents, used during periods of active campaigning were too small to permit much "fixing up." But larger tents, whether the bell-shaped Sibleys, the A tents, or the wall tents, which provided protection from sun and rain during relatively mild seasons when troops were not on the move, gave Rebs and Yanks an opportunity to apply their homemaking instincts. Guns were neatly stacked in the center or near entrances of canvas abodes. Bunks fashioned of boards and filled with leaves, straw, or other soft materials and covered with blankets were placed around the interior to suit the taste and convenience of the occupants. When not used for reclining, bunks served as seats. Additional seating was improvised from kegs, barrels, and cracker boxes. Tables and writing desks were made of boards "liberated" from abandoned buildings or obtained from crates discarded by commissary or quarter master. Canteens, cooking utensils, haversacks, knapsacks and other items of equipment were suspended from tent poles or stacked on the ground. Light came from candles stuck in bayonet sockets.

Homemaking proclivities were indulged to the fullest extent in cold weather when soldiers settled in winter quarters. Winter residences were frequently rectangular cabins made of logs cut from nearby trees, dragged to the building site, notched, and put in place by the soldiers. Slanting roofs were made of boards or split logs covered with pine straw; spaces between the logs were filled with mud. A variation of the log hut was a hybrid structure part wood and part fabric, made by superimposing rectangular tents on log bases. These "winterized" or "stockaded" tents, like the log huts, were usually designed for four men. Sometimes the occupants increased roominess and warmth by excavating interiors to a depth of several feet. In some cases winter dwellings were warmed by stoves, which also were used for cooking, but more commonly heat for comfort and cooking was provided by fireplaces located usually at one end of the room. These were made of small logs chinked with mud and capped by chimneys made of the same materials. Draft was increased by topping chimneys with barrels, but these sometimes caught fire, routing soldiers from their bunks and threatening their abodes with destruction. Some soldiers were content with floors of earth or straw. Others, at considerable labor, covered the soil with split logs or with boards.

The average winter dwelling contained two bunks, one above the other, extending across the side or rear. The occupants made mattresses by filling cloth containers with pine needles, leaves, or straw. Ordinarily they placed knapsacks at the head of the bunks and suspended other equip-

Right: Winter quarters for some were far more luxurious. The 22nd Michigan at Camp Ella in Bishop, Kentucky, had regular barracks to withstand the cold. (GORDON WHITNEY COLLECTION)

Left: Their officers' quarters even boasted a little bit of gingerbread trim. (GORDON WHITNEY COLLECTION)

Left: Wherever and whatever their accommodations, however, the soldiers enjoyed winter. There was little or no fighting and, with some protection from the cold, it was a peaceful time. (USAMHI)

Above: These Confederates of the 1st Texas at Camp Quantico, near Dumfries, Virginia, perform their camp chores with a casual air of contentment. They are the "Beauregard Mess," and this winter of 1861-62 they will be warm. (ROBERT MCDONALD)

Above: Some men used civilian skills to build chimneys and fireplaces. They read books and newspapers and letters from home, and they trained mascots like dogs and birds. (LLOYD OSTENDORP COLLECTION)

ment and extra clothing from nails or pegs driven into the walls. Seats, desks, and tables were made of logs, boxes, kegs, and barrels. Almost every company had a few fastidious members who insisted on providing their winter quarters with wallpaper and adding adornments in the form of mantelpieces, pictures, and fancy pieces of furniture.

When family or friends visited camp, as they sometimes did in the winter season, soldiers took great pride in showing off their homemaking prowess. Many described their comforts in letters to the folk at home. A Georgia private wrote his wife from camp near Fredericksburg in early March, 1863, "You would be surprised to know how comfortable a place I have to live in, a white [from snow] hous and a good fire place and a box, chunk, or the ground wich are all used for seats hear. We all take our seats, some reading, som writing, some laughing, some talking, som set up sleeping and some thinking of home.... Finely [finally] Mr. A. begines to tell whare he herd his first bum and how bad it sceard him and Mr. B. not to be out don tells what dangers he has pased through. Mr. C. he tells his tale.... Mr. E.... says that he thinks that he is the man that ought to have the next furlow.... [After a lively argument over who had the best claim to a furlough] H. commenses singing home sweet hom, all the crowd joines in and the hole wood resounds with the music."

In both winter and summer officers generally lived better than their men, and the higher the rank, with some notable exceptions, the greater their comfort. In winter they had more commodious huts, made usually by the soldiers whom they commanded, and when they lived in tents, they normally had relatively spacious wall tents. Sometimes an officer had a dwelling all to himself, save perhaps for a black servant who performed menial duties. His furniture, clothing, and food usually were superior to that of the rank and file. Normally he had no difficulty in obtaining liquor, a commodity often denied to ordinary soldiers. However, most thirsty privates were able to circumvent the prohibitions when they had funds, but the stuff that they obtained on

Left: Music occupied the time of many, as did cards. Here in the quarters of Dr. David McKay of the Army of the James, unusual luxury is evident. Ample space in an old occupied house, a fireplace, instruments galore, all combine to make the "5 Drons" and their "Fun & Fury" quarters more than habitable. (USAMHI)

Left: The average soldier and officer settled for much less, like the quarters of these officers of the 1st Rhode Island Light Artillery, Battery E. But still they have their books, their maps decorating the wall, and a well-stocked table. (USAMHI)

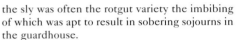

Above and above right: Life in camp was not all relaxation. There were tasks aplenty to keep the men busy and fit. Chopping wood, sweeping, polishing boots, mending socks, and clowning all filled the idle hours. The denizens of "Pine Cottage" did their chores first, then dressed for the camera. (USAMHI)

Right: The "Wigfall Mess" of the 1st Texas Infantry, chop their wood and carry water and wash their dishes. (THE MUSEUM OF THE CONFEDER-ACY, RICHMOND)

Below: The need for wood was endless. (USAMHI)

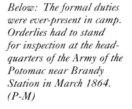

Below: The formal duties were ever-present in camp. Orderlies had to stand for inspection at the head-quarters of the Army of the Potomac near Brandy Station in March 1864. (P-M)

the sly was often the rotgut variety the imbibing of which was apt to result in sobering sojourns in the guardhouse.

Camp life at its best was apt to be monotonous and lonely. Daily drills, Sunday reviews, and periodic parades increased in onerousness with the passing of time. Marches in rain and mud or in heat and dust were irksome and exhausting, and when accompanied by poor rations and polluted water, as they frequently were, they became almost intolerable. Exposure, overexertion, undernourishment, and the ravages of insects and germs produced floods of sickness, and hostile missiles added countless others to the list of the disabled. In the American Civil War the sick and wounded suffered most. Medicines and medical facilities fell far short of needs, especially on the Confederate side.

Both the ailing and the well sought diversion to combat their hardship and boredom. Music was a favorite pastime in both armies. Regimental and brigade bands often gave evening concerts at which they played sentimental, patriotic, and sometimes classical pieces. Occasionally bands would serenade officers, a practice which afforded pleasure to entire camps. General Lee, after listening to an informal band concert in 1864, stated, "I don't believe we can have an army without music." A Rebel private

Left: James F. Gibson's spring 1862 image of the servants of the Prince de Joinville doing his chores for him. (KA)

Above: Artillerists of the 1st Brigade of Horse Artillery, Brandy Station, in September 1863, studied their maps in off moments. (AMERICANA IMAGE GALLERY)

Above: Signal corpsmen refined their skills, if somewhat lazily. A Brady & Company image from 1864. (CHS)

was prompted to remark at the conclusion of a stirring band concert in a Virginia camp, "I felt at the time that I could whip a whole brigade of the enemy." As a rule Billy Yanks, owing to the relatively greater number of musicians and instruments available in Northern units, enjoyed more and better band music than did Rebs. Some of the best music was provided by the Germans, about 200,000 of whom donned the Union blue.

In both armies the instrumental music heard most frequently was provided by individuals and small groups who brought violins, banjos, guitars, and flutes to camp with them and played informally for the entertainment of themselves and their comrades. A Mississippian wrote to a friend early in the war that he and his associates were experiencing lively times in camp. "Every night," he stated, "fiddlers are plentiful.... I wish you would happen in sometime while Will Mason is playing the violin & see some of his capers."

Many regiments had glee clubs who entertained fellow soldiers with a variety of songs. But, as in the case of instrumental programs, the most frequent, and probably the most appreciated vocal performances, were those given by informal groups brought together by the sheer

Left: And there was always drill. (USAMHI)

Left: And more drill. (MHS)

Left: And still more. The New York Excelsior Brigade. (USAMHI)

Right: George N. Barrlard caught this company drilling amid its own quarters, behind a decidedly decorative fence. (NA)

Above: Fresh bread came from the camp bakery, where the bakers let the dough rise in the sun. (INTERNATIONAL MUSEUM OF PHOTOGRA-PHY)

Left: When the drill and the duties were done, how-ever, then came the time for food. Every Civil War sol-dier was an expert at eat-ing. Here Captain James W. Forsythe—later a brigadier general—sits on the staple of the soldier diet, a box of "Army Bread"—hard tack. (NA)

Left: They baked the loaves twenty at a time. (USAMHI)

Below: And doled the loaves out to each mess's cook or servant, along with the ration of meat and vegetables. The meat was rationed by weight. (USAMHI)

Above: No one was too bothered about sanitation. Keeping the bread in the same tent with the animal hay and letting a dog wander over both seemed not out of order. (USAMHI)

Above: The armies brought their own herds with them, killing and butchering fresh beef daily when possible. These beef quarters have been salted and hung for drying. The salt residue lies on the boards below them. It would help preserve the beef—sometimes. (USAMHI)

Above: Cutting the meat for the stew. Brady & Company published this image in 1861. (T. SCOTT SANDERS COLLECTION)

Above: Doling out commissary stores at Camp Essex, weighing, carving, and—with the red tape so beloved of armies—recording who got how much of what and when. (MHS)

Above: Weighing beef on Morris Island, South Carolina. The more tropical the climate, the more likely the soldier was to receive rancid meat—and eat it. (RONN PALM COLLECTION)

love of music combined with a desire to entertain their comrades. A New York artillery captain wrote to a friend in 1863, "We have pretty lively times in the evenings, the Germans of my company get together and sing very sweetly and I try to join in with them."

Reading was another favorite diversion of Rebs and Yanks. What they enjoyed most was reading the letters of their homefolk. "Mail call" from company headquarters always brought throngs of eager soldiers rushing to claim missives from wives, children, parents, and friends. Arrival of mail was about the only incident that would cause men to interrupt their meals. Those whose names were called proceeded happily to some quiet spot to read and reread the latest word from home; those for whom no letters came slipped away in disappointment and envy to resume the drab routine of camp life. "Boys who will lie on their backs with hardly energy enough to turn over," wrote an Alabamian in 1862, "will jump up and hurry to the captain's tent to get it [mail]." A Texan wrote his wife in 1863, "I feel mightily down when the mail comes in and the other boys get letters and I don't." About the same time another Reb wrote his spouse that he "was almost down in histericks to hear from home." Yanks were less frequently disappointed than Rebs by nonreceipt of mail, because mail service in the North, owing to more and better rail and other communications facilities, was much better than in the South. Sometimes letters from rural areas of the South were not delivered in camp for several months. Slowness of Confederate postal service led correspondents to rely increasingly on personal delivery of letters by friends and relatives. Despite uncertainties and delays a large volume of mail reached its destination in both South and North. Unfortunately for the historian, only a small portion of correspondence received in camp was preserved, owing to the inconvenience of keeping it and fear on the part of recipients that it might fall into the hands of foes and become the subject of derisive comment.

Most soldiers enjoyed answering letters. A

Above: Boiled beef for the soldiers, cooked on the camp stove. (USAMHI)

Below: Like soldiers in all armies, Rebs and Yanks complained about their food. But they cooked and ate it nevertheless. (NA)

Above: Not the most nourishing meal, perhaps, but filling. Hardtack and butter on the plate, and bread in hand. Coffee would steam from the cup in good times. (LES JENSEN COLLECTION)

Right: A few potatoes or other vegetables added variety to the salt pork and boiled beef. Always there was hardtack. A private of the 49th New York. (DALE S. SNAIR COLLECTION, RICHMOND)

Above: Lieutenant Colonel F. M. Bache of the 16th United States Infantry and his mess in January 1864. He sits at left, with other members of the Army of the Potomac headquarters staff at Brandy Station. They dine well, served by a servant with a milk glass pitcher. Alexander Gardner's photograph. (USAMHI)

Right: A noncommissioned officers' mess, Company D, 93rd New York, at Bealton, Virginia, August 1863. They dine with less style than the officers, but they still eat well. (MHS)

Right: And the privates eat as they can, and as much as they can. Bread, hardtack, beef, and coffee are their staples. (COLLECTION OF MICHAEL J. MCAFEE)

likely scene during any respite from camp duties was a Reb or Yank off to himself, with paper resting on stump, box, or knee "dropping a few lines" to the folk at home. Health was a favorite subject of comment and many a soldier complained to the homefolk of recurrent bouts with the "the sh-ts," a malady also known as "the Tennessee quick step." Correspondents almost always requested early responses and stressed a desire for information about the doings of children, the progress of crops, the condition of pets and livestock, and details of life in home and community. In the 165 extant letters that Robert M. Gill wrote to his wife Bettie in Mississippi before he was killed at Jonesboro, Georgia, August 31, 1864, one of his most frequent inquiries was about his little daughter, Callie. "Does she remember me?" he asked in one letter. "You must not whip her," he added, "I have a perfect horror of whipping children." The advice that innumerable Rebs and Yanks sent to their offspring was "mind your mother, say your prayers and don't neglect your books."

Next to letters, newspapers provided the most pleasure for soldier readers. Rebs had considerably less access to journalistic literature than did the men in blue because Southern papers did not approach those of the North in numbers, circulation, or coverage of events. Owing to scarcity of newsprint, deterioration of equipment, and inadequacy of financial resources most Southern newspapers declined in size and quality during the conflict, and some became casualties of war. The Memphis *Appeal*

Left: After dinner, port and cigars for these men near Fort Monroe. (NYHS)

Right: And now and then a picnic with sausages and bologna, cider, and sometimes chocolate. (COLLECTION OF MICHAEL J. MCAFEE)

Left: The soldiers supplemented their uninteresting diet with delicacies bought from the sutlers—government-approved vendors—who followed the armies. Here a decidedly seedy-looking lot of them pose amid their wares of liquor and tobacco. (USAMHI)

Right: They opened their stores wherever the tents and winter huts sprang up. Some, like A. Foulke, followed the same unit throughout the war. Brandy Station, Virginia, February 1863. (USAMHI)

Right: The soldiers bellied up to the "bar" for their whiskey and beer. They bought Bibles and books at the same place. (USAMHI)

Left: Fresh oysters were a real delicacy, and often not so fresh. Sutlers were frequently charged with selling rancid victuals. (USAMHI)

had to flee invading Federals so often that it came to be known as "the moving Appeal." Both this paper and the Chattanooga *Daily Rebel* devoted considerable attention to military affairs and were eagerly read by soldiers of the Western armies. The same could be said of the Richmond dailies and Rebs serving in the Army of Northern Virginia. These journals were not driven to use wallpaper for newsprint as were the Vicksburg *Citizen* and the Opelousas, Louisiana, *Courier,* but all of them had their troubles. Circulation in Southern camps suffered from various circumstances including scarcity of money among Johnny Rebs and their families. Papers that found their way to news-hungry Confederates were literally worn out as they passed from hand to hand.

The war created a great boom for Northern journalism, and as circulation increased, both at home and in the army, reporters, photographers, and artists frequented camps to gather news and illustrations, and news vendors regularly made the rounds of military units and hospitals hawking the New York *Tribune, Herald,* and *Times,* the Boston *Journal,* the Philadelphia *Inquirer,* the Cincinnati *Gazette,* the Chicago *Times,* and other metropolitan dailies. Both Yanks and Rebs gave a high rating to the illustrated weeklies that thrived during the war years, including *Leslie's* and *Harper's* and the Richmond-based *Southern Illustrated News.* County and town newspapers were not often sold in camps but soldiers, and especially Billy Yanks, frequently received issues of local journals sent through the mail by publishers or homefolk.

Sometimes regiments and other units issued their own papers, and in rare instances informal groups wrote out news sheets by hand. Both printed and manuscript newspapers contained military information, poetry, gossip, and jokes. After being read in camp they were usually sent to the folk at home.

Magazines such as the *Atlantic* and *Southern*

Above: A "Fruit & Oyster House" in front of Petersburg in 1864. (USAMHI)

Below: Others created virtual shopping centers like this area at Petersburg in early 1865. Sayer's Oyster House sold pipes, cigars, oysters, and soda water. Next door Mr. Shtz sold cakes, and his neighbor sold and repaired boots and shoes. Up on the hill sat an "Eating House," while on the left a clothier sold "Ready Made" army garments. In the center sits the wagon of Bates of New York City, who attached himself strictly to the 7th New York, and behind him stands a wholesale and retail condensed milk "depot." Behind that sits an outhouse. (LC)

Above: Some specialized solely in whiskey and tobacco, where the real money lay. (USAMHI)

Field and *Fireside* had some circulation in camp. Books of fiction, literature, and history never lacked readers in either Northern or Southern camps, but Yanks, owing to better education, more money, and superior distribution facilities had considerably better opportunity to read them than did Rebs. On both sides, but far more often in Northern than in Southern camps, soldiers had access to cheap paperback novels and joke books. Religious organizations flooded camps with tracts, most of them warning readers against the evils of profanity, liquor, and gambling. Among Rebels especially, owing to a dearth of other materials, these tracts always found readers. The most widely read book among both Yanks and Rebs was the Bible.

Religious services provided diversion for many soldiers. Yanks and Rebs often spoke disparagingly of chaplains, and there is considerable evidence to indicate that the better ministers, owing to the poor pay and the great hardships endured by chaplains, preferred service on the home front to that in camp. But "Holy Joes of the Sixties" were often sincere, dedicated individuals whose ministrations were much appreciated by the rank and file. In addition to attending Sabbath services, which usually featured the chaplains' sermons, religiously inclined soldiers often met on their own for prayer meetings led by one of their comrades. In the spring, when the season of active campaigning approached, revivals sometimes swept over the camps, but these occurred more frequently and on larger

Above: Both armies also relied heavily on "foraging," officially sanctioned theft from local farmers who were sometimes—but by no means always—paid in government scrip. G. W. Houghton captured this foraging expedition, decidedly ambitious, leaving to scour the Virginia countryside for edibles. (VHS)

Right: More common was the individual foraging soldier, though there was certainly nothing at all common about this grinning lad, Billy Crump of Company I, 23rd Ohio Infantry. He was orderly to Colonel—later President—Rutherford B. Hayes. In February 1863 he borrowed Hayes's horse and pistol and set off from camp near Gauley Bridge in West Virginia. He traveled twenty miles in two days and came back laden with fifty chickens, two turkeys, one goose, twenty to twenty-five dozen eggs, and between twenty-six and thirty pounds of butter. Here was a good provider. (USAMHI)

scale among Confederates than among Federals. This was due in part to the greater strength among Southerners of evangelistic denominations and to the greater religiousness of their officers, including such high-ranking leaders as Lee, Jackson, and Jeb Stuart. Interestingly, the largest and most fervent revivals experienced by Confederates came after 1862, when owing to the worsening of the military situation and the increasing prospect of exposure to death in combat, Southerners felt a greater need to seek spiritual guidance and comfort.

The religious activity that Yanks and Rebs probably enjoyed most of all was the singing of hymns. Favorites included "Sweet Hour of Prayer," "My Faith Looks Up to Thee," "Rock of Ages," "All Hail the Power of Jesus' Name," "Amazing Grace," "On Jordan's Stormy Banks I Stand," and "There Is a Fountain Filled with Blood." Religious organizations encouraged singing by distributing pocket-size hymn books prepared especially for army use.

When opposing armies were stationed near each other much fraternization occurred. On these occasions Northern newspapers were swapped for those published in the South, and coffee was exchanged for tobacco. Sometimes trade was carried on by means of small boats equipped with sails set in such a manner as to take the vessels across river, lake, or bay separating opposing forces. Throughout fighting areas, Yanks and Rebs swam together, drank together, and even gambled together. Friendly intercourse was sometimes interspersed with communication that was not so cordial. During the siege of Vicksburg, for example, Yanks would call out to Confederates, "Say, Rebs, how do you like your new general?" Southerners would respond, "What do you mean by new general? We've still got old Pemberton." The Federals would retort, "Oh, yes you have, General Starvation." Rebs would come back with the inquiry, "Say, Yanks, have you got yourselves any nigger wives yet? Do you suppose they will improve the Yankee breed any?" The Federal taunt, "Say Reb, haint you got any better clothes than them," once provoked the response, "Who do you think we are, a set of damn fools to put on our good clothes to go out and kill damn dogs in." Then the shooting would resume.

Clowning among themselves, horseplay, teasing, and joking made soldiering more tolerable for many. A person appearing in camp in any unusual garb was almost certain to become the target of much disparagement and ridicule, such as "Come up outer them boots; I know you're in thar; I see your arms sticking out." Or, "Look out, that parrot shell that you're wearing on your head is going to explode." Unpopular officers were sometimes subjected to groans or catcalls as they walked company streets or reclined in their bunks. Some Georgia soldiers once rode their colonel on a rail, letting him dismount only when he promised better behavior.

A Federal officer stationed at Murfreesboro wrote that in March 1863, when General Rosecrans and his staff rode through a camp of Yanks living in pup tents they "were greeted with a tremendous bow-wow. The boys were on their hands and knees, stretching their heads out of the ends of the tents, barking furiously at the passing cavalcade." The general, he added, instead of becoming angry, laughed heartily and

Left: Their hunger satisfied, the soldiers passed their leisure time as best they could. Reading was a favorite in both armies, and literacy was much higher than usually supposed. Those who could not read liked being read to. Gardner caught these news vendors in October 1862. (LC)

Left: In Chattanooga, Tennessee, at the quarters of the 1st Engineers and Mechanics, they read and wrote letters. (MICHIGAN DEPARTMENT OF STATE, STATE ARCHIVES)

Above: A. P. Muben, a somewhat gaily bedecked news vendor, with some of the New York illustrated weeklies so popular with the soldiers. (LC)

Above: In the camp of the 5th Georgia they wrote their letters. (JOE CANOLE, JR.)

Above: The small building in the middle, just left of the tent, is the 13th Massachusetts' library in their camp at Williamsport, Maryland. Few other regiments could boast such an establishment, yet many of the Bay State regiments were almost aggressively literate. (USAMHI)

Above: Field post offices operated with most of the Federal armies, handling a huge volume of soldier mail. Here an unidentified brigadier general hands a letter to the postal clerk. (NA)

Above: In winter quarters such as Brandy Station in February 1864, there were more permanent postal establishments, like this post office with a clerk perched on a mail bag. (USAMHI)

promised the barkers better living accommodations.

Impromptu diversion was afforded by the appearance of a rabbit in camp or along the route of march. Sometimes the excited animal was pressed so long and so hard by yelling soldiers as to be caught. Then an argument was apt to ensue as to what individual or mess was to have the pleasure of eating the captured hare. Hunting, with or without guns, and fishing, with hooks or seines, was always a welcome diversion, not only for the fun that it provided, but also for the enrichment that it gave to issues of hardtack and sowbelly.

Sports and games flourished during periods of leisure. Football was mentioned occasionally in the letters of both Yanks and Rebs but baseball, of the four-base or two-base "town-ball" variety, was a more popular exercise. The ball was often soft and in one version of the game the mode of putting out the runner was to hit him with the ball. Bats were frequently sticks or boards. Scores sometimes were very high. In a game at Yorktown, Virginia, in 1863, the 9th New York Regiment beat the 51st New York by a score of 58-19.

Holidays such as the Fourth of July and, in Irish regiments, St. Patrick's Day, were celebrat-

Above: Neither snow nor rain nor gloom of night—not even the enemy—could stay the delivery of the mail to the soldiers. It was one of the single most important factors in preserving morale. Brandy Station in April 1864. (USAMHI)

Below: A group of IX Corps chaplains pose before their "Baltimore Cotton Duck Extra" tent, near Petersburg. (LC)

Above: Religious revivals frequently swept through the camps even faster than the mail. Devotion, as many soldiers confessed, helped fill idle hours, and sometimes local belles attended as well. Here the 50th New York Engineers built their own church before Petersburg. (P-M)

ed by horse races, boxing, wrestling matches, foot races, leap frog, cricket, broad jumping, and free-for-all scuffles. These festivities were often accompanied by swigging of whiskey or beer on the part of participants and spectators, and at the end of the day guardhouses might overflow with soldiers suffering from black eyes, bruised limbs, and even broken bones.

In winter, when the weather became cold enough to coat lakes and ponds with ice, Yanks found pleasure in skating. Rebs rarely had skates or the skill of using them, but if soles were thick enough they scooted awkwardly over the ice in their shoes. Sleds, often improvised from boards or tubs, carried soldiers down snow-covered hills and merriment was enhanced by occasional spills. Snowball battles were frequent occurrences. Sometimes participants would fight in regiments or brigades, commanded by the same officers who led them in battle. Prisoners were taken and paroled, and the wounded were attended by doctors or nurses. Since contestants occasionally loaded their snow pellets with cores of rock or metal, wounds were sometimes more than superficial. Early in 1863, near Fredericksburg, the 26th New Jersey Regiment and a Vermont unit formed a line of battle and pitched into each other with such fury that "the air was filled with white missles and stentorian cheers went up as one or the other party gained an advantage." After a series of charges and countercharges, each resulting in the taking of prisoners, "victory rested with the Vermonters and the Jersey boys surrendered the field." A Georgia Reb stationed near Fredericksburg wrote his wife in February 1863, "Some times the hole brigade formes and it looks like the sky and the hole elements was made of snow.... General Longstreet and his agitant took regs the other

Right: Father Thomas H. Mooney performs Sunday Mass for the 69th New York. Its colonel, Michael Corcoran, stands with folded arms just left of the cleric. Both North and South claimed divine endorsement. (LC)

Below: When chaplains like this one found themselves conducting services in the presence of shot and shell and weapons of destruction, some were inclined to question whether the deity could possibly condone either side. Fort Darling in April 1865, the chaplain's quarters of the 1st Connecticut Heavy Artillery, photographed by J. Reekie. (LC)

Left: Mass at Camp Cass for the largely Irish 9th Massachusetts Infantry. Only the officers attend this service. (LC)

Left: At Camp Griffin, Virginia, the 49th Pennsylvania worships as Chaplain Captain William Earnshaw uses stacked drums for an altar. (LLOYD OSTENDORF COLLECTION)

Above: With reading and religion exhausted, the soldiers turned to sport. Many opted for something cerebral like chess, but most, like those at the left, preferred cards. (USAMHI)

Right: Gambling filled the long hours of boredom, and not a few pockets as well. Officers of the 82nd Illinois in camp at Atlanta, Georgia, in 1864 gambled with ease and comfort. Outrageous pipes, often handmade, were also the rage in the Western army. (CHS)

Right: When gambling failed there was always horseplay, often at the expense of the poor freedman. (LC)

Left: For the common soldiers, a blanket and a deck of cards were the only necessities. These sergeants belong to the 56th Massachusetts. (USAMHI)

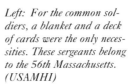

Left: A cockfight could also provide entertainment of a gruesome sort, and plenty of money changed hands on a rooster's feet. Even the brass took part. Brigadier General Orlando B. Willcox affects disinterest, looking at a letter, but he cannot help glancing at the start of a fight staged by former slaves George, on the left, and John, and their chickens. Taken at Petersburg in August 1864. (USAMHI)

day and had a fight with snow balls but the Gen. charged him and took them prisners." A heavy fall of snow in March 1864, at Dalton, Georgia, led to a series of vigorous encounters among Rebs of the Army of Tennessee. A participant in one of them wrote on March 24, "We had a Great Battle yesterday between the 63rd and 54th Va. Regt. It lasted some 2 or 3 hours.... [When] the 54th was like to drive us all out of camp... I... made a charge & drove them out, kept them out until we quit. The officers of the 54th invited me over after the fight . . . to drink with them, complimenting me for Bravery." He added, "I enjoyed the sport fine but it made horse [hoarse] on account of our great charges and cheering." Another Confederate wrote that in a snow fight involving members of New Orleans' Washington Artillery, "every man in our camp, both black and white," participated and that during the fracas, "Capt. C. H. Slocomb lost two front teeth, Lieut. Challeron [got a] black eye," and five privates came out with bloody noses. Among the captured property, he added, "is the flag of the Ga. Regiment, 8 or 10 caps and Hats, frying pan and 4 or 5 pones of corn bread."

Less boisterous than snowball fights but equally enjoyable were the sham courts-martial, the minstrels, and the plays staged by Yanks and

Below: Their funning could take a macabre turn at times. Being so close to death, it helped to make fun of it. (T. GORDON, JR.)

Right: A friendly spar for the camera was a favorite picture to send home. Boxing in camp, however, did not enjoy wide popularity. There was too much real fighting to be done. (DON W. MINDEMANN)

Rebs. In the simulated trials, enlisted men derived special pleasure from assigning officer roles to the rank and file and finding them guilty of such offenses as neglect of duty, drunkenness, immorality, and excessive harshness in discipline. Units such as the Richmond Howitzers and Boston's 44th Massachusetts Infantry formed dramatic associations and presented plays in a manner that won hearty applause from both soldiers and civilians. The 44th Massachusetts gave a program consisting of songs by a quartet, musical selections by the band, a scene from The Merchant of Venice, and a concluding drama entitled A Terrible Catastrophe on the North Atlantic R.R.

Minstrels and comedies were the most popular of all the shows presented in camp. The 9th New York Regiment's Zouave Dramatic Club in June 1862 gave a burlesque Combastus De Zouasio, which a soldier observing rated as well-performed. He liked the singing and dancing and the concluding farce Box and Cox. He reported that the theater was crowded with local aristocrats, soldiers, and officers, among them General John P. Hawkins.

Both individuals and units derived much pleasure from pets. George Baxter of the 24th Massachusetts Regiment wrote from camp in Maryland in December 1861, "Last night I was on guard.... Towards morning a little black kitten came purring around my feet, so I picked her up and put her on my shoulder and continued pacing my beat, with a rifle on one shoulder and a cat on the other." In December 1863 a correspondent of the Army of the Cumberland reported, "One of the boys has carried a red squirrel through thick and thin over a thousand miles. 'Bun' eats hard tack like a veteran and has the freedom of the tent. Another soldier has an owl captured in Arkansas & named 'Minerva'. Another has a young Cumberland Mountain bear; but chief among camp pets are dogs, riding on the saddle bow, tucked into a baggage wagon, mounted on a knapsack [or] growling under a gun.... A dog, like a horse, comes to love the rattle and crash of muskets and cannon." Colonel Lucius Fairchild of the 2nd Wisconsin Regiment wrote from near Fredericksburg in July 1862, "We have... a big half bull dog... named McClellan & stolen from a secesh. He attends all drills... is always at dress parade, sometimes marches up & down in front of the regt with the band & always marches to the center with his officers & up to the Col. All this is done with becoming gravity." A Union private wrote his homefolk from Hilton Head, South Carolina, in 1862, "Co. B has got 3 pets in the shape of yong aligators ... captured ... in the swamp.... Our little dog has a big time with them.... Co. A has a yong coon, Co. K has a crow." Soldiers whiled away many hours at cards, checkers, and dominoes, and almost every camp had a few chess enthusiasts. Meetings of Masons and other fraternal groups afforded diversion to a considerable number of men in both armies. Especially gratifying were the visits of wives and children, but these occasions were all too rare. The same was true of furloughs. A poor compensation for the lack of feminine association were the womanless dances at which soldiers and their bogus sweethearts whirled and stomped to fiddled renditions of such pieces as "Arkansas Traveler," "Billy in the Low Grounds," "The Goose Hangs

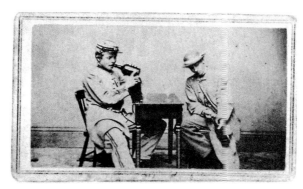

Above: Shamming for the camera was a favorite, and drinking seemed always the chosen topic, perhaps because it was so important a release for the soldiers. An excellent series ranging from the first toast in "Here is to the gal I love," to "Over the Bay," "Going Home," and finally "Good Night." Taken probably by H. Skinner of Fulton, New York, in 1862. (COLLECTION OF WILLIAM WELLING)

Below: Whenever possible, however, camp life was mostly for relaxation. It was a picture that did not change no matter the year, the place, or the army. J. D. Edwards caught these men of the Perote Guards at Pensacola drinking, reading, drawing, gambling. It was a never-ending scene. (TU)

Left: Edwards found the same scene with the 9th Mississippi in April 1861. (MUSEUM OF THE CONFEDERACY, RICHMOND)

Right: General Robert O. Tyler and his staff presented much the same image two years later in Virginia. Tyler stands second from the right. (USAMHI)

Below: Many fortunate officers North and South were joined in winter quarters by their wives, adding a dimension of domestic tranquility denied to most soldiers. (P-M)

High," "The Blue-Tailed Fly," and "Oh Lord God One Friday." These, like other social activities, sometimes were made more festive by copious draughts of "Oh Be Joyful," "Old Red Eye" and "Rock Me to Sleep Mother."

It is not surprising that many Yanks and Rebs sought relief from boredom in gambling. This was usually done with cards, and the most popular card games were poker, euchre, twenty-one, and faro. Soldiers used dice for craps and chuck-a-luck. They also gambled at keno, a game resembling bingo. Raffling was still another popular form of gambling. Rebel Sam Watkins stated that his comrades in the 1st Tennessee Regiment pitted vermin in trials of speed on tin plates. The owner of the louse that first vacated the plate was adjudged the winner. In one series of contests, one soldier's louse won so consistently as to arouse suspicion. An investigation disclosed that the winning Reb had been secretly heating his plate before each contest, thus giving his louse compelling reason to abandon it.

Gambling peaked in periods following payday. "Yesterday was Sunday," wrote a Mississippian shortly after a visit of the paymaster, "and I sat by the fire and saw the preachers holding forth about thirty steps off, and between them and me were two games of poker.... Chuck-a-luck and faro banks are running night and day with eager crowds standing around with their hands full of money. Open gambling has been prohibited but that amounts to nothing."

Visits to nearby towns and cities provided entertainment for many soldiers. Country lads derived special pleasure from these excursions. Zoos, large shops, tall buildings, and horse-drawn omnibuses were all new and exciting to men accustomed to a way of life devoid of all such attractions. Like soldiers of other conflicts, some of them freed for the first time from home restraints and knowing that the future was uncertain, yielded to the lure of a fling at the fleshpots. They visited grog shops and bawdy houses and in some instances paid a high price for their experimentation. The 10th Alabama Regiment, with a mean strength of 1,063, which went from the rural South in the early summer of 1861 to the environs of Richmond, had in July, according to the surgeon's report, a total of 62 new cases of gonorrhea and 6 of syphilis.

When visits to places beyond camp limits

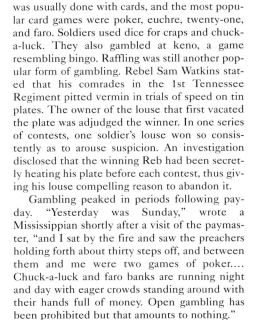

Below: Wives and daughters quickly became a focal point for attention, many men vicariously paying favor to loved ones at home through women with the armies. (USAMHI)

Below: Many read and wrote letters for illiterate soldiers. Some, like the lady on the porch, even brought their babies. Hers has moved during the exposure, causing the blur with feet in her lap. (USAMHI)

Left: The younger and prettier maidens became the belles of the armies, the object of every single officer's suit. This young lady attracts a host from an Illinois battery at Chattanooga in 1865. (CHS)

Above: The women's presence helped their men forget for a time that they were at war, especially when they had quarters like these in a casemate at Fort Monroe. (USAMHI)

Left: For one of these soldiers of Company G, 95th Illinois Infantry, Camp life was more than exotic. It was a constant tension as he attempted to conceal a perhaps scandalous secret. For the soldier on the right, Private Albert Cashier, is in fact a woman. Born in Ireland, her feminine name was Hodgers, but all her life she was known as Albert J. Cashier. She not only successfully maintained her pose, serving well particularly at Vicksburg, but she eluded detection until 1911 when an automobile caused her hospitalization. It took a twentieth-century machine to expose the life-long sham of a patriotic woman who for so long fooled the men of her own century. (SPENCER H. WATTERSON, PONTIAC, ILLINOIS)

were made without leave, as they frequently were, apprehended offenders were subjected to punishment. Brief absences drew light penalties, prescribed by company or regimental commanders. These included extra stints of guard duty, digging ditches, grubbing stumps, riding the wooden horse—a horizontal pole held aloft by two upright beams—standing in a conspicuous place on barrel, box, or stump, and cleaning company grounds. Unit commanders also punished other minor offenses such as petty theft, straggling on the march, excessive drinking, brawling, and neglect of duty. For these breaches of discipline Rebs and Yanks had to carry weights such as logs, rails, or cannonballs, wear placards specifying the offense, such as "I Stole a Shirt" or "I Am a Thief," promenade the parade ground in a "barrel shirt" with arms extending through holes cut in the sides, or wear a ball and chain, the ball being a cannonball weighing six to thirty-two pounds fastened to the ankle by a chain two to six feet long. One of the most painful penal ties imposed by officers was to hang offenders by their thumbs from boughs or beams, with toes barely touching the ground for periods of time varying with the gravity of the disciplinary breach. This was a common punishment for soldiers who spoke disrespectfully to their superiors. Another loathsome punishment often imposed for "back talk" to officers and for other insubordinate behavior was bucking and gagging. This consisted of seating the offender on the ground, tying a stick in his mouth, fastening his hands together with a rope, slipping them over his knees and inserting a pole between the arms and knees. Sometimes artillery officers strapped a recalcitrant with arms and legs extended in spread-eagle fashion to the extra wheel carried on the rear of a caisson. This punishment was cruel enough when the vehicle was stationary and the soldier's head rested at the top of the wheel; but if the wheel was given a half-turn and the caisson driven over rough ground, the pain was excruciating.

Punishments of the sort mentioned above were sometimes dispensed by regimental or garrison courts-martial instead of by unit commanders. These bodies consisted of three officers, and their jurisdiction was restricted to enlisted men and to noncapital cases. They could not assess fines greater than a month's pay or impose hard labor sentences of more than a month's duration.

Left: The soldiers made their camps as much like vacation spots as they could. The quiet moments were the best, like this one caught by Gardner in 1865. (P-M)

Below: Intimate friendships made in camp lasted for life. Brevet Major General Charles H. T. Collis sits at left with a friend. He won the Medal of Honor for Fredericksburg. (NYHS)

Right: Confederates like these of the 1st Texas at Camp Quantico, Virginia, in the winter of '61 formed especially firm associations, bound tightly together by the shared hardships of the later war years. This recently discovered image is published here for the first time. (ROSENBURG LIBRARY, GALVESTON, TEXAS)

Above left: The fellowship… (TONY MARION)

Above: … the outrageous sense of fun… (KA)

Left: … and the smiles of friends made the most memorable of war experiences. Smiling soldiers like Lieutenant John G. Hecksher of the 12th United States Infantry, at left, are rare indeed in Civil War photographs. The men preferred the more somber—nay, glum—aspect of his friend Captain William Sergeant. (P-M)

Below: Camp life was for the generals, too, and they usually enjoyed it even more than their men. Brigadier General George Stoneman sits astride his charger watching men build their winter quarters—or his. (USAMHI)

The most serious offenses, such as murder, rape, arson, desertion, cowardice in battle, striking a superior, and sleeping on sentry post, were tried by general courts-martial, summoned by commanders of separate brigades, divisions, and larger units. They consisted of from five to thirteen officers, and their jurisdiction extended to all types of cases including capital crimes. Army regulations authorized them to issue sentences providing for death, life imprisonment, solitary confinement on bread and water, hard labor, ball and chain, forfeiture of pay and allowances, discharge from the service, reprimand, and, in case of noncommissioned officers, reduction in grade. General courts-martial often specified a combination of legal punishments and sometimes they imposed penalties that violated the spirit if not the letter of the law, such as branding and shaving all or part of the head. The brand, stamped on with indelible ink or burned into the skin of hip, hand, forehead, or cheek, was usually the first letter of the victim's offense, such as "C" for cowardice, "D" for desertion, "T" for theft, and "W" for worthless. The Federals in August 1861 and Confederates in April 1862 enacted legislation prohibiting flogging, but these laws were sometimes ignored.

In both armies deserters, cowards, and other serious offenders who were sentenced to dishonorable discharge sometimes had their scalps shaved, had their buttons or insignia torn off, and were drummed out of camp to the tune of "The Rogue's March"—or in the case of Confederates, to the strains of "Yankee Doodle"—with soldiers fore and aft carrying arms reversed. Some capital offenders were hanged, but most Yanks and Rebs who paid the death penalty were shot by firing squads. Executions, which comrades of the condemned had to witness from a hollow square—a rectangle with one end open—made a tremendous impression. Private Thomas Warrick of Bragg's army wrote to his wife on December 19, 1862, "I saw a site today that made me feel mity bad. I saw a man shot for deserting there was twenty fore Guns shot at him they shot him all to pease… he went home and thay Brote him Back and then he went home again and so they shot him for that. Martha it was one site that I did hate to see But I could not helpe my self I had to do Jest as thay sed for me to doo." A Connecticut soldier reported that two of his comrades fainted while watching thirty executioners fire a fusillade that killed a deserter. Concerning an execution of six other deserters which he was forced to attend the next day, this soldier wrote that he stood within twenty feet of the victim sitting on the coffin nearest him. "They were all fired at the first time," he stated, "& 2 were killed instantly & 3 were shot the second time & the other one died while they were murdering the other three, for I call it murdering & I was not the olney one." Thomas Clark, a Pennsylvania Yank, registered no disapproval when in February 1864 he wrote his sister of the shooting of two deserters in Florida. "It was a great sight," he stated, "for it came on a Sunday and all of our regiment was out.… They where [were] hauled out in an opin wagon sitting on their coffins with a minister with each one of them and they looked and acted like they where going on an excursion. There was twelve men to shoot each one of them. The men was drawn up in a line nine paces from where the prisoners

Above: Major General John Sedgwick, left, sits with Brigadier General George Washington Getty, seated at right, at their Brandy Station tent. (USAMHI)

Above: Major General Israel B. Richardson and servant pose in the summer shade in 1862. (USAMHI)

stood by their coffins. Four o'clock came and the order was given to fire and them and day light was no more. There was nine balls went through one of their hearts and eleven passed through the other ones body. They did not live till the doctors came up to see if they were dead." If this report was accurate, the usual custom was not followed by loading only alternate rifles with live ammunition so that members of the firing squad might not know who fired the lethal shots. Clark attributed his indifference to the fact that the victims were recently recruited substitutes for whom "there was no pity."

Higher authorities on both sides showed a reluctance to approve death sentences. Apparently no Civil War soldier was executed for the capital offense of sleeping on sentry. Among Union forces totaling over 2,000,000 men, only 267 were executed and over half of these were deserters. Aggregate figures for Confederates are not available, but it is known that of 245 cases of court-martial convictions for desertion during the last six months of the conflict, mostly in the Army of Northern Virginia, death was prescribed in only 70 instances. President Davis's general amnesty of February 1865 set aside 31 of these sentences.

But death, by whatever means, became commonplace to Yanks and Rebs as the war progressed. Whatever respite they obtained from it came chiefly in the society and distinctly American character of their life in the camps. There the friendships were made, loyalties built, and memories indelibly imprinted on their minds. Here, at the fire, the tent, the mess table, men North and South displayed the true commonality of all Americans in all wars.

Left: Brigadier General John A. Rawlins, Grant's chief of staff, was joined at City Point, Virginia, by his family in 1864. (USAMHI)

Left: Brigadier General Marsena R. Patrick lived alone, as befitted Grant's chief policeman, provost-marshal general of the Army of the Potomac. (P-M)

Below: Brigadier General Thomas W. Sherman lived in tropical tranquility on Hilton Head, South Carolina, when H. P. Moore took this image on March 8, 1862. (USAMHI)

*Above: And their entertainments were much the same as those of the men they
commanded, including even an occasional sleigh ride. Here at Port Hudson,
Louisiana, in January 1864, Brigadier General Cyrus Hamlin—son of Vice
President Hannibal Hamlin—sits with a companion in the small one-horse
sleigh at left. Behind him are the officers of the black regiment he was raising.
(USAMHI)*

*Above: Music proved a pleasant diversion for all.
Here a member of the band of the 26th North
Carolina Infantry, with his horn. (DALE S. SNAIR
COLLECTION, RICHMOND)*

*Below: This Tennessee fiddler could enliven the cold-
est winter camp with the "Bonnie Blue Flag" or
Dixie. (TENNESSEE STATE MUSEUM)*

*Above: Members of the band of the 26th North Carolina, missing only their
compatriot of the previous image. Taken at Salem, North Carolina, around
1862. (MORAVIAN MUSIC FOUNDATION, INC.)*

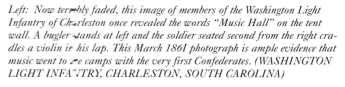

Left: Now terribly faded, this image of members of the Washington Light Infantry of Charleston once revealed the words "Music Hall" on the tent wall. A bugler stands at left and the soldier seated second from the right cradles a violin in his lap. This March 1861 photograph is ample evidence that music went to the camps with the very first Confederates. (WASHINGTON LIGHT INFANTRY, CHARLESTON, SOUTH CAROLINA)

Above: Special ensembles like this group, with tambourine, banjo, guitar, violin, triangle, and bells, sprang up informally from among the members of several regiments. (T. SCOTT SANDERS COLLECTION)

Above: The bands played for all sorts of occasions, the saddest being funerals and farewells to favorite generals being transferred to other commands. The band at left here serenades Major General Frederick Steele as he leaves Arkansas for another post, probably at the end of the war. Steele is standing second from the left between the columns immediately behind the band. (RONN PALM COLLECTION)

Above: A typical Federal regimental band, this one composed of Pennsylvanians, photographed by S. R. Miller. (RONN PALM COLLECTION)

Above: A concomitant to music was dramatics. This engineer battalion formed its own theatrical club, the "Essayons Dramatic Club," giving performances in a theater of their building at Petersburg in 1864. (USAMHI)

Left: Photographers McPherson & Oliver took this image in Baton Rouge in 1863. It shows an improvised theater which at the moment is advertising a "Benefit to Lieutenant M. W. Morris" and presenting the Lady of Lyons and a Favorite Farce. (ILLINOIS STATE HISTORICAL LIBRARY)

Above: Fraternal orders, chiefly the Masons, came with the army. Here Samuel Cooley photographs an improvised "temple" on Folly Island, South Carolina. (USAMHI)

Above: The men trained pets, like the nationally famous "Old Abe," mascot of a Wisconsin regiment with whom it lived through the war. In battle the eagle would fly from its perch and remain aloft until the fighting subsided . (LC)

Above: Dogs were the favorite. This one is supposed to be saying, "I am the dog that went through the army with the 25th Iowa Infantry. (CHICAGO PUBLIC LIBRARY)

Left: Building and elaborate decoration occupied some, especially the ever-industrious 50th New York Engineers, who made their Petersburg headquarters a virtual arbor. (USAMHI)

Left: And, of course, with idle time on their hands, the men would misbehave. That is where the provost came in. Here the Army of the Potomac's provost marshal's camp at Bealton, Virginia, in August 1863. (P-M)

Left: Wherever the army went in numbers, so the provost went also. Mostly the men drank too much or disobeyed orders. (NA,U.S. WAR DEPARTMENT GENERAL STAFF)

Right: When they did, the provost guard spirited them away to the guardhouse. Here the guard for the Army of the Potomac headquarters at Petersburg in 1865. Behind them is the picketed fence of their stockade. (USAMHI)

Below: Minor offenders were fined pay or made to ride the wooden horse and other such essentially humiliating punishments. (ROBERT L. KOTCHIAN)

Above: The worst cases went before courts-martial like this one meeting at Concord, New Hampshire. (USAMHI)

Left: More serious cases spent time at hard labor in the heavy stockades like this United States Military Prison yard at Chattanooga. (NA,U.S. WAR DEPARTMENT GENERAL STAFF)

Left: … so was the punishment. Troops stand drawn into a three-sided square to witness a hanging near Petersburg in 1864. The mounds of earth right of the gallows mark the grave of the condemned already dug. (LC)

Right: Another court-martial, at Chattanooga. If the offense was grave enough . . (TERENCE P. OLEARY, GLADWYNE, PENNSYLVANIA)

Left: And like soldiers everywhere, the men of blue and gray loved to celebrate holidays. Here a Christmas feast appears ready for the men who will tightly jam the benches. Turkeys sit on the tables as well as relishes. The hot vegetables will be brought out and served, and every plate has a slab of bread or cake. (NA)

Right: Another wreath-bedecked hall for Christmas. These diners will be a little less crowded. (USAMHI)

Below: Washington's birthday, February 22, was a holiday in both North and South, and here the "New Forage House" ballroom in Beaufort, South Carolina, stands ready for an 1864 observance. (WRHS)

Right: The speakers' stand for the Beaufort celebration, with flags and bunting aplenty. (USAMHI)

Right: The Fourth of July was the greatest of all in the Union armies, and even some Confederates celebrated the day. Here the 50th New York Engineers revel in the day on July 4, 1864. Joining them, and seated at the extreme left, is Charles Francis Adams, Jr., historian, grandson of President John Quincy Adams, and future president of the Union Pacific Railroad. (USAMHI)

The Conquest of the Mississippi

CHARLES L. DUFOUR

The great river spawned great men to contest her waters

Above: The USS Brooklyn, *the first ship to go on blockade off the mouth of the Mississippi. The warship and the river were to see a lot of each other in the years to come. (NA)*

THE USS *Brooklyn* dropped anchor off the mouth of the Mississippi at 2 P.M. on May 26, 1861, and the Union conquest of the great river, so vital to the Confederacy, was underway.

It was the first implementation of General Winfield Scott's "Anaconda Plan," the purpose of which was not only the military envelopment of the Confederacy but its economic strangulation as well. As early as May 3, Scott had discussed his plan with General George B. McClellan, pointing out that a powerful Union movement, by land and by water, down the Mississippi together with an effective blockade of the river's mouth would "envelop the insurgent States, and bring them to terms with less bloodshed than by another plan."

The effectiveness of the Union blockade was almost immediately felt in New Orleans, the Confederacy's greatest city. On May 30, 1861, a ship loaded with Brazilian coffee was captured by the *Brooklyn* and the next day another New Orleans bound vessel carrying foodstuffs was seized. From the moment the blockade was established, not a single ship reached the Confederate city until Farragut's attacking fleet ran past Fort Jackson and Fort St. Philip in April 1862. Although the Union blockading vessels prevented ships from entering the Mississippi, the river's five passes into the Gulf of Mexico offered avenues of escape to blockade runners from New Orleans and several did make it to sea. The most significant escape was that of the Confederate raider *Sumter* commanded by Raphael Semmes, later of *Alabama* fame, which eluded the blockade on June 30 to prey relentlessly on American commerce vessels for more than six months.

The Confederate government was slow to realize the defenselessness of New Orleans and the absolute necessity of making an all-out effort to prepare the city for invasion. Four months after Louisiana seceded from the Union, a general officer had not yet arrived in New Orleans to take command. During that time, the city had been drained of troops; they had been ordered to Pensacola to reinforce Braxton Bragg. On April 10, two days before the guns sounded at Charleston, Governor Thomas O. Moore of Louisiana complained to Confederate authorities, "We are disorganized, and have no general officer to command and direct." Seven weeks went by before seventy-one-year-old General David E. Twiggs, veteran of more than half a century in the United States Army, reached New Orleans to take command.

Although the Common Council of the City of New Orleans praised Twiggs's "integrity, sagacity, and nerve so essential to a commander," it soon became evident that the enfeebled septuagenarian general was not the man to defend the South's greatest city from Federal attack. President Davis had already received complaints of the "infirmities of General Twiggs," when Governor Moore's plea for "an officer… who, with youth, energy and military ability, would infuse some activity in our preparation and some confidence in our people," reached Richmond in September. In closing this appeal to Davis, Moore begged that "this city, the most important to be preserved of any of the Confederacy, and our coast, the most exposed of all the states, be no longer neglected."

President Davis finally conceded that General Twiggs "has proven unequal to his command," but he shifted the blame for Twiggs's appointment to the people of New Orleans: "As in his selection I yielded much to the solicitation of the

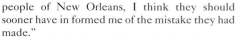

Above: Major General Mansfield Lovell would never be fully appreciated in the Confederacy for his talents. Rather, he would be remembered as the man who lost New Orleans. (USAMHI)

Above: David D. Porter did heavy duty on the Mississippi. At the outset of the war, however, he ridiculed the Confederate success at Head of the Passes as a "ridiculous affair." (USAMHI)

Above: Commodore George N. Hollins, who led the successful Confederate attack on the little Union squadron at Head of the Passes. (LSU)

people of New Orleans, I think they should sooner have in formed me of the mistake they had made."

When Major General Mansfield Lovell was assigned to New Orleans, Twiggs got the implied message and prevented an awkward situation by asking, on October 5, to be relieved from duty for reasons of health. Before leaving for New Orleans, Lovell conferred with both President Davis and Secretary of War Judah P. Benjamin and, with almost prophetic insight, declared that the only proper defense of New Orleans would require a unified command. He argued, but in vain, that the employment of naval as well as army forces should be under his direction. Fearing that Lovell had not fully understood the definition of his command responsibilities, Davis hurried off a letter to him stating, "The fleet maintained at the port of New Orleans and its vicinity is not a part of your command." This decision would prove fatal.

Lovell reached New Orleans on October 17 and found, as he reported to Richmond, "great confusion, irresolution, and want of system in every thing administrative." New Orleans was "almost entirely stripped of everything available in the way of ordnance, stores, ammunition, clothing, medicines etc." There existed a frightening shortage of powder, Lovell reported. So he established two powder mills in New Orleans, and moved a third mill from the Mississippi coast to the city.

Before leaving Virginia, Lovell met with his old army friend General P. G. T. Beauregard, a native of New Orleans who, for ten years before the war, had been in charge of the defenses of Louisiana. Beauregard reiterated to Lovell what he had told Louisiana authorities many months earlier, that Forts Jackson and St. Philip, miles downriver from New Orleans, could not prevent steam vessels from passing unless an obstruction in the river held the ships under the cross fire of the forts for half an hour. Such a barricade, talked about in February but not constructed until the

Left: The CSS McRae, *part of Hollins's "fleet." (NHC)*

Left: The USS Richmond *was rammed by Hollins's ironclad* Manassas, *an action that did more damage to the ironclad than to the Federal warship. The* Richmond *served continually on the river in the years to come. (NHC)*

Above: Naval stations at places like Mound City, Illinois, were organized and readied to construct new ships as well as to refit and repair those already in service. (WRHS)

Above: Ironclads were of interest to the Union naval authorities on the Mississippi. Captain John Rodgers was sent by the Navy Department to supervise the construction of the Benton-*class gunboats at Cairo, Illinois. (NA,U.S. WAR DEPARTMENT GENERAL STAFF)*

summer, had been in place about a month when Lovell reached New Orleans. After inspecting this so-called raft, Lovell undertook to strengthen it.

On arrival, Lovell heard much of a recent Confederate naval victory at the Head of the Passes where a bold attack on a Yankee squadron routed it in what David Dixon Porter later described as "the most ridiculous affair that ever took place in the American Navy."

The heroes of this exploit were Commodore George Hollins and the ironclad *Manassas*, popularly known in New Orleans as the "Turtle." The latter, originally the twin-screw tugboat *Enoch Train*, had been purchased by a syndicate of businessmen for conversion into an ironclad to operate as a privateer against the blockaders. The cigar shaped *Manassas*, covered with railroad iron three quarters of an inch thick, mounted one gun, which operated through a trapdoor forward. It had a heavy cast-iron prow, which extended below the waterline so that the vessel could operate as a ram.

Although the project was supposedly a secret one, reports of the "formidable instrument of destruction" the Confederates were building at New Orleans slipped into the Northern press. Fantastic stories, born of imagination and misinformation, told that the *Manassas* was equipped with a powerful auger which could bore holes in a ship below its waterline and that this "hellish engine" had twenty-four hoses with which boiling water could be played upon the crew of an enemy ship. The "Turtle" was, in fact, much more formidable in the Northern press than it proved in the water. Nevertheless, its owners had high hopes that, operating as a privateer, the *Manassas* would reap a rich harvest of prize money by capturing Union block-

Left: Mound City remained in a bustle of activity during most of the war. (LC)

Above: Its shops and ways echoed to the sounds of machinery and workmen. Here, in the foreground, blocks and tackle and lines are visible on the bank where ships were hauled out of the water for hull-scraping and repair. (USAMHI)

Above: Tugboats like the little Daisy *plied the river constantly off Mound City. (NHC)*

ade vessels. But hardly had the *Manassas* been launched and given its trial runs than Commodore Hollins seized it for the Confederacy against the protests of the syndicate.

On the night of October 11–12, 1861, Hollins's little flotilla, consisting of the *Manassas, McRae, Ivy, Calhoun, Tuscarora, Jackson,* and *Pickens*—New Orleanians called it the "mosquito fleet"—attacked a Union squadron of four warships under Captain John Pope at the Head of the Passes, where the various mouths of the Mississippi leave the main stream.

What followed was a comic opera of naval warfare. The *Manassas* rammed the *Richmond,* and the ten-knot impact disabled the Confederate iron clad while causing panic aboard the Union flag ship. In the confusion and darkness, three Union ships, *Vincennes, Preble,* and *Waterwitch,* on signals from Captain Pope, slipped their cables and began steaming down Southwest Pass, and the *Richmond* followed. A running fight of no actual consequence ensued, but the aftermath was farcical after the *Vincennes* ran aground on the bar. Commander Robert Handy, believing erroneously that Pope had ordered him to abandon ship, did so after ordering the lighting of a slow fuse to the magazine. Fortunately, a Union quartermaster, after lighting the fuse, cut off the burning end and tossed it into the river, and the *Vincennes* was thus saved. "Pope's Run" as the incident became known, was later characterized by Admiral Alfred T. Mahan as "a move which brought intense mortification to himself [Pope] and in a measure to the service."

Fully believing that he had sunk a Union vessel (he announced it as the *Preble*) in this weird affair at the Head of the Passes, Hollins hurried back to New Orleans with the morale-building news of a great victory. But the expedition had little significance beyond creating popular enthusiasm. Elise Ellis Bragg, writing her husband, General Braxton Bragg, said, "Our 'Turtle,' alias *Manassas* made a grand charge and would have done wonders if it had not been disabled. All these things make a sensation, but I fear they help our cause but little, and a dark and gloomy winter seems closing around us."

When General Lovell arrived, New Orleanians were still talking enthusiastically about the action at the Head of the Passes and also of the two giant ironclads *Mississippi* and *Louisiana,* which were

Above: And frequently an entire fleet of ironclads and "tinclads" appeared at anchor in midstream. The USS St. Louis *rests in the center of the image, while in the distance behind its stern can be seen what is probably the USS* Tyler. *(USAMHI)*

Below: Specialized craft like the hospital boat Nashville *were also needed to serve both the navy and the armed soldiers fighting along the river. (LC)*

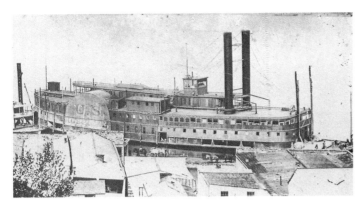

Above: Another hospital ship, the R. C. Wood, *on the wharf at Vicksburg in 1863. (OLD COURT HOUSE MUSEUM, VICKSBURG)*

Above: Cairo, Illinois, also hosted an important naval station. Here its wharf boat lies moored on the shore. (USAMHI)

Above: A river fleet at anchor off Cairo in 1865. (AMERICANA IMAGE GALLERY)

Below: And packet boats carrying mail, like the Golden Era, *shared the stream with gunboats like the USS* Tyler *in the crowded waters off Cairo. Shipbuilder James B. Eads first used his skills to convert a steamer into the gunboat Tyler. (CHS)*

Above: At Cairo, soldiers boarded transports like the USS Brown *for the journey to the front at New Orleans or Vicksburg or Port Hudson. (USAMHI)*

under construction just above the city, and which were expected to be in operation in January.

Meanwhile, the first Union preparations on the upper Mississippi had been made on August 2, when James B. Eads of St. Louis was authorized to construct seven ironclad gunboats of a new type for use on the western rivers. Three river steamers, the *Tyler, Lexington,* and *Conestoga,* had been converted into gunboats, and they became the nucleus of the Union naval forces on the Mississippi until Eads's ironclads were completed.

On October 7, the gunboats *Lexington* and *Tyler,* on a reconnaissance from Cairo, steamed toward Lucas Bend, Missouri, to engage Confederate shore batteries at Iron Bluff, not far from Columbus, Kentucky. On October 12, the same date of the ignominious "Pope's Run" from the Head of the Passes, the *St. Louis,* first Federal ironclad, was launched at Carondelet, Missouri.

Initial land operation by Union forces on the Mississippi proved abortive. On November 7,

Brigadier General U. S. Grant descended from Cairo with 3,000 troops on transports supported by two wooden converted gunboats. Landing on the Missouri side, Grant seized the village of Belmont, across the river from Columbus, Kentucky. Grant held Belmont until Confederate reinforcements from Columbus crossed the river, and then he regained his transports and steamed back to Cairo.

Before 1861 ended, the first significant operation concerned with the conquest of the Mississippi occurred when 1,900 Union troops under Brigadier General John W. Phelps landed on Ship Island, in Mississippi Sound, twelve miles off the mainland and sixty miles from the mouth of the Mississippi.

With the coming of the new year, Union efforts on the upper Mississippi were stepped up. On January 14, three Union gunboats descended to the vicinity of Columbus and shelled Confederate encampments along the river. After the fall of Forts Henry and Donelson early in February, 1862, Columbus became the prime Union objective in the West. The Confederate government, recognizing its extreme vulnerability, ordered the evacuation of Columbus on February 20. Withdrawal of troops, guns, and material began at once and by March 2 the evacuation was completed. All but two of Columbus's 140 guns were moved south to Island No. 10 and its adjacent batteries. The next day, as Federal troops occupied Columbus, another force under General John Pope laid siege to New Madrid, Missouri. After a heavy bombardment of their works on March 13, the Confederates slipped out of New Madrid the next day and retreated to Island No. 10, leaving behind a substantial amount of guns and supplies.

Island No. 10, so named because it was the tenth island in the Mississippi south of its confluence with the Ohio, was assumed by the Confederates to be impregnable. Situated in Madrid Bend, between Tennessee and Missouri, Island No. 10 commanded the river in both directions. Earthworks, constructed for two miles along the banks, made Island No. 10 formidable for an attacking fleet, while virtually impassable swamps made a land attack on Island No. 10 unfeasible.

When Pope seized New Madrid, the Confederate naval force—six gunboats under Commodore Hollins—found itself much outgunned and withdrew to Tiptonville, thirty miles below Island No. 10 by river, but less than five miles by land. The stage was now set for a combined army and navy operation against Island No. 10, with Pope attacking by land while Commodore Andrew Foote's flotilla, headed by Eads's formidable ironclad *Benton*, most powerful warship on the Mississippi, engaged the Confederate bastion from the river. While Pope was impatient to begin operations against Island No. 10 as soon as New Madrid fell, it was not until March 14 that Foote's flotilla left Cairo for the fifty-mile run down to Island No. 10. With seven gunboats and ten mortar vessels, and transports carrying troops to occupy Island No. 10 after its capture, Foote dropped anchor two miles from the Union objective on the morning of March 15. The next day, Foote's mortars opened fire on the Confederate works and on

Left: And he did the same with the USS Lexington. *These gunboats were not very effectively armored, but they were a start.* (USAMHI)

Right: Far more effective was the USS St. Louis, *launched at Carondelet, Missouri, the first Federal ironclad.* (NA, U. S. WAR DEPARTMENT GENERAL STAFF)

Below: Active operations on the Mississippi really begin with Brigadier General U. S. Grant, shown here as a major general. His attack on Belmont was staged from Cairo. (LC)

Left: The first real Union success came at Island No. 10, when Brigadier General John Pope cooperated with Foote's flotilla to force the Confederate bastion to surrender. (NA, U. S. SIGNAL CORPS)

Right: In both defense and offense, cannons mounted on rafts and floated into position were used frequently. on the river at places like Island No. 10. (NHC)

Left: Henry Gurney's image of the mightiest ironclad on the river, the USS Benton, another of Eads's conversions. Foote made it his flagship. This photo was taken at Natchez in 1863 or later. (JOAN AND THOMAS GANDY, NATCHEZ, MISSISSIPPI)

Right: Commander Henry Walke, a Virginian by birth, ran his Carondelet past No. 10's batteries to assist Pope's land assault. (LC)

Right: The USS Pittsburg followed Walke's lead, and Pope's movement was ensured. (LC)

Right: Captures included the Confederate ship CSS Red Rover, a barracks ship which the Federals turned into the first hospital ship in the navy. (USAMHI)

Right: The CSS De Soto was captured as well, to become the USS General Lyon. (NHC)

March 17 the Benton and Foote's other ironclads went into action, at a range of 2,000 yards.

Meanwhile, Pope had realized he needed transports to get his troops across the Mississippi if the joint operation were to be successful. In an official request, he promised that if Foote were to "… run past the batteries of Island No. 10 with two or three gunboats and reach here, I can cross my whole force and capture every man of the enemy at Island No. 10 and on the mainland." Foote immediately rejected Pope's proposal.

Pope's chief engineer, Colonel Josiah W. Bissell, then proposed that a canal be dug through the overflowed swamps to bypass Island No. 10. Pope approved the project when Bissell assured him that he could open a way for vessels of light draft to cut across the neck of land. He authorized Bissell to employ his entire regiment to open the canal. Working feverishly for nearly three weeks, Bissell cut a twelve-mile-long channel, fifty feet wide.

Before Bissell's canal was ready, Foote had a change of mind when Henry Walke, commander of the Carondelet, volunteered to run his ship past Island No. 10's batteries. In a thunderstorm on the night of April 4, the Carondelet ran the fiery gauntlet and reached New Madrid at midnight, a few hours after Bissell's engineers had completed the last stretch of the canal. Three nights later, during another storm, the Pittsburg ran past Island No. 10's guns and anchored at New Madrid. The same night, four shallow-draft steamers passed through Bissell's canal to provide Pope with the transports he needed to get his troops across the river to assault Island No. 10 from the rear.

Island No. 10 had been subjected to constant fire from Foote's ships, and a bold Union raid on

Above: Flag Officer David G. Farragut will be much in evidence on the Mississippi, and nowhere more than in his reduction of Forts Jackson and St. Philip and the capture of New Orleans. (USAMHI)

Left: Fort Jackson. The photograph was supposedly taken in 1862 but is probably early postwar. (WRHS)

Right: The interior of Fort St. Philip looking toward the river, probably also a postwar image. The formidable command these forts exerted on river traffic is evident. (WRHS)

Left: A front view of Fort St. Philip. (WRHS)

Below: And here the much less known Fort Macomb, taken in 1863. The canal ran from Lake Borgne to Lake Pontchartrain in the rear of New Orleans. Colonel Francis Hesseltine and his wife stand with fishing poles in the foreground. (USAMHI)

April 1 by soldiers landing from small boats had succeeded in routing a Confederate guard and spiking six guns—driving soft nails into their touchholes so they could not be fired. Now, with a two-pronged all-out attack imminent, the Confederates began the evacuation of Island No. 10 on April 7. Retreat, however, was futile and seven thousand Confederates, including three generals, hemmed in by Union troops and the swamps, surrendered. On the same fateful date that Island No. 10 fell, the Confederate Army at Shiloh, having been repulsed in the second day's fighting, was preparing its retirement back to Corinth.

With Island No. 10 in Union possession, the only Confederate stronghold on the Mississippi above Memphis was Fort Pillow in Tennessee. Situated on bluffs about eighty miles upstream from Memphis, Fort Pillow consisted of a line of fortifications extended for seven miles along the river. Foote lost no time in putting Fort Pillow under fire and on April 14 he shelled the Confederate works as a preliminary to what he expected to be another combined operation. To Foote's surprise, however, Pope's troops were ordered to Pittsburg Landing, thus making impossible a joint army-navy movement against Fort Pillow.

Meanwhile, at the lower end of the Mississippi, Flag Officer David Glasgow Farragut was readying his campaign against New Orleans. Listed at thirty-seventh among navy captains, Farragut, a vigorously active sixty-year-old, had been in the service for more than half a century. As a boy, he was a midshipman in the War of 1812, and in the Mexican War he served on blockade duty. Secretary of the Navy Gideon Welles was impressed with Farragut, finding him "modest and truthful... self-reliant and brave," and decided he was the man to capture New Orleans. He summoned Farragut to Washington from a desk job in New York in December 1861 and offered him command of the New Orleans expedition.

Early in April, forty-seven days after he reached Ship Island to organize his expedition, Farragut had installed himself at the Head of the Passes with a formidable fleet of 17 warships with a total of 154 guns; a mortar flotilla of 20 schooners, each with a 13-inch mortar and a total of 30 guns; and 7 steamers with 27 guns. Difficul-

Above: Captain Napoleon B. Harrison commanded the USS Cayuga when Farragut ran his fleet past the forts. (USAMHI)

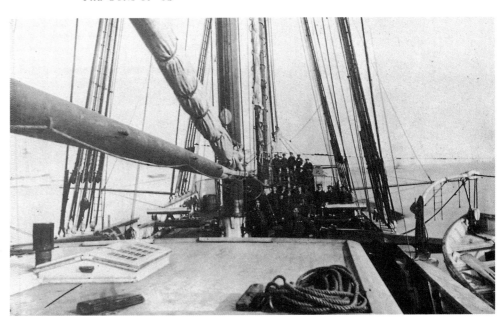

Above: The mortar schooner USS C. P. Williams took part with Porter's mortar fleet in the bombardment of the forts. (WRHS)

Above: And so did the USS Horace Beals. (USAMHI)

Above: These monster mortars could throw a 200-pound shell from 3,000-4,000 yards. These were part of Farragut's fleet, later taken to rest here at the Philadelphia Navy Yard. (USAMHI)

Right: To identify his ships from a distance in the confusion of battle, Farragut ordered numbers painted in letters six feet high on the stacks of each vessel. Number 2 was the USS Winona, which served two years on the Mississippi before joining the blockade off Charleston. (USAMHI)

ties in getting some of his larger ships over the bar caused exasperating delays, but by April 8, Farragut was nearly ready to strike.

Once in the river, Farragut was tireless in his preparations, overlooking no detail needed for success. He sent a geodetic survey team up the river to establish ranges to Forts Jackson and St. Philip from points where David Dixon Porter's mortar boats would be stationed. He had the hulls of his ships smeared with the tawny mud of the river as camouflage; he ordered bags filled with sand to strengthen bulwarks and protect the engines and other machinery; he had gun carriages and decks whitewashed to make easier the location of firing implements in the dark; he ordered iron-link cables suspended on the sides of the ships in the line of the engines; he had nettings made with large ropes spread above the decks to prevent injury from falling timber. Thus Farragut, by his energy, ingenuity, enthusiasm, and confidence not only prepared his ships superbly for the coming ordeal of passing the Confederate forts, but also infused into his officers and crew a high morale.

While confidence prevailed in the Union fleet at the Head of the Passes, New Orleans, with attack imminent, had become a jittery city. Spy fever, which had raged for weeks, was followed by an epidemic of wild rumors which the New Orleans press charged were circulated by "gossip-mongers or evil-disposed persons." The *Picayune* noted that "every day they hear one thousand alarming rumors," while the *Commercial Bulletin* complained that "every possible idea that could enter the head of credulous people seems to have been hatched up and enlarged."

General Mansfield Lovell had more serious matters than hunting spies and dispelling rumors to worry him. Although he was to have no control over the employment of the powerful warships *Louisiana* and *Mississippi*, he recognized them as integral to the defense of New Orleans and he viewed with considerable concern the way progress on the two ships was dragging.

Promised for service by January 1862, it was not until February 6 that the *Louisiana* was launched, with still considerable work left to be done in sheathing the vessel with armor and installing the machinery. The *Mississippi*, which had also been promised for January, was still on the way. Its woodwork was completed and its boilers were in stalled, but it lacked armor and machinery and the central shaft, which was slow in coming from Richmond's Tredegar Works.

Lovell, his hands already tied by Richmond's continued refusal to allow him to head a unified army-navy command, protested on being stripped of 5,000 troops which he was ordered to send to Columbus. To his complaint, Confederate authorities, seemingly totally oblivious of the threat to New Orleans posed by the Union naval build-up at Ship Island, replied that "New Orleans will be defended from above... the forces withdrawn from you are for the defense of your own command."

As if in compensation for withholding from Lovell command of the Confederate Navy at New Orleans, the War Department ordered him to seize fourteen steamboats for a River Defense Fleet, "not to be a part of the Navy... [but] subject to the general command of the military chief." This peculiar arrangement, with the steamboat captains in command of their vessels, was startling to Lovell.

New Orleans' morale sagged when word of the fall of Forts Henry and Donelson reached the city, to be followed shortly by the news that Albert Sidney Johnston's Kentucky line had collapsed with the evacuation of Columbus. Criticism of Confederate leadership, both in Richmond and in the field, was widespread among citizens and in the press. New Orleans was on the verge of panic when Lovell, acting on orders from Richmond, declared martial law in effect on March 15.

Brigadier General Johnson Kelly Duncan, who commanded at Forts Jackson and St. Philip, New Orleans' principal defenses, seventy-five miles downstream from the city, worked his officers and men to the point of exhaustion in preparing the bastions for Farragut's certain attack soon to come. Nearly 1,000 troops garrisoned the forts, which had 115 guns of various calibers—69 at Fort Jackson and 46 at Fort St. Philip.

The barricade, or raft, which had been made more secure by Lovell shortly after his arrival, was supported by enfilading fire from the forts. However, accumulated driftwood and the strong current proved too much for the barrier early in March. The main chains snapped, and the obstruction, so needed to hold enemy ships under the fire of the forts, ceased to exist. A makeshift barrier of parts of the original raft and some schooners, anchored and linked by chains, was hurriedly improvised. The schooners were anchored bow up stream, chained together stem, stern, and midships, with their rigging and cables trailing astern to be hazards to the propellers of enemy ships.

Nervous New Orleans received disheartening news from Shiloh's second day after exulting in the Confederate victory of the first day. The news of the fall of Island No. 10 followed fast, and the city then learned that a storm on April 9 and 10 had again dismantled the raft below the forts. Once more improvisation of a barrier was rushed.

To all of Lovell's worries there was added the continued incomprehensible unawareness in Richmond of the acute danger to New Orleans from Farragut's fleet at the Head of the Passes. Orders had come to send the still uncompleted Louisiana up the river, where President Davis and

Right: Farragut's mighty flagship, the USS Hartford, *its midships sides still showing the chains draped over them as protection from enemy shot during the passage of the forts. A. D. Lytle, the outstanding photographer of Baton Rouge, made this view shortly afterward. (CWTI)*

Left: Farragut and his executive officer Percival Drayton at the wheel of the Hartford. *(USAMHI)*

Left: Men and officers of the Hartford *at the stern pivot gun, a massive Parrott rifle. (USAMHI)*

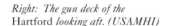

Right: The gun deck of the Hartford *looking aft. (USAMHI)*

Left: The beautiful side-wheeler USS Mississippi, *built in 1839 under the eye of Commodore Matthew C. Perry. She was his flagship in the Mexican War and in his epic voyage to Japan in 1852. Farragut would send it upriver to pass the enemy batteries at Port Hudson the next year, and there it would run aground and be destroyed by its crew. The executive officer was the future Admiral George Dewey. (USAMHI)*

Left: McPherson & Oliver's photograph of the crew of the USS Richmond *at quarters after the capture of New Orleans. (USAMHI)*

Right: Brigadier General Morgan L. Smith, a native of New York, fought for the South and supervised New Orleans' defenses as well as leading troops there. (USAMHI)

Left: The heart of the Crescent City, Jackson Square, showing St. Louis Cathedral and to the right of it, the Presbytere. The Andrew Jackson equestrian statue can be seen, and carved on its pedestal his declaration that the union "must and shall be preserved." (USAMHI)

Secretary of the Navy Mallory amazingly believed the gravest danger to New Orleans lay. To Governor Thomas O. Moore's protest that "the Louisiana... is absolutely a necessity at the forts for the safety of New Orleans, and that it is suicidal to send her elsewhere," President Davis telegraphed back on April 17 the astonishing message: "The wooden vessels are below; the iron gunboats are above. The forts should destroy the former if they attempt to ascend. The *Louisiana* may be indispensible to check the descent of the iron boats."

This was not the only instance of Richmond's inexplicable blindness to the danger to New Orleans from the Union fleet in the river. When Commodore George N. Hollins, commander of the Confederate flotilla at Fort Pillow, asked permission on April 9 to steam down to New Orleans to participate in its defense, Mallory telegraphed back an emphatic refusal. Hollins, not waiting for Mallory's reply, however, reached New Orleans in the McRae and promptly urged by telegram that his fleet join him. Richmond's reply was a summons to Hollins to report at once in the Confederate capitol to head a board examining midshipmen. Thus was the best fighting man in the Confederate Navy on the Mississippi shelved at the most critical moment for New Orleans.

On April 18, Porter's mortar ships began their concentrated fire on the forts and for five days and nights, from a sheltered bend in the river, 13-inch shells were lobbed into Forts Jackson and St. Philip at regular intervals. General Duncan estimated that the Union mortar boats had thrown more than 22,000 shells at the forts before Farragut made his move.

When it became evident that the *Louisiana*, without its motive power in operation, could not go up the river as ordered, Commander W. C. Whittle, navy commander of New Orleans, finally responded to the importuning of Lovell and Duncan to have the ironclad towed down to the forts to serve as a floating battery. Despite the remonstrances of Duncan, the ironclad's captain refused to place the *Louisiana* below the barrier, where it could enfilade the Union mortar boats. He anchored it just above Fort St. Philip where it remained inactive against them. The same day that

Left: Canal Street, running from Royal Street to the river. At the end can be seen the smokestacks of steamboats at the wharves. (USAMHI)

Left: Chartres Street in the French Quarter. (USAMHI)

the *Louisiana* went down to the forts, the *Mississippi*, still far from completed, was launched.

On the night of April 20, Farragut sent Captain Henry Bell with two gunboats to sever the barrier and open a way for the ships to pass through. Bell succeeded in his mission and Farragut, never enthusiastic about the mortar ships' ability to silence the forts, determined to make his run on the night of April 23-24.

Everything was in readiness at the Head of the Passes, but disorganization prevailed among the Confederate defenders. That strange War Department instrument, the River Defense Fleet, refused to take orders from the navy; the navy showed no inclination to cooperate with General Lovell's defense plans; and, to top it, New Orleans was a city verging on panic.

At 2 A.M. on April 24, the *Cayuga* raised its anchors and steamed off into the moonless night, the vanguard of Farragut's attacking fleet. One by one, the warships followed. At 3:30 A.M., the *Cayuga* passed noiselessly through the breach in the barrier, unchallenged by any Confederate vessel and unthreatened by the fire rafts which were supposed to have been illuminated and sent down the river. Immediately, the guns of Fort Jackson and Fort St. Philip opened up as Farragut's other vessels moved into range, firing their broadsides at the forts. The flashes of their guns and the arching course of mortar shells lit the river in a spectacle of awesome grandeur. Three of Farragut's gunboats failed to make it through the breach in the barrier. The *Kennebec* entangled itself in the raft and the *Winona* suffered the same fate, and both freed themselves with difficulty and drifted out of action. The third, the *Itasca*, was badly crippled by gunfire from Fort Jackson and it retired downriver.

At the first fighting, the Confederate River Defense Fleet hurried off ingloriously, but three Rebel ships fought with valor. Hopelessly outgunned and outnumbered, the *Manassas* ("Turtle"), *McRae*, and *Governor Moore* were in the thick of the melee, each drawing the concentrated fire of several Union ships at various stages of the battle. The forts laid down tremendous barrages, but fourteen of Farragut's ships ran the fiery gauntlet successfully, although his flagship, the *Hartford*, was set ablaze by a fire raft while it was aground off Fort St. Philip. For a while, it was touch and go for the *Hartford*, but discipline and engine power prevailed: The fire was extinguished by the crew and the flagship shivered and shook as it freed itself from the mud and steamed out of range of the forts.

At the peak of the battle, the roaring and flashing of the guns created a spectacular scene. One of General Benjamin Butler's officers wrote, "Combine all that you have heard of thunder, add to it all that you have ever seen of lightning, and you have, perhaps, a conception of the scene." To an officer on the Hartford, "it was like the breaking up of the universe with the moon and all the stars bursting in our midst." Farragut himself described it: "It was as if the artillery of heaven were playing upon the earth."

The *Manassas*, which had rammed the *Brooklyn* and *Mississippi* and fought at close quarter half a dozen other Union ships, was finally disabled and scuttled by its crew. The *McRae*, just as active in the unequal fight, had its tiller ropes shot away and made it with difficulty to the protection of Fort Jackson. The *Governor Moore* engaged the *Varuna* in a running battle, rammed the Union

Right: New Orleans' City Hall. Here Farragut raised the Union flag over the conquered city. (USAMHI)

Left: Looking down the levee from Canal Street. The busy traffic, once interrupted by the war, now flows again. Bales of cotton await shipment. (USAMHI)

Right: With the city taken, Major General Benjamin F. Butler and his troops began their controversial occupation. "Spoons" Butler they would call him, after accusations that he stole silver from the citizens. (USAMHI)

Below: Before long New Orleans would be designated the headquarters of the new Department of the Gulf. Here officers serving in the department from several services, army, navy, and marines, gather for a group portrait in March 1863. Seated from the left are Lieutenant Edward Terry of the Richmond, Captain James Alden commanding the Richmond, and Brigadier General Godfrey Weitzel. The rest are staff officers. (USAMHI)

Right: Soon after the fall of New Orleans, Farragut's ships took Baton Rouge and, shown here, Natchez. Then it was time to try for Vicksburg. (USAMHI)

Right: Commander S. P. Lee led the small fleet that first tried to force the surrender of Vicksburg, but unsuccessfully. (USAMHI)

Far right: Farragut soon moved north to join Lee, bringing with him the 3,200 men of Brigadier General Thomas Williams, an almost universally disliked commander. The soldiers would attempt nothing, being shattered by disease. Williams retired to Baton Rouge, and there on August 5 he was killed in the Confederate attack. (USAMHI)

Below: On the way to Vicksburg, Farragut learned of the Union fleet victory at Plum Run Bend, a victory won over ineffectual Confederate ships by gunboats like the USS Carondelet. *(USAMHI)*

ship twice and sank it—Farragut's only loss in the passage of the forts. Beverly Kennon, commander of the *Governor Moore*, fired his ship, threw his sword overboard, and surrendered himself as half a dozen Union gunboats descended upon his horribly cut-up craft. The dead on the *Governor Moore* totaled fifty-seven—nine more than the combined dead in Farragut's fleet and in the two forts.

The Louisiana, still anchored above Fort St. Philip, received heavy firing at close range as Farragut's ships passed up the river, but the ironclad was practically undamaged. David Dixon Porter noted in his journal that had Commander Mitchell, captain of the Louisiana, "possessed the soul of a flea, he could have driven us all out of the river."

The next day, April 25, Farragut pushed up the river to New Orleans. He was amazed at the sight that met his eye: "The levee of New Orleans was one scene of desolation, ships, steamers, cotton, coal, etc., were all in one common blaze," he wrote. "The Mississippi, which was to be the terror of the seas, and no doubt would have been to a great extent... soon came floating by us all in flames, and passed down the river."

Demands that the city surrender met with a scornful refusal by Mayor John Monroe, who pointed out to Farragut that as Lovell had evacuated his militia troops, New Orleans was defenseless and "the city is yours by the power of brutal force."

Meanwhile, down at the forts, mutiny broke out on April 27, compelling Duncan to surrender to Porter. During the signing, the *Louisiana* came drifting by ablaze, and moments later it blew up. All Confederate resistance below New Orleans was now ended. When the news reached Farragut he sent a party ashore to haul down the flag of Louisiana from the city hall flagpole and raise the American flag.

On May 1, Major General Benjamin F. Butler landed his occupation troops and New Orleans' days in the Confederacy were over. Mary Baykin Chesnut prophetically recorded the bitter fact in her diary: "New Orleans is gone, and with it the Confederacy! Are we not cut in two? The Mississippi ruins us if it is lost."

After Butler occupied New Orleans, Farragut was faced with a dilemma: What to do in the light of his original orders. These read: "If the Mississippi expedition from Cairo shall not have descended the river, you will take advantage of the panic to push a strong force up the river to take all their defenses in the rear. You will also reduce the fortifications which defend Mobile Bay and turn them over to the army to hold."

Farragut sent Porter and the mortar boats to Mobile Bay and dispatched Commander S. P. Lee with the *Oneida* and several smaller gunboats up the Mississippi, while he remained at New Orleans with the greater part of his fleet. Baton Rouge and Natchez, both undefended, were captured and the American flag was raised above their public buildings. At Vicksburg, however, Lee's demand for surrender was answered defiantly: "Mississippians don't know and refuse to learn how to surrender to an enemy. If... Farragut or... Butler can teach them let them come and try." Lee gave Vicksburg twenty-four hours to remove its women and children to safety, set up a blockade of the city, and awaited orders from Farragut.

When Farragut learned what was happening upriver, he was anxious to push up the Mississippi with his full command. On May 10, one of the few fleet actions of the war had taken place above Fort Pillow at Plum Run Bend when a much-out gunned Confederate flotilla of eight ships—the Confederate River Defense Fleet—with more valor than judgment attacked seven Union ironclads. With four of his ships disabled by the superior fire power of the Yankees' ships, Captain James Montgomery broke off action and retired downstream to Memphis. On May 23, Farragut's fleet, accompanied by 3,200 troops under Brigadier General Thomas Williams, reached Vicksburg. Two days later, Colonel Charles Ellet's nine rams and two floating batteries, completed for the War Department in only forty days, made liaison with the Western Flotilla, now commanded by Captain Charles H. Davis, who had succeeded the ailing Commodore Foote.

Davis's reaction to Ellet's arrival was politely uncooperative. Ellet informed Davis that he was going to operate against Fort Pillow and asked for one gunboat to accompany him. Failing this, he invited Davis to assign some navy observers to the rams for this "daring and patriotic enterprise." Davis's reply reflected the age-old rivalry between military services: "I decline taking any part in the expedition… I would thank you to inform me how far you consider yourself under my authority; and I shall esteem it a favor to receive from you a copy of the orders under which you are acting." Ellet's reply was conciliatory: "No question of authority need be raised." But to Secretary of War Stanton he wrote, "Commodore Davis will not join me… nor contribute a gunboat… nor allow any of his men to volunteer… I shall therefore… go without him."

The fall of Corinth on June 3 made the Confederate evacuation of Fort Pillow inevitable and exposed Memphis to serious threat. At Memphis, the Confederates were building two powerful ironclads, the *Arkansas* and *Tennessee*, and their seizure was a Union objective. Two of Ellet's rams drew sharp fire from the works at Fort Pillow on June 3, but the Confederates had already begun evacuation, and during the night of June 4 it was completed. The only Confederate defense now between the Union vessels and Memphis was a weak Confederate flotilla at that city.

Union gunboats attacked this flotilla on the morning of June 6 in another of the rare fleet actions on the Mississippi. People of Memphis lined the bluffs to watch the battle when Commodore Davis sent five Union ironclads and four rams—a total of sixty-eight guns—against Montgomery's inferior flotilla of eight makeshift vessels mounting only twenty-eight guns. In the unequal struggle, which featured ramming and close-quarter fighting, the Confederates were decimated. Three Rebel ships were destroyed and four were captured, with only the *Van Dorn* escaping. The Union Navy now controlled the entire Mississippi, except at Vicksburg, Mississippi, and at Port Hudson in Louisiana.

The principal concern of the Union fleet on the Mississippi was the uncompleted Confederate ironclad, *Arkansas*, which, when Memphis was under threat, had been sent downriver to safety.

In the late summer of 1861, the Confederate Navy Department authorized the building of four powerful ironclads, easily the most formidable gun boats on the Mississippi. Devastating to the Confederate cause was the policy of "too little and too late" that prevailed with its gunboat building pro-

Right: The USS Louisville, *too, shown here at Memphis, made light work of the enemy River Defense Fleet at Plum Run Bend. It was, in fact, the largest fleet engagement of the war. (NHC)*

Below: Brigadier General John B. Villepigue commanded the defense of Fort Pillow as best he could, until forced to abandon and destroy his fortifications. (P-M)

Above: Then the Union Navy moved against Memphis. The only thing in their way was a little fleet commanded by the flamboyant M. Jeff Thompson who, though never promoted brigadier general, dressed like one anyhow. (DAVID R. O'REILLY COLLECTION)

Left: Thompson's flotilla was obliterated, all but one captured or destroyed. The Little Rebel *was one of the captured, and it was later put into Federal service. (TERENCE P. O'LEARY, GLADWYNE, PENNSYLVANIA)*

Right: The CSS General Price *had been a cotton-clad—bales of cotton stacked on her sides for protection—when she was sunk at Memphis. Raised and remodeled she became the* USS General Price, *commanded by... (USAMHI)*

Below: ... Acting Volunteer Lieutenant J. F. Richardson. (ROBERT G. HARRIS)

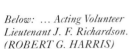

Left: Alfred W. Ellet, later a brigadier general, succeeded to command of the ram fleet when his brother Charles died two weeks after the Battle of Memphis. (USAMHI)

Below: One of the ships of Ellet's ram fleet that destroyed Thompson's little flotilla. (NHC)

Below: And now Memphis belonged to the Union again. The city is shown here viewed from the levee. (USAMHI)

jects. The *Louisiana* and the *Mississippi*, as was stated earlier, were to have been completed at New Orleans by the end of January 1862. But neither was finished when Farragut attacked the forts below New Orleans in April, and the *Louisiana* was blown up and the *Mississippi* set afire.

About the time that work was begun on the *Louisiana* and Mississippi in New Orleans, two other formidable ironclads were started in a Memphis shipyard, the *Arkansas* and the *Tennessee*. Patterned on the *Louisiana* and *Mississippi* and perhaps even more formidable, the Memphis ironclads were to be ready by the end of December 1861.

The descent of the Mississippi by the Union fleet found work on both the *Arkansas* and *Tennessee* lagging, and on April 25, the same day Farragut's warships appeared at New Orleans, the *Arkansas* was launched. It was floated 300 miles down the Mississippi to Yazoo River above Vicksburg and then was towed 200 miles up the Yazoo to Greenwood, where it was expected to be finished shortly. On orders from Richmond, the *Tennessee* was destroyed before launch.

A shortage of workmen, tools, equipment, timber, and other materials needed to complete the *Arkansas* resulted in interminable delays, despite the vigorous efforts of the ship's commander, Lieutenant Isaac Brown, who was charged with the *Arkansas's* completion. Launch day finally came on July 4, but more than six months late, and the *Arkansas* steamed to Yazoo City.

It was Lieutenant Brown's intention to drive his ironclad through the entire combined Union fleet— Farragut had run Vicksburg's fortifications, and had joined Davis above the city—and anchor the *Arkansas* under the protection of the Confederate batteries.

Major General Earl Van Dorn, commanding at Vicksburg, impatiently awaited the *Arkansas*, which he expected to prove a formidable factor in defending the city. It was due on July 14, but it developed that a defective powder magazine admitted steam which dampened the powder. Lieutenant Brown lost a full day drying his powder on canvas spread along the bank. Underway once more, the *Arkansas* ran aground in the darkness.

Instead of reaching the *Mississippi* by daylight, the *Arkansas* was still in the Yazoo when Brown picked up in his glass three Union vessels steaming toward him. They were the ironclads *Carondelet* and *Queen of the West* and the gunboat *Tyler*.

At 6:20 A.M. the *Carondelet* began to fire on the *Arkansas* at less than half a mile away, then turned and headed down the Yazoo, followed by the other two Union vessels. Stern guns opened on the pursuing *Arkansas* as the chase got underway and the Confederate ironclad was badly cut up. Lieutenant Brown was mistakenly believed to have been seriously wounded when struck in the head by a rifle ball. But the *Arkansas's* guns had severely punished the *Carondelet*, shattering its steering equipment and cutting steam-escape, exhaust, and cold-water pipes. The *Carondelet* limped to the bank and did not return the *Arkansas's* broadside and stern guns' fire as the Rebel ironside swept past, still in pursuit of the *Tyler* and the *Queen of the West*. The latter had fled hastily and its commander, James M. Hunter, was later denounced in the *Tyler's* log for his "cowardly and dastardly" behavior. But the *Tyler*, in retreating, kept up its fire as the running fight brought the

two vessels into the Mississippi and on toward Vicksburg.

Suddenly, on rounding a bend, the *Arkansas* came upon the combined fleets of Farragut and Davis—thirty-three ironclads, gunboats, rams, river steamers, and mortar boats—and quickly was furiously engaged. Lieutenant Brown reported later, "The shock of missiles striking our sides was literally continuous, and... we were now surrounded without room for anything but pushing ahead... I had the most lively realization of having steamed into a real volcano, the *Arkansas* from its center firing rapidly to every point of the circumference, without the fear of hitting a friend or missing an enemy."

For about two hours, the *Arkansas* fought its way through the Union fleets and at ten minutes before nine o'clock on July 15 it tied up at the Vicksburg wharf, "smokestack... shot to pieces... much cut up... pilot house smashed and some ugly places through our armor," as Lieutenant Brown later reported.

Elation in Vicksburg was unbounded and General Van Dorn, who had watched the fight from the top of the courthouse, said in his report that Brown "immortalized his single vessel, himself, and the heroes under his command by an achievement the most brilliant ever recorded in naval annals."

Above: Here the Memphis levee itself, with Federal shipping and barges crowding the shore. (USAMHI)

Above: Union Lieutenant John A. Winslow took command of the Memphis naval facilities, turning them to the purposes of Farragut's and Ellet's ships. (USAMHI)

Below: The Memphis Navy Yard, where the mighty CSS Arkansas was constructed. (USAMHI)

Below: Yet much of Memphis sat in ruins, the first Mississippi River city to feel the hand of destruction. (USAMHI)

Below: Vicksburg became even more isolated. Its commander, the dashing Major General Earl Van Dorn, is shown here in an unpublished portrait. He expected the Arkansas to come and redeem the city, and he was not disappointed. (TU)

Right: With Vicksburg secure, Van Dorn sent the Arkansas *downriver to cooperate with Breckinridge in the attack on Baton Rouge, the last real threat to Federal control of the lower Mississippi. Here the waterfront of Baton Rouge, with the state capitol to the right. (LSU)*

Above: Brigadier General Halbert E. Paine command-ed in Baton Rouge after Williams's death in battle, but refused to burn the city when ordered to do so by his superior, Butler. (LC)

Above: Colonel Henry W. Allen was prominent in Breckinridge's attack on Baton Rouge until his leg was shattered by a bullet. He was crippled for the rest of his life. (LSU)

Above: "Dirty Bill" Porter took his Essex *after the* Arkansas, *and later claimed credit for destroying the feared Confederate ironclad. (USAMHI)*

Farragut, not sparing himself in his criticism, wrote Davis, "We were all caught unprepared for him, but we must go down and destroy him.... We must go close to him and smash him in. It will be warm work, but we must do it." That night, Far-ragut made his run. Mortar fire on Vicksburg opened the action at 6 P.M. and forty five minutes later the fleet was underway. At 8: 20 P.M. it had passed the Vicksburg batteries and anchored below the city. But Farragut had not destroyed the *Arkansas;* in fact, only one of his ships, the *Oneida,* actually saw the Rebel ironclad. How ever, the *Arkansas* did not escape damage, for a shot passed through its armor, penetrated the engine room, and disabled the engine and also caused a severe leak. More casualties were added to the morning's toll of ten killed and fifteen wounded.

All efforts to destroy the *Arkansas* failed during the ensuing days—mortar fire directed at the Rebel craft, a direct assault by the *Essex* and *Queen of the West.* Captain Ledyard Phelps of the *Benton* summed it up in a letter to Andrew Foote: "The whole thing was a fizzle. Every day we heard great things threatened only to realize fizzles." Van Dorn, in a telegram to Jefferson Davis, character-ized the attack on the *Arkansas* as a "failure so complete that it was almost ridiculous."

Farragut, chagrined, parted company with the *Arkansas* when he was ordered by the Navy De-partment to return to New Orleans with his fleet. Departing with Farragut was General Williams's force, which was so riddled with illness that barely a fourth of the 3,000-odd troops was ready for duty. Williams retired to Baton Rouge. With only his gunboats left at Vicksburg, Davis deemed it wise to steam upriver to the mouth of the Yazoo. For more than two months—sixty-seven days—Vicksburg had frustrated the efforts of two power-ful Union fleets and more than 3,000 land forces.

The 20,000 to 25,000 shells hurled at the city left Vicksburg undaunted.

Captain Brown took advantage of the respite to visit Granada, Mississippi, where he fell ill. Lieu-tenant Henry Stevens, left in command of the Arkansas, worked feverishly to repair the engines and to increase the ship's armor. General Van Dorn ordered Stevens to take the *Arkansas* down the river to Baton Rouge to support an attack on that city by Major General John C. Breckinridge.

On August 3 at 2 A.M. the *Arkansas* moved from the wharf and headed for Baton Rouge. Throughout the day, the ironclad's engines func-tioned efficiently and an eight-knot speed was

Above: To be sure, the Essex *was a formidable ironclad. She appears here off Baton Rouge (which she helped defend) in March 1863. The* Richmond *and* Mississippi *can be seen off her stern. (USAMHI)*

Above: Church Street in Baton Rouge, during the Federal occupation. (USAMHI)

Above: A. D. Lytle's 1861 image of Baton Rouge, before the destruction of the war came to visit. (LSU)

Below: Another view of Church Street. These views were made by the Baton Rouge firm of W. D. McPherson and his partner Oliver, whose first name is unknown. (USAMHI)

Above: Breckinridge was initially successful, but later he had to abandon Baton Rouge, which showed the effects of the battle. Most of this damage was done by Federal gunboats, chiefly the Essex, *as they attempted to support Williams's beaten troops. (LSU)*

Above: The Louisiana State House, taken by McPherson & Oliver. (USAMHI)

Above: The Louisiana State Penitentiary, captured by Baton Rouge's other outstanding artist, A. D. Lytle. (USAMHI)

Above: L. I. Prince's image of the Baton Rouge Arsenal. (ISHL)

Right: Part of the arsenal grounds, by McPherson & Oliver. (USAMHI)

maintained. But shortly before midnight, the starboard engine broke down, and the *Arkansas* tied up while repairs were made throughout the night. At 8 A.M. on August 5, the *Arkansas* was apparently ready to participate in Breckinridge's attack, which was already underway. When the *Arkansas* was within eight miles of Baton Rouge, the engines went dead again. Once more repairs were rushed and once more the engines broke down. By 9:30 A.M. on August 6, the *Arkansas* seemed ready once again. At that time there appeared, steaming toward the *Arkansas*, four Union gunboats, the *Essex, Cayuga, Katahdin,* and USS *Sumter*. Stevens determined to make a fight of it, but the ironclad's port engine failed as the *Arkansas* headed to engage the enemy. A moment later the starboard engine gave way and the *Arkansas* drifted helplessly toward the advancing Union gunboats.

Both sides opened fire, but ineffectively, and Lieutenant Stevens realized he had no alternative to the destruction of the *Arkansas* to prevent its falling into the hands of the enemy. Ordering the crew ashore and commanding them to take off for the interior, Stevens, with seven officers and petty officers, prepared the *Arkansas* for its end and then abandoned ship, too. For an hour the *Arkansas* floated with the current, its loaded guns firing as the flames reached them, and shortly before noon, it blew up spectacularly.

"It was beautiful," recalled Stevens, "to see her, when abandoned by commander and crew and dedicated to sacrifice, fighting the battle on her own hook."

In a report to the Confederate Congress, Secretary of the Navy Mallory said, "Naval history records few deeds of greater heroism or higher professional ability than this achievement of the *Arkansas*."

With the passing of the *Arkansas*, there passed also the last Confederate offensive challenge on the Mississippi. The Union now controlled the entire river except for the Rebel bastions at Vicksburg and Port Hudson, Louisiana.

Less than a year remained before these last two Confederate strongholds would fall, and the Father of Waters would again go, as Mr. Lincoln expressed it, "unvexed to the sea."

Above: The courthouse as seen by McPherson & Oliver. It was turned into a barracks and later a hospital by the occupying Federals. (USAMHI

Right: Artillery covered as protection against rain on the grounds of the Jackson Barracks. (USAMHI)

Left: Everywhere in the South, when the Union soldiers came, the slaves flocked to their camps. Here the headquarters of the contraband camps in Baton Rouge. (USAMHI)

Left: General Williams's headquarters before the Battle of Baton Rouge. (USAMHI)

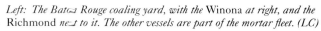

Left: The Baton Rouge coaling yard, with the Winona *at right, and the* Richmond *next to it. The other vessels are part of the mortar fleet. (LC)*

Above: Here Farragut's fleet stands off the city in 1862, on its way north to Vicksburg. The stern of the USS Mississippi *is just visible to the left of the wood pile. The USS* Richmond *is in the center, and the USS* Winona *is to the left of it. (USAMHI)*

Above: The Portsmouth again, with one of the mortar schooners in the distance. (LC)

Above: Often erroneously identified as the Hartford, this image shows the USS Portsmouth on the right and an unidentified warship astern of it. (LC)

Above: A similar view, showing the ruins of a factory at the water's edge. (CWTI)

Above: Two of Porter's mortar schooners lie side by side against the bank at Baton Rouge, while a gunboat, perhaps the Tyler or Conestoga, lies to the left with a damaged stack. (LSU)

Below: The Hartford lies off the Main Street levee in this McPherson & Oliver image.

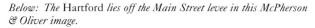

Above: The same view, perhaps from Lytle's window, shows troops disembarking from the Sallie Johnson in the spring of 1863. (USAMHI)

Above: The wharf boat at Baton Rouge, the Natchez, *operated as a warehouse, hotel, and even offered "Fresh Lake Fish" to the soldiers. (USAMHI)*

Above: The Natchez *about to unload supplies from its "warehouse." (USAMHI)*

Above: In March 1863 McPherson & Oliver photographed the Empire Parish *off Baton Rouge. Nathaniel Banks made the steamer his headquarters for a time. (LSU)*

Above: A. D. Lytle's photograph of Federals at leisure on the Mississippi, apparently a celebration. (LSU)

Below: Blacks drafted into service by the Federals worked within sight of the State House. (LSU)

Above: And all around the city the white tents of the soldiers sprouted like mushrooms. (LSU)

Above right: Regiments drilled and reviewed constantly on the old arsenal grounds. (LSU)

Right: And in front of the courthouse. (LSU)

Below: And in front of the Jackson Barracks. (LSU)

Below: One of the final acts of 1862 along the river was the Federal capture of Donaldsonville, Louisiana, in October. Unlike Baton Rouge, Donaldsonville suffered considerably from the fighting. Much of the town lay in ruins. Homes and businesses were burned or battered to pieces. (ISHL)

Below: And in a score of camps on the fringes of the city. Clearly, the Union was here to stay. (LSU)

Left: The Catholic church, damaged. (ISHL)

Left: Everywhere scenes of destruction. (ISHL)

Below: And by the dawn of 1863, nothing was more commonplace along hundreds of miles of Mississippi banks than the sight of Federal soldiers encamped, as here at Morganza, Louisiana. The Mississippi was truly conquered. Only Port Hudson remained, and Vicksburg. (NHC)

Above: But the flag went up and the rebuilding began. (ISHL)

Jackson in the Shenandoah

ROGER G. TANNER

A peculiar professor and a valley whose name meant "Daughter of the Stars"

Above: The men who saved the Valley. Stonewall Jackson and his staff in 1862. The photograph of Jackson was made in Winchester; the composite including all of the portraits is the work of Richmond's distinguished portrait artists Vannerson & Jones. (VM)

IN THE SPRING OF 1862, the Union planned two invasions of Virginia. One is well known: McClellan's seaborne thrust to the Peninsula and Richmond. Less understood is the invasion that was to precede the Peninsula campaign and which was designed to make McClellan's campaign possible. That was the invasion of the Shenandoah Valley.

The Valley lay like a dagger across much of Virginia, running generally north and south between the James and Potomac rivers and bounded by the Blue Ridge and Allegheny mountains. At its northernmost rim, formed by the Potomac, the Valley was actually many miles north of both Washington and Baltimore, so that when Union commanders spread their maps to study the state they were always reminded that the Valley lurked behind them. Confederate forces occupied the northern portion of the Valley, from which they were always in position to thrust across the Potomac. The Baltimore & Ohio Railroad, one of the Union's main east-west highways, was severed by the northern tip of the Valley, as was the Chesapeake & Ohio Canal. The economic impact of the loss of those links was considerable. But worst of all was the fact that Winchester, headquarters of Rebel forces in the Shenandoah, was a scant sixty miles northwest of the Union capital. Geography alone dictated that Confederate forces in the northern Valley must be removed before McClellan launched his Peninsula invasion.

It was initially assumed that ejection of the Rebels posed no significant problem to McClellan's operation. Indeed this was looked upon as an invasion promising major returns for nominal risks. Confederate forces in Winchester were believed to be weak and dispirited after hard campaigning during a savage winter. Federal intelligence reports estimated that Union forces should encounter little difficulty in crossing the Potomac at Harpers Ferry and pushing southward as far as Winchester to destroy Confederate forces there. To ensure success, it was decided that the Federal invasion force would be bolstered by additional thousands of men from McClellan's main army. Once the entire northern Shenandoah had been liberated, garrison forces would be left behind, and the remainder of the invading host would shift east of the Blue Ridge Mountains to take up covering positions around Washington. By protecting Washington these forces would free McClellan to transfer the main Union Army to the doorstep of Richmond.

The two invasions seemed, on paper, to form a sound and perhaps even brilliant plan. And yet, if the invasion of the Valley were disrupted or delayed, the shift of forces eastward would likewise be retarded, which could endanger the Peninsular campaign. Rarely in military history has a major military operation such as the Peninsular campaign depended so substantially for its success upon a seemingly minor and far-removed initial assault.

Rarely, too, has any important military operation been entrusted to one so utterly inexperienced in warfare as Major General Nathaniel P. Banks. Banks was a skilled politician, an ardent abolitionist, and an influential member of the Republican party; during only his second term in the United States Congress he had become Speaker of the House of Representatives. When South Carolina seceded he was retiring from the governor's mansion of Massachusetts; he knew virtually

Above: Major General Nathaniel P. Banks, the perennial loser. Jackson outmaneuvered, out-thought, and outfought him in the Shenandoah, costing Banks 30 percent of his troops in casualties. (LOUIS A.WARREN LINCOLN LIBRARY)

Above: Charlestown, Virginia, in 1862. Here and in the vicinity, the Federals who would face Jackson wintered and readied for the Valley campaign. (USAMHI)

Above: The headquarters of Brigadier General Alpheus S. Williams, who commanded a brigade under Banks in the Valley campaign, taken at Darnestown, Maryland. (USAMHI)

Above: Camps of men of Banks's command at Darnestown. (KA)

nothing of war, but unemployed governors had a way of finding themselves generals in the Civil War, and Banks was slated to lead the Union's drive into the Shenandoah.

That invasion began in February of 1862, as Banks's forces, totaling almost 40,000 men, spilled across the Potomac River and descended upon Winchester. The Federals advanced deliberately, brushing aside what seemed to be only token opposition. On the afternoon of March 11, 1862, Federal divisions converged upon Winchester from two different directions and found the Rebels drawn up in battle formation. A firefight ensued, and there was prospect of battle in the morning, but dawn found the Rebels gone and Winchester fell without a shot.

Banks trailed the Confederates southward from Winchester but was unable to bring them to a fight. They seemed, to Banks, to be running—just as had been anticipated. Within ten days the Rebels had moved far to the south, and Union forces were regrouping around Winchester. Thousands of Federals were already moving east of the Blue Ridge to take up their assigned positions around Washington. Banks even left the Shenandoah for a rest, a rest which was interrupted when, on the evening of March 23, 1862, the telegraph from the Valley began to crackle.

Opposing Banks in the Shenandoah was the Confederate Valley Army, a force of perhaps 4,500 men rostered into three tiny infantry brigades, six small artillery batteries, and 600 poorly disciplined but splendidly mounted cavalrymen led by Colonel Turner Ashby. The Valley Army was commanded by Major General Thomas J. "Stonewall" Jackson, a West Pointer, retired United States

Above: Here in Williamsport, Maryland, the Federals also awaited the order to march south. No one yet knew much about this fellow Jackson. (USAMHI)

Above: The men of the 13th Massachusetts shown here at Williamsport soon had to leave the comfort of their winter quarters. (USAMHI)

Below: The surgeons shown here before their quarters in Williamsport would have plenty of work, thanks to Jackson. (USAMHI)

Above: A brigade headquarters in Banks's command at Martinsburg, Virginia, in March 1862. (USAMHI)

Army Major, and former physics professor at Virginia Military Institute. Jackson was virtually unknown at this point of the war. Except for one brief hour of glory at the First Battle of Bull Run, he had contributed little to the Confederate struggle save a ruthless discipline of his men and a winter campaign in the Alleghenies that had killed or sickened hundreds of them.

But Jackson was full of fight, and that resolve was well adapted to his instructions. His task in the Valley was to keep as many Federal soldiers pinned down there and as far away from McClellan as he could. It was the perfect mission for this fiercely stubborn man. Although outnumbered ten to one he had clung to Winchester even as Banks uncoiled around him; Jackson had even planned an attack on Banks for the night of March 11. He was prevented from striking only when his staff relayed his orders erroneously and moved the army out of position. Jackson retreated, but he left behind his cavalry commander Ashby to cover the rear and to search for openings to attack.

Ashby found an opening as Banks redeployed his forces east of the Blue Ridge to cover Washington in accordance with the overall Union strategy. His mounted scouts detected this eastward shift and relayed word to Jackson. Within hours, Jackson was pushing northward toward Winchester with the bulk of the Valley Army. On March 23, as Banks was reaching Washington for his rest, Jackson was nearing Kernstown, a hamlet three miles south of Winchester. His rapid march had left his troops exhausted and his ranks thinned by straggling; nevertheless, Jackson threw his men into the attack.

What followed was a confused stand-up soldiers' fight called the Battle of Kernstown. The Confederates made good initial headway, then were slowed by unexpected Federal strength. One Confederate wrote his father after the battle, "The crack of rifles and the whistling of balls soon told us what we must expect. Soon volleys of musketry seemed to shake the hills." When one of Jackson's aides reported sighting increasing Federal numbers, the General replied tersely, "Say nothing about it. We are in for it."

Above: Officers of the 2nd Massachusetts in 1861. They and their regiment would feel the full sting of Confederate might in the Shenandoah. (USAMHI)

Left: Colonel John White Geary of the 28th Pennsylvania in an unpublished portrait by McAllister of Philadelphia. Formerly the first mayor of San Francisco and the governor of Kansas Territory, he was, like Banks, a politician turned commander. Unlike Banks, he proved to be a man of genuine military talent. In March 1862 he captured Leesburg before the campaign had fairly begun. (CWTI)

Jackson had blundered into at least 10,000 Federal troops under Brigadier General James Shields. Shields had kept most of his division hidden well enough to fool Ashby's scouts, and then fed them skillfully into the battle. His numbers allowed him to overlap the smaller Southern army on either flank, and by nightfall the Confederates were driven from the field in nearly total rout.

So the Battle of Kernstown ended as a Southern defeat—but a defeat which actually proved some thing of a victory. General Shields was impressed by Jackson's hard fighting; he believed that the Confederates had numbered at least 11,000 men who were the "very flower of the Southern Army."

Shields called for help from Northern forces moving east of the Blue Ridge after the battle; one large division was diverted back to the Valley at once. Shields's reports that the flower of the Southern army had emerged in the northern Shenandoah canceled plans for any further redeployment of Union forces from that area to Washington. Instead, the Union's invasion of the Valley had to begin anew.

Banks returned to the Shenandoah to handle operations there. His army was built up again to 25,000 men and he was directed to drive the Rebels as far south as Staunton. He would be assisted by Federal forces west of the Valley in the Alleghenies. Thus, Kernstown lured the Union to undertake an extended Shenandoah invasion. McClellan henceforth would be operating on one side of Virginia while Banks campaigned on the other; instead of one invasion of Virginia followed by another, the Union was now engaged in a dangerous two-pronged invasion. And every man who was in the Valley would be one man less for McClellan.

Confederate losses at Kernstown totaled almost 25 percent of those engaged; Jackson could not risk battle again for a month. During those weeks, while Federal forces were built up against him, he rebuilt his own battered army. Through March and April he retreated slowly southward up the Valley while he recruited, reorganized, and made his army ready for maneuvers.

Above: Harpers Ferry, Virginia, showing the remnant of the United States Arsenal. Here Banks anchored his army at the outset of the campaign. (USAMHI)

Left: David B. Woodbury's October 1862 image of Federal troops camped on ground which once held the armory buildings. (USAMHI)

Right: The charred remains of a canal boat and steam engine at Harpers Ferry, the scene of repeated destruction in 1862. (USAMHI)

Left: Colonel John Echols was severely wounded leading his 27th Virginia at Kernstown. Three weeks later he was promoted brigadier, and would become—though unsung—one of the finest subordinates in the army. At 6 feet, 4 inches, and weighing 260 pounds, he was a wonderful target. (USAMHI)

Below: Past this sawmill at Kernstown, Jackson advanced against Shields in the Battle of Kernstown, first engagement of the campaign. An 1885 photograph. (USAMHI)

In normal usage, because the top of a map represents the northernmost portion of the area depicted, to go *up* is to go *north* and, conversely, to go *down* is to go *south*. The idiom of the Valley is exactly the opposite because its streams drain generally northward and water routes were the principal early means of transportation. To go *down* the Valley is thus to go *northward* and, conversely, to go *up* is to go *southward*. The Shenandoah's northern region is the *lower* Valley, and the southern region is the *upper* Valley.

Before recounting these movements, a glance at the Shenandoah is essential. Up and down the middle of the region runs the great Valley Pike, a macadamized road which was one of the best highways of its time. Other roads in the area tended to be abysmal, so the principal towns clustered along the pike. From Martinsburg and Winchester in the north, the pike passed through Strasburg, New Market, Harrisonburg, and Staunton in the lower—northern—Valley. Staunton, which linked also with the eastern part of the state by the Virginia Central Railroad, served as Jackson's base of supplies. Another salient feature of the Valley is the great Massanutten Mountain. This is actually an interlocking system of ridges which rises precipitously just east of Strasburg and runs up the Valley for fifty miles. For this distance the Shenandoah is actually two valleys, the Luray Valley between the Massanutten and the Blue Ridge, and the Shenandoah proper between the Massanutten and the Alleghenies. There is only one pass through this tangled green wall, a winding and difficult road between New Market, in the Shenandoah, and the village of Luray, in the Luray Valley. From Luray a passable road ran northward to the little town of Front Royal and southward to the village of Port Republic. In the next few weeks Jackson would fight battles at both ends of that road.

While retreating southward after Kernstown, Jackson had not forgotten his primary mission of keeping Federal forces occupied in the Valley. Nevertheless, sheer Union numbers eventually forced Jackson to almost abandon the Shenandoah. By the end of April he had moved into Swift Run Gap, where he completed the reorganization of the Valley Army. He also received a major reinforcement from east of the Blue Ridge. This was the division of Major General Richard S. Ewell, a fine body of some 8,000 well-trained and well equipped infantry. At the end of April Jackson and Ewell were concentrated within supporting range of each other in the vicinity of Swift Run Gap; their combined forces totaled 14,000 men.

The situation confronting Jackson was complex. Staunton, his base of operations, was threatened from two directions. Union Major General John C. Fremont—the "Pathfinder" of America's westward expansion to California—was approaching Staunton from the Alleghenies with an army of 10,000 to 15,000 men. His advance guard, under Brigadier General R. H. Milroy, was pressing forward vigorously against scattered Confederate strength. Banks, with 25,000 men, was located in Harrisonburg and threatened Staunton from the north. In simplest terms, Jackson's dilemma was how to keep Staunton secure and Fremont and

Left: Jackson, with something of an affinity for stone walls, formed his line of battle on the near side of this one at Kernstown. (USAMHI)

Banks apart but still pinned down in the Valley. The resolution of that dilemma came through a series of dazzling marches and battles rarely equaled in military history.

On April 30, 1862, Jackson slipped out of his camps in Swift Run Gap and headed for Staunton. Ewell's division came across the Blue Ridge and occupied Jackson's camp, attempting thereby to conceal from Banks the start of a Confederate offensive. Winding in and out of the Blue Ridge, Jackson reached Staunton by May 3 with 6,000 men and then plunged westward into the Alleghenies. He soon linked up with the Confederate forces there and drove Fremont's vanguard back. On May 8 Milroy turned to fight near the little mountain town of McDowell. Like Kernstown, the Battle of McDowell was a stand-up soldiers' fight. The mountainous terrain made it impossible to give much direction to the fighting, which broke into small groups of men banging away desperately at each other. Jackson managed to seize the high ground overlooking the Federal camp, and this proved decisive. Though the Rebels suffered heavier casualties than the attacking Federals, they repulsed all attacks, and the next morning found the Union retreat accelerating.

Movement now exploded all around the Valley. Jackson pursued Milroy through the Alleghenies for several days. Banks abandoned Harrisonburg and retreated northward to Strasburg, a signal that the Union again had decided that the Shenandoah invasion was over. Due to Jackson's earlier withdrawal to Swift Run Gap, the Union high command had decided the Shenandoah was secure and Banks could retire to defensive positions along its northern borders and dispatch one division out of the Valley. Unlike the situation in March, however, Banks's redeployment this time was not merely defensive. Instead, Banks was to send Shields's division to Fredericksburg to join forces assembling there which were, in turn, to march south and link up with McClellan outside Richmond. The first step in achieving this redeployment was Banks's withdrawal to Strasburg.

The race began. Jackson hustled his troops back down into the Shenandoah and surged northward after Banks. The movements were rapid; marches of twenty miles a day were typical. The movements were also secret. Jackson had a mania for secrecy and told his subordinates—and his superiors—almost nothing of his location and intentions. His army seemed to simply drop from sight.

That Jackson disappeared during much of the Valley Campaign was true in one literal sense. His movements were such that there is almost no pictorial record of them. Burdened with unwieldy and very heavy equipment, photographers of the day needed a more stationary subject than Jackson's army to bring their talents into play. He simply moved too fast for them to arrive in time to take photographs of his operations. Such pictures as we have are of battlefields and not of the actual battles or marches, with the result that what we know of this campaign comes not from the camera but from the written word.

During May 1862, those words grew increasingly fatigued. "We are very wearied by the march, in fact, virtually worn down. A night's rest appears to do us no good—just as sleepy and languid in the morning as when we sleep in the evening," one Rebel recorded in his diary. Those who had started from Swift Run Gap with Jackson

Left: Captain Pinckney D. Bowles led a company of the 4th Alabama in Jackson's army. Like many junior officers of talent, he gained from the ravages of the bullet, which gave him plenty of opportunity for advancement. He finished the war an unconfirmed brigadier. (USAMHI)

Above: It seemed almost unfair that with so much Confederate talent in the Shenandoah, the Federals enjoyed so little. A case in point is Brigadier General Robert H. Milroy. In 1863 he had almost an entire brigade captured in the Shenandoah, and he did little better against Jackson in the earlier campaign. (USAMHI)

Below: A few days after Jackson's victory at Front Royal, a photographer caught these Confederate prisoners awaiting transport to prison. They keep a respectful distance from their guards and their stacked arms. (LC)

Right: Brigadier General Alpheus S. Williams advanced from brigade to division command at the Battle of Winchester. Few Federals won laurels there. (P-M)

Above: A street in Winchester showing Taylor's Hotel, the building with the columns, where Federal officers made their headquarters in April before the battle. Winchester changed hands in this war fifty-two times. (USAMHI)

Right: Main Street in Winchester, probably taken after the war. Winchester saw more marching armies than any other town in the war. (USAMHI)

Right: Brigadier General William B. Taliaferro, seated left, commanded a brigade for Jackson. He had been in command of the Virginia Militia, as shown here, when it mustered to put down John Brown's attack on Harpers Ferry. (MUSEUM OF THE CONFEDERACY, RICHMOND)

on the last day of April had marched more than 250 miles, most of the way across mountains and over horrible roads. But by force of will and much hard work the Valley Army kept coming. Jackson passed through Massanutten Gap with his forces and those he had collected in the Alleghenies and united around Luray with Ewell's division. He thus assembled all of the Confederates in the Shenandoah, perhaps 17,000 men and 50 cannons. With out a day's rest he turned northward on May 22 and marched to within 10 miles of Front Royal. There would be battle in the morning.

On the morning of May 23, Banks's forces in the Valley were concentrated in two small bodies: 8,000 men at Strasburg, with 1,000 men twelve miles east in Front Royal. Banks's remaining strength was spread along the Manassas Gap Rail road east of the Blue Ridge and beyond supporting distance. Shields's division had completed its shift to Fredericksburg, where it was resting for the march southward to attack Richmond. The Shenandoah had supposedly been secured, a re-deployment of forces out of the Valley had been completed, and all available Federal forces were prepared to move on to Richmond. As had happened after Kernstown, however, Union plans were disarranged.

Around midday on the twenty-third, Jackson's 17,000 men engulfed the Union garrison at Front Royal, comprised principally of the 1st Maryland Infantry. As it happened Jackson also had a regiment recruited in Maryland, and he used it as his shock troops. The Marylanders squared off in a brief but fierce skirmish, interrupted by arrival of a freight train that chugged into town between the opposing battle lines. The Rebels swept up the train, the town, and almost one thousand prisoners. Only a few dozen Federals escaped to bring Banks word of the onslaught.

Banks reacted to the situation poorly, first underestimating and then exaggerating Southern strength. His subordinates urged him to evacuate Strasburg at once, but he refused to do so until midmorning of the next day. He then ordered an immediate retreat, with the result that a near frantic collection of wagon trains, cavalry columns, and infantry poured down the pike for Winchester. The column was subjected to repeated Confederate cavalry raids and occasional shellings. Around Middletown the Federal column was severed, and hundreds of Yankees fled to the south and then the west as Rebels fanned out after them.

Banks, meanwhile, reached Winchester by evening with the bulk of his forces. He put them into line of battle on the hills south of Winchester and began to wire Washington frantically for reinforcements. But there was no time for help to arrive.

The Rebels hit again at first light on May 25, and Banks saw his army dissolve. Within two hours his brigades were swept from their positions in total rout. The Federal flight continued throughout the day, carrying them almost to the Potomac that night.

In two days of running battle, Banks had been swept out of the Valley. Three thousand Federals were prisoners. More than nine thousand rifles, warehouses of urgently needed medical stores, herds of cattle, and tons of other stores had been captured from Strasburg to the Potomac. Confederates gloated that the Federal rout was more complete than that at Manassas; total Southern casualties from Front Royal to Winchester were less

Above: Francis T. Nichols led the 8th Louisiana at Winchester, and there took a wound which cost him his left arm. Promoted to brigadier—as shown here—a few months later, he later lost a foot at Chancellorsville. (NYHS)

Above: A ford on the Shenandoah River, crossed and recrossed by Jackson many times in the course of his campaign. (USAMHI)

Left: A postwar view of the Massanutten Mountain, key to Jackson's brilliant success in the Shenandoah. (USAMHI)

than four hundred killed and wounded. One Rebel veteran summarized this highlight of the war long after when he wrote, "We had no general engagement, and our loss was small; it being a kind of one-sided fight all the time. General Jackson 'got the drop' on them in the start, and kept it."

The effect of Jackson's onslaught was immediate. President Lincoln was seriously disturbed by events in the Shenandoah, and he responded with orders to capture or crush the Valley Army. Studying his map of Virginia, Lincoln noted that Jackson had moved dangerously north of both Fremont and the Union forces around Fredericksburg; the Rebels were, in fact, moving into a trap. Even as the Confederates were herding Banks out of the Shenandoah, Lincoln directed Fremont to drive into the Valley from the Alleghenies, while Shields was ordered to retrace the march he had just made and return to the Valley from the east with 20,000 men. Both halves of this pincer were to enter the Valley well south of Jackson so as to cut off his escape.

Lincoln's bold plan, which was, in effect, a third invasion of the Shenandoah, was purchased at the price of assistance to McClellan. With Shields leading 20,000 men back to the Valley, the remaining Union forces at Fredericksburg were too weak to lunge southward, which is just what Jackson desired. Jackson had fulfilled his mission to keep as many Federal troops as possible tied down in and around the Shenandoah. Overall, some 50,000 to 60,000 Federals across northern Virginia were concentrating on the Valley Army instead of Richmond.

Jackson, meanwhile, pushed northward to Harpers Ferry at the end of May and made a vigorous demonstration before a well-entrenched Union garrison hoping to multiply the shock value of his sudden appearance in the lower Valley. But his own situation was now critical. By May 30,

Above: Jackson's brilliant cavalry leader, Brigadier General Turner Ashby, made major contributions to the defense of the Valley. It cost him his life on June 6, 1862, just two weeks after he received his general's stars. The only known photograph of him in uniform is this one, taken in death. (CHS)

Above: Colonel Beverly Robertson succeeded to command of Ashby's cavalry at his death, and three days later he was made a brigadier. (VM)

Right: Brigadier General John P. Hatch commanded Banks's cavalry in the futile attempt to contain Ashby. Shown here in an 1865 portrait made in Charleston, South Carolina, he failed to distinguish himself. (USAMHI)

Far right: The ever-present Brigadier General Louis Blenker had to make a torturous march with his division in March 1862, going from McClellan's army to join the Federals in the Valley. It took six weeks and the War Department forgot to supply him with anything. Cross Keys was his last battle. He fell from his horse during the war, and in October 1863 he died from the effects of the fall. (P-M)

Below: The battlefield at Cross Keys. (USAMHI)

Right: Colonel Wladimir Krzyzanowski, a Pole by birth, led the 58th New York at Cross Keys. "Kriz" rose to brigade command within a year. (P-M)

Jackson learned he was almost surrounded by Federal columns from the west (Fremont), east (Shields), and north (Banks's reorganizing army and the garrison at Harpers Ferry). Jackson's response was calm and to the point: He ordered his men to turn around and march southward very fast. In two days of heroic effort he covered the fifty miles from Harpers Ferry to Strasburg with all his captured stores and prisoners. He collided with Fremont just outside of Strasburg and drove him back into the Alleghenies, clearing the way for the last of his stragglers to slip through the Union ring.

Throughout the first week of June, the Valley Army withdrew from Strasburg under terrific pressure. Fremont trailed the Rebels along the Valley Pike, while Shields pushed his divisions southward into the Luray Valley. Rain poured down in crackling streams. Units lost their wagon trains, officers lost their commands, regiments became intermingled, and confusion reached epidemic proportions. The courageous cavalry leader Turner Ashby was killed protecting the army's rear in a heavy skirmish. The retreat demanded the courage of a battle and was far more costly. The Valley Army had lost four hundred men fighting its way from Front Royal to Winchester; it lost thousands of stragglers and sick on this retreat. One Rebel wrote, "I never saw a Brigade so completely broken down and unfitted for service as our Brigade.... I am satisfied that the Brigade has lost at least 1,000 men broken down, left on the way and captured."

By June 7, Jackson had turned southeastward from Harrisonburg to slip around the Massanutten to the village of Port Republic. There he would stand between Fremont and Shields, and around this village were to occur scenes as thrilling as any of the Valley Campaign.

These events erupted on the morning of June 8, as a surprise Union cavalry raid stormed into Port Republic and almost captured Jackson and most of his staff. Other Union cavalrymen probed to within a few hundred yards of the huge Confederate wagon train. A courageous stand by a dozen sentries stalled the Union raiders just long enough to allow Jackson to move in reinforcements and eject them.

As if in echo, Fremont's guns began to pound Confederate positions west of Port Republic. Jackson feared that he was about to be struck from two sides at once and built up his positions around the village; he left the handling of Fremont to Ewell's division. Ewell did his job well. In what has become known as the Battle of Cross Keys, Ewell sparred with Fremont throughout the day, repulsing every Union attack and driving the Federals back several miles by nightfall. During the day Shields's advanced guards showed themselves briefly to the east of Port Republic but made no advance.

Emboldened by Fremont's weak showing, Jackson planned the most ambitious battle of the campaign for the next morning. He would maneuver all available men across the two small rivers that joined around Port Republic to crush Shields's advance guard east of those streams, then return to rout Fremont. His timetable allowed only four hours to thrash Shields before he would have to rejoin the thin covering force he would leave behind to bluff Fremont. There was equally little time to prepare the attack; Jackson was able to span the river obstacles with only

Above left: Colonel Thomas T. Munford led the 2nd Virginia Cavalry under Ashby and at Cross Keys. Like many of these Virginians, Munford found that the dashing Valley service appealed to the romantic in him. (CWTI)

Above: Brigadier General Arnold Elzey distinguished himself and his brigade at Port Republic. His horse was killed under him and he took a painful wound in the head. (VM)

Below: Port Republic, in a photograph taken fifty years after the battle in which Jackson effectively completed the Valley campaign in victory. (USAMHI)

Above: Brigadier General George H. Steuart, called "Maryland Steuart," thanks to his birthplace, led a Virginia brigade and was badly wounded at Cross Keys. At Winchester he had declined to obey an order from Jackson because it did not come through the proper chain of command, and this may have cost the Confederates the chance to entirely destroy the Federals. (SOUTHERN HISTORICAL COLLECTION, THE UNIVERSITY OF NORTH CAROLINA AT CHAPEL HILL)

primitive temporary bridges, and this was to cost more valuable time.

Before dawn on June 9, Jackson's maneuver brigades were on the march, and things promptly began to go wrong. Delays were encountered crossing Jackson's hastily erected bridges, batteries came up without ammunition, and the Confederate at tack began piecemeal about 7:00 A.M. It stalled at once and during the next several hours Jackson was outnumbered and on the defensive. Shields's men, recalling Kernstown, attacked furiously and at one point shattered the main Southern line. The dramatic arrival of Ewell with several fresh regiments reversed the flight, but more anxious minutes passed before Jackson finally assembled an overwhelming numerical superiority and drove Shields's forces back handsomely. Kernstown was revenged by the Battle of Port Republic but Confederate losses were severe, and Jackson abandoned any further hope of attacking Fremont. Instead, he coiled his forces along the slopes of the Blue Ridge out of enemy reach. He need not have worried, for both Fremont and Shields retreated the next day.

The Valley campaign comes to an end with those retreats. Jackson made preparations to join Lee around Richmond as soon as he learned of the enemy withdrawals. As he laid his plans, Jackson found himself something of a hero of the South. Since leaving Swift Run Gap on April 30, he had marched almost four hundred miles. He had inflicted approximately seven thousand casualties on the Union, half of them prisoners, and captured enormous quantities of supplies. His own losses had been less than half of those of the enemy, light losses indeed when compared to the ghastly casualty lists from other encounters of this war. Most important of all, the Valley Army's weeks of marching had been weeks of victory which stalled the Union drive on Richmond. Jackson's successes reinspired a South parched for victory. Robert E. Lee expressed the feelings of the Confederacy when he wrote to Jackson, "Your successes have been the cause of the liveliest joy in this army as well as in the country."

The Second Bull Run

DAVID LINDSEY

To Manassas once again, another battle, another defeat

Above: Photographer Timothy O'Sullivan's wagon on the road leading into Culpeper. (USAMHI)

AS UNION Major General George B. McClellan's Peninsular campaign sputtered out in the heavy fighting of the Seven Days Battles, the opposing armies drew apart. McClellan backed off his 100,000-man Army of the Potomac to a new base at Harrison's Landing on the James River, where Federal Navy control assured protection, supplies, and future mobility. The newly named commander of the 75,000-man Confederate Army, General Robert E. Lee, had succeeded in beating back the Union drive on Richmond. Both sides now paused, catching their breath, pondering how to proceed next.

From Washington a disappointed President Abraham Lincoln came in person to McClellan's headquarters to assess the situation. When McClellan handed him a lengthy note giving blunt advice on matters of policy, Lincoln kept his own counsel, while mulling over what to do with his balky general and the well-trained, well-equipped army. In a move to pump new blood and spirit into the eastern theater command, Lincoln now brought bewhiskered Major General John Pope from the west to command a newly organized Army of Virginia that combined the forces of Major Generals Nathaniel Banks, John Fremont, and Irvin McDowell. Pope's credits included some earlier victories in the west, strong antislavery views, and an aggressive attitude toward the enemy. He talked too much and had criticized McClellan's "indisposition to active movements." Also from the west came Major General Henry W. Halleck, clean-shaven and bug eyed, whose large forehead inspired his nickname "Old Brains," to be installed as General-in-Chief of all Union armies.

Where McClellan fitted in the new command picture remained undetermined by Washington. Clearly "Little Mac" was extremely popular with his soldiers, one of whom wrote, "the real man of the army is Little Mac. No general could ask for greater love and more unbounded confidence than he receives from his men.... everywhere among his boys, as he calls them,... he is received with enthusiasm." For himself, McClellan says of his plans for midsummer 1862, "I would have crossed to the south bank" of the James River and seized Petersburg from which "I would have operated against Richmond and its communications from the west, having already gained those from the south." Perhaps. McClellan wrote this years later, knowing with hindsight that General U. S. Grant used precisely that approach in 1864-65. At least one of his soldiers thought it possible, agreeing with McClellan that the administration had not given adequate support, noting, "We want 300,000 men raised and sent down here immediately. We've been fooling about this thing long enough.... The army and the people demand such a vigorous prosecution of the war as shall give some hope of ending it."

But the Lincoln Administration decided otherwise by early August. On August 3 Halleck ordered McClellan "to withdraw your army from the Peninsula to Aquia Creek" on the Potomac, some thirty miles south of Washington. McClellan protested, arguing, "Here is the true defense of Washington; it is here on the banks of the James that the fate of the Union should be decided." But Halleck insisted McClellan get moving. But "Little Mac" as always moved with caution, sending first the wounded, followed by the able-bodied troops, on transports down the James, up Chesapeake Bay and the Potomac to Aquia Creek and

Above: Octagon House in Arlington, Virginia, head-quarters for Major General Irvin McDowell in the early summer of 1862, when Lincoln held his corps back from McClellan on the Peninsula. (USAMHI)

Above: Culpeper's important railroad depot on th Orange & Alexandria. (USAMHI)

Above: Then once again McDowell marched south into Virginia's heartland, past scenes remembered from his campaign of the year before, scenes like Falls Church. (USAMHI)

Left: Inside Culpeper McDowell's soldiers made themselves comfortable for what they hoped might be a long stay. (USAMHI)

Alexandria. All of this took time—too much time as it turned out.

During July Lee watched intently from Richmond seeking to fathom the next Federal move. He learned of Pope's taking command of the new 40,000-man Army of Virginia. If Pope should begin moving south toward Richmond and McClellan should punch again at Richmond from the east, the combined 140,000 Union force would put Lee in deep trouble. To remain inactive was to risk envelopment. Weighing the risks carefully, Lee decided on July 13 to move boldly by sending Major General Thomas J. "Stonewall" Jackson with 12,000 troops sixty miles northwest out of Richmond to Gordonsville. Here where the Virginia Central Railroad crossed the Orange & Alexandria Railroad was the critical point the Confederates had to hold—whether Pope decided to move south or Lee decided to move out from Richmond.

When the Federal command made no immediate response, Lee then sent Major General A. P. Hill's "light division" of 12,000 men forward to join Jackson, saying, "I want Pope to be suppressed." When Jackson probed forward north of

Left: But they would not be there long. In August their wagons loaded to roll toward the enemy. (USAMHI)

Above: There was a new commander in Virginia, Major General John Pope, a hero from the western campaigns who promised he would lead this army to victory. He led the army first toward Cedar Mountain. Pope here appears as a brigadier. (LC)

Right: Cedar Mountain itself sits in the distance, seen here from the Union position. (USAMHI)

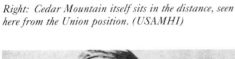

Above: On August 9, 1862, the armies clashed at Cedar Mountain. That same day O'Sullivan caught this battery fording a tributary of the Rappahannock on its way to the fight. (USAMHI)

Below: The battlefield at Cedar Mountain, taken a few days after the fight (NLM)

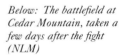

Above: Major General Nathaniel Banks. A failure in the campaign against Jackson in the Shenandoah that spring, he was defeated by Jackson again here at Cedar Mountain. (USAMHI)

Above: The Robinson House near the center of the battlefield at Cedar Mountain. Banks enjoyed some initial success on this line before Jackson smashed him. (USAMHI)

Above: Here the home of the Reverend Mr. Slaughter, an appropriate name for Cedar Mountain. Banks's losses were almost twice those of Jackson. (USAMHI)

Right: Brigadier General John White Geary, hand in blouse, stands with his staff at Harpers Ferry. He fought well for Banks and took two wounds from the field. (LC)

the Rapidan he found a small advance Union force of about 8,000 men under Banks drawn up along a small stream near Cedar Mountain. Characteristically, on August 9 Jackson attacked immediately—probably too soon, since he had only about half his men in position. Banks's troops fought back fiercely, repulsing the first Confederate assaults and pummeling the celebrated Stonewall Brigade (that had won Jackson his nickname at Bull Run a year earlier). But Jackson succeeded in rallying his men, hurried A. P. Hill's division into action, and drove the Federals from the field. After a brief pursuit Jackson withdrew south of the Rapidan.

In itself Cedar Mountain meant little. But over all it meant the military initiative was shifting away from the Federals, who only two months earlier were threatening Richmond. Now Lee, assuming the offensive, would step up pressure on Pope's army. On August 13, learning that McClellan's army was starting to embark from its James River position, he ordered Major General James Longstreet with 25,000 men forward to Gordonsville. Two days later he left some 25,000 soldiers to protect Richmond and he himself moved out to lead the Army of Northern Virginia in person.

General John Pope from his Culpeper headquarters fifteen miles north of the Rapidan River surveyed the military situation. Earlier on arriving from the west, he had issued some bombastic proclamations urging his army to fight tenaciously, not show their backs to the enemy, and not retreat. At mid-August Pope's command of about 55,000 men (including 8,000 of General Ambrose E. Burnside's corps led by Major General Jesse Reno) were encamped north of the Rapidan with the Orange & Alexandria Railroad, their main supply route, running southwest from Alexandria some sixty miles distant. Pope was following Halleck's instructions to remain there until joined by the Army of the Potomac. Some 70,000 to 100,000 of McClellan's troops, withdrawing from the Peninsula via the Potomac and Aquia Creek, were expected shortly to line up alongside Pope's position. At that point, Pope thought, Hal-

Right: Yet Jackson, too, paid a heavy price. Brigadier General Charles S. Winder commanded Jackson's old division in the furious fighting, and in the battle a shell brutally mangled him. He died hours later in this house. (USAMHI)

Left: Officers of the 10th Maine Infantry survey the field of battle some days later. (USAMHI)

Above: Simple homes became field hospitals, this one for Confederate wounded. (USAMHI)

Above: The toll in animals, too, proved heavy. O'Sullivan caught this scene a few days after the fight. (USAMHI)

Right: Men like Brigadier General Samuel W. Crawford—once the surgeon at Fort Sumter—saw their commands almost destroyed. Crawford's brigade suffered 50 percent losses. (NA)

leck would come from Washington and take personal command in the field.

Seeking the weakness in Pope's position north of the Rapidan, with the Rappahannock in his rear, Lee calculated that fast-moving Confederate cavalry could knife swiftly across the Rapidan, drive north, and destroy the rail bridge over the Rappahannock, thus cutting Pope's supply line. But, Lee knew, the strike would have to be lightning fast be cause McClellan's troops would be reaching Pope within about ten days. On August 18 the Confederates tried it, but signals got crossed. Part of the cavalry missed an assignment. A river crossing was left unguarded, and a Federal patrol in a surprise raid south of the river just missed capturing General "Jeb" Stuart but did get his famous plumed hat and silk-lined robe. More important they seized a junior officer carrying Lee's orders. As a result Pope, now aware of Lee's strategy, pulled his troops back to the north bank of the Rappahannock and set strong units at each of the river's fords.

During the intermittent rains of the next few days Lee probed for a crossing of the Rappahannock and pushed farther upstream. Stuart's cavalry crossed after dark on August 22, snaked swiftly through the foothills, and then swinging eastward pounced on Pope's headquarters at Catlett's Station on the Orange & Alexandria Railroad. There Stuart seized a stack of Pope's military papers including an important dispatch book, took personal revenge for the loss of his plumed hat by carrying off Pope's uniform coat, and after trying in vain to fire the rain-soaked rail bridge, withdrew to the Confederate lines.

As the days passed, Lee saw his chance of a quick victory diminishing. From Pope's papers he

Left: The captured were taken back to Culpeper. Here O'Sullivan photographed several Confederates in their rather informal "prison" in Culpeper Court House. (LC)

Below: The Union dead, 314 of them, were buried on the field, in sight of the mountain whose battle killed them. (USAMHI)

Above: Though they lost the battle, the Federals held the field, and here at Cedar Mountain Pope and McDowell made their headquarters. In the background left of the house stands the field wagon for reporters of the New York Herald *who followed the army. (LC)*

Above: On August 18, Pope began to move his army north of the Rappahannock t meet the threat posed by Lee. His engineers had to build several bridges to accomplish the movement. This one crosses the North Fork of the Rappahannock. (USAMHI)

learned that McClellan's V Corps under Major General Fitz John Porter, having landed at Aquia Creek, was marching to join Pope on the upper Rappahannock. Major General Samuel P. Heintzelman's III Corps was scheduled to follow shortly. Lee figured Pope had 70,000 troops within call on August 25 with more on the way. Already outnumbered, Lee would find attack futile if he postponed it even a few days. In fact, it was perhaps already too late for a pitched battle, unless Pope could be maneuvered off balance. Lee was willing to give it a try.

On August 25 Lee sent Jackson with 23,000 "foot cavalry" scurrying out on a long sweep west and north. This division of the army in the immediate presence of the enemy, contrary to all conventional military wisdom, posed a serious military risk. Had Pope pulled all his units together and concentrated on Lee's force remaining south of the Rappahannock, the Rebels might have been badly whipped. But Lee took the gamble, counting on Pope not to move quickly while Jackson circled behind the Bull Run mountains out of sight and around Pope's right flank. If all went well, Jackson would swing in behind and cut Pope's supply and communication lines.

Shedding knapsacks and surplus paraphernalia, Jackson's men sliced swiftly north to Salem Village on the west side of the mountains, then turned east through Thoroughfare Gap in the Bull Run mountains. Having covered a remarkable thirty miles by evening of the first day's march, Jackson proudly watching his columns file forward was heard to murmur, "Who could fail to win battles with such men as these?" The gap, unguarded by Federal troops, was readily negotiated. From its eastern summit the Confederates surveyed the rolling farmland interspersed with woods stretching east ward, with Gainesville lying directly east on the main turnpike that ran northeast to Centreville and southwest to Warrenton. No Federal forces lay in sight on that road. Ten miles beyond lay the Orange & Alexandria rail line, Pope's supply artery and Jackson's target. Pouring out of the mountains, Jackson's troops pushed on swiftly and seized Bristoe Station by dusk on August 26. Capturing most of the astonished garrison, they destroyed the rail bridge over Broad Run, tore up the tracks, cut the telegraph wires, and wrecked two trains. But two trains escaped, one going north to Alexandria, the other south to Warrenton to

Left: The Hazel River, a tributary, afforded a crossing already in place and not destroyed by the Confederates. (USAMHI)

Left: But most bridges had to be built. O'Sullivan took a series of fine images of Franz Sigel's corps crossing this bridge on August 19. (P-M)

Below: Wagons and baggage cross. (LC)

Right: Then horsemen and part of the army's beef herd. (USAMHI)

Left: Many of the Federals camped at Rappahannock Station, where they skirmished with the enemy on August 23. (LC)

Right: Meanwhile, at Catlett's Station, Lee's cavalry captured Pope's baggage, including vital information on reinforcements coming to him from McClellan. (USAMHI)

Left: All that remained were enemy winter huts and earthworks, and at least one outhouse. (USAMHI)

Right: The pace of the campaign accelerated quickly. Jackson, occupying Manassas, evacuated just as Pope was set to attack. All he found was ruins, some like these dating to March 1862 and the first Confederate evacuation. George N. Barnard photo. (LC)

spread the alarm. Jackson's two forward regiments captured Manassas Junction by midnight, and he followed with the rest of his force by morning of August 27.

Manassas Junction, as the main Union supply depot, offered a rich harvest to the tired and hungry Rebels. Here were tons of supplies, hundreds of loaded freight cars, streets of bulging warehouses, fields filled with barrels, boxes, and piles of munitions. After the captured whiskey was carefully destroyed, Jackson's famished men—who had been on short rations for days—tore into the rich stores of food. An enormous picnic resulted as men gorged themselves not only on staples of bread, salt meat, and coffee, but also on canned lobster, oysters, boned turkey, pies, and other delicacies. Shoes, trousers, shirts, toothbrushes, combs, and more were appropriated. The revelry continued all through the day of August 27. Before the bloated army marched that evening, torches were applied to the remaining, unconsumed supplies and munitions, which burned and exploded like fireworks all night.

Meanwhile General Pope with his troops on the north side of the Rappahannock found himself in a position that was both a risk and a challenge—it offered a good opportunity if Pope could seize it, but unless he managed well he would be in increasing danger. Of the three corps comprising his army at the outset, Pope saw McDowell's corps as the only one worth much. Major General Franz Sigel, he thought, was incompetent. Banks's corps, badly mauled at Cedar Mountain, with only 5,000 survivors, was of reduced effectiveness. From McClellan's army, one-armed Major General Phil Kearny brought a reliable division of Heintzelman's corps. Other troops were reported to Pope as at hand or nearby—Heintzelman's other division under Joe Hooker, Reno with most of Burnside's men, and John Reynolds's division from Porter's corps. The rest of Porter's command was reported moving to join Pope. This gave Pope over 70,000 men in the vicinity. If coordinated they could throw overwhelming power against Jackson. At the least they could plug Thoroughfare Gap and thereby prevent Lee and Longstreet's combined force of 30,000 men from using that route to come to Jackson's support. But to do these things, Pope would have to get a good many separate units to do some fast marching under coordinated direction in conditions that would change as the movements of Jackson and Lee changed. Since Pope's wire dispatches to Washington were not reaching Halleck because Jackson had cut the telegraph, Washington had only a faint idea of what was happening in the countryside beyond Manassas Junction. Messages carried by mounted couriers were uncertain. Many slips were possible—Pope could misread enemy movements, his orders to subordinates could be misinterpreted or poorly obeyed, delay and confusion could set in. If any of these things occurred, Lee's gamble would pay off.

From John Buford's effective cavalry Pope learned of Jackson's march west of the mountains—but at first Pope somehow concluded that Jackson was heading for the Shenandoah Valley. Even when he discovered that Jackson's army was coming east through Thoroughfare Gap, Pope seemed unable to deal effectively with the information. Not that Pope was slow or lazy. If nothing else, he was a man of vigor. His response was understandably vigorous. When word reached him of Jackson's sacking of Manassas, Pope pulled his troops back from the Rappahannock to positions running roughly from Gainesville about five miles east of Thoroughfare Gap on the Alexandria-Warrenton turnpike to Warrenton Junction about twenty miles south on the Orange & Alexandria Railroad. This was a well-conceived move.

From Gainesville Pope sent James B. Ricketts's division of McDowell's corps west to cork the bottleneck at Thoroughfare Gap. But from this point forward Pope dispatched curious orders that were often incomprehensible or contradictory or self-canceling. Porter's corps, for example, was marched at top speed for ten miles under a broiling August sun only to be rushed back at the same fervid pace to the point it came from. Heintzelman's III Corps tramped eighteen miles to reach a point only three miles from where it started. Federal troops were being worn down by marching and countermarching on reduced rations, since the Manassas stores had been burned.

Pope pushed other Federal units forward to Manassas Junction to smash Jackson. There they found nothing but smoldering ruins. Leaving after dark the night before, Jackson had sent three columns forward—one across Bull Run and northwest toward Centreville, a second across Bull Run and northwest to Sudley Springs, the third up the west bank of Bull Run. Next day, August 28, he brought all three together near Groveton in a wooded area a short distance west of the Warrenton pike. Puzzled over the invisible Jackson, Pope concluded the enemy was heading north toward the Potomac and ordered troops forward to Centreville to head off such a move. But Jackson wasn't there either. Figuring Jackson was now desperately trying to escape, Pope determined to concentrate his forces on Jackson when he found him.

In making Jackson the sole target of his drive, Pope somehow forgot about Lee and Longstreet. The Federal plug came uncorked from Thoroughfare Gap as Ricketts moved his men back from their forward position there. This was exactly the reverse of what was needed for a Union success. Ricketts should have been strengthened to thwart a juncture between Lee and Longstreet from coming through the pass and joining Jackson. Somehow Pope erroneously developed the notion that McDowell's unit, "ordered to interpose between" Jackson and the enemy's "main body... moving down through Thoroughfare Gap" had "completely accomplished" its mission by driving Longstreet "back to the west side" of the gap. This totally false impression led Pope into mistaken planning for the next day, August 28.

Above: The Barnard & Gibson views taken in March are almost all that survive to give a picture of Manassas. It looked much the same when Pope marched in. (USAMHI)

Left: The fortifications were extensive. (USAMHI)

Left: And so was the clutter and debris. The horse appears to have been hobbled before it was killed, and several pieces of a steer are scattered about it. (USAMHI)

Left: Pope's Federals faced a big task just in cleaning up after the Confederates. (USAMHI)

Right: They occupied the old earthworks. (AMERICANA IMAGE GALLERY)

Right: They restored and refurbished them. (WRHS)

Left: O'Sullivan's July 1862 image shows the eastern range of earthworks at Manassas. (USAMHI)

Below: And this photograph, probably taken by A. J. Russell, reveals Confederate Fort Beauregard. The Federals did not retain the name. (USAMHI)

Arriving at Bristoe by dusk August 27, Pope convinced himself he had Jackson trapped. Out went orders to subordinates to march "at the very earliest blush of dawn" in order to concentrate forces between Gainesville and Manassas and "we shall bag the whole crowd.... Be expeditious, and the day is our own."

In pulling his forces away from Manassas Junction Jackson had ultimately chosen his position well. He brought his various columns together on the western edge of what had been the Bull Run battlefield of a year earlier, under the cover of a wooded area a short distance west of Groveton just off the Warrenton pike. His left was anchored on Bull Run at Sudley Springs, his right on a hill roughly two miles southwest toward Gainesville. His front was protected by a low wooded ridge and a steep embankment of an abandoned railroad line. Here he could rest his men concealed in the shade of the woods, but in a commanding position difficult to assail and with a potential escape route via Aldie Gap in the mountains to his rear. And yet he was close enough for Lee and Longstreet to reach him when they passed through Thoroughfare Gap a dozen miles to the southwest. Here on August 28 Jackson waited in the woods and watched as units of McDowell's corps trudged along the pike to Centreville, past the Stone Bridge to Jackson's left.

Finally as evening approached Jackson determined to make Pope stand and fight rather than let him withdraw to a strong position on the Centreville side of Bull Run. The column of Rufus King's division approached along the pike in the late afternoon heat. "Stonewall" Jackson, after riding out in front of his hidden troops, eyed the Yankees through his glass, then wheeled, galloped back to the ridge, and barked an order. Confederate artillery batteries rolled out and began firing. From the woods Rebel troops charged "with a hoarse roar... like wild beasts at the scent of blood," red battle flags gleaming under the sinking sun. Forming the line of battle they started shooting.

On the Union side Brigadier General John Gibbon's four brigades took the initial shock of the enemy attack. Green, never under fire before, they should have panicked. Instead they wheeled about coolly into their own line of battle and stopped the Rebel attack. Joined by men from Abner Doubleday's brigade, 2,800 Federals faced nearly twice as many Confederates in one of "the hardest close quarter fights of the whole war." The contending battle lines stood face to face "as if they were on parade awaiting inspection, and volleyed away at the murderous range of less than one hundred yards." For two solid hours the deadly firing continued until darkness closed in. By nine o'clock the lines drew apart. On both sides the losses had been staggering. Two of Jackson's generals, William Taliaferro and Richard Ewell, were carried from the field severely wounded. Gibbon's midwestern farm boys, already called the "Black Hat Brigade," won laurels that day and would soon be rightly known as the "Iron Brigade."

By nightfall August 28, Pope, now aware of Jackson's position, decided to destroy Jackson's force the next day. Again orders went to division commanders to move "at the earliest dawn." But as Pope moved his headquarters forward to a hill near the famous Stone House, well-remembered from the first Bull Run battle's intense fighting, he was still fuzzy on several crucial factors. For one, he did not know the current location of McDowell or that Ricketts had moved to Bristoe Station. He still held to his delusion that Lee and Longstreet had been repulsed at Thoroughfare Gap. In addition, his men, after much marching and little eating, were tired and sluggish.

From dawn on August 29 Federal artillery blasted away at Jackson's position in the woods just northwest of the Warrenton pike, while infantry units moved closer. Again, if Pope could get all his forces concentrated, he figured to outweigh Jackson's battered 20,000-man army by three to one. Chance for victory looked bright. Anxious to open the attack, Pope moved hastily while many of his units were still on the road and out of touch.

After the artillery blasts drove in Confederate skirmishers, Sigel's 11,000 men were ordered to attack the center of Jackson's defense line. As a Confederate observer reported, "The Federals sprang forward with a long-drawn 'huzzah' ringing from their 10,000 throats. On they went until half the distance to the [railroad] cut and then the smoke, flash and roar of 4,000 well-aimed guns burst from the Confederate entrenchment, and a wild, reckless and terrifying Southern yell echoed and reechoed through the woodlands." Two more Yankee assaults were made on the center and repulsed.

The attack then shifted to Jackson's left where Pope sent Kearny and Hooker with 12,000 Army of the Potomac veterans aided by Reno's 8,000 seasoned veterans. But organization, timing, and coordination were lacking. Federal units went into action piecemeal, bit by bit, and the full effect of such a massive blow was lost. Besides, the Rebel line here was defended by some of Jackson's best troops under A. P. Hill. The Confederate line bent and at one point snapped temporarily under the impact of six separate attacks, punctuated with vicious hand-to-hand bayonet fighting. Hill's ammunition supply was almost gone and his casualties were enormous, but he managed to hang on as dusk fell.

Meanwhile some 30,000 Union troops nearby had failed to get into action. These men under Porter and McDowell, moving from Manassas toward Gainesville to hit Jackson's right, sighted large clouds of dust ahead. Figuring that Confederate reinforcements were arriving, Porter and McDowell slowed, paused, and shifted course toward Groveton, beyond which fighting raged. Because of their slowness few of McDowell's and none of Porter's troops got into battle before the day's fighting ended. Porter would later be court-martialed and cashiered for holding back here.

Also sitting out the action of August 29 were Longstreet's 30,000 soldiers. They had emerged from Thoroughfare Gap early, marched forward, contacted Jackson's right by noon, and took position just south of the Warrenton pike by 3 P.M., where they blocked Porter's line of advance. Poised to attack the Federal left flank, Longstreet persuaded Lee to wait, arguing that his men needed rest after a long march and that delay might produce new Federal blunders. Toward evening Longstreet sent a reconnaissance unit forward on the pike only to clash with McDowell and to pull back to await the next morning. That night Lee reported to President Davis, "My desire has been to avoid a general engagement, being the weaker force, and by maneuvering to relieve a portion of the country."

Left: Then Pope heard the enemy was at Centreville, and off he went, leaving behind some destruction of his own. Rolling stock of the Orange & Alexandria was burned to the wheels rather than be allowed to fall into Confederate hands. (USAMHI)

Below: Engines were pushed over the railroad embankments. It would take a major effort to right this one. (USAMHI)

Above: And then came another battle at Bull Run. Here Blackburn's Ford is shown on July 4, 1862, a few weeks before the battle. (USAMHI)

Below: Brigadier General William B. Taliaferro took a bad wound in the preliminary fighting at Groveton. (USAMHI)

Right: Some familiar faces were here again. Major General Richard S. Ewell played a minor role at the first Bull Run. Here at the second he was in the thick of the fighting and lost a leg. (VM)

Above: William A. Wallace succeeded to the colonelcy of the 18th South Carolina on the field when its commander was killed. This later image shows him as a brigadier general. (USAMHI)

Above: Major General David R. Jones, called "Neighbor" by friends, was a veteran of the first battle here. During the present campaign he made a major contribution to victory when he took Thoroughfare Gap. (SOUTHERN HISTORICAL COLLECTION, THE UNIVERSITY OF NORTH CAROLINA AT CHAPEL HILL)

Above: And, of course, there was meandering Bull Run. Here the ruins of the Stone Bridge, taken by Barnard & Gibson in March 1862. (USAMHI)

Right: Stone Bridge and the heights beyond once again shook with the sound of guns. (USAMHI)

That night at his headquarters on a hill close to the Stone House at the junction of the Warrenton pike and the Manassas-Sudley road, the husky Pope with the usual cigar in hand reviewed the day's action with some satisfaction. Jackson, as Pope saw it, was badly bruised, was cornered, and could be captured next day. Annoyed by Porter's failure to advance when ordered, he dismissed as nonsense Porter's claim that Longstreet barred his path with three times his numbers. Reporting optimistically, Pope told Halleck, "We fought a terrific battle... which lasted with continuous fury from daybreak until dark.... The enemy is still in our front, but badly used up.... The news just reaches me that the enemy is retreating toward the mountains."

On August 30 Pope's actions defy comprehension. During the morning he planned cautiously in the belief that Jackson, badly cut up, was pulling out of his position leaving only a rear guard— and of course that Lee and Longstreet were not in the vicinity. But if the Federals' task were simply to mop up the remaining Rebels, why wait until midday to start the process? True, Federal troops were tired after much marching and fighting and they had limited supplies; but the same applied to the enemy. As Pope eyed the situation, the railroad embankment, scene of yesterday's heavy fighting, seemed virtually empty, only a few Rebel sharp shooters replying to the Federal outposts' firing. (Jackson had his men out of sight getting some rest on the wooded hillslope above.) Systematically Pope disposed his units, pulling Porter's corps in on the left to close up with McDowell for a two pronged drive along the pike, sending Heintzelman to drive west from the pike against Jackson and "press him vigorously during the whole day."

As Pope was concentrating his forces, Lee kept Jackson firm on his left and had Longstreet fan his five divisions out on the right to form the lower mandible of a giant jaw. Into this maw Union troops were now marched. About noon Stuart reported to Lee that bluecoats were massing in front of Jackson. Lee forwarded the warning to Jackson, who alerted his men, but kept them concealed in the woods.

At noon without warning Federal troops charged forward in three waves—much heavier than the day before. Rebels rushed to man their line along the railroad bank and fought back doggedly. Determined Yankees slogging forward got within a few yards of the defense position. Confederates, running out of ammunition, began heaving rocks at their attackers. Hill's line wavered, broke, then reformed. Jackson signaled an appeal to Lee for reinforcements.

As Porter's units surged forward on the Union left, Longstreet's men coming out from their forest cover absorbed the first fury of the attack, then began pivoting on a hinge close to Groveton and positioned their artillery for enfilading fire. One observer wrote, "gunners leaped to their pieces..., bowling their shots along the serried rows of Federals who up to now had been unaware of the danger to their flank. The effect was instantaneous. Torn and blasted by this fire, the second and third lines milled aimlessly, bewildered, then retreated... whereupon the first line soldiers [seeing]... their supports in flight, also began to waver and give ground." South of the Warrenton pike two New York volunteer regiments guarded the base of a knoll on which a six-gun Union battery was stationed. As Longstreet swept forward these men caught the brunt of the assault. One regiment was quickly overrun. But the second—Zouaves, nattily dressed with white spats, tasseled fezzes, blue jackets, and fancy scarlet trousers—stood firm while the battery flailed the attackers and then limbered—hitched the guns to their teams—and got away, the New Yorkers then withdrawing. The cost was enormous—of 490 Zouaves, 124 lay dead, 223 wounded when it was over.

By 4 P.M. Porter found his men fighting for their lives on their front and left flank with a prospect of being enveloped by Longstreet. A withdrawal began with Longstreet in hot pursuit. As Porter reeled backwards, Lee ordered his whole army to advance—Jackson's units to drive east and south to block Federal retreat along the Warrenton pike to ward the Stone Bridge. Jackson's revived lines surged forward down the embankment and out onto the plain. Shrieking the Rebel yell, they charged against the backdrop of the setting sun, said a Northern observer, like "demons emerging from the earth."

Federal forces rallied on the high ground of Henry House Hill, where Jackson had won his nickname thirteen months earlier. Sigel's and Reno's troops joined Gibbon's "Black Hat" boys to form a firm shield for the retreating Federal units. Some feared the withdrawal might turn to panic and rout, as it had in July 1861 on this very same ground. Riding up to Gibbon, Phil Kearny, empty sleeve flapping in the breeze, cried, "It's another Bull Run!" When Gibbon said he hoped not, Kearny replied, "Perhaps not. Reno is keeping up the fight.... I am not stampeded; you are not stampeded.... My God, that's about all!" At any rate, battling bluecoats on the hill held the charging Rebels long enough for Pope's army to reach and cross the Stone Bridge over Bull Run. The bridge was then blown up. As darkness and rain came on, these troops, grumbling about their inept leaders, slogged on four muddy miles to camp long after nightfall in positions on the heights of Centreville. These were entrenched fortifications left by Confederates from July 1861. What might have been a disastrous Union rout came off as an orderly withdrawal, quite in contrast to first Bull Run. As Pope saw it in his report

Left: McDowell's engineers had to build bridges to span Bull Run a few days before the battle. (USAMHI)

Left: At the southern end of the field, near Union Mills, the Orange & Alexandria crossed Bull Run. (USAMHI)

Left: But the real fighting took place where it had before, around Henry Hill and along the Warrenton Road. Here a part of the battlefield. (USAMHI)

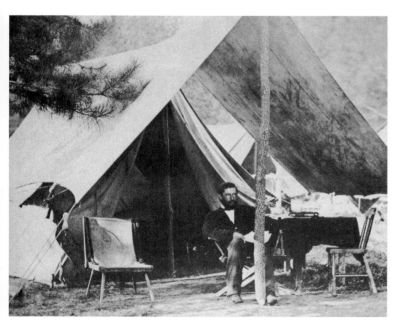

Left: A. J. Myer, the signal officer who could not get his balloon aloft at first Bull Run, operated a more effective signal office for McDowell at the second. Here O'Sullivan's image of Myer in his headquarters in late August. (LC, H. J. MYER COLLECTION)

Right: It must have seemed deja vu *for McDowell. Another Bull Run, another defeat. (USAMHI)*

Above: Sending intelligence to the front, though little good it did. (LC, H. J. MYER COLLECTION)

Left: The 2nd United States Sharpshooters, led by officers like Lieutenant B. S. Calef, saw their first real action at Second Manassas. (USAMHI)

Below: Reuben L. Walker fought with distinction at Second Bull Run, working A. P. Hill's artillery. (VM)

Right: A face familiar to the fields along Bull Run, "Shanks" Evans, hero of the first battle. His command, called the "Tramp Brigade," seemed to be everywhere. A year from now his drinking would get him into trouble. (VM)

Above: Brigadier General Abram Duryée, formerly commander of a flamboyant Zouave regiment, took two wounds in the battle while he led a brigade. (USAMHI)

that night to Halleck, "The battle was most furious for hours without cessation, and the losses on both sides very heavy. The enemy is badly crippled, and we shall do well enough."

But another observer assessed Pope's situation differently, pointing out he had been "kicked, cuffed, hustled about, knocked down, run over and trodden upon.... His communications had been cut; his headquarters pillaged, a corps had marched into his rear...; he had been beaten and foiled in every attempt he had made to 'bag' those defiant intruders; and, in the end, he was glad to find refuge in the intrenchments of Washington."

That night Lee reported proudly if a bit inaccurately to Richmond, "The enemy attacked my left, under Jackson, on Thursday [August 28], and was repulsed. He attacked my right, under Longstreet, on Friday, and was repulsed; and on Saturday I attacked him with my combined armies, and utterly routed" the Federals "on the plains of Manassas."

Casualties on both sides were severe. Lee's losses included 1,481 killed, 7,627 wounded, 89 missing; Pope's, 1,724 killed, 8,372 wounded, 5,958 missing. Some 7,000 Federals appear to have been captured, not counting several thousand wounded left on the field. Over a three-by-five-mile stretch of the Manassas plain, dead and wounded men lay strewn, in some places in heaps. The day after the battle Longstreet's men worked to aid the wounded and bury the dead. Confederate surgeons were so busy with their own as to have no time for Yanks. Shortly Federal ambulances were permitted on the field. Some 3,000 Union wounded were brought to makeshift facilities at Fairfax, where aides, doctors, and nurses were rushed from Washington. Clara Barton, seeking to get medicines and supplies there, estimated that 3,000 wounded men still lay on the straw-strewn ground at Fairfax a week after the battle. "All night," she wrote, "we made compresses and slings, and bound up and wet wounds,

Above: The Stone House on the Warrenton Turnpike would be used as a hospital again, as a year before, when the armies were done fighting around it. (USAMHI)

when we could get water, fed what we could.... Oh, how I needed stores on that field !"

As Pope's wounded were gathered at Fairfax, Union hope, which had been high only a few months before during the drive on Richmond, now lay dashed and broken. All the marching, maneuvering, fighting, dying, sickness, broiling in the Virginia sun had come to nothing by the end of August 1862. Federal troops were back where they had started—resentful, bitter, feeling betrayed and misled by military incompetents. Among Pope's soldiers, noted an officer, "Everyone had an unwashed, sleepy, downcast aspect... as if he would like to hide his head... from all the world." One newsman caught the mood: "We have been whipped by an inferior force of inferior men, better handled than ours."

From the Confederate viewpoint Lee had achieved a miracle—drawing a larger army than his own away from Richmond, running circles around the enemy and then administering a smarting defeat even in the face of superior Union numbers. Southern military fortunes were now at their highest as Lee plunged across the Potomac in early September to invade Union territory. Prospects for European aid to the Confederacy seemed brighter than before, even a possible European intervention that might assure Confederate independence.

In the North a crisis was at hand. Endless lists of wounded and dead filled newspaper pages. Morale sagged. Military leaders and Lincoln's administration were denounced by the surging political opposition. Prospects grew that Republicans would lose control of Congress in the upcoming midterm election, as voters tired of the war. Perhaps some kind of armistice leading to a negotiated peace, some thought, was preferable to continued slaughter and suffering. Obviously Lincoln's plans for wartime emancipation of the slaves—formulated in July—would have to be postponed. Gloom settled over a grim North as the people faced an uncertain future.

And the Widow Henry's house was no more. The war is simply too much for it. (NA, U. S. SIGNAL CORPS)

Above: Few of Pope's high commanders distinguished themselves in the fight. Franz Sigel, commander of a corps, almost never distinguished himself. (USAMHI)

Above: Brigadier General Robert C. Schenck was an exception. He led a brigade in Sigel's corps with distinction until a bullet removed him from further field command . (WRHS)

Right: Samuel P. Heintzelman ended his active field service with an unsuccessful attack on Jackson at Groveton in the opening of the battle. He was photographed here with his staff just a few weeks before the battle. (WRHS)

Above: "Portici," the house that had been headquarters for Johnston in July 1861, saw the armies in its fields once again. (MANASSAS NATIONAL BATTLEFIELD PARK)

Above: A new name attracting much attention was Joseph Hooker, called "Fighting Joe" by the Northern press after his performance on the Peninsula. He led a division for Heintzelman, and would shortly replace Sigel at the head of the I Corps. (USAMHI)

Right: Another Manassas house, again the scene of encamped armies, this time Federals. (USAMHI)

Below: Men of Second Bull Run. Company A, 10th New York Infantry. It was the first regiment hit by John B. Hood's Texans in Longstreet's attack on August 30. A year from now it would be so depleted by battle that it would be redesignated a battalion. (ROBERT MCDONALD)

Right: The 21st Massachusetts. Its officers, like Lieutenant Henry H. Richardson of Company K, are there as well. (USAMHI)

Left: The 73rd Ohio Infantry, shown here leaving Chillicothe in 1862, saw its first battle at Second Manassas. They would go on to march through Georgia with Sherman two years later. Photograph by J. A. Simmonds. (WRHS)

Left: This battle was the undoing of Major General Fitz John Porter. Devoted to "Little Mac," he was used in Pope's vendetta against McClellan and charged with disobedience of orders and disloyalty. In January 1863 he was dismissed from the army. Exoneration did not come until 1886. He appears seated here on August 1, 1862, at Harrison's Landing, less than a month before the battle. (USAMHI)

Left: Micah Jenkins had moved up since leading his 5th South Carolina at First Manassas. He is shown here as a colonel, but a severe wound at this second battle interrupted his career for several months. (LC)

Right: Another promising younger officer, William Mahone, called "Scrappy Billy." Shriveled, dyspeptic, weighing less than one hundred pounds, and furiously combative, he was one of Lee's most active brigadiers. (USAMHI)

Below: Colonel Jerome Robertson took a wound while leading his 5th Texas Infantry in its attack on the 10th New York. He became a brigadier a few months later. His son Felix also became a brigadier. A war criminal, accused of the murder of Negro soldiers at Saltville, Virginia, in 1864, Felix was to be the last surviving Confederate general, living until 1928. (P-M)

Above: David A. Weisiger was officer of the day in Taliaferro's Virginia Militia at the hanging of John Brown. At Bull Run he led a regiment in Mahone's brigade. He was seriously wounded but recovered to become a brigadier as shown here. The Confederacy had no distinction of insignia among the various grades of general—brigadier, major, lieutenant, and full general. All wore three stars in a wreath. (USAMHI)

Above: An unusual bearded portrait of Brigadier General Henry Slocum, promoted to major general just before the battle. He materially aided in covering Pope's retreat after the defeat. (NA)

Left: There was a small engagement at Chantilly, the final echo of the Second Manassas battle, and there one of the Union's most promising officers, Brigadier General Philip Kearny, rode accidentally into enemy soldiers. While attempting to escape he was shot and killed instantly. Winfield Scott called him "the bravest man I ever knew." He lost his arm in the war with Mexico. (USAMHI)

Right: Brigadier General Isaac J. Stevens, once governor of Washington Territory, head of the Breckinridge campaign in 1860, died after the Battle of Second Manassas was virtually done, at Chantilly, on September 1. The Union lost great potential in his death and Kearny's. It recognized the loss in the unusual act of promoting Stevens to major general posthumously. (USAMHI)

Left: And so, defeated, Pope retreated to Centreville, and here he stood briefly. There was no rout this time. A Barnard photo from March 1862. (NLM)

Left: Six months before, jubilant Union soldiers had posed gaily here in the old Confederate earthworks. (USAMHI)

Left: The "Quaker guns" once used by the Rebels to fool the Federals were now a taunt. With the bitter memory of two defeats at Bull Run, Union soldiers were not saddened to continue their retreat to Washington. (USAMHI)

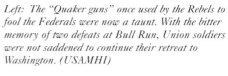

Above: Now these fortifications, designed to protect from an attack from the north, were of little use to them against an enemy that might pursue from the south. (USAMHI)

The War on Rails

ROBERT C. BLACK, III

Spiderlike the rails spread over the land, carrying the war everywhere, and feeding its voracious appetites

Above: The railroad, like the camera, came of age just as the nation went to war. Even as the armies were ready to march, so were the routes and rolling stock ready to carry them. Here a locomotive of the Raleigh & Gaston Railroad in North Carolina, around 1850. The South lay far behind the North in its rail system. (NORTH CAROLINA MUSEUM OF HISTORY)

THE IRON HORSE was not bred, on this continent, for war.

Indeed, American railroads have seldom been planned for military purposes. For over a century and a half they typically have been built to serve the economic convenience, either of the public, or of those interests which found it useful to associate their private aspirations with the public good. No railroad was ever designed to create a Southern Confederacy—or to save the Union. The original lines were established for local reasons; subsequent projects remained oblivious to the possibility of war. That such enterprises should have found themselves engulfed in the first significant railroad conflict in all history was as fortuitous as it was unexpected, and it was inevitable that the railroad facilities of 1861 should in few respects perfectly fulfill the wartime needs of either the United or the Confederate States.

At the dawn of the nineteenth century, Americans still thought of transportation in terms of waterways; even when facing inland, they sought out naturally navigable streams and lakes. Canals and steamboats, which came two decades later, were little more than elaborations upon the water concept. Highways were significant chiefly as land bridges, transcending inconvenient terrain between places of navigation. Railroads, when they appeared, were regarded as a special variety of high way, and they assumed for some time a kind of bridge role—Mohawk & Hudson; Baltimore & Ohio; Richmond, Fredericksburg & Potomac; Western & Atlantic—the western waters were meant. That railroads possessed the capacity to supersede waterways was understood at first by almost no one, and even at the outbreak of the Civil War the idea still lacked universal acceptance. As a result, American railroad enterprise was subject for a long time to local influences, frequently petty in nature, that did much to inhibit the growth of anything like a national system; indeed, neither of the famous sections, Northern or Southern, could boast of anything like a unified network.

There did exist, albeit in embryo form, a number of trans-Appalachian railroad routes that straggled across the map between the east coast and the Mississippi River. Three were unquestionably Northern: the New York Central (Albany to Buffalo) and its connections; the Erie (Piermont, New York, to Dunkirk, New York) and its connections; and the Pennsylvania (Philadelphia to Pittsburgh) and its connections. Another was of uncertain status—the Baltimore & Ohio (Baltimore to Wheeling, Virginia) with connections west, which ran so close beneath Mason's and Dixon's line that it found itself, during much of the Civil War, in a kind of no-man's-land; as a carrier it would serve the Union sometimes, the Confederacy never. Authentically Southern trackage, east to west, coalesced at Chattanooga into the single line of a single company, the Memphis & Charleston, a road destined to early fragmentation. Though Northern superiority in terms of number of "routes" was clear, none of the routes could as yet be classified as trunk lines. The tradition of localism continued to be evident in even so fundamental a matter as the distance between the rails of a track. It is true that many Northern companies had adopted the classic British gauge of 4 feet, 8½ inches; moreover, there was an equally strong tendency in the South to use a gauge of 5 feet. But Northern practice could vary; the Erie was committed to an expansive 6 feet. The South contained considerable mileage of the British sort and in other places fancied an unconventional width of 5 feet, 6 inches. Connecting lines, even of an identical gauge, did not always represent unobstructed arteries. In many instances (but particularly in the South) there existed no physical contact between the roads that served a single city or town. Gaps of this sort were naturally cherished by hackmen and drayers, who saw to it that municipal ordinances discouraged their elimination.

The carriers themselves nursed restrictive notions. Many of them—and once more this was most conspicuous in the South—shrank from releasing their rolling stock to the lines of a "foreign" company. Even in the North, railroad executives were happier when such interchanges involved the property of a third company—the germ of the car-line idea. North or South, the advantages of the through trains were as yet only dimly perceived.

Speaking very generally, it may be said that the railroad equipment of the Civil War period, both Union and Confederate, reflected a kind of American standard; that is, nearly all locomotives were of the 4-4-0 classification—two sets of four wheels front and center, and none under the cab—and burned wood; most rails were of wrought iron and weighed no more than 40 pounds to the yard; while the load limit of the average boxcar was established at about 16,000 pounds. This was only natural; most—though not all—of the engines and cars were manufactured in the North, while most —though not all—of the rails were rolled either in the North or in England. But if the Confederacy entered the Civil War with roughly similar patterns of railroad material, it typically possessed less of everything. The South counted 9,000 line miles of track; the North had 21,000. The Pennsylvania Railroad—in 1861 it ran from Philadelphia to Pittsburgh only!—owned more locomotives—220—than did all the lines of secessionist Virginia. The South Carolina Railroad possessed the greatest number of cars of any Confederate property—849. The leading company in the North was the Delaware, Lackawanna & Western with more than 4,000 cars.

Furthermore, if the Southern railroad plant was deficient at the outset, its capacity to grow, or even to maintain itself, was minimal. Confederate inferiority in the metallurgical arts and the steadily more constrictive effects of the Federal blockage are abundantly documented. But it must also be observed that these factors were rendered much worse by an unimaginative public policy, which prevented the most effective use of what the Confederacy did have.

One must, of course, be fair. At the outset, the United States authorities were as naive with respect to the administration of railroads as were the Confederate. Both opponents had sprung from a common military background, and they now faced each other with a common baggage of notions. Prior to 1861, the steam locomotive had played a scant role in American military activity; army transport had depended upon animal-drawn wagons, moving under the orders of commanders in the field and administered by a quartermaster organization whose traditions were as rigid as they were ancient. Enter the iron horse, offering greatly superior speed and almost unimaginable capacity. That the new beast would be useful was obvious, yet the wagon continued to afford an ad-

Above: Secretary of War Edwin M. Stanton, learning from the bitter lesson of the First Battle of Bull Run, which was lost when the enemy used railroads to combine troops against McDowell, knew the vital role to be played by the railroads. As a result, soon after taking his portfolio, he brought to Washington... (USAMHI)

Above: ... Herman Haupt, a near-genius who graduated from West Point at age eighteen and thereafter dazzled the railroad industry with his achievements. Stanton made him chief of construction of the United States Military Railroads with the rank of brigadier general. He worked wonders. (NA, U. S. SIGNAL CORPS, BRADY COLLECTION)

Above: Tenuous lifelines, like this viaduct on the Baltimore & Ohio at Relay House, Maryland... (MHS)

vantage that the boxcar could not match: it was not confined to a track and therefore, like its motorized descendant, provided a greater flexibility of movement. This flexibility had conditioned, over the centuries, the very mores of military transport. But now, whenever a field commander applied the traditional procedures to a railroad, the anticipated flood of supplies and reinforcements abruptly ceased. Official wrath would thereupon descend upon the railroaders concerned; "wretched" was an early and probably laundered epithet applied by General Joseph E. Johnston to the Confederate management of the Orange & Alexandria, and it is likely that other comments never saw official print.

The causes of such difficulties quickly became obvious to intelligent railroad men. One was understandable: military authorities were prone to dealing with train crews as if they were teamsters enlisted under the Articles of War, ordering them about without thought of the consequences. Another was inevitable: the temptation to regard railroad cars as convenient storehouses, and the disinclination of field units to unload and release them became notorious. Still another was the absence of any well-understood official relationship between the carriers and the military. None of these problems was ever to be perfectly resolved, but experience brought considerable improvement, especially on the Union side.

Of these principal difficulties, the absence of a formal railroad-army relationship was paramount. Until this was assured, there could be no dealing with the storehouses or the *ad hoc* train orders.

During the first year of the war, both administrations, Federal and Confederate, simply muddled through, relying largely upon quartermaster departments of the conventional kind. True, each side commissioned and inserted into the traditional structure certain knowledgeable railroad of-

Above: … and the Orange & Alexandria here at Union Mills on Bull Run, were vital to supply and transportation for the armies. A March 1863 image by A. J. Russell . (USAMHI)

Right: Sometimes they could be protected by a detachment of soldiers, as here near Union Mills in a G. W. Houghton photograph. (VHS)

Below left: But not always. Here, Barnard & Gibson's March 1862 picture of a ruined rail crossing near Blackburn's Ford on Bull Run. (USAMHI)

Below: Posing behind the embankment and pretending to defend the bridge after the fact was of little use. Other means, preventive means, had to be found. (AMERICANA IMAGE GALLERY)

ficials; the Pennsylvania's Thomas Scott and William S. Ashe of the Wilmington & Weldon are primary examples. But in neither organization were these men given appropriate authority: in the administrative bureaus their advice was overlooked; in the field it was flouted.

The Federal authorities finally moved, early in 1862, to attack the railroad problem in a serious way. First came a cleansing at the top: Edwin M. Stanton was appointed Secretary of War in place of the dubious Simon Cameron. Mr. Stanton has not enjoyed a universally favorable press; he could be an unpleasant colleague, and his political honesty remains cloudy to this day. But he was both intelligent and efficient, and he was devoted to the proposition that the Confederacy should be subjected to utter defeat. Shortly after Stanton's arrival, an administration railroad bill was pushed through Congress and received President Lincoln's signature on January 31, 1862. Its text was brief: it granted to the President of the United States the authority to assume, whenever the military situation warranted, full control over any railroad in the country. In the face of such a statute, the subordinate status of the railroad industry was clear.

To enact a law is one thing; to carry it out with imagination and dispatch is another. Even under Stanton an effective implementation required a lengthy period of trial and error. The substance of the act was published as a general order of the Adjutant General's office as early as February 4, and on the eleventh the widely respected general superintendent of the Erie, Daniel C. McCallum, was appointed military director and superintendent of railroads in the United States with very broad powers, based upon the statute and its derivative order. But the troubles persisted; they had penetrated so deep that their elimination would require not only an enlightened supervision but also Herculean labors in the field.

The labors were performed by Herman Haupt, a civil engineer of impeccable reputation, who was charged late in April with the restoration of reliable railroad service in the northern Virginia theater. Haupt was a humorless man, born to controversy. Although a graduate of West Point, he utterly lacked a sense of subordination, and his confrontations with certain braided martinets were memorable. He was, in fact, precisely the kind of man the situation demanded. His professional abilities were vast; they embraced every aspect of rail road construction, maintenance, and operation. He furthermore could usually depend upon the support of both McCallum and Stanton. Amid the Virginia disasters of 1862, he pounded out the fundamentals of an organization, the United States Military Railroads, divided specifically into construction and operating corps, and managed upon carefully stated principles perfected by himself. In the course of his service Haupt underwent repeated fits of the sulks, and after the Gettysburg campaign he stamped home to Massachusetts for good. But his military railroad ideas would be enormously and, for the Federals, happily expanded. They would be much recorded by Yankee photographers.

Though the wartime railroad law conveyed sweeping powers to the Lincoln government, this did not mean that every carrier in the United States was subjected to seizure and operation by the Union Army. So Draconian a process was wisely reserved for emergencies—Gettysburg is

Above: Haupt built blockhouses, frontier-style forts to protect bridges in Virginia and Tennessee. Here one overlooks the Orange & Alexandria crossing of Bull Run. (USAMHI)

Left: Even this was not foolproof, as the same blockhouse, now burned, demonstrates. (USAMHI)

Below: But usually they were effective. Here a more elaborate blockhouse built on the East Tennessee & Georgia line to guard the Hiawassee bridge, largely from raiders like Nathan B. Forrest. (USAMHI)

Right: And here Barnard's 1864 image of a fortified bridge on the Louisville & Nashville crossing of the Cumberland River. Giant fortress doors could close each end of the bridge, turning it into a stronghold. (LC)

Below: It was men like Brigadier General John D. Imboden that Haupt sought to defeat. Though they were usually troublesome to their superiors, on independent command they were skilled at destroying railroad equipment and installations. Imboden wreaked terrible damage on the Baltimore & Ohio in 1863 and 1864. (USAMHI)

Above right: So did Major Harry Gilmor and his 2nd Maryland Cavalry. On an 1864 raid on the B & O he not only stopped a train, but also robbed the passengers, a feat which got him suspended from command. This portrait was made in Columbia, South Carolina, by W. Weain. (USAMHI)

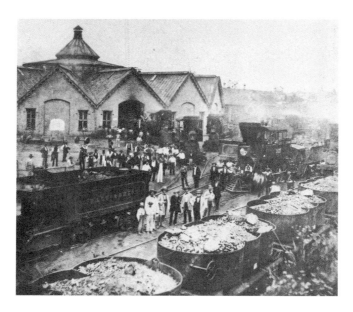

an example—and was routinely applied only to occupied Confederate properties. The statute did, how ever, inspire a healthy cooperation by Northern companies.

Behind the Confederate lines, the railroad situation continued to be in woeful contrast to the improvements on the Union side. Underequipped for the burdens of wartime traffic, hard pressed even to sustain themselves, the Southern carriers were subjected, until nearly the end, to an official policy that can only be pronounced irresponsible. Nothing that was faintly similar to the establishment of McCallum and Haupt was ever achieved. Local, even private, rights were deemed sacrosanct; facts were brushed aside. The South possessed a wealth of natural waterways, especially in the West, but these tended, like the Mississippi, to run in directions favorable to the enemy. The South also enjoyed the means to develop a respectable system of wagon transport, but this was quite inadequate to the supply, over great distances, of the large defensive armies that had become necessary in the face of even larger enemy forces. These, in their turn, had been made possible by both the waterways and the new railroads! Nevertheless, Confederate rails did provide an imperfect skeleton of interior lines, and this just possibly might have been used to so prolong Confederate resistance that the Northern will to fight—always the supreme factor in this war — might have crumbled.

But the Southern leadership failed to make sophisticated use of what was available. It was not until December 1862 that the Richmond government went so far as to bring into its military structure a railroad man of a stature equivalent to that of McCallum and Haupt. This was William M. Wadley, who currently was associated with a half finished enterprise in Louisiana, but who could look back upon a large and fruitful experience with a number of other companies in Georgia and Mississippi. He was, in a professional sense, probably the ablest railroad man in the Southern Confederacy. Wadley was noted for the brevity of his speech and, though not so brusque as Herman Haupt, was deficient in certain military niceties. His Southern loyalties were intense, but he had been born and raised in New England, a circumstance that aroused embarrassing suspicions. But his most serious difficulties were derived from the fact that he had been given rank—a full colonelcy —but no power over either the carriers or over any segment of the military. He tried earnestly to improve matters, but he quickly found himself enmeshed in the thankless role of "ombudsman" between the railroads and the government, neither of which proposed to yield an inch to the other. He did contrive to organize, without clear authority, a quasi-independent Railroad Bureau, with informal lines of communication to a variety of Confederate points. He resigned his commission seven months later, when the Confederate Senate refused, for reasons unspecified, to confirm his appointment.

The activities, such as they were, of the Rail-

Left: The Baltimore & Ohio shops at Martinsburg, Virginia, a favorite target of Confederate raiders. Probably an image from the 1850s. Shown are camelback locomotives and several iron pot coal cars. (BALTIMORE & OHIO RAILROAD)

road Bureau were inherited by Wadley's principal assistant, Captain—later Lieutenant Colonel—Frederick W. Sims. Sims enjoyed neither the background nor the reputation of his predecessor, but he was by no means incompetent, and he was endowed with a happy ability to endure frustration. Like Wadley, he carried responsibility without authority, yet he served to the very end as the Confederacy's principal rail transportation officer, devising ineffective "miracles" and accomplishing nothing of lasting consequence. He was invested at last with the kind of power that he and Wadley should have received at the beginning, but the requisite legislation was approved, with open reluctance, by President Jefferson Davis only on March 9, 1865, precisely a month before Appomattox.

Yet the Confederates could sometimes demonstrate a certain brilliance in their use of railroads. On at least three occasions they managed to improvise a steam-powered mass transit system in order to accomplish a particular strategic purpose.

The first took place in the late spring of 1862, when the divisions of W. H. C. Whiting and Jackson were shunted in bewildering sequence between Richmond and the Valley of the Shenandoah and finally were concentrated upon Lee's left wing in the Peninsula. The episode involved at least 20,000 troops, and though they at times exceeded the capabilities of the Virginia Central Railroad, their commanders did achieve a commendable harmony with its operating personnel. The results, from the Confederate viewpoint, were satisfying.

The second occasion came a few weeks later. It witnessed the removal of the greater part of Braxton Bragg's army from Tupelo, in the northeastern part of Mississippi, and its reconcentration at Chattanooga, Tennessee. Like the Virginia episode it was locally conceived and executed—and was carried out with a minimum of fuss. It was a major undertaking; involved was the movement of more than 20,000 men over the tracks of five railroads by a circuitous route through Mobile, Montgomery, and Atlanta. Yet it was completed in little more than two weeks. The consequences were considerable: the disruption over many months of the entire Federal offensive west of the Appalachians.

The third entailed the famous transfer, in September 1863, of Longstreet's corps from Lee's army in Virginia to Bragg's command in northern Georgia. It was a complex affair, organized under difficult circumstances and carried out under the general supervision of Sims's railroad bureau. Federal activities in eastern Tennessee denied to the Confederates the logical routing via Knoxville, and they were obliged to resort to a series of awkward passages through the Carolinas and Atlanta; the situation was further confused by certain unrelated movements in the direction of Charleston. Nevertheless, the thing was brought off successfully. The weather was pleasant, most schedules were kept, and perhaps half the troops arrived in time to participate in the Battle of Chickamauga. The statistics of the operation remain uncertain; the best estimates suggest that the total number completing the journey cannot have much exceeded 12,000. But their presence undoubtedly contributed to the Confederate victory and to a subsequent glimmer of Confederate hope.

The most significant result of Chickamauga, however, was the Union response to it. Hardly had

Left: A somewhat retouched photo showing the junction of the Baltimore & Ohio and Cumberland & Pennsylvania Railroads with the Chesapeake & Ohio Canal at Cumberland, Maryland. The mules are moving the coal cars into position to dump their contents into the canal barges. Another place exceedingly vulnerable to Confederate raiders. (B & O RAILROAD MUSEUM)

Above: Here the Chattanooga depot at Nashville, Tennessee, shows the effects of a Rebel raid . (HERB PECK, JR.)

Left: And Manassas Junction, Virginia, is repeatedly disrupted by the passing of the armies. (USAMHI)

Left: Keeping the U. S. Military Railroads running would be a massive task for the innovative Haupt. He proved equal to it. Here he paddles a small pontoon boat of his own design, used for inspecting bridge foundations. (USAMHI)

Right: Carrying out Haupt's instructions were engineers like these of the Construction Corps, photographed with their tools in Chattanooga in 1864. (LC)

Below: And commissioned to follow the railroads was one of the few officially commissioned military photographers—perhaps the only one—Major A. J. Russell. Here the headquarters of his operations at Petersburg, near City Point, in the summer of 1864. (ROY MEREDITH)

Below: Haupt moved mountains of material over long distances to maintain old lines and build new ones as needed. Here Russell's image of tons of iron rails at Alexandria, ready to go where needed. (USAMHI)

the plight of the defeated General Rosecrans, now trapped in Chattanooga, become clear when plans were being drafted to rectify the situation with massive reinforcements. The most suitable available units were all in northern Virginia; they must proceed by rail, beginning at once and upon an emergency basis, to the vicinity of Chattanooga. The substantive preparations were completed in a single day: General McCallum, President John Garrett of the Baltimore & Ohio, and Thomas Scott assumed the responsibility for specific segments of the route, which was necessarily long and roundabout. It passed through Washington, Benwood—on the Ohio River in West Virginia—then to Indianapolis, south to Louisville and Nashville, and then to Bridgeport, Alabama, on the Tennessee River. Needed cooperation was ensured by reminding participants of the railroad law of 1862, and behind the law stood a no-nonsense administration and a steadily growing U.S. railroad capability.

The first train puffed away from the Virginia encampments on September 25; the last crept down the winding grade into the Tennessee Valley on the evening of October 6. In eleven and one half days, 25,000 infantry, 10 batteries of artillery, and 100 carloads of miscellaneous equipment had been carried 1,200 miles over the lines of a half dozen railroads without a single serious delay or notable interference by the enemy.

Although the reinforcing of Rosecrans at Chattanooga was the most spectacular incident of its kind over the whole course of the Civil War, it was not, in a technical sense, the most impressive. The United States Military Railroads organization was not to be presented with its supreme challenge until the following spring, when it was charged with the supply, over hundreds of miles of single track, of General William T. Sherman's Atlanta campaign. This represented more than a rigorous exercise in logistics; thanks to the renewed activity of enemy guerrillas, very extensive portions of the route required constant rebuilding. The effort—physical and administrative—was staggering, but Sherman and his 100,000 men never lacked for rations or ammunition. Superintending the miracle were three officers of the Military Railroads—W. W. Wright, Adna Anderson, and E. C. Smeed. The Confederates were simply bewildered, and as they were thrust relentlessly back upon Atlanta they wondered aloud whether the

Yankees were not carrying their bridges and tunnels with them in their knapsacks.

During all this, the officers of the United States Military Railroads were always pleased to have their accomplishments recorded photographically. This pleasant liaison between photographer and military railroader in the Civil War was a natural development; railroad gear "held still" frequently enough to serve as a subject for the slow and inconvenient emulsions of the day; moreover, railroad matters enjoyed, in the 1860s, a distinctive appeal to the picture-buying public.

The photographs that follow remind us of something more than the discussions in the text. They are nearly all Northern images and depict Northern activity. To suggest that there nowhere exists a photograph of an authentic Confederate railroad train would be taking a risk, but such a photo has yet to surface.

The South lacked boiler tubes for its locomotives. It also lacked developer and fixer. Consequently Confederate photographers could not undertake to record everything, and likenesses of loved ones must have always been more sought after than prints of the trains that carried them off to battle. Furthermore, the final catastrophe brought grievous disruption to Southern records in all categories. It was therefore inevitable that surviving views of Confederate railroads should be the work of Northerners and that they should portray scenes of occupation and ruin.

It is a fascinating coincidence that the American Civil War should have been the first conflict to encompass, in an extensive way, the techniques of both photography and railroading. And if railroads contributed to the victory of the Union, contemporary railroad photographs dramatically suggest the reasons.

Left: At Burnside's Wharf on Aquia Creek, the Construction Corps joined the rails with the waters to transport supplies. (NA)

Left: The lines of tracks seem endless. Haupt brought his rails to the very water's edge on the James, below Richmond, in 1865. Photograph by Russell. (USAMHI)

Below: Here, opposite Richmond, even locomotives were brought from ship to roadbed at the war's end. (USAMHI)

Below: In the summer of 1864 Russell captured this scene of the camp of the workers of the Construction Corps at City Point, Virginia, their tents bordering the very ties of their tracks. (USAMHI)

Below right: All along the vital arteries of supply Haupt's men could be found. One, at least, proved indifferent to the camera and, turning his back to it, had a mate shine his shoes. (ROY MEREDITH)

Left: A Russell image of a Construction Corps camp on the outskirts of Richmond after the surrender. The Virginia state capitol appears on the skyline at left. (LC)

Below: A Russell view of rolling stock and camps in Virginia. (NA)

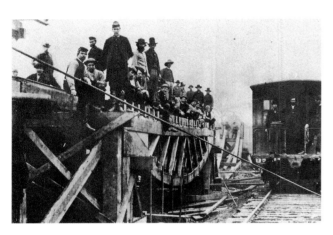

Above: Haupt's innovative mind produced many oddities, including the "shad belly" bridge, easily transportable, and speedily assembled. (ROY MEREDITH)

Right: His "beanpole" bridges made him famous, attracting the admiration of President Lincoln. This bridge over Potomac Creek was built in forty hours, utilizing two old piers from its destroyed predecessor. An A. J. Russell image from May 1864. (USAMHI)

Right: Two days before, this creek was an impassable barrier for trains. Now a train can cross in safety. (LC)

Above: Here in 1863 one such bridge is tested. (ROY MEREDITH)

Above: The Bull Run bridge-a-building. (LC)

Below: And completed. The first train crosses. Russell took this scene in the spring of 1863. (KA)

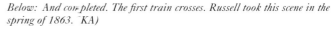

Above: Russell's 1863 print of Bull Run and a bridge under construction in the distance. (KA)

Right: Later there would be time to elaborate and refine the bridge, once it was passing traffic again. The makeshift undergirding of the previous photo is replaced by a sturdy "shad belly" superstructure, complete with ornamental eagle above the entrance. (SOUTHERN RAILWAY SYSTEM)

Left: A similar "beanpole" bridge near Chattanooga. (MHS)

Above: The Howe Turn bridge over the Tennessee at Bridgeport, Alabama, a marvel of Construction Corps engineering. Here, in October 1863, it was just being rebuilt. (MHS)

Below: By January 24, 1864, it is complete, passing regular traffic, and something of a marvel. (MHS)

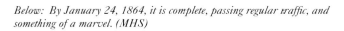

Top and above: And here it is almost finished, with still some temporary shoring at the old piles. (USAMHI)

Left: The same wonders were worked out West. The 1st Michigan Engineers, with Construction Corps help, built the Elk River bridge near Pulaski, Tennessee. It was 700 feet long and 58 feet high. (CHICAGO PUBLIC LIBRARY)

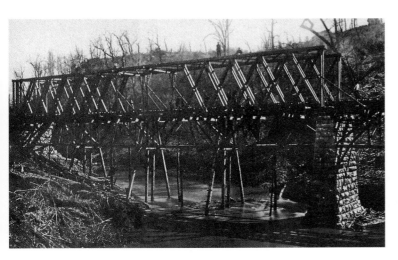

Above: And at every major river and creek between Tennessee and Virginia, similar unheralded feats occurred regularly as Haupt kept the railroads running. (LC)

Above: And a magnificent bridge built over the Tennessee at Chattanooga in 1864, mighty Lookout Mountain brooding in the distance. (MHS)

Left: Conductors and engineers like these actually ran the trains. An A. J. Russell image. (USAMHI)

Right: Their engines were frequently the best that the factories of the North could produce, splendid machines like the Gen. Haupt built by William Mason of Taunton, Massachusetts. (USAMHI)

Left: Their engineers sometimes decorated their locomotives. (USAMHI)

Right: And sometimes the Confederates did the decoration for them. In this Russell photo the men point to enemy shell damage in the stack and tender of the Fred Leach . (USAMHI)

Above: The roundhouse at Alexandria, shown in this Russell image, spun scores of locomotives in the constant traffic moving south. (USAMHI)

Above: Most major cities soon got—if they did not have them already—major rail yards. Alexandria, at the terminus of the Orange & Alexandria, became the most important in the east by virtue of the O & A's necessary part in supplying armies in Virginia. (USAMHI)

Below: The offices of the Orange & Alexandria, photographed by Russell from the top of the roundhouse. (NEIKRUG PHOTOGRAPHICA, LTD.)

Below: Mountains of scrap collected at Alexandria for melting into new rails and wheels. (NA)

Left: Nashville's Chattanooga depot acted as a principal link in the rail system supplying the Federals in the West. (KA)

Above: Lesser depots like this one at Culpeper, Virgirlia, also played their part. (KA)

Above: And always there was the constant motion of engines and ears. Here a puff of smoke and a blur give testimony to one of hundreds of iron horses at its task. (KA)

Left: A variety of special pieces of equipment came out of the needs of war. Here a private car sits on a siding at City Point in 1864. (ROY MERED-ITH)

Left: And here a more elaborate Presidential car, caught by Russell in the Orange Alexandria yard in 1865. It will take Lincoln home to Illinois, in his coffin. (NA)

Below: Iron boxcars like this one were built to safely haul ammunition over the Baltimore & Ohio. (ARCHIVES OF THE B & O RAILROAD MUSEUM—CHESSIE SYSTEM)

Left: Car barges like these operated on the Potomac River, shifting trains where bridges could not cross. (NA)

Above: Haupt was not the only innovator, either. The Confederates, with far more limited means, are believed to have created this railroad battery near Petersburg. Such quickly mobile armored artillery could be very useful, if only the rails went to the right places. (USAMHI)

Left: Improvised rail splices like this made quick repairs to old or sabotaged track. (NA)

Left: The Union, too, put guns on rails, and none greater than the mighty 13-inch mortar "Dictator." It weighed 17,000 pounds and performed well at Petersburg. Only rails could move the behemoth gun. (SOUTHERN RAILWAY SYSTEM)

Right: It is unfortunate that so little survives to illustrate the role of Confederate railroads in the war. What does remain is from the cameras of Union photographers, like this tranquil image of an engine of the Atlantic & North Carolina line. Behind it is a "conductor's car." (USAMHI)

Right: And here at Port Hudson, Louisiana, McPherson & Oliver caught two dilapidated pieces of equipment of the Clinton & Port Hudson Railroad. As in so many other areas, the South simply could not compete with the North's industry in railroading, and as shown, was hard pressed to maintain what it already had. (ISHL)

THE
EMBATTLED
CONFEDERACY

The Onondaga, *a workhorse twin-turreted monitor on the James River. Only two double-turreted monitors saw service during the war, and when Admiral David D. Porter stripped the James fleet for the attack on Fort Fisher in North Carolina in 1864, the* Onondaga *was left to defend the river almost alone.*

The Bloodiest Day: Antietam

JAMES I. ROBERTSON, JR.

Lee the gambler and McClellan the slow do terrible battle in Maryland

The ruins of the Potomac River bridge at Berlin, Maryland. Here and elsewhere in the vicinity Lee began crossing into the North on September 4, 1862. Here the crossing appears a month later, with a Federal pontoon bridge in place. (U. S. ARMY MILITARY HISTORY INSTITUTE, CARLISLE BARRACKS, PA.)

SEPTEMBER 2, 1862, found Virginia virtually free of Federal armies for the first time since the Civil War began. Major General George B. McClellan's huge Army of the Potomac had abandoned the Peninsula east of Richmond following Robert E. Lee's counterattacks in the Seven Days Campaign. A second Federal Army under Major General John Pope had just been all but routed at Second Manassas by the combined forces of Lee and "Stonewall" Jackson. The North's principal assault forces, now sullen and disillusioned, were filing into the fortifications around Washington. The war had returned to where it had begun sixteen months earlier.

Lee then decided on one of his most audacious moves. He would launch an invasion of the North. Based on historical hindsight, this decision appears questionable. Yet less desirable alternatives at the time seemed to justify Lee advancing into enemy territory with a numerically inferior army.

Washington, the North's king in the great chess game of war, was too powerfully defended to be attacked. On the other hand, Lee could not keep his destitute army at Manassas for any length of time. The northern counties of Virginia had been ravaged by war and could not sustain the Confederates. Lee's third choice was to retire to a more defensible site in the Shenandoah Valley or south of the Rappahannock River; but to do so would surrender everything that had been gained at Second Manassas. That left invasion as the most workable alternative, with a number of factors seemingly pointing to success.

The Federal armies were disorganized at the moment and posed no immediate threat. Maryland was a sister state of the South; and if the Army of Northern Virginia could "liberate" the state from Federal occupation troops, Maryland might then cast her lot with the Confederacy—which would have the spontaneous effect of leaving the Northern capital surrounded by seceded territory. An invasion by Lee would also draw the Federals' attention away from Virginia and enable the Old Dominion's farmers to gather the fall crops unmolested. A blow inside the North might trigger widespread demands on Washington for peace. Lastly, such a successful excursion could draw England or France into the Civil War on the side of the South; and foreign recognition seemed the one thing that could most assure victory for the Confederacy.

Therefore, in the pre-dawn darkness on September 4 Lee's columns began wading across the Potomac at the shoals near Leesburg. The Army of Northern Virginia was weaker than it would be at any time during the war, save at Appomattox. Thousands were absent because of wounds, sickness, and exhaustion. Untold others had balked at invasion on the grounds that they had enlisted only to defend their beloved South, and they had simply walked away from the army. The 40,000 ragged Confederates who advanced into Maryland represented barely two thirds of Lee's force. Most of them were barefoot. (Of 300 men in a South Carolina regiment, fewer than 100 were wearing anything akin to shoes.) Yet they were the strongest, the hard core of the Confederacy's main army, and they appeared to one writer as "the scarecrow multitude of lean, vociferous, hairy men who reminded even noncombatants of wolves."

Lee's plan was to strike northward for Harrisburg, Pennsylvania. Capturing that point would break the dual arteries of the Pennsylvania Rail-

Above: The gambler. General Robert Edward Lee took an enormous chance by deciding to invade the North. It was characteristic of the man and of his army. An image from 1862, the year of Antietam. (CIVIL WAR TIMES ILLUSTRATED COLLECTION)

Left: An early postwar view of Frederick, Maryland. On September 6 "Stonewall" Jackson's troops occupied this much-troubled city. It changed hands several times during the war. (USAMHI)

Left: As Lee marched north, another gambler sat in the Executive Mansion in Washington pondering what seemed to be an unending succession of threats and reverses. Lincoln had little time to enjoy the grassy lawns being manicured here in a Brady & Company image from 1862. He had to stop Lee, and the only man who might do it was a high risk... (LIBRARY OF CONGRESS)

road and the Susquehanna River, thereby isolating the Federals' eastern and western theaters of operations from one another. At the same time, the invasion had to be benevolent in tone. The necessity of winning converts in Maryland was such that Lee repeatedly urged his men to show exemplary behavior. That they did so, in the face of raggedness and hunger, is one of the remarkable incidents of the war.

On the morning of September 7 the Confederates paused at Frederick, Maryland. The army was subsisting—as it would throughout the first three weeks of September—on green corn, apples, and an occasional ration of potatoes. Lee himself was in pain. A couple of days earlier he had slipped while mounting his horse. The fall to the ground had broken one hand and badly sprained the other. Yet no time existed for personal discomfort or rest. The army had to move. Maryland had not responded with support for the Confederates. Straggling was on the increase as hard roads tortured already raw feet. Even worse, Lee had received reports that a Federal army was now in pursuit. Indeed, McClellan had been given a second chance. In the latter stages of the Second Manassas Campaign he had found himself at Alexandria, Virginia, a general without an army. Yet Lincoln could not shelve McClellan, whether the President wished it or not. The salvation of the Union at the moment was the Army of the Potomac, and the only general who could make that army respond with any degree of effectiveness was McClellan. So, early in September the dapper little commander once again mounted his black charger, Daniel Webster, and rode to the head of his troops.

The 90,000 men that he greeted at Rockville, Maryland, were not all members of the old Army of the Potomac. Some units had been transferred from Pope's defeated Army of Virginia, while other regiments were entering the field for the first time. Federal soldiers cheered the return of "Little Mac" and morale in the ranks climbed

Above: Major General George B. McClellan. He failed Lincoln badly on the Virginia Peninsula earlier that year and passively contributed to the defeat at Second Manassas. Yet Lincoln offered and "Little Mac" accepted. (USAMHI)

Above: But before he could get to Lee, McClellan had first to pass this stubborn, combative, highly opinionated Confederate, Major General Daniel H. Hill, shown here as a brigadier. At the South Mountain passes this brother-in-law of Jackson's held up the Federal advance for precious hours. (LC)

Right: Colonel Rush Hawkins, organizer and commander of the 9th New York—Hawkins's Zouaves—was more fortunate than Reno. He lived through South Mountain to fight at Antietam. His first love, though, was old and rare books. (NATIONAL ARCHIVES)

Right: An early postwar view of the Wise House on South Mountain, near Fox's Gap. Out in that field Major General Jesse Reno, commanding the Federal IX Corps, took his mortal wound in the fierce fighting of September 14. (USAMHI)

Above: Alexander Gardner's October 1862 image shows some of the chief culprits in McClellan's consistent failures. These are men of the secret service corps at McClellan's headquarters. Standing, in a checked shirt, just left of the tent pole is Allan Pinkerton. A Scot with a considerable reputation as a detective before the war, he was an utter failure at gathering and evaluating military intelligence. He consistently exaggerated the enemy's numbers, making a cautious McClellan even more timid. (COURTESY OF THE CHICAGO HISTORICAL SOCIETY)

Above: Alexander Gardner's view of Main Street in Sharpsburg, Maryland, taken September 21 or 22. Here Lee came to a halt, his northern invasion stopped. Forced to the defensive, he now had to fight for his army's very life. (LC)

overnight. However, the march north and west in search of Lee was characteristic of McClellan: excruciatingly slow and methodical. In this instance McClellan was not entirely to blame. Scores of false reports relative to Lee's whereabouts poured into his headquarters. Worse, General-in-Chief Henry Halleck provided no stability. One day he would warn McClellan that if the Federal Army moved too far northward, Lee could veer around its right flank and threaten Washington. That same day, or the next, Halleck would warn McClellan that if the Federals advanced too far westward, Lee could lunge unmolested into Pennsylvania.

The self-doubts always lurking in McClellan now festered. He wasted days in reorganizing his army, shifting generals here and there, insuring that supply trains, ammunition wagons, and the like were precisely where they were supposed to be. As a result—and during six critical days when the Army of the Potomac should have been in rapid, concentrated pursuit—it advanced a grand total of thirty miles.

In contrast, it took Lee a day at Frederick to analyze his problems and formulate his strategy. He had expected a Federal garrison at Harpers Ferry to abandon that post when the Confederates swept into Maryland. The garrison was still there. It had to be captured, for its 11,000 Federals lay across Lee's line of communications back to Richmond, and they could be an impediment to a Southern withdrawal into the Shenandoah Valley. The possibility also loomed large that units from

Above: Hall Street in Sharpsburg. At the moment that Gardner made his image, St. Paul's Lutheran Church, in the center background, was filled with wounded from the bloodiest day of the war. Gardner's photographic wagon is in the foreground . (LC)

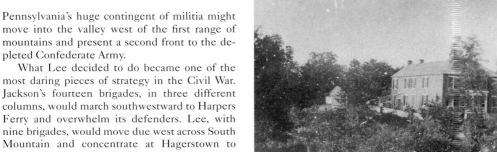

Above: The Federals had been here before. In August 1862, in more placid days along the Antietam, Colonel W. W. Averell of the 3rd Pennsylvania Cavalry sat with fellow officers for the camera. (USAMHI)

Left: But now the whole Federal Army was here, McClellan making his headquarters in the Pry house. Alexander Gardner made this image within a day of the battle. (LC)

Below: The 93rd New York served at Antietam as the headquarters guard for the Army of the Potomac. It kept them from facing the terror of battle with the rest of the army, but they were happy to face Gardner's camera early in October. (USAMHI)

Pennsylvania's huge contingent of militia might move into the valley west of the first range of mountains and present a second front to the depleted Confederate Army.

What Lee decided to do became one of the most daring pieces of strategy in the Civil War. Jackson's fourteen brigades, in three different columns, would march southwestward to Harpers Ferry and overwhelm its defenders. Lee, with nine brigades, would move due west across South Mountain and concentrate at Hagerstown to counter a potential threat from Pennsylvania militia. Daniel Harvey Hill's five brigades would advance only to Boonsborough so as to block both a Federal retreat from Harpers Ferry and a Federal advance toward the South Mountain passes.

These dispositions were spelled out precisely in Special Orders No. 191, which was issued to each of Lee's division commanders, and at dawn on September 10 the Confederates filed out of Frederick. Lee was taking a tremendous gamble: dividing his small army into five parts, with a river separating three of the parts from the other two. Secrecy was imperative for the success of the campaign. However, for the first time in the war, fortune was about to betray Lee.

On September 12, two days after Lee abandoned Frederick, McClellan's army fanned out in the fields surrounding the town. The 27th Indiana was relaxing in a campground formerly occupied by the Confederates when Corporal Barton W. Mitchell spied three cigars wrapped in a piece of paper on the ground. Tobacco was one of the most coveted commodities in the Union armies. Hence, it was a few minutes before Mitchell paid any attention to the wrapping. It was a copy of Special Orders No. 19l, and within an hour it was at McClellan's headquarters. The Federal general was a beneficiary of the greatest security leak in American military history.

McClellan now knew precisely where Lee's army was, what Lee was doing, and what he was likely to do. The massive Federal Army at that moment was nearer each of the Confederate wings (Lee and Jackson) than they were to each

Right: From this site on Elk Mountain McClellan's signalmen watched Lee's movements in his lines along the Antietam. This signal tower was built after the battle. (USAMHI)

Above: The Potomac crossing at Harpers Ferry. Lee wanted the Federal garrison there eliminated to protect his rear. (USAMHI)

Left: Colonel Dixon A. Miles of the 2nd United States Infantry commanded the Federals at Harpers Ferry. Accused of drunkenness during the First Manassas fighting, Miles was relegated to a post of lesser importance—lesser, that is, until Lee invaded the North. He stayed longer than he should have and finally surrendered to Jackson. One of the very last shots fired killed him. (USAMHI)

Above: One of those sent with Jackson to take Harpers Ferry was Brigadier General Ambrose R. Wright, a Georgian who would be seriously wounded at Antietam following the capture of Harpers Ferry. (VALENTINE MUSEUM)

Right: Antietam Bridge, taken by Gardner on September 22. In fact, relatively little happened here, but the photographer found it an alluring subject for his camera. (WAR LIBRARY AND MUSEUM, MOLLUS-PENNSYLVANA, PHILADELPHIA)

other. McClellan would have to move promptly, for the orders were already four days old; and Lee was not one to waste time or to fall behind schedule. If McClellan took advantage of good roads, balmy weather, and advanced rapidly enough, he could annihilate the fractured Army of Northern Virginia. Yet the Federal commander again fell victim to gnawing uncertainty and self-doubt. Were Lee's "orders" purposefully left to be found? Was Lee where he said he would be? Was it all a trap?

Despite the fact that he outnumbered Lee by more than two to one, McClellan was not willing to take risks. With Jackson at Harpers Ferry, Lee at Hagerstown, and only Harvey Hill's division in his front, McClellan nevertheless began a slow movement westward. Throughout Saturday, September 13, the Federals crawled forward. Hill abandoned Boonsborough and began erecting hasty defenses at the passes atop South Mountain. This eminence, the key to the entire Confederate Army, was a long, irregular range of hills that began at the Potomac and continued some thirty five miles northeastward. The two main passes—Crampton's and Turner's gaps—were about five hundred feet above the valley floor.

Hill had no time to reflect that this was his first independent command involving large numbers of troops. He was a dyspeptic, blunt, and caustic general; but as he looked down from the mountain at endless Federal brigades moving toward him, he confessed that he never felt so lonely in all his life. All of the world's soldiers seemed to be coming toward him. However, McClellan's continuing reliance on Allan Pinkerton's unreliable estimates of Confederate strength caused McClellan to conclude that Hill had five times more than the 6,000 Southerners digging in on the mountaintop.

McClellan therefore made careful, cautious plans that consumed a full day. Not until 9 A.M.

Below: Antietam Bridge again, this time looking northeast. McClellan's headquarters in the Pry house was not far distant, and he used this crossing frequently in sending troops into the battle line. (USAMHI)

Above: The Dunker Church on the Antietam battlefield, taken after the battle damage had been repaired. For the thousands of men who contested the ground around it, this simple structure came to symbolize the bloody horror of Antietam. (USAMHI)

on September 14 did the Federal columns start up the slopes. Union troops performed gallantly in scaling the mountainside in the face of sheets of musketry, but the Confederates were just as heroic in holding their position against tremendous odds. It was Thermopylae all over again. It was also the kind of battle that Harvey Hill fought best: hard, close-in combat, with firepower and determination rather than finesse and strategy being the major ingredients. On a more personal note, Hill had no way of knowing that day that one of the Federal brigade commanders assaulting his position was Brigadier General John Gibbon, who had been best man at Hill's wedding a few years earlier.

Intense conflict raged throughout the day as the bulk of two Federal corps swept repeatedly up the mountain, only to be driven back by concentrated fire from thin lines of Southerners massed above. Powder flashes blazed through the battle smoke; hand-to-hand fighting occurred in crevices and along ledges; bodies caromed down the mountain side. One observer likened the Army of the Potomac that day to "a monstrous, crawling, blue black snake, miles long, quilled with the silver slant of muskets at a 'shoulder,' its sluggish tail writhing slowly up over the distant eastern ridge,

Above: Newcomer's Mill on Antietam Creek, by Gardner. (USAMHI)

Above: The Boonsborough Pike crossed the Antietam at the bridge as it ran from Elk Mountain to Sharpsburg. Behind Newcomer's barn, on the left, Lee laid his first line of defense on the ridge on September 15, awaiting McClellan. (USAMHI)

Left: The ruins of the Samuel Mumma house three days after the battle. Here the real fighting in the Battle of Antietam began as the Union I Corps swept against Ewell's and D. H. Hill's Confederates positioned here and nearby. (LC)

Right: Brigadier General George L. Hartsuff led a brigade in Hooker's I Corps in the first attacks against the Confederates, falling with a wound that put him out of action for months. (USAMHI)

Below: Brigadier General William E. Starke fell early in the fight with three separate wounds. He lay dying even as the Federals were pushing his division out of the West Woods. (USAMHI)

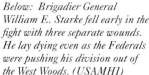

Above: Appearing almost asleep, this dead horse, probably belonging to Colonel Henry Strong of the 6th Louisiana, himself killed in the battle, lies peacefully near the East Woods where Hooker launched his attack. (LC)

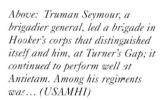

Below: Many fell. Many died. In the fierce fighting along the Hagerstown Pike beside the West Woods and just north of the Dunker Church, hundreds of Confederates of Starke's command sought shelter behind this rail fence. It did them little good. Two days later Gardner found them lying singly... (USAMHI)

Above: Truman Seymour, a brigadier general, led a brigade in Hooker's corps that distinguished itself and him, at Turner's Gap; it continued to perform well at Antietam. Among his regiments was... (USAMHI)

Above: Colonel Hugh W. McNeill's 13th Pennsylvania Reserves, the "Bucktails." McNeill's own bucktail shows in his kepi. He was killed the day before the battle. (USAMHI)

its bruised head weltering in the roar and smoke upon the crest above..."

Around 5 P.M. the Federals gained a momentary toehold at Crampton's Gap before Confederate reinforcements sent them scurrying down the ridge. The battle of South Mountain ended at sundown. Hill had suffered 40 percent casualties in a vicious fight that tactically was a draw. Yet the stand at South Mountain had given Lee a full day to react to McClellan's advance; and, as events were to prove, time was a critical factor.

On the Sunday that Hill made his reputation at South Mountain, "Stonewall" Jackson closed in on the Federals defending Harpers Ferry. Jackson was still sore due to a fall from his horse a week earlier, but his concentration, as usual, was totally on the military situation at hand. Six divisions—the largest force Jackson had ever led—methodically took their positions on the mountains overlooking the Ferry. The tiny Federal garrison was caught in a trap. Late in the afternoon of the fourteenth Jackson's batteries began an uncontested bombardment. At dawn the following day Confederate smoothbores and rifled guns opened a concentrated barrage from three different directions. The cannonade lasted barely an hour before aged and ailing Colonel Dixon S. Miles realized the hopelessness of his situation and ordered his command to strike its colors. Miles was subsequently killed in the final shelling from Jackson's guns.

The Confederates bagged 11,500 prisoners, 73 cannon, 13,000 small arms, 200 wagons, and tons of equipment needed by a Southern army that was as destitute as it looked. A Union correspondent at Harpers Ferry noted that Jackson's appearance "was in no respect to be distinguished from the mongrel, bare-footed crew who follow his fortunes." That same reporter then added grudgingly: "I had heard much of the decayed appearance of the rebel soldiers, and yet they glory in their shame."

Jackson, now alerted by Lee to the necessity of rapid concentration, left Ambrose Powell Hill's division to secure Harpers Ferry while he headed northward to rejoin the other units of Lee's army. Meanwhile, Lee had weighed his options. During

the fourteenth, with Jackson not in control of Harpers Ferry and Harvey Hill waging a no-win contest at South Mountain, Lee had contemplated withdrawal to Virginia. Then came news early on the fifteenth of Jackson's capture of the Ferry. Lee quickly decided to bring the fragments of his army together on the high ground at Sharpsburg, a village midway between Hagerstown and Harpers Ferry. Throughout that day, therefore, Southern brigades converged on Sharpsburg from the north, east, and south. McClellan could have assailed Lee's columns at any time with 60,000 men—which was far more than Lee could have mustered—but he vacillated too long before moving cautiously down the west face of South Mountain.

Lee's decision to stand and fight at Sharpsburg was, with the exception of Gettysburg, the most controversial decision he made during the war. It was bold, since he was weaker in terms of numbers, with the Potomac to his back and only one major avenue of escape. Yet boldness was characteristic of Lee, and boldness was also the only chance for success that the Confederacy possessed.

So the units of the Confederate Army hastily made for Sharpsburg. Major General James Longstreet opposed the site as a battleground; Jackson just as sternly endorsed it. Sharpsburg was a village three miles from the winding Potomac River. Only a ford at Shepherdstown offered escape. What attracted Lee to the site was a formidable defense line: a low, crescent-shaped ridge that extended from northwest to southeast of the town. The Confederate left would rest on the Potomac itself; the right would anchor on Antietam Creek, a sluggish north-south stream too deep for the passage of artillery. Hence, the few bridges over it would be of great strategic importance.

Lack of time and tools prevented the Confederates from preparing elaborate entrenchments at Sharpsburg. Brigades arriving on September 15 and 16 simply threw up what defenses they could. It became a truly remarkable battlefield; the three mile Confederate line was so compact that from a number of vantage points its entire length was visible.

September 16 was the day that McClellan lost

Above: … in groups… (LC)

Below: … and heaped in piles, their Louisiana blood soaking the soil of Maryland. (LC)

Left: After Hooker's initial attack calmed, Major General John Sedgwick led his division of the fresh I Corps against the Hagerstown Pike and the Confederates in the West Woods. (NA)

Above: Captain Joseph Knap's Battery E, Pennsylvania Light Artillery, joined Sedgwick in his attack, taking a position near the Dunker Church. Gardner photographed them two days later, with the open ground between the East, West, and North Woods beyond. (LC)

Above: Men and colors of the 34th New York, Sedgwick's division. Antietam put more than one tear in their tattered banners. (COURTESY OF MICHAEL J. MCAFEE)

Above: The fighting raged for hours, the casualties falling in rows. Near the Dunker Church, with the West Woods behind it, these Confederate artillerymen died defending their battery, probably Captain W. W. Parker's battery of Virginia Light Artillery. (USAMHI)

Above: Brigadier General Roswell Ripley led a Confederate brigade posted behind the Mumma house. He ordered it burned to prevent its affording shelter to attackers, then later fell wounded himself in the fighting in front of the West Woods. (LC)

Above: Brigadier General Samuel Garland also led a brigade that tried to resist Sedgwick's advance. He could not. He was not with them, having been killed in the fight for Fox's Gap three days before. (MUSEUM OF THE CONFEDERACY)

his opportunity. Lee was at most disorganized and at the very least off balance. Fully half his forces were still not on the field. Absenteeism and straggling had put the whole army in the weakest condition it had ever been in. Lee had barely 40,000 men to contest more than twice that number. Never was the opportunity for Federal victory greater. If McClellan had hurled the mighty Army of the Potomac against the improvised and undermanned Confederate line on the sixteenth, it undoubtedly would have snapped, with perhaps fatal consequences. Yet McClellan spent the day perfecting his own lines, getting cannon into proper position, reconsidering moves, and weighing risks. Thus, while skirmishers bickered and artillerists tested their aim, Jackson's men made a hard march and in the late afternoon were reunited with Lee's army at Sharpsburg.

Through a night of drizzling rain the two armies sat and waited nervously for the battle that would come with the dawn. Jackson's brigades formed Lee's left, Harvey Hill held the center, and Longstreet commanded the right. Movements late on the sixteenth gave ample indication that the battle would begin in Jackson's front, a mile north of Sharpsburg. There, on the west side of the Hagerstown Turnpike, stood a patch of trees known as the West Woods. The area was two hundred to three hundred yards wide and surrounded, on three sides, the white, boxlike Dunker Church standing on a slight knoll. Immediately across the turnpike from the West Woods was another clump of trees. Known as the East Woods and similarly about two hundred yards in width, it extended a quarter of a mile eastward. Between the two woods, adjacent to the east side of the road, was a forty acre cornfield with green stalks head-high at that time of the season.

McClellan's battle plan seemed logical enough, given the preponderance of troops at his disposal. The I and XII Federal Corps would spearhead an assault on Lee's left flank. Two additional corps would act in support. This heavy attack would cause the Confederate left to collapse onto the center and block any further Southern advances toward Hagerstown. Simultaneously, the IX Corps on the Federal left would assail Lee's right flank and turn Lee from his escape route. Then, while the two-pronged attack acted as a vise against Lee's army, McClellan would advance with his remaining divisions and crush the Confederate center.

It was an excellent plan, multifaceted but simple. It depended only on superior numbers and coordination—and McClellan failed on both accounts. Wednesday, September 17, 1862, became the bloodiest single day of the Civil War, in large part be cause the Federals attacked piecemeal, thus allowing a critically outmanned Lee to utilize his inner lines of defense to maximum advantage. Antietam Creek (or Sharpsburg, as the battle is also called) consisted of three heavy engagements piled one atop the other. It was a headlong, day-long explosion of combat, void of memorable tactics—concentrated violence in which thousands of soldiers blazed away in fiery collisions stretching across woods, fields, hillsides, and bottomland. American soldiers never fought harder. Death became commonplace as acts of heroism on one side matched gallantry on the other.

The rain stopped shortly before dawn that morning, and a wet mist quickly gave way to clear skies and the promise of a hot day. In command of the first attack (as well as the Federal I Corps) was handsome and ambitious Major General Joseph Hooker, a hard-fighting, hard-living officer. Thirty-five Federal cannon raked the Confederate positions as an overture. Then, at 6 A.M., ten brigades from the I Corps charged down the Hagerstown Turnpike. Opposing this assault by 12,000 Federals were less than 7,000 Confederates under Jackson. Billy Yanks fought their way through the woods and the cornfield. Confederate musketry took a heavy toll; men fell to the ground with each passing second. Yet Hooker's troops almost reached the Dunker Church and the valuable high ground that was the key to Lee's left flank. A Confederate staff officer wrote of the action: "Such a storm of balls I never conceived it possible for men to live through. Shot and shell shrieking and crashing, canister and bullets whistling and hissing most fiend-like through the air until you could almost see them." As Jackson called for reinforcements, the cornfield became a vast slaughter pen. It was a ghastly sight, bloodied now from the carnage. Never in the history of the Army of Northern Virginia were so many high-ranking officers knocked out of action so quickly. At one point a Confederate colonel was in command of a division because all of his superiors were either dead or wounded. Just as Jackson's line seemed on the verge of snapping, fresh troops under Generals Harvey Hill and John B. Hood rushed on the scene. This new Southern attack a Union officer likened to "a scythe running through our line." Around 7: 30 A.M. the battered I Corps slowly withdrew from the field. A fourth of its number, including Hooker, were casualties; and the remainder were mentally up to nothing more that day.

McClellan then turned to Nathaniel Banks's veterans from the 1862 Valley Campaign. Reorganized as the XII Corps, these soldiers were under the command of Major General Joseph K. F. Mansfield. He was a red-faced, white-haired old regular who had graduated from West Point in 1822—before most of his men were even born. Mansfield rushed his brigades forward into action and was among the first to suffer a mortal wound when a bullet tore through his stomach. His men continued their assault and managed to regain part

Above: Brigadier General John B. Hood was in the fighting early, his brigade suffering terrible losses. The 1st Texas under his command lost 82.3 percent of its men as casualties, the greatest loss in any unit in either army during the war. (VM)

Above: The division of Lafayette McLaws was rushed toward the West Woods as Sedgwick attacked. One of McLaws's brigade commanders was a man who, two years before, sat in President Buchanan's cabinet. Howell Cobb of Georgia, once Secretary of the Treasury and a prominent candidate for Confederate President, was now a brigadier general. (UNIVERSITY

Above: Brigadier General John G. Walker's division came to the West Woods, too. He served in the United States Army during the Mexican War, and appears here as a lieutenant in a photo from the 1850s. (TULANE UNIVERSITY)

Right: The converging Confederates caught Sedgwick and shattered his command, forcing him back to the support of the rest of the II Corps, led by Major General Edwin V. Sumner, the oldest corps commander in the Union Army. (CWTI)

Above: Here the Confederates counterattack, driving Sedgwick and Sumner back. (NATIONAL LIBRARY OF MEDICINE)

Right: Brigadier General Winfield Scott Hancock was a brigade commander in the II Corps. After Sedgwick's repulse, he and others were ordered forward to take possession of ground east of the West Woods. The Confederates met them at a sunken road later to be called Bloody Lane. (P-M)

Right: Colonel Turner G. Morehead led his 106th Pennsylvania in Oliver O. Howard's brigade of Sedgwick's division. In the rout of Sedgwick, Morehead's horse was shot from under him. Retreating on foot, he ran back into the face of the advancing enemy to recover his sword. "I am not going to let them damned rebels get it," he exclaimed . (LC)

Below: The hours of bloody fighting for that road took hundreds of lives, among them that of Hancock's division commander, Israel Richardson, seated at center. Hancock succeeded him. (LC)

Above: William Harrow, as colonel of the 14th Indiana, fought his regiment for four hours against Bloody Lane, losing half of his numbers. (P-M)

Right: The lane ran along the property of the Roulette farm. Richardson advanced past the farmhouse to hurl his brigades against the Confederates. (USAMHI)

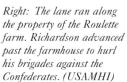

Left: Regular artillerymen from Fitz John Porter's otherwise unengaged corps aided in the attack on Bloody Lane. Captain James M. Robertson led two batteries of the 2nd United States Artillery in the assaults. He stands at right of center. He will become a general after the war. (P-M)

Right: Among the Confederate defenders of the lane, Colonel John B. Gordon of the 6th Alabama took a wound in the head and was only saved from drowning in his own blood by the bullet hole in his hat. (TU)

of the East Woods and the cornfield. Fighting was vicious every foot of the way. Hooker later observed that "every stalk of corn in the northern and greater part of the field was cut as closely as could have been done with a knife, and the slain lay in rows precisely as they had stood in their ranks a few moments before. It was never my fortune to witness a more bloody, dismal battlefield."

This second wave of assaults by Mansfield's corps came in from the northeast, lasted ninety minutes, and also proved fruitless. Confederates firing as rapidly as they could load their guns forced the Federals to relinquish the ground. Had the corps of Hooker and Mansfield attacked in concert and in a concentrated fashion, the outcome would probably have been different. Yet concerted effort and concentration on the part of the Federal Army was lacking throughout the battle.

At 9 A.M., after three hours of killing, McClellan resumed the offensive with a third major attack over the same ground. He ordered the 18,000 troops in the II Corps to assail Jackson from the east-northeast. In command of this corps was Major General Edwin V. "Bull" Sumner, an old Indian fighter with a booming voice and an obsession with rigid discipline. Jackson, meanwhile, had readjusted his lines so that they formed a rough northward-facing arc with the outer points firmly planted.

Sumner's three divisions dashed forward and promptly fell out of alignment, with the result that the sharp point of the attack was blunted before it could pierce the Confederate lines. Major General John Sedgwick's lead division of 5,000 men lumbered into the battle web that Jackson had spun. Half of those Federals were casualties in less than twenty minutes. Sedgwick himself received three wounds that put this superior combat officer out of action for five months.

A lull in the fighting then gave Jackson a chance to launch an attack of his own, with the three fourths of Lee's army now under his command. Shouting Confederates rushed for the cornfield and were almost at the north end when they came under a withering cross fire from fifty cannon concealed several hundred yards away. The Southern ranks were shredded instantly. Jackson called off the assault; this order brought an end to the four hour fight on the left. Three

Left: Confederate dead in the Bloody Lane, taken by Gardner two days after the battle. (LC)

Left: Dead North Carolinians awaiting burial in Bloody Lane. (USAMHI)

Above: After the fighting on the right and center of McClellan's line, he finally sent Major General Ambrose Burnside forward to attack Lee's right flank. Burnside appears here as a brigadier. (KEAN ARCHIVES)

Right: Despite low water that would allow wading the Antietam at several points, Burnside sent his command, brigade by brigade, across this stone span. It would later be called Burnside's Bridge. Here it is viewed from the position of the Confederates who defended it... (LC)

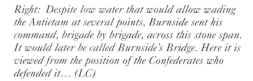

Below: ... and here is how it looked to the attackers who tried to cross it in the face of a wall of fire from Confederates on the ridge beyond. (LC)

Right: The Sherrick farm buildings just west of Burnside's Bridge. Confederates swarmed all around the farm, and when Joseph Sherrick left to escape the battle, he hid $3,000 in gold in his stone wall. He got it back after the battle. (LC)

Federal corps had gone into action one after another. Two were shattered and the third was broken. Federal losses included over 5,000 men. The extent of Southern casualties can be gauged from the fact that after the battle New England soldiers scouting near the Dunker Church chanced upon 146 Confederate bodies lying in a neat, soldierly line. The celebrated Stonewall Brigade, reduced to 250 men by the Second Manassas Campaign, had 88 new holes in its ranks.

Around 10 A.M. the battle shifted southward to what was the Confederate center. This second stage of Antietam Creek would likewise last four hours. Like the rest of McClellan's strategy, this second stage lacked the coordination necessary for total success. The middle of Lee's line at that moment consisted of little more than two brigades (those of Robert Rodes and G. B. Anderson) in Harvey Hill's division. They were posted in a sunken road that ran eastward along a ravine for a thousand yards, then jackknifed southward for the same distance. The Confederates were frantically placing fence rails along the road as defenses when Federals appeared in force on the hilltop above them.

These columns were part of two divisions from Sumner's II Corps (the third division in that corps had literally been wrecked at the Dunker Church). Confederates massed in the road watched in awe as line after line of Federals advanced in paradelike fashion down the hill toward them. "Their gleaming bayonets flashed like burnished silver in the sunlight," a Southern officer noted, and they marched "with the precision of step and perfect alignment of a holiday parade." However, the two Federal divisions actually attacked in what that day was typical disjointed fashion.

The lead division was under Major General William H. French, a hot-tempered, hard-drinking commander whose habit of shutting his eyes tightly when talking caused the men to nickname him "Old Blinkey." French's first wave of troops simply melted away as a result of a heavy volley of musketry from the road. A second wave met the same fate as Federals struggled with the additional obstacle of getting over and around bodies sprawled across the hillside. A third attack produced more casualties for French's battered ranks. Billy Yanks seized whatever protection they could find along the hill; both sides rushed in reinforcements; and a Union officer reported that for three hours "the battle raged incessantly, without either party giving way."

Major General Israel B. Richardson's division then entered the contest in support of French's men. Richardson was a tough veteran of frontier fighting, an unpretentious man who had no use for such military frills as a uniform. He personally led his brigades into action, and he used his sword both to wave his lines forward and to drive skulkers from cover as his profane voice thundered above the action. At one point Richardson shouted: "Where's General _____?"

From the ranks came the reply: "Behind the haystack ! "

"God damn the field officers!" Richardson bellowed as he raced downhill into the battle smoke.

Around 1 P.M. some of Richardson's men succeeded in capturing the high ground near the road's sharp bend. Federals poured an enfilading fire into the 300-odd Confederates still fighting defiantly. The Southerners could not withstand this new fire. Weary, battle-blackened men fell back to a new position. The sunken road was thereafter known as Bloody Lane—and for good reason. A Federal officer who viewed the bodies strewn in the lane commented that a man could walk as far down that road as one could see without stepping on the ground. On the other hand, gaining that road had involved a staggering cost to the Federals. The divisions of French and Richardson suffered combined losses of 509 killed, 2,254 wounded, and 152 missing. Among the slain was Richardson, who died of infection resulting from a bullet wound.

With Lee's center all but broken, the situation was critical. Colonel E. Porter Alexander, a Confederate artillery commander, observed: "Lee's army was ruined, and the end of the Confederacy was in sight." How desperate things were for the Army of Northern Virginia is apparent from two personal incidents. Harvey Hill rounded up 200 stragglers, grabbed a musket, and led a pitiful counterattack that withered in the face of concentrated firepower from the Union lines. Major General James Longstreet, heavyset and somber, was hobbling that day in a carpet slipper because of an infected blister on his foot; nevertheless he helped exhausted gunners man an artillery piece. Yet these acts of devotion did not stop the Federal breakthrough from being complete. Astoundingly, McClellan did that. "It would not be prudent" to deliver another assault, he told Major General William B. Franklin, whose fresh VI Corps—along with Fitz John Porter's entire V Corps—stood poised for the final blow. After the four bloodiest hours to which that day would be witness, McClellan again changed directions and ordered attacks from a different sector. The conflict now moved to its third and final stage.

Left: Once Burnside finally crossed, his men steadily drove back the Confederate defenders. They left their dead, like these on the Sherrick farm, behind them. (LC)

Below: With the threat of dismissal from the army hanging over him as a result of charges about his conduct at Second Manassas, Fitz John Porter sat out the battle on the Antietam, his V Corps being held in reserve. (USAMHI)

Above: Finally forced to leave the field to the enemy, Lee retired from Sharpsburg on September 19. Brigadier General James H. Lane commanded the rear guard as the Confederates withdrew. (VM)

Below: The 139th Pennsylvania arrived on the field on the evening of September 17, too late for the battle. With more Federal reinforcements coming up, Lee would have been foolish to remain. (WESTERN RESERVE HISTORICAL SOCIETY)

Below: Part of Porter's corps, however, did pursue Lee after the Confederates began their withdrawal. The 2nd Maine, shown here in camp at Hall's Hill, Virginia, crossed the Potomac and skirmished with the enemy on September 20. (WRHS)

Right: And cavalry units, which sat out most of the main battle along the Antietam, managed to snipe at Lee's heels as the Confederates crossed at Shepherdstown. Here, stand-ing in the center, is Colonel David M. Gregg and his officers of the 8th Pennsylvania Cavalry. (LC)

Left: Shepherdstown on the Potomac, where McClellan's feeble attempt to pursue Lee made its only real challenge. (LC)

To the south of the battlefield was a stone bridge that spanned Antietam Creek. The road approaching it from the east ran parallel to the stream, then turned abruptly at the bridge and plunged into a funnel-like valley before crossing the bridge. Immediately at the western end of the structure the road veered sharply to the north be-cause of a ridge several hundred feet high that came to within a short distance of the creek's bank. Atop that hill some small Georgia regiments were entrenched under blustery Brigadier Gen-eral Robert Toombs.

Commanding the Federal left was Major Gen-eral Ambrose E. Burnside. A heavily bewhiskered Rhode Islander, he was well liked by all, espe-cially the men in his IX Corps. His four divisions should have acted as a huge sledgehammer against Lee's right. However, instead of employ-ing them en masse against the weak Confederate defenses, Burnside sent them piecemeal into bat-tle that morning. He insisted that the regiments go one at a time across the stone bridge; and as they did, concentrated musketry and canister from the hilltop raked the lines and easily forced each column back from the arched span. Around 1 P.M., as the fight at Bloody Lane came to an end, Fed-eral batteries opened a heavy bombardment at the bridge. The 51st New York and 51st Pennsylvania dashed across the span and established a bridge-head on the west bank of the Antietam. The Georgians, having waged a Thermopylae-like struggle throughout the morning, grudgingly re-tired from the crest of the hill.

For the Union Army the opportunity again ex-isted for a decisive and fatal thrust into Lee's lines. Yet McClellan was tardy in ordering a concerted attack, Burnside was clumsy in executing it, and coordination was once more lacking. Burnside consumed two hours in reorganizing his numeri-cally superior forces, and it was midafternoon be-fore thousands of Federals began moving across the rolling country toward the vulnerable Con-federate flank. Long lines of Billy Yanks brushed aside what remained of Toombs's Georgians, then slammed into D. R. Jones's four brigades—which was all that was left of Lee's army south of Sharpsburg.

Lee quickly shifted artillery pieces and frag-ments of units southward to meet this powerful assault. Longstreet wrote of that moment: "We were already badly whipped and were holding our ground by sheer force of desperation." Indeed they were. By 4 P.M. Sharpsburg was in flames; wounded and demoralized Confederates filled the streets and added a mood of near panic to the frenzy of battle roaring across the countryside; Federal flags were waving in triumph as Burn-side's men advanced to within half a mile of Lee's sole escape route. Less than nine hundred yards separated the Union from complete victory against Lee.

Then occurred one of those rare, dramatic mo-ments that history never forgets. The Federal brigades were so intent in pushing northwestward against Lee's flank that apparently no one saw a column of dust rising in the air to the south. Be-neath that dust was the Confederate "Light Divi-sion" of Major General A. Powell Hill, a hard driving Virginian who sometimes wore red shirts in battle as if to underscore his disdain for danger. After Jackson had captured Harpers Ferry, he had left A. P. Hill's division behind to secure the post. The sound of battle early on September 17 told

Hill that he was badly needed elsewhere; so late that morning he got his troops on the road and started northward. Hill pushed the men hard. Johnny Rebs too exhausted to maintain the pace collapsed along the roadside in droves. Yet Hill urged the men forward, sometimes with the point of his sword. No more than 3,000 of his 5,000 troops reached Sharpsburg; but they marched seventeen miles in seven hours and turned the tide of battle.

Confederates gasping for breath ploughed into Burnside's exposed left flank. Hill himself led the attack, obviously enjoying every second of the in tense fighting (though he was the meekest of men away from battle). Many of his Confederates were wearing blue uniforms captured at Harpers Ferry. This added to the confusion in the unexpected onslaught; shrill screams of the "rebel yell" brought a frightening dimension to weary Federals trying to cope with Hill's attack. It was no use. The conflict in Burnside's sector turned around in a matter of minutes. Federal columns ground to a halt, recoiled, then fell back to the cover of artillery along Antietam Creek. This withdrawal marked the last major action of the day. Night came at last; and when it was impossible to fight any longer, the opposing lines drew apart by mutual consent. In the ensuing darkness there slowly arose a new, more chilling sound: thousands of screams and moans from soldiers too maimed by war to do anything else.

Vicious combat had raged for fourteen hours. Over 100,000 men and 500 artillery pieces had fought a fierce struggle along a 3-mile front. After the long holocaust, Lee's left had been forced back a mile, while his right had retreated half a mile. Those were the day's gains; they paled to in significance when compared to the losses. The Army of the Potomac suffered 12,410 casualties, including 3,000 dead. Lee's losses amounted to 10,700 men. That figure is smaller, to be sure, but it constituted fully a fourth of the Confederate Army. The extent of damage that the Army of Northern Virginia had suffered became obvious that night when Lee held a council of war. All of his lieutenants voiced discouragement. General Hood stated that he simply had no more men left.

"Great God!" Lee exclaimed. "Where is that splendid division you had this morning?"

Below: Then there were the dead to bury, the men who really purchased this field of blood. They lay everywhere. (USAMHI)

Above: While part of the army pursued, much of it bled. Back on the Antietam the Federal surgeons set up their makeshift hospitals. Many sprouted in barns like Dr. Otho Smith's place near Keedysville, taken here by Gardner on September 20. (USAMHI)

Left: Huts were built of straw to provide temporary shelter from the sun. (USAMHI)

Left: Dr. Anson Hurd of the 14th Indiana cared for the wounded from Confederate commands in a hasty field hospital. (USAMHI)

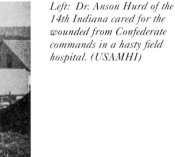

Left: On September 19 Gardner captured burial details working with Federal dead near the North Woods. (USAMHI)

Above: And here is the lonely grave of John Marshall of Company L, 28th Pennsylvania, near the West Woods. (USAMHI)

Left: And the land itself had to recover. St. Paul's suffered heavy damage from artillery fire on both sides. (LC)

Above: And the Federals had time to rest after their greatest test yet in the war. Army blacksmiths had to tend to shodding new stock to replace the hundreds of horses killed. (COURTESY OF THE OAKLAND MUSEUM)

Below: Soldiers like these relaxed in the calm of the waters beside Antietam Bridge, forgetting the pain of just a few days before. (LC)

"They are lying on the field where you sent them," the dejected Hood replied. "My division has been almost wiped out."

Displaying stubborn determination, however, on September 18 Lee waited for McClellan to renew the assaults. Lee had only 30,000 ill-equipped men at hand, while McClellan could boast of more than three times that number. On the field were two Federal corps that had seen no action in the slaughter of the previous day. Yet the hills and dales around Sharpsburg remained deathly still for hour after hour that Thursday. The stench of death fouled the air for miles as the two armies eyed each other warily. Meanwhile McClellan weighed his risks, gathered reports, conferred with his generals, awaited reinforcements, and made vague plans for an attack the next day, or the next, or the next. Across the way Lee's position became more untenable as the day passed, particularly with Federal reinforcements fast approaching. Shortly after sundown bone-tired Confederates slipped away from their lines

Below: The home of Stephen Grove became head-quarters for Fitz John Porter. An officer of his staff could leisurely pose for Gardiner in front of the house and headquarters tents. (USAMHI)

and painfully started southward toward Virginia. An abandoned battlefield greeted McClellan the following morning.

Permitting the Army of Northern Virginia to escape was the worst of McClellan's many failures at Antietam Creek. On the other hand, he must be given some credit in this campaign. He assumed command of demoralized forces early in September; and in the short space of three weeks he had restored morale, reorganized an army, strengthened Washington's defenses, fought two major engagements, forced Lee's retreat to Virginia, and swept Maryland clean of Confederate troops. McClellan felt quite justified in boasting, after Antietam Creek: "I feel that I have done all that can be asked in twice saving the country." Therein lies the tragedy of this general. He never talked of defeating the Confederacy; his only concern was in protecting the Union.

A disappointed Lee found pride in his men as compensation for defeat. "This great battle," he stated, "was fought by less than 40,000 men on our side, all of whom had undergone the greatest labors and hardships in the field and on the march. Nothing could surpass the determined valor with which they met the larger army of the enemy, fully supplied and equipped, and the result reflects the highest credit on the officers and men engaged."

Antietam Creek was not the decisive Union victory that Lincoln had hoped to see, but driving Lee from the North was success enough to prompt Lincoln into an action he had long been considering. On the Monday following the battle, September 22, the President summoned his Cabinet together and announced his intentions of issuing a preliminary emancipation proclamation. The base of the war would thereafter be broadened and its ends appreciably heightened.

Other than Lincoln, few persons at that time sensed that the war's high-water mark may have been reached. Another individual who possibly, and ironically, arrived at the same conclusion was Jefferson Davis. To his Secretary of War shortly after the battle, the Confederate President observed: "Our maximum strength has been mobilized, while the enemy is just beginning to put forth his might."

The Fury of Fredricksburg

PETER J. PARRISH

In a war of mistakes, this battle is the most senseless; even the victor regrets it

THE SMALL VIRGINIA TOWN of Fredericksburg lay in the midst of the fiercely contested hundred miles of territory between the Union and Confederate capitals, almost exactly a halfway house between Washington and Richmond. A quiet town dating from the seventeenth century, with a population of some three or four thousand, it had watched the contending armies swirl around it for more than eighteen months, but the full horror of war had hitherto stopped short of its red brick houses and cobbled streets. However, on November 21, 1862, a Union officer brought to the mayor and Common Council of Fredericksburg a letter from Major General Edwin V. Sumner, commanding the Right Grand Division of the Army of the Potomac. He demanded the surrender of the town; if his request was refused, sixteen hours would be allowed for the evacuation of the civilian population before a bombardment began. The arrival of Confederate troops on the high ground behind the town soon altered the situation, but Fredericksburg now found itself in the no man's-land between two armies readying themselves for battle.

The arrival of the war at Fredericksburg's doorstep followed directly from the first major decision taken by the new commander of the Army of the Potomac, Ambrose E. Burnside. When Lincoln had relieved George B. McClellan of the command of that army early in November 1862, he had surprised many observers by the choice of Burnside as his successor. Sensing his own inadequacy, Burnside accepted the appointment only with the greatest reluctance. But the President's range of choice was extremely limited. If the field of candidates was to be confined to corps commanders in the Army of the Potomac, Lincoln did not want to choose a confirmed disciple of McClellan's, such as William B. Franklin, nor an outspoken critic, such as Joseph Hooker. Despite his poor showing at Antietam, Burnside seemed to have much to commend him. He had shown promise in an independent command in North Carolina and courage and loyalty in the Army of the Potomac. He was in many ways an attractive figure, tall and striking in appearance, honest and straightforward in manner. However, his own self-doubt was amply justified; behind the imposing facade lived a man of limited capacity and limited horizons, as the next few weeks were to show. Like many other officers on both sides, Burnside could perform courageously and creditably up to a certain point, but he was quite incapable of effective command of an army incomparably larger than anything for which West Point training or wartime experience had prepared him. Furthermore, whatever he did, he had little hope of satisfying both the defenders of the deposed McClellan and those who assumed that McClellan's removal would be followed by instant success.

When Burnside took command, the bulk of his army was in the area of Warrenton, just east of the Bull Run Mountains. He organized his huge force of over 120,000 men into three Grand Divisions (each comprising two corps), commanded by Sumner, Franklin, and Hooker. His redoubtable opponent, Robert E. Lee, had also reorganized his much smaller army, now numbering some 80,000 men, into two corps of four divisions each, commanded by James Longstreet and "Stonewall" Jackson. With characteristic audacity Lee had separated the two corps of his much smaller army by

In the wake of Antietam, on October 4, 1862, Lincoln posed with Allan Pinkerton and Major General John McClernand at McClellan's headquarters. The President's patience with "Little Mac" was wearing thin. There was pressure for a new commander. (KA)

Above: A month later Lincoln appointed one: Major General Ambrose Burnside. He was a man with great self-doubts that proved to be well justified. (USAMHI)

Above: But Burnside took his new command and showed a disposition to act. He would turn Lee's flank on the Rappahannock by crossing and taking Fredericksburg, shown here in an 1863 Timothy O'Sullivan image. (USAMHI)

a distance of some fifty miles, with Longstreet at Culpeper Court House, to the south of the Union position, and Jackson still in the Shenandoah Valley.

Burnside quickly decided that he wished to transfer the operations of his army some thirty-five miles to the southeast, in the vicinity of Fredericksburg. This was Burnside's answer to the dilemma which faced all Northern commanders in Virginia. Operations near the coast offered the great advantage of secure supply lines by water but faced the obstacle of a series of rivers obstructing any advance. Operations farther inland faced less serious natural obstacles but depended on a fragile and lengthening supply line. Indeed, Burnside believed that he could not rely upon the rickety, single-track Orange & Alexandria Railroad to sustain his army; he therefore preferred to move farther east, with a view to moving upon Richmond from Fredericksburg. Neither General-in-Chief Henry Halleck nor the President cared much for this plan. Halleck visited Burnside and seems to have succeeded only in confusing both Burnside and himself about the specific movements which the former intended. On November 14 Lincoln finally gave his grudging consent to the plan, adding, in all too accurate words of warning, that "it will succeed if you move very rapidly, otherwise not."

Time was indeed the crux of the matter. If Burnside was to have any chance of success, it was essential that he should get his forces south of the Rappahannock River at or near Fredericksburg before Lee could concentrate his army to resist him. Burnside set his army in motion on November 15 and ordered pontoons to be sent to Fal-

Above: Major General Edwin V. Sumner was ready to cross part of his corps before the Confederates reached Fredericksburg, but Burnside mistakenly withheld his permission—a costly error. Sumner stands at the top, surrounded by members of his staff, at Warrenton, Virginia, just days before his move to Fredericksburg. (USAMHI)

Right: Burnside wanted to make a major crossing in force with the bulk of his army. On November 10, a week before Sumner reached Fredericksburg, Burnside posed at his Warrenton headquarters with several of his generals. Those seated are, from the left: Brigadier General Henry J. Hunt, Brigadier General Winfield S. Hancock, Major General Darius N. Couch, Brigadier General Orlando B. Willcox, and Brigadier General John Buford. Those standing are, from the left: Brigadier General Marsena M. Patrick, Brigadier General Edward Ferrero, Brigadier General John G. Parke, an aide, Burnside, Brigadier General John Cochrane, and Brigadier General Samuel D. Sturgis. (USAMHI)

Right: Surrounding the gathering of the generals was Burnside's headquarters guard, the men of the 93rd New York, and, shown here, Company G. (USAMHI)

Left: Burnside had his headquarters in the quiet village of Warrenton. (USAMHI)

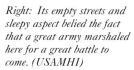

Right: Its empty streets and sleepy aspect belied the fact that a great army marshaled here for a great battle to come. (USAMHI)

mouth, just across the Rappahannock from Fredericksburg, for use in the river crossing. On November 17 his leading contingent, under Sumner, arrived at Falmouth. The railroad from Falmouth to the landing at Aquia Creek was being repaired and supplies were beginning to arrive, but they included no pontoons. Sumner was anxious to cross the river without them, drive out the handful of Confederates in Fredericksburg, and seize the high ground beyond. However, Burnside thought the risks too great, and as the rest of the army came up, it joined Sumner's troops in awaiting the pontoons. They did not arrive until November 25, but by then the opportunity to seize the key positions beyond the Rappahannock without opposition was gone for good. From November 21, Longstreet's corps of Lee's army was digging itself in on the heights behind Fredericksburg, and on November 30 Jackson's corps completed its longer march to the same area.

Before any serious fighting occurred, Burnside had already lost his best opportunity. The blame for the failure to deliver the pontoons on time may have rested with Halleck—or, more generally, it may have reflected the creaking organization and unreliable communications of the Union Army. The responsibility for the delay in crossing the river was essentially Burnside's, and it is permissible to speculate whether the pontoons would have mattered so much if his army had made its sideways move along both sides of the Rappahannock instead of only on its northern side.

With his usual skill in divining the intentions of his opponents, Lee foresaw that Burnside might move towards Fredericksburg, but he could not be sure what would happen next. It was late in the season for further campaigning in northern Virginia, and the weather had already turned wet and cold. Indeed, the battle which was to take place at Fredericksburg in December was the first great winter battle of the war. At first Lee suspected that Burnside's move to Falmouth and the Aquia Creek base might be no more than a prelude to a return to the Peninsular strategy, or even to a waterborne attack at some point farther down the coast, perhaps in North Carolina. However, by the end of November he was convinced that the next great clash between the two armies was to be in and around Fredericksburg.

Lee fully understood the strength of the defensive position which he occupied behind the town, although it had not been his first choice to make a stand there. He appreciated the force of the argument presented by Jackson and others, namely, that while the position could be made defensively impregnable, it offered no scope for a counterattack. Even after the repulse of a Union attack, any Confederate attempt to seize the initiative and cross the river under the guns of the Union Army on the heights beyond would invite disaster. Jackson was all too accurate a prophet when he said that "we will whip the enemy but gain no fruits of victory." Lee would have preferred to fall back to a position on the North Anna River which offered almost equally good defensive possibilities but also much greater opportunity for a counterstroke that might shatter the Union Army. But this would have meant the abandonment of another slice of Virginia territory and would have brought the war dangerously close to Richmond once again. For reasons which were political and psychological rather than purely military, therefore, Lee felt obliged to abandon the idea of a withdrawal to the North Anna. He would

Above: Its value to Burnside lay in the slender iron rails that linked Warrenton with Washington. An August 1862 image by O'Sullivan. (P-M)

Left: Finally Burnside brought his army to Fredericksburg, and from this height he stared across the Rappahannock at his objective. A. J. Russell's image was made the following May. (USAMHI)

Right: Artillery was first employed to soften the Confederate resistance. Here O'Sullivan posed the 5th United States Artillery, Battery D, much as it appeared during the bombardment. (LC)

Above: Perhaps the first casualty of the Fredericksburg Campaign never even saw the battle-field. Brigadier General Francis E. Patterson, the son of the Robert Patterson who so failed in the First Manassas Campaign, had made an error in judgment early in November, and an investigation was impending even as Burnside commenced moving his Grand Divisions. On November 22 he shot himself in the head . (USAMHI)

Left: The only real damage done was to the town itself. This May 1864 image shows the effect of Federal artillery on three houses. (USAMHI)

Above: A home made almost uninhabitable. (P-M)

Above: Several others bare their wounds. (USAMHI)

*Above: There was no question of the Phillips family reoccupying their house.
(USAMHI)*

*Above: A whole city block is ravaged by the rain of iron.
(USAMHI)*

stand—and he would win—at Fredericksburg, but
what would that really achieve?

At Fredericksburg, as on so many Civil War
battlefields, topography shaped the struggle. The
setting was dramatic enough to inspire Lee's oft
quoted words as he watched the spectacle unfolding before and below him: "It is well that war
is so terrible. We should grow too fond of it." The
Rappahannock River, more than 150 yards wide at
this point, swings sharply to the southeast just
above Fredericksburg and flows through a fertile
plain between low hills on either side. The
Stafford Heights on the left bank gave Burnside's
army a position from which its guns could command the river and the town beyond. However,
the Heights, which ran in an irregular arc behind
Fredericksburg on the right bank, were, for most
of their length, far enough back from the river and
the town to be beyond the range of the Union artillery. For considerable stretches, particularly
south of Fredericksburg, these "heights" were no
more than gently rising ground. As at Gettysburg,
such heights or ridges have become clearer in the
mind's eye from innumerable maps and battle nar-
ratives than they appear from the lie of the land itself. At all events, they were prominent enough to
present to the trained military eye an excellent defensive position, and Lee's men had dug themselves in securely by early December.

Faced with this formidable barrier, Burnside
saw three main choices. He could defer any new
move until spring and then perhaps seek new
ground, but this would be politically unpopular,
and Burnside had made up his mind to act. He
could cross the river and pit his men head on
against the Confederate defenses, but the war had
already offered its lessons in the futility of such
frontal assaults on prepared positions. The third
option, either in place of the second or in conjunction with it, was to attempt a river crossing farther upstream, where there were several fords, or
farther downstream, where there were several possible crossing points and where Union gunboats
might offer some support. After visiting Burnside
on November 26–27, Lincoln himself had outlined such a plan for diversions on both flanks in
conjunction with a frontal attack, in the hope of
trapping Lee's army as it was forced to abandon its
prepared positions. But Halleck and Burnside

both thought that such a plan was too complicated and would take too long to prepare. Lee expected an attempted crossing downstream; Burnside did, in fact, prepare for one at Skinker's Neck, some ten miles below Fredericksburg, but he abandoned the idea when Confederate troops moved in to resist any such landing.

Burnside now had nothing else to offer but the idea of a direct frontal attack. Like other and better generals on both sides before and after him, having missed good opportunities and spoiled promising plans by delay, he succumbed to the temptation of the one remaining, and infinitely less promising, option. As a partial explanation, but not an excuse, for Burnside's decision to make a direct assault, it has to be said that his thinking was based upon inadequate information and misleading assumptions about Lee's dispositions. Union scouting had been poor and Burnside's observation balloons did not provide him with a full and balanced picture. He acted on the assumption that Lee's forces, and particularly Jackson's corps holding the southern part of the line, were much more scattered than they actually were. He totally failed to appreciate the high level of concentration of forces which Lee had achieved. In fact, at Fredericksburg the Army of Northern Virginia enjoyed the rare luxury of having several men to defend each yard of its line. In launching his attack on the heights behind Fredericksburg, Burnside thought that he was threatening the left wing of a quite widely dispersed army rather than the concentrated strength of a tough and battle-hardened foe. The mistake was inexcusable, but it explains a good deal of what followed.

Burnside's plan was to use pontoons to establish bridgeheads at two points across the river, one in the town of Fredericksburg itself and the other two miles downstream. Such a division of forces added to the enormous hazards of a river crossing in the face of the enemy, for once across the river the two Union forces, separated by Deep Run and Hazel Run, would have to act independently.

Left: Fredericksburg much as it appeared to Sumner when he first arrived. (USAMHI)

Below: The Lacey house in Falmouth became Sumner's center of operations. (P-M)

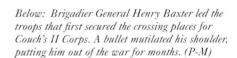

Left: When Burnside was finally ready, the crossing began. On December 11 and 12 Major General William H. French of Sumner's Grand Division crossed the pontoon bridges. (USAMHI)

Below: Brigadier General Henry Baxter led the troops that first secured the crossing places for Couch's II Corps. A bullet mutilated his shoulder, putting him out of the war for months. (P-M)

Below: Shown here just four days before he reached Fredericksburg, Sumner made his headquarters at nearby Falmouth on November 17. (USAMHI)

Above: Lieutenant General Thomas J. "Stonewall" Jackson commanded the II Corps and the entire right half of Lee's line. The Federals would bring battle to him first. (VM)

Above: Spearheading the assault was the division of Major General George G. Meade. He will prove to be one of the ablest, and least appreciated, Union commanders of the war. Here at Fredericksburg he fights his division with ferocious tenacity, almost breaking Jackson's line. (USAMHI)

Right: The Federals had to cross below Fredericksburg, some distance to the left of the scene shown here in this May 1863 image. (P-M)

Below: Meade crossed pontoon bridges like these to assault the Confederate works on the heights. A May 1863 O'Sullivan image. (MHS)

Many of Burnside's subordinate commanders were deeply distrustful of the whole plan—and with good reason—but after all the delays and frustrations of the previous month Burnside's mind was made up.

The crossings began on the night of December 10. There was no significant resistance to the crossing of Franklin's Grand Division downstream, but things were somewhat different at Fredericksburg itself, where Sumner's Grand Division was to establish itself. The sixteen hundred men of Brigadier General William Barksdale's Mississippi brigade held the town itself, and their fire repeatedly drove off the bridge builders. Even a heavy artillery barrage on the morning of December 11 failed to dislodge Barksdale's brigade. Eventually Union troops crossed the river in boats and cleared the town. By evening the two bridgeheads were firmly established, and on December 12 the great bulk of Sumner's and Franklin's men crossed the river without opposition.

Lee had quite deliberately chosen not to contest the river crossing. As he himself explained:

> The plain on which Fredericksburg stands is so completely commanded by the hills of Stafford, in possession of the enemy, that no effectual opposition could be offered to the construction of the bridges or the passage of the river, without exposing our troops to the destructive fire of his numerous batteries.

Furthermore, Lee was quite content to let his enemy come at him on ground of his own choosing. Looking down upon the Union host assembling below, he had ample time to prepare for the coming assault.

His army occupied an immensely strong position. To the south of Deep Run Jackson's corps was drawn up along a low ridge on the edge of the forest, which had concealed so much of its activity from Burnside's airborne observers. His troops looked down an open and gentle slope over which Franklin's men would have to advance. If there was a weak spot in the line, it was created by a coppice jutting out from the rest of the forest. Jackson had concluded that this wood and the swampy ground within it were impenetrable, and had left a gap of some six hundred yards in his line at this point. The northern half of the Confederate position, behind Fredericksburg on Marye's Heights, was held by Longstreet's corps. Here the natural strength of the position was even greater than on Jackson's front. The Heights completely dominated the open ground below. Once the Union troops advanced, they would be at the mercy of the Confederate guns and beyond the protective cover of the Union artillery across the river "A chicken could not live on that field when we open on it," said E. P. Alexander, commanding the artillery on Marye's Heights. To make matters worse for Burnside's men, two other features obstructed any advance towards Marye's Heights. On the outskirts of the town itself the troops had to cross a deep ditch by the only two available bridges, both already damaged to the extent that the soldiers could only pick their way across in single file. Much more serious was the superb defensive position offered below Marye's Heights by a sunken road, on the town side of which was a stone wall, shoulder-high, with earth banked against it. Brigadier General T.R.R. Cobb's brigade, sheltering behind that wall, was to wreak havoc upon successive waves of Union soldiers who knew that they would have to get across that road if they were to achieve anything at all.

Having safely crossed the river, Burnside had no precise idea of how best to tackle the enemy in front of him. His oral orders the night of December 12 and his written orders the next morning were equally vague and did not always tally with each other. Apparently still under the impression that his foe was widely dispersed, he seemed to think that modest attacks by one division on each of the two main sectors would compel Lee to abandon his position.

Thick fog hung over Fredericksburg at dawn on December 13. As it gradually rolled away, the Confederates had a grand view of 80,000 Union troops deploying on the plain below. It was on Jackson's front that the first assault came, but it was launched by only a single division under Major General George G. Meade. Its initial advance was held up by fire on its flank from the two rifled guns of Major John Pelham, commanding Jeb Stuart's horse artillery. When Pelham was at last obliged to withdraw, Meade resumed his advance to the accompaniment of a furious artillery duel between the two sides. He was probing towards the weak spot in Jackson's line in the area of the projecting woodland. His men slogged their way through the marshy undergrowth which Jackson had thought impenetrable. Briefly Meade's men appeared to threaten the heart of Jackson's defenses as they bore down on Brigadier General Maxey Gregg's brigade. Gregg himself was fatally wounded, but two of his regiments held firm. No adequate support arrived to back up what Meade's Pennsylvanians had achieved, and heavy fighting had reduced their numbers by half to around 2,000. Confederate reinforcements came up

Above: Meade's advance was stalled at first by the brilliant handling of just two artillery pieces in the hands of Major John Pelham. Just twenty-two, Pelham resigned from West Point in 1861 to join the South. Lee himself was impressed by the artilleryman. "It is glorious to see such courage in one so young!" he exclaimed. (U. S. MILITARY ACADEMY ARCHIVES)

Above: When Meade pushed past Pelham, he encountered more stubborn resistance from Confederates like the irascible Jubal A. Early, a Virginian who opposed secession and then fought for it wholeheartedly. (PRIVATE COLLECTION)

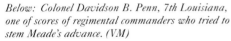

Below: Colonel Davidson B. Penn, 7th Louisiana, one of scores of regimental commanders who tried to stem Meade's advance. (VM)

Above: Leading his Tiger Bayou Rifles of the 14th Louisiana, R. W. Jones looks resplendent in saber, sash, and plumed hat. He will command the regiment by war's end. (TU)

Above: But other great fighters will not last out the battle. Brigadier General Maxey Gregg and his brigade saved the weak spot in Jackson's line, but it cost Gregg his life. (USAMHI)

Right: I Corps veterans like the 30th Pennsylvania, called the 1st Reserves, fought with Meade in the desperate attack on the Confederate left. The Pennsylvanians appear here several months after their Fredericksburg blooding. (USAMHI)

Above: Unfortunately, William B. Franklin, commanding the Left Grand Division, did not support Meade's attack, thereby losing the fruits of Meade's division's bloody advance. Franklin is here shown as a brigadier. (P-M)

Above: Meade's corps commander, Major General John F. Reynolds, a fellow Pennsylvanian, was with him in person during the attack but did not fully employ the rest of the corps. (USAMHI)

Below: While Meade fought doggedly on the Federal left, Major General William F. Smith and his VI Corps spent December 13 mainly waiting in support instead of being used to further the advantage Meade almost secured. Smith stands in the center with his staff. (WRHS)

quickly and turned the tide. Soon the Union troops were in flight, with the Confederates in hot, if unorganized, pursuit. The counterattack eventually ran out of steam—and into Union artillery fire—and the survivors of Meade's division rallied on the riverbank. The Union Army had suffered 5,000 casualties in the fighting on this front. General Franklin was so discouraged by what had happened that he failed to respond to orders from Burnside to renew the attack, although a large part of his force had not yet been engaged. There was no further heavy fighting in this area after 2 :30 P.M.

The Union attacks on the right, towards Marye's Heights, ended in even more costly failure. Partly because of the fog which blanketed the terrain (and no doubt also because of the fog which enveloped Burnside's mind) the first assault on this front did not begin until 11 A.M. At intervals during the remaining five or six hours of daylight, wave after wave of Union attacks spent themselves against the combined strength of the Confederate artillery on Marye's Heights and the infantry in the sunken road below. There was no subtlety, no attempt at deception or diversion, and precious little variety as one frontal attack followed another. Division after division slowly crossed the ditch just outside the town, thus presenting a massed target for the Confederate artillery, and then marched up the wide open slope into a storm of fire.

One Union general, Darius N. Couch, surveying this appalling scene, later recalled that he had cried out: "Oh, great God! See how our men our poor fellows, are falling!" His recollections continue:

I remember that the whole plain was covered with men, prostrate and dropping... I had never before seen fighting like that, nothing approaching it in terrible uproar and destruction... As they charged, the artillery fire would break their formation and they would get mixed; then they would close up, go forward, receive the withering infantry fire... and then the next brigade coming up in sucession would do its duty and melt like snow coming down on warm ground.

In his account of the battle from the other side, General Longstreet used a similar figure of speech: "The Federals had fallen like the steady dripping of rain from the eaves of a house."

There was never any real prospect of breaking the Confederate line. When Lee, momentarily impressed by the incredible persistence of the enemy attacks, expressed some anxiety, Longstreet reassured him:

General, if you put every man now on the other side of the Potomac on that field to approach me over the same line, and give me plenty of ammunition, I will kill them all before they reach my line.

It was a terrible but truthful assessment. As the light began to fade, the attacks were at last called off. There was no Confederate counterattack on this front, and the threatened counterattack by Jackson's corps to the south eventually developed too weakly and too late, and was beaten off by Union artillery. Even when victory on the field of battle was so complete, the winning army was not prepared or organized for a counter-

Right: Men and officers of the 96th Pennsylvania were largely idle with the rest of Smith's corps. Here they cluster around two field guns, the one on the right an unusual repeating gun. (LC)

stroke. Lee probably did not immediately realize the scale of his success; in any event, like Jackson he had known from the outset that their position, however admirable for defense, offered no spring-board for counterattack.

Lee hoped that his opponent would renew the attack the next day. Overnight Burnside's mood swung between black despair and determination to continue the fight. He even talked of personally leading a new assault the next morning, but his subordinate commanders dissuaded him from this wild scheme or from any other plan for a further assault. Indeed, his fellow officers had lost all confidence in their commander, and the Army was in no state for further immediate action. On December 14 and 15 Burnside's army stayed in position under the eyes of the victorious Confederates. Only on December 15 did Burnside send a flag of truce to arrange for the burial of the dead. The ground in front of Marye's Heights was littered not only with the Union dead—often stripped of their heavier clothing by shivering and ill-clad Confederates—but with hundreds upon hundreds of wounded, many of whom lay untended through the two freezing nights which followed the battle.

Total Union casualties—killed, wounded, and missing—were around 12,500, half of them at the foot of Marye's Heights alone. Lee's casualties were less than half that number, a little over 5,000.

On the night of December 15, under cover of a howling storm, the Union Army withdrew back across the Rappahannock without losing another man or scarcely an item of equipment. It was an ironically efficient end to a tragically ineffective operation. Once again the two armies faced each other from the high ground on either side of the river. There they remained until the spring, when another general would launch a very differ-

Below: Major General John B. Hood and his division held the long center of the Confederate line yet were barely engaged. This gallant soldier, with his sad, doleful eyes, chaffed at being inactive. Never a brilliant commander, he had the instincts of a born battler. (MUSEUM OF THE CONFEDERACY)

Above: A company of the 139th Pennsylvania shows what the average infantry company looked like when formed in line. Smith did not engage them. (LC)

Left: Nor did the 67th New York enter the fray. (P-M)

Left: Following Meade's unsuccessful assault, Burnside directed the right of his line to attack through Fredericksburg. The Federals had to advance up these slopes. (NA)

Right: In full view of Confederates posted along these heights behind earthworks. An 1864 image. (USAMHI)

Right: Their destination was the high ground around Marye's house, called Marye's Heights. The bullet scars on the house testify to the fighting that took place. An 1865 image. (USAMHI)

Right: Here and there houses and outbuildings provided shelter for the advancing bluecoats on their way up the slope. (USAMHI)

ent but equally unsuccessful attack upon Lee's position.

For the North Fredericksburg was perhaps the most humiliating and inexcusable defeat of the war. It triggered one of the deepest crises in the four-year struggle—not exclusively or essentially a military crisis but a test of Northern morale, of the Northern will to fight on and win. Army morale slumped and thousands of men went absent without leave. Lincoln distributed a message to the troops, congratulating them upon their courage and offering the nation's thanks. "Although you were not successful, the attempt was not an error nor the failure other than an accident," he wrote in an attempt to defy the plain facts as valiant and unavailing as the Army's attacks on Marye's Heights. The senior officers of the Army waged a war of words among themselves. Some, like Hooker, plied friendly congressmen with their complaints and their gossip; others, like Sumner and Franklin, wrote directly to Lincoln suggesting a return to the James Peninsula; still others, like Brigadier Generals John Newton and John Cochrane, called on Lincoln at the White House to report on the demoralization of the Army as they saw it. Lincoln restrained Burnside from further action and had to face a crisis of command and confidence in the Army during January 1863, until, after charge and countercharge among its senior officers—and the fiasco of the "mud march" up the Rappahannock in another attempt to turn Lee's flank—Burnside was finally removed and replaced by Hooker.

But the crisis was by no means confined to the Army. Coming on top of Republican setbacks in the midterm elections, Fredericksburg raised the curtain on a major political crisis in which Republican senators demanded that Lincoln should re-

Below: And here the most deadly spot of all, the stone wall at the foot of Marye's Heights. From behind this wall Longstreet's Confederates delivered death to hundreds of their enemies. (USAMHI)

Below: But the earthworks at the top gave the defenders excellent cover from which to pour a murderous fire on their attackers. This image of Marye's Heights, probably taken in May 1864, shows well the defenses and the damage left after the battle. (USAMHI)

Above: Lieutenant General James Longstreet, "Old Pete" to his men, solid, dependable, indomitable in defense. He commanded the left half of Lee's army and bore the brunt of the fighting at Fredericksburg. It was while viewing his work that Lee declared that he was glad war was so terrible, else they should grow too fond of it. (USAMHI)

Above: John R. Cooke had just been promoted to brigadier before the battle. He had taken seven wounds by the time of Fredericksburg, but surely the greatest wound of all was that his father was even now a major general in the Union Army. (VM)

Above: One of Longstreet's premier brigade commanders, Brigadier General Joseph B. Kershaw, the flamboyant South Carolinian from First Manassas, felt that that battle should not be called "Bull Run" because it was such an undignified name. (USAMHI)

Above: George T. Anderson became a brigadier the same day as Cooke. He, too, commanded a brigade in Longstreet's corps. This Georgian was known to his men and friends as "Tige," and he could fight like a tiger at that. (VM)

Above: Following Sumner in the attacks on Marye's Heights was Major General Joseph Hooker, already being called "Fighting Joe." Time after time he hurled his divisions against the stone wall and earthworks, and just as many times they were repulsed. He never entirely forgave Burnside for ordering his assault. Already given to politicking in the army, Hooker would soon start campaigning against Burnside. (USAMHI)

Above: Daniel Sickles commanded Hooker's old division in the III Corps and took his promotion as major general just two weeks before the battle. He appears here as a brigadier. He proved to be a good fighter for a general with no qualifications for command other than political influence. (USAMHI)

Above: Another good fighter, though a man intemperate in speech and habits, was Brigadier General Thomas Meagher, the fiery Irishman. He virtually destroyed his famous Irish Brigade in its brutal assaults on Marye's Heights. After the war he would drown when he fell overboard from a river steamer while drunk. (USAMHI)

Above: Men like this dandy from a New York regiment had their finery ripped away in their desperate battle for the Heights, and for life, at Fredericksburg. (NA)

Above: Baxter's Zouaves, the 72nd Pennsylvania, fought for Sumner even when he ordered them into the face of death itself . Seldom was greater heroism more foolishly wasted than at Fredericksburg. (COURTESY OF TERENCE P. O'LEARY)

Right: Their attacks availed them nothing. The battle ended, Burnside could only sit and look across the Rapahannock, and send flag-of-truce parties, like the one shown here, to bury the dead. It had been a wasted battle. (USAMHI)

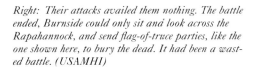

Right: Hawkins's Zouaves, too, and their colonel, Rush Hawkins, standing second from the left, bloodied their fancy uniforms in repeated attacks on Marye's Heights. (NA)

construct his Cabinet on more radical lines and prosecute the war more vigorously. Lincoln warded off the challenge to his authority, but he badly needed military success to lift Northern morale from one of its deepest depressions. The final Emancipation Proclamation, to be issued on January 1, 1863, would scarcely inspire confidence, coming in the wake of electoral reverses, a Cabinet crisis, and a military disaster.

However, Northern morale and Lincoln's pertinacity did survive Fredericksburg, as they had survived so much else. If Confederate victory on the Rappahannock could not break the Northern will to win, it could not achieve much else. The Army of the Potomac would soon be restored to full strength. It continued to enjoy an overwhelming preponderance of men and materiel over its Confederate opponents, and its soldiers had already given ample proof of their resilience and power of recovery in the face of the worst which blundering leadership, faulty organization, and battlefield reverses could inflict upon them. If the North retained the will, it certainly retained the means to fight and win the war. If the South had the ability to win battles, it was already sorely troubled by the depletion of manpower and resources. Battles like Fredericksburg, it was now clear, could not by themselves decide the war. The paradox of Fredericksburg was that it resulted in a victory which revealed the limitations of the victors and a defeat which revealed the strength of the defeated.

Strangling The South

JAMES M. MERRILL

Improvised, often ineffective, the blockade required the building of a new navy

Deceptively peaceful, the parade ground at Fort Monroe swarmed during the war as ships and fleets outfitted and repaired for the arduous duty of patrolling the Confederate coastline, the inlets, harbors, and rivers of rebellion. (USAMHI)

ON THE AFTERNOON of August 22, 1864, the Confederate blockade-runner *Lilian*, hauled away from the cotton press at Wilmington, North Carolina, glided down the Cape Fear River, exchanged signals with the forts at the entrance, dropped anchor, and waited. At nightfall she got under way, her helmsman steering a course due east for the open sea. A shout came from the darkness: "Heave to, or I'll sink you!" Instantly the pilot of the *Lilian* ordered the helm hard to port and attempted to ram the Federal picketboat. The Union craft began firing signal rockets simultaneously with her bow gun. Shells crashed over the *Lilian* without damage, and within an hour she had left all but one of the Federal blockaders far behind. She had barely eluded this vessel when she ran into a cross fire from Yankee steam frigates. After three hours of "frightfully accurate" firing, the Union ships took the badly damaged *Lilian* as a prize and its officers and crew as prisoners of war.

Three years earlier, at the outset of the Civil War, the Union Navy, its ships rotting in dry dock or scattered across the seas at foreign stations, shouldered the task of blockading the Confederate coast from Virginia to Texas. Despite a lack of fighting power in April 1861, the Navy Department dispatched all available seaworthy vessels to Southern ports. The steam frigate *Minnesota* and the sail frigate *Cumberland* anchored at Hampton Roads, the chief base for the North Atlantic Blockading Squadron.

As Lincoln's administration increased the purchase and construction of naval gunboats, the blockading squadrons were materially strengthened. With only 2 ships, in May 1861, guarding the entire coast of North Carolina, a year later 58 craft policed this sector, and at the end of the war the total had reached 142.

In the beginning the Union fleet was obviously unable to make its blockade effective, and as late as 1864 there was still much running of supplies into the South, but Secretary of the Navy Gideon Welles justly believed that his ships were cutting off the Confederacy's trade in most heavy goods.

If the only naval operation during the war had been to blockade the principal ports of the Confederacy, the work of the Navy would have been comparatively easy. However, the outer coastline from the northern boundary of Virginia to Mexico is more than three thousand miles in length; this exterior shoreline along the Atlantic seaboard is merely the outer edge of a series of islands, behind which there are sounds, rivers, and connecting channels and canals, thus forming a protected and almost continuous inland waterway from Virginia to Florida that is navigable for small vessels. Along this outer shoreline there are countless inlets or openings connecting the Atlantic Ocean with the interior waterways. This peculiar topography constantly hampered the Federal blockaders through out four years of war. Although a major port could be effectively policed by Union ships, blockade runners and Confederate privateers could steal through some inlet many miles above or below a principal port and steam unmolested along the sounds to their destinations within the Confederacy. An active coastal commerce, involving the transport of men and supplies to the Southern armies in the field, was carried on in these protected sounds, bays, and rivers, while far out to sea Union blockaders patrolled off the main harbors.

Above: Surprising , considering its vital importance as headquarters of the North Atlantic Blockading Squadron and as a jumping-off place for several expeditions into the South, Fort Monroe was very little photographed during the war. This image s the only one known that captures even a substantial part of the old mas ry fortification. Called Fortress Monroe for years, its name was officially shortened to "Fort" a few years before the war. (NA)

Above: Headquarters of the North Atlantic Blockading Squadron, Fort Monroe, Virginia. Through this sally port passed thousands of soldiers and seamen whose single task it was to deny to the Confederacy the succor of foreign shipping, to assist in the conquest of the Southern coastline. (USAMHI)

To create an efficient blockade the United States Navy either had to station ships off all the inlets and establish an extensive ship-to-ship system of supply or seize the inlets and suitable areas for bases by means of amphibious attack. Obviously the latter plan of using seaborne forces was more practical and was adopted early by the Navy Department. The sea arm of the Union, commanding Confederate waters, was in a position to execute major amphibious assaults against Rebel shore installations. Since the Confederates lacked any semblance of a seagoing Navy, the Federals could concentrate an army in home ports and transport it unmolested to any area along hundreds of miles of enemy coastline.

The building, purchase, or chartering of additional vessels, their conversion for the blockade, and the finding of crews for them became Welles's greatest immediate task, in which time was a major factor. By mid-July 1861 the Navy Department had contracted for the building of 23 gunboats and had purchased or chartered 21 steamers and 3 sailing vessels of various descriptions. These were dispatched to the shipyards in New York and Boston for overhaul.

The early commanding officers of the North Atlantic Blockading Squadron, Commodores Silas H. Stringham, Louis Goldsborough, and Samuel Phillips Lee were careerists with long, spotless, but not brilliant naval dossiers, and they were well schooled in the techniques of the old Navy. Although they did not balk at the use of steam and, on occasion, used it to good advantage, their minds were not elastic enough to permit them to take full advantage of the revolution in naval science (e.g., the transition of sail to steam, wood to iron, and smoothbore to rifled cannon). They resisted employing the newly developed armored vessels to the best tactical advantage and clung tenaciously to the worn-out doctrines of the War of 1812, when ship dueled ship and boarders poured

Above: The wood and coaling yard at Fort Monr e. Here the fleet replenished its constant need for fuel to keep the warships patr ling the Southern coastline. A huge mound of coal is just visible through e archway at left center. (NA)

Left: And while the ships were supplied, so, too, were the tens of thousands of sailors and soldiers campaigning in Virginia and North Carolina. This view shows just one of the streets lined with quartermaster warehouses that crowded around Fort Monroe. (NA)

Right: Part of the backbone of the North Atlantic Blockading Squadron was its armament, much of it tested here at Fort Monroe. Several fifteen-inch Rodmans lie mounted and dismounted here, either before or after testing, while at the far right appear the remnants of a cannon which was tried and failed. (NA)

over the sides with cutlasses and engaged in hand-to-hand combat.

Thrust into positions of great responsibility, these officers followed the rule book of the old Navy. Their experience on routine assignments had not demanded of them a quick grasp of tactical advantage or imbued them with the imaginative intelligence necessary to the solution of new problems. They were men who had already established their professional reputations, and fear of tarnishing their good names made them overly cautious. They hesitated when they should have pushed their advantage. Initial victories were not followed up because they refused to assume personal responsibility for the risks involved.

David D. Porter, who was later to command the North Atlantic Blockading Squadron, does not belong in this category. Younger and more vigorous, he possessed a brashness which the others lacked. His mistakes were not prompted by a lack of confidence or an unwillingness to venture forth. On the contrary, in his first amphibious attack against the North Carolina coast in 1864 his failure was attributable to his overly optimistic evaluation of his own position.

Although the commanders can be criticized, they should not be categorically condemned. Despite their shortcomings, they were competent administrators, and their abilities were equal to organizing and executing their routine blockade assignments. Despite the scarcity of ships and supplies in the beginning, they—especially Stringham, who inaugurated the blockade—should be com mended for the way in which they handled their policing duties.

Right: Mighty cannon like this one stared out from the casemates of the fort, awaiting anyone foolhardy enough to challenge Monroe's dominion over Hampton Roads. This Rodman smoothbore rests on an experimental carriage being tested by the government. (NA)

In early April 1861 Commodore Silas Stringham took command of the *Minnesota* and awaited further instructions. New orders called upon him to organize the Atlantic Blockading Squadron "to protect our commerce, suppress piratical or illegal demonstrations… guard the public interests," and to proceed to establish the blockade of Southern ports. His squadron's command extended from the capes of the Chesapeake to the southern extremity of Florida.

Since this was far too large an area for one com-

Left: Another fifteen-inch Rodman rests heavily on Fort Monroe's parapet, showing the apparatus required to load its mammoth projectiles. (NA)

Right: Captain Hiram Paulding suffered the first major naval loss for the Union Navy when he had to give up the Norfolk Navy Yard in Virginia in April 1861. With it he lost tons of ordnance, hundreds of cannon and spare ships' parts, and the hulk of the Merrimack, soon to be used against the Union as the CSS Virginia. (NA)

Above: The steam frigate USS Minnesota, *flagship of the North Atlantic Blockading Squadron, anchored at Hampton Roads at the war's start. Just four years old in 1861, she would figure prominently in the war, almost being lost to the Confederate ironclad* Virginia *before being saved by the* Monitor *in March 1862. (MHS)*

Above: To begin building the Navy for combat against the enemy, Secretary Welles refitted many ships at the New York and Boston navy yards. Here several naval mortars await being placed on the decks of ships in Boston. (USAMHI)

Above: The sidewheel frigate USS Susquehanna *joined Stringham's blockaders early in the war, and fought well with him in the attack on Hatteras Inlet. Here her officers pose on deck in 1864. The paddlewheel box is visible behind the standing rigging. (NYHS)*

Above: Rear Admiral Silas Stringham was the first commander of the North Atlantic Blockading Squadron. Sixty-four years old, a fifty-two-year veteran of the service, he was loyal, though out of date for the war at hand. Gideon Welles found that "whilst there were doubts and uncertainty on every hand as to who could be trusted, I knew Commodore Stringham to be faithful." (COURTESY OF THE NEW-YORK HISTORICAL SOCIETY)

Left: This is what Stringham was after: sleek blockade-runners seeking to penetrate his curtain of ships to bring supplies to the Confederacy. The ship to the right is the British steamer Giraffe *in dry dock at Glasgow, Scotland, fitting out as a blockade-runner. Renamed the* Robert E. Lee, *she would run the blockade in 1863. (MARINERS MUSEUM)*

Above: Two more steamers at Glasgow destined to be blockade-runners. The vessel at right is the Juno. *(MARINERS MUSEUM)*

Below: A stopping place for the runners before their final journey through the blockade was the British ports in Bermuda. Here the naval dockyard shows a British fleet at anchor during the Civil War. Most are old line ships, sailing vessels on their way to becoming receiving hulks like the one in the foreground. (U.S. NAVAL HISTORICAL CENTER)

Above: In Bristol, England, more blockade-runners were born. Here the Old Dominion *undergoes her conversion for the swift service. Telescoping funnels and smokeless coal, the low lines, and swift speed all worked to her advantage. (CHS)*

mand, a group of naval specialists, working in Washington, suggested to Secretary Welles in July 1861 that the Atlantic Blockading Squadron should be divided in two. This would be advantageous to the efficiency of the blockade since different portions of the Atlantic seaboard possessed differing topographical features and required distinct treatment. They pointed out that the northern, or upper, section was characterized by islands—some small, some large, some narrow, some wide—which separated the sounds and bays from the ocean and were divided at irregular intervals by openings or inlets through which the ocean tides ebbed and flowed. The southern, or lower, section was distinguished by ordinary ports and bays. The North Atlantic Blockading Squadron was to extend from Cape Henry, Virginia, to Cape Roman, South Carolina, a distance of about 370 miles; the South Atlantic Blockading Squadron was to stretch from Cape Roman to St. Augustine, Florida, covering about 220 miles. This recommendation was carried out.

At once Stringham saw that an obstacle to the effectiveness of the North Atlantic Blockading Squadron was the protection afforded Southerners by their coast, much of which was supplied with a double shoreline. Small vessels from Carolinian ports sneaked along the inside passage until they reached an outlet and then dashed for the open seas. Hatteras Inlet was such an obstacle. "The Swash," as the inlet was referred to, was a long, sandy barrier off the coast of North Carolina, six miles south of Cape Hatteras and about ninety

Far left: Captain Smith of the Old Dominion and his officers adopted Confederate naval dress even though their ship was never formally part of the Southern Navy. (COURTESY OF MICHAEL J. MCAFEE)

Left: Lieutenant McClellan of the Old Dominion. (COURTESY OF MICHAEL J. MCAFEE)

miles by water from New Bern, North Carolina. Confederate ships passed from North Carolina cities through internal waterways to Hatteras or neighboring inlets, and then headed for the open seas.

Secessionists recognized these advantages. Fortifications of these outlets were begun, and by the middle of June 1861 the major work had been accomplished on Fort Hatteras, located an eighth of a mile from the channel entrance. Nearby, a second bastion, Fort Clark, was ready for service in late July. The two redoubts, located about three fourths of a mile from one another on the same is land, secured a cross fire upon the entrance to Hatteras Inlet.

Other fortifications were quickly marked off and built at Ocracoke and Oregon inlets, two neighboring outlets to the sea. Confederate priva teers operating from Hatteras Inlet took their toll of Union merchantmen, especially when blockad ing vessels were patrolling other areas. The ma rauders would "dash out," bewailed a Union naval officer, and be "back again in a day with a prize." A large brig and three schooners were a week's catch during July 1861. Blockade-runners contin ued to use the North Carolina inlets. In Washing ton naval strategists concluded that the ports of Norfolk and Richmond could not be successfully blockaded until the Atlantic entrances to Pamlico and Albemarle sounds in North Carolina were shut.

After digesting reports and suggestions from various sources, Assistant Secretary of the Navy Gustavus Vasa Fox worked out plans for an offen sive thrust against Hatteras Inlet. Naval vessels cooperating with a military unit would capture Forts Hatteras and Clark and, accepting the strategists' recommendation, obstruct the channel entrance by sinking schooners loaded with stone. The island was not to be held permanently.

In late August 1861 the expedition got under way for Cape Hatteras. Besides the Army trans ports filled with 860 soldiers commanded by Major General Benjamin Butler, the convoy in cluded the stream frigates *Minnesota* and *Wabash*, the gun boats *Monticello* and *Harriet Lane*, the steam sloop *Pawnee*, the tugboat *Fanny*, the sailing frigate *Cumberland*, and a retinue of small vessels. On the morning of August 27 Cape Hatteras Light was sighted, and after rounding the shoals the squadron dropped anchor. The Federal assault on Hatteras Inlet commenced at 6:40 A.M. on August 28. Because of the heavy breakers along the beach only 320 soldiers were put ashore. Fort Clark was under heavy bombardment from the *Wabash*, *Cumberland*, and *Minnesota*. The Union ships passed repeatedly, belching round after round at the fort while remaining out of range of Confed erate guns. The side-wheeler *Susquehanna*, re turning to Hampton Roads after her tour of duty with the West Indian Squadron, steamed upon the scene and joined the bombardment.

Brutally pasted by naval gunfire, with Yankee troops only three miles away and ammunition nearly exhausted, the Confederates fell back to Fort Hatteras. Federals hoisted the Stars and Stripes over Fort Clark. The *Minnesota*, *Wabash*, and *Susquehanna*, together with the *Monticello*, which had already started firing, opened up on Fort Hatteras.

When darkness arrived the firing ceased. At 5:30 A.M. the following day the squadron weighed anchor and stood towards shore. Warned not to fire

Left: The harbor at Hamilton, Bermuda, saw scores of the runners pass through. Here the British steamer Dee *appears in 1863. On February 5, 1864, she ran ashore off Masonboro Inlet, North Carolina, and was destroyed by the USS* Cambridge *the next day. Her image was captured aboard the block ade-runner* Don *when she was captured by the USS* Pequot *off Wilmington on March 4, 1864. (USAMHI)*

Above: The former Giraffe *as she appeared as the* Robert E. Lee *shortly after her capture. The Union Navy refitted her and renamed her* Fort Donelson. *(LC)*

Left: The blockade-runner A. D. Vance *shortly after her 1864 capture. She, too, entered the Federal service as the USS* Frolic, *remain ing in commission until 1883. (NHC)*

Left: The runner Teaser *photographed off Fort Monroe in December 1864, following her capture. Damage to her paddle box and waterline is clearly evi dent. Most blockade-runners surrendered without a fight when challenged, having vir tually no protection against Federal fire. (LC)*

Right: Another view of the Teaser, extensively damaged. (NA)

upon Fort Clark, the ships steamed in and opened fire on Fort Hatteras.

The ineffective range of Confederate guns, lack of ammunition, and casualties convinced Confederate officers to run up the white flag. Fort Hatteras was surrendered at 11:07 A.M. About 600 Confederates together with their wounded were herded on board a Union transport. Southern casualties numbered 7 dead and 30 wounded.

That evening Stringham and General Butler decided not to level the forts and block the channel as their orders had stated. They recognized that Hatteras would be invaluable as a depot for the blockading squadron, a safe refuge in all types of weather for the coasting trade, and a staging area for future operations against North Carolina and Virginia. To hold the inlet troops and a naval force remained behind. The following day, August 30, the squadron headed northward.

The seizure of Hatteras was successful because of the squadron's accurate fire, with its smothering effect on the forts. But had there been more troops, an adequate plan of attack, and aggressive leaders, the Hatteras expedition could have pushed into North Carolina and created considerable havoc. A Confederate naval officer confided that the enemy erred in not taking possession of the sounds immediately after capturing Hatteras: "There was nothing to prevent it."

Secretary Welles, terming the failure to capitalize on the attack "a misfortune," later pointed out, however, that the victory was the "first effective blow struck by the Navy," and that it was the "commencement of that series of coast movements which from step to step... [was to wrest] almost every port on one long line of sea coast from the insurgents and... [drive] them to the interior."

Above: Captain R. H. Harper of the blockade-runner Hallie. He and his fellow captains ran a dangerous business... (WILLIAM A. ALBAUGH COLLECTION)

Above: ... but the rewards could be enormous, which is what attracted men like Captain A. G. Swaszey to risk the run in his ship Ella. (WILLIAM A. ALBAUGH COLLECTION)

Below: And for the Federals it meant a routine of constant vigilance: standing at the rail, glass in hand, ever watchful for the thin wisp of smoke or the rakish gray hull nearly blending into the horizon that meant a blockade-runner. (USAMHI)

Below: Captain Louis M. Goldsborough came of an old Maryland family with strong naval ties. Though fifty-six years old in 1861, he still succeeded Stribling in command of the squadron and led it in the attack on Roanoke Island. He would be promoted to rear admiral in a few months, but, like Stribling, would eventually ask to be retired in the face of heavy criticism from the press. (USAMHI)

Above: In his efforts to enforce the blockade, Goldsborough used fine new gunboats like the USS Kansas... *(LC)*

Right: ... and converted army transports like the side-wheeler USS Fulton, *shown here on June 20, 1864. (NA)*

The capture of Forts Hatteras and Clark was timely for the Union cause, exclaimed a naval commander, as it was "the first substantial [Federal] victory of the war." Coming soon after the disaster at Bull Run, it raised Union spirits and gained prestige for the Navy.

The Hatteras expedition not only quickened Northern morale but caused alarm in North Carolina and dejection throughout most of the South. The rendezvous area quashed, Confederate marauders from Hatteras no longer preyed upon Union cargo ships plying the coast of North Carolina. In September 1861 fortifications at another inlet, Ocracoke, were captured without a struggle by bluejackets sent from Hatteras. Schooners loaded with stone were sunk at Ocracoke, closing this inlet completely to Confederate commerce and raiders.

Blockade procedures continually varied as the North and South tried to outwit each other. With each passing year blockade and blockade-running techniques became more sophisticated. Swift gray steamers with telescoping funnels glided in and out of Confederate ports. Southern and

Left: Converted New York ferryboats like the USS Morse *took part in the operations at Hatteras Inlet and Roanoke, covered troop landings up the Virginia rivers, and assisted in the blockade patrol. (USAMHI)*

Below: And there were little vessels, like the Seth Low, *which had a special duty. On March 6, 1862, the* Seth Low *left New York with an unusual ship in tow, the USS* Monitor. *Both were on their way to Hampton Roads, the* Virginia, *and the* Monitor's *destiny. (USAMHI)*

Left: Others, like the USS Shawsheen, *scoured the rivers and harbors for "torpedoes," submerged mines that could quickly sink a wooden-hulled vessel. (WRHS)*

Right: Commander John Worden commanded the Monitor. *It was his first ship of the war, he being the first officer to have charge of this new type of warship. He nearly lost his sight thanks to one of the* Virginia*'s shots. (USAMHI)*

Far right: Acting Volunteer Lieutenant Louis N. Stodder served aboard the Monitor, *helping work her turret during the epic fight on March 9. (USAMHI)*

Right: The officers of the Monitor *on July 9, 1862. The turret of the prototype warship rests behind them. Unfortunately no photograph of the entire ship is known to exist. (USAMHI)*

Right: The officers in yet another pose. Paymaster William Keeler, standing wearing spectacles, was with the ship on her last voyage. When she was sinking, he stuffed money and some valuable papers in one of the cannon barrels. A cat jumped into the other. (USAMHI)

Right: Seated on the chair at right is Lieutenant Samuel D. Greene, who took command of the Monitor *when Worden was wounded. Years later Greene would take his own life, reputedly in frustration over an article he was preparing on the* Monitor-Virginia *battle, making him the fight's last casualty. (USAMHI)*

British mariners, navigating the sea-lanes between Rebel coasts and nearby neutral ports—especially Nassau—traded Southern cotton for English cannon.

Once a runner was safely moored in Wilmington, stevedores dumped her freight on the dock and quickly began hauling cotton on board. Dock workers stuffed the bales so closely together in ships' holds that "a mouse could hardly find a room to hide." After the hatches were battened down, a tier of bales was secured fore and aft in every available spot on deck, leaving space only for approaches to the cabins, engine room, and forecastle. A vessel loaded in this way resembled a huge cotton bale with a mast stuck upright at one end.

If blockade-running was "rollicking good fun" for British and Confederate skippers, it was "perfect hell" for Yankee seamen who tried to stop it. For hours crews stood wearily at the guns, waiting, watching, cursing, until the order came to secure. "We go below," grumbled one officer, "and throw ourselves, clothes and all, on the bunk—only to be startled by another gunshot."

Roanoke Island, North Carolina, was recognized by most North Carolinians and a few authorities at Richmond as being of vital importance to the defense of the Old North State and to the Confederacy. Albemarle and Pamlico sounds, strategic to the interior water commerce, connect the Atlantic Ocean and the inlets with the rivers and coastal towns of the North Carolina mainland and with the canals, which lead to Norfolk and Richmond. Located in Croatan Sound, forty-five miles above Federal-held Hatteras Inlet, Roanoke Island commands this chain of sounds, inlets, and rivers. Possession of the island by Union troops would give them undisputed command of the sounds, the sea coast towns, the rear door to Norfolk and, possibly, to the railroads running northward into Virginia.

Realizing the strategic importance of Roanoke Island, Confederate officials hustled a regiment southward from Virginia to occupy and fortify it. Governor Henry T. Clark of North Carolina, sensing the strategic value of the island to the eastern counties, dispatched a disorganized regiment of state troops. Defensive preparations crept forward.

After the fall of Hatteras, naval strategists in Washington recommended that the sounds of North Carolina be occupied permanently by gunboats to break up the foreign and interior trade. At Hampton Roads an expedition of the North Atlantic Blockading Squadron was slowly fitted out. Captain Louis M. Goldsborough, recently assigned to command the squadron, met with President Lincoln and his Cabinet in October to discuss naval tactics in the sounds.

Early in November 1861 Brigadier General Ambrose Burnside, who was then at Annapolis equipping a force for Chesapeake waters, was summoned to Washington, where, in the presence of Lincoln, Secretary of State William Seward, General-in-Chief George B. McClellan and Goldsborough, he was told that his division's objective had been switched to North Carolina. Cooperating with the Navy, his force was to strike such points as would give the Union complete control of Albemarle and Pamlico sounds. Once the thrust into North Carolina was decided upon, Goldsborough returned to Hampton Roads and Burnside to Annapolis. Early in December the naval commander insisted on the capture of

Left: Men of the Monitor *lounge on deck. The two seamen in the right foreground play backgammon. On the turret behind them some of the slight damage done by the* Virginia *is evident. (MARINERS MUSEUM)*

Below: James Gibson caught this image on July 9, 1862, of two officers surveying the turret. At the edge of the deck just to the right of them can be seen a plate slightly loosened where the Virginia *attempted to ram the ironclad but glanced off instead. The pilothouse, the pyramidal object behind the turret, was originally rectangular. Worden was injured there. (USAMHI)*

Above: The cook's fire smoking away, men of the Monitor *await a midday meal. (USAMHI)*

Roanoke Island. Troop ships, cargo schooners, and Staten Island ferryboats arrived at Hampton Roads during the evening of January 10, 1862. On January 11 the attack force, totalling seventy vessels, slid down the channel from Hampton Roads. Orders were explicit. The first objective was Roanoke Island; then, in rapid sucession, New Bern, Beaufort, Fort Macon, and, possibly, Wilmington. On January 13 the fleet anchored in the comparative shelter of Hatteras Inlet.

Goldsborough and Burnside held several "full and free consultations" to work out details for the assault on Roanoke Island. With everything in readiness on February 5, the attack force headed northward toward Pamlico Sound, led by fifteen gunboats and followed by eight of the Army's armed vessels and forty-seven transports with 7,500 men. Foul weather prevented the execution of battle plans on February 6, but at 9:55 A.M. the next day the fleet got under way and steamed toward the narrow opening to Croatan Sound. Slowly the vessels threaded their way through the passage out into the sound. Union and Confederate guns boomed. Goldsborough's vessels hurled "every conceivable kind of projectile"

Above: Worden's successor in command of the Monitor, *the largely unpopular Lieutenant William N. Jeffers, seated before the turret. He commanded the ship in the ill-fated attack on Drewry's Bluff. (USAMHI)*

Above: Lieutenant Catesby Ap R. Jones was executive officer of the Virginia, *a man from an old and honored naval family. When Franklin Buchanan was wounded on March 8, Jones commanded the Confederate ironclad in its battle with the* Monitor *the next day. (NHC)*

Left: Lieutenant John Taylor Wood, grandson of President Zachary Taylor and a career naval officer, served one of the Virginia's guns. He would later become a dreaded commerce raider. (PRIVATE COLLECTION)

Right: Midshipman Henry H. Marmaduke of Missouri was badly injured when the muzzle of his gun was shot away aboard the Virginia. (COURTESY OF JON NIELSON)

Right: Midshipman Hardin B. Littlepage served another of the Virginia's guns in the epic contest. (COURTESY OF ALVAN C. MACAULEY)

Right: Not so fortunate was Lieutenant Joseph B. Smith, commanding the USS Congress. In the hot fighting before his ship was destroyed by the Confederates, he was killed instantly when a shell carried away his head and shoulder. His father had a premonition of his son's death the same day. (USAMHI)

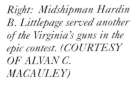

Above: Commodore Gershom Van Brurst commanded the USS Minnesota *in the battle at Hampton Roads, running the vessel aground on March 8. She remained immobile the next day while the* Monitor *successfully kept the* Virginia *away from her. (USAMHI)*

into the Confederate fort. Four thousand Union soldiers disembarked from the transports and waded ashore. Due to heavy rain, operations came to a halt. Burnside and Goldsborough mapped out work for the next day.

A half hour before sunrise on February 8 Union soldiers moved forward. A small naval force maneuvered northward in the sound, removed obstructions, and widened the channel. From the clatter of gunfire on the island, Burnside's position was noted. Once assured that he was not in the line of their fire, other gunboats steamed up and salvoed. After severe fighting, the Confederates surrendered Roanoke Island at 5:25 that afternoon.

News of Roanoke Island thrilled the victory-starved North. This success, coupled with those of General Grant in the west at Forts Henry and Donelson, infused the Union with a spirit, more pronounced than at any time since Bull Run, that the war was soon to be over. During the days which followed the Confederate surrender, Union troops at Roanoke Island improved roads, cleaned up the forts, campgrounds, and hospitals, and built a wharf at Park Point to facilitate the loading and unloading of troops and supplies. Once ammunition ships arrived from the north, the Union force was ready to move. On March 14, 1862, New Bern fell to a Union assault. The port town of Beaufort and nearby Fort Macon succumbed to another effort of the Federal Navy and Army in April 1862. Beaufort, one of the best harbors on the southern coast, was converted into a much needed coaling station and supply base for the North Atlantic Blockading Squadron for its blockade against Wilmington, the only Confederate port of any significance remaining open north of Charleston.

Minor operations in the sounds proceeded without interruption. Union vessels obstructed the entrances to the Dismal Swamp and the Albemarle-Chesapeake canals. The North Carolina towns of Elizabeth City, Edenton, Washington, Winton, and Plymouth were temporarily occupied by Union soldiers and sailors. The back door to Norfolk had slammed shut. The proposed assault against Wilmington was not carried out. The Yankees now held so many points and so long a stretch of coastline that it was impossible throughout May and June 1862 to spare troops for any additional operation, although Goldsborough boasted that he could take the city without the Army's help. The successes of the Goldsborough-Burnside expeditions at Roanoke Island, New Bern, Beaufort, Fort Macon, and other coastal towns impaired the war effort of the Confederacy and North Carolina. Blockade-runners which, prior to March 1862, could pick and choose among several inlets and North Carolina ports had to converge on Wilmington.

In March 1862, after nearly a year of strife, Northerners totaled their successes and discovered that it was the Navy alone, or the Navy acting in conjunction with the Army, that sustained the Union with victories in the eastern theater of operations. Starting from a state of extreme unpreparedness in April 1861, after ten months of struggle the Navy was welded into a potent offensive as well as defensive force. Speaking of the Army, the editor of *Frank Leslie's Illustrated Newspaper* remarked that the successes in the East, "although neither few nor unimportant, have been, for the most part, gained in conjunction with the Navy, which has, not undeservedly, obtained the

Far left: Commander George U. Morris valiantly fought his ship, the USS Cumberland, both before and after she was rammed by the Virginia. Some of the sinking ship's guns were kept in action until the rising water reached their muzzles. (USAMHI)

Left: Brother against brother meant something to Paymaster and Lieutenant Commander J. McKean Buchanan aboard the Congress His brother was Franklin Buchanan, commanding the CSS Virginia. (USAMHI)

Below: Other ironclads did not always prove as impervious to enemy shells as the Monitor. In the abortive attack on Drewry's Bluff the USS Galena suffered severe damage, as shown in Gibson's June 1862 image. She was never an effective ironclad warship. (LC)

larger share of the credit... against these successes, our land forces have had reverses at Big Bethel... Bull Run, and Ball's Bluff."

Early in 1862 the importance of the ironclad warship was underscored in the famous Hampton Roads naval duel. The Confederates had seized the powerful steam frigate the *Merrimack*—sunk by the Yankees during the evacuation of the Norfolk Navy Yard and quickly raised by the Rebels —and a cast-iron ram had been added to her bow. On March 8, 1862, this powerful ironclad, renamed the *Virginia*, steamed down the Elizabeth River to attack the Union blockading squadron in Hampton Roads. With ease the *Virginia* rammed and shelled the *Cumberland*. The *Congress* was then destroyed by hotshot with heavy casualties. Southerners were jubilant as their newspapers predicted the raising of the blockade and the reduction of Washington.

Secretary of the Navy Welles, however, had early in the war contracted for several new types of ironclads; one of these, the *Monitor*, now made her appearance in Hampton Roads. Although the *Monitor* presented a simple appearance, like a "cheese box on a raft," its construction revealed advanced engineering techniques. Her distinguishing features were her small size, her low, flat hull hung a few inches above the waterline, and her central revolving gun turret, which proved impregnable against ten-inch shot at close range.

On March 9 the *Virginia*, returning to attack the *Minnesota* and the rest of the blockading squadron below Fort Monroe, was challenged by the *Monitor*. There followed a hotly fought duel at close quarters in which the *Monitor* protected the *Minnesota* from the onslaught of the Confederate ironclad. Neither vessel did much damage to the other, and after several hours of fighting both quit as if by mutual agreement.

In May 1862, during the Peninsular Campaign, George B. McClellan and his troops marched toward Richmond. They captured Yorktown on May 4, 1862. When Norfolk fell to Union hands, the James River lay open. Goldsborough, still commanding the North Atlantic Blockading Squadron, realized that there was a good chance of the Navy reaching Richmond. The Union iron-

Left: Once portions of the rivers were taken from the Confederates, the ships of the squadron had to patrol them to prevent Rebel crossings and maintain supply and communications. Here at White House, on the Pamunkey River in Virginia, several of these smaller craft go about their tasks. (USAMHI)

Above: One of the converted New York ferries, the Commodore Morris *spent its entire war career on the rivers of Virginia. The ferryboats were unsuited to operations on the ocean. (USAMHI)*

Above: Officers aboard one of the "Commodore" class ferry-gunboats. (CHS)

Right: The USS Commodore Barney *patrolled the James River and the inland waterways of North Carolina. (USAMHI)*

Below: The Commodore Barney's *officers on her foredeck. Cannon and shot now line the deck once used by commuters to New York City. (USAMHI)*

Right: Larger ships like the USS Maratanza, *a side-wheeler gunboat, ventured out of the rivers to take the occasional blockade-runner or Confederate naval vessel. This ship engaged the Rebel gunboat* Teaser *on July 4, 1862, when the* Teaser *tried to run down the James to launch an observation balloon following the Seven Days battles. James Gibson made his image the same day. (LC)*

clad *Galena* drew too much water to reach the Confederate capital, but the approach of the *Monitor* and wooden gunboats might render the city untenable.

Unfortunately for the Union, the ironclads *Galena* and *Monitor*, accompanied by wooden gunboats, were halted by Confederate batteries at Drewry's Bluff, near Richmond. The *Galena* was riddled. Besides severe damage to the hull, she lost thirteen men and eleven were badly wounded. The *Monitor* was uninjured, but due to the comparatively long range at which she fired, her nonrifled guns made little impression on the Confederate works. The engagement at Drewry's Bluff was an undoubted tribute to Confederate energy and ingenuity but a discouraging reverse for the Union Navy. It meant that Army cooperation was essential to take Richmond or any other well-defended port. The Goldsborough-Burnside work in the North Carolina sounds was itself finally halted in early July 1862 when a defeated General McClellan recalled the Army unit to the James River in Virginia.

In fact, the trickiest shoreline to blockade on the Atlantic Coast was that of the Cape Fear River sector, for the river leading to Wilmington had two navigable outlets forty miles apart, both of which were guarded by forts and coastal batteries. As the war continued, the North Atlantic Blockading Squadron began lining up its gunboats in two rows off each of these entrances. The sluggish, barely seaworthy vessels were stationed near the beach, with orders not to chase the blockade-runners out to sea but to flash their position to the swifter Union gunboats farther out. The course the runner was steering was indicated by rocket signals (e.g., one rocket and a white light meant northwestward, and so forth). During the daylight hours in clear weather, when conditions were unsuitable for a runner's escape, the blockading steamers anchored, enabling the captains, officers, and men to sleep. Half an hour before sunset the inshore patrol boats hoisted anchor, got under way and, as twilight fell, moved in toward the beach, keeping a taut watch on Rebel coastal batteries. The speedier Union vessels operating off Wilmington policed an area that extended forty miles offshore. They chased and picked off British and Confederate freighters, signaling the inshore blockade regarding inbound runners.

One afternoon the men on board the blockader *Florida* had their fishing interrupted by a shout:

"Sail ho! two points off the port bow." The officer of the deck sang out to the captain, "That's an Englishman, sir, sure as there's snakes in Virginny." The *Florida* got under way as the captain bellowed to the chief engineer, "Give her all you can." The *Florida* trembled. "The welcome relief from the monotony of months, that had nearly driven men crazy, had come at last," a seaman noted. Changing courses frequently, the *Florida* shortened the distance to the runner until she was within range. Yankee guns blazed. One shot splashed close to the runner's bow. She surrendered.

Approaching the British freighter, the crew of the *Florida* saw sailors jettisoning cargo and papers and preparing to abandon ship. "Train the two pivots on her," the captain of the *Florida* ordered, running out to the bridge and hailing the Britisher: "Throw one more thing… overboard and I'll send a broadside into you, and let you go to the bottom… I shan't pick up a single man." A prize crew was placed on board the runner *Calypso*, and her passengers were transferred to the *Florida*.

Except for such actions, most Civil War duty at sea was monotonous. Some bluejackets who served on board the blockaders described shipboard routine as "pretty stupid." Although the work in the Navy involved neither the degree of peril nor the amount of privation that attended the military campaigns, the awful boredom was broken only by exposure to the elements and blockade-runners dashing out for the open sea. At night no lights or noises were permitted on board the Yankee gun boats, hatches were covered, and lanterns were dimmed with casings. Expecting to sight enemy craft at any minute, crews stood ready to slip cables and man the guns; steam was kept up; officers slept half dressed, with their sidearms within easy reach. A naval lieutenant declared in a letter to home that he was "being used up so fast by the anxieties and climate together" that if he should spend more time on blockade duty he would not be "worth a damn."

Characteristic of any navy at any time, complaints by Union bluejackets increased as the Civil War lengthened from months into years. The men grumbled about everything from the daily routine, hard work, and heat to food, homesickness, and the absence of girls. Journals, letters, courts-martial proceedings, and newspaper accounts all

Left: Gibson's image of the deck of the Teaser *after her capture. In the background stands her captor, the* Maratanza. *(LC)*

Below: The Teaser's *stern gun, a ten-pounder Parrott rifle, did no better. This first "aircraft carrier," complete with silk balloon, was abandoned by its crew. (LC)*

Above: The Teaser's *bow gun, a thirty-two-pounder with reinforced breech, was no match for the* Maratanza, *which put a shot into the Confederate's boiler early in the engagement. (LC)*

Above: The tug-boat Clyde *on the James River. All vessels great and small had work to do in the North Atlantic Blockading Squadron. (NA)*

Above: Most captivating of all the ships patrolling the Southern rivers for the squadron were the monitors. The photographers fell under their spell; more images were made of them than any other class of vessel. Here pose the officers of the USS Sangamon, *like most monitors named for a river. (USAMHI)*

Above: The seamen of the Sangamon, too, stand for the camera. The iron *"breastwork" above the turret was intended to protect lookouts from small arms fire. (NA)*

attest that the commonest grievance of the sailor in the North Atlantic Blockading Squadron concerned monotony. "During the last week," a seaman wrote home, "I have seen enough of the sea. I am not sea sick, but I am sick of the sea." On board the Florida, off Wilmington, a sailor penned the following in his diary:

> I told my mother, she could get a fair idea of our 'adventures,' if she would go on the roof of the house, on a hot summer day, and talk to half a dozen hotel hallboys, who are generally more intelligent, and agreeable, than the average officer.
>
> Then descend to the attic and drink some warm water, full of iron-rust. Then go on the roof again and repeat this 'adventurous process' at intervals, until she was tired out, and go to bed, with everything shut down tight, so as not to show a light.
>
> Adventure! Bah! The blockade is the wrong place for it

For those "raging lions" who believed that wars were won by firing cannon, the quiet and usually uneventful work of the blockade seemed to accomplish nothing.

As the war wore on, the North Atlantic Blockading Squadron, bolstered with more ships and men, executed hit-and-run commando raids along the hostile shores. Assistant Secretary of the Navy Fox recommended to the commander of the squadron, then Admiral Samuel P. Lee, that Union sailors sneak up rivers and destroy runners, arsenals, and saltworks. In late February 1864 a lieutenant effected a daring plot against an installation up the Cape Fear River. Twenty Federal sailors in two boats rowed up the river one cloudy night and disembarked directly in front of a Smithville hotel. Posting a guard for the boats, three officers and one seaman crept up to the commanding general's headquarters, gained entrance, and captured the chief engineer of the river defenses. To their disappointment the Union sailors discovered that the general had gone off to Wilmington. His chief aide, hearing the rumpus and thinking that the 1,000 soldiers in a nearby barracks had mutinied, scampered into the woods and neglected to turn in the alarm. The Federals, meanwhile, hauled away their prisoner so quietly that the Rebel sentries failed to notice. The Yan-

Above: One of the favorite iron monsters on the James, the USS Saugus. *Shown here with a torpedo boom and net in front, it spent nearly its entire career on the James. At war's end, however, it went to Washington to become a temporary prison for the conspirators in the Lincoln assassination. On the hill in the distance behind it is the "crow's nest" signal tower. (USAMHI)*

Above right: Officers of the Saugus. *The varying width of the white stripes on the turrets of this and other monitors was for identification from a distance. (NA)*

Right: The men of the Saugus, *or at least a few of them.* Monitor *crews were not large because of the cramped quarters below decks. (NA)*

Right: The Saugus *in the lead, as a fleet of monitors and other craft patrol the James. The boom across the river in front of the* Saugus *is intended to catch mines that the Confederates would put in the river to float down against Federal ships. The* Sangamon *is just behind, and to its right, in the distance, sits the* Mahopac. *At far left is the twin-turreted* Onondaga. *Between it and the* Sangamon *is the* Atlanta, *once a Confederate ironclad but now in Federal service. (USAMHI)*

kees were out of the harbor before the chief engineer was missed.

Such activities, although minor in importance, roused the anxiety of the Confederate troops in North Carolina. More men were shuttled to coastal areas. Officers reasoned that if boat expeditions could go up to Smithville unnoticed, Unionists could load barges with troops, land on the beaches, and destroy the forts guarding the Cape Fear River.

Besides such hit-and-run raids, the spirits of Union bluejackets were buoyed by the prospects of prize money from captured blockade-runners. Profits from the sale of a prize vessel were first split equally among the captors and the United States Government and, after a 5 percent cut to the squadron commander, the blockader's portion was divided up into twenty equal shares. The skipper took three for himself; the lieutenants, masters, and warrants took four; midshipmen and petty officers took six; and the sailors received the remaining seven.

Competition was keen. Some captains dipped into their own pockets and awarded $50 to the first man spotting a runner, while Congress authorized a $200 bounty to each sailor on board a Yankee gunboat that sank or destroyed an enemy of "equal or superior force" and a $100 bounty for each enemy ship of "inferior force."

When the little tug *Aeolus* pounced on the *Hope* off Wilmington in October 1864, the master won $13,164; the assistant engineer $6,657, or more than four years' pay; the seamen over $1,000 apiece; and the cabin boy $532. Nine days later the *Aeolus* assisted in taking the *Lady Sterling*, which, with her cargo, sold for $509,354.64. Each seaman on board the tug reaped $2,000 from the sale of the Britisher, making $3,000 in prize money for ten days' work.

Officers sitting out the war on the beach bitterly condemned the prize money system for obvious reasons. Admiral Porter also complained that such laws weakened a strict blockade since each man was more interested in looking out for his own interests than in cooperating with his flotilla. Although later in the war Porter condemned the system, when he commanded the North Atlantic Blockading Squadron it was dubbed the "prize money command." Among Union officers, Admiral Lee, who was chief of this squadron for several years, piled up the single largest chunk of prize money, netting $109,689, while the disapproving Porter, running a close second, banked $91,528.

From the beginning of the Atlantic coastal war, Secretary of the Navy Gideon Welles wished to close the port of Wilmington to Confederate commerce. The task was not easy. Natural conditions forced the Yankee squadron to post ships at both openings of the river; because of the weather its gunboats were often in danger of being driven

Left: The Onondaga, *a workhorse twin-turreted monitor on the James. Only two double-turreted monitors saw service during the war, and when Porter stripped the James fleet for the attack on Fort Fisher, the* Onondaga *was left to defend the James almost single-handedly. (USAMHI)*

Left: The Onondaga *on the James, with the USS* Mackinaw *partially hidden at left. (USAMHI)*

Left: The Onondaga, *pound for pound perhaps the finest monitor built during the war. (USAMHI)*

Left: Besides the monitors, special double-ended gunboats, like the USS Mendota, *were also built. Possessing reversible engines, they could steam up or down a narrow river or channel without turning around. She is shown here at Deep Bottom on the James in 1864. (USAMHI)*

Above: The officers of the Mendota. *Commander E. T. Nichols, in white trousers, is seated in the right foreground. (USAMHI)*

Right: The crew of the Mendota *on the foredeck, a Parrott rifle aimed over the starboard side. (USAMHI)*

Below: The view from the crow's nest, with the Saugus *at left and the* Sangamon *at right. (USAMHI)*

Above: On patrol on the James. An unknown gunboat appears in the foreground, and the Mahopac *is visible in the distance. (COURTESY OF BRUCE GIMELSON)*

Above: The little monitor Casco *on the James, near Dutch Gap, in early 1865. Three side-wheel gunboats and another monitor lie astern. (NA)*

ashore. "Cape Fear River," wrote Welles, "is more difficult to blockade than any other port [entrance] on the coast of the United States." The Richmond *Dispatch* claimed that it was "a matter of absolute impossibility" for the Federals to stop Southern blockade-running at Wilmington.

The capture of the Florida sounds in 1862, the closing of Savannah as a port, and the continuous bombardment of Charleston in 1863 by the South Atlantic Blockading Squadron turned the attention of blockade-runners toward Wilmington on the Cape Fear River. By August 1863 the Confederate officer in charge of the blockade-running could report that Wilmington had become the chief supply center of the Confederacy. Forts Fisher and Caswell guarded the approaches to Cape Fear. For one reason or another, plans for an assault against these forts were shelved. In the fall of 1864, however, it seemed necessary, more than ever, to Union strategy that Wilmington should be taken. Secretary Welles confided that the closing of this harbor and the cutting off of communications with Richmond was paramount and "more important, practically, than the capture of Richmond."

Plans for an amphibious assault against Fort Fisher were worked out. In early December 1864, 6,500 troops commanded by General Butler were assigned to the expedition for the assault. Admiral Porter, now commanding the North Atlantic Blockading Squadron, amassed "the most formidable armada ever" and hoped to hand over Fort Fisher "to the Government as a fitting Christmas present." During those early December days Butler and Porter failed to work out any coordinated attack doctrine.

In late December 1864 the army transports, tenders, and small craft—eighty-five in all—steamed out of Hampton Roads. Off the Cape Fear River Porter calculated that Butler and his troops would arrive so that they could land before 8 A.M. on December 24. But at 8 A.M. the trans-

Left: The Saugus, Sangamon, *the former Confederate ironclad* Atlanta, *and the* Onondaga *make one of the endless patrols on the James in the final months of the war. (NA)*

Left: The Mackinaw *and the* Saugus *on the Appomattox River in the summer of 1864. (USAMHI)*

Right: One of the dangers facing these rivercraft of the North Atlantic Blockading Squadron was the torpedoes made by Confederate engineers. Here, late in 1864, Federal engineers disarm enemy mines near Dutch Gap on the James. One such mine rests at the feet of the officer with the long pipe. At the right of the image is the portable darkroom and boxes of equipment of the photographer, Egbert G. Fowx. (LC)

Right: Lieutenant Hunter Davidson, once commander of the ill-fated Teaser, *took charge of the development of the dreaded torpe-does, thus exacting his measure of revenge, for the mines sank more Federal ships than did Confederate guns. (NHC)*

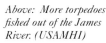

Right: The squadron did more than simply patrol rivers. Daring men and ships engaged the Confederates frequently. More than once they launched raids against the Rebel ironclads that often protected the harbors and upper reaches of the rivers. On October 27-28, 1864, Lieutenant William B. Cushing led a courageous expedition up Albemarle Sound, North Carolina, to destroy the dreaded ironclad CSS Albemarle. *(USAMHI)*

Above: More torpedoes fished out of the James River. (USAMHI)

Below: With a torpedo mounted at the end of a spar on his steam launch, Cushing drove it against the submerged hull of the Albemarle *under darkness and sank her immediately. Here she lies as pho-tographed shortly afterward by Plymouth photographer W. B. Rose. The Federals later raised her. (NHC)*

Below: The Federals put another captured Confederate ironclad, the CSS Atlanta, *into service patrolling the James. She was captured by the monitor* Weehawken *in Wessaw Sound, Georgia, on June 17, 1863, in her first and only battle. Here her new Union officers pose on the foredeck. The characteristic slope-sided casemate of a Confederate ironclad rises behind them. (USAMHI)*

ports were nowhere to be seen. Porter waited until shortly before noon and then decided to start the bombardment against Fort Fisher without the troops. At 11:30 A.M. Porter signaled the squadron to start the attack, with the *New Ironsides* and the monitors *Monadnock, Canonicus,* and *Mahopac* lead-ing the forty-six wooden ships.

Guns blazed from the fort and the fight be-came general. After an hour and a half the Con-federates ceased firing, but Porter's ships maintained the barrage. At sunset a few of Butler's transports came into view, but it was now too late to effect a landing. That night, onboard Porter's flagship, Major General Godfrey Weitzel, who was to lead the attack, arrived to discuss the next day's operation. Porter and Weitzel decided that while the Navy attacked Fort Fisher, the Army would land and assault under the cover of twenty-seven gun boats.

On Christmas Day the *New Ironsides*, the mon-itors, and the wooden gunboats steamed into po-sition and commenced pounding the fort. By midafternoon 2,000 soldiers had landed. What General Weitzel saw when he came up made him shiver. Fort Fisher was the strongest bastion that he had "ever seen or heard of." Noting that the fort had not been "materially injured" by naval gunfire, the general withdrew, boarded a dispatch boat, and reported to Butler that "it would be butchery to order an assault." Five hundred ad-vanced troops had moved to within "150 paces" of Fort Fisher, and had sent back word to move up reinforcements, but a messenger arrived with or-ders to retreat and re-embark.

Porter was incensed. He accused the Army of "cowardice," Weitzel of "having no backbone," and Butler of being "a failure."

When news reached Washington, Northerners wanted to know who was responsible for the fail-ure. *Harper's Weekly* declared that someone had blundered and pointed its finger at Butler, while the New York *Herald* termed the military phase of the expedition "a ridiculous fizzle." In Washing-ton naval strategists "toasted confusion" to Butler and to all "civilian generals."

The lack of harmony between Army and Navy was partially responsible for the failure at Fort Fisher. Neither Porter nor Butler had been vested with overall authority and responsibility for the operation. The attack conclusively demonstrated the defects of a joint command, where neither branch of the service had final responsibility. This

Above: Commander John Newland Maffitt, shown here in a damaged and faded old photograph never previously published, enjoyed three Confederate careers. Besides being commander of the commerce raider CSS Florida, *he also proved a nuisance to the North Atlantic Blockading Squadron as a captain of several blockade-runners, and then, for a time, served as commander of the ironclad* Albemarle. *His adventuring did not stop with the war. He went on to serve foreign governments and Cuban revolutionaries before retiring to North Carolina. (TU)*

Above: While the Confederates could never mount much of a fleet on the rivers, they did emplace batteries along the James and other streams to interdict the passage of Federal traffic. Batteries like this Federal emplacement near Fort Brady on the James commanded a clear field of fire against any hostile vessels, and often had to be taken from the land side before ships could pass. (USAMHI)

deficiency was fortunately rectified in the final amphibious assault of the war.

Three days following the Fort Fisher defeat Admiral Porter, who was still with his squadron off North Carolina, jotted a note to Assistant Secretary Fox. The repulse "is only temporary," Porter said, "for we can take it [i.e., Fort Fisher] at any time—Don't give it up, we will have it yet." On December 30 General Grant at City Point, believing that the Confederates had been lulled into a sense of false security, urged Porter to hold his position, promised an increased force "without the former commander," and took steps to collect more transports.

Porter was happy over Grant's renewed interest. The admiral suggested that the troops rendezvous at Beaufort, North Carolina, where by this time most of his squadron was engaged in loading coal and ammunition. At City Point preparations were being made to get the troops ready for the expedition. Major General Alfred Terry was placed in command of 8,000 troops, most of them veterans of the first Fort Fisher Campaign. Grant told Terry that it was desirable that "a most complete understanding" should exist between him and Porter, and that he should consult with the admiral freely and "get from him the part to be performed by each branch of the public service" so that there would be "unity of action." Grant told Terry to defer to Porter "as much as is consistent with your own responsibilities." Acting on the lesson learned, the army chief was unofficially suggesting that Terry regard Porter as the commander of the joint operation.

On January 8, 1865, Porter and his commanders spied the troopships heading toward Beaufort.

Above: Rear Admiral Samuel P. Lee replaced Goldsborough in command of the North Atlantic Blockading Squadron and intensified efforts against blockade-runners. (USAMHI)

Left: Admiral Raphael Semmes, the commander of the James River fleet for the Confederates at the close of the war, was a man already famed for his high seas adventures. Once captain of the feared commerce raiders Sumter *and* Alabama, *he finished the war in Richmond. He destroyed his fleet rather than see it captured with the fall of the capital, and then accompanied the fleeing Confederate government. (VM)*

Above: Lee's flagship was the USS Agawam, *shown here on the James. (USAMHI)*

Above: She was a powerful ship. Here her crew poses with a massive one hundred-pounder Parrott rifle. (NHC)

Above: Lee continued the capture of hostile shipping, and his sailors continued to share the prize money. The Lady Sterling, *also called the* Hornet *and the* Cuba, *brought over half a million dollars in prize court. She is photographed here by C. W. Yates in Wilmington, North Carolina, in 1865, while serving as the USS* Hornet. *(NHC)*

Right: Eventually Lee, too, was replaced by Admiral David D. Porter. The latter appears here at left, seated beside Major General George G. Meade, in an image taken in May 1865. Though he often conspired against his brother, David G. Farragut, still Porter rose in fame and accomplishment and deserved the new command. He earned it in the operations to take Fort Fisher. (USAMHI)

Below: Moral support for the blockading squadron came from across the Atlantic, from the czar. The Russian frigate Osliaba *came into the harbor at Alexandria, as did other Russian vessels in New York and San Francisco. They were old ships, not terribly useful in a sea battle should the British or French enter the war on the side of the Confederacy, but their presence was nevertheless a symbol of the czar's support for Lincoln. A. J. Russell made this image. (LC)*

They were quickly coaled. Four days later the Federal expedition, composed of 53 naval vessels and 19 transports, started for Fort Fisher. By evening the expedition was off the Confederate stronghold, which Rebel commitments elsewhere had reduced to a force of only 800.

At daylight on January 13, 5 ironclads and 48 wooden vessels steamed to their positions. Headed by the *Brooklyn*, a detachment of vessels maneuvered to within 600 yards of the beach to assist landing operations. *New Ironsides* and the monitors were ordered to anchor 1,000 yards from the fort and "pour in their fire." At 8 A.M. the *New Ironsides* and the monitors opened fire, while a half hour later troops landed up the beach under the command of the Navy. The first 500 soldiers waded ashore unopposed.

In a dense forest a short distance away a Rebel division, numbering 6,000, under General Braxton Bragg had just arrived from Wilmington. It watched the Federal landing, but due to an intervening swamp and "the heavy metal of the fleet," it refused to budge from its hiding place. Bragg rationalized that not even "Grant's army could… storm and carry the fort." Without firing a musket, the division retreated when it later learned that "everything at Fort Fisher was in confusion."

The landing proceeded. The beach was "black with men with their bayonets glittering in the sun shine and their regimental flags fluttering in the breeze." By 3 P.M. 8,000 Federal soldiers had landed. As soon as they dried out, Terry's main force moved inland toward Fort Fisher, located five miles away. During the entire day Porter's fleet pounded the fort. To remedy the miserable showing his ships had made on the previous as-

Left: From his headquarters at Fort Monroe Porter built his armada for the assault on Fort Fisher. Thousands of men and seamen passed over this wharf. The Hygeia Dining Saloon fed hundreds of them. (USAMHI)

Left: Porter himself made his headquarters aboard the USS Malvern. *Here he poses with his staff in December 1864. Standing at far left is William B. Cushing, destroyer of the Albemarle. Porter is in the center with his hand across his chest. (USAMHI)*

Left: Porter called his command "the most formidable armada ever." Here several ships of his fleet ride out a storm off Hampton Roads in December 1864, before leaving for the attack on Fort Fisher. (USAMHI)

Below: Cushing was now a commander, promoted in recognition of his exploits against the Albemarle. *At Fort Fisher he would risk his life for over six hours in a small boat as he sounded and marked the channel for the larger ships to approach the fort. Then he would lead an assault against the ramparts of the fort itself. Here he is only twenty-two years old. His brother, Alonzo, also aged twenty-two, was already killed at Gettysburg. (USAMHI)*

Below: Porter's fleet included Lee's old flagship, the Agawam. *(CHS)*

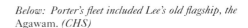

Above: The ironclads were organized into a separate division, commanded by Rear Admiral William Radford. (USAMHI)

Right: Steamers like the USS Rhode Island will tow some of the ironclads to North Carolina waters, since the monitors are unstable in rough seas. Indeed, the Rhode Island was towing the original Monitor when the little ironclad went down in two hundred feet of water off Cape Hatteras in December 1862. (NA)

Above: There are familiar ships here, like the Saugus, shown in the James River a few months later. (USAMHI)

Below: Her officers can look to more action, indeed, more than they have yet seen in their river service. (USAMHI)

Above: The sloop of war Mohican, shown here off the Washington Navy Yard, joined the burgeoning fleet. (CWTI)

sault, the admiral had issued detailed firing instructions.

Urgent pleas went out from the beleaguered fort for reinforcements. In the midst of the bombardment, area commander Major General W.H.C. Whiting arrived at the fort, shook hands with the commanding officer, Colonel William Lamb, and said, "Lamb, my boy, I have come to share your fate. You and your garrison are to be sacrificed."

At nightfall Porter ordered the wooden vessels to haul off and the monitors to keep up their firing. On the beach darkness also overtook the military, who were forced to halt for the night. As January 14 dawned, the wooden vessels took their positions next to the monitors and fired until sundown.

Porter now regarded the fort as "reduced to a pulp." His calculation was correct. Every Confederate gun on the land front had been knocked out, all defensive barriers had been torn up, and not a man had dared "show his head" in that "infernal storm" of shellfire. The Army, meanwhile, was still in the process of unloading its field artillery

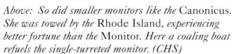

Above: So did smaller monitors like the Canonicus. She was towed by the Rhode Island, experiencing better fortune than the Monitor. Here a coaling boat refuels the single-turreted monitor. (CHS)

Right: Acting Assistant Paymaster Henry M. Meade of the USS Mattabessett went along. He was General Meade's nephew. (P-M)

and was forced to wait throughout the day at a distance of nearly two miles from Fort Fisher.

That evening on board the Malvern Terry and Porter decided to attack the following day, January 15. The naval bombardment was to continue and the assault was scheduled for 3 P.M. The soldiers were to attack the rear of the fort, while armed sailors were to strike the eastern side, or sea face.

In the early morning hours of January 15 the Federal squadron moved in once again and by 10 A.M. it was pounding the fort. The naval assault force, composed of 1,600 sailors and 400 marines, landed two miles up the beach from the bastion. At precisely 3 P.M. a long blast on the Malvern's steam whistle signaled the assault. Naval vessels ceased the bombardment of the stronghold. On board sailors watched their shipmates on the shore jump up, cheering, and run down the open beach. The Rebels, seeing this assault, thought it was the main attack, and nearly the whole force lunged for the sea face. In an instant the entire front wall was "one dense mass of musketeers" who poured a "hot fire" into the advancing bluejackets.

Some Federals reached the parapets of the fort but were mowed down and "slaughtered unmercifully." The wounded limped or crawled out of range, while the dead and dying lay strewn along the beach. The naval charge, though unsuccessful, acted as a decoy for the main military assault and allowed the first detachments of Terry's men to reach the rear parapets unmolested. Army officers were the first to admit that had there been no naval attack, their losses would have been severe. While the attention of the fort was focused on the sea front, the first brigade of soldiers effected a lodgment on the rear parapets and fired into the backs of the Rebels. The defenders turned, but

Left: And the Mahopac will go along. (USAMHI)

Left: So did the USS Santiago de Cuba. She was a merchant side-wheeler at the war's opening, and was then purchased by the Navy Department. With a fine sense of diplomacy, the Navy sent her to patrol the waters around Havana, Cuba, in search of blockade-runners. It was a nice touch, having a ship named for a Cuban city assigned to her shores, especially since the Cubans were rather disposed to favor the Confederacy. (USAMHI)

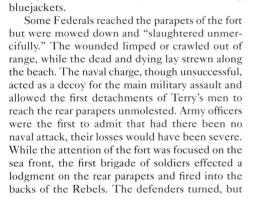

Right: Porter's great "armada" lying off Hampton Roads and ready for the Fort Fisher expedition. Timothy O'Sullivan is probably the artist responsible for this vivid view. Only one of the ships can be identified, the workhorse ironclad New Ironsides. She rests at anchor, the third ship to the right of the vessel in the center of the image. Her bow slopes downward toward the water rather than outward from it. (LC)

Right: Porter's objective, Fort Fisher. O'Sullivan captured these images after the fort was taken on Porter's second try in January 1865. This is the view of part of the face of the earthworks seen from the shore. (USAMHI)

Right: An assault from the ocean would first have to send troops against and over the wooden obstruction, right in the face of cannon fire from the fort. (USAMHI)

Right: The formidable nature of the fort is better seen from the inside. This view of the first three traverses shows the heavy protection afforded each gun. (USAMHI)

the Federals had already gained their initial footing. Other Union brigades rushed forward to support the first.

There was desperate fighting on the parapets. By 5 P.M. the Union soldiers possessed half the land front of Fort Fisher. The fighting for each traverse continued until nearly 9 P.M., when the Confederates, seeing that further resistance was useless, fled from the stronghold. Across Cape Fear River Confederates blew up their remaining installations. The Union had captured Fort Fisher.

On board the gunboat *Gettysburg* an officer assessed the situation: "I firmly believe the Rebels will feel the loss of Fort Fisher more keenly and that our victory here will do more towards the return of peace than anything that has yet been done. We stop supplies." Porter agreed, for he considered the victory "the death blow to the rebellion." To William T. Sherman Porter declared "The door through which the enemy was fed, is closed on them, and all we have to do, is to watch them starve."

By mid-February 1865 Porter and the military units captured Wilmington. Thousands of Tarheels slipped away from the Confederate armies and went home. Late in February General Robert E. Lee declared that the despair of the North Carolinians was destroying his army and that desertions were becoming frequent. The blockade-running bases in the West Indies were hit hard. After the fall of Wilmington one sea captain reported that speculators in Nassau saw that "the bottom had fallen out," and that all of them were in the "depths of despair." Even the stevedores and laborers bewailed the misfortune, for they knew that "the glory of Nassau had departed

Below: O'Sullivan's image of "The Pulpit," the heavily protected bombproof dug right into the earth face of the fort. The calm aspect of the Federal soldiers hardly betrays the excitement and frenzy of the day of their attack. (CHS)

Below: Another traverse, now in ruin after the naval bombardment. (USAMHI)

Above: A British Armstrong gun in place. This is one of many heavily reinforced seacoast guns that the Confederacy obtained from Great Britain despite England's supposed neutrality. (USAMHI)

forever." By March 1865 the blockade-running captains had shifted their base to Havana for the run to Galveston, Texas, and minor ports on the Gulf Coast which still remained open. Except for maintaining the blockade and clearing Confederate harbors of mines, the amphibious assault against Fort Fisher in early 1865 signaled the end of naval operations along the Carolina seaboard.

To accurately gauge the North Atlantic Blockading Squadron's efficiency or its influence on the final collapse of the Confederacy is extremely difficult. Owing to the secrecy required in blockade-running, British and Confederate shipowners and merchants either failed to keep or burned, lost, or completely destroyed cargo statistics, arrival and departure reports, and lists of vessels engaged in the traffic. Years later a historian poring over Confederate newspapers and other documents wrote several articles in The *American Neptune* during the 1940s. Although he neglected to divide the operations of the North and South Atlantic Blockading Squadrons, he concluded in his article on the blockade of the Carolina ports that between 1861 and 1865 more than 2,054 attempts were made to penetrate the Yankee squadrons, a daily average of one and a half runs. Eighty-four percent of the known attempts were successful.

The measure of the blockade's effectiveness, however, lay not in the number of ships seized but rather in the number of cargoes rotting on Liverpool docks and the number of British vessels that never got under way for Nassau. Shipowners who ordinarily would have deposited freight at Carolina wharves were deterred by nightmares of capture, resulting in bankruptcy and, possibly, the poor house. Better by far that the Confederacy should starve than that they should as well. Paper blockade though it might be, the Union's naval embrace of the Southern coastline proved effective against many of its suitors.

Above: An interior view of "The Pulpit." Accommodations were, to say the least, spartan. (USAMHI)

Left: An interior view of the first six traverses on the seaward face of Port Fisher. Littering the sand are cannon shot, probably misses fired by Porter's fleet as they pounded the traverses. (USAMHI)

Left: A banded rifle broken at the muzzle by the heavy fire from the Federal fleet (USAMHI)

Left: Another Armstrong. The carriage has imprinted upon it "Sir W. G. Armstrong & Co. Newcastle-Upon-Tyne." It is a 150-pounder cannon with an 8-inch bore, one of the most formidable guns in the South. (USAMHI)

Right: The land side of the fort was less built up since the Confederates only anticipated an attack from the sea. (USAMHI)

Left: Several ruined carriages and dismounted cannon lie amid these three traverses. (USAMHI)

Right: Another columbiad now peering silently out upon a seascape that is undisputedly Union territory. Once stilled, the mighty guns of Fort Fisher, once the most feared Confederate fortress on the Atlantic, never spoke again. (USAMHI)

Left: A columbiad with its muzzle blown away by a direct hit from one of Porter's ships. (USAMHI)

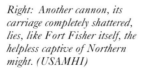

Right: Another cannon, its carriage completely shattered, lies, like Fort Fisher itself, the helpless captive of Northern might. (USAMHI)

Left: The shot furnace et the fort, used for heating solid shot until it was red-hot. Fired against wooden ships, hot shot could start disastrous fires and detonate magazines. (NA)

Left: The entrance to the fort is at left, next to the first traverse. The two dismounted cannon lying at the water's edge are columbiads, with the remains of their carriages next to them. Either the Confederates never had time to get them up on the traverse and mounted or else the Federals' fire cast them back down into the sand and mud. (USAMHI)

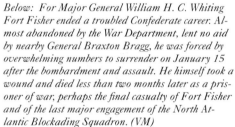

Below: For Major General William H. C. Whiting Fort Fisher ended a troubled Confederate career. Almost abandoned by the War Department, lent no aid by nearby General Braxton Bragg, he was forced by overwhelming numbers to surrender on January 15 after the bombardment and assault. He himself took a wound and died less than two months later as a prisoner of war, perhaps the final casualty of Fort Fisher and of the last major engagement of the North Atlantic Blockading Squadron. (VM)

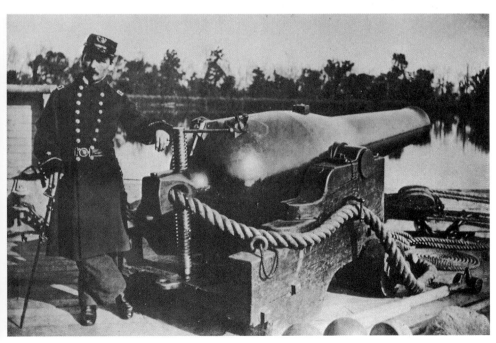

Above: Meanwhile the Yankee ships kept on at their work. Ships like the USS Hunchback, shown here on the James, maintained their ceaseless vigil on the Southern rivers and coastline, seeking to do the Navy's part in putting an end to the Civil War. (NA)

New Bern in North Carolina

A PORTFOLIO

One peaceful southern town
that looked far, far away from the conflict

The quiet streets of a lovely Southern town to which war has come. New Bern, North Carolina, was much contested during the war, commanding as it did the North Carolina Railroad linking Raleigh with the sea, as well as the Neuse River. Yet somehow it always managed to look peaceful, more a Southern still life than a town at war. Its quiet streets rarely betrayed the conflict of which it was a part. (USAMHI)

Left: The headquarters of Major General John G. Foster in New Bern as it looked in 1862 or early 1863. Foster himself stands in front of the second pillar from the left. Private residences like this one bustled with military activity as officers rented or occupied rooms. (SOCIETY FOR THE PRESERVATION OF NEW ENGLAND ANTIQUITIES)

Left: Foster and his staff posed yet again for the camera in front of their decidedly plush headquarters. While active field generals—even Grant, Lee, and Sherman—lived in tents, officers with comfortable occupation assignments like New Bern enjoyed rare amenities. (USAMHI)

Left: Now and then even the men in the ranks enjoyed some of the pleasures of this sedentary duty. They are not gone soft on garrison duty, yet there is an informal, relaxed atmosphere in their jaunty pose. The constant threat of battle and death does not trouble them—or New Bern. The town and its conquerors look comfortable with each other. (USAMHI)

Below: Another peaceful home now host to the men in blue. (USAMHI)

Above: General Foster actually made his residence in this modest dwelling. (USAMHI)

Above: A brigade headquarters at the corner of a New Bern street. The proud colonels stand on the porch, their horses awaiting. In fact, they really had nowhere to go. (SOCIETY FOR THE PRESERVATION OF NEW ENGLAND ANTIQUITIES)

Left: Company H of an unknown regiment, probably from Massachusetts, traded their tents for this fine house. There were servants available for tiny sums, pleasant weather, pretty ladies, and rather little military excitement. Most of the time in New Bern the Yankee soldiers could almost forget the war. (SOCIETY FOR THE PRESERVATION OF NEW ENGLAND ANTIQUITIES)

Below: Company I of the 44th Massachusetts spent nine months in the Union service, almost all of it at New Bern. They appear here on September 25, 1862, at Readville, Massachusetts. Their uniforms will be little soiled in their months in North Carolina. (USAMHI)

Above: Five comrades of Company F, 44th Massachusetts. They proved gentlemanly occupiers. (COURTESY OF MICHAEL J. MCAFEE)

Above: Major J. L. Stackpole sits on the steps of his home, surrounded by his family and a few fellow officers. It could be a scene from back home in Massachusetts: the peaceful street; the carriage lazily awaiting; the shy lady, unwilling to come outside, who sits in the window at right. (SOCIETY FOR THE PRESERVATION OF NEW ENGLAND ANTIQUITIES)

Left: And here "Company E" watches the war pass them by. (SOCIETY FOR THE PRESERVATION OF NEW ENGLAND ANTIQUITIES)

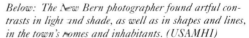

Below: The New Bern photographer found artful contrasts in light and shade, as well as in shapes and lines, in the town's homes and inhabitants. (USAMHI)

Above: The town's public buildings became warehouses. (USAMHI)

Above right: Its little restaurants, like this one, bulged with hungry soldiers. (USAMHI)

Right: While great battles like Fredericksburg and Chancellorsville raged in Virginia, and while Vicksburg starved under siege, New Bern passed along in its tranquil path through the war. (USAMHI)

Left: The occupiers seemed to be everywhere, yet the lack of tents and stockades made them seem less threatening somehow. They hung their blankets out of windows to air just like the citizens. They chopped their firewood and cooled themselves in the breezes just like the civilians. (SOCIETY FOR THE PRESERVATION OF NEW ENGLAND ANTIQUITIES)

Above: Thousands of placid scenes greeted the eyes of New Bern's considerate conquerors. (USAMHI)

Right: The backyards and gardens. (USAMHI)

Left: The former slaves gathered for the camera, their hopes of freedom written on their faces. (USAMHI)

Left: Even faces no longer visible in New Bern could still be seen. When the Confederates left the town, a photographer left behind several images of Southern officers in his gallery. There were old men… (USAMHI)

Right: … rather bemused-looking men… (USAMHI)

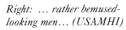

Right: ... those resplendent in their homemade finery. (USAMHI)

Far right: ... and the fully professional-looking soldiers like Colonel J. K. Jordan of the 31st North Carolina. A host of such faces of their enemies peered out at the Federals when they took the town. (USAMHI)

Below: Yet the occupiers' presence still was felt. They brought with them the United States Sanitary Commission to help tend the soldiers' medical and spiritual needs. (USAMHI)

Below right: To be sure, they brought a few tents with them. The officers of the 43rd Massachusetts made their headquarters under canvas. (USAMHI)

Right: They built some earthworks as a defense against possible attack. After all, New Bern was still in enemy country. Here Fort Totten appears as it did in August 1862, being garrisoned by the 3rd New York Artillery. (USAMHI)

Left: They brought their heavy guns to the ordnance yard on Craven Street, where many of them remained unused. (USAMHI)

Left: Meanwhile, New Bern, like so many other small towns in the South under occupation, enjoyed the luxury of being out of the way of the devastating armies. Escaping the death and destruction of the terrible war, New Bern and its people, Northerners and Southerners, lived out an existence somehow out of keeping with the terrible conflict raging all around. They learned of the war by reading of it, by going to F. W. Beers's book and stationery shop to buy Elements of Military Art & History *or* The Mounted Rifleman. *There was no good war, but for New Bern in North Carolina this one was not such a bad one. (USAMHI)*

Slaves No More

DUDLEY T. CORNISH

Negroes, slave and free, had to fight just to take part

The Negro began the Civil War little better off than he had been two centuries before. Though the foreign slave trade was abolished and much internal slave trafficking had been curtailed, all too many Negroes, at one time or another, still passed through slave pens like this one at Alexandria, Virginia, the establishment of Messrs. Price & Burch. (USAMHI)

De massa run? Ha, ha!
De darkey stay? Ho, ho!
It mus'be now de kingdom comin'
An' de year ob Jubilo!

HENRY CLAY WORK, 1862

FOR NEGROES our Civil War was the great divide between slavery and freedom, however limited and partial that freedom turned out to be. Even before the white songwriter had penned his prescient lyrics, Negroes sensed the fundamental meaning and promise of the war. Frederick Douglass, the foremost Negro leader of nineteenth-century America, read the future accurately as early as May 1861 and, with characteristic candor and eloquence, called for the recruitment of a Negro liberating army "to march into the South and raise the banner of emancipation among the slaves." If this proposal seemed as extreme as John Brown's fatal venture less than two years earlier, Douglass was convinced that circumstances in the rousing spring of '61 justified it: "The South having brought revolution and war upon the country, and having elected and consented to play at their fearful game," the Maryland ex-slave reasoned, "she has no right to complain if some good as well as calamity result from her own act and deed."

During a brief foray into historical biography in the 1920s, a white American novelist asserted that "American negroes are the only people in the history of the world, so far as I know, that ever became free without any effort of their own... [The Civil War] was not their business." So far as *he* knew, and his knowledge did not run far. From the very beginning of the war it was their business, and they were involved, North and South, East and West, from beginning to end. Negroes knew what the war was about even before Alexander H. Stephens of Georgia, Vice-President of the Confederacy, had clarified the issue in his "cornerstone speech"; they, however, saw in the war the final solution of the slavery controversy that had rent the Union. Even as their grandfathers found meaning in Thomas Jefferson's electric declaration—"all Men are created equal" and are "endowed by their Creator with certain unalienable Rights,"—so Frederick Douglass's generation felt in its bones that the year of Jubilo had arrived. Tens of thousands of Negroes were eager to help move toward what Abraham Lincoln later called "this great consummation." Hundreds of thousands of others were caught up in the tides of war as the "peculiar institution," of which they were the essential working parts, buckled, strained, and finally collapsed, crushed to death by the tightening coils of Winfield Scott's "Anaconda Plan." To suggest that Negroes saw the war only from the sidelines, as spectators, is to deny the facts and miss the heart of the conflict.

Certainly the American conflict officially began as a "white man's war" on both sides. It was only a matter of time, however, before the logic of the struggle extended its own parameters. It was simply impossible for the 3,953,760 slaves and their 488,070 free brothers and sisters (250,787 in the slave states at that) to ignore the struggle or to be ignored for long in the course of that struggle. President Lincoln made it clear that his primary war aim, indeed, his only war aim for the first eighteen months after the fall of Sumter, was the preservation of the Union. President Jefferson

Above: It was not a pleasant place. (USAMHI)

Davis made it just as clear that his primary war aim was the establishment of Southern independence, with slavery (Alexander Stephens's cornerstone) intact. Accordingly, from the opening rounds of the war Union generals offered to help border state governors put down slave insurrections "with an iron hand." Union troops served occasionally as "slave-catchers" in that same early phase. Spurred by protests, both civil and military, the Union Congress moved to halt both practices in the second spring of the war.

Ironically, Benjamin F. Butler, political general from Massachusetts, based his pragmatic solution to the problem on Confederate use of Negro labor to build fortifications within his field of observation. With the irritating logic that was his hallmark, Butler called fugitives from such military labor "contraband of war" and so added a new word to the American language, a new argument for congressional debate, and a new dimension to the war. Scarcely two weeks after First Bull Run the Union Congress passed its First Confiscation Act, providing for the seizure of all property used "in aid of the rebellion," including slaves. Despite all efforts to ignore slavery as a war issue, Negroes by their very presence—a mobile presence at that—helped make slavery an important issue. Before the war was a full year old slavery had been abolished in the District of Columbia and in all Federal territories, and an additional Article of War prohibited the military "rendition" of fugitives to Confederate masters.

Another political general, John C. Fremont of "Pathfinder" fame, commanding Union forces at St. Louis, stole a march on Lincoln on August 30, 1861, by declaring martial law in Missouri and freeing the slaves of every Rebel in the state! Despite much Northern applause, Lincoln, concerned for border state loyalty, modified Fremont's order to make it conform to the First Confiscation Act. Negroes, and not a few white Unionists, were dismayed at Lincoln's action; James Russell Lowell spoke for a growing minority when he asked, "How many times are we to save Kentucky and lose our self-respect?" Several weeks later Major General David Hunter replaced Fremont in command of the Western Department; as a regular officer and graduate of the U. S. Military Academy at West Point, Hunter was presumed to be safely conservative.

From the first weeks of the war Negroes

Above: The slaves of James Hopkinson on Edisto Island also lived a comfortable existence compared to many of their brethren in less lavish surroundings. (USAMHI)

Above: Joseph E. Davis, brother of the Confederate president, owned these slaves, shown standing in front of the library on Hurricane Plantation, south of Vicksburg, Mississippi. (OLD COURT HOUSE MUSEUM, VICKSBURG)

Right: The Negro cabins on General Thomas F. Drayton's plantation on Hilton Head, South Carolina, in 1862. A genuine little community existed on many of these larger farms, though, in fact, most slaves in the South belonged to masters who had only a handful of chattels. (USAMHI)

Below: On Cockspur Island, Georgia, this Negro cabin provides a closer look at the life of the average slave. (USAMHI)

Above: George S. Cook of Charleston captured this blurred yet starkly contrasted image of a slave "mammy" with the master's child entrusted to her care. The sense of family between white and black was widespread, one of the few happy circumstances of slavery. (COURTESY OF HERB PECK, JR.)

Above: For many, in fact, living space was so rudimentary as to be barely habitable. Here in Fredericksburg, Virginia, a slave family stands before its house, so ramshackle that cold winds could blow through it unimpeded. (USAMHI)

begged for permission to join the Union forces. Applications, proposals, and requests reached the War Department from Boston, New York, Philadelphia, Pittsburgh—even Cincinnati and Cleveland; all were uniformly rejected. Secretary of War Simon Cameron told Jacob Dodson of Washington, when the war was only a fortnight along, that "this Department has no intention at present to call into the service of the Government any colored soldiers." Cameron's personal intention had changed by the end of that year, with the result that Edwin M. Stanton replaced him, and Cameron went to Russia, in part because he had advocated arming the Negro to help save the Union. Meanwhile, articulate Negroes—editors, preachers, teachers, prominent leaders in their communities—agitated the question, arguing that they had a stake in the war, indeed, a greater stake than their white brethren. For the time being, however, John Brown's soul marched in almost exclusively white company; a few hundred lightskinned Negroes actually did enlist in a variety of Union regiments, and not only as cooks and waiters. Those whose racial identity was discovered were uniformly discharged.

From the first weeks of the war other Negroes took advantage of Union incursions into their neighborhoods and began to make their way to Union lines, away from plantations no longer secure and across the bridges leading from Virginia to Washington. Union field commanders first encountered the Negro refugee problem in substantial numbers in Virginia and North Carolina. But the first major disruption of the slave system came at the very end of 1861, when a powerful Army-Navy expedition led by Commodore Samuel F. Du Pont and Brigadier General Thomas W. Sherman descended on the coast of South Carolina and

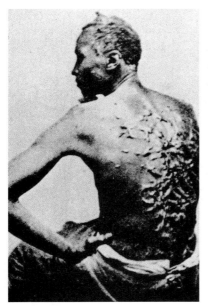

Far left: Slavery had its brutal side as well, when men had absolute power of life and death over their property. Wilson Chinn, a slave from Louisiana who also bore brands on his flesh, poses with instruments of punishment used on unruly Negroes. Such photographs were used during the war to inflame Northern passions and firm resolve against the slaveholders; they helped to exaggerate greatly the stories of cruelties against slaves. (USAMHI)

Left: But some stories were not exaggerations. J. W. Mercer, assistant surgeon of the 47th Massachusetts, examined 400 runaway slaves in Baton Rouge, Louisiana, in the summer of 1863 and found many "to be as badly lacerated as the specimen presented in the enclosed photograph," taken on April 2, 1863 The whip could be brutal in the hands of cruel men. This slave, Gordon, later became a corporal in the Union Army. (USAMHI)

established a beachhead at Port Royal. This beachhead, a sword in the side of the Confederacy, was steadily extended, year after year, down the fringe of the Sea Islands all the way to Florida. Here came the first fatal shock to the peculiar institution—and the first large-scale Union effort to deal with totally unprecedented problems.

With the death of slavery, what was to be done for, to, and with the thousands of slaves whose masters, hearing the guns of Du Pont's squadron smashing the forts at Port Royal, abandoned their rich tidal plantations and headed for safety inland? Under that First Confiscation Act those slaves were the property and responsibility of the Union, and Yankee ingenuity outdid itself in developing schemes and projects suitable to the opportunity. Here began, in Willie Lee Rose's happy phrase, a "rehearsal for reconstruction" which continued throughout the war, with results as various as the programs. While the Union Army had primary responsibility in the Department of the South (and both Army and Navy employed large numbers of former slaves at minimal wages), the Treasury Department got the job of organizing and operating the abandoned plantations; this was a dual assignment with the potential for intramural disputes. Whatever the practical problems of operation, whatever the quarrels between Treasury agents sent down to make cotton and military officers more concerned with making war, what resulted was a curious variety of activities revolving around this first major experiment to apply a wage system to slave labor, the first large-scale effort to shift from the forced labor of the plantation to a semblance of economic self-interest. Responsible for the social and economic well-being of the population on the Sea Islands as well as for the extension of Union military and naval operations in the Department—Port Royal became a major base for the Atlantic Blockade—Union officials, both civil and military, had their work cut out for them.

To counter the abysmal ignorance of the Sea Island population, isolated from the mainland plantations for generations, Edward L. Pierce of Boston, in charge of Treasury Department enterprises, recruited scores of young men and women from the North to establish and operate schools for the freedmen and their families. Negro reaction to this unprecedented opportunity was instant and

Left: The Federals soon dubbed as contrabands the flocks of slaves who escaped from their masters to seek refuge with the advancing armies. Camps for them were set up wherever the columns of the Union advanced. Here a wagonload of contrabands fords the Rappahannock in August 1862, following Pope's army. Timothy O'Sullivan made the image. (P-M)

Left: Contrabands congregated on the plantation of General Drayton once it came under Federal dominion. (USAMHI)

Left: There they continued to harvest and gin the cotton, only now it was for their own benefit rather than that of their onetime masters. (USAMHI)

Above: At Follie's farm, near Cumberland Landing on the Pamunkey River in Virginia, the contrabands posed for James Gibson while McClellan campaigned on the Peninsula. (USAMHI)

Above: At Williamsport, Virginia, in 1862 contrabands attached themselves to the 13th Massachusetts. Often whole families came. At first uncertain what to do with the Negroes, the armies frequently turned them to laboring and other service-oriented tasks. (USAMHI)

Left: These two tattered lads, called "intelligent contrabands," quite probably found their way into service as servants for a soldiers' "mess" or in an officer's tent. (USAMHI)

Below: An unidentified cavalry unit with some of the contrabands who followed them and tended to their needs, including washing and cooking. Many contrabands simply exchanged one form of servitude for another. (COURTESY OF RONN PALM)

overwhelming; letters and reports from "Gideon's Band," as the teachers were soon called, were rich in references to an eagerness to learn, from toddlers to grizzle-headed grandparents. To enrich the Port Royal experiment even more, several New England and New York entrepreneurs came down to put the abandoned plantations on a paying basis, for the most part with promising results. In those Sea Islands off South Carolina and Georgia began the first extensive, imaginative, and, on the whole, encouraging efforts to move a whole people from the old slavery basis of working for "Massa" to the new Yankee basis of working for wages and—though the promise was never quite achieved—on land of their very own. Former slaves worked directly to establish a degree of economic independence for themselves and indirectly against the very underpinning of "Massa's" struggle for political independence. From the start of the Port Royal experiment, Negro men and women (as well as children) began to learn, besides reading and writing and the beginnings of arithmetic, their first lessons in freedom and responsibility, which were both new and frightening. Many of the New England plantation superintendents had to learn new lessons in cotton culture from the former slaves, particularly those who had been captains and drivers in former times. In that same Department of the South, in the late spring of 1862, came another, more startling experiment, one designed to make direct and military use of that "sable arm" of whose strength Frederick Douglass liked to boast.

Meanwhile, across the South, other Negroes found their lives disrupted in many ways as the military needs of the beleaguered Confederacy took precedence over the orderly routine of plantation life. Fortifying the South, including Southern cities, forts, and ports, required prodigious pick-and-shovel work, the felling of trees, and the building of redoubts and gun emplacements. Military leaders requisitioned and even impressed free and slave labor to erect mile upon mile of fortifications—some fifteen miles at Fort Donelson alone. The longer the war continued, the more unpopular these military demands on the Negro population of the South became, especially to slave owners concerned for the health and safety of their people and for the neglected crops back home. Add to this constant problem another that tended to disrupt plantation life even more: the slow but steady advance of Union forces as Scott's "Anaconda Plan" began to uncoil and

Left: Timothy O'Sullivan captured these Negroes at rest outside a cook tent at Culpeper, Virginia, in November 1863. (LC)

Left: Lieutenant W. B. Sears of the 2nd Rhode Island Infantry poses with his servant boy, shown leaning against a camp chair. (USAMHI)

move down the Atlantic Coast, past Hatteras and Port Royal, on down around Florida to Ship Island off the mouths of the Mississippi, and even up that great river in the second spring of the war. At the same time, Union forces in the west were moving down. Brigadier General U. S. Grant won the first significant land victories of the war with the capture of Forts Henry and Donelson in February 1862, followed, with remarkable swiftness, by the fall of Nashville, the first Confederate state capital to welcome Yankee troops. As Union lines extended, slave owners either lost considerable numbers of their "property" or moved them to the interior, out of harm's way. Plantation records from the spring of 1862 on, from Kentucky down through Tennessee to the Gulf, show the gradual collapse of the planters' economy in such poignant entries as "Big Joe went off with the Yankees," followed, say, two weeks later by "Big Joe seen driving Army wagon in N. Orleans." Tens of thousands of Big Joes went off to drive army wagons—and for other reasons.

Lincoln's favorite solutions to the slavery problem were compensated emancipation (financial aid to states which would free their slaves) and colonization, a variety of projects developing from the American Colonization Society after 1817. The first oft-repeated proposal fell on deaf ears even as late as the second year of the war, when the demise of the institution seemed imminent. The second met with very mixed responses, as it had from the founding of Liberia during the presidency of James Monroe. Some prominent Negro leaders, including Henry Highland Garnet and Martin R. Delany, began to advocate emigration to Haiti during the 1850s, especially after the Dred Scott decision doomed their hopes of anything like equality of treatment in the United States. Negroes were divided in their attitudes. Dr. John Rock of Boston spoke for the opposition in 1860: "This being our country, we have made up our minds to remain in it, and try to make it worth living in." A Washington Negro, on the other hand, argued: "Let us emigrate to Hayti, where we shall be free from the white man's contumely, and where we can secure for ourselves and our children after us, a home, a farm, and all the rights which citizenship confers." In June 1861 Fred Douglass came out strongly against emigra-

Left: The Freedmen's Bureau attempted to cope with the ever-swelling numbers of ex-slaves flocking to the Union armies—and did so rather effectively, providing some education and training, as well as spiritual guidance. Here one sees a Freedmen's office at Petersburg, Virginia, late in the war. (USAMHI)

Left: And here is another Freedmen's office, this one in South Carolina, as photographed by Cooley. (NA)

Left: Whole "Freedmen's Villages" like this one at Arlington Heights, Virginia, appeared. Here the inhabitants all pose with books, which many of them probably could not yet read. Perhaps they are bibles, hymnals, or fundamental readers. Whatever, they represented a first step in the noble cause of raising the Negro up from slavery. (USAMHI)

Above: Feeding the thousands of Negroes fell to the Freedmen's Bureau as well. Here, at Beaufort, South Carolina, rations are issued to Negroes. (USAMHI)

Above: Old churches used by the slaves were maintained and new ones were opened. (USAMHI)

Above: And, most important, schools were opened. Here the first schoolhouse built for the instruction of freedmen, at Port Hudson, Louisiana, is the backdrop for several Negro soldiers who are now fighting for their brothers' freedom. (CHS)

Below: The Freedmen's school at Beaufort. (USAMHI)

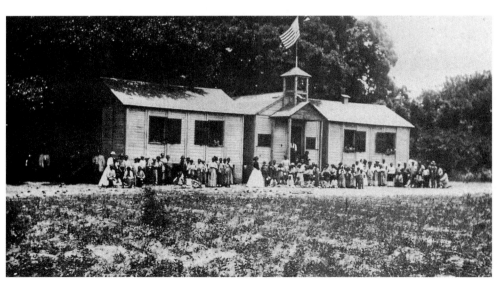

tion: "We are Americans, speaking the same language, adopting the same customs, holding the same general opinions… and shall rise or fall with Americans." By mid-1862 most Negro responses to proposals of colonization took the form of angry denunciations. The New York *Anglo-African* called Lincoln's Central American scheme a message "to stir the hearts of all Confederates" and went on to propose an appropriation "to expatriate and settle elsewhere the surviving slaveholders." Lincoln's one colonization venture was a disastrous failure: Some 450 Negroes from Virginia went to Ile à Vache (off Haiti) in May 1863 to endure smallpox, mutiny, and starvation before the President sent a ship to bring home the survivors in February 1864. Most Negroes, says one historian, "were determined to stay in their native land and struggle their way to equality." Impatient with the hesitating evolution of Union policy, David Hunter, commanding the Department of the South in May 1862, declared the slaves of South Carolina, Georgia, and Florida "forever free." This had the Fremont ring, and it got the Fremont treatment. Lincoln reacted immediately (he had learned about the proclamation through the newspapers!) and called Hunter's decree "altogether void." Even before word of Lincoln's action reached him, Hunter took another radical step: He began to recruit a regiment of former slaves, lamentably using methods little better than impressment. This activity stirred interest throughout the country, stimulating debate in Congress and the press. In the Sea Islands the immediate results were deplorable: Edward Pierce's plantation superintendents penned reports protesting the breakup of families and the disruption of agricultural labor. Undeterred, Hunter pressed his project (and more recruits), selecting noncommissioned officers from the white regiments in his command as company officers to drill the new men and make soldiers of them. In response to congressional inquiries about his regiment of fugitive slaves Hunter explained that his men were not fugitives —their masters were fugitives, and the former slaves had expressed eagerness to overtake their masters in the most effective way—as Union sol-

Above: And the Freedmen's school on Edisto Island, with several of the teachers posing in the doorway. (USAMHI)

Right: Often called Gideonites, the Yankee teachers who went south to educate the former slaves were a dedicated, idealistic band. Whole families devoted themselves to the work. Three Chase sisters pose here with other schoolteachers at Norfolk, Virginia, in 1865. (WRHS)

diers. This occasioned gales of laughter in the House, particularly since Charles Wickliffe of Kentucky had offered the resolution of inquiry. Mean while, George B. McClellan had begun his ill-starred Peninsular Campaign, and Union manpower needs were greater than ever. Despite this military circumstance, Lincoln viewed Hunter's program with profound disfavor, and his War Department declined either to commission the new regiment's officers or to pay its troops. Frustrated, Hunter was forced to let the men go back to their plantations, except for Company A, which remained in camp awaiting better times.

Throughout our military history white Americans have shown much reluctance, even antipathy, to arm Negro men—until harsh military necessity in the form of manpower shortages outweighed other considerations. So it was in the colonial wars and in the American Revolution, with Negro men eventually taking up arms against the French, Indians, and the British—in every American war except the Mexican, when a few Negroes bore arms

Above: A group of Gideonites in Beaufort or Port Royal, as captured by the camera of Samuel Cooley. The southern climate seems to have had a softening effect on the normally dour visage of the Yankee schoolmarm. (WRHS)

Left: Negro soldiers pose with their teachers, their books resting in their laps. Reading alone will not be enough to prepare them for the years of struggle before them. For now they are content to struggle just for their freedom. (LC)

Above: Five little children at New Bern, scrubbed and ready for school. Even with their education they face a hard road ahead. (USAMHI)

*Above: Happy scenes take place for freedom. At Brierfield, the Mississippi planta-
tion home of Jefferson Davis, the Fourth of July in 1864 was cause for decoration
and a Freedmen's picnic. (OLD COURT HOUSE MUSEUM, VICKSBURG)*

*Above: And here, at Emancipation Oak near
Beaufort, a tax collector named Brisbane first read
Lincoln's Emancipation Proclamation to the Negroes
of South Carolina. It was a hallowed place.
(USAMHI)*

*Above: Negroes did more than just study and work.
Thousands saw in the war their chance for a blow
against the institution that had enslaved them for
centuries. A slave, Robert Smalls, together with eight
other Negro men and several women, captured the
Confederate ordnance transport Planter in
Charleston and steamed her out to the blockading fleet
on May 13, 1862. (USAMHI)*

*Right: The steamer Planter,
photographed at
Georgetown, South
Carolina, with several hundred bales of cotton aboard.
Smalls was made a navy
pilot for his exploit and
later became captain of the
vessel. Years later he served
five terms in Congress.
(NHC)*

but the majority went along in their more traditional menial roles. In 1862, however, Union manpower needs finally began to outweigh "other
considerations." Hunter needed more soldiers
than the War Department could provide in his
slowly expanding Sea Island beachhead. Other
Union commanders—in Louisiana after the Navy
had captured New Orleans, and along the bloody
Kansas-Missouri border—needed more fighting
men and, like Hunter, elected to follow Free
Douglass's advice and "call on Africa." Probably
no one ever put the basic premise more bluntly
than Kansas Senator James H. Lane. A Negro, he
asserted, "might just as well 'become food for
powder [i.e., cannon fodder] as my son." If Confederates object to being killed by Negroes Lane
continued with what passed for humor on the
frontier, "let them lay down their arms." Despite
War Department orders to the contrary, Lane persisted in recruiting both Negroes and Indians, secure in the knowledge that he was a thousand
miles from Washington.

Down in Louisiana Benjamin Butler reached
the same conclusion by a more circuitous route. At
first opposed to Negro enlistments, Butler even
drove a subordinate, Brigadier General John W.
Phelps, out of the Army for advocating that course.
Phelps had begun recruiting Negroes and had
drawn up an imaginative program to "organize and
train our African levies." In early August Butler rejected Phelps's proposal and ordered him to put
his Negroes to work, arguing legalistically that
only the President had the authority to employ
Negro soldiers under the Second Confiscation Act
of July 17, 1862. Claiming that he was no slave driver, Phelps resigned and started for his Vermont
home. Long before Phelps saw the Green Mountains, Butler had done a complete about-face: He
invited Negro recruits on August 22, using as legal
cover his authority to enlist former Confederates
who had seen the error of their ways. Among the
defenders of New Orleans had been "a military
organization known as the 'Native Guards' (colored)," and Butler made it clear that his invitation
applied only to it. Thus, Butler temporarily escaped the opprobrium of having armed slaves.
Contemporary observers claimed that Butler's recruiting officers asked few questions, with the result that "the boldest and finest fugitives have
enlisted, while the whole organization is known as
the Free Colored Brigade." Helping to persuade
Butler to this new position and practice, besides
his demonstrable manpower shortages, were ad-
vices from Secretary of the Treasury Salmon P.
Chase and Mrs. Butler, both of whom had pointed
out that anti-Negro soldier sentiment in the North
and West was abating and that the time was ripe
for action. Chase put it well: "And who better to
begin the work than my friend Gen. Butler." Results? Three Negro regiments were mustered into
the Union Army in September, October, and November 1862, regiments which Butler called, with
his usual flair, "Louisiana Native Guards." Their
cadres had come from that formerly Confederate
"military organization," and the vast majority of
their company officers were "free men of color."

Thanks, in large measure, to military necessity
(McClellan's adventure on the Peninsula had
turned into a costly failure, and John Pope's fum-
bling Second Bull Run campaign made the situation even worse) and to congressional authority to
arm Negroes under the Second Confiscation Act,
Secretary of War Stanton not only blessed Butler's

work but also empowered Brigadier General Rufus Saxton, on August 25, 1862, to raise 5,000 Negro troops in Hunter's Department of the South. Using that stubborn Company A as a nucleus, Saxton went to work to build the 1st South Carolina Colored Volunteer Infantry. He invited a young Harvard captain in a Massachusetts infantry regiment to come south as its colonel. So Thomas Wentworth Higginson, certifiable abolitionist and personal friend of the late John Brown, began to collect material for his Civil War classic, *Army Life in a Black Regiment.*

Lane's recruiting grounds were not nearly so ripe for the harvest as Hunter's or Butler's. The census of 1860 showed only 2 slaves in Kansas territory, plus 625 free Negroes—hardly enough for a Civil War regiment of 1,000 men. Lane, a Jayhawker of the first water, was blessed with a fertile imagination and an acquisitive instinct. Selecting his recruiters from abolitionists come West to make Kansas free, he procured sufficient men for the 1st Kansas Colored Volunteer Infantry among fugitives from Missouri and Arkansas. Like Hunter, he selected officers from the noncoms of white regiments. This first Negro regiment to be raised in a free state was mustered into Union service on January 13, 1863. Even before then, in late October, five companies of the 1st Kansas Colored had seen action against bushwackers in Missouri. A week earlier Saxton's "Fust Souf" saw its first action in a long-range raid up the Bell and Sapello rivers, destroying nine saltworks and carrying off lumber and other supplies. That was Company A's reward for patience.

It remained for President Lincoln to put his seal of approval on the war's new dimension. This he did in his Emancipation Proclamation of January 1, 1863: "Such persons of suitable condition, will be received into the armed service of the United States to garrison forts, positions, stations, and other places, and to man vessels of all sorts in said service." With this presidential blessing, however limited, the movement Fred Douglass had advocated in the first month of the war got under way in earnest. The war became a revolution.

At first enterprising states, like Massachusetts and Rhode Island, and ambitious individuals, like Daniel Ullmann of New York and James Mont-

Above: The ex-slaves wanted to be armed to fight, and no one advocated their cause more strongly or effectively than Frederick Douglass, surely the most articulate and widely respected free Negro of his day. (NA)

Above: To Douglass's voice were added those of influential white statesmen and military figures. James H. Lane, the abolitionist firebrand of Kansas, spoke fervently for Negro regiments as a United States Senator. An unstable man, he was to take his own life in 1866. (USAMHI)

Above: White-haired Brigadier General Lorenzo Thomas, Federal adjutant general, shown standing, went West to promote the organization of Negro regiments once their raising was approved. (COURTESY OF DAVID D.FINNEY)

Above: Prominent officers like Brigadier General Cyrus Hamlin, son of Vice-President Hannibal Hamlin, early advocated the use of Negroes in the fighting army, and later commanded the 80th United States Colored Infantry. (CWTI)

Above: Charles Hamlin, like his brother Cyrus, led Negro troops in the war. Many officers did so out of simple conviction. For others, taking a commission in a Negro unit was a speedier way to rise, since finding officers for them was not always easy. (CWTI)

Above: Colonel Robert Gould Shaw felt genuine conviction about Negro soldiers. He gave his life fighting at the head of his regiment, the 54th Massachusetts, at Charleston. Contemptuous Confederates "buried him with his niggers." (LC)

Above: Brigadier General Edward A. Wild, whose name fitted his temperament, lost an arm at South Mountain. In 1863, at New Bern, North Carolina, he raised "Wild's African Brigade." He and his men saw wide service in 1864 and 1865. (USAMHI)

Above: Brigadier General Rufus Saxton raised the 1st South Carolina Colored Infantry and spent the better part of the war recruiting Negro regiments. After the conflict he went into the Freedmen's Bureau. (USAMHI)

Above: Writing under the pen name "Private Miles O'Reilly," Lieutenant Colonel Charles Halpine advocated the inclusion of Negroes in the army for his superior, David Hunter. He wrote the poem "Sambo's Right to be Kilt," and carried out Hunter's first order to organize Negro soldiers. (USAMHI)

gomery of Kansas, secured War Department license to raise regiments, even brigades. Montgomery, frozen out of competition in Kansas, became colonel of the 2nd South Carolina Colored Volunteers. Ullmann recruited a cadre of white officers in New York and then shipped to Louisiana to find his men. There he found Nathaniel P. Banks, Butler's replacement in the Department of the Gulf, already raising his own Negro brigade.

Most enterprising were the efforts of Massachusetts and her abolitionist governor, John A. Andrew. A well-organized recruiting committee sent agents across the North who found volunteers as far west as Chicago and Milwaukee. Douglass joined in the work, giving his full editorial support and two sons. So effective were these tactics that the 54th Massachusetts Infantry soon filled up, and the overflow was enough to form a sister regiment, the 55th. To lead the 54th Andrew selected a young captain, Colonel Robert Gould Shaw, who went to glory six months later on the bloody parapet of Fort Wagner, outside Charleston. The Confederates "buried him with his niggers" with instant effect on the whole Union.

The War Department put the movement on a sound and organized basis in the spring of 1863 by two distinct moves. In late March Stanton sent

Right: Officers of the 4th United States Colored Infantry at Fort Slocum in April 1865. The officers, with rare exception, were white, and "Sambo" is little in evidence. The Negroes might fight, but real equality was another matter. (USAMHI)

Adjutant General Lorenzo Thomas out to the Mississippi Valley, where raw material was plentiful, to push the organization of Negro regiments. In May Stanton set up the Bureau for Colored Troops within his department to centralize activities, monitor officer selection, and provide administrative support. A year later the "African levies" were redesignated as regiments of United States Colored Troops: Higginson's "Fust Souf" became the 33rd U.S.C.T.; Montgomery's 2nd Carolina became the 34th U.S.C.T., and the 1st Kansas Colored became the 79th. Native Guard, Corps d'Afrique, and African Descent regiments lost their picturesque names to become United States forces with no state identity.

Lorenzo Thomas was so diligent in his efforts that he had begun a score of regiments in Arkansas and Louisiana before returning to Washington. He made it plain to reluctant Union commanders that he spoke for the President, and he successfully reduced anti-Negro sentiment among Union troops by offering opportunities for commissions in the new regiments. By the end of 1863 Stanton could report fifty Negro regiments in existence, some of them even in action.

More significant than mere numbers, Stanton could demonstrate that the new auxiliaries had proved their mettle. In three actions in May, June, and July of 1863 Negro regiments showed themselves capable of more than the garrison roles Lincoln had initially assigned them. At Port Hudson on May 27 the 1st and 3rd Regiments, Corps d'Afrique—Butler's 1st and 3rd Native Guards—attacked a strong Confederate position; while they failed to dislodge its defenders after five attacks, they stood up well under fire despite heavy casualties. At Milliken's Bend on June 7 the 9th and 11th Regiments of Louisiana Volunteers of African Descent, both begun by Thomas, stood off Rebel attack, with timely support from a Union gunboat. The third engagement was the July 18 assault on Fort Wagner by Shaw's 54th Massachusetts. That was a military failure, since the Confederates repelled the attack, but only after a hand-to-hand struggle on the very parapet. Shaw died with his leading companies, but the news of his death—and especially of his burial in a ditch with his troops—made him a martyr to the cause. Cabinet officers, congressmen, generals, and journalists thereafter linked the three actions as significant in reducing popular antipathy to permitting Negroes to join the war.

Out on the far frontier on July 17—the day before the 54th Massachusetts won immortality outside Charleston—the 1st Kansas Colored established its military reputation at Honey Springs in present-day Oklahoma. In a "sharp and bloody engagement of two hours duration," as part of Major General James G. Blunt's Army of the Frontier, the Kansas regiment fought well and even captured the colors of a Texas regiment! Of greater importance was the effect of their performance on western sentiment. Blunt stated the case tersely: "The question that negroes will fight is settled; besides they make better soldiers in every respect

Far left: "Contraband Jackson" looks much like the other young Negroes who flocked to the Union banners. He soon became… (USAMHI)

Left: … "Drummer Jackson" of the 79th United States Colored Troops. These photographs were widely circulated as propaganda to encourage Negro enlistments and white support of the Negro regiments. (USAMHI)

Below: Photographs like this one were used as the basis for recruiting posters. "Come and Join Us, Brothers," reads the broadside featuring these well-equipped soldiers. (COURTESY OF JAMES D. SPINA)

Above: In towns all across the country the sable regiments mustered. Here one sees the 127th Ohio, renamed the 5th United States Colored Troops, on Sandusky Street in Delaware, Ohio. (OHIO HISTORICAL SOCIETY)

Above: Guard mounting, probably by the 1st South Carolina Colored Troops at Beaufort. The photographer's shadow is evident in the right foreground. (USAMHI)

Right: Men of Company E of the 4th United States Colored Troops in Fort Lincoln in the defenses of Washington. (USAMHI)

Right: Out West Negro soldiers paraded in captured Vicksburg under their white officers. (OLD COURT HOUSE MUSEUM, VICKSBURG)

Right: Battery A of the 2nd United States Colored Artillery practiced its gun drills with the Army of the Cumberland. (CHS)

than any troops I have ever had under my command." Another less dignified but even more expressive comment came from an officer of the 3rd Wisconsin Cavalry who was identified as an Irish Democrat: "I never believed in niggers before, but my Jasus, they are hell for fighting."

Early in 1864 another Irish officer, Confederate Major General Patrick R. Cleburne, urged the training of "the most courageous of our slaves," arguing that "half-trained negroes have fought as bravely as many other half-trained Yankees." The idea was anathema to most Southerners; Howell Cobb of Georgia found it "the most pernicious idea that has been suggested since the war began… You cannot make soldiers of slaves… If slaves will make good soldiers our whole theory of slavery is wrong." Too late, in January 1865, Robert E. Lee himself sanctioned the policy of arming slaves: "We should employ them without delay." A month before Appomattox President Davis signed a "Negro Soldier Law" authorizing slave enlistments. Too late.

Some 200,000 Negroes served in the Union armies, some as volunteers, some as paid substitutes, some drafted, others ruthlessly impressed from the hordes of contrabands swarming Union camps and columns. They came from New England and New York, Pennsylvania, and all across the North, as well as from every Southern state. What did they do for the Union Army? Everything its white commanders asked them or would let them. They fought in over four hundred engagements, in every theater of the war: from Deep Bottom and Hatcher's Run and Petersburg in Virginia to Poison Spring and Jenkins Ferry in Arkansas; from Olustee in Florida to Brice's Cross Roads in Mississippi; from Fort Fisher, North Carolina, to Fort Blakely outside Mobile. They fought under Major General George H. Thomas at Nashville in the last weeks of 1864; he remarked, as he rode up Overton Hill after the victory: "Gentlemen, the question is settled; negroes will fight." They also dug miles of trenches before Richmond and around Petersburg; they guarded prisoners at Point Lookout and Rock Island and on the Dry Tortugas. They learned to read in company schools, even hiring teachers out of their small pay. For much of the war Negro troops got only ten dollars per month, as against the thirteen their white comrades drew—and officers held back

Above: In Tennessee in 1864 this battery posed all of its members at the gun, standing in pride. It was a long way from a time when Negroes were not trusted with weapons of any sort. Now they had cannon. (COURTESY OF JOSEPH M. BAUMAN)

Above: A Corps d'Afrique battery at Port Hudson, Louisiana. (USAMHI)

three of the Negro soldier's ten for his uniform. One Negro sergeant was executed for mutiny because he refused to allow his company to be paid at the discriminatory rate. Too often Negro troops were issued inferior weapons and horses discarded by white cavalry regiments. Their fate, if captured, was potentially hard: the Confederacy declined to recognize them as soldiers, choosing to consider them as "slaves taken in arms." Some 54th Massachusetts troops, free Negroes from the North, became prisoners at Fort Wagner, and some of them were sold into slavery. "Indiscriminate slaughter" of Union Negroes at Fort Pillow and Poison Spring (both called massacres by the Union) had an ironic effect on their morale: They seldom surrendered after those engagements in the spring of 1864, and they seldom took any Rebel prisoners.

Rough, even barbarous, as were the trials of Negro soldiers, wherever they served the ordeals of the fugitives were worse. Despite the best efforts of army officers, chaplains, and a host of church and civic organizations who sent doctors, nurses, and teachers to the camps, thousands of fugitives found ultimate freedom from disease and even starvation in death. An estimated 200,000 Negro laborers toiled for the Union field forces, driving wagons, digging fortifications, cooking, chopping wood and even cotton on abandoned plantations. Their wages were minimal (and not always paid), whether in South Carolina, Tennessee, or Louisiana, but their efforts helped in at least two ways: to assist the progress of Union arms and to maintain themselves and their families, even at a subsistence level. How many hundreds of Negro scouts and guides helped Union forces—or escaped Yankee prisoners—find their way to safety or a hidden route toward their objective cannot be determined.

It is safe to say that Negroes, both men and women, worked for the cause of the Union—and for their own freedom—in every way imaginable. Susie King Taylor of Savannah escaped to Union lines to become a teacher of the freedmen, a laundress, a nurse, and the bride of a Negro soldier. William Tillman, cook and steward aboard the

Left: The 1st United States Colored Artillery; in fact, it was probably an artillery battery attached to the 1st South Carolina Colored Troops at Beaufort. (WRHS)

Left: Negro soldiers looked as smart on parade as their white counterparts, the white officers standing before them. (NA)

Left: Negro soldiers lived a life similar to that of their white comrades, only for less pay and often with inferior equipment. They were not always the best soldiers, but, given the chance to fight, they did. (COURTESY OF ROBERT MCDONALD)

Left: They had their bands, like this one of the 107th United States Colored Troops, as they appeared in November 1865. The band-master, of course, was white. (USAMHI)

Right: The ill-behaved were punished, put in the guard-house, and made to ride the wooden mule, as shown here at Vicksburg. The dovecote atop the guardhouse seems somehow incongruous with the scene. (USAMHI)

Left: And they had their unruly men, like all armies in all times. The 107th also had its own guardhouse and provost guard, shown here at Fort Corcoran in the Washington defenses. (USAMHI)

Above: And when they transgressed seriously, they faced commensurate punishment. The worst crime a Negro soldier could commit was the molestation of a white woman in occupied territory. A Negro soldier named Johnson allegedly did so, and the scene shown here was the result. With men of his regiment and other spectators drawn up before the gallows, a noose is slipped over his head... (USAMHI)

Right: ... and the trap is dropped. It is June 20, 1864. (USAMHI)

Yankee schooner *S. J. Waring*, recaptured his ship after she had been made a Confederate prize and brought her safely to New York. Robert Smalls of Charleston, assistant pilot of the steamer *Planter*, ran out to deliver her to Union blockaders; he won half the prize money—and during Reconstruction he became a congressman from his native state. Roughly one fourth of the Union Navy were Negroes; an estimated 29,000 by war's end. This was not revolutionary; Negroes had never been barred from naval service, although custom kept them in the lowest ratings—except for an occasional Negro pilot like Smalls, who even became skipper of his own ship—by right of conquest.

Thousands of other Negroes served the Confederacy, although hardly ever as soldiers. They made up the bulk of the South's labor force and worked in virtually every craft: carpenters, foundry workers, coal miners, even drivers of railroad locomotives and canal barges. They were totally involved in the war, chopping cotton, cutting sugar cane, raising corn, protecting the plantation while the white men were "away," bringing their fallen masters home from the front, and even sweating as iron puddlers in the furnaces of Shelby County, Alabama. They sang and they mourned, they struggled against all manner of handicaps and dangers, and they endured, praying for the sweet chariot to swing low, and waiting for Jubilo.

A great American scholar, Benjamin Quarles, the dean of black historians, has summed up the story eloquently: "... the war, with all its bloodshed and sorrow, was an emancipating and uplifting national experience. Its most striking achievement was not its battle conquests on sea and land, but in the momentum it gave to the ideals of the freedom and dignity of man. It made easier every subsequent battle for human rights."

> De whip is lost, de han'cuff broken,
> But de massa'll hab his pay;
> He's ole enough, big enough, ought to know better
> Dan to went an' run away.

Above: But for every case of ignominy there were tens of glorious stories of Negro heroism. Martin R. Delany became one of the very first Negro officers in the army's history when he was made major of the 104th United States Colored Troops. He and several other Negroes were awarded the Medal of Honor for their bravery. (USAMHI)

Above: Thousands served in the Union Navy, as shown here aboard the USS Vermont, *off Hilton Head, in 1863. (USAMHI)*

Above: Wherever the war went, they went as well, sometimes fighting, more often digging and carrying, freeing the white soldiers for the battle. (OHIO HISTORICAL SOCIETY)

Above: But they carried their battle flags proudly, and carried as well the torch of freedom and dignity for the generations of their blood to follow. The color sergeant of the 108th United States Colored Troops leaves little doubt that he is a soldier, and a free man by his own right. (COURTESY OF MICHAEL J. MCAFEE)

Washington at War

A PORTFOLIO

A panoramic view of a divided city
trying desperatlely to cope
with its own growth

Left: Washington in 1863. Symbolically the city and the Capitol that looms over it are, like the Union, not yet complete. Barracks and troop tents below the Capitol show that this is a city at war. Taken from the Smithsonian central tower in 1863. (COURTESY OF THE UNIVERSITY OF ROCHESTER)

Left: The northeast view from the Smithsonian. (COURTESY OF THE UNIVERSITY OF ROCHESTER)

Left: Looking north up Tenth Street. The large Grecian porticoed building in the right background is the Patent Office. To its front right stands the General Post Office. On Tenth Street itself, about half way up on the right side, stands a large building where President Lincoln occasionally attended a play— Ford's Theater. (COURTESY OF THE UNIVERSITY OF ROCHESTER)

Left: Turning the camera to the northwest and continuing his panorama of the capital, the photographer captured the State and Treasury departments in the large building at right center. Just left of it stands the Executive Mansion, now coming to be called the White House. (COURTESY OF THE UNIVERSITY OF ROCHESTER)

Right: Looking due west, the camera sees the still unfinished Washington Monument. On the Virginia shore in the distance, at right center, nearly on the crest of the ridge, is the faint image of the Custis-Lee mansion, called Arlington House, until 1861 the home of Robert E. Lee. (COURTESY OF THE UNIVERSITY OF ROCHESTER)

Right: The Long Bridge crosses the Potomac, leading to Alexandria, southwest of Washington. (COURTESY OF THE UNIVERSITY OF ROCHESTER)

Right: Looking south from the Smithsonian tower. The point of land jutting into the Potomac at left center is Greenleafs Point; the buildings on it are known as the Washington Arsenal. (COURTESY OF THE UNIVERSITY OF ROCHESTER)

Right: Completing the panorama, the camera looks southeast. Unseen, the Eastern Branch provides a waterway leading from the Potomac to the Washington Navy Yard, marked by the tall smokestacks and the long workshop just under the horizon at left center. (COURTESY OF THE UNIVERSITY OP ROCHESTER)

Above: The Treasury Department, where the massive effort of financing and maintaining the Union war effort had its heart. (COURTESY OF AMERICANA IMAGE GALLERY)

Above: The "cash room" inside the Treasury building. By the end of the war the conflict was costing nearly four million dollars a day. (LC)

Above: The nerve center of Mr. Lincoln's army, the War Department. Here Secretary of War Edwin M. Stanton forged the mighty weapon that sought to defeat the Confederacy. The broadside on the tree at left advertises a then popular drama, Guerillas on the Potomac, *a problem much on Stanton's mind, as a matter of fact. (COURTESY OF LLOYD OSTENDORF)*

Above: The Navy Department, where Gideon Welles built a navy and a blockade. The bureaucracy both here and at the War building quickly outgrew the premises. (LC)

Above: The "mall" around 1864. The Smithsonian Institution stands at left amid the park-like plantings along Independence Avenue. The Capitol, its dome near completion, looms in the background. (USAMHI)

Above: The incomplete monument to Washington. Like the Almighty, Washington was invoked as being on the side of both North and South. Clearly, Washington's work, like his monument, was yet undone. (NA)

Left: The Cabin John Bridge over the Chesapeake & Ohio Canal northwest of the city. Built when Jefferson Davis was Secretary of War in the 1850s, his name was removed from the dedicatory plaque in 1861 as a symbolic gesture. (KA)

Above: Civilian residences and boardinghouses all over the city bulged with military personnel. Here one sees the headquarters of Brigadier General Martin D. Hardin, in command of the defenses of Washington from 1864 to the war's end. He is just to the left of the tree at the corner, missing the left arm he lost in a guerrilla ambush. (USAMHI)

Above: Signs of war came early to Washington. Often they came in the persons of those who sought to save the Capitol from the threat of the Confederate presence on the Virginia side of the Potomac. Fiercely loyal Kentuckian Cassius M. Clay raised a company of volunteers in the spring of 1861 to stand guard in the city before the first volunteer regiments arrived. He would become a brigadier general and, later, minister to the court of the czar. (NA)

Above: Private homes became hospitals. Here is "Minnesota Row," three homes on New Jersey Avenue at I Street. The corner home is that of Stephen A. Douglas. The center house belonged to John C. Breckinridge, and the one on the left belonged to Henry M. Rice of Minnesota, for whom the block was named. By May 1864 Douglas was dead, Breckinridge was a Confederate general, and Rice no longer sat in the Senate. Their homes are now the Douglas Hospital. Breckinridge's house would become a residence for General U. S. Grant after the war. (USAMHI)

Above: Men of Company K, 150th Pennsylvania Infantry. Nicknamed Bucktails because of the ornaments worn in their caps, they formed the President's bodyguard in Washington. In a "modern" war it was assumed that the chief of state needed protection. (COURTESY OF RONN PALM)

Above: Timothy O'Sullivan's view of the Armory beef yard, with the Treasury and Executive Mansion in the background. Washington smelled of livestock for four years. In the hot summer months Lincoln had to go to the Soldiers' Home on the outskirts of the city to escape the odors. (COURTESY OF AMERICANA IMAGE GALLERY)

Above: Troops had to eat. Here just one of scores of government mess houses and, to the left, one of many impromptu boardinghouses advertising "sleeping rooms." (USAMHI)

Above: Feeding the troops defending the capital required an office for the quartermaster at the Seventh Street wharf, shown here in May 1865. (USAMHI)

Left: An April 1865 image of the mess house at the U. S. Government Stables. (USAMHI)

Below: A. J. Russell made this 1864 view of the Washington Arsenal on Greenleafs Point. In the distance is the Long Bridge. (USAMHI)

Above: Armory Square, down Constitution Avenue from the Capitol, had its own chapel, complete with onion-shaped bell tower. (USAMHI)

Above: Brigadier General Christopher C. Augur commanded the Department of Washington in the final two years of the war, helping with its defense against Jubal Early's 1864 campaign toward the capital. (KA)

Above: The Arsenal stored, shipped, and put into service the bulk of the ordnance used in the Union armies. Here one sees the cannon and rolling equipment of several batteries of the Excelsior Brigade. (USAMHI)

Right: At any one time the Arsenal yard could always sprout neatly arranged rows of cannon, caissons, limbers, disassembled carriages, and gun tubes. (CHS)

Above: A member of Burnside's Zouaves, taken in Providence before he went to war. (COURTESY OF THE RHODE ISLAND HISTORICAL SOCIETY)

Left: Men of the 10th Rhode Island, Burnside's Zouaves, posing with bayonets fixed. They spent the war as part of the capital defense forces. (COURTESY OF THE RHODE ISLAND HISTORICAL SOCIETY)

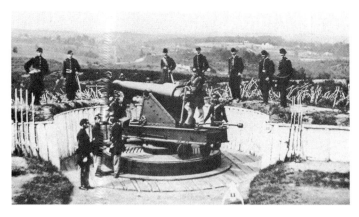

Above: The Federals ringed Washington with a formidable series of defenses. Here Fort Carroll, just across the Eastern Branch from the Arsenal, guards the capital's Maryland approaches. (KA)

Above: Completely on the other side of the city, near Silver Spring, Maryland, sat Fort Stevens. Here is where Early attacked in 1864, facing guns like this 6.4-inch Parrott rifle mounted on a seacoast carriage. (LC)

Left: Fort Richardson sat on the Virginia side, in advance of the approach to the Long Bridge. On this side of the Potomac passes into the defenses always had to be checked, as is being done here by members of the 1st Connecticut Heavy Artillery. (WRHS)

Left: Fort Lyon, considerably more ambitious than many Washington forts, guarded Alexandria from the south, the southernmost major outpost in the Virginia line of defenses. (USAMHI)

Below: Here men of the 34th Massachusetts pose beside a cannon aimed toward the still frequently hostile northern Virginia landscape. (USAMHI)

Left: Fort Slemmer sat north of the city. The men of the 2nd Pennsylvania Heavy Artillery stand in their best warlike pose despite the fact that the fort saw no action. (WRHS)

Above: A. J. Russell's 1864 image of Battery Rodgers in Alexandria. Its fifteen-inch Rodman smoothbore dominates the parapet, though it never fired in anger. (NA)

Above: Officers of the 3rd Massachusetts Heavy Artillery pose at their brigade headquarters in Fort Lincoln, not far from Bladensburg, Maryland. (USAMHI)

Left: Fort Foote, opposite Alexandria, was one of the largest fortifications in the whole defensive chain. Any attack on the capital by water would first have to pass this mighty bastion. (CHS)

Left: Fort Haggerty, just across the Potomac from Georgetown, was one of the smaller installations, yet it still had the sting of four large smoothbores. The man in the left foreground wears the sash of the officer of the day. (COURTESY OF ROBERT J. YOUNGER)

Below left and below: Just east of Fort Haggerty stood the much larger Fort Corcoran, the major defense on the road from Washington to Falls Church, Virginia. (USAMHI)

Above: The Navy Yard bridge over the Eastern Branch, with Uniontown in the distance. A small guard stands post, yet people could get through. John Wilkes Booth was to cross this bridge after shooting Lincoln. *(USAMHI)*

Left: George Barnard caught this image of guards examining a pass at the ferry landing on Mason's Island opposite Georgetown. *(LC)*

Left: An image, probably by Russell, showing Alexandria, with Washington in the distance, in the winter of 1864-65. With hostile Virginia just across the Potomac, the defenders of the capital had to take special precautions to guard access to the city. *(USAMHI)*

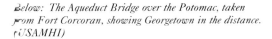

Below: The Aqueduct Bridge over the Potomac, taken from Fort Corcoran, showing Georgetown in the distance. *(USAMHI)*

Left: Another view, by Russell, of the Aqueduct Bridge. *(P-M)*

Right: The Chain Bridge, which crossed the Potomac three miles upriver from Georgetown, was one of the most heavily protected spots. Here a guard box stands at the right, while the guards themselves lounge for the camera. (KA)

Below: William Kunstman of Pennsylvania brought his camera to capture this image of the Chain Bridge. (J. FREDERIC KNECHT COLLECTION)

Above: He stayed to photograph the bridge guards. (J. FREDERIC KNECHT COL-LECTION)

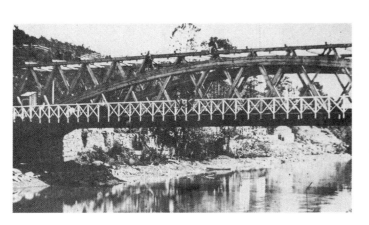

Left: The bridge itself, with two soldiers feigning a spar as they perch on the rail. (J. FREDERIC KNECHT COLLECTION)

Above: The men on the Maryland side waited with small smoothbores to repel any assault across the bridge. (J. FREDERIC KNECHT COLLECTION)

Above: Another photographer caught the men practicing; some are standing with cartridges in their hands, the fuses in place, and lanyards in hand as if ready to fire. (LC)

Left: An old tree was pressed into service for a signal station above the Chain Bridge. (USAMHI)

Left: Kunstman took his camera to nearby Fort Marcy, there to be met by this stern-faced young Horatio of Company A. (J. FREDERIC KNECHT COLLECTION)

Left: The interior of Fort Marcy in a damaged old stereo view by Kunstman. A young Negro soldier, perhaps a servant, stands alone in the center. (J. FREDERIC KNECHT COLLECTION)

Left: Fort Marcy's parade ground, with the men drawn into ranks for review and inspection. Two carriages of spectators look on. (J. FREDERIC KNECHT COLLECTION)

Left: A mighty Parrott rifle looks out over the Virginia countryside from its emplacement in Fort Marcy. (J. FREDERIC KNECHT COLLECTION)

Below: Quarters for the guard on the Virginia side of the Chain Bridge. At far left is the signal station in the tree. (J. FREDERIC KNECHT COLLECTION)

Above: The men defending Washington enjoyed some luxuries denied to their brothers marching with the armies. One was the much greater opportunity to have families with them or nearby, as with these wives and children who posed with their husbands for Kunstman's lens. (J. FREDERIC KNECHT COLLECTION)

Right: The view from the signal tree. Many of Kunstman's photographs survive in poor condition, the glass negatives having been stored away and forgotten for over a century. (J. FREDERIC KNECHT COLLECTION)

Above: Hunting Creek, near Alexandria, and a long bridge with a blockhouse at midstream. (USAMHI)

Above: A closer view of a blockhouse in winter. Most Civil War bridges were defended at both ends. This one, with the defense in the middle, may be unique. (USAMHI)

Left: The entrance to the Long Bridge, the major artery from Washington to Alexandria. "Walk Your Horses" reads the sign on the right. (KA)

Below: The Alexandria side of the Long Bridge looked like a virtual stockade, controlling access for horse and pedestrian alike. (KA)

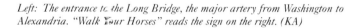

Left: Colonel D. C. McCallum, director of the United States Military Railroads, sits in the center of the group at right, with the railroad span of the Long Bridge before him. (USAMHI)

Left: The Long Bridge in May 1865. With the parallel railroad bridge visible to the left, this span could accommodate enormous traffic. It was the capital's chief link with the armies in Virginia. (USAMHI)

Above: But Washington could also be pleasant duty. The officers of the United States Treasury Battalion, here shown posing in April 1865, could display uniforms unsullied by hard service. (USAMHI)

Above: Brigadier General John H. Martindale served as military governor of Washington in 1863 and early 1864. It was an unenviable task for a soldier because of the constant interference of politicians and the wide Southern sentiment in the city. He left to return to field command. (NA)

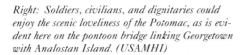

Right: Soldiers, civilians, and dignitaries could enjoy the scenic loveliness of the Potomac, as is evident here on the pontoon bridge linking Georgetown with Analostan Island. (USAMHI)

Left: There was fishing and lounging in the shade along the banks of the Potomac near the Aqueduct Bridge. (USAMHI)

Above: Officers like Brigadier General Daniel Sickles, on leave, could leisurely inspect the Wiard guns at the Washington Arsenal. (USAMHI)

Above: And when Sickles was on leave again, following the loss of his leg at Gettysburg, he could visit with other shelved field officers like Major General Samuel P. Heintzelman, now commanding part of the capital defenses. (USAMHI)

Above: Though war did not come to the heart of the city, still destruction visited from time to time. Here the Smithsonian has burned on January 24, 1865. (SMITHSONIAN INSTITUTION)

Above: But the Smithsonian, like Washington itself, went onward. When Lincoln won re-election in 1864, the safety of the Union was secured. Three years later U. S. Grant became Chief Executive. At heart always a loyal city, the citizens of Washington turned out in record numbers to witness the parade and ceremonies for his inauguration in March 1869. A city at war for four years, it looked confidently toward peace. (LC)

Chancellorsville, Lee's Greatest Triumph

FRANK E. VANDIVER

The greatest gamble, the greatest success; Lee's victory in the open campaign

In the aftermath of the Fredericksburg fiasco, President Lincoln faced the same crisis that had confronted him since the war's beginning. Somewhere he must find the right general for the Army of the Potomac. Fredericksburg had shown that Burnside was not the man. There were many who felt themselves capable, and some loudly proclaimed their self-confidence. The President could confide his private reservations to his secretaries—John G. Nicolay on the left and John Hay on the right—but to the public he expressed only confidence in his new choice of a commander. (USAMHI)

WINTER CAMPS had been fairly comfortable for both the Army of the Potomac and the Army of Northern Virginia. And as spring came in 1863 stirrings began in Blue and Gray lines.

Lee's army had been extensively refitted following the December 1862 Battle of Fredericksburg. "Stonewall" Jackson's II Corps, stretching along the Rappahannock from near Marye's Heights to below Hamilton's Crossing, had recruited and refurbished well; Jackson himself by now shared international renown with Lee. James Longstreet's I Corps had also rebuilt, and the bluff general, with several of his divisions, lingered in North Carolina scavenging and harassing Federal coastal raiders. In the old Fredericksburg lines, made nearly impregnable by months of digging, Lee counted almost 60,000 men.

Across the river the Army of the Potomac also had filled and burnished and had said farewell to yet another luckless leader, Ambrose E. Burnside.

Joseph Hooker came to command at some cost to honor but none to self-esteem. Dapper, often dashing, considered very brave by his troops, Hooker always chafed in subordination. Under Burnside his frustration had been almost overwhelming, and the backwash of Fredericksburg and the so-called "mud march" of January 1863 had fueled Hooker's anger. He had argued with Burnside, complained, and finally openly criticized his commander. Loud and intemperate, Hooker's complaints ran all the way to Washington. When Lincoln at last determined to relieve Burnside, he searched the rolls for a successor. Hooker's reputation for fighting attracted a president longing for aggressive generals. In selecting Hooker, Lincoln weighed his virtues against his carping. The results were conveyed to Hooker in a masterful appointment letter:

> Executive Mansion
> Washington, January 26, 1863

Major General Hooker:

General

I have placed you at the head of the Army of the Potomac. Of course I have done this upon what appeared to me to be sufficient reasons. And yet I think it best for you to know that there are some things in regard to which, I am not quite satisfied with you. I believe you to be a brave and skillful soldier, which, of course, I like. I also believe you do not mix politics with your profession, in which you are right. You have confidence in yourself, which is a valuable, if not an indispensable quality. You are ambitious, which, within reasonable limits, does good rather than harm. But I think that during General Burnside's command of the Army, you have taken counsel of your ambitions, and thwarted him as much as you could, in which you did a great wrong to the country, and to a most meritorious and honorable brother officer. I have heard, in such way as to believe it, of your recently saying that both the Army and the Government needed a Dictator. Of course it was not for this, but in spite of it, that I have given you the command. Only those generals, who gained successes, can set up Dictators. What I now ask of you is military success, and I will risk the Dictatorship. The Government will support you to the utmost of its ability, which is neither more nor less than it has done and will do for all commanders. I must fear that the spirit which you have aided to infuse into the Army, of criticizing their Commander, and withholding confidence from him, will now turn upon you. I shall assist you as far as I can, to put it down. Neither you, nor Napoleon, if he were alive again, could get any good out of an Army, while such a spirit prevails in it. And now, beware of rashness.—Beware of rashness, but with energy, and sleepless vigilance, go forward, and give us victories.

Yours very truly,
A. LINCOLN

Piqued but hardly daunted, Hooker boasted loudly that he would mold a winning army, and throughout the winter he made an impressive beginning. Attention to such vital things as socks, good food, and lodging endeared the general to his troops. Reorganization into traditional divisions and corps, some command adjustments, won approval from veteran commanders. When April brought fighting weather to northern Virginia, Hooker counted some 130,000 men in his ranks, most of them in good spirits and under competent leaders.

Hooker took the initiative. He learned old lessons well and consequently wisely planned to flank Lee's formidable lines by crossing upriver from Fredericksburg, moving rapidly through Virginia's Wilderness, and getting between Lee and Richmond. If his plan worked, Lee would have to fight where Hooker wanted.

Lee's pickets reported long blue lines moving on April 29, 1863. Jeb Stuart's outriders watched the Rapidan and Rappahannock fords—United States, Germanna, Ely's. These were good ones that offered access to various roads penetrating the heavily forested Wilderness.

With the first reports of Yankee movement, Lee reacted by dispatching R. H. Anderson's division toward Chancellorsville. Anderson must watch for the enemy vanguard and hold them back. With luck he might prevent Hooker's emergence from the entangling woods. At any rate, the enemy would be surprised and unable to flank Confederate positions.

Hooker knew he had thought of all contingencies. As his heavy columns marched off toward the river crossings, he kept 40,000 men under Major General John Sedgwick in the Fredericksburg lines to hold Lee's attention. Despite last minute problems which appeared to fuddle Hooker a bit, the general pushed his advance and himself went to cross the Rappahannock on April 30. Caution lifted as action neared. Hooker boasted to a newsman: "The rebel Army... is now the legitimate property of the Army of the Potomac. They may as well pack their haversacks and make for Richmond; and I shall be after them..."

Optimism tinged with experience colored Rebel thoughts. Lee balanced force ratios and remained hopeful. If Longstreet, with the rest of his corps, were at hand, hope would have been brighter. Even so, there seemed a good chance that a detachment could hold Fredericksburg's entrenchments while Lee and Jackson followed Anderson toward the Wilderness.

Wilderness trails were never especially easy, and now, after hard rains, they were boggy and hard on infantry. Hooker's men encountered environmental resistance as soon as they were south of the Rappahannock. Roads were really sluices, narrow and darkened by dripping trees. Federal maps were not entirely accurate. Hooker had intended to move briefly south to the Old Turnpike,

Above: There were still many old familiar faces about the army headquarters despite the new general. Major General Daniel Butterfield became Hooker's chief of staff, a position he would retain for much of the war. (USAMHI)

Above: Major General Joseph Hooker. Now just forty-eight, he had been one of the most highly commended young officers in the war with Mexico. As a result of an accident in a telegraph office, he was called "Fighting Joe Hooker" early in the war and the sobriquet stuck. He bitterly attacked Burnside behind his back, politicking blatantly, and finally won the army command. In giving it, Lincoln warned that the spirit of divisiveness that Hooker had fostered might well turn on him one day. (USAMHI)

Below: The 93rd New York was still the headquarters guard for the Army of the Potomac. Here the regimental staff poses just three months after its one campaign with Hooker. (USAMHI)

Above: Just one month after Chancellorsville, the 8th United States Infantry, provost guard for Hooker's army headquarters, stood for the camera. (P-M)

Above: Lee still faced the Federals across the Rappahannock at Fredericksburg—now much more heavily fortified than the previous December—despite the peaceful aspect of the city in this February 1863 view. Hooker knew he could not launch an attack across the river against positions worse than those faced by Burnside. He would make a diversion here while he crossed most of his army upriver. (US-AMHI)

Above: The terrain Hooker planned to cross was known in Virginia as The Wilderness, a densely wooded, confused, sometimes impenetrable barrier that could confound an army unfamiliar with it. This image, taken in the winter of 1865, shows trees shattered by the battle that Hooker would fight here. (US-AMHI)

near Melzi Chancellor's Farm, and then turn east and clear the trees.

Intentions wavered once Hooker entered the woods. Although his subordinates, especially George G. Meade and William B. Franklin, urged a speedy execution of the original plan, Hooker took refuge at the Chancellor House during the night of April 30 and ordered his men to halt where they were. Some of Hooker's subordinates worried. They recognized loss of initiative and, with it, one of the greatest wasted opportunities of the war. With Longstreet's corps depleted, and with Jubal Early and his division detached at Fredericksburg, Lee appeared to be more vulnerable than ever before! But Hooker hesitated. And, truth to tell, the omens were bad. Trees dripped in a kind of dark foreboding. Sounds were magnified and specters frequent. Axes thudded, muffled and mysterious, as men in blue felled trees for entrenchments.

Near the Chancellor House, where he established his headquarters, Hooker tested the omens and balanced the odds in that strange way he had of arguing with himself. For weeks every thing had been going his way and he had basked and boasted far and wide. Despite the gloomy landscape, recent moves would bring success. If George Meade pressed quickly along the Rappahannock's south bank, Lee would be flanked from the wicked works at Marye's Heights and his army might possibly be divided. In one of his moods of

Above: In March Hooker began his probes across the Rappahannock at points above Fredericksburg. Lee remained in the city, letting his cavalry guard his flanks. Colonel William Morgan, then a major, led his 1st Virginia Cavalry in repeated skirmishes with the Yankees, trying to halt their progress and divine their intent. (PRIVATE COLLECTION)

destiny, Hooker published success to his army on April 30, 1863, in the form of General Orders No. 47: "It is with heartfelt satisfaction the commanding general announces to the army that the operations of the last three days have determined that our enemy must either ingloriously fly, or come out from behind his defenses and give us battle on our own ground, where certain destruction awaits him."

Several Federal commanders must have been both irked and disturbed by this order—irked because of its bombast and disturbed because of its suddenly defensive tone. Where had the aggressiveness of earlier orders and speeches gone? Now, if Lee came out of his lines, the Army of the Potomac would receive attack. Clearly, as Stonewall Jackson guessed, Hooker's zest had gone. Why? What happened in the brooding, wet woodland as Yankee soldiers huddled around campfires and wondered about the quirks of high command—especially when Hooker, on the afternoon of May 1, ordered some of his advancing units to retreat!

A long time later Hooker admitted what happened: "For once I lost confidence in Hooker." He did not realize it for a while and became extremely busy and distracted.

Jackson, too, became busy. With all his divisions, save Early's, which would man the Fredericksburg lines, Jackson marched toward the Wilderness shortly after midnight on May 1. By 8 A.M. he could hear firing from the west and soon found Anderson, who had entrenched a line facing west and northwest, guarding the Old Turnpike, the Plank Road, and the Old Mine Road. With six brigades (three of them from Lafayette McLaws's division) Anderson had skirmished with mysteriously hesitant Union units and kept them at bay. Stonewall became impatient; Hooker ought to be attacked while still clogged in the woods. Anderson, helped by McLaws, was ordered forward on the Old Turnpike. One of Anderson's brigades would lead Jackson's II Corps on the Plank Road—which seemed to offer manuevering room toward Hooker's rumored flank. Jackson urged his men forward and soon noted that Federals retreated before a determined Rebel advance. Lee

Left: Meanwhile, Hooker marshaled his army in and around Falmouth. Many of the regiments had wintered here in now-abandoned winter huts like these. (US-AMHI)

Left: A campaign was coming, and as the army gathered at Falmouth, there was little place for solitude. A soldier took it where he could. (USAMHI)

Right: But the sober reality of war came soon enough. Hooker started to move late in April, and even before the full armies met, men began to die. Lieutenant George Busch of the 98th Pennsylvania was killed opposite Fredericksburg on April 30, 1863, days before the main battle. The horseplay ended abruptly. (US-AMHI)

Below: Spirits rose once more as the pain of the defeat at Fredericksburg subsided. Looking to another "go" at "Bobby Lee," the men in blue could relax with horseplay. This time they would beat the Confederates—of that they were certain. (USAMHI)

Above: Awaiting Hooker's move was General Robert E. Lee, a man with a depleted army less than half the size of the Federals. In 1863 he posed in Richmond for the camera of the firm of Minnis and Cowell, his eyes alight with calm determination. Faced on two fronts, at Fredericksburg and by Hooker advancing in The Wilderness, he made a daring decision. (COURTESY OF DIMENTI STUDIO)

Right: A big part of Lee's gamble would rest on this man, variously known as "Tom Fool," "Old Blue Light," and "Stonewall." Lieutenant General Thomas J. Jackson was to lead his corps in a bold flanking march around Hooker's unsuspecting right. Outnumbered two-to-one, Lee was splitting his army in the face of the enemy. (MUSEUM OF THE CONFEDERACY)

joined Jackson about midday, approved plans for pressing the enemy's right, and galloped off toward his own right, where the enemy's line had not been fully discovered. Jackson rode on to his left, beyond the Catherine Furnace, topped a hill where Jeb Stuart stood watching his horse artillery in action, and the two surveyed the front. Trees clotted their vision; Stuart told of the roads he knew which led toward the Federal right rear. There might be others.

Late in the afternoon Jackson knew that a heavy Union force had entrenched near Chancellorsville; he had one further look at Federal masses and then rode to meet Lee at the Plank Road junction. Federal timidity convinced "Old Jack" that Hooker's offensive had fizzled and that all Yankees would be north of the Rapidan and Rappahannock by morning.

Something had gone wrong with Hooker's offensive—there was no doubt of that. But Hooker still concentrated near Chancellorsville, and his numbers were daunting: Scattered through the trees and clearings, dotted behind works, and clustered around guns were nearly 75,000 men and 208 guns. What could he do with such strength? Calling his commanders to a conference during the night of May 1, Hooker heard two propositions: Find good ground and dig in or attack Lee in the woods, where he was at an equal disadvantage. Retreat was not a real choice—too much boasting had been done and a victory-hungry President Lincoln dogged the Military Telegraph Office for news. The original plan had pretty well "gone up" now that Rebels were in the woods. Attack might be possible, as was a slide south, across Lee's front, toward Richmond, which might still put the Army of the Potomac between Lee's left and the Confederate capital. Hooker ordered General John Reynolds to bring his I Corps from Fredericksburg and then pondered his opportunities.

Lee and Jackson pondered too. Lee disagreed about Hooker's possible retreat during the night. He hoped Jackson was right but felt Hooker could not abandon so notorious an effort. Unless Hooker's right could be turned, things looked sticky—the entire Union left and center seemed firm and strong and attacks on them would likely crumble. If a way around the enemy right could be found, Lee plotted a pincers attack against Hooker's front and rear—Jackson would march around the Union Army and hit it from behind. All that kept "Old Jack" from his greatest opportunity was the need for a protected and secret road curving south and then north back to the Old Turnpike. Was there one? Jackson put the problem to an old chaplain friend, the Reverend Tucker Lacy, who knew the country, and to his trusted topographical engineer, Jedediah Hotchkiss. They vanished in the darkness as May 1 dwindled in camp light and in the odd closeness of killing hordes.

Rumors of numerous Rebel reinforcements—perhaps Longstreet's missing men—flickered through the woods and struck special nerves way out on the Union right, where the XI Corps, Oliver O. Howard commanding, rested in lines mostly facing south. This corps, full of German Americans, was big but not lucky. It suffered often from xenophobic jokes in an army aggressively "American." Many of its officers, though, had Prussian training and knew much about war. Colonel Leopold von Gilsa was one such professional, and he worried increasingly about his brigade as he noted that Hooker's entire right flank was "in the air," unprotected by any natural or other man made barrier. Masses of Rebels were reported by pickets on the western end of the Federal line, yet worries and reports from von Gilsa that passed upward through the chain of command were ridiculed and rejected. The story ran that the Confederates were all clustered to the east and were so outnumbered that they had already begun retreating. That was what everybody saw—the Rebel retreat! What so many Federals saw was "Stonewall" Jackson's corps marching southwest, down past the Catherine Furnace to the Brock Road.

Jackson made the decision to move early on the morning of May 2, when he received word from Lacy and Hotchkiss that a usable, well-screened road leading toward the Yankee right and rear existed. That news came after Jackson and Lee met at a Wilderness campfire—and both generals studied the route. Could Hooker be hit before he shook off his fears and resumed the attack? If Lee divided his force to strike the Federals front and rear, both wings of his army would be smaller than the enemy and each one might be smashed. If Hooker pushed Sedgwick to attack Fredericksburg, Early's force might be wrecked and the Confederates caught in a closing vise. In the firelight Lee looked at his trusted lieutenant and asked: "General Jackson, what do you propose to do?" Still gazing at the map, Jackson pointed to Hotchkiss's sketched route and answered, "Go around here." Lee considered this and queried, "What do you propose to make this movement with?" Jackson had the reply ready, confirmed by hours of thought: "With my whole corps." If the enemy's flank lay as exposed as it seemed, maximum advantage must be taken of the situation—decisive victory lay within the Confederate grasp. A bit surprised, Lee wondered, "What will you leave me?" "The divisions of Anderson and McLaws" came the swift reply—so Jackson would march with 28,000 men and leave Lee 14,000 men to face the bulk of Hooker's strength. Lee's daring matched Jackson's; the attack would be made !

At about 8 A.M. the march began in a warming sunlight. Veteran infantry moved easily and covered ground. Speculation ran through the ranks as to where they were going, but all the gray-clads in the II Corps knew "Old Jack" had a surprise in store for Hooker. Even when they came to an exposed hill and took random shelling, they were confident and happy.

"Old Jack" himself seemed content. At midmorning he sent Lee a request to attack Hooker's front when fighting began behind Chancellorsville, then joined a group of officers at the head of his column. Former cadets or colleagues at the Virginia Military Institute, the officers listened to their commander explain a serious Confederate problem: "The trouble with us has always been to have a reserve to throw in at the critical moment to reap the benefit of advantages gained. We have always had to put in all our troops and never had enough at the time most needed." Hooker, Jackson heard, had more men than he could handle. "I should like to have half as many more as I have today, and I should hurl him in the river!"

Hooker may have had more men than he could handle, but some of his senses were sound that day. Reports coming to him during the morning of

Above: Brigadier General Robert Rodes led the way as Jackson threaded his way over a little-used side road to march around Hooker. He had distinguished himself in every battle he fought, and would continue to do so until a bullet cut him down in 1864. (VM)

Above: Brigadier General Alfred H. Colquitt, who came from Georgia, studied at the College of New Jersey in Princeton and served a term in Congress. On May 2 he led his Georgia brigade with Jackson in the flank march, then wildly attacked Hooker's ill-prepared and surprised right. (LC)

Above: The road on which Jackson led his command in the flanking march. The "plank road" in the foreground, so called because it was paved with board planks, is here joined by the little byroad just beyond the two men in the center of the image. Jackson was riding up this little road when accidental shots fired by his own men felled him. (USAMHI)

Above: Major General Oliver O. Howard, shown here as a brigadier, commanded Hooker's XI Corps. He detected Jackson's flank march but did not comprehend its significance. When "Stonewall" struck, Howard's corps was shattered. (USAMHI)

Above: Howard's corps were largely Germans. Major General Carl Schurz, prominent German revolutionary in the 1840s, led a division which was routed by Jackson's attack. (P-M)

Below: Commanding the 1st Division of the XI Corps was Brigadier General Charles Devens. His division utterly disintegrated, yet he was promoted for his service. Devens stands in the center, surrounded by his staff. (NA)

Right: As Jackson's attack rolled back Howard's corps, the Federals and Confederates both passed by the unassuming little Wilderness Church. Almost exactly one year from now it would figure in a terrible battle once more, continuing the macabre irony of a war in which great battles seemed to be fought on the sabbath and simple churchyards became pastures of death. (US-AMHI)

Right: But the surprise came at a cost to the Confederates, too. That evening, after the surprise attack, "Stonewall" Jackson was riding on the south side of the Plank Road. When he reached this spot, his own men mistook him for an enemy and fired on him. Eight days later he would die. (USAMHI)

a gray column marching southwest stirred speculation. Major General Dan Sickles thought the Rebels were retreating, but Hooker remarked that it was unlike Lee to fall back without fighting. He sent circulars to Major Generals Howard and Henry Slocum warning them to consider the possibility of a flank attack and to keep reserves handy just in case. At the same time, Hooker told Sickles to hit the passing column but to do so cautiously.

Sickles struck the enemy at Catherine Furnace at midafternoon, drove in their skirmishes, and reported the column large and burdened with wagons and guns. He could, Sickles told Hooker, reach the road and engage the whole gray force, but the commanding general still urged caution. Sickles strengthened his line and advanced to the road, where a sharp fight won him many Rebel prisoners—snappy-looking, husky men of the 23rd Georgia. Like most troops disgusted with being bagged, they tried taunting their captors, saying that they had come over to help "eat them eight day rations." One grizzled Rebel listened to a Yankee boast, "We'll have every mother's son of you before we go away," to which he growled, "You'll catch hell before night." Another irked prisoner blurted, "You think you've done a big thing just now, but you wait until Jackson gets around on your right." Blusters from captives go pretty much unnoticed, especially when things are looking up.

Sickles reported that his men were in among Rebel wagons and with a little help could do large damage. Hooker told Howard to send Sickles a brigade. As it happened, when Howard took Francis Barlow's brigade toward the sound of battle, he stripped his corps of its only reserve.

While Hooker waited for good news, expectations ran dismally out on his right. Portents of trouble gathered against the Dutchmen in the XI Corps during the morning. The corps rested, arms stacked, through the lunch hour, but then an odd tension sifted through the ranks. Numerous commanders shook out curtains of skirmishes south of the turnpike on the corps's front. Reports came back of active gray cavalry ahead of parties of hostile infantry, and it looked as though great numbers of Rebels were moving off toward the Federal right. Reports back to corps headquarters earned wise comments about a reconnaissance in force to cover Lee's retreat.

Officers at headquarters were sharp and edu-

Left: Samuel McGowan of South Carolina gallantly led his brigade in the heavy fighting that routed Howard's corps, but he himself took a serious wound in the fray. (VM)

Above: Howard made his headquarters at the home of George E. Chancellor, on the Plank Road. It would soon become a hospital, and its owner would give his name to Lee's greatest victory, as well as the nearby village: Chancellorsville. (USAMHI)

cated about all such high martial matters, but veterans in the ranks knew a retreat when they saw one—and they were not seeing one. The ranks grew restive as the day wore on and the portents became worse.

Several important things worked against the Dutchmen—in addition to Howard's leaving with their reserve. First, they were strung out in a mile long line, for most of the distance only two ranks deep. They faced south and could probably cope with a frontal attack, but a flank attack from the west or northwest would roll them up in a gathering crowd of disaster. Second, by the height of the afternoon old hands knew the Rebels had flanked them. Third, confirmation of that suspicion led to a terrible mounting frustration as nobody high up would listen.

Everything about XI Corps's situation looked bad. It was, in fact, isolated, with its eastern end—where Sickles's had been—resting on open ground near Dowdall's Tavern, a designated strong point with rifle pits and gun emplacements facing south. Westward from there the corps line ran along the road through woods and finally came to an end. There, at the right end of Hooker's whole line, two guns stood in the road and two regiments faced west, each in heavy skirmish order—one rank of men spread thin.

Worst of all, there was political trouble in the corps's right division, with Brigadier General Charles Devens of Boston commanding. Out near the division's far right lay Brigadier General Nathaniel C. McLean's brigade. (McLean had been division commander and was bumped down to make way for Devens.) So, as McLean's men repeatedly reported gray masses moving west, Devens chose to regard them as frightened alarmists and lectured them on the fact that corps headquarters—surely steeped in the fullest wisdom—had sounded no warnings. One of McLean's regimental commanders went to corps headquarters only to be laughed out.

It happened that Leopold von Gilsa's brigade was out on the western end of things; consequently, it also happened that late in the afternoon that wily Prussian veteran received word from his picket line that what looked like the whole Confederate Army was massing and "For God's Sake, make dispositions to receive" them. Von Gilsa took the message to Howard's staff, where the

Right: Colonel Reuben L. Walker was chief of artillery in A. P. Hill's division of Jackson's II Corps. Chancellorsville was a nightmare for artillerists because of the dense terrain. Only the Plank Road allowed good movement of the guns, and it was too often thronged with moving soldiers. This is a heavily retouched portrait photograph. (VM)

Right: Brigadier General Raleigh Colston led a dashing life. Born in France, adopted by a Virginian, a professor at the Virginia Military Institute, and an observer at the March 9, 1862, duel between the Monitor and the Virginia, he followed the war with soldier-of-fortune service in the Egyptian Army. At Chancellorsville he led a division under Jackson. (VM)

Left: Major General David B. Birney was the son of the famous antislavery leader James G. Birney. Standing in the front row center, he commands the 1st Division of Daniel Sickles's III Corps, posted next to Howard when the Confederate flank attack strikes. This image, made toward the end of 1863, shows the divisional banner with the battles of the unit emblazoned thereon. Immediately to the right of the center square one can read the word "Chancellorsville." It was a name hard won. (USAMHI)

Above: Men like this unidentified zouave of the 114th Pennsylvania paid a high price to put that word on their division's flag. (COURTESY OF TERENCE P. O'LEARY)

Above: Poor Francis R. T. Nichols. Only twenty-eight years old, he had already lost his left arm fighting with Jackson in the Shenandoah in 1862. Now a brigadier general, he saw his left foot torn off by a Federal cannonball at Chancellorsville, thus precluding further active service. (VM)

Right: Brigadier General Hobart Ward, seated at left, led a brigade for Birney in the heavy fighting of May 2. A year later he would be relieved of command for alleged intoxication during another campaign in this same Virginia Wilderness. (AMERICANA IMAGE GALLERY)

Above: The 110th Pennsylvania Infantry posed at Falmouth on April 24, 1863, only a week before it went into the inferno of Chancellorsville. A. J. Russell caught the regiment, a part of Sickles's III Corps, anxious for the fight, unaware that Jackson would nearly destroy them. (LC)

news was dismissed with the thought that the forest out to the west was too thick for a line of battle to pass. Vastly bothered, von Gilsa returned to his line to greet "Iron Pants" Dilger, coming over from Carl Schurz's front. He had been sent scouting by his general, who, though not a trained professional, shared the spreading alarm and had shifted part of his front near Wilderness Church to face west just in case. Captain Hubert Dilger, late of the Baden Mountain Artillery, could have saved Hooker.

Defying von Gilsa's warning not to go too far west lest he be captured, Dilger ran into a Rebel battle line, fled for his freedom, and skirted far north, almost to the Rapidan, before he reached Hooker's headquarters. There he failed to get past a supercilious major who showed considerable contempt for alarming words given in a heavy foreign accent. Hooker need not be bothered; go back to XI Corps headquarters. Back there Dilger was berated for unauthorized scouting and was reminded that Lee's army was retreating. Back among his own guns, Dilger cautioned his men to keep the horses handy.

Skirmish firing picked up around 5 P.M., but it went unremarked by great leaders. That skirmish fire Jackson noted as he watched a massive gray battle line form slowly in the late afternoon light. Everything seemed to happen so slowly. The march from Catherine Furnace along Hotchkiss's fifteen-mile route had gone steadily, but heat and rain-sogged roads brought a kind of summer lethargy to his veterans. Sickles's attack had not really stalled the march, but its confusion caused problems for a while.

Jeb Stuart ranged ahead of Jackson's men to probe woods for usable roads. By midafternoon he realized the Brock Road would lead obliquely into the Union lines. Another must be found. The turnpike? Could it be reached in secrecy? Finding Jackson, Stuart rode with him to a knoll near the Brock Road that overlooked the western end of the enemy's lines; the two generals saw entrenchments, guns, and ready infantry. Jackson agreed his men must go farther. Stuart confirmed their road would lead to the turnpike, full aflank the Federals. "Press on, men, press on," Jackson urged. Knowing his customary impatience before impending success, his men marched in growing glee. They were out on "Fighting Joe's" flank, and they were going to ruin his reputation. Where would "Old Jack" put them? He put them across the turnpike in a line that stretched a mile, stretched as far as a man could see in the patches of trees and dense underbrush, and he put them in four divisional lines, clouds of skirmishers out in front. Ahead of them, they knew, lay the XI Corps, and on this second day of May 1863 that would be a corps of Flying Dutchmen.

Robert Emmett Rodes, a young and gifted brigadier, had charge of the forming Rebel lines. At 5:15 P.M. Jackson asked him if he was ready and Rodes said he was. "You can go forward then." The young general signaled his bugler, the notes rang through the woods, and the skirmishers ran forward. The big lines followed, slowly at first, then faster, with increasing momentum, and at last men were tearing through scant growth, running, running with their high, eerie Rebel yell floating on before them.

What the Dutchmen saw first were deer, rabbits, and other animals running at them, fleeing the skirmishers and the yelling. A few braced, but

Russell photographed Company C, of the 110th Pennsylvania, that same day. Some of the boyish faces would never smile again. "No braver or better troops" fought at Chancellorsville, said their brigade commander. For two hours the 110th held a position against superior odds. (MHS)

Above: Sickles's artillery aided materially in staying, at least in part, the thundering advance of Jackson. Private Davis Shephard, shown here mounted next to one of the guns of his 11th New York Light Artillery, saw hard service at Chancellorsville as his three-inch ordnance rifles vainly tried to halt the Confederates. (COURTESY OF ROBERT MCDONALD)

most fled when a long wave of gray dotted with reddened battle flags streamed out of the forest, washed over them, and rolled beyond.

That old muffling effect of the Wilderness trapped the noise of fighting. Hooker spent the afternoon awaiting news from Sickles and urging Sedgwick to take his VI Corps across the Rappahannock in pursuit of Lee's rearguard and trains. This message gave the impression that Hooker firmly accepted the notion of Lee's retreat. At about 6:30 P.M. that fiction dissolved. Hearing noises to the right, one of Hooker's staff walked out in front of headquarters and saw a wild melee of men, horses, wagons, and bouncing guns streaming straight at him down the road. "My God—here they come," he yelled. Hooker and other aides scrambled on horses and rode to try to stem the stampede. "Vere ist der pontoon?" screamed some of the XI Corps's remnants; most just ran without thought. Hooker's little coterie charged the rout, but they were engulfed.

Jolted from his daylong reverie, Hooker came to life now that battle raged. Quickly he ordered trustworthy John Reynolds to get his I Corps forward. Sadly Reynolds reported that a lost dispatch bearer had delayed his move toward Hooker; his men were not yet across United States Ford. There was a hope. The "Old Hooker Division" had been kept close to headquarters. Hooker rode up to its commander, Hiram Berry, and shouted: "General... throw your men into the breach—receive the enemy on your bayonets—don't fire a shot—they can't see you."

Hasty efforts to amass artillery at Fairview Cemetery, facing west, met some success. Howard, all bravery now that disaster loomed, collected some infantry, a few batteries, and put them with Berry's men in a line across the road, west of Hooker's headquarters. Schurz brought up a polyglot force and went to Berry's right; a division of the XII Corps prolonged the left. Guns behind this makeshift line poured shells into the Rebels. Hooker wanted to reinforce his right, but Lee demonstrated so strongly in front of Chancellorsville that an attack seemed imminent and Hooker dared not weaken Winfield Scott Hancock or George Gordon Meade.

Darkness settled over the Wilderness in an uneasy gloom. Sporadic flashes marked isolated

Left: On May 3 Confederate regiments battered ceaselessly against Hooker, while Lee turned his attention to Sedgwick at Fredericksburg. The 16th Virginia and its officers, once the regiment of General Raleigh Colston, fought in Richard H. Anderson's division, assaulted Hooker's center when Jackson struck Howard, and then, on May 3, turned to meet Sedgwick. (MUSEUM OF THE CONFEDERACY)

Left: An artilleryman of the Salem Flying Artillery from Roanoke, Virginia. His battery moved with the 16th Virginia in the attack on May 3. (COURTESY OF DALE S. SNAIR)

Above: On the day after Jackson's attack the fighting continued furiously around the Chancellor House and Chancellorsville. Here the ruins of a once-imposing structure testify to the fury of the fighting. This is an 1865 image. (USAMHI)

Above: Major General Hiram G. Berry commanded a division that had once belonged to Hooker in the III Corps. On the morning of May 3, as the disorganized Federal Army tried to recover from the devastating blow dealt by Jackson, Berry took a mortal wound while fighting with his division. (USAMHI)

Above: He led men like these of the 73rd New York. (USAMHI)

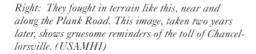

Right: They fought in terrain like this, near and along the Plank Road. This image, taken two years later, shows gruesome reminders of the toll of Chancellorsville. (USAMHI)

fighting, cannonading shook the trees, but heavy encounters stopped. The impetus ebbed from the Rebel attack.

Success stalled Jackson's advance, success and darkness and stiffening resistance. "Old Jack" worked to unscramble units mixed in the headlong rush, bring fresh men forward, replenish munitions, and prepare another thrust. He hoped to crush Hooker between Lee and his own II Corps, perhaps slide a bit to his left, and get between Hooker and vital river crossings.

Reorganization proved complicated; Jackson hated the delay, which gave Hooker time to regroup. Ever eager to move forward, to know where the enemy was, Jackson took a small party of aides and rode ahead of the Confederate lines. Somewhere beyond lay the enemy. Where? Down a dark, shadowy lane he led his little detachment. Slowly, carefully they went until, at last, the clang of axes and voices was heard—the enemy was entrenching just ahead.

Pulling his horse, Little Sorrel, around, Jackson rode quickly back toward the Rebel lines. Rumors were running wild that night—Yankee cavalry roamed everywhere—they were coming down the road straight into a North Carolina regiment! Hasty challenges, quick volleys, and Jackson fell from his saddle, wounded in the left arm and right hand. Hastily put on a stretcher for transfer to the rear, Jackson and his bearers were caught in a terrific cannonade; several bearers fell and Jackson's stretcher crashed to the ground. Major General A. P. Hill, second in command, had just reached Jackson when the barrage struck; he, too, fell wounded. Command devolved, by rank, on Jeb Stuart. Stuart sent a messenger to Jackson's side at

Above: Brigadier General Romeyn B. Ayres led a brigade in George G. Meade's V Corps. Briefly engaged on May 1, he enjoyed the luxury of being relatively idle during the rest of the battle. It did not appeal to the combative veteran of First Manassas. (KA)

Above: Major General Winfield Scott Hancock, who seemed to appear prominently on every field of the Army of the Potomac, did no less so at Chancellorsville. When, finally, Hooker abandoned his position after a few days of idleness following the battle, Hancock covered the withdrawal against excessive odds, and did so successfully. (USAMHI)

Above: But Chancellorsville was a two-part battle. The second part took place at Fredericksburg, an old battleground of 1862. There Hooker had assigned Major General John Sedgwick. (NA)

a field hospital, hoping to receive orders. His left arm amputated, "Old Jack" rose on his other elbow. The battle light gleamed in his shocked eyes and then faded. He said Stuart must do what he thought best.

Too much of Jackson's spirit pervaded the corps to give up the offensive. Stuart reorganized and planned to attack in the morning.

By morning Hooker had some chance not only for survival but even for success. Reynolds's I Corps was at hand to stabilize the right; Meade had put some of the V Corps in next to Reynolds, and Sickles held important high ground at Hazel Grove. The way the Confederates had pushed their attack shoved their right flank out in front of Sickles and exposed their left to Reynolds. Boldness now might turn Lee's gamble into the loss of the war. Hooker looked at Sickles's position and pronounced it too exposed should Lee come up from the south. He told Sickles to retreat to Fairview.

Nothing worse could have been ordered save surrender. Rebels immediately put guns on this high ground, which could enfilade the Union right and left. By holding Hazel Grove the Rebels virtually connected their two wings. Hooker need not, should not, have withdrawn Sickles. With Reynolds at hand, he now counted 76,000 men and the Confederates counted around 42,000, reduced by unknown numbers of casualties; and with Reynolds on the Rebel left, Union numbers were positioned to count. While Jeb Stuart rode along his line exhorting his troops by singing "Old Joe Hooker, won't you come out of the Wilderness," the Federal leader huddled in a mile square of shell-swept ground, waiting to be saved. He

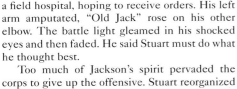

Above: Repeatedly Sedgwick sent his men across the Rappahannock against Marye's Heights. A. J. Russell captured this image of Fredericksburg that very day from across the river. The thirty-two-pounders in the foreground are now idle, but earlier that day they spoke ferociously. (LC)

Above: Indeed, while the fighting for Marye's Heights was going on, Russell operated his camera. The battle is in the far distance, with nothing visible to betray it except the line of smoke just below the horizon. (NEIKRUG PHOTOGRAPHICA, LTD.)

Above: Units like the 31st Pennsylvania, shown here in camp, fought valiantly in repeated assaults before they finally broke through the Confederates' line and started to drive toward Lee's rear. (P-M)

had ordered the harried John Sedgwick to speed to ward Chancellorsville.

During the morning Hooker's men did well and the Union lines held—until a tactical blunder forced further contraction of the Federal position. Desperately Hooker waited for Sedgwick, who was having serious trouble cutting through from Fredericksburg.

About midmorning Hooker walked out on the south porch of his headquarters and a shell from a Rebel gun at Hazel Grove splintered a pillar of the Chancellor House; part of it struck Hooker on the head and knocked him down, stunned. Rumors flowed immediately that he was dead—some wish, perhaps, fathering the thought. He revived quickly, though in considerable pain. Shortly thereafter he gave General Darius Couch limited command of the army, with instructions to retire into a U-shaped tête-de-pont, open end toward United States Ford. By the morning of May 4 Hooker's men were well dug in and waiting. Waiting ruined the last hope of crushing Lee.

Sedgwick had broken through Early's lines at Fredericksburg on May 3 and had pushed on toward Chancellorsville. But Lee noted Hooker's loss of nerve on the third, posted a force to watch

Below: The fighting along the stone wall on Marye's Heights was particularly brutal. Russell took his camera across the Rappahannock to capture the scene less than twenty minutes after the Confederates were driven out. Brigadier General Herman Haupt, chief of construction and transportation on the United States Military Railroads, came with Russell. "I walked over the battle-ground, and examined the heights beyond Marye's house. I then realized the great strength of the position and the impossibility of taking it, if properly defended, by a direct assault in front, as had been attempted by Burnside with disastrous results. My photographic artist, Captain Russell, was with me and secured several large photographic negatives—one very good one of the stone wall, with the rebel dead lying behind it." (USAMHI)

Left: Company K of the 6th Vermont was part of the second regiment to crest Marye's Heights in the final successful attack. (LC)

Above: Brigadier General Albion P. Howe led his division of the VI Corps personally in its attacks on Marye's Heights. Two years later, to the day, he would act as an honor guard over the coffin of Abraham Lincoln. (P-M)

Hooker, and took a big portion of his army toward Sedgwick at Salem Church. Early had skirmished and backed up, tired of retreating, when Lee arrived; together they drove Sedgwick to cover near Banks' Ford and threatened to capture over 20,000 bluecoats.

Lee's attack on the fourth began late and scrambled over difficult ground. Sedgwick held his front until nightfall. Then he got his men across the Rappahannock. That piqued Lee, who had played a daring game of inserting his inferior force between two large enemy elements. He had, by most odds, been lucky to avoid destruction— and yet he always counted on boldness in stressful times. The original decision to let Jackson go around Hooker had been a gamble that paid high dividends; the decision on the third to go against Sedgwick was no less a gamble, and the Salem Church fighting had promised the elimination of an entire Union corps. It had escaped as a result of poor ground and sluggish reaction times in some of his units. This Lee thought a serious lapse, one that wasted another great opportunity. Returning to face Hooker's main body on the fifth, Lee planned to attack on the morrow—but Hooker's bedraggled columns crossed the Rappahannock at United States Ford during the night. His campaign had cost 17,000 Union casualties and achieved nothing save 13,000 Rebel casualties.

Lincoln reacted in anguish. "My God! My God! What will the Country say!" Horace Greeley put it this way: "God! It is horrible—horrible…! 130,000 magnificent soldiers so cut to pieces by less than 60,000 half-starved ragamuffins !"

Historians have said much about Hooker's errors and his moral failure. They have said much, too, about the crowning achievement of Lee and Jackson, about a battle showing the value of maneuver and applied psychology.

Yet Chancellorsville was a Confederate victory fought at too high a price: On May 10, 1863 "Stonewall" Jackson died.

Above: As Sedgwick pursued the retreating Confederates, unaware that Lee would stop him in a few hours and end the battle as a Confederate victory, Russell anxiously moved his camera through the abandoned Southern camps. The briefly victorious Federals celebrated by ransacking the Rebel winter huts, finding liquor, blankets, and souvenirs that most would not have time to take with them. (CHS)

Left: Russell's image of Haupt, at left, surveying the damage to an artillery battery's animals and equipment after the battle. (KA)

Above: Brigadier General Robert F. Hoke would one day tell his North Carolinians that "the proudest day in all your proud careers was that on which you enlisted as Southern soldiers." In defending Fredericksburg he performed proudly, taking a serious wound. (VM)

Above: This 1865 image shows part of the toll of the battle, with Federal dead buried in The Wilderness. Hooker and his campaign had failed despite his bravado. These dead paid the price for his failure. (USAMHI)

Right: Some even escaped burial, or were so hastily interred that war's end found their bones shining in the sun. (USAMHI)

Below: Hooker's supply base at Aquia Creek Landing became untenable as he withdrew his army. (LC)

Right: There was no choice but to evacuate. In June 1863 Timothy O'Sullivan captured several images of the barges and steamers loaded with supplies and materiel for the successful withdrawal. As little as possible would be left for the Confederates. (LC)

Left: Whole trains of cars were loaded on barges, as with the flatcars on the right. It was a massive operation. (KA)

Left: For Hooker it was the only success of the campaign. In June, back in Falmouth, he would pose with his staff. Butterfield is seated at right, followed by Hooker, General Rufus Ingalls, and Major General H. J. Hunt. Within days the sober-looking "Fighting Joe" would be relieved of command even as Lee's Confederates were invading the North. (US-AMHI)

Above: But Lee's victory cost him dear. This early postwar view shows a house near Guiney's Station, a few miles from Fredericksburg. Here "Stonewall" Jackson was brought after he was wounded. His arm was amputated, the wound seemed to be healing, and then pneumonia grasped the great soldier. (DUKE UNIVERSITY LIBRARY)

Right: And in this room, now filled with a shaving horse, rude anvil, planes, and barrel maker's tools, the mighty "Stonewall" died. He had "crossed over the river," and with him went much of the hope of the Army of Northern Virginia. (DUKE UNIVERSITY LIBRARY)

The South at War

CHARLES P. ROLAND

The tragic vision of decline, yet of seemingly indomitable determination

There were many Souths in 1861, but as the war progressed they melded more and more into one, struggling to cope with adversity and survive. There was the South of Richard Habersham's Port Royal plantation, pastoral and carefree… (USAMHI)

THE SOUTHERN POPULATION experienced war at close quarters during the conflict. For four years it raged in their midst. It stirred them to heroic sacrifice and endeavor, but in the end it consumed them. It left its mark in their abandoned homes and cities. It left a deeper mark in the graves of a quarter of the region's men of military age, and in the scarred faces and maimed bodies of countless others. Deepest of all was the mark it left on the heart of the South. A century later the memory of defeat and military occupation remained one of the major distinguishing characteristics of the Southern people.

Few Southerners foresaw the disastrous outcome of the struggle, and those who did foresee and warn of it were ridiculed. Spirits soared at the first call to the colors. The Yankees were too crass and mercenary to be good soldiers, Southerners told themselves, and the world's need for Southern cotton would overcome whatever weaknesses there might be in the regional economy. After traveling through the South in 1861, the English newspaper correspondent William Howard Russell wrote: "With France and England to pour gold into their lap with which to purchase all they need in the conflict, they believe they can beat all the powers of the Northern world in arms."

Lightheartedly the South prepared for war, mustering its state militia companies and forming its volunteer Confederate regiments. A rural and traditionally unregimented society, the South in the beginning supported the Confederate effort with a great spontaneous folk movement. Parties and balls, dinners and barbecues, lotteries and raffles, these and a dozen other forms of entertainment were used to raise money, clothing, and arms for "the cause." Patriotic oratory with a Southern accent and bias gave urgency to these occasions. Even the somberness of troop departures for the front was leavened with gaiety, feasting, dancing, and singing of martial airs, along with the sermons and prayers of the ever-present Southern preachers.

The hard days soon arrived as the Federal blockade isolated southern ports and caused shortages and deprivation of imported necessities. Prices quickly spiraled upward and the Confederate currency was devalued. By 1864 the people in Richmond were saying, with grim humor, that they once took money to the market in their wallets and returned with purchases in baskets; now they took money in baskets and returned with purchases in their wallets.

As the war ground on, the Southern masses underwent extreme hardship. Heads of families were not exempt from Confederate military service, and their wives and children were obliged to endure the travails of war alone. They did so with exemplary fortitude, tilling the land, harvesting the crops, and playing an indispensable role in sustaining the armies and keeping the crippled economy alive.

Those areas beyond the immediate reach of invading Federal armies usually had enough food, but such luxuries as sugar and coffee were soon gone. Salt, an almost essential preservative, was extremely rare. Most medicines were practically unobtainable, and the population had to fall back on outmoded home remedies.

Southern city dwellers experienced shortages more severe than those felt by their rural compatriots. This was the result of a rapid increase in the urban population to work in the war factories

Above: ... and there was the South of busy seaports like Charleston and Savannah, bustling with commerce until the blockade left most of the wharves idle. (NA)

Above: There were scenes like this, captured by George Barnard in 1866, with the docks crowded with bales of cotton awaiting shipment to foreign ports. (KA)

while at the same time the Southern transport system was taxed beyond its capacity in mobilizing and supplying the armies. Also, the slave labor force was disrupted by the struggle, thus reducing the region's supply of necessities. Whole families in Richmond and other cities lived in single rooms, using the fireplaces for both warmth and cooking, and subsisted on corn fritters, boiled potatoes, and beans.

The greatest suffering occurred in the wake of the grappling armies, and this ultimately covered most of the land. The Federals looted Southern food and supplies because, in part, they lived by foraging, and also because of a desire to inflict punishment for the sin of rebellion. The Confederates were to be feared almost as keenly as the invaders. A Louisiana sugar planter complained that Confederate troops had stripped his plantation of virtually every resource for day-to-day living. "From a condition of ease, comfort and abundance," he wrote, "I am suddenly reduced to one of hardship, want & privation." At this time not a Federal soldier had set foot on his place. The population of Georgia late in the war came to dread the appearance of Confederate Major General Joseph Wheeler's cavalry about as much as they dreaded the approach of General Sherman's columns. Victims of friend as well as foe, countless Southern families were left at the door of starvation.

Recreation and entertainment suffered the effects of wartime shortages and of the absence of many of the men. Music and dancing still took place on plantations and in city mansions, but much of the conviviality was now gone. Food and drink became ever more scarce, and in the final months of the conflict "starvation parties" were held where nothing was served but water. Among the rural common people the usual diversions went on, for they cost but little. The chief differences now were the extreme youth of most of the boys who were there to take part, or, sadly, the presence of young men with missing limbs or marred features. The folk amusements included square dancing and singing, picnics and barbe-

Left: Forests of masts betold the riches that lay in the precious fiber so entwined with the Southern economy and way of life—and with slavery. (SOUTH CAROLINA HISTORICAL SOCIETY)

Left: Inland commerce, too, teemed before the war brought it to a near halt. Steamboats like these, photographed at the landing at Chickasaw Bayou, Mississippi, bore a carrying trade that practically disappeared when the Federal gunboats came. (CHS)

Above: It was a South of small country courthouse towns, towns like Warrenton, Virginia, whose chief excitement until then lay in the occasional trial in the courthouse. (USAMHI)

Left: When the armies came to Warrenton in 1862, they found a sleepy market town which had never seen war before. (LC)

Right: Culpeper, Virginia, was much the same until the tented fields bespoke that warring armies had come to stay. (P-M)

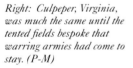

Left: Dusty streets that had known only farmers' wagons became accustomed to the booted heels of the soldier, both friend and invader. (NA)

cues, corn husking, quilting, and spinning bees. Religious revivals were also social occasions. Hunting and fishing, the oldest and most widespread of pastimes among Southern men and boys, remained favorites throughout the conflict and, at the same time, became increasingly important as sources of victuals. The urban poor were less fortunate than the rural poor. Ordinary Southerners living in the cities usually had to be content with such inexpensive activities as neighborly visits, church meetings, open-air band concerts, or military reviews. Ultimately life became too somber for frolics or frivolities anywhere in the stricken South.

As portions of the Confederacy fell to the Union armies, many of the inhabitants, especially among the planter class, left their homes and "refugeed" to Texas or some other temporarily safe place. Taking with them their slaves, valuables, and as many household belongings as possible, they jammed the roads with wagons and carts while the people themselves walked wearily along the edges. They traveled in groups and camped in the fields at night. Their hardships and heartbreak were beyond expression.

State and local governments appropriated funds for the subsistence of soldiers' families. Citizens formed benevolent societies to help the needy. City authorities set up charity markets to collect and distribute produce supplied by planters and farmers of the surrounding areas. Innumerable individuals aided the less fortunate with donations of goods and services. But these measures fell woefully short of the exigencies of the times, and the Confederate government itself attempted no systematic relief of the destitution that spread throughout the population as the war grew in fury.

Loneliness, anxiety, and grief became the constant companions of the people behind the lines. The Confederate postal service broke down almost completely late in the conflict, and the isolation and seclusion of the farms and plantations were maddening. When news did at last arrive, it often contained dread tidings of the death of a loved one in camp or battle. A keen observer of the Confederate scene wrote that nearly as many Southern women died of grief and anxiety as did Southern men of Northern bullets.

The Confederacy had no propaganda department and attempted no organized mobilization of the region's cultural and intellectual resources. Yet because of Confederate patriotism and shared beliefs and values, most of the religious, literary, artistic, and educational leaders of the South lent their talents and energies to the Confederate war effort.

It has been said that the churches are perhaps the best places to look for the origins of cultural nationalism in the Old South. The region was overwhelmingly Protestant, and long before the coming of secession the Southern segments of the two largest national Protestant bodies—the Methodists and Baptists—had broken away and formed themselves into separate denominations. Southern churchmen provided the most telling argument in defense of the institution of slavery— the Biblical argument. Thus the Southern churches were also ideal sources of Confederate political nationalism and wartime morale. Southern preachers and theologians justified secession as a fulfillment of God's will and urged their followers to self-sacrifice in the Confederate cause.

They condemned the North for its alleged atheism and materialism, and they believed the Lord would uphold the arms of His people of the South in their struggle for independence. Preachers "sounded the trumpets" that called the South to war.

With the coming of secession, the other major Protestant churches (Episcopal, Presbyterian, and Lutheran) broke into Southern and Northern wings. Southern Catholics could not follow this course, but they supported the Confederacy as if they had done so. The role of religion in the Confederate effort was to be seen in the lives of many of the Southern leaders. President Davis, reared in a Baptist family but never before formally a church member, became a convert to the Episcopal faith soon after the Confederate government moved to Richmond. He regularly attended services at St. Paul's Episcopal Church and was there on April 2, 1865, when he received General Robert E. Lee's fateful message saying the capital must be abandoned. Many of the chief military figures of the Confederacy were men of strong religious faith. Lee himself was a devout Episcopalian. His great subordinate, Lieutenant General Thomas J. "Stone wall" Jackson, was just as devout a Presbyterian. Thus were the Southern Cavalier and the Southern Puritan joined in the common cause of Southern defense.

The Reverend Robert Louis Dabney, a noted Presbyterian theologian, served on Jackson's staff, and Lee's chief of artillery, Brigadier General William N. Pendleton, was an Episcopal minister who prayed for the souls of his Northern enemies even as he killed them. When commanding a battery early in the war, Pendleton carried the religious military theme to its extremity by naming his guns Matthew, Mark, Luke, and John. Apparently he was oblivious to the incongruity of identifying these engines of death with the apostles of peace. Lieutenant General Leonidas Polk, though a graduate of the United States Military Academy, had long been the Episcopal bishop of Louisiana when the war broke out. At various times during the conflict he reverted to his ecclesiastical role. Affected by the prospect of defeat, many other Confederate generals turned to religion late in the war. On the retreat from Sherman's advance through Georgia, the "Fighting Bishop" took time out from his military duties long enough to baptize Generals Joseph E. Johnston and John Bell Hood.

The Confederate government consciously sought to use religion to strengthen the will of the people. On many occasions throughout the war a day was set apart for special prayers and thanksgiving. Perhaps the most vehement Confederate sentiments ever expressed were those in a plantation overseer's prayer on one of these days. He wrote the following passage in the plantation journal:

This Day is set a part by president Jefferson Davis for fasting and praying owing to the Deplorable condishion ower Southern country is In My prayer Sincerely to God is that Every Black Republican in the Hole combined whorl Either man women o chile that is opposed to negro slavery as it existed in the Southern confederacy shal be trubled with pestilences & calamitys of all kinds & drag out the Balance of there existence in misry & degradation with Scarsely food & rayment enough to keep sole & body to geather and O God I pray the to Direct a bullet or a bayonet to pirce the hart of every northern Soldier that in-

Left: Military wagons filled the streets, with prisoners of war and wounded often billeted in the courthouses and churches, as shown here in Culpeper. (MUSEUM OF THE CONFEDERACY)

Left: The war disrupted the thousands of little railroad siding hamlets that dotted the South. (CHS)

Below: Everywhere the local calm gave way to the overpowering sense of change and displacement of war. (CHS)

Left: Only the shantytowns on the fringes of the larger cities seemed unaffected. Even the armies avoided slums like "Slabtown," located outside Hampton, Virginia. O'Sullivan's camera did not. (USAMHI)

Below: The major Southern cities showed the marks of war in direct proportion to their proximity to the front. Alexandria was the first front, facing Washington across the Potomac. Streets were frequently barricaded to control traffic into and out of the Northern-held but pro-Southern city. (USAMHI)

vades southern Soil & after the Body has Rendered up its Traterish Sole gave it a trators reward a Birth in the Lake of fires & Brimstone. My honest convicksion is that Every man women & chile that has gave aid to the abolishionist are fit Subjects for Hell I all so ask the to aide the Sothern confedercy in mantaining ower rites & establishing the confederate Government Believing in this case the prares from the wicked will prevailith much—Amen—.

Congregations held their own prayer meetings in behalf of Confederate success, and great revivals occurred in the armies as civilian missionaries and preachers circulated among the camps and added their voices to those of the chaplains. That religion played an important role in sustaining the fighting spirit of the Southern people, despite the ultimate outcome of the war, seems beyond doubt. Governor Francis W. Pickens of South Carolina said early in the struggle that the South had made it a holy war. A Confederate congressman said later that the clergy had done more than any other class for the Southern effort. "Not even the bayonets have done more."

This might also be said of the press. Journalism was the most vigorous and most widely read form of writing in the Old South. Many Southern newspapers played an important part in bringing on secession, and by the time the war began almost all

Below: Evidence of the Northern occupiers was everywhere. The provost's building in Alexandria had once been the Marine and Fire Insurance Offices. (WRHS)

Above: Military governors, like Brigadier General John P. Slough, seated at center, ruled in Alexandria and other Southern cities. Many were kind, and most were vilified . (USAMHI)

Southern journals were behind the Confederate cause. But Southern editors were fiercely independent in their views, and they disagreed thoroughly in their attitudes toward President Jefferson Davis and his measures. Nathaniel Tyler's Richmond *Enquirer,* Richard M. Smith's Richmond *Sentinel,* and Richard Yeadon's Charleston *Courier* were so staunch in their support that they came to be looked upon as mouthpieces of the government. Other newspapers were just as strongly hostile. Edward Pollard and John M. Daniel of the Richmond *Examiner* accused Davis of incompetence and tyranny. Robert Barnwell Rhett, the so called "Father of Secession," was relentless in his diatribes against Davis through the columns of his son's newspaper, the Charleston *Mercury.* Such critics probably would have been silenced in the wartime North, but the Confederate government followed a scrupulous hands-off policy that unquestionably allowed its detractors to cripple the popular morale.

Southern creative writers turned out many works extolling the virtues of the people and their cause. Most of these writings were hastily done and too emotional and sentimental to be of lasting quality. But two South Carolina poets, Henry Timrod and Paul Hamilton Hayne, responded to the exaltation and tragedy of the times with verse of genuine merit. Hayne's best wartime composition was "The Battle of Charleston Harbor," which celebrated the heroic episode named in the title. Timrod, remembered as the poet laureate of the Confederacy, praised what he considered to be the peculiar virtues of his region in "The Cotton Boll" and "Ethnogenesis." His "A Cry to Arms" was a poetic bugle call. His most beautiful piece came after the war in his "Ode" to the Confederate dead buried in the Magnolia Cemetery at Charleston. Its opening lines were:

Sleep sweetly in your humble graves,
Sleep, martyrs to a fallen cause,
Though yet no marble column craves
The Pilgrim here to pause.

In seeds of laurel in the earth
The blossom of your fame is blown
And somewhere, waiting for its birth
The shaft is in the stone !

The most respected novelist of the Old South, William Gilmore Simms of Charleston,

Above: None attracted greater condemnation than Major General Benjamin F. Butler. He so managed to antagonize the people of New Orleans that he was branded an outcast by Confederate authorities and was not entitled to the usual courtesies of war should he be captured. He and others like him made potent weapons for Southern anti-Yankee propaganda. (INTERNATIONAL MUSEUM OF PHOTOGRAPHY)

Above: Brigadier General Richard Busteed had bitterly opposed Lincoln's election in 1860, but in 1862 he was entrusted with occupation duty protecting Fort Monroe in Virginia. He would later be a Federal judge in Alabama, and would be accused of fraud. (NA)

Left: The homes, great and small, of Southerners became fair game for Federal officers seeking headquarters. Dr. Murray's home in Fauquier County, Virginia, was captured in this image taken in November 1863 by O'Sullivan after it had been appropriated for the use of some Yankee brass. (P-M)

Above: The Marye house behind Fredericksburg became a Federal office for a time after its bloody part in the battles of December 1862 and May 1863. Rifle pits are still evident in the left foreground of this May 1864 image. (P-M)

Above: General Meade made his September 1863 Culpeper headquarters at the home of a Mr. Wallach. Generally the occupiers took scrupulous care of the properties thus appropriated, paying for damages done by them and their soldiers. (P-M)

Right: In September 1863 these Federals occupied the home of John Minor Botts, a famous Culpeper resident who had been a congressman and bitter opponent of secession. The Confederates imprisoned him in Richmond for his disloyal sentiments. (P-M)

Right: The Fauquier Springs Hotel in August 1862, as seen by O'Sullivan. It was occupied by the advancing Federals during the Second Manassas campaign. (P-M)

Below: It was the same in the West, though generally on a less grand scale. Brigadier General Grenville Dodge had to make his divisional headquarters in Corinth, Mississippi, in this much less imposing home. (CHS)

lived through the Civil War and supported the Confederate cause with some poetry and many vigorous editorials. But the conflict seems to have blighted his genuine literary talents. He wrote no novel on the war. Indeed, little fiction came out of the Confederacy; perhaps there was not enough time for it to mature. Best known was the novel *Macaria; or, Altars of Sacrifice* by the popular novelist Augusta Jane Evans of Mobile. The hero of the story dies on a Civil War battlefield, thus fulfilling the author's theme that the people of the South, like the Greek heroine for whom the story is named, ought to lay down their lives in defense of hearth, home, and independence.

Not surprisingly, the Confederate literature of humor lacked the verve and color that distinguished the tales of the great prewar Southern humorists. Life now was too grim for that. Yet humor did survive the hardships of the war. The Confederacy's chief professional humorist, "Bill Arp" [Charles H. Smith of Georgia], entertained his readers with newspaper barbs addressed to "Mr. Abe Linkhorn." Nor did he neglect Confederate foibles. When the Confederacy became swamped in a confusing mass of treasury notes, he quoted the Secretary of the Treasury as saying he was not sure whether the notes in circulation amounted to six hundred million dollars or six thousand million dollars.

Far more suited to the modern ear was the spontaneous humor of many nonprofessional Southerners of the time. For example, take the bold headline in a Jackson, Mississippi, newspaper late in the war:

RAILROAD ACCIDENT
The 10:00 o'clock train
from Meridian
arrived on time today.

Or witness the naughty but clever poem written in response to a request by one John Harrolson of the Niter and Mining Bureau that the women of

Below: The destruction and displacement caused by the war in the South was on a scale that no one could have anticipated. Tens of thousands of civilians, usually women and children, had to flee the advancing enemy for refugee havens in the interior. They took what they could with them, including granny's pipe. (LC)

Left: Homes not made headquarters all too often became hospitals, like this home on the Manassas battlefield, caught in July 1862 by O'Sullivan. (LC)

Above: Thousands of rural Southern scenes like this unidentified spot bore witness to the destructive force of the contending armies. Southern men in shirtsleeves and suspenders survey the wreckage of what was perhaps a store, a courthouse, or a home, now reduced to rubble, its foundation an echo of a place where Southerners once lived or worked. (CWTI)

Above: Once beautiful places like Fauquier Springs were destroyed, leaving only haunting reminders of their former grandeur. (P-M)

Selma, Alabama, save their chamber pot contents to provide lye for the manufacture of explosives. The last verse went:

> John Harrolson ! John Harrolson !
> Do pray invent a neater
> And somewhat more modest mode
> Of making your saltpetre;
> For tis an awful idea, John,
> gunpowdery and cranky
> That when a lady lifts her shift
> she's killing off a Yankee.

Or take this gem of Southern feminine humor: A South Carolina minister preached a sermon on Joseph in Egypt, closing with the pronouncement that the young Hebrew slave, in refusing to be seduced by his master's wife, had resisted the greatest temptation known to man. At this point a young woman in the audience said in a stage whisper: "Fiddlesticks, everybody knows Old Mrs. Pharaoh was every day of forty." Humor remained a source of Confederate morale when most other sources were gone.

The most enduring of Confederate literature was not written as literature at all in the formal sense. This included the diaries and letters of Southerners describing the tumultuous events of the times and the emotions stirred by them. Most of the diaries were by women; they thus provide insights never before revealed into the hearts and minds of the feminine segment of the Southern population. The most celebrated of the diaries is that of Mary Boykin Chesnut of South Carolina, whose husband was a former United States Senator and served throughout most of the war as an aide to Jefferson Davis. Mrs. Chesnut was able to record with striking candor and freshness the affairs of society at the capital of the Confederacy. She was also able to discern the weaknesses of the short lived republic. Late in the war she said the Confederacy had destroyed itself with internal dissension. One of the most comprehensive collections of family letters was left by the Charles Colcock Jones family of Georgia. They tell the story of Southern travail and heroism with unexcelled poignancy and intimacy.

The Confederacy inherited no strong tradition

Left: Even churches bore the bullet and shot holes of the battle. This one in Fredericksburg looks almost abandoned. (P-M)

Left: Hampton, Virginia, lay largely in ruins after the early fighting of 1862. (US-AMHI)

Left: George Barnard found the main entrance to Hampton Church on July 2, 1862, as much a tombstone as the markers in its cemetery. (NLM)

Right: It had been the oldest Protestant church in America. Now it was a hollow shell. (NLM)

Above left, above, and left: Industry, too, suffered in the South. Never well advanced prior to 1861, Southern industry was overtaxed by the war and was often the target of Union destructiveness. Small companies like the Schofield Iron Works of Macon, Georgia, were hard pressed to meet the demand for weapons and munitions. (COURTESY OF HERB PECK, JR.)

Below: The Confederacy built some of its own industry, though on a very limited scale. The Augusta Powder Works in Georgia was one such plant. (LC)

in the fine arts, nor did it have the time or opportunity to create one. Only in its architecture could the Old South boast of distinguished aesthetic accomplishments—in its great Georgian and neoclassical plantation houses, town houses, and public buildings. The war put an end to the construction of houses and destroyed or damaged many that were already standing. Yet the fine arts did not fail to serve the Southern cause. Theaters were active in all Southern cities, especially in Richmond and Charleston. Shakespearean plays and other classic works continued to be staged. But patriotic or comical themes with hastily contrived and banal plots tended to replace the old favorites. Popular productions of this nature included John Hill Hewitt's *King Linkum the First*, Joseph Hodgson's *The Confederate Vivandiere*, and J. J. Delchamp's *Great Expectations: or, Getting Promoted*. Minstrels and other cheap comedy productions catered to the lower economic and social classes. All offered a means of escape from the terrible burdens of real life. Southern painters and sculptors also turned their talents to patriotic works, depicting war scenes or producing likenesses of well-known Confederate officers. Perhaps the most popular painting done in the Confederacy was William Washington's "The Burial of Latane," which captured the pride and pathos attending the funeral of a young officer killed during Jeb Stuart's daring ride around McClellan's army early in the war.

Music was the most popular and most sustaining art form of the South, being ideally suited to the martial spirit of the age. But the music that most distinguishes the region is its folk music, which at the time of the Civil War was not yet committed to formal composition. Ironically, the most stirring songs of the Confederacy were written by outsiders: the "national anthem" of the Confederacy, "Dixie," by Daniel Emmett of Ohio, as a prewar minstrel tune; and "The Bonnie Blue Flag" by Harry McCarthy, an Irish immigrant. Many other songs caught the emotions of the Southern people at war. Among these were "Maryland, My Mary land," "The Yellow Rose of Texas," and "Some body's Darling," a heartrending piece about a young soldier killed in the line of duty.

Southern schools were quick to feel the damaging effects of the war. Many of the region's most distinguished educators were from the North, and a number of them resigned their positions and left the South when the states where they were teaching seceded from the Union. Perhaps the outstanding example was the resignation of President Frederick A. P. Barnard of the University of Mississippi, who was later to become the president of Columbia College in New York City. A more memorable instance was that of the president of the Louisiana State Seminary and Military Academy, who left his academic post to become one of the most renowned leaders of the Union Army—William Tecumseh Sherman.

But many other college teachers were native Southerners who remained to support their region in the war. Some of them provided essential services to the Confederacy. For example, Professor John W. Mallet of the University of Alabama used his scientific knowledge to invent an improved artillery shell and to supervise the preparation of chemicals for the manufacture of explosives. The famed brother scientists from South Carolina, John and Joseph LeConte, placed their expertise

Above: It was the brainchild of Colonel George Washington Rains, an inventive and dedicated Confederate engineer. His brother was a brigadier general. (COURTESY OF THE AUGUSTA-RICHMOND COUNTY MUSEUM)

Above: Yet there was also a quiet life in the South during the war, a few places seemingly untouched by the sword. Bowling Green Court House in Caroline County, Virginia, seems almost a still life. Restaurant bills of fare, a recruiting poster, and attorney's shingles crowd its pillars and trees. (P-M)

Left: The market square in Norfolk, Virginia, bustles with the same trading activity as before the war. This image by the Kilburn brothers of New Hampshire may have been taken just after the war. (USAMHI)

Left: Armistead and White of Corinth captured Southern laborers going about the same business that they had done for generations, only now sometimes under the watchful eye of a Federal officer. (CHS)

at the disposal of the Confederate Niter and Mining Bureau.

Unable to purchase textbooks, as was the usual custom, from Northern firms, the South set about to supply its own, and soon a number of such volumes were on the market. Though they were inferior to the Northern books because of a lack of good paper and experienced editing, they pleased their readers with sound Confederate sentiments. M. B. Moore's *Geographical Reader for Dixie Children* pictured the South as a Christian land of benign masters and happy slaves. Even the arithmetic books were filled with Confederate indoctrination. They followed the lead of a book produced before the war by Daniel Harvey Hill, then a college mathematics professor and later a Confederate general. In his *Elements of Algebra* Hill included problems with illustrations of Yankee peddlers who allegedly mixed wooden nutmegs with the real ones they sold to unsuspecting Southern housewives. Hill's book also contained an illustration involving Indiana volunteers who ran away from the fighting in the battle of Buena Vista in the Mexican War. Johnson's *Elementary Arithmetic*, published during the Civil War, adopted a similar theme with such illustrations as: "If one Confederate soldier can whip 7 Yankees, how many Confederate soldiers can whip 49 Yankees?"

Southern schools soon lost many of their teachers to the armed forces, and before the war was over most of the college students were also gone. Those of conscription age were not exempt from service; even if they had been exempt, they probably would have volunteered because of their intense Confederate feelings. Ultimately most of the region's colleges closed down; those that remained in operation had a mere handful of faculty and students. Nor did the lower-level schools escape. Many of the region's private "academies,"

Above: There were still quiet moments, as in this image of a man and a woman out shopping in Winchester, Virginia. (WINCHESTER-FREDERICK COUNTY HISTORICAL SOCIETY)

Above: The people who were left behind carried on their lives much as they had before the war. A croquet match on the lawn at Patellus House in Virginia seemed entirely natural in the midst of war. (LC)

Above: There was even the occasional idyllic scene. This is the Big Spring at Huntsville, Alabama, in 1863. It seems more like a genre painting by George Caleb Bingham than a photograph. All that betrays the wartime aspect of the image is the fact that there are no young men, only old men and boys. The rest are off to war. (USAMHI)

Below: The rivers and lakes were still flooded in the spring, as seen here near Huntsville. (CHS)

the mainstay of precollege education in the Old South, were obliged to close for lack of money. The public schools, which in a majority of the Southern states were weak at best, suffered from inferior teaching as unqualified women or old men replaced the regular teachers who were now in uniform. Only in North Carolina, where Superintendent Calvin Wiley was able to prevail upon Governor Zebulon Vance to keep the public schools in his budget, did they continue to operate in a fairly normal way. The Southern educational system barely survived the war. In many places it failed to do so.

Negro Southerners, especially the almost four million slaves who made up the vast majority of the group, received the greatest benefits from the Civil War: They gained their freedom. But during the course of the war they may have suffered more than anyone else. In the Confederate interior before the arrival of the Northern armies, the slaves continued their labors almost as if nothing unusual was afoot. True, their efficiency tended to drop where no white man was still in charge, but generally their productivity remained high. Louisiana slaves harvested and ground the greatest sugar crop in the history of the industry during the first year of the war. At the midpoint of the conflict, long after the issuance of the Emancipation Proclamation, Union soldiers in Louisiana were astonished at the immensity of the corn crops they found being grown by slave labor on plantations recently converted from sugar. According to one of them, the soldiers scoffed at the "ponderous articles" appearing in Northern newspapers saying the Confederacy was about to be starved into submission. Virginia slaves were, to a marked degree, responsible for that state's great behind-the-lines strength during the four years that most of its able-bodied white men were in uniform.

As the Northern forces penetrated into the Confederacy, the slaves flocked away from the plantations and assembled around the Union encampments in a great "jubilee" of freedom. Torn from their moorings and destitute of the means of livelihood, Negroes doubtless would have been ravaged by starvation and disease had not the Union armies provided rations and medical attention for them. Many succumbed in spite of this assistance. A Louisiana planter wrote in pity that the occupants of a nearby runaway camp were living in "the most abject misery Degredation & Filth,"

Above: A lonely mule team could still be seen crossing a brook in Virginia. Some things never changed. (LC)

Above: The Big Spring a year later, taken by Armistead and Taylor of Corinth. The Federals are much in evidence now, and they have considerably improved the spring house. (CHS)

and that they were dying by the hundreds. Such scenes caused some Northern soldiers to predict the demise of the entire race in the South.

Perhaps the most remarkable thing about the behavior of Negroes was that they did not resort to insurrection. The South, as always, seethed with rumors of impending slave violence. Northern abolitionists, as always, expected to see it. Joshua Giddings of Ohio was convinced that the appearance of a force of 40,000 freedom soldiers would set off an upheaval of cataclysmic proportions, a mistaken conviction that the Southern bondsmen were eager to rise like the rebellious slaves of ancient Rome. Southern authorities tightened the restrictions in their slave codes; patrols and home guard military organizations exerted a vigilance not usually found in the lackadaisical South. There were scattered efforts among the bondsmen to stage an uprising. About 134,000 Negroes from the Confederate states were enlisted in the Union armies; large numbers died in uniform. Many individual Negroes committed deeds of sabotage against the Confederacy or otherwise rendered aid to the invaders. Sometimes the Negroes became fractious with their masters. On rare occasions the Negroes resorted to violence; they often pillaged, especially places that had been abandoned by the owners, for the slaves believed the Lord had authorized a latter-day "spoiling on the Egyptians."

But the Negroes did not rebel. Just why they did not do so is difficult to determine. Possibly they were unwilling to take the risk. One of them explained the conduct of his people fatalistically, saying, "I see no use of us going and getting ourselves into trouble. If so be it we are to get free,

Above: People in marshy areas and in the Everglades of Florida still lived on the water and traded on it as before, as in this scene not far from Jacksonville captured by Shaw and Sons of Jacksonville. (CHS)

Left: Confederate women still gathered with their children to talk over their sewing. Here they do so outside the house where General Charles Winder died on Cedar Mountain. (LC)

Below: They met for play and picnics, though sometimes amid scenery that would have seemed foreign prior to the war. Here, in South Carolina, women and children play beside a Confederate "David" torpedo boat. One young man pokes his head out through the top hatch. (VM)

Above: In Florida people still enjoyed the shade of the palm trees and coconuts. (USAMHI)

Above: The church, always important in Southern life, assumed new proportions. With the Almighty on their side, Southerners met to fervently invoke His assistance in the field. Christ Church in Alexandria heard more than one prayer for Jefferson Davis and the Confederacy. (USAMHI)

Right: Of course, not all the Southern clergy were so loyal to the South. "Parson" William G. Prownlow of Tennessee was an ardent pro-Union advocate, even publishing a newspaper called the Whig and Rebel Ventilator. *(NYHS)*

we get it anyhow… We think it betterer to stay home on the plantation, and get our food and our clothes. If we are to get freedom, dar we are ! But, if we run away… where is we?" Probably many slaves refrained from violence because of genuine affection for kind masters. After the war, Mary Boykin Chesnut wrote that the "fidelity" of the Negroes was a principal topic of conversation in South Carolina. "There seems not a single case of a Negro who betrayed his master." Such statements of slave loyalty were gross exaggerations. Yet the slaves did not take advantage of the opportunity to revolt. Through the travail of invasion and the exultation of freedom the South was spared the horrors of a war of the races.

Southern women supported the Confederacy with unexcelled devotion. They upheld the righteousness of a war for Southern independence, encouraged men to enlist, and shamed those who hesitated to do so. They formed "sulk and pout" clubs to indicate their displeasure with "unpatriotic" males; sometimes they sent them petticoats as tokens of contempt. The women vowed to take up arms and go forth into battle if need be to assure the success of the South. Northern soldiers believed them more militant than the men. Henry Timrod paid tribute to their zeal with these lines:

Does any falter? let him turn
To some brave maiden's eyes,
And catch the holy fires that burn
In those sublunar skies.

Oh! could you like your women feel,
and in their spirit march,

A day might see your lines of steel
Beneath the victor's arch.

The greatest contribution made by women to the Confederate effort was in filling the jobs left by the multitude of men who were under arms. In addition to managing plantations and working farms, the women made uniforms for the Quartermaster Department and cartridges for the Ordnance Department. They served as clerks in the government bureaus, taught school, and did hundreds of other tasks normally done by men. Doubtless the women of the Old South were never the delicate butterflies of popular legend. Certainly the women of the Confederacy were not. They played a vital role in supplying their cause with its "sinews of war."

A few Southern women entered the Confederate Army disguised as men. Others served glamorously and importantly as spies. The most famous of these, Belle Boyd, repeatedly came through the Union lines with information that was useful to the Confederate commanders. Mrs. Rose O'Neal Greenhow was drowned in an attempt to get through the Union naval blockade while on an official mission for the Confederacy.

Perhaps the most celebrated heroines of the Confederacy were the women who ministered to the sick or wounded soldiers. They helped to establish the improvised hospitals of the early campaigns, often supplying food and medicine directly from their own homes. At times they risked their lives tending disabled soldiers under fire. Twice wounded on the battlefield in this work, Mrs. Arthur F. Hopkins earned from General Joseph E. Johnston the title "Angel of the South." Ella King Newsom became the "Florence Nightingale" of the Confederate Army. Kate Cumming, Phoebe Pember, and Louisa Susanna McCord were famous as hospital matrons. "Heaven only knows," wrote a foreign observer, "what the soldiers of the South would have done without the exertions of the women in their behalf."

Ultimately the fierce Confederate patriotism of the Southern women yielded before the realities

Left: Education, already backward as compared to the rest of the nation, suffered a setback during the war, yet universities like the University of Virginia managed to continue to graduate students, though fewer and younger, as the war lured the young men from the classroom to the battlefield. Jefferson's rotunda is shown here in what is perhaps an early postwar image. (VM)

Left: The legal machinery and state governments continued to function, even to flourish, in some places. Courthouses and state capitol buildings like this one all across the South continued to be centers of business and politics as they had been before the war. (CHS)

Above: Military schools, always popular in the South, continued with their studies, though the boys tended to be younger than before. The Citadel in Charleston, shown here, sent many a young officer into the Confederate Army. (COURTESY OF JOHN A. HESS)

Above: Public libraries struggled to maintain the literary tradition of the South, often against the greater demands of war. This public library in Beaufort, South Carolina, became a contraband hospital. (US-AMHI)

Right: Yet even for the slaves much of life continued as normal: menial work for little or no compensation. Only the promise of freedom gave them more cheer than most of the their white Southern brethren. (ONONDAGA HISTORICAL ASSOCIATION)

Left: The disruption of the labor force in the South, as slaves fled to contraband camps, left much work to be done by those unused to it—and much that simply remained undone. Here slaves on Joseph Davis's plantation near Vicksburg have set aside their tools to await freedom. (KA)

of war. Their demoralization was a major cause of Confederate collapse. Moved by the appeals of countless women to have their men exempted from conscription, a War Department official wrote: "The iron is gone deep into the heart of society." Letters from distraught wives were a major reason for desertion from Confederate ranks. Most of them described genuine destitution and a growing conviction that all the sacrifice was futile, that the war was irretrievably lost. Which soldier could resist such a letter as the following from his wife? "Before God, Edward, Unless you come home we must die. Last night I was aroused by little Eddie's crying… He said 'Oh, mamma, I'm, so hungry!' And Lucy, Edward, your darling Lucy, she never complains, but she is growing thinner and thinner every day."

The emotions of the Southern people at war surged and ebbed with the tides of victory or defeat on the battlefield. In the beginning the Confederates were gay and hopeful, naively believing the struggle would be quickly won by them. Brilliant early successes—bought, as they were, with heavy sacrifice of life—created a sense of mingled exaltation and grief that was akin to a religious experience in intensity. But enthusiasm waned as the conflict lengthened, the toll in casualties mounted, and the faith in ultimate victory disappeared. Late in the war a Louisiana planter expressed the prevailing mood in the following lines in his diary: "The days (emphatically days of darkness & gloom) succeed each other bringing nothing but despondency with regard to the future… The Lord help us. —Such is war, civil war."

Above: It was a war that affected the young. Cadet Private Thomas Jefferson, a relative of the President and a student at Lexington's Virginia Military Institute, went to war with the VMI Cadets at the age of seventeen. In battle at New Market, on May 15, 1864, he took a mortal wound. (COURTESY OF NEW MARKET BATTLEFIELD PARK)

Above: And the war took the old. An old Rebel sits here with an Enfield musket, providing an eloquent comment on the strain on Southern society when the armed forces had to turn to the aged and the young for manpower. (COURTESY OF HERB PECK, JR.)

Far left: The war affected even the mighty and powerful. Vice-President Alexander H. Stephens saw his nephew go into the Confederate service and posed with him for the camera. (PRIVATE COLLECTION)

Left: State governors and politicians like Milledge L. Bonham of South Carolina often had to lay aside their statesman's black broadcloth to don the Confederate gray in defending their states. (USAMHI)

Above: Families went to war. Corporal William H. Martin of the 7th Louisiana poses with his father, James, a captain in the Algiers Battalion of the Louisiana Militia. The father looks more like a Revolutionary soldier—and was nearly old enough to have been one. (LOUISIANA HISTORICAL ASSOCIATION)

Above: Another elderly member of the Continental Guard, as it was sometimes called. (THE HISTORIC NEW ORLEANS COLLECTION)

Above: Families and friends often had to collect their tin-ware, old clothes, and other castoff items to salvage what could be used, as shown here on the Davis plantation. (KA)

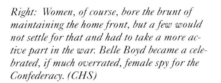

Right: Women, of course, bore the brunt of maintaining the home front, but a few would not settle for that and had to take a more active part in the war. Belle Boyd became a celebrated, if much overrated, female spy for the Confederacy. (CHS)

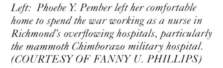

Left: Phoebe Y. Pember left her comfortable home to spend the war working as a nurse in Richmond's overflowing hospitals, particularly the mammoth Chimborazo military hospital. (COURTESY OF FANNY U. PHILLIPS)

Right: The children of President Jefferson Davis felt the pain of war. They are shown here in Montreal just after the surrender. There should have been a fifth child, the son who fell from the Executive Mansion balcony in 1864 and died as a result of the fall. Davis, called from a meeting to be told the news, steeled his nerves and, exhibiting iron self-control, returned to complete the important military conference. The sadness of war touched everyone. (LC)

Right: The children grew up playing at war. John Y. Mason Anderson—son of Brigadier General Joseph R. Anderson, who managed Richmond's Tredegar Iron Works, makers of much of the South's ordnance—played in his little zouave suit of red kepi, pantaloons, blue tunic, and vest. (VM)

Far right: But, always, the most constant reminder of the war for those in the South was the wounded and maimed. Charles Rees of Richmond focused his camera to capture the image of an unidentified officer with his crutches. The war sapped the strength of Southern men and women at home as much as on the battlefield, leaving the entire section on crutches by 1865. It would require a long and painfully slow recovery from the wounds the war inflicted on an entire section of America. (VM)

The Guns at Gettysburg

WILLIAM A. FRASSANITO

A Pennsylvania summer is shattered by the greatest battle of the war

Another campaign is on the way, another battle to come, another meeting between the minions of North and South, and yet one more opportunity for the Army of the Potomac to retrieve its reputation after so many defeats. Perhaps this time there will be a victory. Here, at headquarters near Fairfax Court House, Virginia, in June 1863, the leaders watch and wait. (USAMHI)

BY THE END of May 1863, the war in the eastern theater was progressing well for the Confederacy. Having recently won two major battles at Fredericksburg and Chancellorsville, Robert E. Lee, in consultation with President Davis, determined that the time had once again arrived for a bold thrust northward. Despite high expectations, the immediate goals for the 1863 invasion were nevertheless quite realistic. Of primary concern was the fact that northern Virginia desperately needed a breathing spell. By forcing the war out of Virginia and into enemy territory, a Southern invasion would almost certainly disrupt Union offensive plans for the upcoming summer months, thereby relieving pressure on the Confederate capital at Richmond. Additionally, Virginia farmers would thus be able to tend to their much-needed crops without interruption.

If all went well, and a substantial penetration into enemy territory was achieved, Lee's army would be able to live off of the land, and by threatening and perhaps even capturing one or more major Northern cities, the already downhearted Northern populace might be convinced to support a political peace settlement. Finally, Lee hoped that the invasion might relieve pressure on the vitally important Confederate city of Vicksburg, Mississippi, then struggling for its very survival against Union forces under General Grant.

With the advent of June, Lee's Army of Northern Virginia and Joseph Hooker's Army of the Potomac faced each other at Fredericksburg. Lee's command totaled some 75,000 men. In the wake of Jackson's much-lamented death the month before, it had been reorganized into three infantry corps: I under A. P. Hill, II under Richard S. Ewell, and III under James Longstreet. The cavalry was commanded by J.E.B. Stuart.

Numbering roughly 97,000, the opposing Army of the Potomac was composed of seven infantry corps: I under John F. Reynolds, II under Winfield S. Hancock, III under Daniel E. Sickles, V under George Sykes, VI under John Sedgwick, XI under O. O. Howard, and XII under Henry W. Slocum. The Union cavalry was commanded by Alfred Pleasonton.

Under a veil of secrecy, Lee shifted his army westward on June 3, 1863, first concentrating in the vicinity of Culpeper and then moving into the Shenandoah Valley, where he could march northward while using the mountains as a shield. His cavalry protected the mountain gaps.

Initially unaware of Lee's intentions, Hooker sensed that a major enemy movement was underway following a severe cavalry engagement at Brandy Station on June 9. Urged on by the Lincoln administration, Hooker cautiously followed Lee northward, keeping his army east of the mountains and between Washington and the enemy. On June 15 the vanguard of Lee's forces overwhelmed a Union force under General Robert Milroy at Winchester and continued northward. By June 28 all three Confederate corps had crossed the Mason-Dixon Line; although widely scattered between Chambersburg, Carlisle, and York, they were nevertheless converging steadily on the Pennsylvania state capital at Harrisburg.

In the meanwhile, tension between Hooker and the Lincoln administration reached the breaking point due to Washington's increasing lack of confidence in the Union commander subsequent to the Battle of Chancellorsville. Finally, on June 28, George G. Meade replaced Hooker. June 28 was a critical date in the history of the invasion not only because of this last-minute change in Union commanders but also because it was on this date that Lee first received intelligence that the enemy had crossed the Potomac River and was closing in on his widely dispersed forces. This information came as a surprise to him, for he had been depending on Stuart to keep him informed of enemy movements. Unbeknownst to Lee, his cavalry commander, then involved in a bold raid east of the Union Army, had lost all contact with the main invading force.

Reacting swiftly to this latest intelligence, Lee ordered his detached elements to concentrate at Cashtown, a small hamlet located at the mountains between Chambersburg and Gettysburg. Here Lee would prepare to receive the advance of the Union Army. Thus, by the end of June 1863 Lee's forces, although converging on Cashtown, lay situated generally west and north of Gettysburg, while Meade's Army of the Potomac pressed northward in the direction of Gettysburg from points in the vicinity of Frederick, Taneytown, and Emmitsburg, Maryland. Neither army knew exactly where the other was on June 30, the day advanced Union cavalry units under General John Buford reached the borough of Gettysburg in search of the invading army.

Prior to that summer there was little to distinguish Gettysburg from countless communities of similar size throughout the nation. With a population of 2,400, and located just ten miles north of the Mason-Dixon Line, Gettysburg possessed a moderately thriving carriage industry which had relied heavily on retail markets in Maryland and Virginia before the war. The borough's chief claim to fame, however, rested in its two institutions of higher learning, the Lutheran Theological Seminary and Pennsylvania College (Gettysburg College).

Having reached the town on the last day of June, Buford's cavalry established a picket line beyond the Lutheran Seminary to cover the approaches from the west. By chance a brigade of Confederate infantry under General John Petti-

Left: Here, too, the leaders change. Even as the unvanquished Robert E. Lee is leading his Army of Northern Virginia on an invasion into Pennsylvania, the high command shifts in the Union Army. "Fighting Joe" Hooker will fight no more in Virginia. On June 28, 1863, his command passed to the steady, reliable, and cantankerous Major General George Gordon Meade, standing in the center of this group photographed at Culpeper, Virginia, three months later. The rest are members of his staff who served him well in the coming battle. (USAMHI)

Below: Serving Meade as well were his headquarters guard, the 93rd New York. Theirs was an easy service, for a headquarters guard rarely saw action. Here Company E poses in August 1863 near the Rappahannock. (USAMHI)

Left: As well pleased as Pleasonton could be after Brandy Station, in like measure was Major General James Ewell Brown "Jeb" Stuart chagrined. He was taken much by surprise and was severely criticized afterward for his handling of the battle. Still, the gleam of gentle good cheer never left his eyes. Photographer Minnis, of the Richmond firm of Minnis and Cowell, caught that gleam in this unpublished portrait. (VM)

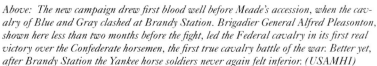

Above: The new campaign drew first blood well before Meade's accession, when the cavalry of Blue and Gray clashed at Brandy Station. Brigadier General Alfred Pleasonton, shown here less than two months before the fight, led the Federal cavalry in its first real victory over the Confederate horsemen, the first true cavalry battle of the war. Better yet, after Brandy Station the Yankee horse soldiers never again felt inferior. (USAMHI)

Above: Brigadier General Beverly H. Robertson, a troublesome subordinate whom Stuart neither liked nor trusted, nevertheless used his own initiative at Brandy Station and helped prevent the episode from being even more embarrassing to Stuart than it already was. (USAMHI)

Above: There were other commands moving in Virginia as Lee's campaign got under way. Down on the Virginia Peninsula the IV Corps stayed behind when McClellan left back in 1862. As Lee marched into Pennsylvania, the Federals there hoped to threaten Richmond and keep reinforcements pinned there instead of going to Lee. Major General Erasmus D. Keyes failed to show enough vigor in the enterprise and found himself put out of the war for good as a result. (WRHS)

Above: Then, in June, as the Confederates marched toward the North, they swarmed over poor Major General Robert H. Milroy and his command at Winchester, Virginia. He managed to stay in the army but never outlived the shame of his defeat. (WRHS)

Right: As soon as he took his new command, Meade began marching toward Pennsylvania to stop Lee. By June 30 elements of the Army of the Potomac reached Emmitsburg, Maryland, a quiet little town of schools and churches.(P-M)

Right: A few days later Alexander Gardner and his team of photographers came to the little town. They found Mount St. Mary's College. (USAMHI)

grew of Heth's division, Hill's corps, had been sent to Gettysburg from the direction of Cashtown to secure supplies that same day. Upon sighting the Union pickets, Pettigrew retired westward to report the enemy's presence.

Early on the morning of July 1, 1863, two Confederate brigades, Archer's and Davis's (also of Heth's division), were dispatched toward Gettysburg to investigate. It was entirely possible that the Northern cavalrymen were nothing more than local militia. The skirmish that ensued quickly escalated into a heated encounter as Buford's troopers offered stiff resistance to the probing enemy reconnaissance.

General Buford, deciding that his position was tenable, and aware that the Union I and XI Corps were then situated just a short distance to the south (in the direction of Emmitsburg), chose to hold his ground and send for help. The Confederates did the same, and before long both armies marched toward Gettysburg in their entirety. Thus it was that a chance encounter between relatively small units ultimately decided the ground upon which the decisive battle of the campaign would be fought. Prior to that morning neither Lee nor Meade had intended to fight at Gettysburg.

For nearly two hours the hard-pressed cavalry men, fighting dismounted, held off repeated enemy assaults in the vicinity of the McPherson farm. Shortly before ten o'clock Buford's force was relieved by the arrival of Reynolds's I Corps. As elements of Wadsworth's division of that corps crossed an unfinished railroad cut north of the Chambersburg Pike and formed a line of battle to engage Davis's Confederate brigade, Archer's

Above: And they found St. Joseph's Seminary, founded by Elizabeth Seton, one day to become America's first saint. (P-M)

Above: But by the time Gardner found Emmitsburg, the armies had found Gettysburg.(USAMHI)

Confederates were renewing their pressure against McPherson's Woods, south of the Pike. Reynolds himself directed the Iron Brigade into McPherson's Woods when he fell to enemy rifle fire. Killed instantly, John F. Reynolds, second in command of the Army of the Potomac and the highest ranking officer from either side to fall at Gettysburg, ironically died during the earliest stages of the three-day battle.

With Reynolds's death, command of I Corps devolved upon Abner Doubleday, whose men continued to maintain their lines against heavy enemy assaults. In a subsequent maneuver against the railroad cut, elements of I Corps succeeded in capturing a large number of Mississippians of Davis's brigade.

At about midday a lull which extended into the early afternoon fell over the field. During this interlude Robert Rodes's Confederate division of Ewell's corps arrived at Oak Ridge, north of the Union line, and soon began to press the extreme right flank of I Corps, held by Baxter's and Paul's brigades of Robertson's division. This threat to the Union right, however, was reduced by the timely arrival of Howard's XI Corps, which, after marching

Left: It was Major General Henry Heth, a Virginian, who led his division toward Gettysburg after learning of the Federal presence there. On July 1 he clashed with them, beginning the bloodiest battle of the Civil War. Before the battle was done, Heth's own blood ran from a dangerous wound. (VM)

Below: The first Federal infantry to arrive on the scene belonged to the I Corps, Major General John F. Reynolds commanding. Here, in this field in front of McPherson's Woods, the I Corps ran headlong into Hill's Confederates and fought desperately for hours to hold his position until Meade could come up. Finally the Southerners forced them back. This view, made two weeks later, shows the scene of the first fighting, with Mathew Brady surveying it. His assistants made this panorama from two separate images. (NA)

Right: The Federals who met Heth were cavalry, horsemen, men in the division commanded by Brigadier General John Buford, a Kentuckian whose cousin was a general in the Confederate cavalry. He held Gettysburg long enough for Meade to begin sending up his army. Buford sits here among members of his staff. (NA)

Right: Wesley Merritt became a brigadier just two days before he led his cavalry brigade in Buford's desperate defense on July 1. His distinguished career in the army continued for another thirty-seven years after Gettysburg. (P-M)

Right: Reynolds did not live to see the retreat. As the fighting raged that morning, he looked back from his saddle toward anticipated reinforcements. A bullet coursed through his head. He was dead before he fell from the saddle. (P-M)

Above: Heth was only the vanguard for the Confederate III Corps, led by the dashing yet peculiar Lieutenant General Ambrose P. Hill. All during the first day's fight Hill directed the battle as it gathered momentum. (OLD COURTHOUSE MUSEUM, VICKSBURG)

Above: Upon Reynolds's fall, command of the I Corps devolved upon Brigadier General Abner Doubleday, who fired the first Federal shot from Fort Sumter and never had anything to do with the invention of baseball. (USAMHI)

through the streets of Gettysburg, formed a line of battle in the open fields just north of Pennsylvania College. Howard's line extended the Union right flank to a small hill known as Barlow's Knoll.

By 2 P.M. the fighting had resumed in earnest, as elements of Hill's and Ewell's powerful corps advanced against the Union I and XI Corps along a nearly two-mile arc traversing the western and northern approaches to Gettysburg. Unfortunately for the Army of the Potomac, Howard's corps was the last to reach the field in time to engage the enemy on July 1. For the Confederates the situation was just the opposite, and by midafternoon Southern reinforcements still arrived in large numbers. At about four o'clock General Jubal Early's newly arrived division of Ewell's Corps struck Union General Francis Barlow's division on the exposed right flank of the XI Corps. Within a short while Barlow's division, and then Howard's entire line, began to crumble.

Retreating into Gettysburg from the northern sector of the field, Howard's men were joined by retreating elements of I Corps, who had almost simultaneously succumbed to Confederate pressure in the vicinity of the McPherson farm. Unfamiliar with the streets and back alleys of the town, and falling back from two different directions, north and west, hundreds of Union soldiers became disoriented as they sought the shelter of Cemetery Hill, a predesignated reserve position located on the southern outskirts of town. In superior numbers the jubilant Confederates followed their distraught foe into the borough streets and succeeded in capturing not only the entire town but some 2,500 Union soldiers as well.

Lee's forces made no attempt to storm Cemetery Hill that evening. Instead, the Confederate commander, having established his headquarters across from the Thompson house on the Chambersburg Pike, began the task of consolidating his lines in preparation for the next day's battle. As the fighting on July 1 drew to a close, Cemetery Hill was fortified by Union forces with the intention of using that point as the nucleus for a new defensive line.

By the next morning Meade had arrived on the field, and the Northern lines were rapidly assuming what has since become known as the "fishhook" formation. Cemetery Hill, defended by the remnants of XI Corps, became the curve of the fishhook, while the heavily wooded Culp's Hill, located just to the east, was occupied by the recently arrived XII Corps. The latter hill became the hook, or right flank, of the Union line. The shank of the formation was eventually occupied by Hancock's II Corps and extended southward along the open fields on Cemetery Ridge. Sickles's III Corps would occupy the extreme Union left.

Little fighting, aside from the scattered fire of opposing skirmishers, occurred throughout the morning and early afternoon of July 2, as both sides prepared for the second day's action. Although it was Lee's design to strike both Union flanks at the same time, the attack was delayed for several hours as Longstreet attempted to maneuver his corps, undetected, into the line of battle on the southern extension of Seminary Ridge, located parallel to the Union positions on Cemetery Ridge.

As Longstreet marched and countermarched his troops behind the Confederate lines, Union General Sickles decided to advance his entire III Corps from its position in the vicinity of the imposing hill known as Little Round Top—the left flank, or eye, of the fishhook—to a more forward position located closer to the Confederate lines. By the time Longstreet was ready to attack, Sickles's new line extended northwestward from the enormous boulders in Devil's Den, through the Rose Woods and the Wheat Field, and then turned sharply northeastward at the Peach Orchard, where it continued along the Emmitsburg Road.

Birney's division held Sickles's left, while A. A Humphreys's division held the right flank of the III Corps line, which at best was placed precariously and was difficult to defend. Not only did Sickles fail to connect his right flank to the left of II Corps, leaving an ominous gap between the two commands, but he also neglected to occupy the most important single terrain feature in his sector, namely, Little Round Top. Only the last-minute efforts of General Gouverneur Warren, Meade's chief of engineers, saved the hill from certain capture by vanguard elements of Longstreet's assaulting force.

The Confederate attack against the Union left began a short while after four o'clock on the afternoon of July 2. The first points to be struck were Little Round Top, which had been occupied by Union infantry just ten minutes before the arrival of Hood's division of Longstreet's corps, and Devil's Den, which fell to Hood's men after a bitter struggle lasting more than an hour. In successive waves the various brigades of Longstreet's corps stormed into the Rose Woods, the Wheat Field, and advanced against III Corps positions at the Peach Orchard and along the Emmitsburg Road.

As the sharp and often confused action progressed throughout the late afternoon hours,

Left: Brigadier General James S. Wadsworth led one of the I Corps divisions that battled valiantly. The corps was more than decimated by the day's fight, and later disbanded. Wadsworth, seated at right, performed admirably, only to fall a year later with a wound almost exactly like Reynolds's. (NA)

Left: Brigadier General Gabriel R. Paul led a New Jersey brigade on that dreadful first day's field. A bullet crashed into his right temple and passed out his left eye, leaving him almost totally blinded for the remaining twenty-three years of his life. (NA)

Above: Francis Barlow was a young brigadier when he fought in the vain attempt to keep the Confederates out of Gettysburg. A bullet left him briefly paralyzed and so dangerously wounded that many believed him dead. Confederate General John B. Gordon personally comforted him as best he could, and years later they became devoted friends.(USAMHI)

Above: The Confederates took losses, too. In the early fighting the Federals captured Brigadier General James J. Archer. He was mortified at being the first Confederate general captured on the field in over a year. When his old friend Doubleday offered his hand and said, "I am glad to meet you," Archer replied coolly, "I am not glad to meet you, sir." (USAMHI)

Above: It was men like Shepherd Green Pryor of the 12th Georgia who finally forced the Federals back. (UNIVERSITY OF GEORGIA LIBRARY, ATHENS)

Right: When the Yankees streamed back from the McPherson's Ridge line, they rushed across these fields into the town of Gettysburg, and from there to the summit of Cemetery Hill, marked by the tall tree on the right at the horizon. Two weeks later Brady's operatives made this view of the scene. (US-AMHI)

Right: The Federals retreated along the Chambersburg Pike, too, shown here while looking from the town toward the Lutheran Theological Seminary at the left. Hill's Confederates pursued them hotly, and after the day's battle was done they proceeded to remove the rails from the fences for firewood. F. Gutekunst of Philadelphia probably made this image. (KA)

Below: The Lutheran Theological Seminary was at first used as a field hospital by the Federals. From its cupola Reynolds had observed the enemy positions. After the rout on McPherson's Ridge it became a Confederate hospital. (LC)

Right: When Lee finally arrived on the field, he, too, probably used the cupola of the Lutheran Theological Seminary as an observatory. (P-M)

Sickles's battered line was reinforced and eventually relieved by elements of Sykes's V Corps, and then by a portion of II Corps. Sickles himself fell, severely wounded near his headquarters at the Trostle farm. Many desperate attempts by individual Union brigades, regiments, and artillery units to check the relentless Confederate tide failed, including the noteworthy action of Edward Cross's Union brigade at the Wheat Field, the counterattack of Brooke's brigade against Semmes's Georgians at the Rose Woods, and the stand of the 9th Massachusetts Battery at the Trostle farmyard. But after nearly four hours of fighting, all Union positions on the initial II Corps line were ultimately overrun.

Indeed, only Little Round Top, the one key terrain feature which should have been occupied by Sickles earlier that afternoon but was not, remained to stem the Southern onslaught. At approximately 7: 30 P.M., as the sun began to fall below the mountains on the western horizon, and as remnants of numerous Union commands streamed back toward the safety of Little Round Top—closely pursued by their victorious but generally exhausted enemy—Crawford's fresh division of Pennsylvania Reserves charged down the slopes of the hill to punch the last gasp of air out of Longstreet's assault. With the onset of darkness, the final defensive line of the Union left flank had been secured.

Despite the limited Confederate successes in capturing Sickles's advanced positions, Lee's overall offensive on July 2 had failed, mainly because of a lack of coordination. Not only had Confederate pressure become piecemeal by the time of the advance of Wright's brigade of Hill's corps in support of Longstreet (against the Union center), but the Southern thrust against the Union right flank at Cemetery Hill and Culp's Hill—intended to commence simultaneously with the at-

Below: The Rebels quickly occupied the town of Gettysburg, and a number of Federals were actually cut off from their commands and captured. One who escaped capture was Brigadier General Alexander Schimmelfennig. Isolated from his division, he took refuge in a small outbuilding which, among its other inhabitants, included a number of pigs. There he was forced to hide for two more days before emerging. Wags in later days referred to the shed as General Schimmelfennig's "headquarters." (P-M)

tack against the Union left—did not get under way until the heaviest fighting on the Union left had already terminated. In fact, it was roughly sundown when elements of two divisions of Ewell's corps began their assault against the hook and curve of the Union right flank.

After fording Rock Creek and moving through the darkening woods at the base of Culp's Hill, Johnson's division advanced up the eastern slope of the hill and soon became engaged with Greene's brigade of the Union XII Corps. Ironically, Greene's New Yorkers stood alone at this critical juncture in the battle, the bulk of the corps having been removed earlier from their Culp's Hill positions to support the Northern effort on the left flank. Thankfully for the Union forces, the hill had previously been fortified by an extensive line of earthworks, strengthened by felled trees and rocks.

Badly outnumbered, Greene's men used their earthworks to great advantage, and although Johnson was able to secure all the abandoned defenses on the southern slopes, he failed to dislodge Greene's line commanding the summit of the hill. Only darkness prevented Johnson from fully appreciating the value of the positions he had, in fact, occupied, which virtually left ajar the door to the Union rear.

Meanwhile, two Confederate brigades of Early's division met with even less success in their attempt to capture the barren and imposing Cemetery Hill. Initially breaking through XI Corps positions at the northern base at about 7: 30 P.M., Avery's North Carolinians suffered severely from a devastating artillery enfilade from nearby

Right: Meade felt uncomfortable with Doubleday in command on the field and sent trusted Major General Winfield Scott Hancock ahead of the army to assume direction of the defense at Gettysburg. Hancock proved to be Meade's strongest arm in the dreadful battle. (USAMHI)

Below and below right: The Tyson brothers made an excellent set of views in August 1863, showing the Hagerstown Road on the right. Hill's Confederates raced along it while pursuing the retreating Federals. Here again they probably burned the fence rails at their campfires during their stay in Gettysburg. (P-M left; RA right)

Left: Classes actually began as usual at the Pennsylvania College on July 1, but the coming battle quickly disrupted the schedule. The buildings soon housed wounded and dying instead of students. (USAMHI)

Above: Late on July 1 the Confederacy's strongest arm, Robert E. Lee, finally reached the field. Now he decided to take the battle to the enemy and drive them from their high ground south of the town. This portrait is by the distinguished Richmond photographer Vannerson. (USAMHI)

Above: The second day's fighting rested largely in the hands of Lieutenant General James "Old Pete" Longstreet, Lee's trusty South Carolinian leading the I Corps. He recognized the value of the two tiny mountains called Big and Little Round Top.(LC)

Left: It was largely thanks to Meade's chief engineer, Brigadier General Gouverneur K. Warren, that the Confederates were denied Little Round Top. He saw its natural advantages and commandeered troops to man it just as Longstreet's divisions began their assault. (USAMHI)

Right: Had the Southerners been able to take and hold the crest, their cannon could have driven Meade from the field. (USAMHI)

Stevens's Knoll. As H. T. Hays's Louisiana "Tigers," who had likewise broken through the initial Union defenses, continued up the steep face of Cemetery Hill, Union reinforcements raced to the aid of the artillery batteries on the crest. After a bitter hand-to-hand struggle, and in the absence of any support from Confederate infantry units stationed near the southern outskirts of town, Hays's men were forced to relinquish their temporary foothold on the Union right. Thus ended the second day's battle, with Meade's basic fishhook formation remaining intact.

Later that night Meade held a council of war at his headquarters on the Taneytown Road to evaluate the progress of the battle thus far, as well as to determine whether or not the positions of the Army of the Potomac were worth maintaining for yet an other day of fighting. They decided to hold the line.

With the return of the detached elements of XII Corps during the night, Johnson's tenuous opportunity for imperiling the Union rear vanished. Beginning at 4:30 the morning of July 3, XII Corps took the initiative by opening on the Confederate lines east and south of the hill. After an engagement lasting nearly seven hours, all of the Union earthworks lost the night before were recaptured. By 11 A.M. the Union right flank stood firmly secured.

For General Lee the failure of his attempts to crush the two Union flanks suggested strongly the tempting possibility that both Union flanks had been fortified at the expense of the Union center, held by Hancock's II Corps. By midday on July 3 the Confederate commander decided to make one last gamble at Gettysburg, a direct frontal assault against Cemetery Ridge. Lee's plan called for a concentrated artillery bombardment to cripple the Union line on the ridge, to be followed by the advance of elements of four infantry divisions: Pickett's, Heth's (now commanded by Pettigrew), Trimble's and Anderson's (in support). All told, the attacking force would number nearly 11,000 men, with Longstreet in overall command. Facing the Confederates across the open fields separating Seminary Ridge and Cemetery Ridge sat II Corps divisions of Alexander Hays, on the Bryan farm, and John Gibbon, near the Codori farm buildings. Supporting these divisions were portions of I Corps, the entire defending force numbering roughly half that of the attackers.

Shortly after one o'clock on the afternoon of July 3, 1863, more than 140 Confederate artillery pieces under the supervision of E. P. Alexander opened fire on the Union center. Upwards of 100 Union guns responded, and for the next two hours the greatest artillery exchange ever witnessed in the Western Hemisphere continued without interruption. As three o'clock approached and Southern artillery ammunition began to run low, orders were issued along Confederate lines to cease fire. The time for the infantry assault had finally arrived.

The subsequent gamble was destined to be far greater than Lee anticipated, for unbeknownst to virtually everyone on the Confederate lines, the majority of Southern artillery rounds completely overshot the main Union defenses. After two hours of bombardment Hancock's positions survived in surprisingly good order. As the dense clouds of smoke from the cannonade slowly drifted away, a few brief moments of anxious quiet descended upon the field.

Then at 3 P.M. an awesome formation of Confederate infantry one mile long abruptly emerged en masse from the woods on Seminary Ridge and began to march, as if on parade, eastward toward what the Confederates hoped would be the disorganized debris of the Union center. The distance between the two ridges averaged slightly less than a mile. In a matter of minutes, as the advancing forces approached the middle of the open fields, artillery batteries from the Union left and right unleashed their fury against both Confederate flanks. Closing their gaps, the advancing divisions continued to push eastward.

It was only when the forward brigades crossed the Emmitsburg Road, roughly two hundred yards west of Hancock's positions, that the main line of the Union II Corps opened fire—shattering the enemy's front ranks with terrible effect. Quickly recovering from this initial shock, the Southern brigades broke into a run and surged up the gentle slope of Cemetery Ridge under a veritable hail of fire, their command structure rapidly disintegrating every step of the way. The next ten or so minutes saw a slaughter rarely equaled in American history, for even before the Confederates reached the low stone wall on the ridge, the Union lines formed into a pocket—elements of Hays's command having swung around into the fields on the Confederate left, and Stannard's Vermont brigade having done the same on the Confederate right.

In the ensuing melee scores of high-ranking officers from both sides, together with literally hundreds upon hundreds of their men, were either killed or wounded. In Pickett's division alone all three brigade commanders were hit: Garnett was killed; Kemper was severely wounded and captured; and Armistead, who led an estimated 150 men over the wall and into the mass of Union infantry surrounding Cushing's battery, was also killed.

Receiving fire from three directions, and with the hopelessness of their situation painfully apparent, vast numbers of trapped Southerners surrendered. Although several thousand members of

Left: During the nighttime hours immediately following the second day's battle, Union soldiers further strengthened the hill by constructing a network of stone walls in anticipation of renewed Confederate assaults the next day. Gibson's photograph shows a portion of these defenses as they appeared on July 6, 1863. (ROBERT J. YOUNGER)

Left: Hastily erected breastworks on Little Round Top's crest gave the Yankees defenses behind which they would ultimately protect themselves from enemy sharpshooters on July 3. Timothy O'Sullivan brought his camera to the summit just four days later. (P-M)

Left: Brady came there a week later. In the distance appears the ground on which the Union center was positioned. (LC)

Right: Brigadier General Evander M. Law of Alabama was one of Longstreet's Confederates. Seated here, in the center, with members of his staff, he led a brigade and then a division in the attacks on Little Round Top. This unpublished image was probably made a few months after the battle. (VM)

Below: Units like the 6th Vermont of John Sedgwick's VI Corps were present to support Sykes. (LC)

Above: Reinforcements rushed to the Little Round Top fight as quickly as Meade and Hancock could send them. Major General George Sykes brought his V Corps to the vicinity but found a greater threat on the way. (P-M)

the attacking force managed to escape to the safety of Seminary Ridge, Longstreet's assault, also known to history as "Pickett's Charge," ended in a dismal failure, with approximately two thirds of the Confederate infantrymen involved having been either killed, wounded, or captured. Casualties in many of the northern units had likewise been appalling, but at the conclusion of the struggle it was their line that held.

Earlier that day J.E.B. Stuart, who had finally rejoined Lee's army following his ill-conceived June raid, was directed to proceed far around Meade's right to harass the Union rear at the same time that Lee's infantrymen were striking the Union center. Three miles east of Gettysburg Stuart's cavalry ran into strong elements of Pleasonton's cavalry corps, and after a sharp encounter in which Union General Custer's Michigan brigade distinguished itself and Confederate General Wade Hampton was wounded, Stuart retired from the field, his lone effort at Gettysburg having been thwarted.

The next day, July 4, 1863, both armies remained on the battlefield, with Meade and Lee each waiting for the other to make the next move. When nothing of significance developed that day, Lee reluctantly concluded that his invasion had reached an impasse. Far from his base of supplies, running low on ammunition, and now facing an impregnable enemy line, Lee saw no alternative but to terminate the invasion. Two of his primary goals—the temporary relief of war-torn Virginia and the disruption of Union offensive plans for that summer—had already been achieved. The other, more wishful goals, which perhaps may have led to a peace settlement favorable to the South, would have to be postponed for another campaign. It was indeed ominous, however, that Vicksburg, Mississippi, would by coincidence fall to General Grant on that same July 4, 1863.

Lee's retreat from Gettysburg commenced late on July 4 and into the early morning hours of July 5. Technically the campaign ended with his successful recrossing of the Potomac River two weeks later. Not only had the Army of Northern Virginia survived the campaign intact but the in-

Right: As the dreadful slaughter was taking place around Little Round Top on July 2, equally severe fighting raged among the boulders of a sharpshooters' nest called Devil's Den. Here, at the foot of Big Round Top, lie several soldiers, probably Confederates, who will not fight again. They lie about as O'Sullivan found them on July 6. (USAMHI)

Right: "The Slaughter Pen" was what they called the area at the foot of Big Round Top and not without reason. (USAMHI)

vasion had so disrupted the Northern war effort in the eastern theater that fully ten months passed before the Army of the Potomac was again able to launch a serious threat against Richmond.

Of the 150,000 soldiers who fought at Gettysburg, 51,000 became casualties during the three days of fighting. In terms of magnitude as well as significance, Gettysburg will forever be ranked among the greatest battles in American history. On November 19, 1863, slightly more than four months after the engagement, the name Gettysburg was further immortalized at the dedication of the Soldiers' National Cemetery when, from a speaker's platform on the summit of Cemetery Hill, Abraham Lincoln delivered his brief but fitting eulogy to those Union soldiers who fell on that field. His promise to them was of equal reassurance to those still living. They had not died in vain.

Left: And in Devil's Den itself James Gibson's camera caught the poignant scene of a young Confederate, hardly out of his teens, dead among the rocks toward which he had charged. (USAMHI)

Above: Just before the struggle for Little Round Top commenced, Major General Daniel E. Sickles foolishly led his III Corps out in advance of the main Union line. Having failed to protect Little Round Top, he now failed to heed orders to come back into line. Instead, he led his corps to destruction in the Wheat Field and the Peach Orchard. He lost a leg in the inferno. (KA)

Above: It was the Confederate division of Major General John B. Hood that struck repeatedly at Little Round Top and then at Sickles in the Wheat Field. Hood suffered a disabled arm in the repeated attacks. (VM)

Above: The II. Corps regiments like the 114th Pennsylvania, a zouave outfit, suffered heavily from the cross fire into which Sickles led them. (USAMHI)

Above: Beyond the Wheat Field, at the southernmost edge of the Rose Farm, raged a heavy fight that left scores of dead Confederates behind. Seminary Ridge, the Southern main line, is in the far distance in this O'Sullivan view taken on July 5.(USAMHI)

Left: After Sickles's wounding, Major General David B. Birney assumed command of the imperiled III Corps and led it ably in extricating itself from Sickles's folly. (USAMHI)

Right: But many Union soldiers remained behind, never to move again. Short on supplies, the Confederates removed the shoes from these fallen Yankees.(USAMHI)

Above: Major General Andrew A. Humphreys won a second star for his leadership of one of Sickles's divisions along the Emmitsburg Road. Soon thereafter he became Meade's chief of staff. He would return to field duty later in the war as one of the ablest corps commanders. (USAMHI)

Right: Many of those attacking the Union center on July 2 were Georgians, and some of their regiments were family affairs. Here are six brothers, all of the 22nd Georgia and all named Jones. At least one of them fell in the fighting this day. (COURTESY OF LUCY C. MULCAHY, ATLANTA)

Right: The 2nd Georgia Battalion served in the same brigade with the 22nd Georgia. They were so dispersed at the opening of the July 2 fight for Cemetery Hill that they ceased to function as a unit. Here are posed the men of "Mess No. 9," at Norfolk, Virginia, in 1862. Their servant, "Pink," stands at right. (NA)

Right: When Birney took over the III Corps, Brigadier General J. H. Hobart Ward, seated at right, assumed command of his division, holding the vulnerable left between Little Round Top and the Emmitsburg Road. He did so admirably. But a year later his presumed drinking got him dismissed from the army. Forty years later he was run over by a train. (USAMHI)

Above: Few stories are more ironic than that of the beloved Colonel Edward Cross of New Hampshire. He went into the Wheat Field fight leading his New Hampshire brigade. Hancock cheered him on, saying it would be the last time he fought without a general's star. "Too late, general," replied Cross. "This is my last battle." Minutes later he was dead. (USAMHI)

Above: A farmhouse unfortunate enough to be in the path of the Confederate advance on July 2 was Abraham Trostle's home. Timothy O'Sullivan found it looking like this a few days later. (P-M)

Above: Everywhere the dead piled up. Here Confederates at the Rose Farm lie in a neat row, awaiting burial on July 5. (USAMHI)

Above: These horses were once the animals of the 9th Massachusetts Artillery. (USAMHI)

Left: There seemed no end to the dead resulting from the terrible fighting. (USAMHI)

Left: One of the most eloquent images of all, Timothy O'Sullivan's July 5 photograph shows a Georgia Confederate disemboweled and dismembered by a Federal shell. O'Sullivan probably placed the shell and rifle in the picture, but no artificial posing was necessary to present an eloquently brutal picture of the terror of the war. (USAMHI)

Left: Portions of the V Corps soon went into the fight to assist the beleaguered III Corps. Brigadier General Samuel W. Crawford, who had been a surgeon in the garrison at Fort Sumter, led a division to the relief of Little Round Top. Here he stands grasping the pole of his headquarters flag a year later. (USAMHI)

Below: The fighting on July 2 raged elsewhere as well, such as in the vicinity of Rock Creek, at Culp's Hill, where the XII Corps held Meade's extreme right. (USAMHI)

Above: Units like the 30th Pennsylvania, with Company A shown here, fought in those fields on their own home soil. Rarely did a Union soldier have that experience, which was commonplace among Southerners. (USAMHI)

Right: A major assault came at Cemetery Hill, the right center of Meade's line. As evening approached, Confederates swept across the fields in the distance of this Brady Company image to attack these slopes. (USAMHI)

Left: The Tysons captured this image of the stone wall along the base of Cemetery Hill, looking toward Culp's Hill. The Confederates hurled themselves against the opposite side of this wall and into the guns of the Yankees. (KA)

Above: Their objective was the crest of the hill named for the cemetery at its summit. Here one sees a Brady Company view of the gatehouse to Evergreen Cemetery. (USAMHI)

Left: Brady's men are believed to have made this view of the ground over which the Rebels attacked. They swept from the right of the picture to the left. (NA)

Below: Federal gun emplacements on Cemetery Hill, showing the hasty defenses thrown up by the Yankee gunners. A photograph by F. Gutekunst. (KA)

Above: Another view of the gateway, by the Tysons. Men hid behind the gravestones, visible in the background, while enemy bullets split and cracked them, showering splinters of marble over the once peaceful "bivouac of the dead." (P-M)

Above: Finally July 3 arrived, marking the last day of the battle and the most desperate. Attacks had failed to take Culp's Hill, Meade's extreme right, though places like the Taney farm, shown here in a Tyson photograph, did fall to the Confederates. (COURTESY OF WILLIAM C. DARRAH, GETTYSBURG)

Above: Breastworks such as these played a vital role in the successful defense of Culp's Hill. Shown here are two of Brady's assistants, gazing in the direction from which the Confederate attacks were made on both the evening of July 2 and the morning of July 3. (ROBERT J. YOUNGER)

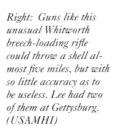

Right: Guns like this unusual Whitworth breech-loading rifle could throw a shell almost five miles, but with so little accuracy as to be useless. Lee had two of them at Gettysburg. (USAMHI)

Above: After the failures elsewhere on the Union lines, Lee now looked to a massive assault on Meade's center as his last hope of success. His chief of artillery, Colonel E. Porter Alexander, massed scores of guns to bombard the Yankee line on Cemetery Ridge. (VM)

Right: Charles W. Squires, seated at left, served with the Washington Artillery of New Orleans. To these men fell the honor of firing the opening shots signaling the commencement of the cannonade. (COURTESY OF W.H.T. SQUIRES, HENDERSON, N.C.)

Below: Behind the Federal lines on Cemetery Ridge Meade made his headquarters in the modest Leister farmhouse. Three days later Gardner made this view, the horses killed in the battle still littering the ground. (LC)

Below right: Here Meade held his council of war the night before and determined to stay and risk another day's battle. (P-M)

Above: Now Major General George E. Pickett led his division, accompanied by two others of Hill's corps, for the grand infantry assault that forever after bore Pickett's name. Both Longstreet and Pickett believed it a mistake. (VM)

Below: Brigadier General James H. Lane led his brigade in the charge and lost almost half of his command. (VM)

Left: Up the slopes of Cemetery Ridge swept the Confederates. They raced past the modest home of free Negro Abraham Bryan, only yards from the crest. The clutter and damage from the fight is still evident in the Brady Company photograph made several days later. (USAMHI)

Right: A dead and decomposed horse lies in Bryan's yard, while a very much alive photographer's assistant poses for dead several days after the fight in this unpublished Brady Company image. (P-M)

Left: Over 1,500 artillery horses were killed in the battle. (USAMHI)

Right: It was Hancock and his II Corps that formed the mainstay of the Cemetery Ridge line, with division commanders like Brigadier General Alexander Hays fighting admirably. (P-M)

Right: The terrible losses to the Confederates could not be replaced. Brigadier General James L. Kemper, who was seriously wounded, fell within a few feet of the enemy line, only to be captured. (VM)

Middle right: Richard B. Garnett had been one of Jackson's best commanders. He led his Virginia brigade in the charge, died in the furious smoke of the fight in front of Meade's line, and was buried with his men in a common grave. (USAMHI)

Above: Supporting Garnett and Kemper was the brigade of General Lewis A. Armistead. With his color-bearer and a few others he actually penetrated the Federal line and just managed to touch a Yankee cannon with his hand before he received a mortal wound. He died a short time later. (VM)

Left: And even a single civilian was killed on July 3. Miss Jennie Wade died instantly when struck by a sniper's bullet earlier that day as she baked bread in her sister's home in the town. (USAMHI)

Below: There were heavy casualties in blue as well. Meade's horse, Baldy, took a bad wound, having already been wounded at both Bull Runs and at Antietam. This last injury put him out of field service for good, though the animal lived on until 1882. He marched in Meade's own funeral in 1872. (P-M)

Below: Brigadier General Joseph R. Davis, nephew of the Confederate President, led his brigade in support of the great assault and helped cover its retreat when it failed. (USAMHI)

Above: Only after the main Battle of Gettysburg was over did the nearby cavalry finally get involved. Brigadier General Hugh J. Kilpatrick led a division of Federal horse, and as the Confederates streamed back toward Seminary Ridge after the failure of the attack, he foolishly sent a brigade in to attack the enemy on another strongly held portion of the field. (COURTESY OF BARBARA CHEATELY, ONTARIO, CALIFORNIA)

Above: The commander of that brigade was Elon J. Farnsworth, a general for just four days. He died in the attack as it was repulsed. (P-M)

Above: A Confederate commander in the mounted fighting was Brigadier General Wade Hampton, who actually held his fire in a duel with a Federal enlisted man until the Yankee could reload his carbine. Then Hampton shot him, only to be wounded grievously himself a few minutes later. (MUSEUM OF THE CONFEDERACY, RICHMOND)

Above: Colonel Laurence S. Baker's leadership of the 1st North Carolina Cavalry in Hampton's command won him promotion to brigadier a few weeks later. Few cavalrymen would boast of their performance in the Gettysburg campaign. (VM)

Above: Three miles east of Gettysburg a larger and exclusively cavalry fight took place on the afternoon of July 3, as Stuart's attempt to penetrate Meade's rear failed. One of the Yankee brigades was led by another new brigadier, George A. Custer. (USAMHI)

Right: Confederate field hospitals full of wounded were left behind by the retreating Lee and quickly surrendered to Meade. At the bottom of this hill the Black Horse Tavern and the barn in front of it contained wounded from Longstreet's corps, in the care of Surgeon Simon Baruch, father of Bernard Baruch. An early post-war view. (SOUTH CAROLINA RELIC ROOM AND MUSEUM, COLUMBIA)

Right: The field hospitals for the Federal wounded grew rapidly as all the injured were brought in, and hundreds of humanitarians flocked from the North to tend them. Here the United States Christian Commission cares for men believed to be from the II Corps. (KA)

Right: Photographer F. Gutekunst of Philadelphia came to make this image of more Christian Commission hospital tents for the II Corps. What had until recently been a cornfield was now a field of pain. (NATIONAL PARK SERVICE)

Above: And everywhere, it seemed, there were men to bury. Here O'Sullivan caught Confederates being laid in shallow graves near the Rose Farm. For them, at least, the war was over. (USAMHI)

Above: Meade finally pursued Lee's retreating army as it trudged back toward Virginia, but it was too late. In Emmitsburg, as Stuart's cavalry covered the retreat, the Southerners stopped long enough to briefly capture the Farmers' Inn and Hotel on July 5. With it they detained one of Gardner's photographers, as Gardner's team was just on its way to photograph the recent battlefield. (USAMHI)

Left: Battery F of the 5th United States Artillery was one of the leading units in the delayed pursuit of Lee. They followed his tracks to the Potomac. (KA)

Below left: Yet finally Lee crossed the great river. On July 19 Meade was himself ready to cross in pursuit, but the bridge at Berlin had been destroyed two years earlier. (USAMHI)

Below: Consequently the engineers threw pontoon bridges across the stream and over they went. But the campaign was done. (USAMHI)

Above: Four months later people again flocked to Gettysburg, this time for the dedication of a national soldiers' cemetery. Hundreds toured the battlefield, itself still not recovered from the fight. Soldiers posed and feigned death in such hellish places as Devil's Den. (LC)

Above: Several hundred spectators assembled to hear the dedication remarks by Edward Everett of Massachusetts and by President Lincoln.(NA)

Below: Lincoln's remarks proved so brief that he had finished and had sat down before the photographer could capture the scene. Instead he caught the President a few minutes later. (His head is encircled in this photograph.) He had spoken of democracy and devotion, of freedom and sacrifice, of the good things in men that must never perish from the earth. (NA)

FIGHTING FOR TIME

Powerful batteries like these thirty-pounder Parrots readied a devastating fire for the final assault when it should come. The besieged Confederates at Port Hudson were about to feel the weight of their iron.
(U.S. ARMY MILITARY HISTORY INSTITUTE, CARLISLE BARRACKS, PENNSYLVANIA)

Jewels of the Mississippi

HERMAN HATTAWAY

Vicksburg and Port Hudson, invincible until Grant

FROM THE OUTSET OF WAR, the Union made control of the entire Mississippi River one of its principal aims. By early 1862 it had seized all but a 110-mile stretch, but at Port Hudson, Louisiana, and Vicksburg, Mississippi, the Confederates held tenaciously to two very strong points: one, a port town twenty-five miles north of Baton Rouge; the other, a commercial city at the mouth of the Yazoo River. Port Hudson sat on an almost precipitous bluff where the river made a sharp turn; Vicksburg, called the Gibraltar of the West, seemed impregnable because of its location on high bluffs and rough surrounding terrain.

Surprisingly, though, the Southern high command paid seemingly inadequate attention to the river. The contrasting attitudes of top leaders reflected both in the priority they assigned to the campaign and in the quality of personnel employed. The North unleashed a major effort, directed by two able commanders: U. S. Grant and William T. Sherman. The Confederacy countered with beclouded policies, a theater commander—General Joseph E. Johnston—who was given insufficient guidance and resources, and a field general who proved inadequate: John Clifford Pemberton.

A native of the North, Pemberton had been born in Philadelphia. Because he ultimately failed to hold Vicksburg, many Southerners afterward considered him either a pariah or a deliberate traitor. He was, in truth, an honest and dedicated man, but his job was too big for him.

Yet, ironically, at Port Hudson, a place of equal importance, the quality of leaders was reversed and the Confederates held secure there until after Vicksburg had fallen. Expertly led by the Rebel Major General Franklin Gardner—who relieved W.N.R. Beall on December 28, 1862—the Southerners arrayed their guns in well-conceived clusters, protected by elaborate earthworks. The Federals floundered under poor

Above: In the subtle, modest eyes of U. S. Grant there is not the look of a man determined not to fail. Yet those eyes were set on Vicksburg in the fall of 1862, and never taken away. He would have his prize if it took a year. In the end, it did. (U.S. ARMY MILITARY HISTORY INSTITUTE, CARLISLE BARRACKS, PA.)

Left: In 1862 the protector of Vicksburg had been the egotistic Major General Earl Van Dorn, a "coxcomb" and "dandy," thought many of his soldiers. The ladies found him attractive, too, until a cuckolded husband killed him on May 7, 1863. (MESERVE COLLECTION, CHICAGO HISTORICAL SOCIETY)

Right: The prize. Vicksburg. The fortress city on the Mississippi. As the Warren County Courthouse dominated the city, so did the city dominate the great river. (USAMHI)

leadership from a former Speaker of the House of Representatives with presidential ambitions, Major General Nathaniel P. Banks.

In late 1862 the onslaught opened at both ends of the Confederate segment of the river. On November 16 a Federal fleet steamed upriver toward Port Hudson and commenced a brief bombardment of the batteries. That action was bloodless and the boats withdrew, leaving things quiet for al most a month, but on December 13 the war vessels returned. Then on the seventeenth the Yankees reoccupied Baton Rouge, which they had abandoned the previous August. Grant, too, before the year's end, launched the first of his efforts against Vicksburg, this one culminating in the Battle of Chickasaw Bayou.

Grant had wanted a three-pronged attack, himself to lead troops overland from Memphis, Sherman to head a downriver naval-supported expedition, and Banks to cooperate with a column from Baton Rouge. But Banks refused to work with Grant, and brilliant cavalry raids by the Rebel Major General Earl Van Dorn caused Grant's own thrust from Memphis to be abandoned. Sherman, though, in late December, steamed south with his 33,000 men aboard sixty transports accompanied by seven gunboats.

Pemberton was not personally at Vicksburg initially. The city's inner defenses were overseen by Major General Martin Luther Smith, and the field forces were led by Brigadier General Stephen D. Lee. Ultimately Pemberton concentrated 12,000 men, but in the beginning the Southerners faced Sherman's force with a mere 2,700 outside the city and another 2,400 manning the interior fortifications.

Sherman's armada went down the Mississippi and twelve miles up the Yazoo River to debark. By December 27 terrain, more than planning, had forced two Union brigades into assault positions at Chickasaw Bayou. There Lee set a trap. A morass of mud and water slowed the Federals and forced them to funnel over a log bridge. The Yankees could get only to within 150 yards of the Rebel main line before withering fire forced the attackers to brake and retreat. Losses were 1,776 Union and 207 Confederate.

Sherman planned another attack, but dense fog settled and a torrential rain instilled fear that a flood might drown the entire command; so he withdrew on January 2, 1863. One Union corporal aptly observed that "Sherman or Grant or both had made a bad blunder."

January passed in relative quiet, but on February 2 the Union ram *Queen of the West* ran past the Vicksburg batteries—proving that it could be done. She was struck twelve times, but not seriously. For the next dozen days this vessel wreaked considerable havoc upon both the Mississippi and Red rivers, until she was lost. She illustrated that the Union possessed a tremendous advantage in the struggle for the Mississippi because the Confederacy never managed to develop sufficient naval strength. There had been a brief moment the previous summer, during the short life of the CSS *Arkansas*, when things might have been rendered differently. But the *Arkansas* had been destroyed by the Confederates to prevent her imminent loss to the enemy. That vessel, and a sister ship that was never finished, were the only new Mississippi River gunboats authorized to be built by the Confederate government. The rest of the

Left: Van Dorn managed to blunt Grant's first campaign against Vicksburg in December 1862. The Federals were here in Oxford, Mississippi, camped about the courthouse and throughout the countryside, when Van Dorn destroyed Grant's supply base at Holly Springs. (CHS)

Left: Meanwhile, Grant had sent William T. Sherman to try to reach Vicksburg by the bayous north of the city. By December 28 Sherman got as far as Chickasaw Bayou, intending to attack the thinly held heights between it and Vicksburg. The next day he struck at Chickasaw Bluffs and suffered a bloody repulse. The Confederates on those commanding heights proved to be stronger than he believed. The defeat ended land operations for the rest of the winter. (USAMHI)

Left: The Navy took the next fire, led by Grant's trusted associate, Acting Rear Admiral David D. Porter, commanding the Mississippi River Squadron. (USAMHI)

Right: Admiral David G. Farragut brought his fleet from New Orleans up past the Port Hudson batteries to cooperate with his stepbrother Porter and with Grant. (USAMHI)

Left: On April 16, 1863, Porter ran part of his fleet, including the newly completed mammoth ironclad Lafayette, past the Vicksburg batteries in order to support the troop crossings below the city. (LOUISIANA STATE UNIVERSITY, DEPARTMENT OF ARCHIVES AND MANUSCRIPTS, BATON ROUGE)

Above: But these could be costly heroics. Ships were hit, and some were lost in the repeated tauntings of the Confederate river batteries. On March 25 the steam ram Switzerland, a ship belonging to the Army, went to the bottom. She appears here earlier off Cairo, Illinois, bristling with guns and soldiers. (CHS)

Above: More formidable rams like the Vindicator survived the passages, and lived to pose one day for the camera with the captured city in the background. (PENNSYLVA-NIA-MOLLUS COLLECTION, WAR LIBRARY AND MUSEUM, PHILADEL-PHIA)

Above: One mighty vessel after another ran past the batteries. (NAVAL HISTORICAL CENTER, WASHINGTON, D.C.)

Above: Colonel J. F. Pargoud, a Frenchman by birth, led his 3d Louisiana Cavalry in resisting Federal landings at Young's Point, Louisiana, when Grant began sending his corps into Louisiana to march below Vicksburg. (NATIONAL ARCHIVES, WASHINGTON, D.C.)

Southern flotilla consisted of altered wooden steam ships.

The Federal Navy conversely possessed a fleet of new boats specifically designed for river warfare. The United States had commissioned seven heavily armed, armored gunboats at St. Louis, each fitted with thirteen large-caliber guns and shielded with oak planking two feet thick on the gun decks. An other vessel, the *Benton*, a converted snag boat, carried sixteen guns and was covered with iron plating. In addition nine Federal rams were built out of old steamers at Cairo, Illinois.

Thus, naval strength proved to be one of the keys to Grant's conduct of his campaign. After Sherman's failure, Grant had the boats bring his army down from Memphis and land it on the Louisiana side, just north of Vicksburg. He immediately set into motion a series of schemes to approach the city from a more desirable direction.

In Grant's canal project, an attempt was made to deflect the waters of the Mississippi from their natural channel so that the naval support could safely bypass the Vicksburg batteries. The diggers dug feverishly but to no avail, while the Confederates remained relatively unconcerned —their engineers having predicted, correctly, that it would come to nothing. A Federal ram

Below: While Grant moved south to attack Grand Gulf in his campaign to approach Vicksburg from the south, Yankee soldiers and sailors made feint attacks north of the city at Haynes' Bluff on the Yazoo. One of the ships involved was the behemoth ironclad Choctaw. (LSU)

Right: The seamen of the Choctaw eventually battered the Yazoo defenses severely, then later became their enemies' saviors by plucking many Confederates out of the river in fighting at Milliken's Bend. (LSU)

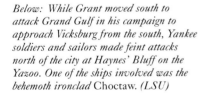

was used in an effort to throw water into the canal with its paddle wheel, but without success.

Then followed the hapless Lake Providence expedition, during which the Union gunboats tried to get into the Red River from above Vicksburg, thereby reaching the precious segment of the Mississippi.

Next came the Yazoo Pass expedition. The Federal Navy moved into Yazoo Pass and tried to get from there into the Yazoo River, via a bayou, but on March 11 were blocked at Fort Pemberton.

Last among the unsuccessful preliminary affairs came complex and fruitless campaigning north of Vicksburg in expeditions on Deer Creek, Steele's Bayou, and Rolling Fork. The Federal gunboats entered bayous north of the Yazoo and tried to maneuver through the narrow, overhung labyrinth of streams.

Grant later asserted that he had only scant hopes that any of these schemes might work. He was saving his major effort for the spring and summer: to have empty vessels, shielded by cotton bales, run southward past the Vicksburg batteries while Grant marched overland with the troops.

MEANWHILE, the Port Hudson campaign also continued in momentary stalemate. On March 14 a prodigious naval bombardment revealed that gunboats alone could not reduce the batteries. Two vessels did run by, but at great cost. The Confederates fired artillery with deadly accuracy, even at night, because they used special reflectors to flash the light from great bonfires they lit on both banks, and they also beamed a number of railroad locomotive headlights onto the river. The shore gunners could "aim almost as well as if it were day."

Although the bombardment continued nearly every night and sometimes during the day, the defenders found time to engage in occasional frivolities. Sometimes they played marbles atop a memorial slab in the nearby cemetery. Or they held footraces for the prize of sleeping on the flat tombs, which, though hard, at least were much drier, and the troops considered them more comfortable, than the damp Louisiana earth.

By mid-April Grant proceeded to force matters to a head at Vicksburg. As a prelude, he employed several diversions. A marauding division under Major General Frederick Steele moved by water from Young's Point to Greenville, Mississippi, and then inland. Colonel Benjamin H. Grierson led 1,000 cavalrymen out of Memphis on a raid that continued all the way into Baton Rouge. Sherman's corps made an elaborate feint from north of Vicksburg, landing at Haynes' Bluff.

On April 16, during the middle of the night, Rear Admiral David D. Porter's fleet ran past the city. Often hit by the Confederate guns, all but one of the boats nevertheless got safely through. They met Grant near Hard Times, west of the river.

On the twenty-ninth the fleet pounded the Rebel gun emplacements across the river and attempted to clear the way for Grant's men to cross. But after six hours, "finding the position too strong," Grant moved his leading force southward to a spot opposite Bruinsburg. Now outnumbering his enemy by more than two to one, Grant was able to cross, push away the Confederates, and force Grand Gulf's evacuation.

Grant pushed one corps rapidly inland toward Port Gibson. A small Confederate force hurried to

Right: A first-rate Confederate officer, Brigadier General John S. Bowen of Georgia, maintained a spirited defense, resisting first at Grand Gulf, and then heroically at Port Gibson on May 1. For his efforts he won promotion, but the ensuing siege of Vicksburg so destroyed his health that he died a week after the surrender. (USAMHI)

Above: As a diversion to assist his movement south of Vicksburg, Grant sent Colonel Benjamin H. Crierson and 1,700 men on a dashing raid into the interior of Mississippi and Louisiana. They rode 800 miles in seventeen days. The raid disrupted Confederate communications and made Grierson a brigadier general, as he appears here. (USAMHI)

Above: Then came the attack on Grand Gulf, where Grant recrossed his army below Vicksburg. Mighty ironclads like the Louisville, *shown here in front of Vicksburg, helped batter the Confederates' meager defenses before the crossing. (KEAN ARCHIVES, PHILADELPHIA, PA.)*

Right: William R. Pywell's image of Big Black River Station, which was right in the center of the Union and Confederate lines. (LIBRARY OF CONGRESS, WASHINGTON, D.C.)

Left: When Grant sent Sherman and 6,000 men on a feint up the Yazoo to Yazoo Pass, ostensibly in the hope of getting around to the eastern side of the city, the little tinclad Rattler *served as flagship. She spent the rest of her career as a raider up and down the Mississippi. (NHC)*

Right: It was at Champion's Hill on May 16 that the Union and Confederate armies finally came together in the first major battle of the campaign. Brigadier General Seth Barton and his brigade held the left of the Southern line, but could not withstand. The rout of Barton threatened the whole Rebel army. (VALENTINE MUSEUM, RICHMOND, VA.)

Above: But there was nothing left but a siege for Lieutenant General John C. Pemberton. He was a Pennsylvanian loyal to the Confederacy, and soon felt himself abandoned by his government and his army. He was not a brilliant commander, but few in his situation could have achieved more. (USAMHI)

Finally the Confederates crossed the river and burned the bridge behind them. Grant could not cross until this and other pontoon bridges went up in its place. This J. M. Moore photograph purports to show Union soldiers in the foreground and Confederate guards and wagons on the other side, but such is not likely to be the case. (OLD COURT HOUSE MUSEUM, VICKSBURG, MISS.)

Above: Colonel Hylan B. Lyon and his 8th Kentucky Cavalry covered the Southern retreat to Vicksburg after the defeat at Champion's Hill, and then later escaped from the siege. (USAMHI)

Left: Vicksburg's railroad depot on the Vicksburg & Jackson line. Until Grant cut off the rail link, this was the destination of the supplies the Confederates stockpiled to resist him. (KA)

Left: The shantytown just below Vicksburg, as seen by a photographer of the city's Washington Photographic Gallery. Much of this vicinity was virtually swept clean in the advancing fortifications of the besieging Federals. (KA)

intercept. Hopelessly outnumbered but aided by the terrain—steep, sharp ridges and gullies covered with thick vines and dense undergrowth—the Southerners fought a plucky defense.

Grant had intended to live off the country, but it was necessary that his forces move rapidly; otherwise they would deplete the immediately available supplies. He quickly realized that he had to reopen supply lines. Organizing this effort delayed him for more than a week while he arranged to run past the Vicksburg batteries an additional 400,000 rations of "hard bread, coffee, sugar, and salt." Ammunition that could not be exposed to fire came by wagon along with additional subsistence stores.

GRANT'S SUCCESS in reaching the east bank below the city caused appropriate alarm in Richmond. Secretary of War James Seddon immediately diverted 5,000 reinforcements to Mississippi and soon after ordered Joe Johnston to assemble 3,000 men and go to take charge in person. Seddon then renewed previous efforts to secure reinforcements from Virginia, but Robert E. Lee effectively resisted the move. Convinced by Lee that the South should not deplete the Virginia forces, President Jefferson Davis and his war secretary turned to General Braxton Bragg's army.

The Union hopes for a successful conclusion to the Vicksburg campaign depended in part upon Major General William S. Rosecrans's remaining sufficiently strong and doing at least enough to ensure effective limits upon any reinforcements that Bragg might send to Pemberton. This Rosecrans accomplished well in his unheralded and under rated Tullahoma campaign.

Meanwhile, Grant's opportunity to move into almost virgin country vastly simplified his logistics. He now luckily enjoyed the fruits of a growing season that was well along in this fertile region where planters had reduced the cultivation of cotton in favor of food crops. In addition to fodder, the countryside abounded in "corn, hogs, cattle, sheep, and poultry." The Mississippi farms thus relieved Grant's long and inadequate road communications, enabling him to "disregard his base and depend upon the country for meat and even for bread." This was

Left: This 1864 panorama of two images offers a wide view of the northeastern portion of Vicksburg, looking toward Fort Hill in the distance. It is seen from the cupola on the Warren County Courthouse. (KA)

Above: Closer to the city the Washington Gallery artist captured a view of an earthwork fortification in the left distance, a flag flying overhead. (KA)

Above: Visible to all, Union and Confederate, was the Warren County Courthouse. At 5:35 one afternoon the Washington cameraman caught the Greek Revival building, which still stands today. Never the scene of fighting itself, the courthouse became in a measure symbolic of the struggle for Vicksburg. (KA)

Right: Row after row of heavily emplaced guns were so situated as to be nearly impervious to Union naval gunnery. That in large measure is why Grant had to take the city from the rear, its landside. This image, probably by French Company of Vicksburg, was made after the city fell. (KA)

Above: The Tuscumbia, *with the USS* Linden—*number 10—in the background, and two of the mortar boats that pounded Vicksburg night and day during the siege. (NHC)*

Left: Schooners with mortars mounted on their decks also entered the bombardment; their high arching shells, with fuses sputtering like rockets in the night, provided not only danger but also an element of entertainment for Vicksburg's citizens. They watched the shells and became rather expert in predicting where they would fall. (USAMHI)

Above: Only a little more successful in the May 22 attack than Sherman was the corps of Major General James B. McPherson, here seated second from the right among his staff. Behind him is the Balfour house, his headquarters in the weeks after the siege. A young general of remarkable promise, he was already a particular favorite with Grant. (KA)

Above: There were other vessels in Grant's combined forces, but none more unique than the Red Rover. *She had been a Confederate troopship at the war's start, then fell to the Yankees with the capture of Island No. 10 in 1862. They converted her into an army hospital ship and later transferred her to the webfoot service, making the* Red Rover *the Navy's first hospital vessel. (NHC)*

Above: The 8th Wisconsin, a fine regiment in its own right, was best known in the army for its eagle mascot, "Old Abe." The bird adopted the regiment, staying with it through most of the war. In battle, said the Badgers, Old Abe went aloft, circling over the fray and screaming at the enemy. When he died after the war, they had him stuffed. A J. M. Moore image. (OCHM)

Above: McPherson's division commanders, men like General John "Blackjack" Logan, got no nearer Vicksburg than did Sherman. (USAMHI)

Below: McPherson's signal corpsmen had little to do but watch and pass an occasional message. A French & Company image. (KA)

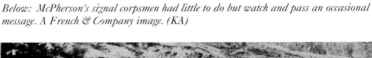

Above: And the division of Brigadier General Marcellus Crocker did not get into the fight at all. (USAMHI)

fortunate, for Grant's line of wagon communications west of the river was tenuous. In the early spring the "roads" that had gradually emerged from the flooded lands amounted to little more than slimy streaks through oozy mud.

Grant's good fortune and good planning in his supply arrangements extended rearward all the way to his base. He had been able to abandon the railroad running north through western Tennessee, so that all his communications above Vicksburg lay on the Mississippi River. He thus foiled one of the main Confederate hopes to defeat him. Johnston had expected, as had Van Dorn the previous winter, again to neutralize Grant with cavalry raids upon supply lines.

Grant was further aided by Pemberton's indecisiveness. Initially Pemberton did perceive that Grant's new position "threatens Jackson, and, if successful, cuts Vicksburg off from the east." To stop Grant, Pemberton realized that his forces, scattered from Port Hudson to north of Vicksburg, must be concentrated. Yet after taking the appropriate initial steps, Pemberton almost immediately quailed and ordered the garrison to stay at Port Hudson.

BY THE MIDDLE of the second week of May, as Grant's resupplied army began its advance, the Confederates stood tragically divided. Grant thus had the opportunity of "threatening both and striking at either." On May 12 an engagement erupted at Raymond, about fifteen miles from the Mississippi capital. The ensuing contest lasted for several hours, each side sustaining some 500 casualties. Gradually the outnumbered Rebels fell back toward Jackson. At the same time Sherman's men clashed with Southern skirmishers along Fourteen Mile Creek. These two struggles induced Grant to choose first to deal with the concentration at Jackson.

Grant used one corps as a covering force to hold Pemberton at bay while the other two Federal corps concentrated against Johnston. Outnumbered almost five to one, Johnston began on the fourteenth to withdraw northward, leaving only two brigades to try delaying the Yankees. Brief, one-sided fighting followed, and in the afternoon Grant's men occupied the capital. Now Grant stood astride Vicksburg's landward communications.

Turning next toward Vicksburg and Pemberton's forces, Grant left a minimal guard to his rear in protection against Johnston's increasing army. Relying primarily upon logistic means, Grant destroyed the Pearl River railroad bridge and the road itself in all directions as far as practicable.

Pemberton meanwhile could have placed Grant in a difficult supply situation if he had been able to hold Grant east of the Big Black River. This Pemberton attempted to do, on the sixteenth, by precipitating a major engagement at Champion's Hill. A little more than four miles east of Edwards Station, Champion's Hill is a crescent-shaped ridge, about seventy-five feet high. Each of the three roads that led eastward from Edwards Station was covered by one of Pemberton's divisions. The Confederate line stretched out about three miles.

Eventually the Federals attacked from the north and northeast in an attempt to roll up the Confederate left flank. The Southerners responded by moving an entire division in a counterclockwise direction, eventually to form a

Above: Tough Western regiments like this one, drawn up for the camera near Vicksburg, pushed their way into, and briefly through, part of the Confederate fortifications to threaten more than half a mile of the Rebel earthworks. A French & Company image of an unidentified Federal regiment. (KA)

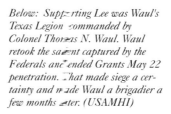

Below: Supporting Lee was Waul's Texas Legion commanded by Colonel Thomas N. Waul. Waul retook the salient captured by the Federals and ended Grant's May 22 penetration. That made siege a certainty and made Waul a brigadier a few months later. (USAMHI)

Below: Only the troublesome and boastful Major General John A. McClernand achieved something of a breakthrough, attacking the eastern defenses of the city. (USAMHI)

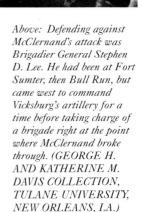

Above: Defending against McClernand's attack was Brigadier General Stephen D. Lee. He had been at Fort Sumter, then Bull Run, but came west to command Vicksburg's artillery for a time before taking charge of a brigade right at the point where McClernand broke through. (GEORGE H. AND KATHERINE M. DAVIS COLLECTION, TULANE UNIVERSITY, NEW ORLEANS, LA.)

Left: Now came the long waiting, the bombardment, and the hunger and disease of summer: the Siege of Vicksburg. Soldiers and civilians on both sides turned mole, living in dugouts and caves. Here the 45th Illinois bivouacked beside the James Shirley house. The Shirley home, the "White House," stood between the lines and miraculously survived the siege. (OCHM)

Above: And to protect Grant from himself—so some said—he relied upon his friend and chief of staff John A. Rawlins, shown here as a brigadier following his promotion in August 1863. Rawlins claimed that he kept Grant from the bottle. (P-M)

Above: As Grant invested the city, he had to guard against an embryonic army building under Joseph E. Johnston, who was trying desperately to relieve Vicksburg. To protect his flank against Johnston, Grant sent the Missouri politician turned soldier Major General Francis Preston Blair, Jr. (USAMHI)

Right: The forty-seven days of siege proved a constant test of resolve and stamina, and a test of blood as well. Brigadier General Isham W. Garrott of Alabama sought to relieve the boredom by himself borrowing an infantryman's rifle and going out on the skirmish line to fire at the Yankees on June 17. The escapade cost him his life just days before his brigadier's commission reached him. (VM)

Above: Meanwhile, Grant brought in reinforcements as he slowly built an irresistible iron wall around Vicksburg. From Virginia he was to receive Major General W. F. Smith and his IX Corps, shown here embarking at Aquia Creek in February 1863. In fact, the IX Corps never reached him at Vicksburg in time to participate in the siege. Alexander Gardner made this image. (LC)

line of battle somewhat in the shape of the number 7. Pemberton expected the main attack along the vertical, but it actually came from the horizontal above.

As the Yankees moved farther and farther to the west, attempting to turn the Rebel left, Pemberton shifted more men northward. The Confederate line eventually stretched more west to east than north to south. And so, fearing greater disaster, Pemberton decided to withdraw, ending the contest.

In this costly battle, the bloodiest of the series of conflicts preliminary to the siege of Vicksburg, Federal effectives numbered about 29,000 and they sustained a total of 2,441 casualties; while the Confederate effectives, probably numbering under 20,000, suffered 3,851 casualties. One Union brigade commander ranked the Battle of Champion's Hill among "the most obstinate and murderous conflicts of the war." And Federal Brigadier General Alvin P. Hovey said to an Illinois soldier, "I cannot think of this bloody hill without sadness and pride."

Pemberton fought a holding action the next day for the Big Black River bridges. He hoped to keep a passage open long enough for the division under Major General William W. Loring, hopelessly cut off and lost, to rejoin the main force. The Confederates occupied a line about one mile long, touching the curving river at both ends. Launching an attack, the Federals quickly discovered a vulnerable point. On the Confederate extreme left the previously prepared earthworks had been washed away by a recent overflow of the river. The Northerners easily moved up to this point and thereby were able to roll up the flank. The Southerners broke in disorder and fled to the environs of the city.

ON MAY 18, THEN, the siege of Vicksburg began. Three days later Banks began a siege of Port Hudson, also. After a minor action on the twenty-first, the Battle of Plains Store, and another on the twenty-second, the Federals began building siege lines. Confederate General Gardner spoke prophetically to the men in one of his batteries: "The enemy are coming, but mark you, many a one will get to Hell before he does to Port Hudson."

Banks had his investment completed by the twenty-third, and thereafter it was constant siege craft. But there was plenty of peripheral action, first at Troth's farm, then at Thompson's Creek, where the Confederates had two war vessels. Both steamers were captured and converted to Federal service. Banks, though, failed to prove himself a particularly capable besieger, and his losses mounted disproportionately high. He already had wasted time, men, and resources aimlessly pursuing all over central Louisiana his strangely chosen personal objectives. Now he reluctantly acknowledged that he did "not know that anything is left me but to direct my forces against Port Hudson," and he revealed an obtuse courage: he also said he feared that this involved "the probable loss of New Orleans."

Indeed, Banks seemed to pay primary attention not to realistic factors but to his personal appearance. His looks had somewhat impressed Admiral Porter, who wrote of Banks: "Rather theatrical in his style of dress, he wore yellow gauntlets high upon his wrists, looking as clean as if they had just come from the glove-maker; his hat was picturesque, his long boots and spurs

Above: Other reinforcements did arrive, swelling the Union numbers. The 2d Michigan came, its last battle the humiliation at Fredericksburg. They would welcome a victory. (BURTON HISTORICAL COLLECTION, DETROIT PUBLIC LIBRARY)

Below: In June Francis J. Herron, at the time the youngest major general on either side, brought his small division to Grant. One of his brigades was led by Brigadier General William Vandever, shown here seated at left with his staff. On the table before them a saber rests atop a map, perhaps of Vicksburg. (FRED EADS)

Below: They held out bravely. Colonel A. W. Reynolds said that "during these forty-seven days, under the terrific fire of the enemy's artillery and infantry, the officers and men of the brigade bore themselves with constancy and courage. Often half-fed and ill-clothed, exposed to the burning sun and soaking rains, they performed their duty cheerfully and without a murmur." (USAMHI)

were faultless." But at least now Banks was to some degree cooperating with Grant by keeping Gardner's garrison from helping Pemberton.

Grant knew that Pemberton might be tenacious in a conventional siege; they had known each other since the Mexican War, when Pemberton had demonstrated a stoically stubborn streak. So, hoping that a prompt attack might catch the enemy unprepared, Grant tried two assaults. In the first, on May 19, the Federals sustained 1,000 casualties, a testament to the strength of the Confederate positions. A second assault, quite large, was hurled on May 22. One momentary breakthrough occurred, at a redoubt defending a railroad cut, but counterattacks closed the breach. Losses were heavy: of 45,000 Federals engaged, 3,199 became casualties, while the Confederates lost fewer than 500 men. Grant tried no more assaults, but he felt confident about the prospects of his siege. "The enemy are undoubtedly in our grasp," he wrote on May 24. "The fall of Vicksburg and the capture of most of the garrison can only be a question of time."

BANKS also tried two fruitless assaults upon Port Hudson: on May 27 and on June 14. In the first the Confederates safely held their fire until the Federals were within forty yards of the lines. "We are laying in our rifle pits," one smug Rebel wrote, "awaiting the hated foe… They will catch it, sure…" And catch it they did!

But the vicious episode gave rise to some exaggerated stories concerning the prowess of the Union's black troops, which the North used for propaganda. Fictitiously, the colored troops were said to have "engaged in mortal hand-to-hand combat, fighting with bayonets: 'one Negro was observed with a rebel soldier in his grasp, tearing the flesh from his face with his teeth…'" A wildly romanticized illustration appeared in *Harper's Weekly.*

Meanwhile, the Rebels were accused of equally fictitious atrocities: the Mississippians supposedly nailed black troops, while alive, to trees around the bluffs. Actually the blacks under Banks fought poorly (although Negro troops valiantly proved themselves on many other fields). They were badly disciplined, ill-managed, and showed cowardice. Many of them were shot by their own disgusted comrades. One officer wrote, "I have heard before of negroes

Above: Closer and closer the advancing earthworks came. Photographers Armstead & Taylor of Corinth made this image of a section of the lines called the gap, and behind it an observation post dubbed Coonskin Tower. To the defenders it became increasingly clear that time was against them. (CHS)

Above: As June came to an end, Grant stepped up his work, launching repeated reconnaissances and small assaults. Here stood Fort Hill, the Confederates' principal earthwork on the river north of the city. On June 25 the Federals attacked and took it. (KA)

Above: By July 3 Pemberton could hold out no more. The next day he surrendered, and jubilant Federals soon occupied the prize they had coveted for so long. At last Yankee soldiers could pose for French in front of the courthouse. (KA)

Above: The photographers eagerly recorded the captures. Vacant lots bulged with Confederate artillery seized as spoils of war. Vicksburg's Methodist Church stands at right. The Catholic Church is in the center under the steeple. (KA)

Left: and Below: Brigadier General George Cosby, like the other Confederates with Johnston, got only as close as Jackson before learning of Vicksburg's surrender. They withstood a Federal attack on the city for a day before they pulled out, leaving Grant undisputed ruler over central Mississippi. (USAMHI)

Above: For a time Grant made his headquarters in this Vicksburg house. (USAMHI)

turning white from fright, and did not believe it; but it is literally true."

The June 14 assault was even more ignominious: the Federals lost 1,805 to a mere 47 Confederate casualties. Why had Banks ordered so reckless a venture? "The people of the North demanded blood, sir," he callously replied. Otherwise the siege dragged on, Gardner's 6,800 men defending well against Banks's 26,000.

The soldiers gave nicknames to the various field pieces. There were names such as Bounding Bet, whose shells typically ricocheted along the ground, skipping and bounding and finally rolling like a bowling ball; and the Lady Davis, also called the Demoralizer, a 10-inch columbiad that the ammunition-short Rebels loaded with whatever they could find, from flatirons to nails. Sometimes such guns belched "cane knives, railroad spikes, bolts, hatchets, ramrods, nuts, wooden plugs fastened together with cotton, and broken pieces of bayonets."

And all the while the troopers burrowed deeper and deeper into the ground "like moles," seeking cover. The hot sun took a heavy toll too. Some of the men grew delirious, or fell asleep in the heat and died. But the siege continued, while sharp shooters and disease—scurvy and malaria—also took their share of lives. Exploding shells shattered the windows of the Port Hudson church, intermixing millions of glass fragments with the field peas stored there by the Confederate commissary. It be came not unusual "to see hungry Confederates spitting out pieces of glass between bites of corn bread."

BUT IN MISSISSIPPI, Grant simply and masterfully outgeneraled his opponents. After things settled down to a siege, the Rebels could do little about it. With modesty and humor Grant afterward gave much credit to Pemberton by characterizing him as his "best friend." Nevertheless, Pemberton's "help" would have availed the Union little without Grant's energy and perceptiveness. Grant exploited the enemy's weakness by first turning against Pemberton and Vicksburg rather than joining Banks against Port Hudson, which Banks had urged and even Lincoln had thought wise.

After the siege began, Johnston received some additional troops from Tennessee and South Carolina, but the Union reinforced Grant much more heavily. Union communications along the Mississippi, protected by gunboats, remained completely secure and Grant had only to wait, while enjoying a tactical security, until Pemberton—trapped against the river obstacle —was forced to surrender because of depleted supplies.

From boats on the river and from troops in the encircling lines, the Vicksburg populace and defenders suffered onslaughts against nerve and will. On June 2 one officer living within the besieged city declared that if the attack went on much longer, "a building will have to be arranged for the accommodation of maniacs," because the constant tension was driving people out of their minds. Union gunboats lobbed into the city huge mortar shells that made impact holes seventeen feet deep.

On the field the situation was described by Confederate Corporal Ephraim Anderson: "The enemy continued to prosecute the siege vigorously. From night to night and from day to day a series of works was presented. Secure and strong lines of fortifications appeared. Redoubts, manned by well practiced sharpshooters,... parapets blazing with artillery crowned every knoll and practicable elevation..., and oblique lines of entrenchments, finally running into parallels, enabled the untiring foe to work his way slowly but steadily forward."

Another Confederate soldier recalled that "fighting by hand grenades was all that was possible at such close quarters. As the Federals had the hand grenades and we had none, we obtained our supply by using such of theirs as failed to explode, or by catching them as they came over the parapet and hurling them back."

And, as Anderson continued, "It soon became evident that there was not an abundant supply of rations... one day,... among the provisions sent up... the only supply in the way of bread was made of peas.... This 'pea bread'... was made

Above: The Signal Corps set up shop in this mansion; their signal wigwag flags hang from the balcony. (USAMHI)

Right: The Quartermaster's people camped behind the city along the old Confederate lines of fortifications. (USAMHI)

Right: Hospitals, like this U.S. Marine Hospital overlooking the river, appeared everywhere. Unfortunately French blurred his own image in making this picture. (KA)

Above: Among the first to take advantage of the capture were, of course, the photographers. The Washington Gallery established itself in the third floor of William Tillman's Saddle & Harness Manufactory. (USAMHI)

Above: Everyone wanted a photograph. French found these rugged Westerners in front of the courthouse. (KA)

Above: The 20th Mississippi Colored Regiment drew itself up for French with Fort Hill in the background. (KA)

Above: Some regiments stood in front of their tents. (P-M)

Below: Grant soon put his men to work refortifying the river batteries as well as the landside lines, for Vicksburg could always be attacked again by men in gray. He built a formidable battery on the river called Castle Fort. From a height of nearly a thousand feet it mounted fifteen guns. (KA)

Below: More guns went into Battery Sherman, guarding Vicksburg's rear on the road to Jackson. They would never fire. (USAMHI)

Above: They posed where they camped, as around "The Castle," an unusual home surrounded by a small moat. Armstead & Taylor found it interesting. (OCHM)

of… 'cow peas,'… a small bean, cultivated quite extensively as provender for animals… the idea grew… that, if reduced to the form of meal, it would make an admirable… bread… But the nature of it was such that it never got done, and the longer it was cooked the harder it became on the outside… but, at the same time, it grew relatively softer on the inside, and, upon breaking it, you were sure to find raw pea meal in the center."

Meanwhile, as the city trembled from the bombardments, the people therein gradually reduced their daily meals to one-half and then to one quarter rations. The Confederate engineer officer S. H. Lockett reported that the men ate "mule meat and rats and young shoots of cane." Dora Miller, one of the entrapped civilians, recalled that during the final days of the siege her servant found rats "hanging dressed in the market." Willie Tunnard, a Confederate enlisted man, wrote that rat flesh, when fried, had a flavor "fully equal to that of squirrels." One Missouri soldier stoutly held that "if you did not know it, you could hardly tell the difference, when cooked," between mule meat and beef.

At last, after forty-seven days of siege, Pemberton and all but two of his officers agreed that they must surrender on July 4, 1863. The Federal losses amounted to 4,910 during the siege, while the Confederates had suffered casualties amounting to 1,872 before they then capitulated totally. The captives numbered 2,166 officers, 27,230 enlisted men, and 115 civilian employees; all were paroled save for 1 officer and 708 men who preferred to go north as prisoners. The Rebel army also yielded its entire complement of equipage: 172 cannon, large amounts of every ammunition type, and some 60,000 shoulder weapons, many of which were of such superior quality that some Union regiments exchanged their own for those they found stacked by their vanquished enemy.

"ALL WILL SING HALLELUJAH! The heroic city has fallen! Vicksburg is ours!" proclaimed a Federal captain. To have to surrender on American Independence Day was bitter indeed for the Southerners, but Pemberton had preferred to do it then, believing that he could get better terms. One citizen who had lived for weeks in a hillside cave said, "I wept incessantly, meeting first one group of soldiers and then another, many of them with tears streaming down their faces." For many hours they listened to "hateful tunes" played by the exuberant Yankee bands. The unreconstructed people of Vicksburg did not themselves celebrate the Fourth of July again until during World War II. But they were relieved, even if also demoralized, that the awful ordeal was over.

The news that Vicksburg had capitulated was sure to be the last thing needed to bring Port Hudson's surrender too. There was hardly any reason to continue to hold only one Confederate garrison on the Mississippi River. And sure enough, just a few days were all that were required: on July 8 Gardner asked Banks for terms. Port Hudson fell, having cost the Union nearly 10,000 men—dead, wounded, or physically impaired from disease or exposure—compared with the Southern losses of only 871. But now the entire Rebel garrison fell prisoner. And "The Father of Waters," as Lincoln gratefully proclaimed, again flowed "unvexed to the sea."

Above: One of those guns was that same 7.44 Blakely used by the Confederates. (USAMHI)

Left: The 17th Illinois Infantry, veterans of the fights at Jackson and Champion's Hill, and the heavy May assaults on Vicksburg, stayed after the surrender to garrison the newly won prize. They stand for the camera here early in 1864, the very picture of the rugged, unkempt, rather unmilitary Western soldier. They were not much on parade. But they could tear the heart out of the Confederacy. (NA)

Right: But it was a long river, with more than one Confederate bastion to guard it. Ships like David G. Farragut's Hartford moved up and down the mighty waterway between Vicksburg and another fortress, Port Hudson. (USAMHI)

Right: Vicksburg, it seemed, was still a fortress city. Only the armies had changed. (KA)

Above: Banks commanded from New Orleans and Baton Rouge, staging his operations against Port Hudson from the latter. At the Baton Rouge arsenal his own guns guarded the river below Port Hudson. (LSU)

Above: The goal was Port Hudson, itself a village of no significance, but along these steep bluffs the Confederates had placed powerful cannon that commanded the river. An image by the Baton Rouge firm of McPherson & Oliver. Some of the cannon bore names, like the Lady Davis, a 10-inch columbiad. (USAMHI)

Below: There, overlooking the Mississippi, his army gathered strength, and lost some of it as well. Men of the 52d Massachusetts who died before the campaign could begin. (ILLINOIS STATE HISTORICAL LIBRARY, SPRINGFIELD)

Above: It was intended to be the prize of another politician-turned-soldier, Nathaniel Prentiss Banks of Massachusetts. When the Confederate fortifications finally fell, it would be largely in spite of him. (USAMHI)

Above: And so could those shore guns sting. Lieutenant Commander A. Boyd Cummings steamed his ship the Richmond against Port Hudson on March 18, 1863. It cost him his life. (USAMHI)

Below: But the Yankee vessels did challenge the batteries from time to time, and they could inflict damage. A well-aimed shot has completely dismounted this Rebel cannon and ruined its siege carriage. (USAMHI)

Below: Even a few "Quaker guns," imitation cannon made from logs, could intimidate a Federal ship. From a distance the sham cannon looked like the real thing. (USAMHI)

Above: The Richmond *itself, almost a double for the* Hartford, *escaped to fight again. (OCHM)*

Above: Scores of lesser ships like the "Red River Packet" St. Maurice *did not challenge the batteries as the warships did, but they steamed constantly up and down the river, bringing more troops and more supplies to the besieging Federals. The* St. Maurice *appears here well laden with barrels and sacks of food. Frequently she carried important dispatches to New Orleans as well. (GLADSTONE COLLECTION)*

Right: The investment of Port Hudson finally came in May, the first attack on the Confederate works being led by Major General Christopher C. Augur, seated in the rocker at his Baton Rouge headquarters. This image was made by the very capable local photographer A. D. Lytle, whose artistry surpassed that of most of the other cameramen on the Mississippi. (LSU)

Left: The first Confederate commander of Port Hudson had been Brigadier General W.N.R. Beall. Later superseded, he remained throughout the siege and, after his capture, was released by the Federals to set up a New York City office for selling captured cotton! (MUSEUM OF THE CONFEDERACY, RICHMOND, VA.)

Right: These Rebel earthworks were almost within a stone's throw of the Federal emplacements along the line of trees in the background. It was to be a long and bitter siege for both armies. (USAMHI)

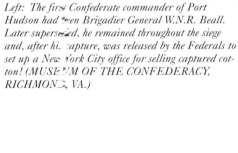

Above: In that May 27 attack, which failed, the 38th Massachusetts occupied this ravine and then held it for the next week in the face of constant Rebel sniping from the trees beyond. In a later assault on June 14, 1863, Federals found themselves trapped by enemy fire for several days and nights. (ISHL)

Below: This Rebel cannon seemed to defy gravity by remaining standing. (USAMHI)

Above: In the big attack of May 27, the Confederates held their ground manfully. This image, taken after the siege, shows one of the most hotly contested points of attack. (USAMHI)

Above: One more shot and it would fall to pieces. (NA)

Left: And it would be costly in men and matériel. Yankee fire almost completely dismounted this gun. (USAMHI)

Left: It would never fire again. (OCHM)

Right: Commanding those Confederates was a man equally gallant, Major General Franklin Gardner. There was a delicious irony in the fact that Pemberton, defending Vicksburg, was a Pennsylvanian and Gardner a New Yorker. His brother fought with the Union, but Gardner's loyalty to the Confederacy was as undoubted as his ability. (CONFEDERATE MUSEUM, NEW ORLEANS, LA.)

Left: Colonel William F. Bartlett had already lost a leg at Yorktown the year before. In the attack on May 27, he rode his horse straight for the Confederate lines and was hit twice. Ignoring his wounds after he fell, he watched his horse bound for the rear, and commented that the animal "jumped like a rabbit." Bartlett would become a brigadier, and rumors circulated that Confederate officers told their men not to fire at the gallant horseman. (USAMHI)

Above: Gardner made his headquarters here just outside the village of Port Hudson. After the garrison fell, it became headquarters for Brigadier General George L. Andrews, who stands in the center, leaning against a post. (USAMHI)

Left: Gardner used this church as a granary for his corn supplies. They dwindled rapidly, and the men resorted to eating rats and other vermin. Gardner, unable to get tobacco, smoked magnolia leaves in his pipe. (ISHL)

Right: Gerdner's soldiers lived as best they could, often in makeshift cabins like these barracks on the edge of the village. (USAMHI)

Right: And on went the siege. Palfrey and his assistants gradually built an ever-tightening grip of saps and earthworks around Port Hudson. They used the materials at hand, trees and cotton bales, as here at the emplacement for Captain Richard Duryea's Battery F, 1st United States Artillery. (USAMHI)

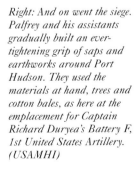

Above: The Confederates ground their corn into meal in these mill buildings during the siege. But finally the sound of the mill at work drew Federal artillery fire that destroyed it. This and several other images of Port Hudson were gathered by Captain J. C. Palfrey, Banks's chief engineer directing the siege work. (USAMHI)

Left: The only supply that the Confederates had in abundance was salt, barrels and barrels of it, along with more barrels of molasses. They left loads of it behind when they surrendered. (CHS)

Below: Even guns from ships were brought ashore. Lieutenant Commander Edward Terry brought these 9-inch guns from the Richmond to make a formidable battery. (USAMHI)

Above: The 1st Indiana Heavy Artillery built an imposing cotton parapet for its guns, but at least one Hoosier found sufficient free time to devote himself to carving a picture of a house on the trunk of the tree in the left foreground and his company number above it. It was in front of this battery that the Union and Confederate lines came nearest to each other. Soldiers threw messages back and forth. (USAMHI)

Right: The 18th New York Artillery used cotton bales as well, shielding their mammoth 20-pounder Parrott rifles. (USAMHI)

Right: This image, made after the siege, shows a Confederate line in the foreground and the Federal parallel just beyond it. That is how close together enemy earthworks came in places. (USAMHI)

Below: It was Captain James Rundel of the 156th New York who brought photographers McPherson & Oliver to Port Hudson to make these and other scenes of the siege. They captured the look of the Citadel, a major Confederate work on the river. Banks and his people were digging tunnels under the Citadel, intending to blow it apart from underground at the same time the infantry attacked. The surrender came just a day before the scheduled explosion. (ISHL)

Above: A massive seventeen-gun Union artillery emplacement near the Citadel had dismounted or destroyed several cannon and forced its occupants to burrow into the earth for protection. The Federal artillery position is in the background. (USAMHI)

Above: The interior of the Citadel. (USAMHI)

Above: Everywhere there was ruin. (USAMHI)

Below: Their works crumbling, their supplies exhausted, their weapons being blown apart, the Confederates could not hold out. (ISHL)

Above: By the time the siege was done, everywhere inside Gardner's lines was a scene of destruction and decay. (USAMHI)

Above: The Trench Cavalier, a massive trench that ran close to the center of the Confederate fortifications. To protect it, the Federals built the parapet of hogsheads in the center, and from behind it, they fired almost directly down and into the trench. (USAMHI)

Above: Powerful batteries like these 30-pounder Parrotts readied a devastating fire for the final assault when it should come. (USAMHI)

Below: Battery A, 1st United States Artillery. Gardner was ringed with cannon wherever he looked. (USAMHI)

Above: Brigadier General Cuvier Grover directed the operations against the Confederate left, including the Trench Cavalier, and as June moved into July, began readying several mines to explode under the Rebel works. Here at his headquarters Grover takes the shade, seen in profile wearing a hat, fourth from the right (USAMHI)

Above: But that morning the General Price, *once a Confederate vessel and now in the Union service, arrived near Port Hudson with the news that Vicksburg had surrendered. (LSU)*

Above: Now the soldiers could rest at last, pitch their tents in the shade of the trees, and try to survive the Deep South summer. (ISHL)

Left: For the tinclad vessels that once braved the batteries of Vicksburg and Port Hudson, ships like the Kenwood, *there was now the routine of patrol duty and an occasional raid. The river was not altogether quiet, but no more fortress batteries on overhead bluffs would threaten Porter's fleets. (USAMHI)*

Above: This mine ran under the Citadel. On July 7 Banks expected to detonate it. (USAMHI)

Left: A Yankee colonel wrapped a copy of the message around a stick and threw it into the Confederate works. There was no arguing with it. A heroic defense could do no more. On July 9 General George L. Andrews led the conquering Federals into Port Hudson. (RONN PALM)

Above: Once more Vicksburg's waterfront bustled with river commerce, with steamboats like the James Watson *and the* White Cloud *vying for room at the levee. (USAMHI)*

Right: The warships, too, plied the waters, even in times of flood, as here with the river seven feet above her banks in 1865. In the background three tinclads, the powerful city-class gunboat Louisville, *and the old woodclad* Tyler *rest easy on the river they helped to win. (KA)*

Above: On July 4, 1864, a year to the day after Vicksburg's surrender, Federal soldiers erected a monument on the place where Grant and Pemberton met to make terms. The earthworks are still visible in the distance. With the war not yet done, still the men who fought sensed something greater than themselves about it all, something that needed commemoration. (KA)

Left: With Vicksburg safely a Union port, the endless procession of steamboats carrying the Lincoln soldiers off to new campaigns and victories commenced. Here early in February, Brigadier General James Tuttle's division, including the brigade of Brigadier General Joseph Mower, arrives aboard the Westmoreland *and other boats, bound for Meridian, Mississippi. (THOMAS SWEENEY)*

Following the Armies

A PORTFOLIO

Wherever they go, the camera follows

Left: The march leads past the fortifications and the posturing officers like Colonel—later General—Régis De Trobriand, who stands atop the carriage sighting along the cannon's barrel. Just to the right, and standing with him, is General Daniel Butterfield, often erroneously credited with authoring the bugle call "Taps." (LC)

Left: Past signal towers near headquarters, past the generals like George Morell, here pointing toward Confederate lines at Miner's Hill, Virginia. (CHS)

Above: Following the armies, the photographer captured them as they went into formation for the march, as here in this early war image. (LEONARD L. TIMMONS)

Right: They might be soldiers, but they were young men, too. More than one has his eyes turned toward the huddled young girls in the foreground, while they earnestly try to appear oblivious. It is a game even older than war. (RP)

Below: Wherever the foot soldiers went, the photographer was not far behind. Often the march led through a nearby town or city. Here Federal regiments stand at ease after passing onto North Market Street in Frederick, Maryland. The bunting and the patriotic displays in some windows indicate that this may be a ceremonial occasion that a photographer captured from J. Rosenstock's second-floor window. (BENJAMIN B. ROSENSTOCK)

Below: A band and mounted troops that accompany the column stand in North Market Street in Frederick, obviously part of a parade. The armies often performed these ceremonial functions. They built morale at home and in the armies as well. (BENJAMIN B.ROSENSTOCK)

Left: But most of the time the march was real. Without the bands and the panoply, the armies marched toward each other, toward fire and battle. Here Federals are camped at the ruins of the bridge at Berlin, Maryland, on the Potomac, in October 1862. They are poised to pursue Lee back into Virginia. (LC)

Below: Army wagons crossing the Union arch of the Washington Aqueduct, where thousands of men and wagons crossed into Virginia. (GLADSTONE COLLECTION)

Below: On the march, James Gardner's image of troopers and pontoon bridge on the Rappahannock, near Fredericksburg, Virginia. (LC)

Above: In the enemy's land new headquarters are established, new scenes for the soldier and the camera. Here the headquarters of the Army of the Potomac near Culpeper, Virginia, in September 1863. Now the army belongs to George G. Meade. (P–M)

Above: Meade established his headquarters in this house, surrounding himself with these officers who became commonplace faces to the men of the army. (P–M)

Left: Several months later Major General John Sedgwick made this handsome Virginia house his headquarters near Brandy Station, Virginia. Wherever the armies went, the generals made good use of local establishments for official purposes. Sedgwick himself stands third from the right. (USAMHI)

Below: Relatives of the leaders were familiar sights on the march. Many served as aides. General Meade's son George was a captain and aide-de-camp to his father. (P-M)

Below: William Kunstman of Pennsylvania took his camera to Virginia to record keystone soldiers in the field. The studio may have been primitive, but the artist posed by it with pride. (MRS. FREDERIC KNECHT)

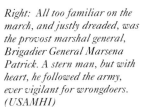

Left: He dressed jauntily and delighted in standing for the camera, as here, at center with two friends. The man at right, Captain F. M. Bache, is another Meade relative. (P-M)

Right: All too familiar on the march, and justly dreaded, was the provost marshal general, Brigadier General Marsena Patrick. A stern man, but with heart, he followed the army, ever vigilant for wrongdoers. (USAMHI)

Above: Familiar, too, were the foreign officers who flocked to the armies to observe for their own curiosity, as well as their governments' information, this American war. Brigadier General Stewart Van Vliet, seated at right, poses for Barnard Gibson with several British and French officers. (BRUCE GIMEL-SON)

Below: Equally colorful, though regarded as far more sinister, were the scouts and guides who led the armies through the South. Those shown here served the Army of the Potomac. Loyal men, renegades, men for hire, all were among their number. Many a soldier mistrusted the true motives of the guides, though most served faithfully. Some became noted in their own right, among them Dan Plue, lying at far left, and Dan Cole, seated at right of center in checked pants. They all looked tough and were. (USAMHI)

Above: Dashing, though not much admired as a leader, was Colonel Hiram Berdan, of Berdan's Sharpshooters. Surely the most colorful of their number was the man at right, Private Truman Head, known for his marksmanship as California Joe. (VERMONT HISTORICAL SOCIETY, MONTPELIER)

Below: In addition to the civilians who served the armies, the military assigned many of its own as scouts and guides. Taken by the romantic nature of their work, they affected the jaunty attire and pose, pistols in belts, of Sir Walter Scott heroes, but were as a rule less effective than their civilian counterparts. (USAMHI)

Left: Someone had to manage the efforts of these scouts and spies while on the march. That was the Secret Service Department, its officers shown here at army headquarters in the field. Their calm pose belies the often dark business they directed, the secrets they knew—or thought they knew. Through the pigeonholes of that desk in their tent passed information that could save or ruin any army. (USAMHI)

Left: Information for the march was also the work of the Signal Corps. Here a signal station in Virginia, between Suffolk and Norfolk, in February 1864. An army traveled in part on its stomach, to be sure, but even more on what it knew. (USAMHI)

Below: Sometimes more permanent locations allowed more elaborate observations. Here signal flags rest behind the scope and tripod as a signalman peers off into presumably enemy territory. (HERB PECK, JR.)

Below: Every hilltop and rise became a potential observation point on the march, for looking ahead and to the flanks for sign of the foe. The ample vistas of the Blue Ridge Mountains and its tributary eminences afforded opportunity to bring out the field glasses and the telescope. (NA)

Below: Observations had to be communicated to the armies and their generals. That became the task of the Military Telegraph Corps. Here, at war's end, the men and equipment pose at Richmond in June 1865, their vital work done. (USAMHI)

Below: Along the routes of march and in the evening camps, the soldiers became accustomed to seeing the poles go up and the singing wires start their work. (USAMHI)

Above: From advanced positions in the field the telegraphers pounded out their messages on the portable field keys. (NA)

Above: Their power came from the battery wagons like this one, which also acted as telegraph stations for communicating with the main army. A soldier marching past knew— or could hope—that he was being helped by the latest information. (NA)

Above: And moving with them was their baggage. Wagons became old friends as they carried the heavier burdens of soldier life. Few became as well known in the Army of the Potomac as this traveled old rambler, U. S. Grant's headquarters wagon. (NA)

Above: When they moved, the soldiers found other friends in the hardware and ingenuity engineers, the men who used canvas pontoons like this one to bridge Southern streams. A March 1864 image of the 50th New York Engineers at Rappahannock Station. (USAMHI)

Left: The roadside scenes of the march were the same everywhere; only the names on the land changed. A Brady Company image taken in Virginia in 1864 shows soldiers filling their water cart from a well. (USAMHI)

Right: Other soldiers draw water for their company from the same well. (USAMHI)

Left: There is relaxation along the march. Even while a soldier looks out from the cupola of Fairfax Courthouse in this 1863 image by O'Sullivan, another rests beside the well to read a newspaper. (CHS)

Left: They rest beside their pontoon bridges, here on the Hazel River in Virginia, near Brandy Station in 1863. (USAMHI)

Below: They rest by the roadside. Here Company B, 170th New York, late in the war. Though the image is certainly posed, still it well reflects the activities of a rest from the march. Cards, letter writing and reading, newspapers, cigars, a nap— all were part of the peaceful moments of the march. (USAMHI)

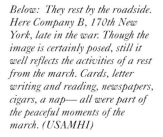

Below: And there was the meal stop, usually right in the road or just beside it. A hasty fire for coffee, a little hardtack from the haversack, perhaps a bit of brandy to flavor the drink, and then a pipe. The soldiers looked forward to these minutes with every step. (RUDOLF K. HAERLE)

Below: Company L, 11th Rhode Island, pauses in a field for bread and cheese, coffee, and perhaps a spoonful of sugar. (LESLIE D. JENSEN)

Above: "Today our mess had their ambrotype taken representing us as taking a meal on picket." So wrote Sergeant Jacob Heffelfinger in his diary on January 3, 1862. He sits right. Picket duty, once the army's march ceased for the day, was a necessary precaution against surprise. It afforded rest as well, and a measure of solitude that was usually absent in armies that sometimes numbered over 100,000. (B. N. MILLER)

Above: Solitary, letter in hand, this early war picket rests his "Jeff Davis" hat on a bayonet. Certainly he has two other picket mates, for their rifles show even if they do not. (ROBERT MCDONALD)

Above: A picket guard at Lewinsville, Virginia, poses at rest for the camera, seemingly unaware of the incongruity of wearing a full field pack while on picket. (CIVIL WAR TIMES ILLUSTRATED COLLECTION, HARRISBURG, PA.)

Right: Finally into camp at the end of the day's march, the soldiers pitched their tents, set their guards, and awaited the night and, sometimes, a few days' rest. A Virginia scene early in the war by Brady & Company. (LC)

Below: An encampment near Blackburn's Ford on Bull Run, captured by O'-Sullivan on July 4, 1862. A bottle or two are in evidence, the meager celebration available on the picket line. (LC)

Below: O'Sullivan captured bathers enjoying a bit of relaxation in the North Anna River in May 1864. Their clothing hangs at the base of the tree at left, guarded by three mates who have not braved the stream. (LC)

Left: In the cold season there is snow. A group of officers enjoy sleighing along the Rappahannock, opposite Fredericksburg, on Washington's Birthday in 1863. Alexander Gardner caught the scene, which includes the noted battlefield artist Alfred R. Waud gesturing with his arm just behind the third mule from the right. (USAMHI)

Below: There was clowning aplenty. Firing mock, or Quaker, guns one minute . . . (USAMHI)

Below: . . . to posing inside a giant Rodman gun in Battery Rodgers near Washington. (USAMHI)

Below: And the next minute clowning in human pyramids. Image by Barnard Bostwick. (GLADSTONE COLLECTION)

Below: Like tourists in all times, the soldiers with hours to spare left the mark of their passing. Here in Falls Church, Virginia, the church wall becomes a catalog of the Federal regiments that have passed by. (USAMHI)

Right: Several men of the 141st New York left their graffiti as reminders of their visit to Falls Church. They, like the scripture on the wall, are on an Exodus of sorts. (USAMHI)

Above: Traveling with the soldiers is an army in itself, the corps of correspondents and artists who brought the war to the people back home. Alexander Gardner made this image on Christmas 1864, showing reporters of the Boston Herald *and other papers, as well as the ubiquitous Alfred Waud, seated second from the right. (RINHART GALLERIES, INC.)*

Above: The field headquarters of the press, chiefly the New York Herald, *was an ever-present sight, complete with the servant in the left background pouring a libation for the thirsty correspondents. (USAMHI)*

Left: The artists, too, were well known to the men. Theodore R. Davis sent north depictions of the battle and campaign scenes so familiar to the soldiers. He and his fur-collared jacket were a common sight in the camps and along the march. (LC)

Right: Alfred R. Waud hardly seems to have had time to produce sketches, spending so much of it in front of the camera. Yet he built the finest body of work of any of the battlefield artists, working for the widely read Harper's Weekly. *(P-M)*

Above: This is how the soldiers knew Waud best, seated on a high place, sketchbook in hand, interpreting them and their war for their families at home and for posterity. O'Sullivan took this photograph of Waud on the Gettysburg battlefield, July 1863. (LC)

Above: The artists and correspondents banded together into an informal "Bohemian Brigade." Here Davis and the noted landscape artist James Walker pose together in Chattanooga, Tennessee, in 1864. (LC)

Left: Walker at work, not an unfamiliar sight to the marching armies. Here, on the slopes of Lookout Mountain overlooking Chattanooga, he works on one of his vivid scenes of the battles for this gateway city in Tennessee. Theodore Davis is perched atop the boulder at right. (CHS)

Below: The soldiers, like Walker, were always interested in a good view. One of the favorite places was Umbrella Rock on Lookout Mountain. (LC)

Left: Of course, following along right behind the armies was the photographer. This artist from Pennsylvania apparently traveled with the 47th Pennsylvania, camera in hand, and his chemicals and paraphernalia on the floor and shelf. (DALE S. SNAIR)

Above: They posed singly with their battle banners. Sergeant Andrew Geddes, 105th Ohio Infantry. (MICHAEL J . MCAFEE)

Right: The officers sat at the edge of Lookout, the Chattanooga valley below them. (KA)

Below: They sat precariously at the rock's very edge, where one poor soldier actually did fall to his death. (TERENCE P. O'LEARY)

Above: They came in groups to pose for R. M. Linn's camera. A reversed tintype. (RP)

Below: And they came in whole bands, to blow their horns above the Tennessee River. Perhaps, appropriately, they played a few bars of "Down in the Valley." (STATE HISTORICAL SOCIETY OF WISCONSIN, MADISON)

Above: The marching armies loved to visit the places of historic as well as scenic significance. Falls Church, where Washington had worshiped, was a favorite. (USAMHI)

Right: The marker commemorating Washington's mother at Fredericksburg caught many passing eyes. (USAMHI)

Left and far left: The slave pens of Price, Birch & Co., Dealers in Slaves, in Alexandria, Virginia, were often visited by soldiers passing through Washington. Some even posed behind the bars of the cells. (USAMHI)

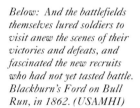

Below: And the battlefields themselves lured soldiers to visit anew the scenes of their victories and defeats, and fascinated the new recruits who had not yet tasted battle. Blackburn's Ford on Bull Run, in 1862. (USAMHI)

Below: The Marshall House in Alexandria, the scene of the martyrdom of Elmer Ellsworth, the Union's first hero, attracted many a curious farmboy become soldier. (USAMHI)

Above: The humble tailor shop of Andrew Johnson in Greeneville, Tennessee. Now Johnson was the loyal governor of Tennessee; he was soon to be Vice-President and, following Lincoln's murder, President . (USAMHI)

Right: The ruins of the stone bridge over Bull Run on the Manassas battlefield. An 1862 image by George N. Barnard. (LC)

Above: The slave quarters on Jefferson Davis's plantation in Mississippi. Alfred Waud made this image in 1866, but it looks much the same as it did in 1863 and later, when Federal soldiers and freedmen thronged the place for souvenirs of the Confederate President. (THE HISTORIC NEW ORLEANS COLLECTION)

Below: A handful of soldiers at Bailey's Cross Roads, Virginia. (WESTERN RESERVE HISTORICAL SOCIETY, CLEVELAND, OHIO)

Above: All across the South the armies passed, leaving their mark, witnessing scenes repeated a hundred times over. E company, 47th Illinois, posing in Oxford, Mississippi, in 1863. (CHS)

Below: They passed scenes of destruction like these wrecked naval cannon. (AMERICANA IMAGE GALLERY)

Above: They saw hapless spies caught at their work and condemned. This man, Johnson, in the white shirt, prays with a parson as he leans against his coffin during his final moments of life. (CHS)

Above: And they saw men die. Here the photographers Armstead & White of Corinth, Mississippi photograph Johnson in death while, rank on rank, Federal cavalrymen pass before him. Already his blood enriches the soil for which he died. (LC)

Above: The armies pass a hundred forgotten cemeteries, like this of the 13th Connecticut near Baton Rouge, Louisiana. Wherever the armies pass, they leave their dead behind. (ISHL)

Above: Their lonely solitary, fallen comrades, alone and at peace in death. (NA)

Above: But always the armies march on. There are rivers to cross, lands to conquer, battles to fight. Crossing the Green River at Bowling Green, Kentucky, these Federals are on their way to preserve the Union. (CHICAGO PUBLIC LIBRARY)

Above: While these Confederates, men of Lee's army, are stopping only briefly in Frederick, Maryland, on their 1862 invasion of the North. They are on their way to Antietam. From his window Rosenstock could observe the sights seen throughout the war-swept land, hear the marching of the booted and bootless feet, and witness the passing of the armies. (BENJAMIN B. ROSENSTOCK)

Raiders of the Seas

NORMAN C. DELANEY

Rebel commerce destroyers take the war around the world

Above: Lincoln's minister to Great Britain, Charles Francis Adams, faced a number of critical problems in keeping the peace between the two great nations, but few were more volatile than the issue of the commerce raiders built or fitted out in Britain for the Confederate Navy. He kept agents everywhere looking for such vessels before they put to sea, and even arranged for photographs to be taken so that the raiders might later be identified. But Adams proved quite unsuccessful in the early years of the war, and one raider after another eluded his grasp. (USAMHI)

THOUGH THE MISSISSIPPI might be "unvexed" after the fall of Vicksburg and Port Hudson, not so the sea it flowed into, for there Confederates carried the American Civil War to distant oceans. In doing so, they seriously disrupted the North's overseas commerce and struck a mortal blow against an already troubled whaling industry. They served to counter the severe injuries inflicted upon the Southern economy by a powerful Northern antagonist. They were the Confederate cruisers—the commerce destroyers.

The authorization by the Confederate Congress on May 10, 1861, for six cruisers to be built in England indicated their awareness that the South was incapable of producing a navy to match that of her enemy. Instead, swift and maneuverable commerce destroyers would be used to strike at the North's vital shipping lanes. Confederate Secretary of the Navy Stephen R. Mallory and other Southern leaders were convinced that recent history was on their side. The United States had played the role of the underdog during both the War of Independence and the War of 1812, yet had scored impressive victories at sea through privateering and cruiser warfare. What Mallory and his supporters failed to recognize, however, was that the successes of cruisers and privateers in the earlier wars had, in the final outcome, made no difference. In 1861 they were convinced that the policy of commerce destruction would contribute to ultimate victory. The South could benefit from privateers and blockade runners, some of which were government owned or chartered, and the government would move promptly to obtain the promising cruisers.

The purpose of the Confederate cruisers was threefold. In addition to crippling enemy commerce, they were expected to panic and demoralize the northeastern coastal population and thus divert hundreds of vessels from the Southern blockade. Even a small number of cruisers—steam-powered and propeller-driven—could contribute significantly to victory. The hit-and-run strategy of the cruisers would be supplemented by the use of privateers, ironclads, torpedoes, and submersible or semisubmersible "Davids." To help in these efforts, the Confederacy had experienced naval officers eager to serve. Millions of dollars for acquiring the cruisers were appropriated from cotton sales abroad and from Confederate bonds and treasury notes.

The problems that still faced Mallory and his department appeared insurmountable. The need to obtain ships—by purchasing or by building them— was urgent. But, even if ships could be obtained overseas, how could they be manned and equipped? Much depended on the policies and attitudes of European powers toward the Confederacy. When Great Britain and France declared their neutrality, Southerners felt disappointed, but they were somewhat encouraged by British and French recognition of the South as a belligerent. The cruisers would be allowed to stop at French ports and those of the British empire but were prohibited from recruiting or taking on military supplies. Those Southerners were naive who believed that the British government would look with favor at the very practice that had been used against them by the United States in earlier wars. In fact, Great Britain in 1856 had, along with other major maritime powers (but not the United States), condemned the practice of warring against commerce.

Confronted with such problems, the South

Left: The officers of the first Confederate commerce raider, Sumter. *Commander Raphael Semmes is seated center. The man standing at center behind him is his executive officer, Lieutenant John McI. Kell, who will stay with Semmes throughout most of the war. (NHC)*

Below: And this is the ship that Semmes commanded, the first publication of a remarkably rare image of the CSS Sumter, *probably taken in Birkenhead or Liverpool after her conversion to the blockade runner* Gibraltar *in 1864. In this small, sleek ship, Semmes and his men sent the first shock of terror through Yankee shippers, portending the havoc he would wreak with his next ship, the* Alabama. *(HENRY E. HUNTINGTON LIBRARY AND ART GALLERY, SAN MARINO, CALIFORNIA)*

needed a man in England with a background in international law as well as in naval building and technology. The identity and purpose of the cruisers, to be secured through private contractors, would have to be carefully guarded until they were safely at sea and under Confederate control. Commander James D. Bulloch, CSN, became the chief architect of the South's naval procurement program in Europe. The veteran officer, who wrote a book describing his role as Confederate agent, has been compared with Robert E. Lee in the magnitude of his labors on behalf of the Confederacy. Bulloch was responsible for the building of two cruisers, the *Florida* and the *Alabama*, the purchase of the *Shenandoah*, and the construction of the Laird rams. Mallory soon realized that Bulloch was indispensable to his overseas operations. Thus, Bulloch, who longed to return to sea duty and had been promised the captaincy of one of his cruisers, never attained his greatest wish. Although he had successfully brought to the Confederacy early in the war the *Fingal*, with an impressive cargo of military supplies, others would gain renown as captains of "his" *Florida, Alabama,* and *Shenandoah.*

Bulloch was successful both in obtaining these ships and in getting them to sea by elaborate subterfuge. Agents and spies employed by the United States minister to Great Britain, Charles Francis Adams, and Thomas H. Dudley, United States consul at Liverpool, were constantly probing for information on the identity and purpose of suspicious vessels under construction. Even photographs and sketches based on descriptions of witnesses were eventually obtained for all the cruisers. Bulloch's *Alabama* was brought to sea as the *Enrica*—all of his cruisers had aliases—only hours before British authorities ordered her detained. Bulloch also devised a method of circumventing Britain's Foreign Enlistment Act by manning, as well as equipping, the cruisers at remote locations. In the case of the *Alabama*, this was done near Terceira in the Azores. Bulloch brought a second ship from England with arms

Below: The whole issue of the cruisers was a constant sore point between the United States and Great Britain. Gideon Welles and his navy had to spend enormous energies putting powerful ships on patrol virtually all over the Atlantic. The mighty USS Tuscarora *spent all of 1862 and much of the next year cruising the English Channel, the Irish sea, and European waters as far south as Gibraltar, looking for the most dread of all Confederate cruisers . . . (P-M)*

Above: . . . the CSS Alabama. *Following his cruise in the* Sumter, *Raphael Semmes took charge of the 290, soon renamed the* Alabama, *in the spring of 1862, and sailed the raider for the next two years. He leans here against a mighty Dahlgren gun, with the trusty Kell standing in the background. (INTERNATIONAL MUSEUM OF PHOTOGRAPHY, ROCHESTER, N.Y.)*

Left: Kell himself took a turn at posing for the camera. The Alabama *was not a neat ship, as evidenced by the clutter on the decks. Semmes regarded many of his seamen with open contempt and despaired of enforcing proper sea discipline. (INTERNATIONAL MUSEUM OF PHOTOGRAPHY)*

and additional sailors and transferred them to the *Alabama*. The ship was then officially commissioned and the men enlisted. Those who refused to serve were allowed to return with Bulloch to England. Captain Raphael Semmes, CSN, assigned command of the *Alabama*, made it clear that he wanted only men willing to serve.

Since his cruisers were equipped with auxiliary steam power, Bulloch arranged for a supply tender, the *Agrippina*, carrying coal, to meet the *Alabama* at secretly designated times and locations. But when this practice proved unreliable and increased the risk of discovery, it was discontinued. Because of the constant danger from enemy warships, cruiser captains needed freedom from any strict schedule. Although given wide discretionary powers, they were under orders to avoid contact with Federal warships and to fight only if escape was impossible.

Raphael Semmes, the most famous of the cruiser captains, commanded both the *Sumter* and the *Alabama*. Semmes was an early advocate of the concept of commerce warfare and helped to convince Mallory of its potential value. Well schooled in international law during thirty-five years of United States naval service, Semmes's abilities were ideally suited to his assignment. The cruise of the *Sumter*—the South's first cruiser—demonstrated to Confederate officials the possibilities of the cruisers they had already authorized. But the small and frail *Sumter*, although successful in taking seventeen prizes in only six months, had worn out her engines and was in no condition to continue as a cruiser.

A second commerce destroyer launched from the Confederacy soon after war began was far less successful than the Sumter. The CSS *Nashville*, commanded by Lieutenant Robert B. Pegram, CSN, operated out of Charleston, South Carolina, and sailed to Southampton, England, in her one brief cruise. With a score of only two prizes, she returned to the Confederacy in February 1862, then served as a blockade runner and a privateer before being sunk by the Federals.

Because cruiser captains could not take their prizes into any Southern port, they disposed of them at sea. American-owned vessels and American-registered cargoes were burned as a matter of course after the removal of all persons on board and the transfer of supplies needed by the Confederates. When American merchant ships were found with cargo belonging to foreign nationals, they were released on ransom bond, documents that stated that the value of the ship would be paid to the Confederacy at the end of the war.

The men engaging in cruiser activities soon became aware that their enemies considered their methods beyond the pale of "civilized" warfare. Early in the war President Lincoln declared that individuals so engaged were "pirates" and could expect to be treated as such when captured. However, the Confederates vowed retaliation if such threats were ever carried out, and the issue remained unresolved. Far from regarding them-

Above: These images of the Alabama *and her officers were either taken at Cape Town, South Africa, or at Luanda, in what is now Angola. Semmes put his vessel into these ports to take on coal, an operation that is taking place while this image of Lieutenants Richard Armstrong and Arthur Sinclair is being exposed. These are the only known photographs of the* Alabama, *and none seem to have survived showing the vessel in its entirety. The only reason these survive is that they were sent ashore along with other valuables before the ship's fateful meeting with the* Kearsarge. *(WHALING MUSEUM, NEW BEDFORD, MASS.)*

Left: Yet Semmes had good officers for the most part, and none in the Confederate Navy saw more service. The man at left is probably Midshipman E. M. Anderson. (INTERNATIONAL MUSEUM OF PHOTOGRAPHY)

selves as pirates, Semmes and other cruiser captains took pride in what they considered to be their honorable treatment of prisoners. These "detainees," who occasionally included women and children, were ordinarily treated humanely until they were eventually transferred to a neutral ship. When he captured the California-bound mail steamer *Ariel,* which included 150 marines among her 700 passengers, Semmes released the ship on ransom bond and paroled the marines as prisoners of war. Yet Semmes had put sailors from his first prizes in irons as retaliation for the similar treatment of his paymaster, Henry Myers of the *Sumter,* who had been seized in Morocco and turned over to United States officials.

Semmes, "Old Beeswax" to his men, gained the most fame of the cruiser captains. His obvious zeal in playing the role of destroyer and his undisguised contempt for Yankee—especially New England— captains contributed to Northerners' hatred of him. Semmes's practice of burning prizes at night to lure unsuspecting Good Samaritan captains contrasted sharply with the conduct of Lieutenant William L. Maury, CSN, of the CSS *Georgia,* who once swore that he would rather be court-martialed than "burn the ship of a man who had come on an errand of mercy." Semmes, dour and humorless with friend and foe alike, with piercing eyes, a waxed mustache, and small imperial-style whiskers, better suited the pirate image. United States naval captains David G. Farragut and David D. Porter were infuriated by Semmes's sinking the USS *Hatteras,* off Galveston, Texas, in a battle that lasted only thirteen

Above: Lincoln's navy sent a small armada of ships after the Alabama. *The* Sabine, *one of the first vessels on the blockade duty, went after her late in 1862. She is shown here in December 1864, off Fort Monroe, Virginia. (USAMHI)*

Above: And the deck under his feet will be that of the USS Kearsarge, *shown here at Portsmouth, New Hampshire, just a few months after her appointment with the Alabama. (GLADSTONE COLLECTION)*

Above: But finally came Captain John A. Winslow, shown here as a commodore. He will be the man to be in the right place at the right time. (USAMHI)

Right: Winslow, standing third from left, and his officers managed to trap the Confederate cruiser in the harbor at Cherbourg. Indeed, there was even some fraternization between the two crews in the neutral port. The local photographer Rondin came aboard the Kearsarge *to make this and other images. (USAMHI)*

Right: He caught Master J. R. Wheeler and Engineer S. L. Smith leaning on their powerful 11-inch forward pivot gun. (USAMHI)

minutes. Such a humiliation was not easily forgotten, even though the *Hatteras*—a former passenger steamer—was a decidedly inferior vessel. Nor could Semmes be forgiven his success in evading his pursuers for so many months at sea.

Semmes's easy victory over the *Hatteras* contributed to his own eventual undoing. Confident that his men could fight and win again, he decided to challenge Captain John A. Winslow, USN, when the powerful USS *Kearsarge* appeared off Cherbourg, France.

The *Alabama* had arrived at Cherbourg on June 11, 1864, after spending twenty-two months at sea. During that time she had covered 75,000 miles and had overhauled almost 300 ships. She had destroyed 55 of these, setting a record unmatched by any other Confederate cruiser. Moreover, a large part of the Northern merchant fleet had by then transferred ownership to foreign flags or had disappeared from the seas entirely. Semmes, soured by his enemy's defamation of him and drained by the demands of months at sea, was about to relinquish his command. He was incensed at those who denounced him as a coward for sailing under false—British and United States —colors and destroying defenseless ships. Semmes preferred to end his career with a dramatic victory, his Confederate flag flying in full view of thousands of spectators. It took Winslow just over an hour to destroy the *Alabama*. Powerful guns in the hands of his well-trained and disciplined crew reduced the *Alabama* to a shattered, sinking hulk. Northerners, exultant over Winslow's victory, nevertheless felt cheated at Semmes's escape to England aboard the yacht *Deerhound*.

Semmes was rewarded by a grateful Congress, which promoted him to admiral and gave him command of the James River Squadron. However, other Southerners may have shared the personal view of diarist Mary Boykin Chesnut when she wrote: "Admiral Semmes, of whom we have been so proud, is a fool after all. He risked the *Alabama* in a sort of duel of ships, and now he has lowered the flag of the famous *Alabama* to the *Kearsarge*. Forgive who may, I cannot!"

The news of the *Alabama's* loss came at a low point for the South. The cruisers provided an important psychological lift for the Southern people. They rejoiced that the South could effectively demonstrate her capacity through the daring exploits of the cruisers. With the *Alabama* gone, the *Florida* remained the only cruiser at sea, and Mallory was eager to acquire others. Two other Confederate naval agents, the renowned oceanographer Commander Matthew Fontaine Maury, CSN, and Commander George T. Sinclair, CSN, went to England to obtain cruisers, but only Maury succeeded in getting his—the *Georgia* and the *Rappahannock*—to sea. However, neither ship was comparable with Bulloch's.

The CSS *Georgia*, under Lieutenant William L. Maury, took only nine prizes during a cruise that began in April 1863 and lasted seven months. She was unsuitable as a cruiser because her iron hull required frequent dry-dockings. Matthew Maury finally secured the CSS *Rappahannock* as her replacement in November 1863. The new ship was no improvement, however. Built in 1857 as the *Victor*, the *Rappahannock* had already been condemned by the British as "rotten and unservicable." After a major overhaul in England, the *Rappahannock* still remained unfit for sea and was brought to Calais for additional repairs. But Emperor Napoleon III was becoming increasingly reluctant to give aid to the apparent loser in the American war. Although he allowed the *Rappa-*

Above: The ship's mighty engine would propel her in the impending battle. A postwar view. (USAMHI)

Right: And Kearsarge's *trusty crew would serve her well. They pose, like the others, in June 1864 for Rondin. On June 19 they will destroy the* Alabama. *(USAMHI)*

Below: While Semmes terrorized Yankee shipping, other agents like Commander Matthew F. Maury tried to outfit and equip cruisers. Maury, a distinguished oceanographer, succeeded to a small degree. (VM)

Right: Maury got the CSS Rappahannock *ready for sea, only to discover that she was "rotten and unservicable." He took her to France, where a photographer in Calais saw her as she is shown here. The French never let her leave port again. It was a terrible blow to her officers. All they could do was wait and hope. (VM)*

Above: But it did not pass by many others—those fortunate enough to serve aboard the CSS Florida, *for instance. Next to the* Alabama *herself, this ship came to be the most feared and sought on the seas. She appears here photographed at Brest, France, probably in 1863, and was in fact the first foreign-built cruiser to be commissioned. (NHC)*

Right: Her first captain, Lieutenant John N. Maffitt, was one of the most dashing Rebel seamen and a man of considerably more humor than Semmes. It was he who ran the ship into Mobile, Alabama, for outfitting, thus bringing disgrace on . . . (WILLIAM A. ALBAUGH COLLECTION)

Above: . . . Commander George H. Preble, who, thanks to events beyond his control, was not able to prevent the Florida *from reaching safety. Even Maffitt later testified that Preble did his very best. Preble found himself dismissed from the service temporarily. (USAMHI)*

Right: When Maffitt proved too ill to retain his command once the raider returned to European waters, he turned the vessel over to Lieutenant Joseph N. Barney. Yet Barney, too, fell ill and relinquished his command to . . . (WILLIAM A. ALBAUGH COLLECTION)

hannock to be dry-docked and repaired, he refused to allow her to leave port.

Sinclair's ship, the *Canton*, designed to be even more formidable than the *Alabama*, presumably would have added much to the success of the cruisers. However, she never got to sea. Receiving irrefutable evidence of the *Canton's* true identity, British authorities seized her for violation of the Foreign Enlistment Act.

Cruiser officers and agents in Great Britain had become personae non gratae by the second half of 1863. The British were embarrassed by the successes of the Confederate agents and the circumvention of the neutrality laws. They were further aggravated by the cruiser captains' use of their foreign ports. Earlier in the war, Nassau authorities had detained the *Florida* for alleged violations of British neutrality and the Foreign Enlistment Act. Although the ship was eventually released, similar incidents continued to exacerbate relations between Great Britain and the Confederate States and, especially, the United States. Numerous charges pressed by the United States government after the war resulted in an international tribunal at Geneva, Switzerland, ruling in 1872 that Great Britain was liable for monetary losses caused by the *Florida*, *Alabama*, *Shenandoah*, and their four satellite cruisers. The British government, accepting responsibility for these violations, paid to the United States the $15.5 million indemnity set by the commission.

Whenever a cruiser succeeded in humiliating the Northern colossus by running the blockade or evading Federal pursuers at sea, Southerners rejoiced. Lieutenant John N. Maffitt, CSN—the dashing "Prince of Privateers"—scored such a triumph when, on September 3, 1862, he brought the *Florida* into heavily blockaded Mobile. This was accomplished despite the fact that Maffitt and all but five members of his crew were stricken with yellow fever. Four months later, Maffitt brought the *Florida* to sea again for a cruise similar to that of the *Alabama*. Finally, at Brest, France, Maffitt—still suffering from his illness—was relieved from command by Lieutenant Joseph N. Barney, CSN, who, also because of ill health, was soon replaced by Lieutenant Charles M. Morris, CSN. The *Florida* finally sailed from Brest after delays lasting almost six months.

At sea, Morris continued to add to the *Florida's*

Above: . . . Lieutenant Charles M. Morris. It was he who commanded the Florida *for the remainder of her days. (WILLIAM A. ALBAUGH COLLECTION)*

Above: Exciting days they were, too. Several Yankee warships plied the Atlantic seeking the Florida, *ships like the sailing sloop* St. Louis, *shown here at Algeciras, Spain, on December 7, 1863. (USAMHI)*

Above: Often the Yankee hunters encountered checkered voyages without ever coming near the Florida. *The USS* Ticonderoga *ran aground off Brazil, ran out of coal and had to rely on sail, was evicted from Grenada by the colonial governor, and had several of its furnace tubes burst—all in a single cruise after the* Florida. *Battle in the open sea would have been a relief after the frustrating fight with elements, machinery, and bureaucracy. (GLADSTONE COLLECTION)*

impressive list of captured prizes, which eventually totaled thirty-seven. But, in the harbor of Bahia, Brazil, Morris's luck ran out. On the night of October 7, 1864, Morris and half his crew were ashore when a surprise attack upon the *Florida* was made by Commander Napoleon Collins, USN, of the USS *Wachusett.* This act promptly raised an international storm. Collins had refused to be thwarted at finding his quarry in a presumed safe haven. He considered that he would have been guilty of inexcusable negligence had he let the "pirates" escape him. Collins gave the order, and without warning, the *Wachusett* rammed the *Florida.* The crew were easily subdued and the ship taken. Collins then had the *Florida* tied fast and, ignoring Brazilian shore fire, towed her to sea. Collins's prize and her crew were brought to the United States, where officials realized that the sovereignty of Brazil had been violated. The *Florida* was ordered returned to Brazil, but she sank in what appears to have been a deliberately caused collision with another vessel at Newport News, Virginia. Secretary of State William H. Seward considered her crew to be "enemies of the human race" and regretted their later release. Collins, although court-martialed and ordered dismissed from the service, was instead restored to his command by Secretary of the Navy Gideon Welles. Welles agreed with Collins's defense that his action, although illegal, was "for the public good."

Much earlier, Lieutenant Charles W. "Savaz" Read, CSN, with a reputation for "coolness and determination," had been requested by Maffitt to serve under him aboard the *Florida.* During the cruise, Read became intrigued with the idea of converting a suitable prize to a cruiser and commanding her. Maffitt also liked the idea and had the prize *Clarence* armed with a 12-pounder howitzer and turned over to Read, in command of twenty sailors. On his own, Read captured a vessel he preferred to the slow *Clarence,* the bark *Tacony.* He transferred his gun and crew and, after burning the *Clarence,* steered for New England. In the next two weeks Read captured fifteen ships. Among those he destroyed were six Gloucester fishing boats. Off Portland, Maine, Read captured the schooner *Archer* and again transferred his gun

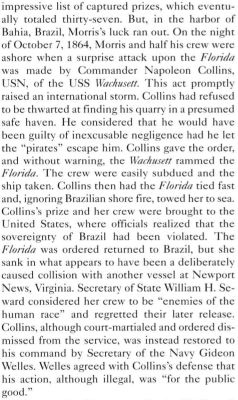

Above left: Her quarry continued to elude the St. Louis *and other ships for months, just as one prize ship after another fell to the raider. Master Richard S. Floyd of the CSS* Florida. *(MC)*

Above: Chief Engineer G. W. Quinn kept the raider's machinery functioning better than on most Confederate ships, and when she put into Brest he posed for the Mage brothers' camera. (MC)

Left: So did his assistant, I. Lake. (MC)

Right: Yet there was better work than standing before a camera. The Florida *stayed at sea as much as possible to visit her damage upon the enemy. When she did put into port, it was only for coaling and provisions. But the French kept her at Brest until February 10, 1864—almost six months after her arrival—before they let her go. Her first stop was Funchal, Madeira, where she anchored to take on coal on February 28. That day or the next a United States official there got a local photographer to make this incredible image of the* Florida, *the large ship in the foreground, her flag sailing bravely in the breeze. The smaller ship in the right foreground is the Confederate blockade runner* Julia. *There are other vessels there as well, and one of them, the large three-masted sailing sloop on the center horizon, is almost certainly the USS* St. Louis, *which had arrived just the day before. This was a neutral port, so the* St. Louis *had to remain at bay until the* Florida *steamed once more into international waters. Yet there is a further irony in this image that captures at once both the hunter and the hunted. For commanding the* St. Louis *was a man with a score to settle, the recently reinstated Commander George H. Preble. This is as close as he ever came to his quarry, however. On February 29 the* Florida *steamed away, while Preble watched helplessly, becalmed. "Oh, for a little steam!" he lamented. Lord Nelson had complained that "the want of frigates" in his squadron would be found engraved on his heart. Poor Preble sadly declared, "I am sure the want of steam will be engraven on mine." (NA)*

Above: Other ships besides Preble's looked in vain for the great raider. The Saco *was one of them, a hard-luck ship with bad boilers and engine. (USAMHI)*

Right: It was Commander Napoleon Collins, shown here as a captain, who finally put an end to the Florida; *yet even he had to resort to questionable means to do it. (NA)*

and crew. Only twenty-one men were accomplishing much of what Mallory had hoped his cruisers would achieve. Governor John Andrew of Massachusetts blasted the Navy Department for the "defenseless condition of the coast." Coastal New England residents were in panic, and scores of vessels took refuge in the nearest port. Some forty ships were directly involved in the search for the raiders, although without seriously weakening the blockade.

In his most daring move, Read brought the *Archer* into Portland harbor at night and surprised the crew of the revenue cutter *Caleb Cushing* at anchor. Unable to get away with his prize, Read released his prisoners and set her ablaze. Finally, before they could return to the *Archer,* Read and his men were captured. They were taken to Fort Warren in Boston harbor, thus ending what has been called "the most brilliant daredevil cruise of the war."

Maffitt was not the only Confederate captain to use a captured prize as a satellite cruiser. Few prizes, however, suited the demands made upon a raider, and captains could ill afford the loss of even a small number of men and guns. Keeping even a minimum crew was a problem that all the captains faced. Some recruits were enlisted from captured prizes, and in some cases men were impressed into Confederate service. Semmes and James I. Wad dell were both guilty of this practice, but only as a desperate measure.

Despite his shortage of men, Semmes converted one of his prizes—the bark *Conrad*—into the satellite cruiser *Tuscaloosa.* For six months this vessel, with fifteen men commanded by Lieutenant John Low, CSN, cruised Atlantic shipping lanes until, at Simon's Bay, South Africa, she was seized for alleged violation of Britain's neutrality laws. The *Tuscaloosa* was eventually released, but by then Low and his men had left for England.

The successes of most cruisers encouraged

Above: Lieutenant Charles W. Read, once an officer on the Florida, *put his experience to good use when he took command of a prize ship and raided the New England coast in a lightning raid that sent shivers through the Union. He appears here as a midshipman in the old United States Navy. (NHC)*

Above: The Alabama, *like the* Florida, *also gave birth to a second-generation cruiser converted from one of her prizes. Semmes put Lieutenant John Low, seated at left, aboard the* Tuscaloosa *and turned him loose in the Atlantic for a six-month cruise. (INTERNATIONAL MUSEUM OF PHOTOGRAPHY)*

Confederate officials during the summer of 1864 to search for replacements. Two blockade runners, *Atlanta* and *Edith*, both at Wilmington, North Carolina, were converted into the cruisers *Tallahassee* and *Chickamauga*. The CSS *Tallahassee*, although swift and easy to maneuver, nevertheless had two serious drawbacks for a cruiser: exposed boilers and insufficient coal storage space. Her resourceful commander, John Taylor Wood, CSN, a veteran of the ironclad *Virginia (Merrimack)*, compensated for these deficiencies by protecting his engines with cotton bales and storing extra coal on deck. He brought the *Tallahassee* through the blockade on August 6, 1864. Wood originally entertained a daring scheme to involve the *Tallahassee* in a surprise night raid into New York harbor to attack its shipping and Navy Yard. Handicapped without a pilot, however, he instead cruised north to Halifax, capturing thirty-three vessels in only a few weeks. Wood's cool official reception at Halifax and the likelihood of his being captured caused him to return to Wilmington. The cruiser was reoutfitted, and as the CSS *Olustee*, under Lieutenant William H. Ward, CSN, she again ran the blockade. Her cruise was brief—only nine days—but before his return to Wilmington on November 7, Ward had destroyed six prizes.

By the time the CSS *Chickamauga*, commanded by Lieutenant John Wilkinson, CSN, left Wilmington on October 28, 1864, it was impossible for any Confederate cruiser to be welcomed in a foreign port. Unable to secure extra coal, Wilkinson returned to Wilmington after three weeks at sea, having burned four of his five prizes. He was back in time to assist in the final defense of Fort Fisher.

Despite enormous odds, Bulloch, still in England, succeeded in obtaining another cruiser, the *Sea King*. Renamed the *Shenandoah*, she was much like the *Alabama* she replaced. Her captain, Lieutenant James I. Waddell, CSN, had no previous cruiser experience, having been waiting as-

Left: Meanwhile, slowly other ships, sometimes even blockade runners, were converted into makeshift cruisers, two of them in Confederate waters. One became the command of Lieutenant John Taylor Wood, a dashing veteran of the CSS Virginia *and grandson of President Zachary Taylor. President Davis was his uncle. This 1854 portrait by J. H. Whitehurst is believed to be Wood, of whom photographs are rare. (CHARLES S. SCHWARTZ)*

Below: And here is Wood's ship itself, the only known photograph of the CSS Tallahassee, *taken in Halifax in August 1864 when she put in for coal after her lightning raid along the New England coast. The authorities were not accommodating, and Wood had to leave port the next day. This remarkable image, showing some slight damage incurred during the cruise, is published here for the first time. (MARITIME MUSEUM OF THE ATLANTIC, HALIFAX, N.S.)*

Above: Bulloch desperately tried to build and send to sea a new class of commerce raiders to assist the cruisers already at work. They would be a formidable race of warships, iron-sheathed, mounting enormous 300-pounder rifles among other armament, and with awesome iron ramming prows just below the waterline. Such vessels, the Confederates believed, could break the blockade and destroy any ship the Yankees sent against them. They built the first one, eventually named the Stonewall, *in France, but it was well into the winter of 1864–65 before she left French waters at last. She steamed for El Ferrol, Spain, for coal and repairs, and there the photographer found her that March. (LC)*

Above: There, too, the USS Niagara *found the* Stonewall. *The Confederate ship put out to sea on March 24 to give battle, but the Federal vessel feared her powerful armament and retired. (LC)*

Right: So the Stonewall *steamed on across the Atlantic unmolested, arriving in Havana in May, where she learned of the end of the war.* Stonewall's *commander gave the untested ship to the governor general of Cuba in return for money to pay off his crew, and Cuba in turn presented the ship to the United States. (NA)*

Right: By July 1865 the mighty ram lay off the Washington Navy Yard, a prize of war. Finally she was sold to Japan, to end her days as the HIJMS Azuma. *(NHC)*

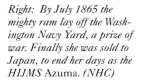

Below left: Sister ships to the Stonewall *wound up in the Prussian and other navies, as did the formidable Laird rams, built on Confederate contract at the Laird shipyards at Birkenhead, England. These ships became such an international point of contention between Britain and the Union that finally they were held up by London authorities and never delivered to the South. Instead, these Confederate rams joined Her Majesty's Royal Navy. One of them, HMS* Wivern, *appears here, the turret that mounted her guns clearly evident. (IMPERIAL WAR MUSEUM, LONDON)*

signment in Europe for several months. Once at sea, the *Shenandoah* was manned and equipped in the manner of the earlier cruisers. Near Madeira, on October 19, 1864, the newly commissioned Shenandoah began what became the most unusual cruise of any Confederate raider. Waddell's orders were to follow sea lanes missed by the earlier cruisers, especially "the enemy's distant whaling grounds." Outwitting hostile officials at Melbourne, Australia, Waddell managed to stow aboard several seamen from that port, in direct violation of the Foreign Enlistment Act. He then cruised to the North Pacific, reaching the Sea of Okhotsk in late May 1865. Finally, in June, he reached the Bering Sea and the Arctic Ocean. There Waddell found his unsuspecting prey—a considerable portion of the American whaling fleet. When told that Lee had surrendered in April and shown newspapers to prove it, Waddell still refused to believe that the war was over. He set twenty of the whalers ablaze, leaving four to carry away his numerous prisoners. His destruction on June 28, 1865—eleven weeks after Appomattox—was the last hostile act of a Confederate force.

Above: It remained to a Confederate cruiser to fire the last shots of the war. Lieutenant James I. Waddell oversaw the conversion of the British vessel Sea King *into yet another commerce raider. On October 19, 1864, he commissioned her . . . (NHC)*

Left: . . . the CSS Shenandoah. *She went to a new assignment, Yankee shipping in the Pacific. In her twelve-month cruise she took thirty-eight prize ships, most of them whaling vessels, and thereby nearly put an end to the American whaling industry in the North Pacific. Her last prizes were taken nearly three months after the war had ended. This remarkable image shows the* Shenandoah *in the Williamstown dry dock at Sydney, Australia, in February 1865, just before she sailed into the Bering Sea and the Arctic Ocean, where most of her prizes were taken. Her proud Confederate flag flies overhead. (NHC)*

Only later, on August 2, when informed of the war's end by a British captain, did Waddell finally accept the reality of defeat. He then decided to sail to England rather than to Australia to surrender. Fearing that he would be branded an outlaw for his last acts of destruction, Waddell disguised his ship as a merchantman and brought her the 17,000 miles to England nonstop. The trip turned into a nightmare. Water and supplies ran short, scurvy developed, and two crewmen died. On November 15, 1865, the *Shenandoah* arrived at Liverpool and Waddell surrendered to amazed British officials. He had brought the cruiser a total of 58,000 miles and had taken thirty-eight prizes, two-thirds of them after the war had ended. Only with Waddell's surrender was the Civil War finally over.

The story of the Confederate cruisers is but one segment of a long and bloody conflict. It involved only a few ships and a few hundred men, most of whom—the ordinary seamen—were not even Southerners. And yet, the cruisers succeeded in destroying two hundred Union merchant ships, fishing craft, and whaling vessels, plus cargoes worth millions of dollars. Despite such injury, however, the North's economy was strong enough to endure every blow from the South. The damage inflicted by the cruisers was like bruises on a powerful giant. The cost of such efforts to the South—in terms of all her resources—was exceedingly high. Secretary of the Navy Welles had clearly seen the means of achieving ultimate victory when he refused to weaken the blockade despite outcries by many Northerners that the cruisers be hunted down and destroyed at all costs. For Lincoln and his advisers to have altered their strategy would have provided Southerners with the relief they so desperately needed from the ever-constricting blockade. As it was, a large number of Federal warships spent frustrating months in pursuit of the elusive raiders, and only the men of the USS *Kearsarge* had the satisfaction of actually locating and destroying a cruiser—the CSS *Alabama* —in a dramatic sea battle.

Left: It was the packet steamer America *that brought the Union the first news of the depredations of the* Shenandoah *(NA)*

Above: And when Waddell himself learned of the war's end some months before, he quickly set course for Liverpool, where he gave up his ship. There, to commemorate their cruise, many of his officers, like John T. Mason, posed for Liverpool photographer C. Ferranti. (MC)

Above: Some, like Raphael Semmes, would carry their hatred of the Yankees to their graves. He and Maury met after the war to sit for this image, two old sea dogs of the Confederacy, whose great war and infant nation were, like their ships, now only a memory. (NHC)

The Siege of Charleston

ROWENA REED

The city that fathered secession suffers the war's longest siege

Above: Hilton Head, South Carolina, headquarters of the Department of the South and nerve center for the war-long siege of Charleston. Here men, matériel, and ships came together to mount the longest sustained investment of an enemy during the entire Civil War. (SOUTH CAROLINA HISTORICAL SOCIETY, CHARLESTON, S.C.)

Above: "Merchant's Row" at Hilton Head, where sutlers and civilian suppliers did their business with the soldiers and sailors. (SOUTH CAROLINA HISTORICAL SOCIETY)

YANKEE RULE OF THE SEA, despite the commerce raiders and the blockade runners, played a large part in the "siege" of Charleston, the longest campaign of the Civil War. Federal attacks on this "cradle of the Confederacy," though erratic, were imaginative and introduced new tactical concepts. Not really a siege, because the city was never invested, the operations in both attack and defense relied upon mass firepower and engineering. The Confederate defense against a superior enemy holding command of the sea was a brilliant achievement, although the Federal failure was due largely to the Lincoln administration's decision to concentrate instead on destroying the main Confederate armies in the field.

Charleston's importance was mainly psychological. There the war began. There the Confederacy would prove worthy of nationhood, or Union hatred of secession would be assuaged. Events there did not decide the issue, but they could have. Loss of Charleston in 1863 might have been more fatal to Southern morale than the fall of Vicksburg. Nevertheless, the Northerners did not, at first, plan to take Charleston and never gave the campaign high priority. It evolved as a by-product of the Federal blockade, itself part of the original "Anaconda Plan" to strangle the Confederacy by shutting off external aid. Established in April 1861, right after the fall of Fort Sumter, the blockade strained the then inadequate Union Navy and required measures for fleet maintenance that led eventually to the siege of Charleston.

Charleston lies between the Ashley and Cooper rivers, on a point of land that juts south into Charleston Harbor itself. Immediately below the city, bounded on the north by the harbor and on the south by the Stono River, sits James Island. It reaches almost down to the Atlantic, separated from the sea only by thin strips of land that run along the ocean face, Folly and Morris islands. The upper tip of Morris Island, called Cummings Point, marks the southern gate into Charleston Harbor. Less than two miles across the harbor mouth lies the northern gate, Fort Moultrie on Sullivan's Island. Between these two gates, lying astride the main channel into the harbor, sits Fort Sumter. A series of forts on James and Sullivan's islands, as well as on Morris Island and in Charleston itself, virtually ringed the harbor with fire.

In the summer of 1861 the Union Blockade Board recommended among other points the seizure of Port Royal, a spacious anchorage midway between Savannah and Charleston, as a station for the blockading squadrons. In early November a large Union fleet commanded by Flag Officer Samuel F. Du Pont reduced the defenses there and occupied the harbor. With him were 12,000 Northern troops under Brigadier General Thomas W. Sherman, who at once established an army base on nearby Hilton Head Island. The easy capture of Port Royal revealed Confederate weakness and threatened the Southern seaports of Charleston and Savannah.

However, Sherman could not move against any point of real importance because he had insufficient water transportation. Nor was Du Pont willing to cooperate in offensive movements. This leading exponent of the blockade thought Charleston of so little importance that he sank old ships loaded with stone in an attempt to close the channels leading to the city. Major General George B. McClellan wanted Charleston as a base for advancing to Augusta and, eventually, to the vital rail junction at Atlanta. But the Northern general-in-chief be came ill in December and was not well until February 1862, by which time his government insisted that all his resources be used against Richmond.

The Confederates took prompt advantage of the Union failure to exploit the lodgment on the southern Atlantic coast. In late November General Robert E. Lee arrived to implement a new system to guard against further Federal movements. Southern policy of siting coastal batteries too far seaward allowed these isolated defenses to be overwhelmed by the superior Union Navy. Lee at once evacuated this peripheral line. Instead, a new line of works was constructed well up the many rivers penetrating that coast to guard vital interior points. With fewer than 14,000 men to garrison Charleston and Savannah, Lee based a mobile defense on the railroad connecting these cities. Detachments stationed along this line could quickly concentrate at any threatened point. Lee's system thus countered Union sea mobility with a greater mobility over a shorter distance by rail. The Confederates also strengthened Charleston's harbor defenses, bridged the Ashley River to improve internal communications, and mounted heavier guns along the city's waterfront. The weakest point in the new system remained the large rivers, like the Edisto, which could lead a sizable enemy force into the rear of Charleston.

Sherman's replacement by Major General David Hunter in April 1862 brought some Union reinforcements and more transportation. Eager to make his reputation by taking Charleston, Hunter persuaded Du Pont to provide some fleet support. In June the Union Navy ascended the Stono River south of James Island, landing a division under Brigadier General Henry W. Benham at Legare's plantation on the left of the Confederate lines, from which point a good road led into the rear of Fort Johnson on the south side of the harbor. But the road was threatened from the direction of Secessionville and the approach to that town restricted by impassable swamps and an earthen battery, Fort Lamar. Benham's unsuccessful frontal assault on this work resulted in large Union casual ties, made worse by the indirect fire of two "cooperating" Federal gunboats, which fell on their own men. Incensed by this fiasco, Hunter absolved himself by filing charges against Benham for supposedly disobeying orders, and spent the remainder of the year reconnoitering and trying to raise regiments of former slaves from the nearby plantations.

Meanwhile, Assistant Secretary of the Navy Gustavus Fox pressured Du Pont to try a naval descent upon Charleston with ironclads. Fox, who had been involved in the futile effort to relieve Fort Sumter in 1861, was obsessed with capturing this "hotbed of secession" and impressed by the apparent invulnerability of the monitor ironclads. A sailor of the old wooden navy, Du Pont loathed the "ugly" iron monitors with their clanking machinery and thought their two heavy guns too few and too slow for contests with forts. In his judgment, only a combined operation with the army to outflank the harbor defenses via the Stono or the North Edisto could succeed. Unfortunately, Hunter proved incapable of cooperating with anybody, and so an unsupported naval attack was ordered by the government.

Du Pont did not like the look of Charleston, and for good reason. In arranging their batteries,

Above: The Port Royal House, comprising a hotel and restaurant, where thousands came and went in the four years of planning and fighting directed at the prize Charleston. (SOUTH CAROLINA HISTORICAL SOCIETY)

Left: After being briefly commanded by Brigadier General Thomas W. Sherman, the Department of the South, and with it the goal of Charleston, went to the sturdy old politico Major General David Hunter. Here, as everywhere in the war, he failed to distinguish himself. (USAMHI)

Above: The only engagement fought while Hunter was in command came at Secessionville, where a subordinate attacked without orders and suffered a defeat. Hunter quickly absolved himself of all blame. (NA)

Above: Regiments like the 104th Pennsylvania took heavy losses for nothing at Secessionville, though Captain John M. Laughlin survived to pose with his model of a seacoast rifle. (RP)

Above: Another who survived, and happily so, was Albert Ordway, a lieutenant of the 24th Massachusetts. After the war he will become one of the most prominent collectors and preservers of war photographs and compiler of many of the major collections extant. (NA)

Left: Yank and Reb did not meet in battle again until April 10, 1863, when skirmishing on Folly Island finally gave the Union a foothold on the very door to Charleston. The Stars and Stripes went up … (USAMHI)

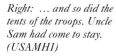

Right: … and so did the tents of the troops. Uncle Sam had come to stay. (USAMHI)

the Confederate engineers under General P.G.T. Beauregard took maximum advantage of the peculiarly favorable configuration of the harbor to construct a complex of mutually supporting defenses, consisting of three interlocking "circles of fire" that extended from the seaward perimeter to beyond the city. Until September 1863, the outer circle— comprising Battery Beauregard and Fort Moultrie on Sullivan's Island, Fort Sumter, a two-tiered brick-casemated fort on an artificial island flanking the main channel, and Batteries Gregg and Wagner on Morris Island—was by far the strongest. For a distance of two thousand yards, the fire of seventy-six heavy guns could be poured upon the main ship channel; while two thousand yards in front of a rope barrier between Sumter and Moultrie, this fire converged to form a "wall" that the Federal squadron had to pass through to remove the obstructions and gain the inner harbor.

Under threat of relief from Command, Du Pont finally agreed to make the attempt as an "experiment," though in the event he was unwilling to risk his ships by pressing the attack vigorously. On April 7, 1863, a Union squadron comprising seven monitors, the large ironclad frigate *New Ironsides*, and the thinly armored, fixed-turret ship *Keokuk* steamed up the channel and engaged Fort Sumter at ranges from one to two thousand yards. The contest was brief and still more discouraging than Du Pont had predicted. Five of the seven monitors were damaged. The *Keokuk*, carried closer to the fort by the tide, was riddled and sank the next day. The *Ironsides* became unmanageable and grounded on a shoal farther off, so her powerful broadside of eight heavy guns fired only once. The disparity of fire was tremendous. While the squadron shot off 139 projectiles, Sumter alone fired over 2,000 rounds and Moultrie half again that number.

Thick smoke prevented the admiral from observing that the few shells that did strike Sumter's thin masonry caused extensive injury. Besides, he was not inclined to look. His judgment had been vindicated and the monitor captains, like John Rodgers and Percival Drayton, who had been confident of success, now backed their admiral by telling the Navy Department that these vessels were useless for offensive purposes. In fact, damages to the monitors were not serious and were easily repaired.

Du Pont's reluctance to resume the attack or to support an army landing on Morris or James islands led to his removal from command. His successor was the former chief of Naval Ordnance, John A. Dahlgren. The Union general-in-chief, Henry W. Halleck, disliked the whole idea of joint expeditions. But in June he was persuaded by the Lincoln administration, who badly wanted Charleston as a moral victory, to allow Brigadier General Quincy A. Gillmore to conduct operations against the city in conjunction with the navy. Gillmore, the North's best engineer, who had earlier demolished Fort Pulaski at Savannah by long range fire, guaranteed to knock down Fort Sumter, opening the channel for a naval coup de main.

Accordingly, Gillmore, with 10,000 reinforcements, arrived in the Department of the South in June. In early July he conferred with Dahlgren about the plan of attack. Benham's repulse the previous year and the squadron's inability to provide fire support long distances from shore made operations on James Island appear unpromising. It was decided instead to approach via Morris Island because the fleet could cover the landings and protect a Union base there against counterattack. The three-stage joint plan called for the capture of Battery, or Fort, Wagner, followed by the destruction of Fort Sumter from breaching batteries erected on Cummings Point. In the final stage the fleet, using the monitors to suppress Moultrie's fire, would remove the obstructions and run into the harbor.

The first stage went well. While Gillmore's batteries on Folly Island pounded the weak defenses on the southern end of Morris Island, and the monitors lying close offshore took them in reverse, two brigades under Brigadier General Truman Seymour rowed across Lighthouse Inlet and over ran these positions on July 10. However, an attempt to storm Wagner the next morning without artillery support was repulsed.

An enclosed earthwork mounting twelve heavy guns and extending completely across Morris Island near its northern end, Wagner was much more formidable than Gillmore had supposed. Its narrow approaches were protected by rifle pits, mines, and a wet ditch. Constructed of fine quartz sand by Colonel D. B. Harris of the Confederate engineers, with its guns in embrasures and its quarters bombproofed, the work was extremely resistant to bombardment. Gillmore, nevertheless, emplaced the siege guns brought for use against Sumter. On July 18 he opened a terrific fire, pounding Wagner for eleven hours with 9,000 heavy projectiles, while the fleet threw 15- and 11-inch shells at close range. Assuming the guns had been disabled and the garrison knocked senseless, Gillmore sent two brigades, led by Colonel Robert G. Shaw and his 54th Massachusetts (colored) troops, to assault the fort. But the defenders, unharmed in the bombproof, retrieved their guns from the sand and repulsed the attack by a storm

Above: But they would stay a long time before the prize was won. Charleston was ringed with a formidable array of forts besides Sumter out in the harbor. Most daunting of all was Fort Moultrie, which dated back to the Revolution. A combination of earthworks, masonry, and palmetto logs, it controlled the main channel into Charleston Harbor. (NA)

Below: In this previously unpublished April 1865 photograph, probably by Savannah artist J. T. Reading, Moultrie's strength is still evident despite the destruction. Gun after gun faced any who dared test its mettle. (AMERICANA IMAGE GALLERY)

Above: Reading catches a 10-inch Brooke gun as it stares out to sea, its store of ammunition still ready. Such guns visited a terrible destruction on the Union fleets that tried to penetrate the harbor. (AMERICANA IMAGE GALLERY)

Right: Here, in April 1865 in Battery Marion in Fort Moultrie, a 7-inch Brooke seacoast gun attracts the attention of men whom it once held at bay. (US-AMHI)

Below: Indeed, this is the single most photographed cannon in Charleston's defenses. The photographers shot it from all angles, and with it the two palmettos incongruously decorating the emplacement. Reading's view. (AMERICANA IMAGE GALLERY)

of grapeshot, canister, and rifle balls, killing and wounding a third of the Union force.

Gillmore now decided to besiege Wagner and built more batteries in the swamps on his left. The ironclads kept down the garrison's fire and guarded the right of the Union lines. By August 8 the siege works were within five hundred yards of the fort. Here progress was stopped by plunging shells from Sumter that were fired over Batteries Wagner and Gregg and fell vertically into the trenches. Gillmore thought it necessary to alter the original plan and destroy Sumter first at long range. In a massive precision bombardment lasting fifteen days, Sumter's gorge wall was practically destroyed. Struck in front and reverse, the rest of the upper casemates fell into rubble. When the firing stopped, only a small section of the northeastern wall remained standing and only one gun, in the western face, was serviceable.

Gillmore tried another expedient to end the campaign quickly. With great exertion and skill, Federal engineers built a heavy emplacement on pilings in the marsh between Morris and James islands. Here they mounted an 8-inch rifled cannon that, at thirty-five degrees elevation with a large powder charge, could throw 200-pound shells five miles into Charleston. When Beauregard refused an ultimatum to surrender the city, the Federals fired this "Swamp Angel" thirty-six times before the gun burst. Fifteen projectiles struck the city, causing some material damage, but no one was killed and the psychological effect was negligible. In the autumn the bombardment was resumed, this time with rifles and mortars firing explosive and incendiary shells. Although damage to buildings was extensive enough to cause civilian evacuation of the lower town, casualties were light. Confederate authorities were believed to have sent Union prisoners of war to be housed under fire in Charleston, to discourage this cannonade. In retaliation, Southern prisoners were kept on Morris Island under the fire of Confederate harbor batteries. Eventually, this futile practice was stopped and the prisoners were exchanged.

Elimination of the plunging fire on the approaches allowed Gillmore to resume the siege of Battery Wagner. By September 7 the trenches had been pushed so close that Wagner's guns were useless. Their stout resistance having won time to strengthen the inner defenses, the Confederates abandoned Morris Island.

Thinking that Sumter had been evacuated also, Dahlgren sent a party of 500 sailors and marines to occupy it the following night. Again the defenders were prepared. The first boats had barely landed under the eastern faces when all the guns on Sullivan's and James islands, along with the Confederate harbor ironclad *Chicora*, opened on them. Bullets and chucks of masonry crashed down from the walls. Within an hour, 125 Federals were prisoners, while the remaining boats beat a hasty retreat. Because of a command dispute with the navy, an army assault force assembled at Cummings Point remained inactive. The boat attack was the climax of Union operations against Charleston. Having accomplished the army's objective by knocking Fort Sumter pretty thoroughly to pieces, Gillmore expected the navy to take the initiative.

Dahlgren recognized his responsibility for the final stage of the joint plan, but he was disconcerted by the limited results of the bombardment and the Union occupation of Morris Island. The

Confederate transfer of Sumter's artillery to the inner defenses eliminated the cross fire on the channel, but the obstructions had to be removed by small boats under full fire from the batteries on Sullivan's Island. Nor was Sumter entirely useless for channel defense. Before the boat attack, the 1st South Carolina Artillery, which had so stubbornly defended the fort, was relieved by the Charleston Battalion of infantry under Major Stephen Elliott, who immediately prepared against another landing. Parts of the shattered work were heavily revetted with earth, sandbags, palmetto logs, and pieces of masonry to afford bombproofs for massing troops to repel assaults. On the exterior slopes, the Confederates placed chevaux-de-frise and wire entanglements as deterrents against surprise. Because a terrific fire could be poured upon Sumter from the increasingly powerful Federal batteries erected on Cummings Point, these obstacles had to be taken up before dawn each day and replaced after sunset.

Elliott intended more than mere defense of a ruined post. Three weeks after assuming command, he suggested to Brigadier General Thomas Jordan, Beauregard's chief of staff, the remounting of some guns on the northeastern face. Four of the lower casemates, shielded by the southeastern wall against reverse fire from Morris Island, were further strengthened in the rear by mounds of log reinforced earth. Three heavy guns mounted in these emplacements crossed their fire just ahead of the obstructions with the fire from Fort Moultrie. Thus, by late October, the ironclads were again exposed to damage in approaching close enough to cover the removal of these obstacles. Barring an other night assault, which neither Union commander considered practicable, the solution appeared to be the complete destruction of the fort.

The second bombardment of Sumter opened on October 26 and continued day and night until December 6. Although heavier than the first and conducted at much closer range, it proved less destructive because of the already battered condition of the masonry and the vigorous exertions of the garrison in adding large quantities of more resistant material. Gillmore's aim was to blow away enough of the southern faces to expose the northern channel faces to his batteries. Unlike direct fire, which caused the material to fall inside the fort, forming a convenient ramp for the defenders to mount the walls, reverse fire threw the debris outside, creating an escalade slope for assault parties.

Despite fairly heavy casualties to the garrison, the bombardment was unsuccessful. While the southern faces were considerably reduced, the three-gun battery remained intact. The 15-inch monitor projectiles, fired over the eastern angle, were far more destructive than the fire of the land batteries—so much so that, at one time, the only remaining magazine, in Sumter's southwestern angle, was seriously threatened.

But Dahlgren was aware only of his own difficulties. The monitors had been in almost constant service since July and needed overhaul. Many leaked badly. Accumulated minor injuries to their turrets and plating added to their unfitness for action, while the crews were decimated by sickness and exhaustion resulting from the extreme heat inside these vessels. The fleet's inability to sustain its fire more than a few hours a day for a few weeks gave the Confederates time to repair damages.

Above: Elsewhere in Moultrie mighty mortars poised ready to send their high-arching shells against any attacker. A previously unpublished 1865 Reading image. (AMERICANA IMAGE GALLERY)

Above: The much-battered remains of the fort at war's end gave testimony to its strength and near impregnability to attack. (USAMHI)

Left: After years of Federal siege, Moultrie could boast stairways that went nowhere. (USAMHI)

Above: Sally ports in walls that no longer stood; yet the bastion never fell in combat. (USAMHI)

Below: But none could match Moultrie. It took four years to see the Stars and Stripes float over it once more. (USAMHI)

Above: To be sure, there were other fortifications on Sullivan's Island, like Fort Marshall on the island's northern tip. (USAMHI)

Above: Four years earlier a Yankee ironclad could pause with safety beside the battered yet formidable fortress. (CHS)

The new monitors scheduled to join Dahlgren for an attempted breakthrough to the city in December were delayed by construction problems, so the navy could do little more than strengthen the blockade.

The second great bombardment having failed to open a way to Charleston, Gillmore asked for a different command. In May 1864 he was called north for operations in Virginia. His successor was Major General John G. Foster, another engineer familiar with the Charleston harbor. Although his instructions were simply to defend ground already held, Foster naturally hoped to accomplish more than his predecessors. The same demands of the Virginia campaign that reduced the Federal forces to about 15,000 men reduced Confederate numbers to barely 5,000 to guard their extensive lines.

Foster first planned to seize Sullivan's Island as the quickest way to open the channel. However, Dahlgren refused to cover landings on the north side. In September 1863 the *Weehawken*, while aground under enemy gunfire, had sustained damages that contributed to her foundering two months later. In November the *Lehigh*, grounded near Cummings Point, was pounded by Fort Moultrie before being hauled off. The admiral considered the treacherous shoals off Sullivan's Island more hazardous than the forts.

Foster next designed a three-phase operation to turn the Southern lines and capture Fort Johnson. On July 2, 5,000 men under Brigadier General J. P. Hatch landed on John's Island and the southern tip of James Island. As expected, the outnumbered defenders withdrew most of the garrison from Johnson, setting the stage for the second phase. That night, 500 men attempted to surprise the fort by water. The plan was excellent, but everything went wrong. The departure from Cummings Point was delayed by the tide, the pilot lost the narrow channel in the dark, and many boats grounded. It was near daylight before the leading boats landed near the fort, by which time the garrison was alert; 5 officers and 135 Federal soldiers were taken prisoner, while the re-

Above: After the failure of the April 1863 naval attack, Quincy Gillmore, hero of Fort Pulaski, gained a foothold on Morris Island, south of Charleston, and began working his way toward the city. (WRHS)

maining boats, retreating without orders, came under fire from Battery Cheves on the eastern shore of James Island. The third phase, an expedition to cut the Charleston & Savannah Railroad, was stopped before it reached its objective. On James and John's islands, Confederate counterattacks led to withdrawal of Union forces.

The Federals turned again to Fort Sumter. While conducting sporadic bombardments, Foster searched for some technique to overcome the stubborn defenders. With aid from the navy, he prepared to float torpedoes and barges containing explosives against the fort, but conditions were never favorable enough to try these devices. Another idea, reflecting Foster's frustration, was to build large row galleys with elevated platforms to storm the walls. Specifications for such ancient contraptions, sent to General Halleck, were rejected with the laconic comment that Foster was to remain on the defensive.

No further initiatives were taken against Charleston until late November, when there were several more unsuccessful attempts against the railroad in conjunction with Major General William T. Sherman's march through Georgia. The fall of Savannah on December 21 and Sherman's advance into South Carolina sealed the fate of Charleston. On February 17, 1865, after sinking their vessels, spiking their guns, and setting fire to many buildings, the Confederates evacuated the city and its defenses under the noses of the Federals, who were then attempting to outflank them via the Stono and Bull's Bay.

And so the siege ended. For twenty-two months Charleston's harbor outposts held against an ironclad fleet and a superior army. While geography, aided by Confederate tenacity and skill, favored the defense, the Federals often failed to press their attacks. Too much reliance was placed on the physical and moral impact of bombardment. Union Army leadership changed too often, and the troops were not the best. The monitors, designed for brief ship-to-ship engagements, held up badly during extended service against shore batteries, and the admirals were too reluctant to risk ships in an all-out push to the city. Finally, the strategic priorities of the Northern high command lay elsewhere. Yet at one time the Charleston campaign was the only Civil War action seriously studied in Europe. It remains one of the war's most interesting chapters.

Above: His first obstacle was Fort Wagner, the Confederate earthwork whose parapet cut completely across the northern end of the island. It had to be taken. (USAMHI)

Above: Doomed as well was Colonel Robert G. Shaw, the twenty-five-year-old leader of the 54th Massachusetts, a colored regiment that took a leading part in the battle. He was killed on Wagner's parapet, and angry Confederates buried him beneath the bodies of his fallen Negro soldiers in a common grave. (USAMHI)

Above: Gillmore gave the job to Brigadier General Truman Seymour, a veteran of the Confederate bombardment of Fort Sumter two years earlier. The attack was doomed to failure, and Seymour himself took a terrible wound that put him out of the war for half a year. (USAMHI)

Above: The immediate commander of the defense of Wagner was Brigadier General William B. Taliaferro, a veteran of the Virginia campaigns and one who had served well under Stonewall Jackson. This previously unpublished portrait shows him as colonel of the 23d Virginia. (CWTI)

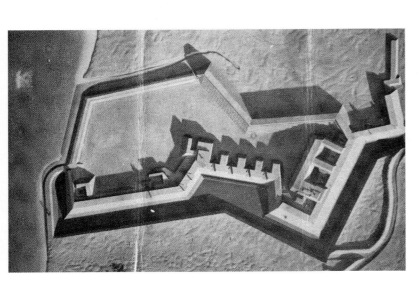

Left: It took over two months before the Rebels finally abandoned Fort Wagner, and by that time Gillmore had thoroughly studied and mapped it. Indeed, he even prepared a model, which was photographed and sent to Washington. (NA)

Above: During those two months regiments like the 39th Illinois waited for the next attack and posed for photographers Haas & Peale. (USAMHI)

Above: The bands played to drive away the summer heat. (USAMHI)

Above: Across the island, behind the works at Battery Wagner, the Confederates also waited and posed for the photographers. This is a rare group shot of Confederates, the 25th South Carolina, formerly Charleston's own Washington Light Infantry. (WASHINGTON LIGHT INFANTRY)

Above: A few wives came to brighten the lonely wait for the 1st United States Artillery, and Samuel Cooley came to capture the scene. (NA)

Above: Meanwhile, unwilling to be idle until Wagner fell, Gillmore planted batteries on Morris Island and began shelling Fort Sumter. Here a 4.2-inch Parrott rifle on a siege carriage fired from the second Swamp Angel battery, the first one having been dismounted when the gun itself exploded. (USAMHI)

Left: Haas & Peale's photograph of the first Swamp Angel after it burst while firing, destroying its carriage and flinging itself up on the sandbag embrasure. (USAMHI)

Above: But the Federals had to get close to Charleston first before big guns would work, and the Confederates had other ideas. The city was a symbol of their cause. (NEW-YORK HISTORICAL SOCIETY)

Above: They would defend it to the last. Here, at top center, is The Citadel, the military school that trained many young Confederate officers. (NYHS)

Above: Major General Jeremy F. Gilmer, chief of the Confederate Engineer Bureau, actually designed some of the city's more formidable defenses. (USAMHI)

Above: There were many who would volunteer to help defend their city, even once-prominent politicos like William Porcher Miles, now a volunteer aide to Beauregard. (LSU)

Above: And others, like Colonel D. B. Harris, actually put Gilmer's plans into practice. (VM)

Above: White Point Gardens, at the foot of the East Battery, an image taken in 1865. Out of almost every backyard grew a gun emplacement. (NA)

Left: And they erected formidable defenses. Here we see the King Street Battery, its grass-covered earth mounds almost giving it the appearance of a city park. (NA)

Above: The Point Battery, its guns, like the city lamp-posts, often illuminating the night sky over Charleston. (USAMHI)

Above: One of many batteries along the city's waterfront, its own "bombproof" magazine built into the earth beneath it. Probably taken by J. T. Reading. (AMERICANA IMAGE GALLERY)

Above: The wharves had their own batteries. (USAMHI)

Above: In time, Gillmore's guns managed to arch their shells into the city. (USAMHI)

Above: So did the other cannon in places like the South Battery, where this was all that remained of a 600-pound Blakely gun. A mighty engine of war was nothing but scrap. (NA)

Above: The tranquil view along the East Battery waterfront belied the noise and turmoil of Charleston under siege. (USAMHI)

Right: But the scars of the bombardment were there. (NA)

Below: And always more guns, in places like Castle Pinckney. (NYHS)

Below: Guns with Charleston at their back, and to their front the enemy. (NYHS)

Above: After the failure of the April 1863 attack on Charleston, a new naval commander, Rear Admiral John A. Dahlgren, arrived on the scene. He renewed the attacks on the city and its forts from the water, and assisted in the final capture of Fort Wagner. (USAMHI)

Below: The attacks of that summer proved harder on the Passaic than on the Confederates. Cooley's assistant E. W. Sinclair made this image, showing some of the turret dents suffered by the ship. (SOUTH CAROLINA HISTORICAL SOCIETY)

Above: Percival Drayton commanded the Passaic that summer and came out of the experience with little enough respect for the wisdom of sending ironclads against fortresses. (NA)

Above: The Passaic *had its smokestack nearly demolished. Here it rests at the Bay Point shops along with other wreckage. (USAMHI)*

Above: The USS Lehigh *joined with the other monitors in Dahlgren's bombardments. It, too, boasted a dent or two when it was later ordered to the James River for service in Virginia, as shown here. (USAMHI)*

Left: One of the most memorable attacks that summer came on September 8, 1863, valued chiefly because Confederate photographer George S. Cook made a rare excursion from his studio and took his camera to Fort Sumter. There, during a bombardment from Dahlgren's fleet, he made a series of magnificent images graphically depicting Sumter and its occupants under siege. Despite poor conditions, he had just set up for a view of the parade ground when a shell believed to come from the Weehawken *exploded just as he exposed a plate. The result was this badly deteriorated image, probably retouched on the original by Cook himself, which also shows a group of Confederates standing and sitting at left. (USAMHI)*

Below: Another view of the shot furnace; defenders pose jauntily for Cook atop it. (SOUTH CAROLINIANA LIBRARY)

Above: A view of the shot furnace, and behind it the officers' quarters, now mere caves amid the dust and ruin. (USAMHI)

Left: Cook took his camera to the parapet, braving enemy fire, to capture this view of three Yankee ironclads firing at Fort Moultrie. It was late in the morning of September 8; the men aboard the Weehawken *had just finished their breakfasts when they opened fire on Sumter. As Dahlgren later reported, "Some movement in Sumter seemed to draw attention from the* Weehawken." *That movement was Cook setting his camera on the parapet. Just after he got this view, the Confederate commander ordered him off, angry that he had drawn enemy fire. The identities of the ships cannot be ascertained with certainty, but the one at the extreme right is probably the* New Ironsides. *(USAMHI)*

Left: In the early hours of September 9 Dahlgren sent parties of volunteers on a daring attempt to land at Sumter in the dark and take it by assault. It failed, and all were captured, including Marine Lieutenant Robert L. Meade, nephew of General George G. Meade. (P-M)

Left: The parade ground now crowded with rubble, wood, and shattered supplies. There is little attempt to maintain a sense of order, though the defenders still line up against the wall for the camera, their uniforms now anything they can find to wear. (USAMHI)

Below: At last Battery Wagner fell, and the new Federal garrison could pose at a dress parade before the parapet that had cost them so dearly in lives. (ROBERT J. YOUNGER)

Below: These heavy Parrott rifles had as their single task the reduction of Sumter to a useless ruin. They very nearly succeeded. (USAMHI)

Above: They cook their meals out in the open over smoking fires, when the enemy's shells are not exploding on the parade ground . (USAMHI)

Above: On August 23, 1863, Gillmore had this photograph of Fort Sumter made from a position near the northern tip of Morris Island. For seven days his guns had been firing at the fort, and the shelling continued for another six hours after this was taken. More than half of the 5,000 shells fired at Sumter found their target. He sent a sketch based on the photo to Washington to show the damage done. (USAMHI)

Above: Eleven weeks later Gillmore had another image made. "I keep up a slow fire on the ruins of Fort Sumter night and day," he reported when he sent in another sketch. The damage done in the previous weeks is obvious. (USAMHI)

Above: Some time later, probably on December 11, 1863, the third and final image in the series revealed the further destruction of the fort. It holds barely the shadow of the shape of the August before; yet the Confederate banner still floats jauntily overhead in this previously unpublished image. (AMERICANA IMAGE CALLERY)

Above: Cooley's November 1864 image of the Morris Island ordnance yard, through which passed the tons of iron hurled at Sumter. (USAMHI)

Above: From the mammoth ordnance yard at Hilton Head came the heavy guns that battered the defenders. (NA)

Above: Gradually Yankee might inevitably wore down the Confederates in Charleston. On July 3, 1864, the bluecoats attacked Fort Johnson and failed. They tried again a week later, only to be driven from James Island altogether for a time. Sumter lies in the distance. (KA)

Right: Later in the war, when the Confederates themselves evacuated the fort, they hacked away at the wooden gun carriages to make them unsafe for firing. (NA)

Above: Another joint Army-Navy attack on Charleston came on September 9, 1864, with more new soldiers and more new ironclads, like the USS Mahopac. *(USAMHI)*

Above: The Confederates held out as best they could, still posing jauntily for the very few photographers who came to see them. These men, probably of Company I, Palmetto Battery, Charleston Light Artillery, pose before their position at Fort Pemberton on the Stono River. The gentleman with arms folded standing before the banner may be their captain, J. R. Bowden. (USAMHI)

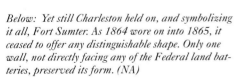

Above: Quarters were not quite what they had been in 1861, but the artillerists could still relax beneath a tree for a game of cards. Of course, there were still slaves to chop wood and wash dishes. (USAMHI)

Below: Yet still Charleston held on, and symbolizing it all, Fort Sumter. As 1864 wore on into 1865, it ceased to offer any distinguishable shape. Only one wall, not directly facing any of the Federal land batteries, preserved its form. (NA)

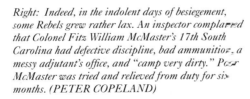

Above: And there was plenty of time for artillery practice, or at least posing for the camera. (USAMHI)

Right: Indeed, in the indolent days of besiegement, some Rebels grew rather lax. An inspector complained that Colonel Fitz William McMaster's 17th South Carolina had defective discipline, bad ammunition, a messy adjutant's office, and "camp very dirty." Poor McMaster was tried and relieved from duty for six months. (PETER COPELAND)

Right: The rest looked like a rocky hillside, guarded from assault at the summit by makeshift portable chevaux-de-frise. Even as early as late 1863, Gillmore believed that he could take the fort by assault but that it was not worth the cost. (NA)

Above: The stakes and the telegraph wire entanglements would cost too many men. (NYHS)

Right: The bombardments forced the defenders to resort to palmetto barricades to patch the gaping holes blasted in the walls. (USAMHI)

Above: It looked like an abandoned medieval ruin. (NA)

Above: The only life visible was often the sentinel in the oft-repaired watchtower. His view was chiefly one of desolation, as was photographer Reading's. (AMERICANA IMAGE GALLERY)

Above: To contain the gradually crumbling masonry and give some kind of order to the fort's walls, the Confederates reinforced them with earth and rubble-filled baskets, which offered an odd contrast to the lonely chimneys rising, and sometimes barrel-capped, from the barracks. (AMERICANA IMAGE GALLERY)

Right: These were the officers' quarters, such as they were, really little more than a jumble of palmettos, baskets, and dirt. (USAMHI)

Above: So rutted and rubbled was the parade ground that boardwalks had to be laid for running guns and wheelbarrows back and forth. (NA)

Below: Yet they held out, their signal gun defiant on the battered parapet. (AMERICANA IMAGE GALLERY)

Above: As Sumter fell, so Charleston had inevitably to fall as well. A beautiful city had been much laid waste. Here sat Secession Hall, where in 1860 the state seceded. (USAMHI)

Below: It was a mingling of textures—the baskets, the rubble, the wire strung on the parapet, the stakes jutting out. The fieldpieces seem almost out of place. (LOUISIANA HISTORICAL ASSOCIATION, SPECIAL COLLECTIONS DIVISION, TULANE UNIVERSITY LIBRARY, NEW ORLEANS)

Above: Here, already being rebuilt in this 1865 view, stands the Circular Church, Secession Hall's neighbor. (USAMHI)

Above: The Northeastern Railroad Depot lay in ruins. (LC)

Below: Hibernian Hall came through the siege relatively secure. (USAMHI)

Below: The Charleston Hotel managed to survive the Yankee shot and shell, only to fall victim to the wrecking ball a century later in 1960. Sometimes a city can face greater enemies than warfare. (USAMHI)

Below: Yet portions of Charleston looked wasted, like the Vendue Range. Once it bustled. (USAMHI)

Right: Meeting Street, with Saint Michael's in the distance. The Confederates painted it black to present less of a target to Federal gunners. The great mound of earth scooped from the street may be a defensive work, or the signs of reconstruction. (NA)

Above: The Mills House Hotel, once home to P.G.T. Beauregard until enemy shells began striking it, showed the effects of the bombardment. (NYHS)

Above: Charleston's old Market House happily missed the rain of iron during the siege; yet it would take time before it again echoed the calls of the vendors on market day. (USAMHI)

Above: At The Citadel, in the city's heart, no more officers would be trained for the Confederate States of America, but it would soon begin schooling young men again for distinguished military careers under the banner of the Union. (NYHS)

Above: Amid the scenes of destruction, there were also signs of renewed life. Mr. McLeish's Vulcan Iron Works was able proudly to proclaim its presence in a sign and a bracket obviously ornamented with a few war "surplus" items like an anchor, a signal gun, and an anvil-like locomotive spring. (LC)

Below: There was much to clean up after the surrender. Here the wreckage of some Yankee ordnance, probably remnants of the first Swamp Angel that exploded. (LC)

Right: Charleston's arsenal bulged with tons of unexpended ammunition and torpedoes, or "infernal machines," plus floating mines. Someone obligingly arranged and marked them for the camera. (USAMHI)

Above: These Blakely guns will never again send hostile shots at fellow Americans. (NYHS)

Above: Most of these will wind up as souvenirs and museum pieces. For now they rest under the taunting gaze of Yankee bunting draped in the trees. (LC)

Right: Americans like these men, Brigadier General John Hatch and his staff. Hatch, seated in the chair, came to Charleston to command the occupation forces. (USAMHI)

Left: His soldiers soon became a common sight, troops like these caught by photographer W. E. James of Brooklyn. (T. SCOTT SANDERS)

Above: The City Hall teemed with bluecoated soldiers. (USAMHI)

Above: They stood sentry before Hatch's headquarters. (USAMHI)

Above: Ships once again came and went without fear to Vanderhoff's Wharf. (USAMHI)

Above: All that remained of the four-year siege of Charleston were the broken guns and the carriages and rubble beneath the Union flag flying over Fort Johnson. (USAMHI)

Left: And out in the harbor, beyond a now silent Fort Moultrie, the brooding hulk of battered but unbeaten Fort Sumter, defiant to the end. (AMERICANA IMAGE GALLERY)

Caring for the Men

GEORGE W. ADAMS

Hospitals, medicines, doctors, and do-gooders

Above: For those unfortunate enough to take an enemy bullet, a piece of shell, or a saber or bayonet wound, this is how the Civil War medical experience often began. These Zouave soldiers are practicing an ambulance drill in Virginia, probably in 1864. The real thing would not have looked so peaceful—or so organized. In battle the officer gesturing into the ambulance would more likely be dodging bullets rather than preening for the camera. (USAMHI)

WHEN THE WAR BEGAN, the United States Army medical staff consisted of only the surgeon general, thirty surgeons, and eighty-three assistant surgeons. Of these, twenty-four resigned to "go South," and three other assistant surgeons were promptly dropped for "disloyalty." Thus the medical corps began its war service with only eighty seven men. When the war ended in 1865, more than eleven thousand doctors had served or were serving, many of these as acting assistant surgeons, uncommissioned and working under contract, often on a part-time basis. They could wear uniforms if they wished and were usually restricted to general hospitals away from the fighting front.

The Confederate Army began by taking the several state militias into service, each regiment equipped with a surgeon and an assistant surgeon, appointed by the state governors. The Confederate Medical Department started with the appointment on May 4 of Daniel De Leon, one of three resigned United States surgeons, as acting surgeon general. After a few weeks he was replaced by another acting surgeon general, who on July 1, 1861, was succeeded by Samuel Preston Moore. He took the rank of colonel and stayed on duty until the collapse of the Confederacy.

Dr. Moore, originally a Charlestonian, had served twenty-seven years in the United States Army. He has been described as brusque and autocratic, a martinet. He was also very hardworking and determined, and he was progressive in his military-medical thinking. Dissatisfied with the quality of many of the surgeons of the state troops, he insisted that to hold a Confederate commission, every medical officer must pass examinations set by one of his examining boards. He disliked filthy camps and hospitals. He believed in "pavilion" hospitals—long, wooden buildings with ample ventilation and sufficient bed space for eighty to one hundred patients. Moore, with the compliance of the Confederate Congress and President Jefferson Davis, began the construction of many such hospitals when field activities demonstrated that the casualties would be high and the war long. Dr. Moore maintained a cooperative relationship with Congress, successive secretaries of war, and President Davis, always subject to the availability of funds from the Confederate Treasury.

In that era of "heroic dosing" Moore foresaw shortages in drugs, surgical instruments, and hospital supplies. He established laboratories for drug manufacture and took prompt steps to purchase needed supplies from Europe. In the course of time, capture of Union warehouses and hospitals played an increasing role in the Confederate supply. As an additional precaution he procured and distributed widely a book on native herbs and other plants that grew wild in the South and were believed to possess curative qualities. As a result, despite frequent shortages of some drugs, the Confederate record was a good one.

Meanwhile, in the old Union, Surgeon General Thomas Lawson, an octogenarian, obligingly died only weeks after Fort Sumter. He was replaced by Clement A. Finley, the sexagenarian senior surgeon who had served since 1818 and was thoroughly imbued with Lawson's parsimonious values. Lawson had wanted to keep the Army Medical Department much as it had been throughout his career, which meant that the eighty-seven surviving members of the medical corps had not had the kind of experience that would be needed in a major war. Yet now they were the senior surgeons of a rapidly expanding army.

Fortunately, immediately after the outbreak of war there was a swarming of humanitarians of both sexes who wanted to be of help to the citizen soldiers. Among the most clamorous was the Women's Central Association for Relief, of New York, all of whose officers were men. Soon there was a strong demand for the creation of a United States sanitary commission, patterned on the British Sanitary Commission, which had been formed to clean up the filth of the Crimean War. The tentative United States commission elected officers; the two most important were the president, Henry W. Bellows, a prominent Unitarian minister, and the executive secretary, Frederick Law Olmsted, superintendent of Central Park. The commission asked for official recognition by the War Department, stating that its purpose was to "advise and assist" that department.

Surgeon General Finley, just beginning his incumbency, had no desire for a sanitary commission, but when that body promised to confine its activities to the volunteer regiments and to leave the regular army alone, he withdrew his objections. Secretary of War Simon Cameron then named a commission of twelve members, of whom three were army doctors.

The United States Sanitary Commission quickly extended itself to 2,500 communities throughout the North, the Chicago branch being especially proficient. The St. Louis people accomplished great things but insisted on remaining independent under the name of the Western Sanitary Commission. The women of the local branches kept busy making bandages, scraping lint, and sending culinary delicacies to army hospitals. The national organization maintained a traveling outpost with the Army of the Potomac to speed sanitary supplies to the field hospitals of that army. In 1862 and again in 1864 the commission provided and manned hospital ships to evacuate Army of the Potomac sick and wounded to general hospitals as far from the front as New York City.

Early in the war, and later when it seemed appropriate, the commission persuaded highly respected doctors to write pamphlets on sanitation and hygiene. These were widely circulated among both medical and line officers. Although often erroneous, these pamphlets presented the best thought of that prebacteriological era and did some good where surgeons could persuade their colonels to take the advice. In the absence of any medical inspectors, the commission induced a number of esteemed doctors to examine recruit camps and to report on cleanliness and on the professional adequacy of surgeons to hold their commissions.

Although the Southerners had some local and state relief organizations, they enjoyed nothing similar to the Sanitary Commission in scope or efficiency; yet in the effects of camp disease and unsanitary conditions, the Confederacy and the Union shared common experiences indeed. The two armies had similar experiences as their forces were being trained, usually in an instruction camp as a gathering place for the troops of each state. Medical officers did not know how to requisition drugs and medical supplies. Commissaries did not know how to requisition rations. It has been said

Right: A folding stretcher used for transporting the wounded from the field to the hospitals and ambulances. (KA)

Left: The ambulance wagons came in a wide variety; many were nothing more specialized for the service than simple flat-bottomed boxes. For a man with a painful wound, a trip of any distance in one of these could be excruciating, even deadly. (MINNESOTA HISTORICAL SOCIETY, ST. PAUL)

Right: These were the men who transported the wounded to the field hospitals. This was the camp of the chief ambulance officer of the IX Corps, in front of Petersburg, Virginia, in August 1864. (LC)

Left: Often the places where the wagons delivered the wounded were as makeshift as the ambulances. The battlefield hospitals and surgeries were usually little more than someone's house, appropriated for the moment. The image shows Mrs. Stevens's house near Centreville. Here Federal wounded from two Bull Run battles were treated. (USAMHI)

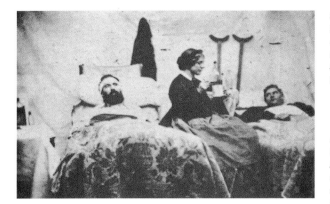

Below: A rude frame house on the Fair Oaks battlefield, used by Hooker's division in 1862. This James F. Gibson image shows eloquently the awful proximity of the battlefield hospital to death. (CHS)

Above: The man who gave form and reason to the management and treatment of wounded on the battlefield was Major Jonathan Letterman, medical director of the Army of the Potomac. He reorganized the field hospital system and instituted mobile hospitals and ambulance service so effectively that his plan has served as a model ever since. (P-M)

Above: The Confederates enjoyed their share of effective physicians as well. Dr. Samuel Stout served as medical director of the Army of Tennessee, with the rank of major. Besides coping with casualties and camp disease, the Confederate surgeon faced an added enemy—shortage of almost every vital medication. (NA)

that "the Americans are a warlike but unmilitary people," and the first months of the Civil War proved the adage. Too many men, when entering the army after a lifetime of being cared for by mothers and wives, had a tendency to "go native" —to ignore washing themselves or their clothing and, worst of all, to ignore all regulations about camp sanitation. Each company was supposed to have a sink, a trench eight feet deep and two feet wide, onto which six inches of earth were to be put each evening. Some regiments, at first, dug no sinks. In other cases the men, disgusted by the sights and odors around the sinks, went off into open spaces around the edge of the camp. The infestation of flies that followed was inevitable, as were the diseases and bacteria they spread to the men and their rations.

Soon long lines of soldiers began coming to sick call with complaints of loose bowels accompanied by various kinds and varying degrees of internal discomfort. The medical officer would make a slapdash diagnosis of diarrhea or dysentery and prescribe an astringent. He usually ascribed this sickness to the eating of bad or badly cooked food. Union Army surgeons were to come to use the term "diarrhea-dysentery," lumping all the cases together as one disease. In fact, in many cases it was only a symptom of tuberculosis or malaria, though amoebic and bacillary dysentery —introduced into the South by slaves brought from Africa—was certainly present as well. It caused enormous sickness and many deaths. The Union Army alone blamed the disease for 50,000 deaths, a sum larger than that ascribed to "killed in action." It was even more lethal in the Confederate Army.

The diets of both armies did not help and were deplorably high in calories and low in vitamins. Fruits and fresh vegetables were notable by their absence, and especially so when the army was in the field. The food part of the ration was fresh or preserved beef, salt pork, navy beans, coffee, and hardtack—large, thick crackers, usually stale and often inhabited by weevils. When troops were not fighting, many created funds to buy fruits and vegetables in the open market. More often they foraged in the countryside, with fresh food a valuable part of the booty. In late 1864, when Major General W. T. Sherman made foraging his official policy on his march from Atlanta to Savannah, his army was never healthier. As the war went on, Confederate soldiers were increasingly asked to subsist on field corn and peas. And the preparation of the food was as bad as the food itself, hasty, undercooked, and almost always fried.

No wonder, then, that at sick call, shortly after reveille, many men who claimed to be sick were marched by the first sergeant to the regimental hospital, usually a wall tent. There the assistant surgeon examined them, then assigned some to cots in the hospital tent, instructed others to be sick in quarters, and restored a few to light duty or to full duty. The less sick and slightly wounded would be expected to nurse, clean, and feed the patients and to see to the disposal of bedpans and urinals.

In the event of an engagement, the assistant surgeon and one or more detailed men, laden with lint, bandages, opium pills and morphine, whiskey and brandy, would establish an "advance" or dressing station just beyond musket fire from the battle. Stretcher-bearers went forward to find the wounded and, if the latter could not walk, to carry them to the dressing station. The assistant surgeon gave the wounded man a stout drink of liquor, expecting it to counteract shock, and then perhaps gave him an opium pill or dust or rubbed morphine into the wound. Later in the war the advantages of a syringe to inject morphine became apparent. The assistant surgeon examined the wound, with special attention to staunching or diminishing bleeding. After removing foreign bodies, he packed the wound with lint, bandaged it, and applied a splint if it seemed advisable. The walking wounded then started for the field hospital, officially the regiment hospital tent, although in 1862 and onward there was an increasing tendency to take over a farmhouse, school, or church if such was available. The recumbent went by ambulances, if there were any, for the ride to the field hospital, usually anywhere from three to five miles from enemy artillery and sometimes much farther.

There, lying on clumps of hay or bare ground, the wounded awaited their turn on the operating table. There was usually little shouting, groaning, or clamor because the wounded were quieted by shock and the combination of liquor and opiate. It was an eerie scene, with a mounting pile of amputated limbs, perhaps five feet high, the surgeon and the assistant surgeon—after a few months both Union and Confederate authorities decided that two assistant surgeons were necessary in a regiment —cutting, sawing, making repairs, and tying ligatures on arteries. The scene was especially awesome at night, with the surgeons working by candlelight on an assignment that might sometimes go on for three or four days with hardly a respite. And there was always the smell of gore.

The surgeons tried to ignore both the slightly wounded and the mortally wounded in the interest of saving as many lives as possible. This meant special attention to arm and leg wounds. Union statistics showed that 71 percent of all gunshot wounds were in the extremities, probably because of fighting from cover behind trees and breastworks. Wounds of the head, neck, chest, and abdomen were most likely to be mortal, so the amputation cases went first on the operating table. The bullet or piece of shell had to be removed, often with the operator using his fingers for a probe. Between the extensive damage done by the Minie bullets used to inflict wounds, and the haste and frequent ignorance in treating them, amputation was all too often the "treatment" prescribed.

Everything about the operation was septic. The surgeon operated in a blood- and often pus-stained coat. He might hold his lancet in his mouth. If he dropped an instrument or sponge, he picked it up, rinsed it in cold water, and continued work. When loose pieces of bone and tissue had been removed, the wound would be packed with moist lint or raw cotton, unsterilized, and bandaged with wet, unsterilized bandages. The bandages were to be kept wet, the patient was to be kept as quiet as possible, and he was to be given small but frequent doses of whiskey and possibly quinine. This was a supportive regime.

The urgency of operating during the primary period—the first twenty-four hours—was to avoid the irritative period, when infection showed itself. The surgeon seldom had to wait more than three or four days for "laudable pus" to appear. This was believed to be the lining of the wound, being expelled so that clean tissue could replace it and the wound could heal. In the rare cases when no pus

Left: Women, too, served officially in the medical service, though in very small numbers. Dr. Mary Edwards Walker was commissioned assistant surgeon, the first woman to hold a commission in the United States Army. She was later awarded the Medal of Honor for her work. (LLOYD OSTENDORF COLLECTION)

Below: Alas, for many a wounded soldier organization and supply were not enough. Arrayed against the twin enemies of enormous, destructive enemy bullets and woeful ignorance of antiseptics, the soldier who was hit in arm or leg stood little chance of keeping the limb. Amputation became a dreadfully commonplace "treatment." Here is a posed scene on an amputating table. This fortunate soldier is only shamming, as the assistant pretends to administer anesthetic and the surgeon holds knife in hand. (LO)

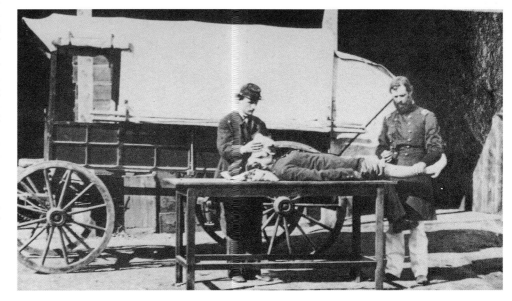

Left: In contrast, what appears to be a genuine amputation scene became an occasion for posing. Taken at Camp Letterman at Gettysburg in August 1863, it shows clearly the bloodstain on the tablecloth and the open wound on the patient's shoulder. As several assistants stand by with the anesthesia and other materials, the surgeon has the good sense to put an apron over his uniform. It was a messy business— with or without the camera. (PEARL KORN)

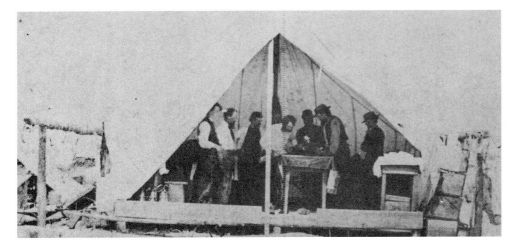

Above: At Morris Island, South Carolina, photographers Haas & Peale captured this image of an operation taking place in July 1863. The very informal attire and lack of posturing on the part of the surgeons may indicate that this is a genuine treatment under way. The patient's shoes lie at the foot of the table, while his own stockinged left foot is just visible on the table's top right. The man in the shadows at the back of the table appears to hold a white cloth or cotton, probably soaked with chloroform, over the patient's face. The absence of tourniquets, sponges, blood basins, and saws and knives suggests that this is not an amputation scene but, more likely, treatment of a broken leg, since the surgeon, in his shirtsleeves and leaning over the table, appears to hold a splint or some other apparatus. The surgeon, incidentally, is Dr. John J. Craven, medical director of the Department of the South, the physician who later attended to Jefferson Davis when he was imprisoned after the war. (USAMHI)

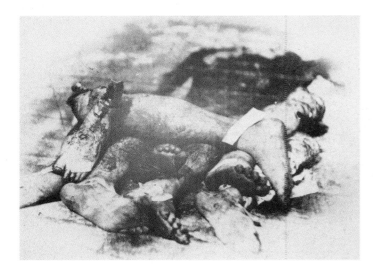

Left: Of this image there can be no doubt. This is no pretended photograph. Eight or nine legs lie where they were stacked after being removed from their owners. The amount of flesh and bone cut away from men in this war can literally be measured in tons. (STANLEY B. BURNS, M.D. AND THE BURNS ARCHIVE)

Left: And another certainty of field hospital medicine was that some would die. At Camp Letterman Dr. Chamberlain and Dr. Lyford established their embalming business, with plenty of clientele awaiting their services. The two gentlemen in the coffins, however, will be spared their knives for the moment. They are posing, having been standing, very much alive, in some other images. (PEARL KORN)

appeared, it was called "healing by first intention" and was a complete mystery. Actually the pus was the sign that Staphylococcus aureus had invaded and was destroying tissue.

As to technique, the amputating surgeons had a choice of the "flap" operation or the "circular," both quite old. The former was quicker but enlarged the wound; the latter, when properly done, opened up a small area to infection. By the end of the war a small majority preferred the flap. The frequency of amputations was much questioned at the time. Yet, considering the condition of the patients, the difficulties of transportation, and the septic condition of the hospitals, amputations probably saved lives rather than limbs.

Men wounded in the abdomen by gunshot frequently died of peritonitis if they had not already bled to death from serious arterial injuries. Wounds of the head and the neck were frequently mortal. Some surgeons in both armies experimented for a while in sealing chest wounds. They would plug the wound with collodion, relieving the dreadful dyspnea—breathlessness—of the patient, but sealing in such infections as entered with the bullet. These cases were likely to be mortal, but the operator seldom knew because the patient was soon evacuated to a general hospital. As for the frightful-looking sabers and bayonets, they inflicted barely 2 percent of the wounds, most of which usually healed.

Surgical fevers disheartened the doctors. Four or five days after a wound operation, the patient would be recovering well, producing copious pus. Then suddenly the pus stopped, the wound dried, and the patient ran a terrific fever. Despite drugs, the patient would very likely be dead in three or four days. The diagnosis was blood poisoning. Erysipelas also affected both armies. With a case mortality of 40 percent, it received serious attention. It was recognized by a characteristic rash, and it was thought by some to be airborne, with the result that both Unionists and Confederates took steps to isolate erysipelas patients in separated tents or wards. The surgeons were in the dark as to how to treat this affliction, but it was noted that if iodine was painted on the edges of a wound, its further extension was stopped.

Civil War surgeons had not only iodine but carbolic acid as well, and a long list of "disinfectants" such as bichloride of mercury, sodium hypochlorite, and other agents. The trouble was that the wound was allowed to become a raging inferno before disinfectants were tried. However, one of the good features of Civil War surgery was that anesthetics were almost always used in operations or the dressing of painful wounds. It was practically universal in the Union, and despite mythology, anesthetics were very seldom unavailable in the Confederacy. The almost universal favorite was chloroform, probably because ether's explosive quality made it dangerous at a field hospital operating table, where there was always the possibility of enemy gunfire.

With the coming of the big battles of 1862, both armies more or less simultaneously evolved larger and better field hospitals. First, regimental hospitals clustered together as brigade hospitals with some differentiation of duty for the various medical officers and with the chief surgeon of the brigade in charge. Soon brigade hospitals clustered into division hospitals, and by 1864 in most field armies there were corps hospitals. There the best surgeons would operate; one surgeon would be in charge of records, another of drugs, another of supplies, and yet another would direct and treat the sick and lightly wounded who were the nurses.

In time for Antietam, the Army of the Potomac, under its medical director Jonathan Letterman, developed the Letterman Ambulance Plan. In this system the ambulances of a division moved together, under a mounted line sergeant, with two stretcher-bearers and one driver per ambulance, to collect the wounded from the field, bring them to the dressing stations, and then take them to the field hospital. It was a vast improvement over the earlier "system," wherein bandsmen in the Union command, and men randomly specified in the Confederacy, were simply appointed to drive the ambulances and carry the litters. Frequently the most unfit soldiers were detailed, which often meant that, not being good fighters, they were little better as medical assistants. Often in the first year of the war they got drunk on medicinal liquor and ignored their wounded comrades in order to hide themselves from enemy fire.

Such improved organization was copied or approximated in the other field armies despite loud opposition from the Quartermaster Corps, which wanted to keep control of ambulances and drivers, and from some field commanders, of whom Major General Don Carlos Buell of the Army of the Ohio was notable for noncooperation.

In general, the Union forces in the West were spared battlefield relief scandals by the fact that major battles were fought on the banks of rivers, whence wounded and sick could be evacuated by riverboats to Mound City, Illinois, St. Louis, and other cities with general hospitals in the safety and secure supply of the North. After the relatively prompt fall of Memphis, that city became the site of several general hospitals. The evacuating boats, however, might be maintained by individual states or by the United States Sanitary Commis-

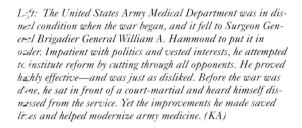

Left: The United States Army Medical Department was in dismal condition when the war began, and it fell to Surgeon General Brigadier General William A. Hammond to put it in order. Impatient with politics and vested interests, he attempted to institute reform by cutting through all opponents. He proved highly effective—and was just as disliked. Before the war was done, he sat in front of a court-martial and heard himself dismissed from the service. Yet the improvements he made saved lives and helped modernize army medicine. (KA)

Right: Women as well revolutionized medical care, and none more so than Dorothea Dix. Prominent before the war in reform movements for the indigent, she became superintendent of nurses for the Union, organizing the small army of ladies who went to the hospitals and the front to care for the men. (USAMHI)

Above: The system of general hospitals established by Hammond and others soon spread across the country. Usually they were placed near enough to the front that wounded and ailing men did not have to travel all the way back to the North for care. The Army of the Potomac's general hospital in 1864-65 stood at its City Point, Virginia, supply base. (USAMHI)

Left: Well-trained corps of surgeons and assistants staffed the general hospitals, often making up for whatever their formal training might have lacked by an abundance of on-the-job training. The image shows a group of surgeons of the Army of the Potomac near Petersburg, Virginia, in October 1864. (USAMHI)

Above: Hospital stewards of the IX Corps near Petersburg, November 1864. (USAMHI)

Above: Camp Letterman General Hospital at Gettysburg, taken by the Tysons during the summer of 1863. That the tents were crowded is evident by the side-by-side placement of beds in the tent in the foreground. (THE OAK-LAND MUSEUM, OAKLAND,CALIF.)

Above: Surgeon Jonathan Letterman sits at left with his assistants in November 1862. Much of the credit for the field hospital system belongs to him. Exhausted after his labors caring for the wounded at Antietam, he retired to a Maryland home for a rest and there met the woman he later married. Behind the impassive face in the image sits a man already in love. (USAMHI)

sion or the Western Sanitary Commission, which led to confusion. The state boats, especially those from Ohio and Indiana, were so persistent in their "raiding" the evacuation hospitals for Buckeyes and Hoosiers that General Grant had to forbid their removing any patients.

After losing control of their rivers, the Confederates made considerable use of railroads in evacuating men from field hospitals to general hospitals. They had no special hospital cars and felt fortunate when they could use passenger rather than freight cars. They became adept at maintaining dressing and supply stations where wounds could be tended and the patients fed. The Union Army, too, increasingly used railroads for evacuating men north. After the Battle of Chattanooga, a real hospital train was regularly used to move the sick and wounded from Chattanooga to Louisville. Some of the cars were equipped with two tiers of bunks, suspended on hard-rubber tugs. At the ends of such cars would be a room for supplies and food preparation. The locomotive assigned to this train was painted scarlet, and at night a string of three red lanterns burned on the front. Confederate cavalry men never bothered this train.

The truth was that the military commanders, both Confederate and Union, hated to see fighting soldiers separated from the army; the fear was they would never return. The South was well aware it was fighting a much larger people. The Union generals were well aware that as the invaders, on the offensive, they needed a majority of the men on the battlefield. They also realized that the deeper they penetrated the South, the greater the number of men needed to garrison important points and to guard ever-longer supply lines. And so there was never an actual separately enlisted and separately trained hospital corps in either army.

When Edwin M. Stanton took over as Lincoln's Secretary of War early in 1862, he realized that Dr. Finley, now a brevet brigadier general, would have to be replaced as surgeon general. Taking the advice of the Sanitary Commission, he appointed William A. Hammond, then a junior assistant surgeon. A Marylander, Hammond had served eleven years as an assistant surgeon before he resigned and became a professor in the University of Maryland Medical School. He was to accomplish many good things and to make many good suggestions during the fourteen months he served as surgeon general. It was obvious to him and to his supporters in the Sanitary Commission that the army needed a group of medical inspectors, chosen for merit and possessing enough rank to give orders to hospital commanders. It was obvious that the makeshift general hospitals—hotels, warehouses, schools, churches—should be rapidly replaced by pavilion hospitals designed for their function. It was obvious that corps and division hospitals should become official and that something like the Letterman Ambulance Plan should be extended throughout the army. It was obvious that the quartermaster should not be able to remove ambulances nor line officers be able to remove experienced attendants from the medical field details.

Eager to educate his department in the best ideas of the time, General Hammond wrote a full-length textbook on military hygiene. He brought about the writing of Joseph J. Woodward's admirable *The Hospital Steward's Manual*. He gave every encouragement to the many medical societies that had sprung up in the army, ordering that interesting scientific specimens should be forwarded to Washington for inclusion in an Army Medical Museum. He began the collection of what has be come the world's largest medical library.

Finley and Hammond secured Congressional authority to augment the regular Army Medical Department by several hundred men, first called brigade surgeons, later surgeons of volunteers, a group that contained unusually prestigious doctors. They were used chiefly as staff assistants. As for the increase in regimental surgeons and assistant surgeons, the Medical Department was to have little say. Higher authority had found it desirable to increase the army by a persistent raising of new regiments rather than by filling up the depleted ranks of the old ones. This maintained the state governors in their unfortunate practices of selecting and commissioning the surgeons and assistant surgeons. The surgeon general could only attempt to reject unfit professionals by extensive use of reexaminations and "plucking" boards.

General Hammond felt frustrated. Secretary Stanton leaned heavily on General Henry Halleck for military advice, and this usually supported the ideas of the old regular army medics who were jealous of Hammond, the interloper who had been promoted over their heads from captain to brigadier general. In addition, Hammond won the enmity of a large proportion of the American medical profession through his banning of the two mercurials, calomel and tartar emetic, from the army drug table. He may have been correct in his idea that these drugs were being overused, but this seemingly arrogant action lost him the sympathy of many medical colleagues.

As a result, Hammond was effectively replaced by Joseph K. Barnes, of the surgeon general's office, in September 1863. It was almost a year before a court-martial of docile surgeons, although finding him "not guilty" on other counts, did vote Hammond guilty of "conduct unbecoming an officer and a gentleman." He had to leave the army.

Even where successful, Hammond was only partially so. After the medical inspector bill passed, Secretary Stanton decreed that half the inspectors were to be "political" appointees. When the ambulance corps bill of 1864 became law, what was essentially the Letterman Ambulance Plan was extended to all the armies. The Army Medical Department was to have the privilege of choosing the enlisted men to be put on ambulance and stretcher-bearer detail, and they could not be withdrawn, but there was still no ambulance corps per se.

Confederate Medical Department organization was very much what Surgeon General Moore thought it should be. Congress gave him a considerable body of medical inspectors and hospital inspectors, the former operating within the field armies and the latter in the general hospitals of each state, with the medical director of each state responsible for its hospitals. There was some debate with the quartermaster general about ambulances, but this was generally over the lack of them. Farm wagons most often constituted the ambulances of the Confederacy. Although Moore had much the same "arrogant" personality traits as did Hammond, he usually obtained prompt obedience to orders rather than conflict. Both armies experimented with "special" hospitals, with ad-

Left: The Army replaced the dismissed Surgeon General Hammond with Brigadier General Joseph K. Barnes, a man of less vision than his predecessor. Barnes profited from Hammond's innovations and continued them, winning for himself and his staff considerable acclaim. A major general at war's end, he stands in the center here with members of his staff, among them Brigadier General Charles H. Crane, seated second from left; Joseph J. Woodward, seated far right; and Edward Curtis, standing far right. It was Barnes who was present at Abraham Lincoln's death, overseeing his care. Woodward and Curtis later performed the autopsy. (NATIONAL LIBRARY OF MEDICINE, BETHESDA, MD.)

Below: The enemy received—or was supposed to receive—the same humane treatment given to friends in these hospitals. A sizaele number of wounded Confederates populated Camp Letterman at Gettysaurg. The crutches and the empty sleeves give testimony to their sacrifice for their cause. This view is believed to have been taken by P. S. Weaver. (USAMFI)

Above: Sometimes the wounded went by steamer, like the medical supply ship Planter, *shown here in the Appomattox River in September 1864. (USAMHI)*

Left: In the West the wounded generally went up the Mississippi by riverboat, some aboard an innovation, the hospital ship. Here the USS Red Rover, *the Army's very first hospital ship, ties up with an ice barge on the Mississippi. She had been a Confederate troopship until captured at Island No. 10 in 1862 and converted into a hospital. (NHC)*

Right: Smaller state and private relief associations also did their part. Here ladies of the Michigan and Pennsylvania Relief Association minister to some wounded and ailing soldiers in a Brady & Company image. (ROBERT J. YOUNGER)

Left: Whether taken north or south, the wounded found much better care for their recovery and convalescence at the permanently established hospitals. In Beaufort, South Carolina, that could mean going to Hospital No. 15, shown here with a local fire brigade posed in front. (NA)

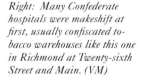

Right: Many Confederate hospitals were makeshift at first, usually confiscated tobacco warehouses like this one in Richmond at Twenty-sixth Street and Main. (VM)

mission limited to patients with the same disorders. The Confederates established several venereal hospitals and some ophthalmic hospitals. The Unionists began a venereal hospital at Nashville and the famed neurological hospital, Turner's Lane, at Philadelphia, where W. W. Keen is believed by some to have founded neurology in America.

In contrast, a "general" hospital did not limit its admissions. The sick and the wounded were evacuated to general hospitals so that empty beds could be made available in field installations when a new rush of wounded was expected. Buildings adapted for use as general hospitals were usually considered unsatisfactory because of the inadequate plumbing, the bad ventilation, and the "crowd poisoning" and "mephfluvia" which that generation thought bred and spread disease. Moore and Hammond believed a large building program of pavilion hospitals in 1862 was the answer. To the best of their abilities both sides carried this out, and followed it by still bigger construction programs in 1863 and 1864. The Union pavilions were longer than their Confederate counterparts. Some were as long as 120 feet, with a width of 14 or 15 feet, with a longitudinal ventilator along the 12- to 14-foot roof. This, along with floor ventilation, made the patients too cold and was later closed by wooden slats.

At the inner end, each pavilion, North and South, had toilets, sometimes flush and sometimes seats over a sloping zinc trough in which water was supposed to run continuously. Reports show that often the water supply was insufficient and that toilets were flushed only after many usings.

Frequently the pavilions were built as though they were spokes spreading from a hub. The buildings at the hub were operating rooms, kitchens, offices, pharmacies and supplies, "dead house," ice house, and other services. The grounds were usually joined by a wooden roadway on which food could be hauled or the wash taken up and delivered by a steam-powered vehicle.

The staff, aside from the medical officers and hospital stewards, was mostly made up of the convalescents. They were frequently weak and weary, often snappish and irritable. They did not like the dirty work they performed. They wanted to go home. The surgeon-in-charge, as the hospital commander was titled, was often in a dilemma. If he returned the patient to his regiment too soon, the man might relapse or die on the road to his unit. If he tried to hold on to the man too long, he might be forcibly returned to his regiment; and if he prevailed upon an inspector to give a medical discharge, he would be losing an attendant who had learned something about his work, and would be forced to rely on a new man who knew nothing. Union and Confederate surgeons-in-charge faced the same problem, although occasionally in Southern hospitals there were hired blacks of both sexes. These people were considered only marginally successful. Some attempts in the North to use cheap male labor as hospital attendants proved unsatisfactory, the men being undisciplined, a "saucy lot" who even stole from the patients.

The brilliant results of Florence Nightingale in cleaning up the Crimean hospitals had been widely noted, with the result that early on it was decided that a corps of female nurses should be added to the army, with Dorothea Dix their superintendent. Miss Dix was widely known as a reformer of jails and as the "founder" of several state mental hospitals. Devoted and hard working, she was disorganized, unyielding in controversy, and deeply in the grip of Victorian ideals of propriety. Allowed to choose the nurses and to set the rules, she announced that her appointees must be at least thirty and plain in appearance, and must always dress in plain, drab dresses and never wear bright-colored ribbons. They could not associate with either surgeons or patients socially, and they must always insist upon their rights as the senior attendants in the wards.

It was not long before outraged surgeons virtually went to war with Miss Dix's nurses, frustrating them, insulting them, trying to drive them from the hospitals. These were strong-minded middle-class American women, accustomed to ruling within the home and to receiving the respectful attention of their husbands and male acquaintances. For the most part they had no nursing training. The surgeons complained that they often substituted their own nostrums for the drugs prescribed and that they sometimes were loud and interfering when attempting to prevent amputations.

As time passed, younger and less self-righteous nurses began to appear in the army, furnished by the Western Sanitary Commission or some other relief agency. Some surgeons learned to suppress their male-chauvinist behavior. In September 1863, the War Department approved a new nurse policy that, although ostensibly a victory for Miss Dix, really defeated her. Under this edict, hospital commanders could send away Dix-appointed nurses but were forced to accept Dix-appointed replacements unless the surgeon general authorized the appointment of someone the surgeon-in-charge preferred. The surgeon general was always willing.

In fact, the female nurses were much liked by the patients and were not so much nurses as mother-substitutes. They wrote letters for their "boys," read to them, decorated the wards with handsome garlands, and sometimes sang. Both armies used small contingents of Catholic nuns in certain general hospitals. They came from the Sis-

Right: Near Richmond, Surgeon General Samuel Moore built a few hospitals, all of them scantily equipped, drafty in winter, and woefully lacking in sanitation. The roofs of the hospital buildings at Camp Winder, for instance, were in desperate need of repair by the end of the war. (VM)

Left: The conquering Federals established their hospitals all across the South. They set up Sedgwick Hospital in Louisiana, shown here, turned houses into hospitals, and arranged medical facilities for ex-slaves. (NA)

Above: They established small complexes of buildings for treatment and care, as at Morehead City, North Carolina. (CHS)

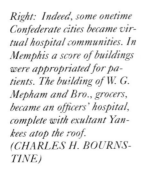

Right: Indeed, some onetime Confederate cities became virtual hospital communities. In Memphis a score of buildings were appropriated for patients. The building of W. G. Mepham and Bro., grocers, became an officers' hospital, complete with exultant Yankees atop the roof. (CHARLES H. BOURNSTINE)

Left: The Jefferson Block Building became Jefferson Hospital. No need to change the name for patriotic reasons here. (CHARLES H. BOURNSTINE)

Right: The Yankees established even better facilities back on conquered land and at the major military installations. Chesapeake General Hospital at Fort Monroe, Virginia, looked more like a resort. (USAMHI)

Left: At Jeffersonville, Indiana, Hammond built Camp Holt, with row upon row of neat wards. (INDIANA HISTORICAL SOCIETY LIBRARY, INDIANAPOLIS)

Right: In Cincinnati the Marine Hospital catered not to marines but to the members of the infantry unit known as the Mississippi Marine Brigade. (NA)

ters of Charity, the Sisters of St. Joseph, the Sisters of Mercy, and the Sisters of the Holy Cross. Having been teachers, some lacked previous hospital experience, but surgeons liked them because they had been bred to discipline. The patients liked them too, but called them all Sisters of Charity.

Hospital food improved perceptively when women matrons took over the supervision of kitchens. These women came from various sources, many supplied by the United States Christian Commission, a large organization that donated delicacies to hospitals but considered the saving of souls, by passing out religious tracts, its principal mission.

Because of the great fame of Clara Barton, and some women like her, an impression prevailed that women functioned in hospitals in the field. This was seldom the case. Miss Barton might best be described as a one-woman relief agency. However, the strong-minded but winning "Mother" Mary Ann Bickerdyke became so popular that in 1864 General W. T. Sherman officially appointed her to his own corps hospital.

Women could be found serving in various ways in Confederate hospitals, too, but the bulk of them were hired black cooks and washerwomen. In the conservative South there was a widespread feeling that a military hospital was no place for a lady. Only in Richmond were there significant numbers of women working in the city's many hospitals.

Richmond was indeed the hospital center of the Confederacy, with twenty hospitals in 1864 after many of the makeshift type had been closed and replaced by pavilion structures. The queen of them was Chimborazo, which had beds for 8,000 men and was often called the largest hospital on the continent. It was organized into four divisions, each with thirty pavilions. There were also five soup houses, five ice houses, "Russian" baths, a 10,000-loaf per day bakery, and a 400-keg brewery. On an adjacent farm the hospital grew food and grazed three hundred cows and several hundred goats. Almost as amazing was Jackson Hospital, which could care for 6,000 patients in similar ways. Elsewhere than Richmond, general hospitals were neither so large nor so grand, but there were many of which the Confederates were proud. By late 1864 there was a total of 154 hospitals, most located close to the southern Atlantic coast. They began to close down, often because of enemy action, early in 1865.

Washington and its environs was the natural hospital center of the Union Army because of its proximity to major battlefields. This proved unfortunate because the city had always been considered a sickly place, chiefly because of the large open canal that stretched across town and into which much sewage was dumped. Also, the metropolitan community had many standing pools in which anopheles mosquitoes bred. The intestinal disease and malarial rate of the hospitals were a natural result.

At the end of 1861 Washington had only 2,000 general hospital beds. The great slaughters of the Peninsular campaign, with the Second Battle of Bull Run immediately after, followed shortly by Antietam, flooded the hospitals of the Washington area and Baltimore and Philadelphia as well. Adaptation went so far as converting the halls of the Pension Office, with cots among the exhibitions, the Georgetown jail, and the House and Senate in the Capitol. From August 31 to the end of 1862, 56,050 cases were treated in Washington. Many of these adaptations were closed in 1863, replaced by modern pavilion hospitals. At the end of 1864 the city contained sixteen hospitals, many of them large and fine. There were seven at nearby Alexandria and one each at Georgetown and Point Lookout, Maryland. Outstanding was Harewood, said to resemble an English nobleman's estate, with professionally landscaped grounds, flower gardens, and a large vegetable garden. Its building consisted of fifteen large pavilions with appropriate service buildings and some tents.

The Western showpiece was Jefferson Hospital at Jeffersonville, Indiana, just across the river from Louisville. Built in the winter of 1863-64 with 2,000 beds, later increased to 2,600, at war's end it had plans for 5,000 beds. Its most interesting architectural feature was a circular corridor 2,000 feet long from which projected twenty-four pavilions, each 175 feet long.

By the last year of the war there were 204 Union general hospitals with beds for 136,894 patients. This proved to be the maximum. In February 1865 the United States began closing down its hospitals.

The many men and women, North and South, who served in the hospital and sanitary services during the war were justly proud of their achievements. The morbidity and mortality rates of both armies showed marked improvement over those of other nineteenth-century wars, particularly America's last conflict, the war with Mexico. In that war 90 percent of the deaths were from nonbattle causes. In contrast, in the Civil War some 600,000 soldiers died, but in the Union Army 30.5 percent of them died in or from battle, and in the Confederate Army the percentage ran to 36.4. Clearly, the physicians and sanitarians had held down the disease mortalities to levels that their generation considered more than reasonable. Better, they made some few halting strides in treatment and medication, and considerable leaps in the organization of dealing with masses of wounded and ailing soldiers. It was a ghastly business for doctors and patients alike; yet without the medicos in blue and gray, much of the young manhood of America at midcentury might not have survived for the work of rebuilding.

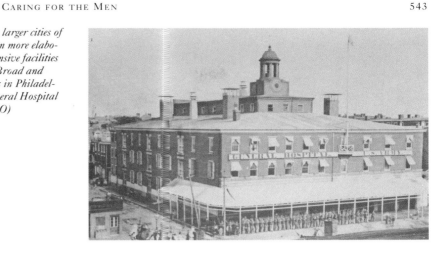

Right: In the larger cities of the North even more elaborate and extensive facilities emerged. At Broad and Cherry streets in Philadelphia this General Hospital appeared. (LO)

Left: In the military posts and forts of New York, hospitals for invalids and convalescents were organized, such as the Fort Schuyler Hospital, shown here on July 27, 1864. (USAMHI)

Right: Alexandria, Virginia, near Washington, burgeoned with such infirmaries. This handsome Italianate house on Wolf Street became a general hospital. (USAMHI)

Below: Washington itself was ringed with hospitals. Harewood Hospital, shown here, was one of the largest. (USAMHI)

Below: Lincoln Hospital was a makeshift arrangement of canvas over frame stretchers. (USAMHI)

Above: The large building in the background is, in fact, the block of homes built in the 1850s by Stephen A. Douglas, John C. Breckinridge—now a Confederate general—and Henry M. Rice. It was called Douglas Row before the war and is now the Douglas Hospital, with a nearby tented adjunct. Just after the surrender, General U. S. Grant will come to live for a time in what had been Breckinridge's home. (USAMHI)

Above: Downtown in Washington's Armory Square another hospital occupies a former public building. Next door sits the United States Steam Fire Brigade, its modern equipment on display in the yard and its canvas hoses drying in the sun on the sidewalk at left. (USAMHI)

Above: These three leg amputees posed together after each lost a leg in the fighting in Georgia. (GLADSTONE COLLECTION)

Above: Armory Square was far more open and pleasant, with military insignia on the walls, the word "Excelsior" over one door, and an inspirational poster at the end of the ward. "The true characteristic of a perfect warrior," it reads, "should be fear of God, love of country, respect for the laws, preference of honor to lawlessness, and to life itself." (USAMHI)

Above: Hospital food, then as later, was always the object of derision, and worse when it was army hospital food. The kitchen at Soldiers' Rest, Alexandria, did the best it could, but institutional food has never been the best. (USAMHI)

Above: The mess room at Harewood Hospital. (LC)

Above: Holidays were the best times. Here, in Armory Square General Hospital, soldiers and nurses probably celebrate either July 4 or the end of the war. (LC)

Above: Once the men were released from the general hospitals, there was cause for celebration as well. Many went to the convalescent camps, where there was greater freedom and sufficient medical care available to get them through to full recovery. This one was in Alexandria, Virginia. (USAMHI)

Above: Quartermaster Ansel L. Snow, seated at center, poses with staff and patients at the Alexandria camp. (RP)

Above: The camp provided entertainment for them with a band. (GLADSTONE COLLECTION)

Above: The Women's Central Association of Relief worked out of New York City's Cooper Union in assisting the United States Sanitary Commission. These ladies appear in their association's main office. Not content only to wait, they also served. (MUSEUM OF THE CITY OF NEW YORK)

Right: Avid organizers like Clara Barton raised money to buy and send medical supplies to the front, as well as to minister to the soldiers' spiritual needs. Barton's operation eventually became the American Red Cross some years after the war. (AMERICAN RED CROSS)

Above: Members of the commission like these, including Major General John A. Dix, organized and operated sanitary fairs in the North to raise funds for their mission. (NA)

Above: The Sanitary Commission operated homes for sick soldiers like this one in Washington, their Lodge for Invalid Soldiers. (AMERICAN RED CROSS)

Left: The Sanitary Commission made its headquarters in Washington on F Street, serving both the Army and the Navy. (USAMHI)

Left: The Sanitary Commission placed its agents with all the armies, but chiefly concentrated on the eastern commands. The Reverend Fred N. Knap served as a special field agent, doing pioneer work in caring for the soldier, work that later became the model for some of the functions of the Red Cross. (AMERICAN RED CROSS)

Above: Here is a Sanitary Commission tent at Camp Letterman, Gettysburg, photographed by the Tysons in August 1863. The surgeons, nurses, and humanitarians frequently made common cause to better the condition of the wounded. (USAMHI)

Above: In the more permanently established camps, the commission built, at its own expense, rest homes for recuperating soldiers. Here at Camp Nelson, Kentucky, sits one such Soldiers' Home. This one even boasted of a fountain in the center of its inner courtyard, thanks to the ample reservoir at the top of the hill. (WRHS)

Above: In late 1863 and early 1864 field headquarters for the commission in the East was near Brandy Station. The rather ubiquitous gentleman in the center with the long gray beard appears in many Sanitary Commission photos taken throughout the war, particularly at Camp Letterman. He is a Dr. Winslow, one of the commission's more ardent leaders. (P-M)

Above: In the field near Petersburg, Virginia, in 1864, a Sanitary Commission office somewhere behind the lines. (LC)

Above: Members of the Sanitary Commission with one of their wagons and with their own flag fluttering in the breeze. Members of the commission went to Geneva, Switzerland, in 1864 to explain their work to the International Humanitarian Convention meeting there. When a treaty calling for basic humanitarian care of soldiers in wartime was negotiated, several provisions reflected the work of the United States Sanitary Commission. (AMERICAN RED CROSS)

Left: The Confederacy, too, sprouted innumerable relief associations, but they, as always, suffered terribly from want of supply, as did the Confederate Medical Department. Surgeon General Samuel Preston Moore did as much as could be expected, even introducing a few innovations of his own, but his cause was a losing one, as was the South's. (VM)

Left: The famous Chimborazo Hospital, one of the largest military hospitals, was built by Moore in Richmond. It could hold thousands of wounded at a time and drew its nurses from the cream of Richmond society. But good care and good intentions could not reverse one of the immutable laws of war: Men die. (LC)

Left: And when they died, they faced either a hasty burial or, for those more fortunate, embalming before their bodies were shipped back to their families. Dr. Bunnell boasted that his cadavers were "free from odor or infection." (USAMHI)

Left: Embalmed or not, the fallen dead's last appointment was with the earth, either in the family plot at home or among other comrades, as here at City Point, Virginia. To be sure, Civil War surgery and medicine saved thousands of lives and made considerable advances in treatment. But they were halting advances, made over the rutted and hillocky road of tens of thousands of graves. (NA)

The Camera Craft

A PORTFOLIO

Innovation, invention, and sometimes art,
spill from the lens

Left: Perhaps because so many of the Civil War photographers themselves sprang from the common people, they often showed a peculiarly apt talent for posing and capturing lowly Americans in distinctly informal scenes. Witness this unusual view of an unidentified muster of recruits or militia. Instead of posing on the village green, they stood in the backyard or side lot of a public house. The men themselves are variously dressed, at least two of them in portions of uniforms, and one self-important gentleman sits in an armchair with his best gun and dog beside him. That is how Americans went to war. (GLADSTONE COLLECTION)

Below: The photographers saw something in the melding of men and war machines with the American landscape. A simple Virginia river crossing at Jericho Mills, on the North Anna, attracted Timothy O'Sullivan. (LC,

Below: So did the Merchant's Cotton Mill at Petersburg, Virginia, the tin roof of the house from which the photographer made the scene intruding into the scene and creating a bizarre contrast to the view beyond. (LC)

Left: Some of the images were simply beautiful in every detail. Johnson's Mill at Petersburg. (NA)

Left: A Federal photographer at New Berne, North Carolina—probably J. Dowling—managed to create almost a genre scene out of men and barrels and boxes and a quartermaster's depot. The barrels contain potatoes, the boxes hardtack, or "army bread." A cook's helper displays fresh bread out a window. (USAMHI)

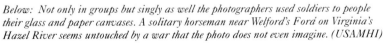

Below: Not only in groups but singly as well the photographers used soldiers to people their glass and paper canvases. A solitary horseman near Welford's Ford on Virginia's Hazel River seems untouched by a war that the photo does not even imagine. (USAMHI)

Below: Soldiers fishing on the Potomac, with the Georgetown aqueduct in the distance and a ferry passing by, offered a compelling scene of peace and calm. (NLM)

Left: Repose offered the most eloquent subject for the lens, and the Civil War soldiers gave the cameramen ample opportunity to catch them at rest. A photographer found these Federals lounging by a pontoon bridge at Deep Bottom on the James River in 1864. (NA)

Below: Lieutenant Thompson at Chattanooga. Nothing seems unnatural. Even the chair and wooden tub seem to grow out of the ground. (KA)

Above: A fading yet still evocative image of one of O'Sullivan's assistants in homespun, lying in a field of wild flowers beside the track of the Orange & Alexandria Railroad. The locomotive fits the scene, the almost pastoral view interrupted only by the jagged earthworks that have spoiled the hillside beyond. (USAMHI)

Right: A sergeant of the 22d New York State Militia sat on a gun carriage, and a Brady assistant at Harpers Ferry found it irresistible. (USAMHI)

Left: A Henry P. Moore view on the Elliott plantation at Hilton Head arranged lights and darks into a vivid portrait of freed blacks in front of the former slave quarters. The moss-laden tree at right almost weeps. (USAMHI)

Left: The living and the dead at Blandford Church near Petersburg, Virginia. (USAMHI)

Left: The onetime scenes of carnage often provided a chance for a special view. George Barnard and James Gibson worked together to capture the ruins of the stone bridge that once crossed Bull Run on the Manassas battlefield. The textures and contrasts give ample evidence of the far from primitive effects possible with the camera of the 1860s and the imaginative eye of the photographer. (USAMHI)

Right: Timothy O'Sullivan's view of Quarles Mill on the North Anna. Almost unseen is the single nude soldier, crouching on a rock at the edge of the stream. (USAMHI)

Right: A magnificent patchwork of patterns made up the outer wall of Fort Sumter in 1865, when George N. Barnard took his camera to Charleston. The regular rhythm of the bricks, interrupted by the latticework of the earth-filled gabions—all drop down to a random system of flagstone at the base. Barnard's work was always superb. (LC)

Above: Even in the more conventional modes of photography the artists experimented. The simple portrait underwent great changes. Lieutenant Colonel O. H. Hart, adjutant of the Federal III Corps, stood with his mount at Brandy Station, Virginia, in February 1864 to offer a lensman a striking pose. (USAMHI)

Above: Generals of course, loved to pose, and none more so than the self-important George B. McClellan. He smiled for the camera… (USAMHI)

Below: … struck a pensive mood… (USAMHI)

Below: … and even offered his back in a decidedly experimental pose. (MJM)

Above: In group portraiture, too, the
artists experimented. Here stand men of
Company B of the 6th New York National Guard, taken in 1863. Yet it is not
a group photograph. Rather, several
smaller group images have been blended
together onto a painted background to
present an almost surreal scene. (STAN-
LEY LEVITT)

Above: If photographer B. Shunk can be believed, he even managed to make this 1863 image
of Harpers Ferry by moonlight. The scene, however, appears too well lit for a night view, unless Shunk exposed his plate for a very long time indeed. (USAMHI)

Above: The innovation took a backseat to grandeur, however, whenever the armies and their photographers came to a place where the landscape demanded undivided attention. Nowhere in the country did the vista command more awe than at Chattanooga. The city fell to the Federals for good in late 1863, but the cameramen became its permanent captors. Lookout Mountain beckoned to them and would not be denied. Here on its summit, above the clouds of mist that often filled the Lookout and Tennessee valleys, the cameras recorded scenes of magnificent scope and beauty. (USAMHI)

Above: R. M. Linn, who established his Gallery Point Lookout on the mountain crest, became a practiced artist in recording the grandeur of the valley, the river, and Chattanooga. (KA)

Left: Thousands came to stand at the precipice, the Tennessee River snaking across the land hundreds of feet below. (NA)

Below: The brilliant George N. Barnard came to Chattanooga to record its scenic environs. Lookout Mountain intrigued him, yet he sought more than mere views from its heights. He found greater scenes in lesser places. (USAMHI)

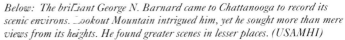

Above: There were tiny ponds and waterfalls everywhere. (USAMHI)

Above: Nearby scenes like Estill Springs, Tennessee... (USAMHI)

Below: Perhaps most lovely was Lu-La Lake. "The waters of this Indian mirror are as pure and clear as possible," Barnard said. The same could be said for his magnificent photograph of the lake. (USAMHI)

Below: The Civil War photographer may have been at his best, however, when he caught a still-life scene such as these vessels on the wharf at Alexandria, Virginia. The image has a peaceful morning air to it, as though the dawn mists have not yet cleared. (USAMHI)

Above: Here is a wedding of images of Fort Carroll, near Giesboro Point in the District of Columbia. A magnificent panorama of the cavalry stables in winter, it offers the look of a country genre painting in still life. Pickets, wheels, branches, and the long stable buildings standing against the snow present a remarkable portrait. The two separate views are here jointed together and published for the first time. (WRHS)

Left: Nothing so moved the cameraman as the solitary sentry on his lonely vigil. This Union enlisted man seems more shadow than substance, more a hole in the winter picture than a part of it. Rarely in the history of war photography has a cameraman achieved a more eloquent image. Like so many of the thousands of views made during the Civil War, the timeless quality and lasting impact of scenes like this attest to the craftsmanship of the photographers of the blue and the gray. (NA)

War on Horseback

DEE BROWN

The dashing dash to "jine the cavalry"

Above: "Boots and saddles." "To horse and away." The eternal lure of the horse-mounted soldier, the dash and romance of it all, captured the imagination of Americans at war, North and South, as no other image. "Draw sabers," this erect bugler blows, his own blade beginning to leave its scabbard. There are gallant charges to come, and more than enough glory for all. (ROBERT MCDONALD)

IN A WAR with so much horror, on the field and in the hospitals, there was a desperate need for romance, for glamour. The cavalry was the glamour arm—handsome young men in flowing motion on graceful steeds, embellished with colorful costumes of capes, jackets, plumed hats, knee boots, and fancy spurs. At least it was that way in the beginning. Also in the early weeks of the Civil War, the cavalry on both sides was compact, slow-moving, heavily accoutred, usually operating with the infantry. Experience brought striking changes, first in the Confederate cavalry, considerably later in the Union. After a few battles in conjunction with the infantry, the horse soldiers began cutting loose from their bases to destroy enemy communications and supplies. They burned bridges and stores, ripped out telegraph lines, and raided far behind the lines in attempts to keep the enemy so busy that he could apply only a part of his potential when battle was joined.

Before the war, professional cavalrymen maintained that two years were required to produce a seasoned trooper, a precept that proved to be more applicable to the North than to the South. For the first two years of conflict the exploits of Jeb Stuart and John Mosby in the East and the daring raids of Nathan Bedford Forrest and John Hunt Morgan in the West far outshone their Union opposites.

One reason given for the early superiority of Confederate cavalry was that in the South the lack of good highways had forced Southerners to travel by horseback from boyhood, while in the North a generation had been riding in wheeled vehicles. Although there may have been some truth in this, rural young men in the North were also horsemen by necessity, but unlike many of the Southern beaux sabreurs, they had to bear the tedious burden of caring for their animals after plowing behind them all day. Young Northerners who knew horses seemed to have little desire to assume the responsibility of taking them to war, and instead joined the infantry. In the South also, long before the war, young men organized themselves into mounted militia companies, often with romantic names. Although these may have been more social than military, the men learned how to drill, ride daringly, and charge with the saber.

Southern cavalry horses were also superior to Northern horses, largely because of the Southern penchant for racing. Almost every Southern town had its track, and the sport developed a superior stock of blooded fleet-footed animals. In the North, muscular and slow-moving draft horses were the preferred breeds.

At the war's beginning there were only six regiments of United States cavalry, dragoons and mounted riflemen, and a considerable number of their officers resigned to serve with the Confederacy. In the opinion of the United States Army's commanding general, Winfield Scott, improvements in weapons had outmoded cavalry. He was inclined, therefore, to limit the number of cavalry regiments for prosecution of the war, and when Lincoln made his first call for volunteers, only one additional regiment of cavalry was authorized.

After George McClellan took command of the Union Army late in August 1861, the policy was quickly reversed. McClellan named George Stoneman chief of cavalry, and by year's end eighty two Union volunteer cavalry regiments were in the process of enrollment and outfitting. Most of them were short of proper weapons, trained riders, and good mounts.

One might suppose that McClellan, who wrote the Army's cavalry regulations and developed a saddle that was standard equipment for half a century, would have handled his horsed soldiers with dash and imagination. Instead, he attached them to infantry divisions, scattering them throughout the Army where they were too often misused by assignment to escort and messenger service. Not until the summer of 1863, when a vast cavalry depot was established at Giesboro Point, did the Union Army have the horse power to challenge the Confederacy's mounted units. Located within the District of Columbia across the eastern branch of the Potomac (Anacostia River), Giesboro was the energy source for the great Union cavalry operations of the last two years of war.

Until that time, however, Confederate cavalry was dominant—a dashing, disruptive, and disconcerting force that kept many a Union commander off balance during the early months of war. In the first major battle, at Bull Run on July 21, 1861, the pattern for Southern cavalry leaders was set by James Ewell Brown "Jeb" Stuart. During the early afternoon of that day, as General Irvin McDowell's advancing Union Army was being brought to a halt by General Thomas Jackson "standing like a stone wall," Stuart led his 1st Virginia Cavalry into the fight. When a column of New York Zouaves tried to stop the Virginians, Stuart sent his Black Horse troop charging in with flashing sabers and rattling carbines. Stuart's horsemen may not have changed the outcome that day, but they certainly added to the terror of the fleeing soldiers in blue.

A West Point graduate in 1854 and a six-year veteran of Indian fighting on the western frontier, Jeb Stuart at twenty-eight was the right man in the right place to create the perfect image of romantic cavalier. He was handsome, he was daring, and he dressed the part—wide-brimmed hat worn at an angle and decorated with an ostrich feather and a gold star, a flowing cape, scarlet-lined jacket, yellow sash around his waist, long gauntlets, golden spurs, and a rose always in his buttonhole.

Two months after Bull Run, Stuart was a brigadier general with five more regiments under his command, and he soon added a battery of

Above: Massed with sabers drawn on the wide parade field, their officers mounted on white chargers in the distance, a Federal cavalry regiment presents all the spectacle of a mode of warfare that was already almost outdated by the 1860s. Here the 13th New York is on inspection at Prospect Hill, Virginia, in July 1865. (LC)

Above: Yet, contrary to its romantic image, the Civil War cavalry was, like every other branch of the service in this very organized war, more organization and administration than dash and glamour. Massive cavalry depots like this one at Camp Stoneman, Giesboro Point, outside Washington, were necessary to house and train the mounts for the armies. (USAMHI)

Below: Indeed, so great was the demand for animals to pass through this mammoth depot that unscrupulous speculators soon did a thriving business in selling spavined and blind horses to the government. (USAMHI)

Below: One of the finest images available showing a Union cavalry training camp. This is Camp Hunter, on the Illinois River, near Ottawa. It was made in the fall of 1861 and shows the 4th Illinois Cavalry in training. The regiment's horses are lined up along the rows of tents, while the men are standing in formation in the distance. It is a rare cavalry outfit that three years from now will be able to boast of a plush encampment like this. (KEN BAUMANN)

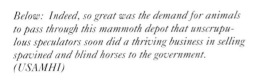

Above: And in the end organization paid off here at Giesboro and throughout the Union mounted war effort. (KA)

Above: It took hundreds of warehouses bulging with supplies and thousands of men like these, soldiers and civilians, to keep the system running. Here is the mess house at one of the government stables in Washington at war's end. (USAMHI)

Right: Mountains of fodder and grass passed through the Army of the Potomac's hay department to keep the animals fed. (NA)

horse artillery commanded by John Pelham. After a winter of relative inactivity by both armies, Stuart's cavalry brigade left Manassas Junction to join in the defense of Richmond, which was threatened by McClellan's growing forces on the Virginia peninsula. Events moved rapidly for the Confederates that spring, with former cavalryman Robert E. Lee replacing the wounded Joe Johnston as commander of the armies in northern Virginia.

Early in June 1862, Lee sent Stuart on a reconnaissance mission that turned into a spectacular ride around the entire invading army of McClellan. With 1,200 of his finest horsemen, Stuart reached the South Anna River on the first day, then turned to the southeast along the Federal flank. After two small skirmishes Stuart made a daring decision to circle the rear of McClellan's army. To cross the Chickahominy, his men had to rebuild a bridge before they could start their return along McClellan's left flank. All the while they were busily capturing and burning supply trains, wrecking railroads, and destroying communications. Ironically, Stuart's opposite cavalry commander in McClellan's army was his father-in-law, Philip St. George Cooke, and at one point the two men were in firing distance of each other. On June 14 Stuart transferred command to Fitzhugh Lee and dashed on ahead to Richmond to inform his commander of weaknesses in McClellan's defenses. Using this information, General Lee ordered Stonewall Jackson to attack the Union Army's rear and flank, as part of the Seven Days Battles, after which McClellan abandoned his long-planned assault on Richmond and withdrew to Harrison's Landing on the James River.

In the West, meanwhile, an entirely different breed of Confederate cavalry leader was attracting much attention. When the war began, Nathan Bedford Forrest, a forty-year-old cotton planter and livestock trader, enlisted as a private at Memphis, Tennessee. In a matter of days his superiors authorized Forrest to raise a battalion of cavalry, and by August 1861 he was in command of several companies of volunteers, many of whom he armed and mounted with his own resources. In a way, Forrest was as theatrical in appearance as Stuart— tall, lithe, finely cut features, swarthy complexion, iron-gray hair, and piercing eyes. Although he lacked the cultured background and military training of Stuart, he was not the illiterate country bumpkin he was sometimes depicted, and his language was the common usage of most West-

Below: Fortifications like Fort Carroll had to be built just to guard all the accumulated matériel that supported the cavalry. Long gone were the days when a few hotspurs leaped upon their horses and that was the cavalry. (USAMHI)

Below: When not on the march, the horsemen lived and looked much like any other soldiers. Their camps, like this one of the 2d Massachusetts Cavalry at Vienna, Virginia, in 1864 sat lightly fortified by felled trees and branches, with only the long, crude stable buildings betraying the fact that horsemen lived here. (USAMHI)

Right: The officers stayed in their little winterized tents near the top of the hill, while the enlisted men shared the larger tents between the stables, man and horse often living in uncomfortable proximity. (USAMHI)

erners of his time. As for his military prowess, Sherman called him "that devil Forrest," and Grant considered him "about the ablest general in the South."

In November 1861 Forrest was raiding as far north as Kentucky. In February 1862 he was at Fort Donelson when the Confederate commanders there decided to surrender to Grant, but instead of surrendering with them, Forrest galloped his men out in a flight to Nashville. In the general retreat from that city, Forrest's cavalry formed a protective rear guard. By early summer he was raiding northward again, capturing Murfreesboro, Tennessee, and its Federal garrison. On October 20 he suffered one of his rare repulses in a skirmish along the Gallatin Pike near Nashville, but later that year he was cutting Grant's communications and harassing his supply lines in western Tennessee.

Also in 1862 another Southern cavalryman began operations in the West. John Hunt Morgan was the cavalier type, a product of the Kentucky Bluegrass, soft-spoken, handsome, a devotee of horses and racing. Long before the war he organized a fashionable militia company, the Lexington Rifles, and around this company late in 1861 he organized the famed 2d Kentucky Cavalry Regiment. Among his recruits was an accomplished telegrapher, George Ellsworth, whose intercepted and faked telegrams became a specialty of Morgan's many cavalry raids. After the fall of Fort Donelson, the Kentuckians withdrew to a Tennessee base, using it for frequent strikes into their home state.

Morgan chose July 4, 1862, to start his first Kentucky raid in force, riding a thousand miles in three weeks, skirmishing, capturing supplies, and recruiting men and horses. Three months later he returned to Kentucky again, this time with Braxton Bragg's army, easily capturing his hometown of Lexington and its Union garrison. Morgan never forgave Bragg for retreating after the Battle of Perryville and abandoning Kentucky to the Federals. On December 21 Morgan left his winter base in Tennessee for a Christmas raid, his most significant accomplishment being the destruction of a vital railroad bridge at Muldraugh's Hill, Kentucky, an act that halted shipments of supplies to Union forces to the south.

While Bragg's army was retreating from Kentucky, another rising Confederate cavalryman, Joe Wheeler, began appearing in official dispatches. Wheeler was only five feet four and in his mid-twenties, but he was a West Pointer. Although he lacked the color and elan of his rivals, Wheeler soon won the nickname "Fighting Joe" and the rank of major general.

Back in the East late in 1862, Jeb Stuart led about 1,800 of his horsemen in a wild three day dash north into Pennsylvania, wrecking railroads and seizing horses and military equipment. On his return he completed another circuit of McClellan's army, which was still positioned along the upper Potomac after the Battle of Antietam.

During that battle a Union cavalry leader provided some evidence of the forthcoming power of

Above: The 3d Pennsylvania Cavalry built its own small village at the headquarters of the Army of the Potamac in the winter of 1864–65. (USAMHI)

Above: And the elegant 13th New York did even better at Prospect Hill. (USAMHI)

Left: They could even boast of rapid communications thanks to their signal station. It was the look of permanence about some of these perennial camp soldiers that often led the weary and cynical infantryman to wonder if anyone "ever saw a dead cavalryman." (USAMHI)

Above: The horsemen often relaxed in some pleasant grove near headquarters, in this case General Alfred Pleasonton's headquarters at Castle Murray, near Auburn, Virginia, in November 1863. (USAMHI)

Above: The headquarters life had the air of home about it, of permanence in a world that was rapidly changing. Officers of the 1st Brigade Horse Artillery at Brandy Station, Virginia, in February 1863. (USAMHI)

Left: Cavalrymen and their constant companions, horse artillerymen, enjoyed the occasional comforts and stimulants of the brigade sutler, in this case the enterprising A. Foulke, who kept himself well fortified in his log store. (USAMHI)

Northern cavalry. He was Alfred Pleasonton, late of the 2d Dragoons, who at the outbreak of war had traveled by horseback from Utah to Washington to offer his services to the Union. Soon he would be in command of a reorganized Federal cavalry corps.

Then came springtime of 1863, midpoint of the Civil War, the year of fullest flowering for the soldiers on horseback, the year of maturation for Union cavalry. By this time both sides had found through experience what weapons and accoutrements best suited them, the methods of fighting that were most successful. The Southerners learned to travel light and live off the country; indeed, the Confederate Congress authorized ranger units that were encouraged to roam independently, raiding Union bases and supply trains for loot to sustain themselves. In northern Virginia, John S. Mosby was the most notable of the ranger leaders. In the West, M. Jeff Thompson was typical of the irregulars who fought in the border states. Thompson sometimes moved his troops on horseback, sometimes in dugout canoes.

Although most cavalrymen favored sabers at the beginning of the war, their use declined in favor of the carbine and the pistol. Records show that fewer than a thousand saber wounds were treated in Federal hospitals during four years of combat. Cavalry commanders also quickly learned to use their horses for swift mobility rather than for direct attacks, bringing their men close to the enemy and dismounting them for combat, with one man in each set of four acting as horse holder.

By 1863 several models of breech-loading carbines were available in quantity for Federal cavalrymen, although opinions differed as to the qualities of the different models. With the new Blakeslee cartridge box known as the Quickloader, a trooper could fire a dozen aimed shots a minute. Yet there were many Southerners, such as Basil Duke of Morgan's cavalry, who were arguing until long after the war in favor of their old-fashioned Enfields and Springfields, which they claimed were more accurate and of longer range than the newer Spencer or Sharp's carbines.

Among the extraordinary feats of cavalrymen on both sides during 1863 was Forrest's interception and capture of Colonel Abel Streight's entire regiment, John Morgan's great raid across the Ohio River into Indiana and Ohio, and Stuart's controversial raid just before Gettysburg, when he inflicted considerable damage upon his enemy but failed to inform Lee of his actions. On the Federal side, in the West Benjamin Grierson, a former music teacher, demonstrated that Yankee cavalry could raid as daringly and as deep behind the lines as Confederates. In a seventeen-day march through the heart of Mississippi, Grierson also demonstrated the value of cavalry in attacking vital supply lines and in drawing off enemy forces from the main battle area, in his case Vicksburg.

Soon after Major General Joseph Hooker took command of the Army of the Potomac early in 1863, he consolidated his forty cavalry regiments into three divisions. For the first time the Union Army had a mobile strike force that could out-

Above: The officers often imported their comforts. Here Major Granger of the 7th Michigan Cavalry entertains friends and family at his quarters. (KARL ROMMEL)

Above: Brigade and regimental bands often took the boredom out of the long fall afternoons at camp. Here at Auburn, Virginia, in October 1863, General Pleasonton sits in the center of the group at left, with Brigadier General Judson Kilpatrick to his immediate right. (LC)

Above: The horsemen brought their own fiddles to liven the camps, as did these cavalrymen in Georgia. (MISSOURI HISTORICAL SOCIETY)

number the Confederates. A new breed of young, aggressive leaders was also coming to the fore with the cavalry corps—notably Hugh Judson Kilpatrick, John Buford, and George Custer.

A preview of what was in store for the free roaming Confederate horsemen occurred on March 17 when Brigadier General William W. Averell challenged Fitzhugh Lee's Confederate brigade at Kelly's Ford on the Rappahannock. What formerly would have been an easy skirmish for the Virginia horsemen turned into a fierce engagement. Averell's men retired from the field, but not until they inflicted double the casualties they received. Among the dead was the Confederate hero of Fredericksburg, "the gallant John Pelham."

The real test came at Brandy Station on June 9. As customary, Jeb Stuart's cavalry was to serve as a screen for Lee's army, which was preparing to invade the North, a march that would culminate in the Battle of Gettysburg. The Confederate cavalry was at its peak, five brigades led by such tested veterans as William E. "Grumble" Jones, Fitzhugh Lee, William H. "Rooney" Lee, and a rising brigadier from South Carolina, Wade Hampton. While waiting for General Lee to move out of Culpeper, Stuart decided to put on a grand review. The various squadrons performed at their glittering best before an audience of beautiful women, various civilian and military officials, as well as a number of distant watchers from Alfred Pleasonton's Union cavalry corps.

General Hooker's balloon observers had reported unusual activity along the Rappahannock, and Pleasonton was ordered to investigate. Among his officers were Buford, Kilpatrick, David McMurtrie Gregg, Alfred Duffie, and George Custer, who was then a captain.

After a careful reconnaissance, Pleasonton decided to attack Stuart by crossing one column at Beverly Ford and another at Kelly's Ford. In numbers the opponents were about equal, 10,000 horse men in blue and 10,000 in gray. The lead units of blue columns crossed the Rappahannock at four o'clock in the morning and caught most of

Right: Farther to the south the picture was the same, only hotter. Men like these Federal cavalrymen at Baton Rouge, Louisiana, built extensive makeshift awnings to protect them from the merciless sun. An A. D. Lytle photograph. (LSU)

Right: Exercise at parade
and mounting often served
only to make a hot day in the
Deep South steamier yet. The
weather put more cavalry-
men out of action than did
bullets and sabers. This Lytle
image, as well as other photographs, have long been erroneously identified as being
taken for the Confederate secret service; but in fact no evidence exists to support the
claim, and the photos have
no real military intelligence
value at all. They show only
the seemingly endless round of
toil and boredom. (LSU)

Above: Two Federal officers, Lieutenants Wright and
Ford, languish before their tent at Westover Landing,
Virginia, in August 1862, obviously in the warm part
of the summer, as evidenced by the fans and the mosquito netting over the cot. But they are still fully dressed
in their heavy woolen uniforms for the camera. (LC)

Right: More sensible was Lieutenant Colonel S. W.
Owen of the 3d Pennsylvania. At Westover Landing in
August 1862 he ignored the camera and opted for a
bottle and a na p. (USAMHI)

Right: Everyone posed, like
these Ohio cavalrymen with
their uncomfortable civilian
friend. (JAMES C.
FRASCA)

the Confederate camps by surprise. Some Confederates hastily retreated, some formed defense
lines, some charged their attackers half-dressed
and riding bareback. At Fleetwood, just east of
Brandy Station, Stuart was finally able to concentrate his forces, and it was here that the greatest
cavalry battle of the war was fought. By this time,
delays and communication failures had collapsed
command organization on both sides so that regiments, battalions, squadrons, and individuals
charged and countercharged in clouds of smoke
and dust. As this was cavalry against cavalry at
close quarters, many a long-unused saber came
into play. After three hours of combat, both sides
were completely exhausted, and many men were
unhorsed from the wild fighting. With the arrival
of Confederate infantry, the Union regiments
began withdrawing across the Rappahannock. Estimates vary as to the number of casualties, but it
is safe to say that about 500 men on each side were
out of combat at the end of the battle.

Brandy Station was not only the greatest cavalry battle of the war; it was the turning point for
Federal cavalry. "Up to that time confessedly inferior to the Southern horsemen, they gained on
this day that confidence in themselves and in their
commanders which enabled them to contest so
fiercely the subsequent battlefields." The man
who said that was not a Union cavalryman but one
of Jeb Stuart's own adjutants.

Succeeding events were portentous for Confederate horsemen. In July John Morgan's raiders
disintegrated during their flight across Ohio; on
the twenty-sixth Morgan was captured and imprisoned. In September, after Bedford Forrest
clashed with General Bragg over the conduct of
the Battle of Chickamauga, he was ordered to turn
his troopers over to General Wheeler. In official
disgrace, but still a hero in the Western Confederacy, Forrest returned to Mississippi to recruit a
new mounted command. But the Southern cavalrymen could not yet be counted out. John
Mosby's rangers were very much in action in
northern Virginia. Joe Wheeler made a daring circuit of General William Rosecrans's Army of the
Cumberland, and in October Stuart gave Kilpatrick and Custer a good scare at Buckland Mills.

As springtime of 1864 approached, with the
war seemingly sunk into stalemate, Union cavalry
leaders planned a daring raid into Richmond. It

Above: And like the entire resplendent 7th New York Cavalry, with Brigadier General I. N. Palmer standing third from the left in front of them. (WRHS)

was a three-pronged affair, with Kilpatrick leading one column, Custer leading a diversionary attack on Stuart's camp near Charlottesville, and twenty one-year-old Ulric Dahlgren (who had lost a leg at Gettysburg) supporting Kilpatrick with a third force. Because of bad timing, the main assault failed. Dahlgren lost his life, Kilpatrick retreated with considerable losses, and only Custer came off well by surprising Stuart's winter bivouac and destroying supplies and capturing horses.

In March Lincoln brought U. S. Grant east to command all Union armies. In early April Grant exiled Pleasonton to the West after informing Lincoln that he was bringing "the very best man in the army" to head the Union cavalry. He was Philip Henry Sheridan, and his arrival signaled the end for Confederate cavalry power in Virginia.

A further blow to the Confederacy's mounted forces occurred on May 11 when Sheridan brought 10,000 of his troopers within a few miles of Richmond, threatening the capital and destroying large quantities of Lee's already dwindling supplies. In an effort to save Richmond, Jeb Stuart attacked with his 4,500 horsemen. A charge led by Custer drove the Confederates back, and while rallying his men, Stuart was mortally wounded.

In the West, however, the indomitable Forrest with his new command continued an unceasing harassment of the Federals. He led a month-long expedition through Tennessee and Kentucky, capturing Union City, Tennessee, on March 24. On April 12 he captured Fort Pillow, Tennessee, an action that is still controversial, some charging that his men massacred black and white soldiers after they surrendered. At Brice's Cross Roads, Mississippi, on June 10, outnumbered more than two to one, Forrest defeated General Samuel Sturgis and sent the Federal column in a panic retreat to Memphis. In August Forrest came close to capturing the Union commanders in Memphis with a daring Sunday morning raid that caught them by surprise. "Old Bedford" closed out the year by assembling a navy of sorts. After capturing two gun boats and two transports, he combined the naval

Right: Even foreigners were caught by the romanticism of the cavalryman. A Frenchman, Louis Rillier de Cansdourt, "jined the cavalry" and served much of the war at the Cavalry Depot in St. Louis, Missouri. It all made for a grand pose. (CHRIS NELSON)

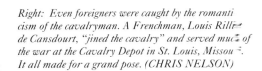

Above: Some of those who sat for the cameras were undeniably cavaliers, the last of an age-old tradition of gallantry ahorse. None filled the role better than General James Ewell Brown ("Jeb") Stuart—bold, fearless, dashing, the peerless Southern cavalier. (VM)

Right: Stuart lost not only a battle at Kelly's Ford but irreplaceable people like the dashing young horse artilleryman Major John Pelham, the "gallant." The whole army sorrowed at the boy captain's death, and it marked the end of Stuart's undisputed preeminence. (VM)

Above: It was Stuart who established the tradition of Confederate invincibility in the mounted arm— until he met up with Brigadier General William W. Averell, shown here as a colonel at Kelly's Ford . (RP)

Above: With Pleasonton, mounted at right, in the fight was a young captain and aide, George A. Custer, mounted here at left, a dandy frequently more resplendent than his commander. He would be heard from in this war. (USAMHI)

Above: B. H. Gault of Company H, 8th Pennsylvania Cavalry, seems all hat and gloves in a uniform distinctly more tailored than the average horse soldier's garb. (CHRIS NELSON)

Above: Men like this lancer, who followed Rush, finally officially managed to lay down their lances in 1863. It gave them a step up from the Middle Ages. (DALE S. SNAIR)

Above: But nothing could take away the cavalier spirit of the horseman, not even defeat at Brandy Station. Men like the giant Heros Von Borke, a Prussian who came to ride with Stuart for the adventure of it, could still find it all a lark. (VM)

Left: Not long thereafter the horsemen of blue and gray met yet again in the greatest cavalry battle of the war. Commanding the cavalry of the Army of the Potomac was General Pleasonton, seated here at center and surrounded by his staff at Warrenton, Virginia, a few months later. (USAMHI)

armament with his shore artillery and shelled everything in sight along the Tennessee River.

Confederate cavalrymen seemed to have a talent for attacking gunboats from their saddles. During Fighting Joe Wheeler's January raid in 1863, his cavalrymen captured a gunboat and three transports on the Cumberland River. On June 24, 1864, Brigadier General Jo Shelby and his audacious Missourians fought three United States steamers on the White River in Arkansas, capturing and destroying the USS *Queen city.*

In the late autumn of that year Shelby joined Major General Sterling Price's expedition into Missouri, the final futile effort to recover that state for the Confederacy. At Westport they felt the sting of Federal cavalry led by none other than the recently deposed commander from Virginia, Alfred Pleasonton. When Price ordered a withdrawal, Pleasonton pursued, but after two heavy engagements the Union commander pulled his troopers away, allowing the beaten Confederates to escape.

Pleasonton's replacement in Virginia, the long armed and short-legged Phil Sheridan, most likely would have shattered Price's cavalry. In the Shenandoah Valley he and Custer were racking up victories and devastating the Eastern Confederacy's breadbasket. On October 19 Sheridan made his famous twenty-mile ride from Winchester to turn the tide of battle against Jubal Early's infantry at Cedar Creek.

By this time other Federal cavalrymen had driven deep into the South. George Stoneman and James H. Wilson were operating in northern Georgia, and Judson Kilpatrick joined Sherman for the march from Atlanta to the sea. Kilpatrick tangled twice with Joe Wheeler's decimated command, but he had so little trouble on the march that he grew careless of security. In South Carolina, March 9, 1865, Wade Hampton's troopers almost captured him in bed, and he was forced to flee without his trousers.

In the meantime, John Morgan had been killed on September 4, 1864, in Tennessee, and on December 13 Stoneman defeated the remnants of his old command. Many units of the once superbly mounted Southern cavalrymen were now reduced to fighting on foot. Wade Hampton and Joe Wheeler were no match for Kilpatrick's powerful cavalry in the Battle of Bentonville in mid-March, 1865. On March 29 Fitzhugh Lee was beginning his last stand in the Appomattox campaign. On April 7 Bedford Forrest fought his last skirmish with Wilson's cavalry in Alabama.

And then on April 8, when the battered survivors of Lee's cavalry units prepared for one final charge near Appomattox, they found themselves facing a solid mass of blue-clad infantrymen, 24,000 strong. The long war practically ended there, and significantly it was a horse soldier in blue who dashed forward under a truce flag to demand immediate and unconditional surrender. The demand was not granted. George Custer had to wait for his commander, General Grant, who on the following day accepted it from General Lee.

Above: Facing Stuart in the summer of 1863 was Brigadier General George Stoneman, here seated at right with members of his staff and with General H. M. Naglee sitting next to him. Though a good officer, Stoneman was replaced by Pleasonton in time for Gettysburg. (P-M)

Above: At Gettysburg it was a cavalryman who brought on the opening of the battle and first realized that this was a good place for the Federals to meet Lee. Brigadier General John Buford, shown here as a captain in 1861, held the line long enough for Meade to begin sending his legions forward. (USAMHI)

Above: Brigadier General Beverly H. Robertson was there, one of the few Confederate cavalrymen with Lee, since Stuart was off on an inconsequential raid that cost Lee dearly. (LC)

Left: And the fighting continued, as did the dying. Just one day after Yellow Tavern, Brigadier General James B. Gordon took a mortal wound while battling Sheridan. These Confederate cavalry generals placed themselves in the thick of the fighting and all too often paid for bravery with death. (USAMHI)

Above: They met their match in the ruthless, relentless Sheridan. When he came to Virginia in the spring of 1864, fresh from victories in the West, he brought bulldog determination and a jugular instinct. He also captained a host of very competent subordinates. Henry E. Davies sits at left, David M. Gregg next to him, with James H. Wilson and Alfred T. A. Torbert on the ground looking at a map while Sheridan gazes past them. Behind Sheridan sits the youthful yet most talented Wesley Merritt, just beginning one of the most distinguished military careers in the army's history. (LC)

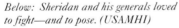

Below: Sheridan and his generals loved to fight—and to pose. (USAMHI)

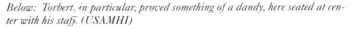

Below: Torbert, in particular, proved something of a dandy, here seated at center with his staff. (USAMHI)

Below: Meanwhile, east of the Blue Ridge Stuart was replaced by another dashing giant, General Wade Hampton of South Carolina, a cavalier who, in a firefight at Gettysburg, declined to shoot at a Yankee cavalryman until the opponent had unjammed his rifle and was able to return fire. (NYHS)

Below: Fighting with Hampton were men who had gone through a lot by the time 1865 approached. General Matthew C. Butler lost a foot at Brandy Station yet stayed with the cavalry to lead one of Hampton's divisions. In 1898, in the war with Spain, he took a commission as a major general in the United States Army and traded his gray for blue. (USAMHI)

Below: Of course, there were two cavalry wars, just as there were two of the other armies, eastern and western. The men who rode in the Deep South and the West were often of a different stripe, leaner, harder, more pragmatic. To be sure, there were the beaux sabreurs like General Pierce Manning Butler Young. A major general at twenty-eight, he led cavalry that resisted Sherman's 1865 advance through the Carolinas. (USAMHI)

Above: One of Wheeler's more competent subordinates was Major General John A. Wharton of Texas. The combativeness of these hotbloods outlived the war all too often. Indeed, on April 6, 1865, while the Confederacy was still gasping for survival, Wharton slapped a colonel in the face during an argument, and the colonel promptly killed him. (USAMHI)

Above: More temperate was Colonel Charles C. Crews, a Georgian who fought with Wheeler right to the end of the war, later claiming that he had been made a general. (USAMHI)

Above: These Confederates in the West and Deep South faced Federals of equal fiber and dash, none more so than Colonel John T. Wilder of the 17th Indiana Cavalry. His regiment carried Spencer repeating carbines, and on June 24, 1863, at Hoover's Gap, Tennessee, they did deadly work against Confederates armed with single-shot weapons. (ELI LILLY AND COMPANY)

Right: Lieutenant General Stephen D. Lee, one of the few Lees not related to Robert E. Lee, commanded Confederate cavalry in Mississippi and Alabama in 1863 and 1864. Already a veteran of Bull Run, Antietam, and Vicksburg, he was still just thirty years old. All the horsemen were young. (LC)

Above: Men of the 5th Ohio Cavalry, who rode across the South with Sherman in 1864, hard men, men of the West. (RP)

Right: General Frank Armstrong was certainly young, a brigadier at twenty-seven and one of Lee and Wheeler's most trusted subordinates. (CM)

Left: In large part because of their youth and impetuosity, these Rebel riders thought to do things not done before by cavalry. For one thing, they stalked and attacked ships! On June 24, 1864, two Confederate cavalry regiments attacked the USS Queen City in the White River, off Clarendon, Arkansas, disabled her paddle wheel, forced her to surrender, and then blew her to bits. (USAMHI)

Left: Another Yankee ship, the Silver Cloud, exacted a measure of revenge in Tennessee by helping drive away from Fort Pillow another daring Rebel raider... (LC)

Above: ... Lieutenant General Nathan Bedford Forrest, perhaps the most storied Confederate cavalryman of them all, and probably the best. (TU)

Above: For a time Forrest and his men had the good fortune to face distinctly inferior Yankee commanders, among them Samuel D. Sturgis, shown here with his family. At Brice's Cross Roads, Mississippi, Forrest gave him such a decisive defeat that Sturgis was virtually shelved for the balance of the war. (NYHS)

Above: In time, however, good leaders came to face Forrest and Wheeler, among them the boy general James Wilson, a favorite of Grant's. Sherman made him his chief of cavalry, and eventually he led 17,000 troopers. In 1865 he finally overwhelmed Forrest and led a triumphant raid through the Deep South, in the process capturing Jefferson Davis. (USAMHI)

Right: Meanwhile, in the East Sheridan and his generals, including Wesley Merritt at left, George Crook in the center, and James W. Forsyth standing between Crook and Custer, laid waste the Shenandoah and then helped Grant trap Lee. (LC)

Below: On April 1, 1865, at Five Forks Lee's cavalry let him down. General Thomas L. Rosser held a fish bake, not expecting any activity that day. (MRS. THOMAS R. COCHRAN, JR.)

Below: Robert E. Lee's son, Major General W.H.F. Lee, the youngest man of that rank in the army, led his cavalry creditably in the fighting but could not withstand Sheridan's might. (USAMHI)

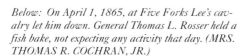

Below: In attendance were, among others, Lee's nephew General Fitzhugh Lee. (USAMHI)

Left: At Five Forks and beyond, well-trained and well-supplied units like the 1st United States Cavalry were simply irresistible. Bravery alone could no longer withstand superior might and equal dash. (USAMHI)

Below: Though for some a little glory still remained even after Appomattox, and for others even stranger fates. General George A. Custer, to whom Sheridan gave much of the credit for cornering Lee and his army. He had just eleven years to live. (USAMHI)

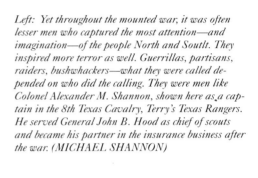

Left: Yet throughout the mounted war, it was often lesser men who captured the most attention—and imagination—of the people North and South. They inspired more terror as well. Guerrillas, partisans, raiders, bushwhackers—what they were called depended on who did the calling. They were men like Colonel Alexander M. Shannon, shown here as a captain in the 8th Texas Cavalry, Terry's Texas Rangers. He served General John B. Hood as chief of scouts and became his partner in the insurance business after the war. (MICHAEL SHANNON)

Right: The scout Dr. Hale on the left and "Tinker Dan" Beatty on the right. These Union guerrillas, like men of both sides, often operated under assumed names. They seemed to gravitate toward colorful sobriquets. (USAMHI)

Left: And they gravitated toward destruction. The Confederate raiders particularly left their mark behind Yankee lines. Here they have taken up rails on the Orange & Alexandria Railroad near Bristoe Station, Virginia, then bent them in the heat of fires from their own ties. A Timothy O'Sullivan image. (LC)

Above: In Virginia, raids like this were as often as not the work of the 43d Battalion of Virginia Cavalry, led by their dashing commander, John Singleton Mosby, standing second from the left among his officers. These partisan rangers were men of daring. (MARYLAND HISTORICAL SOCIETY)

Above: Indeed, led by Mosby, shown here as a lieutenant colonel in 1864, the partisans so dominated a four-county region in northeastern Virginia that it came to be called Mosby's Confederacy. (USAMHI)

Right: In West Virginia the mounted raiders virtually ruled the countryside. Federal outposts like this one at New Creek, West Virginia, could not stop them. (CHS)

Right: All the Yankees could do was to hinder the guerrillas whenever possible, which was not often. For there were other talented men besides Mosby riding against them. Captain Harry Gilmor led a small but effective, and sometimes unruly, command. He will be relieved in 1864 for a time when his men stop a train and rob the civilian passengers. (USAMHI)

Far right: Men of higher rank, and more regular service, occasionally proved to be effective raiders, none more so than Brigadier General John D. Imboden. In 1863 and 1864 his raiding helped materially in protecting the Shenandoah and visiting damage upon the enemy at places like… (USAMHI)

Above: … Charles Town, West Virginia. Here Imboden attacked a Yankee outpost. The Federals barricaded themselves in the courthouse, the same building where old John Brown went to trial. They knocked loopholes in the walls to fire from, but Imboden captured them just the same, leaving the building in near ruin. (LO)

Above: Captain John H. McNeill was even more effective in western Virginia. Until his death in a skirmish, he raided continually, his most dashing exploit being the capture of… (USAMHI)

Far left: … Brigadier General Benjamin F. Kelley and… (USAMHI)

Middle left: … Brigadier General George Crook at Cumberland, Maryland, on February 21, 1865. McNeill stole into town in Union uniform and woke the sleeping generals. (KA)

Left: Albert G. Jenkins lost his life at Cloyd's Mountain, Virginia, in 1864, but not before achieving an enviable reputation as a cavalry raider, on one occasion riding five hundred miles into western Virginia and on into Ohio. As part of Lee's vanguard, in 1863 he occupied and held for several hours Mechanicsburg, Pennsylvania, the northernmost Union town officially captured and occupied by Confederate forces. (USAMHI)

Far left: A host of lesser-known Confederates, men like Colonel John S. Green of the 6th Virginia Cavalry, followed Jenkins, Imboden, and "Grumble" Jones and the other raiders. (WRHS)

Left: And following them were raw and rugged men like this one, armed with an 1855 pistol carbine, two pistols, and the set jaw of determination. (RP)

Right: The Yankees, too, had their raiders, though few were as effective as their opponents. General Hugh Judson Kilpatrick was one, shown here standing in the center, with his staff and his wife on the left, at Stevensburg, Virginia, in March 1864. Just which side suffered more damage from him is debatable. His own men came to call him "Kill-cavalry" for the way he wore them down and wasted them and their horses. Sherman called him a "hell of a damned fool." (US-AMHI)

Below: Kilpatrick, with Colonel Ulric Dahlgren, the son of Admiral John Dahlgren, led a controversial raid on Richmond that failed but did some damage. Kilpatrick raided and destroyed this mill on the James River and Kanawha Canal. (LC)

Right: Another somewhat successful Yankee raider was Brigadier General August V. Kautz. He participated in the capture of John Hunt Morgan and his command in 1863, and the next year joined James H. Wilson in the celebrated but only partially successful ride behind Lee's lines at Petersburg, Virginia, a ride that nearly saw both of them captured. (USAMHI)

Below: It was here in Baton Rouge that the most famous of all Union raiders, Colonel Benjamin Grierson, found safety after a daring ride and hairbreadth escape. During Grant's final campaign on Vicksburg, Grierson provided diversion leading his command south through Mississippi and Louisiana. A. D. Lytle's photograph. (LSU)

Below: Federal cavalrymen like Brigadier General Albert Lee, seated at left, oversaw sporadic raiding into the enemy interior from bases in Baton Rouge and New Orleans as the war went on. (LSU)

Above: And when they did not raid, they sat out the hot, humid summer days at their landscaped and well-appointed quarters. (LSU)

Above: These western raiders were colorful men, men with names like "Doc Rayburn." Captain Howel A. Rayburn led his small command of raiders in the desperate border warfare in Arkansas and Missouri. His opponents called him and his men banditti. (CONFEDERATE CALENDAR WORKS)

Left: But of all Confederate raiders surely the most dashing and the most notorious must be Brigadier General John Hunt Morgan. His raids into Kentucky and the North electrified the Union high command and made him a hero in the South. (VM)

Left: Yet, like all partisans, Morgan could get out of control, and his men, so accustomed to destruction and plunder, could go too far. They did at Mount Sterling, Kentucky, in June 1864. They captured the Federal garrison that had been bivouacked here around the courthouse… (USAMHI)

Below: … and then destroyed the building and robbed the local bank. Morgan never gave a satisfactory explanation, and died just a few months later. (CHS)

Above: Perhaps the best of Morgan's men—and, in fact, a better overall commander than Morgan himself, was the dashing Basil W. Duke. He took over at Morgan's death and after the war proved to be one of the premier writers about the Confederate partisan service. (CWTI)

Above: The damage these Rebel raiders could do was considerable, as here at Johnsonville, Tennessee. (LC)

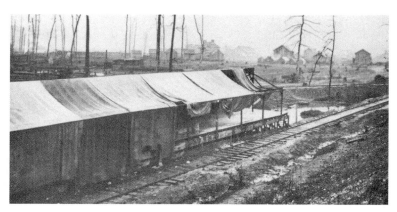

Above: Supply depots like Johnsonville were favorite targets of the partisans, for they could inflict maximum damage without encountering large bodies of enemy soldiers. (LC)

Above: And they liked railroad bridges. They burned nicely and took a long time to rebuild. This one, spanning the Holston River at Strawberry Plains, Tennessee, was destroyed four times by Rebel raiders. (LC)

Above: In eastern Tennessee especially, railroad bridges as a matter of course began to take on the look of makeshift. Here is the bridge across Platt Creek, twelve miles above Knoxville. (LC)

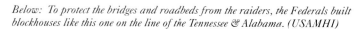

Below: To protect the bridges and roadbeds from the raiders, the Federals built blockhouses like this one on the line of the Tennessee & Alabama. (USAMHI)

Below: To combat the guerrilla depredations in Tennessee and elsewhere, in 1864 Brigadier General Alvan C. Gillem, seated center, took the field. He finally managed to kill Morgan... (USAMHI)

Above: ... but the Union could never stop the work of the raiders. Throughout the war-torn country scenes of road gangs repairing damaged track, like this one after a raid near Murfreesboro, Tennessee, remained commonplace. The work of the Union and the Confederate cavalries went on until the end. (LC)

Above: They rode with sabers drawn. Shown here is Private William Harding, 5th Ohio Cavalry. (ROBERT MCDONALD)

Left: And some with servants to hold their horses. Here is Major Granger of the 7th Michigan. (KARL ROMMEL)

Above: Pistols in their belts. (ROBERT MCDONALD)

Above: Young... (RP)

Above: ... and fiercely determined... (RP)

Above: ... they rode forward, toward the enemy and glory. (ROBERT MCDONALD)

The Sailor's Life

HAROLD D. LANGLEY

The routine, boredom, and sometime adventure of webfoot Reb and Yank

Above: At the mate's call, hundreds of sailors rush to their posts aboard massive steam frigates like this one. Decks crowded, the crews at their guns, a marine detachment standing at attention in their white crossbelts, another of Lincoln's warships is ready to meet the enemy. (WAR MEMORIAL MUSEUM OF VIRGINIA)

CAVALRYMEN were not the only warriors who went into battle as passengers, though they were far more plentiful than their "webfoot" counterparts. Throughout the Civil War the navies of both the North and the South suffered from a shortage of manpower. On both sides the demands of the armies were so persistent that there were never enough sailors, especially experienced men, to complete the crews of all the ships in service. This proved particularly true in the South, where the pool of available seamen was very small under the best of circumstances. Stephen Mallory, the Secretary of the Navy, got the Confederate Congress to pass a law in 1863 whereby any man serving in the army who volunteered for the navy was to be transferred. Mallory claimed that hundreds of men volunteered, but that their military commanders would not release them. In the North, trained seamen were diverted into the army by enlistment bonuses, by local competition to fill regiments, by a desire to try something different, and by the draft. Sometimes it became necessary in both the North and the South to divert soldiers into naval duty. Usually the soldiers were not too pleased by the assignment. Some became disciplinary problems or deserted, but a number adjusted to the demands of the war and gave a good account of themselves.

One part of the Confederate Navy, at least, had no difficulty in attracting men: the ships *Alabama*, *Florida*, *Shenandoah*, and other famous commerce raiders. The commanders of such ships completed their manpower needs by drawing on the crews of the vessels they captured. The Confederates paid high wages and in gold. Those factors and the prospect of being a prisoner made a crucial difference. But the result was that a high percentage of the crews of these famous ships were foreigners.

In the South a young man wishing to join the navy had to have the consent of his parent or guardian if he was under twenty-one years of age. His counterpart in the North needed parental consent if he was under eighteen. No one under the age of thirteen was to be enlisted in the North, or under fourteen in the South. Height requirements for the Union Navy were at least five feet eight inches; those for the Confederacy were four feet eight inches. At the other end of the spectrum, no inexperienced man was to be enlisted in the Union Navy if he was over thirty-three years of age unless he had a trade. If he had a trade, thirty-eight was the age limit. In the South an inexperienced man with a trade could join if he was between twenty five and thirty-five. Inexperienced men without trades were shipped as landsmen or coal heavers. Free blacks could enlist in the Confederate Navy if they had the special permission of the Navy Department or the local squadron commander. Slaves were enlisted with the consent of their owners, and some of them served as officers' servants as well as coal heavers and pilots. Before the war the United States Navy had tried to restrict the number of black men in the ranks to one-twentieth of the crew. During the Civil War, however, the chronic shortages of men led Secretary of the Navy Gideon Welles to suggest to the commander of the South Atlantic Blockading Squadron that he open recruiting stations ashore for the enlistment of blacks or contrabands. As a result of this and other activities, the Union Navy had a high percentage of blacks in the lower ranks. The normal pay scales in both navies ranged from $12 a month for landsmen and other inexperienced hands to $14 a month for ordinary seamen and $18 a month for seamen. Boys were rated as third, second, or first class in ascending order according to their knowledge and physical ability. Third-class boys were paid $7 a month, second class $8, and first class $9.

In both the North and the South it was customary to send the newly recruited men to a receiving ship. These were usually old frigates or other sail-powered ships that were stationed at navy yards in the North and functioned as floating dormitories. In the South old merchant ships were used at Richmond and at other major Southern ports. A recruit arriving on board a receiving ship reported to the officer of the deck. His name and other details went into the ship's books, and he was sent forward. Usually he received only the clothing needed for immediate service. In the North no civilian clothing was allowed, though shortages of uniforms later in the war sometimes made it necessary to modify this rule in the South. When the recruit arrived at the forward part of the receiving ship, he was given a number for his hammock and another for his clothes bag and was assigned to a mess.

While on board a receiving ship the recruit learned the rudiments of navy life. He learned how to address and to respect his officers, petty officers, and shipmates. Much time was spent in various kinds of drills, such as learning to handle sails, rigging, boats, and cutlasses, as well as the procedures for repelling boarders. The manpower demands of the Union and the Confederate navies meant that the amount of time a recruit was on a receiving ship ranged from a few days to a few weeks. Anything not learned on the receiving ship had to be learned in the hard school of active service. Periodically the commander of the receiving ship would receive orders to send a certain number of men to a vessel preparing for active service,

Above: "All hands on deck!" Or perhaps it is another call that the mate blows on his whistlelike pipe. Whatever it is, the Civil War sailor—like his mates in the armies—can look forward to another day of work and play, tedium and excitement. It is the lot of the webfoot men of blue and gray. (LC)

Below: They will answer to the officer of the deck, his speaking trumpet ready to bark orders that send sails flying or steam puffing from the stack. (USAMHI)

Left: It was mostly work in the duty hours aboard ship. Supplies had to be brought aboard in small boats, decks washed, and the ship's sides painted, as evidenced by the lighter patch near the bow of this warship anchored off Baton Rouge. An A. D. Lytle photograph. (LSU)

Below: The steam vessels, great and small, had to take aboard coal to fill their bunkers. Here the monitor Canonicus *is coaling in the James River in the summer of 1864. (USAMHI)*

Above: The engines needed maintenance. The image shows the works of a smaller steam vessel, its engine from the Morgan Iron Works, built in 1861 and sporting steam gauges from the Cosmopolitan Company. It all gleams, even the oiling cans in the brass basket at right. (WRHS)

Right: The engines came from many makers, this one manufactured by the Allaire Works, but basically they looked and operated the same. This one, aboard the steamer Fulton, *also gleams, the signal bell overhead polished and reflecting the light from the hatchway. It was hot work for the seamen trapped below deck with the puffing monsters. (USAMHI)*

Right: Yet there was hot work above as well, and none more tiring than the endless gun drill, particularly endless for a crew that could not meet the time set by its captain or hit its marks. Whether aboard smaller ships like the little USS Hunchback … *(USAMHI)*

or as replacements for a ship that had lost men through death, illness, or desertion.

Once a man reported to a ship in the regular service, he was assigned to various stations at the guns, on deck, in the tops, in a boat, at a mess, and in a hammock. Each had a number to be remembered. So, on a man-of-war, a given recruit or veteran might define his niche in the following way: He belonged to the starboard watch, was stationed in the top of the mizzenmast; he belonged to the third division of the battery, attached to gun number eight, where he was the first loader. In the event of a need to board an enemy vessel, he was the second boarder in his division. When it was necessary to loose or to furl sails, his post was at the starboard yardarm of the mizzen topgallant yard. In reefing sails his position was on the port yardarm of the mizzen topsail yard. When tacking or wearing the ship, his place was at the lee main brace. If the anchor was being raised, his duty was at the capstan. In a boat he pulled the bow oar of the captain's gig. Until all these assignments became second nature to him, the recruit might forget his numbers and have to refresh his memory by consulting the station bill, where everyone's position was recorded.

On gunboats and monitors all the duties associated with masts, rigging, and yards were eliminated, of course. These ships were also much smaller than a steam frigate or some of the merchant vessels converted to warships. But on these smaller ships there were still quarters, guns, and decks to be kept clean, and there were still watches to be kept. On all coal-burning vessels it was a constant problem to keep the ship and the guns clean. The actual work of coaling a ship left black dust everywhere. About the time that the dust was under control, it was time to recoal.

Any man with experience in the merchant service found life on a warship quite different, at least at times. In the merchant service, for example, when raising the anchor, the men at the capstan might sing a sea chantey. In the Navy this and other tasks were performed in silence lest some order from an officer not be heard. Loud talking by the men while on watch was frowned upon for the same reason. In warships of both the Union and the Confederacy, the shipboard routines were performed to the sound of shouted orders, boatswain's pipes, or a drum, depending on the situation covered.

Joining the crew of a warship was apt to be quite a memorable experience for the recruit. Here he found himself among a wide variety of men. There were some older, weatherbeaten types who had been at sea for many years. In contrast to these were the young men of seventeen, eighteen, or younger, away from home for the first time. There were foreigners, including some not many months removed from their old environments in Europe. There were black men, including many who had recently left the slave status. Also caught up in such groups was an occasional North American Indian, or a Pacific islander. In a very real sense a man-of-war was the world in miniature, especially on Union ships. Crews of Confederate gunboats and other vessels that defended Southern harbors, inlets, and rivers were apt to be more homogeneous, especially early in the war.

For the Northern recruit particularly, adaptation to the cross section of humanity that comprised the crew was often difficult. Their early

Right: … or on bigger ones like the Mendota, *the routine was much the same. Only the size of the guns differed. When the men worked the guns on these ships, they wore swords and pistols at their belts. This massive pivot gun is ready to fire. The crew is standing clear, men are ready to haul on the ropes that will pull it back forward after its recoil, and the sailor directly behind the gun carriage holds one hand aloft to signal clear while with the other he grasps the lanyard that will fire the piece. More shot for the next round lie waiting in the shot rack. (USAMHI)*

weeks and months in the Navy might be marked by personality clashes, accusations and counteraccusations, and fights. Marines and officers had the duty of stopping any affrays. The man who struck the first blow might find himself confined to the brig, in irons and on a diet of bread and water for twenty-four hours, as a warning not to persist in such conduct. A man who was wronged by another soon learned to settle his score indirectly rather than by fighting. His tormentor might find the rope of his hammock cut while he was asleep, or have a belaying pin dropped on his toes, or become the victim of other "accidents."

In the Union and the Confederate navies it was the specific duty of the commanding officer to see to it that ordinary seamen, landsmen, and boys were instructed in steering, in heaving the lead to determine the depth of the water, in knotting and splicing ropes, in rowing, in the use of the palm and needle to do sewing, and in bending and reefing sails. Mastery of these duties was necessary if the recruit hoped to qualify for promotion to seaman or to become a petty officer. Coal heavers with any intelligence at all could master the requirements necessary to become a fireman. In addition, the men were continually drilled in exercising the guns, in handling small arms and boats, and in using the boat howitzer. Anything not learned on the receiving ship was thoroughly learned on a ship in regular service. In the Confederacy, whenever the needs of war made it necessary to transfer from one ship to another, the men had to have additional training because no two ships had engines or guns that were exactly the same.

Left: The scene is the same aboard the USS Miami. *The gun crew are armed with .36 caliber Navy pistols and cutlasses. A seaman stands ready to swab out the bore with a brush soaked in water from the bucket. Two other seamen and a marine hold the great long wrenches that will help reset the gun after firing. Another man holds the elevating screw at the breech, and the man at far left holds the lanyard. Everyone is ready to defend that flag. (NHC)*

Left: The routine was the same on the monitors, both inside the turret and with the deck guns outside. They loaded and stood ready … (NA)

Below: … and stood ready and stood clear to fire. Shown here are men of the Lehigh. *(USAMHI)*

Left: Besides the gun practice, a thousand daily chores kept the sailors busy in the long months of blockade and cruising duty. On the gun deck of the USS New Hampshire *barrels are rebound, blocks taken down and refitted, and endless miles of cables spliced, trimmed, and repaired. (P-M)*

In both navies the daily routine was somewhat the same, depending on the size of the ship, the preferences of the captain, the season of the year, and the needs of the moment. Sailors might begin their day as early as 4 A.M. if the ship had to be thoroughly cleaned or was scheduled to be coaled in the morning. Otherwise, a typical day might have gone as follows:

At 5 A.M. the marine bugler sounded reveille. The master-at-arms, or one of his corporals, and the boatswain's mate from the current watch ran around the berth deck shouting at the sleeping men and slapping hammocks. The men were ordered to get up and to lash up their hammocks and bedding into a tight, round bundle. These were then carried up to the spar, or upper, deck. Here the hammocks were stored uniformly behind heavy rope nets, called nettings, along the bulwarks. Storing the hammocks here gave some small additional protection from gunshots and from wood splinters dislodged by cannon fire. The nettings also provided a barrier against boarders. In theory, a well-trained crew was supposed to rise, lash their hammocks, and deliver them to the spar deck in seven minutes. In practice, it may have taken that long to get some men out of their hammocks.

About 5:07 A.M. the crew got out sand, brooms, holystones, and buckets and washed down the decks. Usually the berth deck was scrubbed with saltwater, and the spar deck was holystoned by teams of men working under the direction of a boatswain's mate. In addition to the decks, the brass fittings and other bright work were polished. Metal tracks on which the gun carriages turned were burnished. The guns themselves were cleaned. On ships that carried sails, the rigging, halyards (ropes for hoisting yards or sails), and blocks were checked and maintained as necessary. Once the ship was cleaned, the sailors might fill the buckets with saltwater to wash themselves and to shave, if they so desired.

In a man-of-war, boys assembled at the port gangway at 7:30 A.M. for inspection by the master at-arms. The boys were expected to have clean faces and hands, hair combed, and clothes clean and tidy. Their pants were supposed to be rolled up. After the inspection, each boy was expected to climb to the top of the masthead and come down. Each boy did his best to get up and down first. Sometimes the last boy down had to climb up and down again. The theory behind this routine was that it made the boys agile and gave them a good appetite for breakfast.

At 8 A.M. the boatswain piped breakfast. Cleaning equipment was put away and buckets were returned to their racks. Each man reported to his respective mess, which consisted of from eight to fourteen men. Members of a gun crew, coal heavers and firemen, and topmen would have their own messes, often determined by the watch to which they belonged. Marines and petty officers messed separately, and the boys were distributed among the messes. Each member of the mess took his turn as the orderly or cook, though

Above: There was iron to replace and repair. Ships like the monitor Saugus *carried portable forges, complete with bellows, to turn white-hot iron into ship's parts. Photographer Egbert G. Fowx's trunk of chemicals and makeshift darkroom are visible in the background. (USAMHI)*

Right: Cooks and stewards like these aboard the Fulton *earned their share of obloquy for the wares they produced, trying to turn salt pork, beef, and hard peas with weevils into fit meals. (USAMHI)*

Above: And someone had to watch the ship's accounts. That was the purser. Often regarded as dishonest, and almost always thought a bore, the poor purser stood in low repute. When Herman Melville shipped aboard a United States man-of-war in the 1840s, he found that the ship's purser was only useful in a conversation "by occasional allusions to the rule of three." Purser Mc-Manus of the Fulton. *(USAMHI)*

Above: Of course, the men had to be paid, and that called for the paymaster, this one shown aboard the New Hampshire. *(USAMHI)*

Above: The quartermaster of the New Hampshire. *His lot was the navigation of the ship. (P-M)*

sometimes one person would be hired by his messmates to do the job on a permanent basis. It was the job of the orderly to unlock the mess chest and take out the tableware and cooking utensils, as well as the food allotted to the mess each week by the ship's cook or by the paymaster. The individual kept track of his own knife, fork, spoon, and mug. For breakfast each man was served one pint of coffee without milk, as well as a piece of salt junk, or hard, salted beef. After breakfast the dishes were cleaned and returned to the mess chest.

Then, at 9:30 A.M. came the call to quarters. Guns were inspected to see that they were properly secured and ready for any emergency throughout the day. Once this was done, the men relaxed at their stations by writing letters, reading newspapers or books, or dozing.

Noon was the fixed time for lunch, so at that hour the men reported to their messes. Now they had a piece of beef or pork, vegetables, and coffee. Cheese might enhance the meal from time to time. On blockade duty there were opportunities to acquire fresh provisions from the shore areas, and these broke the monotony of the average meal served at sea.

The crews of the Confederate cruisers usually ate well as a result of their captures of merchant vessels, but for the rest of the Confederate Navy, items like cheese, butter, and raisins, while technically a part of the ration, were never available. Tea and coffee could be obtained from blockade runners, but at a great cost. Even so, the Confederate Navy usually ate better than the Army. One and one-quarter pounds of salted beef, pork, or bacon was issued to each man every day. As late as

Above: Constant vigilance was the business of everyone, on duty or off. Shown here is the lookout station aboard the Vermont *while she stood blockade duty off Charleston. (P-M)*

Below: Of course there were lesser, more personal chores to fill the odd hours. Everyone, from captain to private seaman, had dirty laundry to wash and hang for drying. The USS Sangamon. *(LC)*

Left: There were the quiet moments for the officers, resting against their mammoth guns as they plied the Virginia rivers. Shown here are officers of the Mendota. *One of them has thoughtfully posed a cartridge bag and cutlass on the cannon's screw. (NA)*

1864 the men of the James River Squadron got meat three times a week.

After lunch the men might return to the stations they had left, or portions of the afternoon might be filled by various kinds of drills. Blockade duty proved so monotonous most of the time that commanders had to exercise their ingenuity to keep the men occupied. Training sequences were not the same on any two successive days; thus there was no predicting what would come next on the agenda. As Charles K. Mervine, a boy attached to a blockading squadron ship, wrote in 1863: "The life of a sailor is not one of a real and regular work, his hours of rest may not be uniform but they are more or less regulated. The details of a programe [sic] of any day on shipboard cannot be as fixed as in other forms of labor, yet its original outlines are the same day after day."

At 4 P.M. a light evening meal was served by the various messes. In this and the other meals, the timing was related to the watch sequence of four hours on and four hours off. Mealtimes were when the watch was relieved. From a nutritional point of view, there were objections to this format because in a twenty-four-hour sequence all the meals were crowded into less than eight hours. Since the noon meal was the main meal, men who stood watch at midnight or in the early hours of the morning might be quite hungry.

On blockade duty individual captains could alter the watch routine by splitting the period from 4 P.M. to 8 P.M. into two 2-hour watch segments called dogwatches. This meant that there would be seven watches instead of six in a twenty-four-hour period. If this was done, no watch would have to take the midnight to 4 A.M. shift for two nights in succession. An alternative was to divide the crew into three watches so that each man would be on duty for four hours and off for eight. Still other captains went so far as to use quarter watches, or one-fourth of the working hands, or half of each watch. In this system the watch would be divided into first and second parts, which would constitute the quarter watch. There were, however, those who believed that the use of quarter watches was unwise in dangerous waters.

The watch procedure was also used in coaling the ship. Such work might begin with the port watch and function in a prearranged order. Coaling might begin about 7 A.M. for the Union ships on blockade and be finished by noon, if the crew really worked at it. If they did not, and the work continued into the heat of the afternoon, the process could take as much as twelve hours. Because everything depended upon the time of arrival of the coal ship, there was no consistent time for the operation to begin. If the process began in the late afternoon, it might continue all night.

At 5:30 P.M. the sound of the drum called men to their quarters. Once again guns and stations were inspected to see that everything was ready for the night. This was especially important, for the hours of darkness were the times when the blockade runners were most active. Once the inspection was finished, the boatswain's pipe announced that the hammocks could be removed

Above: A book and the shade of an awning made an afternoon aboard the Hunchback *pass quietly enough. (USAMHI)*

Above: The awninged gun deck of a larger warship kept these officers out of the sun to enjoy their pipes. (USAMHI)

Above: Those fortunate enough to serve aboard passenger steamers pressed into service could enjoy the interior of their ships, such as the saloons like this one aboard the Delaware. *War did not have to be uncomfortable all the time. (WRHS)*

Above: Some, like the fellow at right, even managed to step into their carpet slippers from time to time. (USAMHI)

Above: There were quiet moments for friends to exchange what appear to be cigarettes ... (GLADSTONE COLLECTION)

Above: ... or just to lounge on the deck amid the peaceful paraphernalia of war. (LC)

from the nettings and prepared for sleeping. Then came the period of relaxation for all who were not on watch. The men might write or read letters, or read newspapers and books. At this time and in other free periods during the day they repaired their clothing. Dominoes was a popular pastime. Cards were strictly forbidden. Gambling was also outlawed but went on covertly. It could range from simple games of calling odds and evens, matching money, or bets associated with daily activities, such as how long it would take them to overhaul another ship, to more formal games with dice.

At idle times in the afternoon or evening the men might also listen to music if they were fortunate enough to have a banjo or fiddle player on board. A larger ship might have some semblance of a band. On many vessels minstrel shows or theatricals were staged in the early evening, written and produced by the men themselves. Black crew members performed in minstrel shows along with their white comrades. On ironclads and monitors, of course, space was much more limited, and therefore so was the range of entertainment. In this as in every war, mail from home and from loved ones was looked forward to with great anticipation.

The daily scrubbing the ship received tended to keep the lower decks somewhat damp. This, combined with the daily humidity on the Southern stations, especially in the summer, made for a generally stuffy atmosphere. On monitors and gunboats the heat of the engines warmed the metal plating and the decks. There was also the smell of burning coal and sometimes of sulfur. The men tried to enjoy the fresh air as long as possible before retiring, for during the night the atmosphere on the berth deck sometimes became so oppressive that they had to congregate around the hatches for a breath of air.

Those who wished to smoke went to the forward part of the ship. Cigars and pipes were lit by a taper from a whale oil lamp and carefully extinguished. Hand-rolled cigarettes had been introduced into the United States from Turkey in the late 1850s but did not become popular until many

Left: The sailors, North and South, like the soldiers, turned to music for relaxation, though their songs traditionally ran more to the bawdy than did those of their compatriots in the armies. Minstrels aboard the Wabash, *off Hilton Head. (USAMHI)*

Left: More players aboard the Hunchback, *this time a colored seaman entertaining shipmates. Some smoke, some read, one sailor at left holds a ship's dog, and others peel apples or potatoes. The ship's complement of Negro sailors pose as well, though they stay together and somewhat apart from the rest of the crew. Equality came closer in the navy, but not that close. (NA)*

Right: Yet more minstrels aboard the Wabash, *performing before a painted awning proclaiming their ship and its battles. (NHC)*

Right: The full panoply of sailors at ease. Colored seamen at right patch their worn garments. A game of checkers in the center is played on a fabric board. Acey-deucey, the sailor's backgammon, flourishes elsewhere. And all around is quiet and calm, a peaceful day on the water. If photographs of Confederate sailors were to be found, they would look much the same. (NA)

Below: Of course, the officers could pose on a somewhat higher plane, including perched atop the paddle box. (HENRY DEEKS)

Above: Or in front of the wheelhouse of the USS Philadelphia, *off Charleston. (USAMHI)*

years after the war. Friction matches were strictly forbidden on ships because of the danger of fire, and no uncovered light was allowed in any storeroom or in the hold. Lamps were carefully chosen to avoid any that used explosive oils for fuel.

On some ships it was a common practice to allow time after dinner for general horseplay, tomfoolery, and skylarking as a means of relieving tension. Other captains thought that tension was relieved by scheduled boxing matches in the afternoon. On more sedate ships the hours after dinner were the time for a quiet smoke, for telling or listening to a yarn, or for writing and reading.

Problems relating to the abuse of alcohol were common on all ships and in all ranks. The enlisted man's daily ration of grog, or one gill of whiskey mixed with water, was abolished by act of Congress in September 1862. In the Confederate Navy the enlisted men were entitled to one gill of spirits or a half pint of wine per day. This continued throughout the war, though a man could receive money in lieu of the spirit ration if he chose. Originally this compensation was set at four cents a day, but it rose to twenty cents a day by the final years of the war. The Congress gave the Union sailor an additional five cents a day in lieu of the spirit ration. In both the Union and Confederate navies there were constant efforts to smuggle liquor on board ships, and some of these plans proved successful. Private vessels that sold food to the Union ships on blockade sometimes sold liquor in tins described as oysters or canned meats. Despite such ingenuity, the supply never matched the demand. When a man was discovered drinking or drunk, the usual practice was to place him in irons in the brig. On some ships drunks had saltwater pumped on them until they sobered up.

For the Union ships on blockade duty, tattoo normally sounded at 8 P.M. This was the signal for the men to go to their sleeping quarters and retire. Lights and fires were put out and there was to be no noise. Elsewhere the usual rule was that when the sun set at or after 6 P.M., the tattoo was beaten at 9. When the sun set before 6, tattoo was at 8. For the men of the Union blockading squadrons, going to bed was often accompanied by the latent fear that the ship might be the victim of a torpedo attack before morning. This was especially true after the Confederate submarine *David* succeeded in sinking the U.S. steam frigate *Housatonic*. Sleep might also be interrupted by reports of a blockade runner entering or leaving a harbor. At such times the ship sprang to life as it pursued or overtook a potential prize.

As the control of the Union Navy over the rivers and coastal waters of the Confederacy increased, the opportunities for appropriate Southern countermeasures decreased. Hopes placed in the submarine *David* or the ironclad *Albemarle* as a means of weakening the blockade were soon dashed. Overseas the famous Confederate cruiser *Alabama* went down in a fight with the Union cruiser *Kearsarge* in June 1864. Time was running out for the Confederate Navy.

For the men of the Union Navy the biggest problem was boredom. Despite daily activities of scrubbing, painting, drilling, target practice, entertainments, and the duties directly related to war, time passed slowly. Changing stations, taking on coal and supplies, entering and leaving harbors all added a bit of novelty to a day. But the men eagerly looked forward to short periods of liberty when their ship was at some Union-controlled

Above: Or on the gun deck, or wherever they wanted, for that matter. (DOUGLAS DOUGHTY)

Left: Usually when the photographer came, as here aboard the Lehigh, *the common seamen stood by themselves. (KA)*

port in the South, or was being repaired or overhauled in the North. Any time ashore was an occasion for the pursuit of liquor, women, or both. Men returned from such ventures drunk and often with venereal disease. Fevers and diseases common to the region also took some toll of both Union and Confederate sailors. In battle men could be killed in a horrible fashion by being scalded with steam from shattered engines. Even peaceful steaming on a river could become a hazardous affair when a Confederate sniper opened fire. Shore leave could also be dangerous if a man ventured too far inland or away from Union-held territory. Yet virtually any distraction was a welcome change from the boredom of blockade duty.

Sometimes a man slipped into deep despair over his daily duty. One naval surgeon called this condition land sickness. Those afflicted with it had a terrible urge to smell the earth and to breathe air far removed from the ocean. Sometimes a change of scene and some days ashore solved the problem, but for others the brief change did no good. For such men discouragement and despondency led to real illnesses, and they had to be sent home. It was boredom, and all the other aspects of life in the blockading squadrons, that led a former paymaster's clerk to write that "there was no duty performed during the whole war, in either the land or sea service, that was attended with so much toil, exposure and peril as this duty compelled." All the ship-to-ship fighting put together totaled little more than one week of battle out of four years of war. For the Yankee and Rebel seamen it was indeed a war of watch and wait as they sat imprisoned on their ships.

Above: Sometimes, particularly on the smaller ships, the officers condescended to pose with them, as on the Agawam. *(USAMHI)*

Below: There was time for fun and frolic. The smaller men would crawl inside one of the large bore cannon on the Lehigh, *as in the center, to peer out of the turret. (USAMHI)*

Below: And often the men posed by themselves, like this tired old sea dog next to a 100-pounder Parrott rifle. He looks more like the Ancient Mariner than a sailor aboard the Pawnee. *(CWTI)*

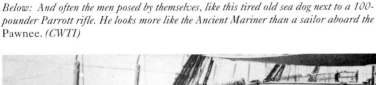

Above: When not relaxing or clowning, almost every man thought of home, of someone he left behind. Sailors, like soldiers, carried photographs of loved ones with them. Lieutenant John McI. Kell of the Alabama carried this image of his wife, Blanche, with him as he and Raphael Semmes terrorized Yankee shipping. Two of the three children would die during the war, and their father would not learn of it until months afterward. There was the hardship that the soldier in the field did not share. Isolated for months at sea, the webfoot was cut off from all news of home and family. It has ever been so in the annals of the sea. (MUNROE D'ANTIGNAC)

Right: Some, like Marine Frank L. Church, managed to find photographers who could work tricks for them. Here Church tickles his own ear with a feather while he poses at sleeping, a remarkably adept trick photograph for the time. (CHURCH FAMILY COLLECTION)

Above: To cheer the homesick, there were excursions ashore. Besides carousing in port, the sailor could take his fowling piece and hunting dogs ashore to bag game, which added a welcome variety to the shipboard menu. Men of the USS Miami. *(USAMHI)*

Above right: Another would-be hunter aboard the Mendota, *and the officer of the deck standing with trumpet ready. (USAMHI)*

Right: In their ship's boats they rowed ashore to hunt, frolic, picnic, or, as here, to visit with the ladies and local civilians. Anything could pass the time. (USAMHI)

Left: And on the Lord's Day they met at ship's service, their souls guarded by men like Chaplain James Gee of the Confederate ship Tacony, the Good Book in hand. (WILLIAM A. ALBAUCH)

Above: Aboard the monitor Passaic off Port Royal, South Carolina, photographer E. W. Sinclair caught the ship's men and officers at divine services. (NA)

Above left: They were young, for the most part, hardy, able, willing, as men of the sea have always been. The boatswain's mate of the New Hampshire. (P-M)

Above middle: Some of them, in a war that brought revolutions in many places, were colored, with the seasoned air of the old salt. (USAMHI)

Above right: Some were no more than boys, boys made men by war. A powder monkey aboard the New Hampshire. (LC)

Left: For all of them, as for these men of the USS Unadilla, life at sea went on from day to day, in and out of danger, marked by their sense of purpose, by their comradeship, and at day's end by the firing of the evening gun. (WRHS)

Prison Pens of Suffering

FRANK L. BYRNE

Simple names like Johnson's Island and Andersonville come to mean hell

Above: All they took with them were the clothes—often rags—on their backs. Two Confederates captured near Norfolk, Virginia, late in 1864. (USAMHI)

OF COURSE, there were prisons in this war far more onerous than the decks of a ship. The prisons of the Civil War in some ways were part of a long tradition and yet, like so much else about the great conflict, they overwhelmed precedents. In previous modern wars, nations had held relatively limited numbers of captives, usually confining enlisted men while putting fewer restrictions on paroled officers. While each war had produced complaints about the mistreatment of prisoners, the duration of their imprisonment had often been shortened by exchange. But in the Civil War, with the Confederacy's independence unrecognized, the two sides found it especially difficult to agree upon terms of exchange, and hence they perforce established long-term prisons. Just as Civil War armies grew beyond the imaginations of antebellum Americans, so the prisons bulged, presenting unexpected problems. The nineteenth-century officials who dealt with them, frequently drawing upon eighteenth century precedents, unwittingly provided a preview of twentieth-century horrors.

The Confederates were first to have to deal with large numbers of prisoners. Even before the firing on Fort Sumter, they had forced the surrender of the United States regulars stationed in Texas, paroling the officers and eventually holding the enlisted men in temporary camps. Following their victory at Bull Run, the Southerners had to provide for over 1,000 prisoners sent back to their capital, which almost by chance became their main prison depot. The officer in charge of the Richmond prisoners was Brigadier General John H. Winder. A West Point graduate, the sixty-one year-old Winder had long served the United States before resigning his commission. He had the respect of President Jefferson Davis, whom he had known of old, and at first he favorably impressed many others among both his friends and foes. But, while he was capable of kindness, especially to those who flattered him, he was also a rigid disciplinarian who became increasingly obsessed with matters of security. At the end of 1861, he became commander of the Confederate capital and quickly antagonized its citizens with his harsh rule. Civilians and prisoners both came to dislike Winder and his staff, dominated heavily by fellow Marylanders and particularly by members of his family.

To house the increasing number of prisoners at Richmond, Winder used several warehouses. One, which became known as Castle Thunder, was used mainly for political prisoners and other Confederate offenders. As in the provost prisons of the North, treatment there was especially stern. In 1862 Winder requisitioned a warehouse occupied by a ship chandlery and grocery company, Libby & Son. While unfurnished, the building did have running water and primitive toilets. Its inmates, being out of the weather, were better off than the men whom Winder encamped in and out of tents on Belle Isle in the James River. But, because the Libby warehouse soon became a facility for officers who wrote a disproportionate share of the accounts of prison life, it became one of the Confederacy's more notorious prisons. Especially well known was the escape through a tunnel of 109 prisoners in 1864. Libby also housed the headquarters of the prisons in Richmond, at which all new prisoners were registered, and therefore most Yankee captives recalled that they had been in "The Libby." Many, however, were soon sent to be imprisoned elsewhere in such diverse ac-

Above: The first step on the long road to imprisonment. Three rawboned Confederates captured in the fighting at Gettysburg await their trip to a Yankee prison. For them the war is over for now, but a greater war, one with boredom and sickness, lies ahead. (USAMHI)

Above: The place was Belle Plain, Virginia, and the Rebels thronged the little valley, clutching their few possessions. (NA)

commodations as a factory in Salisbury, North Carolina, a fort called Castle Pinckney at Charleston, South Carolina, a paper mill in Tuscaloosa, Alabama, and the parish prison at New Orleans. Winder continued to exercise control over prisoners outside Richmond, but without the title that would have put him at the head of a clearly defined prison system.

Meanwhile, the United States government was improvising more systematically. In the fall of 1861 the Federals designated Colonel William H. Hoffman, an officer on parole after the Texas surrender, as commissary general of prisoners. Only a few years younger than Winder, Hoffman also was a graduate of the United States Military Academy and a veteran soldier. In the prewar army, he had learned to manage small garrisons economically and in strict accordance with regulations. Like Winder, he was now faced with the prospect of controlling numbers of men far greater than at any time in his previous experience. If security was Winder's obsession, economy was Hoffman's. Each warden's inmates would suffer in consequence.

Hoffman's initial assignment was to locate and build a central prison. The North, like the South, had begun the war with assorted facilities. Among them was the quondam temporary capitol building in Washington, which, as the Old Capitol Prison, ultimately became the principal jail for political prisoners and other civilians. Also pressed into use were the forts at the Atlantic ports, including McHenry at Baltimore, Delaware below Philadelphia, Lafayette and Columbus at New York, and Warren at Boston. In the West the army took over a former medical college at St. Louis, which became the Gratiot Street Prison. When it overflowed, prisoners began to be kept at the Illinois State Prison at Alton. Hoffman hoped to supersede this hodgepodge with one secure prison.

After inspecting several islands in Lake Erie, Hoffman decided upon Johnson's Island as the site for his prison. A small spot of land in the bay near Sandusky, Ohio, Johnson's Island had the ad-

Above: Standing at intervals along the rim of the prison camp, sentries appear against the sky in this image of the Belle Plain encampment. Most of the prisoners are sleeping under tents for the last time. (USAMHI)

Left: In the early days of the war the next stop for these captured unfortunates was usually a makeshift prison ill-suited for their accommodation. In Richmond and the Confederacy most often that meant a warehouse like this one, soon to be known as Castle Thunder. (USAMHI)

*Right: Castle Thunder was also the
new home of those Southern citizens
deemed "disloyal" or dangerous, for it
has to be remembered that both North
and South faced not only enemies from
without but also from within.
(USAMHI)*

*Above: Many of these ersatz Southern prisons became infamous in their own time, and none more so than the
onetime warehouse and ship chandlery of Libby & Son. This remarkable, previously unpublished image of Libby
Prison was made by Richmond photographer Charles Rees in 1862. Already the windows, now barred, are
jammed with Union prisoners struggling to see what is happening outside. Lined up in front stands the assembled
prison guard. No one will ever overpower them, but the resourceful Yankees will make at least one bold escape by
turning moles. (CHS)*

*Left: Through this door into the so-called fireplace
Federals, led by Colonel Thomas Rose, worked daily
in 1864 to dig a tunnel through the underside of the
building and out under Richmond's Twentieth Street.
In the daring escapade 109 Yankees escaped into the
city streets; 2 of them drowned trying to swim the
James River; and 48 more, including Rose himself,
were recaptured. But 59 made good their escape,
among them Colonel Abel D. Streight. This image was
made years after the war, when Libby was moved as a
war museum to the Chicago World's Columbian Exposition in 1892-93. (CHS)*

vantages of being a mile from the mainland and
free of civilian inhabitants. On it, Hoffman built a
high-fenced camp guarded further by fortifications. For housing he erected one- and two-story
barracks. Prisoners found the resortlike location
pleasant enough in the first summers of the war,
but when winter winds whipped in across the
frozen bay, they shivered, and poets among them
wrote sentimental verses longing for the sunny
South. In 1864 Johnson's Island was the target of
an unsuccessful attempt to free their compatriots
by Confederates based in Canada. Throughout
the war, despite Hoffman's original intent that it
be the main depot for all Rebel prisoners, the island held mostly Confederate officers.

The inadequacy of Hoffman's initial planning
became apparent early in 1862. With the capture
of Fort Donelson, thousands of prisoners fell into
Northern hands. More space was needed for them
than the old veteran had imagined. Hastily he
turned to the camps that had been created to train
Union volunteers. Located at state capitals or in
principal cities, they had good railroad connections, an important consideration in transporting
and feeding the growing horde. Several were on
state fairgrounds with converted prewar buildings;
all had additional barracks and tents. With the addition of board fences and walkways for guards,
the training camps in whole or part became prisons. During the middle of the war, Camp Butler
near Springfield, Illinois, and Camp Randall at
Madison, Wisconsin, were temporarily so used. Of
more lasting significance was Camp Douglas in
Chicago. Undrained, it quickly became so filthy,
according to a Union relief agency, as "to drive a
sanitarian to despair." Yet Quartermaster General
Montgomery C. Meigs rejected as an extrava-
gance Hoffman's proposal to build a sewer. Not
until after the death rate reached 10 percent a
month early in 1863 would Douglas get its drain-
ing. Also important were Camp Morton at Indianapolis and Camp Chase at Columbus. The Ohio
camp also became a major depot for civilian prisoners, especially inhabitants of the border slave
states. In these Northern prisons, as well as in
those of the South, the guards were mostly a random selection of recruits, veterans recuperating
from battle, and home guard units. An exception
was Johnson's Island with a unit expressly recruited for the duty and first known as the Hoffman Battalion, later part of the 128th Ohio.

The buildup of prisoners in the pens of both
belligerents came to a temporary end in July 1862
with the signing of an agreement, or cartel, regulating exchanges. Under it, prisoners were to be
released on parole within days of their capture and
sent across the lines at Aiken's Landing, on the
James River, in the East and Vicksburg in the
West. Hence the prison populations shrank dra-

matically. Soon the South was using mainly Libby and other Richmond buildings to hold the transient prisoners of war and Salisbury for a few hundred civilian captives. In the North, Hoffman was able to concentrate most of his prisoners of war at Johnson's Island, Camp Chase, and Alton. Several former prisons, together with Camp Parole at Annapolis, Maryland, now housed paroled Union soldiers awaiting formal exchange.

For reasons legal and practical, the cartel's operation was soon suspended. The belligerents, after firing off charges of atrocious acts, used threats to withhold prisoners as part of the consequent ritual of retaliation and counterretaliation. The officials who supervised the exchange, Union General Ethan Allen Hitchcock and Confederate Colonel Robert Ould, also quibbled endlessly over the execution of the cartel. Under these pressures the system collapsed, with the regular release of officers ceasing in May 1863 and that of enlisted men two months later. Subsequent attempts to reopen exchange broke down over Ould's refusal to treat as prisoners of war black soldiers who had been slaves in the seceded states. Indeed, Confederate Secretary of War James A. Seddon doubted "whether the exchange of negroes at all for our soldiers will be tolerated. As to the white officers serving with negro troops," he added with ominous import, "we ought never to be inconvenienced with such prisoners." By 1864 the new Union generalissimo, Ulysses S. Grant, added to the legal arguments the contention that it was more humane not to release Confederates who would rejoin their army. "If we commence a system of exchange which liberates all prisoners taken," according to Grant, "we will have to fight on until the whole South is exterminated. If we hold those caught they amount to no more than dead men." Unfortunately for many captives on both sides, Grant's metaphor became literally true as they again accumulated in prisons—this time perhaps for the duration of the war.

Northern and Southern reactions to the challenge of the prisons that were again filling differed significantly. Hoffman immediately supplemented the prisons still open by reactivating the closed camps. He also ordered the building of additional barracks at several of them. By the end of 1863 he had established two entirely new prisons: a fenced group of barracks at Rock Island, Illinois, and a tented camp at Point Lookout, Maryland. The latter, located on a sandy peninsula where the Potomac entered Chesapeake Bay, was convenient to the battlefields in the East and therefore became the largest Union prison, once containing almost 20,000 men. For better control, Hoffman expanded his previous attempts to segregate Confederate officers and enlisted men. Most officers were kept at Johnson's Island or in part of Fort Delaware, while some officers thought to require special security were sent to Fort Warren. The officers of Confederate Raider John Hunt Morgan suffered the special humiliation of being placed in state penitentiaries in Pennsylvania and Ohio—relieved by a spectacular escape from the latter by Morgan and others. In all the Northern prisons, congestion produced problems of feeding, housing, and medical care.

The deterioration of conditions in the South was worse, in part because of a reaction to the problem that was almost a nonresponse. The Confederates hoped that somehow their negotiators could induce the resumption of exchange, which

Above: The rooms in Libby were named by their inhabitants for the battles in which they were captured. Here is the Chickamauga *Room on the first floor. (CHS)*

Above: The Confederates farther to the south took a lot of boys in blue at the first Bull Run fight, and they sent many to Charleston's Castle Pinckney. There was a camaraderie between prisoners and guards here. The guards could lounge in their barracks... (USAMHI)

Above: ... or pose with the prisoners themselves. The Yankees were restricted to the fort's interior parade ground and to casemate dungeons they dubbed Hotel de Zouave and other sobriquets. The guards simply watched them from above. (USAMHI)

Above: At the war's start the Federals, too, went about the prison business in a halting fashion. Colonel, later brigadier general, William Hoffman took the post of commissary general of prisoners and quickly began trying to find accommodations for the Confederates that would fit within the parsimonious budget he set himself. He stands here at right in an image taken in April 1865. (USAMHI)

Above: Early war prisoners he housed in places like Washington's Old Capitol Prison. Once the temporary capitol of the United States, now it housed its enemies, including political prisoners. (USAMHI)

Above: They could peek out through their slatted windows while the prison guard posed below. (AMERICANA IMAGE GALLERY)

Above: And occasionally the camera went inside for an image of a particularly interesting or important tenant, in this case Mrs. Rose O'Neal Greenhow, Confederate spy, here being visited by her daughter. (LC)

would bring back to them the now greater number of Rebels in Yankee hands. They had no wish to provide facilities for the long-term incarceration of their enemies. Therefore, though they confined some of the accumulating prisoners in tobacco warehouses at Danville, Virginia, they allowed most to crowd into the existing Richmond warehouse prisons and into the camp on Belle Isle. Since the Confederate capital was also the center for supplying large armies and a considerable civilian population, a food shortage quickly developed. The Union authorities, receiving reports of hunger among their men in Rebel hands, retaliated in 1864 with reductions in the rations given to Confederates in the North.

Yet shortages and deliberate withholding of rations were not alone responsible for the emaciation and deaths of so many prisoners. Men receiving the full ration of either side might have been less hungry, but they were likely to get sick if they long subsisted exclusively on the bread and meat that were its principal ingredients. Such was the frequent fate of free soldiers when sieges or other circumstances cut off access to vegetables and fruit. Most of the time, prisoners were allowed to buy such supplements from sutlers and others—salvation for many officers but scant help for usually less affluent enlisted men. For the latter in the North, Hoffman authorized buying vegetables with prison funds raised by withholding part of the regular rations. But, with his rigid economy, he tended to order vegetables only after scurvy had actually begun its deadly work. Southerners furnished vegetables even less frequently. As their Union captives sickened, many could no longer digest the rough corn bread. Thus it was less an

Left: Hoffman, like the Confederates, used existing fortresses to house prisoners until he could construct a proper—and cheap—prison. Most infamous of all was Fort Delaware, near Philadelphia. J. L. Gihon took his camera there on July 6, 1864, to capture this unpublished image of several Confederates from Texas, Missouri, Florida, Virginia, Tennessee, and Arkansas. Fort Delaware proved to have one of the highest mortality rates of any Civil War prison. (TERENCE P. O'LEARY)

absolute absence of food than dysentery and diarrhea that killed the bulk of those who died in the South from 1863 to 1865 and turned so many of the survivors into living skeletons.

To relieve the food shortage at Richmond, the Confederates decided to remove most of the prisoners. A further incentive was the Rebels' fear that the prisoners would give aid to any Union attack on Richmond—a fear that impelled them to plant a gunpowder mine under Libby early in 1864 in order to intimidate its officer inmates and keep them from revolting. General Winder sent two relatives to locate and build a prison in southern Georgia. At Andersonville they erected a stockade of timber. Designed originally to hold 10,000 men, it enclosed sixteen acres. At the end of February 1864, even before the fence was finished, rail shipments of prisoners from Richmond began arriving. They found no shelter, and in improvising huts, tents, and burrows they created a disorderly chaos impossible to keep clean. Captain Henry Wirz, the officer nominally in charge of the prison interior, in any event lacked the ability to do much about the worsening conditions. Ill-tempered and profane, ridiculed for his foreign accent, Wirz became the focus of the prisoners' unhappiness and ultimately the target of their hatred. One of his few popular acts was to cooperate with an attempt by prisoners to stop crime, which ended in the trial and public hanging of six prisoners stigmatized as "raiders."

In June 1864, General Winder came to take command of the entire post at Andersonville. Characteristically he centered his attention almost wholly on security rather than on the prisoners' physical condition. He worried not only about an uprising from within the prison but also about the ineffectiveness of the guards and the disloyalty of nearby civilians. In his fear, he even angrily barred local women from bringing vegetables to the scurvy-ridden captives. While prisoners sickened and starved, bartered and robbed, prayed and killed, the Confederates kept watch from the walls of this corral for human beings, occasionally shooting someone who crossed the "deadline." One visitor photographed the grim enclosure. Enlarging it by ten acres did not keep up with the Confederate government's shipments. By late summer almost 33,000 men were in Andersonville; the graves of 13,000 of them memorialized one of the war's greatest horrors.

While a few officers were temporarily at Andersonville, the Confederates moved most of them from Libby to a separate fenced stockade at Macon, Georgia. Not all were able to build shelter, but conditions were generally better than at Andersonville. Prisoners captured farther west were often sent after late 1863 to a former Confederate training camp at Cahaba, Alabama. There a fence enclosed a half-ruined warehouse, which became a depot for enlisted men. It would be less well known than other prisons because so many of its survivors died immediately after release in the explosion of the riverboat *Sultana*. Even more obscure were the several Confederate prison camps beyond the Mississippi. The most important of these was the stockade called Camp Ford at Tyler, Texas. Though isolated and primitive, Camp Ford was healthier than most prisons.

While the South proceeded with the uncoordinated expansion of its prisons, the North continued the more planned enlargement of its system. Besides ordering the construction of new

Above: The fort on Governor's Island, New York, became a prison. (NA)

Above: As did Fort Warren in Boston Harbor. (NYHS)

Above: Indeed, Fort Warren became a favorite spot for a particular kind of prisoner, the blockade runner and the Confederate naval officer. They, in turn, enjoyed a particularly elegant parade ground for their exercise, with Boston in the distance. (NYHS)

barracks at existing posts, Hoffman in 1864 had a fence erected around a camp originally used for Union recruits at Elmira, New York, and early in 1865 he briefly opened a similar facility at Hart's Island, also in the Empire State. The former, used for enlisted men, became the worst Union prison. This was partly because of Hoffman's stress on economy. He and Quartermaster General Meigs repeatedly instructed that barracks be built cheaply. While it was true that Hoffman also ordered flimsy buildings for the Union guards, the Rebel prisoners with their worn clothing, few blankets, and limited fuel suffered more intensely, sickened, and often died. At Elmira, as at Camp Douglas earlier, the Federal authorities were reluctant to spend money to drain the camp. Only after the submission of precise calculations of the gallonage of sewage daily being added to the pond at Elmira did Hoffman belatedly authorize a minor expenditure for materials for a sewer constructed by the prisoners. Besides its pestilential conditions, Elmira suffered from inept administration and several ignorant and brutal surgeons. Unsurprisingly, about a fourth of its some 12,000 prisoners remained in its National Cemetery.

At all Union prisons, a policy of retaliation worsened conditions from mid-1864 to early 1865. Proposing to treat Confederate prisoners as he believed their government treated its captives, Hoffman ordered rations reduced, sutlers' stocks restricted (with sale of food including vegetables often forbidden), and receipt of packages from friends severely limited. The outcome was malnutrition, including more scurvy, and actual hunger. Indeed, at several prisons the inmates organized to hunt and eat rats. In early 1865 the Federal authorities again allowed the sale of extra food and both sides permitted one another to send clothing to prisoners, but this was belated relief. General Hoffman, as he had been brevetted in 1864, finally returned to the United States Treasury the then enormous sum of over $1.8 million, representing more than half the total of the prison funds accumulated by deduction from rations. It represented the unacknowledged price of many prisoners' lives.

While often suffering, inmates of Northern and Southern prisons also had lighter moments. They played cards and otherwise gambled, read books and newspapers, wrote diaries and letters, and conducted classes, theatrical performances, and religious meetings. When extra food was available, some ran eating places or brewed beer. Many made jewelry out of bones and scrap material as souvenirs for loved ones or for sale to guards and civilian visitors. The latter were so curious that they could often be seen at guard posts. At Elmira, entrepreneurs actually built a tower near the walls from which anyone willing to pay could gape at or photograph the prison. Other photographers, mainly in Northern prisons, made portraits for a price within the walls. Since both sides used little of the prisoners' labor, most inmates spent much of the time between roll calls and meals in idleness. Inevitably their main topic of conversation

Above: And so it was only fitting that their prisoners be no ordinary sort. Here sat some of the creme de la creme of the Confederate Navy. (NYHS)

Right: Here some of the better citizens of the South, suspected of treason or simply disliked by the ruling powers in Washington, spent part of the war. Major Jenkins of Florida appears to have brought the better part of his wardrobe with him. (RINHART GALLERIES, INC.)

Above: Among their lodgers was Commander William A. Webb, once in command of the dreaded Confederate ironclad Atlanta. *(WILLIAM A. ALBAUGH)*

Above: The need for a more efficient system for housing prisoners led Colonel Hoffman to lay out a new Federal prison strictly for war prisoners. He placed it on Johnson's Island in Lake Erie. Here the barracks went up, all of them commanded by the guns of Fort Hill. The Ohio shoreline is visible in the distance. (USAMHI)

Above: Four companies of the 128th Ohio, organized to serve as prison guards, soon to be called Hoffman's Battalion; here Company A stands in formation on Johnson's Island. (USAMHI)

Above: In time the island acquired its own artillery command as well, the Ohio National Guard 8th Light Artillery. Part of the stockade surrounding the prison can be seen in the background. (BURTON J. AUSTIN)

was the prospect of obtaining freedom. A few tried to escape; most awaited release.

The Confederate pens in Georgia first disgorged their miserable hordes but not to freedom. Instead, concern about Sherman's invading force caused the Southern leaders to search for safer holding places for the prisoners, who were their only hope of obtaining the release of their own men confined by the Yankees. In the late summer of 1864, the Rebels began to remove the enlisted men from Andersonville and the officers from Macon. After keeping part of them at a temporary camp in Savannah, they moved thousands of the enlisted men to a stockade near Millen, Georgia, which Winder boasted was the world's largest prison. Sherman's March to the Sea quickly ended that dubious distinction, and most of its inmates were shuttled circuitously over the South's collapsing rail system back to Andersonville.

Other prisoners originally at Andersonville and Macon had been sent to Charleston, South Carolina. There the officers were housed at an old hospital that, like most of the city, was in range of Union siege guns. Believing that the Confederates had deliberately put prisoners under fire, the Federal commander sent to Fort Delaware for 600 Southern officer prisoners, whom he confined in a stockade also exposed to artillery bombardment on Morris Island near Charleston. The Confederates then moved their officer prisoners inland to camps at Columbia and the enlisted men to a new prison near Florence, South Carolina. The latter, chosen as usual because of its convenience to railroad transportation, was a stockade outside of which was built up an earthwork. Once again the prisoners were left to improvise quarters while attempting to survive on even scanter rations.

After the disruption of the Confederate prisons in the Deep South, captives had again accumulated at Richmond, mainly on Belle Isle. Unable to feed or shelter them adequately, the Confederate government sent a few to Danville and

Above: Sandusky, Ohio, in the background, looked out upon an island teeming with underfed and ill-clothed Southerners. (USAMHI)

Above: When even Johnson's Island could not accommodate the flow of prisoners, Hoffman turned to onetime Yankee training camps and fairgrounds. Camp Douglas, in Chicago, became a major prison, one of the most popular with photographers. Here a considerable group of Confederates sit for the camera, with what appears to be a fire hydrant in the foreground. (CHS)

abruptly decided to ship the rest to Salisbury, North Carolina. The old fenced camp there had since 1862 held only a few hundred men, mostly deserters and political prisoners. In October 1864, with almost no warning, the Richmond authorities simply dumped some 7,500 men into the pen, with no stream to supply adequate water or carry off sewage. While there were a few huts and tents and an old factory building, many of the prisoners had to dig holes in the earth to escape the North Carolina winter. In their desperation some of the prisoners unsuccessfully made one of the few attempts at a mass outbreak. In less than five months, over a third of a total of 10,000 Salisbury prisoners perished. The proportionate casualties rivaled Andersonville's, but the number of prisoners and hence the total losses were fewer.

At this penultimate moment in the war, the Confederate government responded to the chaotic condition of its prisons by creating a central authority. In November 1864, General Winder finally became commissary general of prisoners, responsible for all facilities east of the Mississippi. He spent much of his brief tenure in office attempting to cope with the inexorable advance of Sherman's men and vainly seeking prison locations permanently safe from attack. Old and exhausted, he died in February 1865 at the Florence prison—followed to his grave by the rejoicing of his embittered captives.

At about the same time, the log jam blocking exchange suddenly gave way. The belligerents had exchanged several thousand sick prisoners in the previous fall and public pressure had mounted to free the rest. Though the Confederates had released some black soldiers who had not previously been Confederate slaves, the issue of the status of ex-slaves still remained. Nonetheless, with the war almost over, Grant decided to agree to a general exchange. At City Point, Virginia, and Wilmington, North Carolina, thousands crossed the lines while fighting continued nearby. With the collapse and surrender of the Confederacy, the remainder of the prisoners on both sides went home and the unhappy camps closed forever. Within them had died over 56,000 men, about 1 in 7 of the Civil War's nonbattle deaths.

Subsequently, the United States sought evidence to blame high Confederate officials for con-

Above: They posed in smaller groups as well. (DAVID R. O'REILLY)

Above: They posed seated and standing. (DAVID R. O'REILLY)

Below: Chicago photographer D. F. Brandon set up a modest studio in the prison to make images such as this pose of ten Kentuckians captured from the command of Raider John Hunt Morgan. *(DAVID R. O'REILLY)*

Above: And some even apparently stood in line, waiting to be in the next image. *(DAVID R. O'REILLY)*

ditions in their prisons and actually tried several subordinates. Only one, Wirz of Andersonville, went to the gallows after the semblance of a trial, whose result was a foregone conclusion. With the stupendous horror of Andersonville as their principal example, former Union prisoners for years wrote books accusing the Confederates of deliberately and cruelly plotting to cause the death of helpless captives. As tempers cooled, defenders of the South were able to get a hearing for the contention that much of the suffering in the South was the result of wartime shortages, while on the other hand the North had with premeditation worsened conditions through its attempts at retaliation. During the Civil War Centennial, those anxious to heal at last the old wounds argued that in fact both sides had done about as well as could have been expected, and that the deaths of prisoners had resulted in large part from the practical limitations of the time and from the war itself. And yet this interpretation is only a little more satisfactory than the earlier explanations. It does not, for example, account for the great differences in conditions and casualties between specific camps and in general between the camps for officers and those for enlisted men. Even in a nineteenth-century civil war, prisons might have been much less fatal. Perhaps a former Confederate and prisoner could be given the last word. As he looked back, Henry Kyd Douglas thought that ill treatment had been exaggerated and that intentional cruelty had been the exception. He concluded, however, that "… there were hardships and suffering among prisoners on both sides from neglect, incompetency, and indifference."

It should hardly have been surprising. North and South had fought a war brought about by "neglect, incompetency, and indifference."

Above: Camp Morton, near Indianapolis, Indiana, took on a distinctly Victorian aspect, complete with gingerbread trim on the buildings. Here the entrance appears in this series of images, most of them previously unpublished. *(UNIVERSITY OF GEORGIA LIBRARY, ATHENS)*

Above: Headquarters Row at Camp Morton could almost have been a small-town street anywhere in the Midwest. *(UNIVERSITY OF GEORGIA LIBRARY, ATHENS)*

Above: This post even had a drum and bugle corps. (UNIVERSITY OF GEORGIA LIBRARY, ATHENS)

Above: And its own artillery company. (UNIVERSITY OF GEORGIA LIBRARY, ATHENS)

Right: And, of course, thousands of prisoners. Their barracks ran along a creek, where they also washed their clothes. In the winter they had little to keep out the cold but their army blankets. Hundreds became ill with diseases and died, one of them being Private Josiah S. Davis of the 45th Virginia. His great-great grandson is the editor of The Image of War. *(UNIVERSITY OF GEORGIA LIBRARY, ATHENS)*

Below: At least Camp Morton did provide a modest attempt at sanitary facilities, unlike so many other prisons. Instead of locating the latrine, or sinks, right in the creek that supplied drinking water, the camp provided the large white latrine in the center of the picture. Still, it was too close to the water, encouraging diseases like the "debility" and dysentery. (UNIVERSITY OF GEORGIA LIBRARY, ATHENS)

Below: Although a cold and lonely place, Camp Morton and its inmates fared far better than those in other places. Camp Morton would never become an infamous name like Fort Delaware or Andersonville. (UNIVERSITY OF GEORGIA LIBRARY, ATHENS)

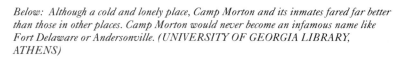

Left: When the rank and file were ready for exchange, the ceremony was a little less formal. Here several hundred Confederate prisoners stand gathered, awaiting their exchange at Cox's Landing on the James River. (USAMHI)

Left: Another heavily used exchange point, before the prisoner exchange system was stopped, was Aiken's Landing on the James, here being patrolled by the double-turreted Yankee monitor Onondaga. (MHS)

Below: Another Rees view of Libby. The commandant stands between the two men in the foreground, hand on his lapel. (VM)

Below: Building like this Petersburg, Virginia, warehouse became temporary prisons. (LC)

Above: In charge of the Federal exchange was Major General Ethan Allen Hitchcock, one of the oldest officers in the service. He was sixty-four when appointed to command the exchange system, and proved contentious to the point that he helped the exchange program break down. An 1865 image by Brady & Company. (KA)

Above: The yards once thronged with prisoners, and in the winter the cold wind blew through the bars and broken windows. (LC)

Above: And so life in the prisons went on, and the numbers began to swell again. A few places enjoyed having their own resident photographers, among them Point Lookout, Maryland. Here Stanley J. Morrow, of the 7th Wisconsin, spent some time recording the scenes of the prison—and his own portrait. (W.H. OVER MUSEUM, UNIVERSITY OF SOUTH DAKOTA, VERMILLION)

Left: Morrow caught the scene of escaped prisoners returned and placed in barrels as punishment. One or two of these men may even be Federals, guards perhaps guilty of some infraction. One of them wears a sign proclaiming "THIEF." (W. H. OVER MUSEUM)

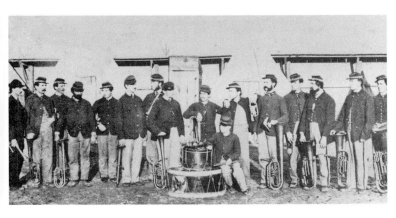

Above: The Point Lookout band, with Morrow himself standing eighth from the left. Whether they were for the entertainment of the guards or the prisoners is uncertain. (W.H. OVER MUSEUM)

Above: The officers in command of Point Lookout, including Brigadier General James Barnes, commandant, standing seventh from the left. (W.H. OVER MUSEUM)

Above: Others who were captured with Morgan were put in state prisons, like these Kentuckians in the Western Penitentiary in Pennsylvania's Allegheny City. They dubbed the photo Happy Family. (RP)

Above: In the South, buildings like this one in Danville, Virginia, became notorious. A postwar image. (USAMHI)

Left and far left: Their water in Danville came from this spring, and their spiritual sustenance from the Reverend George W. Dame. (USAMHI)

Above: But nothing North or South could match in notoriety the place in Georgia first called Camp Sumter. Soon it was known to all as Andersonville. On August 17, 1864, Southern photographer A. J. Riddle took his camera to record this panoramic scene of the southern part of the compound. There were almost 33,000 prisoners confined within its twenty-six acres, all under the watchful—and sometimes cruel—eyes of the sentries atop the stockade. (USAMHI)

Above: The northwest view of the stockade, again by Riddle. The death rate that summer went well over 100 per day; yet there was little intentional mistreatment of prisoners. They enjoyed almost the same substandard diet as their guards. There were simply too many, crowded and with poor sanitation, kept by a Confederacy that did not have the resources to feed them. And that was quite bad enough. (USAMHI)

Above: Another view from the stockade. The long sinks, or latrines, run parallel and next to the stream that provided drinking water. With dysentery rampant, it is no wonder the latrine is constantly crowded. (USAMHI)

Right: Even in the years after the war, the place has not lost its menace. The Confederates abandoned the camp in the days before the war's end. Some time later Fernandina, Florida, photographers Engle & Furlong came to record the crumbling place of horror. The gateway to the stockade... (NA)

Left: … the road leading from the railroad station to the camp, the long road trod by more than 13,000 who never walked back… (NA)

Left: … the southeast stockade, the bakeries at right… (NA)

Left: … and the crumbling stockade itself. Only echoes linger to tell of the misery of the place, as in almost all Civil War prisons. (NA)

Above: Federal soldiers who were captured in the West were retained in the less crowded western prisons, like these men of the 19th Iowa. They are shown here in New Orleans immediately after their release from Camp Ford at Tyler, Texas. Rags and tatters were the uniform of all prisoners. (LC)

Above: The officers of the 19th Iowa looked little better at the time of their release. (LC)

Right: But tatters or no, they were more than happy to be on their way home. (US-AMHI)

Below: Meanwhile, the work of housing the unfortunate continued. At Elmira, New York, General Hoffman built yet another camp, forty acres inside a stockade that ran alongside the aptly named Hoffman Street. The prisoners inside proved to be a curiosity for local photographers like J. E. Larkin, who made this 1864 image, and for the citizens of the surrounding area. (LC)

Below: The civilians were allowed to mount the stockade and look in upon the Confederates inside, here lined up for a roll call of ration issue. Some even made a business of selling goods over the wall to prisoners with money. (MC)

Below: And the armies had to use even the local city jails, as here in Savannah, where quite a few Federals were accommodated during the war. (USAMHI)

Above: Sightseers in the South could take a look, too, both at Union prisoners and at Confederates, as here in Beaufort, South Carolina, where an Episcopal church has been turned into a prison by the conquering Yankees. The tent at right is the prison hospital. (WRHS)

Left: From time to time the men in prison did have to face the threat of being used in the political and military battle between North and South. When it was reported that Confederate authorities in Charleston had placed Union officers in this house on Broad Street, directly in the line of fire from the bombarding Federals, ... (USAMHI)

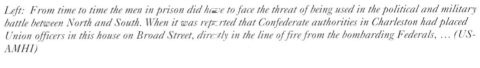

Right: ... the Yankees retaliated by erecting this stockade on Morris Island and populating it with 600 Confederate officer prisoners, right in the line of Southern fire. Both sides backed away from the confrontation before any casualties were suffered. (LC)

Left: With the war over, a fascination erupted in the North. People wanted to see these infamous places they had read about for four years. Libby Prison became the single most photographed building in the former Confederacy. (USAMHI)

Above: The photographers took it from every angle. (NA)

Above: A place that had to be remembered. (VM)

Above: They even gave it a new sign, not that anyone needed reminding. (USAMHI)

Above: Certainly the soldiers, finally released after their time in Libby and the other prisons North and South, needed no reminding. They packed their few prison belongings, donned their tattered uniforms, and went home. Lieutenant William May of 23d Connecticut, after his release from Camp Ford at Tyler, Texas. May edited a prisoners' newspaper, The Old Flag, *for fellow inmates at Camp Ford. (RP)*

Right: And for thousands more there was nothing to remember. They were past their suffering, their war. All that remained for them, as for these hundreds in rank on rank at Andersonville, was to be remembered. (USAMHI)

THE SOUTH BESIEGED

The flagging South's blood, men who could not be spared. Prisoners captured in Virginia in 1864 can do nothing more for their country now, and can only stare at the camera for posterity. Lean and weathered, worn and starved like their infant nation, their war is done. (RINHART GALLERIES, INC.)

The War for Tennessee

EDWIN C. BEARSS

The endless, bloody battles for the state called "Volunteer"

Above: Mr. Lincoln's army was on the move in Tennessee. In a brilliant campaign, Rosecrans had feinted Bragg out of Tennessee's heartland. Now he prepared to drive him into Georgia, and here at Stevenson, Alabama, the right of the advancing Federals established Redoubt Harker to guard rail supply lines. (U.S. ARMY MILITARY HISTORY INSTITUTE)

CIVIL WAR PHOTOGRAPHERS recorded the soldiers and scenes of the sweeping military operations that dashed Confederate expectation in America's heartland and shattered a mighty Southern army. During the six months following the struggle at Stones River, December 31, 1862-January 2, 1863, Union Major General William S. Rosecrans' Army of the Cumberland regrouped and built up strength in and around Murfreesboro in Middle Tennessee, 30 miles southeast of Nashville. Confederate General Braxton Bragg's Army of Tennessee fortified a line covering Duck River barring the direct route to Chattanooga.

Geography and the "iron horse" dictated that Chattanooga, with only 2,545 people in 1860, play a key role in the Civil War. The town was on the south bank of the Tennessee, where the great river knifed its way through a mountain barrier. Possession of Chattanooga, "Gateway to the deep South," was vital to the Confederacy, and a strategic necessity Union leaders could not ignore.

Railroads focused the armies' attention on Chattanooga. It was the terminus of major railroads leading northeast to Knoxville and Richmond, southeast to Atlanta, and northwest to Nashville and Louisville. At Stevenson, Alabama, 40 miles to the southwest, the railroad to Memphis joined the tracks of the Nashville & Chattanooga.

On June 24, 1863, Rosecrans, in response to goading from Washington, took the offensive. There ensued, on the part of the Federals, a brilliantly planned and executed ten-day campaign. After stubborn but brief fights at Hoover's and Liberty Gaps, the bluecoated columns forged ahead. Satisfied that his Middle Tennessee position had become untenable, Bragg determined to abandon the region. Rosecrans' soldiers entered Tullahoma on July 1, capturing a few prisoners, and the Confederates retreated across the Cumberland Plateau and took position behind the Tennessee River. Rosecrans now called a halt, sent his troops into camp, and began stockpiling supplies for a thrust across the Tennessee and on to Chattanooga.

By mid-August, Rosecrans resumed the offensive. His army had regrouped, and ripening corn promised forage for his thousands of horses and mules. His immediate goal was Chattanooga. As in the Tullahoma Campaign, Rosecrans hoped to maneuver the Confederates out of their stronghold by hard marches and an indirect approach.

General Bragg, pending arrival of reinforcements, massed his army in and around Chattanooga. Yankee artillery, north of the Tennessee, opened fire on the town, and Bragg, to counter this threat, recalled most of his troops guarding the downstream crossings. Rosecrans took advantage of Bragg's miscalculations, and divisions crossed and bridged the Tennessee. Pressing rapidly forward after what Rosecrans believed to be a broken and dispirited foe, the XIV and XX Corps entered mountainous northwest Georgia. Thus by September 10 some 45 miles of rugged country separated the wings of Rosecrans' army.

Meanwhile, General Bragg had been reinforced. Major General Simon B. Buckner's 8,000-man corps joined him, and 11,500 troops arrived from central Mississippi. On September 6, Bragg had evacuated Chattanooga and massed his army near La Fayette, 26 miles to the south.

Bragg now moved to take advantage of Rosecrans' blunder and defeat the Federals in detail.

On September 10 he moved to crush Major General George Thomas' advance—Major General James S. Negley's division of the XIV Corps in McLemore's Cove. Plans were frustrated by the inaction of the principal subordinates involved, Lieutenant General Daniel H. Hill and Major General Thomas C. Hindman, and Thomas pulled back. Bragg then turned to assail Major General Thomas Crittenden. Again, a senior corps commander failed and Bragg's plans misfired.

Rosecrans now realized that his army was imperiled. Thomas' XIV Corps and Major General A. M. McCook's XX Corps were recalled and ordered to join Crittenden at Lee & Gordon's Mills, 12 miles south of Chattanooga. Nightfall on September 17 found Rosecrans' infantry corps within supporting distance: Crittenden's at Lee & Gordon's Mills, Thomas' nearby, McCook's in McLemore's Cove, and Gordon Granger's Reserve Corps, called up from near Bridgeport, Alabama, in position at Rossville, guarding the road into Chattanooga.

General Bragg, fuming over his subordinates' failures, marched his columns northward on the east side of Chickamauga Creek. He planned to cross the Chickamauga north of Lee & Gordon's Mills, block the road to Chattanooga, and turn on and either crush Crittenden's XXI Corps or hurl it back on Thomas. By mauling Rosecrans' left, Bragg could reoccupy Chattanooga and possibly destroy the Union Army before it recrossed the Tennessee.

On September 18 three brigades of Lieutenant General James Longstreet's corps detrained at nearby Ringgold. These Army of Northern Virginia veterans, vanguard of a famed corps, had left Virginia nine days before. The Confederacy had employed its interior position and warworn railroads to give Bragg a numerical advantage in the impending struggle.

One of Longstreet's brigades reinforced Brigadier General Bushrod R. Johnson's division as it pressed toward Reed's Bridge. Johnson's column, in Bragg's plan, was to cross the Chickamauga at this bridge and wheel left. Other Confederate divisions and corps, in turn, were to cross at upstream bridges and fords, their movements facilitated by Johnson's advance.

Union cavalry and mounted infantry, guarding the crossings, engaged the Confederates. Alexander's Bridge, upstream from Reed's, was broken down by the horse soldiers, and Major General W. H. T. Walker's corps, advancing on Johnson's left, was compelled to proceed to a downstream ford, where it crossed and reinforced Johnson. The Federals pulled back. By daybreak on the 19th, all of Bragg's army, 66,000 strong, except three divisions, was west of Chickamauga Creek.

Right: On September 9, 1863, Rosecrans also obtained a valuable prize well north of Bragg. Cumberland Gap fell to Federals, thus closing that passage to the enemy and giving the Yankees a back door into eastern Tennessee. (LINCOLN MEMORIAL UNIVERSITY)

Far right: George N. Barnard's image of the pass in Raccoon Mountain near Whiteside, Georgia. An important trestle bridge of the Memphis & Chattanooga Railroad passed through here, and both Confederates and Federals vied for it. These blockhouses are only part of its defenses. (USAMHI)

Above: Here around the Stevenson railroad depot the Yankees built up their supplies for the campaign to come. Mountains of boxes of "army bread" and row after row of salt beef and pork barrels wait on the siding. (BEHRINGER-CRAWFORD MUSEUM, COVINGTON, KENTUCKY)

Above: A magnificent image of an unidentified Federal regiment drawn up for the camera near Stevenson. Hard-bitten Westerners like these would take the war to the enemy wherever they found him. (BEHRINGER-CRAWFORD MUSEUM, COVINGTON, KENTUCKY)

Above: Barnard's camera also caught some of the men who manned those defenses. (WESTERN RESERVE HISTORICAL SOCIETY)

Right: To hinder Rosecrans' advance, the Confederates had destroyed the Howe Turn bridge over the Tennessee River at Bridgeport. Engineers are building a temporary bridge to span the stream. (MINNESOTA HISTORICAL SOCIETY)

Right: The commander of those Confederates, General Braxton Bragg, was on the verge of winning the most shattering triumph in the career of Southern arms. (VALENTINE MUSEUM)

Above: They were all commanded by the smiling Major General William S. Rosecrans, "Old Rosey," whose prospects in the campaign ahead took a decidedly less rosy turn. (USAMHI)

General Rosecrans took advantage of time bought by his mounted troops to redeploy his 58,000-man army to counter Bragg's threat to the Union left. Thomas' corps was called up during the night, and two of his divisions took position on Crittenden's left, covering the roads leading to Reed's and Alexander's bridges.

Early on September 19, General Thomas sent Brigadier General John M. Brannan to reconnoiter the Confederate forces that had crossed the Chickamauga. Feeling their way ahead, the Federals, as they neared Jay's Mill, clashed with Brigadier General Nathan B. Forrest's dismounted cavalry, screening Bragg's right. The Yanks pushed Forrest's people and their supporting infantry back. The Confederates brought up reinforcements, Walker's corps, and the Federals, in turn, recoiled.

As the day progressed, Bragg and Rosecrans continued to call up and commit fresh units. By midafternoon savage combat raged along a three mile front. Around 2:30 the Confederates began advancing successfully. By 4 P.M. the situation looked bleak for the Army of the Cumberland. Bragg's Confederates, if allowed to exploit this success, were in position to block the Dry Valley road —Rosecrans' only remaining link with Chattanooga. Desperately, the Federals held on.

Although darkness closed in, close combat flared for several more hours before the firing and shouting ceased. During the night General Longstreet arrived from Ringgold with two fresh brigades.

Bragg then reorganized his army into two wings preparatory to resuming the attack. Lieutenant General Leonidas Polk was to command the right wing and Longstreet the left.

Bragg called for resumption of the battle at

daybreak on Sunday, September 20. Major General John C. Breckinridge's division on the right was to open the attack, which would be taken up by successive divisions to his left. Misunderstood orders and difficulties in effecting dispositions resulted in several hours delay. It was 9:30 before Breckinridge advanced, and as he did his brigades gained ground and threatened to envelop Thomas' left. A Union counterattack blunted and threw back Breckinridge's grim fighters, mortally wounding one of President Lincoln's Confederate brothers-in-law, Brigadier General Ben Hardin Helm.

Patrick R. Cleburne's division now struck, closing on the Union breastworks. His brigades were mauled as General Thomas called up more reinforcements. After two and a half hours of savage fighting, Polk's wing, having frittered its energy in futile piecemeal attacks on Thomas' barricaded line, recoiled.

It was now 11:15, and Longstreet massed a three-division column under hard-hitting Major General John B. Hood opposite Rosecrans' center. Through a misunderstanding, Rosecrans had just then created a huge hole in his own line opposite Longstreet.

Longstreet's thunderbolt now struck, his column surging through the gap that had opened in the Union line because of Rosecrans' blunder. It shattered their foe. Whole divisions fled the field. Among the dead was the brilliant and beloved Brigadier General William H. Lytle. Rosecrans, McCook, and Crittenden, caught up in the panic, abandoned the field. The right wing of the Union Army, except Colonel John T. Wilder's brigade, which advanced and battered one of Hindman's brigades, was in wild retreat.

General Thomas did not panic. He pulled back and re-formed his right along the crest of Snodgrass Hill. Unwilling to bypass Thomas, Longstreet's troops repeatedly charged up the slopes only to be repulsed. They next moved to envelop Thomas' right and were succeeding when General Granger, marching to the sound of the guns, arrived with two reserve brigades on Snodgrass Hill. Attacking, Granger hurled the Confederates back.

Undaunted, Longstreet returned to the attack, vainly committing his reserve, General William Preston's division. About 4 P.M., Polk's wing resumed battering Thomas' left, and at dusk Thomas withdrew most of his troops to Rossville Gap. On that grim Sunday afternoon Thomas saved the Army of the Cumberland and earned the *nom de guerre* "The Rock of Chickamauga."

Losses in the battle, the war's bloodiest two-day fight, which the Confederates won but failed to follow up, were staggering. Bragg listed 2,312 dead, 14,674 wounded, and 1,468 missing. Rosecrans reported 1,657 dead, 9,756 wounded, and 4,757 missing.

On the night of September 21, 1863, the defeated Union Army was back in Chattanooga. Here, between Confederates in front and natural obstacles to the rear, it was trapped. Bragg's troops advanced and invested the Union forces, occupying Missionary Ridge, Chattanooga Valley, Lookout Mountain, and Lookout Valley.

News of Rosecrans' defeat at Chickamauga had far-reaching repercussions. Two corps, the XI and the XII, were detached from the Army of the Potomac, placed under Major General Joseph Hooker, and rushed west as fast as the railroads

Above: He would win that victory along the banks of Chickamauga Creek in northwestern Georgia. Some of the first skirmishing prior to the battle took place near Lee & Gordon's Mills on the creek. (LIBRARY OF CONGRESS)

Above: The water of Chickamauga Creek would soon be stained with the blood of thousands as the battle commenced. Scores of dead floated peacefully past Lee & Gordon's. (NATIONAL ARCHIVES)

Far left: The bulk of the real battle will be fought on the right, where Lieutenant General Leonidas Polk commands Bragg's right wing. The bishop-turned-general will repeatedly disappoint Bragg, as he does almost everyone except his old friend Jefferson Davis. An unpublished portrait. (COURTESY OF TED YEATMAN)

Left: It was chiefly divisions of the corps of Lieutenant General Daniel H. Hill of North Carolina that set the scene for the Confederate victory. It was his attacks on Rosecrans' left wing that forced the Federal to weaken his center. (VM)

Above: It came at a heavy price. Leading his brigade in one of Hill's attacks, Brigadier General Ben Hardin Helm of Kentucky fell, mortally wounded. He was the brother-in-law of President Abraham Lincoln. (USAMHI)

Above: In the confusion behind Rosecrans' lines, his chief of staff, Brigadier General James A. Garfield, was too busy to write an order for his commander. Rosecrans dictated it to another, and inadvertently it cost him the battle. Garfield, however, would win promotion for Chickamauga and eventually become President. (USAMHI)

Above: There was confusion enough in the Federal army without bungled orders. Major General James S. Negley unaccountably wandered away from the battle line with most of his division and did not heed orders to return. He would never command again, though he claimed for the rest of his days that his disgrace had been engineered by jealous West Point trained officers who despised a man never educated at the Military Academy. (COURTESY OF RONN PALM)

Above: A man who obeyed orders to the letter, however, was Major General Thomas J. Wood. Rosecrans' dictated order told him to move to the left, and Wood obeyed, even though it left a massive hole in the Union line just as… (USAMHI)

could move them. Four divisions were detached from Major General Ulysses S. Grant's Army of the Tennessee, then based at Vicksburg, and sent up the Mississippi by steamboats to Memphis. These units were led by Major General William T. Sherman.

Then Grant, overall commander in the theater, relieved Rosecrans, elevating General Thomas to command the Department and Army of the Cumberland. Grant promptly learned something of Thomas' character. Replying to a telegram from Grant to hold Chattanooga at all hazards, Thomas answered, "We will hold the town till we starve."

The most immediate task facing Grant and Thomas was supplying Chattanooga. Rosecrans began work on a route using the Tennessee River, and now they completed it. While mechanics built the steamboat *Chattanooga*, and other vessels were repaired for service, the generals went about taking and holding Lookout Valley, vital to their supply route. It took secrecy and desperate fighting at Wauhatchie, but by November 1 the route was open. The "cracker line" they called it, bringing vital supplies from the railhead at Bridgeport, Alabama, up the river to Kelley's Ferry aboard the *Chattanooga* and several other ships like her, and then overland to Chattanooga.

Grant now confronted the enemy in his front. But Bragg immediately blundered by allowing Longstreet to take his corps on an ill-advised campaign into East Tennessee toward Knoxville. Learning of this, Grant began to plan an attack on the remaining Confederates.

Early on November 23, to confirm the reports of deserters and spies that two divisions of Buckner's corps were en route to East Tennessee to reinforce Longstreet, Grant directed Thomas to make a forced reconnaissance of the Rebel lines. The Army of the Cumberland—Granger's corps on the left and John N. Palmer's on the right—moved out at 2 P.M., as if on parade, and formed lines of battle in view of watching Confederates. Taking up the advance, the Federals drove in Bragg's pickets and routed the Rebels from a line of rifle pits, capturing more than 200. On the afternoon of the 24th, Sherman's army moved out from its bridgehead in three columns. They overpowered several outposts and, by four o'clock, occupied the north end of Missionary Ridge.

Meanwhile, at 4 A.M. on the 24th, General Hooker put his three divisions in motion. While his pioneers bridged Lookout Creek, Hooker sent Geary's division, reinforced by Brigadier General Walter C. Whitaker's brigade, upstream to cross at Wauhatchie. Screened by a morning fog, Geary's people forded the creek and swept down the slope overlooking the right bank, routing Confederate pickets. Covered by this movement, Hooker's main column bridged and crossed the stream. Supported by enfilading fire of cannon emplaced on Moccasin Point, Hooker's divisions forged ahead, driving a Confederate brigade around the face of Lookout Mountain to the Cravens farm. Though ordered to halt and re-form, Geary, seeing he had the Rebels on the run, pushed ahead until checked by Confederate reinforcements posted behind breastworks beyond the Cravens house. By 2 P.M. the fog had thickened and it was impossible for the combatants to see more than a few yards. This, along with an ammunition shortage, caused Hooker to halt and consolidate his gains. The "Battle Above the Clouds" had ended in a Union success.

Above: Major General Bushrod R. Johnson and his division spearheaded the attack of a Confederate corps aimed precisely at the gap. Johnson, a native of Ohio, was yet one of the most able generals in the Southern service. (COURTESY OF WILLIAM A. AL-BAUGH)

Above: Some of the attacking soldiers in that Confederate assault were hardly more than children, like this youngster of the 9th Mississippi. (COURTESY OF PAUL DE HAAN)

Above: Yet others were experienced and battle-hardened veterans, like Brigadier General John Gregg of Alabama, shown here in an unpublished portrait. He led his brigade into the attack right behind Johnson, taking a wound for his effort. (COURTESY OF LAWRENCE T. JONES)

During the night of the 24th the Confederates withdrew from Lookout Mountain and reported to Bragg on Missionary Ridge. Next morning, a patrol from the 8th Kentucky scrambled up the mountain and at sunrise, the fog having lifted, unfurled the U.S. flag from the point, to the cheers of bluecoated onlookers.

Grant's November 25 program called for Sherman to assail Tunnel Hill, at the north end of Missionary Ridge, at daylight; Hooker to march at the same hour on the road to Rossville, storm Rossville Gap, and threaten Bragg's left and rear; and Thomas to hold his ground until Hooker and Sherman had accomplished their missions.

Sherman began his attack as scheduled. Strong battle lines advanced and occupied a wooded crest within 80 yards of rifle pits held by Cleburne's division. A savage fight ensued. The outnumbered Confederates held firm and stood tall in the face of Sherman's blows. About 2 P.M. two of Sherman's brigades effected a lodgment on the slope of Tunnel Hill but were counterattacked and driven back in disorder.

Hooker was also in trouble, not with the foe, but with Chattanooga Creek. Reaching that stream at 10 A.M., he found the bridge destroyed and the Rossville road obstructed by retreating Confederates. Hooker lost three hours crossing his lead division, which then advanced and seized Rossville Gap. His other divisions followed, and, deploying them in line, Hooker pushed ahead.

Grant, at his Orchard Knob command post, knew that Sherman had been rebuffed at Tunnel Hill and that Hooker had been delayed. To assist Sherman, Grant told Thomas to send his four center divisions to carry the Confederate rifle pits at the foot of Missionary Ridge and there halt and await further instructions. At 3:30 P.M. signal guns on Orchard Knob boomed, and the divisions, covered by a powerful skirmish line, swept forward. The Federals, though subjected to a storm of shot

Above: The attack isolated most of Major General Alexander McCook's XX Corps, and McCook himself, with two of his divisions, fled the battlefield in rout. He never led troops again in the war, and in 1865 was serving as a lowly captain. (USAMHI)

Above: Major General Thomas L. Crittenden fared no better. The Confederate attack shattered one of his divisions and cut him off from the other two. He joined McCook and Rosecrans in following the rout and never held important command again. (WRHS)

Left: Yet there were heroes. Brigadier General William H. Lytle of Ohio was best known then and later as a poet. Here at Chickamauga his division was just moving to the left when the Confederate attack struck. To protect the moving columns of Federals, he turned his brigade back to meet the attack and try to stall it. One brigade faced more than a division of the enemy. In the desperate fight, Lytle was hit by four bullets and died soon thereafter. The Confederates who later found him placed a guard over the body to prevent its being robbed, and gave him an honored burial. That night many Confederates sadly recited the lines of Lytle's most famous poem, Antony and Cleopatra. It began, "I am dying, Egypt, dying." (USAMHI)

Above: It was good ground for a battle, and even after the Confederate breakthrough, the remnants of the Federal army could hold out on hills like this. (NA)

Below: Leading those holdouts was Major General George H. Thomas. Today he would become the "Rock of Chickamauga," valiantly fighting on while nearly surrounded in order to cover the withdrawal of the rest of the army. (LC)

and shell from Confederate batteries emplaced on the commanding heights, routed the Rebels from the rifle pits. After a brief halt and without orders to continue, first one regiment and then others scrambled to its feet and surged up the ridge. They followed so hard on the heels of the Confederates fleeing the rifle pits that the Rebels posted in the works on the crest at many points hesitated to fire for fear of hitting their comrades. Units from Major General Philip H. Sheridan's division reached the crest first, routing Confederate soldiers from their breastworks near Bragg's headquarters. Regiments from the other three divisions ripped the line at other points, and the brigades holding Bragg's center panicked. Many prisoners and cannon were captured. Though the Confederate center was shattered, Lieutenant General William J. Hardee's corps, on the right, grimly held its ground till dark and then retired with Cleburne's division, successfully screening the army's retreat to winter camp at Dalton, Georgia.

Coincident with the November 25 orders for pursuit of Bragg's defeated Army of Tennessee, Grant directed Thomas to send General Granger with 20,000 men to the relief of the force led by Major General Ambrose Burnside, then besieged in Knoxville. In late summer of 1863, Burnside, at the head of the Army of the Ohio, had advanced from bases in central Kentucky. Bypassing heavily fortified Cumberland Gap, Burnside's troops entered Knoxville on September 2. On September 9 the 2,100 Confederates under Brigadier General John W. Frazer, left to "wither on the vine" at Cumberland Gap, laid down their arms.

Burnside was expected to join Rosecrans near Chattanooga, but he moved slowly, and Rose-

Above: Regiments like the 44th Indiana, cut off from their brigades, wandered to Thomas' aid as he built a hasty defense against the ceaseless enemy attacks. (WRHS)

Above: So heavily did the Confederates batter the Yankees that William Preston's division was not even needed until late in the day. He delivered the last major attack on Thomas, with fearful casualties. The general would later be appointed Confederate minister to Mexico. (DEPARTMENT OF ARCHIVES AND MANUSCRIPTS, LOUISIANA STATE UNIVERSITY)

crans' defeat at Chickamauga doomed plans for a rendezvous of the two armies. Then, in early October, 1,500 Southern horsemen led by Brigadier General John S. William,, advancing from Jonesboro, came down the road paralleling the railroad to the vicinity of Bulls Gap. Burnside reinforced his men in that quarter, and, on October 10, at Blue Springs mauled Williams' column and drove it back into southwestern Virginia.

Following the Battle of Wauhatchie, General Bragg had divided his army, sending Longstreet and his corps, reinforced by four brigades of Wheeler's cavalry, to assail Burnside and recapture Knoxville. Longstreet's 10,000 infantry and artillery were shuttled by rail from the Chattanooga area to Sweetwater. General Joseph Wheeler and his cavalry, 5,000 strong, were to cut Burnside's communications and seize high ground at Knoxville. Longstreet, with Lafayette McLaws' and Micah Jenkins' infantry divisions and E. Porter Alexander's reinforced artillery battalion, would cross the Tennessee and make a direct approach on Knoxville.

Wheeler failed. Meanwhile, Longstreet's columns had crossed the Tennessee on November 13 and 14. Spearheaded by a strong vanguard, the Rebels vigorously pushed ahead in a vain effort to force Burnside to fight before he could mass his forces within the Knoxville fortifications. To gain time and enable Burnside's infantry and artillery to strengthen their earthworks, Brigadier General William P. Sanders and his horse soldiers engaged and delayed the Confederate vanguard. With 700 men, he manned and stubbornly held a position covering the Loudon road, about a mile outside the perimeter. The bluecoats held the Rebels until midafternoon on the 18th, when the roadblock was smashed by the South Carolina brigade and Sanders mortally wounded.

Next morning, the Confederates appeared in force. Longstreet, ignoring the need for haste, in-

Above: At last relief came to Thomas when a division of Major General Gordon Granger's Reserve Corps arrived in time to help repulse Preston. (USAMHI)

Above: Leading the first brigade to arrive was Brigadier General Walter C. Whitaker, who marched "to the sound of the guns. (COURTESY OF BARBARA CHEATLY)

Above: Before their successful withdrawal, the last Federal volley fired by Thomas' troops came from the 9th Indiana. Men of Company A pose here. Perhaps their most illustrious private was young Ambrose Bierce, who would later become one of America's most popular essayists and humorists. (NA)

Above: Rosecrans retreated to Chattanooga, and there began to fortify himself. Viewed here from Lookout Mountain, the city appears nearly a year later, with Moccasin Point in the Tennessee River in the foreground. Here for nearly two months the Federals sat and waited. (USAMHI)

vested the city, and his soldiers began digging in. "The earthworks on each side seemed to grow like magic," recalled one soldier. Sharpshooters banged away, and several successful sorties buoyed the defenders' morale.

On the night of the 23rd, Longstreet received a message from General Bragg stating that if it was practicable to defeat Burnside it must be done immediately. The sector selected by Longstreet's chief engineer to be assailed was shielded by Fort Sanders. Longstreet scheduled the attack for sun rise on the 25th, but, on being apprised of the approach of two infantry brigades sent by Bragg as reinforcements, he postponed the assault to await their arrival. With these troops came Brigadier General Danville Leadbetter, an officer of engineers, presumably familiar with the area. Leadbetter's advent resulted in a new reconnaissance and vacillation on the part of Confederate leaders and, as Porter Alexander recalled, "cost us three as valuable days as the sun every shone upon."

Meanwhile, Longstreet had changed his battle plan. Instead of jumping off at sunrise and being preceded by a savage bombardment by Alexander's massed artillery of Fort Sanders, a surprise thrust by four infantry brigades was programmed. The night of November 28–29 was miserable. Temperatures went below freezing and it misted. At 10 P.M. Confederate skirmishers advanced, captured or drove in the enemy pickets, and took possession of abandoned rifle pits within 150 yards of the fort.

The firing alerted the Federals, particularly the 440 soldiers garrisoning Fort Sanders, and the works to the strongpoint's right and left. Cannoneers manning the 12 guns emplaced behind the fort's embrasured parapets stood by their pieces and, during the remaining hours of darkness, fired harassing charges of canister.

At dawn Confederate signal guns barked; several of Alexander's batteries roared into action briefly; and in two columns McLaws' veterans scrambled to their feet and rushed forward. As they neared the fort the van encountered a nasty surprise, telegraph wire entanglements stretched a few inches above ground and secured to stumps and stakes. Though this obstacle was soon passed, it disordered the ranks and caused wild rumors to circulate among supporting units as to impenetrable barriers and a slaughter of the attackers.

From inside the fort and adjoining rifle pits grim Union soldiers blazed away at the oncoming mass with rifle muskets and cannoneers got off several charges of canister. The Confederates rushed on and crowded into the ditch fronting Fort Sanders' northwest bastion. The men lacked scaling ladders, and the parapet slope was frozen and slippery. Soldiers shot through embrasures, causing the Yanks to keep their heads down and to slacken their fire. This enabled some of the Confederates to claw their way up the icy slope and plant three battle flags on the parapet. Men seeking to reach and rally on the colors were killed or captured, and one of the standard bearers was dragged into the fort by the neck.

Confederates milling in the ditch now found themselves under a deadly flank fire of musketry

Left: Rosecrans, disgraced, was to be replaced. Now commanding the Army of the Cumberland would be Thomas, his headquarters here in Chattanooga. (USAMHI)

and canister, as well as shells rolled into the moat as hand grenades. To advance or retreat was equally hazardous, and a number of soldiers began to wave their handkerchiefs. Many of their comrades, however, pulled back slowly at first, but the retreat quickly became disordered and rapid. As McLaws' men withdrew, one of Jenkins' brigades, though Longstreet sought to have it stopped, rushed the fort. Striking the ditch east of the scene of McLaws' repulse, this brigade suffered a similar fate. The assaulting columns were rallied by their officers under cover of the Rebel works, some 600 yards in front of Fort Sanders, and rolls were called. The charges had cost the Confederates 813 casualties: 129 killed, 458 wounded, and 226 missing. Union losses in Fort Sanders were about a score.

Plans for a new and better-organized attack were discussed, but before it could be launched dispatches were received confirming rumors of Bragg's defeat and retreat beyond Ringgold and ordering Longstreet to end the siege and reinforce Bragg.

Preparations were accordingly made to withdraw the troops and, as soon as it was dark, begin the march south. But, after meeting with his generals and being apprised that General Sherman was en route to Knoxville with a powerful column, Longstreet determined to hold his ground in front of Burnside and compel Sherman to continue his march. Longstreet held firm until December 3, when he learned that Sherman's vanguard was within a day's march. During the night the trains started rolling northeastward. Longstreet's troops followed as soon as it was dark on the 4th, retreating to Rogersville. Sherman entered Knoxville on the 6th to be welcomed by General Burnside and his troops, victors in the 16-day siege. The soldiers soon went into winter quarters, and the year's campaigning in Middle and East Tennessee ended.

ONE YEAR LATER, in November 1864, Middle Tennessee again became a focal point in the struggle. General John B. Hood, in the weeks following his evacuation of Atlanta, had succeeded in securing President Jefferson Davis' approval of a plan fated to lead his army deep into Tennessee. Boldly crossing the Chattahoochee, Hood lunged at the Western & Atlantic, the single-track railroad over which General Sherman supplied his "army group." Sherman, detaching a corps to hold Atlanta, hounded Hood's columns across the ridges and hollows of northwest Georgia and into Alabama. Despairing of overtaking and bringing Hood to battle, Sherman was delighted to learn, on November 8, that General Grant had approved Sherman's proposal to return to Atlanta, where preparations would be completed for evacuation of that city and the "March to the Sea."

When Hood failed to turn and follow the Union columns on their return to Atlanta, Sherman directed Major General John M. Schofield and his XXIII Corps to join Thomas in Middle Tennessee. Schofield soon reached Nashville by rail, and part of his corps rushed westward to bolster troops routed from the Johnsonville supply depot by now Major General Nathan B. Forrest's cavalry. Schofield, accompanied by two divisions of his corps, traveled to Pulaski, where, as senior officer, he took command of the troops assembled there to oppose Hood's advance.

Also ordered to join Thomas were Major Gen-

Above: And on October 23, 1863, the new overall commander in the theater arrived, Major General U. S. Grant. This image was made in Nashville around this time by T. F. Saltsman. (COURTESY OF WILLIAM C. DAVIS)

Left: With Grant's arrival there was no question that the siege would be broken. He would not sit and wait here in his headquarters for long. (NA)

Above: Reinforcements came in, among them Major General William T. Sherman with two corps. He made his headquarters here. (NA)

Above: Grant's first chore was to break the strangling hold that Bragg had on his supplies. The "cracker line" is what they called the circuitous route by which Grant re-established his supply. It depended upon the Tennessee River. (USAMHI)

Above: George N. Barnard's photograph of Union soldiers camped at Monument Garden near Chattanooga shows some of the hard-boned Westerners who will fight their way out of Chattanooga. (LC)

eral Andrew J. Smith and his three divisions that had helped smash the Confederates at Westport, near the Kansas border, on October 21-23. Low water on the western rivers delayed the transfer of Smith's "ten wandering tribes of Israel," and the vanguard did not disembark at Nashville until November 30.

General Hood had sought to cross the Tennessee River at Decatur, Alabama, but an aroused defense by the garrison frustrated his plans. Hood then pushed on to Tuscumbia, where by the end of October his men crossed the river and occupied Florence.

On Monday, November 21, Hood put the 50,000-man Army of Tennessee in motion. Screened by Forrest's cavalry, the three infantry corps traveled different roads. Vital days had been lost, and the weather was frightful. There were continuous snow, sleet, and ice storms.

Apprised of the Confederate advance, General Schofield sent his supplies to the rear and evacuated Pulaski. Union infantry reached Columbia on the 24th, in time to reinforce the cavalry and check a dash by Forrest's horse soldiers. Some 48 hours elapsed before all of Hood's infantry arrived in front of Columbia, and by then Schofield had perfected his dispositions for defense of the Duck River crossings.

Hood, seeing that a frontal assault on the Duck River bridgehead could be suicidal, sought to slip across the river and outflank Schofield. On the 28th, Forrest's cavalry hammered backward Thomas' cavalry, who retired toward Franklin, uncovering the Columbia pike.

Leaving Lieutenant General Stephen D. Lee and two divisions of his corps and the army's artillery to entertain Schofield in front of the Columbia bridgehead, Hood, at daybreak on the 29th, began crossing Duck River via a pontoon bridge positioned at a ford uncovered by Forrest's surge. Several of Forrest's brigades spearheaded the Confederate thrust toward Spring Hill, a village on the Columbia pike, eight miles north of Columbia. If the Rebels blocked the road Schofield's army would be confronted by a disas-

Left: Supply steamers like the Missionary *sometimes had to be towed through the shallows as they went upstream. (NA)*

Above: But still they came to tie up at the banks and disgorge their precious cargo. (USAMHI)

Above: They came, like the Chickamauga, *loaded with barrels of salt pork. (NA)*

Right: Or like the Chattanooga, *piled high with sacks of grain. (MHS)*

trous situation. By a hair's breadth, they failed. Schofield, informed that he was outflanked, held Spring Hill long enough to get his army marching safely toward Franklin.

The Confederates, the night being very dark, did little to impede the Union retrograde, though Schofield's columns marched by in view of Hood's campfires.

Except for several dashes by Forrest's cavalry, Schofield's 14-mile retreat to Franklin was not disturbed. General Jacob D. Cox's division was first to reach Franklin on a cold last day of November, and Cox established his command post at Fountain B. Carter's house. The brick dwelling fronted on the west side of the Columbia pike south of town. Schofield arrived and told Cox to deploy the XXIII Corps' two divisions to hold a bridgehead south of Franklin and shield the army as it crossed to the north of the Big Harpeth River on two improvised bridges. Combat veterans all, the soldiers needed no encouragement as they strengthened the earthworks erected some year and a half earlier. More divisions arrived, including General James H. Wilson's cavalry.

An angry and bitter Confederate Army marched north following the Spring Hill fiasco. General Hood was in a foul humor, convinced that failures by subordinates had permitted the Federals to escape a frightful mauling. He was determined to make a final effort to destroy Schofield's army before it gained the security afforded by the Nashville defenses. Hood called for a frontal attack.

It was 4 P.M. when the Rebel battle lines, flags unfurled, stepped out. Few Civil War combat scenes were as free of obstructions to the view. As 15 brigades swept forward at quick step, Union troops posted behind the perimeter anxiously waited. Cleburne's and Brown's people momentarily recoiled when they hit George D. Wagner's advance division, and then stormed ahead. Wagner's brigades broke and bolted for the rear. Confederates raised a shout, "Let's go into the works with them," and the race was on. A number of Cleburne's and Brown's men entered the works to the left and right of the pike hard on the heels of panic-stricken bluecoats.

Colonel Emerson Opdycke hurled his brigade into the breach. Reinforced by two of Cox's regi-

Above: There was usually a cannon aboard, and sometimes even a woman, as here on the Wauhatchie. *(LC)*

Above: And here the Missionary *stands empty but for firewood, ready to return for more. The boiler parts in the foreground give evidence that the Federals had to be prepared for makeshift repairs and spare parts for these vital vessels. (USAMHI)*

Above: Then they were off on the return voyage to get more of the food and material that kept Chattanooga supplied during the siege. Soldiers and civilians were there to watch them go, and to look anxiously for the next steamer. (NA)

ments, Opdycke's men, in furious fighting centering about the Carter house and gin, drove back the Confederates. General Cleburne was among those killed in this savage fighting.

The Rebels attacked with reckless abandon. Brigadier General John Adams led his brigade, and, jumping his horse over a ditch, his steed was killed astride a parapet, and the general pitched headlong among the defenders, mortally wounded. Brown's division assailed the Union center in concert with Cleburne's and grimly clung to a toehold in the ditch fronting the works. Here, Brigadier General Otho F. Strahl stood directing the fire of his men. And here he fell. As darkness, which came quickly, closed in, the combatants, separated by little more than the parapet, banged away, aiming at the flash of the enemy's rifle muskets. Brown had been wounded; two of the division's four brigade commanders, Strahl and States Rights Gist were dead; George W. Gordon had been captured; and John C. Carter was mortally wounded. Battered but still victorious, the Federals withdrew at 11 P.M. when threatened yet again by Forrest on the flank.

The Confederate charge at Franklin, pressed with a savage ferocity, left the field strewn with dead and wounded. Losses among the Rebel leaders were staggering. General Hood reported 6,300 casualties. Five generals were killed, six wounded, one mortally, and one captured. Union losses were 189 killed, 1,033 wounded, and 1,104 missing, of whom more than a thousand were in Wagner's two unnecessarily exposed brigades.

Schofield's tired but confident army reached Nashville on the morning of December 1, where it merged with the forces General Thomas was massing. General A. J. Smith had finally arrived from the Kansas-Missouri border with his three divisions, about 12,000 strong. Major General James B. Steedman had rushed up from Chattanooga by rail, bringing two brigades of blacks and a provisional division of casuals organized from soldiers belonging to Sherman's army group, who had returned from leave too late to participate in the March to the Sea. Most of Steedman's 5,200 officers and men reached Nashville on the evening of the 1st. But one train, having been delayed, was attacked on the 2nd by Forrest's cavalry five miles southeast of Nashville. The locomotive and cars were captured and destroyed. Most of the soldiers, however, cut their way through to Nashville.

Right: It was a tenuous lifeline, always in danger of attacks from Confederate raiders, particularly cavalry led by intrepid soldiers like General Nathan Bedford Forrest. He so loathed Braxton Bragg that he called him "a damned scoundrel" and declared that "if you were any part of a man I would slap your jaws." (USAMHI)

Above: To protect against men like Forrest, Grant had gunboats such as the USS Peosta *patrolling the Tennessee, sometimes convoying the supply ships. (USAMHI)*

Above: Some months after the siege, special gunboats would be commissioned to continue this duty after the armies had left Chattanooga. Here at her moorings sits the USS General Grant. (USAMHI)

Above: Long a landmark in Chattanooga, this old Indian mound became a military office during the siege. "Visitors are requested to register their names at the office," read the sign at the foot of the steps. (NA)

Protecting the approaches to Nashville, a vital Union supply base and communications center since February 1862, were a formidable belt of fortifications. These included redoubts, redans, lunettes, and star forts sited on knobs and hills commanding the roads entering the city from the region south of the Cumberland. These strongpoints were connected by rifle pits.

Thomas positioned his rapidly increasing army in the defenses, while General Hood, despite the Franklin mauling, boldly closed on the southern approaches to Nashville. His reasons for doing so have been challenged, but Hood, however, was a confident man and undoubtedly hoped that a blunder on Thomas' part might yet give the desperate Confederates a victory.

As he closed in on Nashville, Hood deployed S. D. Lee's corps in the center, across the Franklin pike, A. P. Stewart's corps formed on the left, holding the Granny White and Hillsboro pikes, and Cheatham's corps to the right, its flank anchored near the railroad and Murfreesboro pike. One of Forrest's divisions, James R. Chalmers', was detached and guarded the several miles of countryside between Stewart's left and the Cumberland River. Forrest, with the rest of his corps, to effect a partial investment of Thomas' army, swept through the counties to the southeast and guarded the army's right.

Now Hood weakened his army by sending Forrest and William B. Bate's infantry division to harass Thomas' rail communications. Though partially successful, their absence gave the Federals an opportunity. General Grant and the Lincoln administration urged Thomas to take the offensive. On December 2, Grant telegraphed from City Point, Virginia, advising Thomas to attack Hood immediately. Thomas, desirous of boosting the strength of Wilson's mounted arm, which had experienced difficulty coping with Forrest, decided to wait several days. But, on the 8th, the weather, which had been fair with moderate temperatures for more than a week, changed. Sleet and snow blanketed the area, all but paralyzing both armies. Thomas and his generals determined to wait for a thaw before moving out. His situation was not appreciated by Grant and the Administration, and, on the 13th, Major General John A. Logan was ordered to proceed from Washington to Nashville for the purpose of replacing Thomas. Grant, himself, was preparing to leave the nation's capital for

Above: Life during the siege was at first a hardship for the scantily provisioned Federals, and then, once the "cracker line" was operating, the enemy became boredom. Here a jaunty band of neckerchiefed officers pose at the Western & Atlantic Railroad terminal. (COURTESY OF JOSEPH H. BERGERON)

Above: Their musicians relieved what they could of the doldrums. Here the regimental band of the 4th Minnesota, taken at Huntsville, Alabama, soon after the siege. (MHS)

Above: And as soon as the supplies could get in, the "robbers' rows" and sut-lers' shops appeared to relieve the soldiers of their pay. They were barely more than shacks behind their facades. (USAMHI)

Right: There was drill aplenty to keep the men in shape. Here several compa-nies stand in double ranks during skirmish drill, their skirmishers and sharp-shooters thrown forward as if on the advance. There would be plenty of this work for them before long. (USAMHI)

Above: That work would come when Grant decided to take Lookout Mountain. Up these steep and rugged slopes some Federals had to climb and fight on November 24. (MHS)

Middle Tennessee when apprised of the successes scored by Thomas' troops on December 15. This news caused Grant to cancel the orders relieving Thomas and to return to City Point.

On the morning of the 15th, the snow and ice having melted, Thomas' troops moved out. A thick fog hid their march, but the mud slowed their deployment. Thomas' plan called for a feint against Hood's right, to be followed by a powerful thrust designed to envelop the Confederate left.

Advancing via the Murfreesboro pike, Steed-man with two brigades, one of them black, at-tacked Hood's right—Cheatham's corps—between the railroad and pike. Steedman's demonstration focused Hood's attention on this sector. Spearheaded by Wilson's cavalry corps, A. J. Smith's powerful columns trudged out the Char-lotte and Harding pikes and assailed Confederate forces guarding Hood's left. Chalmers' outnum-bered Rebel horse soldiers were brushed aside and a supporting brigade of infantry mauled. In the fighting, as the battle lines wheeled south-eastward, Wilson's cavalry to the right and Smith's infantry on the left, the Federals stormed Re-doubts Nos. 4 and 5. Smith's divisions next ap-proached a stone wall paralleling the Hillsboro pike and defended by men of Stewart's corps. Co-incidentally, Schofield's XXIII Corps, which had supported the attack on Hood's left, took position of Smith's right.

Meanwhile, General Thomas Wood had com-mitted his IV Corps to Smith's left. At 1 P.M. one of Wood's brigades had carried Montgomery Hill, a Rebel outpost midway between the lines in his sector. Wood's battle formations then closed on the rifle pits held by Stewart's people to the right and east of the stone wall. The Confederate line at this point formed a right angle. Assailed by Wood's men coming in from the north and Smith's from the west, Stewart's grim fighters were routed from the salient. Simultaneously, Schofield crossed the Hillsboro pike on a broad front.

Hood, his left shattered, hastened to occupy and hold a new and shorter front. Too late, Hood recognized the folly of the overconfidence that

Above: In command of the attack on Lookout Mountain was a veteran of the Virginia campaigns, Major General Joseph Hooker. Here he stands with his staff with Lookout in the background. Hooker stands at the right, a head taller than the rest, while just behind him, looking away, is General Daniel Butterfield, often erroneously credited with composing "Taps." (USAMHI)

Above: It was bloody and costly fighting. Brigadier General John W. Geary led a division that included his own son. In the battle just west of Lookout, in "Wauhatchie's bloody glen," his son was killed while his father was driving the Confederates off the mountain. (USAMHI)

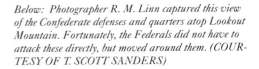

Left: Lookout on the mountain's summit. (USAMHI)

had led him to extend his lines in the presence of an enemy possessing superior numbers. Orders were sent recalling Forrest, but it would be many hours before he could rejoin the army. Sixteen cannon and 1,200 prisoners had been captured, Hood's main line of resistance broken, and his divisions rolled back two miles.

General Thomas met with his corps commanders that evening and made plans for a continuation of the offensive. The night and morning of the 16th were spent by the Federals adjusting their lines and perfecting connections between units.

Then Union skirmishers advanced and found the foe either strongly entrenched or posted behind stone walls. Wood directed the fire of his artillery against Peach Orchard Hill, while Smith's and Schofield's cannoneers swept Shy's Hill with a deadly crossfire. Wilson's cavalry, having dismounted, pushed back Chalmers' outnumbered division. About 3 P.M., while Union artillery pounded the Shy's Hill salient and Wilson's cavalry threatened to sweep Chalmers from the field and turn Hood's left, Wood and Steedman attacked Peach Orchard Hill. Covered by a host of skirmishers, four brigades ascended the slopes. Some of the Yanks gained the Rebel rifle pits, only to be dislodged by a slashing counterstroke by S. D. Lee's troops. The Union brigades recoiled, suffering heavy casualties, including one brigade commander and a number of officers.

Four o'clock was approaching and darkness would soon put a stop to the day's fighting. In the hollow fronting Shy's Hill, Brigadier General John McArthur of Smith's corps had massed one of his brigades. Coincidentally, Wilson's dismounted cavalry continued to gain ground, outflanking

Below: Photographer R. M. Linn captured this view of the Confederate defenses and quarters atop Lookout Mountain. Fortunately, the Federals did not have to attack these directly, but moved around them. (COURTESY OF T. SCOTT SANDERS)

Above: It was a fight in a dense fog much of the time, and some orders could be transmitted only by bugle call. A Confederate cornetist. (COURTESY OF CLYDE E.NOBLE)

Above: The Lookout House on Lookout Mountain, high over the slopes overlooking Chattanooga and the battle that raged for the summit. A lone Federal sentry now stands vigil at its base. (MHS)

Right: The day before the assault on Lookout, Grant sent Thomas forward to take Orchard Knob, the bald rise of ground seen between the two trees. George N. Barnard made this image from the crest of Missionary Ridge, providing the viewer with precisely the view that Bragg's Confederates had as they watched Thomas advance to take the knob. Two days later, from this same vantage, the Confederates watched in awe as the Army of the Cumberland swept across the intervening ground and up the slopes to the very spot where Barnard placed his camera. (USAMHI)

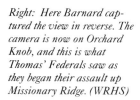

Right: Here Barnard captured the view in reverse. The camera is now on Orchard Knob, and this is what Thomas' Federals saw as they began their assault up Missionary Ridge. (WRHS)

Govan's brigade, forcing back Chalmers, and threatening to envelop Cheatham's left. McArthur's brigade now stormed the steep slopes of Shy's Hill. In a short but desperate struggle, the bluecoats routed the Southerners from the rifle pits. Among the slain was Colonel William M. Shy, of the 20th Tennessee, who gave his name to the hill. Shy's Hill was the key to Hood's position. Cheatham had no reserves to plug the breakthrough. Schofield's corps and Wilson's cavalry and other units of Smith's corps drove ahead. Abandoning their artillery, the Confederates posted west of Granny White pike fled.

As night fell, a drenching rain set in, adding to the confusion, darkness, and misery. Thomas ordered Wood to pursue by the Franklin pike and Wilson via the Granny White pike. Few, if any, Confederates retreated by the latter because of the proximity of Wilson's people. Hurriedly organized and defended roadblocks in the Brentwood Hills gaps and at Hollow Tree Gap, four miles north of Franklin, enabled a few dedicated units to delay Wilson's horse soldiers long enough for the shattered army to cross the Big Harpeth. At Columbia, Forrest rendezvoused with Hood's columns and with his cavalry, and five infantry brigades covered the army's retreat to the Tennessee River. Hood crossed the Tennessee at Bainbridge, Alabama, on December 26 and 27, the campaign done.

Hood had played hell with the Army of Tennessee. A number of units would fight again in North Carolina and others in the defense of Mobile, but the once proud army had been destroyed as a feared fighting machine. Hood had lost the confidence of his officers and men, so, at his request, he was relieved of command by President Davis.

Thomas listed his losses in the decisive two-day Battle of Nashville as 387 killed, 2,562 wounded, and 112 missing. Hood failed to file a return of his casualties, but Thomas' provost marshal listed the number of prisoners captured and deserters received in November and December as more than 13,000. In addition, 72 cannon and 3,000 stands of arms were captured by the Federals. It was an altogether bloody and decisively fitting end to the fight for Tennessee, scene of some of the bloodiest and most decisive combat of the Civil War.

Above: Barnard made this panoramic blending of images at Rossville Gap, the southern end of Missionary Ridge. Here Hooker attacked the left wing of the Confederate line, rushing past the John Ross house at the right and up the slope at left onto the ridge. (BOTH USAMHI)

Left: Men of Gordon Granger's IV Corps practice forming for an assault, sharpshooters and skirmishers in front, artillery in place to give support fire, and the infantry drawn up in wave after wave of double-ranked soldiers. There may be as many as two full brigades in this remarkable image, made at Blue Springs, Tennessee. Granger's corps, including these men, struck at the very center of the Confederate line on Missionary Ridge. (USAMHI)

Above: It was lean and tough Westerners like these who swept up the ridge to drive Bragg's Confederates from the summit. An unidentified regiment. (RP)

Above: In Barnard's view of part of the main run of Missionary Ridge, the lines of Confederate defenses are faintly visible at the crest. Thomas' army marching in full view up that slope unnerved many Southerners and helped lead to the rout that followed. (USAMHI)

Above: Another part of the five-mile line of summit that Bragg tried to defend. His army was so thinly spread that there was only one man for every seven or eight feet in places. (USAMHI)

Above: Yet the men that he had were good ones. Men like the Washington Artillery of New Orleans, shown here in an unpublished image made in New Orleans in 1861. The officer seated is probably Colonel James B. Walton. (CONFEDERATE MUSEUM, NEW ORLEANS)

Above: The men Walton led were hardy Louisianians like these, photographed in 1861 by J. W. Petty of New Orleans. The lines drawn on the image were probably made by designers in 1911 when they defaced the original photo in using it in Francis T. Miller's Photographic History of the Civil War. (USAMHI)

Above: At the northern end of Missionary Ridge another attack was under way while Thomas and Hooker assaulted the center and southern ends. Here General William T. Sherman struck. (USAMHI)

Right: Barnard captured the rugged and difficult terrain over which Sherman had to advance. The crest of Missionary Ridge runs off on the left, while in the distance rises Lookout Mountain. (USAMHI)

Above: Assisting Sherman in his attack were artillerymen such as these, men of Battery B, 1st Illinois, the Chicago Light Artillery. They appear here at war's outset, at Bird's Point, Missouri, in May 1861. They will be battle-seasoned by the time they shell Bragg. (CHICAGO HISTORICAL SOCIETY)

Above: Sherman's objective was Tunnel Hill, where the Chattanooga & Cleveland Railroad passed through this tunnel in Missionary. (NA)

Left: Opposing Sherman was Lieutenant General William J. Hardee. When the rest of the Confederate line on Missionary gave way to Thomas and Hooker; still he held out for a time, covering the retreat. Bragg never had a better subordinate. A heavily retouched prewar portrait taken when Hardee was in United States service. (CIVIL WAR TIMES ILLUS-TRATED COLLECTION)

Left: Major General John M. Palmer commanded the XIV Corps in the November 25 attack, virtually covering the entire battle line. One of his divisions held Thomas' right, another was the center division in the attack up Missionary, and yet a third of Palmer's divisions was with Sherman at Tunnel Hill. (CWTI)

Above: When the Confederates fled in rout from Missionary Ridge, they left behind them not only a signal Federal victory but also forty-two pieces of artillery. Here some 19 of the captured guns stand in line for the conqueror's camera. (USAMHI)

Above: After the victory there was rest for a time, and a sense of revenge for the humiliation of Chickamauga. Federal generals like Brigadier John H. King established their headquarters in comfortable surroundings such as this Italianate masterpiece on Lookout Mountain. (COURTESY OF TERENCE P. O'LEARY)

Left: There was time to lounge and relax once again. (TPO)

Right: Once again they could sight-see, here at Saddle Rock, for instance. "By sitting on this rock under a hot sun," they joked, "you can get a 'Saddle Rock Roast.'" (TPO)

Above: And in Chattanooga now the trains could come and go freely once more, taking men home for furloughs and bringing more back to continue the drive into the Confederacy. (MHS)

Above: Though Grant did not pursue Bragg into Georgia after Missionary Ridge, the Federals did begin even then gathering information for the next campaign in the spring. Out of Chattanooga they sent W. J. Lawton, an intrepid Federal scout who often traveled in the uniform of a Confederate colonel, as he is seen here. In mid-December he penetrated deep into the Confederate lines, learning that after their defeat the Southerners were "low-spirited and demoralized and said they had lost all hope of ever gaining their independence." (USAMHI)

Right: Even while the Chattanooga operations were under way, there was another campaign brewing in Tennessee, and it, like Chattanooga, brought another former commander from Virginia. Hooker fought for Lookout Mountain, and Major General Ambrose Burnside, the loser at Fredericksburg, defended Knoxville. Here he poses, seated, with his former chief of staff, Major General John G. Parke, standing at left. (COURTESY OF BRUCE GIMELSON)

Right: Burnside occupied Knoxville in September, freeing much of eastern Tennessee and allowing thousands of pro-Union Tennesseeans like these refugees to return home. These men were photographed in Knoxville just after their return, and the tattered condition of their clothing testifies to the hardships of their exile. (NA)

Above: Soon after Burnside took Knoxville, Confederate Brigadier General John S. Williams came out of southwest Virginia to harass the Federals. (VM)

Above: Williams fought with elements of Parke's IX Corps here at Blue Springs in October, but was forced back, ending any threat to Burnside for several weeks. Here portions of Parke's corps are encamped, protecting Knoxville's northeastern flank. (LC)

Above: George N. Barnard's view of the bridge of the East Tennessee & Virginia Railroad crossing the Holston River at Strawberry Plains. It was a major approach to Knoxville and well guarded, as the earthwork fort on the hill attests. One of Barnard's assistants—perhaps it is Barnard himself—stands behind an instrument at right. (LC)

Below: This panoramic view, blending two images, shows Knoxville as it appeared during the siege. It is taken from Fort Byington, west of the city, and looks across it. The Holston flows past at right, with Fort Stanley rising above the river at the south end. At the left center rise two hills containing important defensive works, Fort Huntington Smith at the left and Fort Hill to its right in the distance. (BOTH NA)

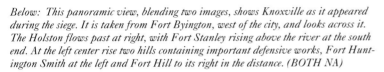

Below: Knoxville appears here in the spring of 1864, looking much the same as during its siege. Taken from the heights below Fort Stanley, this view looks north across the Holston. The Knoxville jail is at left. (LC)

Below: Looking farther to the west, the camera shows the jail at right and, at far left, the University of Tennessee building. In the distant background just to its right is Fort Sanders. (LC)

Above: Another view of the university, this image made at the time of the siege. (USAMHI)

Above: One of the defensive ditches on the perimeter of Fort Sanders, the Union bastion that withstood Longstreet's desperate assault. The university stands in the distance. (LC)

Above: Fort Sanders not long after the siege. A lone soldier stands now where thousands struggled. (LC)

Above: The Confederate chief of ordnance in the Knoxville siege was Lieutenant Peyton T. Manning, but for advice on the best use of his artillery, General Longstreet was more apt to turn to his devoted subordinate… (PRIVATE COLLECTION)

Right: … Colonel E. Porter Alexander, chief of artillery. Through the entire campaign he lost only four guns, thrown into the Holston during the retreat. (TU-LANE UNIVERSITY LIBRARY, NEW ORLEANS)

Far right: Less successful was Major General Lafayette McLaws, one of Longstreet's division commanders. His commander severely censured him for failing to take Fort Sanders, even though McLaws had fought well at Chickamauga. This portrait of McLaws was taken in Augusta, Georgia, in September 1863 during a brief stop in the trip from Virginia to join Bragg at Chickamauga. (TU)

Left: One of the first to die in the siege of Knoxville, Major William M. Gist of the 15th South Carolina was instantly killed on November 19 as he prepared to lead his regiment in a charge. A Federal sharpshooter's aim was true, and a fine Confederate officer lay dead. (MUSEUM OF THE CONFEDERACY)

Below: Silent Fort Sanders after the siege was done. Burnside's chief engineer, Brigadier General Orlando M. Poe, sits at left, facing Lieutenant Colonel Orville E. Babcock, chief engineer of the IX Corps. The success at Knoxville was largely due to their efforts. (USAMHI)

Above: Hood and the Federals met first around the little town of Franklin, shown here in an early postwar image. (USAMHI)

Above: Tennessee was relatively quiet for almost a year, until November 1864 when one last Confederate invasion came out of Georgia. General John Bell Hood planned to leave Sherman behind in Georgia and meet and defeat Thomas and his army around Nashville. Then he could invade Kentucky. It was a bold plan, but boldness was in the character of the one-legged general, shown here around the end of the war. (CHS)

Right: Commanding the three Union divisions in the fight at Franklin was Major General John M. Schofield, just thirty-three years old. Many years later he would recommend that the United States acquire Pearl Harbor in Hawaii. Schofield Barracks, near Pearl Harbor, is named for him. (USAMHI)

Left: Hood's attacks at Franklin were brutal, costly to both sides, and in the end he almost wore out his army. Major General Benjamin F. Cheatham, often accused of drunkenness by Bragg, led one of Hood's corps. He was already under severe censure by Hood for allowing Schofield to retreat to fortified Franklin. (CHS)

Above: Cheatham led his corps in an assault up the Columbia Pike against Federals placed behind the stone wall in the center of the photograph. (USAMHI)

Above: Then the Confederates came up against Schofield's main line, part of it on the Carter farm, just in front of this gin house. (USAMHI)

Above: Brigadier General John C. Brown led his division in attacks on the Carter farm until seriously wounded. (CHS)

Above: Half of Schofield's small army was the IV Corps, commanded by Major General David S. Stanley, seated second from the right. Nathan Kimball, seated at right, led the division that held Schofield's far right. General Thomas J. Wood, of Chickamauga fame, seated second from the left, stayed in reserve in the rear. The other generals are: seated at left, Samuel Beatty; standing, left to right, Ferdinand Van Derveer, Washington L. Elliott, Luther P. Bradley, and Emerson Opdycke. All except Van Derveer were in the battle. (USAMHI)

Above: Opdycke, in particular, was outstanding. His brigade spent thirty minutes bitterly defending a gap that had opened in Schofield's line near the Carter house. He sits in the center here with his regimental commanders. The young officer at far right is only nineteen years old and already lieutenant colonel of the 24th Wisconsin and a Medal of Honor winner. He is Arthur MacArthur, future father of General Douglas MacArthur. (USAMHI)

Above: Some of the bitterest fighting of the war rages around the Carter house, and it tells in the casualties. (USAMHI)

Above: Colonel George A. Smith of the 1st Confederate Georgia Infantry was killed. (VM)

Above: Brigadier General Otho F. Strahl was killed handing guns to his men. "Keep on firing" were his dying words. (USAMHI)

Above: Brigadier General States Rights Gist, like Strahl, led a brigade in Brown's division. He was killed instantly in the attack. (USAMHI)

Left: The cost to Hood's high command was devastating. Besides Strahl and Gist, Generals Hiram Granbury and John Adams were killed, and John C. Carter mortally wounded. But surely the most telling loss of all was the death of the premier division commander in the Army, Major General Patrick R. Cleburne. His was a loss that could never be replaced. (VM)

Right: While Schofield battled Hood at Franklin, General Thomas readied the defenses of Tennessee's capital... (USAMHI)

Left: ... Nashville. George N. Barnard made this image several months after the Battle of Nashville, but it still reveals Federal soldiers encamped on the state house grounds. (KEAN ARCHIVES, PHILADELPHIA)

Below: The state house in Nashville, with the Nashville & Chattanooga Railroad in the foreground . (NA)

Above: The view looking west from the capitol. The log breastworks hastily erected on the capitol building are still in evidence, with loopholes for firing. They were not used, but give evidence of Thomas' determination to hold every inch of ground. (USAMHI)

Above: Looking south from the capitol across the city. Cannon and earthworks still surround the building. (CWTI)

Above: Market Street, off the public square, in downtown Nashville. (USAMHI)

Above: With Hood weakened after Franklin, Grant ordered Thomas to leave his defenses and attack him. But Thomas would not do so until his cavalry was properly mounted. Mounts were always a problem for the cavalry. Here in Nashville, mechanics and smiths work at shoeing horses and keeping wagons in running order. (USAMHI)

Above: It presented a deceptively peaceful picture prior to the fury that was released when Thomas finally did attack on December 15. (USAMHI)

Above: George Barnard captured much of the Nashville scene that day including, here, another view along the outer defense perimeter. Somewhere in the distance Hood's army was being virtually destroyed. (LC)

Left: The next day, December 16, while the battle raged south of Nashville, soldiers left in the outer defenses of the city listened to and watched what they could of the battle. (MHS)

Far left: It was Brigadier General John McArthur's division that attacked and routed Hood's left flank on the first day of fighting. Hood never recovered, and McArthur won another star. (LC)

Left: Lieutenant General Stephen D. Lee had missed the debacle at Franklin, but reached Nashville in time to command the corps holding the right of Hood's deteriorating line. His was the last Confederate command to hold its position as Thomas continued his attacks. (USAMHI)

Left: Brave Confederates like these enlisted men of the Washington Artillery were no match for the greater numbers and fresh troops under Thomas. When New Orleans artist J. W. Petty photographed them in 1861, they were jaunty. After Nashville they and their army were devastated. (USAMHI)

Below: Everyone was a spectator on those two December days. (USAMHI)

Above: Federal Fort Negley, south of Nashville. Hood never got close enough to attack it. (CHS)

Above: Another view of Fort Negley, its gun embrasures glaring, like a smile with missing teeth, toward the Confederates. (USAMHI)

Left: A casemate inside Fort Negley. The light is gleaming on a gun tube inside the ironclad casemate, but the gun will never fire. With the repulse and destruction of Hood, the last threat to Tennessee is at an end. For three years North and South bitterly contested the Volunteer State. Now at last it is decided, and with it rests much of the fate of the Confederacy. (USAMHI)

Squadron of the South

FRANK J. MERLI

Of ships and sea and suffocating the Confederacy

Above: As with the origins of the North Atlantic Blockading Squadron, its Southern counterpart had to depend at war's start upon ships already in service, and often of checkered careers. The USS Niagara, *shown here in September 1863 at Boston, was the steam frigate that helped lay the first transatlantic cable. In 1860 she carried Japan's first diplomatic mission to the United States, then returned to America in April 1861 to find civil war. Immediately she went on the blockade. (LC)*

WHEN PRESIDENT ABRAHAM LINCOLN announced his intent to blockade the Confederate coast, he set on foot a host of problems for his Administration. For one thing, he violated a fundamental maxim of the American view of naval war —that there be no paper blockades. From the days of the Founding Fathers, Americans had insisted that in order for a blockade to be recognized in law it had to be maintained by forces sufficient to prevent entrance to and exit from the ports under blockade. However, in April 1861 the Union Navy simply did not possess enough ships to seal off the 3,500-mile shoreline of the South.

Of course, the President asserted his intent to post a competent force "so as to prevent entrance and exit of vessels from the ports aforesaid." But obviously, with only eight warships in home waters at war's outset, that was bold talk. And before the North could build or buy the ships that would demonstrate its determination to close the South to foreign trade, the European powers would monitor the blockade and assess its impact on their interests.

In the opening weeks of the war—about the time foreign officials started sorting out their responses to conditions in America—a talented Washington naval administrator began devising means to subdue the South by way of its vulnerable seacoasts. Alexander Dallas Bache, great-grandson of Benjamin Franklin, promoter par excellence of technological and scientific innovation, superintendent of the coastal geographic survey, and a supremely gifted political infighter, saw and grasped an opportunity to merge his interests with those of the navy and the nation.

Bache's suggestion for a naval planning board to develop a comprehensive strategy for implementing the blockade therefore found a sympathetic hearing, especially after John C. Fremont, a prominent Republican then in London, warned of "very active" and well-financed Confederate efforts to buy up large numbers of steamers in British shipyards. Secretary of the Navy Gideon Welles and his assistant Gustavus V. Fox remembered the proposal for a centralized naval coordinating committee and set about establishing it. Fortunately, they had at their disposal a number of talented men for the task. In addition to Bache, the Strategy Board, as it came to be called, consisted of Commander Charles H. Davis, Major John C. Barnard, representing the Army Corps of Engineers, and Captain Samuel F. Du Pont, a capable, if sometimes controversial, naval officer who acted as the board's president. Less than a month after its inception, it had prepared a number of important reports, suggesting division of the Southern coastline into four commands, the North Atlantic, South Atlantic, East and West Gulf Squadrons. The navy must seize a base in each, which, besides providing convenient supply and repair facilities for the fleets would also discourage European intervention for the South. They must show Europe that they could control their coastline.

In the autumn of 1861, as Captain Du Pont began massing his Federal armada for its assault on Port Royal, South Carolina, and began assembling and deploying the forces that would become the South Atlantic Blockading Squadron, the chief of Confederate naval procurement in Europe, Captain James D. Bulloch, started planning a challenge to that squadron. Bulloch decided to buy a ship, stock it with much-needed war material, and run it through the blockade. He set about that task with the flair and skill that marked all he did—and he succeeded brilliantly. The *Fingal* was loaded in Scotland, Bulloch and other passengers did not board until after she cleared customs, and after a slow passage the *Fingal* reached Bermuda on November 2. Now she prepared for the final, most perilous steps in the journey to the American coast.

Meanwhile, Union countermeasures began to yield results. On the same day that newly promoted Rear-Admiral Du Pont issued his General Order No. 1 to the commanding officers of the blockading vessels under his command, on October 24, 1861, Secretary of the Navy Welles sent him a warning that the *Fingal* was coming, loaded with supplies for the rebellion. Further, Welles had learned that a Confederate firm in London had purchased the vessel, making her "in reality a Confederate ship." That made her fair game.

After circumventing efforts of the American consul at Bermuda to deplete his crew and deprive him of coal, Bulloch set out for the southern coast on the afternoon of November 7. At a deck conference Bulloch took the men into his confidence, explained his mission, and asked for volunteers. To the question "Will you go?" he received unanimous assent. He then explained his intention to defend the ship against the Savannah blockaders. In the event of an encounter with a blockader, Bulloch intended to take control of the ship and fight it. Would the crew help? Again, to a man, they answered, "Yes."

After settling affairs with the deckhands, Bulloch looked to the most important preparation for a successful dash past the blockaders, the steam engine. As Bulloch explained his plan, Chief Engineer McNair told him that "he had been putting aside a few tons of the nicest and cleanest coal," that if Bulloch could arrange for him to clean his flues and fireboxes, the engines might be made to drive the ship, overloaded as she was, at 11 knots for a brief period.

The last night out, soon after midnight, "as nice a fog as any reasonable blockade-runner could have wanted" enveloped the ship, and under its protection the *Fingal* edged toward land, so as to be inshore of patrol boats. With lights out, engines silent, nerves taut, the crew waited for daybreak. Suddenly, an eerie wail, a sound like an "unearthly steam whistle" threatened to reveal their presence to every Federal vessel for miles around. Then it came again. The offending chanticleer, that bird of morning, did not greet the sun, for it met quick and violent death at the hands of an irate sailor.

At daybreak all was in readiness for the final dash into the harbor. The engineer's preparations proved their worth, as the engines now propelled the ship northward at a steady 11 knots. Even the elements helped, for the fog moved out to sea, forming a curtain between the shore and any patrol boats in the vicinity. Soon the *Fingal* sighted the massive brick walls of Fort Pulaski, crossed the bar, hoisted the Confederate flag, and acknowledged the waving hats and inaudible cheers of the men lining the parapets of that ill-fated fort. Then, close to safety, the *Fingal* ignominiously ran aground. Some hours later, with the help of a rising tide and local tugs, the *Fingal* completed her voyage upriver to Savannah at 4 P.M., November 12, 1861. She brought with her, by Bulloch's estimate, the greatest military cargo ever imported

Left: Warships were not available in abundance to begin Mr. Lincoln's stranglehold on the Southern coastline. This wooden side-wheel tugboat, USS O. M. Pettit, *was purchased by the Navy at the war's start and sent south. She appears here in 1862 off Hilton Head, South Carolina. (USAMHI)*

Left: Ships that accompanied the first offensives directed at the Confederate coast then stayed on post to do blockade duty. The USS Unadilla *was with the Federal fleet that attacked and occupied Beaufort, South Carolina, in November 1861. Thereafter she patrolled those waters, her hearty crew denied another real fight until war's end. (USAMHI)*

Left: The first commander of the South Atlantic Blockading Squadron upon its creation on September 18, 1861, was Rear Admiral Samuel F. I. Du Pont, standing second from the left aboard his flagship USS Wabash *in 1863. He enjoyed a notable career during the Mexican War, then began the Civil War by planning and executing the attack on Port Royal and Hilton Head. (USAMHI)*

Left: Du Pont's mighty ship, the Wabash, *taken in Port Royal Harbor in 1863, from the deck of the monitor USS* Weehawken. *Ironically, the only known image of the* Weehawken *that survives is the stanchion and rope that appears in the lower left of this image. (USAMHI)*

Above: An unpublished portrait of a black seaman aboard the Wabash. *Hundreds of Negroes served in the Union Navy and aboard the blockading ships. (PAUL DE HAAN)*

Above: Commander C. R. P. Rodgers was captain of the Wabash *while Du Pont flew his flag in that ship, commanding it in the attack on Port Royal. In the later siege of Fort Pulaski, Rodgers led the naval force that fought on land in the trenches, and in 1863 took the helm of the ironclad* New Ironsides. *(USAMHI)*

Above: Fort Pulaski was the next major move for the Southern squadron, but first there was extensive preparatory work. Ships like the Coast Guard schooner Arago *did hydrographic work along the shore and in the channels, making some 60,000 casts of the lead in sounding over 300 miles of coastline. Only armed with this knowledge could Du Pont's ships brave the Confederate shores and inlets. (USAMHI)*

Right: The first goal was Tybee Island, which controlled access to Fort Pulaski. Ships like the USS Savannah… *(USAMHI)*

Below: … and the steam sloop Pocahontas *mustered for the November 24, 1861 attack . (USAMHI)*

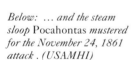

into the Confederacy. Bulloch himself modestly noted that probably "no single ship ever took into the Confederacy a cargo so entirely composed of military and naval supplies." In this, as in so much else connected with his Civil War career, he makes a reliable witness, though his contribution to the Confederate cause is vastly underrated all too often. The original Confederate plan called for Bulloch to stock the *Fingal* with cotton for the credit of the Navy Department abroad and to "return to Europe with her to carry out the further purposes of the government there." But from about November 25, 1861, until February 5—when Bulloch returned to Europe by an alternative route—it proved impossible for the *Fingal* to slip past the blockaders of the Union Squadrons.

During his enforced idleness at Savannah, Bulloch studied the strength and movements of units of the South Atlantic Squadron and assessed Confederate defenses and possibilities of keeping the port open to foreign commerce. His starkly professional reports make grim reading. At the Wassaw outlet Union forces consisted of anywhere from four to seven ships, "frequently as many as eleven"; the enemy seemed fully informed of the *Fingal's* position and of Southern plans to get her out to sea: "Unless there be some changes in the political relations of the United States with the courts of Europe, I consider the port of Savannah as completely closed to commerce for an indefinite time. There are… five ships-of-war at the entrance to the Romerly Marsh, a force too powerful for the simple blockade of the *Fingal*, and this assembling of the enemy's fleet can only be regarded as preliminary to an attack in force upon the city."

But of all of Bulloch's commentaries on conditions in Savannah and of his attempts to get the *Fingal* out past enemy blockaders, one has a particular poignancy. On November 25, 1861, Bulloch told Secretary of the Navy Stephen R. Mallory:

I have the honour to report that the stearn ship *Fingal* has been discharged, and now lies in the Savannah River ready to receive freight.... I cannot refrain from urging the necessity of getting the ship off without delay. Yesterday five of the enemy's gunboats stood cautiously in, and after throwing a number of shells upon and over Tybee Island, a force was landed without opposition. This morning the Federal flag is flying from the lighthouse, and they will doubtless soon have a battery upon the point of the island. The only egress left for the *Fingal* is through Warsaw [sic] Inlet, and it can scarcely be supposed that the enemy will permit it to remain open many days.

Perhaps his pressing concern for getting the *Fingal* back to England and for resuming the vital tasks assigned to him by the Navy Department prevented the usually astute Bulloch from assessing the larger significance of that Federal flag on Tybee Island's lighthouse.

From the USS *Savannah*, at anchor off Tybee Bar at 1 P.M. on November 25, Commander J. S. Missroon reported to Flag Officer Du Pont that at 3 P.M. the previous evening Commander John Rodgers "hoisted the flag of the Union on the martello tower and light-house... [on Tybee Island]." Du Pont lost no time in conveying this good news to his superiors in Washington. "I have," he told Welles, "the honor to inform the Department that the flag of the United States is flying over the territory of the State of Georgia.... I am happy now to have it in my power to inform the Department that the *Flag*, the *Augusta*, and the *Pocahontas* are at anchor in the harbor abreast of Tybee beacon and light, and that the *Savannah* has been ordered to take the same position. The abandonment of Tybee Island on which there is a strong martello tower, with a battery at its base, is due to the terror inspired by the bombardment of Forts Walker and Beauregard, and is a direct fruit of the victory of the 7th." Then Du Pont added a strategic prediction of some importance: "By the fall of Tybee Island, the reduction of Fort Pulaski, which is within easy mortar distance, becomes only a question of time."

Given the supposed impregnability of the massive masonry walls of Pulaski, few, especially among the local southern military commanders, would have agreed with that assessment. But in early 1862 steps were already under way to reduce the sentinel of Savannah.

In its first report of July 5, 1861, the Strategy Board had called for the capture of "a convenient coal depot on the southern extremity of the line of Atlantic blockades, and... if this coal depot were suitably selected it might be used not only as a depot for coal, but as a depot of provisions and common stores, as a harbor of refuge, and as a general rendezvous, or headquarters, for that part of the coast." The place selected by the board for these functions was Fernandina, roughly on the Florida-Georgia border. In addition to the many advantages Fernandina offered as a supply depot, its possession would afford Union forces considerable opportunities to cut off rail and water trade with other parts of the South—it would, in short, serve much the same function at the southern terminus of the blockade that Port Royal and Hampton Roads served in the North. It would give the Squadron effective control over the Georgia coast.

"And," as the board noted, "the naval power that commands the coast of Georgia will command the State of Georgia."

Above: The officers of the Pocahontas... *(USAMHI)*

Above: ... and the men... (USAMHI)

Above: ... and the boat's crew of the ship's cutter were all ready for the attack on... (USAMHI)

Above: ... Tybee Island. They took it without opposition, thus gaining a foothold at the mouth of the Savannah River and a perfect base for the attack on Fort Pulaski, which defended the city. (USAMHI)

Above: It was a place that had been defended before, 304 years before to be exact. The Spaniards erected this martello tower on Tybee in 1557. No longer are there halberds and burnished breastplates, but the soldiers are much the same, like the tower itself, eternal. (USAMHI)

Above: Now came Brigadier General Quincy A. Gillmore, and with him came a plan. He placed heavy batteries of rifled cannon on Tybee Island, and from there would bombard Fort Pulaski into submission. It was the first time that rifles were used against masonry, and the results were devastating. (USAMHI)

Above: Starting on April 10, 1862, Gillmore began to pulverize Fort Pulaski. Shell after shell burrowed into the brick face of the bastion. (USAMHI)

Although Du Pont wished to commence the Fernandina offensive as soon as the Port Royal operation was completed about mid-November 1861, a number of factors combined to delay the start of that operation until early in 1862. Toward the end of 1861 the naval and military commanders, Du Pont and Brigadier General Thomas W. Sherman, had agreed "to some kind of offensive against Savannah," but the ambitious undertaking, requiring logistical resources (especially supplies of coal) and coordination of command facilities not then available, proved "too intricate and hazardous," and it had to be curtailed. As a sort of compromise, the navy set out for Florida, and the army set about preparing for the task of reducing Fort Pulaski, a major obstacle to control of the entrances to Savannah. While Sherman set his plans in motion, Du Pont assembled his armada for the assault on what would become the southern depot of the South Atlantic Squadron.

The long-awaited attack on Fernandina when it came proved an anticlimax. On March 4, Du Pont reported himself in complete possession of the objectives of his mission, having achieved that goal merely by defending his forces against "a few scattered musket shots... from the town." Du Pont's report of the expedition to Secretary Welles contains a capsule comment on the affair that would be difficult to improve upon: "We captured Port Royal, but Fernandina and Fort Clinch have been given to us." If he knew the reason for the "gift" he did not mention it in his report.

After the loss of Port Royal, General Robert E. Lee and other Confederate leaders had reluctantly concluded that the defense of the Atlantic seaboard was impracticable and beyond the capa-

Above: By the end of the day very few Rebel cannon still stood ready to continue the fight . (USAMHI)

Above: More were out of action, like this mortar caught by photographer Timothy O'Sullivan, who made most of the Fort Pulaski views taken that April. (LC)

bilities of military and naval forces of the South. Except in a few special cases, as, for example, Charleston, Confederate forces would withdraw inland, out of range of Union naval bombardment. In early February 1862, General Lee wrote to General James M. Trapier, commander of the Florida military district, that Fernandina might have to be abandoned unless sufficient guns could be found to command the entrance to the Cumberland Sound, "the back door" to the island. By February 24 the Confederate high command realized that no guns could be supplied to the Cumberland forts, and Trapier was authorized to evacuate his defenses. The logic of Southern strategy, not overpowering Union strength, gave Du Pont control of the South Atlantic Coast at no cost. The navy subsequently played only a minor, token role in the later attack on Fort Pulaski, which was predominantly an army operation. Federal troops had occupied Tybee Island, about a mile from the fort, in late 1861, and by early April 1862 they had constructed eleven batteries, including ten 9-inch Columbiads, heavy rifled guns, and emplacements of 13-inch mortar.

Although the attack on Fort Pulaski did not lead to the surrender of Savannah, it did demonstrate another lesson of "modern" war—that walls, however massive and well constructed, could not withstand the pounding of heavy rifled cannons, especially those equipped "with these wonderful projectiles which we now possess," as one Union gunner summed up the encounter. In fact, so poorly defended was the fort that it took Federal forces a mere 30 hours and about 5,275 shots on April 10–11 before the Confederate commander, twenty-six-year-old Colonel Charles H. Olmstead, surrendered. But he raised the white flag only after the fort's flagpole, flying the Stars and Bars, had been shot away three times and the fort's magazine stood exposed to the danger of imminent explosion from enemy fire. His seven and one-half-foot thick walls crumbled under Yankee bombardment.

A reporter for a local newspaper visited the shattered fort soon after its surrender and left this account: "… all the parapet guns were dismounted.… Every casemate gun, except one, [was] dismounted and the casemate walls breached in almost every instance to the top of the

Left: Inside the casemates was a shambles, the rubble so choking the embrasures that even functioning guns could not be reloaded . (LC)

Left: The next day Gillmore resumed his bombardment against weakening resistance. These two gaping holes appeared in the wall, leaving the fort vulnerable to an assault at any time. Its commander had little choice but to surrender. (NEW-YORK HISTORICAL SOCIETY)

Above: In time the industrious Yankee engineers and workmen rebuilt Pulaski into a powerful link in the blockade chain that constricted Savannah. (CHS)

Above: By 1863 the Federals had built up a mighty arsenal and restored much of the fallen masonry, making Pulaski again one of the more attractive casemated forts on the Atlantic coast. (USAMHI)

Above: The 3d Rhode Island Heavy Artillery came to man the mighty seacoast guns that faced Savannah and the ocean. (USAMHI)

Below: The giant smoothbores dwarf a smaller siege gun as the Rhode Islanders go at their gun practice. Two men at front left strain under the weight of a projectile while others pass a powder cartridge from the open chest. (USAMHI)

arch—say between five and six feet in width. The moat outside was so filled with brick and mortar that one could have passed over dry-shod.... The parapet walls on the Tybee side were all gone, in many places to the level of the earth.... The protection to the magazine in the northwest angle of the fort had all been shot away; the entire corner of the magazine next to the passageway was shot off, and the powder exposed, while three shots had actually penetrated the chamber."

The role of the South Atlantic Blockading Squadron was limited and of minor significance. For a time the naval component of the expedition camped on the beach, without being allowed into combat, for all the guns had been manned. Then, after an insubordinate colonel had been relieved of his command and his German troops refused to fight without him, the sailors of Du Pont replaced them and served with distinction. The naval battery, firing three 30-pound Parrott rifled guns and one 24-pound James rifle, proved to be one of the two deadliest components of the Union attack. Commander C. R. P. Rodgers later reported that his rifled guns bore "into the brick face of the wall like augurs," while the columbiads were "striking like trip hammers and breaking off great masses of masonry which had been cut loose by the rifles." The general in command recognized the services of the Navy by including Naval Lieutenant John Irwin in the party that accepted the Confederate surrender of the fort.

This left the *Fingal* trapped in Savannah, and now that presented the Confederate defenders with a glorious opportunity to augment their naval forces. In the spring of 1862 the vessel was turned over to a local shipyard for conversion into an ironclad. In time the blockade runner *Fingal* became the ironclad CSS *Atlanta*, and her story is very much part of the adventures of the South Atlantic Blockading Squadron.

First, the ship was cut down to her deck, which was slightly widened and overlayed with a thick layer of timber and iron. "A casemate was built, the sides and ends inclining at an angle of about 30°." The sides and ends of the casemate were covered with about four inches of iron plate, secured to a backing of three inches of oak over 15 inches of pine. She was armed with two 7-inch rifled guns on bow and stern pivots, and two 6-inch rifled guns in broadside.

As soon as the ship was completed, a public

clamor "to do something" with so magnificent a weapon arose, and the public political pressure prevailed over the calmer, more prudent plans of the naval authorities charged with the defense of the city. "Although the [city] council considered the Confederate armorclad to be competent to al most any achievement," Tattnall knew better. His experience with the *Virginia*, plus his knowledge of the *Atlanta's* deficiencies, convinced him that she would not stand a chance. "I considered the *Atlanta* no match for the monitor class of vessel at close quarters, and in shoal waters particularly." Despite his considerable misgivings about the wisdom of trying to run past the Union guardships, Tattnall agreed to make the attempt. But Union reinforcements of the outlets with the new class monitor *Passaic* stymied Southern plans, at least for the moment. After several shake-ups in the Savannah naval command, Mallory found a man anxious for action. The new commander, William A. Webb, had a reputation with fellow seamen as "a very reckless young officer," one who received his appointment primarily because "he would at once do something." His plans included, among other things, to "raise the blockade between here and Charleston, attack Port Royal, and then blockade Fort Pulaski"—all this without assistance, if need be!

Union intelligence about the maneuvers and plans of the *Atlanta* were "uncanny." When, on the night of June 16, she attempted to surprise the Union forces, a lookout on the monitor *Weehawken* spotted her approach and sounded the alarm at 4:10 A.M. Captain John Rodgers, commander of the Union monitor, was a member of one of America's most illustrious naval families and an experienced officer in his own right, with a reputation for courage and audacity. He commanded an experienced crew that knew its business, cleared for action, and took their ship downstream ready for any contingency, though they and their captain were a bit puzzled by the opening gambit in this game.

Upon entering the Wilmington River, Webb had sighted his quarry, and in his enthusiasm to attack he left the narrow channel and ran aground, a perfect target for the gunners on the *Weehawken*.

Approaching the grounded ship to a range of about 300 yards, Rodgers opened fire with his 11 and 15-inch Dahlgrens, and four out of five shells fell with devastating impact on the near-helpless

Above: Some of their guns they named for popular generals and, like "Burnside," the not so popular. His fellow Rhode Islanders here were perhaps more forgiving than others in the North. (USAMHI)

Below: Governor William Sprague found this namesake at the southwest corner of Pulaski's parapet, commanding a scene that inspired confidence in Union might. (USAMHI)

Below: Officers of the 48th New York garrisoned the fort and posed for the camera along with their colonel, W. B. Barton, standing with his wife. Beyond them lay the mouth of the Savannah River and, in the distance, Tybee Island. (USAMHI)

Below: Inside on the parade ground, the band of the 48th New York and, on dress parade.. (USAMHI)

Above: ... the 48th New York itself, complete with seldom seen white gloves. (USAMHI)

Above: But always in the distance, just ten miles away to the northwest, lay Savannah, and Fort Pulaski must be, like the sentinel, ever vigilant. (USAMHI)

Southern ship. One shot wounded as many as 40 or 50 men. Other shots disabled guns, shot away the pilot house; and Webb's immobility and list prevented him from bringing any of his own guns into effective play. He fired some seven shots, none of them effective. Fifteen minutes of battle —if it can be called that—convinced Webb that he had no choice but to surrender.

Rodgers got a vote of confidence from Congress and a promotion to commodore; the Navy Department believed that its faith in the new monitor class had been vindicated at the bar of history; and Admiral Du Pont could turn over command of the South Atlantic Blockading Squadron to Admiral John A. Dahlgren with a measure of contentment, that, while sweet, did not quite erase the bitterness of his failure to capture the cradle of the Confederacy at Charleston, South Carolina.

From the beginning of the war, Charleston, South Carolina, "the cradle of the Confederacy" and "the hotbed of secession," had possessed a peculiar fascination for Union military and naval planners. Consequently, Washington devoted more resources and time to the subjugation of the city than its military importance justified. However splendid the city might be as a symbol of Confederate defiance, it had no war industries of importance, and its comparatively inadequate rail network with the rest of the South deprived it of any great utility as a way station for blockade-runners.

Yet, Federal naval administrators, especially Assistant Secretary of the Navy Gustavus V. Fox, regarded capture of the city as "the ultimate propaganda prize" for the United States Navy; further, capture of the city would enhance the department's reputation and demonstrate its worth by "attaining a spectacular psychological victory," and in addition a Union victory at the heart of rebeldom would mute press and congressional criticism of the department and confirm the Administration's faith in the invincibility of the newer class of monitors, then coming off the stocks of northern naval yards.

Du Pont wished a carefully prepared and coordinated attack on the city, not because it had any military value, but because failure at so prominent

Above: For the sea-based elements of the Southern squadron, there was much more to blockade duty than looking for runners. Army generals like Benjamin F. Butler might live in the plush cabins of their headquarters boats like the transport Ben DeCord... (USAMHI)

Above: ... but the Navy men had constant work to do. Maintaining the fleet in those Southern waters required extensive on-site facilities, like the machine and carpenters' shops in Station Creek, near Port Royal. (USAMHI)

a place might have disastrous domestic and international repercussions. Impressed by some of the technological improvements in Union ships and guns, Du Pont nonetheless retained substantial reservations about the plans outlined to him by his superiors. More important, he was made to believe that the Navy was expected to take the city: he had "to recognize that this operation was of no consequence to the Army" and no troop reinforcements could be expected for the raw recruits that had been sent to the region. And Du Pont made an important mistake: he never fully convinced his superiors that in fact "he was fundamentally opposed to the method of attack" rather than to merely this or that tactical aspect of the plan.

At noon on April 7, 1863, Du Pont ordered his offensive, with the *Weehawken* in the van, pushing a raft to clear mines and torpedoes from the column's line of approach. The Confederates had not only heavily obstructed the channels but they had marked them with range finders, which greatly increased the accuracy of the fire with which they were able to rake the Union ships as they advanced into range. The *Weehawken*, for example, engaged the enemy for some 40 minutes, sustaining over 50 hits, and as she disengaged she was taking water through a shot hole in her deck. The *Passaic* was hit about 30 times; *Patapsco* became a kind of sitting duck for the Confederate gunners in Forts Moultrie and Sumter and sustained nearly 50 hits; *New Ironsides* escaped certain destruction when an electric torpedo with a ton of gun powder miraculously failed to go off. The last ironclad in line, the *Keokuk*, spent 30 minutes under the undivided attention of the guns of the Confederates, sustaining some 90 hits, many of which lodged below the waterline. Calm weather allowed her to stay afloat overnight, but the next day a roughening of the sea sent her to her grave, but not before the captain and 15 survivors were able to save themselves.

The severe battering that his ironclads had sustained led Du Pont to call off the attack, and though he originally expected to resume it the next day, the reports of his captains changed his mind. As he told Welles, "I was fully convinced that a renewal of the attack could not result in the capture of Charleston, but would, in all probability, end in the destruction of a portion of the ironclad fleet and might leave several of them sunk within reach of the enemy. I therefore determined not to renew the attack, for in my judgement it might have converted a failure into a disaster."

Perhaps Du Pont anticipated some of the northern response to the repulse of his forces, for on April 8 he wrote to Henry Winter Davis and let some of his bitterness show. He told Davis, "Of course, I am ready for the howl—but I never was calmer in my life and never more happy that, where I thought a disaster imminent, I have only had a failure." In letter after letter Du Pont bitterly complained of the monitor mania of his superiors in Washington and of the greed of those civil contractors who pressed the Navy for immediate use of a weapon of unproven effectiveness. In an outburst of anger he once told Davis that "eight musical boxes from Germany off Ft. [Sumter] would have brought about the same effect upon the rebel cause."

Public and departmental dissatisfaction with the results at Charleston led to a shake-up in the naval chain of command. On June 3, 1863, Secre-

Left: Machine shops at Bay Point performed repairs, such as replacing the smoke stack of the monitor Passaic *after it was severely damaged in the April 7, 1863 attack on Charleston. (USAMHI)*

Left: Most of the fleet repairing took place at this floating shop in Machine-Shop Creek, near Port Royal, where two old whaling ships, Edward *and* India, *were converted for the purpose. (USAMHI)*

Left: A constant flow of ships passed into and out of Port Royal, ships like the monitor at center, the transport at left, and James Gordon Bennett's yacht Rebecca *at right. (USAMHI)*

Left: Old ships of the line like the Vermont, *too aged for active service, came south to act as receiving and store ships. (NAVAL HISTORICAL CENTER)*

Above: Captain John Rodgers, standing fourth from left in the center group, commanded the Vermont *at Port Royal and chafed that her massive array of guns remained silent. (USAMHI)*

Above: For officers who had trained for active service, their—perhaps their only—war seemed to be merely one of watch and wait. Even the ship's dog seems bored with the blockade service. (USAMHI)

Right: But certainly some were not bored. Poor Commander George Preble, standing center at the Philadelphia Navy Yard in this early postwar image, was dismissed from the service in 1862 for allowing a Confederate cruiser to run the blockade into Mobile, but then was restored to his rank and sent to Port Royal. He commanded the coal depot for a time, and near the end of the war actually led a "fleet brigade" in fighting on shore. (USAMHI)

tary Welles informed Du Pont that because of his opposition to a renewal of the attack on Charleston the department was relieving him of his command of the South Atlantic Blockading Squadron. The new commander, Andrew Foote, an officer admired by Du Pont, despite the former's advocacy of monitors, unfortunately died before he could assume his new command. His replacement was, from Du Pont's point of view, a less happy one. Admiral John Dahlgren had long intrigued for command of the South Atlantic Squadron, and in his quest he had the advantage of being a favorite of President Lincoln, who much appreciated the loyal support that Dahlgren had tendered in the uncertain early days of the war. In his new post, the armchair admiral hoped to add seagoing laurels to his impressive record of some 20 years as chief of the Bureau of Ordnance. Earlier Du Pont had told another correspondent that "Dahlgren [had been] made an admiral, in part for a gun which is a greater failure than the monitor which carries it."

Dahlgren's repeated attacks on Charleston in the months that followed his appointment fared no better than had Du Pont's, and resulted in greater loss of life and material. Dahlgren launched a series of well-organized but vain attacks on the city but could make no substantial progress in reducing it into submission. It has been estimated that in the course of the Union at-

Below: Real action came to the squadron in 1863, as blockaders, enemy ironclads, and attacks on Charleston kept the fleets busy. On April 7, Du Pont, against his better judgment, attacked Charleston and saw his ironclad fleet severely battered. Ships like the Passaic *visibly displayed their damage. (USAMHI)*

Below: The officers even posed beside their dented turret. (NA)

Above: Yet the Nahant *was revenged a bit. She joined the* Weehawken *in June 1863, with Captain John Rodgers now commanding the latter. (USAMHI)*

Above: The USS Nahant *took 36 hits on its turret, which was completely disabled during the fighting. She appears here shortly afterward in Machine-Shop Creek, with the floating machine shops barely visible in the distant background to the left. The powerful 15-inch Dahlgren and 11-inch Dahlgren smoothbores peering out of the turret were useless to her in the attack. (USAMHI)*

tacks in a few days of the summer of 1863 over 5,000 Federal shells, weighing well over a half million pounds, had rained down on the defenders of Charleston—and still they held out; it is also said that the Union bombardment of Sumter on September 1-2, 1863, was one of the heaviest ever recorded in the annals of war up until that time. Yet the beleaguered city continued to hold out against the best the Union could throw at it, and when the end came, it did not come from the sea.

It is extremely difficult to judge with any precision the impact that the blockading squadrons had on the defeat of the South. The need for secrecy and the danger of capture led to the falsification and destruction of records; the intricacies of international law and the ramifications of British neutrality regulations led to some really imaginative efforts at subterfuge and disguise. Nor is it always possible to unravel the complicated skein of secrecy that the Confederacy wove to cover its operations.

Most important, blockaders had to contend with the greed of those who saw golden opportunities in evading it. "Moreover, once the blockade was in effect, the inflated prices that provisions and war supplies commanded in the Confederacy made it profitable for British shipbuilders to construct fast vessels designed exclusively for blockade-running," and most of these benefited from the technological improvement that steam gave the runner over the blockader. The ports of the South seemed a cornucopia of profit, and even as late as 1864 it is estimated that as many as two of every three ships eluded the most vigilant blockaders. One careful assessment of the efficiency of the blockade of the Carolina ports from 1861 to 1865 estimates that of the more than 2,000

Left: The two of them passed the Frying Pan Shoals Lightship and steamed to Wassaw Sound. The Nahant *is the monitor in the right background. (USAMHI)*

Left: Together they battled and captured the formidable Confederate ironclad Atlanta, *shown here after she was converted to Federal service and sent to the James River in Virginia. (NA)*

Below: Captain W. A. Webb was the Atlanta's luckless commander. He spent the next several months in Fort Warren Prison. (MC)

Above: So did Lieutenant George H. Arledge. (WA)

Above: And 1st Assistant Engineer W. J. Morell. (WA)

Above: And Gunner T. B. Travers. (WA)

Above: And poor Midshipman J. Peters. (WA)

Right: And soon after the capture of the Atlanta *there came a new face to the South Atlantic Blockading Squadron, Rear Admiral John A. Dahlgren, shown here at center with his staff aboard his flagship, the USS* Pawnee. *(NHC)*

attempts to breach the blockade about 85 percent were successful.

No one has ever calculated the profits of foreigners who entered the Confederate trade. Successful captains cleared £1,000 on a round trip from Nassau to Wilmington, and their crews were proportionately well paid. It is reported that one ship earned nearly £85,000 for about three weeks work; and conservative estimates say that profits of £30,000 on each leg of a journey into and out of the Confederacy were not uncommon. It is well known that throughout the war profits remained high, with one Liverpool firm reported to have cleared over £4 million in the trade. Unfortunately, most of these profits accrued to middleman profiteers, for it was late in the war before the Confederate Navy Department established its own system of supply under government sponsorship— and by that time it was too late to have much of an impact on the course of the war.

But the blockade may have cost Lincoln more than it was worth, for it tied up warships that might have been more effective elsewhere. America's greatest naval historian, Alfred Thayer Mahan, reflected upon the naval lessons of the

Above: Once again the crews and their guns readied for an attack. The after 10-inch Dahlgren smoothbore aboard the Wabash, *the gun designed by the new squadron commander. (USAMHI)*

Above: When it was first decided to replace the hapless Du Pont, Washington opted for a naval hero from the West, Admiral Andrew Hull Foote, who relinquished his command of the Mississippi flotilla after the successes at Forts Henry and Donelson and Island No. 10 due to a wound. On June 4, 1863, he received orders to relieve Du Pont, but three weeks later, before he could assume command, he died. (CWTI)

Civil War, and in an all too infrequently quoted passage he observed, "But as the Southern coast, from its extent and many inlets, might have been a source of strength, so, from those very characteristics, it became a fruitful source of injury. The great story of the opening of the Mississippi is but the most striking illustration of an action that was going on incessantly all over the South. At every breach of the sea frontier, warships were entering.

The streams that had carried the wealth and supported the trade of the seceding States turned against them, and admitted their enemies to their hearts. Dismay, insecurity, paralysis, prevailed in regions that might, under happier auspices, have kept a nation alive through the most exhausting war. Never did seapower play a greater or more decisive part than in the contest which determined that the course of the world's history would be modified by the existence of one great nation, in stead of several rival states, in the North American continent."

Possibly the blockade was a waster of resources and opportunities. Certainly the lessons of history are wasted if we recount the story of the South Atlantic Blockading Squadron without asking whether the Federal ships engaged in that duty could have struck a more decisive blow if they had abandoned the coasts for the rivers.

Above: The Wabash's *forward pivot gun, a mammoth 200-pound rifle. Captain H. B. Lowrey, commanding the ship's Marine contingent, stands bearded in the center, while one of his Marines brandishes a much smaller rifle at the far left. (USAMHI)*

Left: Another great Dahlgren aboard the Wabash, *dubbed the "Truth Seeker." (USAMHI)*

Above: The USS Pawnee, *ready for battle. (NA)*

Right: Dahlgren's signalmen aboard the Pawnee *will transmit his orders to the fleet during the impending attack on Charleston. (LC)*

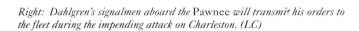

Above: Yet Dahlgren's attacks are no more successful than Du Pont's. The monitor Patapsco's *turret shows the beating it takes. (USAMHI)*

Above: The USS Dai Ching *is no more successful, though later in the year she will go on to capture a blockade-runner before being ordered to Florida. (USAMHI)*

Above: But for the Dai Ching *the war will end on February 3, 1865, when she goes down off Savannah. (USAMHI)*

Right: Again in September, Dahlgren sends his monitors against Fort Sumter, and again without success. For the Patapsco *there are only more dents in the turret. (USAMHI)*

Above: Dahlgren himself went aboard the Montauk for his September bombardment, but its most famous passenger would come nineteen months later, when the body of John Wilkes Booth was brought here briefly before its burial. Here, too, some of the other conspirators in the Lincoln murder were imprisoned. (DAM, LSU)

Above: After the attacks of the summer of 1863, the squadron settled down to the routine of hunting blockade-runners, and effectively at that. The USS Nipsic captured the runner Julia on June 27, 1864. (USAMHI)

Above: The fragile runners could not hope to match powerful guns aboard gunboats like the Nipsic. If they were unable to get away, they surrendered without a fight. (USAMHI)

Above: Sometimes even lightly armed transport ships like the Arago managed to effect a capture or two. (USAMHI)

Above: The Arago, shown in this Samuel A. Cooley view, took part in the celebrated capture of the runner Emma, loaded with cotton, turpentine, and resin. (NA)

Above: The mortar schooner USS Para lent a hand in taking the Emma, though this mighty mortar, "Old Abe," was not called on in the fight, for there was no fight. (USAMHI)

Above: And their ships were the coveted prizes. Frequently they ran them aground rather than surrender, only to see the vessels battered by the waves. Here, on Morris Island, near Charleston, lie the remains of the Ruby. *(USAMHI)*

Above: And here the wreck of the blockade runner Colt, *near Sullivan's Island, in 1865. It was a sad end for these greyhounds of the sea. (USAMHI)*

Above: Gentlemen like this blockade-runner captain, posing calmly with a Confederate banner in Havana, were the wary quarry. (HP)

Above: The squadron extended down to Florida as well, and there Commander John R. Goldsborough patrolled in his USS Florida, *helping in the 1862 capture of Fernandina. (USAMHI)*

Above: There her crew would not see action but simply relieve the Vermont *as a stores and depot ship. It was an ignominious end for these mighty ships of oak. (USAMHI)*

Above: While for others the age-old game of wait went on. The old ship of the line Alabama *was laid down in 1819, but was never launched until April 23, 1861 forty-five years later! She hit the water with a change in name, now the USS* New Hampshire, *and went south to Dahlgren. (USAMHI)*

Above: And so the work went on. Work done by a hundred forgotten vessels and thousands of unsung men. Little armed transports like the Nelly Baker *did their share. (NA)*

Above: So did the giant transports like the Cahawba, *shown here in June 1864, probably at Hampton Roads. (USAMHI)*

Above: There was little the Confederates could send against them except their innovative but ineffective little "Davids," the cigar-shaped torpedo boats that Southerners hoped might sink a few of the Goliaths strangling their ports. One rests here at the Bay Point machine shop, captured by the Federals and photographed by Cooley. (WRHS)

Above: While the "Davids" were not too successful, the Confederate submarine CSS H. L. Hunley *managed to sink the USS* Housatonic *in Charleston Harbor before she went down herself in mysterious circumstances. The USS* Canandaigua *shown here swooped in to pick up the survivors from the first ship in history to be sunk by a submarine. (GLADSTONE COLLECTION)*

Above: Another "David" appears, beached near Charleston, its propeller broken, its torpedo spar extending from its nose. They were makeshift vessels, little better than coffins. (NA)

Above: And at war's end they seemed everywhere along Charleston's waterfront. (NA)

Above: Even in Washington's navy yard they were to be seen tied up next to Yankee monitors. They were the last tangible evidence of the vain efforts of the Confederacy to combat the power of the South Atlantic Blockading Squadron. (NHC)

Partners in Posterity

A PORTFOLIO

Haas & Peale and their incomparable record of siege in South Carolina

IN 1863, AS FEDERAL MINIONS sought relentlessly to take Charleston, their major obstacle was Fort Sumter and the ring of earthwork forts built around the South Carolina city. In a chapter in Volume IV of this series, Fighting for Time, the story of the Siege of Charleston was told. However, there were a pair of photographers there who told much of the story themselves in images far better than words. They were Haas & Peale of Morris Island and Hilton Head. Their 1863 images depicting General Quincy Gillmore's efforts to take Charleston represent almost the total corpus of their Civil War work. Except for a few portraits and random images, Haas & Peale seem to appear in Civil War photography with their arrival at Morris Island, and then disappear again when they have done. Little more is known of them.

Yet if any artists of the war can rest securely knowing that their fame depends upon a single series of images, then surely Haas & Peale have safely made for themselves a niche in posterity with their Charleston views. They are somewhat unique in Civil War photography. Mathew Brady, Alexander Gardner, Samuel Cooley, and others attempted to create and market series of images showing battle and campaign scenes, yet they offered them to the public only in oversized "imperial" prints too unwieldy for casual collecting, stereo views that required a stereo viewer, or else in the small carte-de-visite format that offered little detail for large outdoor scenes. Haas & Peale, however, created a series of over 40 serially numbered views around Charleston in a medium-sized format that offered the advantages of size, chiefly quality, without the disadvantages attendant to the oversize prints.

Alas, it remained for others to gain public acceptance of this new photographic style in the years after the war when the cabinet photograph enjoyed its vogue. But though their innovation did not last, still the work of Haas & Peale has lasted, a reminder of perhaps the most accomplished photographic partnership of the war.

Above: Here on Morris Island, spread out toward the horizon, sprawls the camp of the 9th Maine Infantry. (USAMHI)

Right: They made a virtual tent city, huddled along the shoreline to catch the ocean breezes in the hot, humid summer. (USAMHI)

Left: Undaunted by the heat, General Gillmore and his staff posed in reasonably full uniform for the partners. Gillmore sits at center striking a contemplative pose as he ponders an enormous map captioned "Charleston, South Carolina." Arrayed here and there are a variety of shells and solid projectiles to lend a suitable warlike atmosphere. (USAMHI)

Above: Still, Gillmore, too, could seek some relief from the sun and heat in his tent headquarters on Folly Island. (USAMHI)

Above: There was less relief for the men manning the siege guns that pounded Fort Sumter and the other Charleston forts, however. Here are three 100-pounder Parrott rifles in Battery Rosecrans, all trained on Sumter. (HUGH LOOMIS COLLECTION, KA)

Below: Things do not always go as planned, including cannon shells. One of those 100-pounders had a shell burst before it cleared the muzzle, creating a considerable curiosity for men and officers of the battery. (USAMHI)

Below: An equal curiosity were men from the webfoot service doing shore gun duty. This naval battery of two 80-pounder Whitworth rifles threw its shells, too, at Fort Sumter. Just so no one would forget where they came from, the naval deck carriage of the rifle at right carries the legend "Rear Admiral S. F. Du Pont, Port Royal, S.C." It also carries a pair of boots and some laundry drying in the sun. (USAMHI)

Above: The mammoth 300-pounder Parrott rifle in Battery Strong. (NYHS)

Above: In some places Gillmore built his batteries on artificial islands made of pilings driven into the swamps, or else on little more than built-up sand spits. Here in Battery Hays sat one such gun emplacement, this one for an 8-inch Parrott rifle that is, at the moment, dismounted. (CHS)

Above: The rest of the guns in Battery Hays, however, these 30-pounder Parrott rifles, are more than ready to do service in the bombardment of Confederate Fort Wagner at the end of Morris Island. (SOUTH CAROLINA HISTORICAL SOCIETY, CHARLESTON)

Above: This 300-pounder Parrott in Battery Brown got a bit carried away. (USAMHI)

Left: Its neighbor manages to seem coolly indifferent. (NYHS)

Right: Gillmore peppered Fort Sumter with everything, including these 10-inch siege mortars in Battery Reynolds, here aimed at Fort Wagner. One of the mortar shells can be seen dangling between the two soldiers at extreme left. (NYHS)

Left: These two 100-pounder Parrotts in Battery Meade are attempting to blast a breach in the masonry walls of Sumter. All that they and their fellow batteries will succeed in doing, in fact, is in reducing the fort to a shapeless mound of rubble that will never surrender. (SOUTH CAROLINA HISTORICAL SOCIETY)

Left: Here at the headquarters of the field officer of the trenches, almost anything might be found, stretchers, beer bottles, spare shells, even an "infernal machine," a torpedo or mine. (HUGH LOOMIS COLLECTION, KA)

Left: The telegraph operator, relaying orders and messages back and forth, really needed protection, and here in this bombproof he got it. (NYHS)

Right: Everywhere those who did not live in tents went underground. Here in Fort Wagner, after its fall to Gillmore's army, Federals occupied the bombproofs once used by the Confederates. Earth and sand were happily neutral in this war—they would shield blue and gray alike. (USAMHI)

Right: Life in the lens of Haas and Peale was a little better for the men at sea, even those serving aboard converted Staten Island ferry boats like the Commodore McDonough. At least they could move a bit now and then, steam up to within range of one of the forts, throw a few shells, and then put back out to sea where the breezes cooled the guns and the men. (USAMHI)

Right: The gunboats could not count on navigational assistance from the Charleston lighthouse on Morris Island. In 1863 this is all that was left of it. (USAMHI)

Left: And this is all that is left of a 3oo-pounder Parrott after a shell burst just inside the muzzle. Yet this gun could still be fired, and was. (USAMHI)

Above: When not digging or firing, it was a siege of boredom for Gillmore's little army. These regimental officers had plenty of time to pose for Haas & Peale. (USAMHI)

Above: Now and then, mostly for practice, Gillmore's field batteries drew up in formation, looking formidable, but utterly ineffectual against Sumter's walls or against Fort Wagner's earthworks and bombproofs. Battery B, 1st U.S. Artillery. (USAMHI)

Left: The Beacon House on Morris Island was sufficiently ventilated that heat no longer appeared to be a problem. (USAMHI)

Above: It could get awfully hot out there under the sun. (LC)

Above: But the heat and boredom got to a few, including this unfortunate fellow. He bears a sign proclaiming his offense: "THIEF. This Man, Benj. Ditcher, 55th Mass. Vol's, Stole Money From a Wounded FRIEND." Ditcher had his head shaved, his hands bound behind him, and was paraded through the camp by a guard carrying their rifles upside down and musicians playing the "Rogue's March." Ditcher, like the rest of the 55th Massachusetts, was a Negro, and his "wounded friend" was almost certainly injured in the skirmishing on Folly Island. (CHS)

Above: An orderly delivers a message for the camera on Folly Island. The colonel receiving it is duly formal for the occasion, but the men in the neighboring tent seem unimpressed by the ceremony. (CHS)

Right: Meanwhile the work of reducing Sumter went on, as did Haas & Peale's work of capturing it with their camera. Battery Kirby, with its two 8-inch seacoast mortars. (USAMHI)

Above: One of the "splinter-proofs" to protect gunners from flying chunks of wood and debris as Confederate shells sporadically returned fire. (USAMHI)

Above: In the seemingly endless siege work against Fort Wagner, Gillmore, ever the engineer, created miles of trenches and siege works, pushing parallels ever closer to Wagner. The workmen pushed this rolling sap ahead of them, dug behind it, and thus inched their way toward the fort. (SOUTH CAROLINA HISTORICAL SOCIETY)

Above: Haas & Peale were intent upon capturing it all on their glass plates. (LC)

Above: Meanwhile, the tent city grew ever larger, and the buildup of supplies never stopped. Gillmore was intent upon victory. (LC)

Left: And the irrepressible common soldiers on Morris Island were simply intent upon finding a shady spot wherever they could, even in the shadow of one of their wounded but still dangerous monsters. (USAMHI)

Into the Wilderness

ROBERT K. KRICK

Grant and Lee meet at last, and will not part

Above: The quiet general from the West, come east to face the undefeatable Lee. U. S. Grant was a lieutenant general, the only man of such rank in the Union Army, and now he commanded all of Lincoln's forces in the field. Grant, with his horse Cincinnati, in early June 1864. (NA)

BRANDY STATION and Stevensburg and Culpeper had seen some bitter fighting before the war reached 1864. The locale seemed to attract cavalry forces and mounted charges. In the spring of 1864, however, the whole width and breadth of Culpeper County seemed to be carpeted with Northern canvas. The mighty Federal host was commanded by George G. Meade, but it was to be accompanied on its operations by the general-in-chief of all the Northern armies, U. S. Grant.

On May 4, Grant and Meade launched their long-suffering Army of the Potomac across the Rapidan River into dangerous country. Pontoon bridges carried seasoned veterans and frightened youngsters alike into the Wilderness of Spotsylvania. The river crossings at Germanna Ford and Ely's Ford were historic ones. Lafayette had been here two generations before; this same army had crossed these same fords to disaster just one year and five days earlier.

The Wilderness was a dank and unlovely piece of country, about 70 square miles in extent. Its tangled brush and confusing ravines had enfolded and bemused Joe Hooker's army during 1863's Chancellorsville Campaign. The 1864 edition of the same Federal force might be mired in the same morass, and the Confederate Army of Northern Virginia was just the agency to collaborate with the Wilderness in the undertaking.

R. E. Lee had reunited his army in the month before the Wilderness fighting opened. His I Corps had been on an ill-starred winter campaign in Tennessee, suffering through James Longstreet's failure as an independent strategist. General officers languishing in arrest and deteriorating morale in the ranks gave evidence of the change in the old reliable body. When Lee reviewed the returning corps near Gordonsville, the atmosphere was electric. A hard-nosed brigadier, not given to outbursts of emotion, wrote, "The General reins up his horse, & bares his good gray head, & looks at us & we shout & cry & wave our battle flags & look at him again.… The effect was that of a military sacrament."

Federal columns thrusting through the Wilderness on May 5 were threatened from the west by two separate Confederate corps moving on the Orange Turnpike and the Orange Plank Road. The battle was fought along those two corridors. Dense intervening Wilderness segregated the two fights into bitter enclaves, all but independent of each other. Richard S. Ewell's II Corps and the Union V Corps contested the Turnpike. Fighting raged with particular ferocity around a small clearing known as Saunder's Field or Palmer's Field. The Turnpike bisected the field and a shallow wash ran perpendicular to the road. A Union battery in the .clearing was repeatedly taken and retaken. Infantrymen from both armies sought shelter in the draw. Both sides entrenched with desperate enthusiasm.

Muzzle flashes in the woods ignited leaves, the fire spread to brush and trees, and soon the wounded were burning to death. The sound of cartridge boxes exploding could be heard over the crackling of flames. Federal wounded who could be reached were carried back to surgical stations beyond the Lacy house, "Ellwood," where Stonewall Jackson's arm had been buried twelve months earlier. There were also Federal hospitals farther east toward Wilderness Church and other landmarks from the Chancellorsville Campaign. Skeletons of the unburied dead from that earlier fight were macabre prophets, watching the wounded thousands streaming back.

The costly stalemate achieved during May 5 along the Turnpike was duplicated two miles to the south, along the Plank Road. George W. Getty's division of the U.S. VI Corps stood strong around the intersection of the Plank and Brock roads. The Confederate III Corps followed A. P. Hill up to the fringe of the key intersection and threatened to make it their own, thus isolating the sizable Northern force which had advanced farther south—and setting the stage for destroying the stranded Federals. But the balance of affairs swung away from A. P. Hill and by the end of the day his forces were in dire straits. Hancock's II Corps had pushed the Confederates to the point of breaking when darkness halted operations. One third of Lee's army had not yet reached the field —the I Corps—and its arrival during the night was the only way to forestall disaster.

Grant had spent the 5th near the intersection of the Turnpike with the road from Germanna Ford. He had directed most of the VI Corps under John Sedgwick to strengthen the right flank, above the Turnpike. The troops had moved obliquely into the fray, turning off the Germanna Road near Mrs. Spotswood's house and heading southwest on what was known as the Culpeper Mine Road.

Throughout the 6th of May, Ewell's Confederates and the troops of Sedgwick and Warren struggled inconclusively along the Turnpike. The fragmented gains and losses in the woods yielded a frightful casualty count but no real tactical advantages. John B. Gordon alertly discovered a golden opportunity to turn the Federal right and destroy it; the potential rewards were dazzling. Corps commander Ewell, of the striking personality and the fatal irresolution, equivocated. Not until R. E. Lee arrived in the area during the evening could Gordon get approval to pluck his prize. Gathering darkness constricted the opportunity, but Gordon had little trouble in catching several hundred prisoners—two Union brigadiers among them. The Georgian always believed, using some fragile but persuasive hypothesis, that the lost opportunity was among the greatest that ever slipped through Southern fingers.

Meanwhile, the separate battle along the Plank Road on May 6 had caromed from the brink of Confederate disaster to the brink of Northern disaster and then settled comfortably near a neutral, if bloody, equilibrium. Hancock threw his II Corps into a solid attack early in the morning, exploiting the success he had won the previous evening. Longstreet's corps was not in line, despite Lee's expectations. The Southerners were driven in disorder along the Plank Road all the way back to a small clearing where stood the house and orchard of a widow named Tapp. Lee's army faced disaster. Veteran units, overwhelmed, ran "like a flock of geese."

In this extremity, the first of Longstreet's arriving men filtered into the clearing. Lee's desperation showed through his usually calm mein as he tried to lead the reinforcements into action. They turned his horse back forcibly and promised to restore the situation. The episode was the first of four "Lee to the rear" incidents during a seven-day period. The Federal initiative was blunted, then turned back. Lee grasped the initiative for his own. A flanking movement down an unfinished railroad grade (the same that had figured

Left: He would station himself with the Army of the Potomac and send it into the Wilderness to find Lee and never let him go. Here Grant sits in June 1864, at Cold Harbor, after the Wilderness Campaign is over. Seated beside him is his chief of staff, Brigadier General John A. Rawlins. Standing is Major Theodore S. Bowers. (CHS)

Left: All through that winter and early spring of 1864 the Army of the Potomac prepared itself for the drive into the Wilderness. Part of the army was stationed around Culpeper, Virginia, including the brigade of Brigadier General Alexander S. Webb, standing, hand on sword, in front of his tent. His brigade was almost wiped out by Pickett's Charge at Gettysburg, and in the coming campaign Webb will nearly lose his life. An A. J. Russell image. (USAMHI)

Left: Nearby, just north of Brandy Station, sat the VI Corps. Here Major General John Sedgwick made his headquarters in the home of Dr. Welford. Sedgwick himself stands third from the right. He will not survive the campaign. (WAR LIBRARY AND MUSEUM, MOLLUS-PENNSYLVANIA, PHILADELPHIA)

Left: All around Brandy Station the tents of the waiting Federals sat through the winter. The men were anxious for another chance at "Bobby Lee." (P-M)

Right: Anxious, too, was the immediate commander of the Army of the Potomac, the only man in the army who had ever beaten Lee, Major General George Gordon Meade. Here he stands, fourth from the right, with some of his officers, among them Sedgwick—second from the right—and Brigadier General A. T. A. Torbert, far right, who commands a division of cavalry that will protect Meade's flank in the advance. (P-M)

Right: But there were some old faces in the army that would not be going, and one of them that Meade would not miss was Major General William H. French. Here he stands, fifth from the left, among officers of his III Corps. Meade blamed French for the failure to bag Lee the previous November, and shed no tears when the III was reorganized out of existence and French himself mustered out of active service. (USAMHI)

Right: Finally came May 4, 1864, the great day. Grant ordered the army to move, and the once-teeming winter camps were deserted. James Gardner caught this scene near Brandy Station shortly before the army moved out. (LC)

Right: The first to cross was the V Corps, its wagon train seen here rolling over a bridge at Germanna Ford on the Rapidan. Timothy O'Sullivan photo. (USAMHI)

prominently at Chancellorsville) rolled up the Federal lines "like a wet blanket," in the words of Hancock. At the height of the Confederate surge, Longstreet and General Micah Jenkins were shot down by the mistaken fire of advancing Confederates. In the aftermath, momentum dissipated and the Confederates were obliged to accept a result which forestalled Southern disaster but did not inflict a thorough defeat on the enemy. Longstreet's wounds were thought to be mortal but he recovered and returned to duty in October; Jenkins died during the afternoon.

The Northern army had come across the Rapidan nearly 120,000 strong. Lee was able to counter with about 65,000 men of all arms. That lopsided arithmetic actually grossly understates the case, because the Southern barrel was scraped to its bottom and the Northern barrel was virtually without bottom. Two days of bloodshed in the Wilderness had cost Grant perhaps 18,000 readily replaceable pieces of his army. It had cost Lee less than half that many irreplaceable troops. (Numbers and losses verities—always subject to divergent interpretations—are especially elusive in the 1864 spring campaigns.) Precedent clearly showed Grant the route back across the Rapidan. But the general-in-chief had his eye set on some ghastly and inexorable logic based in the simplest forms of arithmetic—addition and subtraction. On the night of the 7th he prodded the Army of the Potomac into a lunge to the southeast, where there would be unquestioned opportunity to destroy more of the dwindling crop of Southern boys who stood between the North and victory.

Grant's move was toward Spotsylvania Court House, an unobtrusive country settlement composed of three churches and a hotel and a store and a few county buildings. Lee's men raced Grant's for the place, starting long before any other ranking Confederates had deduced what was afoot. Lee's prescience won the race for his side by a matter of seconds. The Federals slogged southeastward along the Brock Road. Southern cavalry resisted the advance from each hedgerow and wood line. Near Todd's Tavern there was a violent clash with Federal cavalry, which was otherwise notably ineffective during this move.

While tired Federal infantry fought and stumbled down the Brock Road, the Confederate I Corps marched most of the night along a parallel route farther west. Richard H. Anderson had had command of the corps since Longstreet's wounding, and he got a very early start. On the morning of May 8, advance elements of Anderson's command were within a mile of the key intersection, which was near a farm called Laurel Hill. Alarms reached them, and they rushed forward just in time to hurl back the first Federal infantry to approach the intersection.

The Union troops were members of Warren's V Corps. The men had been fighting or marching, with little or no rest, for five days. As more of them came up, someone set the bands to playing as faint encouragement, and more assaults were attempted, with the same fatal results. A Confederate officer riding along the lines spied his little brother, an artillerist just through his first action, sheltered behind a dead horse. The boy jumped to his feet, flushed with his newfound valor, and called incongruously across the deadly field, "Bubba, Bubba, I wasn't scared a bit—not a bit!"

Federal reinforcements stumbled into line and

Above: Timothy O'Sullivan recorded the ensuing crossings as the Army of the Potomac supplied the campaign that would drive Lee to cover. Soldiers of the VI Corps cross on pontoon bridges over the Rappahannock at Fredericksburg later in May. (LC)

Above: Awaiting them all was the man who had been the nemesis of so many Federals before them, General Robert E. Lee. There is a deceptive peacefulness about his visage in this image by Richmond photographers Vannerson and Jones. He will be ready for Grant and Meade. (CHS)

Confederate reinforcements arrived opposite them.

Both sides entrenched quickly and deeply. After darkness fell on May 8, the Southern line was stretched to the northeast in a great salient angle which came to be known as "The Mule Shoe" because of its shape. The next morning, as the lines were being consolidated, a Confederate sharp shooter firing from very long range killed John Sedgwick. The corps commander had been purposely standing under fire to encourage his men, saying, "They couldn't hit an elephant at this distance."

On May 10, brilliant young Emory Upton, of New York, led an attack against the Confederate salient's western shoulder. He had recognized the opportunity, sold the plan to his superiors, and executed the attack with skill. The absence of promised support kept the fruits of success beyond reach, but when the Federals were driven back they took along a substantial number of prisoners.

Grant may have concluded that the time was ripe to take Lee head on; or perhaps he decided that that had always been the solution which earlier Federal leaders had missed; or perhaps his ghastly arithmetic suggested that any sort of fighting was going to do the job, and tactical niceties therefore verged on irrelevance. In any event, the successful frontal assault by Upton began a month of frontal assaults in which tens of thousands of Federals were shot with relative ease by sheltered Confederates.

Two days after Upton's temporary success, the Army of the Potomac went right over the top of the Confederates' Mule Shoe earthworks and raised havoc with Lee's entire position. An early morning assault by the Federal II Corps under Hancock shattered the nose of the salient and pushed into the heart of the Southern lines. Near the McCoull house the advance was blunted. Desperate counterattacks pushed the Federals

Left: He will meet them first here, along the Orange Turnpike, four miles west of the Wilderness Church. This is Palmer's Field, and just visible at the base of the trees in the background are the hasty entrenchments behind which Lee awaits Warren. Photo taken late in 1865 or early 1866. (USAMHI)

Left: Charging against these log breastworks, Warren is unsuccessful. His men are caught in a deadly crossfire. An early postwar image. (USAMHI)

Above: One of the defenders is Brigadier General John Marshall Jones, who leads his brigade in defense of those breastworks. During one of Warren's desperate assaults, Jones sat on his horse gazing at the approaching enemy when a bullet ended his life. (VM)

Above: Behind these defenses, the Confederates could withstand everything Warren hurled at them. It was to be a foretaste of the bitter, often inconclusive fighting of the Wilderness. Taken within months of the end of the war. (USAMHI)

Above: During that day's fight on May 5, Warren made his headquarters in the Lacy House, seen in the far distance in this view taken from the Wilderness Tavern. The battle line lay just another mile over the hill. (USAMHI)

Right: Still farther behind the line, though still taking its name from this tangled mass of woods and thickets, stood the Wilderness Church, itself almost lost among the trees. (USAMHI)

Below: Many died that first day, among them Brigadier General Alexander Hays, shown here at his headquarters near Brandy Station. He stands tenth from the right, hand on hip. (COURTESY OF LLOYD OSTENDORF)

back to the tip of the salient and then the fight deteriorated into a brutal brawl at arm's length for some 20 hours. Only earthworks separated the ragged lines as they fought in the rain and mud and blood. Quite early in the struggle a 20-inch-thick oak tree toppled to the ground, having been chewed off by the incessant streams of balls flying in such profusion that the hard wood was gnawed as thoroughly as though by beavers. When Confederate survivors stumbled back to a new line across the base of the salient, their abandoned works had more than justified the *nom de guerre* "The Bloody Angle."

The logistics which controlled the will of generals had dictated a change of base to Grant. His lifeline was shifted from his right rear at Culpeper to his left rear by way of Fredericksburg to the Potomac River at Belle Plain landing. The success of the early morning attack on the salient on May 12 was traceable in part to a coincidence resulting from Grant's change of base. Lee received word of the activity in that direction and for once his uncanny perception of enemy intentions failed him. He feared a major enemy move to the southeast (which eventually came on May 21), and weakened his front line in preparation for a countermove of his own. That fringe benefit was unknown to Grant, but the logistical merits were large. The maritime might of the North steamed to Belle Plain and made it into an overnight city. Confederate prisoners and Federal wounded were funneled out through the landing; recruits and war material and horses passed them en route to the front.

The grisly night of May 12 also brought terrible news to Lee from Richmond. J. E. B. Stuart had been harrying Federal raiders, who were being led toward Richmond by Philip Sheridan. On May 11 a severe cavalry fight had taken place at Yellow Tavern, just north of the capital. Promising young North Carolina Brigadier James B. Gordon had been killed and Stuart himself had suffered a mortal wound. He died in Richmond during the evening of the 12th, while distraught friends and colleagues sang "Rock of Ages" at his request.

Back at Spotsylvania, Grant had Meade moving his army steadily around to its left flank. Warren's V Corps, which had started the battle on the right, moved around to the far left and set up headquarters at the Francis Beverly house, not far from the Court House. Every day there was fighting of varying intensity; sometimes it was localized, sometimes it spread along the lines, but always there was fighting. On May 18, Grant ordered Meade to move against the strongly fortified Confederate main line. Defending artillery so thoroughly swept the attackers that many Confederate infantrymen hardly noticed the whole affair. Meade wrote disgustedly to his wife that finally "even Grant found it useless to knock our heads against a brick wall."

On May 19, Lee sent most of his II Corps, under Ewell, to swing up behind the abandoned Bloody Angle and probe the right rear of the new Federal alignment. The result was an intense struggle around the Harris farm. The Confederates played havoc with some green heavy-artillery regiments, which fought with admirable tenacity, although only recently converted to infantry service. In the confusion many Federal units fired on one another. A disgusted quartermaster watched "Kitching's brigade firing at the enemy; then Tyler's men fired into his; up came Birney's division and fired into Tyler's; while the artillery fired at the whole damned lot." In the final analysis, Ewell had more than he could handle and fell back in confusion under cover of some horse artillery which happened along. The newly blooded Federal heavy artillerists buried their own dead and the Confederate dead around the Harris house and the nearby home of Widow Alsop. Black troops of Ambrose Burnside's IX Corps played a small role in this affair; it was their first action with the Army of the Potomac.

When the armies moved away from Spotsylvania on May 21 they left behind the bloodiest ground in North America. The campaigns in the vicinity from 1862 to 1864 had resulted in more than 100,000 casualties. Grant's route took him

Below: On their way to the battle line, Warren's men and the others to follow came down the Germanna Plank Road to Wilderness Tavern, then marched straight down the Orange Turnpike, shown here running off to the horizon. The tavern stands at left. (USAMHI)

Left: Viewed from the Orange Turnpike, the Wilderness Church nestles at left in the trees, with the Hawkins farm on the right. This was some of the only cleared ground in the vicinity of the battlefield. (NA)

Left: The rest looked like this, these grinning skulls now as much a part of the Wilderness as the leaves and underbrush. (USAMHI)

Below: Sedgwick followed Warren into the battle with the Confederate defenses, his leading division belonging to Major General Horatio G. Wright. Wright, standing in the center beneath the peak of his tent, displays the VI Corps banner behind him. He seems almost to be smiling, and others definitely are. When this photo was made in June 1864 at Cold Harbor, Confederate shell fire was occasionally coming their way, and while the camera was laboriously being adjusted, one wag in the scene commented that he could "Wish a shell would hit the machine." The officers were still smiling when the exposure was made. (USAMHI)

Above: The 56th Massachusetts and the 36th Massachusetts were both repulsed in a bloody assault the afternoon of May 6. At war's end their regimental colors were little better than rags. (USAMHI)

Above: And some of the regiments that fought here were little better. Company I of the 57th Massachusetts went into the fighting on May 6 numbering 86 men. Several weeks later, these nine men, commanded by Sergeant R. K. Williams at right, were all that was left. (USAMHI)

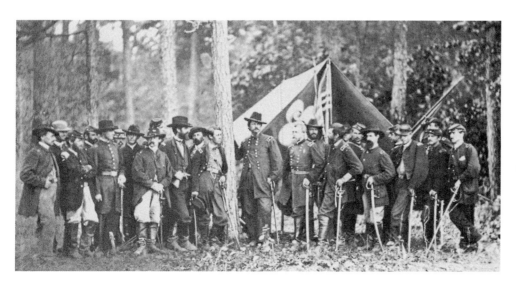

Left: Commanding Meade's II Corps was Major General Winfield Scott Hancock, seen here with his generals and staff. Leaning in front of the tree is Brigadier General Francis Barlow, who began the war as a private. Just to the right of the tree stands Hancock, and next to him is Major General David B. Birney. As the fighting left the Wilderness and moved on to Spotsylvania, Birney and Barlow won glory by capturing over 3,000 Confederates. In the front row next to Birney is Brigadier General John Gibbon. (USAMHI)

past Massaponax Baptist Church in the eastern fringe of Spotsylvania County. A Federal surgeon riding past the church noticed the generals and their entourage seated in the yard of the church on pews. He also watched the ungainly snout of a camera poking out of an upstairs church window recording the high command at deliberations as the Army of the Potomac was being spurred southward on May 21, 1864. The new movement prompted another change of base by the Federals, this time to Port Royal on the Rappahannock River. Grant luxuriated in the flexibility which Union naval prowess gave him.

For two days the armies raced for an advantage, then for five days (May 23–27) they fought and maneuvered along the North Anna River. There were four main river crossing points from west to east: Jericho Mills, Quarles Mills, Ox Ford, and at the Chesterfield Bridge. The commanding heights of the north bank of the river overlooked the south bank and its river flats at all of these points except Ox Ford. Lee skillfully anchored his line at Ox Ford, where the terrain made it all but impossible for the Federals to force a crossing. He then fortified a strong line running away from the river in two lines, covering the absolutely vital rail facilities at Hanover Junction. The line formed an inverted "V," with its apex at Ox Ford.

The Army of the Potomac laid pontoons at the other three crossing points and pushed across in strength. The heaviest skirmishing was in the vicinity of Jericho Mills. Lee pulled his units back into the entrenched line and contemplated a superb opportunity to hurt Grant. The Confederate grip on Ox Ford meant that Lee could move his troops to either side of his line for an attack on a Federal fragment; Federals rallying to the point of attack from the other end of the line would be forced to trek in a huge half circle and cross the river twice. The opportunity was an exciting one, but the prospects for execution revealed the state of Lee's army. Not only was mighty Stonewall gone, but also A. P. Hill was not meeting Lee's needs, Ewell was freshly relieved of his command, and the army could not be put to the task with the verve that had made it famous.

Lee himself was suffering physically during the week and was unable to personally carry the command load at the corps level, although that was to be his lot for much of the remainder of his army's existence. Grant got away from North Anna unscathed. If he noticed the shadows that had been held from his path, and had some understanding of his good fortune, he must have seen reason for optimism; the Army of Northern Virginia had lost its power to assume the offensive, and the most egregious Federal blunders would yield no more than temporary embarrassment.

The next move to the southeast took the Army of the Potomac from the North Anna to the Pa-

Left: The terrain in the Spotsylvania fighting was not any better than the Wilderness, tangled woods filled with Confederate rifle pits and log breastworks. (USAMHI)

Below left: Some, like the brilliant Confederate Brigadier General John B. Gordon, corltinued to win laurels as the campaign progressed . (VM)

Below: Some, like Brigadier General James S. Wadsworth, were left behind, dead in the Wilderness. A Brady & Company photo, probably made in 1862 when Wadsworth was military governor of the District of Columbia. (ROBERT J. YOUNGER)

Above: Colonel Samuel S. Carroll led one of Gibbon's brigades in the Spotsylvania fighting until a wound put him out of action. He won a brigadier's star for his conduct, but spent months recuperating, as shown here. (P-M)

munkey River and beyond to Totopotomoy Creek. The Union columns poured across the Pamunkey at and near Hanovertown. Grant moved his supply base again, down to the White House on the Pamunkey. The house and estate had been owned by General W. H. F. Lee before the war and had connections with Lee's Custis and Washington ancestors. An earlier Federal occupation, during the 1862 Richmond operations, had left the house in ashes. Now it was to serve as the port of entry for another onset.

During the last five days of May there was heavy localized fighting but no widespread action. Through it all, Lee maintained a tenuous grip on the irreplaceable Virginia Central Railroad, barely west of his positions. There was a sharp cavalry fight north of Totopotomoy Creek on the 29th at Haw's Shop and another south of the creek at Old Church the next day. Also on the 30th the Confederates sent John Pegram's excellent brigade forward in an attack near Bethesda Church. Division commander Stephen D. Ramseur was widely blamed for the disastrous result of this attack. James B. Terrill of the 13th Virginia was killed; the Confederate Congress confirmed his nomination as brigadier general the next day.

Right: There were others who would not see Spotsylvania either. Caught in the accidental fire of his own Confederates, the popular and talented young South Carolina Brigadier Micah Jenkins took a bullet in the brain on May 6. In his delirium he urged his men forward, forward. (CHS)

Far right: And shot with Jenkins, though only wounded, was the commander of Lee's I Corps, his old war horse, Lieutenant General James Longstreet, back in Virginia after his ill-fated Knoxville Campaign. The wound put him out of the war for months. Probably an early postwar portrait, taken in New Orleans. (WA)

Above: This is the view that Jenkins and Longstreet were not there to see. Timothy O'Sullivan's image was taken near Spotsylvania Court House. In the foreground are baggage wagons attached to the headquarters of the V Corps, Army of the Potomac. (LC)

Above: Spotsylvania Court House itself, like so many of the places visited by these warring armies, was a simple country village until war made its name terrible. (USAMHI)

Above: The Spotsylvania Hotel, near the Court House, in a late 1865 view. (USAMHI)

Above: Opposite the hotel was so-called "Cash Corner." (USAMHI)

The last meeting of the armies north of the James came at Cold Harbor. During the last night of May both armies completed the gradual slide to the southeast which had been leading to a crossroads called Cold Harbor. A few days short of two years earlier, Lee had fought on this same ground his first major battle as commander of the Army of Northern Virginia, driving McClellan from his position in the Battle of Gaines' Mill. Fitzhugh Lee's cavalry attempted to hold the Cold Harbor crossroads for the Confederates on May 31 but Alfred Torbert's Federal troopers forced Lee away. William F. "Baldy" Smith's XVIII Corps was coming along to help, having been transferred to this front from the scene of the ineffectual operations being bungled by Ben Butler below the James.

The dispute between Fitz Lee and Torbert served as a foundation on which both armies eventually built a network of fortifications. A good opening was lost to the Confederates on the morning of June 1 as a result of some inexperienced leadership and some well-handled Federal Spencer carbines. Late on the 1st, a determined Union assault won some ground from Lee, but at heavy cost. Grant planned a massive attack for June 2 but the delayed arrival of Hancock's II Corps resulted in a postponement until the next morning. Opportunistic Southern initiatives on each flank captured some prisoners during the day; among the Confederate dead was competent, seasoned brigade commander George P. Doles, a thirty-four year-old Georgian.

About 4:30 on the morning of June 3, Grant sent the Army of the Potomac forward in a massive frontal assault which has since come to symbolize the nadir of generalship. The II, VI, and XVIII Corps attacked in directions which left their flanks exposed to vicious enfilade fire as well as head-on punishment. Within a few minutes the attacks had been beaten down, although many of the Northern survivors stubbornly held their ground near the Confederate lines and began to protect themselves with earthworks. The flames and smoke from Southern weapons hid their enemies from the stunned Federals hugging the ground. The roar, they were certain, exceeded the musketry of any other battlefield, even without the artillery thunder. More than 7,000 Union troops had been shot within a few minutes. Four days later Grant requested a truce to tend to the survivors; for ten days the armies lay within 100 yards of each other. The heat and stench and flies and sharpshooters vied for attention. Trench warfare was becoming a way of life. The disgruntled chief of staff of the Federal VI Corps declared that Cold Harbor "was the dreary, dismal, bloody, ineffective close of the... campaign... and corresponded in all its essential features with what had preceded it."

While the armies glowered across the lines around Cold Harbor, events elsewhere in the state affected them. Union General David Hunter's predations in the Shenandoah Valley demanded Lee's attention. On June 13, Jubal Early led the Confederate II Corps away from Richmond toward Lynchburg. Lee was also obliged to weaken his army by detaching Wade Hampton, with two divisions of cavalry, in order to contain a Federal cavalry force raiding under Philip Sheridan. Below the James, Union forces under Benjamin Butler posed a threat to Richmond and Petersburg and the crucial rail net around those cities. On June 9 a scratch force defended Petersburg by the barest

Above: That same day, in the attempt to reach and hold Spotsylvania Court House before Lee could arrive, the Federals sent Brigadier General David McM. Gregg and his Second Cavalry Division on a reconnaissance that was stopped by the arrival of most of Lee's army. Gregg is seated at right. (USAMHI)

Above: Some of the first fighting in the Spotsylvania operations took place here at Todd's Tavern at the junction of the Brock, Catharpin, and Piney Branch roads. Grant tried to use those roads to get around Lee but could not. (USAMHI)

margin against Federal cavalry under August V. Kautz.

The same day that Early marched away toward the Valley, Lee discovered that Grant was moving away from Cold Harbor. In the tangled countryside between the Chickahominy and the James, Lee lost track of his adversary and Grant took advantage of the terrain to outmaneuver the Confederate commander. By June 16 almost all of the Army of the Potomac was across the James River, having crossed on a pontoon bridge of great length and marvelous engineering. From the 15th through the 18th, Petersburg was held by P. G. T. Beauregard against increasingly heavy masses of attackers. Beauregard knew what was happening and pleaded for reinforcements from Lee, but Lee was slow to respond, in part because Beauregard was habitually importunate.

An almost unbelievable series of accidents and failures kept the overwhelming Federal force from taking Petersburg when it was ripe for the taking. Odds ranging up toward ten-to-one were frittered away. The frustrated commander of the Army of the Potomac finally issued peremptory orders for an assault by each corps, regardless of supports which just could not quite be coordinated. When it was made, the precious opportunity had slipped away, and veteran Confederates had arrived to man the earthworks and destroy the attackers. Eager but unseasoned heavy artillerists-turned-infantrymen (the same who had stood so firmly at the Harris farm a month before) continued the attacks. Veterans tried to stop them with "Lie down, you damn fools, you can't take them forts." The damn fools lost more men in one regiment that day than any other Union regiment lost in any battle through the entire war! Grant had suffered about 12,000 casualties while failing to get into Petersburg. It would cost many more, and almost a year of trying, before the town finally fell.

Above left: The first Confederate to arrive on the scene at Spotsylvania was Major General Richard H. Anderson, now risen to replace the wounded Longstreet. Just in time he stopped the Federal drive for the Court House. (VM)

Above: Leading one of Anderson's divisions was Major General Charles W. Field. After the war he took service in the army of the Khedive of Egypt. (USAMHI)

Left: Fighting with him was Brigadier General Harry T. Hays, who received a desperate wound that left him convalescent for much of the rest of the war. (VM)

Above: On May 9, Grant suffered a major loss when Major General John Sedgwick, commanding his VI Corps, was killed by a Confederate sharpshooter. "They couldn't hit an elephant at this distance," he calmly boasted just before the marksman's bullet brought him down. (USAMHI)

Above: The next day, May 10, the desperate and bloody assaults that characterized the Spotsylvania fighting commenced. Warren's V Corps spearheaded much of it. His Second Division commander, Brigadier General Charles Griffin, is seen standing just right of the tent pole. There were few better soldiers in the army. (USAMHI)

Above: Most brilliant of all was the attack led by Colonel Emory Upton, shown here wearing the brigadier's stars that his assault on "The Bloody Angle" won. He was just twenty-four. (NA)

Right: It was some of the most desperate fighting anywhere in the war. Hardly a tree in the vicinity came through it without some memento such as this Confederate shell, found near the position of the 7th Rhode Island. (USAMHI)

Far left: Desperately, Confederates like this private, David Hicks of Virginia, sought to drive Upton back. (AMERICANA IMAGE GALLERY)

Left: Two days later Grant ordered an even more massive attack where Upton's had almost succeeded. It was in an area called "The Mule Shoe," and here it was that Birney and Barlow overran the Confederates and captured several thousand. Reinforcements rushed to "The Mule Shoe," among them Brigadier General Abner Perrin. "I shall come out of this fight a live major general or a dead brigadier," he supposedly declared. He came out a dead brigadier. (P-M)

Left: While the Spotsylvania fighting continued on into the middle of May, Grant constantly built up his supplies for the overland campaign through his supply base at Belle Plain, on the Potomac. Once it had belonged to the Confederates, and their earthworks could still be seen on the hill above the landing. (WRHS)

Below left: But in May 1864 it belonged to the Union, and it teemed with men and wagons. A Brady & Company image taken probably on May 16, 1864. (USAMHI)

Below: Most of the supplies came ashore on the lower wharf. (USAMHI)

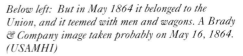

Above: It saw the constant comings and goings of supply steamers as the wagons lined up on the wharf to take on their burdens. (USAMHI)

Above: And then they were off on their way to the Army. (USAMHI)

Above: Brigadier General James J. Abercrombie, seated at right, had just taken command at Belle Plain on May 12 and was still new to it when this and other Belle Plain images were taken. He was one of the oldest officers on active service, born in 1798. He will later be relieved of command at Grant's next supply base when he appears to be "bewildered and lost." (KA)

Above: A. J. Russell's view of the upper wharf at Belle Plain, just the day after engineers built it. Already a barge awaits unloading. (LC)

Above: There was more than supply to contend with. For one thing, Grant was taking thousands of prisoners in the Spotsylvania fighting. Here a host of them wait at Belle Plain for transportation to prison camps in the North. (WRHS)

Above: Then there were the wounded, like these stretched on the Marye House lawn in Fredericksburg. (USAMHI)

Above: In the days ahead, Grant would take even more Confederates, many of them lean and tattered. (RINHART GALLERIES, INC.)

Left: While Stuart was dying, another bold cavalry-man, Brigadier General James B. Gordon, took his own mortal wound. Slowly, Grant was bleeding Lee to death. Portrait by Vannerson and Jones of Richmond. (VM)

Above: There would be more wounded and dead to come. One of the severest blows to Lee came at Yellow Tavern on May 11, when his beloved—if erratic—cavalry chief, Jeb Stuart, was mortally wounded. He was, perhaps, the last of the cavaliers. (VM)

Above: Many were already dead. Here at the Francis Beverly house mounds of earth may testify to the field burials. (WRHS)

Left: The dead seemed uncountable. A Confederate who fell in the attack of May 19, when Lee tried vainly to probe Grant's right flank. (USAMHI)

Right: Another dead Southerner, with nothing before him now but burial, and probably in an unidentified grave. (USAMHI)

Left: O'Sullivan captured the scenes of burial with his camera in May, after the fighting near the Alsop house. As the dead man clutches at the air in rigor, at least one of the burial detail appears to be wearing a mask. The stench would be terrible if the men were not interred quickly. (LC)

Above: The dead Confederates lay lined up for O'Sullivan's camera in rows. There were always onlookers to stare in macabre wonder at the face of death. (USAMHI)

Above: Back in Fredericksburg, artists photographed the interment of Federal dead. At least they would get caskets—rude though they were—and headboards. When there was more time later, they could be removed to permanent plots. A lens from Russell's equipment lies in the foreground. (USAMHI)

Right: In May 1864, when Brady & Company made these images, every blanket in Fredericksburg seemed to have feet. (USAMHI)

Right: Meanwhile, the campaign wore on, as Grant continued to try to get around Lee's flank. As the armies marched, Grant made his temporary headquarters on May 21 at Massaponax Church. (USAMHI)

Left: Here he had aides pull pews out of the church so he could hold an open-air council of war. Happily, a photographer positioned his camera in one of the church's windows and recorded what followed. Grant sits on the pew at upper left, directly in front of the two trees. His cigar is in his mouth. Just left of him is probably his aide and brother-in-law, Colonel Frederick Dent. To the right of Grant sit Charles A. Dana, Assistant Secretary of War, and Chief of Staff Rawlins. General Meade sits at the upper end of the pew at far left. Next to him is an aide, and then sits Lieutenant Colonel Adam Badeau, Grant's military secretary, and then probably Grant's aide, Lieutenant Colonel Horace Porter. The man standing inside the circle of pews at right appears to be reading something aloud, to which Grant is listening. The blur in the background is caused by a constant flow of supply wagons moving to keep pace with the army. (USAMHI)

Above: Grant has moved now and is leaning over the pew at left talking with Meade as they both look at a map. (USAMHI)

Above: And now Grant is seated once more, writing out an order that will keep his army constantly on the move against Lee. (USAMHI)

Above: To help protect his Rappahannock River sup-ply base, Grant also enjoyed the cooperation of the Navy. Here the USS Yankee poses on the river on May 19. (USAMHI)

Above: Now the Federal commander changed his supply base from Belle Plain to Port Royal on the Rappahan-nock River. As his army advanced, Grant was able to make his supply bases advance with him, continuing the endless flow of succor to the marching Federals. (USAMHI)

Right: By May 23, Grant was on the North Anna River, 20 miles south of Spotsylvania, and Lee was waiting on the other side. That day Warren's V Corps began crossing here at Jericho Mill. This is what they saw ahead of them. (USAMHI)

Above: There was only a shallow ford at first, but Warren quickly threw a pontoon bridge over to facilitate the passage of his wagons and artillery. (USAMHI)

Above: The men who drove away the Confederate pickets at the ford were men like this Pennsylvania "bucktail," Private Samuel Royer of Company C, 9th Pennsylvania. Every man in the regiment wore a bucktail in his cap. Royer barely lived out the war, dying June 19, 1865, from the effects of a war wound. (TPO)

Left: Warren's V Corps ammunition train crosses the bridge the day after Jericho Mill was taken. (USAMHI)

Left: And here the 50th New York Engineers work at cutting a wagon road out of the tangled underbrush to make way for Warren's wagons. Every arm of the Army worked in coordination toward the common goal. (USAMHI)

Right: The IX Corps crossed downstream at Quarles Mills, first attacking and overrunning Confederate works at the top of the hill. Then came another bridge, and thousands more Yankees were one river deeper into Virginia. (USAMHI)

Right: Meanwhile, on May 23, as Warren crossed at Jericho, Hancock and his II Corps attacked the redoubt shown on the horizon that guarded the Chesterfield Bridge over the North Anna. They took the redoubt and swept over the bridge. O'Sullivan made this image only a few days later. (USAMHI)

Right: And he took his camera inside the redoubt to capture the view of Yankee cavalry crossing over the bridge toward Hancock's camps in the distance. (LC)

Far left: The Federals soon settled into abandoned enemy works like this, where they could protect their important crossings over the North Anna. (USAMHI)

Left: Yet another destroyed bridge, this one on the North Anna. (USAMHI)

Left: All along the North Anna pontoon bridges sprang up to maintain the flow of foot and wagon traffic that sustained Grant's advance. This one was built by II Corps engineers, downstream from Chesterfield Bridge. (USAMHI)

Below left: But when Lee confronted Grant on the North Anna, the Federals simply pulled back and moved southeast once more, then crossed once again, this time over the Pamunkey River at Hanovertown Ferry. Lee was ready for him once more. (USAMHI)

Below: Meanwhile, Grant once again shifted his supply base, this time from Port Royal on the Rappahannock to White House Landing on the Pamunkey, 15 miles downriver from Hanovertown Ferry. The first troops to arrive found only "inadequate means of landing." Yet by the time this image was made in June, White House was a busily functioning port. (WRHS)

Right: The landing took its name from the White House, which by May 1864 was nothing but lonely chimneys. The man in the felt hat with the beard may be David B. Woodbury, Brady's photographer. (KA)

Right: Here it was that General Abercrombie became bewildered and had to be removed. For his soldiers, however, it was just one more supply base to keep Grant moving. (USAMHI)

Right: And Grant never stopped moving. Here at Old Church, on May 30, Federals skirmished with Lee as Grant's cavalry protected his left flank in the advance. Here a cavalry detail stops outside the Old Church Hotel on June 4. (USAMHI)

Left: On June 2 the fighting around Bethesda claimed another promising young leader, Brigadier General George P. Doles of Georgia. (MC)

Below left: Men like these officers of Doles' 4h Georgia had to look to a new commander. They found him in... (COURTESY OF STEVE MULLINAX)

Below: ... Colonel Philip Cook of the 4th Georgia. Months later he became a brigadier general, as pictured here. (USAMHI)

Above: That same day, at Bethesda Church, Grant and Lee began the fighting that would culminate a few days after in the Battle of Cold Harbor. Colonel James B. Terrill was killed leading one of Lee's regiments near Bethesda. He died without knowing that his promotion to brigadier would be official the next day. Ironically, too, his brother William had been a general in the Union Army, and he, too, fell in battle. (USAMHI)

Below: By June 2, Grant was nearing Cold Harbor. He pushed aside cavalry protection commanded by Robert E. Lee's nephew, General Fitzhugh Lee. (USAMHI)

Below right: Soon the Federals were advancing toward the swampy woodlands like this that bordered the Chickahominy River. Lee was waiting for them. (CHS)

Above: And that led, on June 3, to the dreadful battle of Cold Harbor. Photographer J. Reekie's April 1865 image of part of the Confederate works that stopped Grant's disastrous attacks. (CHS)

Above: Major General William F. Smith with his XVIII Corps had recently arrived, via White House Landing, in time to take part in the attack. His corps, like the others engaged, was dreadfully battered, and he never forgave Meade for sending him into battle at Cold Harbor. (USAMHI)

Above: Brigadier General Goode Bryan missed the fight by just a few hours, his failing health forcing him to turn over his brigade to a senior colonel. A few months later he would have to resign his commission. (USAMHI)

Above: But Confederates like Brigadier General Evander McI. Law were in perfect health and anxious to deliver death to Grant's attacking Federals. Law himself was wounded in repulsing the enemy's charges. (USAMHI)

Below: Not so the 8th Michigan. With drummers like Robert H. Hendershot of Company B, these Wolverines were in the thick of the bloody fight. (TPO)

Left: The men in those assaults were soldiers like these zouaves of the 114th Pennsylvania, here captured by O'Sullivan's camera. They were part of the headquarters guard of the Army of the Potomac, however, and spent more time at parade than in real fighting. (TPO)

Above: What stopped them were Confederate divisions led by men like Major General Henry Heth, said to be the only general that Lee addressed by his given name. (NA)

Above: Brigadier General Joseph Finegan of Florida had just arrived from his home state with a brigade in time to help stem Grant's assault. Few Floridians got the chance to serve with the fabled Army of Northern Virginia. (WRHS)

Above: One of the hundreds who fell in attacking works held by the Confederates was Colonel Peter A. Porter of the 8th New York Heavy Artillery. He died on the field that June 3, killed fighting troops led by his own cousin and childhood playmate General John C. Breckinridge. (USAMHI)

Left: His foolhardy attack at Cold Harbor failed, Grant sent his cavalry on a raid into the heart of Virginia to distract Lee. Confederate cavalry followed, excepting the division of Lee's son, Brigadier General William H. F. Lee. One of "Rooney" Lee's troopers was this man of the 10th Virginia Cavalry, Private Benjamin Franklin Lincoln. His second cousin Abraham was President of the United States. (COURTESY OF DALE SNAIR)

Left: Undeterred, Grant would continue looking for a way to trap Lee and end the war in Virginia. It would not come for another year, but he would never stop trying. Grant stands here at his headquarters at Cold Harbor in early June surrounded by his staff. Colonel Rawlins sits at far left. Brigadier General John G. Barnard, chief engineer of the Union armies at center, hands in lap, and standing just to the right of him is Grant's old friend and military secretary, Lieutenant Colonel Ely S. Parker, a full-blooded Seneca Indian. Parker will be with Grant nine months from now at Appomattox to see the end and to transcribe the terms of surrender. But for both of them, that was still far in the unseen future. (USAMHI)

The Atlanta Campaign

RICHARD M. McMURRY

"Hell has broke loose in Georgia," and Sherman makes it so

Above: Come spring of 1864, it was time for hell to break loose in Georgia. The man to unleash it knew a lot about making war hell, Major General William Tecumseh Sherman. (USAMHI)

IT WAS A LONG WAY from the Wilderness to where the western armies of the Union stood poised along the Tennessee and Mississippi rivers preparing for the summer's campaign into the Confederacy's industrial and agricultural heartland in Georgia and Alabama. Three years of warfare had set the stage for the struggle that, more than any other, would determine the outcome of the war.

The Federals who were to assail the Southern heartland were led by Major General William T. Sherman, a forty-four-year-old, red-headed, red-whiskered, hot-tempered native of Ohio. Sherman commanded the Military Division of the Mississippi, embracing all Northern forces between the Appalachian Mountains and the Mississippi River. For the 1864 campaign he assembled three armies. The Army of the Cumberland (60,000 men) was led by Major General George H. Thomas, a Virginian who had remained loyal to the Union. Major General James B. McPherson, a handsome young Ohioan, led the Army of the Tennessee (25,000 men). The 15,000-man Army of the Ohio was commanded by Major General John M. Schofield, a native of New York.

The Confederate heartland was defended by General Joseph E. Johnston's Army of Tennessee, based at Dalton, Georgia, 30 miles below Chattanooga. Johnston was a Virginian, in his late fifties, whose Civil War career was marred by a bitter personal feud with Confederate President Jefferson Davis. By late 1863, Johnston believed that his greatest enemy was the President; Davis was convinced that Johnston could not be trusted with an army. Pride prevented Johnston from resigning; public pressure forced Davis to keep the popular general in command. Johnston's army numbered about 55,000 and was organized into two infantry corps and a cavalry corps. Lieutenant General William J. Hardee, a grumpy Georgian, commanded one infantry corps; Lieutenant General John Bell Hood, a young Kentuckian turned Texan, led the other. The cavalry was under Major General Joseph Wheeler, a young irresponsible Georgian.

During the winter Johnston and the Confederate authorities debated strategy for 1864. The government wanted to drive the Federals from Tennessee. Johnston, convinced that his army was too weak to advance, preferred to select a strong position, fight a defensive battle, and, if successful, move forward against a defeated enemy. This difference could not be resolved, and the Confederates began the campaign with no clear plan.

The Federals, by contrast, had unified their command under Lieutenant General Ulysses S. Grant, who wanted to use the North's full power by having all Union armies advance simultaneously. While he attacked Lee in Virginia, Grant planned for Sherman to move against Johnston while another force captured Mobile and invaded Alabama, thus extending Federal control to a line running along the Chattahoochee River and on to Montgomery and Mobile. Owing to political factors, the campaign against Mobile was abandoned, and Sherman's drive into Georgia became the Union's major 1864 offensive in the West.

Sherman's forces were based in Chattanooga—a city that had been captured by the Federals in late 1863 and the uppermost point on the Tennessee River from which a railroad ran into the heart of the Confederacy. That railroad, the Western & Atlantic, led southeast some 120 miles to

Atlanta. Geography and the railroad meant that the campaign would take place in Georgia.

Atlanta, meeting place of four railroads, site of major industrial establishments, hospitals, government and military offices, and the key to control of the West, had come into being as a railroad terminus in the early 1840s. Other railroads were built up to link up with the original line, and the city grew to a population of 10,000 in 1860. The influx of refugees, military personnel, and government employees doubled that figure by 1864.

The Federals had many advantages in the campaign. Most important, Sherman and Grant trusted each other and worked together with the support of their government in pursuit of their objective. Johnston's differences with Davis made it impossible for the Confederates to cooperate or even to communicate. Also, Sherman was a more thorough, better-organized, more resourceful, and more flexible leader than Johnston, and he commanded Federal forces in Kentucky, Tennessee, Georgia, Alabama, and Mississippi. There was no overall Confederate commander in the West. Sherman could strike into Alabama against the railroads that supplied Johnston's army, while Johnston could do no more than urge local commanders in Alabama to act. Sherman had, in Thomas and McPherson, chief subordinates of high caliber; Johnston's chief lieutenants, like Johnston himself, were at best mediocre generals. The inability of the Southerners to agree upon a plan, and Johnston's reluctance to take risks and assume responsibility lest he be criticized by Davis, meant that the Federals would have the initiative and determine the character and tempo of the campaign. Finally, Sherman's forces outnumbered Johnston's about 1.5 to 1 when the campaign opened. Although there was no difference in the quality of men in the opposing armies, Sherman's greater strength gave him another advantage. Circumstances so favored the Federals that only leadership of the highest quality could give the Southerners even a hope of victory.

Rocky Face Ridge, a steep height west of Dalton, runs from north to south. Johnston put his army on that ridge and across Crow Valley, north of Dalton. He believed that Sherman would attack this strong position and was confident that the Confederates could repulse any assault.

Sherman, too alert to fall into such a trap, planned to demonstrate against Johnston's position and swing McPherson's army around to the southwest to the railroad that supplied the Confederates at Dalton. Once the Western & Atlantic was broken, Johnston would have to retreat. Originally Sherman planned to move McPherson toward Rome, Georgia, 35 miles southwest of Dalton, to threaten Johnston's railroad. Because McPherson's army did not attain its expected strength, Sherman decided to send him only to Snake Creek Gap, an opening through Rocky Face Ridge about 12 miles below Dalton. A few miles east of the gap was Resaca, where the railroad crossed the Oostenaula River.

Sherman's plan worked almost perfectly. John-

Right: Major General George H. Thomas, the man who had become the "Rock of Chickamauga" back in September 1863, now led the Army of the Cumberland, and here on May 5, 1864, at Ringgold, Georgia, he made his headquarters, readying for the campaign that would shatter the lower South. (USAMHI)

Above: Through that winter of 1863-64, while waiting for the next campaign, the men of Sherman's armies waited at places like Wauhatchie Bridge, guarding his supply lines as he built up his readiness to strike. (USAMHI)

Above: The XV Corps camped around Scottsboro, Alabama, and here its commander, Major General John A. Palmer, made his headquarters. (USAMHI)

Right: And here on May 5 or 6 sat several of Thomas' generals, with the opening of the campaign less than 48 hours in the future. Seated at far left is Brigadier General Jefferson C. Davis, and next to him, with legs crossed, is Brigadier General John M. Brannan, Thomas' chief of artillery. The man writing at the table is Brigadier General Richard W. Johnson. Seated next to him, hat in lap, is Brigadier General John H. King, and Brigadier General William D. Whipple, army chief of staff. Each will see his share of fighting in the days ahead, and Johnson will be severely wounded. (USAMHI)

Below: Ringgold seemed a peaceful enough place in this image, believed to have been taken in 1865 by George N. Barnard. (WRHS)

Above: Not so Buzzard Roost, Georgia. Here on May 8-9, Sherman first met and began to press the Confederate defenses. As Barnard's photo shows so well, even where no major battle was fought, still the passing of the armies left a considerable mess in its wake. (USAMHI)

ston, confident in his Dalton fortifications, was deceived by the demonstrations that Thomas and Schofield staged there in early May. The area to the Confederate left was ignored, and when McPherson reached Snake Creek Gap on May 8 he found it unguarded.

On May 9, McPherson cautiously pushed toward the railroad. Surprised to find numerous Confederates in the area, he drew back to the gap. Johnston had stationed a small force at Resaca to guard the bridge, and by the 9th those men had been joined by advance elements of a 15,000-man force from Mississippi and Alabama that the government had ordered to reinforce Johnston. This force, a third infantry corps, was commanded by Lieutenant General Leonidas Polk, the corpulent Episcopal Bishop of Louisiana who had left military service in 1827. He had resumed his career in 1861 to aid the Confederacy.

Although McPherson had not achieved all for which Sherman had hoped, he had given the Federals a great strategic advantage, and Sherman followed up on his opportunity by shifting Thomas and Schofield to Snake Creek Gap. By nightfall on May 12 only a small detachment of Federals remained in the Dalton area.

Johnston, who had the shorter distance to cover and the use of the railroad, did not abandon Dalton until the night of May 12–13. The Confederates deployed in the rough terrain north and west of Resaca, holding a line that began at the Oostenaula and curved around to rest its right on the Conasauga River. Hood's corps held the right of this line; Hardee's the center; Polk's the left.

On the 13th, Sherman moved against Resaca, his force fanning out, to form a line paralleling that of the Confederates. The first day of the Battle of Resaca was spent in skirmishing. On the 14th, Sherman struck the right center of Johnston's line but was hurled back with heavy loss. Hood lashed out at Sherman's extreme left, and only reinforcements prevented a Confederate victory. Other local attacks took place on the 15th, but Sherman, realizing that such fighting would accomplish little, sent a detachment down the Oostenaula to Lay's Ferry, where it crossed the river and threatened Johnston's railroad. During the night of May 15–16 the Confederate leader crossed the river

Above: It was Major General William B. Bate who held those Confederate works against Sherman's first tentative stabs. He could not hold for long before the Yankee horde. (USAMHI)

Above: Sherman drove for Resaca, Georgia, a tiny hamlet that held the key to the Confederate rear. This image shows Rebel earthworks in the right distance. (USAMHI)

Above: With seasoned veterans like the 33d New Jersey, Sherman fought the Battle for Resaca on May 14–15. (TPO)

Above: Over rugged, fence-strewn ground like this the armies struggled. (USAMHI)

and marched southward, seeking terrain for the defensive battle he wanted to fight.

The opening days of the campaign set the pattern for what followed. Sherman had demonstrated that he could plan complicated operations and the logistical details necessary to support them. When it proved impossible to execute his original plans, he had quickly adapted to new situations. He had held the initiative, and he had used his superior numbers to pin down and outflank the Rebels. He had not, however, pushed aggressively after the Confederates. Johnston had remained passive and twice was maneuvered out of his chosen position. He had neglected Snake Creek Gap and had not defended the south bank of the Oostenaula. In less than two weeks he had abandoned the region north of the Oostenaula (including Rome, an important industrial town) and fallen back into a more open area where Sherman's superior numbers would give the Federals an even greater advantage.

Over the next several days Johnston moved south toward the Etowah River. On May 19 he made an unsuccessful effort to concentrate against a detached part of Sherman's force near Cassville, and that evening he was forced to retreat across the Etowah when his position at Cassville proved vulnerable to artillery. The Rebels took up a strong position about Allatoona Pass. Sherman, after securing his hold north of the river, allowed his men a few days' rest.

On May 23, Sherman crossed the Etowah in open country west of Allatoona. His objective was the small town of Dallas, 14 miles south of the river, from which he could move east to the railroad or southeast toward the Chattahoochee River. "The Etowah," Sherman wrote, "is the Rubicon of Georgia. We are now all in motion like a

Above: Barnard's photograph shows the Confederate rifle pits dug out in the foreground by Joseph E. Johnston's Army of Tennessee. (USAMHI)

Above: Brigadier General Thomas Sweeney, a troublesome Irishman from County Cork, commanded a division of the XVI Corps in the fight at Resaca. A career fighter, he lost his arm at Churubusco in the Mexican War, and a few years hence will lead an "army" of Fenians in an abortive invasion of Canada. (USAMHI)

Above: Helping defend the little railroad town was Confederate Brigadier General William F. Tucker. He survived a desperate wound here that put him out of the war for good, but in 1881 an assassin's bullet cut him down. (VM)

Right: Despite every effort to hold the position, the Confederates had to pull out of Resaca, leaving the village and their defenses to Sherman's victorious Federals. It would be repeated many times in this campaign. (USAMHI)

vast hive of bees and expect to swarm along the Chattahoochee in a few days."

As Sherman's armies closed on Dallas on May 25, they found Confederates posted at New Hope Church, northeast of the town. Overruling his subordinates who believed a strong Rebel force to be in their front, Sherman ordered an attack. The resulting battle of New Hope Church was a victory for Hood's Confederates, who repulsed the Northerners with ease. Two days later another Union attack was defeated at Picketts Mill, northeast of New Hope Church.

Both sides concentrated along the Dallas-New Hope Church-Pickett's Mill line, and for over a week deadly skirmish warfare went on in the heavy woods. The soldiers were made even more uncomfortable by the torrential rains that began on May 25 and continued with but few letups for a month.

Unable to defeat Johnston and experiencing difficulty supplying his men over muddy roads, Sherman began to work his way east, shifting troops from his right to his left. By early June the Northerners had regained the railroad near Acworth. Sherman had again outmaneuvered Johnston and bypassed the Allatoona hills.

By June 10, Sherman had received reinforcements, repaired his railroad, rested his men, and was ready to advance. Johnston, meanwhile, had occupied the hills north of Marietta. Over the next several days Sherman's forces pushed Johnston back to a line running along Kennesaw Mountain and off to the south. On June 14, Polk was killed by Federal artillery fire. Major General William W. Loring took temporary command of his corps.

When the Federals encountered the new Rebel position, Sherman began extending to the southwest to outflank it. Rain and mud slowed movements and hampered efforts to supply units distant from the railroad, but the Federal right slowly stretched southward. Johnston extended his left in an effort to hold his line. By June 22 the armies were strung out along a line that began north of Marietta, swung to the west and then south to a point several miles southwest of the town near Olley's Creek. Skirmishing, artillery fire, and some times large-scale assaults raged along this line.

In late June, when the rains ceased, Sherman changed his tactics. Believing that Johnston's long line would be weak, the Northern leader determined to assault. He planned to attack at three places—the southwestern end of Kennesaw Mountain, Cheatham's Hill west of Marietta, and along Olley's Creek. If the Federals could break through to the railroad, a large part of Johnston's army might be cut off and destroyed.

Sherman attacked on the morning of June 27. After heavy artillery fire, Northern infantry gallantly rushed against the fortifications on Kennesaw and at Cheatham's Hill. Although some Yankees reached the Confederate lines, the Southerners were able to repulse the attacks, inflicting heavy loss on the assaulting forces. Only along Olley's Creek, where Schofield's men managed to gain a position on the south bank, could Sherman claim success.

Schofield's advance gave Sherman a position from which to slice eastward to the railroad or south to the Chattahoochee. A few days after the failure of his attack Sherman began to shift troops to his right, forcing Johnston to choose between

Above: Brigadier General Randall L. Gibson covered the Southern retreat from Resaca. (LSU)

Above: Behind them the Confederates left the battlefield to the victors, and their hastily buried dead to the soil. Rude boards mark the resting spots of those who died in the fight. A Barnard image. (WRHS)

Above: On the armies went, through Kingston. Here for two days they fought before moving on. Barnard followed them in 1865 with his camera. (USAMHI)

Left: Brigadier General Jacob D. Cox led a division of the XXIII Corps in that fighting. He ordered one of his brigades to find and destroy the... (USAMHI)

giving up the Kennesaw line or being cut off from Atlanta.

Johnston, expecting such a maneuver and believing that he could stretch his army no farther, had begun a new line at Smyrna, four miles below Marietta. On the night of July 2–3 he moved to the Smyrna line. Advancing Federals confronted Johnston's new position late on the afternoon of July 3. After a day of skirmishing, Sherman's right threatened Johnston's communications with Atlanta, and during the night of July 4–5 the Southerners fell back to the north bank of the Chattahoochee where they occupied a heavily fortified position.

Realizing that the Rebel line was too strong to be attacked, Sherman sent his cavalry to capture Roswell, 16 miles upriver, and planned to attempt a crossing above Johnston's fortifications. On July 8, while Johnston was distracted by demonstrations downstream, Schofield's men crossed the river, using pontoon boats and the ruins of a dam. By nightfall the Yankees were securely dug in on the south bank. Johnston, during the night of July 9–10, crossed the Chattahoochee and went into position along Peachtree Creek, a few miles from Atlanta. For a week Sherman rested his men and planned his next move.

Johnston had not kept the government informed of the progress of the campaign, and his long retreat had displeased Confederate officials. The authorities were especially worried because it would be possible for the Federals to use the Chattahoochee as a moat while they wrecked Alabama's virtually undefended industrial area. Sherman's presence on the Chattahoochee, even if he advanced no farther into Georgia, would assure Federal success in the campaign and cripple the Confederacy's ability to wage war. If Johnston abandoned Atlanta, the blow to the Confederacy would be devastating. Criticism of Johnston mounted, and Davis, as early as July 12, began to consider replacing him with a commander who could be counted on to fight for Atlanta. On the

Above: …. Mark Cooper Iron Works, outside Cartersville. The factory had supplied arms to the Confederacy, but after Cox's raid it was left a ruin. A postwar image. (GEORGIA DEPARTMENT OF ARCHIVES AND HISTORY)

Above: Finally, Sherman pushed Johnston back across the Etowah River here at Etowah Bridge. Barnard's image shows the fortifications erected by the Confederates to guard the bridge, as well as the beginning of structural supports being erected to keep the Western & Atlantic Railroad crossing operable. (LC)

17th the President, with great reluctance, named Hood to command the Army.

Most historians have been critical of Davis, but their criticism stems more from a knowledge of what happened after Johnston was removed than from an evaluation of the decision itself. Davis faced two different but related questions in July 1864. First, he had to decide if Johnston should be relieved from command. All evidence available to the President indicated that Johnston had mismanaged the campaign and that he would make no real effort to hold Atlanta. Johnston seemed to have no appreciation of the city's logistical, economic, political, or psychological importance. If the Confederacy was to survive, Atlanta must be held and Sherman pushed away from the Southern heartland. Nothing indicated that Johnston had the will, ability, or even intention of trying to do so.

If Johnston were removed, who should replace him? Time dictated that a new commander come from the army at Atlanta. There were only two realistic choices: Hardee and Hood (the III Corps commander, Lieutenant General Alexander P. Stewart, had but recently been named as the permanent replacement for Polk). Hardee, like Johnston, was on bad personal terms with important government officials, had declined to take permanent command of the Army in December 1863, and, it was reported to Davis, had supported Johnston's policy of falling back into Georgia. These factors made Hood the choice by default.

Other factors were also involved. Hood was a bold officer who had led many successful attacks on the enemy. He seems to have worked to undermine Johnston by informing Davis' military adviser, General Braxton Bragg, that Johnston had missed many chances to strike a blow against Sherman. Hood's crippled condition—he had lost a leg and the use of an arm in earlier battles—might have caused Davis some hesitation, but, wounds and all, Hood was the best, indeed the only, alternative to Johnston in mid-July 1864.

WHEN HOOD ASSUMED COMMAND on the morning of July 18, he faced a desperate situation. Sherman was north and east of Atlanta. Thomas' army, with its right on the Chattahoochee, was a hinge on which Schofield and McPherson were swinging to the east to reach the Georgia Railroad, Hood's direct link to the Carolinas and Virginia.

As Thomas' men came down into the valley of

Above: Already, off in the distance down the Western & Atlantic line, Barnard's camera looks toward the next goal, Allatoona Pass. (USAMHI)

Above: Allatoona itself, nestled in the pass, would not see a battle. (USAMHI)

Above: Rather than face fortifications like the earthwork atop the ridge at left, Sherman moved around Johnston and forced the Confederates to pull out of Allatoona. Yet finally the armies would meet in deadly battle at… (USAMHI)

Above: … New Hope Church. Here for nearly two weeks in late May and early June 1864 the armies glowered at each other from positions like these Confederate works. Barnard captured much of it in the summer of 1865. (LC)

Peachtree Creek north of Atlanta, a gap opened in the Federal line. Hood saw a chance to attack the isolated Federal right, and he planned to concentrate the corps of Hardee and Stewart to assail Thomas while his old corps, under Major General Benjamin F. Cheatham, and the cavalry defended Atlanta against Schofield and McPherson. Hood worked through the night of July 19–20 to position his army for this battle.

On the 20th, Hood found the Federals east of Atlanta advancing more rapidly than he had anticipated, and he had to strengthen his eastern flank. The confusion caused by this redeployment delayed the attack. When Hardee and Stewart advanced, they found that Thomas' men had built fortifications. Thus what Hood had intended as a quick blow against an unprepared force became an assault on a strong position. The Confederates, fighting bravely, were repulsed in the Battle of Peachtree Creek.

On July 21, Hood's attention was drawn to the east side of the city. McPherson had advanced along the Georgia Railroad through Decatur to the outskirts of Atlanta. Hood decided to send Hardee's corps south and around to the east to roll up the left of the Federal line and drive it back onto the center and right. That night Hardee's men set off on their march. The roads were narrow and crowded, and the march was slow. Not until early afternoon was Hardee ready to attack. Meanwhile, the advance of the Northern armies had contracted the Federal lines and crowded part of McPherson's army out of place. McPherson ordered these displaced men to his extreme left. Thus, by accident, reinforcements were sent to the point where the attack fell.

Hardee's men struck a line of battle rather than an undefended flank. The resulting Battle of Atlanta raged through the afternoon of July 22, as Hardee's troops, joined by units from the Atlanta defenses, assaulted the Union position. In bitter fighting the Southerners temporarily overran part of the Yankee position, captured several guns and hundreds of prisoners, and killed McPherson. The Confederates, however, were unable to break the Northern line and at night drew back, leaving the Yankees in the position they had held when the battle opened.

By July 26, Sherman had decided upon his next effort. He would extend his army to the west

Above: Amid all the trees and brush and entanglements, it was like fighting in a briar patch. (USAMHI)

Left: Rebels like Uriah Crawford of the 54th Virginia, one of very few Old Dominion units with Johnston's army, were heartily glad to move away from New Hope Church. Alas, for Crawford, he would be captured just two weeks later. (COURTESY OF DELBERT CRAWFORD)

Above: Johnston pulled back to a line along Pine Mountain on June 4, and here skirmishing continued for several days. (LC)

Right: A casualty of that skirmishing was Lieutenant General Leonidas Polk. On June 14 a Federal cannon ball struck him in the chest and he died instantly. He had been an Episcopal bishop, and then a corps commander for the Confederacy. In this remarkable unpublished, and badly faded, portrait he stands wearing the loose pleated uniform blouse that was popular with many generals in the Army of Tennessee. (MC)

Left: It was Brigadier General Absalom Baird's division of the XIV Corps that was skirmishing at Pine Mountain that day. He appears here in 1865, at war's end, wearing mourning crepe for the murdered Lincoln. (KA)

Below: Pine Mountain was only a stop, however, before a bigger and more deadly fight at Kennesaw Mountain. Here, as Barnard's image shows, the armies turned farmers' fences and fields into places of battle. (USAMHI)

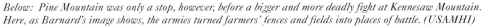
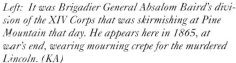

and south of Atlanta to cut Hood's remaining railroads. The Atlanta & West Point Railroad and the Macon & Western ran southwest to East Point, where they forked, the Atlanta & West Point going southwest and the Macon & Western into central Georgia. If the Federals broke those lines, Hood could not hold Atlanta.

Major General Oliver Otis Howard, a native of Maine, had been selected to replace McPherson, and Sherman transferred Howard's Army of the Tennessee from the Federal left to the right. By the afternoon of July 27, Howard's men were west of Atlanta, pushing southward against slight opposition.

Hood, learning of Sherman's movement, sent his old corps, now led by Lieutenant General Stephen D. Lee, supported by Stewart's corps, west from Atlanta on July 28. Hood hoped that Lee would block the Federals, and then, on the following day, Hood would move around their right to attack the rear of the position they had taken confronting Lee.

Lee, finding the Yankees near Ezra Church, attempted to drive them away. He launched a series of sharp, but uncoordinated, assaults on the Northerners, who had hastily built works from logs and church benches. Stewart, coming to Lee's support, joined the attacks. The resulting battle lasted through the afternoon and ended with the Northerners secure in their new position. Hood abandoned his plans for flank attack on July 29.

In his first ten days of command, Hood had thrice lashed out at the Federals. Although none of the battles had fulfilled Hood's expectations, he had demonstrated that he would strike whenever he thought it advantageous to do so. Sherman's movements became more cautious, and as July ended, many Confederates took hope in the belief that Hood's hard fighting had at last stopped the enemy, who seemed always to outflank the Southerners.

THERE WAS NO LARGE-SCALE FIGHTING in the Atlanta area for a month after Ezra Church. Sherman cautiously extended to the southwest, and Hood constructed a parallel line of works covering the railroad. Federal artillery damaged Atlanta but could not drive out the Rebel troops. Both sides resorted to the use of cavalry. Sherman launched several mounted raids against the railroads below Atlanta, hoping to cut Hood's supply line. Although the Federal horsemen inflicted some damage, they were unable to break the rail lines beyond repair.

Hood, on August 10, launched a counterraid, sending Wheeler, with about 4,500 men, to cut the railroad that supplied Sherman. Although Wheeler interrupted operations on the Western & Atlantic, the line was too well protected for the Rebel horsemen to break it thoroughly. Instead of returning to Hood, Wheeler began a raid into East Tennessee, a foolish venture that damaged Hood at a crucial time in the campaign.

In late August, with Wheeler out of the picture, Sherman again attempted to oust Hood from Atlanta. Realizing that only infantry could wreck the Rebels' railroads, the Federal commander, on August 25, began his movement. He sent part of the Army of the Cumberland to hold the Chattahoochee bridges and the railroad while the remainder of his force marched far to the south and west. On August 28, Howard's Army of the Tennessee reached the Atlanta & West Point Railroad at Fairburn, 13 miles southwest of East Point. All that afternoon and through the 29th, Sherman's men so thoroughly destroyed the railroad that only the Macon & Western could supply the Rebels at Atlanta.

Meanwhile, many Confederates had interpreted Sherman's disappearance as a retreat brought on by Wheeler's raid. For a few days optimism reigned among the Southerners. "The scales have turned in favor of the South," wrote an Arkansian, "and the Abolitionists are moving to the rear."

When the Rebels learned of Sherman's presence on the West Point Railroad, they realized that his next objective would be the Macon & Western. Hood, however, without cavalry to ascertain the enemy's strength and intentions, seems to have believed that the force below Atlanta was

Above: It was the greatest fighting yet in the campaign, and the men of the 125th Ohio led the skirmishers in Sherman's attack. The losses were dreadful. This regiment alone suffered 43 casualties just acting as skirmishers. (USAMHI)

Left: There were casualties on both sides, though. Brigadier General Lucius E. Polk, nephew of the slain Leonidas, was put out of the war by a desperate wound at Kennesaw. (USAMHI)

Below left: Yet it was Sherman who suffered the most. Placed behind works like these shown in Barnard's image, the Confederates delivered deadly fire into the attacking Federals. Sherman had to admit defeat. (WRHS)

Below: So did his chief of artillery, Brigadier General William F. Barry. "The nature of military operations in a country like ours is peculiar," he claimed, and unfavorable to artillery. The dense cover forced the guns to work out in the open, exposed, but still they did good work. It cost them. Three division chiefs of artillery were killed in the fighting. (COURTESY OF EUGENE WOODDELL)

Above: The view from behind Johnston's rifle pits on Kennesaw tells the whole story of the dreadful ground over which Sherman had to attack. The broken and battered trees tell the story of the fight's ferocity. (USAMHI)

Above: For fiery Brigadier General Francis M. Cockrell of Missouri, Kennesaw was a tough fight in which his men faced the Federals for an hour within thirty paces of each other. His skirmishers could hear the Yankees, hiding behind rocks, giving the order to "fix bayonets" for the charge. Some of Cockrell's men fired more than sixty times. (GOELET-BUN-COMBE COLLECTION, SOUTHERN HISTORI-CAL COLLECTION)

Left: Despite the victory at Kennesaw, Johnston had to fall back once more as the enemy threatened to get around his flank. Now the Confederates withdrew to the Chattahoochee River, getting ever closer to Atlanta. When Johnston destroyed the bridges in his path, Sherman at once started rebuilding them with lightning speed . (USAMHI)

Right: After the fight at Kennesaw, most of the combat for several days was on the fringes of the armies, at places like Vining's Station. There, on July 4, Brigadier General Alfred J. Vaughan, Jr., had his leg blown off by a Federal shell. He appears here months later, near the end of the war, with the crutch that was his companion for the rest of his life. (HP)

Far right: Finally, Richmond would stand no more of Johnston's retreats. By July 17, Sherman had pushed to within a few miles of Atlanta. Johnston was replaced by an audacious, sad-eyed fighter from Kentucky, General John Bell Hood. He would do no better than Johnston, and at greater cost. (MC)

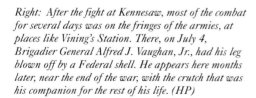

only a raiding party. He did not realize the magnitude of the disaster moving toward the Macon & Western when, on August 30, he ordered Hardee to take two corps (Hardee's own and Lee's) to Jonesboro (14 miles southeast of East Point) to protect the railroad.

On August 30 the Northerners crossed the Flint River and entrenched on the eastern bank. During the night Hardee moved to Jonesboro, where, on the morning of August 31, the Confederates deployed west of the town. That afternoon Hardee assaulted the Federals. The attack was fierce but uncoordinated, and it failed. With more Yankees closing on the town, Hardee drew back and deployed to make a last defense of the railroad. Hood, still not realizing what was happening, concluded that Sherman was going to attack Atlanta from the south. He ordered Hardee to return Lee's corps to Atlanta, leaving only one corps to face the main Union force at Jonesboro.

On September 1 the Northerners fell upon Hardee. Late in the afternoon the Confederate line gave way, and Hardee retreated to the south. Sherman's hold on Hood's last railroad was unbreakable. The Battle of Jonesboro sealed the fate of Atlanta. With the railroad gone, Hood had to give up the city. During the night of September 1–2 the Southerners destroyed what they could not carry away and marched via a circuitous route to join Hardee.

The campaign that began in the north Georgia mountains four months earlier was over. The war would last another nine months, but the capture of Atlanta was a tangible victory demonstrating that the Federals could reach the heart of the South. Hood would go north that fall to meet overwhelming defeat at Nashville in December, while Sherman, leaving Atlanta a burned wreck, marched across Georgia to the sea.

Left: This portrait is believed to be of Hood's chief of staff, Brigadier General Francis A. Shoup, a native of Indiana. He would have to cope with all the paper work of running an army for Hood had no patience for it. (ERNEST HAYWOOD COLLECTION, SHC)

Below: Just three days after taking command, Hood attacked Thomas at Peachtree Creek, proving himself once more to be a vicious fighter, if an unwise one. It was Thomas who emerged the victor, with Atlanta now threatened with encirclement. Barnard's photo shows the graves of those who died on the field. (USAMHI)

Above: Brigadier General James Cantey was absent from his brigade with ill health, but his men led the Confederate attack that for a time stunned Thomas at Peachtree Creek. (CHS)

Above: While the armies began the final battle for Atlanta on July 22, Brigadier General George Stoneman, seated at right, led his cavalry corps on a raid that hoped to capture the notorious prison at Andersonville and free its inmates. Instead, five days later, Stoneman was himself captured. (MICHAEL HAMMERSON)

Right: It was Confederate cavalry led by able officers like Brigadier General William H. Jackson that disrupted Stoneman's plans. (NA)

Far right: Meanwhile, men were dying for Atlanta. In the first day of fighting, Major General James B. McPherson became the only Union Army commander of the war to die in battle. His men saw him ride off to a threatened point during a Confederate attack. A few minutes later his riderless horse returned. (USAMHI)

Below: He fell and died here, among the cannon balls and the macabre, grinning skull of a dead horse. Sherman particularly mourned the loss of one of the most beloved young generals in the service. (GDAH)

Above: At McPherson's death, command of his army went for a time to one of the most able civilians-turned-soldier of the war, Major General John A. Logan of Illinois. The only trouble was, he was not West Point trained. (USAMHI)

Right: Sherman consulted with Major General George H. Thomas, commanding the Army of the Cumberland, and between them they agreed that permanent command of McPherson's army should go to a professional. Thus... (COURTESY OF WANDA WRIGHT)

Far right: ... Major General Oliver O. Howard took over from Logan. (LC)

Far left: That incensed Howard's senior officer, Major General Joseph Hooker, the "Fighting Joe" who lost a major battle at Chancellorsville the year before. Unwilling to serve under his inferior in seniority, Hooker asked to be relieved. For him it was the end of the war. (USAMHI)

Left: With Hooker's departure, command of his XX Corps went for a time to Brigadier General Alpheus S. Williams, a grizzled old fighter and veteran of the battles in Virginia, shown here with his daughter. Thus did the death of McPherson shift commands throughout his army for a time. (USAMHI)

Below left: Meanwhile, for several days after the battle of July 22 the armies watched each other across the lines. Barnard was able to get his camera into some of the abandoned defenses in the summer of 1865. (USAMHI)

Below: He and his instrument could survey some of the scenes of the bloody day's fight. (LC)

Above: Then came the rugged July 28 battle at Ezra Church, Hood's last hope to keep from being driven back into the city. Brigadier General D. H. Reynolds led two Confederate brigades in Hood's attack, intended to keep Sherman from encircling him. A bold officer, born in Ohio, Reynolds fought for five hours in heavy fire before being called back. He suffered 40 percent losses. (MC)

Above: The defenses were well prepared. All around Atlanta ran ditches and rifle pits, with fences, sharpened stakes in the ground... (USAMHI)

Above: ... fortified hilltops... (USAMHI)

Below: Sherman's attackers would have to march across hell to get to the city this way. (USAMHI)

Below: East of the city the Confederates even piled brush on the slopes leading up to their rifle pits. (WRHS)

Below: After the fall of Atlanta, Barnard turned his camera toward the successive waves of vicious obstructions near the Chattanooga railroad line. (CDAH)

Below: Wherever the camera looked, the environs of Atlanta bristled with trenches and rifle pits and stakes in the ground. (GDAH)

Below: It had been the luckless task of Brigadier General Marcus J. Wright to command the District of Atlanta for a time, but before the Federals closed in finally he was sent off to Macon in the center of the state. Before long, the front might be there as well. (A.J. WRIGHT COLLECTION, SHC)

Left: Meanwhile, the Confederates who stayed behind sat in their defenses—like this one—and glowered at the enemy. (GDAH)

Below: It was all they could do, while Sherman slowly encircled them. (USAMHI)

Left: Just two days before the Ezra Church fight, Brigadier General John M. Corse, seated second from the right, took command of the Second Division of the XVI Corps. His division led the way in the flanking movement by which Sherman hoped at last to cut Hood off from retreat. Seated with Corse are the other officers of his division, Brigadier General Richard Rowett, at left, McPherson's old adjutant, General William T. Clark next, and at far right Brigadier General E. W. Rice. This image, made in May 1865, shows all of them at higher grades than they were during the Atlanta Campaign. (USAMHI)

Above: This was the prize they sought. Atlanta in 1864. A Barnard image. (LC)

Above: In the center of the city, not far from the Western & Atlantic depot, stood the Trout House, one of Atlanta's better-known hotels. (LC)

Above: Symbolic of Atlanta, however, was the "car shed" of the Western & Atlantic depot. It was through this depot that Hood's lifeline ran, for Atlanta was the rail communication center of the deep South. (LC)

Above: Barnard did some of the best work of his career once Sherman took Atlanta. This scene, not far from the depot, is one of his most brilliant. (LC)

Above: The Potter house showed to Barnard's camera some of the terrible effects of Federal fire during the bombardment of Hood's defenses. (LC)

Above: The poor Potters' backyard became a major position in the defensive perimeter around the city. It could almost be a scene from the 1914-18 war in Europe. (LC)

Above: When finally Sherman took Atlanta in September, he found there more and more evidences of the defensive strength of the place. It was no wonder that he wisely chose to drive Hood out by encircling him rather than attacking. Kennesaw Mountain had been a costly lesson, but well learned. (LC)

Above: Here, in a Confederate fort on Peachtree Street, Barnard's camera looks south toward the city, over the barrel of cannon No. 211, manufactured in 1863. (LC)

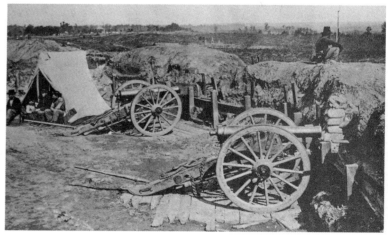

Above: Where once hundreds of Rebels stood ready to fight, now a lone sentry sits atop the earthworks looking off toward his old lines. (LC)

Above: The thought of having to charge across that no-man's-land of entanglements, under unrestricted fire from the enemy, sobered even the most hardened of Sherman's men. They were delighted that he used strategy instead of force. (LC)

Above: By the end of August, Sherman was ready. Brigadier General Thomas E. G. Ransom temporarily led the XVI Corps as the Federals sealed off Hood's last rail link at Jonesboro. (CHICAGO PUBLIC LIBRARY)

Left: Brigadier General Jefferson C. Davis, seated at left, led his corps in the heaviest of the fighting at Jonesboro, yet was so impressed with the valor of the Kentucky Confederate troops opposing him that he personally looked to the welfare of those he captured. He sits in his tent here with Lieutenant Colonel A. C. McClurg. (LC)

Below: Lieutenant General William J. Hardee commanded Hood's unsuccessful attack at Jonesboro. He had to drive Sherman back, or else Atlanta would have to be evacuated. (CHS)

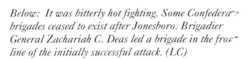

Below: It was bitterly hot fighting. Some Confederate brigades ceased to exist after Jonesboro. Brigadier General Zachariah C. Deas led a brigade in the front line of the initially successful attack. (LC)

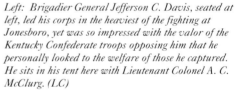

Below: Brigadier General George Maney commanded a division in the battle but managed to make someone in the army high command angry, for he was relieved of his command within minutes of the end of the battle. (MC)

Right: For Brigadier General Daniel C. Govan of Arkansas, Jonesboro was his last battle for quite a while. Captured, he would not return to the service for several months. (USAMHI)

Above: Even with their victory at Jonesboro, the Federals suffered their share as well. Private Henry Cordes of the 18th United States Infantry, seated at right) was part of the 65 percent losses suffered by his regiment. Poor Cordes took a gunshot wound in the left arm and had his limb amputated on the field. (TPO)

Right: The 9th Indiana took part in the chase after Hood's evacuating army. On September 2 they caught up with him near Lovejoy's Station, but the Confederates successfully withdrew deeper into Georgia. It was effectively the end of the Atlanta Campaign. (NA)

Below: Now Sherman could survey what he had conquered, assisted by Barnard's ubiquitous camera. Here on the Georgia Central tracks they found the remains of Hood's ordnance train, destroyed to prevent capture. It was a scene of perfect desolation. (KA)

Below: In the city they found more cars and buildings like the Lard Oil Factory destroyed by Hood's retreating Confederates. (GDAH)

Above: But most of the city proper survived both the fighting and the withdrawal, and in time the grounds around city hall sprouted Yankee winter quarters. (RJY)

Above: Here was the encampment of the 2d Massachusetts. (USAMHI)

Left: Here, probably in the position of Battery K, 5th U.S. Artillery, in Fort No. 7, Sherman and his staff and generals could pose proudly. They are, from left to right: Major L. M. Dayton, aide; Lieutenant Colonel E. D. Kittoe, medical director; Colonel A. Beckwith, commissary; Colonel Orlando M. Poe, chief engineer; Brigadier General William F. Barry, chief of artillery; Colonel W. Warner; Colonel T. G. Baylor, chief of ordnance; Sherman; Captain G. W. Nichols; Colonel C. Ewing, inspector general; an unidentified major; and Captain J. E. Marshall. (USAMHI)

Above: And here was the conqueror, William T. Sherman, astride his charger in the works he fought so long to take. "Atlanta is ours, and fairly won," he wired to Washington. (USAMHI)

Left: Now the once-Confederate works became revitalized forts in the Federal defensive line around Atlanta. Once Confederate Fort No. 7, this is now Yankee Fort No. 7 and looks of toward No. 8. (GDAH)

Below: And Fort No. 8 looks back to No. 7. (GDAH)

Above: Once the building in the background was Hood's headquarters. Now it looks quietly onto Fort No. 10, with guns removed and work parties with shovels enhancing its strength. (USAMHI)

Above: And more work for the men laboring in Fort No. 12, part of a largely new line of defenses. (GDAH)

Above: Far more sophisticated than the Confederate lines around the city, the Federal defensive perimeter would never be tested but stood as a monument to Colonel Poe's capability and the soldiers' hard work. (USAMHI)

Above: Fort No. 19, with Atlanta in the background, protected the Georgia Central line, precautions against a Confederate counteroffensive that never came. (USAMHI)

Right: Before too long it came time for Sherman to leave the city, bound for the sea on his march through Georgia. He could leave nothing useful behind, should the enemy strike for Atlanta. And so the work of destroying began. Here soldiers heat railroad rails before bending them out of shape. Some called the final product "Sherman's hairpins." (LC)

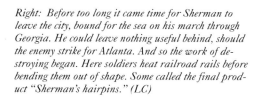

Above: With the ruins of the car shed in the right background, more Yankees lift track from the ties. *(USAMHI)*

Above: Rails heat over fires and boiler parts and other locomotive pieces await their own fate as Sherman destroyed Atlanta as a rail center. *(LC)*

Above: Barnard caught the scene as the roundhouse was reduced to rubble. *(LC)*

Above: Sherman's wagons prepare for the march toward Savannah while the car shed and track beside it live out their last hours before destruction. With one campaign successfully done, the man who made war hell was off for another one. *(CHS)*

Left: Behind him he left a conquered Atlanta, and at the city's court house, the flag of the old Union flew once more. Color Sergeant Johnson, of the 2d Massachusetts, stands with his banner on the court house steps in September 1864. *(MICHAEL J. HAMMERSON)*

Back to the Valley

EVERARD H. SMITH

Some of the faces are new, but the sound of battle is the same in the Shenandoah

Above: The pivotal spot for all operations in the Shenandoah Valley was Harpers Ferry, northern gateway. Here the Shenandoah flowed into the Potomac, and here, too, the Baltimore & Ohio crossed on its way west. The Harpers Ferry Arsenal and Armory, now mere shells of gutted buildings, stand across the river. (USAMHI)

IN 1864 THE SHENANDOAH VALLEY of Virginia again became the scene of major military action, while the Wilderness and Georgia echoed from the guns. Once more, reprising the now familiar theme, a Rebel army muscled confidently into western Maryland and southern Pennsylvania, spreading havoc as it went. Momentarily—as cannon rumbled at Fort Stevens, near Washington, D.C.—it appeared that the very course of the war might be suddenly reversed, and no less an observer than the London *Times* was moved to conclude, "The Confederacy as an enemy is more formidable than ever."

Yet 1864 was not 1862, and the Confederate successes of midsummer proved only transitory. Northern superiority in numbers and resources, combined with a destructive new philosophy of warfare, soon broke the Southern hold on the Valley, and in the process reduced much of that beautiful vale to a smoldering ruin. The Shenandoah became, in fact, a microcosm of the final summer of the Civil War: here, as elsewhere, by the end of the year the Confederacy tottered on the verge of final defeat.

Matters began in April when Major General Franz Sigel, the local Union commander, persuaded Ulysses S. Grant to add a diversionary Valley offensive to his plans for the Old Dominion. A small, wizened German expatriate, Sigel was an officer passionately devoted to the Northern cause but regarded by his men as something of an albatross because of his political connections and foreign background. His strategy, however, was sound: a two-pronged attack on the town of Staunton, with one column, directed by himself, to advance from Harpers Ferry and the other to be led by Brigadier General George Crook from West Virginia.

Unhappily for Sigel, his opponents treated him as the greater threat, and on May 15 they concentrated most of their available forces against him at the Battle of New Market. The Southern ranks included the cadets of the Virginia Military Institute, whose youngest member was barely fifteen. The Rebels also had a superior leader, the charismatic Major General John C. Breckinridge, former U.S. Vice President and veteran corps commander —"that soldierly man," as one of his subordinates remembered him, "mounted magnificently . . . and riding like a Cid." Sigel was driven from the field in rout, provoking Chief of Staff Henry W. Halleck to comment sarcastically, "He will do nothing but run. He never did anything else."

Under heavy political pressure from Washington, Grant quickly replaced Sigel with a new commander, Major General David Hunter. The little German had been no paragon, but his replacement was worse. Sixty-one years old, stocky, with thinning black hair and long Hungarian mustaches, Hunter was an intensely bigoted man whose mind had been dominated by abolitionism. He harbored vindictive feelings toward all Southerners, and his brief stay in the Valley unleashed many passions which had previously been suppressed.

Hunter's swift resumption of the offensive caught Valley defenders by surprise, and the early stages of his campaign were marked by considerable success. A small Rebel army under Brigadier General William E. "Grumble" Jones entrenched at Piedmont in a last-ditch effort to save Staunton, but was soundly defeated on June 5. Next day the Union Army entered the town, and shortly afterward it was joined by General Crook, completing the Federal juncture.

Now Hunter had to plan the next phase of the advance, and he guessed disastrously. Ignoring Grant's sensible suggestion to transport his united army east of the Blue Ridge, then follow the railroad south from Charlottesville to Lynchburg, he elected instead to take the army all the way up the Valley to Buchanan before curling in on Lynchburg from the west. As far as it went, the plan of attack was a good one, enabling him to destroy another important railroad, the Virginia & Tennessee. But it also lengthened his march and gave his opponents adequate time to reinforce the town.

As he progressed, it became increasingly evident that Hunter intended to scourge the Valley with fire as well as the sword. In alleged retaliation for harassment by Rebel partisans such as Lieutenant Colonel John S. Mosby, the homes of numerous Southern sympathizers were put to the torch. Some suspected, however, that the general enjoyed his self-proclaimed role as basilisk. "Frequently, when we passed near houses, women would come running out, begging for protection," noted General Crook. "His invariable answer would be, 'Go away! Go away, or I will burn your house!'" Ultimately such acts of retribution had little impact on the guerrillas, but they set in motion a cycle of violence which gradually escalated as the campaign progressed, affecting both Yankees and Confederates and culminating in, the devastation which left much of the lower Valley a scorched plain.

By June 12, Hunter's slow but insistent advance had become so alarming that the Confederate high command could no longer ignore it. To Robert E. Lee, whose continuing defense of Richmond rested largely on his ability to maintain the railroad network around it, Lynchburg was a transportation hub as vital as Petersburg. Only by detaching part of his own command could he deal with the threat. Hence that evening the II Corps of the Army of Northern Virginia, Lieutenant General Jubal A. Early commanding, departed Richmond for the Valley. Making a virtue of necessity, Lee instructed Early to dispose of Hunter first, then either return to Richmond or effect a Maryland invasion of his own.

Lee could scarcely have chosen a more able, or controversial, lieutenant to execute his orders. "Old Jube," a Valley native, was forty-seven, grizzled, and stoop-shouldered. Afield he affected the dingiest of uniforms, which he covered with an enormous linen duster and surmounted with a white slouch hat and incongruous ostrich plume—withal, as one reporter carefully observed, "a person who would be singled out in a crowd." A man of firm opinions, he inspired similar judgments among his associates, who praised his audacity but criticized his sarcasm and abrasiveness.

A forced march brought the II Corps to Lynchburg just as Hunter's vanguard arrived from the opposite direction. Demoralized by the unexpected turn of events, and unable to retreat back north without being cut off, Hunter immediately withdrew into West Virginia. In so doing he saved his army but took it out of the war for the next three weeks, leaving the Shenandoah completely unprotected.

Of this strategic opportunity Old Jube promptly took full advantage. His army surged down the Valley in a series of marches which in-

Left: Troop trains bringing men from the west passed through Harpers Ferry regularly when the Union controlled the town. These are probably Ohioans, resting on flatcars before continuing their journey, while a train laden with supplies approaches from the left. (SPECIAL COLLECTIONS, U.S. MILITARY ACADEMY LIBRARY)

Above: The Massanutten Mountain broods over the Valley itself, the object of Stonewall Jackson's first great campaigns, and now, in 1864, the scene of yet more bitter fighting. This image was probably made shortly after the war, and shows part of the village of Strasburg. (USAMHI)

Left: Since Stonewall's campaign, there had been only one real battle in the Shenandoah, here at Winchester on June 14–15, 1863. This faded image is believed to have been taken in the so-called Milroy's Fort soon after the fight, and perhaps shows some of the 23 cannon captured from the routed Federal General Robert Milroy's army. (WINCHESTER-FREDERICK COUNTY HISTORICAL SOCIETY)

Above: For months thereafter, the Valley was rather quiet, but affairs in southwest Virginia soon threatened. The Confederate commander, Major General Samuel Jones, was not up to the difficult command, and, in February 1864, Richmond replaced him with… (VM)

Above: … Major General John C. Breckznridge. The youngest Vice President in American history, he had run against Lincoln for the presidency in 1860. Now he was a Confederate officer, charged not only with defending southwest Virginia but also the Valley if it were invaded. (VM)

Above: In May threats came from all over. Union Brigadier General George Crook swooped into southwest Virginia from West Virginia and met part of Breckinridge's command at Cloyd's Mountain. (WRHS)

Above: Breckinridge was not at the battle. Instead, commanding the small Confederate army there was Brigadier General Albert Jenkins. In the battle on May 9, 1864, he lost the fight, his arm, and, within a few days, his life. (NA)

voked the spirit of Stonewall Jackson's old "foot cavalry." After fording the Potomac on July 6, the gray columns circled eastward along a trajectory that directly threatened both Baltimore and Washington, D.C.

This sudden reversal of Federal fortunes precipitated a crisis in the Union chain of command which came appallingly close to costing the United States its capital. Isolated at Petersburg, Grant had no solution to the situation other than the suggestion that his chief of staff should handle the matter. Henry W. Halleck, who was at heart little more than a petulant Washington bureaucrat, and had besides a fine track record for avoiding responsibility, declined action unless his superior initiated it. So nothing was done. Meantime, subordinates pleaded for instructions, refugees thronged the roads leading east and south, and Early calmly occupied Frederick, Maryland, on July 9, exacting a "contribution" of $200,000 from the unhappy town fathers.

Fortunately for the North, one officer possessed sufficient courage to act in the absence of orders. From Baltimore the Rebel invasion had been watched with mounting concern by Major General Lew Wallace, an Ohio political general with the sad eyes of a basset hound and a romantically literary turn of mind. Gathering a greatly outnumbered force at the Monocacy River, Wallace contested Early's passage on the 9th. The forlorn hope ended in defeat, but it delayed the Southern advance for a crucial 12 hours. While the battle was in progress, Grant emerged from his lethargy long enough to dispatch portions of the VI and XIX Corps from Petersburg to Washington. Had Wallace not made his stubborn stand, the commanding general later conceded, Early "might have entered the capital before the arrival of the reinforcements I had sent."

Such an upset was just beyond the pugnacious Rebel leader's grasp, though the might-have-beens remained to haunt Southern apologists thenceforth. The Confederate army reached Washington's northern defense perimeter two days after the Battle of Monocacy. But Early, intimidated by the formidable earthworks he faced, confined his activities to a show of strength, and within hours Grant's veterans had arrived to ensure the safety of the city. The following afternoon Abraham Lincoln visited Fort Stevens, where, to the consternation of Major General Horatio G. Wright, commanding the VI Corps, he casually climbed to the parapet to view the battlefield. Only feet from the President an army doctor collapsed, wounded by a sniper. Swallowing his diffidence, Wright firmly ordered his Commander-in-Chief off the wall (aided, it is alleged, by the youthful Captain Oliver Wendell Holmes, Jr., who shouted unthinkingly at the tall figure, "Get down, you fool!").

The raid on Washington proved the Confederate high-water mark of the summer. When word arrived that Hunter was finally struggling out of the West Virginia wilderness, Early slipped away from the capital unimpeded and regained the sheltering Blue Ridge walls. Still the Confederates were not quite ready to surrender their hard-won initiative. An abortive effort by Hunter to secure the lower Valley ended in near disaster on July 24 when the Rebels pounced on Crook's command at Kernstown. Then, six days later, Early determined to strike back at those who had brought devastation to western Virginia and, in the process, to teach the North a lesson which it would not soon forget.

On the morning of July 30 two mounted brigades under Brigadier General John McCausland entered Chambersburg, Pennsylvania, bearing with them a demand similar to that visited upon Frederick earlier in the month: pay a ransom of $500,000 in currency ($100,000 in specie) or face destruction. Unwilling to believe the threat, the townspeople declined to raise the money—where upon McCausland ordered the entire town fired.

Four hundred buildings, more than half of them homes, were destroyed. As the conflagration raged, some troopers engaged in drunken pillage while others helped residents save their possessions. "The burning of Chambersburg was generally condemned by our regiment at first," admitted a cavalryman, "but when reason had time to regain her seat I believe that they all thought as I thought at first: that it was justice, and justice tempered with mercy.... Now everyone knows that the conciliatory policy has failed—utterly failed—and we are driven *nolens volens* to the opposite mode of procedure."

Clearly, attitudes were hardening on both sides, and this fact was apparent in the momentous change in Union leadership which Grant announced two days after the Chambersburg raid. To Major General Philip H. Sheridan, the new commander, went orders "to put himself south of the enemy and follow him to the death." Presaging future events, the general-in-chief also outlined a specific objective for the campaign: "Such as can not be consumed, destroy," a sentiment expressed with equal cogency in Sheridan's oft-quoted remark that a crow flying over the Valley would have to carry its own rations.

"Restless, full of the combative quality, not politic in language, somewhat reticent, half stubborn and fond of hazard enterprises... he was the embodiment of heroism, dash, and impulse." Thus Grant described Phil Sheridan, the five-foot-five, black-haired, bullet-headed son of Irish immigrants from County Caven. Despite tactical abilities that were never more than modest, Sheridan had won prominence as one of the hardest-fighting generals in the Army of the Potomac. For his forthcoming operations he possessed an army that eventually included seven infantry and three cavalry divisions, plus substantial artillery. His opponent's command mustered no more than five divisions of infantry and two of cavalry, in addition to one brigade of artillery. In terms of manpower the Northern superiority was even more pronounced, probably on the order of two-to-one.

Reflecting his superiors' concern that further Confederate successes would endanger Lincoln in the fall elections, Sheridan proceeded cautiously at first. However, when he finally moved on September 19 against the Southern position at Winchester, just west of Opequon Creek, his juggernaut rolled forward with irresistible momentum. Combined infantry and cavalry assaults smashed the Confederate left flank; Early was sent, in Sheridan's own expressive phrase, "whirling through Winchester." Battered but still defiant, the gray forces entrenched 20 miles farther south at Fisher's Hill, near Strasburg. Here, three days later, Sheridan attacked again, once more outflanking the Confederate left.

Grant now counseled his subordinate, as he

Left: Meanwhile, Breckinridge watched another Federal thrust, south into the Valley. His eyes were the partisan rangers and cavalry scouting all through the Shenandoah, among the most effective being the command of Lieutenant Colonel John Singleton Mosby, the "Gray Ghost of the Confederacy." He appears here near war's end as a full colonel. (VM)

Above: The Yankee army he watched was commanded by Major General Franz Sigel, a man of no military ability but potent political influence. His soldiers proudly declared, being largey Germans themselves, that they "fights mit Sigel." (USAMHI)

Left: Sigel's army was filled with men no more able than himself, men like Brigadier General Jeremiah Sullivan, commanding his infantry. Toward the end of the war he would be relieved of command because no superior wanted him. (USAMHI)

Above: Yet they led good troops, veteran regiments like the 34h Massachusetts, shown here in 1862 outside Alexandria, Virginia. (USAMHI)

Above: Rushing to meet and stop Sigel, Breckinridge enlisted the aid of the Corps of Cadets of Lexington's Virginia Military Institute. Lieutenant Colonel Scott Ship led the boys, some no more than fourteen, in the battle that followed. (NEW MARKET BATTLE-FIELD PARK)

Above: Cadet William Nelson, at nineteen, was among the oldest in the corps who fought at New Market. (VM)

Above: A distinguished yet little known Confederate officer who led one of Breckinridge's brigades at New Market was Brigadier General Gabriel C. Wharton, himself a VMI graduate. (LC)

had Hunter, to occupy the Valley as far south as Staunton and then move eastward toward Charlottesville. But Sheridan resisted, citing logistical difficulties and the dangers of partisan bedevilment. Instead he argued that the ravaging of the lower Shenandoah should remain his primary goal. Accordingly, he sent out raiding parties to destroy as much of the recent harvest as possible. The rest of the army began digging in at Cedar Creek for an indefinite stay. To clear up the details of his strategy, the War Department ordered him to Washington for a brief conference on October 16. For the summons which took him from the front at this critical moment, Sheridan was of course not to blame. Nevertheless, his defensive arrangements at Cedar Creek were open to criticism, for he left his army indifferently posted, its left flank resting unsupported above a defile at the foot of Massanutten Mountain.

Out of the foggy dawn on October 19 rose the spine-chilling wail of the "Rebel Yell" as Old Jube struck the Federal left end-on with the full strength of four divisions. Totally surprised, the Union Army reeled backward along the Valley turnpike for four miles. Sheridan, who learned of the attack just as he was returning from Winchester, spurred furiously toward the battlefield, 14 miles away. En route he passed thousands of fleeing soldiers who turned with a cheer to follow him as he shouted, "About-face, boys! We're going back to our camps! We're going to lick them out of their boots!" In a famous poem published shortly after the battle, T. Buchanan Read exaggerated by half the distance Sheridan's ride covered (and with it the endurance of his charger, Rienzi), but accurately depicted its psychological impact:

He dashed down the line, 'mid a storm of huzzas,
And the wave of retreat checked its course there,
   because

Above: Immediately after the Confederate victory at New Market, Richmond sent Colonel Edwin G. Lee, shown here as a brigadier later in the war, to assume command at Staunton and recruit more troops for the defense of the Valley. It was obvious that the Yankees would come again. (CHS)

Above: In fact, they came within two weeks, led now by a general just as incompetent as Sigel, Major General David Hunter. His destruction of private property, including VMI, would make his name reviled in Virginia. (WRHS)

The sight of the master compelled it to pause.
With foam and with dust the black charger was
    gray;
By the flash of his eye, and his red nostril's play,
He seemed to the whole great army to say:
"I have brought you Sheridan all the way
    From Winchester down to save the day."

By way of anticlimax, when Sheridan arrived he discovered that General Wright had already stabilized the front. Whether Early himself neglected to press the attack, or whether his men simply stopped to plunder the enemy's camps, the impetus of the Southern offensive gradually slowed. The inevitable Northern counterattack precipitated a rout unprecedented even by Valley standards. With dogged tenacity, Early once again assembled his forces farther south, but the final Confederate bid for mastery in the Shenandoah had failed.

Affairs well in hand, Sheridan's men resumed the task of despoliation, their success illustrated by the grim record of the property which they seized or destroyed: 1,200 barns; 71 flour mills; 8 saw mills; 7 furnaces; 4 tanneries; 3 saltpeter works; 1 woolen mill; 1 powder mill; 1 railroad depot; 1,165 pounds of cotton yarn; 974 miles of rail; 15,000 swine; 12,000 sheep; 10,918 cattle; 3,772 horses; 545 mules; 250 calves; 435,802

Above: His adjutant, Colonel David Hunter Strother, was much better liked, and better known by his pen name "Porte Crayon." He drew sketches of army life that were widely published in the North. (USAMHI)

Above: To stop Hunter, Richmond assigned one of Lee's premier fighters, Lieutenant General Jubal A. Early of the II Corps. Cranky, cantankerous, a confirmed bachelor who offended many, still he was more than Hunter's match. (VM)

Above: Hunter was turned back, and with him his chief of cavalry, Major General Julius Stahel, a Hungarian who won the Medal of Honor for his bravery in the Battle of Piedmont in June. (USAMHI)

Above: Less distinguished was the service of Colonel August Moor of the 28th Ohio. Within weeks of Piedmont, he would be out of the service. (USAMHI)

Above: When Early came to the Valley, he brought with him several officers of high merit. He would need them, for barely had he driven Hunter out before he launched his July raid on Washington itself. Confederate cavalry led by Brigadier General Robert Ransom was the vanguard. (USAMHI)

Above: Serving with the Confederate infantry in the raid, and at the Battle of Monocacy, Maryland, which delayed Early, was perhaps the biggest general of the war, Brigadier William R. Peck of Tennessee. He stood six feet six inches tall and won commendation for his bravery in the battle. (USAMHI)

Above: The real hero of Monocacy, however, was a Yankee, Major General Lew Wallace. With inferior numbers, still he managed to stall Early long enough for vital reinforcements to reach Washington and prevent its capture. Years after the war he would write his great book, Ben Hur. (USAMHI)

bushels of wheat; 77,176 bushels of corn; 20,39▨ tons of hay; 500 tons of fodder; 450 tons of straw; 12,000 pounds of bacon; 10,000 pounds of tobacco; and 874 barrels of flour. These depredations di▨ not affect the upper Valley, where Early sti▨ lurked. Even so, between Staunton and the Potomac they were thorough indeed. Thousands o▨ refugees moved north, and a full year after the wa▨ a British traveler found the region standing as desolate as a moor.

While the plundering was underway, Rebe▨ guerrillas continued to plague the invaders, at one point even spiriting General Crook off into captivity. For a while it appeared that the North had a solution to this problem too. Six of Mosby's men were hanged at Front Royal by Brigadier General George A. Custer, a brash young cavalry commander already displaying signs of the faulty judgment which would cost him his life on the Little Big Horn. But anyone could play this game, and after Mosby retaliated in kind both sides mercifully halted the executions. A final stage in the escalation of violence was thereby avoided—yet here in Virginia, as well as elsewhere in the South, rapid progress had been made toward the dreadful 20th century concept of total war.

Sheridan's operations concluded in February 1865, when he overwhelmed the last remnants of Confederate strength at Waynesboro and then rejoined Grant at Petersburg. To contemporaries his campaign was one of the signal accomplishments of the Civil War, and it figured prominently in postbellum song and story. It is true that, in the harsh light of historical retrospection, his exploits fall short of epic proportions. Less than half the Valley suffered from his scorched-earth tactics. Moreover, by nullifying Grant's repeated orders to resume the offensive east of the Blue Ridge, he may well have lost a golden opportunity to end the war six months before Appomattox. All this being said, however, the incompleteness of his

Above: … last-minute reinforcements from Grant's army at Petersburg, among them Brigadier General Frank Wheaton and his division of the VI Corps. Ironically, Wheaton's wife was the daughter of the Confederacy's highest ranking general, Samuel Cooper. (P-M)

Above: Early got as close as Fort Stevens, only a few miles outside the capital. On this ground he fought his hesitating battle that ended the raid. Had he pushed, he might still have broken through despite… (MHS)

Above: It was as close as the ravages of war came to the District of Columbia, and quite close enough for President Lincoln, who was in Fort Stevens during part of the firing. (USAMHI)

Above: This house near Fort Stevens shows the effects of Early's artillery fire during the fighting. (USAMHI)

Right: For a few hours Confederates even occupied the home of Breckinridge's cousin and old friend, Montgomery Blair, at Silver Spring, Maryland. Breckinridge saved the house from looting. (USAMHI)

victory probably did not matter. To his credit, he achieved more than any Union leader before him, for he demolished an important symbol of Southern invincibility. In so doing, he also removed one of the few remaining props upon which rested the fate of the Confederate nation.

Above: Nevertheless, later on Confederate stragglers would vandalize the home of Blair, Lincoln's postmaster general. (USAMHI)

Above: Early, too, took losses, among them the personable young Brigadier General Robert D. Lilley. Back in Virginia, near Winchester, he was so severely wounded that he lost his right arm. Here his empty sleeve is pinned to his blouse. (USAMHI)

Right: Early did not forget the depredations of Hunter in the Valley. In retaliation, he sent Brigadier General John McCausland to demand a payment of half a million dollars from Chambersburg, Pennsylvania. When the town could not produce it, McCausland gave… (COURTESY OF ALEXANDER MCCAUSLAND)

Far right: … Brigadier General Bradley T. Johnson orders to burn the town. (USAMHI)

Below: Johnson applied the torch, and Chambersburg burned. Local photographers, the Zacharias brothers, recorded the aftermath. (MHS)

Below right: All that was left of the Bank of Chambersburg. (MHS)

Above: The skeleton of the Franklin County court house. Chambersburg would eventually receive compensation from Washington for its loss—in the 1970s! (MHS)

Above: But in 1864 there was nothing to assuage the loss. Yankees called it barbarism. Confederates called it revenge. (COURTESY OF MAURICE MAROTTE)

Above: Early's successes in the Shenandoah forced Washington to stop sending political hacks to oppose him. Instead, Grant sent one of his most trusted lieutenants, the ruthless Major General Philip H. Sheridan, small, combative, merciless. He stands at front, fifth from the left, among his staff in 1864. (USAMHI)

Above: Through August and into September, Early and Sheridan feinted at each other. Then on September 19 the Federals attacked, pushing across Opequon Creek and moving toward Winchester. A postwar view of the creek. (USAMHI)

Below: With Early falling back before them, Sheridan's divisions drove toward the Valley pike, shown here looking south toward Winchester. (USAMHI)

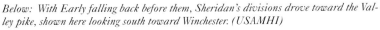

Left: In bitter fighting, one of the best young officers of the Confederate Army, Brigadier General Robert E. Rodes, was killed in action, his division being taken by another promising young officer... (USAMHI)

Above: Yankees, too, started to fall. Brigadier General David A. Russell, who had helped save Washington in July, fell leading a brigade when a shell fragment pierced his heart. He stands at left, with Generals T. H. Neill in the center, and John H. Martindale at right. (USAMHI)

Above: … Brigadier General John Pegram. (COURTESY OF W. HAYS PARKS)

Above: Before long the Confederates were pushed back into Winchester itself, desperately holding out against Sheridan's attacks. An 1885 view, with Milroy's Fort visible on the crest in the distance. (USAMHI)

Above: Brigadier General R. D. Johnston led his brigade with particular bravery in trying to stem the Yankee tide, but Sheridan was too powerful, and Early too scattered. (VM)

Above: From this spot in Milroy's Fort civilians looked out and watched the battle for Winchester as it raged oo in the distance. (USAMHI)

Far left: Brigadier General James McIntosh and his cavalry brigade had helped open the battle. For four hours that morning he held a position against Early's infantry. In the end his battling cost McIntosh a severe wound and a leg. (USAMHI)

Left: For Colonel James Mulligan, it cost more than that. Wounded while leading his brigade, he was captured by the Confederates and died a few days later. (NA)

Above: Around the already ruined Hackwood house the contending armies raged as Sheridan pressed ever closer to Winchester. (USAMHI)

Above: Here, late in the afternoon, elements of Sheridan's XIX Corps poised before the final attack that drove Early out of Winchester. A postwar image. (USAMHI)

Below: Colonel Rutherford B. Hayes won a reputation for himself at Fisher's Hill, and after the war his record helped win him a term in the White House. (P-M)

Left: What put Early's army to flight out of Winchester was the final attack of the day, led by Brigadier General Wesley Merritt. An unpublished image believed to be of the youthful and talented cavalry officer. (COURTESY OF THOMAS SWEENEY)

Above: The armies met next at Fisher's Hill on September 22. Southwest of Strasburg, Fisher's Hill proved to be another Confederate stampede, as Sheridan's attack drove Early from his position on the crest in the center background. Many a Confederate was buried in the little cemetery at left. An 1885 view. (USAMHI)

Above: Viewed from the crest of Fisher's Hill, the Federal positions are off in the distance. By getting around his flank, Sheridan forced Early to retreat and almost cut off escape but for the stubborn rearguard stand of Confederate cavalrymen. (USAMHI)

Right: … Brigadier General W. C. Wickham, who outwitted Sheridan's pursuers and saved Early from possible disaster. (VM)

Far right: Old Jubal smarted under his twin defeats, and through September and into October he planned a counterattack. At Cedar Creek on October 19, 1864, he made it. Spearheading the attack was a bold march around Sheridan's flank led by Major General John B. Gordon, one of the fightingest generals in the Confederate Army. (NA)

Right: Along with Gordon's flank march, Kershaw's brigade crossed Cedar Creek here to assist in the flank attack. It achieved complete surprise and threatened to put the Yankees to rout. A postwar image. (USAMHI)

Left: This hill is where the Federals' unsuspecting left was placed when Early struck. The bluecoats could not stand in the face of a lightning attack. (USAMHI)

Far left: Brigadier General Daniel D. Bidwell fell with a mortal wound while trying to resist Early's assault. (USAMHI)

Left: Confederates like Brigadier General Cullen Battle paid a price for their surprise, however. Leading a brigade in Gordon's attack, Battle took a wound that put him out of the war for good. (USAMHI)

Far left: Only the heroic efforts of men like Brigadier General Lewis A. Grant managed to build a line where the retreating Federals could hold long enough for reinforcements to come and resist Early's drive. (P-M)

Left: Brigadier General Alfred T. A. Torbert's cavalry division also stood in the face of the advancing Confederates, buying enough time for Sheridan to rush to the battlefield and start sending more regiments. A native of Delaware, Torbert actually held a commission in the Confederate Army briefly at war's outset but was at the same time raising the 1st New Jersey. (USAMHI)

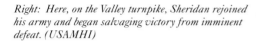

Above: Sheridan was some distance behind the lines when Early struck. Feverishly, he rode his charger forward to take command and rally his army. This postwar image of his horse was made in Leavenworth, Kansas, by photographer E. E. Henry. (USAMHI)

Right: Here, on the Valley turnpike, Sheridan rejoined his army and began salvaging victory from imminent defeat. (USAMHI)

Above: Once more the Federals advanced, across ground like this where they had been placed that morning, unsuspecting the storm that Early would unleash. (USAMHI)

Above: By that afternoon it was Early who was hard-pressed. Here sat his left flank when the revitalized XIX Corps and VI Corps struck in an unstoppable attack that drove the Southerners from the field. Early had his third consecutive defeat. (USAMHI)

Right: Sheridan made his headquarters at Belle Grove mansion, seen here in the distance, a magnificent country house built by the Fairfax family. Here after the battle mortally wounded Confederate Brigadier Stephen D. Ramseur was brought to die. Old friends like Custer and Merritt surrounded him at his deathbed. (USAMHI)

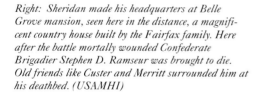

Far left: And that was virtually the end of the Valley Campaign. Through the fall and on into the winter of 1865 the armies glowered at each other, but Early could no longer risk meeting his foe. New officers came to him, men like Colonel Thomas T. Munford, who would command his remnant of cavalry, but they were too few to save the Shenandoah. (VM)

Left: Early himself was relieved in March 1865 and replaced by Major General Lunsford L. Lomax, in command of the Valley District. By then it was a command without an army. (USAMHI)

Left: Through that winter the Federals, too, played a game of watch and wait. For them and for the Valley, the war was almost over. Here, just outside Winchester, the camera captures the headquarters of Colonel Alexander Pennington's cavalry brigade on February 23, 1865. (USAMHI)

Above: And here in Winchester a jaunty Brigadier General George A. Custer sits at the head of the steps, surrounded by his wife and friends. The boy general had distinguished himself in the campaign. (AMERICANA IMAGE GALLERY)

Above: They ha⸱ all distinguished themselves, and with Early dispatched, Sheridan and h⸱ generals could be off for the east of the Blue Ridge, back to Grant, and the ⸱st irresistible surge at Lee. Sitting on the ground are Brigadier Gene⸱l James H. Wilson, at left, Torbert in the center, and Sheridan at right. Seated ⸱hind them are Brigadier General Thomas Davies at left, Brigadier Gene⸱l David M. Gregg in profile, and Merritt at far right. They were a constell⸱on of stars. (KA)

A Campaign That Failed

LUDWELL H. JOHNSON III

Cotton and politics and the Red River make strange war in Louisiana

Above: When an invasion of the Red River was proposed, many, including the man who would lead it, were not enthusiastic. But chief of staff Major General Henry W. Halleck managed to force it to be undertaken. (USAMHI)

THE RED RIVER EXPEDITION, like the Shenandoah campaign part of the Union's nation-wide advance, was perhaps as strange and complicated an episode as the Civil War has to offer. It originated in a combination of motives that included a missionary-imperialist impulse to promote a New England settlement of Texas, fears of French influence in Mexico, President Lincoln's determination to establish a Unionist state government in Louisiana, the machinations of unscrupulous cotton speculators and textile mill interests, the U.S. Navy's thirst for prize money, and the strategic vagaries of Chief of Staff Major General Henry W. Halleck.

The Union plan of campaign called for a powerful column based in New Orleans to advance to the Red River from the south, another force to come down the Mississippi from Vicksburg, a third to march southwestward from Little Rock and the Mississippi Squadron to accompany the main force up the Red River. The objective was to capture Shreveport, headquarters of the Confederate Trans-Mississippi Department, and from there to invade Texas. The campaign was to begin in March 1864, when the Federals needed every available man for the decisive campaigns east of the Mississippi. It was set in motion against the wishes of U. S. Grant, who succeeded Halleck as chief of staff soon after the expedition began. It continued without benefit of an overall commander, met with severe reverses, almost saw the Mississippi Squadron lost or sunk, tied up thousands of troops that otherwise would have been employed with Sherman in Georgia and in an attack on Mobile, and ended in total failure.

Commanding the column coming up from New Orleans was Nathaniel P. Banks, a Massachusetts politician with no prewar military experience who had been repeatedly beaten by Stonewall Jackson in Virginia. Late in 1862, Banks replaced Benjamin F. Butler as commander of the Department of the Gulf, where his principal task was the political reorganization of Louisiana. The Vicksburg column, detached from W. T. Sherman's army, had for its leader the hard-bitten A. J. Smith, who came under Banks' orders when he reached the Red River. Naval forces consisted of the Mississippi Squadron, 23 vessels, mostly ironclads. The admiral of this armada was David Dixon Porter, courageous, vainglorious, and money-hungry, whose sailors were skilled in "capturing" cotton as a prize of war. Frederick Steele led the troops who were to come down from Little Rock. Preoccupied by the task of Republicanizing Arkansas and acutely aware of the logistical pitfalls of a march through south-central Arkansas, Steele would have preferred to make a mere demonstration, but Grant ordered him to move on Shreveport in cooperation with Banks.

Confederate forces were under the general direction of E. Kirby Smith, commander of the Trans-Mississippi Department. Sterling Price, silver-maned former governor of Missouri, led the cavalry contesting Steele's advance. Bearing the brunt of the Federal invasion up the Red was Richard Taylor, son of the late Zachary Taylor and brother to Jefferson Davis' first wife. Highly educated and widely read, Taylor was a very capable amateur soldier who had won his spurs with Jackson in the Shenandoah Valley. He was supremely confident, pugnacious, a leader of men, and an imaginative strategist.

Both Smith and Taylor found it hard to believe

reports of an impending offensive against Shreveport. Surely, said Smith, the enemy could not be so "infatuated" as to divert troops from the central south, where the war would be decided. All doubts were laid to rest when Porter's squadron and A. J. Smith's 11,000 veterans appeared at the mouth of the Red River on March 11. The Federal troops marched inland and overwhelmed the little garrison at Fort De Russy. Porter then carried part of Smith's command to Alexandria, which was occupied on the 15th. When Banks' men reached the town ten days later, Federal forces totaled 30,000 troops, while on the river there were 60 vessels, including transports. To confront this host Taylor had 7,000 men. His only course was to fall back, collect reinforcements, and hope for an opportunity to strike the enemy in detail.

At Alexandria, while Banks was holding elections for the "restored" government of Louisiana, Porter's men rounded up wagons and teams and ranged the countryside collecting cotton. They stenciled "CSA" on the bales to convince the prize court it was Confederate-owned cotton, and under that "USN." One envious army officer told Porter the initials stood for "Cotton Stealing Association of the United States Navy." Porter also had less congenial work to attend to at Alexandria. The river had failed to rise at the usual season, a fact that would give the Navy much grief before the campaign was over, but 13 gunboats and 30 transports managed to scrape into the upper Red, including the huge ironclad Eastport.

When Banks pushed out from Alexandria, Taylor fell back before him. Union infantry entered Natchitoches on April 1, having marched 80 miles in four days. A few miles farther, at Grand Ecore, the main road to Shreveport turned away from the river and, for Banks, away from the shelter of Porter's big guns. On April 6, without waiting to look for a river road, which did exist, Banks plunged into the forbidding pine woods. Porter continued up the narrow, winding river the next day. Taylor withdrew as far as Mansfield, about 40 miles from Shreveport; there he made a stand, deployed his little army, and waited for Banks. Smoldering with anger because reinforcements were so few in number and so long in reaching him, bitterly resenting the gossipers at departmental headquarters who blamed him for the failure to stop the invaders, Taylor was in a dangerous frame of mind.

The Federals tramped through Pleasant Hill and on toward Mansfield. First came the cavalry, then the cavalry's large wagon train, then the infantry. At noon on April 8 the troopers emerged into a clearing, on the far side of which they could see the Rebel skirmish line. Infantry filed into line but did not attack. By four o'clock Taylor's small store of patience was exhausted, and he came down on the enemy with crushing force. Out flanked, the Federals fell back, stiffened as reinforcements arrived, then broke and ran for the rear. When they found the narrow road blocked by the cavalry train, panic spread through the ranks. At last, two miles from the battlefield, a fresh Union division checked the pursuers well after night had fallen. In the darkness, cries of the wounded mingled with joyous shouts as the Confederates plundered the captured wagons. Banks fought most of the battle with about 7,000 men, as compared to Taylor's 8,800. Banks lost 2,235 men, of whom two thirds were captured. Taylor lost 1,000 killed and wounded; there was no report of

Above: The man who would actually command the expedition was Major General Nathaniel P. Banks of Massachusetts, seated at center among his staff. A man of no military experience, and even less ability, he was a political powerhouse, and that got him command. Halleck complained that it was "but little better than murder" to put men like Banks in the field. (MHS)

Above: To back Banks in the Red River Campaign, Washington assembled a mighty ironclad fleet, including 13 ironclads and several more gunboats. A part of that fleet poses here on the Red in May 1864. (USAMHI)

Left: Commanding the naval end of the operation was Admiral David D. Porter, flamboyant, scheming, and anxious to confiscate the abundant cotton on the Red River for the prize money. (USAMHI)

Above: Porter himself made the famous Black Hawk *his flagship. She sits here at anchor in the Mississippi with a small steam tug at her bow. (GLADSTONE COLLECTION)*

Above: Brigadier General A. J. Smith, shown here as a colonel in late 1861, was ordered to cooperate with Banks. He was not very popular with his men, some of whom hissed him when he rode past. And later in the campaign he would suggest arresting Banks for incompetence. (LC)

Above: Quickly the armies gathered, and the fleet assembled. The USS Ouachita *had formerly been a Confederate warship, the* Louisville, *before her capture in 1863. Now she was preparing to steam up the Red. (MHS)*

anyone missing. He captured 20 pieces of artillery and 156 wagons, valuable booty for the lean gray army.

Banks retreated to Pleasant Hill, where he took up a defensive position, strengthened by A. J. Smith's command. Taylor followed, having been reinforced by two small divisions under Thomas J. Churchill. These troops had recently arrived from Arkansas in response to orders from Kirby Smith, who had correctly decided to concentrate against Banks first.

Taylor had followed Stonewall Jackson to some purpose and did not intend to make a simple frontal attack at Pleasant Hill. His plan called for Churchill to envelop the Union left while the rest of the infantry attacked in front. Cavalry would move around the enemy's right flank. If successful, Taylor would cut off all of Banks' avenues of retreat. Churchill's weary soldiers, who had marched 45 miles during the last day and a half, advanced with spirit at three in the afternoon, drove the Federals back, reached the road to Natchitoches, and seemed to have the battle well in hand. However, the Federal left was not where it seemed to be. Churchill had in fact crossed his right in front of A. J. Smith, who attacked at just the right moment. Although it resisted stubbornly, the Confederate right gave way in disorder. Darkness ended the fighting; Taylor had been sharply repulsed.

Banks rode up to Smith. "God bless you, Gen-

Left: Another captured Confederate gunboat was the General Price. *Now she was in the Yankee service, though the commander of the gunboat* Conestoga, *lying astern of her in this January 20, 1864, image by Baton Rouge artist A. D. Lytle, might well have wondered whose side the* General Price *was really on. Seven weeks after this photo of the two was made… (COURTESY OF ROBERT G. HARRIS)*

eral," he exclaimed, "you have saved the army." Later, without consulting Smith, Banks decided to retreat; soon after midnight the army started down the road to Grand Ecore. At Pleasant Hill each side had had approximately 12,000 men engaged. Banks lost 1,400 casualties, Taylor more than 1,600. The "Fighting Politician" had been lucky. With another general there would have been no need to retreat, but probably most of Banks' officers would have agreed with William B. Franklin, commander of the XIX Corps: "From what I had seen of General Banks' ability to command in the field, I was certain that an operation depending on plenty of troops, rather than skill in handling them, was the only one which would have probability of success in his hands."

One arm of the pincers movement on Shreveport was broken when Banks retreated from Pleasant Hill. The other, Steele's army, was advancing on the Confederate stronghold from the northeast; by the time Taylor attacked Banks, the campaign in Arkansas was two weeks old. For the Federals it was a dismal ordeal from start to finish. Steele set out from Little Rock with 6,800 effectives on March 23. A cooperating column of 3,600 men joined him at Elkins' Ferry on April 9, but brought no supplies. The roads were wretched, food and forage scarce, and Price's cavalry swarmed about the column. "Our supplies were nearly exhausted and so was the country," said Steele. "We were obliged to forage from 5 to 15 miles on either side of the road to keep our stock alive." Therefore, on April 12, Steele abruptly changed his direction from southwest to east and made for the town of Camden. There he hoped to accumulate supplies and eventually to resume the offensive.

Ironically, just as Steele was turning back, Kirby Smith decided to strip Taylor of most of his infantry and take them to Arkansas, even though he had learned that Steele was heading for Camden and posed no immediate threat to Shreveport. Taylor argued to no avail for a concentration against Banks and Porter; Kirby Smith was obdurate. He marched off, leaving the fuming Taylor with his cavalry and one small division of infantry. Without doubt this was a strategic mistake of the first magnitude, one that not only affected operations on the Red River, but conceivably had an important bearing on the major campaigns east of the Mississippi.

Kirby Smith left for Arkansas on April 16, the

Left: … with Lieutenant I. F. Richardson in command, seated at right… (COURTESY OF ROBERT G. HARRIS)

Below: … the General Price *collided with the* Conestoga *while both were on their way to the Red River. The* Conestoga *sank, ending a distinguished river career. (NA)*

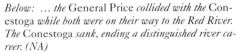

Above: Also along for the campaign was the hospital ship Red Rover. *She, too, had been a Confederate vessel, a barracks ship until captured and converted into the Navy's first commissioned medical ship. (NHC)*

Above: Half of Porter's fleet, it seemed, had changed sides during the war. The Eastport *began its war career as a Confederate warship, an unfinished ironclad completed and put into service by the Yankees. On April 15, 1864, she would strike an underwater mine or "torpedo," and a few days later, crippled, she was sunk to avoid capture. (USAMHI)*

Above: This McPherson & Oliver photograph shows Banks' goal, Alexandria, Louisiana, on the Red River. Federals took it unopposed on March 15 as Porter's fleet steamed up to the wharves. (USAMHI)

Above: The Confederate commander of the Trans-Mississippi Department, General E. Kirby Smith, shown here in an early war photo, was ill prepared or equipped to resist a major invasion. (USAMHI)

Above: His army commander at Alexandria, Lieutenant General Richard Taylor, was the son of President Zachary Taylor and an officer of unusual ability. He also knew he could not resist Banks at Alexandria, so he evacuated. (CHS)

same day that the rear of Steele's column entered Camden. There the beleaguered Federals began their search for food. The capture of a Confederate steamer loaded with corn eased the pinch somewhat, as did the arrival of a wagon train from Pine Bluff with ten days' half-rations. But these successes were more than offset by the loss of a wagon train in a bloody little affair at Poison Spring that cost the Federals almost a third of the escort, and of another in a bigger fight at Marks' Mills, where 1,300 of 1,600 men were lost. The capture of these trains precipitated a crisis: Steele no longer had the means to feed his men and animals. There was only one possible decision: on April 25 Steele ordered an immediate retreat to Little Rock.

With the infantry from Taylor's army now at hand, Kirby Smith took up the pursuit. This was his second serious mistake. The proper course would have been to return swiftly to Louisiana and join Taylor in attacking the Federals before they could extricate themselves from the Red River country. Instead he kept on after Steele, both armies contending with rain and mud, bridging rivers, struggling against hunger and exhaustion. On April 30 he overtook Steele at Jenkins' Ferry, a crossing of the Saline. Fighting across flooded bottom lands, knee-deep in water, assaulting log breastworks, the Confederates made little headway. All during the battle Steele labored to get his trains and artillery across the river. By early afternoon the bloodied Confederates had given up the attack, and the Federals staggered the last miles into Little Rock in peace. The Arkansas phase of the campaign was over.

Back on the Red, Banks had entrenched at Grand Ecore, presenting the strange spectacle of 25,000 men hemmed in by 5,000. Meanwhile, Porter's flotilla had proceeded up the river, headed for Shreveport. When Porter learned of the army's retreat, he managed to turn his vessels around in the narrow, shallow channel and begin the difficult trip downstream. Grinding along the bottom, sticking on submerged stumps, colliding with one another, braving Confederate musketry and artillery fire, they at last reached Grand Ecore safely. This trip, however, was only a foretaste of troubles yet to come.

Banks dismissed his chief of staff and two cavalry generals, scapegoats for his failure, called up reinforcements, and even thought of resuming the offensive. The thought passed quickly; on April 19 he began the retreat to Alexandria. His route took him down a long island formed by the Cane and Red rivers, and Taylor attempted to encircle the enemy as they prepared to leave the island at Monett's Ferry. Had the infantry Kirby Smith marched off to Arkansas still been with Taylor, his plan might well have succeeded; now the odds were too heavy. Pushing the Confederates aside after brisk fighting, Banks' men reached Alexandria on the 25th. They had left behind them a smoking wasteland. "The track of the spoiler," said one observer, "was one scene of desolation.... A painful melancholy, a death-like silence, broods over the land, and desolation reigns supreme."

A. J. Smith's men, not long back from Sherman's devastating Meridian expedition, were the stars of the drama. "The people now will be terribly scourged," promised one of Smith's generals, and scourged they were.

As the navy paralleled the army's withdrawal, Porter was having more trouble. The ponderous *Eastport*, sunk below Grand Ecore by a torpedo and laboriously refloated, proved to be a dangerous encumbrance to the vessels assigned to shepherd her downstream. After grounding repeatedly, *Eastport* finally stuck fast, and Porter had to blow her up. The other boats, including Porter's flagship *Cricket*, had to run an artillery gauntlet five miles above the mouth of Cane River. Two transports were total losses, *Cricket* received 38 hits and, like *Juliet* and *Fort Hindman*, suffered heavy casualties. To make matters worse, when Porter reached Alexandria, he found that the river had fallen, trapping above the falls the backbone of the Mississippi Squadron: *Lexington, Fort Hindman, Osage, Neosho, Mound City, Louisville, Pittsburg, Chillicothe, Carondelet*, and *Ozark*. Should the army continue its retreat, they, like *Eastport*, would have to be destroyed.

On April 21 the War Department heard that the army, badly damaged, had retreated to Grand Ecore. Grant, who had intended to use Banks' force in a campaign against Mobile, gave up all idea of using those troops east of the Mississippi that spring. Banks would be lucky, it seemed, not to lose the army and the fleet. Something had to be done to secure better leadership. Remove Banks, Grant told Halleck, but Lincoln demurred. "General Banks," Halleck told Grant, "is a personal friend of the President, and has strong political supporters in and out of Congress." Lincoln would remove him only if Grant insisted upon it as a military necessity. Ultimately, too late to affect the campaign, a middle way was found: Banks' Department of the Gulf was absorbed in the newly created Military Division of West Mississippi under the command of Edward R. S. Canby. Although nominally retaining his position, Banks would never again take the field.

Ignorant of his impending demotion, Banks was fortifying Alexandria lest his 31,000 men be overwhelmed by Taylor's 6,000. It was an unhappy time for the man whose soldiers derisively called him "Napoleon P. Banks," or sometimes just "Mr. Banks." He could not stay where he was indefinitely, and he could not retreat without abandoning the navy, which was unthinkable. The way out of this dilemma came from an engineer on Franklin's staff, Lieutenant Colonel Joseph Bailey of Wisconsin. Experienced in the logging country,

Above: Within a few days Banks had his army at Alexandria, and as ready to march on as he would ever be. With him was the 19th Kentucky, its headquarters photographed here by Lytle at Baton Rouge a few weeks before. (KA)

Left: With him, too, were men of the 47th Illinois, led by these officers. (COURTESY OF WILLIAM ANDERSON)

Right: With Banks' army there were a mixed bag of officers, including even a professional adventurer, Colonel C. Carroll Tevis, commanding the 3d Maryland Cavalry. His first name was really Washington, but names never were a point of accuracy with him. In the 1850s he served in the Turkish Army under the name Nessim Bey. When made a major in 1854 he changed his appellation to Bim-bachi, and with his next promotion became Quaimaquam! (P-M)

Above: When finally the armies met for the first time, it was at Mansfield, or Sabine Cross Roads, on April 8. Brigadier General J. Patrick Major and his cavalry brigade held the left of the Confederate line. Going into battle, he shouted at his troopers to give the enemy "hell." (GOELET-BUNCOMBE COLLECTION, SHC)

Above: Leading one of the two Southern infantry divisions was Major General John G. Walker, whose Texans outflanked the Federals and drove them back. (LSU)

Above: The next day another battle was fought at Pleasant Hill, and this time Taylor was repulsed. Brigadier General Thomas J. Churchill of Kentucky opened Taylor's attack, but Banks stood his ground. (LC)

Above: Commanding Banks' cavalry in the campaign was Brigadier General Albert L. Lee of Kansas. He had no more military experience than Banks, but better sense. Still, Banks would relieve him of command at the end of the expedition. (USAMHI)

Above: There was another aspect to the Red River Campaign that proved to be ill-fated. Major General Frederick Steele was to move from his headquarters in Little Rock, Arkansas, with a column to support Banks. Steele took his time. Brigadier General Eugene A. Carr, standing at right, commanded his cavalry. Steele stands at left, with giant James Baker of the 13th Iowa between them. (RP)

Bailey proposed to build a temporary dam to raise the water level on the falls. Porter was skeptical, but was in no position to reject any scheme, no matter how improbable. Banks made available the necessary manpower and gave much personal attention to the project. Work began late in April.

Porter and Banks were not the only people unhappy with the campaign so far. Cotton speculators who had trailed along with the expedition expecting a rich haul saw their dreams go up in smoke, or else into the holds of the gunboats. Part of the cotton which had been hauled into Alexandria was seized for use in building the dam, including some owned by one of Lincoln's old friends who had appeared on the Red with the President's permission to go through the lines and buy cotton from the Confederates. "I wish you would take somebody else's cotton than mine," he protested, "that is very fine cotton!"

The Confederates blockading the river below the town inflicted serious losses on Union shipping. On May 4, *City Belle*, with the 120th Ohio on board, was captured, and on the 5th a transport loaded with the 56th Ohio was lost, as were two gunboats, *Covington* and *Signal*. But Taylor's small force was unable to do the one thing that would have meant disaster for the enemy: stop construction of Colonel Bailey's dam.

At the site of this formidable undertaking, the river was 758 feet wide, the water four to six feet deep, and the current a full ten miles an hour. By building from both banks simultaneously and by using every conceivable material, by May 8 Bailey had succeeded in creating a significant rise in the water level. The gunboats would have been able to come down then, but for reasons still unknown Porter had issued no orders to lighten ship by removing guns, ammunition, and stores, to say nothing of the "prize" cotton with which the vessels were gorged. Finally, at the urging of the dam builders, the navy came awake. On the 9th, four gunboats shot the roaring gap in the dam. The others were lightened, and by May 13 all were safe in easy water below the falls. "I have had a hard and anxious time of it," Porter wrote his mother.

Now the army was free to leave Alexandria. Soldiers spread out through the town, smearing wooden buildings with turpentine and camphine and setting scores of fires. A. J. Smith rode amid the flaming buildings exclaiming, "Hurrah, boys, this looks like war!" Some of Banks' staff and head quarters guard tried unsuccessfully to put out the fires. By noon on the 13th the town had been leveled. The burning continued all along the army's line of retreat. On the 16th, Taylor made one last effort to block the invaders, but after holding them back far several hours near Mansura he had to give way before odds of three to one, although he still harried the column's flanks and rear. But Banks marched on, and by May 20 his men had put the Atchafalaya between themselves and the persistent Confederates. The campaign was over.

Above: At Little Rock, Arkansas, Steele marshaled his forces and supplied his army from these warehouses. The men in the ranks supplied themselves from saloons like the one at left, the Star Saloon &o Coffee Stand. (NA)

Above: Brigadier General John M. Thayer led one of Steele's two infantry divisions, little suspecting that their expedition would never reach Banks and would almost end in disaster. (USAMHI)

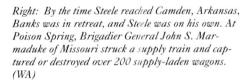

Right: By the time Steele reached Camden, Arkansas, Banks was in retreat, and Steele was on his own. At Poison Spring, Brigadier General John S. Marmaduke of Missouri struck a supply train and captured or destroyed over 200 supply-laden wagons. (WA)

Far right: Major Thomas P. Ochiltree of Texas was one of the staff officers in the Confederate Army led personally by Kirby Smith to strike at Steele in Camden. Steele would hurry back to Little Rock instead. (NA)

Right: Meanwhile, Taylor's depleted army kept Banks at bay at Grand Ecore. Major General John A. Wharton commanded about 2,500 cavalry, nearly half of the "army" with which he held Banks' 25,000 in check. A most able officer, Wharton would be killed only days before war's end when he quarreled with an officer, slapped his face, and was shot in return. This is an unpublished portrait. (VM)

Far right: When Banks finally retreated from Grand Ecore, Wharton pursued him, and Brigadier General Hamilton P. Bee was supposed to use his cavalry to cut off the enemy retreat. At Monett's Ferry, however, Bee was driven off and Banks managed to escape back to Alexandria. (TU)

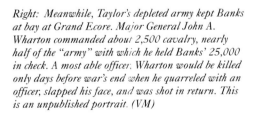

Above: But Alexandria did not mean automatic safety. Though the wharf shown here gives no indication of it, the river's rapids near the city were so low that only four to five inches of water stood in places. The fleet was trapped. (USAMHI)

Above: All these steamers and transports, not to mention the ironclads, might fall into enemy hands or have to be destroyed. (USAMHI)

Above: So heavy was the fire that the Fort Hindman waited an extra day to brave the Confederate fire. A shot struck her steering and she drifted down the river out of control, luckily passing the enemy cannon to safety. (USAMHI)

Above: The unusual ironclad monitor Osage, mounting its turret forward and its stern wheel protected by the iron hump at the rear, appears here on the Red River. She got back to Alexandria without difficulty under the capable leadership of her commander… (NHC)

Above: … Captain Thomas O. Selfridge. When firing the ship's guns, he reportedly sighted them by looking through a hand-held periscope from the turret. (USAMHI)

Above: As the fleet reassembled at Alexandria, waiting for the water to rise or the Confederates to close in, the mammoth Mississippi River ironclads like the Mound City took their stations in the line of warships. This image was almost certainly made on the Red River during the campaign. (NHC)

Left: Here, too, was the USS Louisville, *shown in a photograph taken at Memphis the previous year. (NHC)*

Left: And the unusual little monitor Ozark *had been in service just two months when she joined Porter's fleet. She, too, seemed to be trapped by the low water. (USAMHI)*

Above: The "tinclad" No. 19, the St. Clair, *steamed up from Baton Rouge to help support the fleet while it lay trapped at Alexandria. (LSU)*

Above: But it took the ingenuity of Colonel Joseph Bailey, an engineer, to save the fleet of 33 vessels. He proposed damming the river to raise the water level. He was made a brigadier, as he appears here, for his feat. He saved the fleet. (USAMHI)

Above: Photographers McPherson and Oliver captured the scene as Bailey's dam approached completion. It left just room enough between its wings for the ships to pass through. (USAMHI)

Above: Bailey occupied 3,000 men in building the makeshift dam. Many thought it would not work. (USAMHI)

Right: But Porter would be ever after grateful. "Words are inadequate to express the admiration I feel," said the admiral. "This is without doubt the best engineering feat ever performed." (USAMHI)

Left: Thereafter, it was a race to escape the harassing Confederates. The Covington, *shown here off Memphis in 1863, was attacked even before the fleet left Alexandria, disabled, and captured. (NHC)*

Left: Captured with her was the Signal, *shown here just a few days before assisting with Bailey's dam. The two warships were some compensation to the Confederates for the failure to bag Banks and his army. (USAMHI)*

Left: As for Admiral Porter, he could regard their loss as a small price to pay for saving his fleet, and for saving him any further adventures with Banks. The general would be relieved from field command, and Porter could return to the Black Hawk, *shown here in September 1864, to plan his next voyage. (US-AMHI)*

The Forgotten War: The West

MAURICE MELTON

From the Mississippi to the Golden Gate, the Civil War is everywhere

THE RED RIVER CAMPAIGN was only part of the war in the vast "West." When the issues of the mid-1800s boiled into war, the United States was but half settled. Beyond the Mississippi the West was a mosaic of contrasts—plains, deserts, mountains, seacoasts, bustling cities, wide open spaces, and desolate waste. There were states, territories, and open and unclassified lands. Some areas were settled and relatively civilized, enjoying the traditional social structures of the eastern states. They took the North-South schism seriously, and in some places warfare erupted in intensely personal, no-quarter contests. Other areas were basic American frontier: Indians, outlaws, widely scattered white settlements, and little or no practical government. Wild and raw, the frontier demanded so much for simple survival that the war in the East often went almost unnoticed.

Missouri had been in the thick of the growing sectional split for decades. The act that opened the way to her statehood, the Compromise of 1820, was an effort to balance the opposing forces 40 years before the war. And the partisans who made Kansas bleed in the '50s begot the bushwhackers and Jayhawkers who burned and murdered across the length and breadth of Missouri during four years of official war.

Missouri's early settlers were Southerners. But commerce linked her economy to the North. Her elected officials in 1861 were predominately secessionist, and intended ultimately to ally Missouri with the Confederacy. They nearly succeeded in 1861 when defeat at Wilson's Creek drove Federals out of much of the state.

The Federals returned under Major General Samuel Curtis, who regrouped his forces and drove the Confederates out of Springfield. He followed them into northern Arkansas, where Major General Earl Van Dorn had marshaled a large Confederate force.

Curtis defeated Van Dorn at Elk Horn Tavern. Major General Ben McCulloch was killed and Major General Sterling Price wounded, and Missouri appeared safely in the grasp of the Union. The Federals even held northern Arkansas, from which they could threaten Little Rock, and parts of Louisiana and Texas beyond.

But the border defenses were porous, and control of Missouri was tenuous at best. Price and other Missouri Rebels regularly led military expeditions into Missouri, and fighting raged all over the state from war's outbreak until war's end.

Worse than the regular army campaigns and cavalry jaunts were the bushwhacking raids of the guerrillas. For despite Missouri's 40 years of statehood, her place on the edge of the frontier lent a savage madness to her war. Four years of border warfare in Kansas had fostered hatreds that festered and lingered. By the time the East followed Kansas and Missouri into war, there was a hardened cadre of Kansas militants ready to strike back at Missouri, and Missourians in general had gained a national reputation—unwarranted—as radical slavers, secessionists, and border ruffians.

The most notorious of the Kansans was Senator James H. Lane of Lawrence. Lane demanded extreme retribution against secessionists and slaveholders, and his Jayhawkers robbed and murdered with near impunity in Missouri, turning multitudes of Unionist and neutral Missourians toward the Confederate camp. Lane's raid on Osceola, his plundering and burning of the town,

Above: The confused and troubled nature of the war west of the Mississippi went back long before the Red River Campaign. Texas suffered as much as any state or territory. Her governor in 1861 was the old hero Sam Houston. He opposed secession and resigned when a convention voted the Lone Star State out of the Union. (NA)

and the execution of nine of Osceola's citizens was a typical example of warfare on the border.

The savagery of the civilian conflict brutalized the entire Missouri occupation. The leading guerrilla bands, under William Clarke Quantrill, "Bloody Bill" Anderson, George Todd, and William Gregg, were farm boys mostly, children of families harassed, intimidated, robbed, burned out, or murdered by Federal soldiers or Kansas volunteers. They quickly evolved into the prototype of the hard-riding outlaw bands of the postwar West. The guerrillas used the firepower of their many revolvers, their mobility, and their local support to outmatch detachments of Union troops. Often they dressed in blue uniforms and hailed Federal columns as comrades before opening fire. Theirs was a ruthless, brutal war of extermination.

Major General Henry W. Halleck swelled the ranks of the guerrilla bands with a declaration of no neutrality. Those who were not for the Union, he decreed, would be considered against it. Then, in response to the no-quarter tactics of the guerrillas, he decreed that any civilian caught in arms could be tried and executed on the spot. Executions soon were extended to regular Confederate soldiers captured in Missouri and, occasionally, to townspeople chosen at random in reply to the murder of some local Union man.

The execution of soldiers and civilians, the abridgment of basic civil rights by the military, punitive taxation of towns in areas of heavy guerrilla activity, and finally a state-wide draft of all able bodied men to help fight the guerrillas, all broadened the bushwhackers' base of support. In 1863 the Federals began attacking this base, imprisoning or exiling the friends and families who provided the guerrillas weapons, information, shelter, and sustenance. In August a group of women—including Bill Anderson's sisters and Cole Younger's cousin—were imprisoned in a dilapidated three-story brick building in Kansas City. Within a few days the building collapsed, killing four women and injuring others. The tragedy touched off an uproar in the South and the Midwest, newspapers accusing Federal authorities of undermining the prison.

Quantrill used the bitter emotions of the moment to pull several guerrilla bands together for their greatest effort, a massed raid on Senator Lane's home, Lawrence, Kansas. Within six days of the Kansas City tragedy, Quantrill had nearly 500 raiders at the outskirts of Lawrence. They struck the unsuspecting town at dawn, rampaging through the streets, dragging men from their beds, killing them in their own hallways and yards. Stores and homes were looted and burned, and the guerrillas killed every male they could find who looked big enough to carry a gun. Senator Lane, home on vacation, hid behind a log in back of his house and escaped.

Brigadier General Thomas Ewing's response to the Lawrence raid was drastic. His Order No. 11 virtually stripped the population from a four county area near the Kansas border, requiring everyone residing more than a mile outside a major town to move from the region. Whether Confederate, Union, or neutral in sympathies, people were forced to abandon their homes, possessions, and livelihoods. The order drew harsh criticism, the press both North and South filled with tales of families brutally uprooted and forced, helpless, into the unknown.

Order No. 11 failed to defuse the guerrilla war,

Left: Only seven brave men in that convention stood with Houston and voted against secession. Proud of their stand, they posed for the camera soon afterward, even as Texas readied to join the Confederacy. (AUSTIN-TRAVIS COUNTY COLLECTION, AUSTIN PUBLIC LIBRARY CO3277)

Above: Texans began to flock to the secession banners, and regiments were raised to be sent to Virginia in 1861. These are men of the 1st Texas, taken at or near Camp Quantico, Virginia. (AUSTIN-TRAVIS COUNTY COLLECTION, PICAO3674)

Left: In the early days of 1861, the threat and influence of the war to come stretched even out to California. There Colonel Albert Sidney Johnston was commander of the Department of the Pacific. When Texas seceded, he resigned and came east, to die a year later at Shiloh. (NA)

Above: Fort Union, New Mexico Territory, was headquarters in 1862 for... (NA)

Above: In New Mexico Territory, Colonel—later Major General—E. R. S. Canby commanded, and here blunted one of the earliest Confederate campaigns of the war when Sibley tried to invade New Mexico. Canby, after a distinguished career, would be killed by Indians in 1873. (P-M)

Below: New Mexico Territory, which included modern Arizona, was tenuously held by a string of frontier forts, like Fort Craig shown here in 1865. (NA)

Left: ... Colonel Gabriel R. Paul, who helped support the repulse of Sibley. A year later, now a general at Gettysburg, he lost his sight when a bullet struck his eyes. (USAMHI)

however. In fact, within a few months Quantrill's group destroyed a sizable Federal garrison at Baxter Springs, Kansas, then caught and slaughtered the escort party of Major General James G. Blunt, commander of the District of the Frontier.

Campaigns, raids, and guerrilla actions ranked Missouri third (behind Virginia and Tennessee) in the number of engagements fought during the conflict. The state was the dominant area in the frontier theater of war, and training ground not only for the James and Younger gangs, but for Union scout "Wild Bill" Hickok (who occasionally rode as a spy in Sterling Price's ranks), and for a 7th Kansas recruit named William F. Cody.

UNLIKE MISSOURI, the Territory of Minnesota opened its western lands to white settlement only in the decade before the war. In two 1850s treaties the Federal government forced the Santee Sioux to relinquish nine tenths of their Minnesota lands. In return, they were left a ten-mile-wide strip of reservation, an opportunity to learn the white man's ways of farming, housing, and dress, and cash annuities for 50 years.

Chief Little Crow, courtly, gentlemanly, and a consummate politician, had signed the 1850s treaties. He led a quiet cultural revolution that saw substantial brick homes and tilled fields developed on the reservation. But 1861 brought a bad crop year; 1862 was another. The cash subsidies should have seen the Indians through in comfort, but payments were delayed. Hunger became a fact of life for the Sioux, banned now from hunting on lands that had supported them for generations. For a year and more, poverty deepened and discontent grew. Indian traders stocked food the Indians could subsist on, but because government subsidies were always late, the Indians could do limited business, and only on credit. Sioux who had learned to cipher kept track of their accounts, and found their figures consistently at variance with those kept by the traders. They were not surprised—just angry—when the government refused to accept their figures, paying their annuities directly to the trading posts to settle accounts on the traders' books.

In late August 1862, Little Crow met with Indian agent Thomas Galbraith to complain of the traders' embezzlement, the government's tardy payments, and his people's hunger. When Galbraith relayed these complaints to Indian trader Andrew Myrick, the storekeeper replied, "If they're hungry, let them eat grass and their own dung." The reply spread rapidly through the Sioux reservation and, two days later, four young braves killed four white men and two women.

Little Crow, struggling to make the best for his people in a desperate situation, saw his tribe's doom in the braves' act. For retribution, he knew, would be visited on all Indians. There was no beating the whites in a war: there were far too many and they were too well armed. But there would be no escaping the white man's wrath. In a late-night council, Little Crow outlined for his chiefs the consequences. "You will die like rabbits when the hungry wolves hunt them," he said. Then he added, sadly, "But Little Crow is not a coward. He will die with you."

The next morning Little Crow's braves launched the Sioux Indian War. First they struck the nearby trading post, then surrounding white settlements. Andrew Myrick, the contemptuous white trader, was left stretched dead outside his store, his mouth stuffed full of grass.

Troops at nearby Fort Ridgely heard the firing. They sent out a rescue expedition, but Little Crow was ready. He ambushed the column, killing 23 troopers, and soon attacked the fort itself. For two days the whites beat back Indian assaults. Heavy rains broke early in the battle, pouring so much water that fire arrows died in the shingles and logs of the stockade fort.

Frustrated, the Sioux withdrew and turned on the town of New Ulm, where fierce fighting raged

Above: And like Fort Marcy, at Santa Fe, headquarters of the department. (LC)

Above: It was the goal of Confederate Brigadier General Henry H. Sibley's abortive campaign in the spring of 1862. It was rumored that Sibley was more devoted to alcohol than his duty. (VM)

Left: The invasion stopped here, at Glorieta, near Santa Fe, shown here in a June 1880 image. On March 28, Sibley won a tactical victory here while, in his rear... (COURTESY OF MUSEUM OF NEW MEXICO)

Above: … Major John M. Chivington struck and destroyed the Confederate supply train. That ended Sibley's campaign and made a name for Chivington, who later achieved notoriety of another kind by massacring 500 Cheyennes and Arapahoes at Sand Creek, Colorado, in 1864. (COLORADO HISTORICAL SOCIETY)

Above: Even after Sibley withdrew, New Mexico was still full of colorful characters, none more so than Major W. F. M. Arny, Indian agent for the territory. His Indian finery is in marked contrast to the typical army camp scene in the painted background . (M. J . WRIGHT COLLE:CTION, SHC)

Above: Brigadier General James H. Carleton led his colorful "California Column" east from the Golden State to relieve New Mexico during Sibley's threat. He stayed to take over command of the department and kept it until war's end. (USAMHI)

Above: North of New Mexico, in Nevada and Utah, Colonel Patrick E. Connor tried to control affairs in those territories, mainly keeping the mail and telegraph lines open to California and combatting occasional Indian outbreaks. It won him a major generalcy, as he appears here at the end of the war. (UTAH STATE HISTORICAL SOCIETY)

from house to house. But again armed and aroused whites held off the Sioux.

At St. Paul, Colonel Henry Hastings Sibley gathered the 6th Minnesota Volunteers, 1,400 strong, and brought them west to fight. Sibley maneuvered through skirmishes and ambushes for a month before finally luring the Sioux into a pitched battle, breaking the back of organized Indian resistance in Minnesota. The Sioux scattered, some north to Canada, some west into Dakota. Some stayed, hoping for an arrangement that would allow them to continue existence on their own lands.

Aware from the outset that they could not win, the Sioux had taken a large number of prisoners to barter for terms. Sibley agreed to a truce to talk about prisoner exchange. Using the talks as a diversion, he surrounded the Indian camp, took back the white prisoners, and forced the Indians to capitulate. Over 300 warriors were imprisoned at Fort Snelling, where 36 were convicted and hanged for war crimes. The rest of the tribe was transported to a barren reservation in Dakota Territory, where nearly a quarter of them died the first winter.

The Sioux continued a desultory war in the Dakotas, occasionally raiding back into western Minnesota. In the summer of 1863, Major General John Pope, banished from the white man's war after Second Manassas, was sent north to resolve the Indian problem. He organized a two-pronged expedition and sent it deep into Dakota Territory, Sibley leading one column, Brigadier General Alfred Sully the other. Sibley fought three pitched battles in late July, and Sully destroyed a large Sioux village in August, driving the Indians across the Missouri River. Sporadic incidents continued, however, and another campaign was mounted in the summer of 1864, pushing the Indians into Montana Territory. This was the last major Indian campaign of the war years, but far from the last gasp of the Sioux. They would continue fighting in the northwestern territories for more than a decade.

MANY WESTERN SETTLERS were from the South, and their raucous vocal support of the Confederacy raised fears of dark conspiracies, armed Southern uprisings, and conquest by a great Rebel army from Texas. With the Federal government's preoccupation with the crisis in the East, and a spirit of Southern nationalism apparent in Colorado, Nevada, New Mexico, and California, reasonable men thought they could see the prospect of an American West annexed to the new Confederacy.

The Lincoln administration paid considerable attention to Nevada, for her mines were turning out millions of dollars in gold and silver for the U.S. war effort. Nevada gained territorial status in 1861 and achieved statehood in 1864, just in time to cast Republican votes in the national election.

California was vital to the U.S. war effort, too. Her mining industry, with ten years maturity, was an El Dorado to the Treasury Department. Californians feared for their gold shipments, for Southerners were highly visible around the state's towns and mining camps. They were organizing companies and drilling in the spring of 1861, and some were, as feared, interested in disrupting the state's flow of gold. A delegation approached the commander of the Department of the Pacific, Colonel Albert Sidney Johnston, to enlist his aid in an attack on the gold shipments. But Johnston, still commissioned in the U.S. Army, refused to hear them. He soon resigned, and began a trek east to join the Confederate Army.

Most California secessionists (both Southern-born and California-born) had no intention of joining California to Sidney Johnston's Southern Confederacy. They envisioned, instead, an independent Pacific Republic. California's isolation had fostered the notion of a destiny of her own, and the idea of a Pacific Republic had long been popular. The chaos in the East gave its proponents the opportunity to open a strong campaign for California's independence, and it gained quick popularity in the press. Republicans and Union Democrats combined to fight the movement in the State Assembly, and the firing on Fort Sumter swung opinion heavily in favor of the Union and California's continued place in it.

California was seriously threatened, however, by the early Confederate acquisition of the lower half of New Mexico Territory, which stretched from California to Confederate Texas. New Mexico was naturally divided, a gulf of desert splitting the region into two habitable sections, north and south. The north, with the territorial capital at Santa Fe, was tied to Missouri, where her trails ran. Supplies, news, and settlers all came through Missouri, and that state's decision would determine whether northern New Mexico Territory went Confederate or stayed Union. The southern half was linked in the same way to Texas.

An enmity between the two had already developed, the south feeling that the north dominated territorial government and ignored the south, even to the point of keeping all the troops

Above: Here in Colorado recruits of Company G, 1st Colorado Volunteers, muster on the main street of Empire in 1862. It was a long way to the war, but they would find it. (COLORADO HISTORICAL SOCIETY)

Below: So would the 6th California Infantry, commanded by Colonel Henry M. Black. Their war would be one of few and brief Indian skirmishes. Most of their time they spent garrisoning an island in San Francisco Bay, Alcatraz. (USAMHI)

Below: Up in faraway Oregon the Union had a general, too, Brigadier General Benjamin Alvord, who had nothing to do but keep the peace between settlers and the Nez Perce Indians. Out in the West it was largely a war of boredom for commanders who perhaps dreamed of the glory to be had in Virginia. (EUGENE WOODDELL)

Above: Of course, there were those who had tried for glory in Virginia and failed, and the War Department looked to the West as a convenient place to shelve unsuccessful officers. Thus came Major General Irvin McDowell to command the Department of the Pacific. Defeat at Manassas in 1861 and again in 1862 had been too much for him to survive. He sat out the rest of the conflict in San Francisco. (USAMHI)

Above: San Francisco was not such a bad place to sit. Here lay Fort Point, on the Golden Gate, one of the few casemated seacoast fortifications built before the war that never heard a hostile shot. (NA)

Above: Its guns looked out upon a quiet, thriving harbor, with only a very occasional scare of Confederate sea raiders that never came. (THE BANCROPT LIBRARY)

Above: If Confederates should come, McDowell's command would be ready for them. Artillery drill at the Presidio of San Francisco, during or just after the war. (THE BANCROFT LIBRARY)

in the north, exposing southern New Mexicans to death at the hands of the Apache or robbery and murder by marauding outlaws. So headstrong were the southerners that they had already broken with New Mexico and established their own Territory of Arizona, without a hint of official sanction, well before South Carolina seceded. Then, with new national boundaries drawn and a war having broken out, Arizona leaders met at La Mesilla, an Overland Mail stop above El Paso, and voted to ally their new Arizona Territory with the Confederacy. On the western border, near California, the 68 voting citizens of Tucson passed their own ordinance of secession and elected a delegate to the Confederate Congress.

Union influence crumbled rapidly in both territories. Most of the army officers in the West were Southern, and had resigned. The flow of resigned officers moving east from California, traveling from post to post across New Mexico, made it appear that the majority of the U.S. Army's officer corps was resigning and going south. The loss of military leadership compounded the effects of the daily difficulties under which the western soldier labored—few horses, a chronic shortage of supplies, and pay as much as half a year in arrears.

Brigadier General E. V. Sumner, Sidney Johnston's replacement, established control over California by disarming and disbanding the state's lingering secessionist groups. Then he sent an expedition to garrison Fort Yuma, on the Colorado River crossing from Tucson. In Nevada and Colorado the operating governments held firm against the early clamor of Southern secessionists. And in northern New Mexico, Colonel E. R. S. Canby, an obscure subordinate on the Indian frontier, banded together the demoralized, leaderless troopers scattered across the territory and began organizing a territorial defense.

Canby had no time to lose, for his brother-in-law and former superior, Brigadier General Henry Hopkins Sibley, had gone south and was gathering a small army in Texas to move into northern New Mexico. At the beginning of 1862, Sibley brought his troops north through the Rio Grande Valley, the only invasion route that could sustain a large body of troops. Canby and Sibley clashed at Val Verde, just outside Canby's base at Fort Craig. Unable to destroy Canby or take the fort, Sibley left the Federal force intact in his rear and marched on to Albuquerque. All along the route the Texans pillaged, alienating Southerners who might have welcomed them as liberators and countrymen.

The plundering occurred primarily because of the Confederates' short supplies. Sibley had gathered few rations in west Texas, and his men were hungry. Yet at Albuquerque, Sibley ordered the burning of accumulated Federal stores and food stuffs, and fed his men nothing.

From Albuquerque, Sibley sent Major C. S. Pyron with a column to occupy Santa Fe, where officers again directed the burning of captured stores while troops stood by suffering in hunger.

The territorial governor fled Santa Fe for Fort Union, northeast on the Denver road. The fort was the strongest military post in the territory. Sibley had commanded it once and felt confident of taking it, solidifying Confederate control of New Mexico and Arizona. But Fort Union had been moved and rebuilt since Sibley's day and newly garrisoned by the 1st Colorado Regiment, commanded by Colonel John Slough.

Colonel Canby ordered Slough to hold Fort

Above: Indeed, even the Navy would be ready for any Rebel foolhardy enough to sail into the harbor. In 1863 the Navy Department sent the Aquila *around the Horn, bearing a very heavy cargo for San Francisco—a dismantled monitor! (COURTESY OF CHARLES S. SCHWARTZ)*

Above: Unfortunately, shortly after arrival the vessel sank at Hathaway's Wharf, with the ironclad still aboard. With enormous effort, the Aquila *was raised from the bottom. (CSS)*

Union. Instead, the Colorado regiment took the road to Santa Fe in hopes of surprising the Rebels. Pyron left Santa Fe with intentions of occupying Fort Union, and the two collided in Glorieta Pass.

Slough's lead elements were commanded by the Reverend John Chivington, who had taken a major's commission in the 1st Colorado. Chivington bested Pyron in the initial fighting, and both sides fell back at nightfall and sent for reinforcements. Slough took a day and a night to reach the battlefield with the rest of his force, and the Confederates waited. Finally, after the entire Federal force had reached the field, Pyron attacked. While Slough and Pyron battled in the pass, Chivington led a raiding party behind the Confederates. In a daylong fight Pyron gained dominance on the battlefield, but Chivington's raid to the rear destroyed the Confederates' wagon train. The Rebels thought they had been struck by Canby's army from Fort Craig, abandoned Glorieta, and fell back to Santa Fe.

Canby ordered Slough to break off further action and wait, for Canby soon had his own force in motion and hoped to crush Sibley in a pincer.

Slough resigned in protest at Canby's orders. Chivington assumed his command, and Sibley, caught between the Federal soldiers to the rear and Chivington's Colorado volunteers ahead, committed his army to a pell-mell retreat through the desert. Hungry and short of ammunition, the army degenerated into a leaderless drove struggling for survival. Canby might have captured the lot, but had barely enough rations for his own men

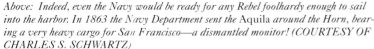

Left: Then began the work of assembling, piece by piece, the ironclad monitor Camanche. *Here proud workers stand on, and under, her bow as she sits in the ways. Local photographers Lawrence and Houseworth made these images, never before published. (CSS)*

Above: In time the ship's hull and below decks were done, with always plenty of spectators around to gawk and get in the way. (NHC)

Right: And finally she was ready to launch. On November 14, 1864, she rides the waves once more, still minus the distinctive turret of the monitor. (CSS)

Right: That came next, as workmen with tools in their hands stand atop the installed gun turret and the pilot house above it. The projection from the top of the turret is perhaps some form of periscope, since no eye slits are visible on the tower itself. (CSS)

Below: Finally, in January 1865, she was completed. The only trouble was, the war was almost over. (R. L. HAGUE)

and none to feed prisoners. Some few Texans did surrender. Some made for California, many of these falling victim to the Apache. Most found their way back to Texas, happy to have survived the desert and the Indians.

The occupation of New Mexico and Arizona was done and Sibley's army had evaporated, leaving Texas' western border open and undefended. The loss of Missouri and northern Arkansas raised rumors of invasion from the north, and the fall of New Orleans nearly sealed off the state from the east. The Mexican border was open, however, and a major trade route developed from San Antonio to Brownsville, then across the river to Matamoros. The Mexican town boomed as a free port, Texas cotton flowing out, war goods for the Confederacy coming in.

IN MARCH OF 1863, Lieutenant General Edmund Kirby Smith assumed command of the Confederacy's Trans-Mississippi, officially composed of Texas, Louisiana, Arkansas, Missouri, and the Indian Territory. The area clung to the east by a slender corridor open across the Mississippi from Vicksburg to Port Hudson. In July these two bastions fell and Kirby Smith's new command was completely cut off.

The general had inherited a department disorganized, dispirited, desperately short on manpower, and virtually leaderless. In an effort to turn the area around and make it productive, self-reliant, and defensible, he called a governors' conference at Marshall, Texas. There, the chief executives of the Trans-Mississippi's states grudgingly relinquished to the military many of their rights, duties, and powers in hopes of seeing the area run with some efficiency. The general now had a domain that would come to be known as "Kirby-smithdom."

The next spring the Trans-Mississippi came under attack. Major General Nathaniel Banks in-

Right: Ready for her maiden voyage, an ironclad that would never see battle or fire a hostile shot, the Ca-manche is about to leave the wharf at the foot of Third Street. She will finally be commissioned in August, months after the war is done. (CSS)

vaded, with support from David Porter's fleet, while Major General Frederick Steele pushed south from Little Rock to join forces. But Banks met defeat at the hands of Richard Taylor, Steele was beaten back to Little Rock, and Porter nearly lost his fleet to low water in the Red River. The Trans-Mississippi, it seemed, had established some defense. But in November the Federals moved again and captured Brownsville, cutting the vital trade route to Matamoros.

Meanwhile, the Indians had re-established control on the western border. Texas frontier troops were absorbed into the Confederate Army and moved east, and from early on, the far West was virtually defenseless. Kiowa and Comanche rampaged in west Texas and the Apache terrorized New Mexico. By the time Brownsville fell they had pushed white settlement out of west Texas and were threatening the middle of the state.

When reaction came it was brutal, in the nature of the untamed West. Texas volunteers caught and slaughtered a tribe of peaceful Kickapoo migrating to Mexico. Ironically, the Indians were fleeing the incessant warfare of the Indian Territory, where factions fought over internal disagreements within the Creek, Cherokee, and Chickasaw tribes. At Sand Creek, Chivington's Colorado volunteers attacked and destroyed a village of Arapaho and Cheyenne, killing men, women, and children. The slaughter was so indiscriminate and savage, even by frontier standards, that it resulted in Chivington's court-martial and blackened the name of his command.

Back in east Texas, Colonel John Ford raised a small army, retook Brownsville, and reopened trade with the outside world. And as the U.S. Navy systematically sealed off the Confederacy's eastern ports in the last year of the war, the fast iron ships running the blockade found their way more and more to the Texas coast and Matamoros.

Free trade and the Trans-Mississippi's manufacturing made life in Texas more bearable than in the rest of the war-ravaged, poverty-stricken South. But farming steadily deteriorated as farmhands, draft animals, and equipment disappeared. Run away inflation reduced the worth of government vouchers to the point that farmers and ranchers finally refused to accept them for their remaining livestock and produce. Commissary agents responded by appropriating horses, cattle, and crops without pay. The Trans-Mississippi, like the eastern Confederacy, was withering on the vine.

With Lee's surrender, strong Federal armies overwhelmed Confederate remnants in North Carolina, south Alabama, and western Louisiana. The last fight of the war flared in Texas, at Palmito Ranch outside Brownsville on May 13, 1865. Northern prisoners told the Texans they were the only ones left fighting. Two weeks later Kirby Smith surrendered the last Confederate army to the western Confederacy's old nemesis, Major General E. R. S. Canby.

Above: It was a long way from the far West to the old Northwest, yet here, too, it was a war of little action and long waiting. No Confederate army ever threatened Fort Wayne, near Detroit, Michigan. For these overcoated soldiers, then, there was only garrison duty and, perhaps, the hope of being ordered off to Virginia. (BURTON HISTORICAL COLLECTION, DETROIT PUBLIC LIBRARY)

Left: Even more removed was St. Paul, Minnesota, nestled peacefully on the bank of the Mississippi. (MHS)

Above: *Soldiers and civilians and local Indians could pass the time together peacefully enough. (MHS)*

Below: *It was even peaceful-looking enough out at Fort Ripley, near the Sioux reservations. (MHS)*

Above: *Powerful Fort Snelling brooded over the mouth of the Minnesota River, assuring protection to the inhabitants. (MHS)*

Above: *In the frontier-like settlements such as Mendota, near Fort Snelling, there was no thought of threat or defense. (MHS)*

Above right: *But then in 1862 the Sioux arose in a bloody campaign that in the end took perhaps 500 white lives, and saw 38 Sioux leaders executed. These settlers rushed toward the forts and larger settlements to escape the Indians, who were enraged at being allowed to starve on their reservations. (MHS)*

Right: *Within days the outbreak spread to South Dakota. These two women with their children were taken captive by a band of Santees and held prisoner for three months before being rescued by friendly Sioux called "Fool Soldiers." (SOUTH DAKOTA STATE HISTORICAL SOCIETY)*

Left: Over 1,000 Sioux were eventually captured and imprisoned here in this camp at Fort Snelling. Instead of drawing attention to their legitimate plight, the Sioux uprising only made their treatment more harsh. (MHS)

Above: This is only one of the jails that held the captives, some of them huddling in their blankets before their guards, one of them, standing at left, an Indian himself . (MHS)

Above: For the rest of the war, places like Fort Rice in the Dakota Territory were built to contain the Indians and prevent more outbreaks. (USAMHI)

Above: Major Charles A. R. Dimon of the 1st U.S. Volunteers commanded the new Fort Rice and poses here with some of the local chiefs during a more tranquil time. They feared him for his harsh, trigger-happy, methods. (USAMHI)

Left: Brigadier General Alfred Sully came to command the District of Dakota in 1863, and in the spring of 1865 made an attempt to make peace with the Indians at Fort Rice. Dimon, now a colonel, ruined his chances. (USAMHI)

Above: And so Sully had to lead another campaign against them. Here the camp of the 6th Iowa Cavalry near Fort Berthold, where Sully hoped again to make terms. He failed, and the problems with the Sioux would go on for decades after the Civil War was done. (MHS)

Above: It was a more conventional war a few hundred miles south of Dakota and Minnesota. Indeed, some of the earliest meetings of Blue and Gray came in Arkansas and Missouri. The first real Confederate hero of the West was Major General Earl Van Dorn, though he lost the Battle of Pea Ridge. A year later he would be murdered by a jealous husband . (MC)

Above: The man who beat Van Dorn at Pea Ridge was Samuel Curtis, seated here in the center of his staff, wearing the uniform of a major general. He later commanded in Missouri, but never again fought a major battle. (MICHAEL J. HAMMERSON)

Above: After Curtis left Arkansas, Major General Frederick Steele replaced him, and in his first act led a campaign that resulted in the capture of Little Rock. (USAMHI)

Above: Curtis had already occupied Helena, Arkansas, and started the work of erecting Fort Curtis, shown here. And before Steele came, there would be other battles in the state. (LC)

Right: Major General Thomas C. Hindman, commanding Confederate forces in the state, led his army against a much smaller Federal command in the northwest part of Arkansas at Prairie Grove. Here Hindman sits in uniform with his children on October 22, 1865. He would be assassinated a few years later. (RJY)

Left: Hindman's army was made up of lean young Arkansas volunteers like these privates. (ARKANSAS HISTORY COMMISSION)

Above: They were attacking the small command of Brigadier General James G. Blunt, a one-time Jayhawker and friend of John Brown of Kansas. (NA)

Above: All that saved Blunt and his little army was the incredible march of Francis J. Herron and his two divisions, who covered 115 miles in three days to reach the battlefield and help defeat Hindman. He sits at center here with his staff, as a brigadier. After Prairie Grove he was promoted, becoming for a time the youngest major general in the war. Photograph by J. A. Scholten of St. Louis. (MICHAEL J. HAMMERSON)

Above: After Prairie Grove, and Steele's capture of Little Rock the following year, Arkansas was made relatively safe for the Union, and Steele could begin the buildup of Little Rock into a major base and supply center. A view across the Arkansas River of several of his supply warehouses. (NA)

Above: Warehouses No.'s 27 and 28 sat right on the river, next to an ice house and bakery. (NA)

Above: The commissary department made its headquarters among a row of dry-goods and auction houses. These images, probably made by artist White of Little Rock, are so clear that the broadsides posted on the walls are legible. They have not been previously published. (NA)

Above: It took a lot of employees to run Steele's quartermaster operation. They lived in these quarters, very comfortable by Civil War standards. The picnic table was a real extra. (NA)

Above: The Federals also established a large general hospital to serve the department. It was, all told, a very well-organized and -constructed post that Steele established in Little Rock, and he needed it. (NA)

Right: The state was never completely safe from Confederate raids. Besides the posts set up in the country, gunboats patrolled the rivers, particularly the Arkansas. The USS Fawn appears here opposite Devall's Bluff on December 31, 1863, only weeks after a skirmish with Rebel raiders. (NHC)

Right: Even Porter's mighty flagship Black Hawk sometimes ventured into Arkansas waters to protect river traffic. (NHC)

Above: Protecting the Federals' western flank, both in Missouri and Arkansas, was Fort Leavenworth out in Kansas. E. E. Henry's image was made around the end of the war. (USAMHI)

Above: And protecting the department from threats within were prisons like this military penitentiary at Little Rock. No region in the country was more threatened by divided loyalties and civilian "treason." (NA)

Above: Here in St. Charles, Missouri, on November 4, 1862, a group of suspected Confederate sympathizers pose for the camera. Missouri would cause more problems of civilian unrest and aid to the enemy than any other border state. (INTERNATIONAL MUSEUM OF PHOTOGRAPHY)

Above: Among other things, the population often harbored or assisted daring and ruthless guerrillas, most notably the partisans led by William C. Quantrill. Here three of Quantrill's men sit for the camera. Fletcher Taylor stands at left. The other two are better known for their postwar deeds. Frank James sits in the center, obviously hamming for the camera with his flashy trousers and a major general's uniform blouse, though he never held any commission. And standing at right is his brother, Jesse James. Missouri was a training ground for their outlaw depredations. (STATE HISTORICAL SOCIETY OF MISSOURI)

Left: Among those depredations was Quantrill's attack at Baxter Springs, Kansas, on October 6, 1863. He and his men brutally murdered scores of Federals in General James G. Blunt's headquarters band, which was with him. The instruments they carry in this image fell into Quantrill's hands, and every one of the bandmen was killed. That was the warfare of the border. (KANSAS STATE HISTORICAL SOCIETY)

Above: The Pacific House, on Fourth and Delaware in Kansas City, Missouri, was headquarters for Brigadier General Thomas Ewing in 1863. There, in an attempt to control the guerrillas, he issued his orders No. 10 and 11, which virtually depopulated four Missouri counties that had harbored Quantrill. A postwar image. (JACKSON COUNTY HISTORICAL SOCIETY)

Above: But nothing but bullets and bars could finally control the Missouri raiders, many of whom used Confederate uniforms as only an excuse for outlawry. Here Jim Anderson, brother of "Bloody Bill" Anderson, sits subdued for a time by Yankee ball and chain. (COURTESY OF CARL BRIEHAN)

Below: Those who could not be captured were often killed. Sometime in 1864 Federals caught up with Captain William H. Stuart. Photographer O. D. Edwards copyrighted and sold images of the guerrilla's bullet-riddled corpse. (COURTESY OF WILLIAM TEMPLEMAN)

Below: A photographer was equally delighted to capture in death a last look at Bloody Bill Anderson, one of Quantrill's most feared and deadliest henchmen. (STATE HISTORICAL SOCIETY OF MISSOURI)

Below: Still others survived the war and their own penchant for pillage. "Little Arch" Clements even took to wearing a crucifix. (LSU)

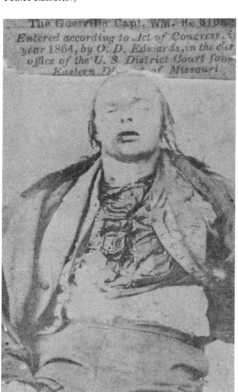

Above: And Smith was served by some able assistants, most notably Lieutenant General Simon B. Buckner, who came in 1864 to be his chief of staff. The bold Kentuckian would live until 1914, and would run for Vice President in 1896. His running mate was Union Major General John M. Palmer. (VM)

Above: Undoubtedly part of the problem in controlling Missouri was that here, as in the far West, Washington sent officers who had failed into exile. In 1864, Major General William S. Rosecrans, disgraced after Chickamauga, took command of the Department of Missouri. (USAMHI)

Above: He faced a formidable foe in command of the Confederate Trans-Mississippi Department, General E. Kirby Smith, veteran of First Manassas and the Kentucky campaign of 1862. He so organized and administered his department that it came in time to be called "Kirbysmithdom." (ATLANTA HISTORICAL SOCIETY)

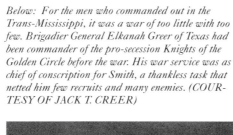

Below: For the men who commanded out in the Trans-Mississippi, it was a war of too little with too few. Brigadier General Elkanah Greer of Texas had been commander of the pro-secession Knights of the Golden Circle before the war. His war service was as chief of conscription for Smith, a thankless task that netted him few recruits and many enemies. (COURTESY OF JACK T. CREER)

Below: Also serving as chief of staff at times was Brigadier General William R. Boggs of Georgia. This portrait was made in 1864 at Smith's headquarters in Shreveport, Louisiana. (TU)

Below: Richmond, too, looked upon the West as a dumping ground for officers who were in the way in Virginia. Major General Benjamin Huger of South Carolina was banished to the Trans-Mississippi on staff duties after his lackluster battlefield performance in the Seven Days' battles. (LSU)

Above: And Smith also got his share of political appointees, though some proved to be happy choices. Henry W. Allen began the war as a Louisiana private. He was made a brigadier general in 1863, and the year later became governor of Louisiana. He proved a strong right arm to Smith in administering Louisiana. Unwilling to live in the United States after the war, he went to Mexico with thousands of other exiles and died there in 1866. An unpublished portrait of General Allen, made probably in 1864. (LSU)

Above: A former governor of Louisiana was Paul O. Hebert, shown here as colonel of the 1st Louisiana Artillery in the summer of 1861. He became a brigadier and was sent for a time to command one of the most neglected places in the Confederacy, the Department of Texas. (VM)

Above: He was later succeeded by Major General John B. Magruder, "Prince John" of Virginia, a little-appreciated officer who brought real talent to Texas and managed his undermanned department skillfully. (CWTI)

Above: It was a state of small towns and modest cities, like Huntsville, where old Sam Houston died in 1863. F. B. Bailey of Navasota brought his camera here to record the court house square. Towns like this could produce only so many soldiers and so much supply, and too much of it was drained off to Virginia. (USAMHI)

Above: With what was left them, however, the Texans did very well. One of the war's great heroes was Lieutenant Richard Dowling. Shown here as a major, the twenty-five-year-old Irishman defended Sabine Pass against four Yankee gunboats with only 47 men and two boats shielded with cotton bales. His victory was so needed and so spectacular that he and his men were awarded the only medals ever presented in the Confederacy. (LSU)

Left: There were few photographers in Texas, and it is not surprising that little survives to show the war in the Lone Star State. Nevertheless, A. G. Wedge of Matamoros, Mexico, probably came to Brownsville on November 6, 1863, when the Confederates had to evacuate the town on the Rio Grande, and he left an important record of the event. (COURTESY OF GARY WRIGHT)

Above: It was a border town as much Mexican as Confederate. (GW)

Below: The riverfront was alive with activity, many people even loading their furniture to take it with them in the evacuation. Bee had only two steamers at his disposal, loading them with supplies to ferry over the Rio Grande to Matamoros, Mexico, for safety. (GW)

Above: Brigadier General Hamilton Bee had a large supply of stores and cotton at Brownsville, and when superior forces of Federals approached, he packed up what he could take with him and destroyed the rest. (GW)

Below: A pontoon bridge across the river helped to carry wagons across. (cw)

Above: The photographer took his camera across the bridge to the Matamoros side to get this rare and somewhat blurred image of the bustle and confusion of the evacuation. Wagons and people are everywhere, and some are even trying to ferry themselves across on the skiff at left. Guards on the bridge are apparently holding it for military traffic alone. (TEXAS SOUTHWEST COLLEGE LI-BRARY, BROWNSVILLE)

Above: By the spring of 1864 the reserves of manpower in Texas were nearly exhausted. Here in Ellis County in late March or early April, First Lieutenant William J. Stokes could display for the camera just ten new recruits for his company. His veterans kneel in uniform, the new men standing behind in their civilian attire. Stokes himself is probably one of the three officers standing. They were all a part of the 4th Texas Cavalry, called the Arizona Brigade, and this rare image is the only one known to exist that shows Texans outdoors in their home state. Equally rare by 1864 are those sparkling new uniforms his veterans wear. (ELLIS COUNTY MUSEUM, INC.)

Above: By late 1864 there were barely eleven depleted brigades in the whole department. Lower Louisiana was defended by just two brigades, one of them commanded by Brigadier General William P. Hardeman, a veteran of the Red River Cam paign. (CWTI)

Above: Many of the troops in the Confederate service claimed a Mexican or Spanish heritage, including these officers of the 3d Texas Cavalry. They are, from the left, Refugio Benavides, Atanacio Vidaurri, Cristobal Benavides, and John Z. Leyendecker. (URSALINE ACADEMY LIBRARY)

Far left: Helping them defend their homeland were colorful characters like the resplendent Captain Samuel J. Richardson, probably the only Confederate of the war outfitted in leopard skin. (MC)

Left: The last real Confederate offensive of the war in the West somehow managed to come out of the belea-guered Trans-Mississippi. Its foundations were laid when the always incompetent Lieutenant General Theophilus H. Holmes resigned as commander of the District of Arkansas in the spring of 1864. (LC)

Above: Major General Mosby Munroe Parsons of Missouri commanded one of Price's two infantry divisions on the advance into Missouri. He, like Price and many others, would go to Mexico after the war. There, on August 15, 1865, he was killed by guerrillas while apparently serving with Mexican Imperial forces. An unpublished portrait. (RJY)

Above: Major General James F. Fagan of Kentucky led the Arkansas cavalry division on the raid. A handsome, capable officer, he commanded the rearguard just before the climactic Battle of Westport on October 23. In the battle itself, his division was scattered. (WRHS)

Above: That made Major General Sterling Price of Missouri his successor. Kirby Smith had little use for Price, but in September he sent him with all the cavalry he could scrape together on a raid deep into Missouri. It would be the last Southern attempt to retake the state. (VM)

Far left: Colonel Archibald S. Dobbin led one of Fagan's brigades, and like the rest was soundly beaten in the battle. He later claimed to have been made a brigadier, and here wears the uniform of a general. (MC)

Left: Along, too, for the campaign was another man who wore a general's blouse without ever being formally promoted, the "Swamp Fox" of Missouri, M. Jefferson Thompson. He had raised armies, commanded a gunboat fleet in battle on the Mississippi, and become one of the most engaging and ubiquitous characters of the Trans-Mississippi. (MC)

Left: And by far the most talented and colorful of Price's generals was Brigadier General John Sappington Marmaduke, the magnificent Missourian leading the second cavalry division. Young, handsome, dashing, a daring horseman, he was also a skilled marksman. In 1863 he fought a duel with fellow General L. M. Walker and left his antagonist dying. Covering the rear of Price's retreating army after Westport, he was captured. While in prison he will be promoted to major general, the last such appointment in the Confederate Army. Twenty years later Missouri will elect him governor. (LSU)

Above: It was one of those "shelved" generals from the East who defeated Price at Westport. Commanding the Federal cavalry, Major General Alfred Pleasonton struck Marmaduke in Price's rear and set off the rout of the Confederates. (P-M)

Above: That was the last threat to the Union in the Trans-Mississippi. By the summer of 1865 the war in the West was over, the Confederates disbanded, and Federals like the band of the 4th Michigan could pose for the camera in San Antonio, Texas, ending the era of the war and beginning the occupation of the South that became Reconstruction. (COURTESY OF PAUL DE HAAN)

Right: Private John J. Williams of the 34th Indiana would not be there to see it, however. On May 13, 1865, in a skirmish at Palmito Ranch, Texas, he became probably the last soldier killed in the Civil War. The first to die in any war are remembered—the poor man who is last is all too soon forgotten. Like the rugged frontier war he fought in out here in the West, Private Williams was doomed to obscurity. (USAMHI)

The End of an Era

The end of the long road at last. For four years the cry in blue had been "On to Richmond!" At last, in April 1865, they were there, the Stars and Stripes flying once more over the Confederate Capitol. The Confederates themselves were gone, their cause, like much of Richmond, in ruins. (NATIONAL ARCHIVES)

The Modern Army

RUSSELL F. WEIGLEY

Years of war, of trial and error, produce at last a fighting machine in the shape of things to come

Managing the U.S. War Department was the humorless but unfailingly effective Secretary of War Edwin M. Stanton. A master of organization, he oversaw the transformation of his department into a virtual war machine. (U.S. ARMY MILITARY HISTORY INSTITUTE)

WHEN Major General William Tecumseh Sherman's Union armies of the West emerged at Savannah to complete their march across Georgia from Atlanta to the sea in December 1864, a full reoutfitting of quartermaster supplies awaited the force of some 60,000 men. "Clothing, shoes, shelter tents, forage, provisions, spare parts of wagons, wagons complete, harness, leather, wax, thread, needles, and tools for all the trades which were plied on the march and in the camp were collected in the harbor of Hilton Head," reported Quartermaster General Montgomery C. Meigs. As soon as naval vessels off the coast reported Sherman's storming of Fort McAllister, a great quartermaster fleet set out for the mouth of the Savannah River with these supplies.

After seeing Sherman's soldiers warmly clothed, the fleet steamed northward again, laden with captured cotton for the Union's mills and the fabrication of more cloth. "All this," the quartermaster general added, "was done in the dead of winter. Light-draft, frail river-steamers trusted themselves, under daring Yankee captains and crews, to the storms of the stormiest coast of the world, and all arrived safely at their destination."

General Meigs considered the replenishing of Sherman's armies the climax of the Union logistical operations of the Civil War, the proof positive that the United States Army had come of age as a finely geared yet immensely powerful machine that could exert its power across almost any distance. Meigs took equal pride in the knowledge that simultaneous with the sailing of the fleet to Sherman, quartermaster vessels were also sustaining other Union detachments all along the Southern coast from Virginia to Texas. To keep in the field the armies with which Lieutenant General Ulysses S. Grant was laying siege to Petersburg and Richmond, the Quartermaster Department had transformed City Point, Virginia, into one of the largest seaports of the world. On an average day forty steamships, seventy-five sailing vessels, and a hundred barges unloaded their cargoes at wharves there running for more than a mile along the James River and extending up the Appomattox River. Behind the wharves sprawled huge warehouses and open storage areas for all kinds of quartermaster stores —the uniforms, tents, forage, and so on that Meigs had also supplied to Sherman at Savannah —as well as the commissary, medical, and ordnance stores that were procured by departments other than Meigs's but transported by the quartermaster to the front—the army's foodstuffs, medicines, and row on row of cannon, pile on pile of rifle bullets and cannon shot and shell. From the City Point depots the United States Military Railroads, a branch of Meigs's department, operated a twenty-one-mile railroad all along the rear of Grant's lines south of the Appomattox. The trains that carried supplies to the lines returned with the wounded, who went first to a two-hundred-acre, ten-thousand-bed military hospital on a high bluff above the Appomattox.

Before the war, City Point had been the eastern terminus of Virginia's Southside Railroad, and the military railroad used seven miles of the Southside's right of way between City Point and Petersburg. But these seven miles had had to be almost completely rebuilt (and the gauge altered from five feet to the newly standard four feet, eight and a half inches), while the bulk of the military

Above: Acting as adjutant general, one of the most important posts in the U.S. Army, responsible for communicating with and directing much of the enterprise of making war, was Brigadier General Lorenzo Thomas. Unlike Stanton, he proved sufficiently ineffective for the Secretary to order him out of Washington in 1863 and keep him on the road thereafter. (USAMHI)

Above: An adjutant was stationed with each army as well, and every general and even colonel had an adjutant to transmit his orders, manage his paperwork, and frequently act as his amanuensis. With the Army of the Potomac, it was Brigadier General Seth Williams, who was later made a major general in recognition of his able services. (WAR LIBRARY AND MUSEUM, MOLLUS PENNSYLVANIA)

Above: It was to be a war far different from that known by the aged Union General-in-Chief Winfield Scott, and though he left active service in 1861, many of the old ideas that he represented lingered on in what was to be a modern war. (USAMHI)

railroad was altogether new, including all the repair facilities to keep the cars rolling. By late 1864, however, railroad operation, construction, and reconstruction were routine activities for the Quartermaster Department. In the West, during Sherman's advance from Chattanooga to Atlanta, eleven bridges were reconstructed and seventy-five miles of completely new track laid, with many more miles of track repaired. The Railroad Construction Corps typically began the rebuilding of a bridge over the Oostenaula River while the old bridge was still burning, the work being slightly delayed "because the iron rods were so hot that the men could not touch them to remove the wreck." When General John Bell Hood's Confederate army subsequently tore up twenty-seven miles of track in a spectacular raid, the Construction Corps had the break repaired in seven and a half days. To ease such rebuilding, the Quartermaster Department took over an uncompleted Confederate mill at Chattanooga for the rolling of rails.

For the accumulating and transporting of the vast quantities of military stores depicted in the photographs of Union Army depots, the mighty industrial capacity of the North obviously underlay such improvisations near the front as the reopened Chattanooga rolling mill and the transformation of City Point into a bustling seaport. Apart from the Union Army's sheer size— probably over two million men served in it during the course of the war and slightly over a million were on its muster rolls when the war ended—the most modern dimension of the army was the lavishness of its subsistence and equipment.

As early as December 1861 Brigadier General Irvin McDowell testified that "a French army of half the size of ours could be supplied with what

Above: Here in Washington, D.C., was the hub of the giant military wheel created by the Union to ride down the rebellion. The War Department stands at left and the Navy Department at right. Calling forth millions of men and hundreds of millions of dollars, they brought victory through organization. (USAMHI)

Right: Washington itself became a major center for army services. Massive government repair shops like these, shown in April 1865, were established to keep the armies moving. (USAMHI)

Above: Hundreds of men were employed at keeping animals shod, not least at the government horse shoeing shop. (USAMHI)

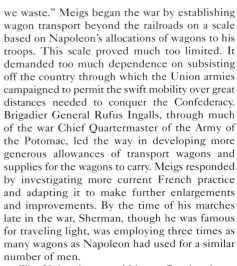

Above: Mechanics at the government repair shops pose for the camera, armed with the weapons of their war—wrenches, mauls, hammers, and leather aprons. (USAMHI)

Right: It was the same at the government trimming shop, where leather and canvas were fitted to make awnings and harnesses and whatever else needed to be "trimmed." (USAMHI)

we waste." Meigs began the war by establishing wagon transport beyond the railroads on a scale based on Napoleon's allocations of wagons to his troops. This scale proved much too limited. It demanded too much dependence on subsisting off the country through which the Union armies campaigned to permit the swift mobility over great distances needed to conquer the Confederacy. Brigadier General Rufus Ingalls, through much of the war Chief Quartermaster of the Army of the Potomac, led the way in developing more generous allowances of transport wagons and supplies for the wagons to carry. Meigs responded by investigating more current French practice and adapting it to make further enlargements and improvements. By the time of his marches late in the war, Sherman, though he was famous for traveling light, was employing three times as many wagons as Napoleon had used for a similar number of men.

The Union Army could be outfitted and sustained on a scale unprecedented in world military history because behind it lay an economy well into the Industrial Revolution and rich in agriculture as well, the whole economy bound together by railroads. The industrial and transportation capacities of the North had advanced far enough for the Union Army to be the first mass army to be supplied on a scale comparable to that of the armies of the twentieth-century world wars.

Saying that about the Union Army, however, like examining the pictures of its supply depots, risks suggesting the cliche that because of the North's economic strength, the South never had a chance of winning the war. The North's industrial and agricultural wealth, and the Union Army's becoming through that wealth the first modern mass army in the plenitude of its resources, probably did not carry quite that much importance for the outcome of the war. Notwithstanding the logistical modernity of the Union Army, the Civil War, unlike World War II, can not be described as a "gross-national-product war," in which the decisive issue was which belligerent could outproduce the other. In World War II the productive capacity of the United States permitted the Allied coalition to bury the Axis under a sheer weight of armaments—an insurmountable tide of tanks, big guns, big ships, airplanes, shells, and bombs. The Union Army in the Civil War, for all its modernity, did not have modern arms. The weapons of the 1860s were still simple enough—mainly muzzle-loading rifles and single-shot cannon—for the Confederacy to produce or otherwise acquire enough of to put up a pretty equal contest on the battle field. The material plenty of the North and of the Union Army applied less directly to the clash of arms than to the enhancement of Union morale and the gradual erosion of Confederate morale.

Nor did the North's economic strength by itself guarantee the lavishness and modernity of the Union Army's sustenance, clothing, and equipment. The experience of Great Britain in the Crimean War less than a decade earlier showed that even the most advanced industrial nation of the nineteenth-century world, seconded by the world's largest merchant fleet and navy in using maritime lines of communication, could not support a modern army in the field if the army's own administration was antiquated and incompetent. British economic power not withstanding, British army strength in the Crimea fell from about 42,000 to about 12,000 effectives in less than a year because British military staffs were too dull-witted and disorganized to maintain the physical health and well-being of the larger force. Thus the Union Army's administrators and logisticians merit considerable credit for translating the economic potential for ample military supplies into reality.

Quartermaster General Meigs deserves the foremost share of this credit. Not a modest man, he described his job of procuring all the Union Army's supplies except ordnance, foodstuffs, and medical items, and transporting everything, including the three latter categories, as the second most important position in the Army, next only to the post of general-in-chief. His assessment was correct. Many of Meigs's lieutenants in the field accomplished similarly impressive work within their spheres, especially Ingalls and the railroad men Colonel Daniel C. McCallum and Brigadier General Herman Haupt. McCallum was director of the United States Military Railroads, Haupt director of railroads in the north eastern theater of war through much of 1862 and 1863.

The Union Secretaries of War contributed much also, even the frequently abused Simon

Right: There were special government shops for repairing and fitting out ambulances, its glum-looking crew wielding their squares and saws, augurs and broadaxes. (USAMHI)

Left: The blacksmiths were probably more numerous than the rest, for they worked in iron, and it was a war fought on iron—iron rails, iron rims, iron horseshoes. (USAMHI)

Above: Nearby the wheelwrights work at making and repairing the wheels that the painters paint. Downtown Washington was a sea of enterprise as the government repair shops proliferated. (USAMHI)

Left: Another small legion of workers fought with brushes, their battlefield the government paint shop. They stand, buckets and brushes in hand, posing with a pile of wheels and boxes awaiting their attention. (USAMHI)

Above: Of course, armies had to be fed, and that called for a legion of white-aproned cooks at the government bakery. The armies in the field usually baked their own bread, so this bakery serviced just the troops around the capital. (USAMHI)

Above: And to keep the men garbed, the office of the U.S. Depot of Army Clothing and Equipage occupied the better part of a city block. A more genteel service bureau, this office could afford a few frills—an ornate eagle painted above its door and a lamp post with stars and CLOTHING DEPOT illuminated in the glass. (USAMHI)

Above: To erect all these buildings, as well as to supply the Union armies with the raw materials of forts and bridges and stockades and more, the government used veritable forests of timber. This government lumber yard was in Alexandria, Virginia, probably photographed by Captain A. J. Russell. (USAMHI)

Cameron. It is true that Cameron presided over the initial outfitting of the Union Army with excessive financial laxity and excessive regard for rewarding political friends. As Quartermaster General Meigs put it, however, in responding to criticisms of the quality of the materials purchased when the Army's numbers of men multiplied twenty-seven times during the first four months—a growth much more rapid than that of either world war—"the troops were clothed and rescued from severe suffering, and those who saw sentinels walking post in the capital of the United States in freezing weather in their drawers, without trousers or overcoats, will not blame the department for its efforts to clothe them, even in materials not quite so durable as army blue kersey." Cameron accomplished more than is sometimes acknowledged toward creating the army of which General McDowell could testify, while Cameron still headed the War Department: "There never was an army in the world that began to be supplied as well as ours is."

Cameron's more efficient successor, Secretary of War Edwin M. Stanton, contributed much to the continuing workability of the whole administrative and logistical system. The contributions of such individuals to Union military supply have to be stressed because success was achieved largely through a triumph of human talents over organizational arrangements that were not much better than those that wrecked the British Army in the Crimea. The various supply bureaus of the United States Army and the related administrative bureaus—the Adjutant General's Department, the Inspector General's Department, the Judge Advocate General's Department, and the Pay Department—along with the Corps of Engineers and the newly created Signal Corps, each habitually had gone its own way with little overall coordination, let alone any combined planning for the development of a coherent supply system for the entire army. Called the General Staff, the heads of these departments in no way constituted the slightest approximation of a modern general staff in the sense of a planning body. It was Stanton's contribution to the making of a modern army that by dominating the War Department, not through the

Below: The lumber went to build experimental "shad-belly" bridges like this one, photographed by Russell. It had just been subjected to 168,000 pounds of weight for nine hours and stood the test. (NATIONAL ARCHIVES)

Above: The wood built platforms like this on which bridge arches were constructed. Built on the upper flat surface, the arches were then . . . (NA)

Above: . . . tipped over on the hinged platform, to be joined into finished sections of bridge. (NA)

medium of organization charts, but by force of an overpowering, even sometimes ruthless personality, he imposed a functional coordination upon the administrative and supply bureaus. Without him, Civil War logistics in the Union Army might well have been as chaotic as those of the later Spanish American War, for the relationships among the bureaus were otherwise the same as in 1898.

Stanton had to deal also with the problem of establishing a modern command system for the combat operations of an army modern in scale. A lawyer by profession, he could intervene to less direct effect in the technical military issues of combat than in administration because combat was too far removed from his own expertise. The regulations of the Army, furthermore, seemed to confine the jurisdiction of the Secretary of War to administration and finance, leaving combat command to the ranking military professional, the general-in-chief—though thus excluding the President's civilian deputy raised questions involving the constitutional principle of civilian control of the military. When to these various difficulties was added the fact that a capable combat commander for an army of from half a million to a million men is never easy to find, most of the war had been fought before the command system of the Union Army matched the effectiveness of the Army's administration and logistics.

In the beginning, the general-in-chief was Brevet Lieutenant General Winfield Scott, who had occupied this lofty post for twenty years and had been a general officer since the War of 1812. A hero of the latter war and of his great campaign from Vera Cruz to the City of Mexico in the Mexican War, Scott had grown fat, dropsical, and tired by 1861. His military brain was still good, and he was the principal designer of the "Anaconda Plan" for strangling the Confederacy by naval blockade as well as pressure by land. But as a strategist Scott had always favored the pre-Napoleonic, eighteenth-century mode of limited war, and even if he had been younger and more vigorous, he might never have developed enough ruthlessness to seek that utter destruction of Confederate armies and resources which was probably necessary to achieve so sweeping a war aim as the complete extinction of Confederate claims to independence.

President Abraham Lincoln therefore acquiesced when a much younger and seemingly

Above: Bridge sections such as this were used to build a new span over the Potomac for the Washington, Alexandria & Georgetown Railroad. They would make a bridge 5,104 feet in length. (KEAN ARCHIVES)

Below: It was a model of wartime engineering. off in the extreme right distance, the Capitol dome looks across to the wonders being done by Lincoln's modern army. (KA)

Above: Furthermore, the builders of the U.S. Military Railroad could erect major depots anywhere they could lay a rail. Here on the James River, at City Point, Virginia, they made the terminus of the road that kept Grant supplied at Petersburg for nearly a year. A Russell image. (USAMHI)

Above: And when boxcars could not go by rail to their final destination, they were put aboard the first "container ships"—steamers and schooners that could hold the cars on their decks. (NA)

Above: Besides rail communications, the Union Army expanded the use of the telegraph to previously undreamed limits for the military. Here in Georgetown, photographer William Morris Smith captures a view of the Signal Corps "camp of instruction," where hundreds of men were trained in Morse code and communication by wigwag flags. (LIBRARY OF CONGRESS)

Right: Signal corpsmen erecting telegraph poles and preparing to string wire. Lincoln's armies, by 1865, could carry instant communication along with them almost anywhere. (AMERICANA IMAGE GALLERY)

much more vigorous soldier, Major General George B. McClellan, maneuvered Scott aside in November 1861. Already commanding the Army of the Potomac, McClellan moved up to be general-in-chief as well. Unfortunately for the Union, McClellan's youth—he was only thirty five—proved to assure no more resolution than Scott had shown when it came to risking bold invasions of the South; and if ruthlessness was needed, McClellan possessed less of that commodity than the old man. McClellan at least recognized, however, that an overall strategy would be necessary for the winning of the war, that it was not enough simply to have tactical ideas for the winning of particular battles; and for this reason, "Little Mac" despite his faults was a better choice for the top Union command than most of the available generals would have been.

Yet McClellan proved to lack a narrower but essential ingredient of generalship—the tactical skills to win the particular battles. Consequently he could not give his strategic design—to push the Confederacy militarily just hard enough to convince the South it could not win, while otherwise conciliating the Southerners with promises of the safety of their property, especially slavery —a real test to demonstrate whether it could work. Lincoln became dissatisfied with McClellan and removed him from the office of general in-chief as early as March 11, 1862, though for the time being he permitted the general to keep command of the Army of the Potomac. Finding, however, no one else with a strategic grasp comparable to McClellan's, Lincoln now undertook the direct, personal exercise of the role of Commander in Chief, giving orders to the armies himself, with Stanton's help.

In the process, Lincoln oversaw the riposte to Major General Thomas J. "Stonewall" Jackson's Valley Campaign, and the maneuvers he designed might have trapped Jackson had the President enjoyed better cooperation from the Union generals on the scene. Jackson's escape, however, helped prove that Lincoln had too many other duties to be able to exercise sufficiently precise direct command over field forces, so the President decided he had to find a new professional general-in-chief, notwithstanding the dearth of strategists. He turned to an officer who had at least written and translated books about strategy,

Major General Henry Wager Halleck. As commander of much of the Western theater of war from November 1861 to Lincoln's choosing him as general-in-chief in July 1862, Halleck had shown only the most limited promise of transforming book learning into strategic accomplishment. Still, he merited some of the credit for his subordinate Grant's Fort Henry, Fort Donelson, and Shiloh campaigns, and all in all he was the most suitable choice on the horizon.

Halleck reinforced the War Department's administrative skills, and his presence assured yet further that the Union Army would be managed and supplied as befitted a modern mass army. But far from exerting a strong strategic grasp, Halleck refused to risk taking responsibility for most of the command decisions on which might turn the outcome of battles or the war. He would give Lincoln and Stanton strategic advice; he would not take strategic command. After July 1862 Lincoln found himself by default still the architect of Union strategy.

Fortunately for the Union, the President had grown to be a strategist of considerable accomplishment—so much, indeed, that in 1926 a British soldier, Colin Ballard, was to write a book called *The Military Genius of Abraham Lincoln*, and some other historians were to bestow accolades almost as enthusiastic as Ballard's. Strategy, the conduct of campaigns and the fitting of them together in a pattern designed to win a war, does not demand nearly so much technical, specialized knowledge of war as does tactics, the manipulation of troops in battle. His strategic vision unclouded by tactical detail, furthermore, Lincoln perceived certain essential principles of the Union war effort more clearly than did almost any professional military man. The professional soldiers had been taught at West Point and from the study of Napoleon's campaigns, for example, that a military force should be concentrated, gathered up to strike a few strong blows or even a single blow against a key objective such as the enemy's political capital or an important road junction. Lincoln recognized, however, that to concentrate Union power against so obvious an objective as Richmond permitted the enemy to concentrate there also in defense, and the effect was to allow the Confederates to make the most of their limited resources. If, on the contrary, the Union used its superior resources not to concentrate but to attack all around the borders of the Confederacy, the enemy did not have the ability to match Union strength everywhere and somewhere around the Confederacy's periphery the defenses were sure to cave in. Similarly, Lincoln recognized clearly that the principal strength of the Confederacy resided in its armed forces and that the main objectives of the Union should not be geographical points even as prominent as Richmond but rather the destruction of the enemy armies.

For all that, Lincoln's lack of professional military credentials, as well as the need for him to attend to a multitude of tasks besides military strategy, undercut his efforts to lead his generals to apply his strategic perceptions. He continued to seek a professional soldier who would share those perceptions and assume strategic and operational command of the Union armies in the manner that only a professional soldier could. When the triumphs of Vicksburg and Chattanooga in 1863 brought Grant to the forefront among Union commanders, Lincoln shared the wide conviction

Above: The photos of the several balloons used by the Union Army observation are well known, but less well remembered are the gas generators used to inflate them. T. S. Lowe's generators Nos. 7 and 8 were government property, just part of an ever-expanding arsenal of weapons. (NA)

Right: So that no waterway might present an impassable obstacle for the marching Union armies, special wagons were designed and equipped with canvas pontoons as well as an anchor to hold the pontoons in place. (P-M)

Above: Whole trains of pontoons, equipped with oars for maneuvering, followed the marching Union armies. (NA)

Right: And when a bridge was not available, "blanket boats" were made by stretching rubberized blankets or canvas over wooden frames, lashing them together, and launching away. It could carry a squad of soldiers and a cannon and limber, as in this Russell photo. (LC)

Right: One photographer, perhaps Russell, recorded the building by Union engineers of a pontoon span near Washington. Here the pontoons are ready for "laying." (USAMHI)

Left: Here another view as the working parties assemble. It is to be a timed test. (USAMHI)

in Congress and among the public that Grant should receive the full rank of lieutenant general, vacant since George Washington, and should displace Halleck as general in-chief, which he did in March 1864. When Lincoln came to know Grant, the conviction deepened. Grant agreed firmly that the destruction of the Confederate armies should be the main objective of Union strategy and that applying pressure against all the enemy armies simultaneously should be a principal means of achieving their destruction.

To what extent the rise of Grant can be said to have given the Union's modern mass armies a modern command system remains nevertheless debatable. Grant decided that as commanding general he would take the field with the Army of the Potomac, directly supervising that army and its commander, Major General George G. Meade, while overseeing other armies less directly via the telegraph and General Halleck. For that purpose, Halleck remained in Washington with the new title of Chief of Staff, but he was not Chief of Staff of the Army in the twentieth-century sense, since he was subordinate to Grant. Halleck's administrative skills and military knowledge made him on the whole an admirable conduit between Grant and the other Union generals. But there were awkwardnesses in these arrangements: in the distance of the chief professional soldier from Washington and in his focusing on one of several armies; in his dependence on a Chief of Staff who remained reluctant to take on responsibilities and who in a legal sense was not ultimately responsible; in Grant's continuing dependence on Secretary Stanton and the chiefs of the supply bureaus to sustain the armies, while

Left: Some 450 men are working at wooden boats and canvas pontoons, some of them joined in giant rafts. In the first twenty minutes they have 1,300 feet ready for the passage of heavy vehicles, including artillery. (USAMHI)

Below: They would do it with huge trains of boats like these beside the camp of the 50th New York Engineers at Rappahannock Station, Virginia, in February 1864. A Timothy O'Sullivan image. (KA)

Above: The bridge assembled in record time, the proud engineers pose in squads along its length. It is a marvel of hasty yet serviceable construction. Again and again in the war, Yankee engineers will "throw" bridges across every stream in their path. (USAMHI)

the bureau chiefs were under Stanton's, not Grant's, command so that the relationship between the powers of the general-in-chief and the Secretary of War remained unclear.

The command system of the Union Army functioned well in the final year of the war because the personalities involved worked well together. Lincoln, Stanton, Grant, Halleck, and Meigs all earned high marks for cooperation with each other. On any organization chart, however, the ultimate Union Army command structure would look like a nightmare. Not least of the problems, there was still the fundamental question as to how Grant's authority as general-in-chief was to be reconciled with the constitutional power of the President as Commander in Chief. This problem was not to be resolved until long after the Civil War, with the creation in 1903 of the twentieth-century version of the Army Chief of Staff as the ranking professional soldier but, unlike a Civil War general-in-chief, claiming no authority to command independent of the President and the Secretary of War.

Whatever the problems of Grant's status, his method of achieving his and Lincoln's objective of the destruction of the Confederate armies added another modern dimension to the Union Army's waging of war. In the campaign of 1864–65, Grant eventually destroyed the principal enemy field force, General Robert E. Lee's Army of Northern Virginia, by the grim expedient of locking it in battle almost every day and inflicting casualties until Lee's army was no more. The campaign became one of deadly attrition, foreshadowing the long-stalemated bloodbath on the Western Front of the First World War, of the Eastern Front of the Second World War, and of the Korean War. At Appomattox, Lee surrendered only some 26,765 men; his army had numbered 66,000 just one year before. To be sure, Grant's strategy of nearly continuous battle imposed tremendous casualties on his own army as well, but the general-in-chief knew that the Union could replenish his ranks while the Confederacy could not replenish Lee's.

Nor was Grant merely the strategic butcher that hostile portrayals have sometimes made him seem. He had demonstrated a superb capacity for agile maneuver in his Vicksburg Campaign before becoming general-in-chief, and he would have preferred to trap and capture Lee's army by maneuver in 1864-65 rather than trade casualties with it. But the combination of Lee's tactical skills and the improved nature of weapons by the 1860s left Grant with no alternative method of destroying the enemy army than its slow attrition in protracted combat.

The final modern dimension of the Civil War, one assuring the resemblance of the Petersburg trench systems to the elaborate field fortifications of later wars, lay in the firepower of the rival armies. Fifteen years earlier, the men who were to be the generals of the Civil War had fought against Mexico a war whose weapons remained much like those of the American Revolution: smoothbore muskets and cannons. The Civil War, in contrast, was a war of rifled muskets and to a large extent of rifled artillery. In the short time between the Mexican and Civil wars, the American adoption of mass-production methods of permitting muzzle-loading weapons to fire rifled projectiles despite the difficulties of loading—particularly the American adoption of the

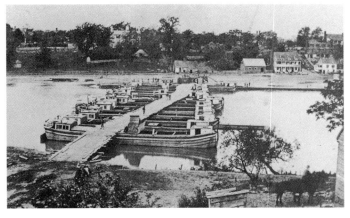

Left: When something more substantial than pontoons were needed, the engineers could make indestructible bridges out of river barges. (COURTESY OF TERENCE P. O'LEARY)

Left: The man in charge of all these ingenious builders was Brigadier General Joseph G. Totten, Chief Engineer of the U.S. army and one of the oldest men in the service. He was seventy-three when the war began and still a man of active mind. He died in 1864 while still on active duty. (USAMHI)

Right: The camps of the engineers were to be found wherever the Yankee armies went. Here at Chattanooga in 1864 sits the camp of the 1st Michigan Engineers and Mechanics, with Lookout Mountain in the distance. (MICHIGAN STATE ARCHIVES, LANSING)

Left: And here in Chattanooga, near the Tennessee River, is a waterworks under construction by Federal engineers in 1864. (NA)

Below: And here it is finished. They did good work. (NA)

Above: Government sawmills like this one on Lookout Mountain, Tennessee, fed the voracious appetites of the engineers. The army simply took the machinery with it wherever it went. (USAMHI)

Above: A good sharp saw-toothed blade, steam-powered, could make as much of a contribution to the Union war effort as a cannon on the field, and sometimes more. (USAMHI)

Right: Wherever the Yankees went, they adapted to their environment, using their skill and engineering ingenuity to the profit of the march to victory. Here at Beaufort, South Carolina, they erected a massive condenser to distill pure water from seawater, leaving vital salt as a by-product. A Samuel Cooley image from November 1864. (NA)

French Captain Claude Etienne Minie's "minie ball"—wrought a revolution in warfare out of all proportion to the seeming smallness of the source.

With smoothbore muskets, effective range had been limited to 200 yards or less. As Grant remarked in his memoirs, "At the distance of a few hundred yards a man might fire at you all day without your finding out." With the Model 1855 or 1861 Springfield rifle and other rifled shoulder arms, effective range leaped to 400 or up to 600 yards. Rifled field artillery attained a maximum effective range of some 2,500 yards. Now a defending force could fire so many accurate shots at an attacker during the time he was within range that any frontal assault against reasonably well trained and resolute troops was almost sure to fail. Even attacks against flanks and rear—in devising which the Union Army's great adversary General Lee was the most skillful tactician since Napoleon—no longer produced quite the devastating effect that they had in Napoleon's day; the firepower of rifled weapons much enhanced the possibility that the victim of such maneuvers might be able to form a new front. Even the best generalship failed to preserve attacking forces from devastating casualties under the defenders' rifles. At Second Bull Run, in August 1862, and Chancellorsville, in May 1863, Lee achieved masterpieces of Napoleonic maneuver against his enemy's flanks, but the Union Army's rifled firepower nevertheless extracted from Lee's forces in those battles casualties of some 19 and 22 percent, respectively. The victor's losses were too high for the victory to yield decisive advantage.

The appalling casualty rates of Civil War battles—at Gettysburg, in July 1863, 23,000 out of some 85,000 for the Union Army, 28,000 out of 75,000 for the Confederate Army—were achieved mainly with single-shot, muzzle-loading shoulder arms and artillery. A relatively small number of breech-loading cannon were used, but problems in satisfactorily locking the breech to permit the firing of adequate powder charges were not yet fully solved. Controversy has always swirled around the question whether the Union Army should have made itself still more modern through a speedier adoption of breech-loading and even repeating muskets and carbines. Both Union and Confederate armies used some such weapons, more often cavalry carbines than infantry rifles because cavalry did not have so much need of long range and sustained firing capacity; breechloaders tended to suffer from gas leakage and fouling of the breech mechanism to the detriment of these qualities.

About 100,000 Sharps carbines and rifles are estimated to have been used by both sides, employing a single-shot breech-loading mechanism patented by Christian Sharps in 1848. By the time of Gettysburg in July 1863, some Spencer breech-loading repeating rifles were in Union service; on July 13, 1863, just after Gettysburg, the Federal Ordnance Department placed its first order for Spencer repeating carbines. Eventually the department ordered 64,685 Spencer carbines and 11,471 Spencer rifles. The seven shot Spencer repeating carbine, using copper rim-fire cartridges, became the standard arm of the Union cavalry by 1864. But like all breech loaders of the era, it still had problems. The cartridge contained only forty-five grains of black powder, so the weapon lacked range and power. When the carbine grew hot, the cartridges tended to stick in the chamber.

In its rejection of breechloaders as the standard infantry weapon, the Ordnance Department was not obtusely conservative. The famous Prussian needle gun, adopted as early as 1843, had less range than standard Union Army muzzle-loaders. Brigadier General John Buford reported that at Gettysburg some of his Union cavalry troopers armed themselves with muzzle-loading infantry muskets in place of their breech-loading carbines; the soldiers knew which was the better weapon in a hard fight.

The rifled muzzle-loading musket and rifled muzzle-loading artillery could do damage enough. They pushed the Civil War armies finally into entrenchments that foreshadowed the Western Front in World War I. They deprived individual battles of decisiveness and transformed the war into a prolonged tactical deadlock resolved only when harsh attrition had brought one of the contestants to exhaustion. They gave the modernity of the Union Army its fullest but most disturbing dimension. Like other modern armies in subsequent modern wars, the Union Army, despite all its resources, could gain the political objectives for which it fought only through the grim strategies of Grant and Sherman. It had to annihilate the enemy armed forces through day-by-day attrition, or it had to carry destruction beyond the enemy armies to the enemy's economy and civilian population.

Above: Here in Beaufort, too, arose the carpenters' shops, this one doing just a little bit of everything. Wagons are repaired, building skylights made, and signs manufactured. Leaning against the wide door at the left is a billboard headed INSTRUCTIONS FOR THE OFFICER OF THE GUARD. More somber reminders of the war sit to the left of it—grave markers for Privates Charles Williams and Blainwell Sweatt. (NA)

Above: Of course, the Beaufort paint shop put the lettering on the signs, and the grave markers. Two more of each rest against the wall here. (NA)

Left: On Hilton Head Island, South Carolina, the U.S. Government established a slaughterhouse to provide freshly butchered meat for the soldiers. The piles of hooves and horns outside attest to recent work. Soldiering, it seemed, was not all glory and fighting after all. They also served who only made steaks. (NA)

Above: All across the North and the South, signs of Union might and organization were evident. In Nashville, Tennessee, the vast Taylor Depot went up. (PRIVATE COLLECTION)

Above: A few blocks away stood the "tent manufactory," not only where canvas tents were made, but also where mass-produced uniforms were cut from patterns. (NA)

Above: In Cincinnati, Ohio, the U.S. Government wagon yard occupied a huge park at Eighth and Freeman streets. (NA)

Above: All of this organization required a lot of fuel for the steam engines, the locomotives, and the ships. Here in Alexandria Russell's camera looks at only a part of the government wharves, with their mountains of cordwood for the fuel burners and another mountain of alfalfa for the hay burners. (USAMHI)

Left: Next door the yard of the Cumberland Coal & Iron Company promised plenty of food for the smoke-belching furnaces aboard the John Brooks and other steamers. (USAMHI)

Above: The man who kept all of these supplies coming to the Union armies was Quartermaster General Montgomery C. Meigs, himself an amateur photographer and an organizer of wonderful efficiency. The men in blue rarely went hungry. (RONN PALM COLLECTION)

Above: Union transport fleets like this one kept all these supplies moving from major centers such as Alexandria to the supply bases established with the advancing armies. Such supply was a marvel of modern logistical design. (NA)

Below: Generals like U. S. Grant had sophisticated docks and wharves built to receive their supplies, understanding that armies did move on their stomachs. City Point, Virginia, in 1864. (USAMHI)

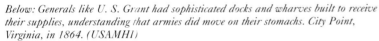

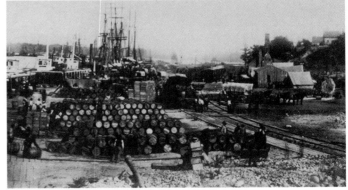

Above: Each army in the field had its own quartermaster as well, and with the army of the Potomac it was the capable Brigadier General Rufus Ingalls. He was the only staff officer with that army to serve from beginning to end of the war, enjoying the esteem of every commander he served under. (USAMHI)

Below: Supplies came straight off the ships and onto the cars of the railroad built by Grant, or into mountainous piles like these barrels of potatoes and salt pork and boxes of hardtack. (P-M)

Above: The James teemed with every variety of ship, once the City Point docks were ready, all bringing in massive stockpiles of supplies. (NA)

Above: The commissary depot at Cedar Level, Virginia, in August 1864 actually looked like a mountain. (USAMHI)

Right: Lesser but still imposing supply depots lay everywhere in the wake of the Union Army. Here at Stoneman's Station, Virginia, in June 1863, sat a depot that tempted Confederate cavalry into dashing raids to destroy or capture much-needed supplies. (USAMHI)

Below right: And from those depots massive wagon trains like this Army of the Potomac supply train at Brandy Station, Virginia, in October 1863, brought the life-sustaining food and materiel to the front. A Timothy O'Sullivan image. (CHICAGO HISTORICAL SOCIETY)

Above: Along with the Union armies themselves moved large herds of cattle for fresh meat. This herd is seen at Giesboro, in Southeast Washington, D.C. So prized was beef during the Civil War that in 1864 Confederate Major General Wade Hampton would lead one of the most daring raids of the war—to capture a cattle herd. (NA)

Above: All the Union services that were so comfortably ensconced back in Washington and the other major centers had their counterparts with the armies themselves. Here at Petersburg, Virginia, in August 1864, an engineer battalion is engaged in making gabions—wicker baskets filled with earth for defenses. (P-M)

Left: Here, too, Union repair shops replaced bad wheels or made new signs. (P-M)

Left: Communities of vendors and mechanics made tiny villages with the armies. Here a church, a sutler, and a photographer advertising his AMBROTYPE & PHOTOGRAPHIC GALLERY stand side by side. (NA)

Above: Keeping the men in the field happy meant keeping the mail running between them and their homes. These field desks are for the Union Army's postal service, for sorting letters and packages. A box of "Honey Soap" is in the large pigeonhole of the desk at the left. (USAMHI)

Below: The soldiers had to keep clean somehow, and for many of them that was something new. Huge laundries like this one at Camp Holt in Jeffersonville, Indiana, made it a little easier for them. (INDIANA HISTORICAL SOCIETY LIBRARY, INDIANAPOLIS)

Above: In the more permanent Union installations, the camp cooks in the kitchen became men of particular importance, as the third fellow from the left in the front row seems to appreciate. He stands hand in apron in the same Napoleonic stance so beloved of the officers. After all, he was a soldier too. (USAMHI)

Right: But all of this was ancillary to the Union Army's constant and pressing need to keep those men, clean or dirty, armed with the weapons necessary to do their job. This infantryman in full field equipment, with Sharps rifle and saber bayonet, is ready for the enemy, thanks to the work of thousands who served behind the lines. (MICHAEL J. MC AFEE COLLECTION)

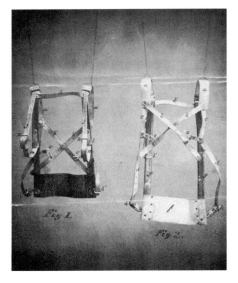

Left: Without that work, these men of the 118th New York, the "Adirondack Regiment," would not be armed with modern Spencer repeating rifles and carbines. (MICHAEL J. MCAFEE COLLECTION)

Left: Above all, the War Department had to be willing to try things that were new, something nineteenth-century armies all too often resisted. Inventors bombarded it with contraptions like Baxter's knapsack supporter, designed to give the wearer full mobility and freedom of movement in the field. (NA)

Left: Inventor Baxter even supplied demonstration photographs with his petition, apparently not realizing that the Civil War soldier rarely if ever went into battle wearing his knapsack. (NA)

Right: Then there was the Adams hand grenade, here attached to the wrist of its inventor, perhaps. It was little more than a hollow shell filled with powder and balls, with a fuse attached. By throwing it, the user set off the timed fuse when the leather strap attached to his wrist jerked a priming pin. It could have been embarrassing if his throw was a little too weak. (NA)

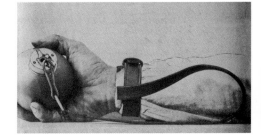

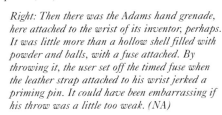

Right: Of more conventional weapons, the War Department considered an untold number, all of them subjected to performance and accuracy tests. The Starr carbine went through tests on October 31, 1864, and was approved for limited use by cavalry. (NA)

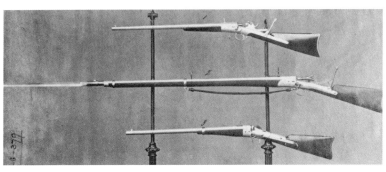

Left: Not so Brand's patent breech-loading firearms. Three versions were offered, the .44 caliber carbine at the top, the .54 caliber rifled musket in the center, and the .54 caliber carbine at the bottom. The weapon at the top was fired some 3,000 times in testing. A self-contained cartridge is shown partially inserted in the breech. For the musket in the center the entire cartridge in the loading and ejecting mechanism are shown. The carbine at the bottom is ready to fire. Inventors would continue designing breechloaders, and all too often a conservative War Department would reject them. (NA)

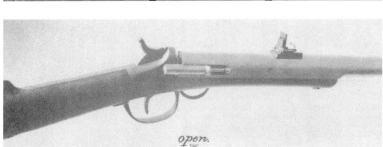

Left: Lee's breechloader was tested in April 1864. The barrel slipped sideways to allow a cartridge to be slid in. The thing projecting backward from the breech provided one solution to the biggest problem with breechloaders— how to eject the spent casing. This one just pushed backward, forcing the shell out. (NA)

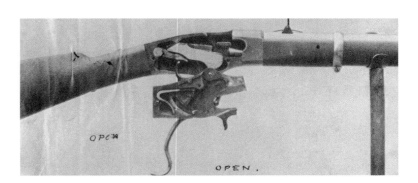

Left: Here the barrel and breech of the Johnson carbine are twisted open, to allow insertion of the cartridge. (NA)

Left: Johnson's breech-loading carbine was even more novel. The whole breech twisted to allow insertion of the cartridge. It is shown here closed. Carbines like this were tested against the standard Sharps carbine. (NA)

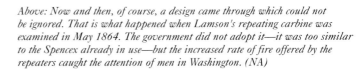

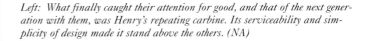

Above: Now and then, of course, a design came through which could not be ignored. That is what happened when Lamson's repeating carbine was examined in May 1864. The government did not adopt it—it was too similar to the Spencex already in use—but the increased rate of fire offered by the repeaters caught the attention of men in Washington. (NA)

Left: What finally caught their attention for good, and that of the next generation with them, was Henry's repeating carbine. Its serviceability and simplicity of design made it stand above the others. (NA)

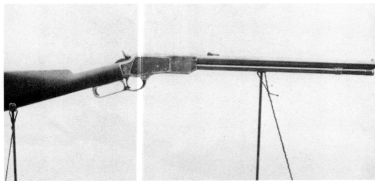

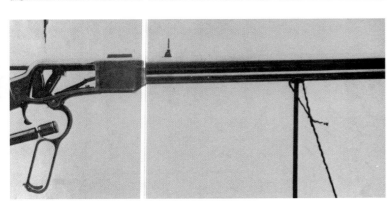

Above right: Equally important to the U.S. Government were the designs coming in for the bigger guns. The yard here at the Washington Arsenal was packed with all manner of cannon during the war, including the Wiard gun supporting the officers at right. (USAMHI)

Above left: Oliver F. Winchester, president of the New Haven Arms Company, who wanted to produce the Henry, was present for its trials. The carbine performed badly that first time out, but in time it would see limited use in the war and afterward it would be the progenitor of the "gun that won the West." (NA)

Left: Because a rifle, no matter what kind, was only as good as its sighting, experiments were made with telescopic sights for sharpshooters' weapons. This one was attached to an American rifle with the massive barrel used for big game like buffalo or for very long-range shooting. (NA)

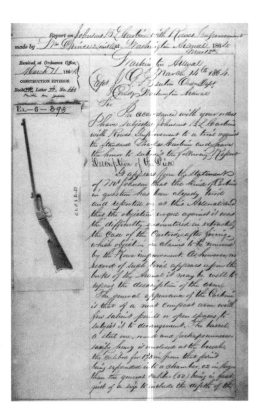

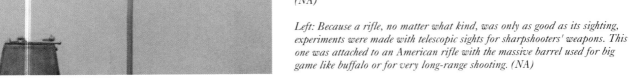

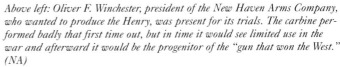

Left: Every army in the field had a chief of ordnance, officers like Union Captain Stephen Vincent Benet, grandfather of the distinguished American poet. They had to take what Washington sent them and keep it serviceable. (USAMHI)

Right: Massive seacoast cannon, like this 15-inch Dahlgren smoothbore, were cast and tested in Washington. Next door to the Dahlgren sits a huge Parrott rifle, its projectiles lined neatly about its carriage. (LC)

Left: The big guns were favorites for play and posing. It took a special gun cradle to transport them by rail, one that could support the 42,500 pounds of iron in such a weapon, not to mention the man inside. (MICHAEL J. HAMMERSON)

Right: Many of them were brought here to Fort Monroe, Virginia, for testing, firing at targets out in Hampton Roads. A cannon like this could hurl its 440-pound shot well over four miles. A Rodman smoothbore. (USAMHI)

Left: It took a special apparatus to move the big guns in the field. William Browne made this 1865 image of a captured Confederate 8-inch Brooke rifle slung from a huge Confederate sling cart. (CHS)

Right: Without one, a mammoth gun tube could not be managed. (USAMHI)

Above: And of course, whatever the size of the guns, the artillery required mountains of projectiles, like those in this scene at the Washington Arsenal made by Captain A. J. Russell, military photographer. Several projectile sizes are evident, including a stack of British Whitworth rifle solid bolts, probably 5-inch, directly in front of the men at left. In the background cannon and mortars and carriages and targets are scattered all about. (AIC)

Right: It was in U.S. Army laboratories like this one, at Sixth and Oxford streets in Philadelphia, that much of the ammunition was designed and even produced. The window at upper right sports a distinctly unmilitary adornment, a window box with plants. (LLOYD OSTEN-DORF COLLECTION)

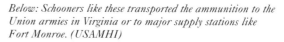

Below: Schooners like these transported the ammunition to the Union armies in Virginia or to major supply stations like Fort Monroe. (USAMHI)

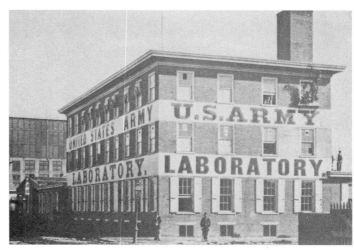

Above: The work of the inventors did not stop at small arms. They looked also to ammunition, with items such as Dodge's cartridge filler. By a series of shiftings and pumpings, powder was automatically placed in the tubes, ready to be topped with bullets and then wrapped in waxed paper. The War Department wisely did not adopt it. (NA)

Below: The so-called wire gun had a barrel made up largely of steel wire wrapped tightly around the bore. It was not an impressive success. (NA)

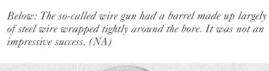

Left: Major testing for experimental new big guns for the Union armies was done either at Fort Monroe or in Washington. Here in the former, a cast-iron 15-inch Rodman sits ready for a series of stress tests. (NA)

Above: And here it is after one charge too many, a still-intact counterpart quietly awaiting its turn in the distance. (NA)

Below: A steel and iron gun fared no better. (NA)

Left: The rifling inside the bore shows handsomely in this "exploded" view of the pieces of the steel and iron gun. The ordnance testers were fascinated with the camera for recording the results of their experiments. (NA)

Above: This cast-iron cannon managed to stand up after 1,600 firings. That was more like it. (NA)

Right: The inventors never gave up. H. B. Mann stands here behind his new breech-loading cannon. This early version is being admired by an onlooker and his dog. Mann would refine it considerably before . . . (NA)

Above: Lee's breechloader fared no better. It went through U.S. Government trials in August 1865, with little hope of a contract now that the fighting was over. In the testing, the supervising officer revealed the prejudice against this type of weapon when he referred to "the arguments against breech-loading guns as a class." Washington learned slowly sometimes. (NA)

Above: . . . submitting it for testing by the U.S. Government in June 1865. By that time the war was done, of course, and Mann was out of luck. Just what he did with his 2,000-pound toy is unknown. (NA)

Above: Broadwell's breechloader was wonderfully simple. The slide sitting on the ammunition box was inserted in the slot in the side of the gun's breech. With the slide pulled out, the shell at left could be inserted into the barrel. Then the slide was pushed in behind it, sealing off the chamber ready for firing. In the distance above the barrel is a target used for testing. (NA)

Left: Broadwell's gun with the slide in place. (NA)

Left: It took constant attention to the projectiles those guns fired to keep the armies in the field well supplied. Shot and shell were experimented with just as much as cannon. The shells at bottom are fitted with experimental fuses, made up of the rings at the center, with the fuse plug at the upper left and right inserted using the tool in the top center. It all had to work. (NA)

Above: The Pevey shell was another such experiment, and one not adopted by the government. The soft tin or lead casing at its base was intended to expand into a gun's rifling grooves, to give the shell a spin as it emerged. (NA)

Left: And here another Pevey shell designed for antipersonnel work—a hollow sphere with powder in the center cavity and iron balls in the outer chamber. American inventors could create decidedly lethal concepts in their pursuit of profits. (NA)

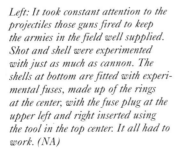

Left: Even the men in uniform, who had the most experience, after all, sometimes turned tinkerer. Philo Maltby of the 14th Ohio Artillery designed this Rotary Sight for siege or seacoast guns. It could adapt to changes in light and was on the whole very refined. Indeed, the examining officer complimented the inventor: "It was constructed by Artificer Maltby in the field with such tools as a soldier in his vocation would there have at his command, and whatever may be said of its adaptability to general service, certainly reflects great credit on his skill and perseverance." Having said that, the officer then concluded that Maltby's was "misdirected ingenuity," condemning all such attempts as "the efforts of a class of persons, ingenius [sic] and well meaning it may be, but who have mistaken the desideratum in the field of invention on which they have entered." The closed mind was already well entrenched in the U.S. military in August 1864. (NA)

Above: Items like the iron siege carriage for heavy guns got a little more attention, but proved to be simply too heavy for horses to pull. (NA)

Above: Real ingenuity came when the imagination tried to fire more than one shot at once. It produced specimens like the volley gun, a simple clustering of 121 barrels inside a cylinder and a breechblock containing 121 charges and bullets. (NA)

Above: The volley gun required a fair amount of special apparatus and, after all, only sent its hail of bullets out into a very limited area. (NA)

Right: Somewhat more to the point was the Requia battery, which actually saw limited service with the Union forces at Charleston, South Carolina. It was just twenty-five barrels side by side, with a strip of brass holding the charges and bullets inserted in the breech. The lanyard-controlled firing hammer is just visible at the rear center. (NA)

Left: If all these weapons of war worked even a fraction as well as their inventors expected, then there were going to be a lot of wounded. And so the designers tried also to perfect the ambulance. E. Hayes & Company of Wheeling, West Virginia, submitted this prototype army ambulance to the U.S. Government in February 1862. Besides being very attractively appointed, it also boasted two water or spirit casks built right into the back panel. (NA)

Above: And for those who did not survive the ingenious means of death being devised for them, the Union laid out cemeteries. It was all part of the job of a modern, organized army that left little to chance. Here in 1864 surveyors are at work laying out a major military cemetery . . . (NA)

Left: . . . on Arlington Heights, Virginia, across the Potomac from Washington. (NA)

Below: Here, on ground which had been the home of Confederate General Robert E. Lee, they began the work of what would become Arlington National Cemetery. From enlistment to arming to death, the organized war was complete. (NA)

"Damn the Torpedoes!"

CHARLES R. HABERLEIN, JR.

Ships of iron, and men to match, battle on an August morning for Mobile

There was a gleam in the eyes of Rear Admiral David Glasgow Farragut. When C. D. Fredericks photographed him in New York, the loyal old Tennessean was laden with glory from his capture of New Orleans and the opening of the Mississippi. In 1864 he wanted another assignment and looked to Mobile, Alabama. (WILLIAM GLADSTONE COLLECTION)

REAR ADMIRAL David Glasgow Farragut returned to the Gulf in January 1864. Refreshed by five months in the North, with his flagship *Hartford* refitted, he was eager to begin the next step in reducing the Confederacy's south coast.

Farragut had begun this work nearly two years previously by boldly running past the fortifications defending New Orleans. With the South's greatest seaport in Federal hands, he had continued with vigorous thrusts up the Mississippi River. Now but one important Rebel port remained on the long Gulf of Mexico shore.

Mobile, Alabama, with its fine rail and water links to the Confederate heartland, was a valuable asset to the South. Located at the head of large, shallow Mobile Bay, the port was well defended. On the mainland an earthwork, Fort Powell, guarded the bay's southwestern "back door." Between Dauphin Island on the west and Mobile Point on the east, on the bay's lower edge, the main entrance was flanked by twin antebellum masonry fortifications, Fort Gaines and Fort Morgan. Since 1861 additional batteries had been added to each. The waterway between them had been largely obstructed by driven pilings and moored mines, or "torpedoes," in the contemporary terminology. A few hundred feet of deep channel remained open, directly under Fort Morgan's heavy guns.

Through this channel passed fast little Confederate steamers with exports of cotton and imports of war-sustaining munitions. The blockade running trade was harassed, but not prevented, by Federal warships lurking offshore and cruising in the sea-lanes. Only direct occupation of the entryway would effectively blockade Mobile. To effect this was Farragut's intention.

Naval assaults on well-defended fortifications would not succeed without cooperating troops, and these were unavailable during the winter and spring of 1864. As the latter season progressed through May, another factor appeared on Mobile Bay: the new Confederate ironclad ram *Tennessee*. Her long-anticipated arrival provoked a brief outbreak of "ram fever" even in the intrepid Farragut. Fretting over the prospect of the Rebel ironclad steaming out into the Gulf, laying waste to the blockaders and perhaps even spearheading efforts to wrest Pensacola, Florida, and New Orleans, Louisiana, from their Northern occupiers, he badly wanted ironclads of his own.

Enemy plans worried the other side, too. Confederate Admiral Franklin Buchanan was ultimately too cautious for a dash into the Gulf. *Tennessee* and her three wooden consorts, the gunboats *Selma*, *Gaines*, and *Morgan*, remained inside the bay, assigned to help defend the forts.

Since his return, Farragut had bombarded the Navy Department with requests for ironclad monitors and army support. He did not delude himself about the response, writing a colleague: "The Government appears to plan the campaigns, and Mobile does not appear to be included just yet.... I shall have to content myself going along the coast and pestering all the people I can get at." The routine blockading and patrolling continued from the Rio Grande to Florida, occasionally punctuated by minor raids and counter raids.

Unknown to the West Gulf Blockading Squadron, Washington had in fact decided on Mobile. The end of the ill-conceived Red River expedition in May and lack of progress in capturing Charleston freed monitors for other employment.

Major General William Tecumseh Sherman's army, marching on Atlanta, needed diversionary support. In June orders went out to four Union monitors to proceed gulfward. Major General E. R. S. Canby, the area's army commander, received instructions from Washington to cooperate with the navy in a Union attack on Mobile.

Hints of these developments reached Farragut within a few weeks. Solid confirmation, in the form of the monitor USS *Manhattan*, steamed into Pensacola harbor early in July. With three more monitors on the way, Farragut and Canby perfected their plans.

Farragut's fleet was to steam past Fort Morgan into Mobile Bay and eliminate the Confederate squadron. Simultaneously, Union Army forces would land on Dauphin Island to assault Fort Gaines. If Fort Powell was taken, so much the better. Once communication was secured between the fleet inside, the logistics system outside, and the troops in between, Fort Morgan would be doomed. Canby put together a 2,000 man contingent with enough transports for the job and appointed Major General Gordon Granger to command them.

In the fleet, ships were coaled, stored, and stripped for action. Superfluous spars and rigging were taken down and stowed. Anchor chain, sandbags, and spare sails were worked in around vital spaces for additional protection. Guns were shifted to the right, or starboard, sides to increase the firepower bearing on Fort Morgan.

Farragut ordered his ships to double up. Each of the more powerful sloops of war would have a gunboat or smaller sloop lashed to its unengaged port side. The lighter ships could then pass into the bay protected by the thicker bulwarks and heavier armament of their partners. In return, the big ships received backup propulsion in case they were disabled.

The four monitors were instructed to stand inshore of—and parallel to—the sloops and gunboats and to bombard Fort Morgan vigorously, to suppress its fire and prevent the *Tennessee* from interfering. All ships were warned to stay east of the black buoys anchored a few hundred yards out from the Fort Morgan shore. These, it was correctly assumed, marked the location of the minefield. The fort's gunfire was less dangerous than a catastrophic explosion of a big torpedo.

Right: The Union had been interested in Mobile and its bay, center for Confederate West Gulf blockade-running operations, for some time. Converted "tinclad" steamers like the USS Elk *patrol led regularly off Mobile's waters. (USAMHI)*

Left: So did Union Major General E. R. S. Canby. After the fiasco of the Red River Campaign in May, his troops needed active and successful employment. A joint move against Mobile with the navy would serve the purpose. (USAMHI)

Above: Union blockaders in the Gulf were hard pressed for adequate bases and sometimes had to use far-flung spots like Florida's Fort Taylor on Key West. (USAMHI)

Above: Farragut, if he could, would make a Yankee base out of Mobile. In July 1864 he staged his mighty fleet in the Gulf, ready to move on Mobile Bay when the moment was right. Flagship of the fleet was his legendary Hartford, *here photographed by McPherson & Oliver, wearing the coat of gray paint used to make her less visible at sea. The first-class sloop appears shortly after her fight in Mobile Bay. (MARINERS MUSEUM)*

Right: Men like Lieutenant Commander George U. Morris, whose first ship, the USS Cumberland, *had been sunk by the Rebel ironclad* Virginia (Merrimack), *commanded the Port Royal in constant blockade duty off Mobile during 1864. (USAMHI)*

Left: Farragut leans against a howitzer on the poop deck of the Hartford, *with the ship's commander, Captain Percival Drayton, leaning against the opposite wheel. The two complemented each other perfectly, Drayton highly organized and efficient and Farragut brilliant, intuitive, and impatient for action. (NAVAL HISTORICAL CENTER)*

Above: Here McPherson & Oliver capture the Yankee fleet as it rests at anchor outside Mobile Bay, above the parapets of Fort Morgan. Though taken sometime after the battle, the photograph gives a fair idea of what the Confederates might have seen the day before the fight. (NA)

Below: Mobile's defenses had been well designed. Confederate Brigadier General Danville Leadbetter was a native of Maine and as an engineer in the U.S. Army and after 1857 as a civilian had spent years here building harbor works. In 1863 he returned to Mobile to supervise the defenses being erected by Southerners. (USAMHI)

Right: The Alabama shorefront bristled with water batteries like this captured Confederate one outside Fort Morgan, photographed by New Orleans artists Moses & Piffet in September 1864. (NA)

Granger's troops went ashore on Dauphin Island as planned, on the third of August, covered by several minor warships. Fort Gaines was immediately invested. However, the Union monitor *Tecumseh* arrived late, forcing postponement of the navy's mission. Farragut was mortified because he could not uphold his end of the plan, but admitted later that the delay was beneficial. During the intervening hours, the Confederates pushed reinforcements into Fort Gaines, where they were easily captured a few days later.

In the wee hours of August 5 the fleet formed up. An unfortunate change of plan, reluctantly adopted by Farragut, assigned the lead to the big sloop *Brooklyn*. Her forward-firing battery was heavier than his flagship *Hartford*'s, and she had a torpedo rake on her bow, presumably capable of fending off any mines encountered. The flagship took second position, followed by the other big sloop, *Richmond*. These three were paired with the fast, light-draft paddle-wheelers *Octorara*, *Metacomet*, and *Port Royal*. Once past the fort, these "double-ender" gunboats would be cast off to drive away the *Selma*, *Gaines*, and *Morgan*, which were of similar force.

Following the lead trio were four more pairs: sloops *Lackawanna* and *Seminole*, sloop *Monongahela* and gunboat *Kennebec*, smaller sloop *Ossipee* and gunboat *Itaska*, and, at the rear, small sloops *Oneida* and *Galena*. The ironclad squadron, parallel and inshore, was led by the single turret *Tecumseh*, followed by the identical *Manhattan*. Each had two 15-inch guns, the most effective weapons available for countering the *Tennessee*. Light-draft monitors *Winnebago* and *Chickasaw*, each with twin turrets and four 11-inch Dahlgren guns, completed the inshore force.

At 6 A.M. the lines of ships stood in over the bar and headed slowly toward Fort Morgan. Under cloudy skies, the westerly wind fluttered battle ensigns out from every masthead and peak. The flood tide would help carry the ships past the fort, and the breeze was just right for blowing dense black-powder smoke directly into Confederate gunners' eyes. Conditions were virtually ideal for Farragut's scheme.

In Fort Morgan, Brigadier General Richard L. Page sent his men to their guns. Nearly twenty heavy smoothbores and rifled cannon and a similar number of medium guns prepared to rake the ships as they approached, bludgeon their sides as they passed, and rake them again as they stood up into Mobile Bay. Admiral Buchanan, on board the *Tennessee*, hovered near the fort's north side, ready to attack any Union ships that got past the batteries. Farther north his three gunboats were positioned to fire freely at oncoming Federals with little risk of effective reply. A short distance out in the channel the torpedoes waited silently.

Fort Morgan boomed out its initial challenge at six minutes past seven. *Brooklyn*'s 100-pounder Parrott bow rifles answered, followed by *Hartford*'s. Other ships opened up as they came into range. Farragut had climbed into the mainmast rigging of his ship, the better to see over the gunsmoke. From there he had good communication with his pilot in the maintop, with *Hartford*'s captain on the quarterdeck, and with *Metacomet*'s commander alongside. Below the admiral the twelve broadside gun crews stood by, ready to throw 9-inch shells as soon as Fort Morgan loomed into their field of fire. On the fore castle, Parrott-rifle gunners were already loading another round.

The monitor *Manhattan*, second in her line, began slow fire from her one serviceable 15-inch gun. The whole ship shuddered as the piece discharged. Thick smoke wafted down into the hull below the turret. From there, smoke penetrated the hot, poorly ventilated machinery spaces, where conditions were so hellish that sweating coal heavers and engineers required frequent relief. Smoke was so intense topside that the captain, in his tiny conning tower over the turret, could see his consorts and target only with difficulty.

The commanders of the faster-firing double turret monitors elected to conn from out in the

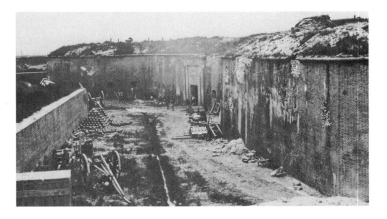

Above: Another front view of the fort shows a row of mortars awaiting emplacement, several Union soldiers with their arms stacked, and on the horizon the badly battered lighthouse. (CHS)

Below: The southwest face looks much the same, battered and damaged, belying the tranquil form of the lounger in the foreground. (CHS)

Left: The front and west side of Fort Morgan shows a little less damage, but the poor lighthouse seems barely able to stand. (USAMHI)

Right: On August 5, 1864, Farragut, seated right, ordered his fleet to steam past Fort Morgan's batteries and into the bay. Drayton, left, was flag captain for the day, commanding the Hartford. *(NHC)*

open, where vision was better. *Chickasaw*'s young captain, George H. Perkins, was so excited that he stood atop one of his turrets "waving his hat and dancing about with delight and excitement." Despite the heavy surrounding cannonade, neither he nor Winnebago's captain were touched.

In the leader, *Tecumseh*, Commander T. A. M. Craven sent off a pair of heavy shells at the very start of the engagement, then reloaded with solid shot and the heaviest powder charges. He was saving his power for the *Tennessee*.

Buchanan watched the Union lines nearing the midpoint of their passage, exchanging a spirited fire with Fort Morgan. He ordered his ponderous ship into motion out into the channel, only a few hundred yards from the *Tecumseh*. Craven turned to port to intercept. Through his conning tower slits he saw a black buoy ahead, seemingly closer inshore than it should have been. Obsessed with stopping the *Tennessee*, he set his course just to the west of the buoy and in the path of the second column of slower-moving ships.

Brooklyn's captain James Alden was surprised and confused by Craven's move. He signaled the flagship: "The monitors are right ahead. We can not go on without passing them. What shall we do?" Farragut was also perplexed. His orders were very clear. Nothing was to prevent the column's advance. Slowing or stopping under the intense fire of the fort risked disaster. The ironclads had been strictly enjoined to keep out of the wooden ships' way. Now, five hundred yards ahead, the *Tecumseh* had turned into his path, and the *Brooklyn* was turning, too.

Suddenly, in what seemed only a matter of seconds, *Tecumseh* shuddered, lurched from side to side, pitched bow down, capsized, and disappeared. Then the *Brooklyn* stopped and began backing hard. Her lookouts had spotted torpedoes in the channel just ahead.

All the careful plans were collapsing, as the battle line began to pile up behind the wayward *Brooklyn*. The ironclads blocked the right-hand route. Above the surface, only the course through the minefield lay clear.

Farragut offered up a hasty prayer for guidance and received the only answer consistent with his character: "Go on!" He called out to those below: "Damn the torpedoes! Four bells!"

Responding to this order, *Hartford*'s engines went ahead full. *Metacomet* backed hard. The two

Above: The USS Hartford's *helm, manned just as it was that morning of the attack, with, left to right, Seaman Joseph Cassier, Captain of the Forecastle John McFarland, Landsman James Reddington, and Quartermaster James Wood. McFarland in particular distinguished himself, receiving the Medal of Honor for outstanding performance of his duty in the battle. (NHC)*

Above: Here men of the Hartford's *after guard pose near one of her 9-inch guns. Directly behind them, rising out of the picture, are the mizzen shrouds where Farragut placed himself during the battle with the ironclad* Tennessee. *(NHC)*

Above: The Hartford's *gun deck, by McPherson & Oliver. The starboard battery of 9-inch Dahlgrens is at the right, these being the guns that engaged Fort Morgan during the passage of the fleet. Here was done terrible carnage among Farragut's gun crews. The two of officers standing at the left are Lieutenants George Mundy and La Rue P. Adams, who commanded most of those guns. Adams himself was wounded. (NHC)*

ships pivoted to port, the double-ender put her engines back ahead, and the two sped past the *Brooklyn* into the lines of torpedoes. At that instant, two shells struck *Hartford*'s battery directly below the admiral's perch, sweeping away most of two gun crews. While the survivors silently removed the bodies of their comrades and brought their guns back into action, other men felt the torpedoes thudding against the hull. Some thought they heard primers snapping.

Nothing happened. Apparently the mine cases were leaky, and their powder had been rendered inert.

Leaving a boat to rescue the *Tecumseh*'s few survivors, *Hartford* and *Metacomet* pressed northward. *Tennessee* tried to ram them, but was evaded amid an exchange of broadsides. Fire from the Confederate gunboats was more serious. All three peppered the *Hartford* freely, since her bow guns could engage but one enemy ship at a time. One of these rifles was soon knocked out. Another shell exploded between the two foremost broadside guns, causing severe casualties. Again *Hartford*'s dead and wounded were quickly removed and the two guns returned to action.

Bearing this murderous fire for several painful minutes, the *Hartford* finally reached a point where her broadside would bear on the enemy. Successive discharges put *Morgan*, *Gaines*, and *Selma* to flight. The *Metacomet* shot off in pursuit, running down and capturing the *Selma* within an hour. The mortally injured *Gaines* beached herself to avoid sinking. Only the *Morgan* survived; sheltering under the fort's protection until nightfall, she escaped up the bay in the darkness.

West of Fort Morgan, it was about 8 A.M. when *Brooklyn* got the situation sorted out and started forward again. Her captain's indecision had left her the center of attention for the Rebel gunners, who made many damaging hits on her battery, hull, and rigging. Astern, the *Richmond* was hardly struck at all. Both rapidly steamed up the channel, engaging the *Tennessee* in turn. Once clear of that enemy, they also sent their consorts off to chase the fleeing Confederate gun boats.

The intense fire of the monitors and leading three sloops apparently drove many of Fort Morgan's gunners under cover, for the next three

Above: Captain James Alden was supposed to take the lead with his sloop Brooklyn, *but he ran into a problem and caused considerable confusion before* Hartford *surged on past him. He and the admiral were never very friendly again. (NHC)*

Above: The USS Ossipee, *photographed at Honolulu in 1867, was a light sloop that Farragut stationed toward the rear of his line as it braved Fort Morgan's guns. She suffered almost no damage at all. (NHC)*

Left: This Winnebago-*class monitor is probably the* Kickapoo, *sistership of the monitors* Chickasaw *and* Winnebago *that brought up the rear of Farragut's line. Neither the admiral nor the monitors' commanders had too much faith in them, and* Winnebago *was nearly put out of action in the battle. The* Kickapoo *joined the fleet at Mobile some weeks after the battle. (U.S. MILITARY ACADEMY, WEST POINT)*

Left: Only one ship was actually crippled by Confederate fire, the sloop Oneida *commanded by Commander J. R. Madison Mullany. He had begged to get into the action that day, and Farragut temporarily assigned him to the* Oneida. *Fire from the CSS* Tennessee *damaged his left arm so badly that it had to be amputated. (NHC)*

Right: One of the greatest heroes of the fight, however, was Ensign Henry C. Nields of Metacomet. *When the USS* Tecumseh *hit a mine and sank, he took a boat out into the channel under heavy fire to rescue her survivors. He saved ten of them. (NHC)*

Above: The most feared enemy for Farragut were not the mines—called "torpedoes"—but the dreaded Rebel ironclad Tennessee, *shown here after her surrender in a photo probably made in New Orleans. Built like almost all Confederate ironclads, she had the strengths and weaknesses of her type. Her four 6.4-inch and two 7-inch Brooke rifles were no match for some of Farragut's heavy cannon. (LC)*

Above: Still, she was a formidable vessel and well handled under the command of a real veteran of ironclad warfare . . . (NHC)

Right: . . . Admiral Franklin Buchanan. He it was who commanded the CSS Virginia *in her fight with the* Cumberland *two years before, taking a wound in the battle. In the fight with Farragut, Buchanan's leg was badly shattered. (NHC)*

pairs of wooden ships passed through with modest damage. Rearguard *Oneida*, smallest of the sloops, received a redoubled fire. In a rain of shot and shell, her starboard boiler was hit and exploded, scalding many of her engineers. The other boiler supplied some steam to the engine, and with the *Galena* gamely pulling at full power, the *Oneida* was able to continue on, pursued by enemy fire until out of range.

Tennessee continued to contest the passage of the follow-up ships. Too slow for successful employment of her ram, she fired as rapidly as a four-gun maximum broadside and unreliable gun primers permitted, making some hits. One hit badly injured long-suffering *Oneida*'s captain. The ironclad received in return a forceful but ineffective ramming from the *Monongahela* and a number of inconsequential shot hits from the wooden fleet. By 8:40 *Tennessee* had been left behind and returned to the fort to assess the situation.

Farragut had achieved his initial objective. His fleet had entered Mobile Bay, still fit for action. The bay was now closed to enemy use. The forts were isolated. Only the *Tennessee* remained as an unpredictable factor, and he could deal with her in due time. His ships anchored in the pocket of deep water northwest of Fort Morgan and prepared to stand down from the tension and horror of the early morning.

Within minutes, however, lookouts saw the *Tennessee* steaming toward them. Admiral Buchanan had decided to expend her modest coal supply in a desperate last attempt to prevent the loss of Mobile Bay. Even if this failed to destroy the Union fleet, he reasoned, his ironsided ship could still return to Fort Morgan and do what she could to buy time for strengthening the upbay defenses.

It was a forlorn hope. Farragut quickly sent *Lackawanna* and *Monongahela* off to intercept and ram the enemy ironclad while the rest of the fleet got ready. Receiving his orders to engage, *Chickasaw*'s Perkins almost somersaulted overboard with joy. Exuberant as he appeared, Perkins' cool conduct in the following hour largely determined the outcome.

The *Monongahela* went full speed at the *Tennessee*, hit her sharply on the starboard side, shuddered to a halt, and backed away. She

Above: Buchanan's chief adversary was Commander James Strong, who brought his sloop Monongahela *in close and repeatedly rammed the Rebel ironclad with his specially prepared prow. This portrait is by Gurney & Son of New York. (CIVIL WAR TIMES ILLUSTRATED COLLECTION)*

Left: And all the while, Fort Morgan's guns were bombarding the Union fleet as it passed. The fort's batteries were so arranged that Farragut had either to risk coming in close to them and taking a heavy shelling or passing through a more distant channel filled with torpedoes. By accident he chose the latter. Fort Morgan itself came in for its share of bombardment later on. (NA)

Right: An elevated view of the fort shows the extensive damage it suffered from the land bombardment on August 22 that followed Farragut's passage. Like all masonry forts in the war, Fort Morgan did not stand up well under siege artillery. (CHS)

received a crushed bow and two shots into the berth deck for her trouble. *Tennessee* seemed unscathed. *Lackawanna* followed with a similar blow to the ironclad's other beam, with like result. The opponents exchanged shots, musketry, insults, and thrown debris as they separated.

Close behind, the *Hartford* also tried to ram, but struck obliquely. Her unshipped anchor took the blow and was bent beyond use. Ironclad and sloop passed port side to port side, a few feet apart. Admiral Farragut watched from an impromptu battle station in the port mizzen shrouds as *Hartford*'s massed 9-inch smoothbores blasted away with solid shot and heavy charges, making a negligible impression on *Tennessee*'s iron casemate. The latter's low-set broadside discharged directly into the *Hartford*'s berth deck, causing heavy casualties among her ammunition party. Farragut's flagship steamed away to try again, but collided with the *Lackawanna*. The battle was over for both of them, though their injuries were not crippling.

The Federal monitors arrived. A Confederate officer watched as "a hideous-looking monster came creeping up on our Port side, whose slowly revolving turret revealed the cavernous depths of a mammoth gun." It was the *Manhattan*. Only one of her 15-inchers worked that day, but it made damaging hits, smashing away armor plate, crushing backing timbers and shocking the enemy with the force of her blows. The *Chickasaw* doggedly clung to the *Tennessee*'s flanks, hammering away at the aft part of her casemate with 11-inch shot. Other ships fired from a distance. In less than half an hour, *Tennessee*'s steering was destroyed, her smokestack knocked away, most of her gunport shutters jammed and her casemate smashed nearly to collapse.

Inside, Admiral Buchanan and a working party were trying to clear one of the after port shutters, so some reply could be made. A shot hit directly opposite them. Despite armor, the concussion and splinters devastated those nearby. Two men were killed and Buchanan's leg so badly broken that he had to be carried below.

Left: The bombardment made a mess of its parapets. (NA)

Right: The so-called citadel of Fort Morgan, viewed from the south by McPherson & Oliver, shows the collapsed roofs and toppled chimneys of a beleaguered fortress. The Confederate gunners did not dare serve their guns on the top tier. (KA)

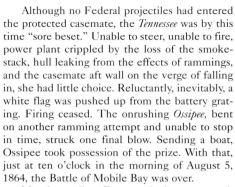

Although no Federal projectiles had entered the protected casemate, the *Tennessee* was by this time "sore beset." Unable to steer, unable to fire, power plant crippled by the loss of the smokestack, hull leaking from the effects of rammings, and the casemate aft wall on the verge of falling in, she had little choice. Reluctantly, inevitably, a white flag was pushed up from the battery grating. Firing ceased. The onrushing *Ossipee*, bent on another ramming attempt and unable to stop in time, struck one final blow. Sending a boat, Ossipee took possession of the prize. With that, just at ten o'clock in the morning of August 5, 1864, the Battle of Mobile Bay was over.

Months earlier, Farragut had commented: "How unequal the contest is between ironclads and wooden vessels in loss of life." How correct he was. His fleet had suffered more than fifty men killed, nearly half of them on his own flag ship, plus over ninety souls carried down with the torpedoed *Tecumseh*. Confederate casual ties were almost trivial by comparison: a dozen killed in the ships, one man dead in the fort.

But battles are not decided on "points." The Southern squadron had been swept away. Within a few days, Fort Powell had been evacuated and Fort Gaines surrendered. On August 23, after General Granger's siege lines reached Fort Morgan's walls and heavy shellfire threatened to destroy its garrison inside inadequate "bombproof" bunkers, General Page capitulated. Mobile city remained in Confederate hands nearly until war's end, but its value to the Confederacy was gone.

Strategically, the Battle of Mobile Bay was a sideshow to the vast campaigns then underway in Georgia and Virginia. Even within the blockading effort, it was not more than a junior partner to the greater undertakings at Charleston, South Carolina, and Wilmington, North Carolina. The numbers of men and ships involved were slight— a few thousand troops and a modest fraction of the navy on the Northern side, even fewer on the Confederate. Mobile's neutralization was simply another ratchet notch in the great Union windlass that was by then inexorably reeling in the South.

However, this August morning with Farragut provides a peerless object lesson in the benefits of close, friendly cooperation between army and navy. Most importantly, it is an unexcelled in stance of inspired leadership and heroic determination. More than a century later, it still commands attention and respect.

Above: Instead, they had to hide below in equally unstable "bombproofs" while the Yankees sent shell after shell at them. (KA)

Left: It proved very frustrating indeed for the fort's commander, Brigadier General Richard L. Page of Virginia. He had been a captain in the Confederate Navy, then switched to the Army. Fort Morgan was to be his only command. He stands here with his family. (WILLIAM ALBAUGH COLLECTION)

Below:Part of the interior of the fort shows a reinforced bombproof and sandbagged parapet, hasty measures to futilely resist the enemy's heavy siege guns. (NA)

Above: The main gate, or sally port, of Fort Morgan. Even though the damage from the bombardment is not yet cleaned up, already the conquering Yankees have built ornamental shot pyramids beside the portals. A giant gun sling stands at far right. (NA)

Left: The parade of the fort looks like a wasteland after its surrender. (NA)

Below: The Civil War almost ended the era of the masonry seacoast fortification, and the damage done to Fort Morgan shows why. Page and his garrison were fortunate to hold long enough to surrender without being buried alive. (NA)

Above: Their guns, like this 8-inch British Blakely, were no match for what the Yankees could throw at them. (NA)

Above: Fort Morgan's southeast bastion in September 1864, the guns now silent, looked out upon nothing but the quarters of some of the victorious Federals. (KA)

Right: The fort's once thundering parapet is now a place for loungers and sightseers. (NA)

Above: There they could see the damage done to this dismounted Columbiad by accurate Yankee fire. (NA)

Above: They could also view the whole scene of destruction and read in it some metaphor for the doom of the Confederacy. (KA)

Left: Fort Morgan was a great scene of devastation, so overwhelming that McPherson & Oliver could not stop photographing it, though some of their shots were becoming redundant. (KA)

Above: Though not itself a target, the lighthouse on Mobile Point, near the fort, was particularly damaged by shots that went high and passed over the fort. In the distance stands a makeshift signal tower, while at the foot of the lighthouse sits the hot-shot furnace. Out on the parapet, men have placed comfortable chairs to enjoy the midday air and sea breezes. (KA)

Right: Somehow the battered lighthouse seems symbolic of the fallen fortress and of the Southern cause for independence that by this time was teetering in precarious balance. (NA)

Right: While Farragut handled the naval end of the victory at Mobile Bay, it was Major General Gordon Granger, a hero of Chickamauga, who besieged Fort Morgan into submission. (USAMHI)

Below: The fort surrendered on August 23, 1864, almost three weeks after the naval battle was over. After the surrender Farragut and Granger met for a camera sitting, having offered in their operations a model of Army-Navy cooperation not often emulated . Granger's commanding officer, Major General E. R. S. Canby, would remark later that "the relations that have existed between the two services . . . have been of the most intimate and cordial character and have resulted in successes of which friends of both the Army and the Navy have reason to be proud."

Above left: It was a welcome rest when the operations for Mobile Bay were complete, and officers of the USS Hartford could relax on deck. All of these men were aboard during the battle. They are ensigns, lieutenants, and surgeons and a captain of marines. It is a well-earned rest. (NHC)

Above right: Later the old USS Potomac, *a sailing frigate more than thirty years old, played host to the captured officers of the Rebel ironclad* Tennessee. *Too old for active fighting, the proud old wooden ship played its support role to the end. (USAMHI)*

Right: As for the CSS Tennessee, *there will be no rest for her. Here she is in New Orleans, being refitted to go into service as the USS* Tennessee. *Having done their best to destroy her, her captors are now ready to add the ship to the ever-growing arsenal of Union naval might. (USAMHI)*

Houghton at the Front

A PORTFOLIO

**The little-known Vermont photographer
G. H. Houghton went to the war in 1862
for an unforgettable series**

AS WITH SO MANY of the war's camera artists, little is known of the Green Mountain photographer G. H. Houghton, of Brattleboro, Vermont. This is all the more unfortunate given the unusually high quality of his work. In at least two trips to the Virginia front in early 1862 and early 1863, Houghton made nearly a hundred images that survive, and probably more that do not. He photographed Vermont soldiers on the Peninsula in what was a considerable change of pace for an artist whose usual work was outdoor scenes of his native state. But Houghton was an unusual artist. Though few hometown photographers went any farther than the army camps when they came to the war zone, Houghton went beyond the camps and took his camera very close indeed to the front. And unlike those of many of his contemporaries, his war views eschewed the modest carte de visite format and appeared instead in large, beautifully detailed prints which he marketed back home in Brattleboro.

A brave, able, and innovative artist, G. H. Houghton of Vermont exemplified the hundreds of unknown photographers who recognized that in this war lay the greatest event of their generation, something worth the effort and the danger to record.

Above: "Photographer's Home," Houghton called this scene. It was one seen throughout the war-torn country— the itinerant artist's tent studio or hastily erected "Picture Gallery," ready to capture for the boys in blue or gray their likenesses. Houghton's establishment here at Camp Griffin, Virginia, was a bit different, however, for he came to record the look of his fellow Vermonters in the field as they battled on the Peninsula in the spring of 1862. (VERMONT HISTORICAL SOCIETY)

Right: Few photographers of the war could surpass Houghton's ability with the lens. There was a tranquillity about his work that belied the deadly business that populated these tents with fighting men around Brigadier General William F. Smith's headquarters at Camp Griffin. (VHS)

Left: Houghton, in fact, began chronicling the career of Green Mountain soldiers even before they left home. Here he records the camp of the 1st Vermont near Brattleboro. (VHS)

Below: And now, down in Virginia, he captures the scene of the 4th Vermont in Camp Griffin, the regiment drawn up, company after company, off to the left, while their band prepares to enspirit them with martial song. (VHS)

Below: Houghton caught the 16th Vermont in their "winterized" tents at Union Mills. (VHS)

Above: The 2d Vermont was here in Camp Griffin, too, less formal for the camera. The man in the center of the standing group appears to hold a newspaper. (VHS)

Left: And the men of the 12th Vermont at Wolf Run Shoals. The men of Company B are ready for a hard winter. The leaves have left the trees, and already the stumps left by ravenous firewood parties testify to the cold. (VHS)

Above: The 3d Vermont camp in Virginia revealed an unusual, if rude, bit of construction, probably a stable for the wagon teams or a commissary store-house. It would not provide much obstruction to the wind. (VHS)

Left: Company A of the 13th Vermont went into camp directly next to a bat-tery it was supporting. Between clearing the woods for a field of fire for the can-non, and foraging for firewood, the for-est is representative of the devastation done to Virginia's woodlands by the war. (VHS)

Below: The 6th Vermont made its headquarters here at Camp Griffin, its bandsmen standing proudly—if somewhat chilly in their great coats—with their instruments. (VHS)

Above: Houghton turned his camera to the places where power stayed, like General Smith's headquarters at a place called Becky Lee's Opening. (VHS)

Right: Smith's favorite campaign horse made a more than fitting subject for the lens, seemingly as casual about the camera as the young "contraband" holding his head. (VHS)

Below: The generals themselves, as always, were happy to pose for Houghton. Brigadier General William F. Smith, standing in the center, a Vermonter, was soon to command a division in the VI Corps. His hat conceals the thin hair that led to his nickname "Baldy." Standing at the right is Brigadier General John Newton, a Virginian who remained loyal to the Union. And at the left is Brigadier General Winfield Scott Hancock. Eighteen years from now he will narrowly lose a bid for the presidency to another former Civil War general, James A. Garfield. (VHS)

Right: Hancock himself made his headquarters under this mulberry tree at Cold Harbor, Virginia. He sits at the left of the shadowy group under its branches. (VHS)

Below right: And he sits at the left here, too, legs crossed and looking casual as he is joined by one of his fellow brigade commanders in Smith's division, Brigadier General William T. H. Brooks, seated next to him. Ironically, in 1864, even before the war was over, Brooks resigned his commission and began farming —in Alabama! (VHS)

Left: Houghton turned his camera to a group of officers in Fort Lincoln that winter as well. Colonel Hiram Berdan, leader of the famed Berdan's Sharpshooters, leans backward (left center) against the cannon tube. Leaning on it with him, his foot on the carriage trail, is Brigadier General John W. Davidson, a native Virginian now commanding a brigade in Smith's division. (VHS)

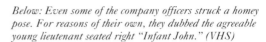
Below: Even some of the company officers struck a homey pose. For reasons of their own, they dubbed the agreeable young lieutenant seated right "Infant John." (VHS)

Above: For all the attention he gave the officers, Houghton was really more interested in the common soldiers. He came to the camp of Company F, 4th Vermont, where the Green Mountain boys agreeably struck the variety of camp poses that the people back home liked to see. (VHS)

Above: Sergeant Rogers' men of Company A, 4th Vermont, look suitably rustic. It is to be hoped that the tiny tent was not supposed to hold all four of them. (VHS)

Above: Houghton caught the teamsters and mechanics attached to Smith's headquarters at their work. All manner of tools—shovels, wagon jacks, axes, and mauls—litter the ground at the left; a portable forge and smithy stands at the far right. (VHS)

Right: Regimental bands like that of the 4th Vermont were always happy to dress up for the camera. (VHS)

Right: Less formally attired, the bandsmen relax in camp amid their instruments and boxes of "pilot bread" (hard tack) like the one making a seat for the soldier at the left. (VHS)

Below: One might have expected a lot of sour notes from all those dour Vermont faces. (VHS)

Right: But dour or no, these Vermonters could look splendid when they wanted to. The 12th Vermont presents an immaculate line for Houghton at Wolf Run Shoals. (VHS)

Left: Company A of the 4th Vermont looks formidable indeed as they pose at charge of bayonet. Yet there is still a lot of innocence in some of those young faces. War has not yet hardened them. (VHS)

Below left: One of Smith's batteries runs through its drill. (VHS)

Below right: And here Houghton views a so-called masked battery of 10-pounder Parrott rifles near the Golding farm on the Peninsula. (VHS)

Left: Houghton, like other photographers, did not focus his lens on actual battle scenes, but he did follow the army's movements a little in Virginia. Here he shows part of one regiment breaking camp near Newport News, the wagons loading tents and equipment for the march. (VHS)

Above: Here an entire battery stands in position, banner flying and officers leaning on their swords. This is dress rehearsal for the sake of the camera, not the way they would look in battle. (VHS)

Above: And here at Lee's Mill, Houghton watches as a battery of Major General Romeyn Ayres's Union artillery crosses an earth dam built by the Confederates. Defenses once occupied by the enemy show in the background. (VHS)

Above: The previous image must have been taken sometime after this one was made, showing the same scene from a different angle. Houghton later claimed that the Rebels were still in their works when he exposed this negative. If so, the graycoats were acting very camera shy. (VHS)

Left: Houghton also looked at some of the country through which his Vermont compatriots tramped and fought, finding some marvelous scenes like this one of Ford's old mill at Wolf Run Shoals. Soldiers are popping out of the windows. (VHS)

Right: He found this slave family at the Gaines house, facing untold changes in their lives in the years to come. (VHS)

Below: Alas, it was the most oft-repeated scene of the war. Men of the 6th Vermont, alive just before the fight at Lee's Mill, are now reduced to names on rude head boards in the Virginia soil. (VHS)

Above: And Houghton found some Vermont boys for whom life's last change had just taken place. Soldiers stand quietly, out of respect for their dead comrades at Camp Griffin. (VHS)

Left: There they would wait until their government or their families could have them brought home. (VHS)

Right: Happily for those who lived, there was a return to home as well, and to a jubilant reception. Here the 4th Vermont comes home to Brattleboro, their uniforms and posture showing that they are hardened veterans now. It is no wonder that the admiring schoolboys cluster and caper around them. They are all local heroes. And so, too, is G. H. Houghton, who went to war with them and brought home the record of their time of trial. (VHS)

The Great March

JOHN G. BARRETT

"From Atlanta to the sea" and on through
the Carolinas, the indomitable Sherman
could not be stopped

Above: On the march again. Major General William T. Sherman would not stop with the capture of Atlanta in early September 1864. There was the rest of Georgia to conquer and a war to win. (NEW YORK HISTORICAL SOCIETY)

IN THE LATE AUTUMN of 1864 Major General William T. Sherman with 62,000 men; 35,000 horses, mules, and cattle; 2,500 wagons; 600 ambulances; and a horde of followers marched across the heart of Georgia, leveling much of the countryside and demoralizing the civilian population. This campaign, from Atlanta to Savannah, known as the "March to the Sea," was but one part of a larger operation which had begun the previous May at Chattanooga, Tennessee, and was to end near Durham, North Carolina, in April 1865.

Only in the mountains of northwest Georgia and around Atlanta did the Federal army meet sustained resistance. Thus the moves from Atlanta to the coast and up through the Carolinas were important for reasons other than victories on the battlefield. Their primary significance rests upon the fact that these campaigns provided a glimpse of what later was called "total war."

Two years earlier, while on duty in western Tennessee, Sherman had evolved his philosophy of total war. Concluding that it was impossible to change the hearts of the people of the South, he decided that he could "make war so terrible" that Southerners would exhaust all peaceful remedies before starting another conflict. He stated that while the Southern people "cannot be made to love us, [they] can be made to fear us and dread the passage of troops through their country." Considering all of the people of the South as enemies of the Union, Sherman planned to use his military forces against the civilian population as well as against the armies of the enemy. He believed this plan of action would demoralize not only the noncombatants but also the men under arms. His program of warfare also called for the destruction of the enemy's economic resources. In bringing the war to the home front he hoped to destroy the South's will to fight. With Sherman war was not "popularity seeking." War was "hell." Still, it was not a sense of cruelty and barbarism that prompted him to formulate his new theory of war. It was more a search for the quickest and surest means to end a bloody conflict.

The first application of this new philosophy of war was to be in Mississippi. In Georgia and the Carolinas, however, Sherman repeated the performance but on a much larger scale.

On November 15, 1864, Sherman's army moved out of Atlanta, which had been in its possession since early September, to begin the March to the Sea. This move was a bold, imaginative stroke, but not one designed to draw off enemy troops. Confederate General John Bell Hood, after losing Atlanta, had hoped, by assuming the offensive in late September and marching for Tennessee, to checkmate his foe. But Sherman, after a futile pursuit, decided to abandon the chase and to move, instead, into the interior of Georgia "to smash things up." So in mid-November one of the curiosities of the war occurred. This date found the two main armies in the Western theater, bitter antagonists for three years, purposely moving in opposite directions, never to meet again.

The Federal army on its March to the Sea was divided into two parts. Major General Oliver O. Howard commanded the right wing which was composed of the XV and XVII Corps commanded respectively by Major Generals Peter J. Osterhaus and Francis P. Blair, Jr. The left wing, under Major General Henry W. Slocum, consisted of Brigadier General Jefferson C. Davis' XIV Corps and Brigadier General Alpheus S. Williams' XX Corps. The cavalry was led by Brigadier General Hugh Judson Kilpatrick.

This army marched from Atlanta in three parallel columns, five to fifteen miles apart, and forming a thirty- to sixty-mile front. Averaging ten to fifteen miles a day, it pushed relentlessly toward the coast. The right wing moved through Jonesboro and then to Monticello, Gordon, and Irwinton. The left wing headed toward Covington, Madison, Eatonton, and Milledgeville, the state capital. In the meantime, Kilpatrick's cavalry struck toward Macon and then withdrew to Gordon and rejoined Sherman at Milledgeville. The general was traveling with the left wing. By November 23 Slocum's entire command was united in and around the capital city. The right wing was close by at Gordon, twelve miles to the south.

In Milledgeville the governor's mansion, which served as Sherman's headquarters, and the capitol were spared the torch by the Federal soldiers. The penitentiary, arsenal, and depot, however, were destroyed by the men in blue, who also took great delight in holding a mock session of the Georgia legislature. They declared the ordinance of secession repealed and voted the state back into the Union.

The next day the march resumed. Sherman accompanied the XX Corps which took the direct road to Sandersville. This small community was reached simultaneously with the XIV Corps two days later. Earlier, Howard's right wing had started its movement along the Georgia Central Railroad toward the coast, tearing up the track as it went. By December 10 all four of the Federal corps had reached the vicinity of Savannah.

When Sherman learned that the city's defenses had recently been strengthened by the arrival of 15,000 troops under Lieutenant General William J. Hardee, he decided that before launching an attack he should first establish contact with the Federal fleet in Ossabaw Sound, south of the city. The quickest route to the water was along the banks of the Ogeechee River which flowed into the sound. But on the south side of the Ogeechee, near its mouth and fifteen miles from Savannah, stood small yet formidable Fort McAllister.

Above: And now his goal would be one of the loveliest cities in all the South, a perfect jewel untouched by the ravages of the war, Savannah. George N. Barnard captured this image of the peaceful river town shortly after the war. (LC)

Above: It was a rested and ready army that Sherman led on its March to the Sea. A close friend from Missouri, Major General Francis Preston Blair, Jr., commanded the XVII Corps. Seated here in the center with his staff, Blair finished the war a bankrupt, having spent himself dry in behalf of the Union cause. (USAMHI)

Left: Leading the XIV Corps was Brevet Major General Jefferson C. Davis, a veteran of the ill-fated defense of Fort Sumter in April 1861, a man who had shot and killed—some said murdered—a fellow Union general in an argument, and a fighter of unquestioned ability. He sits, gloves and sword in hand, among his staff in a photograph made in Washington in July 1865. (USAMHI)

Above: One of the foremost non-West Point-trained officers of the war led the XV Corps after January 8, 1865, as the Union Army made its way north from Savannah. Major General John A. Logan was a politician with a natural bent for war. In this portrait made at war's end, he wears mourning crape for President Lincoln on his sleeve, and a X V Corps badge on his blouse. (CWTI)

Right: The men that these and other generals led would really decide the outcome of the campaign, and they were the raw, toughened Western fighters who had already been blooded at places like Shiloh and Chichamauga. "In my judgment," said Sherman, they were "the most magnificent army in existence." (USAMHI)

Above: Brigadier General Alpheus S. Williams temporarily commanded the XX Corps on the March to the Sea. He wears on his blouse the star badge of his corps. (USAMHI)

Sherman ordered Brigadier General William B. Hazen's division to cross the river and take the fort. The successful assault, lasting barely fifteen minutes, took place late on the afternoon of December 13 under the approving eyes of General Sherman who remained on the north bank of the Ogeechee. Hazen's casualties were three times those of the enemy. Still, he managed to capture the entire Confederate garrison along with fifteen guns.

That night, aboard the gunboat Dandelion in Ossabaw Sound, Sherman wrote Secretary of War Edwin Stanton that he regarded "Savannah as already gained," and so it was. Hardee abandoned the city on the night of December 20, retreating across the Savannah River on pontoon bridges covered with rice straw to muffle the sound of horses and wagons. By the next morning the port city was in Federal hands, and on December 22 Sherman wired President Lincoln: "I beg to present you as a Christmas-gift the city of Savannah, with one hundred and fifty guns and plenty of ammunition, also about twenty five thousand bales of cotton."

For the Federal soldiers the march through Georgia had been "one big picnic." Having destroyed the railroad to his rear, Sherman was dependent upon the countryside for supplies. The army, in order to subsist, was permitted to forage freely as it moved through the fertile lands of the state. Meeting only token resistance from Major General Joseph Wheeler's cavalry and the Georgia militia, the men, as one of them put it, "rioted and feasted on the country," and the order to "forage freely" was interpreted by some to loot and burn. On a sixty-mile front the army had devastated the land as it moved toward the coast.

By all of the accepted rules of strategy, Sherman's veterans should have been transferred immediately to a theater where they "could pull their own weight." The Federal Navy had the ships to transport them to Virginia where Lieutenant General Ulysses S. Grant had General Robert E. Lee bottled up behind fortifications at Petersburg. Grant was desirous of this move but Sherman was not. He wanted, instead, to apply total war to the Carolinas. Every step northward from Savannah, he felt, was as much a

Right: The officers, like these of the 82d Illinois posing in Atlanta, could look civilized enough, indeed resplendent at times. (CHS)

direct attack on Lee at Petersburg as would be operations within sound of the artillery of the Army of Northern Virginia. Furthermore, Sherman was not adverse in the least to the idea of punishing South Carolina for her role in bringing on the war.

When the news of Major General George Thomas' resounding Union victory over Hood at Nashville, Tennessee, reached Grant on December 18, he penned Sherman a confidential note giving him permission to move through the Carolinas. This communication reached Savannah on Christmas eve. An elated Sherman immediately informed his chief that he expected "to be ready to sally forth again" in about ten days.

In Savannah the Federal troops were generally well behaved. Brigadier General John W. Geary's division of Easterners garrisoned the city and, with the exception of a few minor incidents, all depredations ceased. Sherman even went so far as to permit Episcopal churches to omit prayers for the President of the United States, saying at the same time to ministers who asked if they might pray for the Confederate President, "Yes, Jeff Davis and the devil both need it." Also, the general wisely allowed the city officials to retain their posts, and he strengthened the hand of the mayor, Dr. Richard D. Arnold, whom he had known before the war. In fact, the situation was so peaceful in "handsome" Savannah that every day seemed like a Sunday to Sherman.

Above: But the boys in the ranks, unlike their counterparts in the Army of the Potomac, never took the spit and polish of soldiering to heart. They were as content with informality as these men of the 17th Ohio, posing with friends back home. (LO)

Below: They also had to be wary of lightning raids by Confederate cavalrymen like Major General Joseph Wheeler, who accounted for much of the Southern attempt to keep Sherman at bay during the March to the Sea. It was a hopeless task. And it came at a price, for the dashing Wheeler could not control his men. One superior wanted him relieved "for the good of the cause, and for his own reputation." Yet he would go on fighting, and thirty-four years later he would fight again, this time for the United States. In the Spanish-American War, old Joe Wheeler became a Major General of U.S. Volunteers. (LC)

Right: But such an army could march and fight. Indeed, Sherman's wagon trains, like this one photographed near Savannah, were often hard put to keep pace. (USAMHI)

Below: Major General Ambrose R. Wright commanded one of several Confederate defense lines across portions of Georgia, designed in the futile hope of stopping Sherman. Wright was also president of the Georgia state senate, next in line for the governorship, and when Yankee invasion split part of the state away from the capital in Milledgeville, Wright proclaimed himself governor of the remnant. No one paid any attention. (VM)

Right: Another erstwhile politico trying to stop the Yankee invasion was Brigadier General William M. Browne. An Irishman by birth, he had been on Confederate President Jefferson Davis' personal staff, and for a little over a month in 1862 served as temporary Secretary of State of the Confederacy. (LC)

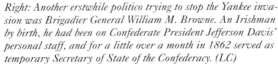

Left: None of the Confederates, amateur or professional, could keep Sherman from the sea. On December 13, 1864, the Federals launched their attack on Fort McAllister, principal coastal guardian of Savannah, and that same day it was all over. (LC)

Right: Though the for''s parapets like this one were well constructed, there were too few defenders inside. Samuel Cooley photographed the fort a few months after its fall. (LC)

During this period of relative tranquillity, preparations for the march north were not neglected. It was a busy time. Nevertheless, very few changes were made in the organization of the army. As during the March to the Sea, it comprised two wings of two corps each. The cavalry remained under Judson Kilpatrick. In the upper command posts there was only one major change. Major General John A. Logan replaced Osterhaus as commander of the XV Corps.

Sherman's plan of campaign called for feints on both Augusta, Georgia, and Charleston, South Carolina, and a march directly on Columbia, the South Carolina capital, and then to Goldsboro, North Carolina, by way of Fayetteville, on the Cape Fear River. Goldsboro was chosen as the destination because that city was connected to the North Carolina coast by two rail lines running, respectively, from Morehead City (via New Bern) and Wilmington, to the south. By this circuit the Federal army could destroy the two chief railroads of the Carolinas, disrupt enemy supply transportation, and devastate the heart of the two states.

Sherman planned to cut himself off completely from his base in Savannah, hence he could expect no government supplies until he reached the Cape Fear River. His wagons could carry only limited provisions. Thus the army

Above: Mortars like this were absolutely useless against Sherman's attack on the fort. It fell with almost the entire garrison within hours. (USAMHI)

Above: The Savannah River, in the distance, flows by Fort McAllister, where Yankee sentinels now stand post. (LC)

Right: Fighting was hand to hand for a time, as the defenders were pushed back into their bombproofs like the openings behind this cannon. The hole behind the cannon is a powder magazine. (LC)

Above: And here an endless procession of workmen is hauling projectiles for big guns like that Columbiad, as McAllister is rearmed and fortified for the Union. (UNIVERSITY OF GEORGIA LIBRARY, ATHENS)

Above: Then commenced the inevitable cleanup, and the conversion of Fort McAllister into a Union strongpoint. A work party is removing a Confederate Columbiad from its carriage. (LC)

Right: Now the Columbiad must guard a Yankee-controlled Savannah River and provide a strong base in his rear. For "Uncle Billy" Sherman is going to turn north toward the Carolinas. (LC)

once again would have to "forage liberally on the country during the march." To regulate the foraging parties, very strict orders were issued. But, as was the case in Georgia, there was a wide discrepancy between the orders and the actions of some of the men. Foraging parties many times degenerated into marauding bands of mounted robbers which operated not under the supervision of an officer but on their own. Most of the pillage and wanton destruction of property in both Georgia and the Carolinas was the work of the "bummers," as this peripheral minority of self-constituted parties of foragers was called.

When Sherman crossed the Savannah River and commenced his march through the Carolinas the latter part of January 1865, the meager Confederate forces that could possibly be brought to oppose him were scattered from Virginia to Mississippi. So by February 7 the major part of the Federal army had penetrated without difficulty well into South Carolina and

Below: From signal towers like this one, Federal messages will pass to the ships in the river or to outposts on the other side. Savannah will be ringed with Yankees. (NA)

Above: It is all Union territory now. When George Barnard turned his lens toward the river soon after the war's close, almost all sign of the conflict had been erased. (LC)

Left: The fighting done, Savannah and its people returned quickly enough to peaceful pursuits. Here at Buena Ventura plantation Barnard might well have wondered if there had ever been a war at all. (LC)

Left: Few occupied cities in Sherman's path suffered so little from their conquerors as Savannah. Sherman put Brigadier General John W. Geary in charge as military governor. Geary, shown here at the table with his staff, his finger pointing, ruled fairly and firmly. He would later become governor of Pennsylvania. (LC)

Right: A Savannah photographer named Beckett captured several views of the city during its occupation, and they attest to its tranquillity. Here is the Pulaski Hotel on Broughton Street . . . (LO)

Right: . . . and here the customs house and post office. (LO)

was encamped along the South Carolina Railroad. Five days later Orangeburg, to the north, was in Sherman's hands.

From Orangeburg the army moved out in the direction of the capital city of Columbia, destroying the railroad as it went. By late afternoon of February 15, only two weeks and a day after the invasion of the Palmetto State had begun in earnest, Sherman's troopers were within four miles of Columbia, called by them the "hell hole of secession." That evening the so-called Battle of Columbia began when a division of the XV Corps quite carelessly camped within range of the Confederate artillery east of the Congaree River and got a mild shelling. The next morning, February 16, Federal skirmishers carried the Confederate defenses around the Congaree River bridge but found only the charred timbers of the structures remaining. On this same date Sherman issued his instructions for the occupation of the city. General Howard was to "destroy public buildings, railroad property, manufacturing, and machine shops" but was to "spare libraries, and asylums, and private dwellings."

By this time Columbia had become a city without law and order. Chaos prevailed. The establishment of martial law on February 17 had not prevented acts of robbery and pillage. Negroes, soldiers, and local citizens either vied with one another for government provisions or turned their attention to the looting of shops and stores.

Early on the morning of the same day Columbia was awakened by a tremendous explosion at the South Carolina Railroad depot, caused in all probability by a looter accidentally igniting the powder stored there. And with the coming of daylight the looting got worse. The state commissary was plundered and in some parts of Main Street, it was reported, "corn and flour and sugar

Above: Colonel Henry A. Barnum became Geary's provost in the city, carefully keeping order and a tight rein on unruly soldiers. Repeatedly wounded during the war, he had actually been proclaimed dead and buried two years before, until someone discovered that they had misidentified the man in the ground . He appears here at war's end in his new rank as brigadier. (P-M)

Left: Savannah city hall at the foot of Bull Street attracted Beckett's camera one day at 12:23 by the tower clock. (LO)

Above: Only a few outward signs show that there was still a war going on. This beautiful Greek Revival building became an ordnance depot for a time . . . (LO)

Above: . . . and Oglethorpe Barracks, once home to Confederate units, now bristles with bluecoats, who would hold Savannah while Sherman marched on, at the end of January 1865, toward the Carolinas. (USAMHI)

Right: Oddly, the Confederates had done little to anticipate defending South Carolina from Sherman. Worse, they had a surplus of generals and a dearth of soldiers. Major General D. H. Hill and others tried to plan a defense of the state, but their counsels were divided and their troops too few and too scattered. (CWTI)

cover[ed] the ground." All the while Lieutenant General Wade Hampton's Confederate cavalry was slowly withdrawing from the city along the Camden and Winnsboro roads.

Columbia, undefended and deranged, was now at the complete mercy of the enemy. Sometime before noon Sherman, with a few members of his staff, rode into the city. Fewer than twelve hours later a large part of South Carolina's capital, including the state house and other public buildings, scores of private homes, several churches, and even a convent lay in smoldering ruins, the result of a great fire that had raged uncontrolled throughout the night. The origin of this conflagration has been the subject of considerable controversy from the day it occurred.

The most likely explanation is that it began from burning cotton. Columbia at this time was a virtual firetrap because of the hundreds of cotton bales in her streets. Some of these had been ignited before Sherman arrived, and a high wind spread tufts of the burning fiber over the city. Also, poorly disciplined troops, many of whom were intoxicated, became incendiaries. In a laconic statement made after the war General Sherman summed up his sentiments on the burning of Columbia: "Though I never ordered it and never wished it, I have never shed any tears over the event, because I believe that it hastened what we all fought for, the end of the war."

The Federal army remained in the city for two days, destroying under orders railroad and

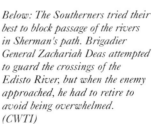

Left: Once again it fell largely to the cavalry to try to retard Sherman's progress. Brigadier General Pierce M. B. Young led his tiny mounted division in repeated attempts to slow the enemy advance, all to no avail. (LC)

Below: The Southerners tried their best to block passage of the rivers in Sherman's path. Brigadier General Zachariah Deas attempted to guard the crossings of the Edisto River, but when the enemy approached, he had to retire to avoid being overwhelmed. (CWTI)

Right: And so, inevitably, on February 17, 1865, Sherman captured Columbia, capital of South Carolina. When he arrived, he found the new state house, still uncompleted. (USAMHI)

Above: And in the wake of occupation came the burning and near destruction of the city. Barnard put his camera on the state house grounds to view the ruins of the city in 1865, a devastation that would unjustly mar Sherman's reputation for a long time to come. (LC)

Right: The state house itself did not survive the conflagration. (LC)

Left: The burned-out offices of the South Carolina Railroad. (SOUTH CAROLINIANA LIBRARY)

Left: The remains of Hunts Hotel, now only chimneys and rubble. (SCL)

public property. The Evans & Cogswell Company, which held the contract for printing Confederate money, was burned, as was the state armory on Arsenal Hill. "They destroyed every thing which the most infernal Yankee ingenuity could devise means to destroy," said one native of Columbia. Then, on February 20, to the accompaniment of hisses and boos from the people along the streets, the troops moved out in the direction of Winnsboro.

This historic old town, as well as Camden to the southeast, and Cheraw to the northeast, suffered much at the hands of the Federal troops. At Cheraw, the army's last stop in South Carolina, Sherman learned that his former antagonist in Georgia, General Joseph E. Johnston, had replaced General P. G. T. Beauregard as commander of the Confederate Army of Tennessee in North and South Carolina. He now concluded that Johnston would unite his widely scattered forces and, at a place of his own choosing, strike one of the Federal corps on the move. Fully aware that the battle he wished to avoid was, in all probability, unavoidable, Sherman put his army in motion for Fayetteville, North Carolina, some seventy miles northeast of Cheraw.

South Carolina was now free of this army which had applied total war in its severest terms within her borders. Lieutenant Charles S. Brown of the 21st Michigan never spoke truer words than when he said: "South Carolina may have been the cause of the whole thing, but she has had an awful punishment."

General Sherman entered North Carolina at the beginning of March with the confident expectation of receiving a friendly welcome from its supposedly large number of pro-Union citizens. Thus he had his officers issue orders for the gentler treatment of the inhabitants, and when the state line was crossed, he circulated new instructions regulating foraging activities. But no orders were drafted prohibiting the burning of the great pine forests within the state.

North Carolina's turpentine woods blazed in fantastic splendor as "bummers touched matches to congealed sap in notches on tree trunks." Seldom did the soldiers pass up an opportunity to fire these pine forests, for the burning rosin and tar created a spectacle of flame and smoke that surpassed in grandeur anything they had ever seen before.

On March 8 North Carolina for the first time felt the full weight of the Federal army, the right wing having crossed the state line on this date. General Sherman, traveling with the XV Corps, made his headquarters near the Laurel Hill Presbyterian Church, a region his soldiers thought looked "real Northernlike," but torrential rains soon turned the roads into a sea of mud and water, making them almost impassable for either man or beast. The most formidable obstacle in the path of the army lay in the dark, swirling waters of the Lumber River and its adjacent swamps. It took a tremendous effort on the part of the Pioneer or Engineer units to get the army through this region. Sherman called it "the damnest marching I ever saw."

To the southeast, in South Carolina, the Federal cavalry under General Kilpatrick crossed the Pee Dee River on March 8. Here Kilpatrick learned that the Confederate cavalry under Wade Hampton was only a few miles behind him and moving rapidly on Fayetteville. Hoping to intercept the enemy, the Federal general set a trap for the Confederates only to have his own camp at Monroe's Crossroads surprised and his troops put to flight on March 9 by the enemy horsemen. To make his own escape, Kilpatrick, clad only in his underclothes, had to spring from the bed of a lady companion, mount the nearest saddleless horse, and disappear into a neighboring swamp.

Since the Federal cavalrymen eventually drove the Confederates out of their camp, there was considerable disagreement over who got the better of the fighting, contemptuously tagged by the Federal infantry as "Kilpatrick's Shirttail Skedaddle." Yet the fact stands that by engaging Kilpatrick in battle, Hampton was able to open the road to Fayetteville which the Federal camp blocked. The Confederate cavalry joined General Hardee's army near Fayetteville the evening of March 10.

The Confederate forces withdrew across the Cape Fear River on March 11, burning the bridge behind them. At the same time the Federal advance entered Fayetteville from the south. The city suffered a great deal as a result of the Federal occupation. Besides the destruction of numerous public buildings, including the United States arsenal which had served the Confederacy for four years, there was considerable pillaging by the bummers before Major General Absalom Baird garrisoned the city with three brigades.

While at Fayetteville Sherman took the opportunity to replace all the rejected animals of his trains with those taken from the local citizens and to clear his columns of the vast crowd of white and black refugees that followed the army. He called these followers "20,000 to 30,000 useless mouths." To Major General Alfred H. Terry at Wilmington, North Carolina, he wrote: "They are dead weight to me and consume our supplies."

By the middle of March Sherman had his entire force across the Cape Fear, and the move on Goldsboro had begun. The general was in a happy frame of mind as he watched his troops march by. The campaign was running smoothly. Goldsboro, he felt sure, would be his in a few days.

From Savannah to Fayetteville Sherman had moved his army in flawless fashion, but from this latter place to Goldsboro his operations were definitely characterized by carelessness in the management of a large command. He placed little importance on Hardee's delaying action at Averasborough on March 16. Also, he allowed his columns to become strung out to such an extent

Left: All that remains of the South Carolina Railroad's freight depot . . . (SCL)

Right: . . . of the bridge over the Congaree River . . . (SCL)

Below: . . . of the state armory on Arsenal Hill, with the photographer's wagon in the foreground. (SCL)

Below: Even the Presbyterian lecture room fell to the flames. (SCL)

Above: Here is what is left of the printing establishment of Evans & Cogswell on West Gervais Street. Confederate treasury notes had been printed here for years. Now even though some of the presses were gotten away safely before Sherman came, the building is as worthless as the scrip it had been printing. (SCL)

Above: When Sherman's march brought him into North Carolina at the beginning of March, he came face to face once more with his old adversary from the Atlanta Campaign, General Joseph E. Johnston. It would be their final confrontation, and Uncle Billy would have it all his own way. (VM)

Above right: The first real fight in North Carolina came at Averasborough on March 16, with the division of Brigadier General William T. Ward of the XX Corps in place for an attack. Ward is seated here with his brigade commanders. Brevet Brigadier General William Cogswell stands at right, next to Brevet Brigadier General Daniel Dustin. And standing at far left is another brevet brigadier, Benjamin Harrison of Ohio. Twenty three years from now he will be elected President. This very image was widely distributed in the 1888 campaign. (USAMHI)

Below: The erratic cavalryman Brigadier General Hugh Judson Kilpatrick helped bring the enemy to bay at Bentonville. Sherman called him "a hell of a damned fool." (USAMHI)

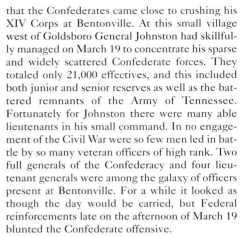

Above: Major General Henry W. Slocum was one of Sherman's favorites and exercised overall command of two corps that pushed back the Confederates at Averasborough. He advanced immediately toward Bentonville, North Carolina. (USAMHI)

Right: And in the battle that followed at Bentonville, on March 19, Slocum made his headquarters in this home, the Harper house. (WESTERN RESERVE HISTORICAL SOCIETY)

that the Confederates came close to crushing his XIV Corps at Bentonville. At this small village west of Goldsboro General Johnston had skillfully managed on March 19 to concentrate his sparse and widely scattered Confederate forces. They totaled only 21,000 effectives, and this included both junior and senior reserves as well as the battered remnants of the Army of Tennessee. Fortunately for Johnston there were many able lieutenants in his small command. In no engagement of the Civil War were so few men led in battle by so many veteran officers of high rank. Two full generals of the Confederacy and four lieutenant generals were among the galaxy of officers present at Bentonville. For a while it looked as though the day would be carried, but Federal reinforcements late on the afternoon of March 19 blunted the Confederate offensive.

More Federal troops reached the field on March 20, and by the next day Sherman had his entire command in the vicinity of Bentonville. That night Johnston withdrew his small force to Smithfield fifteen miles to the north. Rather than pursue his badly outnumbered opponent, Sherman decided to march his victorious troops into Goldsboro. There they were joined by the command of Brigadier General John M. Schofield which had marched up from Wilmington and New Bern.

This completed the task Sherman had set out to do upon leaving Savannah. His army was now united with that of Schofield's. Large supply bases on the North Carolina coast were available by rail and the countryside from Savannah to Goldsboro, in a swath an average of forty miles across, had been laid waste.

Sherman now decided it was time to discuss with Grant the plans for a possible junction of their armies around Richmond. He was a national hero as a result of his Georgia and Carolinas campaigns, and as yet the climactic battle of the war had not been fought. So, with Grant's permission, he could still share with the Army of the Potomac the glory of capturing the Confederate capital.

Late in the day of March 25 Sherman boarded a train for City Point, Virginia, Grant's headquarters. In a festive mood before departure, the general told friends that he planned to see Grant in order "to stir him up" because he had been behind fortifications so long "that he had got fossilized."

Back in North Carolina, at Smithfield, Johnston, uncertain of Sherman's next move, used the time to reorganize his hodgepodge forces. He even held a review for Governor "Zeb" Vance of North Carolina and several ladies from Raleigh. It was thought that the troops "once more" looked "like soldiers." The general was well pleased with the way his men had fought at Bentonville, but in early April, when rumors began to circulate around the camps that Richmond had fallen, morale among the troops started to wane badly. Desertions increased dramatically. Patrols were busy night and day arresting men absent from camp without leave. "Heavens the gloom and how terrible our feelings," wrote a staff officer.

Johnston had no illusions about the future. Shortly after Bentonville he had informed General Lee that "Sherman's force cannot be hindered by the small force I have. I can do no more than annoy him." More and more he became convinced that the only hope lay in bringing the Confederate armies in Virginia and North Carolina together. Even so, Johnston must have thought that hostilities were about to end for at this time he ordered Lieutenant General A. P. Stewart to suspend all executions of deserters. The time for all killing to stop was almost at hand. If the South could go on at all now, the decision rested in the hands of Lee at Petersburg.

Right: The first Confederate force on the scene to meet Slocum was the corps of Lieutenant General A. P. Stewart of Tennessee. Johnston hoped for a surprise attack against Slocum at Bentonville. (VM)

Far right: The first fighting came in the Confederate center, where the North Carolina division of Major General Robert F. Hoke repulsed an attack by the Federals. (SOUTHERN HISTORICAL COLLECTION, UNIVERSITY OF NORTH CAROLINA)

Right: One of Hoke's regiments was the 31st North Carolina, led by dapper Colonel J. V. Jordan. The enemy had long known what he looked like, for this portrait of him was captured in New Bern, North Carolina, when the town and its photographer's studio fell to the Federals in 1862. (USAMHI)

Right: Among the Confederates in the ranks was Private William Washington Cavender of the 1st Georgia Cavalry. Reputed to be an excellent marksman with the pistol, he apparently took his skill seriously enough to point it directly at the camera. (DALE SNAIR COLLECTION)

Left: Sherman had such a surfeit of troops by this time that whole army corps were left out of the fighting. Major General Alfred H. Terry and the X Corps spent most of the campaign marching rather than in battle, much to the derision of the combat veterans from other commands. Against such numbers, the Confederates were almost powerless. (NA)

Left: And so, by the end of March 1865, the Carolinas, like Georgia before them, were conquered. Shortly after the war George N. Barnard came back to Savannah to make a series of images, among them this one of a fountain. Standing in the distance, to the right of the fountain, are two officers, apparently Confederates still wearing their uniforms. If so, it is fitting that one of the photographs with which Barnard concluded his Civil War coverage should include men that he and Sherman had spent so many months pursuing. (IMPERIAL WAR MUSEUM, LONDON)

Petursburg Besieged

RICHARD J. SOMMERS

After three years the Union finally has Lee at bay, but the quarry goes to ground and Grant can only wait

Above: Petersburg, Virginia, major railroad city of the state and key to the capture of Richmond. In June 1864, after months of fighting in the Wilderness and at Spotsylvania, Lieutenant General U. S. Grant and his Union Army were finally close enough to Petersburg to strike. (USAMHI)

CONFIDENT CAPITAL of a nascent nation, Richmond for two years owed her redemption and salvation to General R. E. Lee's Army of Northern Virginia. Lee defended her best by keeping the enemy far afield. By late spring 1864, however, Lieutenant General U. S. Grant's Federals forced Lee back to Richmond's immediate vicinity. Then in the final decisive struggle the two great chieftains grappled for Petersburg, guardian of Richmond's lifeline to the Southern heartland. Through the Cockade City, as Petersburg called herself, ran the railroads linking the capital to the upper Shenandoah Valley and to the blockade runners' Atlantic ports. Whoever controlled Petersburg would control Richmond.

As early as May 1864, while Grant and Lee battled at Spotsylvania, Major General Benjamin F. Butler's Army of the James seized a central position on Bermuda Hundred and briefly threatened both cities. Confederate General Pierre G. T. Beauregard's victory at Drewry's Bluff on May 16 contained that danger, and Petersburg's tiny garrison under Brigadier Generals Henry A. Wise and James Dearing and Lieutenant Colonel Fletcher Archer checked another threat on June 9—a date the city there after celebrated as her time of deliverance. Salvation looked short-lived, though, as Grant's main force assaulted the rail center a week later. Major General William F. Smith's XVIII Corps stormed Petersburg's outer defenses on June 15. Behind him came Major General George G. Meade's Army of the Potomac, which had moved through Charles City Court House and crossed the broad James River at Wilcox's Landing by boat and pontoon bridge. Still, Union hesitancy and Confederate valor, especially that of Major General Bushrod Johnson's division, stopped the onslaught short of Petersburg itself between June 16 and 18.

As he had since May 7, Grant responded to a frontal check by extending his left around the graycoats' right. His severe defeat in the resulting Battle of the Weldon Railroad on June 22—and his recognition that his troops needed rest after seven weeks of incessant fighting—caused him to settle down before the Confederate works east of Petersburg. Grant's war of maneuver was over. The Siege of Petersburg had begun. Here would be decided the fate of the rail center, the capital—perhaps even of Lee's army and the Confederacy itself.

This decision would not come in one great Napoleonic battle. No Civil War battle—except Nashville—achieved those results, and the Petersburg operation did not even aspire to them. Yet Petersburg was not really a siege in the classical European sense, either. Rather it was a grim, relentless effort through which Grant fixed the Southerners in place strategically and tactically to wear them down in a war of attrition. Rather it was, too, a valiant and increasingly desperate effort by Lee to retain tactical mobility, regain strategic mobility, and avert impending disaster. "We must destroy this army of Grant's before he gets to James River," Lee had warned in May. "If he gets there, it will become a siege, and then it will be a mere question of time." Yet as ever, the Virginian did not resign himself to apparent ill fate but strove against the odds to make his own fate. Petersburg would be his greatest such effort—and virtually his last.

For nine and one-half months he and Grant vied for Petersburg and Richmond. Their clash involved battles, of course: flare-ups of heavy but brief fighting punctuating weeks and even months of relative quiescence. But still more it involved supply lines and supplies, permanent fortifications and light fieldworks, and ever expanding fields of operations eventually spanning two rivers and stretching for almost fifty miles.

Supply lines, after all, were what made Petersburg militarily important. A short north-south railroad just west of Bermuda Hundred linked Richmond to Petersburg. Four other railroads fanned out from the city—one northeast toward City Point; one southeast toward Norfolk; one south toward Weldon and Wilmington, in North Carolina; and one—the Southside Railroad—west toward Burkeville and Lynchburg. The two easterly lines fell to Grant when he arrived before Petersburg in mid-June. Not until two months and four tries later, though, did he finally get a permanent choke hold on the Weldon Railroad at Globe Tavern. Even then the graycoats could use the latter tracks northward to Stony Creek Depot, from where they transshipped supplies to Petersburg by wagon. Five Federal drives westward against those wagon roads and against the Southside Railroad set the course for the rest of the campaign. The Yankees finally severed the Southside tracks on April 2, 1865; that night Lee abandoned Petersburg.

Long before Grant reached that final Confederate supply line, he made sure his own forces remained in good supply. The James River, controlled by the U.S. Navy and guarded by six Union garrisons, afforded an unbreakable supply link from Hampton Roads westward to City Point, seven miles northeast of Petersburg, at the mouth of the Appomattox River. The City Point hamlet soon swelled into the well-fortified nerve center of a mighty army. To its rapidly expanded wharves came ships bearing reinforcements, munitions, and supplies. In its environs grew up warehouses for those supplies, hospitals

Above: For the first time in the campaign, Grant managed to steal a march on his adversary . . . (ROBERT J. YOUNGER)

Above: . . . the seemingly unbeatable General Robert E. Lee. Seen here in a portrait by Richmond photographer Julian Vannerson, the Gray Fox seems invincible. (VM)

Above: Grant already held an outpost on the James River about fourteen miles northeast of Petersburg, at Bermuda Hundred, shown here months later as supplies of hay for the Union Army's animals grow into virtual mountains. (USAMHI)

Below: Then, on June 15, Grant completely fooled Lee with a surprise crossing by portions of his army over the James River. Over this speedily erected pontoon bridge at Weyanoke Point, some 2,200 feet long, the IX Corps sped toward unprotected Petersburg. A James Gardner photo. (P-M)

Right: Awaiting them to the east of the city was an old and familiar face, that of General P. G. T. Beauregard. Yankees had fought him at Fort Sumter and First Bull Run and Shiloh, and now, with a handful of defenders, he would meet them again. (USAMHI)

Above: It fell to Major General William F. "Baldy" Smith to make the first Union attack on Petersburg before Confederate reinforcements could arrive. Alas, everything went wrong. (USAMHI)

Left: Beauregard held out, assisted by able subordinates such as Brigadier General Alfred H. Colquitt of Georgia. So sparse were Confederate troops by now that within weeks Colquitt would be ordered off to North Carolina to counter threats there. (VM)

Right: The 25th South Carolina, including whatever remained of this 1861 group from the Washington Light Infantry of Charleston, were among Petersburg's valiant defenders. (WASHINGTON LIGHT INFANTRY, CHARLESTON, SOUTH CAROLINA)

for increasing numbers or sick and wounded, and Provost Marshal General Marsena Patrick's "bull pen" for captured graycoats awaiting transfer to Federal prisons in the North.

Also near City Point Grant established his permanent headquarters and eventually his 1864-65 winter living quarters. From that central location he initiated his onslaughts against Southern positions; some battles he waged on distant sectors without even leaving City Point, though he usually preferred riding to the front to observe events.

From City Point, too, flowed the supplies for his command. Some went to nearby garrisons. Other supplies crossed the lower Appomattox at Broadway Landing and Point of Rocks to Bermuda Hundred. From Bermuda Hundred the supply lines eventually bridged the James— from Jones's Neck to Deep Bottom in June, from Jones's Landing to Aiken's (Varina) Landing in September—to support the growing Northern presence on the Peninsula that threatened Richmond directly. Most supplies meantime headed southwest toward the main body aiming for Petersburg. To haul these supplies, the

Above: Even as Smith's attack was failing and Lee raced to reinforce the city, Major General George G. Meade sped with the bulk of his Army of the Potomac to join in the attacks. This image by Brady & Company was made just days before, on June 12, at Cold Harbor, northeast of Richmond. Meade is seated at center with his legs crossed, surrounded by his staff. Major General Andrew A. Humphreys is on his right, and seated to the right of Humphreys is the army's provost marshal, Brigadier General Marsena Patrick. Standing immediately on Meade's left is his quartermaster, Brigadier General Rufus Ingalls, and the man second to Ingalls' left is Meade's artilleryman Brigadier General Henry I. Hunt. (USAMHI)

Above: James Gardner was present at Charles City Court House on June 14 to capture this image, just as Meade's army was moving through the place on its way to the planned attack. (USAMHI)

Below: When the army reached Wilcox's Landing on the James, it started crossing on steamers. A Brady cameraman made this image probably on June 15, while the crossing was under way. The wharf is crowded with steamers and wagons, as a mighty army is on the move. (WRHS)

Federals operated the captured City Point and Weldon railroads, connected them via the U.S. Military Railroad that provided lateral service along the Union battle line to Globe Tavern, and ran spur lines westward to Poplar Spring Church and Cummings' farm.

These railroads were the final link that brought the North's vast agricultural and industrial resources to City Point, and thence to Grant's soldiers in the field. Superior numbers, backed by superior matériel, could better endure the hot, dry summer when the siege began and the cold winter through which it continued —could better endure the grueling ordeal of close trench warfare and the bitterness of repeated checks—than could the starving, tattered, thinning ranks in gray. In the long run, such superiority could not help but tell. To Grant's credit, he understood how to convert these potential advantages—which, after all, his predecessors in the East had enjoyed, too—into positive achievements.

Over against Federal advantages, the Confederates increasingly suffered from their deteriorating logistical situation. Temporary or permanent loss of supply lines into Petersburg produced immediate problems. Widespread destruction of supplies and communications elsewhere in the Confederacy by Major Generals William T. Sherman, Philip H. Sheridan, and Alfred H. Terry created even graver difficulties. These hostile actions hastened the collapse of the always primitive Southern supply system, and its revitalization in the war's waning weeks came too late to accomplish much. Hungry, ill-clad, outnumbered troops could still win battles but were not likely to win a long campaign—especially against such well-supplied opponents as the Federals.

This increasing disparity lowered some Secessionists' morale. Awareness that their families were also suffering added to their dismay. And the overwhelming reelection of President Lincoln on November 8—with its unmistakable mandate of four more years of unrelenting war—drastically intensified some soldiers' disaffection. Over the winter of 1864 65 their desertion—to the Union forces, to the hills, or to home—increased dramatically. Their departure made the disparity between Southern and Northern armies even worse.

Above: To maintain instant communications with Grant and the rest of the Union Army, a hasty telegraph office was established at the landing. (USAMHI)

Above: But despite all Grant's efforts, Confederates in Petersburg held out long enough for Lee to bring the bulk of his army to the city. Major General Bushrod R. Johnson, a native of Ohio, fought valiantly to halt the first assaults. (DEPARTMENT OF ARCHIVES AND MANUSCRIPTS, LOUISIANA STATE UNIVERSITY, BATON ROUGE)

Above: One of many redoubts placed along the outer Confederate line and captured in the first assaults in June 1864. (P-M)

Left: Yankees, too, were heroic in their efforts to break through the enemy lines. Colonel Joshua L. Chamberlain of the 20th Maine won a battlefield promotion to brigadier general on June 18 in one of the last assaults. (WRHS)

Above: Stopped in front of the city, Grant tried to work around it on the south to cut off Confederate communications via the Weldon Railroad. Here, near Globe Tavern, he was turned back. Captain A. J. Russell made this image late in 1864. (KA)

Above: At City Point Grant built an ordnance wharf that could accommodate the ceaseless comings and goings of the supply steamers. Probably a Russell image. (LC)

Below: Transports like the Neptune *disgorged their supplies directly onto the rail cars that would speed them around Grant's lines wherever needed. Probably a Russell image. (USAMHI)*

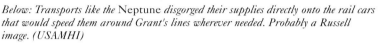

Left: Everywhere there were masts and lines of guns and caissons, a ceaseless activity that continued around the clock. (KA)

Above: So did the supply wagons that would go where the railroad did not. (LC)

Above: The trains await whatever they must carry. (NA)

Left: A row of 12-pounders and their carriages, awaiting transportation to the front. (LC)

Below: Maintaining the mammoth City Point supply base required hundreds of special laborers, and that in turn required a special encampment for them. Here their winter quarters outside the base kept them close to their unending work. (USAMHI)

Yet Lee had always striven against long odds, and to the very end at Petersburg he continued doing so—through daring feints, bold counterattacks, and great reliance on earthworks—to offset his numerical weakness. More than any other Civil War campaign, Petersburg was marked by extensive use of fortifications.

Both that city and Richmond were ringed with permanent defenses when the campaign began. The capital, indeed, had three such rings, plus two forward water batteries on the James at Chaffin's and Drewry's bluffs. When Union Major General Benjamin Butler occupied Deep Bottom, the Rebels dug a trench eastward from Chaffin's to New Market Heights to contain him. His big breakthrough at Fort Harrison on September 29 rendered that trench and much of the Exterior Line of Richmond's permanent defenses untenable—indeed, breached the main camp on Chaffin's Bluff itself. Lee, however, soon stopped that threat and retained the main Richmond works—and the city they guarded—until the final collapse. Yet he could not hurl back the bluecoats, secure in their own field works from Fort Brady through Fort Burnham and thence curving back east toward Deep Bottom.

Comparable stalemate settled over the James itself and Chesterfield County between the two cities. Because the Union Army and Navy had obstructed shallow Trent's Reach to prevent the Confederate Navy disrupting Grant's crossing of the James in mid-June, for the assault on Petersburg, the Yankee vessels were subsequently unable to move upriver above the reach. To bypass those obstructions, Butler dug a canal through narrow Dutch Gap neck between Au gust 1864 and January 1865. Beset with engineering difficulties and annoying but not particularly damaging mortar fire, the canal proved a fiasco, unusable by the Union squadron (though after the war it became the river's main channel),

Left: Soon a more sophisticated telegraphic operation was under way as well, employing a dozen and more key operators, shown here in their rustic summer quarters. (LC)

Left: Grant set up outdoor summer head quarters at City Point, shown here in a Brady & Company image taken in late June or early July 1864. Grant and his staff are seated under the shade of the tree. (USAMHI)

Left: Another Brady image taken at the same time shows Grant seated third from the left. Already there is at least one war trophy: partially furled on a staff leaning against the tree at left is a Confederate battle flag. (USAMHI)

Left: The bluecoats would be at City Point for a long time, though Grant did not know that this summer. Nearly a year later, in spring 1865, his headquarters looked like this in an E. & H.T. Anthony Company image. (RJY)

because the graycoats established three major batteries along the right bank between the existing defenses at Drewry's and Howlett's bluffs to blast the ships if they came. Even more needed by the Rebels were the fieldworks running south from Howlett's to protect the railroad and "cork Butler in his bottle" at Bermuda Hundred. Yet corresponding Federal trenches across the mouth of the "bottle" twice stopped Beauregard's efforts to overrun the area. And Northern batteries, along with river obstructions and the characteristic breakdown of Confederate ironclads, checked the one Southern naval sortie down the James on January 24, 1865.

Meanwhile, the military situation south of the Appomattox in mid-1864 was more fluid, and the ever extending fieldworks there reflected that fact. The initial Northern onslaught on Petersburg on June 15 overran the permanent defenses to the east, but first one, then another line of trenches that Beauregard hastily threw up halted the drive short of the city. Those temporary works connected with the original permanent defenses at Rives's Salient on the Jerusalem Plank Road, the great southeastern angle where the Confederate ramparts bent back westward before turning northward to reach the Appomattox above Petersburg.

Above: Though he was the aggressor here in Virginia, Grant knew that he had to look to his own defense, with the wily Lee as an adversary. Fortifications were built to protect City Point. (P-M)

Below: Even then, City Point felt at least one blast of destruction. On August 9, 1864, an explosion went off, set by Confederate saboteurs. It rocked the ordnance wharves. Russell caught the scene. (USAMHI)

Above: And regiments like the resplendent Zouave 114th Pennsylvania were detailed as provost guard and garrison troops. They pose here in August 1864. (LC)

Right: And it left an enormous mess in its wake. The culprits were never caught. (USAMHI)

Above: Grant himself was listening to an officer who claimed that enemy spies were infiltrating City Point when they heard the explosion. (KA)

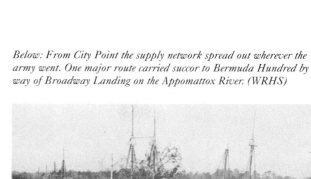

Below: From City Point the supply network spread out wherever the army went. One major route carried succor to Bermuda Hundred by way of Broadway Landing on the Appomattox River. (WRHS)

Left: Much of the ground was like this—too swampy in the winter for passage. An early 1865 image, published by E. & H.T. Anthony Company. (LC)

Below: All this done, there was nothing left for the Federals to do but to start pounding away at Lee. Indeed, even before City Point was well established, Grant's artillery began the work. A Brady photographer made this view of Captain James H. Cooper's Battery B, 1st Pennsylvania Light Artillery, on June 21, 1864. Though long identified as being taken "under fire," Brady's images were made at a time and place when the Confederate lines were about a mile away, and this image was almost certainly posed for the camera. (LC)

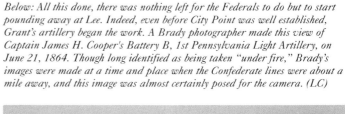

The bluecoats promptly dug their own field works close up against Beauregard's position east of town, from the lower Appomattox to the Jerusalem Plank Road. West of that highway, the fortifications drew apart, out of rifle range. As the Army of the Potomac drove west—to Globe Tavern, to Poplar Spring Church, to Hatcher's Run—it dug trenches to secure each new conquest and link it to previous gains. Moreover, a rear line from the church back northeastward to Blackwater Creek guarded against cavalry raids.

The Confederates, though, made little effort against the Union rear except for sabotaging an ordnance barge to explode at City Point on August 9, rustling a large cattle herd downriver from there on September 15-17, and constantly committing guerrilla depredations. Their main concern, however, lay in protecting their own front, so they dug two lines of fieldworks running southwestward from the city's main fortifications. The forward line guarding the vital supply routes along the Boydton Plank Road and the Southside Railroad remained in Lee's possession until the end. Its eventual capture on April 2, 1865, was what doomed Petersburg.

Right: Brady himself stepped into the picture in this image of the same battery that day. He stands, hands in pockets, just behind the cannon at center. (LC)

Above: Real fighting was done by men like these Zouaves of the 164th New York, the Corcoran Legion. At Deep Bottom, about fifteen miles north of Petersburg, on July 27-28, they met the enemy, only to be repulsed. (USAMHI)

Left: As a result of the stalemate, the Confederates, too, had to settle down to what would be a long siege. Shown here are some of the Southern winter quarters captured in June 1864, now home to grinning Yankees. (P-M)

For fifty-one miles—from west of Richmond on around Petersburg—these Confederate lines eventually stretched. The corresponding Northern front line, thirty miles long, whether field works or permanent defenses, constituted a series of redoubts connected by trenches or infantry parapets. Most such Northern forts were named for officers killed from the Wilderness in May 1864 through Petersburg. The Confederates preferred naming strongholds after living commanders on those sectors—such as Lee himself. The respective practices eventually proved less dissimilar, though. Several of those Confederate generals, too, would lose their lives in or near their redoubts or would ultimately die of wounds received there.

Generals could give their names to forts, but trained engineer officers had to design and refine the works. Moreover, special engineer units—the 1st, 15th, and 50th New York Engineers, the U.S. Engineer Battalion, and the 1st and part of the 2d Confederate Engineers— performed much of the sophisticated technical construction, such as assuring proper slopes and angles and sinking mines and countermines. Most of the actual labor with pick and shovel, however, was provided by fatigue parties of infantry, cavalry, and artillery on both sides and also, on the Southern side, by slaves. Combat troops could establish light works of logs, rails, and earth right on the battlefield. Subsequently, engineer officers and labor parties would strengthen the profile with revetments and gabions, improve angles and fields of fire, and perhaps obstruct approaches with abatis, chevaux-de-frise, or a moat. Such refinements converted the primitive initial sheltering parapets into nearly impregnable fortifications.

Behind those fortifications most soldiers could camp in relative safety and even ease, first in tents, then in winter quarters. But men of both armies holding the sector east of Petersburg

Below: Able defenders like Brigadier General Johnson Hagood turned back Major General Benjamin Butler's May 1864 land attack. (LC)

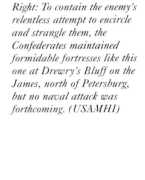

Right: To contain the enemy's relentless attempt to encircle and strangle them, the Confederates maintained formidable fortresses like this one at Drewry's Bluff on the James, north of Petersburg, but no naval attack was forthcoming. (USAMHI)

Right: Following the fighting at Fort Darling, as the earthwork at Drewry's Bluff was called, obstructions placed in the river were intended to interdict ships. (USAMHI)

where shelling and sniping flared daily knew no such respite. Yet even they could seek shelter—against the parapet or in supposedly "bomb proof" dugouts, where they waited out the fire and yearned for transfer to a quieter stretch of line—or, better still, a transfer to reserve or to the unravaged country outside the works.

To view that open country, those reserve positions, and the defenses themselves and to send semaphore messages, signal towers rose over each army's trenches on both sides of the James.

Surer communications clicked along telegraph lines uniting the far-flung sectors to City Point and to Lee's various headquarters: Dunn's Hill, Mrs. Chaffin's, and Edge Hill. Indeed, the relatively static siege was ideal for using telegraph, and within days of units reaching each new position, telegraph wire linked it to the communications net as surely as new earthworks connected it to existing fortifications.

Those fortifications thus provided shelter to the communications and camps behind them and to the garrisons within them. They also afforded platforms for each army's fieldpieces, siege guns, and light and heavy mortars (like the Federal 13-inch seacoast mortar "Dictator") that shelled each other north from the Jerusalem Plank Road to the lower Appomattox. Such artillery fire, however, was generally intended to annoy enemy troops and civilians and to silence enemy fire. Blasting down ramparts, and digging mines—hallmarks of classical European sieges— played little role in the Siege of Petersburg.

Nor were the works—especially the permanent fortifications around the two cities—scenes of heavy fighting. The severe losses and small results from May 5 to June 18, 1864, had made Grant wary of assaulting well-prepared and well-guarded defenses. Thereafter he generally avoided such frontal charges. To him, his own works were not a forward line for delivering direct charges on nearby enemy ramparts. Rather, they were a great entrenched camp, or staging area, from which he could safely launch heavy forays into the relatively unfortified areas beyond either flank. Such forays would either cut the supply lines and capture Richmond or else would at least force the graycoats to leave their works and fight in the open.

Lee was not averse to fighting in the open. His permanent defenses were safe bases from which Beauregard's and Lieutenant General A. P. Hill's infantry and Lieutenant Colonel William Pegram's artillery could sally against the threats, and his fieldworks were ready means for slowing, stopping, or bluffing Union forays until he could counterattack. Also available to him in the open and screening his communications was his usually superior cavalry—an arm that provided extra mobility for meeting threats on several sectors. Such mobility, along with trench defense and surprise attacks, often made three or four Southern brigades the equal or the better of three or four Yankee divisions. Thus, most of the so-called Siege of Petersburg was not a siege at all but a series of forays and counterblows in largely open country.

The defeat of the first Union drive for the Weldon Railroad on June 22 and the rout of Northern cavalry raiders at Reams' Station on June 29 not only converted the mobile maneuver of spring into the static semisiege of summer but also set the tone for the rest of the campaign. For nearly a month the exhausted armies rested.

Above: Old steamers were brought out into the channel and scuttled. (VM)

Above: The officers' quarters were barely a stone's throw from the earthworks. (USAMHI)

Left: They made a virtual barricade across the James. (USAMHI)

Below: In Fort Darling itself, the Confederate officers had dug themselves several substantial gun emplacements, with sunken magazines, bombproofs, and a well. (USAMHI)

Right: Once the fort fell to the Yankees, however, it became a useful bastion for them as well. Federal transports filled with artillery tie up at the tiny dock. (USAMHI)

Above: Elsewhere along the James the Federals secured their hold with water batteries like this one below Fort Brady. (P-M)

Right: Here a large Parrott rifle stares out over the James, not far from Dutch Gap, above Petersburg. (NA)

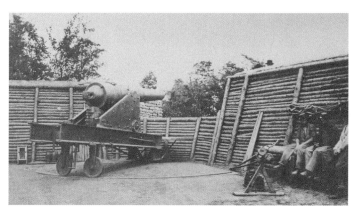

Above: Confederate water batteries were also located near Dutch Gap, mounting formidable guns like this banded Brooke rifle. The Union could not make full use of the James until they could get past obstructions and batteries like these. (USAMHI)

Below: The problem led to one of the war's great, unsuccessful schemes, the Dutch Gap Canal. Butler's Army of the James spent months digging a canal across the narrow neck of land left by a great loop in the river. When completed, it would have allowed ships to bypass enemy water batteries. Captain Russell brought his camera to record the work and probably made this image in August or September 1864. (CHS)

Then, on July 27, three Federal corps under Sheridan and Major General Winfield Scott Hancock crossed the James above Petersburg and burst forth from the Deep Bottom bridgehead toward Richmond itself. Lieutenant General Richard H. Anderson's Rebels, heavily reinforced from Petersburg, stopped that push far short of its goals. Hancock, however, at least succeeded in drawing most of the Confederate army to the Peninsula. He then hastily re turned south of Petersburg to support the impending attack against the weakened South side Railroad.

In a rare frontal blow, Major General Ambrose E. Burnside spearheaded that attack by exploding a mine under Elliott's Salient east of Petersburg in the early morning of July 30. The resulting Battle of the Crater threatened the city with capture, but Yankee blunders, Union Brigadier General James Ledlie's cowardice, the rout of Brigadier General Edward Ferrero's Negro division, a stout defense by Johnson, and repeated counterattacks by Brigadier William Mahone converted the operation into disaster for the Union forces and restored Lee's front.

Upset but undaunted, Grant struck again on August 14. For a second time, Hancock sallied from Deep Bottom, above Petersburg; for a second time, local Rebels under Major General Charles Field, reinforced by troops from the Southside, checked him right away; and for a second time, the Army of the Potomac sought to take advantage of the diversion of enemy units to north of the James. This time, though, Major General Gouverneur K. Warren's V Corps entered the unfortified country west of the Jerusalem Plank Road and cut the key Weldon Railroad at Globe Tavern on August 18. For four days, his Northerners reeled under Beauregard's and Lee's savage counter attacks, but—reinforced in the nick of time by Brigadier General Orlando Willcox's IX Corps divisions—they retained their hold on the railroad. Subsequent efforts by the returned Hancock to tear up track southward from there, however, met disaster at Reams' Station on August 25. Lee, reluctantly reconciled to losing Globe Tavern, thereafter sought to contain the Federals there and to cover the wagon roads leading into Petersburg.

After another interlude of five weeks, Grant drove for those wagon roads and also for Richmond. On September 29 most of Butler's army crossed the James at Deep Bottom and at a new bridge at Aiken's Landing. His right wing under Major General David B. Birney was again checked temporarily at New Market Heights, but this time his upriver column under Major General Edward Ord stormed the outer Confederate defenses at Fort Harrison (later renamed Fort Burnham). This breakthrough on Chaffin's Bluff bade fair to capture the capital, but Unionist errors and the heroic defense by Brigadier General John Gregg and Lieutenant General Richard Ewell checked the disjointed attempts to press on. However, Anderson failed bloodily to retake Fort Harrison the following day. Lee's own effort to roll up the Northern right on the Darbytown Road on October 7 met initial success but eventual defeat. Federals in force were on the Peninsula to stay, and all Lee could now do was to erect new works to contain them. At least, he had little difficulty parrying Brigadier General Adelbert Ames's feeble probe against those works on the Darbytown Road on October 13.

The Union story on the Southside line was similar. On September 30, Brigadier General Charles Griffin punched through the outer defenses at Poplar Spring Church. Major General John G. Parke's halting efforts to continue toward the Boydton Plank Road and the Southside Railroad, though, were routed by Major General Cadmus Wilcox's and Lieutenant General Wade Hampton's skillful counterblows. Yet neither Wilcox, Hampton, nor Major General Henry Heth could recapture the ground initially lost. Meade thus retained another sector, linked it to his previous conquests, and established his headquarters in Aiken's house, nearer to the new front and the scene of future action. From this latest gain, he would launch Major General Romeyn Ayres's limited probe up the Squirrel Level Road on October 8 and three massive onslaughts and a major raid later in the siege.

The first big blow fell on October 27, as Meade and Butler struck simultaneously against both Confederate flanks. Lieutenant General James Longstreet easily blunted Butler's hesitant Army of the James at Fair Oaks. The situation below Petersburg was more touch-and-go. Three Union divisions finally reached the Boydton Plank Road below Hatcher's Run, only to be heavily counterattacked from four sides. In this his final battle, that splendid Union tactician Hancock repulsed every charge, then skillfully extricated his imperiled corps. With him recoiled the whole Army of the Potomac. On both flanks Grant had struck simultaneously; on neither had he accomplished anything.

Left: Again it was probably Russell who made this fall 1864 image showing the work on the canal well under way, the work parties, surveying instruments, and barges and tracks for removing earth all perfectly visible. (NA)

Above: The greatcoats on the working parties attest to the coming of the cold season late in 1864. The workers are almost entirely Negro troops, their white officers standing on the upper level supervising. (NA)

Above: In November Russell made this image showing the last stages of the canal before the remaining earth was blasted away to complete the ditch. Everything is ready, and giant crevices have been sliced through the earth. On January 1, 1865, it needs only the touch of a spark to the powder charges laid and . . . (P-M)

Left: . . . the Dutch Gap Canal is open. (P-M)

Above: In succeeding days and weeks the canal mouth will be widened and deepened to allow traffic to pass through, but in fact the canal will prove to be militarily pointless. It was not completed until April 1865 and by then it was too late to be of use. In later years, ironically enough, the James will shift its course slightly and the canal will become part of the main channel. (USAMHI)

Above: Much of the work was done under nagging but largely fruitless artillery fire from Confederate batteries. One shot did manage to sink this dredge. (LC)

Right: Meanwhile, Butler fretted and fumed here in his head quarters, thoroughly disgusted with his bad fortune, and thoroughly out of favor with Grant. (NA)

This conspicuous failure of his two-pronged assault led Grant to revise his strategy. Thereafter he would mass his forces on the left for a heavy first strike below Petersburg. The initial effort there was simply Warren's destruction of the Weldon Railroad from Jarratt's Station to Belfield in December. Better indication of the new strategy came on February 5, 1865, as Meade again struck for Hatcher's Run. When fighting ended two days later, Warren's V Corps had been roughly handled, but Confederate Brigadier General John Pegram was dead, and Hancock's successor, Major General Andrew A. Humphreys, had permanently extended the Union line to that stream.

Thereafter, Lee and Grant became increasingly aware of the impact of military developments in other theaters on their own operations. Throughout the Petersburg siege, for that matter, both generals had sent troops elsewhere to block threats, win victories, suppress treachery, and enhance prospects around Petersburg. Seven Southern and eleven Northern brigades permanently moved to the Carolinas the winter of 1864-65. Even more did the Shenandoah Valley divert forces from the Tidewater in 1864 (eight of Grant's divisions, five of Lee's). Subsequently, four Gray and five Blue infantry divisions bolstered Lee and Grant from the Shenandoah, and then in early March 1865 Sheridan's two powerful Union cavalry divisions crushed the Confederate Army of the Valley and raided overland from the Blue Ridge to the Peninsula. The two feeble Rebel mounted divisions that rode east from the Shenandoah to resist him hardly offset this mighty build-up of Federal horse at Petersburg.

As this threat to Lee descended from the northwest, even more ominous danger loomed from the south, as Sherman moved irresistibly through the Carolinas, ever closer to Petersburg. Meantime, from north and west, respectively, Hancock's and Major General George Thomas' Union armies threatened Lynchburg. And all the while, Grant tenaciously grappled with the Army of Northern Virginia, determined to pin it down while his subordinates devoured the rest of the Confederacy and then joined him for the final kill.

Lee, as ever, fought back against impending doom. On March 25, 1865, in a daring strike through no-man's land east of Petersburg, Major

General John Gordon's Rebels stormed Fort Stedman. But as with so many breakthroughs in the siege, they could not exploit it, and Parke's and Brigadier General John Hartranft's counterattack soon drove them out. Meantime, Humphreys' and Major General Horatio Wright's corps profited from Gordon's diversion to the center and captured the entrenched picket line on the Confederate right.

Holding that picket line proved advantageous when Grant launched his final offensive on March 29. Sheridan, reinforced by Warren, spearheaded the onslaught south of Hatcher's Run. Humphreys engaged just below that stream, and Wright and Parke stood ready farther north. This time most of the Army of the James, now under Ord, left the Peninsula to join the attack below Petersburg. Brave to the last, the Confederates repeatedly counterattacked this new drive, and time and again they trounced Union divisions. On this occasion, however, the Northerners kept coming. Sheridan routed the last mobile flank guard, Major General George Pickett's command, at Five Forks, April 1. In an even more decisive stroke the following day, Sunday, Wright stormed the works covering the Boydton Plank Road and killed A. P. Hill, long the chief guardian of Petersburg. Later that day, Major General Nelson Miles defeated the last defenders of the Southside Railroad at Sutherland's Station. Only in the fortifications of Petersburg itself did Gordon, Wilcox, and Brigadier General Nathaniel Harris blunt Parke's and Ord's repeated charges until Longstreet's reinforcements could finally arrive from Richmond.

Above: His engineers, like the 15th New York, went into winter quarters such as these and suffered through the cold and damp and mud. The log breastworks with their sandbag firing posts were never used to repel enemy attack. (KA)

Below: To protect themselves from the Confederate shelling, some of Butler's people dug bombproofs into the side of the hill. This image was made on Thanksgiving Day in 1864 while Rebel artillery was firing from afar. It is possibly the work of Captain Russell's assistant Egbert G. Fowx, with whom Russell would later fondly reminisce about the dangers of making photographs while under fire. (USAMHI)

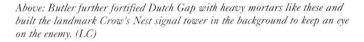

Above: Butler further fortified Dutch Gap with heavy mortars like these and built the landmark Crow's Nest signal tower in the background to keep an eye on the enemy. (LC)

Right: Meanwhile, back on the main Union lines stretching around Petersburg, the work of reducing the enemy continued. On June 20, 1864, a Brady cameraman recorded this image of the 12th New York Battery, now operating in a captured Confederate earthwork, Battery 8. Brady himself appears once again, standing in straw hat in the center. Just two days later this entire battery would be captured in a Confederate attack in another sector. (WRHS)

Above: Slowly the ring of Union fortifications grew. Fort Rice shows the winter huts built to keep the men during the siege. (USAMHI)

Right: Fort Sedgwick went up on the Jerusalem Plank Road, south of Petersburg. It was a massive earthwork incorporating gabions, abatis, and chevaux-de-frise. (USAMHI)

Except for permitting an orderly retreat, though, those reinforcements were too late. This time disaster for the Southern cause was real—and irretrievable. The last wagon road was gone; the last railroad linking Richmond and Petersburg to the outside was gone; and with them was gone the last military justification for holding Petersburg. To stand siege within the city would simply lose the army, too. Yet there was no place else on the James to stand, either. Richmond was now as untenable as the Cockade City.

Overnight, April 2-3, Lee abandoned them both. In his wake, civilian looters burned much of the capital. With daylight came Major General Godfrey Weitzel's and Parke's bluecoats, who at last entered ruined Richmond and battered Petersburg unresisted. Meantime their triumphant comrades in Grant's main body south of the city were in excellent position to intercept Lee's desperate flight toward North Carolina. The Army of Northern Virginia, once mighty, had been too weakened at Petersburg to continue long in the open field. For Lee and his men, within just one week, the road from Petersburg would lead to Appomattox.

Left: The maze of trenches and gabions—earth-filled baskets—soon was dubbed "Fort Hell" by the Confederates. (USAMHI)

Right: There was a lot of engineering going on in both armies and that done by the Federals was chiefly under the direction of Brigadier General John G. Barnard, Grant's chief field engineer. (P-M)

Right: Formidable movable obstructions like these chevaux-de-frise were built to break up enemy assaults. (USAMHI)

Left: Tons of twigs and branches were carefully woven into the gabions that formed the basis of much of the earthworks. (KA)

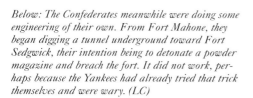

Below: The Confederates meanwhile were doing some engineering of their own. From Fort Mahone, they began digging a tunnel underground toward Fort Sedgwick, their intention being to detonate a powder magazine and breach the fort. It did not work, perhaps because the Yankees had already tried that trick themselves and were wary. (LC)

Above: The sticks were even woven into mats like these, for a variety of purposes, in a rat's maze of tunnels and ditches. (LC)

Right: Besides, these bombproof quarters at Fort Sedgwick were already such a maze of tunnels and holes in the ground that a mine underneath them could hardly go undetected. (LC)

Left: Everywhere men were living in homes carved out of the dirt. Here is a kitchen among the Union bombproofs. (P-M)

Above: And here just one simple soldiers' shelter from flying enemy shells. (P-M)

Below: For the Confederates it was much the same. Here at Gracie's Salient all manner of digging and moving has taken place. To show the proximity of the opposing lines by the end of the siege, the Federal earthworks can be seen in the left distance. (USAMHI)

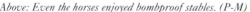
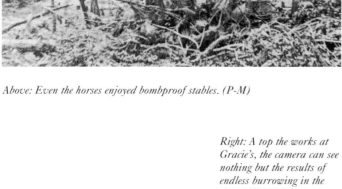

Above: Even the horses enjoyed bombproof stables. (P-M)

Right: A top the works at Gracie's, the camera can see nothing but the results of endless burrowing in the dirt. (USAMHI)

Right: What Union shelling did not ruin, the rain and weather often did, breaking down works and filling the trenches with water and mud. (P-M)

Above: Everywhere the Confederate ditches seemed to stretch to the horizon. (P-M)

Above: Captain Russell's early April 1865 image of one Rebel cannon mounted in the inner line of defenses. In the distance all around it appear more and more lines of works. (LC)

Above: Conditions in the trenches were no different for the Federals. The rain and mud attacked them as well. (USAMHI)

Right: Their work seemed just as endless as, like a colony of ants, they went on with the work of tearing up the soil of Virginia. (USAMHI)

Right: And particularly for the Federal warships that plied the James River nearby. The Union monitor Sangamon rests at her mooring below the Crow's Nest. (WILLIAM GLADSTONE COLLECTION)

Below: Another less tall but more famous signal tower was the Crow's Nest, 136 feet high, near the Dutch Gap Canal. It was a landmark for Yankees all about. (USAMHI)

Right: Farther off, near Bermuda Hundred, yet another tower kept at least a few Yankees high, if not dry. (USAMHI)

Right: When not building, the Yankees were shooting, often mammoth seacoast mortars like this 13-inch behemoth called the Dictator. Its service at Petersburg was neither distinguished nor unusual except for its railroad mounting, but it captured the interest of more than one photographer, and they subsequently made it one of the most famous cannon of the war. O'Sullivan or his assistant David Knox photographed it here on September 1, 1864, mounted on the railroad flatcar that transported it. The officer standing at right center, holding the field glasses, is Brigadier General H. J. Hunt, Meade's chief of artillery. (LC)

Below: And here that same day O'Sullivan or an assistant recorded the scene as the Dictator pointed toward the enemy works beyond the ridge. (USAMHI)

Below: Certainly the most notorious endeavor of the Yankee engineers, however, was the Great Mine. Dug by coal miners in the 48th Pennsylvania, it ran across the no-man's land between the lines and under the Confederate works. It fell to Major General Ambrose Burnside, standing in the center, his hand in his blouse, here with his staff, to make the attack that would follow the explosion of four tons of powder at the end of the 511-foot shaft. He was a poor choice. (NA)

Left: When the charge went off—on July 30, 1864—this "crater" was formed, 30 feet deep, 170 feet long, and from 60 to 80 feet wide. It literally blew a whole section of Confederate works—with their defenders—out of existence. Portions of the shaft are still visible in this 1865 image. (USAMHI)

Burnside's troops rushed in, one brigade commanded by Brigadier General W. F. Bartlett, seated here fourth from the right with his staff at war's end. He already wore an artificial cork leg, and now it was shattered in the attack and he taken prisoner. (USAMHI)

Far left: Occupying the salient that was blown up was Brigadier General Stephen Elliott. He was himself seriously wounded in repulsing Burnside's poorly organized assaults and would not see service again until Bentonville, North Carolina, at the end of the war. (USAMHI)

Left: By the time the Federals were falling into confusion after the explosion, some of them trapped in the crater itself, Brigadier General William Mahone had rushed his Confederate division to the threatened spot. In time he drove the bluecoats out and won for himself a battlefield promotion. (CHS)

Right: After Petersburg's fall a cameraman made this view from the hole, looking off toward the Union lines in the near distance. It shows just how close the opposing parties came in their mole's work. (USAMHI)

Below: The whole Union effort had been a shambles, thanks chiefly to dreadful leadership. Brigadier General James Ledlie, commander of the Federal attack, hid, drinking, in a bombproof while his division went into the slaughter. (NA)

Below: Brigadier General Edward Ferrero, shown seated at the center a few days after the attack, commanded the Negro division that supported Ledlie. Ferrero, too, hid with Ledlie while his command was torn apart. He managed to survive the resulting court of inquiry, though not without censure, but Ledlie would soon leave the service in disgrace. (USAMHI)

Right: The crater itself would survive down to the present, but 5,500 good men of both sides perished or were wounded in the fight for it. Even among regiments like the 40th Massachusetts, assigned as a reserve and never thrown into the actual battle, men fell. This image shows them at drill in the winter of 1862-63 at Miner's Hill, Virginia. It is an important image for another reason. It is one of the two photographs that were the start of the massive 40,000-image collection of the Massachusetts Commandery of the Military Order of the Loyal Legion of the United States (MOLLUS), the largest collection of Civil War images in existence, now at Carlisle Barracks, Pennsylvania. (USAMHI)

Below: In August 1864, still smarting from the setback at the crater, Grant sent part of his army farther out around the Confederate fortifications south of Petersburg and had them strike at Globe Tavern on the Weldon Railroad. (USAMHI)

Above: The subsequent fighting was savage. Confederate Brigadier General Thomas Clingman was so seriously wounded that he never again saw real field service. Regarded as incompetent, he was not sorely missed. (NA)

Left: It was the reinforcing Union division of Brigadier General Orlando B. Willcox, seated second from the right, that finally secured the Weldon line. This image was made in August 1864, a few days before the fighting. (USAMHI)

Left: Grant's September offensive involved swift river crossings. The slender finger of land on the other side in this view of a Union pontoon bridge across the James is Jones' Neck. Captain Russell probably made this image that same month. (USAMHI)

Below: There was another crossing at Aiken's Landing, this one a bridge with a removable section to allow Union steamers to pass through. It is just being opened in this image. (USAMHI)

Left: And here the bridge is ready to allow river traffic passage. The engineers could accommodate anything they set their minds to. (MINNESOTA HISTORICAL SOCIETY)

Left: Over these boards tramped the Union army corps of men like . . . (KA)

Below: . . . Major General Edward O. C. Ord. He was on his way toward Chaffin's Bluff, there to assault. . . (USAMHI)

Above: . . . Confederate Fort Harrison. It was one of the strongest of all Southern forts north of Petersburg. Should it fall, the Federals would have taken a major step on the road to Richmond. A bombproof in the fort after the Federals took it and renamed it Fort Burnham. (KA)

Below: Here, in the rear of Fort Gilmer, near Fort Harrison, sits a 27-foot ditch dug to prevent another underground tunnel like that which led to the Great Mine outside Petersburg. (LC)

Left: Brigadier General John Gregg was one of the defenders of Fort Harrison. Only a week later he was killed in fighting a few miles away. (VM)

Above: Even Confederate ships like the ironclad Richmond supported the defense of the capital by firing from the river on Ord's attacking Federals. Robert Wright was an engineer aboard the vessel. (PAUL DE HAAN)

Above: Brigadier General Adelbert Ames, seated center, poses here with his staff in the winter of 1864-65, not long after his attempt to penetrate Lee's new defenses south of Richmond failed. (SOPHIA SMITH COLLECTION, SMITH COLLEGE,

Left: There were Yankee probes and attacks everywhere, it seemed, and most of them were turned back by skillful and desperate commanders like the Confederate Cadmus M. Wilcox, the major general who later at the siege's end managed to hold off the Federals long enough for his army to escape. (WIRHS)

Above: Late in October 1864 Major General Benjamin Butler became actively engaged north of the James again, but failed. Butler sits on the chair at left center, with Brigadier General Godfrey Weitzel seated on the floor next to him. A Brady operator made the image at Bermuda Hundred in the late summer of 1864. (USAMHI)

Above: While Butler was being repulsed, Meade was fighting a desperate battle near Hatcher's Run, southwest of Petersburg, one of his divisions in the fray being led by Major General Gershom Mott. They narrowly averted disaster before a skillful withdrawal. (USAMHI)

Left: Upon Gracie's death, his command was turned over to Colonel Young M. Moody, a Virginian who would make brigadier in March 1865, one of the last generals appointed in the Confederacy. He stands here at right. (VM)

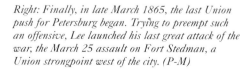

Above: There were hard losses, too, for the Confederates. On December 2 the capable and well-liked Brigadier General Archibald Gracie was killed by a sharpshooter. A New Yorker by birth, he had a large family who remained loyal to the Union. An unpublished ambrotype. (MUSEUM OF THE CONFEDERACY)

Right: Finally, in late March 1865, the last Union push for Petersburg began. Trying to preempt such an offensive, Lee launched his last great attack of the war; the March 25 assault on Fort Stedman, a Union strongpoint west of the city. (P-M)

Above: Leading the attack was one of the last of Lee's premier fighting officers, Major General John B. Gordon. With no formal military training, he yet became one of the ablest battlefield commanders of the war. Fort Stedman was just the last of many courageous assaults for the combative Georgian. (NA)

Within these defenses at Fort Stedman the Federals were taken by surprise by the advancing enemy and nearly put to flight. (P-M)

Right: As he led his brigade against the fort, Brigadier General Philip Cook. suffered a dangerous wound that ended his war service. (VM)

Above: It was in this sector that the Rebels broke through—the line between Fort McGilvery and Fort Stedman. (USAMHI)

Right: But in the end, the Federals behind these Fort Stedman defenses retook what was lost. (USAMHI)

Right: Then on March 29 Yankee divisions led by commanders like Major General Gouverneur K. Warren began to strike at the last available avenue of retreat for the Confederates. (USAMHI)

Far right: There were too few Confederates left to stop them. The attrition in Lee's high command had been dreadful. Just the month before, the brilliant and handsome young Brigadier General John Pegram was killed on Hatcher's Run, three weeks after his marriage. (VM)

Left: Major General Andrew Humphreys, standing hat in hand at the center, led his Union corps in the attack on Hatcher's Run late in March, having become one of Meade's most capable corps commanders. (USAMHI)

Above: Major General Horatio Wright sent his VI Corps into the fight against the Rebels at the same time. (MHS)

Left: There was fighting all along the line as Grant pressed Lee everywhere. Brevet Brigadier General Robert Nugent, seated holding his sword, led his "Irish Brigade" in the fighting on the Southside Railroad on April 2, helping cut off the Confederates' final avenues of escape. (USAMHI)

Right: That same day the IX Corps launched its assaults from Fort Sedgwick, the oft-dubbed "Fort Hell." Captain Russell probably made this view two or three days later, with the battle barely done. (MJH)

Left: Fort Sedgwick fascinated the photographers, who covered every inch of it with their cameras. (USAMHI)

Below: The rains that preceded the final assaults left Fort Sedgwick a muddy mess by the time a cameraman arrived to capture the scene. (LC)

Above: Another Russell image looking along the Union lines from which the attackers sprang on April 2. (USAMHI)

Far left: The fall of Five Forks, some thirteen miles southwest of Petersburg, sealed the fate of the city. There, on April 1, the Yankees had pushed aside the valiant resistance of Brigadier General Eppa Hunton and others, cutting Lee's dwindling lines of retreat. (VM)

Left: Units like the 17th Virginia, commanded by Colonel Arthur Herbert, could not withstand the overwhelming numbers of the enemy. With Five Forks lost, Lee had to abandon Petersburg. (LEE WALLACE)

Below: In the collapse of the Petersburg line, the Confederates lost good men everywhere, but no loss was more disastrous than the death of Lieutenant General A. P. Hill. He had been a pillar of support for Lee. His death was emblematic of the loss of thousands who could not be replaced. (USAMHI)

Above: The loss of Petersburg was a heavy blow to Lee. according to tradition, sometime during the siege of Petersburg the tired old warrior mounted his warhorse Traveller and posed outdoors for an unknown photographer. The war was slowly killing him, but still there is the firmness and stature of the leader about him. This is how his soldiers would ever after remember "Marse Robert". (DEMENTI STUDIO, RICHMOND)

Above: Among the last Confederate commands to hold ot was the brigade of Brigadier General Nathaniel H. Har His men bought time for the rest of the army to make its escape. (USAMHI)

Left: And here, at last, lay Grant's prize. All he had to do was march in. The spires that had for nearly a year been distant landmarks, were now in his grasp. (NA)

Below: James Reekie probably made this image of a street scene in Petersburg. Taken around April 10, it depicts a commonplace sight of train after train of Union supply wagons rolling through the city on their way to the army that followed Lee to Appomattox. (LC)

Left: Captain Russell's image of the principal rail junction in the city, the reason for its military importance and the reason that Lee had to defend the city to the last. Burned cars rest on the tracks at right. The crooked and broken ribbons of rails attest to the inability of the Confederacy to maintain its railroad lines against wear and tear. (LC)

Right: Signs of damage were visible everywhere. The Dunlop house shows where a Federal shell managed to find a nonmilitary target. (USAMHI)

Right: Inside the house all was rubble and ruin. (MHS)

Left: Russell's camera found one bridge that was torched with an engine still upon it, leaving the whole a twisted mess of masonry and iron. (KA)

Right: With Petersburg fallen, the Federal soldiers rushed to the parapets of the Confederate forts to play the tourist and to pose for the cameras. Here Russell found them at Fort Mahone, perhaps as early as April 3. (USAMHI)

Above: Their curiosity seems boundless, that and the relief in at last being able to stand up straight on top of the ground without fear. (USAMHI)

Right: A few had fun posing behind now captured Confederate picket posts like these gabions. T. C. Roche photographed them on April 3. (USAMHI)

Far right: The cannonballs and impedimenta strewn about the ground lent an added touch of realism to scenes that were entirely posed. (USAMHI)

Above: A Confederate artilleryman who has done his best and rests forever. For him, as for all of his comrades, living and dead, the Siege of Petersburg is over. (CHS)

Left: So did the dead, and the photographer found them everywhere, Confederates who died in the attempts to stave off Grant's final onslaught. Roche found this body in the trenches at Fort Mahone on April 3. (MHS)

Below: Lying almost as if asleep, this man died in "Fort Damnation," the nickname for Fort Mahone. The bare feet attest to the dreadful scarcity of shoes in the Southern army. Either he simply did not have shoes when he died or else a fleeing comrade took time out from the evacuation to remove what the dead soldier no longer needed. (CHS)

Above: Only a few yards away from this fallen soldier stands the picket post that Federals posed in for Roche's camera. (RJY)

Left: Roche seemingly could not stop recording scenes of death as he took his camera into Fort Mahone on April 3. They were all over the place. (MHS)

Right: To the victor belongs the glory, but U. S. Grant will spend precious little time riding about his prize on his old warhorse Cincinnati. For Grant's quarry was never a city—it was a man. And though Petersburg has fallen, Lee is still in the field, and with him the Confederacy still lives. (USAMHI)

Richmond, City and Capital at War

EMORY M. THOMAS

Symbol of the Confederacy, the Virginia metropolis fights to the last

Richmond, capital of the Confederacy, for almost four years symbol of Southern independence and determination. It had been a lovely, rather quiet city in 1861 and looks little different in this 1865 view by the Philadelphia partners Levy & Cohen. The state house stands at right, while to the left is the spire of Broad Street Methodist Church and, beside it, an equestrian statue of George Washington. Confederates looked to the example of the "Father of His Country." He was father to theirs as well. (KA)

RICHMOND IN 1860 was an amalgam of mills and magnolias. The place was at once an old Southern town and a young "modern" city.

Located at the falls of the James River, Richmond had been for some time essentially the trading-post community her founder William Byrd II had projected in 1733 and established in 1737. The Virginia legislature during the Revolution had voted in 1779 to move the state capital from Williamsburg to Richmond, and soon after, in 1781, Benedict Arnold honored this distinction by leading a British force into the new capital to raid and burn the town. During the nineteenth century Richmond attracted national attention as the scene of Gabriel Prosser's abortive slave insurrection in 1800, the site of Aaron Burr's treason trial in 1807, and the home of John Marshall and Edgar Allan Poe. The city continued to attract political interest as a state capital and developed a fairly active mercantile economy as a commercial link between the regional countryside and the wider world.

On the eve of the Civil War, though, Richmond was more than a sophisticated trading post. Her principal distinction among Southern cities lay in a somewhat "un-Southern" emphasis upon manufacturing. Much of this activity involved the elemental refinement of local agricultural products, especially tobacco and grain. Twelve mills produced annually three million dollars' worth of flour and meal, and fifty-two tobacco manufacturers processed a gross product worth five million dollars. However important were grains and tobacco to Richmond's economy, the city's iron industry was even more significant. No other city south of the Potomac possessed more than a fraction of Richmond's iron production, which was worth nearly two million dollars in 1860. Joseph R. Anderson's Tredegar Iron Works was the city's largest and most versatile plant and the only establishment in the South capable of producing cannon and railroad rails. Tredegar also led the way in two other atypical southern activities, the attraction of immigrants (mostly German and Irish) and the adaptation of slave labor to industry. In total value of manufactures, Richmond ranked thirteenth among American cities in 1860 and first among cities that soon after composed the Confederacy.

Richmond boasted a relatively sophisticated financial community in 1860—strong banks and insurance companies. The city's slave traders, too, did a brisk business; Richmond ranked second only to New Orleans among the nation's slave markets during the 1850s. At the same time that some Richmonders were manipulating capital with the facility of "Yankees," others were trading with equal facility upon the South's "peculiar institution." And no one seemed to notice the irony.

Despite the urban influence of trade, finance, and manufacturing in Richmond, the place was in many ways still an overgrown town in 1860. The city's population—37,910 total, 23,635 white, 2,576 free Negro, and 11,699 slave—ranked third in 1860 among "Confederate" cities, but twenty-fifth among all American cities. Roughly 38,000 people were not very many, compared to urban centers like New York (1,080,330), Philadelphia (565,529), and Baltimore (212,418). Perhaps even more significant was the dominance of planters and professionals in the upper strata of Richmond social life. As one astute observer noted, "Trade, progressive spirit, and self-made personality were excluded from the plain of the elect, as though germiniferous. The 'sacred soil' and the sacred social circle were paralleled in the mind of their possessors."

Mayor Joseph Mayo served as the city's executive and also as a sort of urban "overseer." The city attempted to act as surrogate master, not only to the slave population, but to the free Negroes, as well. Mayo held court daily to deal with breaches of the city's peace and of Richmond's "Negro Ordinance" which proscribed a rigid code of conduct for both free and bonded Negroes.

Prosperous burgers who occupied a majority of the twelve City Council seats had proven themselves quite capable of running the city. Mayor Mayo was a vigorous man despite his seventy-six years. Whether the men and governmental machinery which ran the small, stable city could rise to the challenges of a swollen, wartime capital was an unanswered question in 1860.

Indeed the question was unasked. Richmond was a conservative city in 1860, and she gave few political indications that she even desired membership in a Southern Confederacy, much less the leadership role implied in be coming its capital. Traditionally the vast majority of Richmond voters were Whigs; Democrats referred to themselves as "the Spartan band." In the presidential election of 1860 Richmonders went Constitutional Union, giving neo-Whig moderate John Bell a two-to-one majority. Then in the selection of delegates to the Virginia convention that considered secession, the city's voters chose two Unionists and one Secessionist. Throughout the winter months of 1861 Virginia's convention sat in the capitol in Richmond and voted moderation while the states of the Deep South seceded and formed the Confederacy at Montgomery.

As the crisis at Fort Sumter between the United States and the Confederate States intensified during the early spring of 1861, the mood in Richmond shifted. By April editorials in all four of the city's newspapers were threatening secession if the Washington government attempted to coerce the seceded states back into the Union. On April 4 the radicals in the state convention failed by only three votes to have a secession referendum put to Virginia voters.

Above: Here Virginia's wartime governors lived and tried their mightiest to manage the state's government separate from that of the Confederacy. In time, Richmond, Virginia, and the C.S.A. seemed indistinguishable. (USAMHI)

Left: One governor, William Smith, spent two years in the Confederate Army as a brigadier general before going to the state house to lead Virginia in the last years of the war. He was called "Extra Billy" because of his penchant for expanding his one-time mail route in return for extra fees from the United States Government back before the war. In battle he wore a beaver hat and carried an umbrella if rain threatened. (VM)

Below: In April 1865 a Northern cameraman, probably Alexander Gardner, made a broad multi-image panorama of the city. Two of his images are joined here, and it presents a scene that would be little different from the look of the capital two or three years before. The state house, as always, dominates the skyline in the left-hand image. (USAMHI, NA)

Left: St. Paul's Episcopal Church stood on Capitol Square, while the square itself was always a popular gathering place for loungers and idle gossipers. (LC)

Right: The view looking west on Main Street. Taken in April 1865, it shows Yankee wagons rolling off in the distance. (LC)

Below: The view from the Confederate "White House" of the Shockoe Valley and the section of Richmond called Butcher Town. It had been, literally, the place where cattle were slaughtered. (NA)

Former Virginia Governor Henry A. Wise then called a kind of counter convention, the "Spontaneous Southern Rights Convention," to meet in Richmond in an effort to stampede the state into radical action.

Then on April 12 came news of the firing on Fort Sumter. Overnight, it seemed, Richmond was transformed. Amid demonstrations of Southern fervor, the state convention passed an ordinance of secession on April 17, and two days later the city exploded in celebration. Ten thousand people, nearly half the white population, poured into the streets, and bonfires, bands, torches, bells, and fireworks hailed the revolution.

A few days later Confederate Vice President Alexander H. Stephens journeyed to Richmond to hasten Virginia's alliance with the Confederacy. In the process he stated, "It is quite within the range of probability that . . . the seat of our government will, within a few weeks be moved to this place." Stephens' remark became prophecy on May 20, when the Confederate Congress voted to move the capital from Montgomery, Alabama, to Richmond.

The presence and influence of Virginia's delegation to the Congress played some role in the decision. Other considerations, however, were also significant. Montgomery in 1861 was small (10,000 people) and ill-prepared to be the seat of a sizable government. Some congressmen were reportedly ready to move anywhere to escape Montgomery's crowded hotels and voracious mosquitoes, and Richmond promised the new government more adequate accommodations and facilities. Perhaps most important, Richmond seemed to offer a war government in proximity to its war. The Confederates assumed that Virginia would become the major battleground in their conflict, and thus moving the government to Richmond seemed a natural way to facilitate the conduct of the war.

Hindsight has offered a set of serious reservations about the wisdom of establishing the Confederate capital at Richmond. Located on the geographical fringe of the nation, the new capital tended to isolate its government from the vast Southern interior. Too, proximity to Washington rendered Richmond a tempting target for Union armies and thus, as one scholar has suggested, a "beleaguered city." And because the South's war eventually included many battle fronts, Richmond's location and defense may have over preoccupied the Confederate government and precluded attention to other theaters which had equal or greater strategic significance. Such latter-day judgments are not unjust, and certainly the Confederacy's prime reason for moving to Richmond (to be close to the war) proved tragically naive.

Yet Richmond was not a bad choice for the capital. To be sure, the location imposed some military strain upon Southern armies; but during the first two years of the war the Tredegar Iron Works were perhaps as crucial to the Confederacy as the government. Southern arms had to hold Richmond whether or not the capital was there. More important, Richmond's role as magnet in attracting Federal armies probably cost the Union more than it did the Confederacy.

The North's "on-to-Richmond" enthusiasm drained men, matériel, and energy that might have been used more effectively elsewhere, and for four years Richmond's defenders defied the

invaders and their hope of quick victory. Far from leading to a quick victory, the hundred miles between capitals became a killing ground on which the North suffered its greatest frustration. Near the end, Richmond's role changed from magnet to "millstone"—hung about the neck of Lee's Army of Northern Virginia. But by then the war had brought about Southern exhaustion everywhere, and though the trenches prolonged the life of Lee's Richmond army, they also trapped them.

In May of 1861, however, the Confederacy lived in blissful ignorance of these gloomy second thoughts, as Jefferson Davis led his government's exodus from Montgomery. Richmond became very quickly the center of intense political and military activity. War was at first parades and picnics in Richmond. "We ought to be miserable and anxious," wrote Mary Chesnut in her famous diary, "and yet these are pleasant days. Perhaps we are unnaturally exhilarated and excited."

The new capital's euphoria certainly lasted through midsummer of 1861, and Richmonders rejoiced over the Southern victory at First Bull Run. But then came the ambulances and trains bearing wounded soldiers and with them an initiation into sobering reality. Richmond became a hospital center in 1861 and continued as one throughout the war. Richmond also became a prison center for captured Federals, and despite efforts to move the captives to prison camps established farther South, Richmond often held 10,000 enemy soldiers on Belle Isle (enlisted men) and in Libby Prison (officers). Wounded friends and captured foes represented only the most obvious challenges faced by Richmond as wartime capital.

Richmond became quickly overcrowded; her population grew eventually to an estimated 100,000, an increase of 150 percent since 1860. The city's crime rate increased as well. Drunken soldiers thought it great sport to seize water melons, throw them into the air, and try to catch them on their bayonets. Gambling houses, "hells," as they were called, flourished despite repeated raids by the city police force, and Richmond became, according to the leading his-

Right: The man in Richmond given charge of these prisons, and all Confederate prisons, was Brigadier General John H. Winder, shown in this unpublished portrait in his prewar uniform as an officer in the United States Army. His task so exhausted him that, like many prisoners in his charge, he died before the war was done. (VM)

Below: More somber to Richmonders was the Virginia State Penitentiary, shown here in an April 1865 image. When the city fell, its 287 inmates escaped, fired the place, and rampaged through the city. (USAMHI)

torian of soldier life in the Confederacy, "the true Mecca of prostitutes." One madam was so bold as to open for business across the street from a YMCA hospital. There "ladies of the evening" advertised themselves from the windows and enticed convalescent soldiers from one bed to another. Although the City Council increased the size of the police force and Mayor Mayo reactivated the "chain gang" for lesser offenders, Richmond remained in the newspaper *Examiner*'s phrase a "bloated metropolis of Vice." Perhaps the most effective method of combating lawbreakers was the policy of the surgeon in-charge of one of the city's military hospitals. Lacking a guardhouse, the officer detained unruly patients and staff in the hospital "dead house" (morgue). Thereafter, he reported, he "never heard anything more from them."

Crowding and crime were both symptom and source of chaotic economic conditions. Richmond did become a center of war industry; the shops and laboratories of Major Josiah Gorgas' Ordnance Bureau multiplied in number and grew in size, as did other government enterprises that produced everything from cannon to currency. Among private enterprises the Tredegar Iron Works, for example, nearly tripled its work force and increased its production to the limit of its ability to secure pig iron. In competition with the wartime prosperity that affected every one from "iron puddlers" to prostitutes, though, was the inflationary spiral of Confederate currency and the scarcity of life's necessities in the city. Wages never kept pace with prices, and crowding compounded the difficulty of supplying the capital with food and fuel. To make matters worse, many of the fields that normally produced food for the city became fields of battle.

Prices rose to the point at which the Richmond *Dispatch* estimated that a family's weekly groceries that cost $6.65 in 1860, cost $68.25 in 1863. Rumors circulated of vast profits made by "extortioners" who hoarded large quantities of provisions and became rich from the sufferings of others. Early spring was the leanest time; new crops were not ready to harvest and stored supplies ran low. In mid-March of 1863, to

Above: Yet there were quieter, more peaceful places. Richmond was a city of churches, and not just the great steepled edifices on Capitol Hill. St. John's Church stood at Broad and 24th streets in the eastern part of the city. A Brady cameraman made this image, and his employer, Mathew Brady himself, stands behind and just right of the tombstone. Here in this church ninety years before, in 1775, Patrick Henry made—or is said to have made— his "Give me liberty" speech. (USAMHI)

Below: Monument Church, or the Monumental Church of Richmond, stood on Broad Street, not far from the Capitol. It was built by private subscription in memory of seventy-two people who died in the 1811 Richmond Theater fire on this site. (USAMHI)

make a bad situation worse, the Confederate Congress authorized the Army to impress foodstuffs. The new law had the effect of unleashing army commissary agents upon the city's marketplaces. Civilian food supplies became quite scarce, and prices of what was available rose alarmingly.

The *Whig* spoke of being "gouged by heartless extortioners and robbed by official rogues," and a War Department official recorded in his diary, "There is a manifest uneasiness in the public mind different from anything I have noticed heretofore."

Then on March 19 and 20, 1863, nine inches of snow blanketed the city and rendered travel in and out of Richmond all but impossible. The weather soon warmed, but as a result roads became quagmires. Those farmers and gardeners who still had food to sell and who were willing to risk impressment at prices now below the market level were all but unable to transport their produce into the city.

On the morning of April 2 a group of working-class housewives gathered at Belvidere Hill Baptist Church. Their neighborhood of Oregon Hill was near the outskirts of the city, and many of their husbands worked in the nearby ironworks. The women talked about their plight and their empty cupboards and then decided to petition the governor for immediate relief. The walk from Oregon Hill to Capitol Square was long, but the day was mild, and as the women walked others joined the march. By the time they reached the governor's mansion the group was sizable, and men and boys had joined the housewives. Governor John Letcher listened to their problems and offered his sympathy, but nothing else. When he had made his offering, Letcher went back inside the mansion, leaving the several hundred people in his front yard to mill about in frustration.

The gathering attracted attention and greater numbers. Soon the gathering became a mob and a leader emerged. Mary Jackson, "a tall, daring Amazonian-looking woman," with a "white

Left: And Richmond's Negroes had their place of worship, too, the First African Baptist Church. It stood just down the street from Monument Church and had one of the South's largest Negro congregations. Many of them pose here on Broad Street for a Brady cameraman. (USAMHI)

Above: The city almshouse stood at the northern edge of the capital. It served as a Confederate hospital during the war until December 1864. Then it became the temporary quarters of the Virginia Military Institute. This Gardner image shows graves in the Shockoe Cemetery in the foreground. (USAMHI)

Right: There were other places where the war did not seem to intrude, places like the tomb of President James Monroe in Hollywood Cemetery. Reekie made this image on April 15, 1865, the same day that the body of another President, Abraham Lincoln, was being carried to the embalmers. (USAMHI)

Above: Richmond was a city playing host to a government at war, and as a result much of the city's normal routine was disrupted and many buildings were converted to wartime purposes. Here the camera views part of the Confederate States Navy Yard at Rocketts, on the James River. The large building in the center is the Quartermaster Department's supply warehouse, one of several buildings in the city devoted to managing supplies for the army. (USAMHI)

Left: Confederate Quartermaster Brigadier General A. R. Lawton was a familiar figure in Richmond and one of the most capable men in the military hierarchy. (MC)

Above: There was a city to run as well as a nation, and here at City Hall, on 11th Street, the affairs of Richmond were attended to by a devoted mayor . . . (USAMHI)

Left: . . . Joseph Mayo. Early in the war he declared that he would never give up his city to an enemy. In April 1865 he actually went riding out into the countryside looking for the Federals to come and accept the city's surrender and help put out the fires. (VM)

feather standing erect, from her hat," urged the people to action. And they followed her white feather away from the governor's mansion toward Richmond's commercial district.

Waving knives, hatchets, and even a few pistols, the mob swept down Main Street shouting for bread. The mob then became a riot. Throughout an area of ten square blocks the rioters broke into shops and warehouses and took food. Some seized the opportunity to take jewelry and clothing as well.

Governor Letcher appeared on the scene and attempted to stop some of the looting, but no one seemed to notice him. Mayor Mayo tried to read the riot act, but no one heard him. Then a company of soldiers, reserve troops from the Tredegar Iron Works, came marching up Main Street. The column drove the advanced rioters back upon the rest and was rapidly clearing the street until someone pulled a horseless wagon across the soldiers' path. The wagon formed a hasty barricade between the troops and the mob, and into the impasse strode the President of the Confederacy.

Jefferson Davis stepped onto the wagon and shouted to the mob. Women hissed while Davis tried to make himself heard. He emptied his pockets, threw his money into the crowd, and then he took out his pocketwatch and gestured at the company of troops. "I will give you five minutes to disperse," he stated, "otherwise you will be fired on."

As if to punctuate the President's demand, the captain of the company commanded, "Load!" The men complied, although no one knew for sure whether they would enforce the President's ultimatum by firing on the crowd of their fellow citizens, some of whom may have been neighbors and relatives. Davis kept his eyes on his watch, and for what seemed a long time no one moved. Then the mob began to drift away, and soon the President and the soldiers were alone in the street. The riot was over.

The City Council met in emergency session the same afternoon and concluded that the riot had been instigated by "outsiders." And instead of hunger the councilmen attributed the riot to "devilish and selfish motives." After resolving that Richmond's "honor, dignity, and safety will be preserved," the city fathers adjourned. During the night artillery batteries unlimbered their pieces on Main Street. The Secretary of War ordered the telegraph office to transmit "nothing of the unfortunate disturbance of today over the wires for any purpose" and made a "special appeal" to Richmond's newspapers "to avoid all reference directly or indirectly to the affair." Thus, on April 3, 1863, the *Dispatch* carried a lead editorial headed "Sufferings in the North."

Although several days later Mayor Mayo was still requesting more troops to prevent further violence, no more bread riots occurred in the capital. The events of April 2 did point out that many Richmonders lived in want. When the City Council met a week after the riot, the members' shock and indignation had worn off. Acting through the Overseers of the Poor, an existing charitable agency, the council directed that needy Richmonders receive food and fuel tickets redeemable at two "free markets."

Two months later the council expanded the relief program by ordering two "visitors" into each of twenty districts to determine need and distribute tickets. Still later the council, faced with declining amounts of food and fuel in the "free markets," established a Board of Supplies to coordinate a search in the countryside for food to be sold at cost in the city. Despite the indifferent success of the board's agent, the city was able to supply food at cost to an average one thousand families per month during the following winter. Eventually the council abandoned the distinction between poor Richmonders and wealthy Richmonders; it ordered the Board of Supplies to secure food "for the city." This exercise in wartime welfare did not prevent some people from being hungry in Richmond. Yet the resourcefulness of the City Council probably prevented many from starving as the pressure of "total war" increased upon the capital.

The sustained strains of home-front war in the Rebel capital severely challenged the hitherto conservative city. It would be easy to say that Richmond's response was often too little too late. Yet there were no solutions to problems that only compounded as the military situation deteriorated. Richmond confronted wounded soldiers, Federal prisoners, refugees, crime, inflation, privation, class conflict, riot, and more. In meeting the challenges of home-front war the city was ever "becoming," always making some new sacrifice in order to endure, and never "being," in the sense of being able to celebrate some point at which she had prevailed.

Richmond did become a national capital. A Prussian visitor probably said it best: "The moral force of the resistance was also centered in Richmond, the capital of the rebellion. . . . The energy of the Confederate resistance that was typified in Richmond impressed me almost as much as the great efforts of the army . . . to hold the field [at Gettysburg] against an overwhelming adversary."

When Major General Thomas "Stonewall" Jackson died as a result of wounds in May of 1863, they bore his body to Richmond to lie in state at the Capitol. A crowd estimated as the largest ever assembled in the city gathered at

Above: The real seat of power in Richmond, however, was here in the old Brockenbrough house, turned into an executive mansion for President Jefferson Davis. Reehie photographed it on April 12, 1865, just nine days after its former occupant had fled . A few days later, President Lincoln had visited the city and sat in Davis' chair here. (USAMHI)

Left: Confederate Vice President Alexander H. Stephens lived here at 12th and Clay streets, on the corner opposite the Executive Mansion. Though neighbors, the two executive of officers spoke as little as possible. (USAMHI)

Below: And here on Franklin Street stood the wartime residence of General Robert E. Lee. The house would become almost as sacred to Virginians as the executive mansion. (USAMHI)

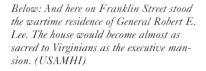

Above: There were many fine homes in the city, like this, the Van Lew mansion. Its occupant, Elizabeth Van Lew, pretended to be eccentric, earning the sobriquet "Crazy Bet," but she also remained loyal to the Union and sometimes sent information through the lines to the Federals. (USAMHI)

In the environs of the city, war industry bloomed during the war, most notably here at the Tredegar Iron Works, chief cannon makers for the Confederacy. Despite a shortage of raw materials, Tredegar was a model of modern efficiency and production in wartime. (USAMHI)

Below: These men worked for the Confederate Nitre and Mining Bureau, trying to collect the raw materials for gunpowder and lead and employing a few Negroes in the process. (MC)

Above: The Richmond arsenal manufactured what guns it could with the shortage of materials. (VM)

the railroad station and followed Jackson's coffin to Capitol Hill. After the prolonged procession of three bands, the hearse, and Jackson's riderless horse through the city, an observer noted, "I should think that every person in the city of Richmond had today buried their nearest and dearest friend." More than the nerve center of government and military command, as "moral force of the resistance" Richmond made a strong bid for the Confederacy's heart as well.

By 1863 the institutions of the capital were also national institutions. Religious denominations printed newspapers, sermons, and tracts in the city and distributed them throughout the South. The Medical College of Virginia was the only medical school in the Confederacy to remain open throughout the war period. And Richmond's press was one of the most active and probably the most influential in the South. During 1863 the Alexandria *Sentinel* moved its office to Richmond and became the capital's fifth daily newspaper. The *Sentinel* and the *Enquirer* were important as quasi organs of the Davis administration; the *Whig* and *Examiner* were equally important as consistent critics of the government. The *Dispatch* continued a more localized focus and pursued a less predictable policy on national issues. Periodicals also grew and prospered in the wartime city. *The Southern Literary Messenger, Southern Illustrated News,* and *Magnolia, A Southern Home Journal,* especially, attracted wide readership, and *The Southern Punch,* modeled on the London humor magazine, offered humor of varying quality to the Confederacy.

Richmond also offered, as the *Whig* reported, "no lack of resources with which to banish dull care." The city's theaters attracted the best entertainers in the South and presented everything from Shakespeare to minstrels. The capital's "official society" led by Varina Davis, the President's wife, entertained its members, even in January 1864, with luncheons of "gumbo, ducks and olives, lettuce salad, chocolate cream, jelly cake, claret cup, champagne, etc." And "insiders" complained of Richmonders' capacity to "swallow scandal with wide open mouths." Less grandiose gatherings were those of the Mosiac Club, whose members, the brightest of the South's intellectuals, gathered whenever one of them fell heir to a quantity of food or drink. Later "starvation parties" came into vogue; host and guests contributed toward musical entertainment and swilled vintage "James River, 1864" for refreshment. No less an authority than General Robert E. Lee encouraged parties in the city for the diversion and relaxation of his troops. And even during the war's last year Mary Chesnut could proclaim from Richmond, "There is life in the old land yet!"

From the beginning, Richmonders were concerned, with reason, for the military security of the capital. In the eastern theater of the war, Confederate armies confronted an enemy whose rallying cry was "on to Richmond."

During the spring and summer of 1862 Richmond was the target of Major General George B. McClellan's Peninsular Campaign, and the war reached the suburbs of the city. Richmond's initial response to this peril was a corporate variety of panic. On March 1 President Davis issued a proclamation of martial law in his capital, and Brigadier General John H. Winder became responsible for conducting military rule within a ten-mile radius of the city. He immediately banned the sale of liquor in Richmond, established a system of passports to control movement to and from the city, and began a series of arbitrary political arrests. On April 22 the Confederate Congress voted itself a pay raise and hastily adjourned. All the while McClellan's army moved closer to the city, making ready for what seemed would be a final thrust. And meanwhile in Richmond, Unionist slogans—"Union Men to the Rescue!" and "God Bless the Stars and Stripes!"—appeared in chalk on walls and fences. Elizabeth Van Lew, an old lady who openly proclaimed her Unionist sympathies, prepared a room in her mansion for General McClellan to be her guest.

Although no one could know it at the time; the crisis in Richmond's fate during the spring of 1862 occurred on May 15. With the USS *Monitor* in the van, Union gunboats were steaming up the James to shell the city. Only hastily prepared obstructions and guns at Drewry's Bluff, about seven miles below Richmond, offered any hope of halting the flotilla. At that point, with so much reason to despair, the city seemed to take heart and assert its will. Governor Letcher called a mass meeting at City Hall to organize citizen-soldiers. As the crowd gathered at five in the afternoon, the guns at Drewry's Bluff opened fire on the enemy ships in the river. Those assembled realized that if the ships got past the river defenses, the Federals would be able to shell the city at will. Then Mayor Mayo arrived and to the tense crowd shouted defiance at the imminent danger. Mayo vowed that should the occasion arise, some other mayor would have to surrender the city. "So help me God, I'll never do it." Next Letcher took the stump. He said he did not know anything about surrender, but were he given the option of giving up the city or watching it shelled, he would respond, "Shell and be damned." Only later that day did the anxious city learn that Drewry's Bluff had held, that the Union ships were returning downriver, and that the immediate danger was past. And later the genius of Lee emerged to drive McClellan's army from the capital's gates.

Although Federal infantry did not so threaten Richmond again until 1864 and 1865, the city had significant scares in 1862 and 1863 from Union cavalry. During the Chancellorsville

Left: In this small factory near Hollywood Cemetery, small-arms ammunition was manufactured for the Confederates in the field. (VM)

Right: Mountains of cannon projectiles stood about the arsenal yard, many of them still in place when the Federals took the city on April 3, 1865. (NA)

Above: Besides munitions, Richmond produced flour in abundance, flour that fed the Confederacy's armies. Here are some of the mills in Manchester, across the James from the capital. (USAMHI)

Right: Another view of one of the Richmond mills. (USAMHI)

Left: The capital was rarely in imminent danger before late 1864. Union Colonel Ulric Dahlgren did lead a daring raid on the city on March 2, 1864, but it failed and he was killed in the attempt. His father was Admiral John A . Dahlgren, inventor of the famous Dahlgren gun. For years afterward the controversy raged over whether or not the colonel had instructed his men to kill Jefferson Davis. (P-M)

Above: Brigadier General Walter H. Stevens was in charge of Richmond's defenses, as well as being Lee's chief engineer. He helped supervise the evacuation of the city on the night of April 2-3, 1865, and was one of the last to cross the Mayo bridge over the James before it was put to the torch. (SOUTHERN HISTORICAL COLLECTION, UNIVERSITY OF NORTH CAROLINA, CHAPEL HILL)

Left: Brigadier General Patrick T. Moore was provost in Richmond, and when the dreadful last day came, it was he who ordered government stores burned . The fires spread, and on April 3 the Yankees marched into a . . . (VM)

Below: . . . devastated city. A whole section of Richmond had been razed to the ground. Though rebuilt almost immediately, for decades to come this area would be known as the "Burnt District." (NA)

Campaign, on May 3, 1863, Richmonders learned that the enemy horsemen were in nearby Hanover County and advancing south toward Richmond. Chaos broke out as bells rang and volunteers hurried out to man the city's fortifications. The commander of Confederate troops in the area announced to a friend that he wished he were dead. The citizen-soldiers were in such a rush to meet the foe that they forgot to carry gunpowder with them for their artillery, and once they remedied that oversight, someone noticed that they had no friction George Stoneman's cavalry came within five miles of the city and turned away. Had they come farther, the 1,500 Federals would have confronted about goo civilians with impotent artillery.

On March 1, 1864, the *Whig* reported that a column of enemy cavalry had been seen behind Lee's lines, but predicted the Federals would "hardly remain long enough to do much damage." As it happened there were two sizable contingents of Union horses converging upon Richmond. Just after noon that day 3,000 troopers commanded by Brigadier General Hugh Judson Kilpatrick appeared on the northern perimeter of the city; they formed for a charge, but then unaccountably withdrew. A bit later in the afternoon the second body of Federal cavalry threatened the city from the west until driven off by Confederate reserves and volunteers. Richmonders correctly concluded that the two thrusts were designed to be a coordinated attack. But only later did the capital learn the full, frightening details of the Federal plan.

The second Union mounted force rode into an ambush as it attempted to withdraw, and its commander, Colonel Ulric Dahlgren, was among those killed in the fray. On Dahlgren's body were found what appeared to be his orders to his command for the ill-fated mission. The colonel had written that he planned to free the captured Federals on Belle Isle, then cross into the city, "exhorting the released prisoners to destroy and burn the hateful city, and . . . not allow the Rebel leader, Davis, and his traitorous crew to escape." Both Confederates and Federals were horrified at such unchivalric intentions, and controversy over the authenticity of the "Dahlgren papers" raged long after the event.

In the summer of 1864 General Ulysses S. Grant attempted to pound Lee into submission. That failing, Grant assaulted Petersburg, the small city about twenty miles south of Richmond. Petersburg was important to Richmond as a railroad junction; if Petersburg fell, only one rail line would remain to connect the Confederacy with its capital. Lee's army held Petersburg; Grant settled down to siege—a campaign of attrition against Petersburg, Richmond, and Richmond's army. Lee accepted the siege; he could see no alternative. His army was too weak, numerically and logistically, to fight "those people" (as Lee termed his enemies) in the open, and trenches might keep the odds nearly even until the Federals tired or erred. Earlier, Grant had vowed "to fight it out on this line, if it takes all summer." It did take all summer, and fall, and winter too; Richmond's army remained steadfast to the end, and some of its finest hours came near the close of its life.

Although the fifty miles of trench networks around the capital remained fairly static, battle-line fighting took place daily. When a Confederate strongpoint fell or a portion of the line wavered, reserve troop units composed of industrial laborers and bureaucrats formed and hurried to reinforce Lee's regulars. Then the work of the industry and government in Richmond ceased for the duration of the emergency, and the Confederacy crumbled a little more. Reliance upon these citizen-soldiers became so frequent that in October 1864, it inspired poetic praise for the "Richmond Reserves":

> Like a beast of the forest, fierce raging
>   with pain,
> The foe in his madness, advances again;
> His eyeballs are glaring, his pulses beat fast,
> While the furies are hastening this effort,
>   his last.
> But the seven-throned queen [Richmond]
>   a calm presence preserves,
> For they've sworn to defend her—the
>   "Richmond Reserves."

However deficient as poetry, the verse displayed an urban consciousness all but unknown three years earlier. And Richmonders who were not poets exhibited a special pride in their city.

On April 1, 1865, the day before Lee evacuated the city, the Sentinel offered this thought: "We are very hopeful of the campaign which is opening, and trust that we are to reap a large advantage from the operations evidently near at hand." Not unlike Brussels on the eve of Waterloo, Richmond during the winter of 1864-65 had erupted into a veritable carnival of parties and weddings—*carpe diem*. One resident remembered that people held "not the brilliant and generous festivals of the olden days in Richmond, but joyous and gay assemblages of a hundred young people, who danced as though the music of cannon shells had never replaced that of the old negro fiddler—who chatted and laughed as if there were no tomorrow."

Below: On April 6, with the rubble barely cool, Alexander Gardner made this panoramic view of the Burnt District, with the state house in the distance. (USAMHI, VM)

Above: Whole blocks of warehouses along the James River were destroyed. (NA)

Above: Levy & Cohen came to record their own views of the ruined city. The large white building still standing was the old U.S. Customs House, which served as the Confederate Treasury. (KA)

Above: Yankee horses wait quietly outside the Confederate Treasury, right next to extensive ruins from the fire that was rather selective in its destruction. (USAMHI)

Right: The people of Richmond were soon up and about again in the city, searching among the ruins for surviving belongings, for lost friends and relatives, or just for some remnant of a way of life now suddenly vanished. (USAMHI)

Above: A paper mill that did not survive. (USAMHI)

Right: Part of the mammoth Gallego Flour Mills, totally destroyed. Pictures of their ruins would stand for more than a century as the perfect image of . . . (USAMHI)

"Tomorrow" came on Sunday, April 2, 1865. Southwest of Petersburg, at Five Forks, the day before, Major General George Pickett's division had been cut off and devoured by the Federals; the thin line of earth and men at Petersburg which stood between Richmond and capture was broken. Lee responded to the situation with his usual professional competence; he endeavored to save his army by abandoning the now untenable capital.

Jefferson Davis was at St. Paul's Church when Lee's telegram arrived from Petersburg. As the Reverend Charles Minnegerode read the ante-Communion service, Davis read the sentence of doom pronounced upon his capital. The President quickly left the church and began the process of evacuating his government. By the time Richmond's churches had concluded their worship, the mass exodus of government officials from the services had confirmed the worst.

Pandemonium broke out that Sunday afternoon. "The office-holders were . . . making arrangements to get off. Every car was ordered to be ready to take them South. . . . The people were rushing up and down the streets, vehicles of all kinds were flying about, bearing goods of all sorts and people of all ages and classes who could go. . .". The City Council met to try to provide protection for private property and to plan the destruction of liquor supplies in the city. Meanwhile, the army prepared to destroy whatever military supplies could-not be moved. Darkness did not slow the frantic activity.

By the early hours of April 3, most of the military and nearly all of the government officials had left. About three o'clock in the morning a fire began. The blaze probably started as part of the Confederacy's attempt to destroy everything that might be of value to the enemy. The flames engulfed the tobacco warehouses, the railroad bridges, the arsenal, and soon raged out of control and burned a large area of the city, from Capitol Square to the James River. As the massive fire blazed, rioting began. Several thousand people tried to reach the stored rations in the commissary depot before the flames. As a committee appointed by the City Council dumped barrels of whiskey into the streets, rioters drank from the gutters.

The evacuation fire, which smoldered in the debris until late June 1865, was devastating. It consumed more than twenty square blocks and all but destroyed the city's commercial district. Every bank, every saloon, and almost every press in the city was destroyed. Between eight hundred and twelve hundred buildings went up in flames, and damage estimates reached thirty million nineteenth-century dollars.

At dawn on April 3 a Confederate rear guard fired the last remaining bridge over the James and dashed away. Soon thereafter Mayor Mayo, who had sworn never to give up the city, rode out of Richmond to try to find someone to whom to surrender. Eventually he found Union Major General Godfrey Weitzel and made arrangements for the restoration of law and order under an occupation regime. At eight o'clock the Federals entered Richmond and marched through the city to Capitol Square.

A few days later President Abraham Lincoln came to survey his prize. And someone wrote a song to celebrate Richmond's capture. Perhaps more than anything else that song expressed what Richmond had meant to the Confederacy:

Now Richmond has fallen, rebellion is done,
Let all men rejoice for the victory is won!
The city where slavery once dwelt in her pride
Is now in our hands and the rebellion has died.
Now Richmond is taken, they'll harm us no more
For treason is crushed and rebellion is o'er.
Our armies have triumphed, the traitors have fled.
We've captured their city, secession is dead.

The last hope of the Confederacy perished in the flames of the fallen capital.

Above: . . . the utter destruction of modern war. (USAMHI)

Right: Though water still flowed over the mill wheel, the machinery no longer turned. Like the Confederacy, it had ground to a halt. (USAMHI)

Left: Everything of military value had to be destroyed. The fleeing Rebels set fire to their railroad bridges like this one on the Richmond & Petersburg line. (USAMHI)

Below: Only portions of the line, like this section connecting Belle Isle with Manchester, remained. (USAMHI)

Left: All else was ruin. (USAMHI)

Right: When the Yankees came, they quickly saved what they could, repaired more, and got the city working again. Pontoon bridges over the James allowed traffic to cross once more. (NA)

Below: City Hall might not bustle for a time, but the Federal soldiers camped across the street ensured that things would be orderly. (USAMHI)

Below: The arsenal yard was a shambles. (USAMHI)

Below: The arsenal itself, shown in this panorama, lay in complete ruins. (USAMHI)

Right: Camps of laborers, many of them Negroes like these, sprang up to do the work of rebuilding the railroads. (KA)

Above: The canal along the waterfront filled once again, but now with U.S. Government transports. (USAMHI)

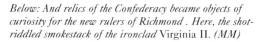

Below: And relics of the Confederacy became objects of curiosity for the new rulers of Richmond . Here, the shot-riddled smokestack of the ironclad Virginia II. *(MM)*

Above: It was a trophy of war now. (USAMHI)

Right: So were scores of pieces of Confederate artillery, lined up at Rocketts for use by the Federals or to be transported to the North. (LC)

Right: Captured guns, still caked with mud from the spring rains, were everywhere. (NA)

Above: And so was their attendant equipment, like this giant gun sling for carrying pieces of heavy artillery. (LC)

Left: There were even a few bits of exotica, like the English Whitworth breech-loading rifle that could fire a solid bolt as far as five miles. (LC)

Below: There was a new governor in the governor's mansion, Francis H. Pierpont, who had helped organize the new state of West Virginia and served during the war as "governor" of those Virginia counties under Federal control. Now he took a seat on the porch of his new mansion, ruling the entire state at last. (KA)

Above: Now the Stars and Stripes flew over Libby Prison, its cells empty of the human misery that made it infamous. (USAMHI)

Right: The burned bridges over the James were rebuilt. (NA)

Above: The Virginia state house, once Capitol of the Confederacy, despite a few broken window panes, went back to the work of housing a state legislature only. Mathew Brady stands fifth from the right on the porch. (USAMHI)

Below: Crowds milled about the Washington monument in Capitol Square once more, where Reekie photographed both Federal soldiers and recently paroled Confederates on April 14, 1865. (USAMHI)

Above:Yankee officers like Major General E. O. C. Ord could pose with his wife and daughter on the 'porch of the Confederate executive mansion. (USAMHI)

Below: And Old Glory waved at last over a burned and battered but surviving Richmond. In a remarkably short time the city would rebuild, moving with the reunited nation into a new era. (NA)

An End at Last

LOUIS MANARIN

When blood and bravery and indomitable will could do no more, the Southern banners were furled

Above: Petersburg theirs, jubilant Federal soldiers caper on the ramparts of Fort Sedgwick, raising their hats and pointing off toward the now silent Confederate lines. (LC)

"AFTER FOUR YEARS of arduous service, marked by unsurpassed courage and fortitude, the Army of Northern Virginia has been compelled to yield . . ." Thus began General Robert E. Lee's farewell address to his army. The decision to yield had not come easy. Only after it became obvious that it would be useless to go on did Lee agree to surrender those who had remained steadfast to the end.

When the end came, it was not unexpected. The Confederate ranks had been thinned by battle, attrition, and the realization that will and determination were not enough. The valiant defense of the Petersburg line, the battle at Sayler's Creek southwest of Richmond, the retreat to the west, and the running attacks of Major General Philip Sheridan's cavalry had taken their toll in dead, wounded, captured, and missing. Many of the last had taken the opportunity to slip away in the confusion of battle and the retreat march.

The night sky on April 8, 1865, presented Lee's men with visible evidence of the military situation. They had been fighting rearguard and flank attacks, but now the sky reflected the red glow of campfires to the east, south, and west. The Federal army had succeeded in moving past the Rebel left flank and across the route of retreat. Only to the north was there an absence of he red glow. Lee's army was almost surrounded.

As the troops bedded down, there was an uneasiness. The army was stretched out and vulnerable to the hit-and-run attacks of the Federal cavalry. Out of the night the blue-clad troopers would swoop down and do their damage and then retire under the cover of darkness. Brigadier General Lindsay Walker's artillerists had successfully repulsed one lightning Federal strike, but when Brigadier General G. A. Custer's troopers struck a second time, about nine o'clock in the evening, they captured twenty four pieces of artillery. The silence from Walker's camp told the Confederates what had happened.

Lee met with Lieutenant General James Longstreet, Major General John Gordon, and Major General Fitz Lee during the evening of April 18 and informed them of the correspondence he had had with Union General U. S. Grant. After reading Grant's letter of April 7 calling for the surrender of the Army of Northern Virginia, Longstreet had counseled his commander with the words "Not yet." In response to Lee's reply asking for clarification on terms, Grant had called for surrender of the army under conditions stating that the men would be on parole until properly exchanged. Surrender was the last option for Lee, and as long as he could, he would keep his army in the field. He proposed to meet with Grant to discuss the restoration of peace, not to negotiate a surrender. He had not received a reply at the time of his meeting with his generals on the evening of April 8. After discussing their options, they agreed that one more effort would be made to break through toward Lynchburg. If they could make it through, the army would turn southward. The plan called for the cavalry under Fitz Lee, supported by the II Corps under Gordon, to drive the Federals back in front, wheel to the left and hold the enemy while the army moved behind their screen.

When the sun came up on Palm Sunday

morning, April 9, 1865, Gordon's men, numbering about 1,600, were in position a half mile west
of Appomattox Court House. On his right,
Gordon saw that Fitz Lee's 2,400 troopers
extended his line. As darkness turned to light,
the Federal earthworks became visible across
the field. If Federal cavalry defended them, then
Gordon and Fitz Lee felt they could force them
back. If the Federal infantry was up, then the
end was at hand.

Major General Bryan Grimes, the fiery North
Carolinian, asked to lead the attack and Gordon
told him to advance all three divisions. The
Federal troopers behind the earthworks gave
way as Gordon's men pressed forward and captured two pieces of artillery. Wheeling to the left,
the jubilant gray-clad infantry opened the road to
Lynchburg. Within an hour, Fitz Lee, on
Gordon's right flank, reported the presence of
Federal infantry. Major General Edward Ord,
with three Union divisions, had marched his
men all day and night and had arrived "barely in
time." Gordon sent for reinforcements, but
Longstreet was being pressured and expected an
attack momentarily on the rear guard. Union regiments appeared on Gordon's right and rear, and
Federal cavalry began to demonstrate on his left
flank as if to drive a wedge between the
Confederate forces. Within three hours the situation had changed from a glimmer of light to
darkness.

When he received reports from his commanders, Lee decided to meet with Grant between
Longstreet's and Major General George Meade's
lines. A truce was ordered and Longstreet was
told to inform Gordon. Upon receipt of the order,
Gordon directed an officer to ride out under a
white flag to inform Ord of the truce. The officer
returned with Custer who demanded immediate
and unconditional surrender in the name of
General Sheridan. Refusing to recognize
Custer's authority, Gordon declined to surrender.
Custer demanded to see Longstreet and Gordon
sent him to the rear under escort. When Custer

Above: It was the Federal victory on April 1, 1865, at Five Forks, southwest of Petersburg, that forced General R. E. Lee at last to evacuate that city and Richmond. Here Rebel prisoners captured in the fight line up on their way to the rear. (USAMHI)

Above: And now the Yankees lay pontoon bridges over the James River for the march into Richmond, occupied at last. A Russell view showing some of the Manchester mills, across the river from the capital. (USAMHI)

Below: Immediately Yankee ships like the Unadilla *start the work of clearing the James of obstructions and "torpedoes," opening it to traffic. (KA)*

Above: Major General Godfrey Weitzel is the general who first takes over the city, send-ing out a telegram that announced on April 3, "We entered Richmond." He stands, boots crossed, on the left of the steps, along with his staff . (VM)

Above: And quickly the traffic commenced. General U. S. Grant's headquarters boat, the River Queen, *can now ply the waters of the James. Aboard this boat the abortive Hampton Roads Peace Conference had taken place back in February 1865. President Lincoln and Grant met aboard the vessel for conferences in March, and on April 4 it brought the President to Richmond for a tour of the captured city. (USAMHI)*

Right: Lincoln transferred to the USS Malvern *for part of the journey to Richmond, entertained by its flag commander . . . (USAMHI)*

Below: . . . Rear Admiral David D. Porter. Porter here wears crape in mourning for the President, who lay dead barely more than a week after his visit. (USAMHI)

Right: Soon the visitors flooded the docks at City Point and Richmond both. Members of Major General George Meade's family crowd the deck of this steamer at City Point, anxious to see the general and to view the scenes of conquest. (P-M)

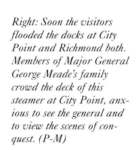

repeated his demand to Longstreet, "Old Pete" also refused to recognize him and ordered him to leave. In the meantime, Gordon had given the word to Fitz Lee, and Lee pulled Brigadier General Thomas Rosser's, Brigadier General Thomas Munford's, and the greater part of his cavalry command out of the action to escape the surrender. Recognizing General Sheridan coming through the lines, Gordon rode out to meet him. Gordon showed him Lee's truce order and both men agreed to a cease-fire until they received word from their commanders.

Grant notified Lee that he could not discuss terms of peace but that he hoped no more blood would be shed. Lee then wrote and asked Grant for a meeting to discuss terms of surrender. Meanwhile, Lee met with Meade, and a truce was declared on that part of the line. Lee then returned through Longstreet's lines to await word from Grant. On the edge of an apple orchard, he stretched out on a pile of fence rails covered with a blanket. Little was said. Officers came up to discuss the situation with members of his staff and Longstreet came to meet with his commander. Lee was worried about the terms. It had been a hard fought struggle and his men had given their all. Now, he was faced with having to admit defeat. Word was passing through his army. Men cried out in rage for one more fight. Tears came to the eyes of many when they received word that the army was going to be surrendered. Others breathed a sigh of relief that it was over. Artillerists on the move were told to turn in to the nearest field and park their guns. Some units had made it through to Lynchburg before the end came, but those that remained did not like the idea of surrendering the powder they had been forced to save.

A little after noon on April 9, a Federal courier rode up to the Confederate camp to accompany Lee to the meeting with Grant. Colonel Orville E. Babcock delivered Grant's reply to Lee's letter. Grant agreed to meet and asked Lee to pick the place. Lee would not delegate the responsibility of arranging the surrender. He asked Colonel Walter Taylor, his adjutant general, to accompany him, but that officer asked to be spared the unpleasant task on the grounds that he had been on two long rides that morning. Lieutenant Colonel Charles Marshall of Lee's staff mounted his horse as did Sergeant G. W. Tucker, who had been at Lieutenant General A. P. Hill's side when he was mortally wounded before Petersburg. Lee, Marshall, and Tucker, accompanied by Babcock, rode toward Appomattox Court House. Marshall was sent forward to find a suitable place to hold the meeting. Tucker was sent with him.

As they rode into the small village, Marshall met Wilmer McLean. This gentleman had lived about a mile from Manassas Junction. After witnessing the battle there in 1861, McLean moved to Appomattox to escape the war. Marshall told him of his mission and McLean showed him an old dilapidated unfurnished house. When Marshall informed him that it was not adequate, McLean offered his home as a meeting place. Marshall sent Tucker back to tell Lee and Babcock while he went into the house to select a room. When they arrived, Lee and Babcock joined Marshall in the parlor. Babcock stationed an orderly outside to direct General Grant.

About a half hour later, Grant rode up. Babcock opened the door and Grant entered the room alone. The two generals shook hands, exchanged greetings, and sat down. After whispered conversation with Grant, Babcock left the room and returned with a number of Federal officers. Among the group were Generals Sheridan and Ord, Brigadier General Horace Porter, Colonel Adam Badeau, and Lieutenant Colonel Ely Parker. They formed a semicircle behind Grant.

After some pleasantries with Grant about service together in the Mexican War, Lee broached the subject of surrender terms. Grant outlined his thoughts calling for the surrender of all equipment and supplies. The men would be paroled not to take up arms until properly exchanged. Lee acknowledged acceptance and Grant put the terms in writing. Lee reviewed them and when Grant asked if he had any suggestions, Lee did mention that the terms did not provide for the horses owned by the men in the ranks. Pointing out that it did provide for the officers, Grant replied that he would not change

Right: But though the enemy capital had fallen, the war was not over. It could never be over so long as this wily and elusive adversary remained at large. Another Julian Vannerson portrait of Robert E. Lee gave little hint that the man behind this peaceful aspect was a champion of war. (VM)

Below: But now he was on the run. As he evacuated Richmond, he took with him what he could and destroyed what he could not. Within days Reekie photographed wreckage left behind. (USAMHI)

Below: It was Major General Philip Sheridan who brought on the Confederate disaster at Five Forks, and thereafter his cavalry dogged the retreating Rebels all along their route. Then, on April 6, he and part of Meade's infantry caught them at Sayler's Creek. (USAMHI)

Left: Meade was after the fleeing Confederates, Meade and his generals. Shown here a few weeks later, they are, from the left, Brevet Brigadier General George Macy, provost; Brevet Major General A. S. Webb, chief of staff; Major General Andrew A. Humphreys, commanding the II Corps; Major General Charles Griffin, commanding the V Corps; Meade; Major General John G. Parke, commanding the IX Corps; Brevet Major General Henry J. Hunt, chief of artillery. The brigadier at right is unidentified. (USAMHI)

Right: Also taken was Brigadier General Montgomery D. Corse. The Yankees simply overwhelmed them. (USAMHI)

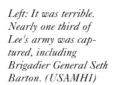

Left: It was terrible. Nearly one third of Lee's army was captured, including Brigadier General Seth Barton. (USAMHI)

Left: The next day Major General Thomas Rosser attempted to hold the vital railroad crossing of the Appomattox River at High Bridge, west of Petersburg. A desperate little fight ensued. (VM)

Right: Brigadier General James Dearing engaged Federal Brigadier General Theodore Read in a pistol duel that left Read dead and Dearing dying, the last Confederate general to die of wounds in battle. (USAMHI)

the terms but he would instruct his officers to allow any man who claimed to own a horse or mule to keep it for farming.

Grant instructed that his letter be copied and Lee directed Marshall to draft a reply. While the writing was being completed, Grant introduced his officers to Lee. It was not a pleasant experience for Lee, and as soon as the formalities were over, he brought up the matter of Federal prisoners. Grant agreed to accept them. When Lee requested that a train from Lynchburg be allowed to pass so he could supply his men with provisions, it was learned that the train had been captured by Sheridan the night before. Grant offered to send Lee food, and after discussion as to the amount, he directed that 25,000 rations be sent to Lee's men.

Lee made some changes in Marshall's draft of the letter accepting the surrender terms. Borrowing a piece of paper, Marshall copied the letter and Lee signed it. Marshall sealed the letter and presented it to Colonel Parker who gave him Grant's surrender terms letter. The exchange of letters formally completed the surrender of the Army of Northern Virginia. Before leaving, Lee asked that Meade be notified of the surrender to avoid any possible flare-up of fighting. He also requested that the two armies be kept separate for the time being. Grant agreed and dispatched men to notify Meade. It was close to 4 P.M. when Lee and Grant shook hands again, and Lee bowed to the other officers and left the room. On the porch, he called for his horse, and as he mounted, Grant came down the steps. The Union general removed his hat and his subordinates followed. Lee acknowledged their gesture by raising his hat. Without a word, he turned Traveller and rode out of the yard.

Lee knew that Grant had given favorable surrender terms. What could have been a humiliating experience was made more bearable by the genuine courtesy and respect displayed on both sides. As he rode into his lines toward his camp at the apple orchard, Lee's veterans began crowding around asking if the army had been surrendered. With tears in his eyes, he told them that it had been. Expressions of anger, frustration, and sorrow came from the men. Upon Lee's arrival at the camp, he notified Colonel T. M. R. Talcott, commanding the Engineers, that the rations would be coming in. Lee then walked away to be by himself. He paced up and down to relieve the pressures pent up inside of him. His solitude was interrupted by visiting Federal officers who wanted to meet him. After receiving a letter from Grant appointing commissioners to arrange the details of the surrender, Lee mounted Traveller to return to his own headquarters. Along the road he was met by more men from his army. The word of the surrender had passed quickly and the road was lined on both sides. Officers on horseback stood behind the lines. When he arrived at his headquarters, others were waiting to see him, to talk to him, to shake his hand. That evening, while seated around the campfire, Lee instructed Marshall to draft a farewell address to the army.

The next day, April 10, Lee dispatched orders to his subordinate commanders to prepare final reports on the last campaign. When he found that Marshall had not prepared the draft of the farewell address, he told him to go into his ambulance where he would not be disturbed.

Longstreet, Gordon, and Brigadier General William N. Pendleton were appointed by Lee as commissioners to draft the surrender procedures. Grant had appointed Major Generals John Gibbon, Charles Griffin, and Wesley Merritt. These men met in the McLean house the same day to make arrangements for the formal surrender, the transfer of public property, private horses, and mules, and the lease of transportation to officers. It was also agreed that the terms would embrace all men within a twenty five-mile radius of the courthouse and units that were operating with the army on April 8, except those that were over twenty miles from Appomattox on the ninth. Each parole was to be signed by the soldier's commander or his staff officer, not by the Federal provost marshal. The signed parole was sufficient for passage through Federal lines. By a separate order, Grant authorized free travel on Federal transports and military railroads.

During the morning of April 10, Grant had attempted to ride over to meet with Lee but was stopped by Confederate pickets. When he heard of this, Lee mounted Traveller and rode out to meet his former adversary. The two men greeted each other by lifting their hats. Grant expressed a desire to prevent further bloodshed and suggested that if the other Confederate armies would surrender then peace would come. He felt that Lee could use his influence and prestige to bring this about, but Lee felt it was not his decision but President Jefferson Davis'. After about a half hour, the two men parted. On his way back to camp, Lee met General Meade. The two conversed and then rode back to Lee's headquarters.

When Marshall finished his draft of the farewell address, Lee reviewed it. He struck out one paragraph that he felt was too harsh and changed some of the words. The address was then copied and given to Lee for his signature. Once signed, copies of General Order No. 9 were made, signed by Lee, and distributed to his subordinate commanders. They had it transmitted to the men in the ranks. Copies were made by officers and men and brought to Lee for his signature.

The next day, April 11, the campaign reports came into Lee's headquarters from his subordinate commanders, and he began to prepare his own final report. Muster rolls were made out for all Confederate units and copies were forwarded to both headquarters. A total of 28,231 men of all arms of the service were reported. The paroles, which had to be printed, were received. Formal surrender of the artillery and cavalry occurred on this day. Union Major General John W. Turner's division, of the Army of the James, witnessed the transfer of equipment and animals as the members of Confederate artillery units left their guns parked for the last time. Those who claimed horses or mules were allowed to keep them. Upon receipt of their paroles, they said good-bye to comrades and began the trek home. The remaining Confederate cavalry of Major General W. H. F. "Rooney" Lee's division laid down their swords and fire arms before Major General Ranald Mackenzie's troopers. With their paroles in hand, they rode off, not to take up arms until properly exchanged.

The Confederate commissioners had asked that the infantry be allowed to stack arms, cartridge boxes, and flags in their camps, but Grant would not consent. The surrender could not be a symbolic gesture of walking away from the

Right: High Bridge and the nearby wagon road bridge were supposed to be burned by the Confederates once they had crossed over them. (USAMHI)

Below: However, Colonel T. M. R. Talcott of Lee's staff was unable to get the fires set in time, and the Yankees rushed the bridge and put them out. Everything for Lee was going awry now. (VM)

Below: The next day, April 8, Lee hoped to find provisions for his starving army awaiting him here at Appomattox Station. He found nothing. (LC)

Above: After Sayler's Creek, Lee was in danger of having more generals than privates. On April 7 Brigadier General Henry A. Wise joined him. Former Virginia governor and a brother-in-law of the General Meade now dogging them, Wise led a battered division out of the trap at Sayler's Creek. When Lee teased him, saying he could be shot for what he said about a superior officer who ran away, Wise replied "Shot! I wish you would shoot me. If you don't, some Yankee probably will within twenty-four hours." (USAMHI)

Left: Now the generals who had lost their commands began to find their way into his lines. Major General Bushrod Johnson lost his, or so he thought, at Sayler's Creek. His men fought their way out under Wise. (USAMHI)

Above: Brigadier General William P. Roberts, the youngest general in the Confederacy, was only twenty-three and lost his command at Five Forks. Lee had no more men to give him at Appomattox. (USAMHI)

Above: Lee was trapped. Desperately he allowed Major General Bryan Grimes to make a last attack on the morning of April 9. He could not cut his way out, and that left no alternative but for Lee to meet Grant to discuss terms of surrender. (USAMHI)

Right: By April 9 the last avenue of escape for Lee was cut off, largely thanks to the swiftness of one of Sheridan's best division commanders, Brigadier General George A. Custer. He would never again experience the glory he knew at Appomattox. Eleven years later he would die looking for it at Little Big Horn. (USAMHI)

instruments of war. It had to be an act of relinquishing equipment and flags and the act had to be witnessed. Declining to give up their battle flags, some units tore them up and distributed pieces to the members. Some flags were smuggled out by men who refused to surrender and slipped away during the night. Some were secreted under the clothing of men who took part in the final ceremony.

On the morning of April 12, the Confederate infantry prepared to carry out the final act. The units formed in ranks, with officers and flags in position. General John Gordon's command started down the ridge first. As the Confederate column came up the hill, Brigadier General Joshua L. Chamberlain, commanding the Federal division, gave orders for the bugler to sound carry arms, the marching salute. Gordon responded by saluting Chamberlain and ordering his men to carry arms. Victor saluted vanquished and they returned the honor. Goldon's men marched beyond the Federal column and halted. The ranks were dressed and the order was given to fix bayonets. The command to stack arms came next, and the men moved across the road and stacked their arms. Cartridge boxes were hung from the muskets and battle flags were rolled up and laid on the stacks.

The units re-formed in the road and marched past the courthouse and halted. Here they broke ranks, shook hands, and bade each other farewell as the other units moved through the cordon to stack arms. Some men returned to camp, but most of them turned toward home. Men from the same area usually left in small groups under command of the ranking officer. They carried with them the news that the Army of Northern Virginia had been surrendered. Lee officially notified President Davis of this in his report of April 12, and although he did not witness the surrender, Lee remained on the field until the act was completed. With his own parole in hand he turned his face toward Richmond, and with members of his staff he started the long journey back.

In fact, on April 10 news of Lee's surrender reached Davis at Danville, in southern Virginia, where he had paused on his flight from Richmond, and late that day he left by rail for Greensboro, North Carolina. The Confederate cavalry and artillery units that had escaped before the army was surrendered made their way to Lynchburg, in the west, where, after consulting the Confederate Secretary of War John C. Breckinridge, they disbanded. Some units made their way south intent on joining General Joe Johnston in North Carolina, while others struck out for home. As word of Lee's surrender crossed the mountains and men from his army brought the word, other units began to dissolve or disband. Major General Lunsford Lomax's command, operating between Lynchburg and Danville began to disintegrate as the Virginia units left the ranks. Word of Lee's surrender caused Colonel William Nelson to disband his artillery battalion at Pittsylvania Court House and to distribute the horses among the men. The Federal cavalry entered Lynchburg on April 13 and on April 15 General Lomax and Brigadier General William L. Jackson disbanded their commands at Buchanan, in the Shenandoah Valley. Federal Major General Winfield Scott Hancock extended Grant's terms to all soldiers of the Army of Northern Virginia in the valley if they would

come in and receive their paroles. At Millwood, on April 21, Colonel John Singleton Mosby disbanded his Rangers. Effective resistance was at an end in Virginia by the end of the month.

Meanwhile, at Greensboro, President Davis met with Generals Johnston and P. G. T. Beauregard and his Cabinet on April 12. Johnston's army was at Hillsborough while Major General William T. Sherman's was preparing to enter Raleigh. Johnston recommended negotiation but Davis felt that it would only result in surrender. Outvoted, Davis agreed to authorize Johnston to meet with Sherman. While they were discussing conditions in North Carolina, the last major city of the Confederacy fell. Mobile, Alabama, was occupied by Union troops under Major General E. R. S. Canby. Confederate forces under Major General D. H. Maury had evacuated the night before toward Meridian, Mississippi, with hopes of joining Johnston's army in North Carolina.

Sherman's men occupied Raleigh on April 13 and pressed on to Durham Station the next day. On the fourteenth Johnston communicated with Sherman and sought a temporary suspension of hostilities pending discussions of peace. After negotiations as to time and place, they agreed to meet on April 17 on the road between Durham Station and Hillsborough. Sherman left Raleigh by train for Durham Station, and there he met Brigadier General Hugh Kilpatrick who provided a Union cavalry escort. As Sherman's party set out with a cavalryman in the lead carrying a flag of truce, Johnston and Lieutenant General Wade Hampton were moving toward Durham Station with an escort. Hampton's orderly carried the flag of truce.

Right: . . . accompanied by his military secretary, Lieutenant Colonel Charles Marshall . . . (TULANE UNIVERSITY, NEW ORLEANS)

Below: . . . Lee entered this parlor. A postwar image shows the now bare room where Lee and Grant met to make peace. For the Army of Northern Virginia, four years of arduous service were done. (NA)

When the two groups met, Johnston and Sherman shook hands and introduced their aides. Johnston noted that he had passed a small farmhouse, so he and Sherman rode back down the road to James Bennett's log farmhouse. Lucy Bennett met them at the door, and after granting their request to use the house, she retired with her four children to one of the outbuildings. The two men closed the door to the one room house and discussed amnesty and surrender terms in private. Unable to reach a decision on all points, they agreed to meet again the next day. On the eighteenth Confederate Secretary of War Breckinridge joined the discussion and it was then that Sherman drew up a memorandum of agreement.

In their discussion the three men went beyond the original intent of the meeting and considered terms for a general armistice, dealing with reconstruction policies that were not in fact within Sherman's authority to establish. Sherman believed he was expressing President Lincoln's wishes in his terms. But Lincoln was dead, murdered on April 14, and Andrew Johnson now sat in the White House.

The agreement did put an end to the fighting, even though the other terms would be rejected by the Federal authorities. With the exception of Major General James H. Wilson's Union cavalry raids in Georgia and Alabama and Major General George Stoneman's in western North Carolina, most of the remaining engagements east of the Mississippi were minor skirmishes. Jefferson Davis moved to Charlotte where he approved Johnston's agreement with Sherman. Unknown to Davis at the time, Sherman was being informed that the agreement had been disapproved by Washington and he was directed to resume active campaigning within forty-eight hours if Johnston did not surrender.

At Johnston's request, Sherman met with him again at the Bennett place on April 26. By the terms of the agreement of that day, Johnston's army was to be mustered at Greensboro and there the ordnance supplies were to be turned in and the men were to be paroled. Brigadier General John M. Schofield,

Above: The gallant cavalryman Major General Wesley Merritt was another. For him the Civil War was only the beginning of a brilliant career that went on for thirty-five more years and included service in the Spanish-American War. (CWTI)

Above: On April 12, 1865, when the Confederate infantrymen formally marched up and stacked their arms for the last time, Grant detailed Brigadier General Joseph J. Bartlett to receive them. With that symbolic act, the war in Virginia was done. (P-M)

Right: The collapse was everywhere. Down in North Carolina, Major General William T. Sherman finally brought Confederate General Joseph E. Johnston and his army to bay near Durham Station. In this modest home, the Bennett place, Johnston and Sherman met to arrange the surrender of yet another Confederate army. (LC)

who was to be Federal departmental commander, agreed to six supplemental terms when Johnston objected to the general terms. He assured Johnston that there would be sufficient transportation, that each brigade could keep one seventh of their arms until they reached their state capital, that both officers and enlisted men could retain their private property, that troops from Texas and Arkansas were to be provided water transportation, and that all naval forces within the limits of Johnston's command were also included. The men were to be supplied with ten days' rations so they would not have to live off the country side. The agreement, signed by Johnston and Schofield, brought an official end to hostilities in North Carolina.

Johnston announced the termination of hostilities to the governors of the Confederate states and the Confederate Army. When word was received that the Army had been surrendered, men began leaving. Major General Joseph Wheeler vowed he would not surrender and he left with those of his command who would follow him to attempt to find President Davis. Wade Hampton, who was not personally with Johnston's army at the time, declared that he was not included in the surrender and would not stay. When his cavalrymen left, he rode after them and ordered them to return. While they did so, he rode to join President Davis. For those units remaining with the Army, muster rolls were prepared and paroles were issued. Those units at Bush Hill, Randolph County, were paroled on June 29 and each man received $1.25 in silver as final pay. This was part of the approximately $38,000 in Confederate Treasury silver that Johnston ordered to be distributed equally to officers and men. Those units at Greensboro were paroled on May 1 and 2, and on the latter day, Johnston's farewell address, General Order No. 22, was read to the troops.

Meanwhile, those units that had remained in northeastern North Carolina had been isolated. Some simply disbanded when they received word of Lee's surrender or of the first Johnston-Sherman agreement. Brigadier General Laurence

Johnston's army was a shadow. Regiments had been so depleted that men like this private from the 33d Tennessee were members of units composed of five and six regiments combined and still understrength. (HERB PECK, JR.)

Above: The generals in North Carolina were as battered as the army. Brigadier General Laurence S. Baker could hardly wear his uniform for all the wounds he bore, and still he was on active service. (VM)

Left: Out in Mississippi the story was the same. Near Vicksburg the Federals set up a special camp for the exchange of prisoners, realizing that the war was all but over. Here in April 1865 a photographer caught what was probably one of the very last such meetings as Confederate officers confer under flag of truce with their Yankee counterparts. (VITO-LO-RINHART GALLERIES, NEW YORK CITY)

Below: Officers without commands, like Brigadier General William R. Peck, simply came into Federal lines to take their parole. A mammoth six feet six inches tall, Peck made quite a catch. (STEVE MULLINAX)

Above: Everywhere the signs of impending Union occupation sprang up. In Huntsville, Alabama, Brigadier General Emerson Opdycke established his headquarters in this house, obviously there to stay for a while. (USAMHI)

S. Baker withdrew his force from Weldon on April 13. When he heard of Lee's surrender, he decided to disband his force and to make an attempt to join Johnston's army with those who would follow. Efforts to penetrate beyond the Union scouting parties and pickets failed, so he sent word to the Union commander at Raleigh that he would surrender his force under the first Johnston-Sherman agreement. His offer to surrender was accepted and his men were paroled at Bunn's House, Nash County, on April 20, 1865.

Other units refused to surrender and simply took their arms and went home. One section of Company C, 13th Battalion North Carolina Light Artillery had been on detached service with the Army of Northern Virginia and had made it to Lynchburg before Lee's surrender. Instead of disbanding, they made their way south and joined the other section of the company attached to Johnston's army near Greensboro. When word of Johnston's surrender came, the men of the first section, fearing they would be covered by its terms and thus not properly exchanged, left camp and were not reported on the company's final muster roll.

As Johnston's army began disbanding after April 26, Lieutenant General Richard Taylor and

Above: Nearby Major General David Stanley set up his IV Corps headquarters. (USAMHI)

Left: There was no one in Alabama to stop them. On May 4 the last Confederate army east of the Mississippi surrendered to Major General E. R. S. Canby near Mobile. (USAMHI)

Right: The last army was that of Lieutenant General Richard Taylor, son of President Zachary Taylor and brother-in-law of Jefferson Davis. (DAM, LSU)

Canby formulated surrender terms on May 2 based on the Appomattox agreement. Two days later, at Citronelle, Alabama, General Taylor surrendered the forces in the Department of Alabama, Mississippi, and East Louisiana. Major General Sam Jones, commanding at Tallahassee, Florida, surrendered the forces under his command on May 10, the day President Davis was captured near Irwinville, Georgia.

Small groups continued to surrender east of the Mississippi, but because the main forces in that area had surrendered, President Johnson proclaimed "armed resistance . . . virtually at an end." West of the Mississippi, Brigadier General M. Jeff Thompson surrendered at Chalk Bluff, Arkansas, on May 11. He, too, agreed to the Appomattox terms. The last remaining Confederate army in the field was under General E. Kirby Smith. The Army of Trans-Mississippi was surrendered under Appomattox-type terms agreed to during a meeting at New Orleans on May 26. At that meeting Lieutenant General S. B. Buckner represented General Kirby Smith and Major General Peter J. Osterhaus represented General Canby. When General Kirby Smith approved the agreement on June 2, the army was surrendered. Except for some troops under Brigadier General Jo Shelby, who refused to accept the surrender terms and led his men into Mexico, Confederate military resistance was at an end.

On the high seas, the CSS *Shenandoah* continued to attack Union whaling vessels until word was received on August 2 that the war was over. Lieutenant James Waddell, commanding the *Shenandoah* set sail for Liverpool, England, where he surrendered his ship to British authorities on November 6, 1865. It was not until April 2, 1866, that President Johnson proclaimed the insurrection at an end in Georgia, South Carolina, Virginia, North Carolina, Tennessee, Alabama, Louisiana, Arkansas, Mississippi, and Florida. On August 20, 1866, he extended his proclamation to include Texas, the last of the Secessionist states. The terms set down by Grant and Lee had set the tone for those to come. They were magnanimous, not harsh, but firm. They acknowledged respect for the vanquished and the need to begin jointly the rebuilding of the Union.

Above: Here at the Baton Rouge, Louisiana, arsenal, the artillery of Taylor's army sits, row upon row, after the surrender. (DAM, LSU)

Right: The havoc and destruction continued even after Taylor's surrender. On May 25 some twenty tons of Confederate powder exploded in a warehouse in Mobile, leveling a fair-sized area and doing $5 million in damage. (USAMHI)

Right: The only substantial Confederate force left in the field was the Trans-Mississippi, and on May 26 it too succumbed. Colonel Thomas P. Ochiltree of Texas could affect a brigadier's uniform that he was not entitled to wear, but all his protestations of inevitable victory could not affect the outcome of the war for his army. (MC)

Left: Perhaps realizing that they were the end of an era, the last organized army to surrender, the ranking officers of the Trans-Mississippi met to preserve their portrait for posterity in one of the most remarkable Confederate photographs in existence. Seated second from the left is the army commander, General Edmund Kirby Smith. Seated to his right, is Brigadier General Henry W. Allen, forced to use a cane after a wound suffered at Shiloh, now governor of Confederate Louisiana. He helped Smith negotiate the surrender terms. Seated at Smith's immediate left is his chief of staff, Brigadier General William R. Boggs. The identity of the remaining officers is unknown, but they are presumably members of Smith's staff. The presence of Allen makes it probable that this image was made at the time the surrender negotiations were under way. If so, it is the last image made of Confederate generals on active service. (CONFEDERATE MUSEUM, NEW ORLEANS)

Left: Even as the armies were surrendering, the Federals were reclaiming the South. Charleston fell to them back in February 1865, and now Yankee soldiers filled the streets of the former seed bed of secession. The Post Office was put back in business. (JAMES G. HEAVILIN)

Below: And the grounds of the Charleston Arsenal once more held Union guns—Parrott rifles used in the siege of Charleston—mixed with captured Confederate cannon. Flags and bunting draped from the trees reveal that this image was probably made on April 14, the fourth anniversary of the fall of Fort Sumter. (NYHS)

Below: Dignitaries flocked to Charleston on that day for the special ceremonies. For their edification, they could view row upon row of cannon and ammunition. (CHS)

Above: But above all they could go out to Fort Sumter. The Federal fleet in the harbor sent its most colorful flags up the halyards to celebrate the day. (LC)

Left: And old and ailing Major General Robert Anderson, now retired, who had lowered the Stars and Stripes on April 14, 1861, was there. (USAMHI)

Right: After the speeches and ceremony Anderson raised on the Fort Sumter flagpole the very same Stars and Stripes that he had taken down four years before. With the war now all but done, all that remained was the ceremony and the symbolism, working to give some meaning to all that had happened. (T. SCOTT SANDERS)

Left: Yet the final surrender would not come for months. Lieutenant James Waddell, commanding the Confederate commerce raider Shenandoah, did not learn of the surrenders until August. And on November 6, 1865, seven months after Lee surrendered and almost six months after Smith, Waddell gave up his ship to British authorities in Liverpool. That, at last, was an end to it. (MC)

Below: The guns at last were silent, never to speak again. (NA)

Below: And at his home in Richmond, on April 16, 1865, General Robert E. Lee posed for his portrait for the last time in the uniform he had ennobled. Mathew Brady importuned him to pose, and in the end the general consented. For all the wear that the years and the cares have inflicted, there is still in his eyes the look of a man who may have been worn down to defeat but who was never beaten. Already he is on his way to becoming an immortal hero to all Americans. (NA)

Right: But for a few, even the admission of defeat is too much. Old Edmund Ruffin of Virginia, the fire-eating Secessionist who fired one of the first shots at Fort Sumter in 1861, who hailed John Brown's raid on Harpers Ferry in 1859 because it would bring on secession, and who loathed all things Northern and Yankee, refused to yield. On June 17, 1865, after everyone had surrendered, Ruffin wrote in his diary: "And now . . . with what will be near to my latest breath, I hereby repeat . . . my unmitigated hatred to Yankee rule—to all political, social, & business connection with Yankees, & to the perfidious, malignant, & vile Yankee race." Then he put a rifle muzzle in his mouth and pulled the trigger. Having fired one of the war's first shots, he fired as well one of its last. (VM)

The "Late Unpleasant-ness"

WILLIAM C. DAVIS

The war done, there was peace to wage, and battles anew with the hatreds remaining, and challenges ahead for a nation reuniting

Above: In the midst of jubilation came terror, a last act of hate to poison the peace. Here, in the theater of John T. Ford, on the evening of April 14, 1865, President Lincoln came to see a play. (LC)

IT WAS ALL BUT DONE, the long unimaginable nightmare over. General Robert E. Lee's once seemingly invincible Army of Northern Virginia was reduced to a shadow, and surrendered on the grassy roadside of Appomattox. In North Carolina the South's other major eastern army was at bay and its commander, General Joseph E. Johnston, was suggesting to his antagonist Major General William T. Sherman that they meet to explore the possibilities of peace. Mobile, the Confederacy's last great city, had fallen. The flag of the Union flew once more over the unrecognizable ruins of Fort Sumter, where the whole dreadful business began. The small Southern armies farther west still held out, but the avenues of escape open to them were dwindling. The Confederate government was in flight after the fall of Richmond, and to more and more of its soldiers the awful truth became evident that there was nothing left to keep fighting for. It was all over.

But like the dying moments of a robust man worn down by illness, there could still be a last, sudden outburst, some final surge of desperate energy before death. The Civil War would not quietly die in its sleep. There was a final act of bitter, blinding, senseless hate to perform, and who better to stage it than an actor. For months John Wilkes Booth, nationally famed player, sometime oil speculator, inveterate rakehell with the ladies of Washington and New York, had been planning his greatest performance. He would never take up arms to defend the South he so loudly espoused, but late in 1864 he devised a theatrical scheme to kidnap President Lincoln and spirit him away to the Confederacy as hostage for the release of Confederate prisoners held in the North—even for Southern independence itself. How much of the plan sprang from genuine patriotism and how much came from the simple egotistical impulse of a born posturer may never be known. What is certain is that repeated attempts were foiled through accident or ineptitude. Then came Lee's surrender and the symbolic end of the war. All else would be anticlimax, and now Booth's plan seemed pointless. But rather than abandon his schemes, he simply gave their goal a new and more sinister direction. Now Lincoln must die, not to save the Confederacy but in vengeance for having conquered it.

Booth chose a theater for his stage, of course, and the April 14, 1865, evening performance at Ford's Theatre of *Our American Cousin.* The Lincolns were to attend. The dreadful act of that night is engraved indelibly upon every American consciousness. At about 10:20 P.M. actor Harry Hawk down on the stage delivered one of the most amusing lines of the farce, calling an actress a "sockdologizing old mantrap!" There was an outburst of laughter in the theater. Perhaps Lincoln, sitting in a box to the right of the stage, laughed as well. Ironically, the four letters at the end of that line, "trap," formed the last human syllable he would ever hear. At that very instant he was himself sitting in a trap. As Hawk delivered the line, Booth stepped silently into the box, unseen, directly behind the President. He held a small derringer pistol in front of him, its muzzle no more than six inches from the back of Lincoln's head. Before the laughter died down, he pulled the trigger.

A round bullet, an ounce or more of lead, burst from the muzzle and struck Lincoln an

Above: The President and his wife sat in the box at the right, their guests in the one at the left. A portrait of George Washington and a United States Treasury guard flag decorated the railing. (USAMHI)

Below: Across the street, to the Peterson rooming house, they carried the President, and into this back room. Here, all through the night, he labored for breath, unconscious. Here at 7:22 A .M., April 15, he died . Within minutes after the body was carried out, photographer Julius Ulke brought his camera into the still undisturbed room. Here he made at least two images that would remain lost for nearly a century. They showed the bed in which the President died, the coverlet that left his bare feet protruding as they laid the long and lanky Kentuckian diagonally on the mattress. And they showed the pillow soaked with Lincoln's blood as it oozed from his head wound. From humble beginnings he had come, and so he went, in a humble rooming house. Yet it was no place for the death of a President. (LO)

inch or two behind his left ear. Starting to flatten as it pounded its way through his skull, driving bits of hair and tissue and bone before it, the missile entered the brain, shock waves from the impact sending fractures racing around both sides of the skull. Already Lincoln's head was virtually destroyed. Meanwhile the bullet careered onward through the cerebellum, causing Lincoln to raise his right arm convulsively, though by then the deadly lead had continued in its path, destroying the million and more instinctive and learned reflexes that had made Lincoln a good rail-splitter and a miserable dancer.

The cerebellum was largely a ruin when the bullet smashed into the hypothalamus and thalamus, probably destroying all of Lincoln's senses except smell. Here, too, lay all the seats of ancient instincts for flight from danger, but now it was too late to fly. Finally the fatal ball plunged on into the forepart of the cerebral cortex, erasing as it went untold memories—the faint recollections of his beloved mother, the truth of his supposed love for Ann Rutledge, the pain of the loss of two of his sons, and the in calculable burden of leading his nation through war to the peace that lay at hand. Finally Booth's messenger of hate halted its path somewhere behind the right eye. The President was unconscious. Out of pure physical reflex, the body would struggle on, holding to life until the next morning. Carried from Ford's Theatre to a rooming house belonging to one William Peterson across 10th Street, it would ooze blood onto pillows and gasp at breath for several hours. But all that had made Lincoln what he was had died before the laughter trailed away from Hawk's portentous last word, "mantrap."

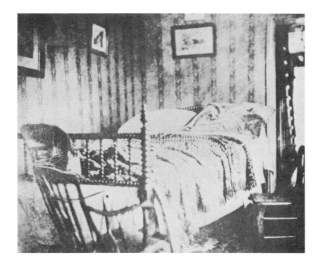

Below: The White House went silent in shock, and the Union prepared for a long mourning. (USAMHI)

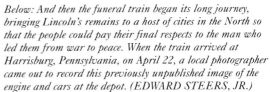

Below: And then the funeral train began its long journey, bringing Lincoln's remains to a host of cities in the North so that the people could pay their final respects to the man who led them from war to peace. When the train arrived at Harrisburg, Pennsylvania, on April 22, a local photographer came out to record this previously unpublished image of the engine and cars at the depot. (EDWARD STEERS, JR.)

Above: The funeral parade up Pennsylvania Avenue in Washington, D.C., began the formal outpouring of grief. A wing of the Capitol appears in the right distance. (USAMHI)

Left: City Hall in New York City, on April 24, is thronged with people eager for a last look at the kindly visage of Father Abraham. (INTERNATIONAL MUSEUM OF PHOTOGRAPHY AT GEORGE EASTMAN HOUSE, ROCHESTER, N.Y.)

Right: This is what they saw. The only known image of Lincoln in death was made as he lay here in City Hall, flanked by his honor guards, Rear Admiral Charles Davis on the left and Brevet Brigadier General Edward D. Townsend on the right. Jeremiah Gurney, Jr., made the image, which shows Lincoln's face dimly visible in the open casket and, resting on top of the coffin, the flowered initials "AL." Secretary of War Edwin M. Stanton objected to the photograph because he found it macabre and ordered it suppressed and the negative destroyed, but this one print survived, to be discovered again in 1952. (ILLINOIS STATE HISTORICAL LIBRARY, SPRINGFIELD)

Left: Albany, New York, hung with crape, awaits the arrival of the funeral train. (ALBANY INSTITUTE OF HISTORY AND ART)

The North lurched into mourning, a grief more prolonged than any in its history. So great a tragedy coming in train with so great a triumph almost unnerved many Americans, even some in the South. The public outpouring of lamentation from pulpit and press was staggering. Lincoln's body literally went on tour for funerals in New York, Philadelphia, Baltimore, and elsewhere. For twenty days the casket traveled before at last it came to rest in Springfield, Illinois, the city he had moved to as a young man.

Back in Washington, Ford's Theatre was closed and the Peterson house across the street became a tourist attraction. A Massachusetts soldier, Charles Nightingale, returning from the war, visited the place and stepped into the room where Lincoln died. Neatly placed on the simple bedstead he saw "the bloody pillow upon which the nation's martyr passed from time to eternity." Nightingale, as so many others, could not but be moved. "I shall never forget my feelings as I stood there gazing with feverish excitement upon that blood-stained pillow," he wrote a few days later. "They were of awe and madness, indescribable, deep."

For two weeks after the murder the dark days continued. The manhunt for Booth and his accomplices spread throughout the nation. Some who had been his confederates in the kidnapping scheme were quietly arrested. So was Mary Surratt, mother of one of the plotters and keeper of a Washington boardinghouse where kidnapping—and some said murder—plans were hatched. Finally, on April 26, Booth was cornered in a shed near the Rappahannock River in Virginia. Refusing to surrender himself, he fell to a bullet fired in the dark, perhaps from one of his pursuers, perhaps from his own gun. He died shortly after dawn, the same day that General Johnston surrendered at last to General Sherman in North Carolina and the war east of the Alleghenies came virtually to an end. The next day, as if to add a final terrible coda to the most doleful fortnight in living memory, the steamer *Sultana*, loaded with 2,000 or more Union soldiers, most of them recently released prisoners who had survived Confederate prison camps and

Right: And back in Springfield, Illinois, Lincoln's home is draped in black in preparation for the last of the funeral ceremonies before he is laid to rest. (CHICAGO PUBLIC LIBRARY)

Above: Meanwhile, the rest of the Union will not rest until justice is done to Lincoln's murderer and his accomplices. When all the accused are apprehended, they will stand trial before this military commission, posing here in Mathew Brady's Washington studio. They are, from the left, Colonel Charles H. Tompkins; Major General David Hunter, president of the commission; Major General August Kautz; Brevet Brigadier General James Ekin; Major General Lew Wallace; John A. Bingham; Brigadier General Albion Howe; Brigadier General Thomas M. Harris; Judge Advocate General Joseph Holt; Brigadier General Robert S. Foster; Colonel Henry L. Burnett; and Colonel D. R. Clendenin. (NA)

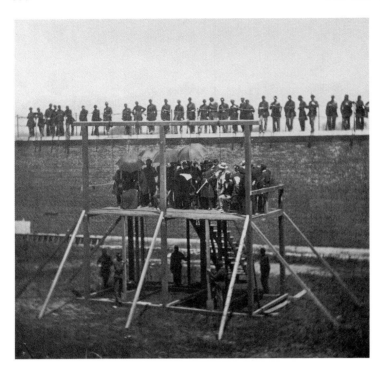

Left: Their verdict reached on June 30, 1865, the commission sent four conspirators to the gallows. Here on July 7, in the yard of the Old Penitentiary in Washington, D.C., they mounted the scaffold. They sat down while Brigadier General John Hartranft read aloud their sentences and the order for execution. He stands beneath the umbrella in the center of the group, paper in his hand. Seated at the far right is George Atzerodt, charged with attempting to murder Vice President Andrew Johnson. Immediately next to him sits David Herold, who had fled with Booth and helped in his foiled escape attempt. Sitting just behind the center post is Lewis Paine, who tried to assassinate Secretary of State William Seward; just visible on his head is a straw hat that he had playfully snatched from the head of a bystander before he mounted the steps. Seated at far left is Mrs. Mary Surratt, who kept the boardinghouse where the conspirators met. (LC)

Right: Now they stand, their hands and legs being bound and the nooses put in place. Chief executioner Christopher Rath is personally placing Paine's noose. Everyone grudgingly admired the courage of the young man. "I want you to die quick," Rath was saying to Paine. "You know best," replied the condemned. (LC)

Below: The trap is sprung and justice is done. (LC)

were going home from the war, exploded on the Mississippi as she steamed north of Memphis. At least 1,200 died and perhaps hundreds more that were unaccounted for. It was up to that time the worst single marine disaster in history, and once more, so recently euphoric over victory, the North was plunged into gloom and mourning.

The Union badly needed something to cheer it from its despair. After all, it had won the war, preserved itself, put down rebellion, ended slavery, and—some claimed—prevented the death of democracy for all time. There were a million heroes in blue to honor for their services before they took discharge, and Washington decided to stage a mammoth celebration both to do the Union veterans justice and to lift the nation from its grief. A Grand Review was scheduled for May 23-24, 1865.

The first day the noble old Army of the Potomac marched from the Capitol down Pennsylvania Avenue and past the White House. This was the aristocrat of Federal armies, marching smartly, well dressed, tempered by repeated defeats and vindicated by final victory. All the memories of the Seven Days, of Second Manassas and Antietam and Fredericksburg, of humiliation at Chancellorsville and revenge at Gettysburg, filed past the stands as rank upon rank of blue marched out of time and into posterity. The next day came Sherman's armies from North Carolina, Westerners mostly, roughly dressed, rawboned, ill-disciplined, lackluster on parade, yet bringing with them the greatest string of victories of any army on the continent. Two days later the last remaining Confederate army surrendered in Louisiana, and it was all done.

To be sure, there were still a few Confederate holdouts, not least the remnant of the Richmond government. Having fled their burning capital, President Jefferson Davis and his Cabinet hopped from place to place, establishing temporary capitals as they tried to stay ahead of their pursuers and rally their remaining soldiers.

They reached North Carolina only in time to consult with Johnston while he asked Sherman for terms, and then the flight continued. Along the way, members of his Cabinet who had stood by him for years one by one dropped out of the party to make their own separate peace with the victors, until by May 4, at Washington, Georgia, there were none remaining but his Secretary of War, John C. Breckinridge, and his Postmaster General, John H. Reagan. While Breckinridge set out to lead their pursuers on a false trail, Davis left to make a last bid to escape the country. But near Irwinville, Georgia, on May 10, the President's party was surprised by Federal troops and captured without struggle. Of all the high officers of the government, only Breckinridge and Secretary of State Judah P. Benjamin finally escaped to safety.

Retribution was inevitable, yet slow in coming and on a lesser scale than for any other civil conflict in human memory. The first to feel it would be those involved in the President's murder. In June 1865, in a long and controversial trial, eight defendants, including Mrs. Surratt and the Maryland doctor Samuel Mudd who treated Booth during his flight, were put on the dock charged with conspiracy to assassinate Lincoln. Though all probably had knowledge of or involvement in the kidnapping schemes, it is

Above: As the bodies still dangle from their ropes, the boxes for their burial are stacked beneath them as the crowd starts to melt away. The gallows will be sawed into souvenirs. (LC)

Left: Lincoln's death leaves a new President in his stead. Andrew Johnson of Tennessee, Lincoln's second Vice President, a man who will try to follow in Father Abraham's steps, without much success. (USAMHI)

Below: There is more tragedy to come even when the fighting is stopped. With thousands of Federal prisoners being freed from Confederate prison camps, steamers like the Sultana *were brimmed with passengers as they transported men up the Mississippi from Vicksburg to the North. On April 27, just the day after this image of the ship was made, her boiler exploded in midstream north of Memphis and the vessel went down in the darkness. With over 2,000 men aboard, she took nearly three fourths of them down with her. It was the worst ship disaster in the nation's history. (LC)*

Left: While the military surrenders were taking place in early April, there was a small band of Confederates trying to flee the country—President Jefferson Davis and his Cabinet. (LC)

Above: Brigadier General Henry H. Walker commanded the Confederate troops in the Danville, Virginia, area, and Davis ordered him to go to North Carolina and join General Joseph E. Johnston's army, not knowing that even then Johnston was preparing to sue for terms. (VM)

Above: One by one the officers and Cabinet members with Davis dropped along the wayside, to attempt their own individual escape or else to surrender and take their chances. Vice President Alexander H. Stephens simply went home and awaited his arrest, accepting it calmly. (CM)

still uncertain which if any of them had foreknowledge of Booth's eleventh-hour decision to kill the President. In the end, four who could not be directly connected with the assassination were sentenced to long prison terms. Four others, including Mary Surratt, were sentenced to the gallows. Their hangings on July 7 drew international attention, more because of the execution of a woman than for any other reason.

And for a time the executions seemed to satisfy much of the North's need for vengeance against the South. Indeed, incredible as it seems after four years of the costliest and bloodiest war yet fought in the hemisphere, only one Confederate would actually be brought to trial and charged with crimes. Major Henry Wirz, the hapless and admittedly unsympathetic commandant of the infamous Confederate prison camp near Andersonville, Georgia, was accused of willfully torturing and starving, even murdering, defenseless Union prisoners under his command. No one will ever completely sift truth from fancy in his story, though it is probable that he was no worse and no better than any other unfortunate Southern officer assigned to oversee tens of thousands of captured Federals packed into cramped quarters with too little food and almost no sanitation. But Andersonville had become in the North a symbol of Rebel cruelty and barbarism on an emotional scale so great that a scapegoat was inevitable—some small taste of Southern blood to balance the scale against the deaths from starvation and disease of thousands of Union men. On November 10, 1865, Wirz went to the scaffold, in relative terms probably an innocent man. Yet, ironically, he was symbolic of the incredible tolerance and magnanimity of the victors, for—however unjust—his would be the only execution of an enemy soldier for war crimes, a restraint unparalleled in the history of civil conflict.

Perhaps there was little time for retribution because the men of both armies, North and South, were too busy returning home to find what remained of the life they had left four years before. It was a staggering problem. In 1865 the Union had just over 1,000,000 men under arms, spread literally from Atlantic to Pacific, Maine to Texas. Just the transportation needed to get Massachusetts men home from Texas and Hoosiers back from Virginia, taxed every resource of rail and water. The Union armies could not be disbanded all at once, either. First, new recruits would be released. Then men in hospitals, then men whose enlistments expired earliest. The disbanding and discharge was already under way in the East before the last Confederate army in the West had yet surrendered. And when the soldiers were finally mustered out, they were sent home with money in their pockets, some $270,000,000 of it.

How different it was for the defeated Confederates, and yet it could have been far worse. Following the magnanimous course of Grant at Appomattox, there were no punishments or recriminations when the other Southern armies capitulated. Men and officers were made only to take their paroles, surrender their arms, and go home. Federal supply trains were opened to their former foes, men who claimed to own horses were allowed to take them, and the still-proud Confederates were simply permitted to find their way home. The few who refused either to take parole or admit defeat fled to the hills, intent upon continuing the war in partisan fashion, but they were few indeed, accomplished nothing, and either abandoned their efforts or, as in Missouri, abandoned their patriotic pretensions and simply became brigands.

For weeks following the surrenders, the roads of the South were filled with passing Confederates, ragged men, often in tears, occasionally stopping to ask food or water and to pass the news of the surrenders. Grant and Sherman arranged some transportation for those who lived far to the West, but most of them walked, sometimes for weeks, before they found their homes. A New York journalist in the South watched the exodus, and could not conceal that he was "daily touched to the heart by seeing these poor homesick boys and exhausted men wandering about in threadbare uniforms, with scanty outfit of slender haversack and blanket roll hung over their shoulders, seeking the nearest route home."

The receptions that met the men in blue and gray when they found their homes were as different as the flags they had fought for. Throughout the North there was jubilation, a joy that could not entirely be stilled even by the Lincoln tragedy. As regiment after regiment came marching home, great cities and tiny courthouse towns bedecked themselves with bunting and flags to give their boys a cheering welcome. One last time the hardened veterans marched in parade down their home streets. Many stood in rank for a final photograph, to be reproduced by the score and treasured for years to come. Officers and men, equals once more, shook hands, slapped backs, laughed, and more often wept, as they said farewell not only to their war service, but also to the most exciting days of their lives. The conflict lay behind them now, and so, with it, they left much of the best of their youth.

There was joy in the South as well, of a different kind. The war was lost and no one could be joyful about that, but at last it was over and the men were coming home. Everyone could take some comfort at least from that. But there were no parades in Richmond or New Orleans. The regiments arrived in bits and pieces, not as whole units, and the men quietly went to their homes, or what remained of them. In a region worn and starved to gauntness by the past four years, there was little enough for survival, much less for lavish receptions. Many Confederates found their homes fallen to ruin from neglect or destroyed by Northern raiders or Southern vandals. The families they had left in 1861 had often been forced to flee as refugees, often moving hundreds of miles to stay ahead of the enemy. Cut off from contact for months, some soldiers would have to spend more months, even years, trying to find the loved ones left behind.

Yet in at least one way, soldiers of both the Union and Confederacy were the same. They could take comfort from the fact that they had lived to go home again. So many others did not. Hundreds of thousands lay buried in the soil of Tennessee and Virginia and Pennsylvania and so many other places. Many had been hastily interred after battle. Even more had succumbed to accidents and disease. Tens of thousands on both sides had died in prisons. As quickly as possible, families on both sides began the often heartbreaking and frustrating work of trying to find the remains of their sons and husbands, to bring them home. It was a great silent exodus,

Above: General Braxton Bragg, on the other hand, stayed with the presidential party almost to the end, acting as Davis' chief military adviser. An unpublished portrait made probably by the Montgomery, Alabama, photographer A. C. McIntyre in 1862. (CM)

Above: In the end the last Cabinet officer standing by Davis was his Secretary of War, John C. Breckinridge, also a major general. He commanded the escort as the fleeing President moved through the Carolinas and into Georgia. (USAMHI)

Left: Here in Abbeville, South Carolina, in the home of Armisted Burt, Davis held his last council of war. He wanted to continue the war; Breckinridge and the others told him it was over. (USAMHI)

Below: Finally, near Irwinville, Georgia, the pursuing Federals closed in and captured Davis. Lieutenant Colonel Benjamin Pritchard led his 4th Michigan Cavalry against Davis' camp and thereby won himself a brevet rank of brigadier. Pritchard sits third from the left. (DUDLEY H. PRITCHARD)

Above: The President and his band were brought to Macon, Georgia, where photographer A. J. Riddle made this May 13, 1865, image of the ambulance and wagon which carried Davis and his party. Pritchard's troopers fill the street in front of Major General James Wilson's Federal headquarters. Prison awaited Davis, though he would never be tried or convicted of treason. (USAMHI)

Left: Some were more fortunate than Davis. Secretary of War Breckinridge did successfully escape in a hair-raising adventure through Florida and across the Gulf Stream that saw him dodging Federal patrols, turning pirate, and nearly perishing in a storm at sea. The month-long ordeal showed in his face when, a few days after reaching Cuba, he sat for this photograph, probably by Charles D. Fredericks' Havana studio. (WILLIAM C. DAVIS)

wagons and trains and steamers carrying a veritable host of mute, moldering passengers, whose bodies were making a final journey that their spirits had made long before.

In the defeated and impoverished South, there was neither money nor inclination to establish formal cemeteries for the Confederate dead, beyond those already dictated by circumstance near the battlefields. But in the North, even before the end of the war, a movement began for the creation of national military cemeteries to honor the fallen brave. Lincoln had spoken at the dedication of one in Gettysburg, Pennsylvania, on November 19, 1863. Others were established at Alexandria, Virginia; at Vicksburg, Mississippi; and most notably at Arlington, Virginia. Here on the southern bank of the Potomac, on grounds that once were part of the estate of Robert E. Lee, one of the most beautiful cemeteries in the nation was established shortly before war's end. Lee would never return here again, but thousands who died fighting him would rest beneath his land.

Just as they memorialized their dead, so did the men of the Union begin almost immediately to memorialize what they had done. Well before the war ceased, local officials at Gettysburg and Antietam and elsewhere began envisioning parks, lands at the battlefields to be set aside to preserve the memory of what had occurred there. And by 1864 there were even a few markers and monuments starting to sprout on the landscape, all of them Northern. In the winter of 1864-5 men of Brigadier General William Gamble's brigade built two red sandstone pyramids on the field near Manassas, Virginia, each commemorating the men in blue who fell in the battles of First and Second Bull Run. On June 10, 1865, with the war done, several hundred soldiers and dignitaries came to formally dedicate the monuments, the first of hundreds of such scenes in the years to come.

Confederates, too, joined in the drive to preserve the memory of what they had tried to achieve, though understandably in a region depressed by the war, the immediate impetus was more economic than historical. At Petersburg, Virginia, within months after Lee's surrender, an enterprising former Confederate was operating probably the first battlefield museum in the country, charging twenty-five cents for visitors to view relics of the great Battle of the Crater.

Above: With all the tragedy that attended their victories, the Federals needed some means of celebrating their triumph. The War Department called for a Grand Review of Major General George Meade's and Major General William T. Sherman's armies in Washington on May 23-24. Viewing stands were erected for the dignitaries along Pennsylvania Avenue. The stand draped with flags was for President Johnson, the Cabinet, the generals, and special guests. (NYHS)

Right: Crowds gathered early all along the route, anxious to cheer the brave men who had delivered the Union and put down the Rebellion. (USAMHI)

A quarter could be a lot of money in a stricken region. Every resource in the South had been stretched to exhaustion by the war, and those not used up by the Confederates themselves had most likely been destroyed or damaged by the invading Federals. Transportation was at a standstill. Rolling stock and tracks had either been ruined from lack of maintenance or parts taken up and melted to make cannon, or wrecked by raiders. There were virtually no sound river steamers to get waterborne commerce moving again. The telegraph lines were down, and there was little good news for them to carry in any case. While some regions were almost untouched by the war, others had seen their fields ravaged by overplanting and the demands of feeding armies, and their cities ruined by bombardment, razed by fires, or turned squalid from overcrowding by refugees. At war's end Southerners were not only largely a displaced people; the South was almost a displaced region. Lee and the other most sensible Confederate leaders knew this without having to look and offered the wisest counsel they could. Go home, they told their men, go home quietly, without bitterness, and go to work rebuilding. Accept the verdict of the war and put it behind.

The most prominent Confederate of them all would never accept the outcome of the conflict. Yet as the postwar era began, Jefferson Davis was awaiting a verdict of his own. He and several other Confederate politicians who had held office in the old Union, were under indictment for treason, which should hardly have been a surprise. In most other nations of the nineteenth-century world, they would have been stood against a wall and shot. But here a peculiar mix of tolerance, exhaustion, and uncertainty produced an entirely different sort of denouement for the leaders of the rebellion. Of them all, only Davis would come close to trial, and in even his case it would become evident that the Union government did not really know what to do.

Below: THE PUBLIC SCHOOLS OF WASHINGTON WELCOME THE HEROES OF THE REPUBLIC. HONOR TO THE BRAVE—so read one of hundreds of signs that greeted the soldiers. This one is on the Capitol building, as crowds of men, ladies, and school children line the street. In the background, the building's columns are still wrapped in mourning for the dead Lincoln. (USAMHI)

Above: They were not disappointed. In the most magnificent parade the capital had ever seen, thousands upon thousands of blue-clad soldiers marched from the Capitol down Pennsylvania Avenue toward the Executive Mansion. Captain A. J. Russell took his camera into the Capitol dome to record this outstanding view of one brigade marching down the avenue. (USAMHI)

Above: At the other end of the street, near Willard's Hotel at right, Alexander Gardner or an assistant made scene after scene of the passing heroes. An unidentified major general lifts his hat in salute before his command passes by. (USAMHI)

Right: The first infantry to pass in review on May 23 was the IX Corps of Major General John Parke. The general and his staff ride at the front. (USAMHI)

Below right: Major General A. A. Humphreys and his II Corps soon followed, Humphreys a blur of motion in the lead. (USAMHI)

Left: Hour after hour the soldiers and their wagons and cannon passed along the street, marching to the beat of their drums and the sound of the special march composed for the occasion. (NYHS)

Below: The flag flew at half staff, but it and all the crape could not dampen the spirits of this two-day orgy of patriotism and celebration. (USAMHI)

At first Washington officials believed—or wanted to believe—that Davis and his leaders had been involved in the Lincoln murder. Indeed, there is some evidence that prosecutors may even have tried to persuade deponents at the assassination trial to perjure themselves to implicate Davis, but the attempt failed. For two years Davis was kept a prisoner at Fort Monroe, Virginia, but the Federal authorities would never bring him before a jury. By 1867 friends had arranged for his release on bail, and passions had cooled to the point that the government actually believed that trying Davis for treason could be an embarrassment. He would certainly be convicted if tried, and then what should they do with him? The law prescribed execution, but that would only enrage the South, thus far rather docile in defeat, and probably cause controversy with European nations that had entertained some sympathy with the Confederacy. In the end the Federal authorities simply let the case lapse, and Davis remained a free man, bitter and unwilling to the end to admit defeat. The few other imprisoned leaders went free as well. It was a remarkably bloodless aftermath to the bloodiest war in American history.

Yet the South was not to pass from war to peace without paying some price, gentle though it may have been compared to that paid by other defeated peoples. Reconstruction of loyal state governments had already begun under Lincoln as Southern territory came once more under Federal control. "We must extinguish our resentment if we expect harmony and Union," Lincoln had told his Cabinet the very day he was shot. Emissaries including General U. S. Grant traveled through the South to gauge the temper of the people, and most concluded with Grant that Southerners accepted the verdict of the war and wanted to rejoin the Union as quickly as possible.

For nearly two years there was surprisingly little interference in Southern affairs, as white Southerners once more elected men of their own

Above: Every new regiment marching down Capitol Hill did so to resounding cheers from the men and boys and the ladies waving their handkerchiefs. (P-M)

Right: Johnny was at last marching home again. (P-M)

Left: Sometimes the enthusiastic bystanders walked out into the avenue itself to get a closer look. (USAMHI)

Below: The dignitaries, meanwhile, sat patiently through the endless hours of passing troops (NYHS)

Below: The victories of the armies were printed on the bunting hanging from the roof of the reviewing stand—SPOTSYLVANIA, ANTIETAM, CHATTANOOGA, and more. In this image made on the second day of the review, as Sherman's army passes by, General Meade sits at the far right of the central part of the stand. Next to him, holding a newspaper, is General Sherman. Secretary of the Navy Gideon Welles sits in the center of the group, just to the left of a bouquet of flowers, and at the far left of the advanced gallery Secretary of War Stanton turns his head to talk with an unseen Lieutenant General U. S. Grant. (KA)

kind to their legislatures and tried to send them to Congress. But during that time it became increasingly evident that an old pattern was reemerging. The same men who had led the South before the war were in charge once again and attempting to act as if the war had not happened. Once again they were claiming for their states the right to decide in matters in which the Republican majority in Congress believed Congress' right was paramount. Worse, though the slaves had all been freed, Southern states were enacting "Black Codes" which in effect returned them to a kind of servitude by enormously restricting their freedoms. In April and June 1866, when it came time to debate the civil rights act and the Fourteenth Amendment to the Constitution, which, among other things, guaranteed the vote to Negroes, the South balked, and the radical wing of the Republicans, who had always favored stern treatment of the former Confederate states, decided that the South had not learned its lesson. Triumphant in Congress, the Radical Republicans succeeded in instituting for the next decade a plan of "reconstruction," the excesses of which have been exaggerated in the ensuing century but which nevertheless did visit upon the Southern mind and spirit a wound never yet erased.

The day of the "carpetbagger" had come— the Yankee opportunist went South to profit from cheap land and labor while native Southerners barely survived. There is truth to some of the carpetbagger legend, though the reverse of the coin is that these entrepreneurs brought with them an influx of capital and energy which played a strong role in reviving the Southern economy.

Republicans went South, and some Southerners joined with them—the "scalawags"— to run the Reconstruction state governments. Most Southern states at one time or another after the war fell under Republican rule. Often it was good, honest government, but in some few celebrated cases it was corrupt and abusive. Despite the long-held myth that the former slaves came to control several states, the fact is that in only one state, South Carolina, did Negro representatives hold a majority and that for only a single term in one house. There were no Negro governors, nor were the great mass of freed slaves a serious social threat to their former masters. Nevertheless, so fearful were Southerners of

Above: Soon Major General John A. Logan followed, behind him the Army of the Tennessee stretching back to the horizon. (USAMHI)

Above: Then came the XX Corps, as the endless procession lasted on through the day. (USAMHI)

Right: With their marching done, the officers of the armies gathered before the camera of Alexander Gardner for a final group portrait, the last time they would all be together. General Sherman sits here in the center, with the generals and other members of his staff . (LC)

Above: On this second day, Major General Henry W. Slocum rode at the head of his Army of Georgia. (USAMHI)

Above: Brigadier General Jefferson C. Davis led the XI V Corps, his horse a mere blur in the image, along with what appears to have been a bystander running across the street. (USAMHI)

their former chattels, that groups like the Knights of the White Camellia, the White Brotherhood, and of course the Ku Klux Klan arose to intimidate the Negroes and preserve white supremacy. Even prominent Confederate leaders condemned the violence and lawlessness of these vigilante groups, though their rise is hardly surprising. Having just suffered the humiliation of being the first and only Americans ever defeated in a war—and Southerners had always prided them selves on their military prowess—they were in its aftermath faced simultaneously with economic collapse, social and political revolution, and the sudden appearance in their midst, as free men, of millions of Negroes who had every reason to despise Southern whites. The white Southerners were in their way every bit as terrified as the Negroes they sought to intimidate.

Of course, there were many—perhaps as many as 10,000—who simply refused to take part in the South's travail, or who felt they dare not. Beginning with the flight of some of the Cabinet members and generals in 1865 and continuing on through the late 1860s, thousands of Southerners abandoned the country to go into exile, fearful of indictments against them, unwilling to live again under Yankee rule or bent on starting new lives elsewhere. By far the majority of them went to Mexico where whole colonies of expatriates were founded. Many of the generals took service there with the Emperor Maximilian, while their families tried to carve out new lives in the revolution-torn country. It did not work, however, and within a few years most of them had returned to the South.

Similar colonies were set up in Brazil and in other South and Central American countries. A small band of ex-Confederates dwelled in Havana for years after the war, and many more went to Europe. Judah P. Benjamin, Davis' Secretary of State, remained in England for the rest of his life, becoming a successful barrister and Queen's Counsel. Major General William W. Loring left the United States in 1869 and entered the service of the Khedive of Egypt, ironically serving in the same army as some

Left: General Grant stands at the center with his staff, including Lieutenant Colonel Ely S. Parker, seated second from the left, a Seneca Indian who served as Grant's military secretary. It was he who transcribed Grant's terms to Lee at Appomattox. Brevet Major General John Rawlins, Grant's chief of staff, sits on Grant's immediate left, and Adjutant General Seth Williams sits on the other side of Grant. (AIG)

adventuring ex-Union officers. And many, like the escaped Breckinridge, simply wandered abroad until the indictments against them were lifted, anxious simply to return home and start their lives anew. Breckinridge himself went from Cuba to Canada to Europe and back to Niagara, Canada, once more, patiently looking across the border to the United States and longing for the day of his return. He and the thousands of others may have been Confederates for four years, but they had been Americans a lot longer, and very few would not return to their homes eventually.

In the United States Southerners looked to many things to help them rebuild their personal and sectional fortunes. Recognizing the utter destruction of their transportation systems in the war and needing to modernize and rebuild in order to once more get their crops to market, a boom wave of railroad building commenced throughout the South, often financed by Northern entrepreneurs. To lend a cachet of authority to the enterprises, a host of former Confederate military luminaries became active or figurehead officers of the new lines. Joseph E. Johnston, Nathan B. Forrest, Breckinridge, P. G. T. Beauregard, and many more became railroad presidents, and most took an active role in leading the struggle to rebuild. When states like Louisiana instituted lotteries to rebuild their treasuries, men like Beauregard and feisty old Major General Jubal A. Early supervised them. And scores of former Confederates entered the life insurance business as several new firms were capitalized to sell policies and raise investment funds for rebuilding. Of course the old Confederates could not stay out of politics either. Though they had to take a loyalty oath and those who had been under indictment had to formally apply for restoration of their rights of citizenship, in a short time their voices were once more heard in state legislatures and the halls of Congress. No longer did they have the power to cripple or halt the national government as before, but in alliance with Northern Democrats and others tiring of Radical Republican rule, they finally came back to the point where in the disputed 1876 presiden-

Above: General Meade and his staff sit for Gardner, Meade in the center. Artillery chief Major General Henry Hunt sits at Meade's immediate right. (MHS)

Right: Then it was time to celebrate around the Union. Philadelphia dresses itself up to receive its sons once more. (FREE LIBRARY OF PHILADELPHIA)

Left: *The generals, too, went home, though not all of them for good. Galena, Illinois) decorated one of its main streets for the return of a man who was once one of its most obscure citizens, Lieutenant General U. S. Grant. GENERAL: THE "SIDE-WALK" IS BUILT reads the banner, perhaps referring to some bit of civic progress while Grant was busy with the war. (CARL H. JOHN-SON, JR.)*

tial election, they controlled the deciding electoral votes. Thus they made their bargain. Republican Rutherford B. Hayes, with fewer popular votes than his Democratic rival, Samuel J. Tilden, would be President, but Re construction would end. With Federal soldiers withdrawn from the South and control of civil affairs once more entirely in the hands of Southerners, the final political vestiges of war and defeat were removed. Now it remained to heal the emotional wounds.

The old Union—the states of the North—was not idle in the decade after the war. It continued to grow in power and prosperity, virtually forcing the rest of the world to take notice of the infant Yankee giant come to adulthood in the family of nations. All the industrial world had watched the war, and now it saw the manifestations of a newly confident, even belligerent, United States rising to its potential. Yankee trade expanded throughout the globe and virtually dominated its own hemisphere. The bright new and mighty squadrons of American warships cruised the world's seas, demonstrating Union naval power and modernity. American influence in the affairs of other nations began to be felt, and her old friend and older adversary Great Britain was once again made to feel the sting of defeat by her Yankee cousin. Already fearful that the cocky and powerful Americans would renew the age-old drive to wrest Canada from her, Britain was forced to submit to international arbitration in 1872 over the Alabama claims, American demands for millions of dollars in reparations for the damage done to Union ship ping by Confederate raiders fitted out in British ports. The British paid their penalties manfully, and the long Anglo-American friendship, though often strained, would continue.

Above: An Ohio regiment lines up for the last muster in Cleveland, a glad time, yet not without sorrow. Most of these young Americans would never again experience anything to compare with their days at war. (LC)

Right: *On July 26, 1865, the 23d Ohio was mustered out of service, and its officers met here at the monument they had already erected to the regiment in Cleveland after its service at Antietam, Maryland, in 1862. It is perhaps the first—certainly one of the first—regimental monuments erected, and it marks as well the rise to prominence of two future American Presidents from the regiment. Brigadier General Rutherford B. Hayes, once colonel of the 23d Ohio, stands immediately left of the monument, his head just visible above the shoulder of the man in front of him. And the officer standing second to the right from the marker is probably Major William McKinley. Few regiments could claim such distinguished alumni. (USAMHI)*

Left: There were those who would never go home. Now that the battlefields were silent, the work of removing the hastily buried dead and reinterring them could begin in earnest. It was an odious and difficult task. (USAMHI)

Below: But it was worth the effort, and quickly the nation gave its honored dead a fitting resting place. Here is a soldiers' cemetery in Alexandria, Virginia. Many of the dead could not be identified; only numbers appear on their grave markers. (USAMHI)

If as a result of the war the Union became a world power, so, too, did the conflict ensure its grasp on territory already claimed as its own. The years of fighting had a profound impact upon the settlement of the great expanse of unsettled, uncharted West. A few campaigns, even a few small battles, had been fought for control of the hundreds of thousands of miles of plains and mountains. The Indians could hardly profit from the great war taking place in the East. At best it gave them a brief rest from the inevitable push to dispossess them. Yet even before the war ended, the massive migration of whites began, and directly as a result of the conflict. Besides the soldiers who came West and besides the civilians and camp followers who inevitably clustered about the army camps, there came also thousands of men who had little choice. No one knows how many deserted from both armies during the war, but very few of them could be expected to go home to probable capture and certain disgrace. They went West instead. Hardly the most desirable of settlers, they almost ensured that the next few years would be lawless and wild in a land of men without creed. And when the end of the war left thousands more too accustomed to the practice of raiding and near-lawless adventuring to quit, it was inevitable that they, too, should go West. As a result the so-called Wild West was the direct offspring of the Civil War, and not unnaturally it would fall also to veterans of the war to go to the new settlements to preserve law and order. The James brothers had been Confederate guerrillas. "Wild Bill" Hickok had served the Union. For them and many more the days of the Old West were little more than a continuation of the adventure of the war.

Below: At Arlington National Cemetery, on grounds that were once the property of Robert E. Lee's family, thousands more were laid to rest. Ironically, Privates J. Kelly and J. Richards, beneath the two stones at front center, both died on their country's birthday, July 4, 1864. (USAMHI)

Below: And the work of marking and memorializing the battlefields began, with Bull Run (Manassas) being fittingly the first. On June 10, 1865, William Morris Smith made this image of the ceremonies dedicating the battle monument on Henry House Hill. (LC)

For every bully boy and bravo who crossed the plains, however, thousands of other more peaceable settlers came, tired of the East, ruined by the war, or simply anxious for something better than what they had. These are the people who "won" the West, not from the Indians or the bandits but from the land itself. Southerners and Northerners alike made the trek, and it went far toward reconciliation that they built towns and counties and states together. All that land out there just waiting gave them something to fight for in common, something to help rebuild the

*Right: There were speeches to
listen to, and this crowd is
reasonably attentive.
Standing hands on hips at
the right is Major General
Samuel P. Heintzelman,
who fought in the battle here
at Bull Run in 1861. Next
to him, arms folded, is
Major General Montgomery
C. Meigs, quartermaster general of the Union armies,
and next to him, at his left,
is Brigadier General
Alexander B. Dyer. (AIG)*

*Right: And here the generals and bystanders stand
for the camera, beneath the plaque that offers the
monument IN MEMORY OF THE PATRIOTS.
(NA)*

*Above: There were difficult years ahead for the South.
Happily, there were few reprisals against individuals
as a result of the war. Champ Ferguson of Tennessee
would suffer one of them, however. Guilty of murdering several white and Negro Federal soldiers in
1864, he was tried in Nashville in the summer of
1865. This portrait was made the day before his
hanging. (HP)*

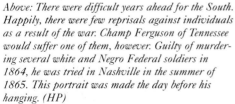

*Right: Elsewhere in Virginia, the survivors of a shat-
tered Confederacy will have to wait awhile before they
can erect their monuments. They are even hard put
just now to care adequately for their dead. Here in
Richmond's Hollywood Cemetery, in April 1865, the
mounds of earth testify to fresh burials, and the rude
headboards testify to the utter inability to provide
more than the barest ceremony for these fallen men.
That would change in time. (LC)*

Right: Only one Confederate officer was brought to trial for "war crimes," Major Henry Wirz, the commander of the infamous prison camp at Andersonville, Georgia. Despite his probable lack of intent in bringing about the deaths of thousands of Union prisoners, the horrors of Andersonville had to be avenged. On November 10, 1865, reporters gather in Washington, D.C., to witness Wirz's execution. (LC)

Below: Alexander Gardner brought his camera to capture the scene as, with the Capitol dome in the background, the trap is released and Wirz plummets to his death. (LC)

Left: As his lifeless body swings at the end of the rope, the dead of Andersonville are revenged . (LC)

Below: Jefferson Davis was indicted for treason in May 1866, but no trial was forthcoming. These were the jurymen before whom he was to be tried, yet the trial never came. In 1867, after exactly two years in prison, Davis was released on bail. (VM)

fraternal bonds that war had severed. Were it not for the West, reconciliation might have taken far longer than it did.

Of course, time would be the greatest healer of them all. As the years passed and the soldiers got older and gentler, so too did the passions. By the end of the century nostalgia and forgiving memory had already erased much of the bad, covering what remained in a patina of romance and myth. Veterans of both sides banded together in fraternal organizations—the mighty Grand Army of the Republic, the proud United Confederate Veterans. Intended originally as political action groups, they came in time to look more toward the care of the aging veterans, the infirm, those disabled by the war. Around the country, North and South, homes for the indigent and helpless veterans appeared. In annual conventions, the old generals and leaders came forth again and again to talk to their comrades of past glories and present patriotism. Through the dim, teary-eyed vision of the old fading soldiers, the memories grew less and less distinct, and all the more treasured.

In time they all had to go, to follow in death all those uncountable legions already departed on the nation's battlefields. Ironically, of the great men, Lee was the first to depart. The war killed him as surely as if a bullet had struck him down. He lived only until 1870, when he was only sixty-four, a symbol of peaceful acceptance of the war's verdict, a champion of reconciliation. Grateful and tolerant to the last, he threatened one of his professors at Washing ton College with dismissal if the man ever spoke disrespectfully of General Grant in his presence. The mourning was universal throughout the South and even in the North at the great warrior's passing, noble to the very end.

Left: For a time, elections were left once more in the hands of Southerners, but more and more Northern Republicans would come to enlist the new votes of the freed slaves to win office. Actual rule by the carpetbaggers was greatly exaggerated by ex-Confederates, but it did happen. The number of Federal uniforms in this Baton Rouge, Louisiana, electioneering wagon, speaks to the support given one candidate by the Northern conquerors. (DAM, LSU)

His old adversary Grant outlived him by fifteen years, with a nobility that, in its way, matched that of Lee. Lifted in 1872 to the highest office in the gift of the American people for his victory, Grant the President endured scandal and disgrace and financial disaster, to end his days still universally admired as a simple, honest soldier. His heroic struggle in his last days to complete his memoirs and provide for his family touched men everywhere. He beat the cancer that killed him only by days, leaving behind one of the finest memoirs ever written by a soldier and an example of courage which even his for mer enemies admired.

Of course there were those who held their bitterness to the end. Jefferson Davis would never admit defeat, never accept the war's lessons. To the last of his days he sought to win with his pen what his sword had lost. Though they never loved him as they did Lee, still his people admired and respected their old President. When he died in 1889, the last of the great political leaders of the war, even the North was respectful.

But the people were always the more touched by the generals and soldiers, the men who really fought the war, and they were the ones who seemed more readily able to forgive and forget. Nothing could be more touching than the last days of the archrivals Sherman and Johnston. They had not met prior to the war. Their acquaintance began at First Bull Run. They met again in the Vicksburg Campaign and then all across Georgia on the road to Atlanta. In the war's last days they faced each other in the Carolinas until finally Johnston surrendered. There after the two became cordial friends, in the manner of thousands of others, and when the great Sherman finally passed away in 1891, his old friend and enemy Johnston was there as an honorary pallbearer, standing bareheaded in the pouring rain. A friend admonished the old Confederate to put his hat on, but he would not. If the positions had been reversed, he said, and Sherman were standing there mourning a dead Johnston, the Federal would not have put his hat on. And so the old Confederate took cold and was dead of pneumonia within weeks.

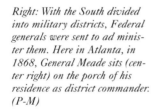

Left: Then came the occupation of the South by Federal troops and the years of Reconstruction. A regiment of Union troops in Memphis, Tennessee, in June 1865. (HP)

Right: With the South divided into military districts, Federal generals were sent to ad minister them. Here in Atlanta, in 1868, General Meade sits (center right) on the porch of his residence as district commander. (P-M)

Far left: The former Confederates fought back however they could, in the legislative halls and in out-of-the-way places by night, seeking to intimidate both the Negroes and the whites who collaborated with them. They rode out of the darkness dressed in frightening robes and hoods. (LO)

Left: In time the disorganized raiders formed more formal secret societies, the most notorious coming to be called the Ku Klux Klan. Here, on December 20, 1871, one of their members who had been captured and turned state's evidence poses in his regalia at Holly Springs, Mississippi. (HP)

More and more the remaining vestiges of the old war reminded Americans of their common bonds and virtues rather than their onetime controversies. Grand reunions of veterans blue and gray were held to celebrate the anniversaries of dates once held terrible. At Gettysburg in 1913 and again in 1938, mammoth reunions paid for by the nation brought thousands of old soldiers forth once more to walk the field of battle where some had fought and relive the old times. All across the country national military parks were established to memorialize what both sides stood and fought for. In time they all came to realize that it had been a very American war, exemplifying, North and South, all of the best and worst in themselves as Americans.

And throughout it all, from Appomattox on, for generations forward, down to the last living veteran, the constant companion of the Civil War experience, the camera, was there recording the passing of an era. Like America itself, the photographers after the war moved on, to the West, out into the world. They, like their nation, had given their youth, their best years, to the epic struggle of North and South. But they were not finished by that war. They and their craft would move ahead while their achievement made it possible for future generations always to look back.

They were all timeless men in their way, preserved in the images for all time. They had lived the spirit of their era, of an age now gone by but which can never die, thanks to them. They were all men, now long dead, who will yet live forever.

Right: The great Confederate cavalry chieftain Lieutenant General Nathan B. Forrest for a time served as Grand Wizard of the Klan, but around 1868 ordered it disbanded when he perceived that it was leading only to ineffective violence. (DAM, LSU)

Far right: Some, like Wade Hampton, once a great cavalryman, fought in the political arena to combat Reconstruction. Hampton became governor of South Carolina in 1876, was reelected in 1878, and then served two terms as a U.S. senator. (CM)

Right: Other former Confederates tried in different ways to survive Reconstruction and rebuild themselves as well. General P. G. T. Beauregard was proud enough of his service as late as 1872 to be still autographing his wartime portrait. He and other generals looked to railroading to bring the South into the industrial age. (VM)

Left: Thousands who could not face life in a defeated South emigrated to other countries, most notably Mexico. The family of Major General Sterling Price suffered a shipwreck on its way to Mexico in 1865. They pose here with other survivors, Mrs. Price seated at the center. (MISSOURI HISTORICAL SOCIETY, ST. LOUIS)

Below: Awaiting them in Mexico in 1865 were some of the generals who had exiled themselves rather than surrender. Standing left is Major General John B. Magruder and next to him is Brigadier General William P. Hardeman. Seated from the left are Major Generals Cadmus Wilcox, Sterling Price, and Thomas C. Hindman. All would eventually return to the United States when the Mexican colonization attempt failed. (NA)

Above: Others went to Canada. Here, standing at the far left, is the Confederacy's last Secretary of War, Major General John C. Breckinridge, posing with his family in front of Niagara Falls in 1867. Still under indictment for treason, Breckinridge did not dare return to the United States, though he wanted to desperately. The best he could do was come here to Canada to live, so he could look across the Niagara River and see the country from which he was self-exiled. In 1869 he finally returned after amnesty was declared by President Johnson. (WCD)

Right: Meanwhile, the Confederates' old adversaries were spreading out and leaving the country, though for other reasons. Irishmen like Brigadier General Thomas Sweeny, born in County Cork, began to look to Canada as a place to attack England so as to force her to free their native Ireland. Sweeny and other so-called Fenians invaded Canada in 1866, but the whole movement failed comically. (THOMAS SWEENEY)

Above: President of the Fenians was Colonel John O'Mahony of the 40th New York. (WC)

Right: The Union itself was expanding, looking to stretch its influence beyond its borders. The shipbuilding begun during the war continued. War vessels like the USS Ammonoosuc, *a cruiser here under construction at the Boston Navy Yard in 1864, would be completed after the war to join one of the most modern fleets in the world. (MM)*

Left: The mighty USS Madawaska, *largest commissioned vessel in the Navy, was renamed* Tennessee *in 1869 and made flagship of the Adriatic and North AtlanticSquadron. (USAMHI)*

Below: Here at Rio de Janeiro, Brazil, the USS Guerriere, *flagship of the South Atlantic Squadron, sits at anchor. (USAMHI)*

Above: The powerful USS Kearsarge *cruised the Pacific, stopping here in Sydney, Australia in 1869 (NHC)*

Right: And the powerful monitor USS Miantonomoh *was sent on a major European tour in 1866-67, to learn what she could of naval facilities there and to impress Europeans with the new naval might of the United States. She certainly did the latter. "The wolf is in our fold," lamented the London* Times. *She appears here at Malaga, Spain, early in 1867. (NHC)*

Left: So much did the Union now feel its muscle that it took Great Britain to task in 1869 for serving as outfitting agent for Confederate ships like the raider Alabama. *In the deliberations over claims for damage done to Union shipping by that vessel and other raiders, these Yankee commissioners. . .(WG)*

Below: . . . negotiated in 1872 with these British leaders for the eventual payment of $15 million to the United States. (WG)

Left: The Yankees were moving West, too, expanding their influence in their own continent. Here at Fort Sanders, Wyoming, in 1866, there was a notable gathering of luminaries. Former Major General Grenville M. Dodge stands at far left; he had now left the Army and was building the Union Pacific Railroad. Second to the right from Dodge is Major General Philip Sheridan, and second to the right from him is Major General John Gibbon; both Sheridan and Gibbon were now facing hostile Indians on the Plains.

Wearing a white hat and leaning on the fence to the right of Gibbon is Lieutenant General U. S. Grant, now commanding general of the Army, and the man in white vest standing in the very center of the photo is Major General William T. Sherman. Standing at far right is Major General John A. Rawlins, and next to him is Colonel Adam Badeau. The white-bearded man in cape and top hat is Brevet Major General William S. Harney, now retired. They were all on a tour of inspection of the route of the Union Pacific. (GENE PANTANO)

Left: Some tried to profit as best they could from their war experiences. The actress Pauline Cushman made a shabby career of sorts by appearing in her uniform and telling the story of her dramatically unsuccessful days as a Federal spy. (NYHS)

Above: For other former Union generals the years after the war were less exciting, less active. Major General Ambrose Burnside sits at center, with Major General Robert Anderson seated at the right. It is 1865 and Burnside would go on into industry and politics. Anderson would be dead in 1871, worn out by the war. (VITOLO-RINHART GALLERIES, NEW YORK CITY)

Left: But for many of the other veterans, there was nothing left but a lifetime on public or private charity. This New Jersey soldier gave a lot for his country. (WILLIAM C. MC

Below: The nation tried to do what it could in return, and indeed few war veterans were ever cared for better than the Union's boys in blue. Here in the National Home for Disabled Volunteer Soldiers in Dayton, Ohio, an excellent library was provided for the soldiers' entertainment. An 1876 image by the Mote Brothers. (RJY)

Left: Gradually the old leaders grew older. Age is marking Generals Heintzelman and Sheridan as they sit here, second and third from the left. And Admiral David Farragut is weighted with years as well as gold braid. Gradually they will die away. Farragut will be the first of this group to go, in 1870. (CHICAGO PUBLIC LIBRARY)

Above: And his once proud warship the USS Hartford will, like Farragut, grow old. In 1876 she came to Philadelphia for the great Centennial Exposition. (P-M)

Left: Other veteran ships like the USS Idaho will simply be laid up in the navy yards, with nothing left to do. (NHC)

Above: For the once proud monitors USS Shawnee *and USS* Wassuc *the same fate lay ahead, to be tied up at the Boston Navy Yard with nothing to look forward to but salvage for scrap. (CHS)*

Right: Even the USS Miantonomoh, *after its world cruise, would wind up at a slip on the Charles River next to the two monitors. (NHC)*

Above: As the years went on, the colors faded and the old Confederate leaders slowly began to wane and disappear. Here at White Sulphur Springs, Virginia, in the 1870s, General Joseph E. Johnston stands to the right, with family and friends. Major General Jeremy Gilmer stands on the opposite side of the trunk; at far left of the picture stands Brigadier General John S. Preston; and the man seated at right is Major General George Washington Custis Lee, son of . . . (VM)

Right: . . . General Robert E. Lee. Photographer A. H. Plecker of Lynchburg captured this image of Lee and Traveller during the summer of 1866. The general was aging rapidly. (AIG)

Left: By 1869, when he sat for this unpublished Brady portrait, Lee was just sixty-two and had barely a year to live. (WCD)

Below: In October 1870 the great general was dead. On October 14 this procession carried his remains from his residence in Lexington, Virginia, to the chapel of Washington College, of which he had been president since 1865. (WASHINGTON AND LEE UNIVERSITY, LEXINGTON, VIRGINIA)

Below: The next day the funeral services were held in the chapel, while the crowds outside gathered to pay their respects. Gray-clad cadets of the Virginia Military Institute at Lexington stand in the center. For Virginia and the South it is a farewell to their most memorable era, and to their greatest national hero. (WASHINGTON AND LEE UNIVERSITY)

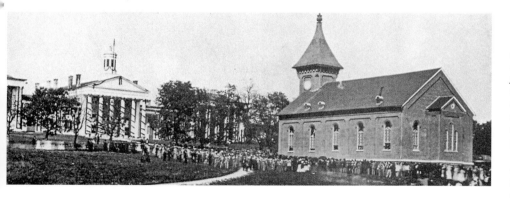

Below left: There are more heroes left to die. On July 22, 1885, with two clouded terms as President and four years as one of the greatest generals of his age behind him, U. S. Grant is dying of cancer in a cottage at Mount McGregor, New York. He had just finished the heroic task of writing his memoirs against the most immutable deadline of all, his own death. (CHAPMAN R. GRANT)

Below right: The next day the general's chair was empty, draped in black. Another era ended. (CHAPMAN R. GRANT)

Left: "Little Aleck" Stephens, troublesome Vice President of the Confederacy, lived until 1883, unrepentant to the last, and uncompromising. (WA)

Left: For Jefferson Davis, there was at least the small satisfaction of outliving all of the other major leaders of the war—Lincoln, Grant, Lee. Here he stands on the steps of his home Beauvoir in Mississippi. (TU)

Left: He devoted the last years of his life to writing his history of the Confederacy, trying to win with the pen what he had lost by the sword. He, too, never fully admitted defeat or error and never entirely forgave his old foes. (CONFEDERATE RELIC ROOM AND MUSEUM, COLUMBIA, SOUTH CAROLINA)

Above right: Here in this study at Beauvoir Davis began the work of creating his version of the Lost Cause myth. Here he wrote his Rise and Fall of the Confederate Government, *his personal apologia and the first in the unending stream of works by former Confederates designed to prove that even if the South did not win the war, it should have done so. The echoes that began in this modest, book-lined room are sounding still. (LC)*

Right: But he, too, had to answer the final call. In 1889, in New Orleans, the Confederacy's one and only President lay dead, and with him went much of the history and the enduring myth of the Lost Cause. (CONFEDERATE RELIC ROOM AND MUSEUM)

Left: In 1876 trees and grass grew on the heights overlooking Fredericksburg, Virginia, where in 1862 they sprouted only guns. An image by Edward L. Wilson & W. Irving Adams. (DUKE UNIVERSITY LIBRARY, DURHAM, NORTH CAROLINA)

Right: At Gettysburg, Pennsylvania, greatest battlefield of them all, the soldiers were laying cornerstones for monuments as early as July 4, 1865, when the 50th Pennsylvania Infantry gathered here for a dedication. At the end of that month they were mustered out of service. (OAKLAND MUSEUM, OAKLAND, CALIFORNIA)

Right: As the years went on, the monuments and markers multiplied. By the 1880s Little Round Top already bristled with them. Gettysburg was on its way to becoming the best-marked battlefield in the world. (USAMHI)

Right: The soldiers came back after the war to establish homes like this Gettysburg house, as orphanages for the children left behind by men who fell for the cause. Grant himself stands second from the right in this 1867 image. The Soldiers' Orphans Home at Gettysburg operated until 1887. (LC)

Left: Enterprising Southerners beat out their old adversaries in realizing the tourist potential of the battlefields. It was late in 1865 when a Virginian opened a small museum here at the Crater at Petersburg. (TU)

Right: The Crater became a popular tourist attraction, each visitor paying twenty-five cents to view the artifacts and look at the great hole made by the Yankee mine in July 1864, during the siege. When this image was made in 1867, visitors were a daily occurrence. (LEE A. WALLACE, JR.)

Below: For all of them, the men and generals and photographers and the people who stayed at home and waited, it had been the most momentous experience of their lives. Never again would they and their country endure such a trial, and emerge so ennobled. They had lived the last days of American innocence. (KA)

Left: The old soldiers themselves got older, the memories fading along with the old animosities. The veterans gathered in reunions, North and South, and even the once-maligned Negro soldiers were often welcome. Old Jefferson Shields was Confederate Major General Stonewall Jackson's wartime cook and now a frequent visitor at Stonewall Brigade reunions. This image was made around 1905, forty years after the war ended. (LEONARD L. TIMMONS)

Above: As the parades went on year after year, there were fewer and fewer of the old heroes to fill the wagons. Here in 1913, fifty years after Gettysburg and Vicksburg, the old gentlemen are looking ever closer to the grave. (LEONARD L. TIMMONS)

Above: Many of the soldiers had gone to war as beardless boys; they emerged as men, in a modern nation bright with promise for the future. Behind them now lay the hatreds, the blood . . . (HP)

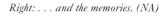

Right: . . . and the memories. (NA)

Index

Commonly known abbreviations are used for frequently repeated terms, e.g., HQ for headquarters, POWs for prisoners of war, RR for railroad.

Contributors

Listed in alphabetical order

George Washington Adams established himself many years ago as perhaps the leading authority on Civil War medicine with the publication of *Doctors in Blue: The Medical History of the Union Army in the Civil War*. Educated at Harvard University, Dr. Adams taught at his alma mater and at Massachusetts Institute of Technology before becoming Dean of Colorado College.

John G. Barrett has spent three decades on the faculty of the Virginia Military Institute at Lexington, is a Guggenheim fellow, and is the author of several acclaimed Civil War books, including *Sherman's March Through the Carolinas*, *The Civil War in North Carolina*, and *North Carolina Civil War Documentary*.

Edwin C. Bearss is chief historian of the National Park Service and the author of many important books on the Civil War, including *Decision in Mississippi*, *Forrest at Brice's Cross Roads*, and *Hardluck Ironclad*, about the sinking and salvage of the Civil War ironclad *Cairo*.

Robert C. Black is a retired professor of history at Colorado Women's College whose special interest has always been transportation. He is the author of *The Railroads of the Confederacy*.

Dee Brown became an internationally known author with the publication of his bestselling history of the Indian, *Bury My Heart at Wounded Knee*. But, in fact, he had been a prolific writer of fiction and nonfiction for many years before, his works including Civil War studies such as *Grierson's Raid*, the story of the North's most dashing cavalry expedition of the war.

Frank L. Byrne is one of the few Civil War scholars ever to turn their attention to the prisons of the war. A professor of history at Kent State University, he has written numerous articles on the subject, and continues active research in the field while publishing books on such topics as prohibition and temperance history.

Albert Castel has specialized in the war west of the Alleghenies in his books and articles, among them *General Sterling Price and the Civil War in the West*, *Kansas—A Frontier State at War*, and *William Clarke Quantrell*.

Dudley T. Cornish, professor of history at Pittsburgh State University, is the author of the classic work *The Sable Arm: Negro Troops in the Union Army, 1861–1865*.

Joseph P. Cullen served for many years as a historian with the National Park Service. The author of numerous articles on the Civil War, he also wrote the National Historical Society's *Concise History of the American Revolution* and *The Peninsula Campaign*.

William C. Davis, who conceived and edited this work, was for many years editor and publisher of *Civil War Times Illustrated* and other historical magazines. Among his many works are *Breckinridge: Statesman, Soldier, Symbol*, *The Orphan Brigade*, *Battle at Bull Run*, and *The Imperiled Union, 1861–1865*.

Norman C. Delaney has made the story of the Confederate commerce raiders the object of intense investigation for many years. A professor at Del Mar College of Corpus Christi, Texas, Delaney is the author of *John McIntosh Kell of the Raider Alabama*.

Charles Dufour, past president of the Louisiana Historical Association and one of the founders of the Civil War Round Table, is a New Orleans native and retired newspaperman, and the author of eight books, three of which dwell on the Civil War.

William A. Frassanito, chief photographic consultant for this work, is one of the foremost historians and interpreters of Civil War photographs.

Charles R. Haberlein, Jr. is Photographic Curator and Historian at the Naval Historical Center in Washington, D. C., the nation's finest collection of naval illustrations. He has been of inestimable assistance with naval matters in the production of this work.

Warren W. Hassler, Jr., longtime professor of history at Pennsylvania State University, is a highly regarded and prolific historian in the field of American and Civil War military history.

Herman Hattaway of the University of Missouri at Kansas City won the Jefferson Davis Award for the best book in Confederate History with his biography of General Stephen D. Lee.

Leslie D. Jensen, Curator of Collections at Richmond's Museum of the Confederacy, is a specialist in Confederate uniforms and equipment.

Ludwell H. Johnson III has been for many years a professor of history at the College of William and Mary and a noted specialist in the Civil War. Among his works are *The Red River Campaign, Politics and Cotton in the Civil War* and *Division and Reunion: America 1848–1877*, a provocative and decidedly pro-Confederate history of the Civil War era which has challenged many long-accepted ideas about the conflict.

Virgil Carrington Jones has long been associated with the naval history of the war through his trilogy *The Civil War at Sea*.

Maury Klein is the biographer of General E. P. Alexander, Lee's chief of Artillery, as well as Jay Gould. He has also published works on the Louisville & Nashville Railroad and the Great Richmond Terminal.

Robert K Krick is a historian with the National Park Service, and the author of several books on the Confederate Army, including *Lee's Colonels, A Biographical Register of the Field Officers of the Army of Northern Virginia*, and *Parker's Virginia Battery*.

Harold D. Langley, curator and supervisor of the Division of Naval History of the Smithsonian Institution's National Museum of American History, has a considerable reputation as a student of the American Navy in the years prior to the Civil War. Among his works are *Social Reform in the U.S. Navy, 1798–1862* and an edition of the papers of Henry L. Stimson.

David Lindsey, professor of history at California State University, Los Angeles, since 1936, is the author of numerous books, including *Americans in Conflict: The Civil War and Reconstruction*.

Louis Manarin, state archivist at the Virginia State Library in Richmond, has long been associated with research and writing on the Confederacy and the Civil War. Among his works are *Richmond Volunteers and The Bloody Sixth*, as well as *North Carolina Troops 1861–1864: A Roster*.

Maurice Melton is a specialist in Confederate Naval History, and the author of *Confederate Ironclads*. He serves on the board of advisors for the Confederate Naval Museum at Columbus, Georgia.

Frank J. Merli is a professor of history at Queens College. His book *Great Britain and the Confederate Navy 1861–1865* is one of the preeminent works of modern times on Civil War diplomacy and the much-neglected naval side of the conflict.

Richard M. McMurry is a historian specializing in the Civil War and the Confederacy. Among his books are *The Road Past Kennesaw: The Atlanta Campaign of 1864* and *John Bell Hood and the War for Southern Independence*.

James M. Merrill, a Guggenheim and Mershon Fellow, served as a lieutenant in the United Sates Navy, which inspired his interest in Civil War naval and maritime operations. Among his books are *Battle Flags South: The Civil War on Western Rivers*, *Rebel Shore: Union Sea Power in the Civil War*, and *Sailor's Admiral*, a biography of William F. Halsey.

Peter J. Parrish, author of *The American Civil War*, is professor of modern history at the University of Dundee, Scotland.

Frederic E. Ray is art director of *Civil War Times Illustrated* and *American History Illustrated*, as well as serving as a photographic consultant for this work. His *Alfred R. Waud, Civil War Artist*, is one of the foremost biographies of the legion of battlefield artists who followed the armies.

Rowena Reed, professor of history at Dartmouth College, is the author of *Combined Operations in the Civil War*, a major reassessment of Army–Navy cooperation during the war and the opportunities won or lost because of it.

James I. Robertson, Jr. has written and edited numerous books and articles on the Civil War years. He served as executive director for the United States Civil War Centennial Commission from 1961 to 1965. One of his outstanding contributions is the two-volume *Civil War Books: A Critical Bibliography*.

Charles P. Roland, professor of history at the University of Kentucky, served as assistant to the chief historian for the Department of the Army. Among his books are *Louisiana Sugar Plantations During the American Civil War* and *The Confederacy*.

Everard H. Smith has long specialized in the story of the campaign for the Shenandoah Valley in 1864. A cum laude graduate from Yale, he took his Ph.D. at the University of North Carolina and is currently teaching history and political science at High Point College in North Carolina.

Richard J. Sommers, Archivist at the U. S. Army Military History Institute, is one of the foremost authorities on the military aspects of the Civil War. He has long been a contributor of articles to magazines and journals concerned with the period, and he is the author of the acclaimed *Richmond Redeemed: The Siege at Petersburg*, the winner of the first Bell I. Wiley Prize for distinguished research and writing in the field of the Civil War.

William N. Still, professor of history at East Carolina University, Greenville, North Carolina, has written numerous articles as well as *Iron Afloat: The Story of Confederate Ironclads and Confederate Shipbuilding*.

W. A. Swanberg has written on a wide range of subjects in American History, from the Civil War to biographies of Jim Fisk and Theodore Dreiser. His Civil War works include *Sickles the Incredible*, a biography of General Daniel Sickles, and *First Blood—The Story of Fort Sumter*.

Robert G. Tanner, an attorney, is the author of *Stonewall in the Valley*. His main interests lie in the Shenandoah Valley campaign of 1862.

Emory M. Thomas is professor of history at the University of Georgia. Among his works on the Confederacy and Reconstruction are *The Confederacy as a Revolutionary Experience*, *The Confederate Nation*, *The Confederate State of Richmond: A Biography of the Capital*, and *The American War and Peace, 1860–1877*.

Frank E. Vandiver, president of Texas A&M University, was a recipient of the Harry S Truman award from the Kansas City Civil War Round Table and has written numerous books and articles on the Confederacy, most notably his biography of T. J. Jackson, *Mighty Stonewall*.

Russell F. Weigley is one of America's most distinguished military historians. A professor at Temple University, he is the author of *Quartermaster General of the Union Army*, a biography of General Montgomery C. Meigs, *History of the United States Army*, and *Eisenhower's Lieutenants: The Campaign of France and Germany, 1944–1945*, among many other distinguished works.

Bell I. Wiley was preeminent among Civil War historians, with more than fifty books to his credit. The story of the common people of that era was his chief interest, and his two works *The Life of Johnny Reb* and *The Life of Billy Yank* have become classics. He also served as chairman of the Board of Advisors of the National Historical Society.

T. Harry Williams achieved a reputation as one of the foremost American historians of our time. His biography *Huey Long* won him the Pulitzer Prize and the National Book Award. He was, however, best known for his work on the Civil War, including *Lincoln and the Radicals*, *Lincoln and his Generals*, *P.G.T. Beauregard*, *The Union Sundered*, and many more.

ABBREVIATIONS

A key to abbreviations used in photo captions

AIG — America Image Gallery, Gettysburg, Pennsylvania

CHS — Chicago Historical Society

CM — Confederate Museum, New Orleans

CSS — Charles S. Schwartz

CWTI — Civil War Times Illustrated Collection, Harrisburg, Pennsylvania

DAM, LSU — Department of Archives and Manuscripts, Louisiana State University, Baton Rouge

GDAH — Georgia Department of Archives and History, Atlanta

GW — Gary Wright

HP — Herb Peck

ISHL — Illinois State Historical Library, Springfield

JM — Jack McGuire

JMB — Joe M. Bauman

KA — Kean Archives, Philadelphia

KHS — Kentucky Historical Society, Kentucky Military Museum, Frankfort

LC — Library of Congress

LJW — Larry J. West

LO — Lloyd Ostendorf Collection

LSU — Louisiana State University, Dept. of Archives and Manuscripts, Baton Rouge

MC — Museum of the Confederacy

MHS — Minnesota Historical Society

MJH — Michael J. Hammerson

MJM — Michael J. McAfee

MM — Mariners Museum, Newport News, Virginia

NA — National Archives

NHC — U.S. Naval Historical Center

NLM — National Library of Medicine, Bethesda, Maryland

NYHS — New York Historical Society, New York

OCHM — Old Court House Museum, Vicksburg, Mississippi

PHS — Pensacola Historical Society, Pensacola, Florida

P-M — Pennsylvania-MOLLUS Collection, War Library and Museum, Philadelphia

RJY — Robert J. Younger

RP — Ronn Palm

SCL — South Carolina Library, University of South Carolina, Columbia

SHC — Southern Historical Collection, University of North Carolina, Chapel Hill

TU — Louisiana Historical Association, Special Collection Division, Tulane University Library, New Orleans

USAMHI — U.S. Army Military History Institute, Carlisle Barracks, Pennsylvania

VHS — Vermont Historical Society

VM — Valentine Museum, Richmond

WA — William Albaugh Collection

WCD — William C. Davis

WG — William Gladstone Collection

WRHS — Western Reserve Historical Society, Cleveland, Ohio